THE

Sunset

COOKBOOK

THE
Sunset
COOKBOOK

over 1,000 fresh, flavorful recipes
for the way you cook today

Oxmoor
House.

contents

acknowledgments

This is the cookbook I have long wanted to have in my own kitchen. It is the be-all, end-all for anyone who loves to cook with fresh ingredients, appreciates easy techniques, and has a taste for adventure.

I started seriously envisioning this cookbook more than 10 years ago, when I became editor of *Sunset* magazine. I could see how passionate our readers were about our recipes, the joy and pleasure they take in cooking with us every month. Through the years, I'd corner my book publishing colleagues at meetings and parties to pitch the idea for this landmark guide to cooking "our way." Back then our book business was entirely focused on *Sunset's* other renowned subjects of home design and gardening, so I got polite nods all around. "But it will be incredible," I vowed. "The book you want to give everyone you know who loves food!" I realized I might have to wait for a few fellow food lovers to join my campaign to make it happen....

Luckily, that campaign was reignited by Margo True, who became *Sunset's* food editor in 2006. A passionate, energetic lover of cooking and all flavors and tastes of the West, Margo shaped and edited the book beyond my wildest dreams. It was her vivid proposal, in fact, that won over the business side, too. My heartfelt thanks and gratitude to our food lovers at the very top: Barb Newton, Jim Childs, and Richard Fraiman, who said "yes" to *The Sunset Cookbook*.

Margo would be the first to say that this book was a monumental team effort, and the result of many years and types of creativity. Our thanks to:

- Former *Sunset* magazine food editors Jerry Anne Di Vecchio and Sara Schneider, and previous staff writers, including Linda Anusasananan. They defined Western cooking for millions of readers and set the standard for excellence.

- Elaine Johnson and Amy Machnak, our *Sunset* food staff, and test kitchen coordinator Stephanie Dean for contributing recipes, sidebars, and tasting notes to the process. Thanks to Stephanie, too, for combing through our archives as well as coordinating the recipe testing for this book. Many thanks to Sara Schneider, now *Sunset's* wine editor, for contributing excellent wine essays.

- Our staff of test kitchen "retesters" who take a recipe we think already works and make it perfect.

- *Sunset* creative director Mia Daminato, photo director Yvonne Stender, and editor Sue Smith for the luscious photography. Oxmoor House senior designer Emily Parrish and Allison Sperando for the beautiful layout.

- *Sunset* brand manager at Oxmoor House, Fonda Hitchcock, for keeping us on track from beginning to end. The editorial staff of Oxmoor House, especially editorial director Susan Payne Dobbs, managing editor Laurie Herr, and project editor Vanessa Lynn Rusch, for patiently working long distance and long hours. Hats off to proofreader Lauren Brooks, indexer Mary Ann Laurens, production manager Terri Beste-Farley, and interns Georgia Dodge and Perri Hubbard.

- Marie Pence, for organizing our digital files, and project manager Linda Bouchard, for getting the big ship of this cookbook on the right course at the outset.

- Pam Hoenig, project editor, for whipping a mountain of material into shape at breakneck speed, with enduring good grace and an uncanny ability to see the big picture and tiny details all at once.

- Copy editors Tam Putnam and Julie Harris, who swept up after us in so many places.

- The San Francisco chefs who gave us great advice on whole-animal cooking: Staffan Terje of Perbacco, Ryan Farr of 4505 Meats, and Chris Cosentino of Incanto. Roberto Guerra, owner of La Caja China company, for guidance on using the roasting box. The helpful staff at Avedano's butcher shop in San Francisco, who supplied us with pork fat and tips for rendering lard: Dittmer's meat market in Mountain View, for the lamb and pig, Shujau Siddiqi, of Halal Market in Santa Clara, for his advice about goat, and goat ranchers Gary and Tracy Silva, as well as Dusty Copeland of Copeland Family Farms.

- The generous folks at Cook's Seafood and Melissa's World Variety Produce.

And, of course, many thanks to the *Sunset* readers and chefs who have contributed wonderful recipes to this book and over the years.

Katie Tamony
Editor-in-chief, *Sunset* magazine

introduction

This is my idea of a perfect dinner: I'm in Ojai, California, at my parents' place, and our whole family and a group of our friends are sitting on the back patio under the oak trees, with the mountains just in view. It's springtime, and the sweetness of orange blossoms drifts in from the trees that curve up the driveway.

Nobody's dressed too fancy. We're all relaxed, happy to see each other, and sipping good red wine from Casa Barranca, the new winery that is very conveniently located just a mile or so away, and some crisp whites from Napa that my cousin Pete brought down. The food comes mainly from the Ojai farmers' market via my mom's kitchen, and some of it is from her garden. We're eating a big leafy salad, with greens so fresh they practically seem alive, and tangy-sweet oranges from one of the trees, and avocados that are like butter, but better. Mom's wonderful chicken and sausage paella is flavored with the herbs she grows, which somehow have more intensity in Ojai than they do anywhere else, probably because of the sun. Dessert might be a Meyer lemon cake that my sister and I have collaborated on, or homemade ice cream. I lean back and think, Life is sweet.

I love living in the West not only because my family is here, or because it's supremely beautiful in a wide-open, endless-vistas sort of way. I also love the food, and the way we cook and eat at home—which is to say outside whenever we can, without a lot of fuss, and starting with good ingredients. It's not hard to find those in the West, since most of our country's fruits and vegetables are grown here. Every region has its own beautiful, abundant food, which more than anything else defines how we cook: salmon, shellfish, berries, hazelnuts, and mushrooms in the Northwest; lamb, beef, buffalo, peaches, and potatoes in Colorado and Idaho; chiles, blue corn, heirloom beans, and pine nuts in the Southwest; pineapple, fish, taro, coffee, and vanilla in Hawaii; and lettuces, artichokes, olives, dates, walnuts, and almonds in California, plus milk and citrus. As if that weren't bounty enough, we also have wonderful artisanal cheeses—with more being crafted every year—and the best wine regions in the nation supplying bottles for our tables.

With all that, we're two-thirds of the way to a great dinner. The rest is up to us.

For generations, *Sunset* has been showing home cooks how to use those superb ingredients to make food that's easy, but exciting. We published a recipe for pesto in 1946, probably the first magazine in the U.S. to do so, and wrote about farmers' markets soon after they began to sprout in the late 1970s. We helped newcomers to our region figure out the potential of avocados and unlock the secrets of the artichoke. In our 110-year history, we've documented and eaten just about everything that grows, roams, or swims in the West, from walnuts to wahoo.

In the past decade, our food landscape has grown exponentially richer, and the way we navigate it has changed too. *Sunset's* goal with *The Sunset Cookbook* is to give you the kind of recipes you need right now, but also ones that spark your imagination and lead you to discovery.

Vegetables Galore

Farmers' markets have cropped up in just about every city and town, and along with providing first-rate staple crops like carrots, onions, and celery, they've introduced unfamiliar, thrilling edibles like broccoli romanesco, green garlic, and Thai basil. Some supermarkets are following their lead, offering Asian long beans and cactus pads right there with the bagged broccoli. We're signing up to buy food directly from farms, through CSAs, and having fun figuring out what to do with the box that arrives each week. And we're gardening like never before, planting and eating our own tomatoes, lettuces, and string beans, and exploring a fascinating variety of heirloom seeds.

That's why we've devoted three full chapters of this book to vegetables—salads, side dishes, and vegetarian main courses. Salads are practically a way of life here, especially in California, where they're what's for dinner as often as they are the starter or side. Vegetables as side dishes are indispensable, both for our health and because they taste good.

They're crucial too in vegetarian main courses, giving color, flavor, and variety to an ever more interesting array of meatless meals. Which, by the way, aren't just for vegetarians any more—lots of us are eating less meat than we used to, or routinely skipping it, in part because vegetables have gotten so good. No one has to be reminded to eat their veggies in the West.

Taste Adventures

We're also more open-minded, curious eaters than we used to be, even five years ago. Food on TV has something to do with it, as does the proliferation of innovative restaurants (and food carts). So does the fact that we're multigenerationally multicultural. Cultures that immigrated to the Spanish-Mexican and Native American West are now firmly established—Chinese, Japanese, Russian, Dutch, Portuguese, Scandinavian, Indian, Thai, Vietnamese, Filipino, Korean, Persian, Basque—and the way we cook and eat is ever more integrated. It comes naturally, almost without thinking. We love planked salmon, a venerable Native American technique, but these days the fish might be seasoned with teriyaki. It's no big deal for us to snack on Japanese edamame with our cocktails, fry up Mexican chorizo for our eggs, or put Korean *kimchi* on a burger; we have fun rummaging through our shared pantry, and the recipes in this book do the same.

Because we know that you're curious cooks, we've also gathered recipes and techniques from the cutting edge of Western food and then figured out how to make them work at home. We've explored the frontiers of vegetable cooking (*page 276*), ordered and roasted whole animals (it's surprisingly easy and totally delicious; *see page 496*), and experimented with buffalo, goat, and venison.

That said, you'll find plenty of classic Western recipes in these pages (see the essential list, *below*). Sometimes nothing is as good as an awesome fish taco, or a juicy hunk of beef tri-tip grilled Santa Maria style, or a big bowl of succulent *chile verde*, pork shoulder braised with green chiles until it's so tender you can eat it with a spoon.

24 Iconic Western Dishes

These foods are all inextricably embedded in Western cooking and eating. The page references are to our favorite versions, arranged in order of their appearance. (*For a longer list of key Western recipes, see page 743.*)

- Guacamole (*page 25*)
- Date shake (*page 75*)
- Mai Tai (*page 76*)
- *Pho* (Vietnamese noodle soup; *page 98*)

- *Chile verde* (*page 123*)
- Cioppino (*page 126*)
- Citrus and avocado salad (*page 135*)
- Caesar salad (*page 143*)
- Crab Louis (*page 163*)
- Cobb salad (*page 169*)
- San Francisco–style burrito (*page 192*)
- Fish tacos (*page 196*)
- California-style pizza (*pages 198–199*)
- California roll (*page 337*)

- Dungeness crab (*page 339*)
- Abalone (*page 349*)
- Green chile chicken enchiladas (*page 367*)
- Tamales (*page 418*)
- Buffalo (*page 431*)
- Barbecued oysters (*page 444*)
- Barbecued turkey (*page 479*)
- Santa Maria barbecue (*page 486*)
- Plank-roasted salmon (*page 506*)
- Sopaipillas (*page 593*)

Grilling 24/7

Cooking in the open was a constant of the Old West—for Native Americans, for the settlers on the Oregon and Santa Fe trails, for the cowboys working the herds. We've never fully moved indoors. Our relatively good weather lets us cook and eat outside much of the year, and most of us have, if not a view of mountains or ocean, at least a backyard or a deck where we can enjoy the sun and the fresh air. That's part of why we love our grills so much; we don't have to go inside to cook. Also, there's the fun of grilling, which (especially if it's charcoal) is not unlike a sport. You're playing with fire, coaxing it to cook your food just right.

And when it's just right, it's so right…pork ribs falling off the bone, crisp-skinned sausages split from the heat, shrimp with a hint of char. You will notice that our grilling chapter, which starts on *page 432*, is twice the size of any other chapter in the book, and covers everything you could possibly think of to cook on a grill, from appetizers to dessert. It should give you lots of reasons to linger outside.

Fast Food, Made Right

There's never enough time during the week to get everything done, especially if you have kids, so we've taken pains to put all our favorite fast, easy, accessible weeknight dinners—both those developed in our test kitchen and sent in by our readers—in this book (for a list, see the Weeknight Meals index, starting on *page 745*). We don't open cans and boxes of processed food, the easiest shortcuts; our commitment (because we believe it's yours too) is to start with good, nutritious, fresh foods. The other trap of fast cooking is sameness and dullness. We've spent hours dreaming up recipes that are as fun to cook as they are quick to prepare (check out Crazed Mom's Easy Steak and Garam Masala *Naan*-wiches, *page 461*, or Halibut Kebabs with Grilled Bread and Pancetta, *page 505*, two of my favorites).

The time estimate on each of our recipes assumes you are starting with whole ingredients. It takes into account the chopping, peeling, and slicing usually mentioned in the ingredient list—so it's actually a figure that means something, because it refers to more than just the cooking steps. You have probably seen recipes, published elsewhere, that attempt to persuade you that they can be made in 10 minutes or less. If you've ever wondered whether you're being bamboozled (especially if it's a main course), try this little exercise. Read through the recipe, guesstimate how long each step will take you, and add to that how long it will take to prep the ingredients. Most recipes require at least 10 minutes just for prep.

Slow Food, for Sanity

But life isn't all about speed and efficiency and multitasking. Sometimes you need to slow down to register that life is even happening. So this book also has recipes that induce a more meditative rhythm. Make bread or a big pot of stew; bake a cake or start a pot roast. Then check your pulse. It's probably slower.

A Healthy Way to Eat

On the whole, we Westerners care a lot about health and well-being. At *Sunset*, we believe that the best way to stay healthy is to eat smaller portions of a lot of different kinds of foods, especially vegetables, fruits, and whole grains; exercise your body; and make sure that every now and then you eat the things you love, even if they're really fattening or full of sugar—gooey cheeses, chocolate, ice cream, doughnuts, whatever—because life should have joy. The trick is to think of them as special-occasion foods, because that's what they've been for most of human evolution (when we had them at all), and our bodies simply can't cope with daily onslaughts of richness.

It also helps to be aware of how many calories a dish has, if you're trying to lose weight, and other nutritional information like sodium, if you're watching your salt intake. So we provide a short list of nutritional data beneath every recipe. (For an explanation of each component on the list, and how much the average person needs of it, *see page 18*.)

We're also starting to understand that our health in the larger sense goes way beyond those handy little numbers. It encompasses our whole system of food production. We're beginning to see that nutritious meat involves the well-being of the animal, how a beef steer crammed into a feedlot to be fattened on grain might not be as robust as a steer out on pasture, eating the grass that is its natural food. Or that routinely dosing factory-raised chickens with antibiotics to make them grow faster and prevent them from getting sick might not be great for us either. Or that the health of an entire species—salmon, for instance—depends on how we choose to harvest and eat it. Our goal with these issues, as with the little nutritional numbers we supply for each recipe, is to give you information you might find useful, so that you can make up your own mind.

Wine on the Table

Every year, we enjoy wine more. Living, as we do, surrounded by some of the world's best wineries, it's inevitable. Wine is part of our lifestyle, and we believe that its rightful place is on the table, making food taste better and vice versa. To help steer you toward the most mouthwatering matches, we've included wine-pairing essays all through this book (plus a sidebar on the West's excellent craft beers). We end with a special wine chapter *(page 726)* that sets forth the basics of enjoying and understanding this great contribution to how we eat and live.

How We Chose and Tested the Recipes

We combed through hundreds of recipes, picking out ones that fit how we eat today (mainly from more recent years) and slotting them into chapters until we'd amassed about a thousand. (It seemed like a good round number.) Then we added in the recipes that *Sunset* readers have requested most, winnowing out those that seemed too firmly entrenched in their era to fit our mission for this book (sorry, Zucchini Grande Olé!). And then we raked the list with critical eyes: Did we have the key Western recipes? Did we have enough great weeknight choices? What about vegetarian options—were they covered? We attacked the list up, down, and sideways.

Once we'd identified the gaps, we went archive-diving to find recipes to fill them. We had to have a recipe for *pho* (Vietnamese noodle soup), and we needed a few nice big festive roasts from the grill, and where were the muffins? Muffins are to breakfast what wheels are to a car, and we had a paltry two recipes. We found most of the missing pieces by flipping through our 110 years' worth of issues. The rest we developed from scratch.

We had the list (now far too long). Our next task: to eliminate by testing. Some of these recipes were decades old, and though they sounded great, who knew how they'd be today, in a world of changed ingredients—and tastes? Would they seem fresh and exciting?

At *Sunset*, we have our own particular system, in place since the 1960s, for testing recipes. Once we've created something that seems ready for publication, we turn it over to the people we call the "retesters." The retesters are good home cooks with no formal culinary training, who come into *Sunset's* test kitchen to play the role of the *Sunset* reader. Their job is to cook the recipe exactly as it is written: no "fixing." (This is a hard impulse to resist.) Most of our retesters have worked for *Sunset* for years, and we rely on them utterly; they catch mistakes we never would have noticed, and ask questions that never would have occurred to us. Recipes are tested, then revised, and tested as many times as required (always by a different retester) until no questions remain.

The retesters tackled the mountain of recipes. We lived through months of two kitchens going full blast, of tables piled end to end with food. One particularly memorable afternoon, we faced a tidal wave of meaty food—giant tamale pie, venison with three different sauces, a roast chicken, enchiladas, a whole herb-crusted ham, and a rack of ribs, plus cocktails. It was the second tasting of the day. After, we sat slumped around the table, glassy-eyed and semi-conscious. Then a retester brought in three grilled tri-tips. We rose to duty, and then went home and collapsed.

We were surprised by what emerged from all of this testing. There was a time in our past when herbs were apparently considered super-potent and used so sparingly as to be barely detectable, at least by today's tastes (forget about chiles). We found a beef tenderloin recipe that we knew had potential, tripled the fresh herbs and garlic, and grilled it instead of roasting; it was delicious *(see page 488 for the recipe)*. Some of the recipes were startling, like a Day-Glo persimmon chiffon pie that somehow made us think of toothpaste, and a chicken, steamed in a pot, that looked like a naked baby. Others were amazing: We hit a motherlode of fabulous bread and pastry recipes from the 1960s, including Kugelhopf *(page 553)*, Quick Stollen *(page 554)*, and Make-ahead Glazed Orange Rolls *(page 540)*.

Gradually, after all our pokings and proddings, additions and subtractions, the list settled into its current form, waiting only for you to cook from it.

An Open Invitation

Hundreds of the recipes in these pages came from you, our readers, and we invite you to continue being part of this book by sending praise—which we naturally love to hear—and also criticisms to our Facebook page *(facebook.com/Sunsetmagazine)*. A book this size is bound to have mistakes and omissions, and your helpful suggestions will make future editions that much better. We truly want to know what you think, because food, like language, is a communal creation, and is richest and most alive when everyone's involved.

Margo True
Food Editor, *Sunset* magazine

how to use this book

Measure the Ingredients (Most of the Time)

Some of the most wonderful food I've ever eaten has come from cooks who stood at the stove and stirred in handfuls of this and that. Measuring cups and spoons were nowhere to be seen. However, these cooks *were* measuring—by sight and feel and experience.

The trouble arrives when you try to duplicate what an instinctive cook has done. Either you need to have learned at her elbow, by watching and tasting (the best method), or you have to rely on a record—i.e., the recipe—in which those handfuls have been set down as specific amounts. Assuming it's a well-written and tested recipe, following the measurements will summon up the original dish.

At *Sunset*, we take pains to measure precisely (unless it doesn't greatly affect the outcome, in which case we give a range or leave the amounts up to you). We have a fairly standard measuring style, but are describing it here so that you have the best chance of duplicating what we created for you in our test kitchen.

MEASURING EQUIPMENT IN GENERAL. Buy decent measuring cups and spoons from a cookware store. Cheap ones can be wildly inaccurate and will throw off your cooking.

MEASURING LIQUIDS. Use liquid measuring cups, which come in 1-, 2-, and 4-cup sizes; they're made of glass or clear plastic and have a spout. Measurement marks are on the sides, and there's plenty of space above the highest marking so that you can measure a liquid accurately without it spilling over. To measure, put the cup on a level surface, pour in the liquid, and read the marking at eye level. Standard measuring spoons are fine for small amounts of liquid.

MEASURING DRY INGREDIENTS. Use standard metal or plastic dry-measure cups, which usually come in nested sets of ¼-cup, ⅓-cup, ½-cup, and 1-cup measures, and standard measuring spoons, which usually come in sets of ¼-, ½-, and 1-teaspoon measures, plus 1 tablespoon. If a recipe includes any special measuring instructions, like "firmly packed" or "sift before measuring," be sure you do—it will make a big difference in the final volume.

A few constants in our recipes:

Flour. Gently spoon the flour into the cup, piling it high; level it off with a metal spatula or a straight-sided knife. Don't measure flour by scooping it out of the canister.

Solid shortening or lard. Pack it into the cup with a metal spatula and run the spatula through the shortening to pop any air bubbles. Pack again and level off.

Shredded cheese. Spoon it into a dry measuring cup until even with the rim—don't pack it.

MEASURING BY WEIGHT. This is by far the most accurate way to measure, but most home cooks are more comfortable measuring by volume. However, we do call for measuring whole ingredients by weight, since it's a shopping aid: there are scales in every grocery store and weight measurements on most packages. At home, to double check, it helps to weigh again (packaged-goods producers sometimes throw in extra). The best tool is a digital scale, because it's very precise and gives readouts in both ounces and grams.

Know the Ingredients

These are the pantry basics we rely on constantly in this book. Explanations of other ingredients, if they're needed, appear with the relevant recipes.

BALSAMIC VINEGAR. Certified balsamic vinegar from the Modena and Reggio Emilia regions of Italy (*aceto balsamico tradizionale*) is ambrosial stuff, made by aging the vinegar in casks of different woods for at least 12 years. However, it's not widely available and is very expensive. Decent uncertified vinegars, such as Cavalli or Elsa brands, can be found in gourmet grocery stores. When we call for "good-quality balsamic vinegar," this is what we mean. It has no additives (such as caramel coloring), a pleasingly syrupy consistency, and an acceptably rich flavor.

BROWN SUGAR. Usually we'll specify light or dark. If we don't, then either works equally well.

BUTTER. We mean salted, because that's what most people have in their refrigerators. That said, unsalted butter allows us to control exactly how much salt goes into a dish (salted butters have varying amounts). For some baked goods, we specify unsalted when a precise amount of salt is critical for the best flavor. When a recipe calls for softened butter, take it out of the fridge at least 40 minutes before using, or microwave for 5 to 10 seconds for a whole stick, less for a smaller piece. If you don't use butter often, wrap it airtight and keep it in the freezer; it keeps for up to 4 months.

CHEESE. Full-fat. We do use cheeses that are naturally lower in fat (like goat cheese, for instance), but we prefer not to use naturally high-fat cheeses, like cheddar, that are processed to reduce their fat content. Their flavor and texture suffer, and they behave differently in cooking.

CREAM. When we call for whipping cream, we mean either regular whipping cream, which is 30% to 36% milkfat, or heavy whipping cream, which is 36% milkfat or more. Both produce a thick, stable whipped cream, but heavy cream has a richer flavor and a more silken texture. If it matters which you use, we tell you in the recipe. Look for pasteurized cream, not ultra-pasteurized, which tastes cooked instead of fresh and also doesn't whip quite as well.

Half-and-half, a homogenized mixture of milk and cream, is 10% to 12% milkfat. **Sour cream** is a tangy, thick, cultured light cream with a milkfat of 18%. **Mexican cream,** called *crema*, is also a cultured product, with a gentler flavor and a pourable consistency. **Crème fraîche,** a French-style cultured cream, is silky and thick, with a delicately nutty flavor.

CREAM CHEESE. Full-fat. We don't recommend low-fat or nonfat cream cheeses. They are unlike full-fat in taste and texture, and they don't behave the same way in cooking, so using them can ruin your dish.

EGGS. Large (about 2 oz. each in the shell), unless otherwise noted.

FISH SAUCE. An essential seasoning in Southeast Asia and the Philippines, drawn from vats of whole small fish fermented in brine (ancient Romans had a similar sauce, called *garum*). There are many different styles of fish sauce, some saltier and funkier than others. We prefer the lighter, less pungent Thai fish sauce (*nam pla*) and Vietnamese fish sauce (*nuoc mam*).

FLOUR. Unbleached all-purpose, unless otherwise indicated. Buy fresh flour at least once a year, because it does get stale (you'll notice a big difference in your baked goods if you use fresh). If you'll use up a package of flour within a few months, it will be fine at room temperature in an airtight container. Otherwise, put the package in a heavy-duty resealable plastic bag and keep it in the fridge for up to six months or in the freezer for up to a year.

MILK. Whole, unless otherwise indicated.

OLIVE OIL. If we ask for extra-virgin olive oil, the highest grade, we usually mean for it to be drizzled on at the last minute rather than used for cooking, because heat breaks down the flavors of the oil. Use any olive oil as soon as you can after buying. Unlike wine, olive oil does not improve with age; most oils last not much more than a year, and only if kept in a dark place away from heat. That's why the best olive oil producers put the harvest date on their bottles, so you know exactly how old it is. Another piece of label information to look for: the seal of the California Olive Oil Council (COOC) for oils produced in the state, which means the oil has passed a rigorous tasting to qualify as extra-virgin. (Olive-oil labeling is not strictly regulated, so it's not uncommon for producers to pass off inferior stuff as extra-virgin.)

Olive oil is a lower grade and less expensive than extra-virgin. This is what we use when we want olive oil for cooking. It still flavors the food, but has no special qualities that we'll regret losing in the heat.

PEPPER. We always mean freshly ground black pepper, unless otherwise specified. The minute it's ground, black pepper begins to lose flavor, so when you buy pre-ground pepper you may very well be spending money on a little jar of dust. Better to buy peppercorns whole and put them in a sturdy, comfortable-in-the-hand grinder that produces a lot of pepper per grind, like the Peppermate *(peppermate.com)*.

SALT. Although there are all kinds of terrific gourmet salts on the market, we mostly use three kinds in our cooking: table salt, kosher salt, and sea salt. (*See Shaking Out the Salts, on page 67,* for more information on types of salt, including specialty salts.)

Table salt dissolves quickly and disperses evenly because of its fine grains, and because of that is usually our choice for baking. Usually it contains iodine and ingredients that keep it from clumping.

Kosher salt has larger grains than table salt, and we like using it for savory cooking because it's easy to pinch and sprinkle. Also, it has a cleaner taste than table salt and is almost always additive- and iodine-free. By volume, it's not as salty as table salt (use 1¼ tsp. kosher for every 1 tsp. table salt). When we call for kosher salt, we mean a flake-shaped salt like Morton. Diamond Crystal brand kosher salt has pyramid-shaped hollow crystals, making it much more voluminous than other kosher salts and ideal for salt crusts (as in the salt-baked striped bass recipe on *page 310*).

Sea salt is made by evaporating ocean water. Its taste and texture vary enormously depending on the producer, the body of water, and how much of the natural minerals are left in; we've had some sea salt that's been so thoroughly purified that it might as well have been table salt, and other salts that tasted earthy or even floral.

SOUR CREAM. Full-fat. Low-fat and nonfat sour creams bear no relation in taste or texture to full-fat sour cream, and we don't recommend them in cooking.

SUGAR. White granulated, produced from either sugar beets or sugarcane, unless otherwise specified.

YEAST. Active dry yeast, sold in packets or jars. A microscopic, single-celled living organism abundant in nature, yeast is also cultivated and then dried. Each little nubbin of active dry yeast is actually thousands of desiccated yeast cells clumped together. When you mix yeast with warm water (not hot, as 140° water kills it), the cells "wake up." When you add flour, the yeast begins feeding on the sugars in the starch and multiplying, meanwhile producing the carbon dioxide gas that makes bread rise. Keep yeast in an airtight container in the fridge or freezer.

YOGURT. Plain full-fat, unless otherwise specified, and regular (unstrained) style. We often use Greek (strained) yogurt, but will specify if we do.

A Guide to Our Nutrition Footnotes

Each of our recipes comes with an analysis of its main energy-yielding components, based on USDA guidelines: fat, protein, and carbohydrates, plus a tally of its sodium, saturated fat, and cholesterol content, since these have been targeted as substances to limit. Generally, the analysis is for a single serving. If an ingredient is listed with a substitution, only the first-listed ingredient is analyzed.

Optional ingredients, and those for which no stated amount is given, aren't included in the calculations.

CALORIES. A measure of the energy that food provides. How many calories you need to maintain your current weight depends on your height, on how active you are, and on your basal metabolic rate, which is a completely individual measure of how your body burns energy. As a benchmark for the calories an average person requires per day, the USDA suggests 2,000. Many women need less, and sedentary people need quite a bit less.

CALORIES FROM FAT. The current advice from the USDA's Dietary Guidelines for Americans *(health.gov/dietaryguidelines)* is that no more than 35% of your daily calories come from fat. However, take this with a grain of salt, as it's intended to apply to all the foods that you eat over the course of a day. Don't let this dissuade you from any one individual recipe, and bear in mind that the numbers can be misleading: Take, for instance, a nice big green salad tossed with vinaigrette. Because the main ingredients are so low in calories, most of the calories will come from the vinaigrette, and the numbers will make the salad seem like a high-fat food.

PROTEIN. A chain of amino acids that are the building blocks for all sorts of functions and structures within the body. The USDA recommendation is for 50 grams per day, based on a 2,000-calorie diet. Most Americans eat far more protein than they need.

FAT. While fat can and should be part of a healthful diet, the type of fat makes a difference. Of the four main types of fat, monounsaturated and polyunsaturated—which come primarily from fish, nuts, seeds, fruits, and vegetables—promote heart health. Saturated fats, which come from animal sources, can raise "bad" (LDL) cholesterol. Trans fats, mostly coming from the hydrogenation of oils, do this too, and also lower "good" (HDL) cholesterol. Both are linked to heart disease, but trans fats are coming under particular scrutiny. For now, the official recommendation is that no more than a third of fat calories should come from saturated or trans fats.

Trans fats have only recently been added to nutrition labels by the government. We don't have enough food-source information to run the calculations on our recipes, so trans fats information isn't part of our nutritional data—yet.

CARBOHYDRATES. These are the easiest of the main energy-yielding nutrients for our bodies to break down for energy. Carbs are the only source of fiber, which helps digestion and moderates glucose levels. Whole-grain sources of carbohydrates have much higher levels of fiber and nutrients than refined sources. The USDA suggests 300 grams of carbohydrates per day, plus 25 to 30 grams of fiber.

SODIUM. A major mineral, it is essential for nerve transmission and muscle contraction. Salt (sodium chloride) is the main form of sodium in our diets, and too much of it can contribute to high blood pressure. Processed food is mainly to blame for the high-sodium diets so common today. The recommended daily maximum for sodium is 2,400 mg. (about 1 tsp. of table salt), but that recommendation is likely to be lowered in the near future to 1,500 mg.

CHOLESTEROL. A compound found in all animal products. High levels of "bad" cholesterol—low-density lipoproteins (LDL)—are linked to heart disease. The relationship between dietary cholesterol (in the foods we eat) and blood cholesterol (in our bodies) is, frankly, not totally understood. The current guideline is to consume no more than 300 mg. a day of dietary cholesterol.

A Few Words about Your Oven, Stovetop, Microwave, and Pots and Pans

No two **ovens** cook the same way. Some have heating elements on the top, some on the bottom. Some are off by 25° or more, and others are perfectly calibrated. **Stove burners** vary in their heating capacity, too. On top of this, different **pots and pans** conduct heat differently, depending on what they're made of and how they're shaped. Your kitchen and its tools are unique to you, and are part of what makes your cooking like no one else's.

What all these variables also mean is that recipe cooking times can only ever be guidelines. The most important clue to doneness, besides your own experience as a cook, is the recipe's description of what the food should look and/or feel like when it's finished.

When it comes to pots and pans, the biggest tip we can give you is that it's really worth it to buy good-quality **cookware**. It will instantly improve your cooking and is a pleasure to use. **Nonstick pans** have to be treated a little differently from not-nonstick. High heat will damage the nonstick coating, and some coatings can release harmful PFOA gases when heated too high. Never use them for broiling or in the oven—and, on the stovetop, don't heat them past medium if they're empty, or medium-high if they're filled with food (or oil, for heating). **Microwave ovens** range in power levels and options for heating. We stick to the simplest method: Microwave the food on full power, whatever that is for you, until you get the desired result.

features of this book

STORIES ABOUT FOOD. Every ingredient and every recipe comes from somewhere; no food exists alone in space. Learning even a little about your food—where and how it was grown, who grew it or came up with the recipe—increases your appreciation of it as well as your ability to assess its quality. That's why you'll find stories about key Western ingredients and dishes all through this book. Once you've read about how the navel orange transformed California *(page 669)*, for instance, or about how two states lay claim to Frito Pie *(page 127)*, you'll see that ordinary foods are often, in fact, extraordinary.

VARIATIONS. Once we've cooked a dish, even if we really enjoyed it, we often like to change it up the next time we make it, and we know a lot of you cook the same way. So, in many cases, we've suggested variations on a recipe for future meals.

INGREDIENTS AND SOURCING INFORMATION. We have a short explanation of ingredients, starting on the next page, but it's purposely confined to the essentials you'll use constantly in these recipes. Whenever a less familiar food needs defining, or is available only by mail-order or at a specialty store, we give the relevant information in the form of a tip that follows the recipe, or sometimes in a sidebar nearby for your convenience.

MAKE-AHEAD TIPS. Whenever possible, we tell you how to make all or part of a recipe ahead, so it fits your schedule.

NUTRITIONAL INFORMATION. Every recipe comes with a brief rundown of its main nutritional components, giving you information you might want if you're monitoring some aspect of your diet.

WINE-PAIRING GUIDANCE. You'll find suggestions throughout the book, as well as a wine chapter at the back *(page 726)* that answers your most common wine-drinking questions, spotlights the most popular wine types in the West, and takes you on a virtual tour of our most important wine regions.

TOPICAL RECIPE INDEXES. To help you quickly find the kinds of recipes you look for often, we've put together a few helpful indexes: Lean & Healthy Recipes *(page 748)*, Weeknight Meals (recipes you can make in 45 minutes or less, *page 745*), and Essential Western Recipes *(page 743)*. Also, we've compiled our vegan-friendly recipes into a Vegan Recipes index *(page 751)*.

HIGH-ALTITUDE BAKING TIPS. In the West, where so much of the terrain is mountainous, it is really tough to bake successfully—especially the higher up you are. Our section on *page 812* shows you how to adjust flatlander recipes so that you can produce a lovely, level cake and a crisp-crusted pie, among other things.

appetizers
& first
courses

Fresh, imaginative, and boldly flavored, these little bites and beginnings can introduce a dinner—or, in combination, be dinner itself.

Appetizers at their best make two important things happen right away: They let your guests know that they're welcome in your house and that they're going to eat well—a reassuring combination.

So we've given you a collection of appetizers that do both, with choices that suit the kind of host you happen to be. Do you like to kick back and watch a movie with friends? Try Caramelized Maui Onion Dip *(page 23)*, made not from a package of instant soup but from scratch, and so worth the extra effort; or big bowls of fresh custom-flavored popcorn (Gouda Garlic Popcorn or Indian-spiced Popcorn, *page 28*). Or do you like to offer a few elegant dishes that your guests will linger over? Fava Bean Crostini *(page 33)*, crisp-coated Baked Stuffed Olives *(page 32)*, or fresh Pacific Oysters on the Half-shell topped with icy, refreshing Grapefruit Granita *(page 47)* would do the trick. Maybe you like your evenings to have a theme? Then set out home-made Dim Sum *(page 42)* before serving a Chinese-style dinner. And if you think appetizers are much more exciting than any main course, go through the chapter, pick several recipes, and serve them as dinner.

As much as we love the richer tidbits, we know it's smart to have some starters that are low in fat and calories. So we've included several, but made sure they tasted truly wonderful and uncompromised. (To see them listed separately, turn to our Lean & Healthy index on *page 748*.)

Whatever the time of year, the occasion, or your style of throwing a party, you'll find a lot to choose from in the pages that follow.

Appetizers & First Courses

Pepita–Roasted Tomatillo Dip

For a special presentation, try serving this smooth, rich-tasting dip in a hollowed-out squash.

MAKES About 1½ cups | **TIME** 25 minutes

3 fresh tomatillos (about 6 oz. total), husks removed
½ cup pumpkin seeds *(pepitas)*
2 medium garlic cloves, peeled
2 tbsp. fresh lemon juice
⅓ cup extra-virgin olive oil
½ cup loosely packed cilantro leaves
½ tsp. salt, plus more to taste
Tortilla chips

1. Put tomatillos in a small baking pan and broil 4 to 6 in. from heat, turning once, until skins are lightly charred, 5 to 8 minutes.
2. In a small, heavy skillet over medium heat, toast pumpkin seeds until golden brown, 2 to 4 minutes.
3. In a blender, whirl tomatillos, pumpkin seeds, garlic, lemon juice, oil, cilantro, and salt until combined but still slightly chunky. Scrape into a small bowl; add more salt to taste. Serve with chips.
Make Ahead: Up to 1 day, chilled.

PER TBSP.: 36 cal., 86% (31 cal.) from fat; 0.3 g protein; 3.4 g fat (0.5 g sat.); 1.3 g carbo (0.2 g fiber); 49 mg sodium; 0 mg chol.

Hazelnut Hummus

This nutty and very regional take on hummus is from reader Juliette Mulholland of Corvallis, Oregon.

MAKES 2 cups | **TIME** 30 minutes

1 cup hazelnuts (about ¼ lb.), toasted *(see How to Toast Nuts, page 134)*, or ¼ cup hazelnut butter
1 can (14 oz.) chickpeas (garbanzos), rinsed and drained
3 tbsp. extra-virgin olive oil
1 garlic clove, chopped
1 tbsp. chopped parsley
2 tbsp. fresh lemon juice
Salt and freshly ground black pepper
1 tbsp. hazelnut oil (optional)

In a food processor, grind hazelnuts until smooth. Add chickpeas, olive oil, garlic, parsley, and lemon juice, and purée until smooth. Add water, 1 tbsp. at a time, to thin to desired consistency. Add salt and pepper to taste. Drizzle with hazelnut oil if you like.
Make Ahead: Up to 2 days, chilled.

PER TBSP.: 42 cal., 81% (34 cal.) from fat; 0.9 g protein; 3.8 g fat (0.3 g sat.); 1.9 g carbo (0.6 g fiber); 14 mg sodium; 0 mg chol.

Caramelized Maui Onion Dip

Remember packaged onion-soup-mix dip? This is like that, but infinitely better. Make the addictive stuff at least an hour ahead of time to let the flavors develop, and serve it with enough potato chips to scoop up every last bit.

MAKES 2 cups | **TIME** 30 minutes, plus 1 hour to chill

2 tbsp. olive oil
2 Maui onions (or other sweet onions; *see Maui Onions below*), halved and thinly sliced (about 5 cups)
1 cup sour cream
½ cup buttermilk
1 tsp. kosher salt

1. Heat oil in a large nonstick frying pan over medium heat. Add onions and cook, stirring occasionally, until brown, sticky, and caramelized, about 20 minutes. If the pan starts to burn, reduce heat to medium-low and add 1 tbsp. water, stirring well. Transfer onions to a small bowl and chill until cold, about 1 hour.
2. Reserve 1 tbsp. onions. In a food processor, pulse remaining onions, the sour cream, buttermilk, and salt just until combined. Transfer to a serving dish, top with reserved onions, and chill at least 1 hour.
Make Ahead: Up to 2 days, chilled.

PER 2-TBSP. SERVING: 69 cal., 62% (43 cal.) from fat; 1.5 g protein; 4.8 g fat (2.1 g sat.); 5.6 g carbo (0.8 g fiber); 94 mg sodium; 6.6 mg chol.

Maui Onions: Sweet and Juicy

Grown in rich volcanic soil on the Hawaiian island for which they're named, juicy, golden yellow Maui onions are sweeter and less pungent than regular onions because of their lower sulfur content. Maui onions, however, must be used quickly; they don't keep as well as regular onions. Stores usually label Maui onions by name.

Hot Artichoke Dip

Some recipes never go out of style. Creamy artichoke dip, hot from the oven, is always a party pleaser. Along with crusty bread, use cooked artichoke leaves.

MAKES 3 cups; 16 to 18 servings | **TIME** 1 hour

1 cup freshly grated parmesan cheese, divided
1 package (8 oz.) cream cheese, at room temperature
1 cup sour cream or mayonnaise
1 tsp. finely chopped dill
1 can (13.75 oz.) artichoke hearts, drained, or 1 package (10 oz.) frozen artichoke hearts, thawed
Toasted baguette slices

1. Set aside 1 tbsp. parmesan. In a bowl with a mixer, beat remaining parmesan, the cream cheese, sour cream, and dill until well blended and creamy. Finely chop artichoke hearts and stir in.
2. Preheat oven to 325°. Spoon mixture into a shallow 3- to 4-cup baking dish. Sprinkle with remaining 1 tbsp. parmesan. Bake, uncovered, until lightly browned and hot in center, 30 to 45 minutes.
3. Serve with baguette slices for scooping up dip.
Make Ahead: Up to 1 day, chilled. Reheat at 325°.

PER SERVING (ABOUT 2½ TBSP.) WITHOUT BREAD: 110 cal., 77% (85 cal.) from fat; 4.5 g protein; 9.4 g fat (5.1 g sat.); 2.4 g carbo; 192 mg sodium; 27 mg chol.

Avocado-Lime Dip with Vegetable Sticks

You can also serve the dip with tortilla chips, carrot sticks, or cherry tomatoes.

MAKES About 1 cup dip; 6 servings | **TIME** 30 minutes

½ lb. green beans, ends trimmed
1 firm-ripe avocado (10 oz.), pitted and peeled
½ cup plain nonfat yogurt
2 tbsp. fresh lime juice
1 tbsp. loosely packed mint leaves (optional)
1 garlic clove, peeled
½ tsp. kosher salt
1 jicama (½ lb.), peeled and cut into ½-in.-thick sticks

1. In a 2- to 3-qt. pan over high heat, bring about 1 qt. water to a boil. Add green beans and cook until tender to the bite, 3 to 6 minutes, depending on their thickness. Drain and immerse immediately in ice water until cool, about 2 minutes; drain again.
2. In a blender or food processor, combine avocado, yogurt, lime juice, mint if using, garlic, and salt; purée until very smooth.
3. Spoon dip into a bowl and serve with green beans and jicama sticks.

PER SERVING: 92 cal., 54% (50 cal.) from fat; 2.7 g protein; 5.5 g fat (0.9 g sat.); 10 g carbo (3 g fiber); 184 mg sodium; 0.4 mg chol.

Getting the Most From Your Avocado

Even in season, avocados can be pricey. Here's how to choose and prepare them to extract the most flavor possible.

1. Select an avocado that is just ripe. Squeeze it with your whole hand; it should have the same slight "give" as chilled butter. If it's squishy, the fruit is too ripe.
2. Preserve the tastiest part, the dark green layer under the skin. First, remove the pit: Cut lengthwise around the middle and twist the halves apart. Thunk a chef's knife into pit and twist it **(A)**. To get the pit off the knife, slide it against the inner rim of the kitchen sink. If you're mashing the avocado, scrape it out of its peel with a spoon. If you want perfect slices or dice, score skin down center with a paring knife and carefully pull off peel **(B)**.

A

B

Gabriel's Guacamole

At Gabriel's, in Santa Fe, New Mexico, the guacamole—made tableside in a traditional Mexican *molcajete* (stone mortar)—is seasoned according to customer preference. Here is the base recipe: Add more garlic, jalapeño, onion, salt, lime juice, and/or cilantro to your taste.

MAKES 2 cups | **TIME** 10 minutes

2 firm-ripe medium Hass avocados, pitted, peeled, and diced
¼ tsp. *each* minced garlic and jalapeño, plus more to taste
¼ cup chopped tomato
1 tsp. finely chopped onion, plus more to taste
Salt
2 tsp. *each* fresh lime juice and finely chopped cilantro, plus more to taste
Tortilla chips

In a medium bowl or a *molcajete*, coarsely mash avocados, garlic, and jalapeño with a wooden spoon or a pestle until avocados are creamy but still very chunky. Add tomato, onion, and salt to taste, and stir. Sprinkle with lime juice and cilantro, then stir and taste once more. Add more seasonings if you like. Serve with tortilla chips.

PER ¼-CUP SERVING: 75 cal., 80% (60 cal.) from fat; 1.0 g protein; 6.7 g fat (0.9 g sat.); 4.3 g carbo (3 g fiber); 17 mg sodium; 0 mg chol.

Sake-Soy Guacamole

Serve this guacamole—loosely based on a recipe from Hawaiian chef Alan Wong—with radishes and other vegetables or taro chips.

recipe pictured
on page
49

MAKES 1½ cups | **TIME** 20 minutes

2 firm-ripe medium avocados, pitted
1 serrano chile, seeds and ribs removed and finely chopped
2 tbsp. *each* fresh lime juice and minced shiso leaves (optional; *see Quick Tips below*)
1½ tbsp. *each* soy sauce and finely grated fresh ginger
1 tbsp. *each* sake and finely chopped green onion
1 tbsp. sesame seeds, toasted (*see Quick Tips below*)

Scoop avocado flesh into a medium bowl and mash with a fork (leave slightly chunky). Stir in remaining ingredients except sesame seeds. Sprinkle with seeds.
Quick Tips: Shiso is an aromatic herb; look for it at Asian markets. To toast sesame seeds, heat them in a dry pan over medium heat until golden, stirring occasionally.

PER TBSP.: 30 cal., 80% (24 cal.) from fat; 0.4 g protein; 2.7 g fat (0.4 g sat.); 1.4 g carbo (0.4 g fiber); 66 mg sodium; 0 mg chol.

Tangy Watercress Pesto

Set this out with a basket of bread and a platter of vegetables: radishes, sugar snap peas, blanched asparagus, and steamed artichokes. Add poached shrimp, hard-cooked eggs, and boiled new potatoes, and call it dinner.

MAKES About 2 cups | **TIME** 10 minutes

½ cup pine nuts, toasted (*see How to Toast Nuts, page 134*)
1 large garlic clove
4 cups loosely packed watercress sprigs
1 cup finely shredded parmesan cheese
½ cup *each* crème fraîche or sour cream and extra-virgin olive oil
¼ cup fresh lemon juice
½ tsp. salt

1. In a food processor, combine pine nuts and garlic; whirl until finely chopped.
2. Add watercress, parmesan, crème fraîche, oil, lemon juice, and salt; purée until smooth.
Make Ahead: Up to 2 days, chilled.

PER TBSP.: 69 cal., 87% (60 cal.) from fat; 1.9 g protein; 6.7 g fat (2 g sat.); 0.8 g carbo (0.3 g fiber); 89 mg sodium; 5.1 mg chol.

Roasted Green Chile Chipotle Salsa

Reader Debby Bennett of Hilo, Hawaii, got the inspiration for this recipe from a salsa she was served in Tijuana.

MAKES About 2 cups; 8 servings | **TIME** 20 minutes

1 white onion, quartered
1 poblano chile or 2 Anaheim chiles (5 oz. total)
1 lb. fresh tomatillos, husks removed
3 large garlic cloves
2 or 3 canned chipotle chiles in adobo sauce, plus 1 tbsp. sauce
¼ cup cilantro leaves
1 tbsp. fresh lime juice
Salt
Tortilla chips

1. Put onion, fresh chile, tomatillos, and garlic on a baking sheet. Broil 4 to 5 in. from heat, turning once, until blackened, 8 to 10 minutes total. Let cool.
2. Peel, stem, and seed broiled chile and cut into chunks. In a blender or food processor, purée broiled onion, chile, tomatillos, and garlic along with chipotle chiles with sauce, cilantro, and lime juice until coarsely puréed. Season to taste with salt. Serve with tortilla chips.

PER ¼-CUP SERVING: 40 cal., 16% (6.3 cal.) from fat; 1.5 g protein; 0.7 g fat (0.1 g sat.); 8.2 g carbo (1.9 g fiber); 165 mg sodium; 0 mg chol.

Smoky Salmon Chive Spread

The use of nonfat Greek yogurt evokes the silkiness of mayo without the fat. Of course, the spread is good with full-fat yogurt, too—just depends on the occasion.

MAKES 2 cups | **TIME** 15 minutes

2 cans (7.5 oz. each) salmon, preferably Alaska king or sockeye, well drained
1 container (7 oz.) nonfat Greek yogurt
2 oz. hot-smoked salmon, finely chopped
¼ cup finely chopped red onion, plus slivers for garnish
3 tbsp. chopped chives
2 tsp. Dijon mustard
½ tsp. freshly ground black pepper
Kosher salt
Seeded crisp lavash or other crackers

1. Remove bones and skin from canned salmon; break into chunks.
2. In a medium bowl, mix yogurt, hot-smoked salmon, chopped onion, chives, mustard, and pepper with a fork until well combined. Gently stir in canned salmon, season to taste with salt, and top with slivered onion. Serve with lavash.
Make Ahead: Up to 3 days, chilled (you may need to moisten with a bit more yogurt before serving).

PER 1½-TBSP. SERVING: 39 cal., 31% (12 cal.) from fat; 6.3 g protein; 1.4 g fat (0.1 g sat.); 0.9 g carbo (0.1 g fiber); 43 mg sodium; 1.5 mg chol.

Zaatar Straws

A savory Middle Eastern spice mix, *zaatar* typically includes sesame seeds, thyme, marjoram, and sumac and is often sprinkled onto pita bread spread with a thick, strained yogurt called *labneh*. Here, it is sprinkled on quick-to-make puff-pastry straws and paired with a creamy, garlicky yogurt dip.

MAKES About 20 straws | **TIME** 40 minutes

Flour for rolling pastry
½ lb. puff pastry, chilled
About 2 tbsp. extra-virgin olive oil
3 or 4 tbsp. *zaatar*, divided *(see Quick Tip, right)*
Egg wash (1 egg whisked with 2 tbsp. water)
Garlicky Yogurt Dip *(recipe follows)*

1. Preheat oven to 375°. Flour a work surface and a rolling pin. Set puff pastry on surface, sprinkle lightly with flour, and roll out into a rectangle about 8 by 12 in. and ⅛ in. thick. Arrange pastry so that it's horizontal, and trim edges even.
2. Brush pastry all over with oil. Sprinkle left half of pastry liberally with half the *zaatar* and fold right (unsprinkled) pastry half over *zaatar*, as if closing a book. Lightly sprinkle top of pastry with flour and roll back out into a rectangle almost as large as the one you began with. As before, brush pastry with oil, sprinkle half with remaining *zaatar*, and fold unsprinkled

Food-friendly Bubbles

Sparkling wine has an image problem: Its reputation for celebration overshadows the fact that it's one of the best food wines, period. Usually, after a few toasts, people abandon bubbles and move on to still wines.

Don't do it! With beautiful acidity, low alcohol levels, no heavy oak, and all that vibrant effervescence, sparkling wine—especially the West Coast's fruit-rich New World style—is more flexible with wine-challenging foods than any single still variety.

Sparklers Are Versatile
Nowhere is that more evident than across the range of appetizers and first courses that we love in the West.

With our melting pot of local products and ethnic flavors—salty, spicy, and tangy—sparklers truly shine. Their tart, yeasty bubbles are a great foil for salt, spice, and vinegar; a counterbalance to richness (cheeses, puff pastry, fried foods); and a dead-on match for smoky, toasty, and nutty dishes.

Mix and Match Styles
Adding to the fun, sparkling isn't just one style of wine. It's made in various combinations of two main grapes: Chardonnay and Pinot Noir. A *blanc de blancs* ("white of whites") is all Chardonnay; a classic brut some blend of the two; and a

blanc de noirs ("white of blacks") all or mostly Pinot. So you have a spectrum of flavors to play with, from Chardonnay's tart apple and citrus (great potential alongside Oysters on the Half-shell with Tangerine–Chile Mignonette, *page 48,* or Caramelized Maui Onion Dip, *page 23*) to Pinot's red berry, spice, and loam (try it with Chinese Pork Radicchio Wraps with Hot-Sweet Dipping Sauce, *page 44,* or earthy Mushroom Potstickers, *page 43*).

And don't confine the bubbles to this chapter. They won't let you down through soups, salads, tacos, pasta, seafood, poultry, and beyond.

half over *zaatar*. Roll puff pastry with the pin a few times to seal.

3. With a sharp knife, cut pastry lengthwise into ⅓-in.-wide strips. Twist each strip loosely a couple of times and put on an ungreased baking sheet (push ends onto sheet to keep straw from untwisting; you may need two sheets). Dab tops of strips lightly with egg wash.

4. Bake straws until medium golden brown, 12 to 15 minutes. Let cool 1 minute, then loosen gently from sheet with spatula. Serve warm or cool, with dip.

Quick Tip: *Zaatar* is available at Middle Eastern markets and gourmet grocery stores.

Make Ahead: Up to 1 day, stored airtight at room temperature.

PER STRAW WITH ABOUT 2½ TSP. DIP: 117 cal., 58% (68 cal.) from fat; 2.3 g protein; 7.5 g fat (1.7 g sat.); 10 g carbo (0.3 g fiber); 88 mg sodium; 12 mg chol.

Garlicky Yogurt Dip: Mince 4 **garlic cloves**, sprinkle with ½ tsp. **kosher salt**, and mash to a paste against a cutting board with flat side of a large chef's knife. In a serving bowl, mix garlic mash with 1 cup **thick Greek-style yogurt** or *labneh* and stir in 1 tbsp. finely chopped **flat-leaf parsley**. Makes 1 cup.

Salt-and-Pepper Crackers

Why bake your own crackers? One reason might be to blow the socks off your guests. Another would be to find out what a fresh-baked cracker tastes like: flavorful and floury, with bright sparks of salt and flecks of fresh black pepper throughout.

MAKES 4 dozen crackers (2 in. each) | **TIME** 50 minutes

2 cups flour, plus more for rolling
1 tbsp. sugar
1 tbsp. salt, plus more for sprinkling
⅛ tsp. freshly ground black pepper, plus more
    for sprinkling
2 tbsp. butter, chilled and cut into small pieces
⅔ cup milk

1. Preheat oven to 425°. In a large bowl, combine flour, sugar, salt, and pepper. Add butter and rub with fingers to work it into flour mixture until no discernible pieces remain. Stir in milk. (Or you can pulse flour, sugar, salt, and pepper in a food processor to combine, add butter, pulse until no discernible pieces remain, and whirl in milk.) Turn mixture out onto a floured work surface and knead; form into a ball.

2. Divide dough ball in half. Working with one half at a time, pat each into a rectangle on a sheet of parchment paper. With a lightly floured rolling pin, roll rectangles paper-thin and transfer each, on its piece of parchment, to its own baking sheet. Sprinkle with salt and pepper. Cut lightly (not necessarily all the way through) into 2-in. squares. (Cut off uneven sides or simply have some uneven crackers.)

3. Bake 10 minutes. Switch position of sheets and continue baking until dough is starting to brown but is still mostly white or golden, about 5 minutes. Let cool on pans. Break into crackers.

Make Ahead: Up to 2 days, stored airtight at room temperature.

PER CRACKER: 27 cal., 20% (5.4 cal.) from fat; 0.7 g protein; 0.6 g fat (0.4 g sat.); 4.6 g carbo (0.1 g fiber); 152 mg sodium; 1.8 mg chol.

Savory Spiced Shortbreads

These buttery, curry-flavored shortbreads are perfect with cocktails—particularly those made with whiskey, bourbon, or rye.

MAKES 3 dozen crackers | **TIME** 30 minutes, plus 1 hour to chill

¾ cup butter, at room temperature
2 tbsp. sugar
1 tsp. *each* salt and curry powder
½ tsp. *each* ground cumin and freshly ground black
    pepper
¼ tsp. *each* turmeric and cayenne
1¼ cups flour, plus more for rolling

1. In a large bowl with a mixer (or in bowl of a stand mixer fitted with a paddle attachment), beat butter and sugar until light and fluffy. Add salt, curry powder, cumin, black pepper, turmeric, and cayenne. Beat until well combined. Scrape down mixer and sides of bowl. Beat in flour until well combined.

2. Turn dough out onto a large piece of waxed paper on a work surface. Roll dough into a 2-in.-thick log about 12 in. long. Wrap in waxed paper and chill until firm, at least 1 hour.

3. Preheat oven to 325°. Cut chilled dough into ¼-in.-thick slices. Lay slices at least ½ in. apart on ungreased baking sheets. Bake until set but not brown, about 12 minutes. Cool on wire racks.

Make Ahead: Dough, up to 2 days, chilled; baked crackers up to 2 months, stored airtight at room temperature.

PER SHORTBREAD: 53 cal., 66% (35 cal.) from fat; 0.5 g protein; 3.9 g fat (2.4 g sat.); 4.1 g carbo (0.1 g fiber); 104 mg sodium; 10 mg chol.

Red Onion and Gorgonzola Flatbreads

Because it's easy to work with, this semolina flatbread from reader Erin Burke is a great way to try your hand at yeasted dough.

MAKES 32 small flatbreads | **TIME** 1 hour, plus 1 hour to rise

1 package (2¼ tsp.) active dry yeast
2 cups all-purpose flour, plus more for rolling
1 cup semolina flour, plus more for sprinkling
¼ cup olive oil, divided
2 tsp. salt, divided
1 red onion
1 tbsp. fresh rosemary leaves, minced
2 tbsp. balsamic vinegar
½ tsp. red chile flakes
¼ lb. gorgonzola or other blue cheese, crumbled

1. In a large bowl, dissolve yeast in 1 cup warm water (100° to 110°). Let stand until foamy, about 5 minutes. Stir in flours, 2 tbsp. oil, and 1 tsp. salt. (Dough will be stiff.) Cover bowl with plastic wrap and let stand in a warm place (about 80°) to rise until one and a half times its original volume, about 1 hour.
2. Meanwhile, halve onion lengthwise, peel, and thinly slice. In a bowl, combine onion and rosemary with remaining 2 tbsp. oil, the vinegar, remaining 1 tsp. salt, and the chile flakes. Cover and set aside.
3. Preheat oven to 450°. Lightly sprinkle two baking sheets with semolina. Turn risen dough out onto a lightly floured work surface. Knead dough just until it feels smooth, about 10 times. Divide into 32 balls. Set 16 balls aside and cover with plastic wrap. With a lightly floured rolling pin, roll out the others as thinly as possible. Put 8 rounds on each baking sheet. Top each with a scant 1 tbsp. onion mixture and 1½ tsp. blue cheese. Bake until browned and sizzling, about 15 minutes. Repeat with remaining dough balls, onion mixture, and cheese. Serve hot or warm.
Make Ahead: Dough rounds may be rolled out (step 3) and chilled on baking sheets, up to 1 day, or frozen up to 2 weeks. Bring dough to room temperature before proceeding. Toppings may be made 1 day ahead.

PER FLATBREAD: 80 cal., 34% (27 cal.) from fat; 2.4 g protein; 3 g fat (1 g sat.); 11 g carbo (0.5 g fiber); 195 mg sodium; 3.1 mg chol.

Gouda Garlic Popcorn

Why pay a premium for flavored popcorn when making it yourself is so simple? See below for an Indian-spiced variation.

SERVES 6 | **TIME** 10 minutes

1 tbsp. vegetable oil
½ cup popcorn kernels
2 cups finely shredded smoked gouda cheese
Garlic salt

1. Coat bottom of a wide, lidded pot with oil. Add popcorn kernels and set pot, covered, over high heat. Pop corn, shaking pot often. Remove from heat.
2. Sprinkle popcorn (still in pot) with gouda and garlic salt to taste, tossing well.

PER SERVING: 211 cal., 56% (119 cal.) from fat; 11 g protein; 13 g fat (6.9 g sat.); 12 g carbo (2.3 g fiber); 310 mg sodium; 43 mg chol.

Indian-spiced Popcorn: Pop corn as directed in Gouda Garlic Popcorn. Transfer to a large bowl. In same pot, melt ¼ cup **butter**; add 1 tsp. **garam masala** and a little **cayenne** and **turmeric**. Drizzle over popcorn. Sprinkle with salt to taste.

PER SERVING: 145 cal., 65% (94 cal.) from fat; 1.8 g protein; 11 g fat (5.1 g sat.); 11 g carbo (2.4 g fiber); 55 mg sodium; 20 mg chol.

Hasty Hots

This very easy snack has been a *Sunset* reader favorite for decades.

SERVES 12 | **TIME** 15 minutes

1 slender baguette (½ lb.), cut in half crosswise
½ cup *each* diagonally sliced green onions, mayonnaise, and grated or finely shredded parmesan cheese

1. Preheat broiler. Slice each baguette half lengthwise and put, cut side up, on a 12- by 15-in. baking sheet. Broil about 3 in. from heat until toasted, 2 to 3 minutes.
2. Meanwhile, mix green onions, mayonnaise, and parmesan. Spread mixture on bread.
3. Return to broiler and broil until lightly browned, about 1½ minutes. Let cool about 2 minutes to crisp. Cut each piece into thirds.

PER SERVING: 142 cal., 57% (81 cal.) from fat; 4.4 g protein; 9 g fat (1.9 g sat.); 11 g carbo (0.6 g fiber); 259 mg sodium; 6.8 mg chol.

Sicilian Bruschetta

Caponata, a sweet, tangy Sicilian eggplant-pepper relish, becomes downright addictive spooned over toasts with mild, creamy ricotta cheese.

MAKES 5 cups; 12 servings, plus leftovers
TIME 50 minutes

1 loaf (1 lb.) crusty Italian bread such as ciabatta, cut into ⅓-in.-thick slices
About 6 tbsp. olive oil, divided
1 large eggplant, cut into ½-in. dice (about 4 cups)
2 tbsp. minced garlic
1 cup *each* chopped celery, red bell pepper, and green olives
¼ cup *each* red wine vinegar and tomato paste
½ cup raisins
½ cup pine nuts, toasted (*see How to Toast Nuts, page 134*)
2 tsp. *each* kosher salt and sugar
¼ cup *each* chopped basil, oregano, and flat-leaf parsley leaves
1 cup ricotta cheese

1. Preheat oven to 350°. Lay bread on a baking sheet and brush with about 2 tbsp. oil. Bake until toasted and light golden brown, about 5 minutes. Set aside.
2. Heat 2 tbsp. oil in a large nonstick frying pan over medium-high heat. Cook eggplant, stirring often, until softened and starting to brown, about 8 minutes. Transfer to a bowl and set aside.
3. In same pan, cook garlic in remaining 2 tbsp. oil, stirring, until fragrant, about 1 minute. Add celery, bell pepper, and olives, stirring to combine, and cook until softened, 5 to 8 minutes. Stir in ¼ cup water, the vinegar, tomato paste, raisins, and pine nuts and cook until heated through. Stir in reserved eggplant and the salt and sugar, then mix in herbs.
4. Serve caponata with ricotta on the toasted bread.
Make Ahead: Caponata and toasts up to 2 days; chill caponata and store toasts in a resealable plastic bag at room temperature.

PER SERVING: 275 cal., 59% (162 cal.) from fat; 8.2 g protein; 18 g fat (3.2 g sat.); 29 g carbo (2.8 g fiber); 715 mg sodium; 10 mg chol.

Caramelized Pear and Sage Crostini

Sweet pears and sharp blue cheese create an exciting yet homey appetizer. Serve with a Pear Sidecar *(page 80)*, sparkling wine, or a slightly sweet white wine.

MAKES 16 crostini | **TIME** 30 minutes

¼ cup butter, divided
3 ripe Bartlett pears, cored, peeled, and chopped
½ tsp. salt
½ white or whole-wheat baguette
6 sage leaves, chopped
¼ cup crumbled mild blue cheese
¼ tsp. freshly ground black pepper

1. Preheat oven to 375°. Melt 3 tbsp. butter in a large frying pan over medium heat. Add pears and salt. Cook, stirring occasionally, until pears are soft, about 10 minutes.
2. Meanwhile, cut baguette into 16 slices (¼ in. thick). Spread slices with remaining 1 tbsp. butter and arrange on a baking sheet in a single layer. Bake slices until well toasted, 10 to 15 minutes.
3. When pears are soft, stir in sage and remove from heat. Top toasted baguette slices with pear mixture and blue cheese. Sprinkle with pepper. Serve warm.
Make Ahead: Can toast baguette slices up to 1 day ahead; store in a resealable plastic bag at room temperature.

PER CROSTINO: 90 cal., 40% (36 cal.) from fat; 1.8 g protein; 4 g fat (2.3 g sat.); 12 g carbo (1.1 g fiber); 217 mg sodium; 9.3 mg chol.

Chile-Cheese Fondue

If you use an electric fondue pot, turn the heat to medium while you're mixing and melting fondue, then turn to the lowest setting while serving.

SERVES 8 | **TIME** 25 minutes

1 to 1¼ cups milk
½ lb. *each* jack or pepper jack cheese and sharp cheddar cheese, shredded
2 tbsp. cornstarch
1 tsp. crushed cumin seeds
1 can (4 oz.) diced green chiles, drained
1 baguette (½ lb.), cut into ¾-in. cubes, and/or tortilla chips

1. In a 1½- to 2-qt. fondue pan (flameproof ceramic or porcelain-glazed cast iron) or heavy-bottomed pot over medium heat, warm 1 cup of milk until bubbles form and slowly rise to surface, about 5 minutes.
2. In a bowl, mix cheeses, cornstarch, and crushed cumin. Add cheese mixture, a handful at a time, to hot milk, stirring until fondue is smoothly melted and beginning to bubble. Stir in green chiles.
3. Set pan over an ignited alcohol or canned solid-fuel flame (if pan is ceramic, put a heat diffuser between it and heat source). Adjust heat so fondue bubbles very slowly. Check occasionally to be sure fondue is not scorching on bottom.
4. If eating with bread cubes, spear them with fondue forks or thin skewers and twirl in sauce. If fondue gets too thick, stir in more heated milk, a few tbsp. at a time.

PER SERVING: 347 cal., 54% (188 cal.) from fat; 17 g protein; 21 g fat (13 g sat.); 21 g carbo (1 g fiber); 605 mg sodium; 64 mg chol.

Morel Mushrooms

Morel mushrooms are in season in the spring and early summer in the Northwest, and have distinctive conical, honeycombed caps. The earthy, somewhat smoky flavor of fresh morels is unparalleled, but they're just as good dried, too.

Be sure to clean morels well before using, since they can be sandy. Here's how: Swish fresh morels around in a bowl of water and let them soak for 15 minutes. Lift out, leaving the grit behind. Change the water, swish around again, lift out, and pat dry. Dried morels can be rinsed and then reconstituted by soaking in hot water for 30 minutes. Lift the morels out and use the flavorful liquid in cooking if you like (pour it out carefully so that you leave the grit behind in the bowl).

Morel Mushroom and Oloroso Sherry Gratin

This rich dish is served at the bar at Eva Restaurant, in Seattle, when morels are in season—or whenever chef Amy McCray is in the mood for morels. It is presented in a small *cazuela* (a Spanish earthenware casserole); we increased the portion to make a generous appetizer for four. Chef McCray's husband and Eva's wine director, James Hondros, suggests sipping the same sherry you use to prepare the gratin or a Spanish Rioja.

SERVES 4 | **TIME** About 45 minutes

½ lb. fresh morel or cremini mushrooms (*see Quick Tips below*)
3 tbsp. butter
⅓ cup minced shallots (about 2 oz.)
2 tbsp. minced garlic
½ cup oloroso sherry (*see Quick Tips below*)
1 cup whipping cream
1 cup finely shredded (about 2 oz.) manchego cheese (*see Quick Tips below*)
½ lb. crusty artisan-style bread, sliced and toasted

1. Trim and discard discolored stem ends from morels. To clean, follow instructions in Morel Mushrooms (*left*). Cut mushrooms in half lengthwise (if using cremini mushrooms, cut into quarters).
2. In a 10- to 12-inch frying pan over medium heat, melt butter. Add shallots and garlic and cook, stirring often, until limp, about 5 minutes. Add mushrooms and cook, stirring often, until juices released by mushrooms have evaporated, 5 to 6 minutes. Add sherry and increase heat to medium-high. Boil until sherry is reduced by about half, about 3 minutes. Add cream and boil, stirring occasionally, until sauce thickly coats mushrooms and is reduced by about two-thirds, 4 to 5 minutes.
3. Spoon mushroom mixture into a shallow 3- to 4-cup ceramic baking dish. Sprinkle top evenly with manchego cheese. Broil 4 to 6 in. from heat until cheese is melted and bubbling, about 2 minutes. Serve with toasted bread slices.
Quick Tips: If you can't find morels, cremini mushrooms will make a different but delicious dish. Oloroso is an aromatic, nutty sherry made in both dry and sweet styles. If you can't find manchego cheese, use another sharp-flavored, aged white cheese, such as dry jack.

PER SERVING: 511 cal., 60% (306 cal.) from fat; 12 g protein; 34 g fat (21 g sat.); 40 g carbo (2.7 g fiber); 532 mg sodium; 105 mg chol.

Baked Dates in Cheddar-Rosemary Pastry

Sweet and savory, crisp and chewy, the small bites from reader Yoshie Wong of Steilacoom, Washington, set the stage for the rest of the meal. Cut leftover pastry into strips or squares and bake alongside the dates; they make delicious crackers.

MAKES 48 hors d'oeuvres | **TIME** 30 minutes, plus 1 hour to chill

½ cup butter, chilled and cut into small pieces
¾ cup finely shredded sharp cheddar cheese
1 tbsp. minced rosemary leaves
1⅓ cups flour, plus more for rolling
½ tsp. salt
¼ tsp. cayenne
2 tsp. cider vinegar
48 pitted Medjool dates

1. Pulse butter, cheddar cheese, rosemary, flour, salt, and cayenne in a food processor until mixture resembles cornmeal. Add vinegar and 2 tbsp. very cold water and pulse just until mixture holds together. Lay a piece of plastic wrap on a work surface and turn dough out onto it. Form dough into a 6-in. square, cover with more plastic wrap, and chill at least 1 hour.
2. Preheat oven to 400°. Put chilled dough on a lightly floured surface and roll out into a 12-in. square with a lightly floured rolling pin. Cut square into 48 strips (1- by 3-in. each). Wrap each date with a pastry strip, then arrange on two baking sheets. Bake until pastry is light golden, about 15 minutes. Serve hot.
Make Ahead: Dough, up to 2 days, chilled.

PER HORS D'OEUVRE: 85 cal., 27% (23 cal.) from fat; 1.2 g protein; 2.5 g fat (1.6 g sat.); 15 g carbo (1.3 g fiber); 55 mg sodium; 7 mg chol.

■ Medjool Dates

FROM THE PANTRY

The biggest of all dates (up to 3 in. long), with finely wrinkled, delicate skin, Medjool dates are chewy-tender and dense. They're available at most grocery stores, as well as at health food stores and Middle Eastern markets—and at farmers' markets in California and Arizona, where they are grown. For more on Western-grown dates, *see page 690*.

Caramelized Onion-Apple Bites

These savory hors d'oeuvres, from reader Allison Rose of Seattle, can be assembled in advance—ideal for relaxed entertaining.

MAKES 32 triangles | **TIME** 1½ hours

3 tbsp. unsalted butter
1 lb. yellow onions, thinly sliced
½ tsp. salt, plus more to taste
2 Granny Smith or other tart apples, peeled, cored, and thinly sliced
¼ tsp. freshly ground black pepper
1 sheet frozen puff pastry, defrosted just before use
3 oz. fontina cheese, shredded
1 tbsp. minced thyme leaves

1. Melt butter in a large frying pan over medium-high heat. Add onions and salt. Cook, stirring occasionally, until onions are soft, about 5 minutes. Add apples and stir to coat. Reduce heat to medium and cook, stirring often, until onions are medium brown, about 30 minutes. Stir in pepper and salt to taste. Set aside and let cool, about 10 minutes.
2. Preheat oven to 375°. Unwrap puff pastry sheet. Cut sheet into 16 squares, then halve those squares diagonally to make 32 triangles. Arrange them, not touching, on a baking sheet. Place a spoonful of cooled onion-apple mixture on each triangle. Top with a sprinkle of fontina cheese and thyme.
3. Bake until puffed and golden, 15 to 20 minutes. Serve hot.
Make Ahead: Topping (through step 1), up to 2 days ahead, chilled. Triangles can be prepared through step 2 the morning of a party, covered, and chilled; pop into the oven when guests arrive. Triangles can also be frozen, wrapped well, up to 3 months (do not defrost before baking).

PER TRIANGLE: 72 cal., 60% (43 cal.) from fat; 1.4 g protein; 4.8 g fat (1.6 g sat.); 5.9 g carbo (0.5 g fiber); 77 mg sodium; 6 mg chol.

Baked Stuffed Olives

Olives are filled with a rich and savory pork mixture, coated in bread crumbs, and baked to a salty crispness. They're inspired by the fabulous stuffed olives of Ascoli, a city in the Le Marche region of Italy.

MAKES 48 olives | **TIME** 1¾ hours

48 very large pitted green olives, preferably Ascoli (*see Quick Tips, right*)
4 garlic cloves
¼ cup flat-leaf parsley leaves
¼ lb. ground pork (*see Quick Tips, right*)
1 tsp. *each* salt and freshly ground black pepper, divided
½ cup *each* finely shredded parmesan cheese and flour
¼ tsp. cayenne
2 eggs
2 cups fine dried bread crumbs or panko (Japanese-style bread crumbs)

1. Drain olives in a colander, then in a single layer on several layers of paper towels to further drain and dry.
2. In a food processor, pulse garlic until minced, scraping down sides as needed. Add parsley; pulse until minced, scraping down sides as needed. Add pork, ½ tsp. each salt and pepper, and the parmesan. Whirl to blend.
3. Using your fingers or a small spoon, stuff each olive with ¼ to ½ tsp. pork mixture. Re-form olive around mixture if necessary. (The breading and baking will keep them together once they're cooked.)
4. Preheat oven to 375°. In a resealable plastic bag, combine flour, remaining ½ tsp. each salt and pepper, and the cayenne. Put stuffed olives in bag and toss to coat. Remove olives and place, in a single layer, on a dry surface, shaking off excess flour.
5. In a medium bowl, beat eggs with 2 tbsp. water. Next to eggs, set a large plate or shallow bowl and fill with bread crumbs. On other side of bread crumbs, set a large baking sheet.
6. Dip floured olives, a few at a time, in egg mixture and let excess drip off; then roll olives in bread crumbs, tap off excess, and set coated olives on baking sheet. This process is easier if you keep one hand "dry" (to put floured olives in egg mixture and take coated olives out of bread crumbs) and one hand "wet" (to move olives from egg to bread crumbs).
7. Bake olives until golden and sizzling, about 20 minutes. Serve warm.
Quick Tips: Ascoli olives are available at Italian markets and some gourmet markets. If you can't find them or any other very large pitted green olive, use very large pimiento-stuffed olives and remove the pimientos. You can use ¼ lb. pork tenderloin cut into pieces in place of the ground pork. Add it to the garlic and parsley and pulse to grind it a few times before adding salt, pepper, and parmesan.
Make Ahead: Through step 6, frozen, for up to 2 months. Bake, straight from the freezer, in a 375° oven on a baking sheet until browned and hot, about 30 minutes.

PER OLIVE: 41 cal., 37% (15 cal.) from fat; 1.7 g protein; 1.7 g fat (0.5 g sat.); 4.5 g carbo (0.3 g fiber); 201 mg sodium; 11 mg chol.

Mini Pumpernickel Grilled Cheese and Pickle Sandwiches

These little sandwiches were inspired by a visit to Winchester Cheese Co., in Riverside County, California, makers of fine gouda from an old Dutch recipe.

MAKES 12 mini sandwiches | **TIME** 20 minutes

24 slices cocktail-size pumpernickel bread
¼ lb. aged gouda cheese (such as Winchester Sharp), thinly sliced
2 dill pickles, thinly sliced, or about 1 cup dill pickle slices, blotted dry with paper towels
2 oz. thinly sliced smoked ham, cut to fit on pumpernickel slices
3 tbsp. butter

1. On each of 12 slices of bread, arrange a layer of gouda slices, cover with a layer of pickle slices, and top with a slice of ham. Top ham with another slice or two of cheese and cover with a piece of bread.
2. Divide butter between two large frying pans and heat over medium heat until butter melts and foam subsides. Divide sandwiches between pans and cook, turning once, until cheese is melted and each side is crisp, about 3 minutes per side.
3. Cut sandwiches in half diagonally; serve immediately.
Make Ahead: To cook large batches for a party, assemble sandwiches through step 1 a few hours before cooking and chill on a baking sheet, wrapped in plastic wrap. Before serving, brush melted butter onto outsides of sandwiches and broil, turning once.

PER MINI SANDWICH: 103 cal., 54% (56 cal.) from fat; 4.6 g protein; 6.2 g fat (3.6 g sat.); 7.4 g carbo (1 g fiber); 437 mg sodium; 21 mg chol.

Avocados with Warm Bacon Parsley Vinaigrette

Crunchy bacon brings out the smokiness of a good Hass avocado, and the sharp vinaigrette helps cut its richness.

recipe pictured on page 50

SERVES 4 as a first course | **TIME** 20 minutes

⅓ lb. thin-sliced bacon
2 firm-ripe avocados, pitted, peeled, and each cut into
    4 to 6 wedges
3 garlic cloves, minced
2 tbsp. fresh lemon juice
1 tsp. sugar
Kosher salt and freshly ground black pepper
2 tbsp. chopped flat-leaf parsley

1. Cook bacon in a large frying pan over medium-low heat until crisp. Drain on paper towels; let cool. Remove pan from heat and discard all but 2 tbsp. bacon fat. Divide avocado wedges among plates.
2. Heat reserved bacon fat over medium heat. Add garlic, ¼ cup water (carefully, because it will sputter a little), the lemon juice, and sugar and simmer 1 minute, stirring. Season with salt and pepper. Stir in parsley and crumble in bacon. Immediately pour over avocado wedges and serve.

PER SERVING: 270 cal., 83% (225 cal.) from fat; 5.2 g protein; 25 g fat (5.7 g sat.); 8.6 g carbo (2.5 g fiber); 211 mg sodium; 14 mg chol.

Prosciutto-wrapped Asparagus

The sauce for this recipe from reader Roxanne Chan of Albany, California, is reminiscent of deviled eggs; it makes an elegant accompaniment for the asparagus.

SERVES 4 as a first course | **TIME** 30 minutes

16 asparagus spears
¼ tsp. salt, plus more to taste
¼ cup sour cream
1 hard-cooked egg, peeled and finely chopped
1 tbsp. chopped flat-leaf parsley
2 tsp. fresh lemon juice
½ tsp. Dijon mustard
¼ tsp. finely shredded lemon zest
⅛ tsp. freshly ground black pepper
4 thin slices prosciutto

1. Snap woody ends off asparagus spears. In a large frying pan, bring ¾ cup water to boil. Add salt and trimmed asparagus, cover, and cook until asparagus is tender, about 4 minutes. Drain, pat dry, and let cool.
2. In a small bowl, combine sour cream, chopped egg, parsley, lemon juice, mustard, lemon zest, and pepper. Add salt to taste.
3. Lay 4 asparagus spears on each slice of prosciutto; roll 1 up. Repeat to form three more bundles. Serve with sauce.

PER SERVING: 88 cal., 63% (55 cal.) from fat; 6.5 g protein; 6.1 g fat (3 g sat.); 3.5 g carbo (0.6 g fiber); 336 mg sodium; 69 mg chol.

5 Easy Apps

1. Buttered Radishes
Cut a thin wedge out of each **radish** and fill the space with **unsalted butter**. Dip in **kosher salt**.

2. Fava Bean Crostini
Remove **fava** beans from pods and boil 4 minutes in salted water; drain and immediately rinse with cold water. Pierce loose shell around each cooled bean with a sharp knife or your fingernail and pop it out. Mash beans with a fork. Stir in some chopped **mint leaves**, season with salt, and spread on **toasted bread**.

3. Pancetta-Wrapped Figs
Wrap **fresh figs** in a strip of **pancetta**. Cook in a frying pan over medium heat, turning, until fat renders and pancetta crisps. (Or thread several wrapped figs onto thin metal skewers and grill.)

4. Roasted Grapes
Roast bunches of **grapes** on a baking sheet in a 350° oven, turning occasionally, until juices caramelize, 40 to 45 minutes. Serve with **baguette toasts** and a hunk of **creamy blue cheese** on the side.

5. Tuna Wasabi Crisps
Toss drained **canned tuna** with the vinaigrette of your choice; put on a **rice cracker** and dollop with store-bought **wasabi mayo**. (For the most sustainable choice, look for troll- or pole-caught tuna from U.S. waters that is also dolphin-safe. If the tuna meets these criteria, you'll see them spelled out on the can.)

■ Brussels Sprouts

FROM THE GARDEN

They look like mini-ature cabbages, and brussels sprouts are, in fact, members of the cabbage family. They're at their peak of flavor in the late fall and early winter. Farmers' markets often sell them on the stalk—a giant, odd-looking branch that looks a bit like a Christmas tree (the sprouts snap off easily). Store sprouts in the refrigerator in a paper bag for up to 3 days; if they're kept any longer, they'll develop a strong flavor.

Roasted Brussels Sprout and Prosciutto Skewers

These mini skewers, which look like little green lollipops, are low in fat and for that reason are handy to include in a party hors d'oeuvre spread. It's nice to intersperse the lean with the rich so your guests have choice. You'll need 24 decorative toothpicks.

MAKES 24 skewers | **TIME** 30 minutes

24 small brussels sprouts (¾ to 1 lb.)
1 tbsp. *each* olive oil and maple syrup
¾ tsp. salt
¼ tsp. freshly ground black pepper
¼ lb. thinly sliced prosciutto

1. Preheat oven to 450°. Line a rimmed baking pan with foil.
2. Trim brussels sprouts at base and remove any damaged or leathery outer leaves. In a large bowl, whisk oil, maple syrup, salt, and pepper to blend. Toss sprouts in oil mixture to coat well. Put sprouts in pre-pared pan in a single layer.
3. Roast, tossing every 5 minutes, until sprouts are browned but tender-crisp, 10 to 12 minutes total. Remove from oven and let cool 10 minutes.
4. Meanwhile, cut each prosciutto slice into strips about 1 in. wide. Gently wrap each roasted sprout lengthwise in a prosciutto strip. Insert a toothpick through prosciutto into the base of each sprout. Serve at room temperature.
Make Ahead: Up to 1 day ahead, make through step 3; chill. Bring to room temperature before proceeding.

PER 2-SKEWER SERVING: 47 cal., 43% (20 cal.) from fat; 3.7 g protein; 2.2 g fat (0.5 g sat.); 3.8 g carbo (1.2 g fiber); 410 mg sodium; 5 mg chol.

Baby-artichoke Antipasto

Baby artichokes grow on the same plant as large artichokes; they're just the smaller buds. Serve the artichokes and fresh mozzarella balls with garlicky aioli and crusty bread.

SERVES 8 | **TIME** 45 minutes, plus overnight to chill

2 cups reduced-sodium chicken broth
2 tsp. kosher salt, plus more to taste
3 bay leaves
16 small thyme sprigs
3 or 4 small garlic cloves, halved
1 tsp. black peppercorns
2 lemons
24 baby artichokes
½ lb. fresh mozzarella balls *(see Quick Tip below)*
2 tbsp. extra-virgin olive oil
Freshly ground black pepper
Red-pepper Pine Nut Aioli *(recipe, right)*

1. Put broth, 2 cups water, salt, bay leaves, 8 thyme sprigs, the garlic, and peppercorns in a large pot. Halve 1 lemon, squeeze juice from the halves into pot, and drop in juiced rinds.
2. Break off green outer leaves of artichokes until you reach tender yellowish inner leaves (be ruthless; you'll remove about half the leaves). Trim ½ in. from thorny tips and trim stem to about ½ in. Drop into broth mixture.
3. Bring artichokes in broth mixture almost to a boil. Reduce heat and simmer, covered, until leaves are tender when pierced with a sharp knife, 20 to 30 min-utes. Let cool to room temperature, covered; then chill artichokes in broth overnight.
4. Let artichokes come to room temperature, about 1 hour. Drain artichokes, cut them in half lengthwise, and remove cooked thyme sprigs. Divide artichokes and mozzarella balls among plates, drizzle with oil, and season with salt and pepper to taste. With a zester or a razor-sharp grater, such as a Microplane, shred about 1 tsp. zest from remaining lemon and scatter over plates along with remaining thyme sprigs. Serve with aioli.
Quick Tip: Mozzarella balls come in various sizes. Those labeled *ciliegine* (Italian for "little cherries") can be used whole; cut larger balls into chunks.
Make Ahead: Up to 3 days, through step 3, chilled.

PER 3-ARTICHOKE SERVING: 203 cal., 49% (99 cal.) from fat; 13 g protein; 11 g fat (5 g sat.); 19 g carbo (9.3 g fiber); 960 mg sodium; 25 mg chol.

Red-pepper Pine Nut Aioli

Nutty, rich, and garlicky, this makes a great dip for any vegetable antipasto. It's good on a pork or roast beef sandwich too.

MAKES 1½ cups | **TIME** 15 minutes

½ cup chopped roasted red peppers
¼ cup pine nuts, toasted (*see How to Toast Nuts, page 134*)
2 garlic cloves, minced
1 tsp. kosher salt
1 egg (*see Quick Tip below*)
2 tsp. fresh lemon juice
½ cup *each* canola oil and mild olive oil

1. Purée red peppers and pine nuts in a food processor until smooth. Scrape into a medium bowl and set aside. Mash garlic with salt to a paste and add to processor with egg and lemon juice; purée until smooth. Drizzle in oils, drop by drop at first and then in a slow stream once mixture has begun to emulsify. Purée until mixture is thick.
2. Add to red-pepper mixture and fold in until thoroughly combined. Cover and keep chilled until ready to serve.
Quick Tip: If you're worried about eating a raw egg, don't use it. Instead, after puréeing the red peppers and pine nuts in step 1, blend in 1 cup mayonnaise and the garlic paste, then season with lemon juice.
Make Ahead: Up to 4 days, chilled.

PER 2-TBSP. SERVING: 185 cal., 97% (180 cal.) from fat; 1.2 g protein; 20 g fat (2.2 g sat.); 1.2 g carbo (0.2 g fiber); 180 mg sodium; 18 mg chol.

■ Pine Nuts

FROM THE PANTRY

Tiny, rich pine nuts—treasures embedded deep in the pine cone—come from several types of pine trees grown in various parts of the world, including the American Southwest, where the seeds have nourished the Hopi, Navajo, and other Native American peoples for thousands of years. Sometimes labeled pignoli, pinyon, or piñon, pine nuts are sold in varyint sizes; most are costly, because the trees aren't farmed—they grow only in natural stands. To find pine nuts in the shell, go to *pinenut.com*; for more on Western nuts, *see page 617.*

Marinated Artichokes

These flavorful artichokes are an ideal first course for a warm-weather menu.

SERVES 8 | **TIME** 1 hour, plus 30 minutes to cool

1 lemon
4 lbs. regular or baby artichokes, stems trimmed to about ½ in.
¼ cup extra-virgin olive oil, divided
3 garlic cloves, coarsely chopped
1 tbsp. finely shredded orange zest
½ tsp. red chile flakes
½ tsp. salt, plus more to taste
1 tsp. cracked black peppercorns
2 tbsp. *each* sherry vinegar and chopped flat-leaf parsley

1. Finely shred zest from lemon and reserve; you should have about 1 tbsp. Cut lemon in half and squeeze juice into a large bowl, discarding any seeds; fill bowl halfway with water.
2. Break off green outer leaves of artichokes until you reach tender yellowish inner leaves. Trim thorny tips and pare away fibrous green layers from bottoms and stems. Cut each artichoke into quarters lengthwise; with a spoon, scoop out and discard fuzzy centers. Cut quarters into ½-in. wedges (if using baby artichokes, leave quarters whole). As you work, drop pieces into bowl with water and lemon juice.
3. Drain artichokes. In a 10- to 12-in. nonstick frying pan over medium-high heat, heat 2 tbsp. oil, the garlic, lemon and orange zest, and chile flakes, stirring, until mixture is fragrant, about 2 minutes. Stir in artichokes, salt, and cracked pepper. Reduce heat to medium and pour in ½ cup water; cover and cook until water has been absorbed and artichokes are tender when pierced with a sharp knife, about 15 minutes.
4. Remove from heat and stir in vinegar and remaining 2 tbsp. oil. Pour into a shallow bowl; cool to room temperature. Before serving, stir in parsley and add salt to taste.
Make Ahead: Up to 2 days, chilled.

PER SERVING: 107 cal., 60% (64 cal.) from fat; 3.1 g protein; 7.1 g fat (1 g sat.); 11 g carbo (4.9 g fiber); 231 mg sodium; 0 mg chol.

Spicy Fried Chickpeas

Hot and a bit crisp, these quick little snacks are good with almost any drink. Serve them right away; time is not their friend, and they're best when still warm from the oil.

SERVES 6 | **TIME** 25 minutes

1 can (15 oz.) chickpeas (garbanzos)
Vegetable oil for frying
1 tsp. *each* kosher or fine sea salt and freshly ground
    black pepper
¼ tsp. *each* chipotle chile powder and ground coriander
⅛ tsp. cayenne

1. Drain and rinse chickpeas. Spread in a single layer on a clean kitchen towel or paper towels and pat dry.
2. In a large pot over medium-high heat, bring 2 in. oil to between 350° and 375° (use a deep-fry or candy thermometer to test temperature, or simply drop a chickpea in: When it sizzles, the oil is ready).
3. Meanwhile, in a medium bowl, combine salt, pepper, chipotle powder, coriander, and cayenne. Set aside.
4. With a large spoon or strainer, lower chickpeas into oil. They will bubble vigorously, so be careful (wearing long sleeves will help protect your arms from spatters). Cook until bubbling calms down and chickpeas are hot and crispy (test one for doneness), about 3 minutes. With a slotted spoon or strainer, transfer chickpeas to several layers of paper towels and drain 1 minute.
5. Toss chickpeas with spice mixture. Serve immediately.

PER SERVING: 88 cal., 57% (50 cal.) from fat; 2.5 g protein; 5.6 g fat (0.6 g sat.); 7.1 g carbo (2 g fiber); 403 mg sodium; 0 mg chol.

■ Dandelion Greens

FROM THE GARDEN

The dandelion greens offered in grocery stores are milder than the more minerally garden weed. Either way, look for young, tender leaves. Like other leafy greens, dandelion greens are an outstanding source of vitamins A and K. To tame the greens' natural bitterness, pair them with dried fruit, toasted nuts, and olive or nut oil.

Winter Greens Turnovers

Turnovers are a wonderful addition to your hors d'oeuvre repertoire. Filled with mellow Swiss chard, cheese, and bitter dandelion greens, these have an earthy flavor and crisp exterior.

MAKES 20 turnovers | **TIME** 1½ hours

3 tbsp. olive oil
1 medium onion, diced
3 garlic cloves, minced
1 bunch Swiss chard, ribs and stems discarded and
    leaves coarsely chopped
1 bunch dandelion greens (*see Dandelion Greens, left*),
    stems discarded and leaves chopped
½ cup shredded parmesan cheese
¼ cup whole-milk ricotta cheese
1 egg
½ tsp. *each* salt and freshly ground black pepper
½ cup butter
7 sheets thawed filo dough (12- by 17-in. each)

1. Heat a large frying pan over medium-high heat; add oil. Add onion and cook, stirring, until translucent, about 3 minutes. Add garlic and cook 2 minutes more. Add Swiss chard and dandelion greens in large handfuls and cook, stirring, until any liquid is evaporated.
2. Transfer mixture to a medium bowl and stir in parmesan, ricotta, egg, salt, and pepper.
3. Preheat oven to 350°. Melt butter in a small saucepan. Unroll filo and cover with a moist towel. Working with 1 sheet of filo at a time, arrange sheet so a short side is facing you. Cut sheet lengthwise into three even strips and brush each strip liberally with butter. Place 1 heaping tbsp. of greens at the bottom of each strip of filo, slightly off center. Fold the dough to make a triangle, then continue folding and turning (as if you were folding a flag) to make the turnover. Brush top with butter and put on an ungreased baking sheet. Repeat with remaining filo, greens, and butter.
4. Bake finished turnovers until puffed and brown, about 30 minutes. Serve hot.
Make Ahead: Through step 3, frozen for up to 2 weeks. Bake, straight from the freezer, a little longer than 30 minutes.

PER TURNOVER: 115 cal., 66% (76 cal.) from fat; 3.1 g protein; 8.4 g fat (3.9 g sat.); 7.5 g carbo (1.4 g fiber); 246 mg sodium; 26 mg chol.

Cauliflower Panko *Pakoras*

recipe pictured on page 56

This is our interpretation of the Indian fritter. Instead of frying batter-dipped cauliflower, which is the traditional way, we coat it with panko (light and crunchy Japanese-style bread crumbs), bake it, and then pair the crisp morsels with a zippy cilantro sauce.

SERVES 8 | **TIME** 30 minutes

½ cup flour
1½ cups panko, divided
½ tsp. *each* garam masala (*see Quick Tip below*), baking soda, and salt
¼ tsp. *each* ground cumin, turmeric, and cayenne
¼ tsp. freshly ground black pepper
1 tbsp. fresh lemon juice
¾ cup club soda
2 egg whites
2 bags (12 oz. each) cauliflower florets, cut into bite-size pieces
1 tbsp. vegetable oil
Cilantro Mint Dipping Sauce (*recipe follows*)

1. Preheat oven to 475°. In a large bowl, whisk together flour, ½ cup panko, the garam masala, baking soda, salt, cumin, turmeric, cayenne, and black pepper. Whisk in lemon juice and club soda. Set aside.
2. In a small bowl, use a clean whisk to beat egg whites until foamy. Whisk whites into flour mixture.
3. Using your hands or a spatula, add cauliflower to batter and combine until all florets are coated. Put remaining 1 cup panko in a medium bowl. Lift florets, one at a time, out of batter and toss to coat with panko, tapping off any excess.
4. Place florets on a large nonstick baking sheet coated with oil. Bake until browned and crispy, about 20 minutes.

Quick Tip: Find garam masala in the spice section of many supermarkets. If you cannot find it, substitute ½ tsp. of the following mixture: 1 tsp. cinnamon, ½ tsp. *each* ground cumin and freshly ground black pepper, and ¼ tsp. *each* ground cardamom, nutmeg, cloves, and cayenne.

PER SERVING WITHOUT SAUCE: 111 cal., 19% (21 cal.) from fat; 4.9 g protein; 2.3 g fat (0.2 g sat.); 18 g carbo (2.6 g fiber); 286 mg sodium; 0 mg chol.

Cilantro Mint Dipping Sauce: In a food processor, pulse 1 stemmed **serrano chile**, 2 cups **cilantro leaves**, and 12 large **mint leaves** until reduced in volume by half. Add 2 tbsp. water, 2 tbsp. **vegetable oil**, 1 tbsp. **fresh lemon juice**, and ½ tsp. **salt**. Purée until smooth, adding 1 more tbsp. water if needed. Makes ½ cup.

PER TBSP.: 33 cal., 97% (32 cal.) from fat; 0.2 g protein; 3.5 g fat (0.4 g sat.); 0.6 g carbo (0.4 g fiber); 147 mg sodium; 0 mg chol.

Filo Tomato Tart

The tart from reader Sandy McKee of Omaha, Nebraska, is stunning and simple—a winner as a party hors d'oeuvre or a picnic main course.

MAKES About 20 squares (3 in. each) | **TIME** 45 minutes

7 sheets thawed filo dough (12- by 17-in. each)
Cooking-oil spray or vegetable oil
5 tbsp. unsalted butter, melted
7 tbsp. shredded parmesan cheese, divided
1 cup *each* very thinly sliced onion and shredded mozzarella cheese
8 Roma tomatoes, cut into ⅛-in.-thick slices (*see Quick Tip below*)
1 tbsp. fresh thyme leaves
Salt and freshly ground black pepper

1. Preheat oven to 375°. Line a large baking sheet with parchment paper and spray paper with cooking-oil spray (or brush lightly with vegetable oil). Unroll filo and cover with a moist kitchen towel. Working with 1 sheet of filo at a time, lay sheet on parchment and brush lightly with a little melted butter. Sprinkle all over with 1 tbsp. parmesan. Repeat layering five more times (with filo, butter, and parmesan), pressing each sheet firmly so it sticks to sheet below. Lay the last filo sheet on top, brush with remaining melted butter, and sprinkle on remaining 1 tbsp. parmesan.
2. Scatter onion across filo, top with mozzarella, and arrange tomato slices in a single layer, overlapping slightly. Sprinkle with thyme and salt and pepper to taste.
3. Bake until filo is golden brown, 30 to 35 minutes. Cool 10 minutes, then serve.

Quick Tip: Cut the tomatoes very thin so the juice evaporates while baking, or the dough will be soggy.

PER SQUARE: 76 cal., 60% (46 cal.) from fat; 2.5 g protein; 5.1 g fat (2.9 g sat.); 5.2 g carbo (0.5 g fiber); 88 mg sodium; 14 mg chol.

Mini Corn Dogs

These are daintier, fluffier versions of the behemoths you find at state and county fairs, but they're still great with mustard and ketchup. You'll need 40 sturdy toothpicks.

MAKES 40 mini corn dogs | **TIME** 45 minutes

1 cup cornmeal
¾ cup flour
2 tbsp. plus 1 tsp. sugar
1½ tsp. kosher salt
¾ tsp. baking powder
¼ tsp. *each* baking soda and cayenne
1¼ cups buttermilk
4 cups vegetable oil
1 package (16 oz.) mini sausages

1. Combine cornmeal, flour, sugar, salt, baking powder, baking soda, and cayenne. In a medium bowl, mix buttermilk and 3 tbsp. water. Add dry ingredients to buttermilk mixture and stir (mixture will be lumpy). Let rest 10 minutes.
2. Heat oil to 375° (check with a candy or deep-fry thermometer) in a high-sided 8-qt. pot. Insert a toothpick into end of each sausage, leaving at least 1 in. of toothpick exposed. Remix batter slightly, and transfer to a small, deep container.
3. Dip each sausage into batter, holding toothpick end, then carefully drop into hot oil, frying only three at a time. Turn with a slotted spoon until golden. Transfer to a plate lined with paper towels.
Make Ahead: Fry up to 3 hours ahead, then reheat in a 400° oven until hot and starting to brown slightly. They will not be as crisp as when freshly fried.

PER MINI DOG: 106 cal., 68% (72 cal.) from fat; 2.3 g protein; 8.3 g fat (1.6 g sat.); 6.3 g carbo (0.2 g fiber); 209 mg sodium; 7.8 mg chol.

Baby Ballpark Dogs

Here's a fun twist on pigs in a blanket. Pâte à choux (the same dough used for cream puffs) is quick and easy to make, but you'll need a little practice to pipe it neatly into hot-dog bun shapes.

MAKES 15 mini hot dogs | **TIME** 1 hour

Cooking-oil spray
¼ cup butter
1 cup flour
4 eggs
1 package (12 oz.) mini cocktail franks
Yellow mustard in a squeeze bottle
½ cup finely shredded cheddar cheese
¼ cup pickle relish

1. Preheat oven to 400°. Coat two baking sheets with cooking-oil spray and line with parchment or waxed paper.
2. In a medium saucepan, melt butter over high heat, then add 1 cup water and bring to a boil. Add flour and cook, stirring vigorously with a wooden spoon, until a ball forms. Continue to cook until a film begins to form on bottom of pan, about 1 minute.
3. Transfer dough to bowl of a stand mixer fitted with a paddle attachment. On low speed, add eggs 1 at a time, incorporating each before adding the next.
4. Spoon dough into a large resealable plastic bag. Cut a corner of the bag to make a ½-in. opening. Gather bag above dough, twist, and push dough to opening. On prepared baking sheets, pipe dough into two slightly separated parallel lines, about 2 in. long (the dough lines should be same length as a mini frank and almost as thick). Then pipe a small amount of dough between the pair of lines to create an H. Place a frank between and parallel to the pair of lines, pressing down slightly. Repeat with remaining dough and franks, spacing about 2 in. apart.
5. Bake until puffed and golden brown, about 15 to 20 minutes.
6. Cool hot dogs until slightly warm, then squeeze a small ribbon of mustard onto length of each dog, top with a sprinkle of cheese, and spoon about ¼ tsp. relish onto center.
Make Ahead: Through step 4 and chill, covered, up to 1½ hours prior to baking.

PER MINI DOG: 169 cal., 64% (108 cal.) from fat; 6.3 g protein; 12 g fat (5.9 g sat.); 8.3 g carbo (0.2 g fiber); 283 mg sodium; 85 mg chol.

the Great American Cheese Revival

For most of the 20th century, industrially produced cheeses—smooth blocks (or slices) of standardized tastes and textures—dominated America's grocery store shelves. You had to really hunt to find the interesting small-scale cheeses produced at the time, like California's Vella Dry Jack, blues from Oregon's Rogue Creamery, and Washington State University Creamery's Cougar Gold. Good cheese generally meant European imported.

The West Leads the Way

In the late 1970s, an American cheese revolution began, and it started out West. Riding a swell of new interest in natural, seasonal, local food, a few cheesemakers dedicated to artisanal cheese—that is, made by hand in small batches—became stars. On her farm in Oroville, Washington, Sally Jackson produced excellent sheep's-milk cheese. Sadie Kendall crafted what were probably the first French-style surface-ripened goat cheeses in the country, in the central California town of Atascadero. And Laura Chenel, in Sonoma, north of San Francisco, began selling her fresh goat's-milk cheeses to cheese shops and restaurants in the Bay Area, including Chez Panisse. It was Chenel, in figuring out how to efficiently produce and sell cheeses year-round, who blazed a path that other artisan cheesemakers could follow. And they did, by the dozens, all over the country.

Small Cheese, Big Flavor

Their successes inspired others, and now there are more than 400 artisan cheesemakers in the United States. In the West, cheese is booming. In Washington state alone, the number of small cheesemakers doubled between 2005 and 2010. Some areas, like California's Marin and Sonoma counties, have become internationally famous for the quality of their cheeses. Cheese guilds in California, Washington, and Oregon support distinctive local products; there are cheese festivals in at least four Western states; and Western cheeses increasingly shine in competitions, even in Europe: At the 2007 World Cheese Awards in London, California's Fiscalini cheddar took the Wyke Farms Trophy, the first non-British cheese to do so, and Marin French Cheese Company's brie beat all the French bries in 2005.

We still have plenty of mass-produced cheese in the West. The difference now is that we have choices. Good cheese can come from right here at home.

Eight Favorite Western Cheesemakers

This list does not even begin to represent the range of terrific cheesemakers working in the West. We've focused on those whose cheeses are widely available across the country. Use the list as your launching pad into the world of Western cheese.

• **BEECHER'S HANDMADE CHEESE,** Seattle (*beechershandmadecheese.com*). If you visit Pike Place Market, you can watch Beecher's cheeses being made, then buy one of a dozen different kinds. Beecher's shop sells other Northwest cheeses too.

• **BELLWETHER FARMS,** Sonoma County, California (*bellwethercheese.com*). Eight individual cheeses made from sheep's and cows' milk, plus harder to find (but sensational) sheep's-milk yogurt.

• **COWGIRL CREAMERY,** Point Reyes, California (*cowgirlcreamery.com*). Cowgirl makes 10 wonderful cow's-milk cheeses. You can find them in cheese stores as well as in its own shops—which also sell artisanal cheeses from across the West and around the world—at San Francisco's Ferry Plaza Building, in Point Reyes (where visitors can also take a tour), and in Washington, D.C.

• **CYPRESS GROVE CHEVRE,** Arcata, California (*cypressgrovechevre.com*). Ten cheeses, with Humboldt Fog—one of the best-selling artisan cheeses in America—out in front.

• **FISCALINI CHEESE CO.,** Modesto, California (*fiscalinicheese.com*). Famous for its farmstead cheddars, especially an aged bandage-wrapped cheddar, and for the firm, nutty San Joaquin Gold.

• **HAYSTACK MOUNTAIN GOAT DAIRY,** Longmont, Colorado (*haystackgoatcheese.com*). Three aged raw-milk cheeses and a variety of fresh cheeses, including soft-ripened ones.

• **MARIN FRENCH CHEESE,** Petaluma, California (*marinfrenchcheese.com*). The oldest continually operating cheese-maker in America, it opened in 1865, selling fresh cheese to booming San Francisco. It has produced soft-ripened camembert- and brie-style cheeses for more than 100 years.

• **ROGUE CREAMERY,** Central Point, Oregon (*roguecreamery.com*). Not only does Rogue make six incredible blue cheeses, it sponsors all kinds of events for cheeseheads, including the annual Oregon Cheese Festival.

Chile-spiced Sweet Potato Tamales

These tamales are from Denver chef Sean Yontz.

MAKES 12 to 15 tamales | **TIME** 1½ hours, plus 1 hour to steam

¼ cup butter, at room temperature
2 tbsp. firmly packed brown sugar
1 tbsp. cinnamon
1½ lbs. orange-fleshed sweet potatoes (often labeled "yams"), halved lengthwise
¼ cup fresh lard or additional butter
1 cup chicken broth
1¼ cups masa harina *(see Quick Tips below)*
1 tbsp. baking powder
2 canned chipotle chiles in adobo sauce, minced
Salt and freshly ground black pepper
20 dried cornhusks, soaked *(see Quick Tips below)*

1. Preheat oven to 350°. In a small bowl, mix butter, brown sugar, and cinnamon. Set sweet potato halves, cut sides up, in a baking dish, and rub cut sides with butter mixture. Bake until soft when pressed, about 1 hour.
2. Scoop flesh from sweet potatoes (discard skins) into a bowl; mash with a fork until smooth.
3. In a 1- to 2-qt. pan over low heat, melt lard. Pour in broth and stir until warm. Add broth mixture to sweet potatoes; mix well. Gradually add masa harina, stirring until well blended. Stir in baking powder and chipotles and season with salt and pepper to taste.
4. Tear 3 or 4 soaked cornhusks into long, thin strips. Lay a whole soaked husk on a work surface, smooth side down, with one long edge facing you. Spoon a scant ⅓ cup filling lengthwise down center of husk. Fold bottom edge over filling and roll up tamale. Tie each end with a thin strip of husk. Repeat until all filling is used.
5. In an 8- to 10-qt. pan, set a rack at least 1 in. above 1 in. of water; bring water to a boil over high heat. Place tamales on rack, lower heat to maintain a simmer, cover, and steam until filling is firm, about 1 hour, adding boiling water to pan as needed to maintain 1-in. depth. Remove tamales and let stand at least 10 minutes before serving.
Quick Tips: Masa harina (dehydrated corn dough; also labeled masa flour, corn flour, or instant corn masa mix) and dried cornhusks are available in Mexican markets. Separate husks and discard silks; soak husks in hot water until pliable, about 20 minutes.
Make Ahead: Through step 5, up to 1 day ahead; chill. Reheat in steamer 15 to 20 minutes.

PER TAMALE: 132 cal., 47% (62 cal.) from fat; 2.2 g protein; 6.9 g fat (3.3 g sat.); 16 g carbo (1.3 g fiber); 164 mg sodium; 12 mg chol.

Green Corn Mini Tamales with Cheese and Chiles

In Mexico and the Southwest, the ripening of sweet summer corn is the signal for a special treat: green corn tamales. The tamales aren't literally green—they get that name because they cook in their own green husks. Mild and slightly sweet, the tamales taste like a delicate corn pudding. The fresh husks tend to separate into narrow, vertical sections, limiting the filling to one or two bites—just right for appetizers. Kathleen and Jeffrey Hamilton of Tucson, Arizona (who gave us this recipe), once put on a feast serving 30 dozen of these tiny things. A raisin-studded version follows.

MAKES 36 tamales | **TIME** 2 hours, 40 minutes

5 to 7 ears (4 to 5 lbs.) unhusked corn
¼ cup fresh lard *(see In Praise of Real Lard, page 649)*, melted
2 tsp. sugar
1 tbsp. salt
⅓ cup (half a 4-oz. can) canned whole green chiles cut into thin slivers
¾ cup shredded jack or pepper jack cheese

1. With a strong, sharp knife or cleaver, cut through husk, corn, and cob, removing about ¼ in. of cob on both ends of each ear. Peel off husks without tearing them. To keep moist, put in resealable plastic bags and set aside. Pull silk from corn and discard; rinse corn.
2. With a knife or a corn scraper, cut kernels from cobs to yield 4 cups loosely packed. Purée kernels in a food processor. Mix with lard, sugar, and salt. For a corn-chile-cheese filling, dice chiles and stir them and cheese into corn mixture (for a corn filling with toppings, reserve cheese and chiles to add later).
3. Lay one large husk on a work surface, with a long edge facing you. In the center of the husk, near the firmer, stem end, place 1⅓ tbsp. corn-chile mixture if using (or for corn filling with toppings, place 1 tbsp. filling on husk and add 1 tsp. cheese and 1 or 2 slivers of chile). Fold one long side of husk over to cover filling, then fold other long side over. Fold up flexible end of husk to seal in filling. (If you run out of full-length husks, you can use two smaller inner husks, overlapped.) Gently stack tamales, folded end down, in a steamer basket; support them against other tamales so ends stay shut. You can stack the steamer to capacity, but tamales should fit loosely so heat can circulate.
4. Set a rack into a 5- to 6-qt. pan, add 1 in. water to pan, and heat until rapidly boiling. Place steamer on the rack and steam until tamales in center are firm to the touch (pull one out and unwrap to test), about 1½ hours.

Add boiling water to pan as needed to maintain water level. Serve tamales hot. You can keep them warm over the hot water, covered and off the stove, for several hours if you like.

Make Ahead: Cool thoroughly, put in a single layer on baking sheets, and freeze; when frozen solid, transfer to plastic bags and freeze up to 6 months. To serve, let thaw, then steam until hot, about 15 minutes.

PER TAMALE: 43 cal., 55% (24 cal.) from fat; 1.5 g protein; 2.7 g fat (1 g sat.); 4.4 g carbo (.5 g fiber); 95 mg sodium; 3.4 mg chol.

Spiced Green Corn Mini Tamales: Replace cheese and chiles with ¾ cup **raisins** and ½ tsp. **cinnamon**.

PER TAMALE: 45 cal., 40% (18 cal.) from fat; 1 g protein; 2 g fat (0.6 g sat.); 6.9 g carbo (0.6 g fiber); 81.6 mg sodium; 1.4 mg chol.

Blue Cheese Puffs

These are incredibly easy, with big results—they're airy and only lightly cheesy. They're great with chicken salad and a California sparkling wine.

MAKES 2 dozen puffs; 8 servings | **TIME** 40 minutes, plus 15 minutes to stand

¼ cup butter
¾ cup flour
3 eggs
⅔ cup crumbled good-quality blue cheese (*see Quick Tip below*)

1. Preheat oven to 400°. Butter a 12- by 15-in. baking sheet.
2. In a 2- to 3-qt. pan over high heat, bring ¾ cup water and the butter to a full rolling boil. Remove from heat, add flour all at once, and stir until mixture is a smooth, thick paste with no lumps. Add eggs 1 at a time, stirring vigorously after each addition until dough is no longer slippery. Stir in cheese, then let stand for 15 minutes.
3. Evenly space 24 mounds of dough (about 1 rounded tbsp. each) on prepared baking sheet. Bake until puffs are dry and richly browned, about 30 minutes.
Quick Tip: Good choices include Point Reyes Farmstead Cheese Original Blue and Oregonzola and Rogue River blues from Rogue Creamery.
Make Ahead: Up to 1 day, stored airtight at room temperature, or frozen up to 2 weeks. Let baked puffs cool completely before wrapping airtight. To reheat frozen puffs, let thaw, then bake at 350° until warm, about 3 minutes.

PER 3-PUFF SERVING: 165 cal., 60% (99 cal.) from fat; 6 g protein; 11 g fat (6.5 g sat.); 9.4 g carbo; 289 mg sodium; 106 mg chol.

Deviled Eggs with Bacon

The contrast of crunchy bacon with the smooth creaminess of the egg is part of what makes the stuffed eggs from San Francisco restaurateur Pat Kuleto so very good. The miso-flavored variation is a creation of the *Sunset* test kitchen.

MAKES 12 deviled egg halves | **TIME** 30 minutes

6 eggs
2 slices bacon, coarsely chopped
¼ cup sour cream
1 tbsp. Dijon mustard
Hot sauce
Salt
Chopped flat-leaf parsley

1. Place eggs in a 3- to 4-qt. pan and add enough cold water to cover by 1 in. Bring to a simmer over high heat, then reduce heat so bubbles break surface only occasionally. Cook 15 minutes. Drain eggs, cover with cold water, and let stand until cool, about 10 minutes.
2. Meanwhile, in an 8- to 10-in. frying pan over medium-high heat, cook bacon until crisp and brown, stirring, about 3 minutes. With a slotted spoon, transfer bacon to paper towels to drain. Crumble when cool. Discard all but 1 tbsp. bacon fat from pan.
3. Peel eggs and cut in half lengthwise. Remove yolks and put in a small bowl. Mash yolks with a fork, blending in reserved 1 tbsp. bacon fat, the sour cream, and mustard. Add hot sauce and salt to taste.
4. Mound yolk mixture in egg white cavities. Sprinkle with bacon and parsley just before serving.
Make Ahead: Fill eggs up to 1 day ahead; arrange in a single layer, cover, and chill. Wrap bacon and parsley separately, chill, and garnish eggs before serving.

PER DEVILED EGG HALF: 62 cal., 69% (43 cal.) from fat; 3.6 g protein; 4.8 g fat (1.8 g sat.); 0.5 g carbo (0 g fiber); 85 mg sodium; 110 mg chol.

Miso Deviled Eggs: Hard-cook eggs as directed in step 1. Peel and cut in half lengthwise. Remove yolks and put in a small bowl. Vigorously mash yolks with 2½ tsp. **miso**, 1 tbsp. **sesame oil**, and 2 tbsp. **plain yogurt or milk**. Taste and add more miso if you like. Stir in ¼ cup thinly sliced **green onion**. Spoon mixture into whites. Sprinkle eggs with 2 tsp. **toasted sesame seeds**. Makes 12 deviled egg halves.

PER DEVILED EGG HALF: 56 cal., 66% (137 cal.) from fat; 3.5 g protein; 4.2 g fat (1.1 g sat.); 1 g carbo (0.2 g fiber); 80 mg sodium; 106 mg chol.

Dim Sum at Home

Cantonese-style dim sum—savory and sweet snacks, eaten with tea—arrived in America in the 1840s with a large wave of Chinese immigrants, seeking fortune in the California Gold Rush. San Francisco's Chinatown, the first in the country, likely opened teahouses not long after, according to Chinatown historian Shirley Fong-Torres, and from those small beginnings grew the great urban dim sum palaces we know today, where waiters push steaming carts past diners eager to snag yet another dumpling or fried tidbit. We're used to thinking of dim sum as a purely restaurant experience. But it's possible—and fun—to make some simple dumplings yourself too, and invite a few friends to help you eat (or even make) them. These can be prepared together for a meal with green tea or individually as hors d'oeuvres. Here's how to fill and shape potstickers and *shu mai*.

Potstickers

Fold the wrapper, edges dampened, up in a half-circle around the filling; pinch closed. At one end, form a ⅛-in. pleat and pinch it flat. Pleat to other end.

Shu mai

Brush edge of wrapper with egg and pull up around filling in a bowl shape; pinch pleats into place around filling and either flatten pleats or leave as is.

How to Steam Dim Sum

Measure your steamer basket and choose a pot with a diameter at least 2 in. more. To keep dumplings from sticking, cut a circle of parchment paper 1 in. smaller in diameter than the basket (so steam can flow up around the edges) and fit it in. Pour water into the pot to a depth of 1 in. and bring to a boil over high heat. Fill the basket with dim sum first, then set it in the pot. Cover and cook, adding hot water as needed.

Naked Shrimp and Chive Dumplings

These simple dumplings are just the filling, no wrapper. Serve with soy sauce, ponzu, or other dipping sauce.

MAKES 24 dumplings | **TIME** 30 minutes

½ lb. shrimp, peeled and deveined, divided
1 bunch chives, minced (about ⅓ cup)

1. In a food processor, whirl half of shrimp until not quite a smooth paste. Add remaining shrimp and pulse to chop coarsely. Pulse in chives. Divide mixture into 24 pieces. Roll each piece into a ball.
2. Place balls in stacked parchment-lined steamers (or steam in batches in one basket; *see Dim Sum at Home, left*). Steam dumplings until cooked through, about 10 minutes. Serve immediately.
Make Ahead: Through step 1 up to 8 hours ahead; chill.

PER DUMPLING: 20 cal., 15% (3 cal.) from fat; 3.9 g protein; 0.3 g fat (0.1 g sat.); 0.2 g carbo (0 g fiber); 28 mg sodium; 29 mg chol.

Pork and Shrimp Dumplings
(Shu Mai)

Shu mai typically have flattened pleats, but you can leave them unflattened if you want a star shape.

MAKES 24 dumplings | **TIME** 45 minutes

½ lb. ground pork
¼ lb. shrimp, peeled, deveined, and chopped
3 green onions, trimmed and finely chopped
2-in. piece fresh ginger, finely shredded (about 2 tbsp.)
1 tbsp. rice wine, sake, or fino sherry
1 tbsp. soy sauce
24 gyoza (potsticker) wrappers (3½ to 4 in. each)
1 egg, beaten

1. In a bowl, mix pork, shrimp, green onions, ginger, rice wine, and soy sauce.
2. On a work surface, lay out gyoza wrappers. Top each with about 1 tbsp. pork-shrimp mixture. Brush edges of wrapper with beaten egg and form dumplings (*see Dim Sum at Home, left*). Put *shu mai* in stacked parchment-lined steamers (or steam in batches in one steamer basket).
3. Steam dumplings until cooked through, about 10 minutes. Serve immediately.
Quick Tip: Gyoza wrappers (which are round, instead of square like won ton wrappers) can be found in the refrigerator section of most supermarkets.

PER DUMPLING: 49 cal., 43% (21 cal.) from fat; 2.7 g protein; 2.3 g fat (0.8 g sat.); 3.3 g carbo (0.1 g fiber); 82 mg sodium; 21 mg chol.

Mushroom Potstickers

Instead of the traditional ground pork, our potstickers are stuffed with finely chopped mushrooms, giving them a rich, earthy flavor.

MAKES 36 potstickers | **TIME** 1½ hours

1½ oz. dried mushrooms, such as maitake, wood ear, or oyster (*see Quick Tips below*)
3 to 4 tbsp. vegetable or canola oil, divided
½ lb. fresh shiitake mushrooms, stems discarded and caps finely chopped
1 tbsp. minced shallot
1 garlic clove, minced
½ tsp. salt
1 tbsp. soy sauce, or more to taste
2 tsp. Asian (toasted) sesame oil, or more to taste
1 egg, beaten
36 gyoza (potsticker) wrappers (3½ to 4 in. each; *see Quick Tips below*)

1. Put dried mushrooms in a bowl, cover with 2 cups boiling water, and let stand until tender, about 30 minutes. Drain, reserving soaking liquid; finely chop mushrooms.
2. Heat 1 tbsp. vegetable oil in a large frying pan over medium-high heat. Add shiitakes and cook, stirring occasionally, until they start to release their liquid. Add shallot, garlic, and salt. Cook, stirring, until fragrant, about 30 seconds. Add rehydrated mushrooms and ½ cup strained soaking liquid (reserve rest of liquid). Cook, stirring, until liquid has evaporated, 3 minutes.
3. Transfer mixture to a large bowl and let cool to lukewarm. Stir in soy sauce and sesame oil; add more if you like. Stir in egg.
4. On a work surface, lay down a wrapper. Put about 1 tbsp. mushroom mixture in center. Dampen edges of wrapper with water, fold in half, and seal (*see Dim Sum at Home, left*). Put dumpling on a baking sheet or dry work surface. Continue with rest of wrappers and filling.
5. In a large nonstick frying pan, heat 2 tsp. vegetable oil over medium-high heat. Place as many dumplings in pan as will fit without touching. Cook until bottoms of dumplings are brown, 2 to 3 minutes. Add ¾ cup reserved soaking liquid or water, cover, and cook until liquid is absorbed and bottoms are sizzling again, 3 to 5 minutes. Transfer to serving dish and repeat with remaining dumplings and oil. Serve hot or warm.
Quick Tips: You can find dried maitake and wood ear mushrooms in Asian markets and oyster mushrooms and gyoza wrappers in well-stocked supermarkets.

PER POTSTICKER: 35 cal., 40% (14 cal.) from fat; 0.4 g protein; 1.5 g fat (0.2 g sat.); 4.2 g carbo (0.3 g fiber); 88 mg sodium; 5.9 mg chol.

Tofu–Pine Nut Lettuce Wraps

These protein-rich wraps make a fun party appetizer or a light meal. Be sure to use extra-firm tofu.

SERVES 8 to 10 as an appetizer; 3 or 4 as a main course
TIME 20 minutes

¾ lb. extra-firm tofu
3 tbsp. unseasoned rice vinegar
2 tbsp. soy sauce
1 tbsp. sugar
2 cups coarsely chopped flat-leaf parsley
1 tbsp. vegetable oil
Salt
½ cup pine nuts, toasted (*see How to Toast Nuts, page 134*)
16 to 20 iceberg or butter lettuce leaves
¾ cup hoisin sauce

1. Rinse tofu and pat dry. Cut into ¼-in. cubes.
2. Put tofu, vinegar, soy sauce, and sugar in a 10- to 12-in. frying pan over medium-high heat and cook, stirring, until tofu is hot and liquid is absorbed, 2 to 3 minutes. Add parsley and oil; cook, stirring, just until parsley begins to wilt, about 30 seconds. Add salt to taste.
3. Just before serving (warm or cool), stir in toasted pine nuts and transfer to a bowl. Pile lettuce into a basket and spoon hoisin sauce into a small bowl. Spoon tofu mixture into lettuce leaves, add a little hoisin sauce, and wrap up to eat.

PER APPETIZER SERVING: 156 cal., 44% (68 cal.) from fat; 5.9 g protein; 7.5 g fat (1.1 g sat.); 15 g carbo (1.2 g fiber); 594 mg sodium; 0 mg chol.

■ Extra-firm Tofu

FROM THE PANTRY

Because the moisture has been pressed out of it, extra-firm tofu (also called *nigari tofu*) stands up well to stir-frying as well as to grilling and sautéing.

Chinese Pork Radicchio Wraps with Hot-Sweet Dipping Sauce

Chinese cooks are masters of savory tidbits served in lettuce cups, an idea that inspired this recipe.

SERVES 8 to 10 | **TIME** 1¼ hours, plus 1 hour to chill

1 garlic clove, peeled
½ cup plus 2 tbsp. soy sauce
½ cup vegetable oil
¼ cup sugar
¼ tsp. Chinese five-spice powder
1 pork tenderloin (1 to 1½ lbs.), fat and membrane trimmed
¼ cup prepared Chinese plum sauce
1 tbsp. prepared Chinese-style mustard
2 or 3 drops Sriracha chili sauce, or more to taste
2 heads radicchio, cores trimmed and leaves separated
3 green onions (white and pale green parts), trimmed and thinly sliced lengthwise into ribbons
1 daikon radish, ends trimmed and shredded lengthwise into ribbons; or 20 red radishes, sliced into matchsticks

1. In a food processor, blend garlic, ½ cup soy sauce, the oil, sugar, and five-spice powder. Put pork tenderloin in a shallow dish or resealable plastic bag and slowly add soy mixture. Turn pork over to coat in marinade. Cover and refrigerate at least 1 hour and as long as overnight.
2. Preheat broiler to high. Transfer pork to a roasting pan lined with foil; discard marinade. Broil 6 to 8 in. below heat until meat begins to brown on top, about 10 minutes. Turn pork over, move roasting pan to center oven rack, and reduce heat to 350°. Roast meat until an instant-read thermometer inserted in thickest part registers 150°, about 30 minutes (meat should be slightly pink; cut to check). Transfer to a cutting board, loosely cover with foil, and let rest 10 minutes.
3. Meanwhile, in a small bowl whisk together plum sauce, mustard, remaining 2 tbsp. soy sauce, and the Sriracha; transfer sauce to a serving dish.
4. To assemble wraps, slice tenderloin very thinly and arrange one slice on each radicchio leaf. Top with green onion and radish ribbons. Tuck up bottom of each leaf and fold sides inward to eat. Drizzle with or dip into sauce.

PER SERVING: 161 cal., 45% (73 cal.) from fat; 14 g protein; 8.1 g fat (1.6 g sat.); 8.7 g carbo (0.5 g fiber); 706 mg sodium; 33 mg chol.

Green Onion and Fontina *Arancini*

Italian *arancini*—balls of rice (often stuffed with meat, vegetables, and/or cheese) coated with bread crumbs and fried—make great party or snack food. No one can resist hot melted cheese.

MAKES About 25 rice balls | **TIME** 1¼ hours

Vegetable oil for frying
1 egg
4 cups (½ batch) **Parmesan Risotto** *(page 231)*, chilled until cold
2 green onions (white and pale green parts), trimmed and very thinly sliced
3 oz. fontina cheese, cut into ½-in. cubes
½ cup fine dried bread crumbs
Salt

1. Pour oil into a large, wide, heavy pot to a depth of 3 in. and heat until oil measures 350° on a deep-fry thermometer.
2. Meanwhile, in a glass measuring cup, beat egg; pour half into a large bowl (save the rest for another use). Add chilled risotto and green onions to egg in large bowl and stir until well combined.
3. With wet hands, form 2 tbsp. risotto mixture into a ball and make a well in the center with your thumb. Put a cube of fontina in well and push risotto mixture up around it to form a ball. Set ball on a baking sheet and repeat with remaining risotto mixture and fontina.
4. Put bread crumbs in a shallow dish. Roll balls in crumbs; return to baking sheet. Line another baking sheet with paper towels.
5. Fry first ball as a test: Cook, turning, until golden all over, 2 to 4 minutes. Drain on lined baking sheet and cut to see whether cheese has melted. If it hasn't, raise temperature a little or cook a little longer. Fry balls in batches of five or six, turning, until golden all over, 2 to 4 minutes per batch. Using a slotted spoon, transfer as done to lined baking sheet. Season with salt to taste and serve immediately, or keep warm in a 200° oven up to 30 minutes.
Make Ahead: Through step 3 up to 8 hours ahead; chilled.

PER RICE BALL: 41 cal., 41% (17 cal.) from fat; 1.5 g protein; 1.9 g fat (0.7 g sat.); 4.5 g carbo (0.4 g fiber); 104 mg sodium; 5.2 mg chol.

Garlic-stuffed Mushrooms

The vast amount of garlic here is tempered by being slowly cooked in cream, resulting in a rich, mild garlic stuffing.

SERVES 4 to 6 | **TIME** 1½ hours

2 garlic heads, cloves separated and peeled
1 cup heavy whipping cream
1 tsp. salt
1 cup panko *(see Panko below)* or fine dried bread crumbs
24 large button or cremini mushrooms, cleaned *(see Quick Tip below)* and stemmed
2 tsp. olive oil
¼ tsp. freshly ground black pepper

1. Preheat oven to 400°. Oil a baking sheet.
2. In a small saucepan over low heat, slowly cook garlic and cream until garlic is soft enough to mash with a spoon, 45 to 55 minutes. (Cream will be reduced and thick.) Remove from heat and mash garlic into cream with a fork, making a rough purée. Stir in salt and panko and mix thoroughly.
3. Lay mushroom caps, top sides down, on prepared baking sheet. Brush edges with oil and fill centers with garlic cream. Bake until starting to brown, about 15 minutes. Let stand 5 to 10 minutes. Lift mushrooms from any released liquid. Sprinkle with pepper.
Quick Tip: To clean mushrooms, wipe them with a dry brush and a damp paper towel. Particularly dirty specimens should be swished around in a bowl of cold water for a minute, then dried on paper towels.
Make Ahead: Garlic cream, up to 1 day, chilled. Mushrooms, stuff up to 2 hours ahead; chill. Or bake them 2 hours ahead; reheat in a 350° oven until warm, 10 to 15 minutes.

PER SERVING: 231 cal., 66% (153 cal.) from fat; 4.9 g protein; 17 g fat (9.4 g sat.); 17 g carbo (1.8 g fiber); 438 mg sodium; 54 mg chol.

■ Panko

FROM THE PANTRY

Panko are Japanese-style coarse bread crumbs, and they create an extra-crunchy, light crust on fried or baked foods. Cooks love them because they're crispier than regular bread crumbs, and they've jumped from Japanese recipes into all manner of American dishes. Find them in well-stocked supermarkets (in the Asian section or with other bread-crumb products) and in Asian grocery stores.

Heaven on a
Half-shell

Let's talk West Coast oysters: Pacifics, the most prolific, found up and down the coast; Olympias, Washington's native oyster; Kumamotos, which, like Pacifics, originated in Japan; and European flats. Washington in particular is celebrated for its oysters—two of the biggest shellfish companies in the world, Coast Seafoods and Taylor Shellfish Farms, have oyster hatcheries in the state.

Oyster Tasting

PACIFIC (*CRASSOSTREA GIGAS*)

• **Basics:** Though the large Pacific oyster, the most harvested and consumed oyster in the world, is a native of Japan, it has been harvested here since 1919. Like wine grapes, oysters have different characteristics depending on where they're grown. For example, the Pacifics from Samish Bay have wide, almost fan-shaped shells. Those from Hood Canal are smaller and straighter, with deep cups. And oysters raised in southern Puget Sound can get enormous, with an elongated shape that is greatly prized in Hong Kong and other Asian markets.

• **Availability:** Year-round. Triploid Pacifics, hatchery-bred oysters that don't reproduce, are excellent even from June through September, when other oysters are unpleasantly flabby as a result of spawning.

• **Taste:** Oysters take on the character of the waters in which they're raised, and Samish Bay oysters tend to be salty, whereas Hood Canal oysters are sweet, and oysters raised in southern Puget Sound and Willapa Bay are pleasantly redolent of algae and mud.

KUMAMOTO (*CRASSOSTREA SIKAMEA*)

• **Basics:** The medium-size Kumo, as it's called, has been cultivated in Washington since the 1940s; the oyster is more widely available here now than in Japan's Kumamoto Prefecture, for which it is named.

• **Availability:** Kumos are at their best from October through April.

• **Taste:** Sweet and buttery—this is the perfect oyster for beginners.

OLYMPIA (*OSTREA LURIDA*)

• **Basics:** The tiny Olympia is the only oyster species native to the West Coast. Overharvesting and pollution from pulp mills almost caused the Olympia to go extinct in the late

1950s, but the past 30 years have brought cleaner water and improvements in harvesting techniques, which in turn enabled the population to make a significant recovery.

• **Availability:** Olympias are best from November through April.

• **Taste:** Salty, slightly metallic.

EUROPEAN FLAT (*OSTREA EDULIS*)

• **Basics:** The European flat oyster, sometimes referred to as Belon, was introduced to Washington during the 1950s. This medium-size oyster has a rounder shell than Pacifics and Kumos.

• **Availability:** European flats are best from November through April.

• **Taste:** Sweet and metallic.

Getting Sauced

When raw oysters are really fresh, why gild the lily? Well, it's all a matter of taste, and if you are ready to move beyond bottled cocktail sauce or a squirt of fresh lemon, try any of these potions.

Asian Balsamic Sauce: Combine equal parts **balsamic vinegar** and **soy sauce**, then stir in thinly sliced **green onions**.

Gingered Vinegar Sauce: Combine 4 parts **unseasoned rice vinegar** and 1 part **Thai or Vietnamese fish sauce** (*nam pla* or *nuoc mam*), ¼ tsp. minced **fresh ginger** for each tbsp. vinegar, and enough **sugar** to mellow the mixture's sharpness.

Shallot and Black Pepper Vinaigrette: Combine 4 parts **white wine vinegar**, 2 parts water, and 1 part minced **shallots**. Add a generous grinding of **black pepper**.

Green Chile–Cucumber Salsa: Combine 6 parts finely diced **cucumber**, 2 parts **seasoned rice vinegar**, and 1 part *each* minced **cilantro** and minced **jalapeño chiles**.

Horseradish and Chive Sauce: Combine 6 to 8 parts **fresh lemon juice** and 1 part *each* **prepared horseradish** and finely chopped **chives** or the tops of **green onions**.

Lime with Red Chiles: Combine 2 parts *each* **fresh lime juice** and **Thai or Vietnamese fish sauce** (*nam pla* or *nuoc mam*), 1 part minced **fresh ginger**, and ½ tsp. **sugar** for each tbsp. lime juice. Then add **red chile flakes** to taste.

How to Shuck an Oyster

If you're just learning, take your time—don't rush it. Stay relaxed and focused, and after a few dozen you'll get the hang of it. You need a thick kitchen towel and an oyster knife, which has a special short, blunt, strong blade. You can find the knife in most cookware shops.

1. Set the oyster on a work surface (don't hold it in your hand unless you're experienced and very confident), with the curved half on the bottom, and the narrow, hinged tip pointing in your direction. Fold the towel a couple of times and use it as a pad to hold the oyster down with one hand.

2. With your other hand, insert the tip of the knife into the oyster's hinge (you may have to poke around a little to find an entry) and twist your knife firmly to pop open the shell.

3. Slide the knife beneath the oyster and cut it free from the lower shell. Be careful not to spill the juices.

If you proceed slowly and carefully—and save your cocktail for sipping after the shucking rather than during—you should be fine. (Another word of warning: People with compromised immune systems should avoid shucking and eating raw oysters.)

Buying on the Half-shell or Shucked

Most fishmongers sell oysters on the half-shell to order (ask that they keep the liquid in the shells) or shucked completely. Make sure the sell-by date on shucked oysters, which are usually sold in a jar, is current. Whether jarred or on the half-shell, oysters should be refrigerated as soon as possible and used within two days of purchase.

Oysters on the Half-shell with Grapefruit Granita

recipe pictured on page 52

In a recipe from MeMe Pederson, co-owner of the San Francisco catering company Taste, peppery, vodka-laced granita sets off the briny sweetness of West Coast oysters (*see Heaven on a Half-shell, left*). If you're offering the oysters as part of a buffet, serve them on crushed ice with the granita in a bowl alongside, also on ice.

MAKES About 2 cups granita with 3 dozen oysters
TIME 15 minutes, plus 3 hours to freeze granita

1 cup fresh grapefruit juice (from 1 or 2 large grapefruit, preferably pink)
3 tbsp. Champagne vinegar
½ tbsp. sugar dissolved in ½ tbsp. hot water
½ tbsp. vodka
½ tsp. *each* finely chopped tarragon and flat-leaf parsley
½ tsp. freshly ground black pepper
Rock salt or crushed ice
3 dozen chilled small to medium oysters on the half-shell

1. Combine all ingredients except rock salt and oysters, pour into a loaf pan (to a depth of about 1 in.), and freeze 1 hour. Rake and crush mixture with tines of a fork and freeze for another hour. Rake and crush mixture again and freeze 1 hour more.

2. Spread rock salt on a platter. Rake and crush granita a final time into fine crystals. Set oysters on rock salt and top each oyster with a spoonful of granita.

Make Ahead: Granita, up to 3 days, frozen. Re-rake with fork before serving.

PER OYSTER WITH GRANITA: 12 cal., 25% (3 cal.) from fat; 0.8 g protein; 0.3 g fat (0.1 g sat.); 1.3 g carbo (0 g fiber); 13 mg sodium; 6.2 mg chol.

Oysters on the Half-shell with Tangerine-Chile Mignonette

A mignonette sauce usually involves black pepper and shallots. We've added a sweet dimension to ours.

MAKES 8 servings | **TIME** 10 minutes

2 tsp. finely shredded tangerine zest
⅓ cup fresh tangerine juice
3 tbsp. unseasoned rice vinegar
1 red jalapeño chile, seeds and ribs removed and minced
1 tbsp. minced shallot
⅛ tsp. freshly ground black pepper
2 dozen oysters on the half-shell (see *Heaven on a Half-shell, page 46*)

1. In a small bowl, mix tangerine zest and juice, vinegar, jalapeño, shallot, and pepper.
2. Nest oysters in crushed ice on a rimmed tray. Set bowl of tangerine-chile mignonette alongside oysters on tray. To eat, spoon a little sauce onto each oyster.
Make Ahead: Mignonette, up to 3 days, chilled. Have oysters shucked at the market up to 1 day ahead; set, cup side up, on a rimmed tray; cover and chill.

PER 3-OYSTER SERVING: 36 cal., 28% (9.9 cal.) from fat; 3.1 g protein; 1.1 g fat (0.3 g sat.); 3.2 g carbo (0 g fiber); 48 mg sodium; 23 mg chol.

Thai Coconut-Chili Clams and Mussels

Chef Lisa Henderson serves this at Latitude restaurant in Vancouver, British Columbia. We lightened the broth with a white wine; if you prefer it richer, replace the wine with another can of coconut milk. (Don't double the recipe—you'll end up with too much liquid.)

SERVES 4 | **TIME** 45 minutes

1 lb. clams in shells, suitable for steaming, scrubbed
1 lb. mussels, scrubbed and debearded
2 tbsp. olive oil
½ cup minced shallots
1½ tbsp. minced fresh ginger
1 tbsp. minced garlic
1 can (13.5 oz.) coconut milk
1 cup dry white wine (see *note above*)
⅓ cup Asian sweet chili sauce (see *Quick Tip, above right*)
2 tbsp. fresh lime juice
⅓ cup slivered basil leaves
Salt
⅓ cup thinly sliced green onions
Lime wedges

1. Discard any clams and mussels that don't close when you tap their shells.
2. Pour oil into a 10- to 12-in. frying pan over medium-high heat; when hot, add shallots, ginger, and garlic and cook, stirring often, until shallots are limp, 2 to 3 minutes. Stir in coconut milk, wine, and chili sauce and bring to a boil.
3. Add clams, cover, and cook for 5 minutes. Add mussels, cover, and simmer, reducing heat if necessary, until the shells have opened, 2 to 3 minutes longer. Discard any closed clams or mussels. Gently stir in lime juice and basil; add salt to taste.
4. Sprinkle with green onions and serve with lime wedges.
Quick Tip: Asian sweet chili sauce is sometimes labeled "for chicken."

PER SERVING: 395 cal., 64% (252 cal.) from fat; 9.1 g protein; 28 g fat (19 g sat.); 19 g carbo (0.7 g fiber); 283 mg sodium; 15 mg chol.

Mussels with Corn-Tomato Salsa

Peruvian food is becoming increasingly popular on the West Coast. This is a specialty of Callao, the chief seaport of Peru, as served at Andina restaurant in Portland, Oregon.

SERVES 4 | **TIME** 30 minutes

1 cup cooked corn kernels
½ cup *each* diced onion and tomato
½ cup loosely packed cilantro leaves, plus a few for garnish
2 tbsp. fresh lime juice
1 tbsp. vegetable oil
1 tbsp. *salsa rocoto* (see *Quick Tip below*) or Sriracha chili sauce
Salt and freshly ground black pepper
30 mussels, scrubbed and debearded
1 cup white wine
1 lime, cut into wedges

1. Combine corn, onion, tomato, cilantro, lime juice, oil, and salsa rocoto. Season with salt and pepper.
2. Discard mussels that don't close when tapped. In a large pot with a tight-fitting lid over high heat, bring wine to a boil. Add mussels, then cover and cook until they open, about 3 minutes. Drain. Discard any closed mussels.
3. Shuck mussels, leaving them on the half-shell. Top each mussel with a spoonful of corn salsa. Serve warm, garnished with lime wedges and cilantro leaves.
Quick Tip: Salsa rocoto is a made from *ají rocoto*, a chile similar to a red jalapeño. Find it in Latino markets.
Make Ahead: Up to 1 day, chilled.

PER 6-MUSSEL SERVING: 102 cal., 35% (36 cal.) from fat; 5.8 g protein; 4 g fat (0.5 g sat.); 12 g carbo (1.8 g fiber); 131 mg sodium; 10 mg chol.

Sake-Soy Guacamole,
page 25

**Avocados with Warm Bacon
Parsley Vinaigrette,** *page 33*

Classic Tiki Mai Tai,
page 76

Oysters on the Half-shell
with Grapefruit Granita,
page 47

Ultimate Crabcakes,
page 62

Rangpur Lime Shooters,
page 79

Sesame Ahi Poke,
page 68

Cauliflower Panko *Pakoras,*
page 37

Fresh Bloody Mary,
page 76

Peach Martinis with Chiles
from the Garden, *page 78*

Vietnamese Shrimp Lettuce
Wraps with Spicy Lime Dipping
Sauce, *page 64*

Sunset Margaritas,
page 80

Savory Japanese Crab Custard (Crab *Chawan Mushi*)

Classically, this Japanese custard is made with clams, but here it gets a Northwest spin with Dungeness crab.

SERVES 4 as a first course | **TIME** 40 minutes

4 eggs
3 tbsp. dry sherry
2 tsp. soy sauce
1 tsp. sugar
½ tsp. salt
1⅓ cups warm prepared *dashi-no-moto* or chicken broth *(see Quick Tip below)*
6 oz. shelled cooked crab (¾ cup; *see Dungeness Crab 101, page 340)*
2 tbsp. thinly sliced green onion
1 tsp. minced fresh ginger

1. In a bowl, beat eggs to blend with sherry, soy sauce, sugar, and salt. Whisk in dashi, then stir in crab, green onion, and ginger.
2. Divide egg mixture among four custard cups or ramekins (8-oz. size). Cover cups tightly with foil.
3. Pour 1 in. water into a 5- to 6- quart pan (about 10 in. wide and 4 in. deep); set a rack in pan over water. Bring to a boil over high heat; reduce heat to a simmer and set custard cups, slightly separated, on rack. Cover pan and simmer until custards barely jiggle in the center when cups are gently shaken (lift foil to check), 8 to 10 minutes.
Quick Tip: Reconstitute dashi-no-moto as directed on package for noodle soup; cool slightly.

PER SERVING: 151 cal., 34% (52 cal.) from fat; 18 g protein; 5.8 g fat (1.6 g sat.); 2.7 g carbo (0.1 g fiber); 669 mg sodium; 255 mg. chol.

■ *Dashi-no-moto*

Dashi-no-moto (powdered soup base made from fish, mushrooms, and seaweed) is sold in Asian markets and well-stocked grocery stores. It's very handy when you don't have time to simmer up a batch of *dashi* (broth made from dried kelp and flakes of dried bonito, a type of tuna). For a recipe, *see page 95.*

Crab and Smoked Trout Cakes with Herb Salad

Try a citrusy version of Pinot Gris with this dish—the wine is like a final squeeze of lemon on the salad.

SERVES 4 | **TIME** 50 minutes

½ lb. (about 1 cup) shelled cooked Alaska king or Dungeness crab *(see Dungeness Crab 101, page 340)*
3 oz. smoked trout, skin removed and finely chopped (about ½ cup)
½ cup finely chopped green onions
2 tbsp. plus 2 tsp. fresh lemon juice, divided
2 tbsp. mayonnaise
1 tsp. whole-grain Dijon mustard
1 egg
1½ cups panko (Japanese-style bread crumbs), divided
1 tbsp. plus 2 tsp. olive oil, divided
1½ cups chervil sprigs
½ cup *each* tarragon and cilantro leaves
Salt and freshly ground black pepper

1. Pick out any shells in crab. In a bowl, combine crab, trout, green onions, 2 tbsp. lemon juice, the mayonnaise, mustard, egg, and ½ cup panko. Mix well. Form mixture into eight 2½- by ½-in. cakes. Pour remaining 1 cup panko onto a plate and coat each cake with crumbs, pressing in gently.
2. Pour 1 tbsp. oil into a large frying pan over medium-high heat. When hot, add cakes in a single layer and cook, turning once, until golden brown on both sides, about 10 minutes total.
3. In a medium bowl, mix chervil, tarragon, and cilantro. Toss with remaining 2 tsp. each lemon juice and oil; season with salt and pepper to taste. Serve trout cakes with salad.
Make Ahead: Form cakes up to 6 hours ahead and chill. Coat with panko and fry just before serving.

PER SERVING: 317 cal., 45% (144 cal.) from fat; 22 g protein; 16 g fat (2.6 g sat.); 19 g carbo (1.1 g fiber); 520 mg sodium; 119 mg chol.

FROM THE PANTRY

Ultimate Crabcakes

These crabcakes, from reader Frederick Basgal of Menlo Park, California, are the kind crab lovers dream of—crab-packed mounds bound together by a creamy purée of egg and scallops rather than bread crumbs. Basgal's inspiration for the purée came from a crabcake recipe by California chef Hubert Keller.

recipe pictured on page **53**

MAKES 6 crabcakes | **TIME** 40 minutes

¼ lb. sea scallops *(see Quick Tip below)*
2 tbsp. lightly beaten egg
3 tbsp. heavy whipping cream
1 lb. (3 cups) shelled cooked Dungeness crab *(see Dungeness Crab 101, page 340)*
2 tbsp. *each* diced (¼ in.) red and yellow bell peppers
2 tbsp. finely chopped cilantro
3 tbsp. finely chopped chives, divided
2 tsp. green hot sauce, such as Tabasco
¼ tsp. *each* salt and cayenne
2 tbsp. olive oil
Devil Sauce *(recipe follows)*

1. In a food processor, pulse scallops and egg just until scallops are chopped. With motor running, pour in cream and purée until smooth. Scrape scallop mixture into a medium bowl. Stir in crab, bell peppers, cilantro, 2 tbsp. chives, the hot sauce, salt, and cayenne, breaking up most large chunks of crab.

2. Lay an 18-in. sheet of parchment paper on a work surface. Scoop six mounds of crab mixture onto parchment. Shape each into an even cake about 1¼ in. thick, using your fingers or, for neater sides, a 2 ½-in.-diameter ring mold.

3. Pour oil into a 12-in. nonstick frying pan and heat over medium-low heat. Using a thin, flexible spatula, carefully transfer cakes to pan. Cook, turning once, until nicely browned and no longer wet in center, about 10 minutes total.

4. Place each crabcake on a warm plate, dollop with Devil Sauce (or serve it on the side), and scatter with remaining 1 tbsp. chives.

Quick Tip: Avoid scallops that have been plumped up by a dip in sodium tripolyphosphate (STP) solution, which is also used with ham. These scallops, when cooked, will ooze a copious amount of milky white liquid, preventing them from getting a nice brown crust. Scallops that haven't been treated with this solution are usually sold as "dry" scallops.

PER CRABCAKE WITHOUT SAUCE: 168 cal., 49% (83 cal.) from fat; 19 g protein; 9.2 g fat (2.6 g sat.); 1 g carbo (0.1 g fiber); 357 mg sodium; 113 mg chol.

Devil Sauce: In a small bowl, stir together ¾ cup **mayonnaise**, ½ tsp. **ground coriander**, and 1 tsp. **red hot sauce**, such as Tabasco. Taste and add more hot sauce if you like.
Make Ahead: Up to 1 week, chilled.

PER 2-TBSP. SERVING: 197 cal., 100% from fat; 0.3 g protein; 22 g fat (3.3 g sat.); 0.7 g carbo (0 g fiber); 161 mg sodium; 16 mg chol.

Sweet-Hot Coconut Shrimp

Good for parties, because you can prepare them ahead, then cook them fast. You'll need 8 to 10 wooden skewers.

SERVES 8 to 10 | **TIME** 40 minutes, plus 1 hour to marinate

1 lb. large shrimp (21 to 30 per lb.), peeled and deveined
½ cup coconut milk
Sweet-Hot Chile Sauce *(recipe follows)*
2 cups thinly sliced English cucumber

1. In a bowl, mix shrimp, coconut milk, and 2 tbsp. sweet-hot chili sauce. Cover and chill at least 1 hour or up to 1 day.

2. Thread shrimp onto 8 to 10 soaked wooden skewers *(see Quick Tip below)*. Set on a rack in a 10- by 15-in. broiler pan.

3. Broil shrimp 3 to 4 in. from heat, turning once, until shrimp are opaque but still moist-looking in center of thickest part (cut to test), 5 to 6 minutes.

4. Arrange cucumber slices on a platter. Set shrimp on top. Drizzle about 3 more tbsp. chile sauce over shrimp. Serve shrimp hot or cool, with remaining chile sauce in a small bowl on the side.

Quick Tip: Soak wooden skewers in water for 30 minutes before using.
Make Ahead: Marinate shrimp and make chile sauce up to 1 day ahead and chill. Skewer shrimp up to 6 hours ahead and chill.

PER SERVING: 83 cal., 23% (19 cal.) from fat; 9.8 g protein; 2.1 g fat (1.2 g sat.); 6 g carbo (0.3 g fiber); 108 mg sodium; 69 mg chol.

Sweet-Hot Chile Sauce: In a 1- to 2-qt. pan, mix 1 cup **unseasoned rice vinegar**, ⅔ cup **sugar**, 1 tbsp. minced **garlic**, 1¼ tsp. **red chile flakes**, and 2 tbsp. **Thai or Vietnamese fish sauce (nam pla or nuoc mam)** or ½ tsp. **salt**. Stir occasionally over high heat until mixture is reduced to about ¾ cup, 12 to 15 minutes. Let cool. Makes about ¾ cup.

PER TBSP.: 51 cal., 5% (2.7 cal.) from fat; 0.5 g protein; 0.3 g fat (0.1 g sat.); 12 g carbo (0.1 g fiber); 100 mg sodium; 0 mg chol.

Crunchy Shrimp Won Tons with Green-onion Dipping Sauce

Reader Gloria Bradley won the appetizer category of our Best of the West recipe contest with these perky-looking won tons. Be careful, though: They gush juice when you bite into them, so be sure to have napkins handy.

MAKES 24 won tons | **TIME** 45 minutes

1 cup low-sodium soy sauce, divided
⅓ cup coarsely chopped cilantro, plus leaves and tender stems from 24 sprigs
1 tbsp. finely shredded lemon zest
2 tbsp. plus 2 tsp. minced fresh ginger
2 tbsp. Asian (toasted) sesame oil, divided
24 large shrimp (21 to 30 per lb.), peeled with tails left on and deveined
Vegetable oil for frying
24 square won ton wrappers (about 3½ in. each)
¼ cup fresh orange juice
3 tbsp. fresh lemon juice
2 tbsp. orange marmalade
3 tbsp. finely chopped green onion

1. In a large bowl, whisk together ½ cup soy sauce, the chopped cilantro, lemon zest, 2 tbsp. ginger, and 1 tbsp. sesame oil.
2. Add shrimp to bowl and stir to coat. Cover with plastic wrap and marinate 15 to 20 minutes at room temperature. Drain shrimp in a colander, spread out on paper towels, and pat dry.
3. Pour vegetable oil into a deep, heavy pot to a depth of 3 in. and heat to 375° on a deep-fry thermometer. Meanwhile, spread out won ton wrappers. Working with 1 wrapper at a time, put several cilantro leaves and stems along wrapper edge nearest you. Top with a shrimp, arranging it so that the tail extends beyond the wrapper. Fold wrapper edge that is opposite the tail over shrimp. Brush far edge of wrapper with water and, starting with near edge, roll wrapper loosely around shrimp, forming a package. Press seam to firmly seal.
4. Preheat oven to 200° and put a shallow rack in a baking pan. When oil reaches 375°, fry won tons in several batches so as not to crowd them, flipping midway through cooking, until medium golden brown, 1½ to 2 minutes. Lift shrimp out with tongs, draining excess oil, and transfer to baking pan; keep shrimp warm in oven.
5. In a small bowl, whisk together remaining ½ cup soy sauce, 1 tbsp. sesame oil, and 2 tsp. ginger, and the orange and lemon juices, marmalade, and green onion. Serve won tons hot, with dipping sauce on the side.
Make Ahead: Sauce, up to 1 day, chilled.

PER WON TON: 96 cal., 51% (49 cal.) from fat; 4.4 g protein; 5.4 g fat (0.7 g sat.); 7.1 g carbo (0.2 g fiber); 370 mg sodium; 24 mg chol.

Bourbon-glazed Shrimp

This recipe, from reader Brad Hightow of Oakland, California, won Best Seafood Dish in a local barbecue contest. Hightow recommends using a high-quality bourbon. You'll need 24 skewers or toothpicks.

SERVES 8 | **TIME** 35 minutes

1 tsp. vegetable oil
1 garlic clove, minced
2 tbsp. bourbon
1 tsp. Worcestershire sauce
¼ tsp. hot sauce
3 tbsp. butter, cut into small pieces
Salt and freshly ground black pepper
24 large shrimp (21 to 30 per lb.), peeled and deveined
6 slices bacon, each cut into quarters (halved lengthwise and then crosswise)

1. In a 2-qt. pan, heat oil over medium-high heat. Add garlic and stir until golden, 1 to 2 minutes. Remove pan from heat and add bourbon, Worcestershire, and hot sauce. Light contents with a long match and let the flames burn out. Return to low heat and add butter, one piece at a time, stirring to incorporate into sauce. Add salt and pepper to taste.
2. Preheat broiler. Meanwhile, lay each shrimp on its side, place a piece of bacon along its back (cut bacon to fit lengthwise if necessary), and wrap bacon lengthwise around shrimp. Secure with a skewer or toothpick. Arrange shrimp in a single layer on a 10- by 15-in. broiler pan. Brush liberally with bourbon sauce. Broil 5 in. from heat 3 to 4 minutes, turn, brush with more sauce, and broil until cooked through, another 2 minutes. Discard any extra sauce.

PER SHRIMP: 91 cal., 54% (49 cal.) from fat; 9.4 g protein; 5.4 g fat (2.3 g sat.); 0.5 g carbo; 161 mg sodium; 69 mg chol.

Vietnamese Shrimp Lettuce Wraps with Spicy Lime Dipping Sauce

recipe pictured on page **59**

These colorful wraps mimic Vietnamese spring rolls.

SERVES 8 to 10 | **TIME** 1 hour

¾ lb. jumbo shrimp (16 to 20 per lb.), peeled and deveined
¼ tsp. *each* salt and freshly ground black pepper
1 package (3.75 oz.) cellophane noodles (*see Quick Tip below*)
2 tbsp. unseasoned rice vinegar
½ to 1 tsp. red chile flakes
2 tbsp. fresh lime juice
2 garlic cloves, minced
1 tbsp. sugar
¼ cup Thai or Vietnamese fish sauce (*nam pla or nuoc mam*)
2 heads Boston or butter lettuce, cores trimmed and leaves separated
1 large carrot, shredded lengthwise into ribbons
¼ cup *each* basil, cilantro, and mint leaves
¼ cup dry-roasted peanuts, finely chopped

1. Put shrimp, salt, and pepper in a pot and add cold water to just cover shrimp. Bring water to a boil, then reduce heat to a simmer and cook until shrimp are bright pink and tails are curled, about 1 minute. With a slotted spoon, transfer shrimp to a colander and let cool.
2. Put cellophane noodles in a medium pot and cover with hot water. Cover pot and set aside until noodles are softened, at least 15 minutes. Drain noodles and (using kitchen scissors) cut into 2- to 3-in. pieces. Return noodles to pot, drizzle with vinegar, and toss. Cover and set aside.
3. In a small bowl, mix chile flakes and lime juice and let stand several minutes. Add garlic, sugar, and fish sauce; whisk until sugar is dissolved. Transfer sauce to a small serving bowl.
4. To assemble wraps, arrange some noodles in the middle of each lettuce leaf and top with one shrimp. Top with carrot, basil, cilantro, mint, and peanuts. Tuck up the bottom of each leaf and fold sides inward to eat. Drizzle with or dip into sauce.
Quick Tip: Cellophane noodles—also called bean thread or glass noodles—are available at Asian grocery stores and most large supermarkets; rice-stick noodles or vermicelli may be substituted (follow package directions to prepare).

PER SERVING: 121 cal., 23% (28 cal.) from fat; 8.2 g protein; 3.1 g fat (0.5 g sat.); 15 g carbo (1.4 g fiber); 374 mg sodium; 42 mg chol.

Crispy Shrimp with Arugula and Lemony Mayo

A crowd-pleasing appetizer from Maria Helm Sinskey, cookbook author and co-owner of Robert Sinskey Vineyards in Napa Valley. The shrimp can be plated with the greens as a sit-down first course or served without greens as stand-up finger food.

SERVES 8 | **TIME** 35 minutes, plus 1 hour to chill

LEMONY MAYO
2 egg yolks
2 tbsp. fresh lemon juice, plus more to taste
1 tbsp. Dijon mustard
½ tsp. sugar
½ tsp. kosher salt, plus more to taste
Few grinds of black pepper
¼ cup extra-virgin olive oil
About ¾ cup canola oil
1 tsp. finely shredded lemon zest
CRISPY SHRIMP & SALAD
¾ cup flour
4 egg whites, lightly beaten
1½ cups fine dried bread crumbs or panko (Japanese-style bread crumbs)
4 tsp. kosher salt, divided, plus more to taste
½ tsp. cayenne (optional)
About 5½ tbsp. extra-virgin olive oil, divided
24 jumbo shrimp (16 to 20 per lb.), peeled with tails left on and deveined
4 cups arugula or tender watercress sprigs
1½ tbsp. fresh lemon juice
Freshly ground black pepper

1. Make lemony mayo: In a food processor, blend egg yolks, lemon juice, mustard, sugar, salt, and pepper. With motor running, drizzle in olive oil and then canola oil; mixture should be thick and shiny (you may need a little more or less canola oil). Add lemon zest. Taste and add more salt and lemon juice as needed. Chill until cold, at least 1 hour. Makes 1¼ cups.
2. Make crispy shrimp: Preheat oven to 475°. Pour flour, egg whites, and bread crumbs into separate shallow bowls. Stir 1 tsp. salt into flour. Stir 1 tbsp. salt and the cayenne if using into bread crumbs.
3. Pour ¼ cup olive oil into a large rimmed baking pan; spread to cover bottom. Dredge shrimp in flour, shaking off excess; dip in egg whites, letting excess drip off; roll in bread crumbs. Press each shrimp in oil, then turn to coat other side, adding more oil to pan if necessary to coat all shrimp. Set, slightly separated, in pan.
4. Bake shrimp until browned on the bottom, about 8 minutes, then turn over and bake until golden brown

all over and opaque but still moist-looking in center of thickest part, 5 to 8 minutes longer.

5. Make salad and serve: Mix arugula with lemon juice, remaining 1½ tbsp. olive oil, and salt and black pepper to taste. Divide arugula salad among plates and set shrimp alongside, with a dollop of mayo on each plate for dipping.

Make Ahead: Bread shrimp earlier in the day and chill, uncovered (the coating dries out and the shrimp get crisper). Make mayo up to 1 day ahead and chill.

PER SERVING WITH MAYONNAISE: 555 cal., 66% (369 cal.) from fat; 22 g protein; 41 g fat (4.7 g sat.); 26 g carbo (1.3 g fiber); 988 mg sodium; 168 mg chol.

Bay Shrimp on Belgian Endive

Cookbook author Peggy Knickerbocker adapted the venerable San Francisco dish crab Louis to create these fresh and crunchy morsels. The leftover aioli (if there is any) is delicious spread on sandwiches.

SERVES 20 to 36 hors d'oeuvres; 10 to 12 servings
TIME 30 minutes

1 egg
½ tsp. kosher salt, plus more to taste
1 small garlic clove, minced
2 tsp. Dijon mustard
1 cup mild extra-virgin olive oil
½ to ¾ tsp. red chile flakes
2 tbsp. fresh lemon juice
1 lb. cooked bay shrimp, rinsed and drained
4 tbsp. finely chopped flat-leaf parsley
1 tsp. finely chopped thyme leaves
3 or 4 large heads red or green Belgian endive, or
    a combination
Freshly ground black pepper

1. To make aioli, blend egg, salt, garlic, and mustard in a food processor until smooth. Add oil, drop by drop at first and then in a slow stream once mixture has begun to emulsify. Blend until mixture is thick, then add red chile flakes and lemon juice and pulse to combine. Chill aioli, covered with plastic wrap.

2. Mix shrimp with parsley, thyme, and salt to taste. Add just enough aioli (5 to 6 tbsp.) to bind the shrimp.

3. Cut bases off endive and separate leaves (save small ones for another use, such as salad). Arrange leaves on a platter and top each with 1 tbsp. shrimp mixture and a grind of pepper.

Make Ahead: Aioli, up to 3 days, chilled.

PER SERVING: 228 cal., 83% (189 cal.) from fat; 9.5 g protein; 21 g fat (3.2 g sat.); 1.1 g carbo (0.6 g fiber); 353 mg sodium; 100 mg chol.

Peruvian Ceviche

This version of Peru's national dish comes from Doris Rodriguez de Platt, owner of Andina restaurant in Portland, Oregon.

SERVES 4 | **TIME** 1 hour

1½ lbs. very fresh skinned ono, mahimahi, or bluenose
    bass fillets, cut into ½-in. dice *(see Quick Tips below)*
½ small red onion, halved and slivered
¾ cup fresh lime juice
½ tsp. salt
1 fresh habanero chile (optional), halved, seeds and ribs
    removed, and thinly sliced
1 tbsp. *ají amarillo* sauce (optional; *see Quick Tips below*)
½ cup cilantro leaves, chopped
1 orange-fleshed sweet potato (often labeled "yam"),
    boiled until tender, peeled, and sliced
1 ear corn, husked, boiled 2 minutes, and cut into
    4 pieces
4 butter lettuce leaves

1. Rinse diced fish and slivered onion in cold water and dry thoroughly.

2. In a large bowl, combine fish, onion, lime juice, salt, habanero if using, and ají amarillo sauce if using. Cover and refrigerate 20 minutes.

3. Just before serving, stir in cilantro. Serve with sweet potato, corn, and lettuce leaves on the side.

Quick Tips: Ono (also called wahoo) has white, delicate flesh. Shop at a trusted market with sushi-safe fish (professionally frozen to subzero temperatures to kill parasites), tell the fishmonger you plan to eat it raw, and keep the fish as cold as possible until you serve it. *Ají amarillo* is a yellow chile with a slightly sweet flavor and plenty of heat. It is sold in jars or as a puréed sauce at many Latino markets.

PER SERVING: 226 cal., 6.6% (15 cal.) from fat; 33 g protein; 1.7 g fat (0.4 g sat.); 19 g carbo (2.2 g fiber); 458 mg sodium; 124 mg chol.

■ Belgian Endive

FROM THE GARDEN

A member of the chicory family, Belgian endive is a small, cigar-shaped head of compact, pointed leaves that's grown in darkness to keep it pale. The leaves are creamy white with yellow-green or red tips. Belgian endive has a slightly bitter flavor and crunchy leaves that are good for stuffing, scooping, or dipping; you can also cut them crosswise and toss them in with salad greens. They turn brown as soon as they're sliced, though, so cut them at the last minute.

Ceviche Perlita

Claud Mann—chef and cohost of the TBS show *Dinner & a Movie,* co-publisher of *Edible Ojai* magazine, and resident of Ojai, California—makes this dish all summer long. His wife's father, who grew up in Acapulco, invented it and called it Perlita, or "little pearl," for his daughter Perla. The title also refers to the bright bits of fish in the ceviche.

SERVES 8 to 10 | **TIME** 1 hour, plus 3 hours to marinate

¾ **lb. very fresh skinned halibut or sea bass fillets, cut into ¼- to ½-in. dice** *(see Quick Tip, right)*
3 **tbsp.** *each* **fresh lime and lemon juice, divided**
2 **tbsp. extra-virgin olive oil**
1 **tsp. dried oregano, preferably Mexican**
2 **tbsp. juice from a jar of sliced pickled jalapeños (sometimes labeled "nacho jalapeños"), plus ¼ cup pickled jalapeños, minced**
½ **sweet medium white onion, finely chopped**
¾ **cup grape tomatoes or 1 medium firm-ripe tomato, cut into ¼-in. cubes**
½ **cucumber, peeled, seeded, and cut into ¼-in. cubes**
¼ **lb. pitted green olives (preferably not brined in vinegar; if they are, rinse before using), finely chopped**
½ **cup very finely crumbled** *cotija* **(firm Mexican cheese) or feta cheese (about 3 oz.)**
1 **serrano chile, stemmed and minced**
2 **tbsp. chopped cilantro**
1 **firm-ripe avocado**
Kosher salt
Thick tortilla chips
Mexican hot sauce, such as Cholula

1. In a medium bowl, combine fish and 2 tbsp. each lime and lemon juice. Cover and refrigerate at least 3 hours and up to 6, stirring occasionally.
2. Meanwhile, mix oil, oregano (rubbed between your palms first if flecks are large), and pickled jalapeño juice in a large bowl.
3. Drain fish in a colander, discarding juice, and add to oil mixture. Toss to coat.
4. Add pickled jalapeños, onion, tomatoes, cucumber, olives, cheese, serrano, and cilantro. Peel avocado, pit, cut into ½-in. cubes, and toss gently with remaining 1 tbsp. lemon juice; add to bowl and toss ceviche gently and thoroughly. Season with salt to taste and remaining 1 tbsp. lime juice. Serve with tortilla chips and hot sauce.

Quick Tip: The citric acid in lime and lemon juice firms fish and makes it opaque, so ceviche looks and tastes cooked but isn't. Shop at a trusted market with sushi-safe fish (professionally frozen to subzero temperatures to kill parasites), tell the fishmonger you plan to eat it raw, and keep the fish as cold as possible until you serve it.

PER SERVING: 164 cal., 66% (108 cal.) from fat; 11 g protein; 12 g fat (2.9 g sat.); 4.8 g carbo (1.2 g fiber); 576 mg sodium; 20 mg chol.

Hawaiian Steamed Mahimahi Wraps (Mahimahi *Laulau*)

Glossy, green Hawaiian *ti* (pronounced *tee*) leaves are traditionally used in flower arrangements as well as for wrapping food. Here they are the wrappers in a recipe for tasty morsels of lime-and-ginger-spiked mahimahi from Greg and Lynn Boyer of Oahu.

SERVES 12 | **TIME** 1½ hours

About 8 large fresh ti leaves or 1 package (1 lb.) thawed frozen banana leaves *(see Quick Tip, right)*
1½ **lbs. mahimahi fillets**
2 **tsp. kosher salt**
1 **large carrot**
1 **red bell pepper, seeds and ribs removed**
8 **green onions (white and pale green parts only)**
1 **tbsp. butter**
4-**in. piece fresh ginger, minced**
2 **limes, cut into wedges**
About 1½ tbsp. Hawaiian red clay salt *(see Shaking Out the Salts, right)* **or sea salt**

1. If using ti leaves, cut each leaf in half along center rib and discard rib. If using banana leaves, soak in warm water to soften. Tear 12 long, narrow strips from 1 or 2 leaves and boil 30 seconds; drain. Cut remaining leaves with the grain into 24 strips, each about 12 in. by 3 in.
2. Cut fish into 12 pieces (each about 2 in. square) and sprinkle both sides with salt. Chill 30 minutes.
3. Meanwhile, cut carrot, bell pepper, and green onions into 2-in. lengths and then cut into thinnest possible slivers. Melt butter in a frying pan over medium heat. Add vegetables and ginger; cook, stirring often, until softened but not browned, 3 to 4 minutes. Remove from heat.

4. Arrange two strips of ti or banana leaves, shiny sides down, one on top of the other in a cross shape. Place one mahimahi piece in center of cross, then top with a generous tbsp. vegetable mixture. Beginning with lower strip, fold leaves over filling, alternating strips and using each new strip to fold loose end of previous strip over filling. Tuck end of last strip beneath packet, then tie closed with a boiled leaf strip. Repeat with remaining leaf strips, fish, and vegetables.

5. Set a rack or steamer basket in a large pot and add water to about ½ in. below top of rack. Bring water to a boil over high heat. Place fish packets in a single layer on rack or in basket (steam in batches if necessary).

Cover pot tightly and steam until fish is just barely opaque in the center, 6 to 10 minutes (do not overcook; cut to test). Tip packets to drain any water. Serve hot or warm, with lime wedges and Hawaiian red clay salt.

Quick Tip: Find ti leaves online or at florists' shops (ask for leaves that have not been sprayed), or substitute banana leaves, available frozen in Asian and Latino food markets (they aren't as flexible, but will work).

Make Ahead: Wrap laulau up to 4 hours ahead and chill (steam for an extra minute or 2).

PER SERVING: 67 cal., 19% (13 cal.) from fat; 11 g protein; 1.4 g fat (0.7 g sat.); 2.3 g carbo (0.6 g fiber); 391 mg sodium; 44 mg chol.

Shaking Out the Salts

The variety of salts on the market is staggering, and choosing the right one can make a big difference in your cooking. Here's a quick guide to regular salts—and some gourmet ones too.

Table Salt

The familiar, fine-grained standby. Anti-caking agents keep it free-flowing. Iodine, a mineral essential for proper functioning of both thyroid and brain, may be added too. Table salt is either mined from the earth or evaporated from seawater.

USES: All-around cooking; preferred by bakers because it measures uniformly and dissolves quickly.

Kosher Salt

A coarse-grained salt used for koshering (drawing blood out of) meat and favored by many cooks for its clean taste and pinchable texture.

USES: General cooking, salt crusting, brining, and coating the rims of margarita glasses. If substituting for table salt, you'll need twice as much

Diamond Crystal brand (its pyramid shape adds volume) or just slightly more flake-shaped Morton.

Sea Salt

Made from evaporated seawater. Refined sea salt is the least expensive; it has the dryness and uniform flavor of table salt, but without any additives. Unrefined sea salts are moist, irregular crystals that retain trace minerals, subtle flavors, and, sometimes, colors from the source. Connoisseurs particularly prize French *fleur de sel* ("flower of salt"), delicate crystals that form on top of evaporation ponds, and coarser *sel gris* ("gray salt"), from the lower layers.

USES: Sea salt is available in fine to coarse grains. Fine-textured refined or unrefined works well for all-purpose cooking and seasoning. Unrefined medium to coarse-grain sea salt makes flavorful toppings that stick well to dough, fish, and meat. Try expensive artisanal finishing salts at the table, where you can appreciate their nuances.

Flake Salt

Large, pretty crystals with a delicate crunch. The thin, hollow pyramid shape (which breaks easily into flakes) allows this salt to perch on food so you get a pop of saltiness when you bite into it.

USES: Sprinkle over a Caprese salad or dot over a scoop or two of rich ice cream.

Flavored Salt

The best contain naturally derived flavors and range from smoky to citrusy to chile-hot. Originally for ceremonial use, *Hawaiian red salt*—white sea salt with 'alaea clay added—is gaining a following with cooks for its brick red color and earthy flavor. *Black Hawaiian salt*, with charcoal blended in, has a somewhat smoky flavor. Find flavored salts online and in specialty-foods stores.

USES: Great on steaks and vegetables.

Northwest Smoked Salmon Crêpes

Nancy Hess of Portland, Oregon, used her own home-smoked local salmon for the filling in a recipe that won the appetizer category in our Best Thanksgiving Recipes contest. "A holiday in our house is not complete without these crêpes," says Hess.

MAKES 36 to 42 filled crêpes | **TIME** 2¼ hours

CRÊPES
3 eggs
1 cup *each* milk and flour
2 tbsp. butter, melted
2 to 3 tbsp. canola oil
FILLING
5 oz. hot-smoked salmon (*see Quick Tip, above right*)
⅔ cup mayonnaise
⅓ cup sour cream
1 cup finely shredded parmesan cheese, divided
2 tsp. fresh lemon juice
¾ tsp. *each* Worcestershire sauce and chopped dill
⅛ tsp. *each* white pepper and hot sauce
Seasoned salt
2 tbsp. butter, melted
Paprika
Dill sprigs

1. Make crêpes: In a blender, combine eggs, milk, flour, and melted butter; blend until smooth. Heat oil in a 10-in. nonstick frying pan over medium heat. When hot, swirl to coat, then pour any excess oil into a small heatproof bowl. Immediately pour in ⅓ cup crêpe batter and tilt to coat bottom. If there are a few holes, drizzle with a little batter to fill in. Cook crêpe until edge is lightly browned and surface looks dry, 30 to 60 seconds. Run a spatula under crêpe edge to loosen. Turn over and brown other side lightly, 10 to 20 seconds. Tip pan over a plate to release crêpe. Repeat to cook remaining batter, adding more oil as needed and stacking cooked crêpes.
2. Stack two crêpes and, with a 2¾- to 3-in. round cookie cutter, cut into closely spaced rounds. Repeat to cut remaining crêpes; discard scraps.
3. Preheat oven to 350°. Make filling: Remove any skin and bones from salmon. With your hands, break salmon into fine pieces; you should have about 1 cup. In a bowl, mix mayonnaise, sour cream, ½ cup parmesan, the lemon juice, Worcestershire, chopped dill, white pepper, and hot sauce. Stir in salmon and seasoned salt to taste.

4. Mound about 1½ tsp. salmon filling on one half of each crêpe round; fold it over to make a half-moon shape. Set crêpes, slightly overlapping, in a buttered 10- by 15-in. baking pan. Drizzle with melted butter and sprinkle with remaining ½ cup cheese and a little paprika.
5. Bake until crêpes are golden and bubbly, 15 to 25 minutes. Transfer to a serving platter or plates and garnish with dill sprigs.
Quick Tip: Hot-smoked salmon is firmer and flakier than cold-smoked salmon (lox).
Make Ahead: Crêpes (without filling) up to 3 days ahead; chill. Bring to room temperature before separating. Can fill the crêpes (through step 3) up to 1 day ahead and chill.

PER CRÊPE: 76 cal., 71% (54 cal.) from fat; 3.3 g protein; 6 g fat (2.2 g sat.); 3.1 g carbo (0.1 g fiber); 112 mg sodium; 26 mg chol.

Sesame Ahi Poke

Poke, the much-loved Hawaiian raw-fish salad, has many variations; this is a relatively simple one. It should always be prepared with the highest-quality fish, often found at Japanese markets.

recipe pictured on page 55

SERVES 4 | **TIME** 25 minutes

1½ lbs. sashimi-grade ahi tuna steaks, cut into ½-in. dice (*see Quick Tips below*)
1 tbsp. *each* minced fresh ginger and Asian (toasted) sesame oil
⅓ cup sliced green onions
3 tbsp. low-sodium soy sauce
2 tsp. sesame seeds, toasted (*see Quick Tips below*)
Taro chips

Combine all ingredients except chips in a medium bowl. Serve immediately with chips on the side.
Quick Tips: Ahi is not prone to parasites, so can safely be eaten raw without special handling. Still, seek out sashimi grade for the best quality. To toast sesame seeds, heat them in a dry pan over medium heat until golden, stirring occasionally.

PER ½-CUP SERVING WITHOUT CHIPS: 58 cal., 22% (13 cal.) from fat; 10 g protein; 1.4 g fat (0.3 g sat.); 0.5 g carbo (0.1 g fiber); 118 mg sodium; 19 mg chol.

Tuna Tartare in Spicy Sesame Oil

Chef George Morrone serves a version of this Asian-Southwest fusion tartare at Lalime's restaurant in Berkeley, California.

SERVES 8 as a first course | **TIME** 1 hour

4 green and/or red jalapeño chiles (3 to 4 oz. total; 2 green and 2 red, or all green)
½ cup Asian (toasted) sesame oil
⅓ cup pine nuts, toasted (*see How to Toast Nuts, page 134*)
1½ cups diced firm-ripe plums
1 tsp. minced garlic
¾ tsp. salt
3 tbsp. finely slivered mint leaves, divided
1 lb. sashimi-grade ahi (bigeye or yellowfin tuna), rinsed and patted dry (*see Quick Tip below*)
1 tsp. to 1 tbsp. ground dried ancho or California chiles
16 slices firm white sandwich bread

1. Stem and halve jalapeños lengthwise. Pour sesame oil into a 1- to 2-qt. pan over low heat. With a spoon, scrape seeds and ribs into sesame oil (reserve jalapeños). Cook oil until warm, 3 to 5 minutes. Remove from heat and let stand until oil is as spicy as you like, about 15 minutes for mild, 2 hours for hot. Pour oil through a fine strainer into a large bowl. Discard chile seeds and ribs. Set aside about 2 tsp. oil.

2. Mince jalapeños and put in bowl with oil, along with pine nuts, plums, garlic, salt, and 2 tbsp. mint.

3. Trim any sinew from ahi. Finely chop fish. Stir into plum mixture. Season to taste with ground chiles.

4. Cut crusts from bread and reserve for other uses. Toast bread, then cut into triangles.

5. Mound ahi mixture on plates. Spoon reserved 2 tsp. chile oil over ahi and plates. Sprinkle with remaining mint. Serve with toast points.

Quick Tip: Ahi is not prone to parasites, so can safely be eaten raw without special handling. Still, seek out sashimi grade for the best quality.

PER SERVING: 388 cal., 44% (171 cal.) from fat; 20 g protein; 19 g fat (2.8 g sat.); 34 g carbo (2.5 g fiber); 549 mg sodium; 26 mg chol.

Spiced Beef Tenderloin

This silky beef requires a bit of advance planning because you're essentially curing the meat—but it's very easy to do. (If you cut the marinating time to 1 day, the results will be good but not quite as silky or flavorful.) Serve with crusty rolls and chutney if you like.

SERVES About 25 | **TIME** 2 hours, plus 4 days to cure

2 tbsp. black peppercorns (or a mix of black and green peppercorns)
6 tbsp. firmly packed dark brown sugar
2 tbsp. plus 2 tsp. kosher salt
1½ tsp. *each* ground ginger, allspice, nutmeg, coriander, and cardamom
¾ tsp. ground cloves
1 whole beef tenderloin (about 5 lbs.), tied with kitchen twine as a roast (*see Quick Tip below*)
4 garlic cloves, coarsely crushed
2 tbsp. vegetable oil, divided

1. Grind peppercorns in an electric spice grinder (or clean coffee grinder) to a medium grind. In a small bowl, combine pepper, brown sugar, salt, ginger, allspice, nutmeg, coriander, cardamom, and cloves; whisk to combine. Rub meat sparingly with crushed garlic slivers, then rub all over with spice mixture.

2. Cut tenderloin crosswise in half. Wrap each half very tightly with several layers of plastic wrap (so that it looks swaddled), put in a rimmed pan, and refrigerate 4 days.

3. Preheat oven to 400°. Heat 1 tbsp. of oil in a large frying pan (not nonstick) over high heat. Add one piece of meat and sear until well browned on all sides, 7 to 10 minutes. Transfer to a rimmed baking pan and repeat with remaining 1 tbsp. oil and beef. Transfer baking pan to oven and cook meat until thermometer inserted in thickest part registers 135°, 20 to 30 minutes. (Halves may not cook at the same rate; after meat has been in the oven 20 minutes, begin taking temperature of both pieces every 5 minutes.) Transfer to a carving board, tent with foil, and let rest 15 minutes. Remove kitchen twine.

4. Cut meat into very thin slices (less than ¼ in., if possible) and serve warm or at room temperature.

Quick Tip: Many butchers will trim the tenderloin of silverskin and excess fat and tie it as a roast for you. If you do it yourself, tie the roast at 2-in. intervals with separate pieces of kitchen twine to give it an even shape as it cooks.

Make Ahead: Roast beef up to 2 days; chill. Bring to room temperature before serving.

PER 2-SLICE SERVING: 246 cal., 66% (162 cal.) from fat; 16 g protein; 18 g fat (6.9 g sat.); 4 g carbo (0.1 g fiber); 665 mg sodium; 57 mg chol.

cocktails
& other
drinks

From icy martinis and margaritas to fresh fruit smoothies to soul-warming coffee concoctions, here are sips for every occasion.

It's no stretch to say that the world of drinks in the West has never been more exciting. The sleek, urbane classics of the '50s and '60s—like martinis and bloody Marys—never really left, and umbrella-festooned tiki drinks have surfed back into style, as fun as ever (if you've never had one, try our mai tai on *page 76*). Pre-Prohibition cocktails such as the sidecar and whiskey sour have also come roaring back. Add to that a fresh new style of using local and seasonal fruits and vegetables—plus flavoring syrups, liquors, and spices from all over the globe—to create entirely different and delicious cocktails and you can understand the fancy name that bartending sometimes goes by these days: mixology. (Two of our recent favorites from this style: Kumquat Digestifs, *page 78*, and Peach Martinis with Chiles from the Garden, *page 78*.)

Outside the cocktail hour, we've included dozens of recipes for purely refreshing drinks packed with Western fruit: persimmon smoothies, thirst-quenching Mexican *aguas frescas*, limeades, lemonades, iced teas, Asian-style bubble teas, and, of course, the simple, utterly wonderful California Date Shake (*page 75*), made with rich, chewy Medjool dates. And because we Westerners are serious about our coffee, we end with a few well-made coffee drinks that are as full of flavor as they are of caffeine.

Cocktails & Other Drinks

Layered Fruit Smoothies

With spectacular bands of strawberry pink and golden yellow, these cool and creamy smoothies make an impressive drink to serve for brunch.

SERVES 2 | **TIME** 25 minutes

1 ripe mango, peeled, pitted, and coarsely
   chopped
1¼ cups plain low-fat yogurt, divided
¼ cup honey, divided
1 tbsp. fresh lime juice
¼ tsp. finely shredded lime zest
1 ripe banana, chopped
10 medium strawberries, hulled
1 tbsp. fresh lemon juice
¼ tsp. finely shredded lemon zest

1. In a blender, purée mango, ¾ cup yogurt, 2 tbsp. honey, the lime juice and zest, and 2 ice cubes until smooth. Divide mango-lime smoothie between two clear straight-sided glasses and set aside.
2. Rinse blender, then purée banana, strawberries, lemon juice and zest, and remaining ½ cup yogurt, 2 tbsp. honey, and 2 ice cubes until smooth.

3. Layer banana-strawberry smoothie onto mango smoothie, gently spooning strawberry mixture around inside edge of each glass to create a clean horizontal line.

PER SERVING: 408 cal., 7% (30 cal.) from fat; 9.6 g protein; 3.3 g fat (1.7 g sat.); 94 g carbo (5.4 g fiber); 109 mg sodium; 8.5 mg chol.

Persimmon Breakfast Smoothies

Look for acorn-shaped Hachiya persimmons to add a bit of cinnamony flavor to your morning smoothie.

SERVES 2 | **TIME** 5 minutes

2 Hachiya persimmons *(see Persimmons: Fall's*
   Most Beautiful Fruit, below)
¾ cup plain low-fat yogurt
½ cup milk
¾ cup orange juice

1. Cut tops off persimmons and scoop out pulp (should yield about 1 cup).
2. In a blender, purée persimmon pulp, yogurt, milk, orange juice, and 1 cup ice cubes until smooth.

PER SERVING: 253 cal., 14% (36 cal.) from fat; 8.5 g protein; 4 g fat (2.1 g sat.); 50 g carbo (6.2 g fiber); 91 mg sodium; 12 mg chol.

Persimmons: Fall's Most Beautiful Fruit

Leaf-barren persimmon trees filled with smooth, bright orange orbs of fruit are one of the first signs of fall in much of the West. Most of the persimmons grown commercially are Japanese, first introduced to California in the 1870s. With the rapid influx of Asian immigrants to the state, the fruit's popularity boomed, and California now grows most of the persimmons in the country.

Hachiya vs. Fuyu
Two types are primarily available: Hachiya, an elongated acorn-shaped fruit that should be eaten only when jelly-soft (otherwise it's overwhelmingly astringent), and Fuyu, a squat, juicy, tomato-shaped variety eaten when firm. Every now and then at a farmers' market, you might see some of the rarer types: Hyakume (cinnamon persimmon), a crisp variety with flesh that's flecked with brown; so-called chocolate varieties, which have dark flesh and a slight chocolate flavor; and the deep reddish orange Giant Fuyu.

How to Eat a Persimmon
To eat a Hachiya, chill it, cut off the top, and spoon out the flesh. Hachiya pulp makes very good smoothies and is wonderful in baked goods. For a crisp type such as Fuyu, peel it if you like (the skin is slightly bitter), seed if necessary, and thinly slice crosswise—or just bite into it as you would an apple. Add the firm persimmons to salads, tuck slices into cheese or ham sandwiches, or dress them with a squeeze of citrus for breakfast.

How to Pick a Persimmon
Look for brightly colored, unbruised fruits at farmers' markets and grocery stores starting in October and continuing through early December.

Cranberry–Green Tea Smoothie

Green tea and cranberries fill this high-energy smoothie with powerful antioxidants. Frozen fruit is ideal for smoothies, because it chills the drink without diluting it as melting ice would. And individually quick-frozen (IQF) technology has made it possible to produce high-quality frozen fruit, with a nutritional value on par with that of fresh fruit. To make a pineapple–green tea smoothie, substitute 1 cup frozen pineapple chunks for the blackberries and strawberries.

SERVES 1 | **TIME** 10 minutes

½ cup *each* **frozen cranberries and blackberries**
¼ cup **frozen blueberries**
5 **frozen whole strawberries**
1 **ripe banana, peeled**
½ cup **brewed green tea, cooled to room temperature**
¼ cup **plain soy milk**
2 tbsp. **honey or firmly packed light brown sugar**

In a blender, purée all ingredients until smooth.

PER SERVING: 378 cal., 5% (18 cal.) from fat; 5.2 g protein; 2 g fat (0.2 g sat.); 92 g carbo (11 g fiber); 38 mg sodium; 0 mg chol.

Melon *Agua Fresca*

Lightly sweetened and bursting with the sweet flavor of ripe fruit, *aguas frescas* are the perfect summertime refresher. Be sure to use very ripe melons. Papaya and strawberry variations follow.

MAKES About 2½ qts.; 10 servings | **TIME** 10 minutes, plus 1 hour to chill

5 cups **cubed peeled, seeded watermelon, cantaloupe, or honeydew melon (from about 3 lbs. melon)**
½ to ¾ cup **sugar**
⅓ to ½ cup **fresh lime juice**

1. In a blender, purée melon, ½ cup of sugar, and 1 cup water until very smooth.
2. Pour into a large pitcher (at least 3 qts.). Whisk in ⅓ cup of lime juice and 7 cups water, then more sugar and lime juice to taste. Chill until cold, at least 1 hour and up to 1 day. Serve over ice.

PER 1-CUP SERVING: 64 cal., 3% (1.8 cal.) from fat; 0.6 g protein; 0.2 g fat (0 g sat.); 16 g carbo (0.5 g fiber); 7.5 mg sodium; 0 mg chol.

Papaya *Agua Fresca*: Substitute 5 cups cubed, peeled, seeded ripe **Mexican papayas** (from about 3 lbs. papayas) for the melon. Look for large, ripe papayas (the skin turns orange as the fruit ripens). Don't worry about blemishes; often the ripest, sweetest Mexican papayas have bruises or dark spots on the skin.

PER 1-CUP SERVING: 76 cal., 1% (0.9 cal.) from fat; 0.6 g protein; 0.1 g fat (0 g sat.); 19 g carbo (0.8 g fiber); 4.1 mg sodium; 0 mg chol.

Strawberry *Agua Fresca*: Substitute 5 cups hulled **strawberries** (about 1½ lbs.) for the melon and prepare as directed for Melon *Agua Fresca* through step 1. Press blended strawberry mixture through a fine mesh strainer (discard residue from strainer) into a tall pitcher before continuing with step 2.

PER 1-CUP SERVING: 63 cal., 4% (2.7 cal.) from fat; 0.5 g protein; 0.3 g fat (0 g sat.); 16 g carbo (0 g fiber); 2.1 mg sodium; 0 mg chol.

Brazilian "Lemonade"

Lemons aren't much seen in Brazil, where this drink originated and where it's called *limonada Suiça* ("Swiss lemonade"). It's actually made with limes. A limeade that's ever so slightly creamy with the addition of condensed milk, this version comes from reader Kelley Gee of Rexburg, Idaho. Think of it as Key lime pie in a glass, without the crust.

MAKES About 1½ qts.; 6 servings | **TIME** 10 minutes, plus 1 hour to chill

3 **limes, quartered**
⅓ cup **sugar**
3 tbsp. **sweetened condensed milk**

1. Put all ingredients in a blender. Add 4 cups cold water and blend on high speed until limes are slightly chopped.
2. Strain into a pitcher and then, with strainer still resting above the pitcher, slowly pour about 1 more cup water (depending on how sweet you want the drink) through the strainer over lime pieces to extract residual sugar and juice. Chill until cold, at least 1 hour.

PER 1-CUP SERVING: 83 cal., 10% (8.1 cal.) from fat; 1 g protein; 0.9 g fat (0.5 g sat.); 20 g carbo (0 g fiber); 13 mg sodium; 3.3 mg chol.

Lemongrass-Ginger Iced Tea

The delicate floral aroma of this drink makes it appealing for sipping in the garden; the low caffeine levels in green tea mean you can enjoy it all day long—and the antioxidants are a plus.

SERVES 4 | **TIME** 15 minutes, plus 2½ hours

1 stalk fresh lemongrass, tough outer layers pulled off, stem end trimmed, and cut into 2-in. lengths
½ cup sugar
7 thin slices fresh ginger
5 tea bags green tea

1. Crush lemongrass with flat side of a large knife.
2. In a 2-qt. pan, bring 5 cups water, the sugar, ginger, and lemongrass to a boil. Remove from heat and add green tea; let steep until flavor is as strong as you like, about 4 minutes. Discard tea bags; let tea cool, about 30 minutes.
3. Pour through a fine mesh strainer into a pitcher. Cover and chill until cold, at least 2 hours. Pour into tall glasses filled with ice.
Make Ahead: Up to 2 days, chilled.

PER SERVING: 102 cal., 0% (0.3 cal.) from fat; 0.1 g protein; 0 g fat; 26 g carbo (0.1 g fiber); 0.6 mg sodium; 0 mg chol.

Cherry Limeade

Use sweet, juicy Bing cherries for the best flavor.

MAKES 5¾ cups; 4 to 6 servings | **TIME** 10 minutes

1½ lbs. fresh cherries, stemmed and pitted
1 cup fresh lime juice
½ cup sugar

1. In a blender, purée all ingredients until smooth.
2. Press purée through a fine mesh strainer into a pitcher (at least 2 qts.), extracting as much liquid as possible; discard residue. Stir in 3 cups cold water and serve over ice.

PER SERVING: 143 cal., 6% (9 cal.) from fat; 1.3 g protein; 1 g fat (0.2 g sat.); 35 g carbo (1.5 g fiber); 6.7 mg sodium; 0 mg chol.

California Date Shake

One of the great foods of the Sunshine State, the date shake is exactly what you want to be slurping while visiting baking-hot date country near Palm Springs. Our favorite shake is the one at Shields Date Gardens, in Indio. Shields uses its own date "crystals"—dehydrated Deglet Noor and Blonde dates (the latter is one of its signature varieties). You can order these online (shieldsdategarden.com) or substitute fresh, as we've done here. This shake is sensational with a shot of rum stirred in.

Makes 1 shake (1⅓ cups) | **TIME** 10 minutes

4 pitted Medjool dates (about 3 oz.), coarsely chopped
¼ cup very cold milk
1¼ cups high-quality vanilla ice cream

In a blender, blend dates and milk until smooth and super-frothy. Add ice cream and pulse a few times, until just blended.

PER SHAKE: 614 cal., 30% (182 cal.) from fat; 9.2 g protein; 20 g fat (12 g sat.); 105 g carbo (6.8 g fiber); 157 mg sodium; 79 mg chol.

Hot Cranberry-Ginger Punch

This bright, zippy cranberry and ginger punch will take off winter's chill, whether you tote it in a thermos on a cross-country skiing expedition or have it simmering on the stove. Add a bit of extra sugar for the kids.

MAKES 1 qt.; 4 servings | **TIME** 35 minutes

1 qt. cranberry juice blend
2 oz. fresh ginger, thinly sliced (about ¼ cup)
⅓ cup fresh lime juice
⅓ cup sugar, plus more to taste

1. In a 2- to 3-qt. pan over medium heat, combine cranberry juice and ginger slices. Bring to a simmer and cook to infuse flavor, about 20 minutes.
2. Stir in lime juice and sugar; stir until sugar has dissolved. Taste and add up to ¼ cup more sugar if desired. Pour through a fine mesh strainer into a thermos or heatproof pitcher (discard solids). Serve hot.

PER 1-CUP SERVING: 212 cal., 1% (2.9 cal.) from fat; 0.2 g protein; 0.3 g fat (0 g sat.); 54 g carbo (0 g fiber); 6.4 mg sodium; 0 mg chol.

Guava-Lime Coolers

Grenadine adds a pretty coral tinge to this easy, festive drink from Greg Boyer, a landscape designer in Oahu, Hawaii, but it can be omitted. Use 100 percent guava juice for best flavor, not sweetened guava nectar.

MAKES About 2 qts.; 12 servings | **TIME** 10 minutes

7 cups guava juice
3 cups white (light) rum
⅔ cup fresh lime juice
¼ cup grenadine (pomegranate-flavored syrup)
Lime slices or wedges, or fresh guava slices

1. In a large pitcher, mix guava juice, rum, lime juice, and grenadine.
2. Pour over ice cubes in cocktail glasses and garnish with slices of lime or guava.

PER SERVING: 232 cal., 0% from fat; 0.1 g protein; 0 g fat; 26 g carbo (0 g fiber); 4.7 mg sodium; 0 mg chol.

Classic Tiki Mai Tai

recipe pictured on page **51**

The mai tai is a creation of the West, invented in the 1940s by Vic Bergeron of Trader Vic's fame. The original featured aged rum, lime juice, and orange liqueur, with a bit of orgeat (almond-flavored syrup). This one is only slightly tweaked. Go as fanciful as you like with the garnishes.

SERVES 1 | **TIME** 5 minutes

2 tbsp. *each* **white (light) rum and gold rum**
1 tbsp. *each* **orange curaçao, orgeat, rock candy syrup (see Quick Tips below), and fresh lime juice**
2 tbsp. dark rum

1. Into a cocktail shaker, pour white and gold rums, curaçao, orgeat, rock candy syrup, and lime juice. Fill with ice cubes, cover, and shake vigorously.
2. Strain into an ice-filled 8- to 12-oz. glass. Slowly pour dark rum onto top of drink.
Quick Tips: Rock candy syrup is simple syrup with a hint of vanilla; look for it and orgeat where other cordial syrups are sold.

PER SERVING: 320 cal., 0% from fat; 0 g protein; 0 g fat; 27 g carbo (0 g fiber); 15 mg sodium; 0 mg chol.

Fresh Bloody Mary

recipe pictured on page **57**

Try making this with summer-ripe heirloom tomatoes. Look for varieties like Kellogg's Breakfast, which is OJ-yellow and has lots of juice and a bright, tart flavor.

MAKES 1 generous or 2 smaller servings | **TIME** 10 minutes

½ lb. ripe tomatoes
¼ cup gin or vodka
1 tbsp. fresh lemon juice
¼ tsp. Worcestershire sauce
¼ tsp. salt, or to taste
1 pinch to ⅛ tsp. celery seeds
Hot sauce
Celery sticks and green onions, trimmed
Freshly ground black pepper

1. Cut tomatoes in half crosswise. Press tomatoes, cut side down, through a colander or a coarse mesh strainer set over a bowl to collect juice (you'll need about ¾ cup); discard skins.
2. Mix the ¾ cup tomato juice, gin, lemon juice, Worcestershire, salt, celery seeds, and hot sauce to taste. Pour into an ice-filled glass or two. Garnish with celery and/or green onion. Sprinkle with pepper.

PER GENEROUS SERVING: 182 cal., 2% (4.5 cal.) from fat; 2.1 g protein; 0.5 g fat (0.1 g sat.); 13 g carbo (3.8 g fiber); 665 mg sodium; 0 mg chol.

Pineapple Drops

This tangy and sweet drink pairs well with the rich flavors of barbecue. You'll need 6 cocktail skewers.

SERVES 6 | **TIME** 5 minutes, plus 2 hours to chill

1½ cups *each* **pineapple juice and vodka**
3 tbsp. fresh lime juice
About 1 cup sugar
Couple of lime wedges
Fresh pineapple, peeled, cored, and cut into ¾-in. chunks (about 12)

1. In a pitcher, mix pineapple juice, vodka, and lime juice, then chill until cold, at least 2 hours.
2. Pour sugar onto a large plate. Rub rims of six martini glasses with lime wedges. Dip rims in sugar. Divide vodka mixture among glasses. Push a few pineapple chunks onto each skewer and set one in each glass.

PER SERVING: 169 cal., 0% from fat; 0.3 g protein; 0 g fat; 10 g carbo (0 g fiber); 1.3 mg sodium; 0 mg chol.

Craft Beer in the West

Until about 30 years ago, beer in this country was dominated by corporate perpetrators of beer crime. The likes of Anheuser-Busch had appropriated a noble style—pilsner—watered it down, pumped it full of carbon dioxide, and earned this country a reputation for insipid brew but dynamite beer commercials.

But in the mid-1960s, small brewers across the country and especially the West began making inroads. Fritz Maytag bought San Francisco's Anchor Brewing Company, with an agenda of preserving old beermaking traditions. A decade later, New Albion Brewery was founded in Sonoma, California; it closed seven years later, but not before inspiring a spate of homebrewers to follow suit—in effect launching a movement of full-flavored artisan beers. Nationwide, there are now more than 1,500 craft brewers. When it comes to the number of breweries per capita, three of the top five states are in the West: Colorado, Oregon, and Montana. And it is Colorado that boasts the most beers on tap at any given event, at the Great American Beer Festival.

Choose Your Style

The range of beer styles is dizzying (even in the '80s, Alan Eames, in *A Beer Drinker's Companion*, claimed that there were more than 117 in the world). But they fall into only two main categories: ales and lagers. In broad terms, the differences between the two are a matter of the kind of yeast used and the temperature at which the beer was fermented. Ales are fermented at warmer temperatures, producing rich, fruity aromas and flavors. Lagers are fermented at cooler temperatures and tend to be leaner and subtler.

THE ROLE OF MALT AND HOPS. In both categories, the brewer's first tool for variety is malt—grain (usually barley) that has been soaked in water and allowed to sprout; it's then roasted and turned into a mash. The level of roast on the malt determines a beer's color, and the amount of malt its body and alcohol level. The second main tool is hops, which bring bitterness to balance the sweet malt (a good thing in ale) as well as an aromatic herbal quality (which a lager needs). Within each category—ales and lagers—you'll find light- to dark-colored styles. But

don't be fooled into thinking dark beers are necessarily high in alcohol: Guinness, for instance, is not.

Made for Food

The proliferation of top-quality beer styles has challenged the quality of the casual foods we've traditionally consumed with the beverage. A ballpark dog needs to be a good one if it's a great bock you're drinking. And pubs have stepped up: "Gastropub" is the operative term now, for establishments that offer creative versions of longtime favorite beer food, plus full-on gourmet cooking.

THINK BEER NOT WINE. Beyond pubs, beer-and-food pairing is a hot frontier. When it comes to the highly seasoned, robust cuisines that have moved onto our tables in the West, let beer pick up where wine leaves off. When too much vinegar kills your wine, when chiles and garlic and spices are looming large (in Mexican, Chinese, Southeast Asian, and Indian dishes)—look to a lager. A couple of quintessential Western dishes make wonderful beer partners: Northwest planked salmon (the sweet, smoky fish reaches out

to toasty malt) and Southern California fried-fish tacos (a crisp, hoppy, foaming lager is like a spritz of lemon). And the gentle carbonation in beer works as a great foil for the creamy texture of cheese.

A FEW PAIRING POINTERS. Are there other rules for pairing? Just common sense. Go for lighter-bodied, milder lagers and ales with delicate foods, and darker, richer versions of either for heartier dishes. Think about beer's malt level as similar to a wine's fruitiness (which stands up to spicy heat in food), and its hoppiness as similar to the acidity and herbal quality in wine (which match with vinegar, herbs, and vegetables). A tangy, chile-hot Thai noodle dish, then, works well with a fairly generously malted and hopped lager—a full-bodied pilsner, for example.

This renaissance of top-quality beer has, in a sense, elevated the spirit of celebration, relaxation, and togetherness of our pubs, picnics, and beach parties. The cold one you pour can now match any culinary adventure on your plate. It's an integral part of good food in the West.

Kumquat Digestifs

Make this delicious after-dinner drink for a little bit of summer sunshine in winter, when kumquats are in season. It's also tasty poured over ice cream. Select kumquats that are bright orange and firm; avoid any that are green-tinged.

MAKES 2½ cups; 10 servings | **TIME** 20 minutes, plus 3 weeks to infuse

½ cup sugar
2 cups vodka
10 kumquats, cut in half lengthwise, plus 5 to 6 whole
Several thyme branches

1. In a medium saucepan, heat sugar over medium heat with ½ cup water, stirring, until sugar is dissolved. Let cool to room temperature.
2. Stir in vodka. Pour mixture into a decanter and add kumquats (halves first) and thyme. Chill at least 3 weeks to infuse.
3. Serve ice-cold in shot glasses.

PER ¼-CUP SERVING: 177 cal., 1.3% (2.3 cal.) from fat; 0.6 g protein; 0.3 g fat (0 g sat.); 15 g carbo (1.9 g fiber); 3.4 mg sodium; 0 mg chol.

Ginger-Rosemary Lemon-drop Cocktails

Dory Ford, former executive chef at Portola Restaurant at the Monterey Bay Aquarium in California, found his inspiration for this refreshing drink in the herb garden. For a nonalcoholic ginger lemonade, increase the water in the concentrate to 3 cups and the sugar to ¾ cup.

SERVES 8 | **TIME** 45 minutes

1⅓ cups sugar, divided
About 1¼-in.-square piece unpeeled fresh ginger, cut into ⅛-in.-thick slices
2 rosemary sprigs (5 in. each), plus 8 sprigs (1½ in. each) for garnish
1 cup fresh lemon juice (from about 6 lemons)
1 lemon
1½ cups citron vodka

1. Make lemon concentrate: In a medium saucepan, bring ⅔ cup sugar, ginger, 5-in. rosemary sprigs, and 2½ cups water to a boil. Reduce heat to a simmer and cook, stirring occasionally, about 10 minutes. Remove from heat; let steep at room temperature 20 minutes. Strain into a medium bowl, discarding rosemary and ginger, and stir in lemon juice.

2. Pour remaining ⅔ cup sugar onto a plate. Slice 2 thin slices from lemon and quarter the slices. Insert a 1½-in. rosemary sprig through center of each quarter. With a wedge cut from remaining lemon, rub rims of eight cocktail glasses. Twist rims gently in sugar to coat.
3. Fill a large pitcher half-full with ice cubes. Pour in vodka and lemon concentrate and stir vigorously. Strain into glasses. Float a rosemary-skewered lemon quarter in each.
Make Ahead: Concentrate, up to 1 week, chilled.

PER SERVING: 206 cal., 0% (0.9 cal.) from fat; 0.4 g protein; 0.1 g fat (0 g sat.); 30 g carbo (0 g fiber); 1.7 mg sodium; 0 mg chol.

Peach Martinis with Chiles from the Garden

recipe pictured on page **58**

This cocktail—created by chef Jesse Z. Cool of Flea St. Café, in Menlo Park, California, and the Cool Café, in nearby Palo Alto—is one to be enjoyed in the heart of summer, using juicy, ripe peaches. She likes to serve it with freshly shucked oysters and warm olive bread smeared with a soft blue cheese. You'll need six small skewers or toothpicks.

SERVES 6 | **TIME** 12 minutes

6 to 12 slices ripe white peach
6 slices red or green jalapeño or Thai chile
Kosher salt
6 to 12 tsp. dry vermouth
1½ cups high-quality gin or vodka

1. Fill six martini glasses with ice, then water; let stand until glasses are very cold, about 5 minutes (or chill them, empty, in the freezer).
2. Meanwhile, for each drink, push 1 or 2 peach slices and 1 chile slice onto a small skewer or toothpick. Sprinkle peaches lightly with salt.
3. Empty glasses and pour 1 to 2 tsp. of vermouth into each. Swirl to coat glass, then pour off and discard most of the vermouth.
4. Fill a 3-cup martini shaker with ice cubes and add gin. Cover and shake until cold, 4 to 6 times. Strain into glasses. Garnish each with a peach-chile skewer.

PER SERVING: 147 cal., 0% from fat; 0.1 g protein; 0 g fat (0.3 g fiber); 0.8 mg sodium; 0 mg chol.

Herbaltinis

The lively cocktail from reader Carry Porter of Kirkland, Washington, gets its kick from freshly squeezed orange and lime juices, as well as crushed fresh mint and rosemary.

MAKES 1½ qts.; 8 to 12 servings | **TIME** 20 minutes

24 mint sprigs (4 in. each)
12 rosemary sprigs (3 in. each)
¾ cup superfine sugar
2 oranges (6 oz. each), chilled and quartered
2¼ cups gin, chilled in freezer
1 cup plus 2 tbsp. fresh lime juice (from about 7 limes), chilled
1½ cups club soda, chilled
Mint leaves

1. In a 2 ½- to 3-qt. pitcher, combine mint and rosemary sprigs and sugar. With a long-handled wooden spoon, muddle (or crush) herbs and sugar together. Squeeze juice from oranges into pitcher, then drop quarters in. Press a few times with spoon to release oil from orange peels. Stir in gin, lime juice, and ½ cup ice water. Mix until sugar is dissolved. If using martini glasses, chill in freezer.
2. To serve, slowly pour chilled club soda into pitcher, pouring down the side. Stir gently to blend. Pour through a strainer into chilled martini glasses or ice-filled glasses. Float a mint leaf on top of each.
Make Ahead: Up to 4 hours, chilled in pitcher; however, since crushed mint turns dark after about 20 minutes, strain mixture just before guests arrive, return it to the pitcher, and add a handful of fresh mint leaves.

PER SERVING: 159 cal., 1% (0.9 cal.) from fat; 0.2 g protein; 0.1 g fat (0 g sat.); 16 g carbo (0.1 g fiber); 1.1 mg sodium; 0 mg chol.

Grapefruit Margaritas

Serve this beautifully hued cocktail in pitchers at your next patio party.

MAKES 1½ qts.; 6 servings | **TIME** 5 minutes, plus 1 hour to chill

3 cups fresh Ruby grapefruit juice
2 cups tequila
1 cup triple sec
¼ cup sugar
1 Ruby grapefruit

1. In a 2 qt. pitcher, combine grapefruit juice, tequila, and triple sec. Chill until cold, at least 1 hour.

2. Pour sugar onto a large plate. Cut grapefruit in half and rub rims of double old-fashioned glasses (8 oz.) with cut side of one half, then dip rims in sugar to coat.
3. Fill glasses with ice cubes. Pour margaritas over ice, taking care not to disturb sugared glass rims.
Make Ahead: Up to 1 day, chilled.

PER ¾-CUP SERVING: 284 cal., 0% from fat; 0 g protein; 0 g fat; 27 g carbo (0 g fiber); 0.6 mg sodium; 0 mg chol.

Rangpur Lime Shooters

recipe
pictured
on page
54

Rangpur limes are thick-skinned, orange-hued hybrid mandarins, originally from Rangpur, in what is now Bangladesh. They thrive in California. The limes are fruity, aromatic, and bracingly sour, like a mix of tangerine and lime. Think of these shooters, from chef Cal Stamenov of Marinus restaurant at Bernardus Lodge in Carmel Valley, California, as really good margaritas that you can pick up with your fingers.

SERVES 6 | **TIME** 20 minutes, plus 2 hours to chill

2 envelopes unflavored gelatin
1 cup fresh Rangpur lime juice (see Quick Tip below); or ⅔ cup fresh lime juice plus ⅓ cup fresh tangerine juice
¾ cup sugar
½ cup white (silver) tequila
Flaky sea salt, such as Maldon (optional)
Rangpur lime wedges (optional)

1. In a small saucepan, sprinkle gelatin over ½ cup water. Let stand until softened, about 5 minutes. Add citrus juice and sugar; cook, stirring, over medium-high heat until steaming, 3 to 5 minutes. Nest pan in a bowl of ice water and stir until cool; stir in tequila.
2. Line a 8½- by 4½-in. loaf pan with plastic wrap, letting wrap hang over ends. Pour citrus mixture into pan, cover with another piece of plastic (not touching mixture), and chill until firm, at least 2 hours.
3. Uncover pan. Holding ends of plastic wrap, lift gelled mixture on wrap onto a cutting board. Cut into 18 cubes. Transfer to a plate. If you like, sprinkle with a little salt and garnish with lime wedges.
Quick Tip: Find Rangpur limes at specialty-foods markets mainly in winter.
Make Ahead: Up to 1 week, chilled.

PER 3-SHOOTER SERVING: 167 cal., 0% from fat; 2.2 g protein; 0 g fat; 29 g carbo (0 g fiber); 5.3 mg sodium; 0 mg chol.

Pear Sidecar

This sweet (but not too sweet) drink should be made one at a time in a cocktail shaker. Energetic shaking and a proper drink-to-ice ratio—possible only in a shaker—are key: The ice dilutes and softens the "edges" of the cocktail, encouraging otherwise sharp flavors to meld together.

SERVES 1 | **TIME** 10 minutes

¼ **cup pear brandy**
2 **tbsp. unsweetened pear juice or nectar**
1 **tbsp.** *each* **fresh lemon juice and Simple Syrup**
    (opposite page)
1 **or 2 pear slices, about ½ in. thick**

1. Fill a cocktail shaker with ice. Pour brandy, pear juice, lemon juice, and simple syrup over ice. Cover and shake vigorously for 1 minute.
2. Strain and pour into a chilled martini glass. Garnish with a slice or 2 of pear.

PER SERVING: 252 cal., 1% (1.8 cal.) from fat; 0.2 g protein; 0.2 g fat (0 g sat.); 41 g carbo (0.9 g fiber); 4.6 mg sodium; 0 mg chol.

Brandy Shakes

Hugo Matheson, chef-owner of the Kitchen restaurant in Boulder, Colorado, mixes these up for friends of his who love brandy freezes. Feel free to experiment with other flavors of ice cream and less brandy if you like. These are knock-your-boots-off boozy—and delicious.

SERVES 6 | **TIME** 5 minutes

1 **qt. high-quality vanilla ice cream, slightly softened**
1 **cup brandy**

Put ice cream and brandy in a blender and blend until smooth. Pour into glasses.

PER ¾-CUP SERVING: 335 cal., 43% (144 cal.) from fat; 3.5 g protein; 16 g fat (9.8 g sat.); 22 g carbo (0 g fiber); 55 mg sodium; 60 mg chol.

Sunset Margaritas

A drizzle of pomegranate juice down the side of the glass makes this orange margarita look at least faintly like a sky at sunset. It's usually poured at *Sunset's* Celebration Weekend event, our big annual open house.

recipe pictured on page 60

SERVES 2 | **TIME** 5 minutes

⅓ **cup** *each* **tequila and triple sec**
3 **tbsp. orange juice**
2 **tbsp. fresh lime juice**
4 **tbsp. pomegranate juice**
2 **twists lime zest**

1. Put 1 cup ice cubes in a pitcher. Pour in tequila, triple sec, orange juice, and lime juice. Stir well and divide between two cocktail glasses.
2. Using a spouted pourer or a large spoon, carefully pour 2 tbsp. pomegranate juice down side of each glass. Garnish each with lime twist, crushed slightly just before adding.

PER SERVING: 225 cal., 0% (1.4 cal.) from fat; 0.3 g protein; 0.2 g fat (0 g sat.); 20 g carbo (0.2 g fiber); 3.8 mg sodium; 0 mg chol.

Infused Sake

Robert Robinson, former general manager at Ponzu in San Francisco, likes to add fresh pineapple or mango to sake. As the fruit steeps, it gradually transfers flavor and color to the clear rice wine, enhancing sake's fruity and floral qualities.

SERVES 6 | **TIME** 10 minutes, plus 5 days to infuse

1 **bottle (750 ml.) sake**
1 **cup sliced peeled fresh pineapple or sliced, peeled,**
    and pitted firm-ripe mango

1. In a wide-mouthed 1- to 1½-qt. jar, combine sake and fruit. Cover and chill until sake has a subtle fruit flavor, about 5 days.
2. Lift out fruit with a slotted spoon and discard. Serve cold—the sooner, the better.
Make Ahead: Infused sake (without fruit) up to 1 week, chilled.

PER SERVING: 170 cal., 0% from fat; 0.6 g protein; 0 g fat; 7.5 g carbo (0 g fiber); 2.7 mg sodium; 0 mg chol.

Pisco Sour

Greg Hoitsma, bartender at Andina restaurant in Portland, Oregon, is known for his ever-changing seasonal cocktails, but the pisco sour, invented in Peru around 1900, is always on his list. Hoitsma recommends using a pisco (Peruvian grape brandy) that has a bit of bite to it to create the balance in this creamy, frothy, limy drink.

SERVES 1 | **TIME** 5 minutes

¼ cup (2 oz.) pisco
1 tbsp. *each* sugar and fresh lime juice
1 tsp. pasteurized egg whites
Aromatic bitters
Lime wedge

In a blender, whirl 3 ice cubes, the pisco, sugar, lime juice, and egg whites until smooth (you'll no longer hear ice cracking against side of blender). Serve straight up in a martini glass with a dash of aromatic bitters and a wedge of lime.

PER SERVING: 224 cal., 0.7 g protein; 0.2 g fat (0 g sat.); 33 g carbo (0 g fiber); 9 mg sodium; 0 mg chol.

Tarragon Bubble Fling

The fresh, savory herbs infused in this sparkling-wine cocktail make it an ideal match for classic appetizers like herb-coated goat cheese and smoked salmon.

SERVES 1 | **TIME** 2 minutes

2 tbsp. tarragon-flavored Herb-infused Simple Syrup *(recipe follows)*
About ½ cup (4 oz.) *blanc de blancs* sparkling wine, chilled
Tarragon sprig

Pour simple syrup into a chilled Champagne flute, fill flute with sparkling wine, and garnish with tarragon sprig.

PER SERVING: 194 cal., 0% from fat; 0.1 g protein; 0 g fat; 28 g carbo (0 g fiber); 5.9 mg sodium; 0 mg chol.

Simple Syrup: In a 2-qt. glass measuring cup, combine 1 cup *each* **water** and **sugar**. Microwave, stirring once, until sugar is dissolved, about 2 minutes. Chill until cold, about 1 hour. Makes about 1¼ cups.

Herb-infused Simple Syrup: When sugar is dissolved, stir in ½ cup loosely packed **fresh herbs** such as tarragon or basil, then chill until cold. When cold, strain into another glass measuring cup; discard herbs.

Red, White, and Sparkling

Dark-red liqueur slips beneath the white wine cocktail; sparkling wine provides a layer of bubbles on top.

SERVES 1 | **TIME** 3 minutes

6 tbsp. (3 oz.) Pinot Grigio or Pinot Gris, chilled
1 tbsp. *each* Simple Syrup *(below, left)* and fresh lemon juice
2 tbsp. cassis liqueur or black raspberry-flavored liqueur, such as Chambord
About 2 tbsp. *blanc de noirs* sparkling wine

1. Pour Pinot Grigio, simple syrup, and lemon juice into a cocktail shaker filled with ice. Cover and shake just until chilled, about 5 seconds, then pour into a chilled martini glass.
2. Carefully pour liqueur down side of glass and let it settle on bottom. Gently pour sparkling wine on top and serve immediately.

PER SERVING: 232 cal., 0% from fat; 0.1 g protein; 0 g fat; 26 g carbo (0.1 g fiber); 6 mg sodium; 0 mg chol.

White Peach Sangria

This refreshing sangria gets its sweetness (and a double dose of peach flavor) from peach schnapps and sliced fresh peaches.

SERVES 10 | **TIME** 15 minutes, plus 2 hours to chill

1 bottle (750 ml.) Riesling or other aromatic white wine
2 cups thin wedges firm-ripe white peaches (about ¾ lb.)
½ cup peach schnapps
1 cup loosely packed mint sprigs
1 bottle (750 ml.) brut-style sparkling wine, chilled

1. In a large pitcher or small punch bowl, combine Riesling, peaches, peach schnapps, and mint sprigs. Cover and chill until cold, at least 2 hours.
2. Pour in sparkling wine, stir gently, and serve immediately in chilled white wine glasses.

PER SERVING: 170 cal., 1% (1.3 cal.) from fat; 0.5 g protein; 0.2 g fat (0 g sat.); 12 g carbo (0.7 g fiber); 4.7 mg sodium; 0 mg chol.

Coconut Eggnog

Try this rich Puerto Rican–style eggnog with or without the rum.

SERVES 12 | **TIME** 20 minutes, plus 4 hours to steep/chill

1 pt. half-and-half
4 cinnamon sticks (3½ in. long)
1 tsp. whole cloves
5 egg yolks
1 can (14 oz.) sweetened condensed milk
1 can (13.5 oz.) coconut milk
1¼ cups light or dark rum (optional)
Ground cinnamon

1. Heat half-and-half, cinnamon sticks, and cloves in a saucepan, stirring, until boiling. Remove from heat and let stand for 1 hour. Strain and return to pan.
2. Whisk egg yolks and condensed milk into half-and-half. Cook over medium heat, stirring constantly, until mixture reaches 160° on a candy thermometer (don't allow it to boil). Stir in coconut milk. Let cool, then chill at least 3 hours.
3. Blend half of mixture at a time in a blender until frothy. Pour into a bowl and stir in rum if using. Ladle into glasses and sprinkle with cinnamon to taste.
Make Ahead: Up to 3 days, chilled.

PER SERVING: 248 cal., 57% (142 cal.) from fat; 5.8 g protein; 16 g fat (11 g sat.); 21 g carbo (0.1 g fiber); 70 mg sodium; 119 mg chol.

Orange-scented Mulled Wine

Warm coriander and pungent cardamom—instead of the usual cinnamon—give traditional mulled wine a spicy, floral twist.

SERVES 9 | **TIME** 20 minutes, plus 30 minutes to steep

1 large orange
Seeds from 8 cardamom pods
1 tbsp. coriander seeds
3 tbsp. chopped crystallized ginger
8 to 9 tbsp. sugar, divided
2 bottles (750 ml. each) dry red wine
¼ cup triple sec (optional)
Thin orange slices (optional)

1. With a vegetable peeler, pare 8 thin strips zest (4 in. by ½ in. each) from orange. Juice orange.
2. Wrap cardamom and coriander seeds and ginger in a piece of cheesecloth and tie with kitchen twine.

3. In a nonreactive saucepan, crush orange zest and 7 tbsp. sugar with a wooden spoon to release oil from zest. Add orange juice, wine, and spice packet. Cover and bring to a simmer over high heat, about 5 minutes. Remove from heat and let stand, covered, 30 minutes. Discard spice packet and orange zest.
4. To serve, heat wine, covered, over medium heat just until steaming. Stir in triple sec if using and remaining 1 to 2 tbsp. sugar to taste. Ladle into heatproof glasses. Garnish with orange slices if you like.

PER SERVING: 213 cal., 1% (1.3 cal.) from fat; 0.3 g protein; 0.1 g fat (0 g sat.); 23 g carbo (0.5 g fiber); 8.8 mg sodium; 0 mg chol.

Warm Star Pear Cider

This delicious hot pear cider, created by Mimi Booth of Ukiah, California, is made with honey (her husband is a beekeeper in Mendocino County). It's steeped with tangy dried hibiscus blossoms as a nod to the region's Latino cooking traditions.

SERVES 8 | **TIME** 15 minutes

½ cup dried hibiscus blossoms (*see Quick Tip below*)
4 cups pear nectar
2 cups red wine
¼ cup fresh lemon juice
2 star anise pods, plus more for garnish
⅓ cup honey
Thin pear slices (optional)

1. Boil 2 cups water. In a small heatproof bowl, pour boiling water over hibiscus blossoms and let steep 5 minutes.
2. Meanwhile, in a nonreactive saucepan, warm pear nectar, wine, lemon juice, and 2 star anise pods over low heat.
3. Strain hibiscus infusion into a large pitcher, add pear nectar mixture, and stir in honey. Serve warm in mugs. Garnish each serving with a whole star anise and pear slice if you like.
Quick Tip: Find dried hibiscus at Latino markets, under its Spanish name, *jamaica*.

PER SERVING: 169 cal., 0% (0.3 cal.) from fat; 0.3 g protein; 0 g fat; 33 g carbo (0.8 g fiber); 8 mg sodium; 0 mg chol.

Warm Apple Pie Cocktails

These really do taste exactly like warm apple pie, but with a kick.

SERVES 6 | **TIME** 5 minutes, plus 30 minutes to steep

1½ qts. fresh unfiltered apple juice
3 cinnamon sticks (2½ in. long)
12 whole cloves
6 whole allspice
1½ cups spiced rum
Sweetened whipped cream

1. Combine apple juice and whole spices in a saucepan and bring to a simmer. Remove from heat and let stand 30 minutes.
2. To serve, reheat juice, then strain into heatproof mugs. Add ¼ cup rum to each and top with whipped cream.

PER SERVING: 244 cal., 1% (3.4 cal.) from fat; 0.3 g protein; 0.4 g fat (0.1 g sat.); 0.3 g carbo (0.7 g fiber); 11 mg sodium; 0 mg chol.

Rhubarb-Rose Bubble Tea

Bubble tea, a drink partly filled with fat, chewy "bubbles" made from tapioca starch, originated in Taiwan in the 1980s and quickly spread around the globe. It found a thirsty audience in many parts of the West, especially California and especially in Asian-style cafes, and makers came up with all kinds of flavor combinations. Ours is a bit less sweet than the cafe standard and uses fresh ingredients rather than powders. Find thick straws (a fun part of the sipping experience) at Asian markets and well-stocked grocery stores.

SERVES 2 | **TIME** 30 minutes

1½ cups sliced rhubarb
½ cup sugar
½ cup green-tea-flavor or black tapioca pearls (see Quick Tips, above right)
½ cup cool double-strength jasmine tea
½ to 1 tbsp. rose water or orange-blossom water, such as Monteux (see Quick Tips, above right)

1. In a small saucepan, mix rhubarb and sugar with 1 tbsp. water. Cook, covered, over medium heat, stirring occasionally, until rhubarb is very soft, about 10 minutes. Purée in a blender and leave there to cool slightly.

2. Meanwhile, in a medium saucepan, cook the tapioca pearls in about 4 cups boiling water according to package directions until soft but still chewy, about 6 minutes. Drain, rinse, and drain again. Divide between two large glasses (14 oz. each).
3. To blender with rhubarb, add 2 cups ice cubes, the tea, and rose water; purée. Pour into glasses and add a fat straw to each.
Quick Tips: Look for tapioca pearls at Asian markets and in the supermarket's Asian-foods aisle. Find rose or orange-blossom water at gourmet grocery stores.

PER SERVING: 350 cal., 1% (1.7 cal.) from fat; 0.9 g protein; 0.2 g fat (0.1 g sat.); 88 g carbo (2 g fiber); 4.2 mg sodium; 0 mg chol.

Mango-Coconut Bubble Tea

This is a bubble-tea twist on the mango *lassi*, a classic Indian drink made with mango and yogurt. If you can't find a good fresh mango, use canned mango pulp—and if your mango is very fibrous, purée it first, then strain and purée again with the ice cubes, tea, coconut milk, and sugar.

SERVES 2 | **TIME** 15 minutes

½ cup black tapioca pearls (see Quick Tips below)
3 cups diced peeled fresh mango
½ cup cool double-strength black tea
¼ cup canned coconut milk
4 tbsp. sugar

1. In a 2-qt. pan, cook tapioca pearls in about 4 cups boiling water according to package directions until soft but still chewy, about 6 minutes. Drain, rinse, and drain again. Divide between two large glasses (16 oz. each).
2. In a blender, chop 1 cup ice cubes; purée ice with half of the following: mango, tea, coconut milk, and sugar. Pour into a glass. Repeat for second drink. Add a fat straw to each drink (see Quick Tips below).
Quick Tips: Find fat straws, along with the tapioca pearls, at Asian markets and well-stocked grocery stores.

PER SERVING: 463 cal., 15% (70 cal.) from fat; 2 g protein; 7.8 g fat (6.5 g sat.); 103 g carbo (5.5 g fiber); 9.8 mg sodium; 0 mg chol.

Brandied Hot Chocolate

On a chilly day, this grown-up version—rich with bittersweet chocolate and punched up with French brandy—will heat you up from your head to your toes.

SERVES 4 | **TIME** 10 minutes

1½ cups (about 6 oz.) grated bittersweet chocolate
½ cup dried low-fat milk powder
4 cups whole milk
4 tbsp. Armagnac
Whipped cream or marshmallows (optional)

1. In a small bowl, mix grated chocolate with milk powder.
2. In a medium saucepan, heat milk over medium heat, then stir in chocolate mixture. Whisk until chocolate has melted and mixture is smooth and hot.
3. Pour 1 tbsp. Armagnac into each of four mugs, then fill each with hot chocolate. Serve hot, garnished with whipped cream or marshmallows if you like.

PER SERVING: 608 cal., 39% (235 cal.) from fat; 34 g protein; 26 g fat (14 g sat.); 63 g carbo (3 g fiber); 438 mg sodium; 24 mg chol.

Hot Spiked White Chocolate

A portable dessert that warms your hands as you sip.

SERVES 1 | **TIME** 10 minutes

¾ cup milk
2 tbsp. *each* white chocolate chips and vanilla vodka
1½ tbsp. miniature marshmallows
⅛ tsp. unsweetened cocoa powder

1. Heat milk in a small saucepan over medium heat until very hot. Add chocolate chips and whisk until melted.
2. Pour vodka into a heatproof glass, add warm milk, top with marshmallows, and dust with cocoa.

PER SERVING: 304 cal., 38% (115 cal.) from fat; 7.3 g protein; 13 g fat (7.6 g sat.); 25 g carbo (0.1 g fiber); 96 mg sodium; 23 mg chol.

Layered Mocha

Sip hot chocolate through layers of hot espresso and thick, cold cream in this deconstructed mocha. It's based on the classic *bicerin* (bee-cheh-*reen*), from Caffè al Bicerin in Turin, Italy, and it fits right into our coffee-loving culture in the western United States. Serve in heatproof glasses to see the layers, and stir in more sugar to taste.

SERVES 4 | **TIME** 30 minutes

½ cup *each* heavy whipping cream and chopped semisweet chocolate
2½ tbsp. sugar, divided, plus more to taste
1 cup hot brewed espresso
1 tsp. unsweetened cocoa powder (not Dutch-processed; optional)

1. Pour cream into a bowl and chill until very cold, about 15 minutes. Fill four heatproof glasses (6 to 8 oz. each) with boiling water.
2. In a small saucepan over high heat, bring ¾ cup water to a boil. Reduce heat to low and whisk in chopped chocolate until smoothly blended. Add 1 tbsp. sugar. Stir over medium-low heat until mixture thickens slightly and coats spoon in a thin layer, 3 to 5 minutes. Cover and keep hot.
3. Whip cream with 1 tbsp. of sugar until thick, but before peaks form (cream should still be pourable). Mix remaining ½ tbsp. sugar with hot espresso.
4. Pour out water from glasses. Pour one-quarter of hot chocolate into a glass. Hold a spoon, concave side down, at about a 45° angle so tip of spoon touches inside of glass slightly above chocolate. Very slowly, pour one-quarter of espresso over back of spoon. Repeat for each glass. Spoon thick cream onto espresso. Sift a bit of cocoa over cream if you like.

PER SERVING: 235 cal., 65% (153 cal.) from fat; 1.5 g protein; 17.3 g fat (11 g sat.); 22 g carbo (1.2 g fiber); 15 mg sodium; 41 mg chol.

■ Cocoa

FROM THE PANTRY

Unsweetened cocoa, or cocoa powder, is made from roasted, ground cacao seeds that have had much of their fat removed. There are two types of cocoa: natural (nonalkalized) and Dutch-processed (alkalized). Both are unsweetened, but their flavors differ subtly. Natural cocoa tastes fruity, tart, and acidic, and is simply untreated cocoa. It's rarely labeled "natural," so you'll just see "cocoa" on the label. Dutch-processed cocoa is treated with an alkali to reduce its harshness and acidity. This type of cocoa has a rich, dark color and a mellow, toasted flavor.

How the West Won Coffee

The West has long had a special relationship with coffee. In 1825, coffee plants were brought from Brazil to the island of Oahu. Today, Hawaii is the only U.S. state that grows coffee commercially, with the beans produced in the Kona districts of the Big Island being best known.

Coffee and the Gold Rush
A couple of decades after that giant leap for coffee in the West, a 15-year-old named James A. Folger, working for California's first coffee mill, the Pioneer Steam Coffee and Spice Mills in San Francisco, started carrying coffee samples to the gold fields—introducing exhausted Gold Rushers to the joys of beans already roasted and ground. He eventually bought the company and renamed it J.A. Folger & Co.; it became one of the first national coffee brands.

European Influences
Caffe Trieste began serving Italian espresso in San Francisco in 1956. The era of artisanal coffee and hip coffee shops was born 10 years later, when Alfred Peet, who had grown up working in the coffee business in Holland, opened Peet's Coffee in Berkeley, popularizing a dark-roast style. He later trained the founders of a new little company called Starbucks and initially supplied them with Peet's fresh-roasted beans. The game-changer Starbucks, whose first store opened in Seattle in 1971, went on to become America's largest coffeehouse chain, with more than 11,000 stores at last count.

The story, of course, continues to percolate. Small in-house roasters like San Francisco's Blue Bottle and Portland's Stumptown Coffee Roasters win accolades and devoted followers, not just for their beans and individual drip coffees, but also for focusing on free-trade standards and relationships with growers around the world.

Vietnamese Iced Coffee

Traditionally, this dessert coffee is brewed by the cup. A small metal coffee filter (found in many Asian markets) filled with fine-ground coffee is placed on a mug containing a generous spoonful of sweetened condensed milk. Water, poured into the filter and coffee, slowly drips into the milk. By dessert time, all the water has drained, and the coffee is poured into a glass filled with ice. Find a bubble drink variation below.

SERVES 6 | **TIME** 15 minutes

¾ to 1 cup low-fat sweetened condensed milk
1½ cups fine-ground French roast or espresso roast
coffee

1. Pour ¾ cup condensed milk into a coffee pot or pitcher. Put ground coffee into a filter cone and set it onto pot.
2. Pour 3 cups boiling water, in batches, into filter until it all drips into pot.
3. Mix coffee and milk. Taste and add more milk if you like. Pour into six ice-filled glasses.

PER SERVING: 122 cal., 11% (14 cal.) from fat; 3.1 g protein; 1.5 g fat (1 g sat.); 23 g carbo (0 g fiber); 42 mg sodium; 5 mg chol.

Vietnamese Bubble Coffee: In a medium pan, cook ½ cup **black tapioca pearls** (find at Asian markets and in the supermarket's Asian-foods aisle) in about 4 cups boiling water according to package directions until pearls are soft but still chewy, about 6 minutes. Drain, rinse, and drain again. Make Vietnamese Iced Coffee as directed, but divide coffee between four heat-proof glasses (8 oz. each) and don't add ice. Drink with a fat straw (also at Asian markets and supermarkets) or use a spoon to scoop up the bubbles. Serves 4.

Keoke Coffee

George Bullington, the late co-owner of Bully's, in La Jolla, California, is credited with inventing this body-warming drink in the late 1960s for his restaurant's bar. His staff dubbed it George's Coffee, until one of the cooks, a Hawaiian, came up with the name that stuck: *Keoke* is Hawaiian for "George."

SERVES 2 | **TIME** 5 minutes

4 tbsp. *each* **brandy, crème de cacao, and coffee-flavored**
liqueur, such as Kahlúa
3 cups hot brewed coffee
4 tbsp. whipped cream (optional)

Pour 2 tbsp. each brandy, crème de cacao, and coffee liqueur into two mugs. Add half of coffee to each. Top with whipped cream if you like.

PER SERVING: 245 cal., 0% from fat; 0.4 g protein; 0 g fat; 19 g carbo (0 g fiber); 7.1 mg sodium; 0 mg chol.

soups, stews & chili

Essential comfort food, these fresh, aromatic dishes are easy to make and full of the flavors of the West.

Few other foods have as big a payoff as soup. At its most basic, it's inexpensive and straightforward to make; you can whip up a big batch and eat it all week long. And a well-made soup is a wonderful way to use up ripe produce from your garden or the market. You'll find plenty of suggestions here for simple soups that are eloquent with the flavors of the season—corn, tomatoes, artichokes, beets, pumpkin, mushrooms.

When you want something more substantial, try one of our big-bowl soups, like Whole-grain Pasta Soup with Greens and Parmesan (*page 94*) or Caramelized-vegetable and Meatball Soup (*page 96*). Some are traditional recipes from different nationalities that have settled in the West. The Vietnamese beef noodle soup *Pho Bo* (*page 98*) and Mexican Tortilla Soup (*page 97*) are two of our favorites. Others are adaptations that substitute local ingredients and use time-saving techniques to fit our busy lives. That's how we came up with Japanese Potsticker Soup (*page 97*), on the table in 25 minutes, and Chinese Pork and Asparagus Soup (*page 100*), ready in 30.

It's only a few steps from a hearty soup to a stew, and we've included some of those too, in all their fragrant, tender, long-simmered glory. Try Paprika Short-rib Beef Stew (*page 108*), with shards of meat falling off the bone into a rich, paprika-scented broth; New Mexico's *Carne Adovada* (*page 123*), packed with earthy red New Mexican chile and hunks of pork; or Classic Cioppino (*page 126*), the fabulous seafood stew invented by Italian fishermen in San Francisco more than a century ago.

We end the chapter with a quintet of chilis that will prove to you, with every spoonful you eat, why they're worth making from scratch.

Soups, Stews & Chili

soups, stews & chili

Tiered Tomato Soup

This soup is a glory of flavor and color, with a ruby red stratum of tomato soup crowning a spring green layer of avocado purée. Clear, straight-sided glasses or wineglasses (12- to 16-oz. each) show off the layers best, but large martini glasses also work.

SERVES 6 to 8 as a first course | **TIME** 30 minutes, plus 1 hour to chill

2 lbs. ripe tomatoes
Salt
3 or 4 tbsp. white wine vinegar, divided
2 firm-ripe avocados (½ lb. each)
¾ cup chicken broth
¼ cup sour cream
3 tbsp. fresh lime juice
1 cucumber (¾ lb.)
3 tbsp. minced shallots
1 tsp. minced tarragon

1. Core tomatoes; cut into chunks. Purée in a blender or food processor until smooth, then rub through a fine strainer into a bowl; you should have about 3 cups. Discard residue. Season purée to taste with salt and 2 or 3 tbsp. vinegar. Cover and chill until cold, at least 1 hour.
2. Peel and pit avocados; cut into chunks. In a blender or food processor, purée avocados, broth, sour cream, and lime juice until smooth. Add salt to taste. Put in a bowl and cover surface with plastic wrap; chill until cold, at least 1 hour.
3. Peel cucumber; cut in half lengthwise and scoop out and discard seeds. Dice into ⅛-in. pieces; you should have about 1 cup. In a small bowl, mix cucumber, shallots, the remaining 1 tbsp. vinegar, and the tarragon. Cover and chill until cold, at least 30 minutes.
4. To serve, stir avocado mixture to blend and pour equal portions into glasses. Whisk tomato mixture to blend and gently pour over avocado. Top with cucumber mixture.

PER SERVING: 117 cal., 65% (76 cal.) from fat; 2.5 g protein; 8.4 g fat (2.1 g sat.); 11 g carbo (2.4 g fiber); 31 mg sodium; 3.5 mg chol.

Chilled Pineapple Gazpacho

recipe pictured on page 117

A delicious, intensely flavored soup, this gazpacho demands fresh pineapple juice. You may be tempted to use canned, but trust us—it's just not the same. Chef and *Sunset* reader Jason Edwards invented the soup for his wife, Irene, who was on a raw-food diet at the time, but it appeals to everyone who tries it, regardless of gastronomic persuasions.

SERVES 4 as a first course | **TIME** 30 minutes, plus 2 hours to chill

1 slightly underripe pineapple (*see Quick Tip below*), peeled, cored, and cut into chunks
½ cup peeled, diced red bell pepper (¼-in. pieces)
½ cup peeled, seeded, diced cucumber (¼-in. pieces)
¼ cup finely chopped red onion, rinsed in cold water and patted dry with paper towels
¼ to ½ serrano chile, minced (remove seeds and ribs first if you want less heat)
1 tbsp. chopped cilantro, plus whole leaves for garnish
1 or 2 tbsp. fresh lime juice
½ tsp. sea salt, or to taste

1. Juice the pineapple in a juicer or purée in a blender and strain. Pour juice into a medium bowl. Stir in bell pepper and cucumber. Add onion, chile, and chopped cilantro. Sprinkle with lime juice and season with salt.
2. Cover and chill until very cold, about 2 hours. Serve garnished with cilantro leaves.
Quick Tip: Pick a pineapple that isn't too fragrant or yellow.
Make Ahead: Up to 1 day, chilled (add onion and chile no more than 2 hours before serving).

PER SERVING: 70 cal., 3% (2 cal.) from fat; 1 g protein; 0.2 g fat (0 g sat.); 18 g carbo (2.2 g fiber); 283 mg sodium; 0 mg chol.

Tomato-Cucumber Gazpacho

This simplified version of gazpacho, developed by the staff of Parcel 104 restaurant in Santa Clara, California, is a light, refreshing way to use the very ripest (and almost too ripe) tomatoes. For a more rustic presentation, dice the vegetables instead of puréeing them.

SERVES 8 as a first course | **TIME** 30 minutes

2 lbs. very ripe tomatoes, seeded and roughly chopped
1 English cucumber or 1 lb. Persian cucumbers, peeled and roughly chopped
1 red bell pepper, seeds and ribs removed and roughly chopped
¼ cup extra-virgin olive oil
1 tbsp. salt, plus more to taste
1 tbsp. sherry vinegar
Freshly ground black pepper
¼ cup diced red onion (optional), rinsed in cold water and patted dry with paper towels

1. In a blender, purée tomatoes, cucumber, bell pepper, oil, salt, and vinegar until smooth. (You may need to blend in batches.) Season with additional salt and pepper to taste.
2. Divide soup among small cups; garnish with a sprinkling of onion if using.

PER ½-CUP SERVING: 182 cal., 74% (135 cal.) from fat; 2.5 g protein; 15 g fat (2.1 g sat.); 14 g carbo (3.4 g fiber); 1,769 mg sodium; 0 mg chol.

Chilled Corn Soup

A summer soup that is pure essence of corn. Blanching the basil, an herb that tends to blacken once it's cut, keeps it jewel green. For a smoky flavor, roast or grill the corn in its husk instead of boiling it.

MAKES About 6 cups; 4 servings | **TIME** 20 minutes, plus 3 hours to chill

9 medium ears fresh yellow corn, husked
Salt
½ cup tightly packed basil leaves
¼ cup extra-virgin olive oil

1. Plunge ears of corn into a large pot of boiling water and boil, covered, 2 to 3 minutes, until heated through. Remove from water; when ears are cool enough to handle, slice off kernels with a sharp paring knife. In two batches, purée kernels in a blender with 4 cups water. Strain purée into a bowl, pressing to squeeze out the corn liquid, and throw away the kernel mash.

Add salt to taste and chill soup until cold, at least 3 hours.
2. Meanwhile, plunge basil into boiling water for 2 or 3 seconds. Drain immediately, plunge leaves into ice water, and drain again. Purée basil in a blender with ½ tsp. salt and the oil.
3. Serve soup cold, drizzled with basil oil.

PER SERVING: 337 cal, 44% (147 cal.) from fat; 8.4 g protein; 17 g fat (2.3 g sat.); 48 g carbo (6.9 g fiber); 38 mg sodium; 0 mg chol.

Creamy Artichoke Soup

A classic California soup, earthy and smooth.

MAKES About 5 cups; 4 servings | **TIME** 1 hour

6 fresh or frozen artichoke hearts
1 tbsp. salt, plus more to taste
3 tbsp. butter
1 onion, chopped
2 tbsp. flour
4 cups chicken broth
3 tbsp. whipping cream
Freshly ground black pepper
Chopped chervil (optional)

1. If using fresh artichokes, trim leaves, stems, and fuzzy chokes from artichokes (save leaves for other uses).
2. Bring a large pot of water to a boil and add salt. Drain the hearts and add to boiling water (if using frozen, just add to boiling water). Cook until tender, 4 to 5 minutes. Drain.
3. In a pan over medium-high heat, melt butter. Add onion and stir until golden. Stir in flour; cook, stirring often, 3 to 5 minutes. Add broth and artichoke hearts; stir until mixture boils and thickens, 15 to 20 minutes.
4. Purée mixture in a blender until smooth, in batches. Strain through a medium-mesh strainer into a pan and heat through. Add cream and salt and pepper to taste. Serve garnished with chervil if using.

PER SERVING: 364 cal., 52% (188 cal.) from fat; 16 g protein; 21 g fat (9.5 g sat.); 37 g carbo (16 g fiber); 2,324 mg sodium; 63 mg chol.

soups, stews & chili

Romesco Soup

We turned romesco—a classic Spanish sauce made of ground tomatoes, peppers, onions, garlic, olive oil, and almonds—into soup. It tastes like a cream soup but actually contains no cream. Powdered milk and the silky texture of cooked onions and roasted peppers make it rich and smooth; the lentils add thickness. This is quite a spicy soup; if you'd like it to be gentler, use regular sweet paprika instead of the hot.

MAKES 7 cups; 4 or 5 servings | **TIME** 1 hour

2 tbsp. olive oil
2 medium onions, halved and thinly sliced
½ tsp. salt, plus more to taste
6 garlic cloves, minced
½ tsp. hot smoked Spanish or Hungarian paprika
½ cup hulled red lentils, sorted for debris and rinsed
3 jars (12 oz. each) roasted red peppers, drained and rinsed
1 can (28 oz.) diced tomatoes
1⅓ cups chicken or vegetable broth or water, or more as needed
⅔ cup nonfat dried milk
1 tbsp. good-quality red wine vinegar, plus more to taste
¼ cup sliced almonds, toasted (*see How to Toast Nuts, page 134*)
Roasted almond oil or extra-virgin olive oil for drizzling (optional)

1. Warm olive oil in a large pot over medium-high heat. Add onions and salt and stir to combine. Cover, reduce heat to medium, and cook, stirring occasionally, until onions are very soft, 5 to 10 minutes; reduce heat, if necessary, to keep onions from browning.
2. Add garlic and cook, uncovered, until soft, about 3 minutes. Stir in paprika and cook 1 minute. Add lentils, peppers, tomatoes, and broth. Bring to a boil, reduce heat to maintain a steady simmer, cover, and cook until lentils are extremely soft, about 30 minutes.
3. In three batches, carefully purée hot soup in a blender until very smooth, at least 3 minutes per batch. Add dried milk and vinegar to last batch. Stir batches together and taste for salt and vinegar, adding more if needed; add a little more broth if soup seems too thick.
4. Serve topped with a sprinkle of almonds and a drizzle of almond oil if using.

PER 1½-CUP SERVING: 289 cal., 27% (77 cal.) from fat; 13 g protein; 8.5 g fat (1.1 g sat.); 45 g carbo (6 g fiber); 962 mg sodium; 1.6 mg chol.

Fennel and Comice Pear Soup

Fennel, also called sweet anise or finocchio, is crunchy and has a lovely anisey flavor. It has three distinct parts: the stalks, the feathery fronds (which can be used as an herb), and the pale green bulbs. Comice pears are large, plump, and very sweet and juicy. Together they make a perfect fall or winter first course.

SERVES 6 to 8 as a first course | **TIME** 30 minutes

2 heads fennel
1 yellow onion, chopped
2 tbsp. butter
2 Comice pears, peeled, cored, and coarsely chopped (*see Comice Pears, below*)
4 cups chicken or vegetable broth, or more as needed
Salt, white pepper, and freshly ground black pepper

1. Trim base and stalks from fennel, reserving a few feathery fronds for garnish. Coarsely chop bulbs.
2. In a medium pan, combine chopped fennel, onion, butter, and 2 tbsp. water; cover and cook over medium-high heat until vegetables are limp, 5 to 7 minutes. Add pears and broth; cover, reduce heat, and simmer until pears are soft, about 5 minutes.
3. Purée mixture in a blender, in batches if necessary, until smooth.
4. Return soup to pan to reheat. If it's too thick, add a little more broth. Season with salt and white pepper to taste. Serve sprinkled with reserved fennel fronds and black pepper to taste.

PER 1-CUP SERVING: 106 cal., 36% (38 cal.) from fat; 4 g protein; 4.3 g fat (2.3 g sat.); 15 g carbo (3.8 g fiber); 100 mg sodium; 8.7 mg chol.

■ Comice Pears
— FROM THE GARDEN

So plump it's almost swollen-looking, the Comice pear is renowned for its subtle sweetness, juiciness, and fine-grained texture. You can usually identify it not only by its chubbiness but also by its deeply indented blossom end. Look for Comices from September through March. (For more about Western pears, *see page 706*.)

Four-Onion Soup

Sweet Western onions, red onions, leeks, and shallots add layers of rich onion flavor to the French classic. For this recipe, you'll need ovenproof soup bowls.

SERVES 4 to 6 | **TIME** 1½ hours

2 lbs. red onions
1 lb. *each* sweet onions, such as Walla Walla or Maui, and leeks
½ lb. shallots
3 tbsp. butter
1 tsp. salt, plus more to taste
6 cups beef broth
1½ cups dry red wine
2 tsp. chopped thyme leaves
Freshly ground black pepper
¾ cup *each* shredded Swiss cheese and coarsely shredded dry jack or parmesan cheese
4 to 6 slices (1 in. thick) crusty French bread

1. Cut red and sweet onions in half lengthwise; peel and thinly slice crosswise. Cut off and discard dark green tops and root ends from leeks. Cut leeks in half lengthwise and swish around in a large bowl of water to rinse off dirt; transfer to a colander, leaving dirt behind, and rinse again in fresh water if necessary. Slice leeks thinly crosswise. Peel shallots and thinly slice crosswise.
2. In a 4- to 6-qt. pan over medium-low heat, melt butter. Add onions, leeks, and shallots. Sprinkle with salt. Cook, stirring occasionally and adjusting heat as necessary to prevent scorching, until onions are very soft and deep golden brown, about 1 hour.
3. Stir in broth, wine, and thyme; add pepper and more salt to taste. Bring soup to a simmer and cook, stirring occasionally, to blend flavors, about 10 minutes.
4. In a small bowl, mix Swiss and jack cheeses. Set ovenproof soup bowls on a baking sheet. Ladle hot soup into bowls. Float a slice of bread on each bowl of soup, then sprinkle each with shredded cheese. Broil soup about 8 in. from heat until cheese is bubbly and starting to brown, 2 to 3 minutes. Serve hot.
Make Ahead: Soup base (through step 3), up to 3 days, chilled. Reheat before proceeding with step 4.

PER SERVING: 499 cal., 29% (144 cal.) from fat; 23 g protein; 16 g fat (9 g sat.); 61 g carbo (5.5 g fiber); 1,019 mg sodium; 44 mg chol.

Spiced Pumpkin Soup with Ginger Browned Butter

Warm spices and caramelized onions underscore the natural sweetness of pumpkin and butternut squash in this comforting soup. The easy swirl of ginger butter on top at the end adds a bit of flavor and a lot of style.

SERVES 8 | **TIME** 1¾ hours

2 lbs. *each* Sugar Pie or other baking pumpkin, and butternut or acorn squash *(see Quick Tip, right)*
8 cups reduced-sodium chicken or vegetable broth, divided
7 tbsp. butter, divided
2 medium onions, chopped
1 tsp. salt, plus more to taste
4 garlic cloves, chopped
2 tbsp. plus 1 tsp. grated fresh ginger
1 tsp. ground ginger
¼ tsp. freshly grated nutmeg
⅛ tsp. *each* ground cloves and freshly ground cardamom seeds (from about 4 pods)
2 carrots, chopped
½ cup firmly packed light brown sugar

1. Preheat oven to 375°. Cut pumpkin and squash in half lengthwise. Scoop out seeds and any stringy parts. Put flesh side up in a large roasting pan with 1 cup broth. Cover pan with foil and bake until vegetables are tender when pierced with a fork, about 1 hour.
2. Meanwhile, melt 3 tbsp. butter in a large pot over medium heat. Add onions and salt. Cook, stirring occasionally, until onions are soft and start to look creamy, about 5 minutes. Reduce heat to low or medium-low and cook, stirring every few minutes, until onions turn a caramel color and become quite sweet, about 30 minutes. Set aside.
3. When pumpkin and squash are tender, scoop out flesh and set aside; discard skins. Reserve any liquid in bottom of pan.
4. Return pot with onions to medium-high heat. Add garlic and 2 tbsp. fresh ginger. Cook, stirring, until fragrant, about 2 minutes. Add ground ginger, nutmeg, cloves, and cardamom. Cook, stirring, 1 minute. Add remaining 7 cups broth, the carrots, cooked pumpkin and squash, and reserved liquid from roasting pan. Bring to a boil, then reduce heat and simmer until carrots are tender, about 15 minutes.
5. Purée vegetables and broth in a blender, in batches, until completely smooth. (For a silky-smooth soup, you can pour puréed soup through a strainer.) Return to pot and stir in brown sugar. Season with salt to taste. Keep warm over low heat.

soups, stews & chili

6. Put a small bowl or measuring cup next to the stove. Melt remaining 4 tbsp. butter in a small frying pan over medium-high heat. Add remaining 1 tsp. fresh ginger. Cook, stirring occasionally, until butter starts to foam. Stir mixture constantly until it starts to brown. Pour mixture into waiting bowl or measuring cup. Serve soup with a swirl of ginger browned butter in each bowl.

Quick Tip: You can substitute 3½ lbs. packaged, peeled and cubed butternut squash for the pumpkin and squash. Skip steps 1 and 3, decrease the amount of broth to 7 cups, and add the squash with the broth and carrots to the onion mixture in step 4. Cook until all vegetables are tender, about 25 minutes.

PER SERVING: 248 cal., 36% (90 cal.) from fat; 5.6 g protein; 10 g fat (6.3 g sat.); 37 g carbo (3.2 g fiber); 982 mg sodium; 27 mg chol.

Watercress Vichyssoise

A member of the mustard family, watercress has a pleasing pungency and beautiful emerald green color. Use the small-leafed, dark green watercress for the pepperiest bite (larger-leafed, paler hydroponic watercress tends to be more subdued). Add a dollop of crème fraîche, fromage blanc, or sour cream to each serving if you like.

MAKES 6 cups; 4 servings | **TIME** 50 minutes

1 lb. leeks
2 tbsp. olive oil
¼ tsp. salt, plus more to taste
½ tsp. freshly ground black pepper, plus more to taste
4 cups reduced-sodium chicken or vegetable broth, or more as needed
1 lb. Yukon Gold potatoes, peeled and chopped
1 lb. watercress, tough stems trimmed

1. Trim root ends from leeks and cut leeks in half lengthwise. Swish around in a large bowl of water to rinse off dirt; transfer to a colander, leaving dirt behind, and rinse again in fresh water if necessary. Cut into ½-in. slices.
2. Heat oil in a large pot over medium-high heat. Add leeks, salt, and pepper and cook until leeks are limp, stirring often, about 5 minutes. Add broth and potatoes. Bring to a boil, covered; reduce heat and simmer until potatoes are tender when pierced, 10 to 15 minutes. Add watercress and cook until wilted, about 30 seconds.
3. Purée vegetables and broth in a blender, in batches if necessary, holding lid down with a kitchen towel. Pour back into saucepan and thin with more broth if you like; reheat until hot. Season with more salt and pepper.

PER 1½-CUP SERVING: 221 cal., 34% (76 cal.) from fat; 11 g protein; 8.5 g fat (1.5 g sat.); 27 g carbo (2.7 g fiber); 334 mg sodium; 25 mg chol.

Mushroom-Potato Soup with Smoked Paprika

Smoked paprika adds a satisfying hint of woodsmoke. For an even deeper mushroom flavor, you can substitute shiitake, oyster, or mitake (also called maitake or hen of the woods) for the button mushrooms.

SERVES 6 to 8 | **TIME** 1 hour

2 oz. dried porcini mushrooms
1½ lbs. fresh button or cremini mushrooms
3 tbsp. olive oil
1 onion, halved lengthwise and thinly sliced
1½ tsp. salt
3 oz. pancetta, chopped
1 tbsp. sweet smoked Spanish paprika (see *Quick Tip* below)
1 cup dry white wine
2 cups chicken broth
3 russet or Yukon Gold potatoes (1½ lbs.), peeled and chopped
Salt and freshly ground black pepper
6 to 8 tbsp. crème fraîche or sour cream

1. In a small bowl, pour 1 cup boiling water over dried porcini. Set aside until softened.
2. Cut stems off button mushrooms. Finely chop stems; set aside. Halve caps, slice, and add to stems. With a slotted spoon, lift out porcini, pressing excess liquid into bowl, and transfer to a cutting board. Finely chop porcini and add to stems and caps. Reserve soaking liquid.
3. Heat oil in a large pot over medium-high heat; add onion and salt. Cook, stirring, until onion is soft, about 3 minutes. Add pancetta and cook until onion looks a bit creamy, about 2 minutes. Add paprika and cook until very fragrant, 2 minutes. Turn heat to high and add mushrooms. Cook, stirring constantly, until mushrooms start releasing their liquid, 3 to 5 minutes.
4. Add wine and cook until liquid is reduced by half, about 3 minutes. Add reserved porcini soaking liquid (pouring carefully to leave behind the sandy dregs), broth, 2 cups water, and potatoes. Bring to a boil, then reduce heat to low and simmer, uncovered, until potatoes are tender, 10 to 15 minutes.
5. Season with salt and pepper to taste. Serve with a dollop of crème fraîche in each bowl.

Quick Tip: Smoked Spanish paprika is available at well-stocked and specialty grocery stores.

PER SERVING: 265 cal., 51% (135 cal.) from fat; 8.3 g protein; 15 g fat (6.1 g sat.); 25 g carbo (4.2 g fiber); 713 mg sodium; 17 mg chol.

Whole-grain Pasta Soup with Greens and Parmesan

In a recipe this simple, every ingredient shines, so be sure to use the best-quality cheese and chicken broth you can find (homemade broth would be best). This soup is meant to be eaten as soon as it's made; after a few hours in the broth, the pasta will turn soft and gummy.

SERVES 6 to 8 | **TIME** 30 minutes

10½ cups reduced-sodium chicken broth or Homemade Chicken Broth *(recipe follows)*
3 cups very thinly sliced kale leaves (stems removed)
½ lb. whole-grain angel hair pasta or thin spaghetti, broken into small pieces
6 oz. parmesan cheese, preferably parmigiano-reggiano
2 tsp. fresh lemon juice
Red chile flakes (optional)

1. In a large pot over high heat, bring broth to a boil. Add kale, reduce heat to medium-high, and cook 2 minutes. Add pasta and cook until tender but not soft, 4 to 7 minutes or according to package instructions.
2. While pasta is cooking, use a vegetable peeler to shave parmesan into strips about 3 in. long and ½ in. wide (dimensions do not need to be exact).
3. Just before serving, stir in lemon juice. Top bowls with parmesan curls and a sprinkling of chile flakes if using.

PER SERVING: 236 cal., 22% (52 cal.) from fat; 19 g protein; 5.8 g fat (4 g sat.); 29 g carbo (4.4 g fiber); 1,059 mg sodium; 17 mg chol.

Homemade Chicken Broth

Making your own chicken broth is worth it in many ways: You cleverly use the last scraps of the chicken, which is both economical and conscientious; you scent your kitchen with a meaty, warm, herbaceous fragrance; and you have broth that's superior to what you can buy, and a lot less salty too. Freeze it in 2- or 3-cup portions so you always have it around for impromptu soup-making.

MAKES About 3 qts. | **TIME** 3 hours, plus 6 hours to chill

5 lbs. uncooked chicken or turkey pieces and/or bones (skin and fat discarded), or a mixture of bones from roasted poultry and uncooked meat scraps
1 onion (½ lb.), coarsely chopped
1 carrot (¼ lb.), cut into chunks
2 stalks celery (¼ lb. total), leafy tops left on, cut into chunks
½ cup flat-leaf parsley sprigs
5 black peppercorns
1 bay leaf
1 thyme sprig or ¼ tsp. dried thyme

1. In a 6- to 8-qt. pot over medium-high heat, combine all ingredients. Add cold water just to cover. Bring to a simmer, then lower heat to maintain simmer and cook, occasionally skimming and discarding foam from surface, until liquid is golden and has a deep chicken flavor, about 2 hours. Do not let broth boil; the surface should barely be disturbed by small bubbles. If a layer of fat forms on the surface, skim off and discard. If liquid drops below the level of chicken and vegetables, add more cold water just to cover.
2. Set a fine mesh strainer over a large bowl nested in ice water in the sink. Ladle or carefully pour broth through strainer into bowl. Let broth drip from solids without pressing on solids to extract more liquid (otherwise you'll end up with a murky broth). Discard solids. Stir broth occasionally until cool, 10 to 20 minutes; cover and chill until broth is cold and any fat on the surface is firm, at least 6 hours and up to 1 day.
3. With a spoon, skim fat from surface of broth and discard.
Make Ahead: Up to 4 days, chilled; up to 3 months, frozen. To freeze, pour into resealable plastic bags, leaving space for broth to expand as it freezes, or into ice cube trays (enclose them in a resealable bag); label each batch with the current date.

PER CUP: 19 cal., 18% (3.4 cal.) from fat; 3 g protein; 0.4 g fat (0 g sat.); 0.8 g carbo (0 g fiber); 106 mg sodium; 3.8 mg chol.

Golden Beet and Beet Greens Soup

Make the most of fresh farmers' market beets with this soup, which uses the delicious leaves as well as the beets themselves.

SERVES 4 | **TIME** 1¼ hours

3 golden beets with leafy tops (1½ lbs.)
1 tbsp. olive oil
1 red onion (6 oz.), sliced lengthwise
2 garlic cloves, minced
4 cups reduced-sodium vegetable or chicken broth, or more as needed
½ tsp. salt
¼ tsp. freshly ground black pepper

1. Trim leafy tops off beets, leaving 1 in. of stems attached. Wash beets and leaves, discarding tough stems. Put beets in a medium saucepan and cover with water. Bring to a boil, covered; reduce heat and simmer until beets are tender when pierced, 35 to 45 minutes. Drain and let cool. Remove skin and stems, then cut beets thinly crosswise. Cut beet leaves crosswise into thin shreds. Set aside.

2. Heat oil in a large pot over medium-high heat. Add onion and garlic and cook until lightly browned, about 4 minutes. Add broth and sliced beets. Bring to a boil. Stir in reserved beet greens and cook until wilted, about 1 minute. Add more broth if you like. Season with salt and pepper.

PER SERVING: 112 cal., 29% (32 cal.) from fat; 2.4 g protein; 3.6 g fat (0.5 g sat.); 18 g carbo (3.9 g fiber); 931 mg sodium; 0 mg chol.

Asian Greens and Tofu Soup

This nourishing soup gets most of its flavor from *dashi,* a light Japanese broth made from kombu seaweed and flakes of dried bonito tuna; it's savory without tasting fishy. We like to use a combination of Asian greens, but tender spinach makes a fine substitute.

SERVES 6 | TIME 1 hour

Homemade *Dashi (recipe follows)*
½ cup white or yellow miso
4 cups coarsely chopped mixed Asian greens, such as tatsoi and Chinese broccoli
3 cups coarsely chopped bok choy (leaves and stems)
2 bunches (about 16) green onions, thinly sliced
2 tsp. grated fresh ginger
1 package (12.3 oz.) extra-firm silken tofu, patted dry and cut into ½-in. cubes
Sriracha chili sauce or other Asian-style hot sauce
Sesame oil (optional)

1. In a small bowl, mix 2 cups hot dashi with miso, stirring until there are no lumps, then stir back into rest of dashi.
2. Bring liquid to a gentle simmer (do not boil) and stir in greens, bok choy, green onions, and ginger. Once greens have wilted, stir in tofu and let simmer, uncovered, 5 minutes. Offer with hot sauce and sesame oil if using.

PER SERVING: 115 cal., 24% (28 cal.) from fat; 10 g protein; 3.1 g fat (0.4 g sat.); 14 g carbo (4.2 g fiber); sodium N/A; 0 mg chol.

Homemade *Dashi*: Soak 2 pieces **kombu** (4 in. each) in 8 cups cold water for 20 minutes. Bring to a boil and add ½ cup **dried bonito flakes**. Remove from heat, let sit 5 minutes, then strain through a fine-mesh strainer into a large saucepan. Makes 7 cups.
Quick Tip: Kombu and dried bonito flakes are available at Asian markets and many grocery stores.

PER CUP: 6 cal., 0% from fat; 0.6 g protein; 0 g fat; 0.7 g carbo (0.3 g fiber); 32 g sodium; 0.6 mg chol.

Mexican Chicken and Chayote Soup

Memories of his mother's cooking in Veracruz, Mexico, inspired Eligio Hernández of Newman, California, to create this light but satisfying soup. Chayote (also called mirliton or christophene) is a mild-flavored pale green, pear-shaped relative of melon, cucumber, and squash. You can substitute zucchini.

SERVES 4 | TIME 45 minutes

1 chayote (¾ lb.)
1 tbsp. vegetable oil
1 white onion (6 oz.), chopped
3 garlic cloves, chopped
2 jalapeño chiles, seeds and ribs removed and thinly sliced
1 tsp. cumin seeds
4 cups chicken broth
1 can (14.5 oz.) diced tomatoes
1 can (15 oz.) chickpeas (garbanzos), drained and rinsed
4 boned, skinned chicken breast halves (6 oz. each)
1 firm-ripe avocado (½ lb.), pitted, peeled, and sliced
2 tbsp. chopped cilantro
Lime wedges
Salt
Cooked rice

1. Cut chayote into ½-in. cubes (you can cut through the edible seed).
2. Set a 5- to 6-qt. pan over high heat. When hot, add oil, onion, garlic, chiles, and cumin seeds; stir until onion begins to brown, 2 to 3 minutes. Add broth, tomatoes (with their juice), chickpeas, and chayote; bring to a boil.
3. Add chicken in a single layer, pushing down to submerge in liquid. Return to a boil, then cover pan tightly and remove from heat. Let stand until chicken is no longer pink in center of thickest part (cut to test), 15 to 17 minutes. With tongs, lift chicken out. Return soup to a boil over high heat; if chayote is not tender, simmer, covered, until tender when pierced. Cut chicken breasts crosswise into thick slices, leaving pieces next to each other; with a wide spatula, transfer each sliced breast half to a wide bowl.
4. Ladle soup into bowls. Distribute avocado slices and cilantro over chicken and garnish with lime wedges to squeeze over servings. Add salt to taste. Serve with hot rice to spoon into soup.

PER SERVING: 455 cal., 28% (126 cal.) from fat; 54 g protein; 14 g fat (2.1 g sat.); 28 g carbo (5.3 g fiber); 478 mg sodium; 99 mg chol.

Caramelized-vegetable and Meatball Soup

This soup is built on root vegetables roasted until sweet, dense, and crisply browned. Roast meatballs at the same time, then add with broth to the pan with vegetables, and you have soup straight from the oven. While you're at it, warm some bread in the oven too.

MAKES 3 qts.; 6 to 8 servings | **TIME** 1¾ hours

1 small butternut squash, peeled, halved, and seeded
3 medium Yukon Gold potatoes, peeled
2 *each* large carrots and parsnips, peeled
15 to 20 garlic cloves, peeled
3½ tbsp. olive oil, divided, plus more for shaping meatballs
2½ tsp. kosher salt, divided, plus more to taste
1½ tsp. freshly ground black pepper, divided, plus more to taste
1 lb. ground turkey (not breast only; *see Quick Tip, above right*)
1 tbsp. fennel seeds
1 egg, lightly beaten
2 large leeks
1 large head fennel, trimmed and bulb cut into ¼-in.-thick slices (reserve feathery fronds for garnish)
8 cups reduced-sodium chicken broth

1. Preheat oven to 425° and arrange racks in upper and lower thirds of oven. Cut squash, potatoes, carrots, and parsnips into 1-in. pieces and put in a large oiled roasting pan; add garlic. Toss with 2½ tbsp. oil, 1½ tsp. salt, and 1 tsp. pepper and spread out in a single layer, leaving as much room as possible around the pieces. Roast vegetables on lower rack until browned and tender, about 40 minutes (stir after they've browned underneath, about 25 minutes).

2. Meanwhile, make meatballs: With wet hands, mix turkey, fennel seeds, egg, and remaining 1 tsp. salt and ½ tsp. pepper together in a medium bowl. Oil your hands and shape turkey mixture into 1-in. meatballs; set on an oiled rimmed baking sheet as you go, using more oil as needed to coat them well. Roast meatballs on upper rack 15 to 20 minutes, turning a couple of times to brown well on all sides.

3. Trim root ends from leeks and cut leeks in half lengthwise. Swish around in a large bowl of water to rinse off dirt; transfer to a colander, leaving dirt behind, and rinse again in fresh water if necessary. Cut into ¼-in. slices. Heat remaining 1 tbsp. oil in a large pot over medium-high heat. Add leeks and fennel, season with salt and pepper to taste, and cook until softened, about 5 minutes. Pour in broth and bring to a boil over high heat, covered. Lower heat and simmer vegetables until meltingly soft, about 25 minutes.

4. When vegetables in oven have caramelized and meatballs are browned, remove both from oven. Transfer meatballs to roasting pan. Pour a ladleful of hot broth into baking sheet and scrape up browned bits; pour into roasting pan along with all contents of pot and gently scrape up vegetables' browned bits. Return to oven and bake 5 minutes to let flavors mingle.

Quick Tip: Avoid buying white-meat-only ground turkey for the meatballs; it's too dry and your meatballs will fall apart (and be tasteless besides).

PER 1½-CUP SERVING: 330 cal., 33% (108 cal.) from fat; 18 g protein; 12 g fat (2.3 g sat.); 39 g carbo (6.7 g fiber); 1,045 mg sodium; 68 mg chol.

Coconut-Lime Chicken and Rice Soup

To prepare this even faster, buy a rotisserie chicken from a good deli (a 2-pounder will yield about 4 cups of meat). For more of a kick, add ¼ to ½ tsp. red chile flakes to the broth mixture in step 1.

MAKES 2½ qts.; 6 servings | **TIME** 40 minutes

5 cups chicken broth
⅓ cup fresh lime juice
¼ cup thinly sliced fresh ginger
2 garlic cloves, crushed with flat side of a knife
3 tbsp. *each* soy sauce and firmly packed brown sugar
2 cans (13.5 oz. each) reduced-fat coconut milk
4 cups bite-size pieces cooked chicken
1 red or green jalapeño chile (optional), stemmed and thinly sliced crosswise
3 cups cooked medium-grain white rice
½ cup thinly slivered basil leaves
Lime wedges

1. In a 4- to 5-qt. pan, combine broth, lime juice, ginger, garlic, soy sauce, and brown sugar. Bring to a boil over high heat, then cover, reduce heat, and simmer until flavors are blended, about 20 minutes.

2. With a slotted spoon, lift out and discard ginger slices and garlic cloves. Add coconut milk, chicken, and jalapeño slices if using to broth mixture. Heat soup over medium-high heat, stirring, just until hot, 5 to 6 minutes; don't let boil.

3. Divide hot rice among soup bowls. Sprinkle with basil and spoon soup over the top. Garnish with lime wedges to squeeze into soup to taste.

PER SERVING: 459 cal., 27% (126 cal.) from fat; 39 g protein; 14 g fat (6.3 g sat.); 44 g carbo (0.4 g fiber); 696 mg sodium; 83 mg chol.

Tortilla Soup

To get to know her neighbors better, Johanna Sedman of Berkeley, California, started hosting a soup night once a month. This is one of her creations. Its charm lies in the toppings, which guests can customize to their liking.

MAKES About 4½ qts.; 12 servings | **TIME** 1 hour

1 tbsp. vegetable oil, plus more for frying
2 large onions, chopped
8 garlic cloves, minced
1½ tbsp. kosher salt, divided
1 tsp. ground cumin
½ tsp. red chile flakes
12 cups reduced-sodium chicken broth
1 can (28 oz.) diced tomatoes
Juice of 2 limes, divided
1 package (8 oz.) small corn tortillas, cut into
   ¼-in.-thick strips *(see Quick Tip below)*
2 lbs. boned, skinned chicken breasts, cut into
   ¼-in.-thick strips
1 cup chopped cilantro
Sliced avocado, sour cream, shredded Monterey jack
   cheese, additional chopped cilantro, and/or sliced
   green onions for topping

1. Heat oil in a large pot (at least 5 qts.) over medium heat. Add onions and cook, stirring a few times, until translucent, 5 to 7 minutes. Stir in two-thirds of garlic, 1 tbsp. salt, the cumin, and red chile flakes and cook 2 minutes. Add broth, tomatoes (with their juice), and half the lime juice and increase heat to a gentle simmer; cook 20 minutes.

2. Meanwhile, pour about 1 in. of oil into a small frying pan set over medium-high heat. When oil is hot but not smoking, add a third of the tortilla strips and cook until golden brown and crisp, about 2 minutes. With a slotted spoon, transfer strips to a paper towel–lined baking pan. Repeat with remaining tortilla strips in two batches. Sprinkle with 1 tsp. salt. Set aside.

3. Purée soup in batches in a blender until smooth. Return soup to pot and resume simmering. In a bowl, toss chicken with remaining lime juice, garlic, and ½ tsp. salt. Marinate at room temperature for 10 minutes, then add to soup and simmer until chicken is just cooked through, about 5 minutes. Stir in cilantro.

4. Serve with tortilla strips and toppings for your guests to add as they like.

Quick Tip: No time to make tortilla strips? Store-bought chips will do in a pinch.

PER SERVING: 243 cal., 32% (78 cal.) from fat; 21 g protein; 8.9 g fat (1.3 g sat.); 21 g carbo (1.8 g fiber); 1,565 mg sodium; 37 mg chol.

Herb Ravioli Soup

Ravioli made with thinly rolled pasta adds delicacy to this pretty soup, but it's good with the sturdier type too. We've included a variation that uses gyoza (Japanese potstickers) instead of the ravioli.

SERVES 6 | **TIME** 25 minutes

2 tbsp. extra-virgin olive oil
1 medium yellow onion, coarsely chopped
1 cup diced carrots (about 2 medium)
Freshly ground black pepper
6 cups chicken broth
1 lb. chicken ravioli
1 cup fresh or frozen peas
2 tsp. *each* chopped oregano and thyme leaves
1 tbsp. chopped flat-leaf parsley
1 to 2 tbsp. grated parmesan cheese

1. Heat oil over medium heat in a medium pot until hot. Add onion and carrots and cook, stirring, until onion is translucent and slightly golden and carrots are beginning to soften, about 7 minutes. Season to taste with pepper.

2. Add broth to pot, raise heat to high, and bring to a boil. Add ravioli and return broth to a boil. Cook ravioli according to package directions until tender to the bite. During last 4 to 5 minutes of cooking, add fresh peas (if using frozen, add at the very last minute), oregano, and thyme. Season to taste with pepper and stir in parsley.

3. Serve with a sprinkling of parmesan.

PER SERVING: 320 cal., 28% (90 cal.) from fat; 16 g protein; 10 g fat (2.4 g sat.); 42 g carbo (4.4 g fiber); 1,062 mg sodium; 37 mg chol.

Japanese Potsticker Soup:
Omit onion in step 1. Add 3 slices **fresh ginger** (each ¼ in. thick) with the broth in step 2; bring to a boil. Add **fresh peas** if using; cook 2 minutes. Add 1 lb. **chicken gyoza** and return broth to a boil. Stir in 2 tbsp. **soy sauce**. Cook gyoza until almost tender to the bite, 2 to 3 minutes. Add frozen peas if using; cook 1 minute more. Remove ginger slices. Season soup to taste with **black pepper** and stir in 2 tbsp. **parsley** (omit oregano and thyme). Top with ¼ lb. **mung bean sprouts** and 4 thinly sliced **green onions** (omit parmesan).

PER SERVING: 227 cal., 44% (99 cal.) from fat; 12 g protein; 11 g fat (2.3 g sat.); 22 g carbo (3.3 g fiber); 1,285 mg sodium; 21 mg chol.

Chicken and Corn Summer Chowder

This one-pot meal is both rich and light, with a fresh, bright topping of avocado, tomato, cilantro, and lime.

recipe pictured on page **109**

SERVES 6 | **TIME** 50 minutes

2 slices bacon, chopped
1 onion, chopped
3 tbsp. flour
1 lb. Yukon Gold potatoes, peeled and chopped
6 cups reduced-sodium chicken broth
4 cups shredded cooked chicken (from a 2½- to 3-lb. roasted chicken)
Kernels cut from 3 ears corn (about 3 cups)
¼ to ½ cup heavy whipping cream
2 ripe medium tomatoes, seeded and chopped
1 firm-ripe avocado, pitted, peeled, and chopped
1 cup loosely packed cilantro leaves
2 limes, cut into wedges
Freshly ground black pepper

1. In a large, heavy pot over medium-high heat, cook bacon until fat renders and meat starts to brown. Add onion, reduce heat to medium, and cook, stirring often, until soft, about 3 minutes. Sprinkle with flour and cook, stirring, until flour smells cooked (you should get a whiff of baked piecrust) but hasn't started to brown, about 3 minutes.
2. Add potatoes and broth. Bring to a boil. Reduce heat to keep mixture simmering and cook until potatoes are barely tender, about 5 minutes. Add chicken and corn and bring to a boil. Reduce heat to low and stir in cream to taste. Heat through, about 2 minutes.
3. Serve garnished with tomatoes, avocado, cilantro, a squirt or two of lime juice, and pepper to taste.

PER 2-CUP SERVING: 504 cal., 41% (207 cal.) from fat; 37 g protein; 23 g fat (7.9 g sat.); 40 g carbo (4.8 g fiber); 733 mg sodium; 109 mg chol.

Vietnamese Beef Noodle Soup (Pho Bo)

No street or home in Vietnam is without some version of *pho*, the country's quintessential breakfast soup. Beef noodle is a classic type. For a simpler version, *see Quick Tips, right.*

SERVES 6 | **TIME** 2¼ to 2½ hours

½ cup thinly sliced fresh ginger (about 3 oz.)
1 cup thinly sliced shallots (about ¼ lb.)
3 star anise pods (or 2 tsp. pieces) or 1 tsp. anise seeds
1 cinnamon stick (3 in. long)
1½ lbs boned beef chuck, fat trimmed
2½ qts. beef broth
¼ cup Thai or Vietnamese fish sauce (*nam pla* or *nuoc mam*), plus more to taste
1 tbsp. sugar
Salt
2 cups bean sprouts (5 to 6 oz.), rinsed
¼ cup very thinly sliced red or green chiles, such as Thai, serrano, or jalapeño
½ cup Thai or small regular basil leaves
½ cup cilantro leaves
3 limes, cut into wedges
½ lb. boned beef sirloin steak, fat trimmed and very thinly sliced (*see Quick Tips, above right*)
6 cups Cooked Rice Noodles (about ⅛ in. wide; *recipe follows*)
½ cup thinly sliced yellow onion
¾ cup thinly sliced green onions
Hoisin sauce and Asian red chili paste or sauce (optional)

1. Wrap ginger, shallots, star anise, and cinnamon stick in two layers of cheesecloth (about 17 in. square); tie with heavy cotton string. In an 8- to 10-qt. pan, combine beef chuck, broth, 2½ qts. water, fish sauce, sugar, and spice bundle. Cover and bring to a boil over high heat; uncover, reduce heat, and simmer until beef is tender when pierced, 1½ to 1¾ hours.
2. With a slotted spoon, transfer meat to a board. Remove and discard spice bundle. Skim and discard fat from broth. Add salt and more fish sauce to taste. Return broth to a simmer.
3. Meanwhile, arrange bean sprouts, chiles, basil, cilantro, and limes on a platter. When beef chuck is cool enough to handle, thinly slice across the grain.
4. Immerse sliced sirloin in simmering broth (use a wire basket or strainer, if available) and cook just until brown on the outside but still pink in the center, 30 seconds to 1 minute; lift out (with basket or a slotted spoon).

soups, stews & chili

98   The Sunset Cookbook

5. Mound hot noodles in deep bowls (at least 3-cup capacity). Top with beef chuck, sirloin, and onions. Ladle broth over portions to cover generously.

6. Serve with platter of accompaniments and hoisin sauce and chili paste (if using) to add to taste.

Quick Tips: To slice the sirloin as thinly as possible, freeze it flat for 30 to 45 minutes, then cut it crosswise into 2- to 3-in.-long strips. For a simpler version of *pho bo,* omit the beef chuck, increase the boned sirloin steak to 2 lbs., and increase the beef broth to 3 qts.; for steps 1 and 2, simmer broth (omit water) with the spice bundle and add fish sauce, sugar, and salt to taste.

Make Ahead: Sliced meat, up to 6 hours, chilled; broth (steps 1 and 2), up to 1 day, chilled (cover beef chuck and broth separately). Bring broth to a boil before serving.

PER SERVING: 592 cal., 17% (99 cal.) from fat; 42 g protein; 11 g fat (4 g sat.); 81 g carbo (1.3 g fiber); 768 mg sodium; 97 mg chol.

Cooked Rice Noodles *(Bun)*: Dried rice noodles range in width from about 1⁄16 to 1⁄4 in.; their cooked yield varies slightly, so be sure to look for the width specified in the recipe. In a 6- to 8-qt. pan over high heat, bring 3 to 4 qts. water to a boil. Add 12 to 14 oz. **dried rice noodles** (*mai fun,* rice sticks, or rice vermicelli) and stir to separate; cook until barely tender to the bite, 2 to 3 minutes. Drain. If not using immediately, rinse well to keep noodles from sticking together and drain again. Makes 6 to 8 cups; 6 to 8 servings.

PER SERVING: 144 cal., 0% from fat; 0 g protein; 0 g fat; 36 g carbo (0 g fiber); 75 mg sodium; 0 mg chol.

Pho: Vietnamese Culture in a Bowl

Pho, the beloved meat-and-noodle soup of Vietnam, has firmly established itself in the United States—particularly in the West, where large numbers of Vietnamese have settled. Noodle shops abound in urban areas like Los Angeles, Seattle, San Francisco, and San Jose, and in many rural areas as well, selling huge, fragrant, steaming bowls of *pho* (pronounced *fuh*): *pho bo* (beef), *pho ga* (chicken), *pho heo* (pork), and *pho bo tai* (rare beef slices).

A Commingling of Cuisines
Pho originated in Hanoi at the turn of the last century, probably inspired by *pot-au-feu,* the beef stew of Vietnam's French colonial rulers, and incorporating Chinese-style rice noodles. In those early days, it was a rich, intense beef broth embellished only with the noodles and sliced beef. As it spread to South Vietnam—an area with more and richer ingredients at its disposal—*pho* took on spices and herbs and diversified in style to include chicken and other ingredients. It's this bounteous style of *pho* that crossed the ocean to the United States, brought by immigrants fleeing the fall of Saigon in 1975.

It's All in the Broth
The key to a good *pho bo* is its broth. Beef bones full of marrow are simmered for hours with ginger, onion, fish sauce, star anise, cloves, and salt to develop rich, meaty, umami flavor. When the broth is ready and steaming hot, it is poured over very thin cooked flat rice noodles and thin, tender slices of raw or cooked beef.

Customize Your Bowl
Served on the side are the condiments, including black pepper, bean sprouts, hoisin sauce, chili sauce, fresh chiles, wedges of lime, and heaps of Thai basil leaves (*rau que*) and the cilantro-like saw-leaf herb (*ngo gai*). Herbs are added as you eat rather than all at once, which keeps the herbs fresh and also prevents the broth from cooling too much. Traditionally a breakfast dish, *pho* is in such demand that it is now available night and day here and in Vietnam.

Beef and Star Anise Noodle Soup

This rich, hearty dish is based on the Sichuan beef noodle soup at Queen's House in Mountain View, California.

SERVES 4 | **TIME** 30 minutes, plus 1 hour to marinate and 3 hours unattended oven time

2 lbs. beef short ribs
¼ cup soy sauce
2 tbsp. *each* minced fresh ginger and garlic
4 dried Thai chiles
4 star anise pods, broken
3 tbsp. vegetable oil
5 cups reduced-sodium beef broth
Salt and freshly ground black pepper
½ lb. baby bok choy, stalks separated
21 oz. fresh or 12 oz. dried thick wheat noodles, such as udon

1. In a medium bowl, combine ribs with soy sauce, ginger, garlic, chiles, and star anise. Cover and chill at least 1 hour and up to 1 day, stirring occasionally.
2. Preheat oven to 300°. In an 8-qt. pot with ovenproof lid, heat oil over high heat until almost smoking. Lift ribs from marinade (save marinade) and brown on all sides, 4 to 6 minutes total.
3. Add marinade, broth, and 2 cups water to pot; cover and bring to a boil. Cook in oven until meat is extremely tender, about 3 hours.
4. Remove bones from ribs and discard. Cut larger rib meat into pieces. Skim excess fat from surface of broth if you like. Return meat to broth. Season to taste with salt and pepper. Add bok choy; let sit, covered, a few minutes to wilt.
5. Meanwhile, bring a 2-qt. pot of water to a boil. Add noodles and cook until tender to the bite, about 3 minutes for fresh and 8 minutes for dried. Drain noodles but don't rinse. Divide among bowls. Top with rib pieces and bok choy and ladle about 1½ cups broth into each bowl.
Make Ahead: Ribs (through step 3), up to 2 days, chilled. To continue cooking, remove any solid fat on top and remove bones and cut meat into pieces. Reheat meat in broth over medium heat, add bok choy, and proceed with step 5.

PER SERVING: 871 cal., 23% (198 cal.) from fat; 49 g protein; 22 g fat (6.3 g sat.); 120 g carbo (5.8 g fiber); sodium N/A (varies depending on noodles); 67 mg chol.

Chinese Pork and Asparagus Soup

Melt-in-your-mouth pork and tender-crisp asparagus combine in a savory, ginger-spiked broth.

SERVES 4 | **TIME** 30 minutes

6 oz. dried uncooked chow mein noodles
5 cups reduced-sodium chicken broth
1 tbsp. finely grated fresh ginger
3 tbsp. reduced-sodium soy sauce
1 pork tenderloin (about 1 lb.), fat trimmed
1 lb. asparagus, bottoms trimmed and cut into 1-in. pieces
¼ cup thinly sliced green onions
Sriracha chili sauce

1. Cook noodles according to package directions; drain, then set aside.
2. Meanwhile, in a large saucepan, combine broth, ginger, and soy sauce and bring to a simmer over medium heat.
3. Thinly slice pork, then add to broth along with asparagus. Stir to separate meat slices and cook until pork is no longer pink, 3 to 4 minutes. Stir in green onions and noodles. Serve with Sriracha.

PER SERVING: 398 cal., 38% (153 cal.) from fat; 33 g protein; 17 g fat (3.1 g sat.); 31 g carbo (2.7 g fiber); 1,404 mg sodium; 68 mg chol.

Everybody Loves Sriracha

Sriracha hot sauce may be named after a Thai city (Sri Racha), but the incendiary red sauce—otherwise known as rooster sauce, for the white rooster adorning each clear plastic bottle—is made in suburban Los Angeles by Huy Fong Foods.

Its creator, Huy Fong founder David Tran, says he invented his exhilarating red jalapeño purée seasoned with garlic powder, sugar, salt, and vinegar not just for Asians but for all cultures. He's succeeded: Today it's squirted into everything from Vietnamese *pho* to Korean beef tacos to steakhouse glazes to burger sauces, a burst of sweet-tangy heat that crosses culinary borders with ease.

Wild Rice and Mushroom Soup

A little cream goes a long way in this earthy, supremely comforting soup. You can substitute bacon for the pancetta if you like.

SERVES 8 | **TIME** 1½ hours

¾ cup wild rice (*see Quick Tip, right*)
1 tbsp. salt
1 oz. dried porcini mushrooms
1 leek
5 tbsp. butter at room temperature, divided
¼ lb. pancetta, finely chopped
½ lb. button mushrooms, finely chopped
2 tbsp. flour
½ cup dry white wine
4 cups reduced-sodium chicken or vegetable broth
3 tbsp. minced flat-leaf parsley
½ tsp. freshly ground black pepper
⅔ cup heavy whipping cream

1. Put wild rice, salt, and 8 cups cold water in a medium pot. Bring to a boil, lower heat to maintain a steady simmer, and cook until rice is tender, about 45 minutes. Drain and set aside.
2. Meanwhile, put porcini in a small bowl and pour in 1½ cups boiling water. Let sit until soft, about 15 minutes. Trim root end from leek and cut leek in half lengthwise. Swish around in a large bowl of water to rinse off dirt; transfer to a colander, leaving dirt behind, and rinse again in fresh water if necessary. Thinly slice white and light green parts.
3. In a large pot, cook 1 tbsp. butter and the pancetta over medium-high heat until meat renders some of its fat and turns a lighter pink. Add button mushrooms and leek. Cook, stirring occasionally, until mushrooms release their liquid, about 10 minutes.
4. Meanwhile, lift porcini from liquid with a slotted spoon (reserving liquid), chop finely, and add to pot.
5. Sprinkle mushroom mixture with flour and cook, stirring constantly, until flour starts to stick to bottom of pot (scrape it up as much as possible while stirring). Add wine, reserved liquid from soaking porcini (pouring slowly so as to leave any grit behind), and broth. Bring to a boil; lower heat to maintain a steady simmer and cook 15 minutes.
6. Meanwhile, combine remaining 4 tbsp. butter, the parsley, and pepper. Set aside.
7. Add reserved wild rice to mushroom mixture and cook 10 minutes. Stir in cream and cook until hot, about 1 minute.
8. Serve hot, with a dollop of parsley butter on each serving.

Quick Tip: Look for whole wild rice grains; they cook more evenly and keep their nutty-chewy texture better than split or broken grains do.

PER SERVING: 305 cal., 62% (189 cal.) from fat; 8.1 g protein; 21 g fat (12 g sat.); 20 g carbo (2.5 g fiber); 818 mg sodium; 55 mg chol.

Broccoli Rabe and Ham in Ginger Broth

Spicy greens meet sweet, tender ham in a wonderful quick soup.

SERVES 4 | **TIME** 30 minutes

5 cups chicken broth, or more as needed
6 thin slices fresh ginger
2 large garlic cloves, crushed
1 fresh red chile, stemmed and cut into rings, divided
¼ lb. cooked ham, cut into wide, thin strips
½ to ¾ lb. broccoli rabe (rapini) or Chinese mustard greens (gai choy), ends trimmed and cut into 2-in. lengths

1. In a large saucepan over high heat, bring broth, ginger, garlic, and 2 to 4 chile rings to a boil. Cover and simmer until broth is infused with flavor, 8 to 10 minutes. With a slotted spoon, remove ginger, garlic, and chile if you like.
2. Add ham and greens to broth; add more broth, if needed, to cover greens. Bring to a boil, covered, and cook until greens are barely tender, 2 to 3 minutes.
3. Top each bowl with a few more red chile rings if you like.

PER SERVING: 85 cal., 34% (29 cal.) from fat; 9.7 g protein; 3.2 g fat (0.9 g sat.); 6 g carbo (0.3 g fiber); 1,639 mg sodium; 23 mg chol.

■ Broccoli Rabe

FROM THE GARDEN

Though related to broccoli, broccoli rabe (also called rapini) has more punch—a bitter bite typical of members of the chicory and mustard families. It looks like a skinnier, leafier, leggier broccoli, with tiny green flower buds at the stalk tips that open into little yellow blossoms. Broccoli rabe is terrific cooked with plenty of olive oil to temper its pepperiness.

Chinese Hot-and-Sour Soup

Berkeley, California, resident Johanna Sedman prepares this soup occasionally for a monthly soup party she hosts for her neighbors. This version is a bit milder than the restaurant standard, but that's what we like about it. The flavors are balanced and fresh, and the acidity functions as an accent, not a one-note blast.

MAKES About 4½ qts.; 18 servings | **TIME** 1½ hours

2 lbs. pork top loin, cut crosswise into ⅛-in.-thick strips
¼ cup plus 2 tbsp. soy sauce
2 tbsp. grated fresh ginger
¾ cup unseasoned rice vinegar
¼ cup cornstarch
2 tbsp. sugar
1 tsp. salt
¼ cup peanut oil
1 can (8 oz.) sliced bamboo shoots, drained and rinsed
12 cups chicken broth
¾ lb. shiitake mushrooms, stems discarded and caps thinly sliced
¾ lb. firm tofu, drained and cubed
4 eggs
½ tsp. Asian (toasted) sesame oil
1 tbsp. freshly ground black pepper (*see Quick Tip, above right*)
Chopped cilantro and sliced green onions (white and pale green parts)

1. In a medium bowl, toss pork with ¼ cup soy sauce and the ginger. Marinate 20 minutes. In another bowl, stir together remaining 2 tbsp. soy sauce, the vinegar, cornstarch, sugar, and salt; set aside.
2. Heat peanut oil in a large pot (at least 5 qts.) over medium-high heat until hot. Add pork and marinade and cook, stirring constantly, until pork loses its pink color, about 4 minutes. Stir in bamboo shoots and cook 1 minute.
3. Increase heat to high, add broth, and bring to a boil. Add mushrooms, reduce heat to a simmer, and cook about 20 minutes.
4. Add tofu and simmer 5 minutes. Add soy-vinegar mixture and simmer 5 minutes more; the liquid will thicken.
5. In a small bowl, beat eggs with sesame oil. Slowly pour eggs into soup in a thin stream while stirring soup very slowly in one direction. Add pepper, stir briefly, then simmer 5 minutes. Serve sprinkled with cilantro and green onions.

Quick Tip: The heat from the black pepper in this soup intensifies as it sits. If you plan to make the soup ahead of time or want a milder flavor, use 2 tsp. during cooking; then taste the soup before serving and add more pepper if you like.

PER 1-CUP SERVING: 244 cal., 66% (162 cal.) from fat; 15 g protein; 18 g fat (5.7 g sat.); 18 g carbo (0.7 g fiber); 890 mg sodium; 80 mg chol.

Brussels Sprouts and Sausage Soup

The easy soup from reader Ellen Tafeen, of Portola Valley, California, makes a substantial and delicious main course, especially if you serve it with a loaf of hearty rye bread and a fresh green salad.

SERVES 4 | **TIME** 45 minutes

1 lb. brussels sprouts
½ lb. andouille sausage
1 tsp. olive oil
3 large red potatoes
2 bay leaves
1 tsp. caraway seeds
4 cups reduced-sodium chicken broth

1. Trim brussels sprouts at base and remove any damaged outer leaves. Cut sprouts in half lengthwise. Set aside.
2. Cut sausage into ¼-in.-thick slices. Put oil and sausage in a medium pot over medium-high heat and cook, stirring occasionally, until sausage is well browned, about 7 minutes.
3. Meanwhile, cut potatoes into roughly ½-in. pieces.
4. When sausage is browned, add bay leaves and caraway seeds to pot. Cook, stirring, until fragrant, about 1 minute. Add potatoes, broth, and 1 cup water. Bring to a boil. Add brussels sprouts. Partially cover pot and reduce heat to low or medium-low to maintain a steady simmer. Cook soup until potatoes and brussels sprouts are tender, about 15 minutes.

PER SERVING: 344 cal., 37% (126 cal.) from fat; 19 g protein; 14 g fat (4.3 g sat.); 40 g carbo (8.1 g fiber); 1,054 mg sodium; 35 mg chol.

Shrimp, Chile, and Pasta Soup
(Sopa Seca de Camarones y Fideos)

Fideos (vermicelli) are much loved in Mexico, where they form the basis of thick, delicious soups. Usually the soups are served as a first course, but our hearty shrimp version is a meal in a bowl. A *sopa seca*, (or "dry soup") falls midway between soup and stew.

SERVES 4 | **TIME** 35 minutes

2 dried ancho or pasilla chiles (each 4 to 5 in. long; see Quick Tip below)
3 tbsp. olive oil
6 oz. dried vermicelli or fideos, broken into thirds
½ tsp. *each* anise seeds and cumin seeds
1 medium onion, chopped
2 large garlic cloves, minced
4 cups reduced-sodium chicken broth
1 lb. medium shrimp (31 to 42 per lb.), peeled with tails left on and deveined
Kosher salt
½ cup sour cream (optional)
Diced avocado (optional)
¼ cup chopped cilantro

1. Wipe chiles clean with a damp cloth. Break off stems, then shake out and discard seeds. In a small bowl, cover chiles with hot water and let stand until softened, 5 to 10 minutes. Drain and coarsely chop.
2. Meanwhile, pour oil into a 12-in. nonstick frying pan over medium-low heat. Add pasta; stir and turn often with tongs until almost golden, 3 to 5 minutes. Stir in anise and cumin seeds, onion, and garlic. Lift pasta so it mostly sits on top of onion mixture, then cook onion mixture, stirring often, until softened, 4 to 5 minutes.
3. Stir in chiles and broth. Bring to a simmer over medium-high heat, then reduce heat to medium and simmer 3 minutes; add shrimp and simmer until pasta is tender to the bite, 3 to 4 minutes more. Season to taste with salt.
4. Top each serving with a spoonful of sour cream and some avocado if using and sprinkle with cilantro.
Quick Tip: Good dried chiles are soft, flexible, and smell a bit like prunes. Avoid hard, brittle specimens—they're old and less flavorful.

PER SERVING: 420 cal., 30% (126 cal.) from fat; 32 g protein; 14 g fat (2 g sat.); 42 g carbo (3.7 g fiber); 737 mg sodium; 164 mg chol.

Carrot Soup with Crab

recipe pictured on page **111**

Serve this soup, a fine showcase for Dungeness or Alaska king crab, to brighten a winter day.

SERVES 4 as a first course | **TIME** 1¼ hours

2½ tbsp. butter
1 medium onion, chopped
1 lb. carrots, sliced
1 large bay leaf (or 2 small)
2 tbsp. white rice
1 tsp. salt
½ tsp. *each* freshly ground black pepper and finely shredded lemon zest
6 oz. shelled cooked Dungeness crab (from a 1½-lb. crab; see *Dungeness Crab 101, page 340*)
1 tbsp. *each* fresh lemon juice and minced chives
Chopped chives

1. In a 5-qt. pot over medium-high heat, melt butter. Add onion, carrots, bay leaf, rice, salt, and pepper. Cook, stirring, until onion is light golden, about 6 minutes. Add 5 cups water and bring mixture to a boil, then reduce heat and simmer 25 minutes. Remove bay leaf.
2. Working in batches, purée soup in a blender until smooth. Return soup to pot, stir in lemon zest, and keep warm.
3. In a small bowl, toss crab with lemon juice and minced chives. Put an equal mound of crab mixture in the center of each soup bowl, then ladle soup around crab. Garnish with chopped chives.

PER SERVING: 181 cal., 39% (71 cal.) from fat; 11 g protein; 8.1 g fat (4.6 g sat.); 18 g carbo (3.6 g fiber); 859 mg sodium; 49 mg chol.

Halibut and Chickpea Soup

This light, clear soup derives its liveliness from fresh rosemary and ripe tomatoes. Serve with crusty bread.

SERVES 6 | **TIME** 30 minutes

1 tsp. olive oil, plus more for drizzling
¾ cup chopped onion
1 tsp. fennel seeds, crushed
1 small rosemary sprig (about 4 in.)
4 ripe red tomatoes (about 1 lb.), roughly chopped
1 can (14 oz.) chickpeas (garbanzos), drained and rinsed
½ cup dry white wine
6 cups reduced-sodium chicken broth
1 lb. boned, skinned white-fleshed fish fillets, such as Pacific halibut or Pacific cod
1 tsp. *each* salt and freshly ground black pepper
½ cup chopped flat-leaf parsley

1. Heat oil in a large saucepan over medium heat until hot. Add onion and cook until softened, stirring occasionally, about 3 minutes. Add fennel seeds, rosemary, tomatoes, chickpeas, wine, and broth; cover and bring to a boil.

2. Meanwhile, cut fish into 1-in. chunks. Add to boiling broth. Reduce heat and simmer until fish is cooked through and pulls apart when poked with a fork, about 3 minutes. Remove rosemary sprig, then stir in salt and pepper. Serve with a drizzle of oil to taste and a sprinkling of parsley.

PER SERVING: 224 cal., 30% (68 cal.) from fat; 22 g protein; 7.6 g fat (0.9 g sat.); 14 g carbo (3.6 g fiber); 1,083 mg sodium; 24 mg chol.

Warm Soba Noodle Bowl

A popular Japanese winter dish, warm soba with toppings is just the thing for lunch on an overcast day. The broth is made with *dashi,* the staple soup base whose delicate flavor comes from dried bonito tuna flakes and seaweed.

SERVES 4 | **TIME** 40 minutes

2 eggs
6 cups liquid *dashi (see Quick Tip, above right)* or Homemade *Dashi (page 95)*
4 shiitake mushrooms, stems removed and caps thinly sliced
1 tbsp. *each* mirin and soy sauce
1 lb. dried soba noodles
20 thin slices peeled daikon
1 sheet nori seaweed, cut into ¼- by 1-in. strips
2 green onions, trimmed and finely sliced diagonally

1. Put eggs, still in shells, in a small pot of cold water. Bring to a boil, remove from heat, cover, and let sit 15 minutes. Drain; rinse with cold water.

2. In a medium saucepan, bring dashi to a boil. Reduce heat to low and add mushrooms, mirin, and soy sauce.

3. Bring a 3-qt. saucepan of water to a boil. Add soba and cook, stirring to separate noodles, until softened, about 5 minutes. Drain but don't rinse. Divide noodles among bowls.

4. Pour 1½ cups dashi over noodles in each bowl. Arrange mushrooms and daikon over noodles, dividing evenly so each bowl has a neat row of both. Peel eggs and cut each in half lengthwise, placing 1 half in each bowl. Divide nori and green onions among bowls.

Quick Tip: You can find liquid dashi in containers in Japanese groceries and some gourmet stores. It's more widely available as a dry concentrate called *dashi-no-moto;* reconstitute according to package directions.

PER SERVING: 436 cal., 6.9% (30 cal.) from fat; 20 g protein; 3.3 g fat (0.9 g sat.); 88 g carbo (0.4 g fiber); 1,534 mg sodium; 106 mg chol.

Salmon Egg-drop Soup

Going into cold-and-flu season, reader Jeanette Taplin of Foster City, California, wanted a tasty soup with lots of virus-fighting power. After reading about the health benefits of salmon, ginger, and spinach, she came up with this quick version of the Chinese egg-drop soup.

SERVES 4 | **TIME** 25 minutes

3 cans (14.5 oz. each) chicken broth
3 tbsp. coarsely chopped fresh ginger
¾ lb. boned, skinned salmon fillet, cut into 1-in. chunks
2 cups loosely packed stemmed spinach leaves (about 2 oz.)
2 eggs, beaten to blend
¼ cup chopped green onions
Salt and freshly ground black pepper

1. In a 4- to 5-qt. pan over high heat, bring broth to a boil. Add ginger, reduce heat to maintain a simmer, cover, and cook to flavor broth, about 10 minutes. Remove ginger chunks with a slotted spoon or a fine-mesh strainer.

2. Add salmon to broth and simmer until opaque but still moist-looking in the center (cut to test), about 5 minutes. Add spinach and stir just until wilted.

3. Increase heat to bring broth back to a boil and slowly stir in eggs. Stir in green onions and season with salt and pepper to taste.

PER SERVING: 246 cal., 44% (108 cal.) from fat; 31 g protein; 12 g fat (2.6 g sat.); 1.9 g carbo (0.6 g fiber); 191 mg sodium; 156 mg chol.

soups, stews & chili

Green Tea Soup with Brown Rice and Black Cod

A simple broth of green tea poured over brown rice and fish makes an easy and healthful weeknight meal. We're partial to the extra-chewy texture of short-grain rice for this soup, but any reheated leftover rice will do. To shave off even more time, you can use precooked fish. Shredded leftover chicken or diced tofu also works.

SERVES 4 | **TIME** 1¼ hours

2 cups short-grain brown rice
1 tsp. salt, divided
1 package (about 0.8 oz.) toasted, seasoned nori
  (see Quick Tips below)
2 green onions, trimmed
2 tsp. vegetable or canola oil
1 lb. black cod fillets (see Quick Tips below)
8 tea bags of genmaicha (see Quick Tips below)
1 tsp. black sesame seeds (see Quick Tips below)
Tamari (rich, thick Japanese soy sauce) or soy sauce
  (optional)
Asian (toasted) sesame oil (optional)

1. In a medium saucepan, bring rice, ½ tsp. salt, and 4 cups water to a boil. Cover, reduce heat to a simmer, and cook until rice is tender to the bite, about 50 minutes. Remove rice from heat, uncover, and fluff with a fork.
2. Meanwhile, cut nori into ¼-in.-wide strips and set aside. Thinly slice green onions crosswise.
3. Preheat broiler. Generously oil a baking sheet. Put fish on sheet and turn over to coat both sides. Sprinkle with remaining ½ tsp. salt. Broil 3 to 4 in. from heat until cooked through (flesh flakes easily and is opaque in center), about 5 minutes. Transfer fish to a plate and set aside. (Skip this step if you're substituting cooked fish or chicken for the cod.)
4. When rice is cooked, bring 8 cups water to a boil. In a large teapot, measuring cup, or pitcher, pour water over tea bags. Let steep 5 minutes.
5. Meanwhile, divide cooked rice among large soup bowls. Place a fourth of the cod on each bed of rice. Pour 2 cups hot tea over each. Sprinkle with green onion and sesame seeds. Serve with bowls of nori, tamari, and sesame oil (if using) on the side.
Quick Tips: Toasted, seasoned nori and black sesame seeds are available at Asian markets and some supermarkets. Black cod is also known as sablefish or butterfish. Find genmaicha (green tea with roasted brown rice) at Asian markets and specialty-foods stores.

PER SERVING: 465 cal., 12% (58 cal.) from fat; 26 g protein; 6.4 g fat (0.5 g sat.); 82 g carbo (6.3 g fiber); 656 mg sodium; 49 mg chol.

Leek and Fennel Chowder with Smoked Salmon

You'll want to eat this spring soup by the big bowlful.

MAKES 4¾ qts.; 8 to 10 servings | **TIME** 1 hour

3 lbs. leeks
2 heads fennel (2½ to 3 lbs. total)
¾ cup thinly sliced chives
2 tbsp. butter
5 cups chicken broth
1 bay leaf
3 lbs. thin-skinned potatoes, cut into ½- to ¾-in. cubes
5 cups milk
½ cup flour
½ tsp. salt, plus more to taste
⅛ tsp. freshly ground black pepper, plus more to taste
1 lb. thin-sliced smoked salmon (see Quick Tip below), cut
  into strips 2 to 3 in. long and ½ in. wide

1. Trim and discard root ends and dark green tops from leeks. Cut leeks in half lengthwise and swish around in a bowl of water to rinse off dirt; transfer to a colander, leaving dirt behind, and rinse again in fresh water if necessary. Thinly slice crosswise.
2. Trim off and discard root ends and stalks from fennel; reserve 2 or 3 sprigs of feathery green fronds for garnish, and finely chop enough of remaining fronds to make 3 tbsp. In a bowl, mix chopped greens with chives; cover and chill. Chop fennel bulbs.
3. In a 6- to 8-qt. pan over medium heat, melt butter. Add leeks and chopped fennel bulbs, cover, and stir occasionally until vegetables are very limp, 10 to 12 minutes. Add broth and bay leaf. Bring to a boil over high heat.
4. Add potatoes to broth and return to a simmer; reduce heat, cover, and simmer, stirring occasionally, until potatoes are tender when pierced, 15 to 20 minutes.
5. In a bowl, whisk milk, flour, salt, and pepper until smooth. Add to broth mixture and stir over high heat until boiling, about 5 minutes. Add more salt and pepper to taste. Garnish soup with reserved fennel fronds. Offer smoked salmon and chive mixture to add to taste.
Quick Tip: Use either soft, cold-smoked salmon (also called lox or Nova-style) or firmer, hot-smoked salmon (also called kippered), or offer both for an interesting mix.
Make Ahead: Chowder, up to 1 day ahead; cool, then cover and chill. Chill salmon, chives, and fennel sprigs separately. Reheat chowder, covered, over medium to medium-high heat, stirring often.

PER SERVING: 357 cal., 28% (100 cal.) from fat; 27 g protein; 11 g fat (5.5 g sat.); 40 g carbo (8.6 g fiber); 1,499 mg sodium; 42 mg chol.

Chicken Stew with Olives and Lemon

Boneless chicken thighs are just as convenient as breasts, and they have an added advantage: Their succulent texture and robust flavor stand up well to braising. Give them the flavors of Italian salsa verde—bright parsley, tart lemon, piquant capers, and green olives—for a fresh, fast dish. For a spicier version and one using fish, see the variations that follow.

SERVES 4 | **TIME** 45 minutes

1 lb. skinned, boned chicken thighs, patted dry
2 tbsp. flour
1½ tsp. *each* salt and freshly ground black pepper, plus more to taste
2 tbsp. olive oil
2 large garlic cloves, minced
1 tbsp. capers, drained and minced
Finely shredded zest and juice of 1 lemon
½ cup dry white wine
1¾ cups chicken broth
1 lb. Yukon Gold potatoes, cut into ¾-in. cubes (see Quick Tip, above right)
1 package (8 oz.) frozen artichoke hearts, thawed and quartered if large
1 cup finely chopped flat-leaf parsley
1 cup pitted medium green olives
Lemon wedges

1. Cut each chicken thigh into 2 or 3 chunks. In a resealable plastic bag, combine flour, salt, and pepper. Add chicken, seal, and shake to coat.
2. Heat oil in a large pot over medium-high heat until hot. Add chicken (discard excess flour) in a single layer and cook, turning once, until browned on both sides, 4 to 5 minutes total. Transfer to a plate.
3. Reduce heat to medium. Add garlic, capers, and lemon zest and stir just until fragrant, about 30 seconds. Add wine and simmer, scraping up browned bits from bottom of pot, until reduced by half, about 2 minutes. Add broth, potatoes, and chicken and return to a simmer. Lower heat slightly to maintain simmer, cover, and cook 10 minutes.
4. Add artichokes to pot and stir. Cover and cook until potatoes are tender when pierced, 8 to 10 minutes. Stir in parsley, lemon juice to taste, and olives. Season with salt and pepper to taste. Serve with lemon wedges on the side.

Quick Tip: To save prep time, cube the potatoes or mince the garlic and capers while the chicken browns. Then, while the stew simmers, you can chop the parsley and juice the lemon.

PER SERVING: 385 cal., 37% (144 cal.) from fat; 29 g protein; 16 g fat (2.6 g sat.); 32 g carbo (6.8 g fiber); 2,171 mg sodium; 94 mg chol.

Spicy Olive-Tomato Chicken Stew: Add **red chile flakes** instead of lemon zest (omit lemon juice), and substitute 1 can (14.5 oz.) **petite diced tomatoes** (with their juice) for the white wine. Omit potatoes and use **black olives** instead of green.

Halibut-Artichoke Stew: Replace chicken with **halibut chunks**, omitting step 1 and skipping the browning in step 2 (simply sauté garlic, capers, and lemon zest in oil). Sprinkle fish with **salt** and **pepper**, add to stew with artichokes, and cook until opaque in center.

Lemony Lentil Stew

Even the lentil skeptics in *Sunset's* test kitchen loved this bright, zingy Ethiopian-style stew.

SERVES 6 | **TIME** 35 minutes

2 tbsp. butter
3 garlic cloves, minced
2 cups yellow or brown lentils, sorted for debris and rinsed
4 cups chicken or vegetable broth
1 tbsp. *each* minced fresh ginger and finely shredded lemon zest
¼ cup fresh lemon juice
Salt and freshly ground black pepper
Chopped cilantro and lemon wedges

1. Melt butter in a 3-qt. pan over medium-high heat. Add garlic and stir until just beginning to brown, about 1 minute. Add lentils and stir to coat with butter, then add broth. Simmer, covered, until lentils are tender but not mushy, 20 to 30 minutes. They will thicken as they cool.
2. Stir in ginger, lemon zest and juice, and salt and pepper to taste. Serve sprinkled with cilantro and offer lemon wedges on the side.

PER SERVING: 276 cal., 20% (50 cal.) from fat; 20 g protein; 5.5 g fat (3 g sat.); 39 g carbo (7.4 g fiber); 118 mg sodium; 13 mg chol.

soups, stews & chili

Speedy Chicken Posole with Avocado and Lime

This dish, using canned hominy, takes a fraction of the time needed for regular posole. Serve with warm corn tortillas.

SERVES 4 or 5 | **TIME** 45 minutes

3 large poblano chiles (1 lb. total)
6 garlic cloves
1 large onion
2 cans (14.5 oz. each) white hominy
1½ lbs. boned, skinned chicken thighs
½ tsp. kosher salt
2 tsp. dried Mexican oregano (*see Quick Tip below*), divided
2 tbsp. olive oil
3 cups reduced-sodium chicken broth
3 tbsp. ground red New Mexico chiles (*see Quick Tip below*)
Sliced avocado, lime wedges, cilantro sprigs, and sour cream for garnish

1. Preheat broiler. When hot, broil poblanos on a baking sheet until blackened, turning as needed, about 15 minutes.
2. Meanwhile, in a food processor, mince garlic. Cut onion in chunks and pulse with garlic until chopped. Drain hominy.
3. Cut chicken into 1- to 1½-in. chunks and sprinkle with salt and 1 tsp. oregano. Heat oil in a 5- to 6-qt. pan over high heat. Brown half the chicken lightly, stirring occasionally, about 5 minutes. With a slotted spoon, transfer meat to a plate. Repeat with remaining chicken.
4. Reduce heat to medium-high. Add onion mixture and remaining 1 tsp. oregano to pan and sauté until onion is softened, about 3 minutes. Meanwhile, in a microwave-safe bowl, microwave broth until steaming, about 3 minutes. Add ground chiles to pan and cook, stirring, about 30 seconds. Add broth, hominy, and chicken. Cover and bring to a boil, then reduce heat and simmer to blend flavors, 10 minutes.
5. Remove stems, skins, and seeds from poblanos and discard; chop poblanos.
6. Stir poblanos into posole and cook 1 minute. Ladle into bowls; top with garnishes.

Quick Tip: Find Mexican oregano at well-stocked grocery stores, along with ground red New Mexico chiles.

PER SERVING: 436 cal. 39% (169 cal.) from fat; 32 g protein; 19 g fat (4.2 g sat.); 36 g carbo (7.2 g fiber); 715 mg sodium; 89 mg chol.

Japanese-style One-pot Supper

Reader Marlene Kawahata of Palo Alto, California, sent in this truly substantial yet super-fast dinner.

SERVES 4 | **TIME** 20 minutes

3 oz. dried bean-thread noodles (*saifun* or cellophane noodles; *see Quick Tip below*)
5 cups reduced-sodium chicken broth
½ cup mirin (*see Quick Tip below*) or cream sherry
¼ cup soy sauce
1 tbsp. sugar
3 to 5 thin slices fresh ginger
¾ lb. skinned, boned chicken thighs, cut into 1-in. chunks
1 small red bell pepper, seeds and ribs removed and cut into thin strips
¼ lb. sugar snap or snow peas (*see Sugar Snap Peas, below*)
¼ lb. button mushrooms, sliced
½ lb. firm tofu, drained and cut into 1-in. cubes
3 green onions, trimmed and cut into 1-in. lengths
Sriracha chili sauce

1. In a small bowl, soak bean-thread noodles in boiling water until soft, about 5 minutes. Drain and cut into 6- to 10-in. lengths.
2. In a 5- to 6-qt. pot or a 12-in. frying pan (with sides at least 2 in. high), bring broth, mirin, soy sauce, sugar, and ginger to a boil over high heat. Reduce heat and simmer, covered, 5 minutes.
3. Arrange noodles, chicken, bell pepper, peas, mushrooms, tofu, and green onions in separate piles in the pot. Cover and simmer, without stirring, until chicken chunks are no longer pink in center (cut one to test), about 5 minutes. Set pot on the table so people can serve themselves, with Sriracha on the side.

Quick Tip: Look for dried bean-thread noodles, mirin, and Sriracha in the Asian section of the supermarket.

PER SERVING: 363 cal., 15% (53 cal.) from fat; 28 g protein; 5.9 g fat (1.3 g sat.); 42 g carbo (2.5 g fiber); 1,827 mg sodium; 71 mg chol.

■ Sugar Snap Peas

FROM THE GARDEN

These crisp beauties have a fleeting season—they're at their peak of sweet tenderness in the spring and early summer. The peas, pod and all, are delicious eaten raw but are good briefly cooked with other ingredients. They provide a nice crunchy element. To trim snap peas (as well as snow peas), cut or snap off ends and pull up sharply to remove any string on the pea. Discard ends and strings.

Singapore-style Turkey Stew

This recipe is a family favorite of reader Paul Firth of Cool, California. Firth adapted it from reader Roxanne Chan's recipe for Singapore chicken stew with spinach.

SERVES 4 | **TIME** 45 minutes

1 lb. ground lean turkey
½ tsp. *each* Chinese five-spice powder *(see Quick Tip below)*, red chile flakes, and salt
2 tbsp. flour
1 tbsp. vegetable oil
2 garlic cloves, minced
1 tbsp. grated fresh ginger
1 can (13.5 oz.) coconut milk
1 can (14.5 oz.) chicken broth
1 head bok choy (12 oz.), stem ends trimmed and cut crosswise into 1-in.-wide ribbons
1 can (14 oz.) baby corn, drained
2 Roma tomatoes (about ½ lb. total), cored and chopped
¼ cup *each* drained canned sliced water chestnuts and thinly sliced green onions
1 tbsp. fresh lime juice
3 tbsp. chopped cilantro

1. In a large bowl, mix turkey, five-spice powder, red chile flakes, and salt. Shape mixture into 1-in. balls. Pour flour onto a large rimmed plate and roll balls in flour to coat lightly.
2. Pour oil into a 4- to 5-qt. nonstick pan over medium heat. Add meatballs in a single layer. Cook, turning frequently, until lightly browned all over and barely pink in center (cut to test), 7 to 10 minutes. Using a slotted spoon, transfer to a plate.
3. Add garlic and ginger to pan and stir just until fragrant, about 30 seconds. Add coconut milk, broth, and meatballs; bring to a simmer. Adjust heat to maintain a simmer, cover, and cook until meatballs are no longer pink in center, about 8 minutes.
4. Stir in bok choy, corn, tomatoes, water chestnuts, green onions, and lime juice and cook, stirring occasionally, until bok choy leaves are wilted and stems are barely tender to the bite, about 5 minutes. Sprinkle with cilantro and serve from pan.
Quick Tip: If you can't find Chinese five-spice powder, substitute equal parts ground anise seeds, cinnamon, cloves, and ginger.

PER SERVING: 463 cal., 66% (306 cal.) from fat; 27 g protein; 34 g fat (21 g sat.); 16 g carbo (4.4 g fiber); 534 mg sodium; 85 mg chol.

Paprika Short-rib Beef Stew

This fragrant and satisfying dish from reader Mickey Strang, of McKinleyville, California, gets a double dose of flavor from the addition of hot Hungarian paprika and smoked Spanish paprika.

SERVES 8 | **TIME** 3½ hours

½ cup flour
2 tbsp. hot Hungarian paprika *(see Quick Tip below)*
2 tsp. sweet smoked Spanish paprika *(see Quick Tip below)*
1½ tsp. salt, divided, plus more to taste
1 tsp. freshly ground black pepper, plus more to taste
4 lbs. beef short ribs
4 strips thick-cut bacon
1 medium onion, chopped
4 garlic cloves, finely chopped
1 bottle (12 oz.) beer
1 can (14.5 oz.) whole peeled tomatoes, chopped and juice reserved
2 lbs. Yukon Gold or russet potatoes

1. Preheat oven to 300°. Combine flour, hot and smoked paprikas, 1 tsp. salt, and the pepper in a large bowl or large resealable plastic bag. Working in two or three batches, toss short ribs with flour mixture and set aside.
2. In a large Dutch oven or other heavy ovenproof pot over medium-high heat, cook bacon until fat renders. Transfer with a slotted spoon to paper towels and reserve. Pour off all but 1 tbsp. fat from pot. Add short ribs and brown on all sides, 3 to 5 minutes per side. Transfer short ribs to a plate and reserve. Chop reserved bacon and set aside.
3. Add onion and remaining ½ tsp. salt to pot and cook, stirring, until soft, about 3 minutes. Add garlic and cook, stirring, until fragrant, about 1 minute. Add beer and, using a wooden spoon or spatula, scrape up any browned bits on bottom of pan. Add tomatoes (with their juice) and reserved bacon. Increase heat to high and bring mixture to a boil. Return short ribs to pot, cover, and bake 2 hours.
4. Peel potatoes and cut into 1-in. pieces. Add to short ribs, cover, and bake until potatoes are tender and meat pulls away easily from the bone, about 30 minutes. Season with salt and pepper to taste. Spoon off excess fat.
Quick Tip: Hungarian and smoked Spanish paprikas are available at well-stocked and specialty grocery stores.

PER 1½-CUP SERVING: 724 cal., 65% (468 cal.) from fat; 31 g protein; 52 g fat (22 g sat.); 32 g carbo (2.3 g fiber); 679 mg sodium; 112 mg chol.

soups, stews & chili

Chicken and Corn Summer
Chowder, *page 98*

Spicy Avocado-Poblano
Salad, *page 142*

Carrot Soup with Crab,
page 103

Classic Cioppino,
page 126

Lemon Cashew Chicken
Salad, *page 169*

Vietnamese Calamari
Herb Salad, *page 166*

Fresh Corn and Avocado
Salad, *page 139*

Asian Pear, Persimmon, and
Almond Salad, *page 139*

Chilled Pineapple Gazpacho, *page 89*

Baked Goat Cheese with
Spring Lettuce Salad, *page 145*

Devilish Chorizo Chili
with Hominy, *page 128*

Green Chile Pork Stew
(Chile Verde), page 123

Smoky Beef Stew with Blue Cheese and Chives

Bacon, smoked paprika, and chipotle chile powder (from dried smoked jalapeños) give this stew layers of smoky flavor.

SERVES 8 | **TIME** 4 hours

2 tbsp. vegetable oil, divided
4 lbs. beef chuck, fat trimmed and cut into 1½-in. pieces
4 strips hardwood-smoked bacon, chopped
2 large onions, cut into ½-in. wedges
1 tsp. salt, plus more to taste
¼ cup flour
1 tbsp. sweet smoked Spanish paprika (*see Smoked Spanish Paprika, right*)
1 tsp. chipotle chile powder
2 bottles (750 ml. each) dry red wine
2 lbs. russet or Yukon Gold potatoes, peeled and cut into large pieces
1 lb. carrots, cut into ¼- by 2-in. sticks
1 tbsp. butter
½ cup crumbled blue cheese
Freshly ground black pepper
¼ cup minced chives

1. Heat a heavy, large ovenproof pot or Dutch oven (not nonstick) over medium-high heat. Add 1 tbsp. oil. When hot, add a quarter or a little less of the beef. The first piece should sizzle when it hits the pot; if it doesn't, remove it and wait for oil to get hotter. Pieces should not touch—you want plenty of room so juices evaporate quickly and meat can brown. Cook until well browned and a bit crusted, about 5 minutes each side, adjusting heat so meat sizzles but does not burn. Pieces are ready to turn when they release from the bottom easily. Transfer meat to a bowl and repeat with remaining meat and oil as needed, for a total of four or five batches. This takes about an hour when done properly.
2. Preheat oven to 350°. Add bacon to pot and cook until fat renders and bacon starts to brown. Using a slotted spoon, transfer bacon to bowl with beef. Add onions to pot and stir in salt. Cook, stirring, until onions begin to soften, about 2 minutes. Transfer onions to bowl with beef. Add flour to pot and cook, stirring, until it starts to turn golden and smells faintly of piecrust, about 2 minutes. Add paprika and chipotle chile powder and cook, stirring, until fragrant, 30 seconds.
3. Add wine and increase heat to high. Using a wooden spoon or spatula, scrape up any browned bits from bottom of pot. Add reserved beef, bacon, and onions. Bring mixture to a boil. Cover and bake until meat is tender, about 1½ hours.

4. Return pot to stove. Add potatoes and bring to a boil. Add carrots and bring back to a boil. Adjust heat to maintain a simmer. Cook, uncovered, until vegetables are tender, about 30 minutes.
5. Stir in butter and add salt to taste. Serve garnished with blue cheese, pepper to taste, and chives.
Make Ahead: Through step 3, up to 1 day, chilled. Add 15 minutes to the cooking time for the potatoes since the liquid will take longer to boil.

PER 1½-CUP SERVING: 795 cal., 40% (315 cal.) from fat; 51 g protein; 35 g fat (13 g sat.); 35 g carbo (4 g fiber); 766 mg sodium; 170 mg chol.

■ Smoked Spanish Paprika

FROM THE PANTRY

Made from peppers dried over a wood fire and then finely ground into a velvety red powder, smoked Spanish paprika has a complex, smoky fragrance and flavor. There are three types available (if you want smoked, read the label to make sure that is what you are getting; all of these varieties are also available in sun-dried—not smoked—form): **sweet paprika** (*pimentón dulce*), which is earthy and mild; **bittersweet paprika** (*pimentón agridulce*), rich, complex, and slightly smoky; and **hot paprika** (*pimentón picante*), which is medium-hot but slightly sweet. The recipes in this book mainly call for either sweet or hot. Smoked paprika pairs well with hearty, robust foods such as beef, lamb, and grilled mushrooms. The most famous smoked paprika is *pimentón de La Vera*, made from peppers grown and smoke-dried over oak wood in the La Vera region of western Spain.

Beef-Ale Stew and Green Onion–Buttermilk Dumplings

Rich with ale and caramelized onions, this stew provides a thick, hearty base for the fluffy white dumplings that are dropped in at the end of cooking.

SERVES 6 to 8 | **TIME** 4½ hours

4 lbs. beef chuck, fat trimmed and cut into 1½-in. pieces
6 tbsp. plus 2 cups flour, divided
3¾ tsp. salt, divided
1 tsp. freshly ground black pepper
2 tbsp. vegetable oil, divided
2 bottles (12 oz. each) ale
2 large onions, thinly sliced
½ lb. mushrooms, quartered
3 large carrots, halved lengthwise and cut into 1-in. lengths
½ cup thinly sliced green onions (green part only)
½ tsp. baking soda
4½ tbsp. cold butter, cut into small pieces
¾ cup buttermilk, or more as needed
1 egg

1. In a large bowl, toss beef with 3 tbsp. flour, 1 tsp. salt, and the pepper. In a large pot over medium-high heat, heat 1 tbsp. oil. Add enough beef to pot to form a single layer (about a third of beef), being careful not to overcrowd pot. Brown meat on all sides, about 7 minutes total, then transfer meat to a large bowl. Brown remaining beef in two batches and transfer to bowl. If meat or pan juices start to scorch, reduce heat.

2. Add 1 bottle of ale to pot. Using a wooden spoon or spatula, scrape up any browned bits on bottom. Pour ale from pot over reserved beef and return empty pot to medium-high heat. Add remaining 1 tbsp. oil to pot. Add onions and 2 tsp. salt. Cook, stirring often, 2 minutes. Cover pot and reduce heat to low. Cook, stirring occasionally, until onions have a hint of gold color, about 20 minutes.

3. Remove lid, raise heat to medium-high, stir in 3 tbsp. flour, and cook, stirring often, 3 minutes. Add mushrooms, reserved beef and ale, remaining bottle of ale, and the carrots. Bring to a boil. Cover and lower heat to a gentle simmer. Cook, stirring occasionally, until beef is tender, about 3 hours.

4. About 40 minutes before serving, make dumplings: In a medium bowl, stir together remaining 2 cups flour and ¾ tsp. salt, the green onions, and baking soda. Using a pastry blender or your fingers, work cold butter into flour mixture until it resembles cornmeal with some pea-size pieces. In another bowl, whisk together buttermilk and egg. Gently fold wet ingredients into dry, mixing until a very shaggy dough forms. If more liquid is needed, add additional buttermilk 1 tbsp. at a time. Gently form dough into 12 equal balls and drop into stew. Cover pot and cook until dumplings are fluffy and cooked through, 20 to 30 minutes. Let sit 15 minutes before serving; stew will thicken as it cools.

PER SERVING: 732 cal., 39% (288 cal.) from fat; 58 g protein; 32 g fat (13 g sat.); 50 g carbo (4.2 g fiber); 1,675 mg sodium; 220 mg chol.

Rick's Pork and Vegetable Hot Pots

When preparing his stew at home, Rick Yoder, owner of Seattle's Wild Ginger, cooks it ahead and reheats individual servings in Chinese clay pots.

SERVES 4 | **TIME** 1½ hours

1 tbsp. vegetable oil, divided
1 lb. boned pork shoulder (butt), fat trimmed and cut into ¾-in. chunks
2 garlic cloves, minced
1 onion (½ lb.), cut into ¾-in. chunks
2 carrots (6 oz. total), thinly sliced
¼ lb. mushrooms, quartered
2 tbsp. *each* hoisin sauce and Shaoxing rice wine or dry sherry
1½ cups chicken broth
¾ lb. slender eggplant, stemmed and cut into ¾-in. chunks
1 red bell pepper (½ lb.), seeds and ribs removed and cut into ¾-in. chunks
1 tsp. Asian (toasted) sesame oil
Soy sauce
Thinly sliced green onions

1. Heat 2 tsp. oil in a 5- to 6-qt. pot or wok over high heat; swirl to coat pan. Add pork and garlic. Stir-fry until lightly browned, 10 to 15 minutes. Pour pork and garlic into a bowl.

2. To pot, add remaining 1 tsp. oil, the onion, carrots, and mushrooms. Stir-fry over high heat until onion begins to brown, about 10 minutes.

3. Add hoisin sauce, rice wine, broth, and pork. Cook until boiling, stirring to release browned bits from bottom of pot. Cover and simmer over low heat 10 minutes; stir often.

4. Add eggplant and bell pepper to pot. Mix, cover, and simmer over low heat until pork is very tender when pierced, 30 to 40 minutes longer; stir occasionally.

5. Add sesame oil and soy sauce to taste. Serve topped with green onions.

PER SERVING: 332 cal., 38% (126 cal.) from fat; 26 g protein; 14 g fat (4 g sat.); 24 g carbo (4.6 g fiber); 306 mg sodium; 77 mg chol.

soups, stews & chili

Green Chile Pork Stew
(Chile Verde)

This spicy, long-simmered pork dish is a fixture in New Mexico, Arizona, and Colorado cooking, and each state has its own version. (New Mexicans use their famous green chiles, naturally.) Ours is a bit of a combination.

recipe pictured on page **120**

SERVES 6 to 8 | **TIME** 2½ hours

4 lbs. boned pork shoulder (butt), fat trimmed and cut into 2-in. cubes
2 to 3 tbsp. vegetable oil, as needed
3 onions (2 lbs. total), cut into ¼-in. wedges
5 large garlic cloves, minced
3 tbsp. ground cumin
1 can (28 oz.) peeled whole tomatoes
1 can (14.5 oz.) chicken broth
1½ lbs. Anaheim or poblano chiles (about 10), peeled (*see Quick Tip below*) and chopped; or 4 cans (7 oz. each) whole green chiles, drained and chopped
2 tbsp. chopped oregano leaves
Salt and freshly ground black pepper
Chopped cilantro
Lime wedges

1. In a 6- to 8-qt. pan, combine pork with ⅓ cup water. Cover and cook over medium-high heat, stirring occasionally, until meat is very juicy, 15 to 20 minutes. Uncover, increase heat to high, and cook, stirring often, until liquid is evaporated and meat is browned, 20 to 30 minutes. Lift out meat and set aside.
2. Reduce heat to medium. If you have leftover rendered pork fat in the pan, discard all but 3 tbsp.; if not, add oil. Add onions, garlic, and cumin; stir and cover. Cook, stirring occasionally, until onions are soft, about 8 minutes.
3. Return meat and any accumulated juices to pan. Add tomatoes (with their juice) and broth. Break up tomatoes with a spoon. Bring almost to a boil, then reduce to a gentle simmer, cover, and cook 1 hour.
4. Stir in chiles and oregano. Cover and cook until pork is very tender when pierced and flavors are blended, about 15 minutes. Season to taste with salt and pepper. Sprinkle with cilantro and serve with lime wedges to squeeze over chile.
Quick Tip: To peel chiles, remove stems, slice in half lengthwise, then remove ribs and seeds. Lay cut side down on a cookie sheet and broil 4 to 5 in. from heat until black and blistered, 5 to 8 minutes. Let chiles cool, then peel.

PER SERVING: 454 cal., 38% (171 cal.) from fat; 50 g protein; 19 g fat (6.2 g sat.); 21 g carbo (3.6 g fiber); 362 mg sodium; 152 mg chol.

Red Chile and Pork Stew
(Carne Adovada)

In New Mexico, ground dried red chiles are used to both season and thicken sauces. They are sold according to heat level, from mild and sweet to quite spicy, so be sure to buy a batch that suits your taste. (Don't be intimidated by the large quantity called for in this recipe; this ingredient is nothing like cayenne or supermarket "chili powder.") Ground Chimayo chiles have a particularly intense, flowery aroma (for sources, *see Quick Tip below*). Serve with warm corn or flour tortillas if you like.

SERVES 6 | **TIME** 2¾ hours

3 tbsp. vegetable oil, divided
2 medium onions, chopped
6 large garlic cloves, minced
3 tbsp. flour
1½ tsp. *each* salt and ground cumin
1 tsp. freshly ground black pepper
3½ lbs. boned pork shoulder (butt), fat trimmed and cut into 1½-in. cubes
1 cup ground dried red New Mexico chiles, preferably Chimayo
4 cups reduced-sodium chicken broth
1 bay leaf

1. Preheat oven to 350°. Heat 2 tbsp. oil in a large, heavy-bottomed, ovenproof pot over medium-high heat. Add onions and garlic and cook, stirring, until onions are golden, about 6 minutes. Remove from heat and transfer onions and garlic to a bowl with a slotted spoon.
2. In a large bowl, stir together flour, salt, cumin, and pepper. Add pork and toss to coat. Return pot to medium-high heat, add remaining 1 tbsp. oil, and, working in batches, lightly brown meat on all sides, 5 to 7 minutes per batch. Transfer meat to a separate bowl as you go.
3. Return onions and garlic to pot. Sprinkle with ground chiles and cook, stirring, 2 minutes (mixture will be thick). Add broth and, using a wooden spoon or spatula, scrape up any browned bits from bottom of pot.
4. Transfer contents of pot to a blender (in batches if needed) and purée until smooth. Return sauce to pot and add bay leaf and reserved pork.
5. Cover pot, put in oven, and cook 1 hour.
6. Set lid slightly ajar and continue cooking until pork is fork-tender, about 1 hour more.
Quick Tip: Look for ground dried red Chimayo chile powder in Latino markets or online at *cibolojunction.com* or *santafeschoolofcooking.com*.

PER SERVING: 577 cal., 47% (270 cal.) from fat; 57 g protein; 30 g fat (8.5 g sat.); 20 g carbo (5.4 g fiber); 1,171 mg sodium; 177 mg chol.

Shot-and-a-Beer Pork Stew

This recipe came from Tacolicious, a San Francisco restaurant that started as a taco stand at the city's Thursday Ferry Plaza Farmers Market. Owner Joe Hargrave makes the pork at home as a stew. The chiles fall apart as the dish cooks, giving the meat a mellow, earthy spiciness.

SERVES 6 | **TIME** 3¾ hours

2 large dried chipotle chiles
2 large dried ancho chiles
1 bottle (12 oz.) Mexican lager, such as Tecate
¼ cup white (silver) tequila
3½ lbs. boned pork shoulder (butt), fat trimmed and cut into 2-in. cubes
2 tsp. kosher salt
1 tbsp. vegetable oil
1 medium onion, chopped
3 garlic cloves, chopped
¾ lb. ripe tomatoes, chopped
2 tsp. *each* ground cumin and dried oregano, preferably Mexican *(see Quick Tip below)*
Cabbage and cilantro slaw with lime vinaigrette, lime wedges, crumbled *cotija* cheese, and tortilla chips for accompaniments

1. Wipe chipotle and ancho chiles clean with a damp cloth. In a dry, heavy saucepan over medium heat, toast chiles until fragrant and puffy, turning occasionally to keep them from burning, 3 to 5 minutes. Let cool slightly, then remove stems, seeds, and membranes. Pour beer and tequila over chiles to soften.
2. Meanwhile, season pork cubes with salt. Heat oil in a heavy, large ovenproof pot over medium-high heat until hot. Brown half the pork at a time, turning as needed, 8 to 10 minutes per batch. Transfer browned pork to a bowl.
3. Add onion and garlic to pot; cook until soft, stirring often, about 5 minutes. Stir in beer mixture, tomatoes, cumin, oregano, and pork. Add water if needed to barely cover pork. Bring to a boil over high heat; cover.
4. Preheat oven to 350°. Bake stew until pork is falling-apart tender, about 3 hours. Skim fat. Serve stew with accompaniments.
Quick Tip: Look for Mexican oregano in the Latino foods aisle of the supermarket or at a Latino food market; it's stronger and more fragrant than Mediterranean oregano.
Make Ahead: Up to 2 days, chilled.

PER SERVING: 618 cal., 58% (360 cal.) from fat; 50 g protein; 40 g fat (14 g sat.); 15 g carbo (4.4 g fiber); 517 mg sodium; 186 mg chol.

Lamb Stew with White Beans and Artichokes

Baby artichokes are actually fully mature artichokes (albeit small and tender ones) that have grown low on the stalk in the shade of the frondlike leaves of the artichoke plant. Unlike their larger siblings, baby artichokes are rendered entirely edible with just a little trimming. Here they combine deliciously with slow-cooked lamb shoulder.

SERVES 6 | **TIME** 2¼ hours

1 tbsp. olive oil
2 lbs. boned lamb shoulder or other stewing cut, fat trimmed and cut into 1½-in. chunks
4 garlic cloves, minced
1 can (14.5 oz.) chicken broth
1 cup dry white wine
¾ cup dried tomatoes
¼ tsp. *each* salt and freshly ground black pepper
2 lbs. baby artichokes (about 3 in. long)
2 cans (15 oz. each) cannellini (white) beans, drained and rinsed
½ cup pitted kalamata olives
¼ cup chopped flat-leaf parsley
2 tbsp. chopped thyme leaves

1. Heat oil in a 5- to 6-qt. pan over medium-high heat. Add lamb and stir occasionally until browned, about 10 minutes. Add garlic and cook until fragrant, 1 minute longer.
2. Add broth, wine, tomatoes, salt, and pepper, and bring to a boil. Lower heat to maintain a simmer; cover and cook until lamb is tender when pierced, about 1½ hours.
3. Meanwhile, rinse and trim artichokes *(see Trimming Baby Artichokes, right)* and cut in half. When lamb is tender, stir in beans, olives, parsley, thyme, and artichokes. Cover and cook until artichokes are tender when pierced, 20 to 25 minutes longer.

PER SERVING: 470 cal., 33% (153 cal.) from fat; 44 g protein; 17 g fat (4.5 g sat.); 38 g carbo (15 g fiber); 1,030 mg sodium; 100 mg chol.

soups, stews & chili

Trimming Baby Artichokes

Choose baby artichokes that are heavy for their size, with firm, moist-looking stems. Because cut artichokes darken when exposed to air, many recipes advise putting them in a bowl of lemon juice and water—but we have found that this doesn't make a significant difference in their color after cooking. We only bother with the lemon water if we're eating the artichokes raw (usually very thinly sliced). Here's how to cut baby artichokes down to size.

1. For a neat presentation, cut off the stem at the base of the artichoke, using a sharp knife. You could also trim the tough outer surface of the stem and leave it on, if you like.

2. Peel back and snap off the leaves all around the base of the artichoke until you reach the tender layer of leaves that are yellow at the bottom and green at the top. You'll remove a lot of leaves.

3. Cut off the top third of the remaining leaves (the pointy green part). With a sharp paring knife, trim off all the remaining green, fibrous material from around the base of the artichoke.

Spicy Seafood Stew

Quinoa soaks up the juices of this flavorful combination of fish, shrimp, and squid while adding a mild, nutty flavor and fluffy, faintly crunchy texture.

SERVES 4 | **TIME** 50 minutes

1 tbsp. olive oil
1 onion (½ lb.), halved and thinly slivered lengthwise
2 garlic cloves, minced
1 can (32 oz.) diced or crushed tomatoes
½ lb. red or white thin-skinned potatoes (about 1 in. wide), quartered
1 or 2 green chiles, such as jalapeños, seeds and ribs removed and minced
½ tsp. *each* ground cumin, chili powder, and salt
¾ lb. medium shrimp (31 to 42 per lb.), peeled and deveined
½ lb. tilapia or other white-fleshed fish fillets, cut into 1-in. chunks
¼ lb. squid (calamari) rings (optional)
2 tbsp. chopped cilantro
Cooked Quinoa *(see Quick Tip below; recipe follows)*

1. Heat oil in a 5- to 6-qt. pan over medium-high heat until hot but not smoking; add onion and garlic and stir often until onion is very limp, 8 to 10 minutes. Add tomatoes, 1½ cups water, potatoes, chiles, cumin, chili powder, and salt; increase heat to high and bring to a boil. Reduce heat until liquid is simmering gently, cover, and cook until potatoes are tender when pierced, 20 to 25 minutes.
2. Stir in seafood. Cover and simmer until shrimp, fish, and squid (if using) are opaque but still moist-looking in the center of thickest part (cut to test), 3 to 4 minutes. Stir in cilantro. Spoon hot quinoa onto rimmed plates; top with stew.
Quick Tip: To have the quinoa and stew ready at the same time, start the quinoa once you've added the potatoes in step 1.

PER SERVING WITHOUT QUINOA: 262 cal., 24% (62 cal.) from fat; 32 g protein; 6.9 g fat (0.8 g sat.); 19 g carbo (4.4 g fiber); 823 mg sodium; 156 mg chol.

Cooked Quinoa: In a 3- to 4-qt. pan over high heat, bring 3 cups water to a boil. In a strainer, rinse 1½ cups **quinoa** under running water; drain thoroughly. Add quinoa and ¼ tsp. **salt** to pan with boiling water. Adjust heat to maintain a simmer, cover, and cook until water is absorbed and quinoa is tender to bite, 20 to 25 minutes. Makes 5 cups; 4 servings.

PER SERVING: 238 cal., 14% (33 cal.) from fat; 8.4 g protein; 3.7 g fat (0.4 g sat.); 44 g carbo (3.8 g fiber); 156 mg sodium; 0 mg chol.

San Francisco's Fabulous Fish Stew

Great dishes are often born of memory and whatever ingredients happen to be on hand. Such was the case with *cioppino*, the emblematic fish stew of San Francisco. During the mid-1800s, the city's immigrant Italian fishermen used what was left of the day's catch to cook a thick purée of fish and vegetables, much as they had in their home port city of Genoa. They called it *ciuppin*, dialect for "little soup."

Over time, Sicilians replaced the Genoese on the fishing boats, and in their cooking pots *cioppino*, as it came to be called, acquired peppers and tomatoes, and the fish was left in chunks. Today *cioppino* is a sumptuous, garlicky, tomatoey stew brimming with several different kinds of available fish, shellfish (Dungeness crab, shrimp, clams, and/or mussels), wine, herbs, and olive oil—transcending its origins as a poor man's dish.

Classic Cioppino

recipe pictured on page **112**

This tomato-based seafood stew takes its inspiration from the communal feasts Italian fishermen created on San Francisco docks. Serve it with crusty sourdough bread and a crisp Semillon or Chardonnay with good acidity.

SERVES 4 to 6 | **TIME** 1 hour

1 head fennel (¾ lb.)
3 tbsp. olive oil
1 onion (½ lb.), chopped
2 garlic cloves, minced
¼ cup chopped flat-leaf parsley, divided
3 cans (14.5 oz. each) diced tomatoes
2 cups dry white wine
⅓ cup tomato paste
1 tbsp. dried basil
½ tsp. *each* dried oregano and red chile flakes
1 dozen clams in shell suitable for steaming (discard any that are not closed), well scrubbed
2 cooked Dungeness crabs (about 2 lbs. each), cleaned and cracked (*see Dungeness Crab 101, page 340*)
1 lb. large shrimp (21 to 30 per lb.), peeled and deveined
Salt and freshly ground black pepper

1. Trim off and discard tough stalks and base of fennel head. Core and chop bulb.

2. In a 6- to 8-qt. pan over medium-high heat, stir fennel, oil, onion, garlic, and 2 tbsp. parsley until onion is limp, 8 to 10 minutes.

3. Add diced tomatoes (with their juice), wine, tomato paste, basil, oregano, and red chile flakes. Bring to a boil over high heat. Cover and simmer over low heat until flavors are well blended, about 15 minutes.

4. Add clams and crabs. Cover and bring to a boil over high heat, then reduce heat and simmer, covered, for 5 minutes (transfer any opened clams to a bowl and cover to keep warm). Stir in shrimp, cover, and simmer until clams finish popping open, shrimp turn pink, and crab is hot, 6 to 9 minutes longer; remove seafood as it finishes cooking. Discard clams that have not opened.

5. Season cioppino with salt and pepper to taste and ladle into bowls with seafood. Serve sprinkled with remaining 2 tbsp. parsley.

PER SERVING: 309 cal., 29% (90 cal.) from fat; 35 g protein; 10 g fat (1.4 g sat.); 21 g carbo (4.3 g fiber); 798 mg sodium; 176 mg chol.

Thai Red Curry Fish Stew

Versions of red curry abound in Thailand, but most are flavored with a paste of red chiles, garlic, shallots, galangal (similar to ginger), and shrimp paste and have coconut milk as their base. Light coconut milk works well in this stew, and prepared Thai red curry paste, found in most supermarkets, makes it a snap to put together.

SERVES 6 | **TIME** 45 minutes

1½ cups jasmine rice
½ tsp. salt
1 large orange-fleshed sweet potato (often labeled "yam")
2 cans (13.5 oz. each) light coconut milk, divided
2 tbsp. Thai red curry paste (*see Quick Tips, above right*)
1 tbsp. minced lemongrass (*see Quick Tips, above right*)
2 kaffir (also called *makrut*) lime leaves (*see Quick Tips, above right*)
2 tbsp. *each* Thai or Vietnamese fish sauce (*nam pla or nuoc mam*) and firmly packed dark brown sugar
1½ lbs. firm fish fillets, such as halibut or tilapia
6 oz. fresh spinach leaves, stems trimmed
1 cup *each* loosely packed Thai basil (*see Quick Tips, above right*) and mint leaves
Lime wedges

1. Bring 6 cups water to a boil in a medium saucepan. Add rice and salt. Cover and reduce heat to low. Cook 15 minutes, then turn off heat and let sit 5 minutes. Fluff with a fork and cover to keep warm.

2. Meanwhile, bring 1 in. water to a boil in a large saucepan. Peel sweet potato and cut into ½-in. cubes. Put in a steamer basket over boiling water. Cover and steam until tender, about 10 minutes. Set aside.

3. While sweet potato is cooking, spoon about ¼ cup from top (the thick opaque layer) of coconut milk in each can and put in a 4- to 5-qt. pot or deep sauté pan. Add curry paste and whisk until smoothly blended. Cook mixture, stirring, over medium heat until nearly dry, 3 to 5 minutes. Reduce heat to medium-low and add remaining coconut milk, the lemongrass, lime leaves, fish sauce, and brown sugar. Simmer, uncovered, 5 minutes.

4. Meanwhile, cut fish into 1½-in. cubes. Increase heat to medium; add fish and spinach. Cover and cook until fish is no longer translucent, 5 to 7 minutes.

5. Chop basil and mint and stir into stew along with sweet potato cubes. Serve over rice, with lime wedges on the side.

Quick Tips: The spice level in prepared red curry pastes varies depending on the brand, so taste before using. Start with 2 tbsp., then add more if you like. Find lemongrass, lime leaves, and Thai basil at Asian markets and specialty-produce stores, or substitute 2 tsp. finely shredded lime zest in step 3 for the lemongrass and lime leaves and use regular basil instead of Thai.

PER 1½-CUP SERVING CURRY AND 1-CUP SERVING RICE: 707 cal., 17% (117 cal.) from fat; 38 g protein; 13 g fat (5.5 g sat.); 113 g carbo (4.9 g fiber); 965 mg sodium; 36 mg chol.

The Story of Frito Pie

Although Frito pie is often said to have been born in New Mexico, at the Woolworth's lunch counter in Santa Fe, history favors Texas.

Charles Elmer Doolin of San Antonio founded the Frito Company in 1932, and a couple of years later, Frito pie appeared. This humble but delicious concoction of chili poured over Frito chips—often right in the bag, with shredded cheese, lettuce, tomato, and onion on top—may or may not have been invented by Elmer's mom, Daisy Dean Doolin, but one thing is sure: Generations of Texans knew Frito pie before it surfaced in New Mexico in the early 1960s.

You can argue, though, that Santa Fe has put its own stamp on the dish, serving it with either green or red chile made with the state's prize crop.

The Diner's Frito Pie with Barbara Cozart's Red Chili

Here's a sit-down, feed-a-crowd version of a Southwest classic from the Diner, a once-popular stop (now closed) in Tres Piedras, 30 miles northwest of Taos, New Mexico. Former owner Barbara Cozart prepared her chili using only locally grown red chiles from the Espanola Valley.

SERVES 6 | **TIME** 30 minutes

2 lbs. ground lean (7% fat) beef
1½ tbsp. garlic powder
1 tsp. salt, plus more to taste
2 tbsp. flour
1 can (15 oz.) black beans (optional), drained and rinsed
¼ cup ground dried New Mexico chiles or chili powder
1 bag (15 oz.) Fritos corn chips (about 4½ cups)
6 tbsp. finely chopped onion
1½ cups shredded longhorn cheddar cheese
2 cups finely shredded iceberg lettuce
¾ cup chopped tomato

1. In a 5- to 6-qt. pan over medium-high heat, cook ground beef with garlic powder and salt, stirring, until beef is crumbly and well browned, 6 to 8 minutes.

2. With a large slotted spoon, push beef mixture to one side and tilt pan so liquid runs to opposite side. Stir flour into liquid until well blended, then mix with beef mixture. Add 2 cups water, black beans if using, and ground chiles; stir until mixture boils and thickens, about 8 minutes.

3. Spread Fritos in wide, shallow bowls, using about ¾ cup in each, and sprinkle chopped onion on top. Divide chili among bowls and top with cheese, lettuce, and tomato. Add more salt to taste.

PER SERVING: 776 cal., 53% (414 cal.) from fat; 44 g protein; 46 g fat (14 g sat.); 45 g carbo (3.9 g fiber); 1,088 mg sodium; 117 mg chol.

Smoky Beef-and-Bacon Chili

Bacon, fire-roasted tomatoes, and spicy smoked paprika give an easy-to-make chili a deep, complex flavor. While it's great right after you make it, it's even better the next day. Serve with warm cornbread for a complete meal.

SERVES 6 | **TIME** 1 hour, 10 minutes

2 slices thick-cut bacon, finely chopped
1 large onion, finely chopped
1 large garlic clove, minced
1½ lbs. lean ground beef
1½ tbsp. chili powder
1½ tsp. *each* ground cumin and sweet smoked Spanish paprika *(see Quick Tip below)*
½ tsp. to 1½ tsp. cayenne
1 tsp. salt, plus more to taste
1 can (14.5 oz.) crushed fire-roasted tomatoes *(see Quick Tip below)* or regular crushed tomatoes
1 can (8 oz.) tomato sauce
1 cup beer (India Pale Ale or pilsner)
1 tsp. Worcestershire sauce
1 can (14.5 oz.) pinto beans, drained and rinsed
Sour cream, sliced green onions, and/or shredded cheddar cheese for topping

1. In a large, heavy-bottomed pot over medium-high heat, cook bacon, stirring until it just begins to brown, about 4 minutes. Add onion, lower heat to medium, cover, and cook, stirring occasionally, until translucent, 4 to 7 minutes. Uncover pot, stir in garlic, and cook 1 minute.
2. Increase heat to medium-high and add ground beef; cook, breaking up meat with a wooden spoon and stirring gently, until beef loses its raw color, 6 to 8 minutes. Stir in chili powder, cumin, paprika, cayenne, and salt and cook 1 minute. Add tomatoes, tomato sauce, beer, and Worcestershire and bring to a boil. Reduce heat to medium-low, cover partially, and cook 30 minutes.
3. Add beans and cook 10 minutes, uncovered. Season to taste with more salt. Serve with toppings on the side.
Quick Tip: Smoked Spanish paprika and fire-roasted tomatoes are available at well-stocked and specialty grocery stores.

PER SERVING: 465 cal., 62% (288 cal.) from fat; 26 g protein; 32 g fat (12 g sat.); 19 g carbo (4.3 g fiber); 1,078 mg sodium; 94 mg chol.

Devilish Chorizo Chili with Hominy

recipe pictured on page **119**

Not only is this chili easy to make ahead, it actually improves with time. If you like your chili very spicy, add an extra teaspoon of chipotle powder.

SERVES 8 | **TIME** 50 minutes

2½ lbs. uncooked Mexican chorizo *(see Quick Tip below)*
1 lb. ground lean beef
2 large onions, chopped
5 garlic cloves, minced
2 cans (7 oz. each) diced green chiles, drained
¼ cup chili powder
1 tsp. ground chipotle chile powder
2 tsp. *each* chopped oregano leaves and ground cumin
1 can (28 oz.) crushed tomatoes
1 bottle (12 oz.) ale or other hearty beer
2 cans (15 oz. each) yellow hominy, drained and rinsed
Salt

1. Squeeze sausages from casings into a 6- to 8-qt. pan over high heat; discard casings. Add beef, onions, and garlic. Cook, stirring occasionally and breaking meat into small pieces, until meat is browned and onions are soft, about 10 minutes. Spoon off and discard fat.
2. Add green chiles, chili powder, chipotle chile powder, oregano, and cumin. Cook, stirring, 1 minute. Stir in tomatoes, ale, and hominy. Bring to a boil; then reduce heat until chili is simmering gently, cover, and simmer 30 minutes, stirring occasionally. Season with salt to taste.
Quick Tip: Buy the best-quality chorizo you can find, preferably from a butcher or Mexican market, and avoid the type of chorizo that is very soft, very orange, and sold in plastic casings; it tends to break down too much in cooking and can have an unpleasant flavor. Substitute another spicy uncooked sausage if you can't find good chorizo. Note that Mexican chorizo is very different from Spanish chorizo, which is cooked.
Make Ahead: Up to 2 days, chilled.

PER SERVING: 512 cal., 54% (279 cal.) from fat; 27 g protein; 31 g fat (11 g sat.); 32 g carbo (6.6 g fiber); 1,523 mg sodium; 90 mg chol.

soups, stews & chili

Pumpkin and Pork Chili

Although it's fast to make, this recipe delivers complex, hearty flavors. It's a good choice for your weeknight cooking repertoire.

SERVES 4 | **TIME** 1 hour

1 tbsp. olive oil
¾ lb. pork tenderloin, fat and membrane trimmed, cut into ½-in. cubes
1 onion (about ½ lb.), chopped
3 garlic cloves, minced
2 cans (12 oz. each) tomatillos, drained
1½ to 3 tbsp. canned diced jalapeño chiles
4 cups cubed (½ in.) pumpkin, such as Sugar Pie or Baby Bear (see Quick Tip below)
2 cans (15 oz. each) small white beans, drained and rinsed
1 tsp. ground cumin
½ tsp. ground chipotle chiles or chili powder
¼ tsp. salt
⅓ cup chopped cilantro
2 tbsp. fresh lime juice

1. Heat oil in a 5- to 6-qt. pan over medium-high heat until hot. Add pork and cook, stirring frequently, until browned, 2 to 3 minutes. Transfer pork to a plate. Add onion and garlic to pan; cook, stirring frequently, until onion is softened, about 8 minutes.
2. Meanwhile, in a blender, purée tomatillos and jalapeños until smooth.
3. Add 1 cup water, tomatillo mixture, pumpkin, beans, cumin, ground chiles, and salt to pan. Reduce heat to maintain a simmer, cover, and cook, stirring occasionally, 10 minutes.
4. Stir in pork. Cook, covered, until pork is no longer pink in center (cut to test), 10 minutes longer. Stir in cilantro and lime juice.
Quick Tip: To cut pumpkin into cubes, halve vertically and scrape out seeds. Cut halves into 1-in.-wide wedges. Peel each slice, then cut flesh into cubes.

PER SERVING: 378 cal., 18% (68 cal.) from fat; 28 g protein; 7.6 g fat (1.6 g sat.); 48 g carbo (9.8 g fiber); 790 mg sodium; 55 mg chol.

Slow-cooker Turkey and Hominy Chili

Serve this with warm cornbread.

SERVES 6 to 8 | **TIME** 6¾ to 7¾ hours on low, 4¾ to 5¾ hours on high

1 onion (½ lb.), chopped
1 red bell pepper (½ lb.), seeds and ribs removed and chopped
6 garlic cloves, minced or pressed
1 jalapeño chile, seeds and ribs removed and minced
1 tbsp. chili powder
1½ tsp. *each* dried oregano and ground cumin
2 or 3 turkey thighs (about 3 lbs. total)
1 can (15 oz.) hominy (yellow or white), drained and rinsed
1 can (28 oz.) crushed tomatoes in purée or chopped tomatoes
Shredded jack cheese
Canned sliced black ripe olives, drained
Thinly sliced green onions
Salt and freshly ground black pepper

1. In a 4½-qt. or larger slow-cooker, mix onion, bell pepper, garlic, jalapeño, chili powder, oregano, and cumin.
2. Pull off and discard skin from turkey thighs; trim off and discard fat. Lay thighs on vegetables in cooker. Pour hominy and tomatoes over turkey.
3. Cover and cook until turkey pulls easily from bone, 6 to 7 hours on low, 4 to 5 hours on high. If possible, turn meat over about halfway through cooking.
4. With a slotted spoon, transfer turkey to a plate. Skim and discard any fat from cooking liquid. When turkey is cool enough to handle, in about 10 minutes, discard bones and tear meat into large chunks. Return meat and juices to cooker; cover and cook until hot, 10 to 15 minutes.
5. Top as desired with cheese, olives, and green onions. Season with salt and pepper to taste.

PER SERVING: 209 cal., 21% (43 cal.) from fat; 22 g protein; 4.8 g fat (1.4 g sat.); 19 g carbo (3 g fiber); 359 mg sodium; 73 mg chol.

salads

Anything goes when it comes to salads. We use everything our farms and markets give us, and let our imaginations lead the way.

How far we've come since the days of the iceberg wedge with blue-cheese dressing! (Not that we don't still love it.) The fields of greens carpeting huge swaths of the West—including California's Salinas Valley, the "Salad Bowl of the World"—produce an unbelievable variety of lettuces and other vegetables for us cooks to play with. Iceberg has been joined by romaine, green and red leaf, oak leaf, and butter lettuces, as well as all the other leaves that aren't technically lettuce, but who cares? We toss them into our salads anyway, because they taste good: spinach, arugula, tatsoi, frisée, radicchio, mizuna, baby mustard greens, orach, mache, and whole herb leaves too—even weeds like dandelion and purslane.

And those are just the greens. We have such good vegetables and fruits in the West that they entice us to put them in the salad bowl too. Tomatoes, cucumbers, sure—but why not beautiful raw beets and artichokes, thinly shaved, or fresh pea shoots, or juicy kernels of corn? Or cooked vegetables like roasted red peppers and grilled asparagus, which add other dimensions of flavor and texture? Fruit also has a place in salads; its acidity and sweetness give a salad zest and zing. Or make your salad bloom with flowers (*page* 144).

Just about any kind of protein works in a salad. Nuts add crunch and richness. Good cheese can be fantastic. Top your salad with meat or fish, and you've made dinner.

Add culture to the salad bowl, and you open up near-infinite possibilities for seasonings and techniques. Our recipes borrow from nearly from every group of people that has settled in the West. One of our favorites is Vietnamese Calamari Herb Salad (*page* 166), a mix of hot, crisp fried calamari and whole leaves of cooling herbs. Chipotle coleslaw (*page* 155) uses smoky Mexican chipotle chiles to transform a standard slaw. Carrot Manchego Salad (*page* 152) turns ordinary sliced carrots into a side dish that evokes Moorish Spain.

So then what, exactly, is a salad, if everything can go into it, and from everywhere? From our point of view, it's simple: Anything with a dressing is a salad. When you toss or drizzle your ingredients with dressing, you unite them.

Despite our love of invention, we happily return to our classic Western salads too—the Cobb, the Caesar, the taco salad. But we never forget that they began the same way we make salad today: with good ingredients and an urge to create something new.

salads

Composed Fruit Salad with Ginger-Lime Syrup

Most fruit salads are served as chunky mixes—appealing to the mouth but less so to the eye. A composed, or arranged, salad is an elegant alternative. This one has a stylish green-and-gold palette. A zingy ginger-lime syrup to pour on top makes the flavors sing.

SERVES 8 | **TIME** 40 minutes

1 cup sugar
10 quarter-size slices fresh ginger
8 slices (¼-in.-thick) lime, divided
2 tbsp. fresh lime juice
3 qts. sliced or chopped fresh yellow and green fruit (mangoes, yellow watermelon, cantaloupe, honeydew melon, nectarines, golden raspberries, yellow and green kiwi fruit, green grapes, and/or golden plums)

1. In a 1- to 1½-qt. pan, combine 1½ cups water, sugar, ginger, and 5 lime slices. Simmer over medium-low heat until liquid is infused with ginger flavor, about 7 minutes. Remove from heat. Stir in lime juice; strain and cool.

2. Arrange fruit on a platter, grouping by color. Pour ginger-lime syrup into a small pitcher and drop in remaining 3 lime slices. Serve with fruit.

PER SERVING: 216 cal., 3% (6 cal.) from fat; 1.9 g protein; 0.7 g fat (0.1 g sat.); 55 g carbo (4.7 g fiber); 13 mg sodium; 0 mg chol.

Grape, Toasted Almond, and Sweet Onion Salad

Both juicy and crunchy, this autumnal salad makes a refreshing counterpoint to rich food. Give it a try at your next Thanksgiving feast.

SERVES 8 to 10 | **TIME** 20 minutes

¾ tsp. salt
1 tbsp. plus 1 tsp. fresh lemon juice
5 tbsp. roasted almond oil
1 package (12 oz.) salad mix with sturdy greens, especially radicchio
1 sweet onion such as Walla Walla or Maui, halved lengthwise, then cut into half-moons
2 cups seedless red grapes, each halved
1 cup sliced almonds, toasted (see Quick Tip and How to Toast Nuts below)

1. In a small bowl, whisk salt, lemon juice, and oil together.

2. Combine greens, onion, grapes, and almonds in a large serving bowl. Toss with dressing right before serving.

Quick Tip: Almonds should have a mild aroma and fresh taste. Store them airtight in the fridge or freezer to preserve the volatile oils responsible for flavor.

PER SERVING: 152 cal., 68% (103 cal.) from fat; 2.9 g protein; 12 g fat (0.9 g sat.); 12 g carbo (2.2 g fiber); 184 mg sodium; 0 mg chol.

How to Toast Nuts

Most nuts taste much better toasted, and they're crunchier, too. The exceptions are nuts used for coating or topping food that will be baked or roasted; if you pretoast these nuts, they will probably burn and turn bitter. The following toasting method applies to all nuts (including pine nuts), whether whole, halved, slivered, sliced, skin-on, or blanched.

Spread out nuts on a baking pan in a single layer and toast in a 350° oven until golden, 5 to 15 minutes. If the nuts have skins on, break one open to check the interior color. You can toast nuts in a nonstick frying pan too, but they won't toast as evenly or as deeply.

Toasting Hazelnuts

Skin-on hazelnuts need to be rid of their fibrous skins to be at their most delicious. To do this, toast them, then wrap them in a kitchen towel while still hot and rub them against each other to remove as many skins as possible (you won't be able to get off all the skins because they cling persistently; between one-fourth and two-thirds skinned is fine).

salads

How to Cut Citrus into Segments

1. With a small, sharp knife, cut ends off fruit. Then set fruit on one cut end on a board. Cut away peel and outer membrane in wide strips, following curve of fruit with knife.

2. Holding fruit over a small bowl to catch juice, cut between inner membranes and fruit to release segments. Drop segments into bowl and squeeze juice from membranes into another bowl. (Use juice if recipe calls for it, save for another use, or drink it.)

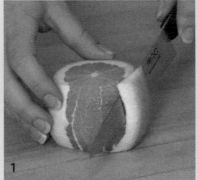

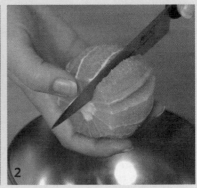

Crunchy Coconut-Berry Salad

With its tropical ingredients—jicama, coconut, and lime—this fruit salad is ideal alongside Hawaiian-style pork or shrimp skewers. Mint and honey give it a sweet freshness. It's also good for a special-occasion brunch; try it with banana pancakes or waffles.

SERVES 6 | **TIME** 20 minutes

¾ cup unsweetened sliced dried coconut (*see Quick Tip below*)
¼ cup fresh lime juice
2 tbsp. honey
3 cups mixed fresh berries (blackberries, blueberries, raspberries, and/or sliced strawberries)
1 cup diced peeled jicama
3 tbsp. loosely packed mint leaves

1. In a 6- to 8-in. pan, stir coconut often over medium-high heat until lightly browned, 2 to 3 minutes. Pour from pan and set aside.
2. In a large serving bowl, whisk together lime juice and honey. Add berries and jicama. Tear mint leaves into small pieces and scatter over salad. Add toasted coconut and mix gently.
Quick Tip: Unsweetened sliced dried coconut (also called flaked coconut or coconut chips) is sold in natural-foods stores. You can substitute sweetened shredded coconut if you like.

PER SERVING: 119 cal., 42% (50 cal.) from fat; 1.4 g protein; 5.5 g fat (4.6 g sat.); 19 g carbo (4.3 g fiber); 8.7 mg sodium; 0 mg chol.

Ruby Grapefruit, Avocado, and Spinach Salad

Fresh ginger, fish sauce, and rice vinegar add a Southeast Asian twist to this wintertime favorite.

SERVES 4 | **TIME** 10 minutes

3½ cups baby spinach
3 ruby grapefruit (1 lb. each), segmented (*see How to Cut Citrus into Segments, above*), juice reserved
1 firm-ripe avocado (about ½ lb.), pitted, peeled, and thinly sliced
2 tbsp. *each* unseasoned rice vinegar and Vietnamese fish sauce (*nuoc mam*)
2 tsp. minced fresh ginger
2½ tsp. sugar

1. Arrange spinach on salad plates. Arrange grapefruit segments and avocado on spinach.
2. Measure 3 tbsp. grapefruit juice (save any extra for other uses) into a small bowl and whisk with vinegar, fish sauce, ginger, and sugar to blend. Spoon dressing over salads.

PER SERVING: 173 cal., 39% (67 cal.) from fat; 4.2 g protein; 7.4 g fat (1.2 g sat.); 26 g carbo (4.8 g fiber); 395 mg sodium; 0 mg chol.

Marionberry, Blue Cheese, and Arugula Salad

The marionberry, or marion blackberry, is an especially flavorful and fragrant type of blackberry. If you can't find this type, other blackberries will work fine.

SERVES 4 | **TIME** 15 minutes

3 tbsp. extra-virgin olive oil
1 tbsp. fresh lemon juice
1 tbsp. fresh thyme leaves, divided
¼ tsp. dry mustard
¼ tsp. *each* salt and freshly ground black pepper, plus more to taste
6 oz. arugula (about 13 cups)
6 oz. marionberries or other blackberries (1½ cups)
2 oz. mild blue cheese, crumbled

1. In a salad bowl, whisk together oil, lemon juice, 1 tsp. thyme, the mustard, salt, and pepper.
2. Add arugula and gently toss until leaves are coated with dressing. Add berries and gently toss. Divide among salad plates. Top each salad with blue cheese. Sprinkle with remaining 2 tsp. thyme and season with salt and pepper to taste.

PER SERVING: 175 cal., 77% (135 cal.) from fat; 4.5 g protein; 15 g fat (4.2 g sat.); 7.8 g carbo (2.7 g fiber); 353 mg sodium; 11 mg chol.

Watercress-Endive Salad with Blood Oranges and Pomegranates

San Francisco caterer MeMe Pederson often serves this bright-tasting, colorful salad with dates stuffed with fresh goat cheese.

SERVES 12 | **TIME** 1 hour

1 tbsp. minced shallot (1 large shallot)
3 tbsp. Champagne vinegar
1 tbsp. Dijon mustard
½ cup plus 2 tbsp. extra-virgin olive oil
1 tsp. *each* finely chopped tarragon and flat-leaf parsley
1 tsp. kosher salt
6 bunches watercress or arugula, large stems removed (*see Quick Tip in Classic Cobb Salad, page 169*)
3 heads Belgian endive, thinly sliced crosswise (*see Quick Tip, above right*)
8 large blood oranges, segmented (*see How to Cut Citrus into Segments, page 135*)
½ to ¾ cup pomegranate seeds
1 cup slivered almonds, toasted (*see How to Toast Nuts, page 134*)

1. Whisk together shallot, vinegar, and mustard. Drizzle in oil, whisking, then whisk in tarragon, parsley, and salt.
2. In a large bowl, toss watercress, Belgian endive, and oranges with 4 to 5 tbsp. vinaigrette, or just enough to coat. Divide among salad plates and garnish each salad with pomegranate seeds and toasted almonds.
Quick Tip: Slice Belgian endive right before serving, as it tends to discolor when exposed to air.
Make Ahead: Vinaigrette and individual salad ingredients (with the exception of Belgian endive), up to several hours, chilled. Toss together right before serving.

PER SERVING WITH VINAIGRETTE: 176 cal., 56% (99 cal.) from fat; 3.9 g protein; 11 g fat (1.2 g sat.); 18 g carbo (4 g fiber); 92 mg sodium; 0 mg chol.

PER TBSP. VINAIGRETTE: 77 cal., 100% (77 cal.) from fat; 0 g protein; 8.8 g fat (1.3 g sat.); 0.2 g carbo (0 g fiber); 145 mg sodium; 0 mg chol.

Arugula Salad with Nectarines and Mango Chutney Dressing

Oregon cookbook author Janie Hibler came up with this combination, using a slightly tart and spicy dressing as a bridge between the flavors of sweet white nectarines and peppery greens. Feel free to use yellow nectarines or peaches if you can't find white nectarines.

SERVES 8 | **TIME** 25 minutes

½ lb. baby arugula (about 3 qts. loosely packed)
4 ripe white or yellow nectarines, pitted and cut into ½-in.-thick slices
¼ cup extra-virgin olive oil
2 tbsp. *each* fresh lime juice and mild mango chutney such as Major Grey
½ tsp. kosher salt
⅓ cup thinly sliced sweet onion such as Walla Walla or Maui
⅓ cup chopped toasted hazelnuts (*see How to Toast Nuts, page 134*)

1. Gently mix arugula and nectarines in a large salad bowl.
2. Purée oil, lime juice, chutney, and salt in a blender until almost smooth; pour over salad. Scatter onion and hazelnuts over greens and toss together.

PER SERVING: 144 cal., 63% (90 cal.) from fat; 2.1 g protein; 10 g fat (1.2 g sat.); 13 g carbo (2 g fiber); 89 mg sodium; 0 mg chol.

salads

Spiced Orange Salad

The combination of oranges and onions first appeared in *Sunset* in the early 1930s, inspired by salads from the Middle East and Africa and by the abundance of both crops in the West. For this salad, we prefer juice oranges such as Valencias; their slices hold together better than those of navel oranges.

SERVES 6 | **TIME** 15 to 20 minutes

¾ tsp. ground cumin
½ tsp. *each* paprika or mild ground dried chiles and
  kosher salt
¼ tsp. *each* freshly ground black pepper, chopped
  thyme leaves, and curry powder
⅛ tsp. cinnamon
¼ cup white wine vinegar, plus more to taste
1 tbsp. olive oil
1 tsp. sugar
6 oranges (2½ lbs. total)
1 mild red onion (6 oz.), thinly sliced (*see Quick Tip*
  below)
½ cup finely slivered mint leaves, plus whole leaves
  for garnish
2 tbsp. chopped cilantro, plus whole leaves for garnish
Salt
½ cup black olives such as Niçoise or kalamata

1. In a small bowl, combine cumin, paprika, kosher salt, pepper, thyme, curry powder, and cinnamon.
2. In another small bowl, mix vinegar with the oil and sugar. Stir in spice blend. Set aside.
3. With a small, sharp knife, cut peel and white membrane from oranges. Slice the oranges crosswise into ¼-in.-thick slices and discard seeds.
4. In a wide, shallow bowl, gently mix orange slices, onion, slivered mint, and chopped cilantro. Pour in dressing and mix gently. Taste and add salt and more vinegar if desired.
5. Scatter olives, mint leaves, and cilantro leaves over the top.
Quick Tip: If you have a super-pungent red onion, put the slices in a bowl of cold water and soak 15 to 30 minutes, changing the water if necessary.

PER SERVING: 138 cal., 37% (51 cal.) from fat; 1.7 g protein; 5.7 g fat (0.7 g sat.); 22 g carbo (4.6 g fiber); 370 mg sodium; 0 mg chol.

Peach and Mint Caprese with Curry Vinaigrette

Los Angeles food stylist Valerie Aikman-Smith likes to make this refreshing version of the classic Italian salad at the height of summer, "when everyone is sick of tomatoes." If your plates aren't white, start your layering with the mozzarella—its creamy paleness will look pretty against a color. Use good peaches, and splurge on buffalo mozzarella if you can; it's creamier and tangier than cow's-milk mozzarella. (It's very perishable, though, so check the sell-by date and use it fast.)

SERVES 8 | **TIME** 40 minutes

½ tbsp. Madras curry powder
½ cup *each* extra-virgin olive oil and Champagne vinegar
½ tsp. mild honey
4 balls (½ lb. each) mozzarella cheese, preferably
  buffalo's milk
4 large firm-ripe yellow or white peaches
10 to 12 sprigs *each* mint and basil
Sea salt or kosher salt
Freshly ground black pepper

1. In a dry (not nonstick) skillet, toast curry powder over medium heat, stirring constantly, until fragrant, a shade darker, and just starting to smoke, about 2 minutes. Transfer to a bowl; let cool briefly. Whisk in oil, vinegar, and honey. Set aside.
2. Slice mozzarella into ½-in.-thick pieces and set aside. Peel peaches, cut in half lengthwise, and remove pits. Set each half flat on a cutting board and slice into ½-in.-thick half-moons; set aside. Pluck mint and basil leaves from stems (reserving 8 mint sprigs) and set aside.
3. Set out small plates or flattish bowls and build a loose tower of salad on each: Lay a couple of pieces of peach in the center, top with a leaf or two of mint and basil, drape on a piece of mozzarella, and repeat layering two or three times. Top each stack with 2 peach slices and a mint sprig. Drizzle with curry vinaigrette, season with salt and pepper to taste, and scatter a few mint and basil leaves on each plate.
Make Ahead: Vinaigrette, up to 1 week, chilled; mozzarella, peaches, and herbs, up to several hours, chilled (toss peaches with a bit of vinaigrette to prevent browning). Drain cheese in a colander before serving.

PER SERVING: 481 cal., 71% (342 cal.) from fat; 21 g protein; 38 g fat (22 g sat.); 10 g carbo (1.7 g fiber); 922 mg sodium; 80 mg chol.

Build a Better Salad

The simple, foolproof method for a great tossed salad? Start with one or more ingredients from the first category, then pull some from at least a few of the remaining groups, reducing amounts as you move down the list.

• **LEAVES:** Actually, you can make a beautiful salad with nothing more than lettuces and herbs. Think about mixing different flavors, shapes, and textures: peppery arugula with mild, tender butter lettuce; crunchy romaine with slightly chewy parsley. To see whether you'll like a certain combo, taste tiny shreds together first.

• **VEGETABLES:** Anything good to eat raw will work: mushrooms, radishes, carrots, green onions, tomatoes, cucumbers, fresh peas. Mix in cooked vegetables for added layers of texture and flavor: white beans, chickpeas (garbanzos), potatoes, sautéed shallots, roasted peppers, artichokes, and beets, for instance.

• **FRUITS:** Their sweetness and acidity perk a salad right up. Standbys are strawberries, pears, figs, oranges, apples, and persimmons. Dried fruits create little explosions of flavor: slivered apricots, raisins, currants, cranberries, and cherries. And don't forget lemon and lime zests.

• **RICH TASTES:** Used sparingly, they're the treasures in the pile of green: meats (bacon, prosciutto, sausage, smoked salmon); cheeses (parmesan or pecorino shaved with a vegetable peeler, crumbled blue cheese or feta, soft gobs of goat cheese); nuts (toast for best flavor and crunch; *see How to Toast Nuts, page 134)*; and avocados, the butter of the vegetable kingdom.

• **SOUR AND SALTY TASTES:** Like meats, cheeses, and nuts, these should also be used just as accents since they're so flavorful. Try olives, capers, anchovies, and preserved lemon.

Roasted Apple, Bacon, and Frisée Salad

This salad is a happy marriage of sweet, sour, and salty. The warm dressing wilts the frisée slightly, so dress the salad right before you serve it.

SERVES 4 to 6 | **TIME** 40 minutes

2 large Braeburn or Fuji apples, peeled, cored, and cut into ¼-in.-thick slices
1 tbsp. extra-virgin olive oil
2 tbsp. maple syrup
½ tsp. *each* salt and freshly ground black pepper, plus more to taste
2 medium shallots, very thinly sliced and separated into rings
3 tbsp. sherry vinegar
4 slices thick-cut bacon, cut crosswise into ¼-in.-wide strips
2 large bunches frisée, outer leaves removed, or 5 heads endive, sliced crosswise

1. Preheat oven to 400°. In a small bowl, combine apples, oil, maple syrup, salt, and pepper. Toss to coat, then transfer apple slices to a nonstick baking sheet and bake for 15 minutes. Stir, then continue to cook until golden brown and tender, 10 to 15 minutes more. Set aside.
2. Meanwhile, in a small bowl, combine shallots and vinegar. Set aside.
3. In a heavy frying pan over medium heat, cook bacon until crisp and brown, about 7 minutes; drain on paper towels. Pour off all but 3 tbsp. of bacon fat and return pan to low heat.
4. Remove shallots from vinegar and set aside. Add vinegar to hot bacon fat, whisking until dressing is emulsified.
5. Arrange frisée in a bowl and add apples, bacon pieces, and shallots. Pour warm dressing over greens and toss to coat.

PER SERVING: 163 cal., 61% (99 cal.) from fat; 2.9 g protein; 11 g fat (3.2 g sat.); 14 g carbo (1.6 g fiber); 356 mg sodium; 11 mg chol.

salads

Asian Pear, Persimmon, and Almond Salad

A mix of vivid chartreuse and bronze lettuces really sets off the fruits' fall colors. For more information on persimmons, *see page 73.*

recipe pictured on page **116**

SERVES 4 | **TIME** 20 minutes

¼ cup fresh lime juice
1 tsp. roasted almond oil or extra-virgin olive oil
2 tbsp. honey
¼ tsp. kosher salt
⅛ tsp. cayenne
2 oz. small, whole tender lettuces or salad mix (about 1 loosely packed qt.)
1 large Asian pear, cut into thin wedges
2 firm-ripe Fuyu persimmons, cut into thin wedges
⅓ cup sliced almonds, toasted (*see How to Toast Nuts, page 134*)

1. In a medium bowl, whisk lime juice, oil, honey, salt, and cayenne until blended.
2. In another medium bowl, gently mix lettuces with 1 to 2 tbsp. dressing. Add pear, persimmons, and almonds to bowl with remaining dressing and mix gently to coat.
3. Divide lettuce among salad plates. Spoon fruit mixture on top.

PER SERVING: 182 cal., 27% (50 cal.) from fat; 2.6 g protein; 5.5 g fat (0.5 g sat.); 35 g carbo (6 g fiber); 75 mg sodium; 0 mg chol.

Western Waldorf

A fresh take on the classic mayonnaisey Waldorf, this salad works as a side dish, a main course (if you add chicken), or even—with a spoonful of plain yogurt—as a light dessert.

SERVES 6 | **TIME** 20 minutes

¼ cup unfiltered apple juice
1 tsp. roasted walnut or almond oil or extra-virgin olive oil
⅛ tsp. *each* kosher salt, cinnamon, and freshly ground black pepper
2 Pink Lady apples (or another sweet-tart variety such as Jonathan or **Piñata**)
½ cup coarsely chopped walnuts, toasted (*see How to Toast Nuts, page 134*)
2 large tangerines, segmented (*see How to Cut Citrus into Segments, page 135*) and halved
1 cup seedless red or green grapes, each halved

1. In a small bowl, whisk apple juice, oil, salt, cinnamon, and pepper until blended.
2. Core apples, cut into thin wedges, and cut wedges in half crosswise. In a medium salad bowl, combine apples, walnuts, tangerines, and grapes. Pour dressing over fruit and nuts and mix gently to coat.

PER SERVING: 136 cal., 49% (66 cal.) from fat; 1.9 g protein; 7.3 g fat (0.7 g sat.); 18 g carbo (2.7 g fiber); 27 mg sodium; 0 mg chol.

Fresh Corn and Avocado Salad

This recipe from reader Kathy Kane, of Menlo Park, California, is a celebration of summer—sweet corn, sun-ripened tomatoes, and intoxicating fresh basil— tied together with the buttery smoothness of avocado.

recipe pictured on page **115**

SERVES 6 | **TIME** 30 minutes

6 ears corn, husked
2 cups halved cherry tomatoes
½ cup thinly sliced red onion
1 large firm-ripe avocado, pitted, peeled, and cut into ½-in. cubes
⅓ cup chopped basil leaves
2 tbsp. Champagne vinegar
1 tsp. Dijon mustard
¼ cup extra-virgin olive oil
¼ tsp. *each* kosher salt and freshly ground black pepper

1. In a large pot of boiling water, cook corn until warmed through, 3 to 5 minutes. Drain and rinse under cold running water until cool.
2. Meanwhile, combine tomatoes, onion, avocado, and basil in a large bowl. In a small bowl, whisk vinegar, mustard, oil, salt, and pepper until blended.
3. Cut corn kernels off cobs and add to salad, then pour in vinaigrette and toss gently to combine.

PER SERVING: 245 cal., 62% (153 cal.) from fat; 4.5 g protein; 17 g fat (2.5 g sat.); 25 g carbo (4.4 g fiber); 92 mg sodium; 0 mg chol.

Spinach-Pomegranate Salad with Pears and Hazelnuts

The use of hazelnut oil amps up the toasted-nut flavor in this salad.

SERVES 6 | **TIME** 30 minutes

¾ **cup unsweetened pomegranate juice**
1 **tbsp. fresh lemon juice**
2 **tsp. roasted hazelnut oil or extra-virgin olive oil**
½ **tsp. kosher salt**
¼ **tsp. minced thyme leaves**
⅛ **tsp. freshly ground black pepper**
5 **oz. spinach leaves (about 2 loosely packed qts.)**
¾ **cup finely shredded radicchio (from 1 head)**
½ **cup pomegranate seeds (see Pomegranates: California Rubies, below)**
½ **cup coarsely chopped toasted hazelnuts (see How to Toast Nuts, page 134)**
1 **large firm-ripe Bartlett pear**

1. In a small saucepan, boil pomegranate juice until reduced to ¼ cup, 5 to 6 minutes. Let cool. Whisk in lemon juice, oil, salt, thyme, and pepper.
2. In a large salad bowl, gently mix spinach, radicchio, pomegranate seeds, and hazelnuts with dressing. Divide among plates.
3. Quarter pear and core. Thinly slice crosswise, then stack slices and cut into matchsticks. Arrange pear on salads.

PER SERVING: 124 cal., 56% (69 cal.) from fat; 2.2 g protein; 7.7 g fat (0.6 g sat.); 13 g carbo (2.3 g fiber); 118 mg sodium; 0 mg chol.

Escarole Salad with Chopped Egg and Anchovy Vinaigrette

Escarole is ideal for a buffet because the large, hearty leaves don't wilt when dressed. This salad, from San Francisco cookbook author Peggy Knickerbocker, is crunchy even the next day.

SERVES 10 to 12 | **TIME** 30 minutes

3 **to 4 bunches escarole, tough green outer leaves discarded (a third to half of each head; save for another use, such as soup)**
2 **garlic cloves, finely chopped**
½ **tsp. salt**
¼ **tsp. freshly ground black pepper**
6 **anchovy fillets, chopped, plus 2 whole fillets**
2 **tbsp. fresh lemon juice**
⅓ **to ½ cup extra-virgin olive oil**
3 **hard-cooked eggs, cooled, peeled, and grated on large holes of a box grater**

1. Soak escarole in cold water and dry by rolling in a kitchen towel. Tear each leaf into 2 or 3 large pieces and chill while you make dressing.
2. In a mortar or food processor, pound or purée garlic, salt, and pepper until garlic is a paste. Add chopped anchovies and pound or process to a paste. Add lemon juice and oil and whisk or process to combine.
3. Pour dressing over escarole leaves and toss thoroughly to coat. Arrange on a large serving platter and scatter with grated egg. Slice whole anchovies lengthwise into thin strips and arrange on top.

PER SERVING: 120 cal., 75% (90 cal.) from fat; 3.9 g protein; 10 g fat (1.8 g sat.); 4.1 g carbo (2.4 g fiber); 253 mg sodium; 60 mg chol.

Pomegranates: California Rubies

Beginning in late August, California enters pomegranate season. Nearly the entire U.S. production of these beautiful and strange fruits, with their thick, leathery red skins and hundreds of juicy, gemlike seeds, is grown in the state (with some in Arizona). Foothill, the first harvested variety, has a mild taste and pink seeds. Early Wonderful, which appears in mid-September, is more tart, with light red seeds.

Wonderful, the biggest crop, comes on the scene from late September to Christmas. It's the sweetest, with dark red seeds.

Ever since pomegranates were found to be high in antioxidants several years ago, their popularity has soared, especially in juices—because the seeds can be a bit of a chore to pick out of the fruit. However, there are times when nothing but the

seeds will do—they're wonderful in rice and meat dishes and in fruit salads, and are fun to eat on their own. To make seeding easier and also splatter-free, cut the pomegranate into chunks in a bowl of water and, working with your hands underwater, break the seeds free from the spongy white pith. The rind and bits of pith will float to the top, where they can be scooped off.

salads

Hazelnut Herb Salad

Tarragon, chives, and parsley temper the richness of the hazelnuts in this salad from Maria Hines, chef and owner of Tilth, in Seattle.

SERVES 10 to 12 | **TIME** 35 minutes

1 cup hazelnuts, toasted (*see How to Toast Nuts, page 134*)
¾ tsp. salt, divided, plus more to taste
1 bunch chives
Leaves from 5 tarragon sprigs
Leaves from 3 flat-leaf parsley sprigs
¼ cup *each* roasted hazelnut oil and extra-virgin olive oil
1 egg yolk
¼ tsp. dry mustard
1 tbsp. fresh lemon juice
¼ tsp. freshly ground black pepper, plus more to taste
3 heads butter lettuce such as Bibb

1. Roughly chop hazelnuts and set aside.
2. Fill a medium saucepan with water and bring to a boil. Add ½ tsp. salt, the chives, tarragon, and parsley. Cook 30 seconds; drain. Rinse herbs with very cold water and use your hands to squeeze out as much water from them as possible. Chop herbs and put in a blender.
3. Add both oils to blender and purée until mixture is smooth, 2 to 3 minutes.
4. In a small bowl, whisk egg yolk and mustard together. Add a drop of the herb-oil mixture and whisk until fully incorporated. Repeat with the remaining herb-oil mixture, adding only ½ tsp. at a time, to create a thick, mayonnaise-like dressing. Whisk in remaining ¼ tsp. salt, the lemon juice, and pepper. Add more salt and pepper to taste if you like.
5. Tear lettuce leaves into bite-size pieces and put in a large bowl. Toss gently but thoroughly with dressing. Garnish with reserved hazelnuts.
Make Ahead: Dressing, up to 2 days, chilled; hazelnuts, up to 2 days, airtight at room temperature.

PER SERVING: 152 cal., 95% (144 cal.) from fat; 2.1 g protein; 16 g fat (1.5 g sat.); 2.6 g carbo (1.2 g fiber); 197 mg sodium; 18 mg chol.

America's Salad Bowl

Lettuce is happiest in a place that's not too hot and not too cold. Between California and Arizona, the West provides the perfect conditions to grow lettuce year-round, producing 98 percent of the nation's crop. From April through November, lettuces thrive in California's Salinas Valley; November through March, operations shift to the state's Imperial Valley and the area around Yuma, Arizona. But the story of the West as America's salad bowl is as much about innovation as climate.

Greens on Ice
The iced-shipping industry developed in California in the 1920s and '30s alongside the orderly rows of lettuce in the Salinas Valley, extending their market. Boxcars filled with lettuce heads covered in a snowy mound of ice could be sent all the way to the East Coast, where the dominant crisphead type got nicknamed "iceberg."

In 1989, the industry was again transformed when one of Salinas's pioneering companies in iced-lettuce transport, now named Fresh Express, created and mass-marketed bagged, ready-to-eat, washed lettuces.

Lettuce Types
Of the four main types of lettuce, two dominate today's market. Crunchy, mild, tightly compacted *crisphead* (including iceberg), often served in a wedge drizzled with blue cheese dressing, is both maligned and loved. More robust-flavored, upright-growing *romaine* has taken off in popularity, thanks to Caesar salads. Other types are *butterhead* (or *butter*)—a less compacted round lettuce with light green to red soft-textured and mild leaves—and *loose leaf*, also soft and mild, with leaves that branch from the stem. Loose-leaf lettuces come in assorted colors (red, bronze, dark green, chartreuse) and textures from smooth and flat to frilly; oak leaf may be the best-known variety.

Bagged and bulk-sold salad mixes have evolved to include a wide range of small young to larger torn lettuces, other salad greens, herbs, and even flowers. For example, mesclun—a mix of small, young greens first grown in Provence and popularized in the West by Alice Waters at Chez Panisse in the 1970s—may include spicy arugula and licoricy chervil with lettuces.

The latest "innovation" in lettuces is heirlooms. Farmers' markets and some grocery stores are bringing back old varieties such as deeply notched, bronze-tinged Brunia, a French loose-leaf type, and Forellen schluss, a maroon-spotted Austrian romaine lettuce whose name is German for "speckled like a trout."

Papaya and Avocado Salads with Hawaiian Vanilla Vinaigrette

These delicately floral, fruity salads are built on individual lettuce leaves, making them easy to pick up and eat by hand. Hawaiian papayas are small and pear shaped, with finely grained yellow-orange flesh; they tend to have more flavor than the larger Mexican papayas.

SERVES 12 | **TIME** 30 minutes, plus 1 hour to macerate

½ cup olive oil
6 tbsp. Champagne vinegar
1 tsp. sugar
½ tsp. kosher salt
1 Hawaiian (or other) vanilla bean
24 medium butter lettuce leaves (from about 3 heads)
2 Hawaiian papayas, peeled, seeded, and sliced (*see Quick Tip below*)
2 large firm-ripe avocados, pitted, peeled, and sliced

1. In a small bowl, whisk together oil, vinegar, sugar, and salt. Cut vanilla bean in half lengthwise, scrape seeds from one half with the back of a paring knife, and add seeds and scraped pod to vinaigrette (reserve other half of pod for another use). Set aside at room temperature for at least 1 hour to let the vanilla flavor develop. Discard scraped pod.
2. Arrange lettuce leaves on a large platter in a single layer. On each leaf, lay 1 or 2 papaya slices and 1 or 2 avocado slices. Drizzle vinaigrette over salad.
Quick Tip: Ripen papayas at room temperature until the skin is mostly yellow and flesh "gives" a little when squeezed. Be careful not to buy overripe ones (all too common on supermarket shelves); they'll taste fermented.
Make Ahead: Vinaigrette, up to 1 day, chilled; allow to come to room temperature before using.

PER SERVING: 171 cal., 79% (135 cal.) from fat; 1.3 g protein; 15 g fat (2.2 g sat.); 9 g carbo (1.4 g fiber); 55 mg sodium; 0 mg chol.

■ Hawaiian Vanilla

FROM THE PANTRY

The tropical weather of Hawaii transforms its vanilla blossoms into the most aromatic beans in the world. The high price of the vanilla beans results from the fact that every vanilla orchid must be pollinated by hand on the one day each year when the flower opens.

Spicy Avocado-Poblano Salad

Roasted chiles, crunchy jicama and radishes, silky avocado, crumbly cheese, and a spicy-sweet dressing make this salad an explosion of flavors and textures. Have it with pork chops or a juicy steak.

recipe pictured on page 110

SERVES 4 | **TIME** 50 minutes

4 medium poblano chiles (about ¾ lb. total)
2 tbsp. fresh lime juice, divided
1 tsp. kosher salt
¼ tsp. honey
⅛ tsp. cayenne
3 tbsp. avocado, safflower, or canola oil
2 large firm-ripe avocados
½ lb. jicama, peeled, halved, and thinly sliced into half-moons
¼ cup crumbled *cotija* (dry, salty white Mexican cheese; sometimes called *queso añejo*) or parmesan cheese
¼ cup pumpkin seeds (*pepitas*), toasted (*see Quick Tip below*)
4 radishes, cut into matchsticks

1. Preheat oven to broil. Broil poblanos 4 in. from heat in a rimmed baking pan, turning as needed, until blackened all over, about 10 minutes. Let sit on pan until skins are loosened, 15 to 20 minutes.
2. Whisk together 1 tbsp. lime juice, salt, honey, cayenne, and oil.
3. Halve, pit, and peel avocados. Lay each avocado half cut side down, rest your hand gently on top, and slide knife through avocado horizontally to make ¼-in.-thick slices. Drizzle with remaining 1 tbsp. lime juice.
4. Skin, stem, and seed poblanos. Cut into irregular 1- to 2-in. pieces.
5. On salad plates, arrange a layer each of poblano pieces, avocado slices, and jicama; drizzle with some dressing. Add another layer each of poblanos and avocados, drizzle with more dressing, and tuck remaining jicama slices into salads from the side. Sprinkle with cheese, pumpkin seeds, and radishes.
Quick Tip: Toast pumpkin seeds in a small (not nonstick) frying pan over medium heat until popped and golden brown, stirring occasionally, 2 to 4 minutes.

PER SERVING: 327 cal., 74% (243 cal.) from fat; 5.5 g protein; 27 g fat (4.4 g sat.); 20 g carbo (6.1 g fiber); 397 mg sodium; 4 mg chol.

salads

Stacked Caesar Salad with Parmesan Rafts

Here is an architectural Caesar—our homage to a legendary salad. To alleviate concerns about salmonella, we've eliminated the raw egg; a quick buzz in the blender emulsifies the remaining components into a creamy dressing. This salad is most dramatic when made with whole inner romaine lettuce leaves (often sold as "romaine hearts").

SERVES 4 to 6 as a main course | **TIME** 1 hour

1 sourdough baguette (about 2-in. wide; ½ to ¾ lb.)
About ¾ cup extra-virgin olive oil, divided
1⅓ cups finely shredded parmesan cheese (about ¼ lb.), divided
⅓ cup fresh lemon juice
9 canned anchovy fillets, drained
4 tsp. minced garlic
¾ tsp. freshly ground black pepper
½ tsp. salt, plus more to taste
4 qts. tender inner romaine lettuce leaves (max. 8 in. long, 1⅓ lbs. total)
1 cup parmesan cheese curls (3 oz. total; *see Quick Tip below*)

1. Preheat oven to 325°. Make parmesan rafts: Cut baguette into diagonal slices ¼ in. thick. Lightly brush both sides of each slice with oil, using 3 to 4 tbsp. total. Arrange in a single layer in two shallow 12- by 17-in. baking pans. Bake 5 minutes. Sprinkle slices evenly with 1 cup shredded parmesan. Bake until cheese is melted and bread is golden, 10 to 12 minutes.
2. In a blender, blend remaining 9 tbsp. oil, remaining ⅓ cup shredded parmesan, the lemon juice, anchovies, garlic, pepper, and salt until smooth.
3. Put lettuce in a large bowl and parmesan rafts in another. Drizzle two-thirds of dressing over lettuce and remainder over rafts. Mix rafts to coat with dressing; with your hands or two spoons, gently lift and mix lettuce to coat.
4. Divide a third of lettuce among dinner plates. Arrange a third of parmesan rafts loosely on top, and add a third of parmesan curls. Repeat with remaining lettuce, rafts, and curls to add two more layers. Season salads to taste with salt.
Quick Tip: To make the curls, pull a vegetable peeler across the wide side of a block of parmesan (it's easier if the cheese is at room temperature).

PER SERVING: 521 cal., 67% (351 cal.) from fat; 20 g protein; 39 g fat (10 g sat.); 25 g carbo (2.8 g fiber); 1,234 mg sodium; 28 mg chol.

The Story of Caesar Salad

Tijuana, Mexico, July 4, 1924, Caesar's Place. As the restaurant fills with holiday diners, Italian-born chef and restaurant owner Caesar Cardini runs short on ingredients for the day's salad. He improvises with what's on hand: romaine leaves, parmesan cheese, olive oil, lemon juice, a raw egg, Worcestershire sauce, and croutons (anchovies came later). The salad is a hit with the Hollywood set who frequent Cardini's restaurant, and they take their reverence for Caesar back home. Served plain or topped with everything from grilled chicken to fried ginger, the salad becomes a hallmark of California cuisine.

Frisée, Tangerine, and Sesame Salad

Tangerines provide a welcome flavor spark in winter.

SERVES 4 | **TIME** 20 minutes

Finely shredded zest from 1 tangerine
3 tbsp. fresh tangerine juice
2 tbsp. vegetable oil
1 tsp. finely shredded fresh ginger
½ tsp. Asian (toasted) sesame oil
¼ tsp. salt, plus more to taste
3 tangerines, segmented (*see How to Cut Citrus into Segments, page 135*)
¼ red onion, thinly sliced and rinsed
1 small head frisée, torn into bite-size pieces
1 tsp. toasted sesame seeds (*see Quick Tip below*)
2 tbsp. pomegranate seeds (optional)

1. Combine tangerine zest and juice, vegetable oil, ginger, sesame oil, and salt in a small bowl (add more salt to taste if you like).
2. In a medium serving bowl, toss tangerine segments with onion, frisée, and tangerine-ginger dressing. Sprinkle with sesame seeds and pomegranate seeds if using.
Quick Tip: Toast sesame seeds in a nonstick frying pan over medium heat, shaking and stirring often, until golden brown, 5 to 7 minutes.

PER SERVING: 122 cal., 58% (71 cal.) from fat; 1.4 g protein; 8.2 g fat (0.9 g sat.); 13 g carbo (1.9 g fiber); 160 mg sodium; 0 mg chol.

Our Favorite Salad Flowers

Nasturtiums and Johnny-jump-ups are the flowers you'll see most often in the produce section of specialty-foods stores and farmers' markets (choose unsprayed, organic petals and blooms; avoid flowers from florists and nurseries). The best way to have other choices is to grow them. If you're growing your own flowers from seedlings, be sure to buy organic plants—and don't spray them as they grow.

• **BACHELOR'S BUTTONS** (*Centaurea cyanus*): Flowers are spiky-looking but soft, and come in blue, purple, pink, rose, or white. They have a cucumberish flavor and a fun, frilly texture. Eat whole or as petals.

• **BORAGE** (*Borago officinalis*): Blue, starlike flowers with a delicate cucumber taste and hints of melon.

To eat, pull out the hairy sepals in the center. The leaves are edible as well.

• **CALENDULAS** (*Calendula officinalis*): Daisylike blooms are usually orange or yellow and have a mildly tangy, chrysanthemum-like taste. They're best eaten as petals.

• **CARNATIONS** (*Dianthus*): These cottage garden flowers, also known as pinks, are sweet and spicy. Eat only the petals, and taste each flower before using, as they can sometimes be bitter. Clove pink (*D. caryophyllus*) and cottage pink (*D. plumarius*) are especially nice.

• **HERB FLOWERS** (*basil, chives, rosemary*): They taste like the leaves, but often with a touch of sweetness. Many are tiny and delicate, so pick them right before using or snip the

entire blossom stem and put it in water until ready to use.

• **NASTURTIUMS** (*Tropaeolum majus*): This is truly the tastiest flower—peppery and mustardy with a touch of honey. Colors range from yellow to reddish orange and can also be variegated. The petals are thin and fragile and seem to melt on the tongue. The peppery leaves are edible too.

• **STOCK** (*Matthiola*): Blossoms have a warmly spicy flavor, like a combination of cloves and cinnamon, and come in many colors. Use flowerets.

• **VIOLAS,** including pansies (*Viola x wittrockiana*) and Johnny-jump-ups (*V. tricolor*): All violas are edible, with a faint lettucelike taste and velvety texture. (Pansies are the largest; the littlest are Johnny-jump-ups.)

Blooming Salad

You can take salad to a whole new level by adding edible flowers.

SERVES 6 | **TIME** 20 minutes

2½ tbsp. grapeseed, safflower, or canola oil
1 tbsp. unseasoned rice vinegar
½ tsp. kosher salt
¼ tsp. freshly ground black pepper
1 tsp. minced tarragon
1 Persian cucumber or ⅓ English cucumber
About 50 sugar snap peas
¼ cup loosely packed chervil sprigs (optional)
3 oz. mâche clusters (about 3 loosely packed cups)
¼ lb. salad mix (about 1½ loosely packed qts.)
4 medium radishes, sliced in half lengthwise
Unsprayed organic edible petals and blossoms (*see Our Favorite Salad Flowers, above*)

1. Whisk oil, vinegar, salt, pepper, and tarragon together in a small bowl.
2. Thinly slice cucumber. Split 30 of the fatter pea pods and remove the peas; set aside. Gently rinse chervil (if using), mâche, and salad mix and gently spin twice in a salad spinner to thoroughly dry the leaves.
3. Put greens in a large bowl and toss gently but thoroughly with 3 tbsp. dressing (leaves should be barely coated); add more dressing if necessary.
4. Divide greens among plates. To each salad, add a few slices of cucumber, some sugar snap peas (both whole pods and individual peas), and some radishes. Drizzle with any remaining dressing if you like and top with whole flowers and flower petals.

PER SERVING: 67 cal., 77% (51 cal.) from fat; 1 g protein; 5.7 g fat (0.5 g sat.); 3.2 g carbo (0.5 g fiber); 101 mg sodium; 0 mg chol.

salads

Green Salad with Papaya Seed Dressing

Greg and Lynn Boyer of Oahu gave us this version of the classic Hawaiian salad. The creamy-looking dressing gets its texture and zing from sweet onions and peppery, crunchy papaya seeds.

SERVES 10 to 12 | **TIME** 15 minutes

⅓ cup *each* unseasoned rice vinegar and canola oil
½ small sweet onion such as Maui or Walla Walla, chopped
1½ tsp. sugar
½ tsp. *each* salt and dry mustard
1½ tbsp. papaya seeds
1 large sweet onion such as Maui or Walla Walla, thinly sliced into rings and rinsed with cold water
1 lb. mixed salad greens
2 firm-ripe avocados, pitted, peeled, and sliced

1. In a blender, blend vinegar, oil, chopped onion, sugar, salt, and mustard until smooth. Add papaya seeds and pulse until seeds look like coarsely ground peppercorns.
2. In a large bowl, combine onion rings, salad greens, and three-quarters of avocado slices; pour dressing over salad and toss gently to coat. Arrange salad on a large platter and top with remaining slices of avocado.

PER SERVING: 145 cal., 74% (108 cal.) from fat; 1.8 g protein; 12 g fat (1.4 g sat.); 8.4 g carbo (1.7 g fiber); 122 mg sodium; 0 mg chol.

Salad Greens, Ready When You Are

If you take 10 minutes to wash your greens when you get them home from the market, they'll be ready to use for a fast salad (and you won't have to pay lots more for bagged, prewashed greens). Immerse the leaves in water and swish gently to remove any grit, then lift out to drain in a colander or spin dry. Arrange leaves in a single layer on paper towels or a kitchen towel, roll them up, and put in a plastic bag; roll bag closed. Chill up to 1 week.

Baked Goat Cheese with Spring Lettuce Salad

This salad has been on the cafe menu at Chez Panisse, in Berkeley, California, for more than 25 years. You can skip marinating the cheese, but it won't be nearly as flavorful.

recipe pictured on page **118**

SERVES 4 | **TIME** 30 minutes, plus 12 hours to marinate

¾ lb. fresh mild goat cheese
Leaves from 4 thyme sprigs, chopped
Leaves from 1 small rosemary sprig, chopped
1½ cups extra-virgin olive oil
1 cup panko (Japanese-style bread crumbs)
½ baguette, cut into eight ¼-in.-thick slices
1 tsp. sherry vinegar
½ tsp. kosher or sea salt
¼ tsp. freshly ground black pepper
2½ tbsp. roasted walnut or extra-virgin olive oil
½ lb. baby lettuces or salad mix
½ cup walnuts, toasted (*see How to Toast Nuts, page 134*) and coarsely chopped

1. Cut goat cheese into eight 1-in.-thick disks and put in a container just big enough to hold them in a single layer. Sprinkle cheese with thyme and rosemary and pour olive oil on top. Cover and chill at least 12 hours. One hour before baking, pop them in the freezer to firm up.
2. Preheat oven to 400°. Remove cheese from marinade and roll all sides in panko, pressing gently so crumbs adhere. Arrange on a large baking sheet and bake until golden, about 15 minutes, turning over halfway through. Add baguette slices for last 5 minutes of baking.
3. Whisk together vinegar, salt, pepper, and walnut oil. Put lettuces in a large bowl, drizzle with just enough dressing to coat, and toss gently and thoroughly.
4. Divide lettuces among salad plates, sprinkle with walnuts, and to each plate add two goat cheese disks and a baguette slice. Serve immediately.
Make Ahead: Goat cheese can marinate for up to 1 week, chilled.

PER SERVING: 703 cal., 65% (459 cal.) from fat; 25 g protein; 51 g fat (16 g sat.); 38 g carbo (3 g fiber); 804 mg sodium; 39 mg chol.

Endive Salad with Bacon, Gorgonzola, and Avocado

This salad from reader Samantha Saffir, of Santa Monica, California, makes great use of endive and ripe avocados. We like to toss it together for a casual presentation, but if you want to dress it up for a dinner party, keep the endive leaves whole, arrange them on a platter, fill them with the avocado-bacon-gorgonzola mixture, and drizzle with the vinaigrette.

SERVES 4 to 6 | **TIME** 20 minutes

5 slices (about 5 oz.) thick-cut bacon
4 large heads Belgian endive, trimmed and coarsely chopped
2 firm-ripe avocados, pitted, peeled, and chopped
½ cup crumbled gorgonzola cheese
2 tbsp. minced shallot
1 tbsp. sherry vinegar
¼ cup extra-virgin olive oil

1. In a large frying pan over medium-high heat, cook bacon, turning once, until crisp and brown, about 6 minutes total. Drain bacon on paper towels, then crumble into small pieces.
2. In a medium salad bowl, combine bacon, endive, avocados, and gorgonzola. Set aside. In a small bowl, whisk together shallot and vinegar. Gradually drizzle in oil, whisking until dressing is emulsified. Pour vinaigrette over salad and toss to coat. Serve immediately.

PER SERVING: 322 cal., 87% (279 cal.) from fat; 7 g protein; 31 g fat (7.4 g sat.); 8.3 g carbo (2.8 g fiber); 295 mg sodium; 17 mg chol.

Asparagus and Butter Lettuce Salad

The texture of butter lettuce keeps this salad light and delicate, but you can use any tender, sweet lettuce in its place.

SERVES 4 | **TIME** 30 minutes

1 bunch asparagus (about 1 lb.)
2 heads butter lettuce such as Bibb
3 tbsp. extra-virgin olive oil
5 tsp. fresh lemon juice
½ tsp. *each* honey and salt
¼ tsp. *each* finely shredded lemon zest and freshly ground black pepper
⅛ tsp. dry mustard
¼ lb. *perline* (tiny balls) mozzarella cheese *(see Quick Tip, above right)*
2 tbsp. pine nuts

1. Hold the woody end of an asparagus stalk and bend until it snaps off. Repeat with remaining stalks and discard woody ends. Cut trimmed spears on the diagonal into ⅛-in. slices, leaving tips about 1 in. long.
2. Remove and discard outer leaves of lettuce heads. Tear remaining leaves into bite-size pieces. Set aside.
3. In a small bowl or measuring cup, whisk together oil, lemon juice, honey, salt, lemon zest, pepper, and mustard until creamy-looking.
4. In a large bowl, toss lettuce with 3 tbsp. dressing. Divide lettuce among salad plates. Toss asparagus pieces with remaining dressing and spoon over lettuces, dividing evenly. Sprinkle salads with perline and pine nuts.
Quick Tip: You can find perline mozzarella at specialty-foods stores and Italian markets, or substitute a ¼-lb. piece of fresh mozzarella cut into ¼-in. pieces.

PER SERVING: 240 cal., 75% (180 cal.) from fat; 11 g protein; 20 g fat (6.4 g sat.); 7.2 g carbo (2 g fiber); 411 mg sodium; 25 mg chol.

Slow-roasted Portabellas on Parsley Salad

Large, meaty portabella mushrooms create an almost steaklike impression, especially when drizzled with good balsamic vinegar.

SERVES 4 | **TIME** 45 minutes

4 portabella mushrooms *(see Quick Tips below)*, stems removed
1 tbsp. extra-virgin olive oil, divided
2 cups flat-leaf parsley leaves
1½ tsp. good-quality balsamic vinegar *(see Quick Tips below)*, divided
Coarse sea salt or kosher salt
Parmesan curls (use a vegetable peeler)

1. Preheat oven to 250°. Brush mushroom caps with 1 tsp. oil and put, top side down, on a baking sheet. Bake until shrunken slightly, about 30 minutes.
2. In a medium bowl, toss parsley leaves with 1 tsp. oil and ½ tsp. vinegar. Add salt to taste.
3. To serve, divide salad among plates. Slice portabellas and arrange on salad. Drizzle with remaining 1 tsp. each oil and vinegar. Sprinkle with salt and add parmesan curls on the side.
Quick Tips: To clean mushrooms, wipe them with a small dry brush (such as a clean nail brush) and a damp paper towel. Particularly dirty specimens should be swished around in a bowl of cold water for a minute, then dried on paper towels. For this recipe, use a good-quality balsamic vinegar—not the thin kind (which usually lists caramel and sugar on the label),

salads

but one with rich flavor and syrupy texture. True Italian balsamic vinegar—*aceto balsamico tradizionale*—from Modena and Reggio Emilia is the best, but it's very expensive. You can find decent and affordable approximations in well-stocked grocery stores; Elsa and Fini are good brands to look for.

PER SERVING: 70 cal., 49% (34 cal.) from fat; 3.5 g protein; 3.8 g fat (0.5 g sat.); 7.9 g carbo (3 g fiber); 19 mg sodium; chol N/A.

Spicy Sunflower Salad with Carrot Dressing

Using a mix of small-to-large and delicate-to-crunchy greens makes this salad lively. Be aware that raw sprouts can occasionally contain bacteria that cause foodborne illness, so children, the elderly, and those with weakened immune systems should avoid eating them.

SERVES 6 | **TIME** 30 minutes

2 cups fresh carrot juice
3 tbsp. fresh lime juice
1 tsp. Sriracha chili sauce or ¼ tsp. cayenne
1 tsp. Asian (toasted) sesame oil
¼ tsp. kosher salt
½ cup shelled sunflower seeds
½ large orange or yellow bell pepper
6 oz. sunflower sprouts (1½ qts. loosely packed) or 5 oz. mixed baby lettuces (2 qts.)
1½ cups loosely packed mild or spicy sprouts such as clover or radish
1½ cups loosely packed pea shoots or micro greens (*see Try Some Tiny Greens, right*)
⅓ cup long, fine shreds of carrot, preferably shredded with a mandoline
Salt

1. Preheat oven to 350°. In a wide, 3- to 4-qt. saucepan, boil carrot juice over medium-high heat, stirring often, until reduced to ¼ cup, 12 to 15 minutes. Pour into a small bowl and let cool. Whisk in lime juice, Sriracha, sesame oil, and salt. Set dressing aside.
2. Toast sunflower seeds in a shallow pan in oven until light golden, shaking pan occasionally, 4 to 8 minutes. Let cool.
3. Trim off membrane and curved ends of bell pepper. Cut pepper lengthwise into very thin strips.
4. In a large bowl, combine bell pepper, sprouts, pea shoots, and carrot shreds, using your hands to toss and separate everything until evenly mixed. Pour seeds and dressing on top; mix gently. Season with salt to taste.

PER SERVING: 129 cal., 49% (63 cal.) from fat; 4.6 g protein; 7 g fat (0.8 g sat.); 15 g carbo (0.7 g fiber); 88 mg sodium; 0 mg chol.

Tomato Salad with Chile and Lime

This salad reminds us of fresh salsa. It would be right at home at a Mexican-themed buffet or on the table with beef fajitas or pork or shrimp tacos.

SERVES 8 | **TIME** 25 minutes

2 lbs. ripe tomatoes
1 large mild green chile, such as poblano
3 tbsp. olive oil
2 tbsp. fresh lime juice
½ tsp. salt, plus more to taste
¼ tsp. dry mustard

1. Core and halve tomatoes. Remove seeds (either scoop them out with a spoon or squeeze them out) and cut tomatoes into bite-size pieces. Put tomatoes in a large bowl.
2. Remove stem and seeds from chile. Finely chop chile and add to tomatoes. Set aside.
3. In a small bowl, whisk together oil, lime juice, salt, and mustard until emulsified.
4. Drizzle dressing over tomatoes and chiles and toss gently to combine. Add more salt to taste if you like. Serve at room temperature.

PER SERVING: 72 cal., 68% (49 cal.) from fat; 1.1 g protein; 5.4 g fat (0.7 g sat.); 6 g carbo (1.5 g fiber); 155 mg sodium; 0 mg chol.

Try Some Tiny Greens

Sprout selection varies from market to market, but choices are usually interchangeable in recipes—so have fun exploring options. Farmers' markets may have great choices too.

• **WISPY SPROUTS:** Delicately crunchy; seeds are often still attached. Try mild alfalfa and clover, more robust broccoli, and spicy radish and onion. Some growers package them as a mix for a blend of flavors.

• **STURDY SPROUTS** (also sold as "shoots"): More mature sprouts with bigger first leaves attached. Buckwheat and pea sprouts are sweet and tender; sunflower is crunchy, with a flavor like the seeds.

• **MICRO GREENS:** Very mild little seedlings of mizuna, tatsoi, mustard, kohlrabi, cabbage, broccoli, arugula, amaranth, and others. They are often sold as a blend.

Icebox Salad

The top layers of chopped vegetables keep the dressing from soaking and wilting the bottom layer of lettuce. Believe it or not, this salad improves after a few hours in the refrigerator. The dressing works its way into the peas, cucumbers, and radishes; the flavors meld; and the vegetables become sweeter. This is perfect for a summer cookout or picnic—and it feeds a crowd.

SERVES 12 | **TIME** 45 minutes, plus 2 hours to chill

2 cups plain low-fat yogurt
1 small head romaine lettuce
10 oz. sugar snap peas
1 bunch radishes (about 12)
1 English cucumber
4 green onions
1 package (10 oz.) frozen peas or 2 cups shelled
   fresh peas
3 tbsp. olive oil
¾ tsp. salt
¼ tsp. freshly ground black pepper
2 tbsp. minced dill
4 large mint leaves, minced
½ cup finely chopped chives (about 1 bunch)

1. Line a fine-mesh strainer with two layers of cheese-cloth and put strainer over a bowl. Put yogurt in strainer, cover with plastic wrap, and chill 30 minutes.
2. Meanwhile, tear romaine into bite-size pieces. Arrange lettuce evenly in a 9- by 13-in. baking pan or other 2-qt. dish.
3. Chop sugar snap peas and arrange evenly on top of lettuce. Trim and thinly slice radishes. Arrange them on top of sugar snap peas.
4. Peel cucumber, halve lengthwise, and, using a spoon, scoop out and discard pulpy flesh and small seeds in the center. Cut each cucumber half lengthwise again and chop. Arrange cucumber on top of radishes. Trim green onions, thinly slice white and light green parts, and sprinkle evenly over cucumber.
5. If using frozen peas, put in a colander or strainer and run under hot water for 1 to 2 minutes to thaw. If using fresh peas, follow cooking instructions in the *Quick Tip, above right.* Dry peas thoroughly on paper towels and sprinkle evenly over green onions.
6. Transfer yogurt to a bowl (discard liquid beneath strainer). Stir in oil, salt, and pepper, then stir in dill and mint. Spread yogurt mixture evenly over salad and sprinkle with chives. Cover with plastic wrap and chill at least 2 hours and up to overnight. Serve cold, cut into 12 pieces.

Quick Tip: To prepare fresh peas, bring a large saucepan of water to a boil. Add peas and 1 tsp. salt. Boil for 1 minute, drain, and plunge peas into ice water to stop cooking. Drain.
Make Ahead: Up to 1 day, chilled.

PER SERVING: 95 cal., 39% (37 cal.) from fat; 4.7 g protein; 4.2 g fat (0.8 g sat.); 10 g carbo (2.5 g fiber); 205 mg sodium; 2.3 mg chol.

Snow Pea Salad with Sesame Dressing

Crunchy, simple, and good, this is an excellent side for any grilled food with Asian flavors.

SERVES 4 to 6 | **TIME** 15 minutes, plus 1 hour to chill

1 lb. snow peas, trimmed
3 tbsp. vegetable oil
2 tbsp. soy sauce
1½ tbsp. Asian (toasted) sesame oil (*see Asian*
   [Toasted] Sesame Oil, below)
2 tsp. grated fresh ginger
1 tsp. sugar
½ tsp. hot Chinese mustard
2 tbsp. thinly sliced green onions, divided
1 tsp. sesame seeds

1. Blanch snow peas in boiling water until they turn a brighter green, 15 to 30 seconds. Drain immediately, rinse under cold running water, then drain again. Pat dry.
2. Stack several snow peas and slice on the diagonal into ¼-in.-wide strips. Repeat to slice remaining peas.
3. In a large bowl, whisk vegetable oil, soy sauce, sesame oil, ginger, sugar, and mustard until well combined. Add sliced snow peas and 1 tbsp. green onions; mix to coat. Cover and chill until cold, at least 1 hour.
4. Just before serving, mound salad on a platter and sprinkle with remaining 1 tbsp. green onions and the sesame seeds.
Make Ahead: Through step 3, up to 1 day, chilled.

PER SERVING: 132 cal., 75% (99 cal.) from fat; 2.5 g protein; 11 g fat (1.4 g sat.); 7.2 g carbo (2 g fiber); 352 mg sodium; 0 mg chol.

■ Asian (Toasted) Sesame Oil

FROM THE PANTRY

The dark oil extracted from toasted sesame seeds is rich, nutty, and mesmerizingly fragrant. For maximum flavor, get a brand that is 100 percent sesame oil; cheaper blends are less intense. Heat dissipates the oil's flavor and aroma, so it's best added to a dish as a finishing touch.

salads

Green Bean, Hazelnut, and Mint Salad with Lemon Dressing

With its bright, pesto-like flavors, this is one of our favorite ways to serve green beans.

SERVES 6 | **TIME** 30 minutes

8 cups packed green beans (about ¾ lb.), trimmed
2 tbsp. chopped mint leaves
1 tbsp. finely shredded lemon zest
2 tsp. fresh lemon juice
½ tsp. salt
¼ cup roasted hazelnut oil or extra-virgin olive oil
¾ cup hazelnuts, toasted *(see How to Toast Nuts, page 134)*

1. In a 4- to 6-qt. pot over high heat, bring 3 qts. salted water to a boil. Add green beans and cook until just crisp-tender, 4 to 7 minutes. Drain in a colander and plunge beans into a bowl of ice water to cool. Drain again and set aside.
2. In a small bowl, stir together mint, lemon zest and juice, and salt. Drizzle in oil, whisking constantly.
3. In a large bowl, gently toss green beans with dressing and hazelnuts. Serve at room temperature.
Make Ahead: Up to 3 hours, at room temperature.

PER SERVING: 188 cal., 86% (162 cal.) from fat; 2.8 g protein; 18 g fat (1.3 g sat.); 6.2 g carbo (2.3 g fiber); 197 mg sodium; 0 mg chol.

The New Three-bean Salad

No mushy canned kidney beans here—and the flavors get even better if you start the salad a day ahead.

SERVES 8 to 10 | **TIME** 40 minutes

Finely shredded zest of 2 lemons
¼ cup *each* **fresh lemon juice and grapeseed or canola oil**
½ tsp. kosher salt, plus more to taste
½ tsp. sugar
1 bag (10 oz.) frozen shelled edamame
1 can (15 oz.) chickpeas (garbanzos), drained and rinsed
10 oz. green beans, trimmed and cut into 1-in. pieces
6 green onions, trimmed and thinly sliced diagonally

1. In a serving bowl, whisk together lemon zest, lemon juice, oil, salt, and sugar. Set aside.
2. In a large saucepan fitted with a steamer basket, bring 1 in. water to a boil over medium-high heat. Steam edamame, covered, 3 minutes. Add chickpeas and steam, covered, until heated through, 4 to 5 minutes. Pour both into a colander, then pat dry on a kitchen towel. Add to bowl with dressing and toss to coat.

3. In the same saucepan, bring another 1 in. water to a boil. Fill a large bowl with ice water and set aside. Steam green beans, covered, until tender-crisp, 4 to 5 minutes. Drain, then plunge into ice water. Let sit 30 seconds, drain, and pat dry on towel.
4. Add green beans and green onions to chickpea mixture, toss to coat, and add more salt to taste if you like.
Make Ahead: Through step 3, up to 1 day; wrap chickpea mixture and green beans separately; chill. Bring both to room temperature before proceeding. Dressed salad can stand at room temperature up to 1 hour before serving.

PER SERVING: 123 cal., 55% (68 cal.) from fat; 5.1 g protein; 7.5 g fat (0.6 g sat.); 10 g carbo (3.3 g fiber); 110 mg sodium; 0 mg chol.

Edamame-Orzo Salad

Here's a simple and tasty East-West fusion: Italian orzo pasta tossed with Japanese edamame.

SERVES 4 | **TIME** 30 minutes

2 cups frozen shelled edamame *(see Edamame, below)*
½ cup orzo
¼ cup finely chopped red bell pepper
2 tbsp. roasted walnut oil or vegetable oil
2 tbsp. fresh lemon juice
1 tsp. minced garlic
1 tsp. finely shredded lemon zest
½ tsp. kosher salt

1. Cook edamame and orzo according to package directions; drain.
2. Combine edamame, orzo, bell pepper, oil, lemon juice, garlic, lemon zest, and salt.
Make Ahead: Up to 3 days, chilled.

PER SERVING: 210 cal., 43% (90 cal.) from fat; 8.9 g protein; 10 g fat (0.7 g sat.); 22 g carbo (3.5 g fiber); 248 mg sodium; 0 mg chol.

■ Edamame

FROM THE GARDEN

Fresh soybeans (edamame), good as a snack and in salads, are packed with nutrients. Each ½-cup serving contains 4 grams of fiber and only 3 grams of fat, all of which are the heart-healthy mono- and polyunsaturated kinds. The beans are also high in soy protein, which may help reduce cholesterol when part of a low-fat diet.

Our Favorite Heirloom Beans

Wonderful beans like Red Appaloosa are no longer impossible to find, thanks to the efforts of heirloom seed savers and growers like New Mexico's "Bean Queen," Elizabeth Berry; Seed Savers Exchange in Iowa; Seeds of Change near Santa Fe; and Seed Bank in Petaluma, California. You can buy a variety of heirloom beans online or at specialty-foods stores or farmers' markets. Some we look for:

• **BLACK VALENTINE:** Small jet-black bean with a meaty texture and neutral flavor.

• **CANNELLINI:** White bean with a creamy texture and a delicate, sweet, nutty flavor.

• **FLAGEOLET** (also called Green Flageolet): Very slender, white to pale-green bean with a mild taste and buttery, melting texture.

• **FLOR DE MAYO:** Small red bean with a medium-firm but creamy texture and subtly sweet flavor.

• **NEW MEXICO APPALOOSA:** Mottled black-and-white or red-and-white bean with a smooth, creamy texture and mild, earthy flavor.

• **SCARLET RUNNER:** An inch-long purple bean with black markings; a meaty, starchy texture; and a sweet chestnut flavor.

• **WHITE AZTEC:** Thumb-size, plump white bean with a flavor and texture reminiscent of potatoes.

Citrus and Bean Salad

Katharine Kagel of Cafe Pasqual's, in Santa Fe, created this recipe for heirloom legumes.

MAKES 7 cups; 8 servings | **TIME** 1½ hours, plus at least 2 hours to soak beans

2 cups (14 oz.) dried beans such as Red Appaloosa, Flor de Mayo, or Scarlet Runner *(see Our Favorite Heirloom Beans, above)*
2 cups finely chopped red onion, divided, plus ½ cup thinly sliced
2 tbsp. minced garlic
1 tsp. salt, plus more to taste
1 cup minced flat-leaf parsley
¼ cup *each* olive oil and fresh lemon juice
2 tsp. freshly ground black pepper
3 oranges (1½ lbs. total), peel and membrane removed, sliced crosswise
1 tbsp. *each* long, fine shreds orange zest and lemon zest
1 tsp. long, fine shreds lime zest

1. Soak beans as directed in *Dried-bean Basics, page 242.*
2. In a 6- to 8-qt. pan, bring 2 qts. water, beans, 1½ cups chopped onion, and the garlic to a boil over high heat. Reduce heat and simmer, covered, for 40 minutes. Add salt and simmer, covered, until beans are just tender to the bite, 30 to 90 minutes more, depending on age of beans.
3. Drain beans and let cool in a bowl. Gently mix in remaining ½ cup chopped onion, the parsley, oil, lemon juice, and pepper. Arrange orange slices on a platter.

Spoon beans over orange slices. Garnish with onion slices and citrus zests and add salt to taste.

PER SERVING: 289 cal., 24% (68 cal.) from fat; 13 g protein; 7.6 g fat (1 g sat.); 45 g carbo (8.2 g fiber); 292 mg sodium; 0 mg chol.

Warm Chickpea, Red Pepper, and Spinach Salad with Harissa

To create this bright-tasting but sultry salad, San Francisco chef Dan Petrie starts with classic Moroccan roasted vegetables, then adds fresh spinach and a sherry vinaigrette.

SERVES 6 | **TIME** 1 hour

1 tbsp. sherry vinegar
1½ tsp. Dijon mustard
1 tsp. *each* kosher salt and freshly ground black pepper, divided, plus more to taste
2 to 4 tsp. *harissa (see Quick Tip, above right)*, divided
3 tbsp. extra-virgin olive oil
1 *each* medium red and medium yellow bell pepper
2 tbsp. olive oil
1 medium eggplant, cut into ½-in. cubes
1 can (15 oz.) chickpeas (garbanzos), drained and rinsed
1 bag (6 oz.) baby spinach
12 large mint leaves, stacked and cut crosswise into thin ribbons
⅓ cup minced red onion, rinsed and drained

1. Preheat broiler. Whisk together vinegar, mustard, ¼ tsp. each salt and pepper, and 2 tsp. harissa in a bowl. Gradually whisk in extra-virgin olive oil. Taste; add more harissa if you like a hotter dressing. Set aside.

2. Put peppers on a baking sheet and broil 4 in. from heat, turning periodically, until charred on all sides, about 20 minutes. Put peppers in a paper bag about 15 minutes to allow trapped steam to loosen their skins. Remove charred skins, stems, and seeds; cut peppers into ½-in. pieces.

3. Meanwhile, heat olive oil in a large nonstick frying pan over medium heat. Add eggplant and cook, stirring often, until softened and beginning to color, about 12 minutes. Add chickpeas, 2 tbsp. water, and remaining ¾ tsp. each salt and pepper; cook, stirring, to blend flavors, about 3 minutes. Stir in chopped peppers. Remove from heat and let stand until vegetables are warm but not hot.

4. In a large bowl, toss spinach, mint, and onion with half the vinaigrette. Add chickpea mixture, drizzle with additional dressing, and toss again to coat. Season with more salt and pepper.

Quick Tip: Look for harissa, a North African chile-and-spice paste, in the international section of many supermarkets. Heat level varies greatly from brand to brand, so try a little before using.

PER SERVING: 197 cal., 59% (117 cal.) from fat; 4.6 g protein; 13 g fat (1.7 g sat.); 19 g carbo (5.6 g fiber); 360 mg sodium; 0 mg chol.

Chickpea Panzanella with Capers

Sunset reader Gretchen Brunner, of Seattle, shared this recipe for Italian-style bread-and-tomato salad, given some substance with chickpeas. It's a great way to use stale bread.

SERVES 5 or 6 | **TIME** 25 minutes

¾ lb. day-old crusty whole-grain bread, cut into
    1-in. chunks
2 large ripe heirloom tomatoes, cut into 1-in. chunks
2 cups loosely packed arugula
½ cup thinly sliced red onion
1 can (15 oz.) chickpeas (garbanzos), drained and rinsed
2 tbsp. capers
½ cup extra-virgin olive oil
3 tbsp. red wine vinegar
12 basil leaves, cut crosswise into thin strips
½ tsp. kosher salt
1 tsp. freshly ground black pepper

In a large bowl, combine all ingredients, tossing well to coat.

PER 2-CUP SERVING: 386 cal., 51% (198 cal.) from fat; 10 g protein; 22 g fat (2.7 g sat.); 38 g carbo (6.7 g fiber); 580 mg sodium; 0 mg chol.

Roasted Artichoke Salad with Lemon and Mint

Unlike larger artichokes, tender "baby" artichokes are entirely edible once you trim them. Look for them in late winter and early spring.

SERVES 4 | **TIME** 45 minutes

3 lbs. baby artichokes (about 3 in. long), trimmed (*see Trimming Baby Artichokes, page 125*) and quartered
3 tbsp. olive oil, divided
¼ tsp. *each* salt and freshly ground black pepper
2 tbsp. fresh lemon juice
3 tbsp. chopped mint leaves
2 oz. parmesan cheese

1. Preheat oven to 450°. In a 12- by 18-in. baking pan, mix artichokes with 2 tbsp. oil, salt, and pepper to coat.

2. Bake, stirring occasionally, until artichokes are browned and crisp at edges and tender when pierced, about 15 minutes.

3. Spoon artichokes into a bowl and add lemon juice, mint, and remaining 1 tbsp. oil; mix thoroughly. Using a vegetable peeler, shave parmesan over salad. Serve warm.

PER SERVING: 270 cal., 47% (126 cal.) from fat; 15 g protein; 14 g fat (3.7 g sat.); 31 g carbo (15 g fiber); 714 mg sodium; 9.6 mg chol.

2 Ways with Arugula

Arugula's peppery bite complements sweet, rich ingredients such as figs or roasted onions. It also holds its own alongside strongly flavored foods like olives.

QUICK IDEA NO. 1: Use in sandwiches instead of lettuce. Great with chicken, turkey, or steak and nutty cheeses like gruyère.

QUICK IDEA NO. 2: Toss with sliced ripe plums, toasted almonds, sliced sweet onion, and a vinaigrette of sherry vinegar and extra-virgin olive oil.

Roasted Beet Salad with Oranges and *Queso Fresco* (*Ensalada de Betabel*)

This salad from Thomas Schnetz, cookbook author and chef-owner of Doña Tomás, in Oakland, California, is all about vivid colors and flavors, with sweet beets playing off tangy lime and orange.

SERVES 8 | **TIME** 1½ hours, plus 30 minutes to cool

4 beets (2½ in. wide, with root and stem ends intact), preferably different colors
5 tbsp. extra-virgin olive oil, divided
Kosher salt
2 limes
2 tbsp. *each* finely chopped shallots and red wine vinegar
4 medium oranges, segmented (*see How to Cut Citrus into Segments, page 135*), juice reserved
Freshly ground black pepper
6 cups arugula
½ cup cilantro leaves
4 to 6 oz. *queso fresco* (*see Quick Tip below*), crumbled

1. Preheat oven to 375°. Scrub beets, pat dry, rub with 1 tbsp. oil, and sprinkle generously with salt. Put beets on a foil-covered baking sheet and bake until tender when pierced, about 1 hour. Refrigerate, uncovered, until cool enough to handle, about 30 minutes. Cut off roots and stems, then rub beets with paper towels to remove skin; discard skin. Cut beets in half lengthwise, then slice into half-moons about ¼ in. thick; set aside.
2. Using a razor-sharp grater, such as a Microplane, or the fine shredder holes of a box grater, finely zest limes into another bowl. Juice limes and add juice to zest. Add shallots, vinegar, and juice from oranges. Whisking constantly, slowly drizzle remaining ¼ cup oil into bowl. Add beets, toss to coat, and season to taste with salt and pepper. Cover bowl airtight and let stand at room temperature at least 15 minutes.
3. Arrange arugula on a platter. Sprinkle with cilantro. Pour beets and dressing over leaves and scatter with orange segments and cheese.
Quick Tip: Queso fresco is a very mild fresh Mexican cheese carried by many supermarkets; if you can't find it, use a mild feta cheese.
Make Ahead: Roasted and cooled beets, up to 3 days, chilled; through step 2, up to 3 hours.

PER SERVING: 192 cal., 61% (117 cal.) from fat; 5 g protein; 13 g fat (4.3 g sat.); 16 g carbo (2.7 g fiber); 171 mg sodium; 13 mg chol.

Carrot Manchego Salad

A citrus vinaigrette with notes of honey, cumin, and sherry accents the carrots; they're salted and drained first to remove their liquid, so it doesn't dilute the dressing. Salting also makes the carrots slightly tender. Toasting and grinding whole cumin seeds tempers the bitter overtones of raw cumin.

SERVES 6 | **TIME** 30 minutes, plus 1 hour to salt

9 or 10 medium carrots, sliced into thin coins on a mandoline or with slicing attachment of a food processor (5 cups)
About 2¼ tsp. salt, divided
1 small garlic clove, peeled
1 tsp. cumin seeds
2 tbsp. *each* fresh orange juice and sherry vinegar
½ tsp. *each* mild honey and freshly ground black pepper
2 tsp. minced cilantro, plus several cilantro leaves for garnish
5½ tbsp. fruity extra-virgin olive oil
3 oz. manchego cheese (*see Quick Tip below*), shaved with a vegetable peeler
10 Bibb lettuce leaves

1. Toss sliced carrots with 2 tsp. salt and put in a colander. Put a plate on top of carrots, weigh down with a 1-lb. can, and set in sink to drain for 1 hour.
2. Meanwhile, chop garlic, sprinkle with a pinch of salt, and mash into a paste on a cutting board with flat side of a chef's knife.
3. In a small frying pan, toast cumin seeds over medium heat until fragrant, about 1 minute, then grind finely with a mortar and pestle (or put cooled seeds in a resealable plastic bag and crush with a meat mallet or a small heavy frying pan). In a small bowl, whisk together garlic, cumin, orange juice, vinegar, honey, pepper, remaining ¼ tsp. salt, and the minced cilantro; drizzle in oil, whisking.
4. Rinse carrots and turn onto a clean kitchen towel. Gently dry with another towel. In a large bowl, toss carrots with half the vinaigrette and the shaved cheese. Divide lettuce leaves among plates and drizzle lightly with remaining vinaigrette. Layer carrots on top and crown with cilantro leaves.
Quick Tip: Manchego, a firm sheep's-milk cheese from Spain, is available at specialty-foods stores. We prefer using one with a good, strong flavor (ask for a taste before you buy it). A mild pecorino will also work.

PER SERVING: 218 cal., 74% (162 cal.) from fat; 4.7 g protein; 18 g fat (5.3 g sat.); 11 g carbo (3.1 g fiber); 312 mg sodium; 15 mg chol.

salads

Celery Victor with Watercress and Capers

This simple and delicious poached vegetable dish hails from the days before raw greens defined a salad. To bring it into the modern era (and because the combination tastes good), we've added watercress and capers.

SERVES 6 | **TIME** 30 minutes, plus 2 hours to chill

3 celery hearts (each about 2½ in. wide; *see Quick Tip below*)
3½ cups chicken broth
⅓ cup *each* extra-virgin olive oil and tarragon vinegar or white wine vinegar
4 cups loosely packed watercress sprigs (about ¼ lb.), stems removed *(see Quick Tip in Classic Cobb Salad, page 169)*
2 tbsp. drained capers
Salt and freshly ground black pepper

1. Trim and discard tough stem ends from celery hearts, keeping stalks attached to bases. Trim tops to make stalks about 8 in. long; discard tops. With a vegetable peeler, pare coarse strings from backs of outer stalks. Cut each heart in half lengthwise; tie each half tightly around the center with cotton string.
2. Combine celery and broth in a 5- to 6-qt. pan (at least 10 in. wide). Bring to a boil over high heat; cover, reduce heat, and simmer until celery is tender when pierced, 12 to 15 minutes, turning bundles over halfway through cooking.
3. Combine oil, tarragon, and vinegar in a 1-gal. resealable plastic freezer bag. With tongs, transfer celery from broth to bag (save broth for other uses). Set upright and let cool, unsealed.
4. Seal bag and turn to coat celery with dressing. Chill until cold, at least 2 hours, turning bag occasionally.
5. Divide watercress among plates. Lift celery bundles from dressing; remove and discard strings. Place a bundle on each mound of watercress and sprinkle with capers. Spoon remaining dressing from bag over salads if you like, and add salt and pepper to taste.
Quick Tip: Many supermarkets sell tender hearts of celery, but if they aren't available, pull off the large outer stalks from regular bunches of celery and use the tender, pale green inner stalks (save the outer stalks for other uses).
Make Ahead: Through step 4, up to 1 day, chilled.

PER SERVING: 138 cal., 82% (113 cal.) from fat; 3.4 g protein; 13 g fat (1.9 g sat.); 3.1 g carbo (1.6 g fiber); 248 mg sodium; 15 mg chol.

Victor Hirtzler & Celery Victor

With a red fez set rakishly atop his head and a persona larger than life, chef Victor Hirtzler—a native of Strasbourg, France; a former taster for Czar Nicholas II; and once chef to King Carlos I of Portugal—reigned over the kitchen at the Hotel St. Francis in San Francisco from 1904 to 1926. Among the astonishingly varied European-inspired creations Hirtzler named after himself, Celery Victor (circa 1910) is the most enduring.

Warm Daikon and Smoked Trout Salad

Daikon, a white Asian radish, is sweet and earthy with a mild nip. Here it pairs beautifully with the rich flavor of smoked trout. Peel off the root's thin skin and any root hairs before using.

SERVES 4 | **TIME** 20 minutes

1 tbsp. olive oil
5 oz. daikon, halved lengthwise and sliced into half-moons
3 garlic cloves, thinly sliced
¾ lb. escarole, chopped
2 skinned smoked trout fillets, broken into chunks
Kosher salt and freshly ground black pepper
Lemon wedges

1. Heat oil in a large, heavy-bottomed pot over medium-high heat. Add daikon and garlic to pan. Cook, stirring often, until tender-crisp, about 7 minutes (add a little water if daikon starts to stick).
2. Add escarole and cook, stirring, until wilted, about 2 minutes. Gently mix in trout. Season to taste with salt and pepper. Squeeze lemon on top to taste.

PER SERVING: 162 cal., 40% (64 cal.) from fat; 18 g protein; 7.2 g fat (1.5 g sat.); 6.5 g carbo (4.6 g fiber); 36 mg sodium; 81 mg chol.

Warm Kabocha Squash Salad

The warm salad from L.A. chef and restaurateur Suzanne Goin uses kabocha squash, also known as Japanese pumpkin. The dark orange kabocha is sweeter than butternut squash, with a moist, fluffy texture and a slighty nutty flavor that plays nicely against the bitter dandelion greens.

SERVES 6 | **TIME** 45 minutes

CANDIED PUMPKIN SEEDS
2 tsp. butter
½ cup pumpkin seeds (*pepitas*)
¼ tsp. ground cumin
⅛ tsp. *each* **cinnamon, paprika, cayenne, and salt**
1 tbsp. honey
SQUASH SALAD
1 kabocha squash (about 1¾ lbs.)
¼ cup extra-virgin olive oil, divided
1 tbsp. fresh thyme leaves
¾ tsp. salt, divided, plus more to taste
½ tsp. freshly ground black pepper, plus more to taste
3 tbsp. sherry vinegar
½ lb. dandelion greens, ends trimmed
½ lb. thick-cut applewood-smoked bacon, cut into ½-in. pieces
¼ cup thinly sliced shallots
3 oz. pecorino romano cheese

1. Prepare candied pumpkin seeds: In a medium frying pan over medium heat, melt butter. Stir in pumpkin seeds, cumin, cinnamon, paprika, cayenne, and salt. Cook, stirring constantly, until pumpkin seeds are lightly browned, about 2 minutes. Stir in honey and cook, stirring, 1 minute. Remove from heat and spread in a single layer on a plate. Let cool until no longer sticky, 12 to 15 minutes.
2. While seeds are cooling, prepare squash: Preheat oven to 475°. Cut squash in half vertically and scoop out seeds. Cut halves into ½-in.-thick wedges. Trim and discard peel from each wedge. In a 12- by 17-in. baking pan, mix squash with 2 tbsp. oil and thyme until coated. Sprinkle generously with ½ tsp. salt and pepper. Arrange pieces in a single layer and bake until squash is slightly browned and tender when pierced, 15 to 20 minutes.
3. In a small bowl, whisk together vinegar, remaining 2 tbsp. oil, and remaining ¼ tsp. salt. Put greens and squash in a large bowl.
4. In a medium frying pan over medium-high heat, cook bacon, stirring occasionally, until lightly browned and crisp, about 5 minutes. Transfer to paper towels to drain. Discard all but 2 tbsp. fat from pan. Add shallots to pan and cook, stirring constantly, over medium-high heat until limp, about 4 minutes. Remove from heat and carefully stir in vinegar mixture. Pour mixture over greens and squash; mix gently to coat.
5. Divide salad among plates. Using a vegetable peeler, shave pecorino cheese over top of each. Sprinkle salads with bacon and candied pumpkin seeds. Season with salt and pepper to taste.
Make Ahead: Candied pumpkin seeds, up to 3 days, stored airtight at room temperature.

PER SERVING WITH PUMPKIN SEEDS: 360 cal., 70% (252 cal.) from fat; 14 g protein; 28 g fat (8.1 g sat.); 18 g carbo (3.7 g fiber); 736 mg sodium; 26 mg chol.

Crunchy Napa Cabbage Slaw

This Chinese-accented slaw is one of our all-time favorite potluck recipes (and among those most frequently requested by readers). It goes really well with barbecued brisket or ribs.

MAKES About 14 cups; 14 to 16 servings | **TIME** 1 hour

8 cups (about 1 lb.) coarsely shredded napa cabbage
¾ lb. snow peas, trimmed and thinly sliced
1⅓ cups *each* **thinly sliced radishes and green onions**
1⅓ cups loosely packed cilantro leaves
3 tbsp. *each* **white wine vinegar and sugar**
1 tbsp. soy sauce
1 garlic clove, minced
½ tsp. *each* **Asian (toasted) sesame oil and ground ginger**
¼ tsp. cayenne
1 cup mayonnaise
⅔ cup slivered almonds, toasted (*see How to Toast Nuts, page 134***)**

1. In a large bowl, combine cabbage, snow peas, radishes, green onions, and cilantro.
2. In a small bowl, combine vinegar, sugar, soy sauce, garlic, sesame oil, ginger, and cayenne; stir until sugar dissolves. Gradually whisk in mayonnaise until blended.
3. Add dressing and toasted almonds to cabbage mixture; mix gently to coat.

PER 1-CUP SERVING: 185 cal., 78% (144 cal.) from fat; 2.9 g protein; 16 g fat (2.2 g sat.); 8.7 g carbo (1.8 g fiber); 172 mg sodium; 9.3 mg chol.

salads

■ Cabbage

Cabbage is a member of the Brassica family (along with broccoli, brussels sprouts, and cauliflower), which contain phytochemicals that have been shown to reduce the risk of certain types of cancer. It can be stored in the refrigerator for up to 3 months because its tightly wrapped leaves lock out oxygen. A quick rinse sufficiently cleans cabbage; prepare it by removing and discarding the tough outer leaves.

Chipotle Coleslaw

We love the smoky flavor of this chile-fired slaw from New Mexico grilling experts Bill and Cheryl Alters Jamison. It's great piled on pulled-pork sandwiches (for a recipe, see *Achiote-and-Orange Pulled Pork, page 494*).

SERVES 6 to 8 | **TIME** 30 minutes

½ cup *each* mayonnaise and sour cream
3 tbsp. distilled white vinegar
1 tbsp. molasses (not blackstrap)
1½ tsp. sugar
1 small canned chipotle chile, minced, plus 2 tsp. adobo
 sauce from can
1 tsp. kosher salt, plus more to taste
6 cups *each* packed shredded green and red cabbage
 (*see Cabbage, above*)
7 green onions (green and pale green parts), trimmed
 and thinly sliced
1 cup tightly packed chopped cilantro, divided

1. In a medium bowl, stir together mayonnaise, sour cream, vinegar, molasses, sugar, minced chile, adobo sauce, and salt.
2. In a large bowl, toss together cabbage, green onions, and ¾ cup cilantro. Pour dressing over vegetables, toss well, and refrigerate at least 30 minutes.
3. Before serving, add more salt if you like and scatter remaining ¼ cup cilantro over top.
Make Ahead: Through step 2, up to 4 hours, chilled.

PER SERVING: 215 cal., 67% (144 cal.) from fat; 3.7 g protein; 16 g fat (4 g sat.); 17 g carbo (4.7 g fiber); 473 mg sodium; 16 mg chol.

Thai-style Cabbage Slaw

Lime juice, chopped mint, and cilantro makes this new take on slaw really refreshing.

SERVES 8 to 10 | **TIME** 15 minutes

3 tbsp. fresh lime juice
2 tbsp. Thai or Vietnamese fish sauce (*nam pla* or
 nuoc mam)
1 tbsp. sugar
½ to ¾ tsp. red chile flakes
6 cups finely shredded red or green cabbage
½ cup slivered red onion, rinsed and drained
½ cup *each* chopped mint and cilantro leaves
½ cup chopped roasted salted peanuts
Salt

1. In a large bowl, mix lime juice, fish sauce, 2 tbsp. water, sugar, and chile flakes to taste. Stir in cabbage and onion.
2. Just before serving, stir in mint, cilantro, peanuts, and salt to taste.
Make Ahead: Through step 1, up to 2 hours, chilled.

PER SERVING: 72 cal., 50% (36 cal.) from fat; 3.3 g protein; 4 g fat (0.6 g sat.); 7.2 g carbo (2 g fiber); 158 mg sodium; 0 mg chol.

Fennel-Pepper Slaw

We like this slaw after it has been chilled in its dressing overnight, but it's also good after an hour. For cutting paper-thin fennel slices, nothing beats a mandoline.

SERVES 6 | **TIME** 25 minutes

3 tbsp. *each* fresh lemon juice and olive oil
1 tbsp. *each* Dijon mustard and honey
Salt and freshly ground black pepper
2 small heads fennel (about 1¾ lbs. total)
3 *each* red, yellow, and/or orange bell peppers, seeds
 and ribs removed and slivered lengthwise

1. In a small bowl, whisk lemon juice, oil, mustard, and honey to blend. Add salt and pepper to taste.
2. Trim stem end and stalks from fennel; chop enough feathery green fronds to make 2 tbsp. and reserve. Cut heads in half lengthwise, then shave into paper-thin strips or cut into thin slivers.
3. In a bowl, combine fennel strips and bell peppers. Drizzle with dressing and mix gently to coat; cover and chill at least 1 hour and up to 1 day. Just before serving, sprinkle with reserved fennel fronds.

PER SERVING: 114 cal., 55% (63 cal.) from fat; 1.5 g protein; 7 g fat (0.9 g sat.); 13 g carbo (3.6 g fiber); 111 mg sodium; 0 mg chol.

The Secrets to Delicious Potato Salad

• **Use the right potatoes.** For potato salads that have mayonnaise or cream in the dressing, use starchy potatoes such as russets, which cook up nice and fluffy and, even when just tender, fall apart a bit once cooked; the bits of starch blend well with the dressing. Slightly less starchy potatoes such as Yukon Golds, Yellow Finns, or fingerlings work well too. Choose red potatoes and other waxy varieties for warm potato salads because they stand up better to the heat of the dressing.

• **Cook potatoes until they are just tender to the bite.** You want them to keep their shape and not turn to mush once dressed.

• **Toss cooked potatoes with vinegar or lemon juice while they are still warm,** so they absorb the tang; then let them cool before tossing with dressing and eggs or any other ingredients.

• **Serve potato salad as soon as possible after it's made.** We were stunned by the difference between a just-made potato salad and one that had been chilled for a few hours. Freshly cooked potatoes retain their flavor and texture; dressings taste bright and vibrant; and any vegetables or aromatics remain crisp and distinct.

Yukon Gold and Fresh Herb Potato Salad

The tangy salad from Oregon cookbook author Janie Hibler is all about good potatoes, olive oil, and herbs.

SERVES 8 to 10 | **TIME** 1 hour

4 lbs. Yukon Gold potatoes (about 3 in. wide)
6 tbsp. fruity extra-virgin olive oil
3 tbsp. Champagne vinegar
¾ tsp. kosher salt, plus more to taste
1½ tbsp. *each* chopped basil and flat-leaf parsley
1 tbsp. minced chives
Freshly ground black pepper

1. Pour about 1 in. water into a large pot and set a steamer basket in bottom (*see Quick Tip below*). Bring to a boil. Add potatoes, reduce heat, and simmer, covered, until tender when pierced, 25 to 30 minutes. Transfer potatoes to a colander in sink, rinse with cool water, and let stand until cool enough to handle.
2. Peel potatoes and slice crosswise into ½-in.-thick pieces. Put in a large serving bowl.
3. In a small bowl, whisk together oil, vinegar, and salt and drizzle over warm potatoes. Sprinkle with basil, parsley, chives, and pepper and additional salt to taste, mixing gently to coat.
Quick Tip: Potatoes cook most evenly in a steamer basket, but if you don't have one, fill a pot halfway with water and simmer potatoes.
Make Ahead: Up to 1 day, chilled (salad will become even more flavorful). Before serving, bring to room temperature, then stir.

PER SERVING: 208 cal., 37% (76 cal.) from fat; 3.9 g protein; 8.4 g fat (1.2 g sat.); 29 g carbo (2 g fiber); 97 mg sodium; 0 mg chol.

Bacon-Olive Potato Salad

Pair this warm potato salad filled with briny olives and capers with grilled or roasted chicken or pork. If you're a fan of capers, add more of them.

SERVES 6 to 8 | **TIME** 30 minutes

2 lbs. red-skinned potatoes
1 tbsp. salt
½ lb. thick-cut bacon, chopped
¼ cup cider vinegar
⅔ cup *each* pitted green olives and kalamata olives
4 large shallots
3 tbsp. brined capers
2 tbsp. chopped flat-leaf parsley

1. Cut potatoes in half lengthwise, then into ¼-in.-thick slices. Put potatoes in a large pot, cover with cold water, and bring to a boil. Add salt, reduce heat to maintain a slow boil, and cook potatoes until tender to the bite, about 8 minutes. Drain potatoes and put in a large bowl.
2. Meanwhile, in a large frying pan (not nonstick) over medium-high heat, cook bacon until brown and crisp. Add vinegar and, using a wooden spoon, scrape up any browned bits on bottom of pan. Keep warm over low heat.
3. In a food processor, pulse olives, shallots, and capers until chopped. Add bacon to olive mixture, stir, and pour over potatoes. Add parsley and toss to combine. Serve warm or at room temperature.
Make Ahead: Up to 1 hour, at room temperature. Avoid reheating if possible.

PER SERVING: 270 cal., 60% (162 cal.) from fat; 4.8 g protein; 18 g fat (6.3 g sat.); 21 g carbo (2.3 g fiber); 725 mg sodium; 19 mg chol.

salads

Chanterelle-Potato Salad with Pancetta, Shallots, and Thyme

Potato salad goes uptown with the addition of fresh chanterelles in a recipe from Dory Ford, former executive chef at Monterey Bay Aquarium's Portola Restaurant. You'll have about 1 cup of vinaigrette left over; it's excellent on any salad and on fish, and keeps up to 2 weeks, chilled.

SERVES 8 | **TIME** 1 hour, 40 minutes

¼ cup white wine vinegar
⅔ cup vegetable oil
⅔ cup extra-virgin olive oil, or more as needed to dress potatoes
1 chopped shallot plus 1 minced shallot
2 tsp. kosher salt, divided
¾ lb. fresh chanterelle mushrooms or 10 oz. oyster mushrooms
6 oz. slab pancetta or thick-cut bacon, diced
3 lbs. baby Yukon Gold potatoes, halved lengthwise (if potatoes are longer than 2 in., cut into quarters)
4 medium garlic cloves, minced
2 tsp. fresh thyme leaves
¾ tsp. freshly ground black pepper, divided
2 tbsp. butter
⅓ cup Chardonnay or other white wine
2 tbsp. chopped tarragon
1 tbsp. chopped chives

1. Put vinegar, vegetable and olive oils, chopped shallot, and ½ tsp. salt in a blender and blend at medium speed until mixture is pale yellow and emulsified.
2. Preheat oven to 375°. Wipe chanterelles with a damp cloth or scrape with a knife to remove dirt; cut away dry, woody parts. Tear mushrooms into 1-in. pieces. If using oyster mushrooms, remove stems. Set mushrooms aside.
3. Cook pancetta in a large frying pan over medium-high heat until crisp and browned, about 7 minutes. Transfer with a slotted spoon to paper towels, reserving 3 tbsp. drippings (add olive oil as needed to make 3 tbsp.).
4. Toss potatoes with reserved pancetta drippings, garlic, thyme, 1 tsp. salt, and ½ tsp. pepper. Divide potatoes between two 9- by 13-in. baking pans. Bake, stirring every 10 minutes, until tender, well browned, and crispy, 25 to 35 minutes.
5. Meanwhile, melt butter in a large frying pan over medium-high heat. Add minced shallot and cook until soft, about 1 minute. Add mushrooms and cook, stirring occasionally, until browned, 5 to 6 minutes. Add

Chardonnay, remaining ½ tsp. salt, and remaining ¼ tsp. pepper; scrape up browned bits from bottom of pan and cook until liquid evaporates, about 2 minutes.
6. In a large bowl, toss together potatoes, mushrooms, pancetta, tarragon, and chives. Drizzle vinaigrette over potato mixture. Serve warm.

PER 1-CUP SALAD WITHOUT DRESSING: 380 cal., 54% (206 cal.) from fat; 9.2 g protein; 24 g fat (5.8 g sat.); 34 g carbo (2.9 g fiber); 832 mg sodium; 26 mg chol.

PER TSP. DRESSING: 34 cal., 100% (34 cal.) from fat; 0 g protein; 4 g fat (4.4 g sat.); 0 g carbo (0 g fiber); 13 mg sodium; 0 mg chol.

Bread-and-Butter Pickle and Potato Salad

For many of us, this creamy potato salad, with a little kick supplied by the pickle juice and cider vinegar, tastes like a big bowl of home.

MAKES About 11 cups; 12 to 14 servings | **TIME** 1 hour

4 lbs. Yukon Gold or red thin-skinned potatoes (about 2¼ in. wide)
2 tbsp. yellow mustard seeds
1 cup finely chopped bread-and-butter pickles, plus ½ cup juice from jar, strained
1 cup mayonnaise
¼ cup cider vinegar
2 red bell peppers (1 lb. total), seeds and ribs removed and diced
¾ cup minced flat-leaf parsley, divided
Salt and freshly ground black pepper

1. In a 6- to 8-qt. pan, combine potatoes and 3 qts. water. Cover and bring to a boil over high heat. Reduce heat and simmer, covered, until potatoes are tender when pierced, 20 to 30 minutes. Drain well and let stand until cool enough to touch, 15 to 25 minutes.
2. Meanwhile, in a small bowl, soak mustard seeds in about ½ cup hot water until soft, about 5 minutes. Drain.
3. In a large bowl, mix mustard seeds, chopped pickles, pickle juice, mayonnaise, and vinegar.
4. Peel warm potatoes, cut into about ¾-in. cubes, and drop into dressing. Add bell peppers; mix gently. Let cool to room temperature, at least 15 minutes. Add ½ cup parsley and salt and pepper to taste; mix gently.
5. Right before serving, sprinkle with remaining ¼ cup parsley.
Make Ahead: Through step 3, up to 1 day, chilled.

PER SERVING: 250 cal., 28% (71 cal.) from fat; 4.8 g protein; 7.9 g fat (1.1 g sat.); 40 g carbo (3.1 g fiber); 265 mg sodium; 5.6 mg chol.

Warm Fingerling Potato and Smoked Trout Salad

Serve alone or with salad greens or green beans.

SERVES 4 as a main course | **TIME** 30 minutes

2 tbsp. salt-cured or drained canned capers (*see Quick Tip below*)
2 lbs. fingerling potatoes (1 by 2 in. wide) or other thin-skinned potatoes (2 in. wide), halved lengthwise
½ lb. boneless smoked trout fillets
⅓ cup olive oil
¼ cup fresh lemon juice
½ tsp. freshly ground black pepper
1 tart green apple, such as Granny Smith, cored and thinly sliced
1 tbsp. chopped dill
Sour cream (optional)

1. If using salt-cured capers, put in a small bowl, cover with water, and let soak 10 minutes to remove salt; rinse and pat completely dry. (For brine-packed capers, rinse well and pat dry.)
2. In a 4- to 6-qt. pan over high heat, bring 2 to 3 qts. water to a boil. Add potatoes and cook, uncovered, until tender when pierced, about 15 minutes. Drain.
3. Meanwhile, pull off and discard skin from trout. Break the fish into bite-size pieces.
4. Set a 1- to 1½-qt. pan over medium-high heat. When hot, add oil; when it begins to ripple, add capers (use a pot holder and stand back—the oil may splatter). Cook, stirring once, until capers have opened and are light brown and crisp, about 1 minute. Pour into a fine-mesh strainer over a 1-cup glass measuring cup; reserve oil. Pour capers onto paper towels to drain.
5. In a large serving bowl, whisk oil from capers with lemon juice and pepper. Stir in potatoes. Add trout, apple, and dill and mix gently. Sprinkle fried capers over top. Serve with sour cream on the side if using.
Quick Tip: Large salt-cured capers, sold in specialty-foods shops, open up dramatically when fried, but smaller, brine-packed ones will work too.

PER SERVING: 451 cal., 48% (216 cal.) from fat; 18 g protein; 24 g fat (3.9 g sat.); 43 g carbo (4.7 g fiber); 759 mg sodium; 14 mg chol.

California Couscous Salad

Inspired by her favorite tabbouleh recipe, reader Suzanne Calderon, of Oceanside, California, substituted couscous for the usual bulgur wheat and came up with this light, crunchy salad.

SERVES 6 | **TIME** 20 minutes

1¾ cups (14 oz.) chicken or vegetable broth
1½ cups (¾ lb.) couscous
⅓ cup *each* olive oil and fresh lemon juice
Salt and freshly ground black pepper
1 medium red bell pepper, seeds and ribs removed and finely chopped
1 small red onion, finely chopped
½ cup sliced almonds, toasted (*see How to Toast Nuts, page 134*) and chopped
½ cup finely chopped cilantro
Cilantro sprigs and lemon slices (optional)

1. In a small pot over high heat, bring broth and ¼ cup water to a boil. Add couscous, cover, and remove from heat. Let sit 5 minutes. Fluff with a fork.
2. In a large bowl, whisk together oil and lemon juice. Pour over couscous and toss to coat. Add salt and pepper to taste.
3. Stir in red pepper, onion, almonds, and chopped cilantro. Garnish with cilantro sprigs and lemon slices if using. Serve at room temperature.

PER SERVING: 349 cal., 41% (144 cal.) from fat; 8.9 g protein; 16 g fat (2 g sat.); 42 g carbo (2.4 g fiber); 151 mg sodium; 0 mg chol.

■ Couscous

FROM THE PANTRY

Couscous, regarded by many as a grain, is actually pasta made from semolina (coarsely ground durum wheat). Pearl couscous, also known as Israeli couscous and *maftoul*, has larger-size grains than regular couscous and takes on the consistency of macaroni when prepared. It cooks longer than regular couscous because it's bigger, but its size allows it to absorb plenty of liquid and flavor. Look for this import in specialty and Middle Eastern markets.

salads

Beef Taco Salad with Black Beans and Crunchy Tortilla Strips

As Mexican food became part of mainstream Western dining, creative cooks began incorporating elements of popular dishes like tacos into salads. *Sunset* reported on this development in 1954 with Mexican tostadas—"open-face sandwiches [that] serve as salads." By the 1970s, taco salad had grabbed the West's imagination, and during that decade we published nearly a dozen versions; this one is from 2001. It's been a perennial favorite.

SERVES 4 to 6 as a main course | **TIME** 50 minutes

3 corn tortillas (about 6 in. wide)
2½ tbsp. olive oil, divided
¾ tsp. *each* salt and chili powder
¾ lb. boned tender beef steak such as top loin, fat trimmed and patted dry
1 tbsp. distilled white vinegar
½ tsp. ground cumin
¼ tsp. cinnamon
3 qts. finely shredded romaine lettuce
1 can (15 oz.) black beans, drained and rinsed
1 cup shredded (¼ lb.) sharp cheddar cheese
1¼ cups Classic Guacamole (*recipe follows*)
½ cup sour cream
¼ cup sliced green onions
2 cups store-bought or homemade tomato salsa (*see Salsa Ranchera, page 568*)

1. Preheat oven to 425°. Stack tortillas and cut into ⅛- to ¼-in.-wide strips. In a 12- by 17-in. baking pan, toss strips with 1 tbsp. oil, the salt, and chili powder. Bake tortilla strips, stirring occasionally, until crisp, 5 to 8 minutes. Remove from pan and let cool.
2. Meanwhile, cut steak across the grain into ¼-in.-thick slices. Stack a few slices at a time and cut into strips about ¼ in. wide and 3 to 4 in. long. Set meat strips aside. In a small bowl, mix vinegar, cumin, and cinnamon.
3. Heat a 10- to 12-in. frying pan over high heat. When hot, add remaining 1½ tbsp. oil and quickly swirl to coat bottom. Add beef all at once and stir just until browned on surface and still pink in center (cut to test), about 1 minute. Add vinegar mixture and stir just until liquid is evaporated, about 1 minute.
4. Mound lettuce in center of a large, shallow bowl. Surround with tortilla strips. Layer beans, cheddar, then steak evenly over lettuce. Top with guacamole and sour cream and sprinkle with green onions. Gently spoon salad onto plates; serve with salsa.

Make Ahead: Shredded lettuce, up to 1 day, chilled airtight; tortilla strips, up to 1 day, stored airtight at room temperature.

PER SERVING WITH GUACAMOLE: 576 cal., 61% (351 cal.) from fat; 27 g protein; 39 g fat (16 g sat.); 30 g carbo (8.7 g fiber); 1,236 mg sodium; 83 mg chol.

Classic Guacamole: Pit and peel 2 firm-ripe **avocados** (1 lb. total). In a bowl, using a fork, coarsely mash avocados with 1 tbsp. each fresh **lime juice** and chopped **cilantro** and 1 tsp. minced **garlic**. Add **salt** and **cayenne** to taste. Serve, or chill airtight up to 2 hours. Makes 1¼ cups.

PER TBSP.: 27 cal., 85% (23 cal.) from fat; 0.3 g protein; 2.6 g fat (0.4 g sat.); 1.3 g carbo (0.3 g fiber); 1.8 mg sodium; 0 mg chol.

Crisp Lettuces with Noodles, Tofu, and Peanuts

Use a crunchy lettuce like Sierra or a red romaine like Ruben's Red—or a mix of iceberg and romaine.

SERVES 4 | **TIME** 35 minutes

½ lb. capellini or angel hair pasta, broken into about 2-in. lengths
3 tbsp. seasoned rice vinegar
2 tbsp. peanut oil
1 tbsp. *each* Asian (toasted) sesame oil and Asian chili oil
1 package (8 oz.) savory baked tofu such as five-spice flavor, cut into ½-in. cubes
½ lb. crisp lettuces, cut crosswise in ¼-in.-wide strips
1 cup loosely packed cilantro leaves
1 cup chopped salted roasted peanuts
Soy sauce

1. Fill a 5- to 6-qt. pan three-quarters full of water and bring to a boil over high heat. Cook pasta according to package directions; drain.
2. Meanwhile, in a large serving bowl, stir together vinegar, peanut oil, sesame oil, and chili oil.
3. Add hot noodles to bowl. Gently stir to coat with oil mixture, then add tofu, lettuce, cilantro, and peanuts and toss lightly. Season each serving to taste with soy sauce.

PER SERVING: 646 cal., 50% (324 cal.) from fat; 29 g protein; 36 g fat (5 g sat.); 56 g carbo (6.7 g fiber); 623 mg sodium; 0 mg chol.

Shrimp, Lemon, and Spinach Whole-grain Pasta Salad

We lightened up this pasta salad by replacing the usual mayonnaise dressing with Greek-style low-fat yogurt, which is strained so that it's thick and rich-tasting.

SERVES 4 to 6 as a main course | **TIME** 35 minutes

¾ lb. whole-grain rotini, rotelle, or fusilli pasta (*see Quick Tip below*)
1 lb. medium shrimp (31 to 42 per lb.), peeled and deveined
¼ cup olive oil, divided
1 medium red onion, chopped
3 large garlic cloves, minced
¾ tsp. salt, plus more to taste
½ tsp. red chile flakes
¼ tsp. ground cumin
2 cups loosely packed baby spinach leaves
1 can (15 oz.) chickpeas (garbanzos), drained and rinsed
1¼ cups plain low-fat Greek-style yogurt
⅓ cup chopped mint leaves
2½ tbsp. fresh lemon juice
2 tsp. finely shredded lemon zest

1. Cook pasta in a large pot of boiling salted water according to package instructions. Drain and set aside.
2. Meanwhile, toss shrimp with 2 tbsp. oil, onion, garlic, salt, red chile flakes, and cumin; marinate at room temperature 10 minutes.
3. Preheat a medium frying pan over medium heat, then add shrimp and marinade. Cook, stirring often, until shrimp are pink and firm, 3 to 4 minutes.
4. In a large bowl, toss together pasta, shrimp mixture, spinach, chickpeas, yogurt, mint, lemon juice and zest, and remaining 2 tbsp. oil. Season to taste with salt. Serve warm or at room temperature.
Quick Tip: Not all pastas marketed as "whole grain" are created equal; the percentage and type of whole grain varies from brand to brand. Be sure to look at the ingredient list on the box; also check to see whether the box carries the logo of the Whole Grains Council.

PER SERVING: 405 cal., 27% (108 cal.) from fat; 23 g protein; 12 g fat (3 g sat.); 54 g carbo (10 g fiber); 475 mg sodium; 81 mg chol.

Shrimp, Watercress, and Millet Salad

This salad is a power-packed combination of grains and greens, with the millet providing nutty flavor as well as thiamin, niacin, and a host of minerals and the peppery watercress supplying lots of vitamins A, C, and K.

SERVES 4 | **TIME** 30 minutes

¼ cup hulled millet
1 tsp. plus 2 tbsp. extra-virgin olive oil
2 tbsp. fresh lemon juice
1½ tsp. finely shredded lemon zest
½ tsp. kosher salt
3 cups loosely packed watercress (about 1 bunch), stems removed (*see Watercress, below*)
1 cup loosely packed mint leaves, chopped
⅓ cup finely chopped red onion, rinsed and drained
1 cup cooked bay shrimp

1. In a small saucepan, bring millet, 1 tsp. oil, and ¾ cup salted water to a boil. Reduce heat and simmer, covered, 20 minutes. Remove from heat and let stand 5 minutes.
2. Meanwhile, in a small bowl, whisk together lemon juice and zest, remaining 2 tbsp. oil, and the salt.
3. Put millet in a serving bowl. Pour in dressing and toss gently. Add watercress, mint, onion, and shrimp and toss gently to mix.

PER SERVING: 179 cal., 47% (84 cal.) from fat; 11 g protein; 9.3 g fat (1.4 g sat.); 14 g carbo (4.6 g fiber); 325 mg sodium; 69 mg chol.

■ Watercress

You'll find two types of watercress in markets. The first is the standard cultivated type, with deep green, small leaves and tough, thick-stemmed sprigs. Only the tender green leaves and small stems are really palatable, so this type of cress requires a bit of prep work. The payoff: The leaves are peppery and full-flavored. (To prep, *see Quick Tip in Classic Cobb Salad, page 169.*)

The second type is hydroponic, sold in plastic shells with the roots still attached. Kept in water, these greens stay fresh longer. And because the cress is harvested earlier, the stems are tender and edible. The flavor is relatively pallid—or mild, depending on your point of view. Either type is loaded with vitamin C and antioxidants, so whichever you choose, you'll be adding a lot of nutrients (and practically no calories) to your plate, along with color and flavor.

salads

FROM THE GARDEN

5 Quick and Easy Salad Ideas

1. Watermelon and Feta
Combine chunks of **watermelon** and creamy **feta cheese** along with **toasted pine nuts**, chopped **flat-leaf parsley**, a simple **lemon vinaigrette** (1 part fresh lemon juice to 3 parts canola oil, plus salt to taste), and lots of freshly ground black pepper.

2. Fava and Pecorino
Take **fava beans** out of the pods, boil them in salted water for 1 to 2 minutes, rinse to cool, and then pop them out of their skins (slit skins with a small knife or your fingernail). Toss **peeled favas** with a **fruity olive oil** and small chunks or shavings of young **pecorino cheese**.

3. Brussels Sprouts Slaw
Toss thinly sliced raw **brussels sprouts** with very thinly sliced **radicchio**, **toasted pine nuts**, crumbled **sharp goat cheese**, and a **red wine vinaigrette** (1 part fruity red wine vinegar to 3 parts extra-virgin olive oil, a bit of minced shallot if you like, and salt and freshly ground black pepper to taste).

4. Curried Chicken with Grapes and Almonds
Toss halved **grapes** with shredded **cooked chicken**, **toasted almonds**, and sliced **green onions**. Moisten salad with a **curry vinaigrette** (equal parts white wine vinegar and olive oil, plus curry powder, salt, and freshly ground black pepper to taste).

5. Sugar Snap Peas and Asparagus
Cut blanched **sugar snap peas** (strings removed) into ½-in. lengths and combine with blanched **asparagus** (cut into similar-size pieces) and halved **cherry tomatoes**. Dress with an **herb vinaigrette** (1 part fresh lemon juice to 3 parts extra-virgin olive oil, along with salt and minced dill, chives, or parsley) and sprinkle a little shaved **parmesan cheese** on top.

Melon and Shrimp Salad

John Beardsley, who has been a chef at several San Francisco restaurants, makes good use of kaffir (*makrut*) lime leaves here, following both Southeast Asian traditions and his own creative direction.

SERVES 4 to 6 | **TIME** 20 minutes

1 tbsp. sugar
1 tbsp. minced fresh ginger
1 kaffir (also called *makrut*) lime leaf (2½ to 3 in. long; see Kaffir Lime Leaves, right)
¼ cup fresh lime juice
2 tbsp. Vietnamese fish sauce (*nuoc mam*) or soy sauce
1 cantaloupe (about 1½ lbs.)
1 honeydew (about 1½ lbs.)
½ lb. shelled cooked small shrimp (41 to 60 per lb.)
1 jalapeño chile, seeds and ribs removed and minced
1 tbsp. *each* slivered basil leaves and finely chopped cilantro
2 tbsp. finely chopped salted roasted peanuts

1. In a microwave-safe bowl, mix sugar, ginger, and 1 tbsp. water. Cut lime leaf crosswise into thin slivers; add to bowl. Microwave until hot, about 30 seconds. Add lime juice and fish sauce, stir, and let dressing stand. (If you are substituting lime and lemon zest for the lime leaf, combine with the sugar, ginger, and water but don't heat the mixture.)

2. Cut off and discard peel from both melons, then cut in half and scoop out and discard seeds. Cut each melon into 1-in.-thick slices and arrange on a platter.
3. Put shrimp in a colander and rinse under cold water; drain on paper towels. Scatter shrimp over melon. Stir minced jalapeño into dressing, then spoon dressing over melon and shrimp. Sprinkle basil and cilantro over salad and top with peanuts.

PER SERVING: 119 cal., 19% (23 cal.) from fat; 10 g protein; 2.6 g fat (0.8 g sat.); 15 g carbo (1.3 g fiber); 307 mg sodium; 74 mg chol.

■ Kaffir Lime Leaves

FROM THE GARDEN

Fresh kaffir lime leaves are sold at Asian markets and some other specialty-foods stores; they can be frozen 2 to 3 months. If you can't find any, substitute ¼ tsp. *each* finely shredded lime zest and lemon zest for each lime leaf called for in recipe. Kaffir (or *makrut*) limes, with leaves shaped like figure eights, are native to Southeast Asia.

Green Goddess Salad

This version of Green Goddess salad is from Peter DeMarais, executive chef of San Francisco's Palace Hotel from 1993 to 2005 (his great-grandfather was also a chef there). DeMarais's interpretation uses fresh herbs with a bolder hand than the original, and the inclusion of chervil in the dressing adds a subtle licorice flavor (if you can't find chervil, increase the tarragon to 1 cup).

SERVES 6 as a main course | **TIME** 45 minutes

1 head iceberg lettuce (1 lb.)
1 head radicchio (⅓ lb.)
1 can (15 oz.) artichoke bottoms, drained
1¼ lbs. cooked bay shrimp
1½ cups cherry or pear tomatoes (red, yellow, or a combination), halved if larger than 1 in.
Green Goddess Dressing (recipe follows)
Paper-thin red onion rings
Tarragon sprigs

1. Cut iceberg lettuce lengthwise through core into 6 equal wedges. Cut radicchio lengthwise into 6 equal wedges. Arrange 1 lettuce wedge and 1 radicchio wedge on each dinner plate.
2. Place 1 artichoke bottom, cup side up, beside lettuce on each plate; reserve any extra for other uses. Mound shrimp in artichokes on plates, letting shrimp spill over edges. Arrange tomatoes alongside.
3. Spoon about half the Green Goddess dressing over salads. Top with onion rings and tarragon sprigs. Serve remaining dressing on the side.
Make Ahead: Dressing, up to 1 week, chilled.

PER SERVING: 446 cal., 63% (279 cal.) from fat; 27 g protein; 31 g fat (4.8 g sat.); 15 g carbo (3.7 g fiber); 944 mg sodium; 210 mg chol.

Green Goddess Dressing: In a blender or food processor, combine 1 cup **mayonnaise or sour cream**, 5 cups loosely packed **spinach leaves** (6 oz.), 1 cup loosely packed **parsley leaves**, ½ cup loosely packed **tarragon leaves**, ½ cup loosely packed **chervil leaves** (optional), 1 tbsp. *each* fresh **lemon juice** and chopped **shallot**, and 1 can (2 oz.) **anchovies**, drained. Blend until very smooth. Makes 2 cups.

PER TBSP.: 56 cal., 89% (50 cal.) from fat; 0.8 g protein; 5.6 g fat (0.8 g sat.); 0.9 g carbo (0.3 g fiber); 96 mg sodium; 4.8 mg chol.

The Creation of a Goddess

In 1923 the play *The Green Goddess* opened in San Francisco. To celebrate the play's success, a dinner party was held at the grand Palace Hotel, for which executive chef Phillip Roemer created a special salad dressing to spoon over artichoke bottoms filled with shrimp, chicken, or crab. In keeping with the era's tastes, the dressing incorporated just a suggestion of green herbs and anchovies, and plenty of mayonnaise. Created as an homage, the dressing eventually became more famous than the play.

Crab, Shrimp, and Mango Salad with Yuzu Vinaigrette

At Marinus restaurant, at Bernardus Lodge in Carmel Valley, California, chef Cal Stamenov serves a deluxe all-crab first-course version of this recipe. The yuzu, prized in Japanese and Korean cooking, looks like a squat lemon and has an ultra-aromatic floral flavor that makes it a knockout with seafood and mango.

SERVES 4 as a main course | **TIME** 35 minutes

Finely shredded zest from 2 yuzus or 1 Meyer lemon (see Quick Tips, above right)
3 tbsp. fresh yuzu juice, or 4 tsp. *each* fresh Meyer and Eureka (regular) lemon juices, divided
¼ tsp. kosher salt
⅛ tsp. freshly ground black pepper
¼ cup fruity extra-virgin olive oil
⅓ cup mayonnaise
1 tsp. *each* minced fresh ginger and soy sauce
2 firm-ripe mangoes
½ lb. *each* shelled cooked crab and cooked bay shrimp (or use all shrimp; see Quick Tips, above right)
5 oz. baby arugula (2 qts. loosely packed)
4 kaffir (also called *makrut*) lime leaves (see Quick Tips, above right), minced, or finely shredded zest from 2 limes

1. In a medium bowl, combine zest, half the juice, the salt, and pepper. Gradually whisk in oil. Set aside.
2. In a small bowl, stir together mayonnaise, ginger, soy sauce, and remaining juice until smooth. Chill until ready to use.
3. Cut cheeks (fleshy sides) from mangoes, peel, and thinly slice fruit crosswise. Cut remaining fruit from pits; peel it and thinly slice.
4. In a medium bowl, mix crab and shrimp with 2 tbsp. vinaigrette.

5. In another bowl, gently mix mangoes and arugula with remaining vinaigrette. Spoon salad onto plates and top with crab-and-shrimp mixture. Sprinkle with lime leaves. Serve soy-ginger mayonnaise on the side to dot over salads.

Quick Tips: Some specialty markets have yuzus, and most well-stocked grocery stores in the West carry Meyer lemons in late fall and winter. If you can't find yuzus or Meyer lemons, substitute Eureka (regular) lemons. Buy shelled crab from a good fish market, or shell meat from a 2-lb. cooked crab. Look for sustainable wild-caught Oregon pink shrimp. You can find lime leaves at Asian markets and some other specialty-foods stores; they can be frozen 2 to 3 months.

PER SERVING WITH 1 TBSP. SOY-GINGER MAYONNAISE: 446 cal., 63% (279 cal.) from fat; 25 g protein; 31 g fat (4.5 g sat.); 21 g carbo (2 g fiber); 558 mg sodium; 178 mg chol.

Deviled Crab Louis

Whoever Louis—or Louie—was (no one's quite sure), the Hotel St. Francis in San Francisco was serving his addictive combination of Dungeness crab, iceberg lettuce, and chili-mayo dressing in 1910. Our updated version reflects the broader choices of greens now available, and salsa and smoky chipotle chiles replace the chili sauce for a more interesting interplay of flavors. But a little mountain of sweet, fresh crab—a far pricier ingredient now than a century ago—still crowns the dish.

SERVES 4 as a main course | **TIME** 1¼ hours

8 romaine or iceberg lettuce leaves (10 in. long)
1 head Belgian endive (white or red; 3 oz.), leaves separated
2 qts. finely shredded romaine or iceberg lettuce, or a combination (see *Quick Tip, above right*)
¼ cup chopped flat-leaf parsley
Deviled Louis Dressing (*recipe follows*), divided
1 lb. shelled cooked Dungeness or Alaska king crab
2 firm-ripe tomatoes (¾ lb. total), cored and each cut into 8 wedges
2 hard-cooked eggs, peeled and each cut into 4 wedges
Salt and freshly ground black pepper
2 tbsp. chopped chives, plus at least 4 whole chives for garnish
Lemon wedges

1. Line dinner plates or wide bowls with whole lettuce leaves, then Belgian endive leaves.

2. In a large bowl, combine shredded lettuce and parsley. Add ⅔ cup deviled Louis dressing and mix gently. Divide among lettuce-lined plates.

3. Remove and discard any bits of shell from crab. Mound crab in center of shredded lettuce mixture; arrange tomato and egg wedges around edges. Sprinkle salads with salt, pepper, and chopped chives and garnish with whole chives. Serve with lemon wedges and remaining dressing.

Quick Tip: To cut fine shreds of iceberg lettuce, cut head in half through core; cut out and discard core. Cut each half in half again lengthwise, then set each quarter on one cut side and slice thinly lengthwise. To cut fine shreds of romaine, stack a few leaves at a time, roll lengthwise into a cylinder, and slice thinly crosswise.

Make Ahead: Shredded lettuce, up to 1 day, chilled; dressing, up to 1 week, chilled.

PER SERVING: 297 cal., 37% (109 cal.) from fat; 31 g protein; 12 g fat (2.2 g sat.); 16 g carbo (4.4 g fiber); 713 mg sodium; 198 mg chol.

Deviled Louis Dressing: In a blender, purée 1 cup **tomato salsa** (medium to hot) and 3 to 4 tsp. chopped **canned chipotle chiles** until smooth. Pour into a bowl and stir in 2 cups **mayonnaise**, 6 tbsp. fresh **lemon juice**, and 1 tbsp. **sugar**. Season with **salt** and **freshly ground black pepper** to taste. Makes 3½ cups.

PER TBSP.: 35 cal., 71% (25 cal.) from fat; 0.2 g protein; 2.8 g fat (0.4 g sat.); 2.7 g carbo (0.1 g fiber); 89 mg sodium; 2.2 mg chol.

How to Hard-cook Eggs

First of all, don't boil them. Cooking eggs at too high a temperature and for too long results in two common problems: greenish yolks and cracked shells. Here's an easy way to avoid that: Place eggs in a single layer in a saucepan with enough water to cover the eggs by at least 1 inch. Cover the pan and bring just to a boil; immediately turn off the heat. Let the eggs stand, covered, for 15 minutes. Run the eggs under cold water until completely cool. Gently crack each shell and peel under running water, starting with the large end. Use eggs older than 7 days—they are easier to peel.

Meyer Lemon Crab Salad

This simple, refreshing salad from reader Elizabeth Farquhar of Logsden, Oregon, combines two exceptional West Coast winter ingredients: crab and fresh citrus. Serve as a starter course or lunch main course.

SERVES 6 | **TIME** 15 minutes

¾ lb. shelled, cooked Dungeness crab *(see Dungeness Crab 101, page 340)*
¼ tsp. finely shredded Meyer lemon zest *(see Quick Tip below)*
¼ cup fresh Meyer lemon juice
2 tbsp. finely chopped shallot
1 tbsp. Asian (toasted) sesame oil
½ tsp. salt, plus more to taste
¼ tsp. freshly ground black pepper, plus more to taste
1 cup watercress leaves and small sprigs (large stems removed; *see Quick Tip in Classic Cobb Salad, page 169*)

In a medium bowl, toss crab with lemon zest and juice, shallot, sesame oil, salt, and pepper. Add more salt and pepper to taste. Serve on a bed of watercress.

Quick Tip: Because they're typically a bit soft, chill Meyer lemons before you zest them; the cold, firm peel will be easier to cut. For the same reason, juice them after zesting, not before.

PER SERVING: 83 cal., 36% (30 cal.) from fat; 12 g protein; 3.3 g fat (0.5 g sat.); 1.3 g carbo (0.2 g fiber); 356 mg sodium; 57 mg chol.

Mixed Seafood Salad (*Insalata ai Frutti di Mare*)

This seafood salad is part of the Calabrian Christmas Eve feast that cooking teacher Rosetta Costantino, of Emeryville, California, prepares with her family every year to honor their southern Italian food traditions. It's a juicy dish, so serve bread for dipping.

SERVES 8 | **TIME** 1½ hours, plus 2 hours to marinate

1 lb. *each* mussels and Manila clams
1 lb. large shrimp (21 to 30 per lb.), peeled and deveined
1 lb. cleaned fresh or thawed frozen squid (whole tubes or whole tubes and tentacles; *see Quick Tip, right*), cut into ¾-in. rings or pieces
½ cup extra-virgin olive oil
½ cup fresh lemon juice, plus more to taste
3 garlic cloves, minced
2 tbsp. finely chopped flat-leaf parsley
1 tsp. kosher salt, plus more to taste
Freshly ground black pepper

1. Scrub mussels with a stiff brush under cold running water. Pull off any fibrous beards. Throw away any mussels with open shells (set them aside for a few minutes first to see if they begin to close; if they do, you can use them).

2. Put clams in a bowl, cover with cold water, and soak 15 minutes. Lift out and scrub with a stiff brush under cold running water. Rinse bowl and put clams back in. Cover with fresh cold water, soak 15 minutes, and lift out, leaving any sand in bowl. Keep rinsing clams until no sand remains in bowl. As with mussels, throw away any clams whose shells have not shut.

3. Bring a large pot of salted water to a boil over high heat. Set a bowl of ice water nearby. Boil shrimp just until pink, about 2 minutes. Using a strainer, transfer shrimp to ice water to stop cooking.

4. Add squid to boiling water. Once pot has returned to a boil, cook squid until tentacles curl back and rings are opaque, 45 seconds to 1 minute. Drain well, pat dry with paper towels, and add to bowl of shrimp.

5. Put 1 tbsp. water (to just cover the bottom) in a 4-qt. saucepan and add cleaned mussels. Cover and cook over high heat until mussels open, 1 to 1½ minutes. Pick out and throw away any mussels that fail to open. Transfer cooked mussels to a clean bowl and let cool 20 minutes.

6. Add cleaned clams and 1 tbsp. water to pan and steam, covered, over high heat until they open, 1½ minutes. Pick out and throw away any clams that fail to open. Let cool 20 minutes in pan.

7. Add cooled mussels and clams in their shells to bowl of squid and shrimp (leave liquid behind).

8. In a small bowl, whisk together oil, lemon juice, garlic, and parsley. Whisk in salt and several grinds of black pepper. Pour dressing over seafood and stir gently to bathe with dressing. Let salad marinate at cool room temperature for 2 hours, tossing occasionally so flavors blend.

9. Just before serving, taste and season with additional lemon juice or salt if you like. Serve in shallow bowls, with plenty of the marinade spooned over.

Quick Tip: Squid are frequently sold cleaned and cut up as tubes (mantles), tubes and tentacles, or rings (sliced tubes). If you discover any uncleaned tubes, just pull out and discard the long, clear quills and rinse out tubes.

Make Ahead: Through step 8, up to 1 day, chilled. Bring to room temperature before serving.

PER SERVING: 248 cal., 58% (144 cal.) from fat; 21 g protein; 16 g fat (2.4 g sat.); 5.2 g carbo (0.1 g fiber); 390 mg sodium; 210 mg chol.

salads

Spicy Scallop and Bean-thread Noodle Salad

Bean-thread noodles (also known as *saifun* or cellophane noodles) are thin, wiry dried noodles made from the starch of mung beans. They turn puffy and crisp when deep-fried and clear when cooked in water, as they are here. In this salad, the neutral-flavored noodles absorb the pungent seasonings of chile, ginger, garlic, and vinegar.

SERVES 3 or 4 as a main course | **TIME** 30 minutes

½ lb. Chinese long beans or slender green beans
1 red bell pepper (½ lb.)
½ lb. dried bean-thread noodles (*see Quick Tip below*)
¾ lb. bay scallops
1 tbsp. minced garlic
2 tsp. *each* minced fresh ginger and vegetable oil
½ tsp. red chile flakes
3 tbsp. *each* soy sauce and balsamic vinegar
2 tsp. sugar
¾ cup thinly sliced green onions

1. In a 5- to 6-qt. heavy-bottomed pot over high heat, bring 2½ to 3 qts. water to a boil. Meanwhile, trim stem ends from green beans, then cut beans into 3-in. lengths. Remove seeds and ribs from bell pepper, then cut into thin slivers 2 to 3 in. long.
2. Add beans to boiling water and return to a boil. Remove from heat and add bean threads and scallops; cover and let stand until scallops are barely opaque in center of thickest part (cut to test) and bean threads are barely tender to the bite, 3 to 5 minutes. Drain, rinse under cold running water until cool, and drain again thoroughly. Rinse and dry pan.
3. In the same pan over high heat, cook garlic and ginger in oil, stirring, just until garlic begins to brown, about 1 minute. Stir in chile flakes and remove from heat. Add soy sauce, vinegar, and sugar. Add noodle mixture, bell pepper, and green onions; mix gently.
Quick Tip: The noodles will be slippery after cooking; if they seem unmanageable, cut them into shorter lengths with scissors.

PER SERVING: 352 cal., 8% (29 cal.) from fat; 17 g protein; 3.2 g fat (0.4 g sat.); 64 g carbo (3.3 g fiber); 923 mg sodium; 28 mg chol.

Orange-Ginger Calamari Salad

This easy salad combines the sparkling flavors of lime and ginger. It was adapted from one created by Mark Dommen when he was executive chef of Julia's Kitchen at the now-closed Copia: The American Center for Food, Wine, and the Arts in Napa, California.

SERVES 4 | **TIME** 1 hour

1 lb. cleaned fresh or thawed frozen squid (*see Quick Tip below*) or bay scallops
3 oranges (10 oz. each), segmented (*see How to Cut Citrus into Segments, page 135*), juice reserved
3 tbsp. *each* grapeseed or canola oil and fresh lime juice
2 tbsp. minced shallot
1 tbsp. minced fresh ginger
2 tsp. sugar
½ tsp. salt, plus more to taste
Freshly ground black pepper
2 qts. (10 oz.) bite-size pieces butter lettuce leaves
1 cup matchstick-size pieces (3 in. long) peeled jicama
⅓ cup finely shredded mint leaves

1. In a 5- to 6-qt. pan over high heat, bring 2½ to 3 qts. water to a boil. Meanwhile, if necessary, cut squid tubes crosswise into ¼-in.-thick rings; leave tentacles whole. Rinse and drain squid or scallops.
2. Stir squid or scallops into boiling water; cover tightly and remove from heat. Let stand just until squid feels firm when pressed, about 1 minute (do not overcook or squid may turn rubbery), or scallops are barely opaque but still moist-looking in center (cut to test), about 2 minutes. Drain, rinse in cold water, and drain again thoroughly. Put seafood in a large bowl.
3. Pour orange segments and reserved juice into a fine-mesh strainer set over a 1- to 1½-qt. pan. Reserve segments. Bring juice to a boil over high heat and maintain boil, stirring occasionally, until reduced to 2 tbsp., 2 to 6 minutes. Remove from heat. Stir in oil, lime juice, shallot, ginger, sugar, salt, and pepper to taste.
4. Add juice mixture, orange segments, lettuce, jicama, and mint to seafood; mix gently. Add more salt and pepper to taste.
Quick Tip: Squid are frequently sold cleaned and cut up as tubes (mantles), tubes and tentacles, or rings (sliced tubes). If you discover any uncleaned tubes, just pull out and discard the long, clear quills and rinse out tubes.
Make Ahead: Through step 3, up to 1 day; chill ingredients separately.

PER SERVING: 311 cal., 35% (108 cal.) from fat; 21 g protein; 12 g fat (1.5 g sat.); 31 g carbo (6.9 g fiber); 351 mg sodium; 265 mg chol.

Vietnamese Calamari Herb Salad

In Vietnam, seafood and meats are often paired with lots and lots of fresh herbs. Here, the intense, fresh flavors of mint, basil, dill, parsley, and cilantro make a clean-tasting counterpoint to rich, lightly crunchy calamari.

recipe pictured on page 114

SERVES 8 as a first course | **TIME** 1½ hours

¾ cup fresh lime juice (6 to 8 large limes)
2 tbsp. sugar
¼ cup Thai or Vietnamese fish sauce (*nam pla* or *nuoc mam*)
1 *each* red and green jalapeño chiles, seeds and ribs removed and minced
2 cups *each* loosely packed mint, basil, dill, flat-leaf parsley, and cilantro leaves
½ cup chopped red onion
½ cup sliced celery (¼ in. thick)
1 cup salted whole cashews
4 cups vegetable oil
1 lb. cleaned fresh or thawed frozen squid tubes and tentacles (*see Quick Tips, above right*)
½ cup *each* all-purpose flour and rice flour (*see Quick Tips, above right*)
1 tsp. kosher salt, plus more to taste
¼ tsp. cayenne

1. In a small bowl, combine lime juice, sugar, fish sauce, and chiles. Set dressing aside.
2. In a large serving bowl, combine mint, basil, dill, parsley, cilantro, onion, celery, and cashews. Set aside.
3. In a 4-qt. pot about 10 in. in diameter, heat oil until it registers 360° on a deep-fry thermometer.
4. While oil is heating, slice squid tubes in half lengthwise with a sharp knife. Lay each half flat, inside up, and gently score three or four lines across it with the point of a knife; turn it 90° and score three or four lines across the first score marks to make a grid pattern (think tic-tac-toe). Put in a small bowl with tentacles. Set aside.
5. In another small bowl, combine all-purpose flour, rice flour, salt, and cayenne. Drop squid pieces into flour mixture, turning to coat well. Shake off any excess.
6. Working in three batches, fry squid 4 to 5 minutes per batch, until pieces are curled and light brown. Using a slotted spoon, transfer fried calamari to a large plate lined with several folded paper towels and sprinkle lightly with salt to taste. Allow oil temperature to return to 360° between batches.

7. Add warm calamari to herb mixture and pour half the dressing over it. Toss gently just until coated. Serve immediately, with remaining dressing on the side.
Quick Tips: If you discover any uncleaned squid tubes, just pull out and discard the long, clear quills and rinse out tubes. Rice flour can be found in the Asian foods section of most supermarkets.

PER 1½-CUP SERVING: 352 cal., 51% (180 cal.) from fat; 16 g protein; 20 g fat (3.3 g sat.); 29 g carbo (4.9 g fiber); 632 mg sodium; 132 mg chol.

Tuna Salad with White Beans

With a soup and some thickly sliced toast, this salad makes a fine snack. It's great after a day at the beach when you're feeling drowsy and are in need of clean, stimulating flavors.

SERVES 4 | **TIME** 15 minutes

1 can (6.5 to 7 oz.) good-quality oil-packed Pacific albacore tuna
1 can (15 oz.) cannellini or other white beans, drained and rinsed
4 stalks celery, chopped same size as beans
2 tbsp. *each* minced red onion and extra-virgin olive oil
Salt and freshly ground black pepper

In a medium bowl, mix together tuna, beans, celery, onion, and oil. Season with salt and pepper to taste.

PER SERVING: 212 cal., 41% (86 cal.) from fat; 18 g protein; 9.6 g fat (1.4 g sat.); 14 g carbo (5.3 g fiber); 440 mg sodium; 15 mg chol.

■ Canned Tuna

FROM THE PANTRY

For the most sustainably harvested tuna, look for Pacific albacore that's pole- or troll-caught and dolphin- and turtle-safe (if it is, the can label will proudly state that fact). The gold star for sustainable seafood is the Marine Stewardship Council logo, which signifies the best (and traceable-to-the-source) choice for wild-caught fish. Our favorite brand of canned tuna is the extremely flavorful American Tuna (*american tuna.com*). For more on canned fish, *see Canned Fish Basics (page 328)*.

salads

Seafood Cobb Salad

A big fan of Cobb salad, reader Wendy Nankeville, of Novato, California, adapted it for seafood.

SERVES 4 as main course | **TIME** 40 minutes

¼ cup *each* fresh lime juice and olive oil
1 tbsp. *each* Dijon mustard and balsamic vinegar
2 tbsp. minced cilantro
1 tsp. *each* minced garlic and sugar
½ tsp. ground cumin
2 qts. shredded romaine lettuce
1 lb. (about 3 cups) cooked shelled crab, shrimp, or scallops *(see Quick Tip, right)* or a combination
¾ cup diced ripe tomato
⅔ cup finely diced red onion
1 firm-ripe avocado (6 oz.), peeled, pitted, and diced
¾ cup crumbled blue cheese
Salt and freshly ground black pepper

1. In a large bowl, mix lime juice, oil, mustard, vinegar, cilantro, garlic, sugar, and cumin.

2. Add romaine and lift with two forks to coat with dressing. With a slotted spoon, transfer lettuce to individual wide bowls.

3. Add shellfish to dressing remaining in large bowl and mix gently. Spoon shellfish and dressing onto lettuce in each wide bowl, arranging in a 2-in.-wide band across the center.

4. Arrange equal bands of tomato, onion, avocado, and blue cheese on each salad. Season to taste with salt and pepper.

Quick Tip: To cook scallops, bring 1 qt. water to a boil in a 2- to 3-qt. pan. Rinse scallops, add to boiling water, remove from heat, cover, and let stand until opaque but still moist-looking in center of thickest part (cut to test), about 2 minutes. Drain.

PER SERVING: 498 cal., 61% (306 cal.) from fat; 37 g protein; 34 g fat (12 g sat.); 13 g carbo (3.4 g fiber); 1,048 mg sodium; 202 mg chol.

How to Pair Wines with Salads

Simple salads are hard on wine. Greens don't warm up to it on their own; add vinegar, and your wine can go flat and harsh in a jiffy. Fortunately, two serendipitous trends in the West make wine and salad pairing a tasty adventure.

Complexity Is Key
Here, salad is rarely simple. We often eat it as a main course, throwing in toasted nuts, cheese, grilled vegetables, and exotic ingredients—which make great partners with the right wine.

White Is the Way to Go
On the wine side, the style that's often "right"—crisp white—is available in a wider range than ever.

Sauvignon Blanc, one of the highest-acid still whites, is a good go-to salad wine. Generally herbal and fruity at once, it stands up to vinaigrettes, green vegetables, and herbs and is a slam-dunk with tangy goat cheese (you couldn't do better than a Sauv Blanc with the classic Baked Goat Cheese with Spring Lettuce Salad, page 145). Other great choices are crisp versions of Pinot Grigio/Gris (they're the same variety), Pinot Blanc, Viognier, and Riesling (more and more lovely ones, from bone-dry to off-dry, are being made on the West Coast). And two others warrant a try—sparkling wine, because you can't go wrong with it; and unoaked Chardonnay, in the spirit of exploring new territory (these are fermented in stainless steel tanks rather than oak barrels, to produce lighter, fruitier wines).

Tips for Making a Salad Wine-friendly
A few simple tricks result in salads that are genuinely wine-worthy.

USE A GENTLE ACID in the vinaigrette, such as sherry or rice vinegar, citrus juice, and/or wine. (Rule of thumb: Your food should never be higher in acid than your wine.) Meyer Lemon Crab Salad *(page 164)* would go well with a *blanc de blancs* sparkler (made exclusively from Chardonnay grapes).

ADD FAT in the form of mayonnaise, cheese, avocados, nuts, and/or plenty of good quality olive oil. Our Crunchy Napa Cabbage Slaw *(page 154)* isn't shy on wine challenges (radishes, green onions, cilantro, soy sauce, garlic, cayenne), but the almonds and mayo bridge to a fruity white like Riesling, as does the avocado in Spicy Avocado–Poblano Salad *(page 142)*.

ADD PROTEIN. Whether used in small ways, as with the pancetta in the Chanterelle–Potato Salad *(page 157)*, or big, as with the shellfish in our Seafood Cobb *(above)*, protein brings the pairing into balance. Try a miner-ally but rich-fruited Pinot Gris in the first case, a dry Riesling in the second.

ADD CHAR. Grill the vegetables, toast the nuts, roast the garlic. Cooking takes the edge off harsh ingredients, and the sweet caramelization builds a connection to fruit-driven wines.

WHEN PASTA, GRAINS, AND LEGUMES ARE ADDED to the salad, go for full-bodied, textured wines—Viogniers, Chardonnays, and sparklers.

An interesting salad and the right glass of wine can come together in a seamless meal. Your work is done.

Best-ever Chinese Chicken Salad

This version of the salad has all the great flavor of the original but with additional fresh ingredients.

SERVES 6 to 8 as a main course | **TIME** 45 minutes

2 tbsp. *each* unseasoned rice vinegar and light
  brown sugar
1½ tbsp. soy sauce
1 tbsp. Sriracha chili sauce
1½ tsp. grated fresh ginger
¼ cup canola or grapeseed oil
Salt
½ lb. asparagus, bottoms trimmed and cut diagonally
  into 1-in. pieces
2 navel oranges or 1 can (11 oz.) mandarin orange slices,
  drained
About 1½ cups vegetable oil for frying
4 fresh won ton wrappers (about 3½ in. each), cut into
  ¼-in.-wide strips (*see Quick Tips below*)
6 cups finely shredded cabbage
2 cups cubed cooked chicken
1 large firm-ripe avocado, pitted, peeled, and cubed
4 green onions, trimmed and sliced diagonally
2 tbsp. sesame seeds, toasted (*see Quick Tips below*)

1. In a bowl, whisk together vinegar, brown sugar, soy sauce, chili sauce, and ginger. Slowly drizzle in oil, whisking constantly. Season with salt. Set dressing aside.
2. In a 2- to 3-qt. pan over high heat, bring about 1 qt. water to a boil. Add asparagus and cook until crisp-tender, 2 to 3 minutes. Drain, then plunge asparagus into ice water to stop the cooking. Drain and set aside.
3. Cut off and discard ends from oranges. Following curve of fruit, cut off peel and outer membrane. Slice oranges crosswise into ¼-in.-thick rounds, then cut rounds into quarters. Set aside.
4. Pour oil into a 3- to 4-qt. pan (oil should be about ½ in. deep) and set over medium-high heat. When oil reaches 350°, add won ton strips and fry, stirring, until golden brown on both sides, about 30 seconds total. With a slotted spoon, transfer to paper towels.
5. In a large serving bowl, toss cabbage, chicken, and asparagus with dressing. Top with avocado, orange slices, and won ton strips, then garnish with green onions and sesame seeds.
Quick Tips: You can use store-bought crispy won tons or chow mein noodles instead of frying your own. Toast sesame seeds in a nonstick frying pan over medium heat, shaking often, until golden brown, 5 to 7 minutes.

PER SERVING: 308 cal., 56% (171 cal.) from fat; 15 g protein; 19 g fat (3.1 g sat.); 20 g carbo (4 g fiber); 317 mg sodium; 36 mg chol.

Chinese-style Chicken Salad Comes West

Historians point an uncertain finger to California for the first public appearance of Chinese chicken salad. Chef Lee of the New Moon Restaurant, which opened in Los Angeles in 1950, claims to have brought the recipe from Hong Kong. And in San Francisco in the early 1960s, Cecilia Chiang served Chinese chicken salad at the Mandarin. *Sunset*'s first recipe for it, published in 1970, came from Ming's of Palo Alto. Former owner Dan Lee reported that the restaurant started serving the top-selling dish sometime between 1958 and 1960. "We based it on a Chinese dish called finger-shredded chicken," he recalled. No matter its specific origin, it's gone on to become an American classic.

Warm Chicken BLT Salad

No need for sides with this filling supper salad.

SERVES 4 as a main course | **TIME** 30 minutes

1 lb. boned, skinned chicken breast halves (3 to 4)
14 oz. butter lettuce (2 heads), leaves separated and
  torn into 3-in. pieces
1¼ cups cherry or small pear-shaped tomatoes (red
  and/or yellow), cut in half
1 firm-ripe avocado (¾ lb.), pitted and peeled
8 slices (10 oz.) applewood-smoked or regular bacon,
  chopped
¼ cup *each* extra-virgin olive oil and tarragon vinegar or
  white wine vinegar
¼ tsp. *each* salt and freshly ground black pepper, plus
  more to taste

1. Cut chicken into 1- to 1½-in. pieces.
2. Put lettuce and tomatoes in a salad bowl. Cut avocado into quarters lengthwise; thinly slice crosswise. Add to salad.
3. In a large frying pan over medium-high heat, cook bacon, stirring often, until browned and crisp, 8 to 10 minutes. With a slotted spoon, transfer bacon to paper towels to drain. Discard all but 1 tbsp. fat from pan.
4. Add chicken to pan; cook, stirring often, over medium-high heat until no longer pink in thickest part (cut to test), about 5 minutes. Remove pan from heat and stir in oil, vinegar, and salt and pepper, scraping any browned bits from bottom of pan. Add chicken and bacon to salad and mix gently. Add more salt and pepper to taste.

PER SERVING: 474 cal., 65% (306 cal.) from fat; 33 g protein; 34 g fat (6.9 g sat.); 11 g carbo (3 g fiber); 485 mg sodium; 85 mg chol.

salads

Classic Cobb Salad

Late one night in 1937, a hungry Bob Cobb, manager of Hollywood's Brown Derby, wandered into the restaurant's kitchen. Scrounging from the refrigerator, he created what would become the Derby's signature salad—or so the story goes. Theater promotor Sid Grauman, who was with him that night, liked the greens topped with chopped chicken, roquefort cheese, and bacon and soon began requesting it. The Cobb was added to the menu and became a huge hit with customers. The original restaurant (a conspicuous Bunyan-size domed hat) is now closed, but the salad lives on at restaurants across the country.

SERVES 4 to 6 as a main course | **TIME** 1½ hours

1 lb. sliced bacon, preferably applewood smoked, coarsely chopped
⅓ cup extra-virgin olive oil
¼ cup tarragon vinegar
1 tbsp. *each* Dijon mustard and minced shallot
½ tsp. freshly ground black pepper
¼ tsp. salt
1 qt. loosely packed watercress sprigs (¼ lb.), tough stems removed *(see Quick Tip, above right)*
4 qts. finely shredded lettuce (use half butter lettuce and half iceberg or all iceberg)
2 firm-ripe tomatoes (⅔ lb. total), cored and chopped
1½ cups thinly sliced skinned cooked chicken
⅔ cup crumbled (3 oz.) pungent blue cheese such as Oregon Blue, roquefort, or gorgonzola
2 hard-cooked eggs, peeled and chopped
1 firm-ripe avocado (½ lb.), halved, pitted, peeled, and thinly sliced crosswise

1. In a large frying pan over medium-high heat, cook bacon, stirring often, until browned and crisp, 10 to 15 minutes; spoon out and discard fat in pan as it accumulates. With a slotted spoon, transfer bacon to paper towels to drain; discard remaining fat.
2. In a 1-cup glass measure or small bowl, mix oil, vinegar, mustard, shallot, pepper, and salt.
3. Set aside 4 to 6 watercress sprigs; coarsely chop remaining sprigs. In a very large bowl, combine chopped watercress and lettuce. Add all but ¼ cup dressing and mix gently to coat.
4. Divide lettuce mixture among wide, shallow bowls. On each, in wedges shaped like pie slices, arrange equal portions of bacon, tomatoes, chicken, blue cheese, eggs, and avocado.
5. Spoon remaining dressing over toppings. Garnish salads with reserved watercress sprigs.

Quick Tip: To trim the tough stems from a bunch of watercress, hold it upside down and "shave" it by running a sharp knife down the sides of the bunch. Reserve the shaved leaves. Remove the now-exposed tough stems from the outside of the bunch, then slice off all the lower stems at once and discard. You'll be left with mainly tender sprigs, and picking out the few remaining tough stems won't take long.

PER SERVING: 458 cal., 71% (324 cal.) from fat; 25 g protein; 36 g fat (10 g sat.); 12 g carbo (3.5 g fiber); 768 mg sodium; 129 mg chol.

Lemon Cashew Chicken Salad

Here's an unusual, fresh-tasting chicken salad that's low in fat, thanks to the thick, creamy yogurt that replaces half the mayo. Serve on lettuce if you like, or use it to fill a sandwich, maybe with sweet onion for crunch—or, in summer, a slice of ripe tomato.

recipe pictured on page **113**

SERVES 6 | **TIME** 45 minutes

1 tsp. *each* cumin seeds and coriander seeds
3 medium lemons
1½ tbsp. butter
3 tbsp. minced fresh ginger
1 to 3 tbsp. finely chopped jalapeño chile
½ tsp. salt
⅓ cup *each* mayonnaise and Greek yogurt
½ cup *each* chopped cilantro and green onions
4 cups shredded white and dark chicken meat (from a 2½- to 3-lb. rotisserie chicken)
Chopped toasted cashews *(see How to Toast Nuts, page 134)*

1. In a medium frying pan over low heat, toast cumin and coriander seeds until fragrant, 3 to 5 minutes. Transfer seeds to a spice grinder and process until finely ground. Finely zest lemons with a razor-sharp grater, such as a Microplane, or the fine shredding holes of a box grater and set aside zest. Juice 1 lemon and set aside 3 tbsp. juice.
2. In the same frying pan used to toast seeds, melt butter over medium heat. Add ginger, jalapeño, and salt; cook, stirring occasionally, until jalapeño is soft, 3 to 5 minutes. Remove from heat and set aside.
3. In a large bowl, stir together mayonnaise, yogurt, lemon zest and juice, ginger-jalapeño mixture, and ground spices. Add cilantro, green onions, and chicken; stir to coat well with dressing. Taste and adjust seasonings as needed. Sprinkle with cashews and serve.

PER SERVING: 273 cal., 66% (180 cal.) from fat; 20 g protein; 20 g fat (6 g sat.); 4.2 g carbo (0.6 g fiber); 860 mg sodium; 101 mg chol.

sandwiches, burritos & pizza

A compendium of casual, handheld foods so good you'll be tempted to skip the takeout kind.

What is it that's so compelling about food you can hold? No matter how grown up you are, eating with your hands taps into some kind of early pleasure center. You understand more about a food when you touch it: the stretchiness of a good pizza, the warmth and ooze of a bean burrito, the buttery crispness of a grilled cheese sandwich. It builds anticipation for every bite.

And there's so much good handheld food to choose from in the West. We offer some favorites here, from sandwiches as simple as bacon, basil, and tomato (*page 175*) to a post-Thanksgiving extravaganza of turkey, caramelized shallots, cranberries, and blue cheese (*page 176*). And we are profoundly grateful for the tortilla, without which we would never have cultural icons like Baja Fried-fish Tacos (*page 196*)—or burritos (*page 191*), tostadas (*page 194*), and quesadillas (*page 197*).

Pizza is red-hot in the West now, with Phoenix, San Francisco, and Los Angeles among the cities raising our standards. Make your own dough if you like (*page 200*), but you can get decent store-bought dough, crank your oven to its hottest, and bake delicious pizza in less than half an hour. The only major handheld food missing here is burgers, which you'll find in the chapters Vegetarian Mains (*page 276*) and The Fire Outside (*page 432*).

Sandwiches, Burritos & Pizzas

Roast Beef and Two-chile Grilled Cheese on Onion Rolls

We love the heat in this sandwich from reader Alicia Lopez, of Boise, Idaho, but if you want it less spicy, cut back on the chipotle in the mayo and on the green chiles.

MAKES 4 sandwiches | **TIME** 25 minutes

¼ cup mayonnaise
1 tbsp. minced canned chipotle chiles in adobo sauce (about 4 chiles)
4 onion rolls
2 tsp. olive oil, plus more for coating rolls
½ lb. pepper jack cheese, thinly sliced
½ lb. thinly sliced rare roast beef
4 canned mild green chiles, split, seeded, and patted dry

1. Stir together mayonnaise and chipotles and set aside.
2. Preheat a panini press (*see Quick Tip below*.) to 350° (medium heat). Brush outsides of rolls with oil. Split rolls. Spread each bottom half with 1½ tsp. chipotle mayonnaise, then top each with 2 slices cheese; 2 or 3 slices roast beef; 1 mild chile, opened up flat; and 2 more slices cheese.
3. Spread each top half of rolls with 1½ tsp. chipotle mayonnaise and place on top of sandwiches. Grill 2 sandwiches at a time until crisp and bubbling, 3 to 4 minutes. Let sandwiches cool slightly, then slice with a serrated knife and serve.
Quick Tip: If you don't have a panini press, cook sandwiches in a frying pan or cast-iron skillet with a heated cast-iron skillet on top of them.

PER SANDWICH: 597 cal., 56% (333 cal.) from fat; 33 g protein; 37 g fat (14 g sat.); 33 g carbo (1.4 g fiber); 1,167 mg sodium; 89 mg chol.

Our 10 Favorite Grilled Cheese Combos

1. Pesto and fresh mozzarella on rustic Italian bread; tomato and prosciutto optional
2. Avocado and jack
3. Gouda and thinly sliced dill pickles on rye (for a party recipe, see *Mini Pumpernickel Grilled Cheese and Pickle Sandwiches*, page 32)
4. Raisin bread, tart apple, and cheddar
5. Ripe tomato and any kind of cheese
6. Bacon and any kind of cheese
7. Fig preserves and Swiss or gruyère
8. Tuna, pepper jack, and thinly sliced red onion
9. Spicy-sweet mango chutney and sharp white cheddar
10. Ripe, oozy brie and grilled eggplant

Grilled Pastrami, Swiss, and Sweet Onion Marmalade on Rye

Make the marmalade ahead so you can whip up these sandwiches—from reader Jennifer Brumfield, of Bellingham, Washington—in just a few minutes. Any leftover marmalade is terrific on pork chops and roast beef.

MAKES 2 sandwiches | **TIME** 1 hour

1 tbsp. *each* salted butter and vegetable oil
2 medium red onions, thinly sliced
1 large garlic clove, minced
½ cup sugar
½ tsp. salt
1 tsp. freshly ground black pepper
½ cup *each* red wine vinegar and dry but fruity red wine, such as Zinfandel or Grenache
4 slices extra-sour rye or caraway rye bread
2 tbsp. unsalted butter, softened
4 thin slices pastrami, uncured if available
¼ lb. Swiss cheese, coarsely shredded
2 tbsp. whole-grain mustard

1. Make marmalade: Melt salted butter with oil in a large heavy frying pan over medium-high heat. Add onions, garlic, sugar, salt, and pepper, stirring well to combine. Reduce heat to medium and cook, stirring occasionally, until onions have softened and browned, about 20 minutes. Add vinegar and wine. Cook, uncovered, stirring occasionally, until most of liquid has been absorbed and onions are soft and sticky, about 10 minutes. Let marmalade cool slightly.
2. Make sandwiches: Evenly spread one side of each bread slice with ½ tbsp. unsalted butter. Spread unbuttered side of 2 slices with 1½ tbsp. marmalade each, then top with pastrami and cheese. Spread mustard on unbuttered side of remaining 2 bread slices and place each, buttered side up, on pastrami- and cheese-topped slices.
3. Heat a large nonstick frying pan over medium heat. Add sandwiches and cook, turning once, until golden brown on both sides and cheese is melted, about 5 minutes total.
Make Ahead: Marmalade, up to 2 weeks, chilled.

PER SANDWICH: 660 cal., 46% (306 cal.) from fat; 33 g protein; 34 g fat (19 g sat.); 51 g carbo (4.4 g fiber); 1,623 mg sodium; 112 mg chol.

Hoi An–style Oven-crisped Pork Sandwiches (*Bánh Mì Thit Hoi An*)

This version of *bánh mì* comes from Hoi An, a charming old fishing village in central Vietnam. Choose a sweet baguette with a light, slightly soft interior and a thin, crisp crust.

recipe pictured on page **177**

MAKES 6 sandwiches | **TIME** 45 minutes

1 tsp. Chinese five-spice powder
1 tbsp. vegetable oil
¼ cup chopped shallots
1 garlic clove, minced
¾ lb. ground lean pork
3 tbsp. soy sauce
1½ tsp. sugar
Salt
3 baguettes (½ lb. each; *see note above*)
2 tbsp. Asian red chili paste or Sriracha sauce, plus more to taste
½ lb. roasted, boned, fat-trimmed pork loin or cooked ham or chicken, thinly sliced
2 cups thinly sliced English cucumbers (about ½ lb.)
3 cups salad mix (¼ lb.)
½ cup Thai or regular basil leaves, cut into 1-in. pieces
½ cup Fried Sliced Shallots (optional; *page 211*)

1. In an 8- to 10-in. frying pan over medium-high heat, stir five-spice powder until fragrant, about 30 seconds. Stir in oil, shallots, and garlic. Add ground pork and cook, stirring often and breaking apart with a spoon, until meat is crumbly and no longer pink, about 15 minutes. Add soy sauce, sugar, and salt to taste.
2. Preheat oven to 375°. Cut baguettes in half crosswise, then split lengthwise almost all the way through, leaving halves attached at one side. Spread 1 tsp. chili paste on one cut side of each baguette section. Spoon about a sixth of warm ground pork mixture, including juice, over chili paste. Tuck a sixth of pork slices into each sandwich. Set sandwiches, slightly separated, on a 12- by 15-in. baking sheet.
3. Bake just until filling is warm and crust is crisp, about 5 minutes. Remove sandwiches from oven and fill each with a sixth of cucumbers, salad mix, basil, and fried shallots if using. Add more chili paste and salt to taste.
Make Ahead: Through step 2, up to 1 hour, covered loosely and kept at room temperature.

PER SANDWICH: 596 cal., 29% (171 cal.) from fat; 35 g protein; 19 g fat (4.2 g sat.); 70 g carbo (4.3 g fiber); 1,290 mg sodium; 64 mg chol.

Bánh Mì: The Vietnamese Sandwich

Especially in regions with large Vietnamese populations—like California's San Gabriel Valley and the cities of San Jose, Seattle, and Portland, Oregon—*bánh mì*, the Vietnamese-style baguette sandwich, has become a standby. It always has pork in some form, chiles, fresh herbs, spices, and usually marinated vegetables. It can also include a layer of smooth chicken-liver or pork pâté. For another version, *see Vietnamese-style Turkey Subs (page 176)*.

Escarole, Egg, and Prosciutto Sandwiches

Escarole retains its crunch for hours and has a faint and pleasing bitterness.

MAKES 4 sandwiches | **TIME** 20 minutes

3 oz. thinly sliced prosciutto, cut into ½-in.-wide strips and separated
1 tbsp. olive oil
1 tsp. minced garlic
2½ qts. coarsely chopped escarole (from a ½-lb. head)
2 tsp. minced marjoram leaves
6 eggs, lightly beaten
4 squares focaccia (each 1 in. thick and 3 in. wide; ¾ lb. total), split in half and toasted
Salt and freshly ground black pepper

1. In a 10- to 12-in. nonstick frying pan over medium-high heat, cook prosciutto in oil, stirring, until browned, 5 to 7 minutes. With a slotted spoon, transfer to paper towels to drain. Reduce heat to medium.
2. Add garlic to pan and cook, stirring, about 30 seconds. Stir in escarole, marjoram, and ¼ cup water. Cover and simmer until escarole is tender to the bite, about 5 minutes. Drain off any remaining water.
3. Uncover pan and pour in eggs. Cook, stirring often, over medium heat until eggs are softly set, 2 to 4 minutes. Stir in reserved prosciutto.
4. Set focaccia bottoms on plates; spoon egg mixture over them. Season to taste with salt and pepper. Cover with focaccia tops.

PER SANDWICH: 429 cal., 40% (171 cal.) from fat; 27 g protein; 19 g fat (5.8 g sat.); 41 g carbo (2.6 g fiber); 904 mg sodium; 346 mg chol.

Bacon, Basil, and Tomato Sandwich

This sandwich is best enjoyed in summer, using a meaty heirloom tomato or two and basil picked right from the garden.

MAKES 1 sandwich | **TIME** 15 minutes

1 piece (about 3½ by 5 in.) ciabatta bread or a crusty roll
2 to 3 tbsp. mayonnaise
4 to 6 large basil leaves
4 to 6 slices ripe, juicy tomato
Salt and freshly ground black pepper
2 slices bacon, cooked until crisp

Split ciabatta bread in half lengthwise. Toast lightly. Spread cut sides with mayonnaise. Cover bottom half with basil leaves and tomato slices. Sprinkle with salt and pepper to taste. Top with bacon. Cap with top half of ciabatta.

PER SANDWICH: 420 cal., 39% (165 cal.) from fat; 13 g protein; 18 g fat (3.9 g sat.); 52 g carbo (1.8 g fiber); 975 mg sodium; 23 mg chol.

Fried Chicken Sandwiches with Spicy Slaw

The rich fried chicken pairs perfectly with the bright-tasting chile-spiked slaw.

MAKES 6 sandwiches | **TIME** 1 hour

2 cups finely shredded red and/or green cabbage
1 medium carrot, coarsely shredded
¼ cup *each* mint and cilantro leaves, coarsely chopped
½ tsp. minced serrano chile
1½ tbsp. *each* fresh lime juice and olive oil
2½ tsp. kosher salt, divided, plus more to taste
1 cup flour
⅓ cup yellow cornmeal
1 tsp. cayenne
1 cup buttermilk
1 egg
1½ lbs. skinned, boned chicken breasts, cut at an angle across grain into 1-in.-thick strips
Vegetable oil for frying
6 long soft sandwich rolls, split
Mayonnaise

1. In a bowl, combine cabbage, carrot, mint, cilantro, and chile. Stir in lime juice and olive oil and season to taste with salt. Set slaw aside.
2. In a pie pan, mix flour, cornmeal, 1½ tsp. salt, and the cayenne. In a medium bowl, whisk buttermilk and egg

to combine. Dredge chicken in flour mixture, dip into buttermilk mixture, then return to flour mixture, turning to coat all sides.
3. Pour 1 in. vegetable oil into a 5- or 6-qt. pan over medium-high heat. When oil reaches 350°, add chicken in a single layer (work in batches if necessary) and cook until well browned all over and no longer pink in center (cut to test), about 6 minutes per batch. As chicken is done, transfer to paper towels and sprinkle lightly with remaining 1 tsp. salt.
4. Spread sandwich rolls with mayonnaise. Divide chicken among rolls and top generously with slaw.

PER SANDWICH: 554 cal., 29% (162 cal.) from fat; 37 g protein; 18 g fat (3.1 g sat.); 58 g carbo (4.1 g fiber); 1,151 mg sodium; 103 mg chol.

Tangy Lemon-Cucumber Chicken Salad Croissants

A bouquet of herbs, plus lemon and cucumber, blends with the meatiness of roast chicken to make a stellar sandwich. Using a crisp cucumber is key; it keeps the croissants from getting soggy.

MAKES 8 to 10 mini sandwiches; 4 or 5 regular-size sandwiches | **TIME** 35 minutes

¼ cup extra-virgin olive oil
3 tbsp. fresh lemon juice
1 tbsp. finely shredded lemon zest
1 tbsp. *each* chopped dill, chives, flat-leaf parsley, basil, and mint leaves
1 tbsp. chopped brined capers
¼ tsp. salt
½ tsp. freshly ground black pepper
3 cups shredded roasted chicken (*see Quick Tip below*)
½ English cucumber, seeded and diced (about 1 cup)
6 green onions (including some green tops), trimmed and sliced
8 to 10 mini croissants or 4 or 5 regular-size croissants

1. In a small bowl, whisk together oil, lemon juice and zest, dill, chives, parsley, basil, mint, capers, salt, and pepper.
2. In a large bowl, toss together chicken, cucumber, and green onions. Add dressing to chicken mixture and stir to coat.
3. Halve croissants lengthwise. Fill bottoms with salad and cap with tops.
Quick Tip: A 2½- to 3-lb. rotisserie-cooked chicken will give you about 3 cups of meat.

PER MINI SANDWICH: 243 cal., 56% (135 cal.) from fat; 12 g protein; 15 g fat (5.1 g sat.); 15 g carbo (1.3 g fiber); 600 mg sodium; 61 mg chol.

Vietnamese-style Turkey Subs

This interpretation of *báhn mì* is a great way to use leftover dark meat, because it stands up well to the pungent dressing. A slightly off-dry Riesling is an excellent match for the sandwich's intense flavors. *Báhn mì* can include a layer of chicken-liver or pork pâté. If you'd like to add pâté, spread it over the chili paste before you add the turkey.

MAKES 4 sandwiches | **TIME** 1 hour

3 cups finely shredded cabbage *(see Quick Tips below)*
½ cup finely shredded carrots
½ cup unseasoned rice vinegar, divided
1 tsp. sugar
½ tsp. salt
⅓ cup widely sliced green onions
1 tbsp. *each* **fresh lime juice and chopped fresh ginger**
2 tsp. chopped garlic
½ tsp. Chinese five-spice powder
4 cups shredded cooked turkey (mostly dark meat)
1 thick, light-textured baguette, cut into 4 sections, or
  4 long rolls such as *bolillos (see Quick Tips below)*
4 tsp. Asian chili paste
¼ cup cilantro leaves

1. In a bowl, mix cabbage and carrots with ¼ cup vinegar, the sugar, and salt; let stand about 30 minutes.
2. In a blender, combine remaining ¼ cup vinegar with green onions, lime juice, ginger, garlic, and five-spice powder. Blend until smooth. Pour mixture into a medium bowl. Add turkey and mix to coat.
3. Split baguette sections lengthwise almost all the way through, leaving halves attached at one side. Spread 1 tsp. chili paste on one cut side of each. Mound turkey mixture on top, then add cabbage mixture and cilantro leaves.

Quick Tips: The bagged shredded green cabbage sold as "angel hair" works well for this slaw. *Bolillos* are Mexican or Salvadoran rolls with a crusty exterior, soft interior, and torpedo shape; find them at Latino bakeries and grocery stores.

PER SANDWICH: 542 cal., 23% (126 cal.) from fat; 49 g protein; 14 g fat (4 g sat.); 53 g carbo (4.4 g fiber); 966 mg sodium; 123 mg chol.

Turkey Sandwiches with Shallots, Cranberries, and Blue Cheese

This sandwich combines some very familiar Thanksgiving flavors (turkey and cranberry) with enough surprising ones (shallots and blue cheese) to make you forget you're eating leftovers.

MAKES 4 sandwiches | **TIME** 30 minutes

2 tbsp. olive oil
10 shallots, thinly sliced
¾ tsp. salt, plus more to taste
5 tbsp. soft blue cheese
⅓ cup mayonnaise
4 crusty sandwich rolls, such as ciabatta, sliced in half
  and toasted
½ cup cranberry sauce
8 slices cooked turkey breast (about ¼ in. thick)
4 leaves romaine lettuce

1. Heat oil in a small frying pan over medium heat. Add shallots and salt, stir, reduce heat to medium-low, and cover. Cook, stirring occasionally, until shallots are soft and browned, about 15 minutes (if shallots appear to be browning too quickly, reduce heat to low). Taste shallots and add more salt if necessary.
2. Meanwhile, in a small bowl, stir together blue cheese and mayonnaise until smooth.
3. Spread top half of each roll with cranberry sauce. Generously spread bottom halves with mayonnaise mixture and layer with turkey slices, lettuce, shallots, and the top bread halves.

PER SANDWICH: 524 cal., 52% (270 cal.) from fat; 33 g protein; 30 g fat (5.3 g sat.); 39 g carbo (1.3 g fiber); 998 mg sodium; 91 mg chol.

■ Shallots

FROM THE GARDEN

Shallots differ from onions in that many varieties produce a cluster of several bulbs to a plant. Shallots also have finer layers and contain less water. Because of the low water content, their flavor is more concentrated than that of onions. They can burn and toughen easily, though, so use caution when sautéing. They are often a better stand-in for the drier, small red onions used in Asian cooking (India in particular) than our moist onions.

Hoi An-style Oven-crisped Pork Sandwiches (*Bánh Mi Thit Hoi An*), page 174

California Niçoise Sandwiches,
page 189

Thousand-seed Pilaf,
page 234

Baja Fish Tacos,
page 196

Giant Butternut Squash Ravioli,
page 224

Penne with Oyster Mushrooms,
Prosciutto, and Mint, *page 208*

Linguine with Gorgonzola, Potatoes, Green Beans, and Sage, *page 209*

Delfina's Broccoli Rabe Pizza,
page 199

Molten Cheese Gnocchi,
page 225

Caramelized Carrot Risotto,
page 230

Pappardelle with Chicken and
Winter Greens, *page 213*

Golden Gate Grilled Turkey
and Cheese, *page 189*

Golden Gate Grilled Turkey and Cheese

The sandwich from reader Britta Glade of Orinda, California, is like a Monte Cristo—only better. The parmesan crust is pure genius.

recipe pictured on page **188**

MAKES 2 sandwiches | **TIME** 30 minutes

2 tbsp. butter, softened
1 tsp. minced garlic
½ tsp. red chile flakes
1 egg, lightly beaten
¼ cup milk
1 cup coarsely shredded parmesan cheese
4 freshly cut slices from a sourdough loaf
6 oz. thinly sliced turkey
½ firm-ripe avocado, pitted, peeled, and thinly sliced
1 tbsp. chopped cilantro
2 slices muenster cheese

1. In a small bowl, combine butter, garlic, and chile flakes. In a medium bowl, whisk egg and milk. Spread parmesan on a plate.
2. In a large frying pan, melt half the garlic butter over medium heat. Dip 1 bread slice in egg mixture, coating one side only. Dip coated side into parmesan. Put in frying pan, cheese side down. Repeat with 1 more bread slice. Arrange turkey, avocado, cilantro, and muenster on both slices, dividing evenly.
3. Dip remaining bread slices into egg on one side and then into parmesan. Set on sandwiches in pan, cheese side up. Continue cooking sandwiches over medium heat until undersides are golden brown, 3 to 4 minutes. Lift sandwiches and add remaining garlic butter to pan; flip and cook until second side is golden brown, another 3 to 4 minutes.

PER SANDWICH: 866 cal., 54% (468 cal.) from fat; 62 g protein; 52 g fat (26 g sat.); 38 g carbo (2.7 g fiber); 1,668 mg sodium; 272 mg chol.

California Niçoise Sandwiches

Though inspired by the classic French salad, this fancy tuna sandwich takes a Western turn with sourdough and avocados.

recipe pictured on page **178**

MAKES 6 sandwiches | **TIME** 30 minutes

1 baguette-style loaf, about 20 in. long and 3 to 4 in. wide *(see Quick Tips below)*
½ cup mayonnaise
1 garlic clove, minced
2 tsp. finely shredded lemon zest
2 cans (6.5 to 7 oz. each) oil-packed tuna, drained *(see Quick Tips below)*
1½ tbsp. *each* chopped tarragon and red wine vinegar
Salt and freshly ground black pepper
½ cup thinly sliced radishes
1 ripe medium tomato, thinly sliced
2 hard-cooked eggs, peeled and sliced into thin rounds
½ firm-ripe avocado, pitted, peeled, and thinly sliced
½ cup chopped pitted kalamata olives

1. Slice loaf in half lengthwise. Scoop out about three-quarters of bread from top and bottom halves to create pockets; save scooped-out bread for another use, such as bread crumbs, if you like.
2. In a small bowl, whisk together mayonnaise, garlic, and lemon zest. Spread generously over inside of loaf's top half.
3. In a medium bowl, stir together tuna, tarragon, vinegar, and salt and pepper to taste. Spoon into bottom half of loaf.
4. Top tuna mixture with radish slices, then tomato, egg, and avocado slices. Spoon olives over all and top with the other loaf half. To serve, slice into six equal portions.

Quick Tips: We love this sandwich on crusty sourdough, but it can be a bit messy to eat. For a tidier bite, try soft Italian-style bread. For the most sustainably harvested tuna, look for Pacific albacore that's pole- or troll-caught and dolphin- and turtle-safe (if it is, the label will say). Our favorite brand is the extremely flavorful American Tuna *(americantuna.com)*.
Make Ahead: Up to 3 hours, chilled.

PER SANDWICH: 495 cal., 51% (252 cal.) from fat; 25 g protein; 28 g fat (4.7 g sat.); 35 g carbo (2.7 g fiber); 881 mg sodium; 92 mg chol.

Crab, Shrimp, and Corn Salad on Sourdough Baguette

The sweet, delicate flavors of fresh crab and bay shrimp shine in simple recipes such as this one.

MAKES 8 to 10 sandwiches | **TIME** 25 minutes

2 sourdough baguettes, each cut into 4 or 5 pieces (4 in. long)
½ lb. shelled cooked crab, thoroughly drained and patted dry
½ lb. cooked bay shrimp, patted dry
¾ cup fresh corn kernels (sliced from 1 or 2 ears of corn)
1 medium red onion, diced (about 1 cup; *see Quick Tip below*)
1 red or orange bell pepper, seeds and ribs removed and diced (about 1 cup)
½ cup roughly chopped flat-leaf parsley
¼ cup extra-virgin olive oil
3 tbsp. Champagne vinegar
¼ tsp. salt
½ tsp. freshly ground black pepper

1. Cut baguette pieces in half lengthwise. Scoop out about three-quarters of bread from top and bottom halves to create pockets; save scooped-out bread for another use, such as bread crumbs, if you like.
2. In a large bowl, toss together crab, shrimp, corn, onion, and bell pepper.
3. In a small bowl, whisk together parsley, oil, vinegar, salt, and pepper. Pour dressing over crab and shrimp mixture and stir to coat filling.
4. Fill bottom halves of baguettes with salad and set top halves on salad.
Quick Tip: For a milder onion flavor, rinse diced onion with cold water and pat dry before adding to salad.

PER SANDWICH: 214 cal., 34% (73 cal.) from fat; 14 g protein; 8.1 g fat (1.2 g sat.); 22 g carbo (1.8 g fiber); 388 mg sodium; 74 mg chol.

■ Fennel

Look for small, heavy, white fennel heads (sometimes also labeled "fresh anise") that are firm and free of cracks, browning, or moist areas. The stalks should be crisp, with feathery, bright green fronds. Store fennel bulbs in a perforated plastic bag in the refrigerator for up to five days. After that, the bulbs begin to toughen and lose flavor. The stalks and fronds are just as edible as the bulb; use the stalk the same way as the bulb and the fronds as you would an herb (they also make a pretty garnish).

Tuna, Lemon, Fennel, and Black-olive Salad on Sourdough Rolls

This tasty spin on ordinary mayo-celery tuna salad was inspired by the pole-caught tuna sandwich at the San Francisco branch of 'Wichcraft, a New York sandwich shop. The lemon slices are softened by a good salting and are delicious with the tuna and olives.

MAKES 8 to 10 sandwiches | **TIME** 30 minutes

1 small lemon
½ head fennel, base and stalks trimmed (*see Fennel, below left*)
¼ tsp. salt
8 to 10 sourdough or French bread rolls
30 oz. canned oil-packed tuna (*see Quick Tip below*), drained
2 tbsp. extra-virgin olive oil
1 tbsp. chopped brined capers
¼ cup *each* chopped pitted kalamata olives and roughly chopped dill

1. Slice lemon very thinly using a knife or mandoline. Quarter lemon slices, removing any seeds. Very thinly slice fennel bulb the same way. In a medium bowl, toss together lemon, fennel, and salt and let sit 20 minutes.
2. Slice rolls in half lengthwise. Scoop out about three-quarters of bread from top and bottom halves to create pockets; save scooped-out bread for another use, such as bread crumbs, if you like.
3. In a medium bowl, toss together tuna, oil, capers, olives, and dill. Gently stir in lemon-fennel mixture. Fill sourdough roll bottoms with tuna salad, dividing evenly, and cap with tops.
Quick Tip: Use the best olive oil–packed tuna you can find; its rich flavor will reward you in these sandwiches. For the most sustainably harvested tuna, look for Pacific albacore that's pole- or troll-caught and dolphin- and turtle-safe (if it is, the label will say). Our favorite brand is the extremely flavorful American Tuna (*americantuna.com*).

PER SANDWICH: 266 cal., 42% (113 cal.) from fat; 22 g protein; 13 g fat (1.2 g sat.); 17 g carbo (1.6 g fiber); 787 mg sodium; 34 mg chol.

How to Clean and Fillet Sardines

1. Remove guts. Wearing plastic gloves if you like, lay each fish on its side on a work surface. Insert a small, sharp knife ¼ in. above belly, just behind the gills, and cut lengthwise along belly to tail to open. Pull out guts and rinse fish.

2. Scale. Gently scrape fish from tail to head with your fingertips to loosen scales.

3. Trim. With kitchen scissors, cut off dorsal (top) fin and tail. Rinse fish and work surface.

4. Fillet. At collar below head, score a crosswise slit on each side of fish just to the bone. Hold fish head with one hand. With index and middle fingers of your other hand, make a scissor shape; slide "blades" of your fingers into slits on either side of fish. Slide your fingers along backbone to the tail, pushing fillets off the bone (they come off easily).

5. Cut fillets. Cut in half lengthwise and pull off any pin bones.

Sardine BLTs with Herbs and Lemon

Consumed with great gusto all over the Mediterranean, fresh sardines are finally starting to get the respect they deserve in the United States. This recipe is a good one for entry-level eaters of fresh sardines, since the fish's bold flavor is tempered by bacon, herbs, and lemon.

MAKES 4 sandwiches | **TIME** 30 minutes

½ cup mayonnaise
3 tbsp. chopped flat-leaf parsley
2 tbsp. chopped chives
Finely shredded zest of 1 lemon
2 tsp. fresh lemon juice
8 slices bacon
8 sardines (1⅓ lbs. total), cleaned and filleted (*see Quick Tip, above right*)
4 crusty rolls, split and toasted
About 2 cups loosely packed arugula
8 tomato slices

1. Mix mayonnaise, parsley, chives, and lemon zest and juice in a small bowl; chill.

2. Cook bacon until crisp in a 12-in. frying pan, then transfer to paper towels to drain. Reserve fat in pan.

3. Cook sardines skin side down in fat (in two batches if needed) over medium-high heat until opaque, tipping

pan often and spooning fat over fish. Drain fish on paper towels.

4. Spread rolls with parsley-chive mayonnaise. Layer arugula, tomatoes, bacon, and sardines in rolls and cut in half.

Quick Tip: Ask your fishmonger to clean and fillet the sardines for you, or do it yourself.

PER SANDWICH: 552 cal., 41% (228 cal.) from fat; 23g protein; 25 g fat (14 g sat.); 40 g carbo (2.1 g fiber); 1,142 mg sodium; 71 mg chol.

Chicken, Black Bean, and Goat Cheese Burritos

A relatively low-fat and fast-to-make burrito. The fresher your tortillas, the easier the burrito will be to wrap.

MAKES 6 burritos | **TIME** 30 minutes

1 lb. skinned, boned chicken breast halves
1 tsp. ground cumin
½ tsp. *each* salt (optional) and freshly ground black pepper
4 flour tortillas (10 in. wide)
1 can (15 oz.) black beans
1 tsp. canola oil
½ cup (3 oz.) soft fresh goat cheese, broken into small chunks
About 1 cup store-bought fresh green salsa, plus more for serving

1. Preheat oven to 350°. Cut chicken breast halves across the grain into 3- by ½-in. strips. In a bowl, coat strips with cumin, salt if using, and pepper.

2. Seal tortillas in foil and warm in oven until hot, about 10 minutes.

3. Meanwhile, put beans and their liquid in a 1-qt. pan and cook over medium-high heat, stirring occasionally, until bubbling, about 5 minutes.

4. In a 10- to 12-in. nonstick frying pan over medium heat, heat oil until shimmering. Add chicken and cook, stirring often, until meat is no longer pink in center, about 8 minutes.

5. Lay tortillas flat. Fill each with chicken, beans (including enough liquid to moisten), cheese, and 2 to 3 tbsp. salsa. Fold over sides and roll up tightly to enclose. Serve with more salsa.

PER BURRITO: 339 cal., 26% (87 cal.) from fat; 26 g protein; 9.7 g fat (3.5 g sat.); 38 g carbo (4.8 g fiber); 882 mg sodium; 48 mg chol.

Salmon Burritos with Chile-roasted Vegetables

We replaced the usual rice with pan-roasted sweet potato, onion, and zucchini, giving this burrito a healthy dose of fiber—as well as heart-protecting micro-nutrients such as carotenoids (in the sweet potatoes), flavonoids (onions), folic acid (cabbage), and omega-3 fatty acids (salmon).

MAKES 6 burritos | **TIME** 45 minutes

2 tbsp. olive oil
2 tsp. fresh lime juice
4 garlic cloves, minced
1½ tsp. *each* ground dried chiles and salt
1 lb. boned salmon fillet (about 1 in. thick)
1 large orange-fleshed sweet potato (often labeled "yam"), peeled, quartered lengthwise, and sliced ¼ in. thick
1 zucchini, halved lengthwise and sliced ⅓ in. thick
1 red onion, halved lengthwise and cut into ¼-in.-thick wedges
1 poblano chile, seeds and ribs removed and chopped
6 whole-wheat flour tortillas (10 in. wide), warmed (see *Quick Tip below*)
Chopped cilantro, shredded cabbage, low-fat sour cream, and lime wedges

1. Preheat oven to 425°. Line two 12- by 15-in. baking pans with foil.
2. Whisk together oil, lime juice, garlic, ground dried chiles, and salt. Brush flesh side of salmon with 2 tbsp. lime-chile marinade. Set aside.
3. In a medium bowl, toss sweet potato, zucchini, onion, and poblano chile with remaining marinade. Arrange vegetables in a single layer in baking pans.
4. Roast vegetables for 10 minutes, then add salmon, skin side down, to one pan and return to oven. Continue roasting until potatoes are tender when pierced and salmon is opaque but still moist-looking in center of thickest part (cut to test), 7 to 10 minutes.
5. Remove skin from salmon and slice fillet into six equal portions.
6. Spoon vegetable mixture onto warm tortillas. Top each with a piece of salmon and a little cilantro, cabbage, and sour cream. Fold over sides and roll up tightly to enclose. Serve with more sour cream and lime wedges.
Quick Tip: To heat tortillas, wrap in a kitchen towel and microwave until warm and soft, about 1 minute.

PER BURRITO: 325 cal., 39% (126 cal.) from fat; 19 g protein; 14 g fat (2.5 g sat.); 30 g carbo (3.4 g fiber); 852 mg sodium; 45 mg chol.

Sunset's Burritos Grandes

San Franciscans love giant burritos packed with a dinner plate's worth of food, and these are outstanding. For less indulgent burritos, omit the guacamole, sour cream, and cheese, and make six instead of four. You'll need two 18-in.-long metal skewers or four 10-in. ones for grilling the meat.

MAKES 4 large or 6 regular-size burritos | **TIME** 1 hour, plus 15 minutes to marinate

2 oz. (4 to 6) dried ancho, New Mexico, or California chiles (see *Quick Tip, far right*)
⅓ cup tequila
¼ cup fresh lemon juice
3 garlic cloves, peeled
1 tbsp. olive oil
½ tsp. dried oregano
1 tsp. salt, divided
1¼ lbs. pork shoulder (butt), fat trimmed
½ cup long-grain white rice
¼ cup canned tomato sauce
1 can (15 oz.) pinto or red beans
4 large (13 in.) or 6 regular-size (10 in.) flour tortillas
1¼ cups store-bought or homemade guacamole (*recipe follows*)
⅓ cup *crema* (Mexican cultured cream; see *Quick Tip, far right*) or sour cream
1 cup crumbled *cotija* cheese (also called *queso añejo*; see *Quick Tip, far right*) or shredded jack cheese
½ cup chopped cilantro
1⅔ cups Classic Salsa Fresca (*recipe follows)* or store-bought red salsa, divided

1. Wipe chiles clean with a damp cloth and remove stems and seeds. Chop in a blender until finely ground. Add tequila, lemon juice, ¼ cup water, garlic, oil, oregano, and ¾ tsp. salt; blend until smooth.
2. Cut pork across grain into slices ½ in. thick and 3 to 4 in. long. In a bowl, add meat to marinade. Chill at least 15 minutes and up to 24 hours.
3. Lift meat from marinade and thread strips onto skewers. Lay skewers parallel and about 2 in. apart on a baking sheet. Pat marinade onto meat.
4. Prepare a charcoal or gas grill for direct medium-high heat (*see Direct Heat Grilling, page 436*). Lay skewered meat on oiled cooking grate (close lid on gas grill). Cook, turning often, until meat is well browned and crusty, about 20 minutes.
5. Meanwhile, in a 1½- to 2-qt. pan over high heat, bring ¾ cup water, the rice, tomato sauce, and remaining ¼ tsp. salt to a boil. Reduce heat and simmer, covered, until liquid is absorbed, 15 to 20 minutes.

6. About 5 minutes before meat is done, put beans and their liquid in a 1-qt. pan and cook over medium-high heat until bubbling, about 5 minutes.

7. Lift cooked meat to a platter and cover with foil. Heat 1 or 2 tortillas at a time on grill until lightly browned but still soft, turning once, 30 to 40 seconds. Stack on platter beneath foil to keep warm.

8. Preheat oven to 200°. Warm serving plates in oven. Remove meat from skewers to a board and cut into ¼-in.-wide strips. Lay tortillas flat. Toward one side of each, fill with guacamole, crema, pork, beans (including most of liquid), rice, cheese, and cilantro; divide 1 cup salsa among burritos. Fold over sides and roll up tightly to enclose. Work quickly during assembly to keep burritos hot, and serve on warm plates; if burritos cool off, you can wrap each one in lightly oiled foil and heat in a 350° oven for 10 to 20 minutes. Serve remaining salsa in a bowl to add to taste.

Quick Tip: Buy ancho chiles, *crema*, and *cotija* cheese at a Mexican market or other specialty-foods store.

PER LARGE BURRITO: 930 cal., 41% (378 cal.) from fat; 45 g protein; 42 g fat (9.9 g sat.); 81 g carbo; 1,250 mg sodium; 114 mg chol.

Guacamole: Pit and peel 2 firm-ripe **avocados** (1 lb. total). In a bowl, coarsely mash avocados with a fork or pastry blender. Stir in 1½ tbsp. fresh **lime juice**, 1 tbsp. chopped **cilantro**, and ½ tsp. **ground cumin**. Add **garlic salt** to taste. Makes about 1¼ cups.

PER TBSP.: 27 cal., 85% (23 cal.) from fat; 0.3 g protein; 2.6 g fat (0.4 g sat.); 1.3 g carbo; 1.9 mg sodium; 0 mg chol.

Classic Salsa Fresca: In a bowl, combine 1½ cups chopped ripe **tomatoes**, ¼ cup sliced **green onions**, 1½ to 2 tbsp. minced **jalapeño chile**, and 1 tsp. fresh **lemon juice**. Season to taste with **salt**. Makes 1⅔ cups.

PER TBSP.: 2.7 cal., 0% from fat; 0.1 g protein; 0 g fat; 0.6 g carbo; 1.1 mg sodium; 0 mg chol.

Tortillas: Bread of the West

These humble flatbreads have a long history in the West, especially those made of corn—which makes sense, given that corn has been cultivated in the New World for at least 5,000 years. Native Americans had been making them for centuries by the time the Spanish arrived, bringing wheat. By the mid-1800s, wheat-flour tortillas were common around the colonial city of Santa Fe and likely in California too.

Those two types, corn (including blue corn) and flour, continue to be our main tortilla choices today. Sizes range from 2 inches to the thin, 18-inch giants popular in the Mexican state of Sonora. Here are some of the more common sizes and their uses.

Corn Tortillas
These are made of dried corn kernels—usually very starchy flint corn—boiled in water with slaked lime (called *cal* in Mexico) to soften and loosen the hard hulls, or skins, of the kernels. The hulls are removed, and the wet, softened corn is ground into dough (*masa*), patted out into tortillas, and griddle-baked.

2 TO 3 INCHES IN DIAMETER: *Tortillerías* sometimes sell these tiny specimens. They're great fried crisp and topped with shreds of meat, salsa, and Mexican cheese for appetizers.

5 TO 6 INCHES: The standard size. These tend to be thin as well as small, so two are usually stacked together, often as wrappers for soft tacos.

7 TO 8 INCHES: A bit thicker, these wrap nicely around fillings to make enchiladas. Folded in half or torn into large pieces, they make good scoops for posole and any number of stews. They're also often fried to make hard-shelled tacos or tostadas.

GORDITAS: These ¼-inch-thick tortilla-like creations are made with masa, lard, and/or mashed potatoes. They're often fried till crisp-edged, then split and stuffed with pork or other fillings.

Flour Tortillas
Unlike corn tortillas, flour tortillas contain fat (usually lard or vegetable shortening), so they're more pliable.

7 TO 8 INCHES: This size is ideal for folding around fajita fillings and enjoying warm alongside *chile colorado* or other stews. They're also used for soft tacos.

10 INCHES: Standard size for burritos.

11 TO 13 INCHES: These super-size tortillas are big enough to wrap around a hefty portion of fillings to create a true handheld meal.

Fresh Is Best
Regardless of size or grain type, a tortilla is best when it's very fresh—as in, made that day—while it's still soft and tastes faintly sweet, like grains. If tortillas have never made you sit up and take notice, it's worth seeking out ones that do—at a *tortillería* or a grocery store that sells fresh ones made without preservatives.

Yucatecan Tostadas (Salbutes)

Salbutes—crisp little handheld tortillas topped with shredded turkey, avocado, pickled onions, and cabbage or lettuce—are a popular street food in the Yucatán region of Mexico. Serve them for lunch or as a palate-refreshing snack after Thanksgiving. The sauce is quite hot, so use it sparingly. (If you love heat, use 1 habanero chile, as is done in the Yucatán, instead of the 2 serranos; you can also leave the seeds and ribs in the serranos to amp up the heat.)

MAKES 8 tostadas; 4 servings | **TIME** 45 minutes

1 red onion, halved and thinly sliced
1 cup distilled white vinegar
1 tsp. salt, divided
¼ tsp. freshly ground black pepper
Vegetable oil for frying
8 corn tortillas (4 in. wide; *see Quick Tips, above right*)
3 tbsp. olive oil
1 medium white or yellow onion, halved and thinly
   sliced
½ tsp. dried oregano, preferably Mexican *(see Quick Tips, above right)*
2 cups shredded cooked turkey
1 cup chicken broth
2 serrano chiles, seeds and ribs removed and minced
2 tbsp. fresh lime juice
1 tbsp. orange juice
1 firm-ripe avocado, pitted, peeled, and sliced
About 1½ cups shredded green and/or red cabbage

1. In a small pan over high heat, cover red onion with cold water and bring to a boil. Remove from heat and drain. Put red onion in a small bowl with vinegar, ½ tsp. salt, and the pepper. Set aside to marinate at least 30 minutes at room temperature.
2. To a small frying pan over high heat, add 1 in. of vegetable oil and heat to 375°. Fry 1 tortilla at a time until golden and crispy. Drain on paper towels.
3. Heat olive oil in a large frying pan over high heat. Add sliced white or yellow onion and ¼ tsp. salt. Cook, stirring, until onion is soft, about 4 minutes. Add oregano and cook until fragrant, about 1 minute. Add turkey and broth. Bring to a boil, lower heat to a steady simmer, and cook, partially covered, for 10 minutes to let flavors blend.
4. Meanwhile, in a small bowl, combine chiles, lime juice, orange juice, and remaining ¼ tsp. salt. Set aside.
5. To assemble, divide turkey-onion mixture among tortillas, then top each with avocado, cabbage, and drained pickled red onion (you will have extra onion; *see Quick Tips, above right*). Serve with serrano-citrus sauce.

Quick Tips: You can substitute larger tortillas if that's all you can find, but the *salbutes* will be harder to pick up and eat. Mexican oregano is stronger and more aromatic than the more widely available Italian or Greek oregano; look for it at Mexican markets and well-stocked grocery stores. Use leftover pickled red onion on sandwiches or salads.
Make Ahead: Through step 1, up to 1 week, covered and chilled.

PER 2-TOSTADA SERVING: 530 cal., 54% (288 cal.) from fat; 27 g protein; 32 g fat (5 g sat.); 38 g carbo (5.6 g fiber); 470 mg sodium; 54 mg chol.

Crisp Chicken Tacos (Tacos de Pollo)

No need to use stale store-bought shells to make these crispy tacos from Thomas Schnetz, cookbook author and chef-owner of the Oakland, California, restaurant Doña Tomás. His easy method turns fresh corn tortillas into crunchy pockets filled with a simple, savory filling. You'll need 16 wooden toothpicks.

MAKES 16 tacos; 8 servings | **TIME** 1 hour

3 cups packed shredded cooked chicken meat (*see Quick Tip, above right*)
2 cups shredded (½ lb.) jack cheese
Kosher salt
About 2 cups vegetable oil, divided
16 corn tortillas (5 to 6 in. wide)
1 cup coarsely chopped cilantro
Tomato-Cucumber Salsa *(recipe follows)*

1. In a bowl, mix chicken with jack cheese and season to taste with salt.
2. Pour 3 tbsp. oil into a medium frying pan over high heat. When hot, add 1 tortilla at a time, heating just enough to soften but not crisp, about 10 seconds per side. As heated, stack on paper towels, cover with a kitchen towel, and keep warm in oven. Add more oil to pan as needed.
3. Mix cilantro with chicken filling. Working with 1 tortilla at a time, distribute about ¼ cup packed chicken filling down the center. Fold tortilla in half over filling and thread 1 toothpick through top edges to seal.
4. Preheat oven to 200°. Pour at least ½ in. oil into same pan and set on high heat. When hot, add 4 to 6 tacos (depending on pan size; do not overcrowd). Tacos should sizzle when they hit oil. Cook, turning as needed, until shells are crisp and golden brown, 1 to 2 minutes per side. Lift tacos from pan with a slotted spoon, draining oil back into pan. Lay tacos in a single layer on a baking sheet lined with paper towels and keep warm

sandwiches, burritos & pizza

in oven. Fry remaining tacos in the same way, adding more oil as needed. When all tacos are cooked, pull out and discard toothpicks. Serve with tomato-cucumber salsa on the side.

Quick Tip: A typical rotisserie chicken yields just enough meat for this recipe.

Make Ahead: Through step 3, up to 4 hours, chilled. Fry just before serving, or fry up to 6 hours ahead and recrisp in a 300° oven for 15 minutes before serving.

PER TACO: 238 cal., 53% (126 cal.) from fat; 14 g protein; 14 g fat (4.1 g sat.); 14 g carbo (1.7 g fiber); 147 mg sodium; 43 mg chol.

Tomato-Cucumber Salsa

MAKES 4 cups | **TIME** 25 minutes

2 lbs. ripe tomatoes
½ cup chopped white onion
1 tbsp. chopped garlic
2 serrano chiles, seeds and ribs removed and chopped (see *Quick Tip below*)
3 tbsp. red wine vinegar
2 cups diced peeled English cucumber
Kosher salt

1. Immerse tomatoes in boiling water to cover for 5 seconds (if ripe) to 15 seconds (if firm). Lift out and drain. Core tomatoes and pull off skin; discard cores and skins. Halve tomatoes crosswise; squeeze out juice and seeds and discard.
2. In a food processor, combine seeded tomatoes, onion, garlic, chiles, and vinegar. Pulse until finely chopped. Transfer to a bowl.
3. In processor, pulse cucumber until coarsely chopped. Add to tomato mixture and season with salt to taste.

Quick Tip: Serrano chiles can be very hot, so add to taste.

Make Ahead: Up to 3 days, chilled.

PER TBSP.: 4.2 cal., 0% from fat; 0.1 g protein; 0 g fat; 0.9 g carbo (0.2 g fiber); 1.5 mg sodium; 0 mg chol.

■ Chile or Chili?

Chiles (with an "e") are a single variety of hot pepper—fresh or dried—and nothing else. Most chili (with an "i") powders and flakes are a blend of spices, including ancho chiles (dried poblanos), cumin, garlic, and oregano. Tex-Mex dishes use chili powder; true Mexican and New Mexican dishes use chile powder or flakes for pure flavor with mild heat. (Chili also refers, of course, to the meat-and-beans stew.)

Garlicky Shrimp-Cilantro Tacos
(*Tacos de Camarones al Mojo de Ajo*)

Sweet onions and shrimp meet the gentle heat of garlic and chiles in these tacos, also from Thomas Schnetz, chef-owner of Oakland's Doña Tomás.

MAKES 16 tacos; 8 servings | **TIME** 35 minutes

¼ cup vegetable oil
1 lb. white onions, thinly sliced
2 or 3 serrano chiles, seeds and ribs removed and thinly sliced (see *Quick Tips below*)
¼ cup butter
3 tbsp. finely chopped garlic
2½ lbs. large shrimp (21 to 30 per lb.), peeled, deveined, and halved lengthwise
1 cup coarsely chopped cilantro
Kosher salt
32 corn tortillas (5 to 6 in. wide), warmed (see *Quick Tips below*)
2 limes, cut into wedges

1. Heat oil in a large frying pan over high heat. Add onions and chiles and cook, stirring frequently, until onions are lightly browned, about 10 minutes. Transfer vegetables to a bowl and set aside.
2. Melt butter in the same frying pan over medium-high heat, add garlic, and stir until sizzling, about 1 minute. Add half the shrimp to pan. Cook, stirring often, until shrimp are bright pink and no longer wet-looking in thickest part (cut to test), about 5 minutes; transfer shrimp to bowl with reserved vegetables. Add remaining shrimp to pan and cook as above, then return cooked shrimp and vegetables to pan and stir everything together until hot, 2 to 3 minutes. Add cilantro and salt to taste.
3. Serve shrimp in a large bowl alongside warm tortillas (use 2 tortillas, stacked, per taco), accompanied by lime wedges to squeeze over the top.

Quick Tips: Serrano chiles can be very hot, so add to taste. To heat tortillas, wrap in a kitchen towel and microwave until warm and soft, about 1 minute.

Make Ahead: Vegetables, up to 2 hours, at room temperature. Reheat before continuing.

PER TACO: 243 cal., 32% (77 cal.) from fat; 15 g protein; 8.5 g fat (2.5 g sat.); 28 g carbo (3.1 g fiber); 197 mg sodium; 95 mg chol.

Baja Fish Tacos

A good fish taco, a cold Corona, and the beach—these equal summer up and down the coast of California.

recipe pictured on page 180

MAKES 6 to 8 tacos | **TIME** 45 minutes

1 cup *each* dark beer and flour
1 tsp. salt
Vegetable oil
1½ lbs. firm, white-fleshed fish fillets such as Pacific cod or tilapia, cut into 1-in.-wide strips
12 to 16 corn tortillas (6 in. wide), warmed (*see Quick Tip, right*)
Cabbage and Cilantro Slaw (*recipe follows*)
Chipotle Tartar Sauce (*recipe follows*)
Lime wedges

1. In a bowl, whisk beer, flour, and salt until well blended.
2. Preheat oven to 200°. Pour about 1 in. of oil into a 10- to 12-in. nonstick frying pan (with sides at least 2 in. high); heat over medium-high heat until oil measures 360° on a deep-fry thermometer. With a fork, dip each piece of fish into beer batter, then lift out and let drain briefly. Slide fish into oil, a few pieces at a time, and cook until golden (adjust heat to maintain 360°), turning if necessary to brown on all sides, 2 to 4 minutes per batch. With a slotted spoon, transfer cooked fish to a paper towel–lined baking sheet. Keep warm in oven while frying remaining fish.
3. To assemble each taco, stack 2 warm tortillas and top with a couple of pieces of fish, then a spoonful of slaw. Serve with tartar sauce on the side to add to taste and lime wedges to squeeze over top.
Quick Tip: To heat tortillas, wrap in a kitchen towel and microwave until warm and soft, about 1 minute.

PER TACO WITHOUT SLAW AND SAUCE: 537 cal., 57% (306 cal.) from fat; 20 g protein; 34 g fat (18 g sat.); 39 g carbo (3.9 g fiber); 573 mg sodium; 53 mg chol.

Cabbage and Cilantro Slaw: In a large bowl, mix 1½ qts. finely shredded **cabbage** (about 10 oz.), ⅓ cup chopped **cilantro**, 3 tbsp. fresh **lime juice**, 2 tbsp. **vegetable oil**, ¼ tsp. **red chile flakes**, and **salt** to taste. Makes 4¼ cups.

Chipotle Tartar Sauce: Rinse 2 tbsp. **canned chipotle chiles** in adobo sauce and discard seeds and veins. In a blender, purée chiles with 1 cup **mayonnaise** and ¼ cup each **sweet pickle relish** and **chopped onion** until smooth. Makes 1⅓ cups.

The Great Fish Taco Migration

The fish taco can be reduced to a very simple equation: Fish + Tortilla = Fish Taco. From this perspective, there is little question that people have been eating fish tacos in the coastal areas of Mexico for a long time. It probably goes back thousands of years to when indigenous North American peoples first wrapped the offshore catch into stone-ground-corn tortillas.

The Baja Connection
More recently, somewhere in Baja California, sometime in the last century, someone concocted what is considered to be the prototypical modern fish taco. This delicacy consists of a lightly battered mild white fish (usually shark) deep-fried until crisp, then served in a corn tortilla (often two) with shredded cabbage, a sauce based on mayonnaise or *crema* (Mexican cultured cream), a bit of salsa, and a spritz of lime. It's different from other types of Mexican tacos—it's actually sort of like tempura—and some speculate that the arrival of Japanese fishermen in Baja in the 1920s may have had a lot to do with the birth of today's fish taco.

Moving North
When did the idea migrate north? The inspiration came in 1974, when Ralph Rubio and some friends from San Diego State went down to San Felipe, in Baja. Rubio was fond of the fresh fish tacos made by a vendor there named Carlos. One night Rubio suggested that Carlos open up a stand in San Diego. Carlos replied that he didn't want to leave Mexico. "I vividly remember the conversation," says Rubio today. "It was late at night, I'm drinking Coronas with my buddies, and the thought hit me: If he doesn't want to open a stand, why don't I just get the recipe?"

Carlos provided Rubio with a recipe, though he didn't specify exact amounts of ingredients. From there, Rubio experimented with various fish, batter mixes, and sauces and, with the backing of his father, opened his first restaurant in 1983 in an old, failed hamburger stand near San Diego's Mission Bay.

By 2010, Rubio's Fresh Mexican Grill was operating, licensing, or franchising more than 190 restaurants in the West. In the '80s, not long after opening his first place, Rubio went back to San Felipe to see the legendary Carlos and give him some money as thanks. But Carlos had moved—some said to the rival fish-taco center of Ensenada. One thing is for sure: his recipe has made untold thousands of taco-eaters happy.

sandwiches, burritos & pizza

Cola Shredded-beef Tacos

Toasting the dried chiles first intensifies their flavor. This recipe is adapted from one in the cookbook *Amor y Tacos*, by San Diego–based chef Deborah Schneider.

MAKES 12 tacos; 6 servings | **TIME** 4¼ hours

3 medium dried ancho chiles *(see Quick Tips, right)*
2 large dried guajillo chiles *(see Quick Tips, right)*
2 tbsp. canola oil, divided
¼ cup finely chopped red onion
2 large garlic cloves, sliced
½ tsp. cumin seeds
1 cup canned diced tomatoes
1 tsp. dried oregano, preferably Mexican *(see Quick Tips)*
2 tsp. kosher salt, divided
2 lbs. chuck roast, fat trimmed and cut into 4 pieces
1 bay leaf
1½ cups Mexican Coca-Cola (cane-sugar sweetened) or another cola (not diet; *see Quick Tips*)
12 or 24 corn tortillas (6 in. wide; use 24 if they're thin and floppy), warmed *(see Quick Tips)*
Chopped avocado, red onion, and cilantro; thinly sliced pickled jalapeños; and *crema* (Mexican cultured cream; *see Quick Tips*) or sour cream

1. Wipe chiles clean with a damp cloth, then stem and seed them and tear into pieces. Heat 1 tbsp. oil in a heavy medium saucepan over medium heat. Add onion and garlic and cook, stirring, until softened, 1 to 2 minutes. Add chiles and cook, stirring, until fragrant, 1 to 2 minutes. Add 1½ cups water, the cumin seeds, tomatoes, oregano, and 1 tsp. salt. Bring to a boil; reduce heat and simmer, covered, until chiles are softened, 10 minutes. Purée in a blender until very smooth.
2. Meanwhile, season beef with remaining 1 tsp. salt. Heat remaining 1 tbsp. oil in a 5- to 6-qt. pot over medium-high heat. Brown beef all over, turning occasionally, 10 to 14 minutes (you may need to do this in batches). Discard fat, if any.
3. Pour chile sauce into pot and add bay leaf, cola, and a little water if needed to barely cover meat. Cover, reduce heat, and simmer until beef is very tender, about 3 hours.
4. With a slotted spoon, transfer beef to a plate. Let cool slightly, then tear into shreds, discarding any fat or gristle. Meanwhile, boil sauce over medium-high heat, stirring occasionally, until slightly thickened and reduced to about 3 cups, 10 to 30 minutes. Stir in beef and heat a few minutes until hot. Remove bay leaf.
5. With a slotted spoon, transfer beef with some sauce to a bowl. Spoon beef into tortillas (double tortillas if they're thin), tuck in accompaniments, and serve with remaining sauce if you like.

Quick Tips: You can find the dried chiles, Mexican Coca-Cola, *crema*, and Mexican oregano at a Latino market. To heat tortillas, wrap in a kitchen towel and microwave until warm and soft, about 1 minute.
Make Ahead: Through step 3, up to 2 days, chilled. Reheat before proceeding.

PER 2-TACO SERVING: 587 cal., 54% (315 cal.) from fat; 32 g protein; 35 g fat (11 g sat.); 40 g carbo (6.5 g fiber); 607 mg sodium; 107 mg chol.

Chicken *Tinga* Quesadillas

Tinga is a classic slow-braised meat dish that Vicky Rangel, of Mountain View, California, remembers from her childhood in Michoacán, Mexico. She developed a quicker version, used here in quesadillas.

MAKES 4 quesadillas | **TIME** 1 hour

¼ lb. Mexican chorizo sausage, casing removed and crumbled
1 onion (10 oz.), thinly sliced
1 or 2 canned chipotle chiles in adobo sauce
1½ cups shredded cooked chicken
1 can (8 oz.) tomato sauce
Salt
4 flour tortillas (8 in. wide)
1 tbsp. corn or canola oil
1 cup shredded jack cheese (¼ lb.)
¼ cup chopped cilantro
Red or green salsa

1. Preheat oven to 450°. In a 10- to 12-in. frying pan over medium-high heat, combine chorizo, onion, and 3 tbsp. water. Cover and cook 5 minutes, stirring occasionally. Uncover and stir over high heat until onion begins to brown, 3 to 5 minutes longer.
2. Finely chop chiles. (Scrape out chile seeds first if you want less heat.) Add chiles, chicken, and tomato sauce to onion mixture. Stir over medium heat until simmering, about 2 minutes. Add salt to taste. Spoon into a bowl.
3. Lay tortillas on a work surface and brush one side of each tortilla lightly with oil; turn tortillas oiled side down. Sprinkle half of each tortilla with a quarter each of the jack cheese, chicken mixture, and cilantro. Fold each tortilla over filling.
4. Lay folded tortillas, slightly separated, on a 12- by 15-in. baking sheet. Bake until browned, 7 to 9 minutes. Transfer quesadillas to plates. If desired, cut in half. Top with red or green salsa to taste.

PER QUESADILLA: 528 cal., 46% (245 cal.) from fat; 35 g protein; 27 g fat (11 g sat.); 34 g carbo (3.5 g fiber); 1,171 mg sodium; 95 mg chol.

Shortcut Barbecued Chicken Pizza

Reader Meredith McGowan of Valencia, California, likes devising original combinations to top her family's favorite dish—pizza. McGowan makes dough from scratch, but prebaked pizza crusts, available in many supermarkets, are an easy time-saver.

MAKES 2 pizzas (8 in. each); 4 servings
TIME 45 minutes to 1 hour

1 lb. boned, skinned chicken breasts
⅓ cup store-bought or homemade barbecue sauce (for a recipe, *see Chipotle Barbecue Sauce, page 466*), divided
Salt and freshly ground black pepper
4 slices bacon, cut into 1-in. pieces
2 baked pizza crusts (7 to 8 in., 5 oz. each)
¼ cup cream cheese
¼ cup canned diced green chiles, drained
½ cup shredded jack cheese
¼ to ½ tsp. red chile flakes

1. Preheat oven to 350°. Put chicken in an 8-in. square baking pan and coat with about 2 tbsp. barbecue sauce. Sprinkle with salt and pepper to taste. Bake until no longer pink at center of thickest part (cut to test), about 20 minutes. Remove chicken from oven and increase temperature to 400°. Let chicken stand until cool enough to handle.
2. Meanwhile, in a 10- to 12-in. frying pan over high heat, cook bacon, stirring often, until browned and crisp, about 5 minutes. With a slotted spoon, transfer to paper towels to drain.
3. Tear cooled chicken into bite-size chunks. In a small bowl, mix with remaining 3 tbsp. plus 1 tsp. barbecue sauce.
4. Put pizza crusts on a 12- by 15-in. baking sheet. Spread each with half the cream cheese. Spoon chicken in sauce evenly over both crusts; top with bacon, green chiles, jack cheese, and chile flakes.
5. Bake pizzas until cheese is browned and bubbling, 15 to 20 minutes. Transfer to a board and cut into wedges.

PER SERVING (½ PIZZA): 561 cal., 31% (176 cal.) from fat; 49 g protein; 20 g fat (8.2 g sat.); 44 g carbo (2.1 g fiber); 1,044 mg sodium; 132 mg chol.

Delfina's Pizza Dough

From Pizzeria Delfina in San Francisco comes the best homemade pizza dough we've ever tried—smooth, supple, and easy to work with. You can use regular flour, but for a truly awesome, springy-yet-crunchy crust, go for high-gluten Italian "00" (finely milled) flour. Use this dough for Delfina's Broccoli Rabe Pizza (*recipe follows*) or Delfina's Carbonara Pizzas (*page 200*) or any other thin-crust pizza.

MAKES Enough dough for 6 pizzas (12 in. each)
TIME 2 hours, plus 4 hours to rise

1 tsp. (slightly rounded) fresh yeast
1½ tsp. extra-virgin olive oil
1 lb., 14 oz. (about 6 cups) "00" flour, preferably Caputo (*see Quick Tips below*), or all-purpose flour
1½ tbsp. kosher salt (*see Quick Tips below*)

1. Put yeast, oil, and 2 cups plus 1 tbsp. cold water in the bowl of a stand mixer; mix, using dough hook, on lowest speed until yeast has completely dissolved, about 5 minutes. Add flour and mix another 8 minutes. If you must mix by hand, stir ingredients together with a wooden spoon until blended; then turn dough out onto a lightly floured work surface and knead until smooth and stretchy, at least 15 minutes.
2. Cover bowl or dough loosely with a dampened kitchen towel and let dough rise 20 minutes in a warm (about 80°) place.
3. Add salt and mix on low speed until incorporated and dissolved, about 7 minutes; or, if mixing by hand, sprinkle dough with salt and knead 10 minutes.
4. Turn dough onto a lightly floured work surface and cut into six equal portions. Roll each into a tight ball. Set on a lightly floured baking sheet.
5. Cover tightly with plastic wrap and let rise at least 4 hours at warm room temperature. Dough balls have risen properly when they are soft, pillowy, and full of air.
Quick Tips: Find "00" flour in well-stocked supermarkets and Italian markets. For best results, measure flour by weight rather than volume. Though 1½ tbsp. may seem like a lot of salt, the dough won't taste too salty as long as you use coarse-grained kosher salt, not fine-grained table salt.
Make Ahead: Dough can be formed into balls and set on a lightly floured baking sheet (step 4), then tightly covered with plastic wrap and chilled overnight (dough will rise slowly in the refrigerator). After dough balls have risen, you can freeze them for up to 2 weeks. Let chilled or frozen dough come to room temperature before proceeding.

sandwiches, burritos & pizza

Delfina's Broccoli Rabe Pizza

Fresh mozzarella, salty caciocavallo cheese straight from Campania, and peppery broccoli rabe make this one of our favorite pizzas. *Pizzaiolo* Anthony Strong drizzles on a bit of cream before shoving the pizza in the oven, to keep the cheese from burning.

recipe
pictured
on page
184

MAKES 3 pizzas (12 in. each); 24 slices | **TIME** 1 hour

10 oz. fresh mozzarella cheese packed in liquid
⅓ cup liquid from mozzarella container
¼ cup packed coarsely shredded caciocavallo or parmesan cheese
¼ cup *each* heavy whipping cream and buttermilk
½ tsp. kosher salt, divided
1 lb. (about 1 large bunch) broccoli rabe (rapini)
2 garlic cloves, well smashed
¼ cup olive oil, plus more for drizzling over pizza
About ¼ tsp. red chile flakes, divided
Freshly ground black pepper
3 balls room-temperature Delfina's Pizza Dough (*see preceding recipe*)
⅓ cup black olives (oil-cured or Gaeta, soaked in water and drained if very salty), pitted and torn in half

1. Heat a pizza stone or baking sheet on lowest rack of oven at 550° (or as high as oven will go) for at least 30 minutes. With flat side of a chef's knife, mash a third of the mozzarella into a pulverized mass. Dice remaining mozzarella into ½-in. cubes. In a medium bowl, mix both mozzarellas with mozzarella liquid, caciocavallo, cream, and buttermilk. Season with ¼ tsp. salt.
2. Cut broccoli rabe into 1-in. sections, discarding tough lower stems.
3. In a large frying pan over very low heat, cook garlic in oil, stirring often, until it starts to turn transparent, about 5 minutes. Add ¼ tsp. chile flakes and toast for a second, then add broccoli rabe. Stir in remaining ¼ tsp. salt and several grinds of pepper.
4. Increase heat to medium-high and cook broccoli rabe, stirring, until liquid starts to evaporate and broccoli rabe is tender-crisp, 5 to 7 minutes (don't cook it into mush). If liquid is gone and broccoli rabe is still too crunchy, add ¼ cup water and cook until tender-crisp, repeating if necessary.
5. Working with one ball of dough at a time (keep remaining balls tightly covered), set dough on a well-floured pizza peel or rimless baking sheet and stretch it into a 12-in. circle (*see How to Stretch Pizza Dough, page 200*). Flop stretched-out dough onto peel.
6. Spread about ⅔ cup cheese mixture over dough. Top with ½ cup broccoli rabe, a generous pinch of chile

flakes, and 2 tbsp. olives. Give peel a good shake every few seconds to keep dough from sticking.
7. Plant tip of pizza peel (or long edge of baking sheet) on pizza stone and shove pizza quickly onto it. Bake until pizza is puffy and browned, 5 to 6 minutes. Drizzle with oil.
8. Repeat with remaining two dough balls and topping.
Make Ahead: Cheese mixture and broccoli rabe topping, up to 1 day, chilled.

PER SLICE (⅛ PIZZA): 157 cal., 43% (68 cal.) from fat; 5.5 g protein; 7.5 g fat (3 g sat.); 15 g carbo (0.5 g fiber); 540 mg sodium; 17 mg chol.

3 Ways with Store-bought Pizza Dough

You can buy refrigerated pizza dough in almost any supermarket. Bring the dough to room temperature, stretch it (*see How to Stretch Pizza Dough, page 200*), then try one of our quick and easy flavor combinations. Set a pizza stone or baking sheet on the lowest rack of the oven and preheat the oven as high as it will go (at least 450°). Slide your pizza right onto the stone or baking sheet and take it out when it's blistered and golden—anywhere from 5 to 15 minutes.

1. Enchilada Pizza
Spread **red enchilada sauce** over the stretched-out pizza dough, leaving a ½-in. border. Top sauce with drained canned **black beans**, chopped **jalapeño chile**, chopped **green onions**, shredded **jack cheese**, and crumbled *queso fresco*. Bake until bubbly and golden, then sprinkle with chopped **cilantro**.

2. Manchego and Artichoke Pizza
Top the stretched-out pizza dough with shredded **manchego cheese**, drained and thinly sliced jarred **artichoke hearts**, quartered pitted **kalamata olives**, slivered **red onions**, seeded and sliced **pepperoncini**, more manchego, and **freshly ground black pepper**, leaving a ½-in. border of dough around pizza. Bake until crust is golden and cheese melts.

3. Tomato, Mint, and Feta Pizza
Brush the stretched-out pizza dough generously with **olive oil**. Bake 5 minutes. Leaving a ½-in. border, scatter dough with thinly sliced, seeded **Roma tomatoes**; minced **oregano** and **mint leaves**; minced **garlic**; finely shredded **lemon zest**; and crumbled **feta cheese**. Drizzle with olive oil and bake until crust is golden. Drizzle with more olive oil.

How to Stretch Pizza Dough

Using a rolling pin to stretch dough will ruin the rim and flatten the air bubbles that give the crust its rise. Anthony Strong, of San Francisco's Pizzeria Delfina, showed us how to stretch dough by hand. Remember to start with dough at room temperature.

1. Tap down the center of the dough ball with your fingertips to gently deflate it. Next, push dough outward from the center with your fingertips.

2. Pick up the dough circle. With your fingers under the rim, turn it like a steering wheel.

3. Drape the dough over the backs of your hands and gently stretch outward.

Delfina's Carbonara Pizza

We like to eat this pizza for breakfast too. To keep the egg from getting overcooked, crack it on just before the pie is done.

MAKES 3 pizzas (12 in. each); 24 slices | **TIME** 1 hour

8 or 9 green onions
9 oz. guanciale (cured pork cheek) or pancetta, coarsely chopped
3 balls room-temperature Delfina's Pizza Dough *(page 198)*
1½ cups coarsely shredded pecorino romano
Freshly ground black pepper
9 tbsp. heavy whipping cream
3 eggs

1. Heat a pizza stone or baking sheet on lowest rack of oven at 550° (or as high as oven will go) for at least 30 minutes.
2. Cut green onions into long slivers, soak in cold water for 20 minutes, and drain in a colander. Set aside.

3. Meanwhile, bring a small pot of water to a boil, add guanciale or pancetta, and boil until softened, about 5 minutes. Drain and set aside.
4. Working with one ball of dough at a time (keep remaining balls tightly covered), set dough on a well-floured pizza peel or rimless baking sheet and stretch it into a 12-in. circle *(see How to Stretch Pizza Dough, above)*. Flop stretched-out dough onto the peel.
5. Spread about ½ cup pecorino romano over dough. Top with a third of green onions, then a third of guanciale. Grind on some pepper and drizzle with 3 tbsp. cream. Give peel a good shake every few seconds to keep dough from sticking.
6. Plant tip of pizza peel (or long edge of baking sheet) on pizza stone and shove pizza quickly onto it. Bake 2 minutes, then remove pizza from oven with peel or baking sheet, crack an egg into the center, return pizza to oven, and bake 3 minutes more. Just before serving, drag a knife through the egg to spread it around.
7. Repeat with remaining dough balls and topping.

PER SLICE (⅛ PIZZA): 160 cal., 46% (74 cal.) from fat; 6.5 g protein; 8.2 g fat (4 g sat.); 14 g carbo (0.6 g fiber); 680 mg sodium; 48 mg chol.

sandwiches, burritos & pizza

Pizzetta 211 Margherita Pepperoni Pizza

Instead of basil leaves on its margherita, Pizzetta 211 in San Francisco uses a pesto-like basil oil—and adds excellent pepperoni if you ask. The extended mixing time for the dough develops the gluten in the flour and produces a pizza crust with a nice stretchy rim.

MAKES 4 pizzas (10 to 11 in. each); 32 slices
TIME 2¾ hours

2 tsp. active dry yeast
2½ cups flour, divided, plus more for sprinkling
About 2 tsp. sea salt
About 7 tbsp. extra-virgin olive oil, divided
2 garlic cloves, thinly sliced
1 can (14.5 oz.) crushed or diced tomatoes, preferably organic, whizzed briefly in a food processor to a chunky purée
1 cup loosely packed basil leaves
⅔ lb. fresh mozzarella cheese, preferably *fior di latte*, cut into ½-in. cubes (about 2 cups)
About 1 tsp. dried oregano
8 or 9 slices spicy salami (about ¼ lb.)

1. In a medium bowl, whisk together 1 cup room-temperature water and the yeast. Let stand 15 minutes at room temperature.
2. In bowl of a stand mixer, using a dough hook, mix 2 cups flour, 2 tsp. salt, 1 tbsp. oil, and the yeast mixture on medium speed until well incorporated, scraping down sides of bowl as needed. Add remaining ½ cup flour and mix until dough is very smooth and elastic, about 30 minutes. If you must mix by hand, stir dough ingredients together with a wooden spoon until blended; then turn out onto a floured work surface and knead until very smooth and elastic, at least 40 minutes.
3. Meanwhile, make tomato sauce: In a medium pot, heat 2 tbsp. oil over medium heat until hot but not smoking. Add garlic and swirl in hot oil until it starts to smell good, about 15 seconds. Stir in puréed tomatoes and simmer, uncovered, to thicken and cook off "canned" flavors, at least 25 minutes. Set aside.
4. While sauce is cooking, put remaining ¼ cup oil and the basil in a food processor and whirl to finely chop basil, scraping down sides of bowl as needed. Stir 1 tbsp. basil oil into tomato sauce as it's cooking, along with a pinch of salt. Pour remaining basil oil into a small bowl and cover surface with a thin layer of olive oil to preserve the color.
5. Divide kneaded dough into four portions. Roll each portion into a tight ball. Dust each with flour, set it on a floured baking sheet, and cover loosely with plastic wrap.

Let dough rise in a warm (about 80°) place until almost doubled in size (do not let rise longer than 1 hour).
6. Put a pizza stone or baking sheet on bottom rack of oven and preheat to 550° (or as high as oven will go) for at least 30 minutes.
7. Working with one ball of dough at a time (keep remaining balls tightly covered), set dough on a well-floured pizza peel or rimless baking sheet and stretch it into a 10- to 11-in. circle (*see How to Stretch Pizza Dough, page 200*). Flop stretched-out dough onto the peel.
8. Spoon 3 to 4 tbsp. tomato sauce onto dough, leaving at least a ½-in. border around pizza.
9. Plant tip of pizza peel (or long edge of baking sheet) on pizza stone and shove pizza quickly onto it. Bake until crust looks dryish but not browned, 3 to 6 minutes. Remove pizza from oven and sprinkle on about ½ cup mozzarella cubes in clusters, then a generous pinch of oregano, then a quarter of salami. Return to oven and cook until crust is golden brown and firm but not rock hard, 2 to 5 minutes more. Transfer pizza to a cutting board and drizzle with basil oil.
10. Make and bake the rest of the pizzas the same way.
Make Ahead: Dough can be formed into balls, set on a lightly floured baking sheet, and tightly covered with plastic wrap (step 5), then chilled overnight (dough will rise slowly in the refrigerator). After dough balls have risen, you can freeze them for up to 2 weeks. Let chilled or frozen dough come to room temperature before proceeding.

PER SLICE (⅛ PIZZA): 107 cal., 49% (52 cal.) from fat; 3.7 g protein; 5.9 g fat (2.1 g sat.); 8.6 g carbo (0.6 g fiber); 280 mg sodium; 125 mg chol.

Two Pizza Tools That Really Matter

A PIZZA STONE, available at cookware shops, creates the super-heated surface you need for a genuinely great crust. As soon as the pizza hits the stone, it will start to puff up. You can get decent results, though, by using a preheated baking sheet instead. (Don't use soap when cleaning a stone—it will sink into the stone's pores and flavor the next pizza.)

A PIZZA PEEL, also available at cookware shops, provides a nice smooth surface on which to shape the crust. Flour it well, and don't wash it afterward; just brush off the excess. The flour that remains fills in the wood's pores and gives the peel a more nonstick quality. The beveled edge helps you smoothly slide the dough onto the pizza stone or baking sheet, and its long handle protects your forearms from getting too close to the heat of the oven.

Emilia's Sausage, Mushroom, and Red Pepper Pizza

Keith Freilich, owner and operator of Emilia's in Berkeley, California, roasts his own peppers for this pizza, but you can use jarred if you're short on time. The dough rises just fine overnight in the fridge, so you can divide the pizza-making process over 2 days if you like.

MAKES 2 pizzas (12 in. each) | **TIME** 2½ hours, plus 6 to 8 hours for dough to rise

¼ cake fresh yeast *(see Quick Tip, below right)*

2½ cups unbleached flour, divided

1 tsp. fine sea salt, divided

2 tbsp. plus 2 tsp. extra-virgin olive oil, plus more for drizzling (optional)

1 lb. cremini mushrooms, sliced

2 minced garlic cloves, plus 1 whole clove

3 roasted red bell peppers, roasted in oven or grilled *(see Roasted Red Peppers with Garlic and Olive Oil, page 245)* or store-bought jarred (drain and rinse if jarred)

1 cup good-quality canned plum tomatoes

Leaves of 2 or 3 marjoram sprigs, minced

¼ lb. fresh mozzarella cheese packed in liquid, cut into ½-in. cubes

¼ lb. low-moisture mozzarella cheese, coarsely shredded

½ lb. Italian sausages, casings removed and formed into ½-in. balls

Freshly ground black pepper

Finely shredded parmigiano-reggiano

10 to 12 basil leaves, torn into pieces

1. On morning of the day you wish to make pizza for dinner, create a sponge: In bowl of a stand mixer, dissolve yeast in 1 cup minus 1 tbsp. cold water, then mix in 1½ cups flour. Cover and set aside at room temperature for 3 to 4 hours.

2. In the afternoon, mix ½ tsp. salt into sponge, then remaining 1 cup flour. Attach dough hook and knead 25 to 30 minutes. Let dough rest, covered, 30 minutes. If you must mix by hand, stir ingredients together with a wooden spoon until blended; then turn out onto a floured work surface and knead until smooth and stretchy, at least 35 minutes.

3. Divide dough in half and form into two balls. Set balls on a smooth, clean surface and cover each with an inverted bowl at least 10 in. in diameter. Let rise in a warm (about 80°) place until puffed up and about twice their original size, 3 to 4 hours.

4. In a large nonstick frying pan, heat 2 tbsp. oil over medium heat. Add mushrooms and ¼ tsp. salt and cook, stirring, until their liquid has almost completely evaporated. Stir in minced garlic, cook 1 minute, and remove from heat.

5. Remove stems, ribs, seeds and skins from peppers and cut flesh into ¼-in. strips.

6. Mince remaining garlic clove, then mash with flat side of a chef's knife into a paste. Pulp tomatoes with a food mill or a food processor (use shredder blade) and transfer to a bowl. Stir in remaining ¼ tsp. salt, the garlic paste, remaining 2 tsp. oil, and the marjoram.

7. Set a baking stone on lowest rack of oven and preheat to 550° (or as high as oven will go) for at least 30 minutes.

8. Working with one ball of dough at a time (keep remaining ball tightly covered), set dough on a well-floured pizza peel or rimless baking sheet and stretch it into a 12-in. circle *(see How to Stretch Pizza Dough, page 200)*. Flop stretched-out dough onto the peel.

9. Prick center of dough quickly with a fork and slide onto pizza stone in a smooth, fluid motion. Bake 2 minutes, then pull out with pizza peel.

10. Add toppings quickly, so dough doesn't stick to peel. (As you work, slide dough back and forth every minute or so with a quick jerk of peel to help keep it from sticking; if it does, lift dough and sprinkle more flour underneath, then jerk again.) First, sprinkle half of each kind of mozzarella onto pizza. Then release your inner Jackson Pollock, spooning on half the sauce with a flicking motion. Add half the roasted peppers, mushrooms, and sausage. Grind on black pepper to taste.

11. Slide pizza back onto the stone and bake until crust is puffy and golden, 8 to 10 minutes. Take it out with the peel, sprinkle on some parmigiano-reggiano, and scatter some torn basil leaves over top. Drizzle with additional oil if using and dig in.

12. Repeat with remaining dough, sauce, and toppings.

Quick Tip: Find fresh yeast in the supermarket's refrigerator section next to the cheeses and butter.

Make Ahead: Dough can be formed into balls (step 3), tightly covered with plastic wrap, and chilled overnight (dough will rise slowly in the refrigerator). After dough balls have risen, you can freeze them for up to 2 weeks. Let chilled or frozen dough come to room temperature before proceeding.

PER SLICE (⅛ PIZZA): 209 cal., 44% (92 cal.) from fat; 9 g protein; 10 g fat (4 g sat.); 20 g carbo (1.4 g fiber); 339 mg sodium; 24 mg chol.

The California Pizza Phenomenon

Up until the 1980s, Americans had three main styles of pizza: New York (big and cheesy, with large, foldable slices), New Haven (thin-crusted, from a coal- or wood-fired brick oven), and Chicago (deep dish). Toppings consisted mainly of tomato, cheeses, and herbs, plus white clams in the New Haven version. Then a wave of wild new pizza rose up in California and was surfed across the country.

It began, as most great pizza does, with the oven. Tommaso's, a venerable Italian restaurant in San Francisco's North Beach neighborhood, had installed the West Coast's first wood-burning brick pizza oven when it opened in 1935. That oven—and travels to Italy—inspired Alice Waters, in 1980, to showcase a pizza oven in her brand-new Café at Chez Panisse, above her main restaurant in Berkeley. The inventive cooks there began to use toppings never seen before on pizza, like goat cheese and duck sausage, drawing on the flavors of France as well as Italy. The Panisse pizzas were an instant sensation.

California Pizza Goes Mainstream

Around the same time, a cook named Ed LaDou at San Francisco's Prego Ristorante was fooling around with unusual toppings (interviews with LaDou suggest he was a bit of a rebel, and had been playing with pizza for years at other places too). One night, LaDou sent out an off-the-menu combo of mustard, ricotta, pâté, and red pepper to a customer who was none other than chef Wolfgang Puck. Lucky LaDou: When Puck opened Spago in Hollywood in 1982, modeling it after the Café at Chez Panisse, LaDou was on board as the head pizza chef.

At Spago, LaDou and Puck took pizza to another dimension, topping it with everything from smoked salmon with crème fraîche, capers, and dill (the famous "Jewish pizza") to barbecued chicken. Three years later, LaDou helped launch California Pizza Kitchen, bringing with him 250 recipes. CPK's meteoric success—it now has restaurants in more than 30 states and 10 foreign countries—took California pizza into the mainstream, as did Puck's launch of his own frozen pizza line.

Today, California pizza has an anything-goes connotation, its toppings ranging from full-meal medleys like Thai peanut chicken, seven-vegetable tofu, and black beans and pork with chile to elegant little crusts with nothing but the best local artichokes and rosemary. Once a trend, creative combinations are now part of our pizza-eating life.

Pesto-Chicken Calzones

The ultimate after-work, no-fuss meal. These calzones are packed with flavor—and vitamins—thanks to the broccoli. For a version with red peppers and prosciutto, see the variation below.

MAKES 4 calzones | **TIME** 45 minutes

1 lb. store-bought or homemade pizza dough (*see Quick Tip below*), at room temperature
1⅓ cups shredded mozzarella cheese
½ cup pesto
1 cup cooked chopped broccoli
1 cup shredded cooked chicken (about ¼ lb.)
Olive oil

1. Preheat oven to 450°. On a lightly floured work surface, divide dough into four pieces. Using your hands, stretch each piece into a 6-in. round. If dough shrinks, let it rest about 5 minutes, then stretch again. (*See How to Stretch Pizza Dough, page 200.*)

2. Divide mozzarella among dough rounds, then top with pesto, broccoli, and chicken.

3. Gently pull half the dough over filling to make a half-moon shape. Fold bottom edge over top edge and pinch firmly to seal. Brush calzone tops lightly with oil. Transfer to a large baking sheet.

4. Bake calzones until golden brown, 20 to 25 minutes. Let cool about 5 minutes, then transfer to plates.

Quick Tip: For homemade dough, use Delfina's Pizza Dough (*page 198*) or dough for Pizzetta 211 Margherita Pepperoni Pizza (*page 201*) or Emilia's Sausage, Mushroom, and Red Pepper Pizza (*page 202*).

Make Ahead: Through step 3, then freeze on a baking sheet. When frozen, wrap each calzone with foil and keep in freezer for up to 1 month. Bake frozen calzones at 375° until browned and cooked through, 30 to 35 minutes.

PER CALZONE: 586 cal., 38% (225 cal.) from fat; 31 g protein; 25 g fat (9 g sat.); 61 g carbo (3.6 g fiber); 1,545 mg sodium; 65 mg chol.

Red Pepper, Fontina, and Prosciutto
Calzones: Follow the directions above, substituting 1¼ cups (5 oz.) shredded **fontina cheese**; ½ cup sliced **roasted red peppers**; ¼ cup chopped **basil leaves**; 3 oz. thinly sliced **prosciutto**, chopped; and 3 oz. **goat cheese**.

PER CALZONE: 548 cal., 39% (216 cal.) from fat; 30 g protein; 24 g fat (13 g sat.); 57 g carbo (1.8 g fiber); 1,896 mg sodium; 81 mg chol.

pasta, noodles & grains

They're the kitchen standbys: inexpensive, nutritious, and versatile. If you have pasta or grains in your cupboard, you're already halfway to dinner.

Pasta needs so little embellishment to give pleasure. A bowl of hot, freshly cooked spaghetti, with good butter and wisps of parmesan melting down into it, has a kind of simple magnificence that lifts the spirits. Especially at the end of a hectic day, putting together something easy and rewarding like that—or pasta with a quick pesto (*page* 208) or with anchovies and bread crumbs (*page* 218)—is a relief. Yet when you're in the mood for something more elegant, pasta steps up to the plate too: Try roasted duck with pappardelle and green-olive sauce (*page* 216), or Giant Butternut Squash Ravioli, flavored with almonds and sage (*page* 224).

Pasta in the West means Asian-style as much as it does Italian: delicious bean-thread noodles, which turn transparent when cooked, soaking up the flavors of whatever they're paired with (as in our Korean Clear Noodles with Beef and Mixed Vegetables, *page* 212); Chinese egg noodles, the key to a good lo mein (*page* 214); or pristine white rice noodles, so tasty with soups, grilled fish (*page* 218), meats, and tofu.

Meanwhile, grains just keep getting more interesting. We're putting wheat berries, quinoa, and bulgur into everything from salads to sides to main courses, and loving the way they taste (take a look at vibrant Tangerine Quinoa Pilaf, *page* 235). And we're exploring the ever-widening world of rice, cooking up brown rice, basmati, jasmine, and sushi-style (and discovering some surprises: Sushi rice, for example, makes great risotto—*see page* 230).

Pastas and grains suit every mood, every occasion, and every culture that we are in the West, and this chapter offers all of these.

Pasta, Noodles & Grains

Linguine with Caramelized Baby Artichokes and Prosciutto

Unlike larger artichokes, which have tougher, thicker leaves and inedible, thistly chokes, baby artichokes are entirely edible once trimmed.

SERVES 4 | **TIME** 1 hour

1 garlic clove, peeled
¼ lb. artisan-style bread (crust removed), cut into 1-in. cubes
2 tbsp. olive oil, divided
1½ tbsp. butter
3 cups thinly sliced leeks (*see Quick Tip, above right*)
¼ tsp. *each* salt and freshly ground black pepper
2 lbs. baby artichokes (about 3 in. long), trimmed and quartered (*see Trimming Baby Artichokes, page 125*)
1 cup chicken broth, divided, or more as needed
2 tbsp. fresh lemon juice
½ cup dry white wine
¾ lb. linguine
2 oz. thinly sliced prosciutto, cut into ½-in.-wide strips
¼ cup chopped flat-leaf parsley

1. In a blender, chop garlic until minced. Add half the bread cubes and pulse until coarse crumbs form. Pour onto a plate; repeat with remaining bread cubes. Pour ½ tbsp. oil into a 10- to 12-in. frying pan over medium-high heat. When hot, add crumbs; cook, stirring often and lowering heat if crumbs threaten to scorch, until crisp and golden, 10 to 15 minutes. Set aside.
2. Put butter and remaining 1½ tbsp. oil in a 10- to 12-in. frying pan (with sides at least 2 in. high) over medium-low heat. When butter is melted, add leeks, salt, and pepper, and cook, stirring occasionally, until leeks are very limp and starting to brown, 10 to 15 minutes.
3. Add artichokes, ¾ cup broth, and the lemon juice; increase heat to medium and bring to a simmer. Cover; cook until artichokes are tender when pierced, about 10 minutes. Uncover and cook until liquid has evaporated and mixture begins to brown, 5 to 10 minutes longer.
4. Stir in wine, scraping up browned bits from bottom of pan. Cook until liquid has almost evaporated, about 1 minute. Stir in remaining ¼ cup broth; if mixture appears too dry, add a little more broth.
5. Meanwhile, in a 5- to 6-qt. pan over high heat, bring about 2 qts. water to a boil. Add linguine and cook, uncovered, until tender to the bite, 9 to 12 minutes; stir a few times to separate strands of pasta. Drain and stir into artichoke mixture along with prosciutto, parsley, and bread crumbs.

Quick Tip: To clean leeks, cut off and discard root ends and dark green leaves. Cut in half lengthwise and swish in a large bowl of water to rinse; transfer to a colander, leaving dirt behind. Thinly slice crosswise.

PER SERVING: 662 cal., 22% (144 cal.) from fat; 26 g protein; 16 g fat (4.6 g sat.); 110 g carbo (14 g fiber); 1,034 mg sodium; 24 mg chol.

Spaghetti with Garlic and Parsley

This recipe (as well as the clam sauce variation, *below*) is a nice example of how just a few ingredients can come together to create an intensely flavorful dish. If you've got a garden full of basil, feel free to use it instead of the parsley.

SERVES 2 as a main course or 4 as a side dish
TIME 20 minutes

½ lb. spaghetti or spaghetti rigati (*see Quick Tip below*)
¼ cup extra-virgin olive oil
3 or 4 garlic cloves, minced
1 tbsp. minced canned anchovies
¼ to ½ tsp. red chile flakes
½ cup chopped flat-leaf parsley
Salt
Shredded parmesan cheese

1. In a 5- to 6-qt. pan over high heat, bring about 3 qts. water to a boil. Add spaghetti, stir to separate, and cook, uncovered, until tender to the bite, 9 to 12 minutes (5 to 6 minutes for rigati). Drain pasta, reserving about 1 cup cooking water. Rinse and dry pan.
2. In same pan, over medium-low heat, combine oil, garlic, anchovies, and chile flakes; cook, stirring until garlic is soft and anchovies disintegrate, 3 to 4 minutes.
3. Add pasta and parsley to pan and mix well, adding as much of reserved cooking water to moisten as desired. Heat, stirring, until pasta is hot, 1 to 3 minutes. Add salt to taste. Mound in a serving bowl or on individual plates; add parmesan cheese to taste.
Quick Tip: Spaghetti rigati has tiny grooves that help hold sauce.

PER MAIN-DISH SERVING: 692 cal., 40% (279 cal.) from fat; 18 g protein; 31 g fat (4.5 g sat.); 87 g carbo (3.5 g fiber); 345 mg sodium; 5 mg chol.

Spaghetti with Clam Sauce: Follow recipe above, adding 1 can (7 oz.) **chopped clams** (with juices) along with pasta and parsley in step 3. Serve with **lemon wedges** instead of parmesan. Serves 3 as a main course.

PER SERVING: 513 cal., 37% (189 cal.) from fat; 21 g protein; 21 g fat (3 g sat.); 60 g carbo (2.3 g fiber); 268 mg sodium; 26 mg chol.

Pesto's *Sunset* Premiere

Back in 1946, when authentic Italian food was still exotic in this country, *Sunset* ran its first recipe for pesto.

This was remarkable, given that the era is better known for the introduction of Betty Crocker cake mix (1947) and frozen french fries (1948). Spaghetti was beginning to lose its foreign accent, but pesto was unknown to most, having received its first American mention just two years earlier in the *New York Times*. According to Lynne Olver, food historian and editor of *foodtimeline.org*, that item was a brief recommendation for a brand of imported canned pesto paste. So *Sunset's* pesto recipe was likely the first in a major American publication.

Pellegrini and Pesto

For that bit of good fortune, we tip our hats to Angelo Pellegrini, the Tuscan-born English professor and Renaissance man whose writings on food, gardening, and living well (including his best-known book, *The Unprejudiced Palate*, first published in 1948 and back in print) made him one of the West's most beloved food authorities. *Sunset* had a long relationship with Pellegrini, who lived in Seattle until his death in 1991, and it's his pesto recipe that first graced our pages.

Pesto, he wrote, "is an extraordinarily pleasant experience both for the nostrils and the palate. Its only disadvantage is that it may unduly whet the appetite. I once knew a man in Florence who wagered he could eat 2 pounds of pasta al pesto… after a normal dinner. The prize was a barrel of Chianti. He won the wager and lived to drink the wine!"

Pellegrini's pesto recipe gave no exact amounts, just a little bit of this, a little bit of that. In June 1959, we returned to pesto with a more standardized recipe, which you'll find below.

Long after *Sunset* embraced pesto, the sauce was still unknown to most American cooks. "Fresh basil was not to be seen in the markets until the 1970s," says Jerry Anne Di Vecchio, who served as *Sunset's* food editor from 1980 to 2001. "That's when pesto came into its own." In the 1980s and '90s, the sauce finally became a favorite of both chefs and home cooks.

Classic Pesto

Catering to modern tastes, we've reduced the ¾ cup oil in the recipe we published in 1959 to a little more than ¼ cup. The flavors remain true.

MAKES ⅓ cup | **TIME** 10 minutes

½ cup basil leaves
4 large or 6 medium garlic cloves, peeled
⅓ cup shredded romano cheese
3 tbsp. pine nuts
2 tbsp. minced flat-leaf parsley
½ tsp. salt
¼ cup plus 1 tbsp. extra-virgin olive oil

Put basil in a mortar with garlic, romano cheese, pine nuts, parsley, and salt. Pound until smooth, then add olive oil and mix until smooth. Or purée all ingredients in a blender.

PER TBSP.: 76 cal., 78% (59 cal.) from fat; 3.1 g protein; 6.5 g fat (1.6 g sat); 2.3 g carbo; 0.6 g fiber, 278 mg sodium; 5.2 mg chol.

Penne with Oyster Mushrooms, Prosciutto, and Mint

You can substitute button or cremini mushrooms for the oyster mushrooms.

recipe pictured on page 182

SERVES 2 to 4 | **TIME** 40 minutes

1 tbsp. plus 1 tsp. kosher salt
½ lb. penne
3 tbsp. olive oil
1 lb. oyster mushrooms, tough stems removed and caps sliced *(see Quick Tip, above right)*
2 garlic cloves, thinly sliced
½ cup chicken broth
1 cup finely shredded fontina cheese, preferably Italian
½ cup chopped mint leaves
2 slices prosciutto, chopped
Freshly ground black pepper

1. Bring a large pot of water to a boil. Add 1 tbsp. salt and the penne and cook, uncovered, until just tender to the bite. Drain; set aside.
2. In the same pot, heat oil over high heat until shimmering. Add mushrooms and remaining 1 tsp. salt and cook, stirring constantly, until mushrooms stop releasing liquid and start to brown, about 10 minutes. Reduce heat to medium-high and add garlic. Cook, stirring, until fragrant,

about 2 minutes. Stir in broth and penne and cook until broth is absorbed. Stir in fontina until it melts and coats the pasta. Take off heat and stir in mint. Serve immediately, topped with prosciutto and pepper.

Quick Tip: To clean mushrooms, wipe with a dry brush and a damp paper towel. Swish particularly dirty ones in a bowl of cold water for a minute; dry on paper towels.

PER SERVING: 540 cal., 37% (198 cal.) from fat; 25 g protein; 22 g fat (7.2 g sat.); 65 g carbo (5.8 g fiber); 1,169 mg sodium; 39 mg chol.

Linguine with Gorgonzola, Potatoes, Green Beans, and Sage

Speedy cooking at its best. Variations on the green beans and herbs follow.

recipe pictured on page **183**

SERVES 6 | **TIME** 30 minutes

2 medium Yukon Gold potatoes
1 tbsp. salt
1 lb. linguine
10 oz. green beans, trimmed and cut into 2-in. lengths, or 1 bag (10 oz.) frozen cut green beans
6 sage leaves, plus more for garnish
½ lb. gorgonzola dolce or other soft blue cheese, such as Fourme d'Ambert *(see Quick Tip below)*
2 tbsp. butter
½ tsp. freshly ground black pepper, plus more for garnish

1. Peel potatoes and cut into ¾-in. pieces. Bring 2 qts. water to a boil. Add potatoes, salt and linguine. Stir, cover, and return to a vigorous boil. Add green beans, cover, and bring back to a boil. Uncover and cook until linguine is tender to the bite, about 5 minutes.
2. Meanwhile, chop sage. In a large serving bowl, mash cheese, butter, sage, and pepper together. Set aside.
3. Reserve ½ cup cooking water, then drain pasta and vegetables, shaking off as much water as possible. Pour on top of cheese–butter mixture. Toss to combine until cheese melts and coats pasta. If resulting sauce is too thick, add reserved cooking water, 1 tbsp. at a time. Serve hot, topped with more sage leaves and pepper if you like.
Quick Tip: If you can't find gorgonzola dolce or other soft blue cheese, use 6 oz. regular blue cheese (such as gorgonzola or Danish blue) and increase butter to ¼ cup total.

PER SERVING: 505 cal., 30% (153 cal.) from fat; 19 g protein; 17 g fat (11 g sat.); 69 g carbo (2.7 g fiber); 1,085 mg sodium; 44 mg chol.

Variations
• Replace green beans with 6 oz. **spinach**, cut into thin ribbons or chopped; add to pasta water for last minute of cooking.

• Instead of green beans, in a large frying pan over high heat, cook 1 head **radicchio**, thinly sliced, in 2 tsp. **olive oil** until wilted, about 3 minutes. Add to cooked pasta before tossing with cheese.
• Use **thyme**, **oregano**, or **basil** instead of sage.

Filipino-style Stir-fried Noodles with Vegetables and Tofu *(Pancit)*

Our version of the Filipino favorite is based on one at House of Sisig, in Daly City, California.

SERVES 6 | **TIME** 1 hour

3½ oz. rice vermicelli
½ lb. medium-thick fresh wheat noodles *(see Quick Tip below and A Brief Guide to Asian Noodles, page 215)*
2 tbsp. plus ¼ cup vegetable oil, divided
2 tbsp. chopped garlic, divided
1 medium onion, thinly sliced
2 cups shredded green cabbage
1 carrot, finely shredded
1 package (12 oz.) firm tofu, patted dry and cut into ½-in. cubes
3 tbsp. soy sauce
1½ tsp. freshly ground black pepper
1 cup reduced-sodium chicken or vegetable broth
1 lemon, cut into wedges

1. In a medium bowl, cover vermicelli with boiling water. Let stand until tender, 5 to 8 minutes. Drain; rinse with cold water. Cut into 10-in. lengths and set aside.
2. Bring a 4-qt. pot of water to a boil. Add wheat noodles and cook until tender, 2 to 4 minutes; drain and set aside.
3. Heat 2 tbsp. oil in a large wok over medium heat. Fry 1 tbsp. garlic until light golden, 30 seconds. Strain garlic and oil into a bowl and set both aside.
4. Add remaining ¼ cup oil to hot wok and swirl to coat. Add remaining 1 tbsp. garlic and cook until fragrant, about 30 seconds. Add onion and cabbage; increase heat to medium-high. Cook, stirring occasionally, until vegetables begin to soften, about 3 minutes. Add carrot; cook, stirring, until it softens, about 1 minute.
5. Increase heat to high. Add tofu, reserved noodles, soy sauce, pepper, and broth to wok. Cook, stirring occasionally, until tofu is heated through and liquid has reduced by about half, about 5 minutes. Stir in reserved 2 tbsp. garlic oil. Sprinkle fried garlic on noodles and serve with lemon wedges on the side.
Quick Tip: Look for the words "pancit Canton" on the label.

PER SERVING: 437 cal., 51% (225 cal.) from fat; 12 g protein; 25 g fat (10 g sat.); 42 g carbo (3.8 g fiber); 829 mg sodium; 0 mg chol.

Vietnamese Herb Noodle Salad (*Bun Voi Rau Thom*)

This traditional Vietnamese salad, made with noodles and generous handfuls of fresh, pungent herbs, is infinitely adaptable, a bed for everything from pork chops to braised eggplant. The recipe comes from cookbook author Ann Le, who grew up in Westminster, California—also known as Little Saigon, home to the largest population of Vietnamese outside of Vietnam. Prepare it with your choice of the toppings and garnishes and let people assemble their own salads.

SERVES 4 as a main course | **TIME** 45 minutes

½ lb. rice vermicelli or *mai fun*
1 cup *each* loosely packed mint, basil, and cilantro leaves or sprigs
3-in. chunk cucumber, peeled, halved, seeded, and cut into 1½-in.-long matchsticks
1 cup mung bean sprouts, rinsed
1 lime, cut into wedges
TOPPINGS
Grilled Beef with Lemongrass and Garlic *(recipe follows)*
Vietnamese-style Peppery Grilled Shrimp *(page 211)*
Sautéed Tofu with Oyster Sauce and Cilantro *(page 211)*
GARNISHES & DIPPING SAUCE
2 green onions, trimmed and thinly sliced
¼ cup Fried Sliced Garlic *(page 211)*
3 tbsp. crushed unsalted dry-roasted peanuts
Vietnamese Dipping Sauce *(page 219)*

1. Cook vermicelli according to package instructions. Drain, rinse with cool water, put in a bowl, and cover with a kitchen towel.
2. Set herbs, cucumber, sprouts, and lime wedges on a platter. Set out cooked toppings on platters. Serve garnishes and dipping sauce in small bowls.
3. Before serving, check noodles; if gummy, rinse again and drain. Let people assemble their own salads. Traditionally, it's noodles first, followed by herbs (to be roughly torn over salads), cucumber, and sprouts; then toppings; then garnishes and a squeeze of lime juice and/or a sprinkling of dipping sauce.

PER SERVING WITHOUT COOKED TOPPINGS OR DIPPING SAUCE: 220 cal., 4% (9 cal.) from fat; 6.1 g protein; 1 g fat (0.1 g sat.); 48 g carbo (5.2 g fiber); 16 mg sodium; 0 mg chol.

Grilled Beef with Lemongrass and Garlic

You can use a grill pan or broiler instead of a grill. (Broil the onions first, about 10 in. from heat, then the beef, about 6 in. from heat.) You'll need two 8-in. metal skewers.

SERVES 4 | **TIME** 30 minutes, plus 2 hours to marinate

1½ tsp. sugar
1 tbsp. freshly ground black pepper
2½ tbsp. minced garlic (3 or 4 large cloves)
1½ stalks fresh lemongrass, stem ends trimmed, tough outer layers pulled off and inner cores minced (about 3 tbsp.)
3 tbsp. Thai or Vietnamese fish sauce (*nam pla* or *nuoc mam; see Fish Sauce, right*)
3 tbsp. olive oil, divided
1 lb. beef tri-tip or round, cut across the grain into ¼-in.-thick slices
2 yellow onions, quartered
2 tbsp. *each* loosely packed cilantro sprigs and crushed unsalted dry-roasted peanuts

1. In a wide, shallow bowl, whisk together sugar, pepper, garlic, lemongrass, fish sauce, and 2 tbsp. oil. Add beef, toss to coat, and refrigerate 2 hours.
2. Rub remaining 1 tbsp. oil over onions. Thread onions onto skewers.
3. Prepare a charcoal or gas grill for direct medium-high heat *(see Direct Heat Grilling, page 436)*. Using a wad of oiled paper towels and tongs, oil cooking grate. Lay onion skewers on grill and cook (close lid on gas grill) until softened, about 15 minutes, turning skewers every 5 minutes or so.
4. When onions are cooked halfway, lay beef slices on grill and cook (close lid on gas grill), turning once, 3 to 5 minutes.
5. Arrange beef and onions on a platter and garnish with cilantro and peanuts.

PER SERVING: 428 cal., 61% (261 cal.) from fat; 26 g protein; 29 g fat (7.9 g sat.); 16 g carbo (2.3 g fiber); 516 mg sodium; 74 mg chol.

Vietnamese-style Peppery Grilled Shrimp

You can use a grill pan or broiler instead of a grill. You'll need six 6-in. wooden skewers.

SERVES 4 | **TIME** 25 minutes, plus 15 minutes to marinate

2 tbsp. finely chopped fresh lemongrass (tender inner core)
5 tbsp. minced garlic (about 10 large cloves)
½ tsp. Sriracha chili sauce
3 tbsp. Thai or Vietnamese fish sauce (*nam pla or nuoc mam; see Fish Sauce below*)
2 tsp. sugar
3 tbsp. olive oil
2 tbsp. fresh lime juice
1 tbsp. freshly ground black pepper
¼ cup finely chopped green onions
1 lb. medium shrimp (31 to 42 per lb.), peeled with tails left on and deveined
⅓ cup loosely packed mint leaves, stacked and cut crosswise into thin slivers

1. Soak skewers in water for at least 30 minutes before grilling to prevent them from scorching. In a medium bowl, whisk together lemongrass, garlic, chili sauce, fish sauce, sugar, oil, lime juice, pepper, and green onions. Add shrimp and toss to coat. Let marinate 15 minutes at room temperature or up to 1 hour in the refrigerator.
2. Prepare a charcoal or gas grill for direct high heat (*see Direct Heat Grilling, page 436*). Using a wad of oiled paper towels and tongs, oil cooking grate. Thread shrimp onto skewers and grill until curled, pink, and opaque, 2 to 3 minutes per side.
3. Remove skewers from grill and garnish shrimp with slivered mint.

PER SERVING: 258 cal., 45% (117 cal.) from fat; 22 g protein; 13 g fat (2 g sat.); 13 g carbo (1.6 g fiber); 598 mg sodium; 140 mg chol.

■ Fish Sauce

Fish sauce, widely used in Southeast Asian cuisine as a condiment and flavoring for various dishes, is a salty, light-brown liquid made from fermented fish, water, and salt. It's best used sparingly—just a spoonful makes a world of difference. Combine fish sauce with sugar and lime juice to make a dipping sauce for vegetables and spring rolls, or use it as a base to add pungent flavor to dishes. We recommend Thai or Vietnamese fish sauce (*nam pla or nuoc mam*) in our recipes; each is milder and lighter than Filipino fish sauce.

Sautéed Tofu with Oyster Sauce and Cilantro

To gussy up this recipe, double the sauce and add sliced mushrooms, carrots, or bok choy.

SERVES 4 | **TIME** 10 minutes

2 tbsp. oyster sauce
1 tsp. freshly ground black pepper
1 tbsp. sugar
2 tbsp. Thai or Vietnamese fish sauce (*nam pla or nuoc mam; see Fish Sauce below*)
1 tbsp. olive oil
1 package (14 oz.) extra-firm tofu, drained, cubed, and patted dry
¼ cup loosely packed cilantro sprigs

1. In a small bowl, whisk oyster sauce, pepper, sugar, and fish sauce.
2. Heat oil over medium heat in a medium nonstick skillet and add tofu. Cook 1 minute, stir gently, and add oyster sauce mixture. Cook, stirring occasionally, until tofu is hot and sauce has reduced a little, about 5 minutes. Top with cilantro.

PER SERVING: 167 cal., 54% (90 cal.) from fat; 13 g protein; 10 g fat (1.5 g sat.); 8.4 g carbo (0.6 g fiber); 665 mg sodium; 0 mg chol.

Fried Sliced Garlic or Shallots: In a medium frying pan, heat ⅓ cup **olive oil** over medium heat. Thinly slice 8 medium **garlic** cloves lengthwise or use 1 cup thinly sliced **shallots** and fry until just golden, 2 to 3 minutes for garlic, 6 to 10 minutes for shallots. Using a slotted spoon, transfer to paper towels to drain. Makes about ¼ cup garlic and about ½ cup shallots.
Quick Tip: Garlic is at its best when it's really fresh. Look for plump, firm bulbs and avoid any with little green shoots poking up. Store in a cool, dry place.

PER TBSP. GARLIC: 39 cal., 79% (31 cal.) from fat; 0.4 g protein; 3.4 g fat (0.5 g sat.); 2 g carbo (0.1 g fiber); 1 mg sodium; 0 mg chol.

PER TBSP. SHALLOTS: 45 cal., 69% (31 cal.) from fat; 0.5 g protein; 3.4 g fat (0.4 g sat.); 3.4 g carbo (0.2 g fiber); 2.4 mg sodium; 0 mg chol.

Korean Clear Noodles with Beef and Mixed Vegetables (*Chap Chae*)

A noodle dish from Phyllis Chai, of San Jose, California.

SERVES 6 | **TIME** 1 hour

6 oz. dried bean-thread noodles (*saifun; see A Brief Guide to Asian Noodles, page 215*)
8 dried shiitake mushrooms (1 oz.)
6 oz. beef flank steak
¼ cup Asian (toasted) sesame oil, divided
5 tbsp. soy sauce, divided
2 tbsp. sliced green onion plus 3 whole green onions
3 tsp. sugar, divided
1 garlic clove, pressed or minced
1 yellow onion (½ lb.), sliced into ¼-in.-thick slivers
1 cup coarsely shredded carrots
1 cup diagonally sliced (¼ in. thick) green beans
¼ tsp. freshly ground black pepper, plus more to taste
Salt
1 tbsp. toasted sesame seeds (*see Quick Tip, above right*)

1. In a 3- to 4-qt. pan over high heat, bring 2 qts. water to a boil. Immerse noodles in water and stir to separate; cover and remove from heat. Let stand until noodles are soft, 3 to 5 minutes. Drain well. With scissors, cut into 6-in. lengths.

2. Rinse mushrooms and put in a small bowl with enough hot water to cover; let stand until soft, about 15 minutes. Lift mushrooms from soaking liquid (reserve liquid for another use or discard) and squeeze dry. Cut stems off mushrooms and discard. Cut mushroom caps into ¼-in.-wide strips.

3. Chop beef into ¼-in. pieces. In a bowl, mix meat with 1 tsp. sesame oil, 2 tbsp. soy sauce, the sliced green onion, 1 tsp. sugar, and the garlic until well coated. Cover and chill at least 30 minutes and up to 2 hours.

4. Meanwhile, trim root ends from whole green onions; cut into 2-in. lengths.

5. In a 12-in. nonstick frying pan or a 5- to 6-qt. nonstick pan over medium heat, cook 2 tsp. sesame oil and the yellow onion until slightly softened but not limp, about 4 minutes. Transfer to a large bowl. Return pan to medium heat and add 1 more tsp. sesame oil, the carrots, and green onion lengths. Cook, stirring often, until green onions are slightly wilted, about 2 minutes; add to bowl. Return pan to medium heat and add 2 more tsp. sesame oil, the mushrooms, and green beans; cook until mushrooms are lightly browned, about 4 minutes. Add to bowl.

6. Return pan to medium heat; add 1 tbsp. sesame oil and the beef mixture. Cook until lightly browned, stirring often, 4 to 6 minutes; add to bowl. Return pan

to heat and add drained noodles, pepper, and remaining 3 tbsp. soy sauce, 1 tbsp. sesame oil, and 2 tsp. sugar; cook until noodles are hot, 2 to 4 minutes. Pour into bowl with vegetable-beef mixture. Mix well, adding salt and pepper to taste. Pour into a bowl; sprinkle with sesame seeds.

Quick Tip: Find already toasted sesame seeds in the Asian foods section of the supermarket, or toast them yourself in a dry frying pan over medium heat until golden, about 5 minutes.

PER SERVING: 299 cal., 39% (117 cal.) from fat; 8.2 g protein; 13 g fat (2.7 g sat.); 39 g carbo (3.3 g fiber); 892 mg sodium; 15 mg chol.

Beef with Tomatoes, Pasta, and Chili Sauce (*Tallarín Saltado*)

While researching a story on Peruvian cooking, we came across *tallarín saltado*, a popular fusion dish that combines Asian stir-fry techniques with beef, fresh tomatoes, Asian chili sauce, and Italian spaghetti. It was a hit here at *Sunset*: The dish is fast and easy, and you can substitute other meats, vegetables, or kinds of pasta. Below is our favorite combination, using broccoli and fusilli, followed by several variations. For a less spicy dish, decrease or leave out the chili sauce.

SERVES 4 | **TIME** 35 minutes

½ lb. fusilli
2 tbsp. vegetable oil
1 lb. beef sirloin, halved lengthwise and cut into ¼-in.-thick slices (*see Quick Tip, above right*)
1 large onion, halved lengthwise and cut into thin wedges
3 cups broccoli florets (about 1 in. each)
3 tbsp. soy sauce, plus more to taste
1 tbsp. Sriracha chili sauce, plus more to taste
1 tbsp. chopped cilantro, plus more for garnish if you like
¼ tsp. freshly ground black pepper
3 ripe medium tomatoes, cut into 1-in.-thick wedges

1. Bring a large pot of salted water to a boil. Add fusilli and cook, uncovered, until tender to the bite, 5 to 10 minutes. Drain and set aside.

2. Meanwhile, heat oil in a large frying pan over medium-high heat until hot but not smoking. Add beef and cook until it starts to brown, about 3 minutes. Stir and let it continue to brown for 2 or 3 minutes more. Transfer beef to a plate, reserving oil in pan, and set beef aside.

3. Add onion to pan and cook, stirring often, until it begins to brown, 2 or 3 minutes. Add broccoli and cook until bright green, 2 or 3 minutes. Add soy sauce, Sriracha, cilantro, and pepper. Cook, stirring frequently, about 3 minutes. Add tomatoes and reserved beef and cook until tomatoes begin to release their juice, 2 or 3 minutes longer. Add fusilli, stir, and cook until most of liquid has evaporated or been absorbed by pasta, 2 or 3 minutes. Season to taste with additional soy sauce or Sriracha. Serve hot with a sprinkling of cilantro if you like.

Quick Tip: Slicing the beef is easier if it has been chilled for 20 to 30 minutes in the freezer.

PER SERVING: 596 cal., 39% (234 cal.) from fat; 34 g protein; 26 g fat (7.9 g sat.); 58 g carbo (6.4 g fiber); 1,276 mg sodium; 76 mg chol.

Chicken or Seafood *Tallarín Saltado*: Use 1 lb.
boned, skinned **chicken breasts**, cut into ¼-in.-thick strips, or 1 lb. medium **shrimp**, peeled and deveined, instead of the beef.

Use a different vegetable: Add a green vegetable
(such as **green beans** or **zucchini**) in addition to or instead of the broccoli. You can also toss in a thinly sliced **red or green bell pepper** or 1 cup thinly sliced **green cabbage** (add at the same time as the onion).

Switch out the pasta: Try it with **penne** instead of
fusilli. Or, for a more authentically Peruvian version, use **spaghetti**.

Shredded or Grated?

Often these two terms are taken to be interchangeable, but there's a difference between an ingredient that's grated and one that's shredded. Grated food is very fine, almost powdered, and the ingredient generally has to be fairly dry or hard before it can be successfully grated (think of bread crumbs or aged parmesan). A true grater: the punched-out holes on a box grater. Shredded food is, very simply, in the form of shreds, whether wispy or thick. Why do we care about terminology? Because it makes a difference in cooking; grated food blends in more evenly with whatever you're mixing it with, whereas shredded food has more of a presence in a dish, as its pieces are larger.

Most of the cutting surfaces on a box grater (despite its name) produce shreds, as does the extremely handy Microplane. Lemon zest (the colored part of the peel) is almost always finely shredded for recipes; soft cheese is often coarsely shredded; and fresh nutmeg is always grated.

Pappardelle with Chicken and Winter Greens

This bright-tasting pasta makes good use of radicchio and chard, two sturdy greens packed with vitamins and flavor.

recipe pictured on page **187**

SERVES 6 | **TIME** 1 hour

1 lb. green Swiss chard
½ medium head radicchio
1 medium lemon
2 tbsp. olive oil
3 large garlic cloves, thinly sliced
½ cup reduced-sodium chicken broth
⅓ cup *each* dry sherry and heavy whipping cream
1 cup shredded asiago cheese, divided
3 cups shredded white and dark chicken meat (from one
    2½- to 3-lb. rotisserie chicken)
Salt and freshly ground black pepper
½ lb. pappardelle

1. Bring a large pot of well-salted water to a boil over high heat. Meanwhile, trim stems and ribs from chard (save for another use, such as soup, if you like). Cut leaves crosswise into ⅓-in.-wide ribbons. Peel any rubbery outer leaves from radicchio and cut out tough core; discard both. Slice remaining leaves crosswise into ⅓-in.-wide ribbons. Finely shred zest of lemon and set aside zest. Juice lemon and set aside 3 tbsp. juice.

2. Heat oil in a 12-in. frying pan over medium heat. Add garlic and cook until just fragrant, 1 to 2 minutes. Increase heat to medium-high. Add broth, sherry, chard, radicchio, and lemon zest. Turn to coat and cook until chard is just tender to the bite, 2 to 3 minutes. Add cream and half of asiago; stir to combine. Stir in chicken and cook until warmed through. Stir in lemon juice and season with salt and pepper to taste.

3. Meanwhile, cook pappardelle in boiling water, uncovered, until tender to the bite. Drain and add to frying pan; use tongs to combine. Transfer pasta to a serving bowl, sprinkle with remaining asiago, and serve.

Quick Tip: If you like your chard tender rather than tender-crisp, cook it longer in step 2 (fish out a piece from the pan and taste it).

PER SERVING: 448 cal., 40% (180 cal.) from fat; 27 g protein; 20 g fat (9.1 g sat.); 35 g carbo (2.4 g fiber); 846 mg sodium; 94 mg chol.

Rice Noodles with Chicken and Vegetables

A delicious meal in a bowl from Peter and Wendy Lee, of Millbrae, California, this is an example of how light, flavorful, and easy home-style Chinese cooking can be. Use Chinese black (Chinkiang) vinegar and/or Sriracha chili sauce to season each bowl to taste.

SERVES 4 to 6 | **TIME** 45 minutes

4 cups chicken broth
6 to 7 oz. rice noodles (*mai fun; see A Brief Guide to Asian Noodles, opposite page*)**, rinsed**
1 tsp. plus ¼ cup vegetable oil, divided
1 egg, beaten
1 skinned, boned chicken breast half (¼ lb.), cut into very thin matchsticks (2 in. long)
2 tbsp. Japanese noodle soup base, such as Kikkoman Memmi (*see Quick Tip, above right*)
1 tbsp. Shaoxing rice wine
2 cups carrot matchsticks (2 in. long)
2 cups thinly sliced fresh shiitake mushroom caps
5 cups (10 oz.) finely shredded green cabbage
Salt

1. In a medium pan over high heat, bring broth to a boil. Add rice noodles, stir to submerge, and remove from heat. Let stand until tender to the bite, about 15 minutes. Pour noodles into a colander set over a bowl to drain; reserve broth.
2. Meanwhile, set a 10-in. nonstick frying pan over medium heat and add 1 tsp. oil; when hot, pour in egg and swirl to make a paper-thin pancake. Cook until set, about 1 minute. Slide pancake from pan onto a board and let cool, then cut into thin strips.
3. In a small bowl, mix chicken with noodle soup base and rice wine. Pour 2 tbsp. oil into a 14-in. wok or 12-in. frying pan (with sides at least 2½ in. high) over high heat. When hot, add chicken mixture and cook, stirring, until no longer pink in center, about 45 seconds. Add carrot sticks and cook, stirring, until tender-crisp, 1 to 2 minutes. Add mushrooms and cook until beginning to brown but still firm to the bite, 45 seconds to 1 minute. Add cabbage and cook, stirring, until barely wilted, about 30 seconds longer. Transfer chicken and vegetables to a bowl.
4. Reduce heat to medium-high, add remaining 2 tbsp. oil to wok, and pour in softened noodles. Stir vigorously to separate, then cook until heated through, 2 to 3 minutes. Add chicken-vegetable mixture and stir until heated through and mixed well, adding a little of the reserved broth if mixture seems too dry; reserve remaining broth for other uses. Stir in salt to taste. Pour noodles into a serving dish and top with strips of egg.
Quick Tip: If you can't find Kikkoman Memmi noodle soup base, substitute 2 tbsp. soy sauce, 2 tsp. Chinese black (Chinkiang) or unseasoned rice vinegar, 1 tsp. sugar, and ½ tsp. Vietnamese fish sauce (*nuoc mam*).

PER SERVING: 241 cal., 28% (68 cal.) from fat; 9.4 g protein; 7.5 g fat (1.5 g sat.); 35 g carbo (3 g fiber); 507 mg sodium; 49 mg chol.

Vegetable and Chicken Lo Mein

From Ann Cooper (director of nutrition services for Colorado's Boulder Valley School District), this makes for a great packed lunch, hot or cold.

SERVES 4 | **TIME** 45 minutes

¾ lb. fresh Chinese egg noodles (lo mein; *see Quick Tip below*)
1 tsp. Asian (toasted) sesame oil
¼ cup hoisin sauce
2 tbsp. soy sauce
2 tbsp. canola oil, divided
1 tbsp. minced fresh ginger
4 tsp. minced garlic
⅓ cup thinly sliced green onions
1 cup *each* **coarsely shredded carrots, thinly sliced celery, and thinly sliced red onion**
1½ cups chopped cooked chicken or diced firm tofu
¾ cup mung bean sprouts, rinsed
3 tbsp. chopped cilantro

1. Bring a large pot of salted water to a boil and cook noodles, uncovered, until tender to the bite, 4 to 5 minutes. Drain and mix with sesame oil. In a small bowl, combine hoisin and soy sauce.
2. Pour 1 tbsp. of canola oil into a 12-in. nonstick frying pan over medium heat. Add ginger, garlic, green onions, carrots, celery, and red onion, and cook, stirring often, just until softened, 2 to 4 minutes. Add chicken and bean sprouts and cook, stirring, just until warm. Turn out into a bowl and cover to keep warm.
3. Wipe frying pan clean. Pour remaining 1 tbsp. canola oil into pan over medium heat. Add noodles; cook, turning occasionally, until light brown, 3 to 5 minutes.
4. Pour hoisin mixture and chicken mixture over noodles, add cilantro, and mix gently.
Quick Tip: You can substitute fresh angel hair pasta for Chinese egg noodles; use 9 oz. and cook in step 3 for only 45 seconds.

PER SERVING: 592 cal., 24% (144 cal.) from fat; 30 g protein; 16 g fat (2.5 g sat.); 81 g carbo (4.8 g fiber); 1,226 mg sodium; 128 mg chol.

A Brief Guide to Asian Noodles

Most Asian noodles originated in China (the probable birthplace of pasta, period) and spread outward, assuming varied forms. Look for dried noodles in the international section of the supermarket or in an Asian market. Find fresh noodles refrigerated at Asian markets.

• **BEAN THREADS** (also called *saifun* or cellophane noodles). Thin, wiry dried noodles made from the starch of mung beans. Must be soaked in hot water until soft before cooking. They turn clear and slippery when simmered in water and crisp when deep-fried. Neutral in flavor, they absorb seasonings from the surrounding dish.

• **EGG NOODLES.** Usually coiled into single portions, dried egg noodles are made from wheat flour and eggs. Boil until tender, drain, then deep-fry or add to soups or stir-fries. Fresh egg noodles are best if quickly boiled to soften. They can be braised, steamed, stir-fried, or deep-fried. Many have yellow food coloring added.

• **RICE NOODLES** (also called rice sticks, *mai fun*, or *mi fun*). Most plentiful in the big rice-growing countries of China, Thailand, and Vietnam. Dried white noodles, made from rice flour, vary from whisker-thin to about ¼ inch wide. Soak them in very hot water until opaque and tender before adding to dishes. When fried, they puff up and get crisp. Fresh rice noodles don't need to be soaked. Both dried and fresh have a mild rice flavor.

• **SOBA.** A staple of Japanese cuisine, these thin, tan noodles are made mainly from buckwheat flour and have a robust, earthy flavor and pleasing resilience. Boil them until they are softened but still slightly chewy. Soba are very good in warm soups or cold noodle salads.

• **WHEAT NOODLES.** Ubiquitous in northern China, where wheat thrives. Dried wheat noodles come wrapped or tied in neat little bundles. Boil them until al dente (as you would Italian pasta). Dried wheat noodles are good in soups or stir-fries. Fresh wheat noodles are available in many forms and a range of thicknesses. Add them directly to soups, stews, and braised dishes.

Sunset Turkey Tetrazzini

We took classic tetrazzini—a dish invented in San Francisco in the early 1900s to honor soprano Luisa Tetrazzini, who lived in the city for a time—and punched it up with fresh leeks, portabella mushrooms, and radicchio.

SERVES 8 | **TIME** 1 hour

3 leeks
5 tbsp. butter, divided
2 portabella mushroom caps, cubed
1½ cups (¼ lb.) sliced button mushrooms
5 tsp. salt, divided
¼ tsp. nutmeg
1 lb. medium egg noodles
3 tbsp. flour
2 cups chicken broth
½ cup dry sherry
1 cup half-and-half
½ cup grated parmesan cheese
2 cups cubed or shredded (½-in. pieces) cooked turkey
⅓ cup chopped flat-leaf parsley, plus extra for garnish
¾ cup chopped radicchio leaves

1. Cut off and discard root ends and dark green leaves of leeks. Cut leeks in half lengthwise and swish around in a large bowl of water to rinse; transfer to a colander, leaving dirt behind, and rinse again in fresh water if necessary. Thinly slice crosswise into half-moons.

2. Melt 2 tbsp. butter in a 14-in. frying pan or 5-qt. saucepan over medium heat. Add leeks, mushrooms, 1 tsp. salt, and the nutmeg; cook, stirring often, until vegetables are soft and beginning to brown, about 12 minutes. Using a slotted spoon, transfer leek mixture to a bowl and set aside. Set aside pan with any cooking juices in it.

3. Bring a large pot of water to a boil. Add 3 tsp. salt and the egg noodles and cook until they are barely tender to the bite. Drain noodles and set aside, covered.

4. While noodles are cooking, melt remaining 3 tbsp. butter in same frying pan or saucepan. Sprinkle in flour and cook, stirring, until mixture looks glossy and golden brown, about 3 minutes. Whisk in broth and sherry and simmer until thickened, about 3 minutes. Remove from heat and whisk in half-and-half, parmesan, and remaining 1 tsp. salt. Reduce heat to low, return pan to heat, and stir in leek mixture, turkey, and parsley.

5. Just before serving, stir in radicchio. Serve over cooked noodles and garnish with parsley.

PER SERVING: 455 cal., 32% (144 cal.) from fat; 24 g protein; 16 g fat (8.6 g sat.); 53 g carbo (2.8 g fiber); 1,148 mg sodium; 115 mg chol.

Duck Legs in Green-olive Sauce with Cracklings and Pappardelle

Duck is especially delicious when cooked so that the skin gets crisp; follow our method here and you might just start eating more duck. The briny green olives help cut the richness of the meat and taste great besides. The recipe also works well with chicken—and will cook in about half the time *(variation follows).*

SERVES 6 | **TIME** 2½ hours, plus 30 minutes to cure

6 whole duck legs (thighs and drumsticks attached, about 3 lbs. total; *see Quick Tips, right*)
¼ cup *each* sugar and kosher salt
1 medium onion, chopped
2 cups reduced-sodium chicken broth
1 can (8 oz.) tomato sauce
2 tsp. dried thyme
1 cup cracked green olives, drained
1 tbsp. brined green peppercorns, drained
3 tbsp. orange-flavored liqueur, such as Cointreau
1 tsp. finely shredded orange zest
¾ lb. pappardelle or wide egg noodles
3 tbsp. fine dried bread crumbs
¼ cup finely chopped flat-leaf parsley *(see Parsley below right)*

1. Pull and carefully cut skin from duck legs without cutting meat; set skin aside. Trim fat from meat and save for another use if you like *(see Quick Tips, above right)*. Mix sugar and salt in a large bowl; add duck legs and rub with mixture. Cover duck legs and chill at least 30 minutes and up to 1 hour.
2. Meanwhile, preheat oven to 350°. Lay duck skin flat on a work surface, fat side up. With a sharp knife, slice off any thick areas of fat so fat is even; discard trimmings. Stretch skin flat, fat side down, in a single layer in a rimmed baking pan. Bake until skin is crisp and deep golden, 25 to 30 minutes; occasionally turn pieces over. With tongs, transfer crisp skin (cracklings) to paper towels to drain. Reserve 3 tbsp. duck fat; save the rest for another use. Coarsely chop cracklings; set aside.
3. Rinse duck legs well, rubbing gently to help release salt. Pat dry.
4. Pour 2 tbsp. reserved duck fat into a 12-in. frying pan over medium-high heat. Lightly brown half of duck legs, turning as needed, 5 to 8 minutes total; reduce heat if pan starts to scorch. Repeat with remaining duck. Transfer duck to a shallow 2½- to 3-qt. baking dish.

5. Add onion to pan and cook, stirring, until soft, 4 or 5 minutes. Add broth, tomato sauce, thyme, olives, and peppercorns. Reduce heat and simmer about 10 minutes, stirring occasionally, to blend flavors. Add orange liqueur and orange zest. Pour over duck, cover dish tightly with foil, and bake until duck is very tender when pierced, about 1½ hours.
6. About 15 minutes before duck is done, bring a large pot of salted water to a boil. Cook pasta, uncovered, until tender to the bite. Drain pasta and return it to cooking pot.
7. In a large frying pan over medium-high heat, cook remaining 1 tbsp. duck fat, the bread crumbs, and cracklings, stirring, until crumbs are lightly toasted, 2 to 3 minutes.
8. Skim and discard fat from duck sauce. Mix about ½ cup sauce into pasta. Arrange pasta on a large platter and top with duck legs. Spoon remaining sauce on top and sprinkle with parsley and crackling mixture.
Quick Tips: Order duck legs from your butcher. Save the fat trimmed from the duck legs, melt it in a frying pan over low heat, and combine it with the fat from making cracklings in step 2. Strained and combined with olive oil or butter, it's a delicious medium for frying potatoes.

PER SERVING: 738 cal., 37% (270 cal.) from fat; 60 g protein; 30 g fat (7.5 g sat.); 55 g carbo (3.5 g fiber); 1,724 mg sodium; 217 mg chol.

Chicken in Green-olive Sauce with Pappardelle: Substitute 12 **chicken thighs** (about 4½ lbs. total) for the duck legs. In step 1, increase **sugar** and **salt** to 6 tbsp. each. In step 4, use 2 tbsp. **canola oil** to brown the thighs. Baking time will be about 45 minutes. Cook **pasta** after chicken is tender. Reduce the sauce in step 8: Pour it into a saucepan and boil until reduced to 3 cups, about 5 minutes.

■ Parsley

FROM THE GARDEN

No garden should be without parsley. It's the workhorse of the herb world and can go in just about every dish you cook. Parsley's mild, grassy taste doesn't overpower the other ingredients. We prefer flat-leaf parsley *(above)* for cooking because it stands up better to heat and has more flavor.

Malaysian Noodles with Crab and Sausage (Penang Char Kway Teow)

Street hawkers in Penang, Malaysia, are famous for this dish. It's fast to prepare, making it a good choice for a weeknight dinner.

SERVES 4 | **TIME** 30 minutes

7 oz. wide, flat rice noodles (see A Brief Guide to Asian Noodles, page 215)
3 tbsp. vegetable oil
2 garlic cloves, finely chopped
1 to 2 tbsp. sambal (Indonesian or Malaysian chili paste; see Quick Tips below)
2 lop chong (Chinese sausages), cut into ¼-in. slices (see Quick Tips below)
6 green onions, trimmed and cut into 2-in. lengths
2 tbsp. soy sauce
4 eggs
½ tsp. freshly ground white pepper (see Quick Tips below)
6 oz. mung bean sprouts, rinsed
½ lb. shelled cooked Dungeness or other crab

1. In a large bowl, cover noodles with boiling water. Let stand until tender to the bite, 5 to 8 minutes. Drain; rinse with cold water.

2. Heat a large wok over medium heat. Add oil and swirl to coat. Add garlic and cook until fragrant, 30 seconds. Stir in sambal (start with 1 tbsp.); mixture will spatter, so stand back after adding.

3. Increase heat to medium-high and add sausages. Cook, stirring occasionally, until sausages are light golden, 1 to 2 minutes. Add green onions and cook, stirring, until they begin to soften but are still quite crisp, 1 to 2 minutes. Add noodles and soy sauce, stirring to coat.

4. Make a well in center of pan. Crack in eggs (push noodles aside if they fall into center) and cook until whites begin to set, about 3 minutes. Break yolks with a spoon; scramble eggs and toss with noodles. Add white pepper, 1 tbsp. water, the bean sprouts, and crab; cook, stirring, until bean sprouts are tender-crisp, about 2 minutes.

Quick Tips: You'll find sambal and lop chong at Asian grocery stores. Grind white pepper in a clean coffee grinder; its fresh taste is worth the effort.

PER SERVING: 521 cal., 43% (225 cal.) from fat; 28 g protein; 25 g fat (5.7 g sat.); 45 g carbo (1.9 g fiber); 1,074 mg sodium; 283 mg chol.

Smoked Salmon Vermicelli

This elegant pasta has only a few ingredients, but together they make an incredibly satisfying supper. The dish requires nothing more than a big green salad as accompaniment. If you want to take it over the top, spoon fat pearls of salmon caviar or tiny, crunchy tobiko (flying-fish roe) onto each serving.

SERVES 4 | **TIME** 20 minutes

2 tbsp. unsalted butter
1 small onion, cut into thin half-moons
1 cup whipping cream
1½ tbsp. finely shredded lemon zest
¼ cup fresh lemon juice
½ tsp. kosher salt and freshly ground black pepper, plus more to taste
½ lb. vermicelli
½ lb. hot- or cold-smoked salmon, cut into pieces
½ cup finely chopped flat-leaf parsley (see Parsley, opposite page)

1. Bring a large pot of salted water to a boil. Meanwhile, in a large, high-sided frying pan over medium heat, melt butter. Add onion and cook, stirring, until soft but not browned, about 3 minutes. Stir in cream, lemon zest and juice, salt, and pepper. Reduce heat to medium-low and cook until mixture has thickened slightly, 4 to 5 minutes.

2. Add pasta to boiling water and cook, uncovered, until tender to the bite. Drain, reserving 1 cup cooking water.

3. Add salmon to cream mixture and stir to combine. Pour pasta into frying pan with salmon-cream mixture and toss to coat, adding some of reserved cooking water as needed to moisten pasta. Add parsley and toss to combine. Season to taste with salt and pepper.

PER SERVING: 546 cal., 51% (281 cal.) from fat; 20 g protein; 31 g fat (18 g sat.); 48 g carbo (2.7 g fiber); 716 mg sodium; 111 mg chol.

Spaghetti with Anchovies and Bread Crumbs (*Spaghetti con Acciughe e Mollica*)

At her home in Oakland, California, Rosetta Costantino—who teaches Italian cooking—serves this dish as part of the Christmas Eve menu, as is traditional in her native Calabria; but it's good any time. Chiles add spark to the sauce, with toasted bread crumbs sprinkled in for crunch.

SERVES 8 | **TIME** 50 minutes

6 salt-packed anchovies (*see Quick Tip below*) or
    12 high-quality anchovy fillets in olive oil, divided
1 lb. spaghetti
½ cup extra-virgin olive oil
6 large garlic cloves, minced
1 or 2 small fresh or dried hot red chiles such as
    peperoncini or Thai, thinly sliced
2 tbsp. minced flat-leaf parsley
¾ cup Toasted Fresh Bread Crumbs (*recipe follows*),
    divided

1. If using salt-packed anchovies, rinse under cold running water. With your fingers, pry them open along back and lift out backbone to yield 2 fillets. Rinse fillets again to remove any fine bones; pat dry on paper towels. If using anchovy fillets in olive oil, lift out of jar or tin, leaving oil behind (no need to rinse). Finely chop 6 fillets; set aside. Cut remaining 6 fillets into 4 or 5 pieces each; set aside.
2. In an 8-qt. pot over high heat, bring 5 qts. well-salted water to a boil. Add pasta and cook, uncovered, until tender to the bite, about 10 minutes, stirring a few times to separate pasta strands.
3. Meanwhile, put olive oil, garlic, finely chopped anchovies, and chiles in a deep 12-in. frying pan (with sides at least 2 in. high) or wide pot and cook over low heat, stirring, until anchovies dissolve. Stir in parsley and remaining anchovies; turn off heat.
4. When pasta is almost done, set aside 1 cup of cooking water, then drain pasta and transfer to pan of anchovy sauce. Toss quickly; add some reserved cooking water if pasta seems dry. Set aside 2 tbsp. bread; add remainder to pasta and toss until coated with crumbs.
5. Divide pasta among warm bowls and sprinkle each serving with some reserved bread crumbs.
Quick Tip: Italian and specialty stores carry whole salt-packed anchovies—typically sold by the piece—which are meatier and more flavorful than oil-packed.

PER SERVING: 411 cal., 42% (171 cal.) from fat; 9.6 g protein; 19 g fat (2.8 g sat.); 51 g carbo (1.9 g fiber); 440 mg sodium; 1.7 mg chol.

Toasted Fresh Bread Crumbs

Crunchy toasted bread crumbs are a traditional substitute for cheese on pasta in southern Italy. The secret to making evenly browned bread crumbs is to cook them in a skillet and stir without pause.

MAKES About ¾ cup | **TIME** 30 minutes

4-in. (¼ lb.) piece Italian-style bread with crust, such as
    pugliese
2 tbsp. extra-virgin olive oil

1. Preheat oven to 300°. Cut bread into cubes; scatter on a baking sheet in a single layer. Bake until cubes feel dry on outside but still moist inside, about 15 minutes.
2. When bread cubes are cool, put in a food processor and pulse into fine crumbs. Set aside ¾ cup firmly packed bread crumbs; save remaining for another use.
3. Heat oil in a 10-in. frying pan over medium heat just until warm (not hot). Add reserved bread crumbs and stir to coat with oil. Cook, stirring constantly, until bread crumbs are golden brown and crunchy, about 5 minutes.

PER TBSP.: 46 cal., 53% (24 cal.) from fat; 0.9 g protein; 2.7 g fat (0.4 g sat.); 4.8 g carbo (0.3 g fiber); 55 mg sodium; 0 mg chol.

Grilled Catfish with Noodles (*Cha Ca*)

At the Noodle Ranch in Seattle, former head chef Nga Bui set a hot, spicy fish fillet on a bed of rice noodles and greens for a light, refreshing meal in a bowl. The grilled catfish fillet also makes a tasty sandwich.

SERVES 6 | **TIME** 1 hour, plus 30 minutes to marinate

⅓ cup minced shallots
3 tbsp. Thai or Vietnamese fish sauce (*nam pla or
    nuoc mam*)
1 tbsp. red or yellow curry powder
1½ tsp. ground ginger
1 tsp. turmeric
½ tsp. cayenne
2 garlic cloves, pressed or minced
6 boned, skinned catfish or tilapia fillets (about 6 oz. each)
About 2 tbsp. vegetable oil
4 cups bite-size pieces iceberg lettuce
3 cups mung bean sprouts (6 to 8 oz.), rinsed
½ cup *each* mint and cilantro leaves
6 to 8 cups cooled Cooked Rice Noodles (*Bun; page 99*)
½ cup *each* chopped roasted, salted peanuts and dill
⅓ cup thinly sliced green onions
½ cup Fried Sliced Shallots (*page 211*)
Vietnamese Dipping Sauce (*recipe follows*)

1. In a small bowl, mix minced shallots, fish sauce, curry powder, ginger, turmeric, cayenne, and garlic. Rub shallot mixture all over fillets and stack in a bowl. Cover and chill 30 minutes and up to 1 day.

2. Prepare a charcoal or gas grill for direct high heat (*see Direct Heat Grilling, page 436*). Brush both sides of catfish fillets lightly with oil. Grill fish (close lid on gas grill), turning once, until barely opaque but still moist-looking in center of thickest part (cut to test), 4 to 8 minutes total. Serve hot or cool.

3. Meanwhile, divide lettuce, bean sprouts, mint, and cilantro among deep, wide bowls. Mound noodles over lettuce, sprouts, and herbs.

4. Lay a grilled fish fillet on each mound of noodles. Sprinkle peanuts, dill, green onions, and fried shallots over top. Serve with dipping sauce to drizzle on to taste.

PER SERVING: 705 cal., 38% (270 cal.) from fat; 36 g protein; 30 g fat (5.2 g sat.); 72 g carbo (3.1 g fiber); 1,316 mg sodium; 56 mg chol.

Vietnamese Dipping Sauce (*Nuoc Cham*): There are many versions of this classic sauce; this is one of our favorites. In a small bowl, mix ½ cup water, ½ cup **Thai or Vietnamese fish sauce** (*nam pla* or *nuoc mam*), ¼ cup *each* unseasoned **rice vinegar** and **fresh lime juice**, 2 tbsp. **sugar**, and 2 **garlic cloves**, minced. Add 1 to 1½ tsp. minced **hot red chile** (such as Thai, serrano, jalapeño, or Fresno) **or Asian red chili paste** to taste. Can make up to a day ahead; chill. Makes 1½ cups.

PER TBSP.: 18 cal., 30% (5.4 cal.) from fat; 0.8 g protein; 0.6 g fat (0.1 g sat.); 2.3 g carbo (0 g fiber); 199 mg sodium; 0 mg chol.

■ Red Curry Powder

FROM THE PANTRY

Red curry powder is a blend of chile, garlic, lemongrass, and other spices, and is the basis of many Thai and Malaysian dishes. Find it in the spice section of many supermarkets; if it's unavailable, use the more common yellow powder. Feel free to use jarred red and yellow curry pastes too, which often taste fresher. The spice level of each brand varies, so taste before using; start with the minimum.

Shrimp Pad Thai

Quick and delicious, pad Thai is ubiquitous street food in Thailand. The dried shrimp, added along with the fresh, bring intensity and texture to the dish.

SERVES 8 | **TIME** 35 minutes

¾ lb. rice vermicelli
⅓ cup peanut or vegetable oil
1 tbsp. minced garlic
½ lb. medium shrimp (30 to 35 per lb.), peeled and deveined
5 green onions, trimmed and cut into 2-in. pieces
1 tbsp. dried shrimp (*see Quick Tip below*), minced
2 cups mung bean sprouts, rinsed, divided
⅓ cup Thai or Vietnamese fish sauce (*nam pla* or *nuoc mam*)
2 tbsp. *each* ketchup and sugar
1 tsp. red chile flakes
2 eggs, lightly beaten
½ cup cilantro leaves
⅓ cup chopped roasted unsalted peanuts (optional)
6 to 8 lime wedges
Sriracha chili sauce (optional)

1. In a large bowl, cover vermicelli in very hot water and let stand until soft, about 15 minutes, stirring often to prevent sticking.

2. Meanwhile, heat a large wok or frying pan over high heat. Pour in oil and carefully swirl to coat sides. Add garlic, peeled fresh shrimp, and green onions and cook 2 minutes, stirring often. Stir in dried shrimp, 1 cup bean sprouts, the fish sauce, ketchup, sugar, and chile flakes. Push shrimp mixture to one side of pan and carefully pour eggs onto other side, trying to coat pan evenly. Let cook undisturbed 1 minute, then quickly scramble with other ingredients.

3. Drain noodles and add to egg mixture. Cook until noodles start to brown slightly, 3 to 4 minutes, stirring once or twice.

4. Transfer to plates. Top with remaining 1 cup bean sprouts, the cilantro, and peanuts if you like. Serve with lime wedges and Sriracha if you like.

Quick Tip: Dried shimp and the other Asian ingredients listed here are available at Asian markets and often in the Asian foods section of well-stocked supermarkets.

PER SERVING: 321 cal., 34% (108 cal.) from fat; 13 g protein; 12 g fat (2.2 g sat.); 41 g carbo (1.4 g fiber); 643 mg sodium; 97 mg chol.

Pasta with Scallops and Lemon

One busy night, reader Robin Grant of Oakland, Oregon, had little on hand besides a lemon and some scallops. With fresh basil from her garden and some dried pasta, the ingredients became an appealing weeknight meal.

SERVES 4 | **TIME** 30 minutes

¾ lb. penne
1 onion (about 6 oz.), diced
3 garlic cloves, minced
2 tbsp. olive oil
1 tbsp. finely shredded lemon zest
¼ cup fresh lemon juice
1 tbsp. butter
1 lb. scallops (about 1½ in. wide)
⅓ cup chopped basil leaves
Salt and freshly ground black pepper

1. In a 5- to 6-qt. pan over high heat, bring about 4 qts. water to a boil. Add penne and cook, uncovered and stirring occasionally, until tender to the bite, 10 to 12 minutes. Drain.
2. Meanwhile, in a 10- to 12-in. frying pan (with sides at least 2 in. high) over medium heat, cook onion and garlic in oil until limp, 3 to 5 minutes. Add lemon zest and juice, butter, and scallops. Bring to a simmer and cook until scallops are opaque but still moist-looking in center (cut to test), about 6 minutes.
3. Add pasta and basil to scallop mixture and stir until heated through. Add salt and pepper to taste. Transfer to a wide, shallow bowl to serve.

PER SERVING: 524 cal., 21% (108 cal.) from fat; 31 g protein; 12 g fat (3 g sat.); 72 g carbo (3.1 g fiber); 223 mg sodium; 45 mg chol.

Farmed vs. Wild Scallops (and Other Mollusks)

Scallops, clams, oysters, and mussels are the ideal farmed seafood. In the wild, they may be harvested using hydraulic dredges, which rip up the ocean floor. Farming involves either raising the mollusks on beaches and hand-raking to harvest, which has very little impact on the beach itself; or growing them on strings hanging from floating platforms or in metal-mesh sacks laid on floating racks, neither of which does any environmental damage whatsoever.

Moreover, these little bivalves eat plankton, so do nothing to deplete other fish populations. And best of all, they're filter feeders, leaving the water cleaner than it was before.

Italian Crab and Pasta

Back in 1890, the Italian grandparents of reader Dorene Centioli-McTigue failed to find the right fish for their Christmas Eve pasta their first year in Seattle. What they did encounter was plenty of Dungeness crab, so they created a new tradition: cracked crab and pasta in a homemade tomato sauce. Their granddaughter serves it to this day. Provide nut or crab crackers and plenty of napkins or wet towels.

SERVES 6 | **TIME** 1 hour

6 tbsp. olive oil
3 Dungeness crabs (about 2 lbs. each), cooked, cleaned, and cracked *(see Dungeness Crab 101, page 340)*
2 cans (28 oz. each) Italian-style peeled whole tomatoes
3 garlic cloves, crushed
¼ cup thinly slivered fresh basil leaves or 1 tbsp. dried
1 lb. angel hair pasta or fresh linguine
¼ lb. shelled cooked crab
Salt and freshly ground black pepper
3 to 4 tbsp. chopped flat-leaf parsley

1. Pour oil into a 12-in. frying pan (with sides at least 2 in. high) or 6- to 8-qt. pan over medium heat. When warm, add crabs in shell and cook, stirring occasionally, until juices leak into pan, 5 to 7 minutes. With tongs, transfer crab pieces in shell to a large serving bowl; cover and keep warm in a 200° oven.
2. Add tomatoes (with their juice), garlic, and basil to pan. Scrape up any crab bits from bottom of pan. Cover and bring to a boil over high heat, stirring occasionally. Boil gently, uncovered, stirring occasionally, crushing tomatoes with a potato masher or spoon, and reducing heat as sauce thickens, until sauce is thick and reduced to about 4½ cups, about 30 minutes. Remove from heat. Spoon about a third of sauce over crabs in shell; cover loosely and return to oven.
3. About 15 minutes before sauce is done, in a 6- to 8-qt. pan over high heat, bring 3 to 4 qts. water to a boil. Add pasta, stir to separate, and cook just until barely tender to the bite, 3 to 4 minutes for angel hair, about 2 minutes for fresh linguine. Drain.
4. Over low heat, add shelled cooked crab to remaining tomato sauce; heat, stirring occasionally, until hot, 1 to 2 minutes. Add salt and pepper to taste. Pour drained pasta into sauce and mix well.
5. Mound pasta in a wide, shallow serving bowl. Remove crab from oven and sprinkle both crab and pasta with parsley.

PER SERVING: 587 cal., 28% (162 cal.) from fat; 38 g protein; 18 g fat (2.4 g sat.); 69 g carbo (4.2 g fiber); 794 mg sodium; 128 mg chol.

Spicy Baked Penne with Sausage and Chard

Reader Wendy Skidmore of Los Altos, California, relies on dishes that are simple and quick, made with ingredients she usually has on hand. This hearty baked penne is a delicious example.

SERVES 4 | **TIME** 50 minutes

½ lb. penne
2 tsp. olive oil
2 links hot Italian sausage (½ lb. total), casings removed
2 garlic cloves, minced
2 cups chopped Swiss chard leaves (*see Swiss Chard below*)
1 can (14.5 oz.) diced tomatoes
¼ tsp. *each* salt and freshly ground black pepper
2 cups shredded mozzarella cheese (½ lb.)
¼ cup finely shredded parmesan cheese

1. Preheat oven to 350°. In a 5- to 6-qt. pot over high heat, bring about 4 qts. water to a boil. Add penne and cook, uncovered, stirring occasionally, until tender to the bite, 10 to 12 minutes. Drain and dry pot with a kitchen towel.
2. Pour oil into dried pot over medium-high heat. Add sausage and garlic; cook, stirring and breaking apart with a spoon, until sausage is crumbled and brown, about 10 minutes.
3. Add chard and cook, stirring often, until wilted, about 5 minutes. Stir in tomatoes (with their juice), salt, pepper, and pasta. Pour mixture into a 2- to 2½-qt. baking dish. Sprinkle mozzarella and parmesan over the top.
4. Bake until cheeses are browned and bubbling, 25 to 30 minutes.

PER SERVING: 636 cal., 50% (315 cal.) from fat; 30 g protein; 35 g fat (15 g sat.); 50 g carbo (2.6 g fiber); 1,079 mg sodium; 91 mg chol.

■ Swiss Chard

FROM THE GARDEN

This earthy-flavored green has crinkly leaves and stems that come in any color from yellow to red to deep green. It's sold in bunches, with each bunch being about half stems and half leaves. If you buy a bunch with large leaves, it will be easier to clean. Spinach is a good substitute for Swiss chard leaves. Most recipes just call for the leaves, but the stalks are perfectly edible; chop and sauté until tender.

Pasta Paella

Paella is one of Spain's great one-pan dishes, but in its best known form, it's too much work for a quick week night supper. This lesser-known version uses thin pasta instead of rice and is much quicker to make. Add a green salad and you have a simple, unusual dinner for any night of the week.

SERVES 4 | **TIME** 35 minutes

2 tbsp. olive oil
½ lb. angel hair or capellini pasta
1 onion (½ lb.), chopped
3 garlic cloves, minced
¼ tsp. turmeric
1½ cups chicken broth
1 can (14.5 oz.) diced tomatoes
1 package (8 oz.) frozen artichoke hearts, thawed
1 dozen small clams in shells, suitable for steaming (about 1 lb.; optional), scrubbed
½ lb. large shrimp (21 to 30 per lb.), peeled and deveined
½ lb. boned halibut fillet, cut into ½-in. chunks
1 cup frozen petite peas
Salt
Lemon wedges

1. Pour oil into an 11- to 12-in. frying pan over medium-high heat. Break pasta into 3- to 4-in. lengths and drop into oil; cook, stirring often, until golden, 6 to 8 minutes. Add onion, garlic, and turmeric; cook until onion is limp, 3 to 4 minutes. Stir in broth and tomatoes (with their juice); cover and bring to a boil over high heat.
2. Spread mixture level. Evenly distribute artichoke hearts and clams, if using, over pasta. Cover, reduce heat to medium, and cook for 5 minutes. Evenly distribute shrimp, fish, and peas over pasta. Cover and cook until clams have opened and fish is barely opaque in center of thickest part (cut to test), 5 to 8 minutes longer.
3. Uncover and cook until pasta has absorbed most of liquid and is beginning to brown on bottom, 2 to 4 minutes. Add salt to taste. Garnish with lemon wedges to squeeze over seafood. Serve from pan.

PER SERVING: 497 cal., 20% (99 cal.) from fat; 39 g protein; 11 g fat (1.5 g sat.); 61 g carbo (7.9 g fiber); 382 mg sodium; 104 mg chol.

Green Lasagna Swirls

We got into a playful mood with lasagna noodles, and this is the result—perky shapes and a high proportion of chewy-tender noodles to greens.

SERVES 5 to 7 | **TIME** 1¼ hours

1 package (½ lb.) dried lasagna (1¼ in. wide)
2 cups chopped onions (about ½ lb.)
2 tbsp. *each* butter and flour
1½ cups chicken broth
1 cup milk
3 cups (about ¾ lb.) freshly shredded parmesan cheese, divided
Basic Sautéed Greens (*recipe follows*)
2 tbsp. minced fresh marjoram leaves or 2 tsp. dried marjoram
1 tbsp. minced fresh sage leaves or 1 tsp. dried rubbed sage
¼ tsp. ground nutmeg
1 cup ricotta cheese
2 eggs, lightly beaten
Salt and freshly ground black pepper

1. In a 5- to 6-qt. pan over high heat, bring 3 qts. water to a boil. Add lasagna and cook, uncovered, stirring occasionally, until tender to the bite, about 10 minutes. Drain, immerse in cold water until cool, then drain again.
2. Meanwhile, in a 2- to 3-qt. pan over medium heat, cook onions in butter, stirring frequently, until softened, 8 to 10 minutes. Add flour and cook 1 minute, stirring. Gradually whisk in broth and milk, raise heat to medium-high, and continue whisking until mixture boils. Remove from heat and stir in 2 cups parmesan. Spread half the sauce in a shallow 3-qt. baking dish.
3. Drain greens; save liquid for other use. Finely chop greens. In a bowl, mix greens, marjoram, sage, nutmeg, ricotta, ¾ cup parmesan, and the eggs.
4. Preheat oven to 375°. Lay lasagna noodles flat on a work surface. Spread about 2½ tbsp. greens mixture evenly over each, then cut in half lengthwise and roll each up from one end. Stand rolls upright, side by side, on sauce in baking dish. Spread remaining sauce evenly over rolls. Seal pan with foil.
5. Bake lasagna rolls until bubbling in center, about 45 minutes. Uncover and sprinkle with remaining ¼ cup parmesan. Broil 5 to 6 in. from heat until parmesan begins to brown, about 4 minutes.
6. Season to taste with salt and pepper.
Make Ahead: Through step 4, up to 1 day, chilled (bring to room temperature before baking).

PER SERVING USING SPINACH: 620 cal., 46% (285 cal.) from fat; 43 g protein; 32 g fat (16 g sat.); 43 g carbo (4.7 g fiber); 1302 mg sodium; 146 mg chol.

Basic Sautéed Greens

Use mustard greens, beet greens, spinach, Swiss chard, or a mix of all four—or choose from *A Gallery of Greens, below*.

MAKES 2 to 2½ cups | **TIME** 15 to 35 minutes

1 lb. mustard greens, beet greens (leaves only), stemmed spinach, or Swiss chard (*see Swiss Chard, page 221*)
1 tbsp. olive oil
2 garlic cloves, thinly sliced
Kosher salt and freshly ground black pepper

1. Discard yellowed or wilted leaves from greens. If greens aren't washed, immerse in cold water and rinse well; drain.
2. For beet greens or Swiss chard, trim and discard discolored stem ends, then thinly slice stems; trim and discard stems from other greens. Coarsely chop leaves from all greens.
3. Pour oil into a 6- to 8-qt. saucepan over medium-high heat. When hot, add garlic; stir until limp, about 15 seconds. Add greens with the water that clings to leaves (if greens are dry, add ¼ cup water); stir often

A Gallery of Greens

Supermarkets carry most of these greens, and at farmers' markets, you'll find an even wider selection. We've divided the greens according to their sturdiness.

Tender
Spinach: Sweet but slightly astringent.

Medium
Beet greens: Earthy.
Collard greens: Robust, slightly bittersweet.
Mustard greens: Pungent and peppery; mellow with cooking.
Ornamental kale: Nutty, with cabbagelike heads.
Swiss chard: Mild and slightly smoky (green variety) to earthy (red). Can be green, red, or rainbow-colored (red, pink, orange, yellow, and green).
Turnip greens: Mellow and slightly sweet.

Firm
Kale: Robust and herbaceous.
Lacinato kale: Also called dinosaur kale, lacinto kale, *cavolo nero*, or Tuscan kale. Dark green (almost black), with bumpy, narrow leaves; very flavorful.
Purple kale: Very sturdy, minerally, and slightly bitter.

until greens are wilted, about 2 minutes. For spinach, proceed to step 5.

4. Add ½ cup water, reduce heat to medium, and simmer, covered, until greens are tender to bite, 5 to 12 minutes for medium-textured greens, and up to 25 minutes for firm ones. If all liquid evaporates during cooking, add about ⅓ cup more water.

5. Season to taste with salt and pepper.

PER ½-CUP SERVING OF GREENS: 70 cal., 51% (36 cal.) from fat; 4.8 g protein; 4 g fat (0.6 g sat.); 6.4 g carbo (3.6 g fiber); 129 mg sodium; 0 mg chol.

Lasagna with Sausage Ragù

This lasagna, with its meaty ragù and creamy, nutmeg-scented béchamel, is a subtle departure from the familiar cheese-laden lasagna favored by many Americans. It's actually closer to authentic Italian lasagna. We simplified the ragù, however, by using sweet Italian sausage instead of the traditional beef, pork, and/or veal.

SERVES 6 to 8 | **TIME** 3 hours

7 tbsp. butter, divided
1 tbsp. vegetable oil
½ cup *each* **diced (¼ in.) onion, carrots, and celery**
1 lb. sweet Italian sausages, casings removed
1½ tsp. salt, divided
4 cups whole milk, divided
½ cup dry white wine
1 can (28 oz.) peeled whole tomatoes, finely chopped or crushed with your hands, juice reserved
Freshly ground black pepper
¼ cup flour
¼ tsp. freshly grated nutmeg
¾ lb. lasagna noodles (*see Lasagna Noodles, right***)**
1 cup grated good-quality parmesan cheese

1. In a large, heavy-bottomed saucepan, melt 2 tbsp. butter in oil over medium heat. Add onion and cook, stirring often, until golden, about 5 minutes. Add carrots and celery and cook, stirring often, 5 more minutes. Add sausage and ½ tsp. salt, breaking up meat with a wooden spoon, and cook until sausage loses its raw color.

2. Add 1 cup milk and cook over medium heat, stirring, until completely absorbed, 10 to 12 minutes. (The milk will appear quite curdled at this point; don't be alarmed.) Add wine and cook until reduced by half, about 3 minutes. Add tomatoes and their juice; bring to a boil over medium-high heat, then lower heat and gently simmer, uncovered, 2 hours. Season with salt and pepper to taste.

3. Meanwhile, after ragù has cooked 1½ hours, make béchamel by melting remaining 5 tbsp. butter in a medium heavy-bottomed saucepan over medium heat. Add flour and cook, stirring constantly, until it turns light golden brown, about 5 minutes. Slowly drizzle in remaining 3 cups milk, whisking constantly. Bring to a simmer and continue to cook, whisking, until thickened, about 10 minutes. Season with remaining 1 tsp. salt, the nutmeg, and pepper to taste.

4. Preheat oven to 375°. Cook lasagna noodles according to package directions, being careful not to overcook. Drain and lay flat on kitchen towels, making sure noodles do not overlap. Butter bottom of a 9- by 13-in. baking dish and coat with about ½ cup of ragù. Add a single layer of noodles (for most brands this is four sheets per layer). Spread on one-third of béchamel; top béchamel with one-quarter of remaining ragù, then one-quarter of parmesan. Repeat layering two more times, covering final layer with remaining ragù and parmesan.

5. Cover lasagna with buttered foil and bake 20 minutes. Uncover and bake until top browns slightly, about 10 minutes longer. Let stand 15 minutes before serving.

PER SERVING: 721 cal., 55% (396 cal.) from fat; 28 g protein; 44 g fat (20 g sat.); 54 g carbo (2.7 g fiber); 1,617 mg sodium; 111 mg chol.

■ Lasagna Noodles

FROM THE PANTRY

Imported, commercially produced dried lasagna noodles (the kind you boil first) work well in this recipe, but if you can find fresh noodles at a specialty-foods shop, try those instead. Just boil the noodles a few at a time for 2 minutes, plunge in an ice bath, and dry before assembling lasagna.

Giant Butternut Squash Ravioli

Paired with crunchy almonds and earthy sage and parmesan, butternut squash makes an unforgettable filling for these oversize ravioli from L.A.-based cookbook author Martha Rose Shulman. *See Quick Tip, below right,* for an option that saves a bit of time.

recipe pictured
on page
181

MAKES 24 to 30 ravioli; 8 servings | **TIME** 4 hours

FILLING
1 butternut squash (about 3½ lbs.), peeled, seeded, and cut into 2-in. chunks
1 tbsp. extra-virgin olive oil
Salt and freshly ground black pepper
¾ cup ground toasted almonds (see *How to Toast Nuts*, page 134)
1 tbsp. minced sage leaves
1¾ cups grated parmesan cheese
½ tsp. freshly grated nutmeg

ASSEMBLING & SERVING
Fine semolina
Fresh Pasta Dough (*recipe follows*), rolled into sheets as directed, or 2 lbs. store-bought fresh ravioli or lasagna sheets
4 cups reduced-sodium chicken broth
2 tbsp. butter
2 tsp. extra-virgin olive oil, divided
1 tbsp. minced flat-leaf parsley
Freshly shredded parmesan

1. Make filling: Preheat oven to 425°. Put squash chunks in a rimmed baking pan, drizzle with oil, and season generously with salt and pepper. Toss to coat. Bake, stirring squash every 20 minutes, until very tender, 35 to 45 minutes.
2. Carefully spoon hot squash into a food processor and purée until very smooth. Scrape squash into a large bowl and let cool. Stir in almonds, sage, parmesan, and nutmeg. Add salt and pepper to taste.
3. Assemble ravioli: Line a rimmed baking pan with parchment paper and sprinkle with semolina; set aside. On a work surface, lay one pasta sheet with a long side facing you. Spoon 2-tbsp. mounds of squash mixture filling along the center of pasta sheet, starting 2 in. from a short end and repeating at 4-in. intervals. Around mounds of filling, brush pasta with water. Place a second pasta sheet over the first, starting at a short end and easing pasta over filling, gently pressing out air and sealing pasta around each mound as you go.
4. Trim long sides of pasta sheet with a pastry wheel or knife so sheet is 4 in. wide. Cut ravioli between filling to make 4-in. squares. Transfer ravioli to parchment-lined pan and cover with plastic wrap; gather and wrap pasta scraps too. Continue forming ravioli, rerolling scraps according to directions for Fresh Pasta Dough and stacking one more layer of parchment over first (add another pan if needed), until you've used all the filling; you should have 24 to 30 ravioli and may have leftover pasta dough. (If dough scraps become too dry to reroll, crumble into food processor and pulse with 1 tsp. water at a time until moistened.)
5. In a saucepan, boil broth until reduced by a third. Add butter; keep warm.
6. To serve: Preheat oven to 150° and set wide soup plates or rimmed dinner plates in oven to warm. Bring 2 large pots (8 to 10 qts. each) of generously salted water to a rolling boil and add 1 tsp. oil to each. Divide ravioli between pots, reduce heat so water boils gently, and cook ravioli, occasionally pushing them down into water, until tender to the bite (test a corner of one to check), 5 to 7 minutes.
7. Set out soup plates. Using a slotted spoon, transfer 3 ravioli from water to each plate. Ladle broth over ravioli, sprinkle with parsley, and serve with parmesan.
Quick Tip: Buy 2¾ lbs. peeled chunks of butternut squash instead of a whole squash.
Make Ahead: Filling, through step 2, chilled overnight. Ravioli, through step 4 up to 1 day, chilled; or freeze on pans until firm, transfer to resealable plastic bags, and freeze up to 3 weeks. Cook ravioli straight from fridge or freezer.

PER SERVING: 572 cal., 35% (198 cal.) from fat; 22 g protein; 22 g fat (6.4 g sat.); 75 g carbo (7 g fiber); 877 mg sodium; 123 mg chol.

Fresh Pasta Dough

Semolina gives the dough a slight and very satisfying chewiness.

MAKES Dough for 24 to 30 giant ravioli | **TIME** 1 hour, plus 30 minutes to rest

2⅔ cups all-purpose flour
1⅓ cups fine semolina (see *Quick Tip, above right*)
1 tsp. salt
4 eggs
4 tsp. extra-virgin olive oil

1. Put flour, semolina, and salt in a food processor and pulse to combine. In a glass measuring cup, whisk ⅓ cup water, the eggs, and oil to blend. With motor running, pour egg mixture into flour mixture. Process until dough comes together. If it seems dry, add 1 tbsp. water.

2. On a lightly floured work surface, knead dough until smooth (it will be very stiff), 5 to 7 minutes. Wrap airtight and let stand at room temperature about 30 minutes.

3. Set rollers of a pasta machine at widest setting. Cut dough into eight equal pieces. Flatten one portion (keep others covered) and feed through rollers, then fold dough in thirds crosswise. Repeat rolling and folding, feeding narrow end through rollers, until dough looks very smooth and sheets are about 5 in. wide, about five times; if dough gets sticky, lightly dust with flour, and if sheets are too narrow, fold and re-roll. Then, without folding, roll dough once at each successively thinner setting until it's as thin as possible; when dough gets too long to handle, cut in half and continue rolling the halves.

4. Set finished pieces on sheets of flour-dusted parchment paper. Let stand, uncovered, until a bit drier, about 5 minutes. Stack sheets between parchment and wrap airtight; set aside. Repeat with remaining dough.

Quick Tip: Find fine semolina in the baking aisle of well-stocked supermarkets.

Make Ahead: Through step 2, up to 1 day, covered and chilled. Bring to room temperature before using.

Molten Cheese Gnocchi

Think of molten chocolate cake and you'll get the idea here: Each gnocchi has a melted cheese center. It's easy to pop down several of these gnocchi before your brain registers how rich they are—so savor them slowly.

recipe pictured on page **185**

MAKES About 100 gnocchi; 6 to 8 main-course or 10 to 12 first-course servings | **TIME** 3 hours

2 lbs. russet potatoes (3 large)
4 cups (about 9 oz.) finely shredded aged gouda cheese (such as Winchester Sharp; *see Quick Tips, right*), divided
¾ cup heavy whipping cream
1 egg, lightly beaten
1 tsp. salt
1 to 2 cups flour
1½ tbsp. butter, melted
1 tsp. freshly ground black pepper
2 tbsp. finely chopped flat-leaf parsley

1. Preheat oven to 350°. Set potatoes on a baking sheet and slash each deeply lengthwise down the center. Bake until potatoes are tender and look slightly dried out, 1¼ to 1½ hours.

2. In a small bowl, mix together 3 cups cheese and the cream. Set aside.

3. As soon as potatoes are cool enough to handle, cut them in half and spoon out baked flesh; discard skins. Put potatoes through a potato ricer (*see Quick Tips below*) into a large bowl. Mix in egg, salt, and 1 cup flour, adding just enough additional flour to make the dough pliable and not sticky (too much flour will make gnocchi heavy). Turn dough out onto a lightly floured work surface; with floured hands, knead dough 10 to 12 times.

4. Divide dough and cover one batch with a damp kitchen towel. Roll other batch into a ¾-in.-thick rope and cut into ¾-in.-long pieces. Roll each piece into a ball, then flatten into a 2-in. circle with your fingers or the bottom of a well-floured drinking glass.

5. Bring a large pot of salted water to a boil. Top each dough circle with ½ tsp. cheese-cream mixture. Gather up dough around filling and pinch to close, then roll into a small, smooth ball. Repeat rolling, filling, and forming with second batch of dough.

6. Preheat broiler. Divide melted butter between two 2-qt. baking dishes (or use one 4-qt. baking dish and all the butter). Working in batches, drop gnocchi into boiling water, being careful not to crowd them. Boil gnocchi until they rise to the surface, 4 or 5 minutes; cook 8 to 10 seconds longer, then transfer with a slotted spoon to the baking dish(es), making sure water drains off gnocchi.

7. Turn gnocchi to coat in butter. Sprinkle with pepper and remaining 1 cup cheese. Broil 4 in. from heat until browned on top, about 5 minutes. Sprinkle with parsley.

Quick Tips: We like to use farmstead gouda from Winchester Cheese Company in Riverside, California, where the cheeses are made following a master recipe that founder Jules Wesselink learned in his native Holland. If you don't have a ricer, you can use the fine disk on a food mill, but it will take longer and the gnocchi won't be as fluffy.

Make Ahead: Through step 5, frozen (freeze in a single layer on a cookie sheet to harden, then transfer to resealable freezer bags).

PER MAIN-COURSE SERVING: 443 cal., 47% (207 cal.) from fat; 16 g protein; 23 g fat (14 g sat.); 43 g carbo (2.9 g fiber); 686 mg sodium; 113 mg chol.

Ricotta-Basil Gnocchi

Semolina—coarsely ground durum wheat—gives these gnocchi, from reader Gemma Sciabica, of Modesto, California, a chewy texture. Gemma, author of four cookbooks about olive oil, is married to Joseph Sciabica, founder of the renowned olive oil company Nick Sciabica & Sons.

SERVES 6 | **TIME** 1¼ hours

1 container (15 oz.) whole-milk ricotta cheese
½ cup shredded romano cheese, plus more to taste
¼ cup minced basil leaves
2 eggs
2 tbsp. olive oil
½ tsp. freshly ground black pepper, plus more to taste
About 2⅓ cups fine semolina (*see Quick Tip below*)
1 tbsp. salt, plus more to taste
3 cups marinara sauce, heated (store-bought or homemade; *see recipe for Marinara Sauce in Vegetable Ribbon Pasta Shells, page 288*)

1. In a large bowl, mix ricotta, romano cheese, basil, eggs, oil, and pepper until well blended. Add 2 cups semolina and stir until evenly moistened.
2. Scrape dough onto a board lightly coated with semolina and knead until it forms a smooth ball that's no longer sticky, about 20 turns, adding more of remaining semolina as needed to prevent sticking.
3. Cut dough into 10 pieces. With your fingers, roll each into a ½-in.-thick rope. Cut ropes into 1-in. pieces and lay, slightly separated, on baking sheets lightly coated with semolina.
4. In an 8- to 10-qt. pan over high heat, bring 5 qts. water and the salt to a boil. With a wooden spoon, gently push gnocchi into water; cook, stirring occasionally, until tender to the bite, about 10 minutes. Drain.
5. Spoon marinara sauce into a bowl and mound gnocchi on top. Add romano, salt, and pepper to taste.
Quick Tip: Find fine semolina in the baking aisle of well-stocked supermarkets.

PER SERVING: 546 cal., 36% (198 cal.) from fat; 23 g protein; 22 g fat (8.8 g sat.); 65 g carbo (4.8 g fiber); 1,206 mg sodium; 114 mg chol.

■ Ricotta Cheese

FROM THE PANTRY

Ricotta ("recooked" in Italian) cheese is made from reheated whey—the liquid that separates out from the curds when cheese is made. In Italy, it's made from the milk of cows, sheep, goats, and domestic water buffalo (very rich); in the U.S. ricotta is mainly from cow's milk, though a handful of producers here do make the other types. The soft curds add a subtle, rich taste to recipes.

Orzo with Fried Shallots

A savory side adapted from a recipe by cookbook authors and chefs Caprial and John Pence, of Portland, Oregon.

SERVES 6 as a side dish | **TIME** 20 minutes

1 tsp. salt, plus more to taste
1 lb. orzo
1 tbsp. extra-virgin olive oil
3 tbsp. butter
4 shallots (6 oz. total), slivered
3 garlic cloves, chopped
4 green onions, trimmed and thinly sliced
Freshly ground black pepper

1. In a 5- to 6-qt. pan over high heat, bring about 3 qts. water and 1 tsp. salt to a boil. Add orzo and cook until barely tender to the bite, 5 to 9 minutes. Drain well. Pour into a bowl and mix with oil. Rinse and dry pan.
2. In the same pan, over medium heat, melt butter. Add shallots and cook, stirring often, until they start to brown, 3 to 4 minutes. Add garlic and orzo; mix well and cook just until pasta is warm, 2 to 5 minutes.
3. Remove from heat and stir in green onions and salt and pepper to taste.

PER SERVING: 375 cal., 22% (84 cal.) from fat; 11 g protein; 9.3 g fat (4.1 g sat.); 62 g carbo (2.3 g fiber); 327 mg sodium; 16 mg chol.

Mushroom Orzo "Risotto"

Orzo absorbs liquid and flavor much like rice, but it doesn't need to be stirred obsessively for an al dente, creamy result.

SERVES 4 as a main course | **TIME** 1 hour

3 tbsp. butter, divided
¾ lb. mushrooms, sliced
¾ cup chopped shallots or onion
2 cups orzo
3 cups chicken broth
½ cup dry sherry
⅓ cup freshly grated parmesan cheese, plus more to taste
Salt and freshly ground black pepper
Chopped flat-leaf parsley

1. Melt 1 tbsp. butter in a 12-in. frying pan over high heat. Add mushrooms and shallots; cook, stirring often, until mushrooms are lightly browned, 9 to 12 minutes.
2. Reduce heat to medium and add remaining 2 tbsp. butter and the orzo; stir often until pasta is light golden, about 2 minutes.

3. Add broth and sherry. Bring to a boil over high heat, then reduce heat and simmer, stirring often, until pasta is tender to the bite and most of liquid is absorbed, 9 to 11 minutes. If mixture becomes too thick before pasta is done, add a little more broth.

4. Stir in parmesan and salt and pepper to taste. Spoon orzo into wide bowls and sprinkle with a little parsley and more parmesan cheese to taste.

PER SERVING: 524 cal., 21% (112 cal.) from fat; 23 g protein; 13 g fat (7.2 g sat.); 77 g carbo (3.2 g fiber); 892 mg sodium; 30 mg chol.

Nutted Brown Rice Pilaf

Nuts bring flavor, richness, and protein to this hearty side dish. We like to serve it with roast pork or as a vegetarian main dish, accompanied by sautéed greens and roasted sweet potatoes.

SERVES 8 as a side dish | **TIME** 1¼ hours

2 tbsp. olive oil
1 onion, finely chopped
½ tsp. salt, plus more to taste
⅓ cup *each* slivered almonds, pistachio halves and/or pieces, and chopped walnuts
3 garlic cloves, minced
1 tsp. ground coriander
½ tsp. *each* ground cumin and freshly ground black pepper
1 cup long-grain brown rice or basmati brown rice (*see Brown Rice, above right*)
1 cup dry white wine
2½ cups reduced-sodium chicken or vegetable broth
2 tbsp. minced flat-leaf parsley (optional)

1. In a large frying pan with a tight-fitting lid, cook oil, onion, and salt over medium heat until onion has softened, about 8 minutes. Increase heat to high and add almonds, pistachios, and walnuts. Cook, stirring, until nuts start to toast. Onions may brown a bit, which is fine, but reduce heat if they start to burn. Add garlic and cook until fragrant, about 30 seconds.

2. Add coriander, cumin, and pepper. Cook, stirring, until fragrant, about 30 seconds. Add rice and stir to combine. Add wine and cook, stirring, until absorbed, about 2 minutes. Add broth and bring to a boil. Cover, reduce heat to low, and cook until rice is tender to the bite, about 50 minutes.

3. Fluff with a fork, and add salt to taste. Serve sprinkled with parsley if you like.

PER ½-CUP SERVING: 227 cal., 52% (117 cal.) from fat; 6 g protein; 13 g fat (1.4 g sat.); 24 g carbo (2.3 g fiber); 329 mg sodium; 0 mg chol.

■ Brown Rice

FROM THE PANTRY

Toothsome and satisfying, brown rice is rice that hasn't been messed with. Any type of white rice—long-grain, short-grain, basmati—begins as brown rice, which means its outer layer of bran has not yet been removed. The bran is what gives brown rice its higher quotient of fiber, fatty acids, B vitamins, and magnesium (among other vitamins and minerals) compared with white rice, and is responsible for its dense, chewy texture—great in salads, soups, stuffings, and casseroles. Brown rice takes longer to cook (about 50 minutes), so we often steam up a large batch and freeze portions, since it defrosts nicely in a microwave or at room temp—or in the refrigerator overnight. We especially like the brown rice from two California growers: Massa Organics (*massaorganics.com*) and Lundberg Family Farms (*lundberg.com*), both in the Sacramento Valley.

Pearl Couscous with Fresh Peas and Mint

Also known as Israeli couscous, pearl couscous has an appealing tender-chewy texture. Try serving this dish with grilled lamb.

SERVES 6 to 8 as a side dish | **TIME** 15 minutes

3 cups chicken or vegetable broth
2 cups pearl couscous
1 cup fresh peas (*see Quick Tip below*)
½ cup chopped mint leaves
Salt and freshly ground black pepper

1. Bring broth and 1 cup water to a boil in a medium pan. Stir in couscous and peas. Lower heat to medium and cook, stirring frequently, until couscous and peas are tender, 5 to 10 minutes.

2. Stir in mint and cook 1 minute. Add salt and pepper to taste.

Quick Tip: Frozen peas may be substituted for fresh; if you use frozen, stir them in at the last minute, along with the mint.

PER SERVING: 224 cal., 0% (4 cal.) from fat; 9.3 g protein; 0.5 g fat (0.1 g sat.); 45 g carbo (3 g fiber); 253 mg sodium; 0 mg chol.

Saffron Couscous

This easy, fragrant side dish pairs well with Grilled Chicken Kebabs with Romesco Sauce (*page 475*).

SERVES 4 as a side dish | **TIME** 20 minutes

3 tbsp. butter
⅛ tsp. crushed saffron threads
1 medium onion, cut into thin half-moons
1 tsp. salt
1 cup reduced-sodium chicken broth
10 oz. (1½ cups) couscous
⅓ cup chopped flat-leaf parsley

1. In a medium frying pan (with sides at least 2 in. high) over medium heat, melt butter. Add saffron and cook, stirring, 1 minute. Add onion and salt and cook, stirring, until translucent, about 7 minutes.
2. Add broth and 1 cup water and bring to a boil. Add couscous, stir, cover, and remove from heat. Let stand 5 minutes.
3. Fluff couscous with a fork, then gently stir. Sprinkle with parsley and serve.

PER SERVING: 364 cal., 23% (82 cal.) from fat; 10 g protein; 9.1 g fat (5.5 g sat.); 59 g carbo (3.2 g fiber); 823 mg sodium; 23 mg chol.

■ Saffron

FROM THE PANTRY

So potent it takes only a pinch or two to perfume an entire dish, saffron is one of the most prized spices in the world. And one of the most expensive. Saffron threads are the bright red stigma of the crocus plant *Crocus sativus*. One crocus flower has three stigmas, and it takes 13,000 stigmas—about 4,330 flowers—to produce one ounce of saffron. In the main saffron-producing nations—Spain, Iran, and India—the threads are gathered by hand and dried over a low fire. It's a worthy and delicious investment. A tip: Unless you use a lot of saffron, buy a bottle and split it (and the cost) with a friend.

Garlic and Gilroy

"The Garlic Capital of the World"—that's what Gilroy, California, proudly calls itself. Although China actually leads in global production, sunny little Gilroy processes more garlic than anywhere else on Earth, and it certainly grows the most garlic in America. Locals revel in the deep, pungent aroma that hangs over the town as freshly picked garlic is pickled, minced, and powdered into umpteen different garlic products (you can even smell it driving past on the freeway with your windows up).

At the end of the harvest, for three days in late July, more than 100,000 garlic lovers pour into Gilroy to watch the Great Garlic Cook-off (winners are crowned with garlic wreaths), snack on garlic concoctions ranging from delicious (garlic fries) to strange (garlic ice cream), meet Miss Gilroy Garlic and her court, and listen to live music. And, of course, buy garlands of exceptionally fresh, juicy garlic. (For details on the festival, go to *gilroygarlicfestival.com*.)

Garlic-fried Jasmine Rice

In Tim Luym's native Philippines, this is a breakfast staple; he served it for dinner at his now-closed Poleng Lounge in San Francisco. He loves the chewier texture of brown jasmine rice compared with white.

SERVES 4 as a side dish | **TIME** 45 minutes, plus 2 hours to chill

1½ cups brown jasmine rice
1½ tbsp. plus 1 tsp. canola oil
1 tbsp. minced garlic
Kosher salt and freshly ground black pepper

1. Rinse rice thoroughly in a fine-mesh strainer under running water, then pour into a medium saucepan with 1¾ cups water. Bring to a boil over high heat. Reduce heat and simmer, covered, until water is absorbed, 15 to 18 minutes. Remove pan from heat and let stand, covered, 10 minutes.
2. Pour rice into a rimmed baking pan. Let cool, then chill, uncovered, until firm and dry, at least 2 hours.
3. Heat 1½ tbsp. oil in a 12-in. frying pan over medium-high heat. Add rice and heat, stirring gently, until hot, 1 to 2 minutes. With a wooden spoon, clear a space in center of pan; pour in remaining 1 tsp. oil and stir garlic into oil. Let garlic sizzle for about 30 seconds, then stir into rice to combine. Season to taste with salt and pepper.
Make Ahead: Through step 2 up to 1 day, chilled.

PER SERVING: 306 cal., 21% (64 cal.) from fat; 5.7 g protein; 7.1 g fat (0.8 g sat.); 54 g carbo (2.5 g fiber); 5.3 mg sodium; 0 mg chol.

Pork and Asparagus Rice Bowl

Cooking the pork and asparagus separately keeps their flavors distinct. Read the recipe through before starting, so you'll be ready to do prep work while the rice and eggs are cooking. *(See variations at right.)*

SERVES 4 to 6 | **TIME** 45 minutes

4 eggs
2 cups medium-grain or sushi rice
¼ tsp. salt
1 lb. ground pork
¼ cup sake
2 tbsp. plus 1 tsp. tamari or soy sauce
4-in. piece fresh ginger, divided
3 garlic cloves
6 green onions
2 bunches asparagus
2 tbsp. vegetable or peanut oil, divided
1 cup chicken broth

1. Put unshelled eggs in a saucepan; cover with cold water. Bring to a boil over high heat. When water boils, cover, turn off heat, and let stand 14 minutes. Fill a bowl with ice water. Transfer eggs to ice water and set aside.
2. While eggs are cooking, in a second medium saucepan, bring rice, salt, and 3 cups water to a boil. Cover, reduce heat to low, and cook 15 minutes. Take off heat, still covered, and let stand 5 minutes.
3. While rice is coming to a boil and eggs are standing, mix together pork, sake, and 2 tbsp. tamari in a small bowl. Peel and grate ginger. Put 1 tbsp. ginger in with pork; put remainder in a small bowl and set aside.
4. While rice is cooking, peel and roughly chop garlic; trim and chop green onions. Add both to bowl of ginger. Trim tough stem ends off asparagus, cut into 1½-in. pieces, and set aside.
5. While rice is standing, heat 1 tbsp. oil in a large frying pan over high heat. Add pork mixture. Cook, stirring occasionally, until pork is cooked through, about 4 minutes, breaking up any clumps of meat.
6. Meanwhile, fluff rice with a fork and divide among 4 to 6 bowls; set them near the stove. Top rice with pork and pan juices.
7. Return pan to heat and add remaining 1 tbsp. oil and the reserved ginger, garlic, and green onions. Cook, stirring, until fragrant, about 1 minute. Add asparagus and remaining 1 tsp. tamari and stir to combine. Add broth, cover, and cook until asparagus is just tender to the bite, 2 to 3 minutes.
8. While asparagus cooks, pat eggs dry, peel, and cut into ¼-in.-thick slices. Divide asparagus and pan juices

among bowls of rice and pork. Top each serving with slices of egg and serve immediately.

PER SERVING: 690 cal., 39% (270 cal.) from fat; 31 g protein; 30 g fat (9.3 g sat.); 70 g carbo (2.6 g fiber); 802 mg sodium; 235 mg chol.

Variations
• Substitute 1 lb. **ground turkey** for the pork.
• Use **medium-grain brown rice** for a nutty and healthful departure from white rice (increase cooking time for rice to 30 minutes).
• In step 7, use any one of the following vegetables instead of the asparagus: 20 oz. **fresh spinach**, rinsed and any tough stems removed (reduce chicken broth to ¼ cup); 1 lb. **green beans**, trimmed and cut into 1½-in. pieces; 2 medium heads **broccoli**, cut into 1-in. florets (increase cooking time to about 4 minutes); or 4 heads **baby bok choy**, separated into leaves.

Spicy Thai Fried Rice with Shrimp

Day-old leftover rice gives this fragrant fried rice the best texture, but you can also make it with rice cooked and cooled the same day. Reader Anne Biedel of Kihei, Hawaii, who gave us the recipe, finds the fish sauce adds a barely detectable pungency, similar to anchovies in Caesar salad.

SERVES 4 | **TIME** 35 minutes

2 tbsp. olive oil
1½ tsp. minced garlic
½ cup thinly sliced green onions
4 tsp. minced seeded jalapeño chiles
3 cups cooked jasmine or long-grain white rice, cold
1 to 2 tbsp. sugar
2 tbsp. *each* soy sauce and Vietnamese fish sauce (*nuoc mam*)
1¼ cups cooked bay shrimp or diced cooked pork or chicken (about ½ lb.)
1 cup *each* chopped cilantro and basil leaves
1 tsp. Asian (toasted) sesame oil

1. Pour olive oil into a 12-in. nonstick frying pan over medium-high heat; add garlic, onions, and chiles and cook, stirring frequently, until onions have softened, 2 to 4 minutes.
2. Add rice, sugar to taste, soy sauce, and fish sauce; reduce heat to medium and cook, stirring frequently, until ingredients are well coated and hot, 3 to 4 minutes.
3. Add shrimp, cilantro, basil, and sesame oil; cook until shrimp are heated through, about 3 minutes.

PER SERVING: 345 cal., 25% (86 cal.) from fat; 18 g protein; 9.5 g fat (1.4 g sat.); 50 g carbo (1.4 g fiber); 953 mg sodium; 111 mg chol.

Caramelized Carrot Risotto

Delicate mascarpone cheese harmonizes with the sweet caramelized carrots in this beautiful risotto. To make it even prettier, you can cut the carrots into ¼-in. dice (it's time-consuming, but the carrots will look like little jewels).

recipe pictured on page **186**

SERVES 6 to 8 as a side dish or first course
TIME 1¼ hours

2 tbsp. vegetable oil, divided
3 tbsp. unsalted butter, divided
6 medium carrots, diced small (about 3 cups)
½ tsp. salt, plus more to taste
1 tsp. sugar
5 cups reduced-sodium chicken broth
⅓ cup minced onion
1½ cups risotto rice (*see the Right Rice for Risotto below*)
½ cup dry white wine
¼ cup mascarpone cheese or heavy whipping cream
¾ cup finely shredded parmesan cheese, divided
2 tbsp. finely chopped flat-leaf parsley, divided
1 tsp. roughly chopped thyme leaves
⅛ tsp. white pepper to taste

1. Heat 1 tbsp. oil and 1 tbsp. butter over medium heat in a medium heavy-bottomed pot; add carrots and stir with a wooden spoon until well coated. Add ½ cup water, salt, and sugar; cover and cook until tender, about 5 minutes. Uncover and cook, stirring occasionally, until water evaporates and carrots are just starting to brown, a few minutes more. Reserve half of carrots. In a blender, purée other half with ¾ cup hot water.
2. In a medium pan, bring broth to a simmer and keep at a simmer, covered, over low heat.
3. Heat remaining 1 tbsp. oil and 2 tbsp. butter over medium heat in same (unwashed) pot used for carrots. Add onion and cook, stirring, until translucent, about 3 minutes. Add rice, stirring with a wooden spoon to coat with butter and oil, 1 minute. Add wine and cook, stirring, until wine is absorbed. Add carrot purée and cook, stirring, until mixture no longer looks soupy.
4. Add hot broth, ½ cup at a time; cook, stirring after each addition, until broth is almost absorbed. Continue adding broth, stirring until each addition is absorbed before adding the next, until rice is tender to the bite (about 20 minutes; at least 1 cup broth will remain).
5. Fold in reserved carrots (save 2 tbsp. for garnish), mascarpone, ¼ cup parmesan, 1 tbsp. parsley, and the thyme. Add up to 1 cup additional broth (¼ cup at a time) if risotto is thicker than you want it to be. Season with salt to taste and white pepper.
6. Divide risotto among bowls and sprinkle with remaining ½ cup parmesan and 1 tbsp. parsley and reserved carrots. Serve immediately.

PER SERVING: 302 cal., 42% (126 cal.) from fat; 9.1 g protein; 14 g fat (7.1 g sat.); 33 g carbo (4.1 g fiber); 696 mg sodium; 25 mg chol.

The Right Rice for Risotto

Risotto's characteristic creaminess and chewiness come from the rice itself, as risotto rice is no ordinary rice. It contains two starches: an amylopectin exterior, which softens fast—especially under the pressure of constant stirring—to create a creamy sensation in the mouth; and an amylose interior, which stays relatively firm during cooking to give you that ideal al dente bite.

• **ARBORIO** is the starchiest of the three popular risotto types, and the most prone to getting gummy as it cooks. The interiors of the grains tend to be chalky and crumbly. Arborio is widely available.

• **OUR FAVORITE: CARNAROLI** has longer, narrow grains that cook the most evenly and have the best texture—creamy without being gluey and a good chewy interior.

• **VIALONE NANO** grains are smaller, oval shaped, and produce a delicate risotto with a nutty flavor.

• **SURPRISE: SUSHI RICE!** Medium-grain Nishiki brand is creamy and chewy, and so much like Arborio that half our tasting panel couldn't tell the difference. Plus it costs less than any Italian risotto rice.

Parmesan Risotto

Slowly stirring hot broth into creamy white rice is a soothing exercise that produces a really comforting yet sophisticated dish. Following this recipe are two variations on the theme.

SERVES 8 as a side dish | **TIME** 50 minutes

3 qts. reduced-sodium chicken broth
2 tbsp. olive oil
2 tbsp. plus 1 tsp. butter
1 medium onion, chopped
2½ cups risotto rice (*see the Right Rice for Risotto, opposite page*)
¾ cup dry white wine
½ tsp. salt, plus more to taste
½ cup freshly shredded parmesan cheese, plus more for serving
½ tsp. freshly ground black pepper
¼ cup chopped flat-leaf parsley

1. Bring broth to a simmer in a medium pot. Keep at a simmer, covered, over low heat.

2. Heat oil and 2 tbsp. butter over medium heat in a heavy-bottomed 8-qt. pot. Add onion and cook, stirring occasionally, until translucent and beginning to turn golden, about 10 minutes. Add rice and cook, stirring constantly, until grains are slightly translucent at the edges, about 3 minutes more.

3. Add wine and salt and cook, stirring, until wine is completely absorbed by rice. Add hot broth, ½ cup at a time, and cook, stirring constantly after each addition until broth is completely absorbed by rice; reduce heat to medium-low if mixture starts to boil. Continue adding broth and stirring until rice is just tender to the bite, 15 to 30 minutes (you will have broth left over). Keep rice at a constant simmer.

4. Remove rice from heat and stir in parmesan, pepper, parsley, remaining 1 tsp. butter, and salt to taste. If risotto is thicker than you want it to be, stir in 1 to 2 cups remaining broth. Serve immediately, with more parmesan on the side for sprinkling.

PER 1-CUP SERVING: 307 cal., 27% (83 cal.) from fat; 10 g protein; 9.2 g fat (3.7 g sat.); 46 g carbo (4.3 g fiber); 1,008 mg sodium; 14 mg chol.

Prosecco and Oyster Mushroom Risotto: Follow steps 1 and 2 of Parmesan Risotto. Substitute ¾ cup **prosecco** for dry white wine. While rice is cooking, melt 2 tbsp. **butter** in a large frying pan over medium-high heat. Add ¾ lb. **oyster mushrooms**, halved (stems removed; caps quartered if very large and left whole if very small), and ¼ tsp. **salt**. Cook, stirring occasionally, until tender. Stir sautéed mushrooms into risotto along with the parmesan and other flavorings.

PER 1-CUP SERVING: 343 cal., 31% (108 cal.) from fat; 11 g protein; 12 g fat (5.5 g sat.); 48 g carbo (4.9 g fiber); 1,110 mg sodium; 22 mg chol.

Gorgonzola and Radicchio Risotto: Follow steps 1 and 2 of Parmesan Risotto. While rice is cooking, cut 1 small head **radicchio** into shreds. Heat 1 tbsp. **olive oil** in a large skillet over medium heat and add radicchio and ¼ tsp. **salt**. Cook, stirring occasionally, until radicchio is wilted and tender, 2 to 4 minutes. Substitute ⅓ lb. **gorgonzola dolce** (or other mild, creamy blue cheese), broken into pieces, for parmesan; stir gorgonzola and wilted radicchio into risotto along with other flavorings.

PER 1-CUP SERVING: 366 cal., 37% (135 cal.) from fat; 12 g protein; 15 g fat (6.7 g sat.); 47 g carbo (4.6 g fiber); 1,229 mg sodium; 26 mg chol.

■ Parmesan

FROM THE PANTRY

Although many fine cheeses are made in the West, parmesan, the pride of Italy, can't be replicated here. It's indispensable in all kinds of dishes and wonderful on its own, in shaggy hunks. Look for wedges with the words (or bits of the words) "parmigiano-reggiano" stenciled into the wax; they're your guarantee that the cheese is true parmigiano-reggiano, made in the provinces of Parma and Reggio Emilia. It is the most famous and delicious of Italy's *grana* style of cheeses (*grana* refers to the appealingly grainy texture of the cheese); there are several others, including the very tasty (and more affordable) *grana padano*, also sold here. Grate or shred parmesan just before using for the best flavor, and let it come to room temperature before you eat it by the hunk.

Chanterelle Mushroom Risotto

The richly flavored fall risotto is adapted from one served by Matthew Bousquet at his Restaurant Mirepoix in Windsor, California. Begin roasting the mushrooms before you start making the risotto.

SERVES 6 as a main course | **TIME** 1 hour

ROASTED CHANTERELLES
½ lb. chanterelle mushrooms, trimmed and cut into
   1-in. pieces
1 shallot, thinly sliced
2 tbsp. olive oil
1 tbsp. butter, melted
1 tsp. fresh thyme leaves
¼ tsp. *each* salt and freshly ground black pepper
RISOTTO
¼ lb. bacon, diced
2 tbsp. olive oil
1 onion (½ lb.), halved lengthwise and thinly sliced
1 tbsp. minced garlic
¼ tsp. *each* salt and freshly ground black pepper
1 bunch (10 to 12 oz.) red Swiss chard
2 cups risotto rice *(see the Right Rice for Risotto,
   page 230)*
1 cup dry white wine
6 cups chicken broth, or more as needed
¼ cup finely shredded parmesan cheese
2 tbsp. butter

1. Roast the chanterelles: Preheat oven to 400°. In a 12- by 15-in. baking pan, mix mushrooms, shallot, oil, butter, thyme, salt, and pepper. Bake, stirring occasionally, until mushrooms are tender and beginning to brown on edges, 12 to 15 minutes.
2. Make risotto: In a 12-in. frying pan (with sides 2 in. high) or a 5-qt. pan over medium-high heat, cook bacon, stirring, until browned and crisp, about 5 minutes. Transfer to paper towels to drain. Discard all but about ½ tbsp. bacon fat from pan.
3. Add oil to pan over medium-high heat. When hot, add onion, garlic, salt, and pepper. Reduce heat to medium and cook, stirring frequently, until onion is very soft and browned, 20 to 25 minutes (if onion starts to scorch, reduce heat further and stir in 2 tbsp. water).
4. Meanwhile, trim and discard stem ends of chard. Thinly slice stems crosswise and coarsely chop leaves. In a 5- to 6-qt. pan over high heat, bring about 3 qts. water to a boil. Add chard and cook, stirring occasionally, until stems are tender-crisp to the bite, 3 to 4 minutes. Drain, put in a large bowl of ice water until cool, and drain again.

5. Add rice to onion and cook, stirring, until opaque, about 3 minutes. Add wine and cook, stirring, over medium heat until wine is absorbed, 1 to 2 minutes. Add hot broth, 1 cup at a time, and cook, stirring after each addition until broth is almost absorbed, 20 to 25 minutes total (rice should be tender to the bite).
6. Stir in parmesan, butter, bacon, chard, and roasted mushrooms. If risotto is thicker than desired, stir in a little more broth. Spoon risotto into wide, shallow bowls and serve immediately.
Make Ahead: Step 1, up to 4 hours; hold mushrooms at room temperature.

PER SERVING: 457 cal., 39% (180 cal.) from fat; 18 g protein; 20 g fat (6.6 g sat.); 52 g carbo (5.8 g fiber); 577 mg sodium; 23 mg chol.

Wild Rice Pilaf

Nutritious wild rice (actually a grass) has three times as much fiber as white rice and almost twice as much protein—and an appealingly nutty, almost smoky taste. The grains of top-grade wild rice are nearly an inch long; lesser grades are shorter or sometimes broken. All will taste good, but in a pilaf, the long grains look more beautiful.

SERVES 8 to 10 as a side dish | **TIME** 1¾ hours

2½ cups wild rice
2 tbsp. butter
1 cup *each* finely chopped onion and celery
2½ cups *each* reduced-sodium chicken broth and apple
   cider or juice
½ cup slivered almonds, toasted *(see How to Toast Nuts,
   page 134)*
¼ cup finely chopped kumquats (about 8) or finely
   chopped dried apricots
⅓ cup minced flat-leaf parsley
Kosher salt and freshly ground black pepper

1. Rinse wild rice well with cool water; drain.
2. In a 12-in. frying pan or a 4- to 5-qt. pan over medium-high heat, melt butter. Add onion and celery and cook, stirring often, over medium-high heat until vegetables are lightly browned, about 10 minutes.
3. Stir in wild rice, broth, and cider. Bring to a boil, covered; reduce heat and simmer until grains begin to split and rice is tender to the bite, 1½ to 1¾ hours. Drain any liquid.
4. Stir in almonds, kumquats, parsley, and salt and pepper to taste.

PER SERVING: 254 cal., 22% (57 cal.) from fat; 9.6 g protein; 6.3 g fat (1.8 g sat.); 42 g carbo (3 g fiber); 60 mg sodium; 6.2 mg chol.

Shrimp with Bacon-Cheese Polenta

Our version of shrimp and grits comes with bacon, which adds a smoky meatiness to the entire dish. It's particularly flavorful when cooked in a cast-iron skillet—the hotter surface creates lots of crusty brown bits.

SERVES 4 to 6 as a main course | **TIME** 45 minutes

½ tsp. salt, plus more to taste
1 cup polenta
8 slices thick-cut bacon
2 bunches green onions (about 16)
3 ripe medium tomatoes
¼ tsp. freshly ground black pepper
3 garlic cloves, peeled
1¼ lbs. shrimp, peeled and deveined
½ cup dry white wine
2 tbsp. butter
1 cup finely shredded (¼ lb.) white cheddar cheese

1. In a medium saucepan, bring 3½ cups water to a boil. Add salt. Pour in polenta in a thin stream, whisk-ing constantly, and cook while whisking until mixture comes to a steady simmer. Reduce heat to maintain a gentle simmer, cover, and stir every 5 minutes until polenta is thick and creamy and pulls away slightly from sides of pan when stirred, 20 to 40 minutes.
2. Meanwhile, in a large frying pan over medium-high heat, cook bacon until fat renders and edges start to brown and crisp. While bacon cooks, trim stems and ends of green onions, leaving onions as intact as possible. Drain bacon on paper towels, chop, and set aside.
3. Remove all but 1 tbsp. bacon fat from pan. Add whole green onions and cook over medium heat until soft and starting to brown, about 3 minutes; turn and brown other side, about 3 minutes more. While green onions cook, halve tomatoes crosswise and sprinkle cut sides with the pepper and salt to taste. Chop garlic. Set both aside.
4. Transfer green onions to a baking sheet or platter and cover to keep warm. Put tomato halves cut side down in pan with bacon fat and cook until they start to brown, about 3 minutes. Turn tomatoes and cook until heated through and a bit soft, about 3 minutes more. Transfer to baking sheet with green onions and cover to keep warm.
5. Add garlic to pan and cook, stirring, until fragrant, about 1 minute. Add shrimp and cook, stirring con-stantly, until starting to turn pink, 1 to 2 minutes. Pour in wine and cook, stirring and scraping up any

browned bits from bottom of pan, until shrimp is cooked through, about 2 minutes. Remove from heat.
6. Stir butter, cheese, and bacon into polenta. Divide polenta among plates and top with shrimp and remaining liquid in pan. Set a tomato half and several green onions beside polenta.

PER SERVING: 523 cal., 44% (228 cal.) from fat; 38 g protein; 25 g fat (12 g sat.); 31 g carbo (3.8 g fiber); 888 mg sodium; 225 mg chol.

Polenta with Pancetta and Sage

Look for Italian brands of polenta or cornmeal labeled "polenta"; avoid instant (it's gluey). Cooking time depends on how you like your polenta. In our tests, 20 minutes produced creamy polenta with tender, separate grains; after 40 minutes, the mixture was thicker, with softer, less distinct grains.

MAKES About 4½ cups; 4 to 6 side-dish servings
TIME 50 minutes

1 tsp. olive oil
½ cup (3 oz.) chopped pancetta or bacon
1 tbsp. chopped sage leaves
1 cup polenta
Salt and freshly ground black pepper

1. Heat oil in a 2½- to 3-qt. pot over medium-high heat until hot. Add pancetta and cook, stirring occasionally, until crisp and beginning to brown, about 5 minutes. With a slotted spoon, transfer half of pancetta to paper towels to drain.
2. Add sage to pot and cook, stirring, until fragrant, about 30 seconds. Carefully add 5 cups water (it may splatter a little) and bring to a boil.
3. Stirring constantly, pour in polenta in a slow, thin stream, pausing occasionally to break up any lumps.
4. Reduce heat and simmer, stirring often, until polenta is thick and creamy and pulls away slightly from sides of pan when stirred, 20 to 40 minutes; adjust heat as necessary to maintain a simmer. Add salt and pepper to taste.
5. Ladle polenta into bowls and top with reserved pancetta.

PER SERVING: 252 cal., 33% (83 cal.) from fat; 5.2 g protein; 9.2 g fat (3.1 g sat.); 36 g carbo (4.7 g fiber); 97 mg sodium; 9.5 mg chol.

Green-chile Grits

A recipe from reader Judy Johnston, of Mesilla, New Mexico, re-creates Southern grits in a thoroughly Western way.

SERVES 4 as a side dish | **TIME** 1 hour

3 fresh Anaheim or New Mexico green chiles
4 cups chicken broth
1 cup quick-cooking grits
2 tbsp. butter
2 cups finely shredded cheddar cheese
2 eggs, beaten

1. Broil chiles 4 in. from heat, turning once or twice, until skins are charred all over. Let stand until cool enough to handle, then peel skins and discard stems and seeds. Dice chiles.
2. Preheat oven to 350°. In a 3- or 4-qt. pan over high heat, bring broth to a boil. Add grits, reduce heat to medium, and cook, stirring, until broth is absorbed, 5 to 6 minutes. Stir in butter, cheese, and chiles.
3. In a small bowl, whisk ½ cup cooked grits into beaten eggs. When blended, stir egg mixture back into saucepan with rest of grits. Pour mixture into a greased 2-qt. baking dish. Bake until just set, 25 to 30 minutes.

PER SERVING: 494 cal., 55% (270 cal.) from fat; 24 g protein; 30 g fat (17 g sat.); 33 g carbo (2.3 g fiber); 552 mg sodium; 185 mg chol.

Minty Tabbouleh with Preserved Lemon

Tabbouleh gets a zingy makeover, thanks to aromatic mint and salty, tangy preserved lemon. Our version complements grilled meats of all sorts.

SERVES 8 as a side dish | **TIME** 30 minutes, plus 30 minutes to chill

1 cup bulgur wheat
1 tsp. salt, plus more to taste
2 cups packed mint leaves (from about 2 bunches), divided
¼ cup *each* extra-virgin olive oil and fresh lemon juice
2 garlic cloves, minced
1 tsp. freshly ground black pepper, plus more to taste
2 preserved lemons *(see Quick Tip, above right)*
8 cups loosely packed flat-leaf parsley leaves (from about 4 bunches)

1. Put bulgur and salt in a large bowl. Pour 1½ cups boiling water over bulgur, cover bowl, and let stand 20 minutes.

2. Meanwhile, in a blender or food processor, purée 1 cup mint leaves, the oil, lemon juice, garlic, and pepper until smooth, scraping down sides as necessary. Pour dressing over bulgur, stir to combine, cover, and chill at least 30 minutes and up to overnight.
3. Meanwhile, remove and discard pulp from preserved lemons. Rinse rind and chop finely. Stir into bulgur mixture. Finely chop parsley and remaining 1 cup mint leaves (or pulse them in batches in a food processor). Add to bulgur mixture and stir to combine thoroughly. Add more salt and/or pepper to taste.
Quick Tip: Find preserved lemons at Middle Eastern markets and specialty-foods stores.
Make Ahead: Up to 2 days, chilled.

PER SERVING: 165 cal., 42% (69 cal.) from fat; 5.1 g protein; 7.7 g fat (1.1 g sat.); 23 g carbo (9.4 g fiber); 623 mg sodium; 0 mg chol.

Thousand-seed Pilaf

recipe pictured on page **179**

We've used red quinoa in this recipe to enhance the beauty of the dish. It would be fine with beige, too—or a combo of all three colors of quinoa (red, beige, and black). They all taste the same.

SERVES 8 to 10 as a side dish | **TIME** 40 minutes

1 tsp. *each* cumin seeds, mustard seeds, dill seeds, and coriander seeds
½ tsp. *each* celery seeds and caraway seeds
1 tsp. olive oil
⅔ cup *each* quinoa, couscous, bulgur wheat, and kalijira rice *(see Quick Tip, above right)*
6½ cups reduced-sodium chicken or vegetable broth
1 tbsp. finely shredded lemon zest, plus long curls of zest for garnish if you like
2 tbsp. fresh lemon juice
⅓ cup minced flat-leaf parsley, plus leaves for garnish
Kosher salt and freshly ground black pepper

1. Combine cumin, mustard, dill, coriander, celery, and caraway seeds in a 12-in. frying pan or a 4- to 5-qt. pot. Add oil. Cook, stirring often, over high heat until seeds smell fragrant and begin to pop, about 2 minutes.
2. Meanwhile, thoroughly rinse and drain quinoa. Add quinoa, couscous, bulgur, and rice to pan. Cook, stirring, until grains are lightly toasted, 2 to 3 minutes.
3. Add broth and bring to a rapid boil, covered. Remove from heat and let stand until liquid is absorbed, 15 to 20 minutes.
4. Stir in lemon zest and juice, minced parsley, and salt and pepper to taste. Spoon pilaf into a bowl and top

with lemon zest curls and parsley. Serve hot, warm, or at room temperature.

Quick Tip: Kalijira is a very small-grained basmati-type rice, usually available at Indian grocery stores. If you can't find kalijira, replace it with another ⅔ cup quinoa, couscous, or bulgur.

PER SERVING: 195 cal., 7.7% (15 cal.) from fat; 11 g protein; 1.7 g fat (0.2 g sat.); 35 g carbo (4 g fiber); 66 mg sodium; 0 mg chol.

Quinoa with Toasted Pine Nuts

This easy side dish, which goes with just about anything, shows off the simple, nutty appeal of the fluffy little grainlike quinoa.

SERVES 6 | **TIME** 30 minutes

1 tbsp. canola oil
1 cup quinoa, thoroughly rinsed *(see Quinoa, right)*
1¾ cups chicken or vegetable broth
¼ tsp. kosher salt, plus more to taste
⅔ cup pine nuts, toasted *(see How to Toast Nuts, page 134)*
½ cup chopped green onions
2 tbsp. chopped cilantro

1. Heat oil in a heavy-bottomed 4- to 5-qt. pot over medium-high heat. Add quinoa and cook, stirring, until it smells toasted, about 3 minutes. Add broth and salt. Bring to a boil over high heat, covered; reduce heat and simmer, stirring occasionally, until quinoa is tender and completely translucent, about 15 minutes.
2. Remove from heat and let stand 5 minutes. Stir in pine nuts, green onions, and cilantro; season with salt to taste.

PER SERVING: 235 cal., 55% (129 cal.) from fat; 7.8 g protein; 14 g fat (1.1 g sat.); 20 g carbo (2.5 g fiber); 195 mg sodium; 0 mg chol.

Tangerine Quinoa Pilaf

The bright, sweet taste of tangerine juice and zest is wonderful with the slightly crunchy quinoa.

SERVES 4 as a side dish | **TIME** 35 minutes

1 cup reduced-sodium chicken broth or water
½ cup fresh tangerine juice
1 cup quinoa, thoroughly rinsed *(see Quinoa below)*
Finely shredded zest of 1 tangerine
2 tbsp. dried currants
¼ cup pine nuts, toasted *(see How to Toast Nuts, page 134)*
1 tbsp. minced chives
Kosher salt

1. In a medium pan, bring broth and tangerine juice to a boil. Add quinoa, cover, reduce heat to low, and simmer until tender, about 20 minutes.
2. Fluff quinoa with a fork and stir in tangerine zest, currants, pine nuts, and chives. Season with salt to taste.

PER SERVING: 247 cal., 31% (76 cal.) from fat; 9 g protein; 8.5 g fat (0.7 g sat.); 35 g carbo (3.7 g fiber); 100 mg sodium; 0 mg chol.

■ Quinoa

FROM THE PANTRY

A quick-cooking, high-protein grain native to the Andes of South America, quinoa (pronounced *keen*-wah) grows in Colorado too. The mild, nutty taste and fluffy-but-chewy texture make it a nice choice for pairing with spicy foods. It's available in many supermarkets right alongside rice—look for ordinary pale beige quinoa as well as gorgeous red and black quinoas. Quinoa is a good source of protein and fiber, and it's gluten-free. It cooks very quickly (15 minutes) and is a great substitute for rice (it even cooks well in a rice cooker). The grain is naturally coated with a bitter, resin-like substance called saponin, which is mainly rinsed off before packaging—but it's a good idea to rinse it again prior to cooking.

vegetables on the side

Discover new ways to use the bounty that surrounds you, whether it be from the farmers' market, the grocery store, or your own backyard.

Given the variety, freshness, and quality of Western produce, it's no wonder we're besotted with vegetables. Great local farms, farmers' markets, specialty markets—from Indian to Chinese to Latino—and well-stocked grocery stores have totally changed how we shop and what we buy. We can get extraordinary "ordinary" vegetables (just-picked corn, sun-ripened heirloom tomatoes) as well as the uncommon stuff, like egg-size Thai eggplant or Chinese long beans. Add in the boom in backyard gardening, and we're living *la vida* vegetable.

That's why most of the recipes in this chapter are on the adventuresome side. You already know how good a backyard tomato is with just salt and olive oil and maybe a few basil leaves. You could boil corn in your sleep. But how about tomatoes simmered in a spicy Indian yogurt sauce *(page 246)*? Or fresh corn cakes *(page 247)*? Cauliflower takes on a new dimension when it's roasted *(page 265)*, beets baked in an herbed salt crust *(page 274)* will perfume your entire kitchen as they cook, and addictive Avocado Fries *(page 275)* give you a whole new way to love an old favorite.

We never stop looking for easy vegetable recipes, either, because we know that good produce often doesn't need much done to it. For a list of our quick picks—really more suggestions than recipes—*see page 247*. (The Bacon-Rosemary Persimmons are great with pork chops, by the way, and we love the Sesame-Garlic Peas with skewered grilled shrimp.)

Maybe there are vegetables you're on the cusp of trying but haven't had the right recipe to get you started—those baby artichokes you often see at the

farmers' market, for instance. Try our easy recipe on *page 240*, and they'll go
from mysterious to delicious. Maybe you find brussels sprouts intriguing
but alien-looking. We recommend Shaved Brussels Sprouts with Pancetta
(*page 266*)—so good you'll have a warm and friendly feeling toward sprouts
the next time you buy them. Chinese long beans, dark green beans that
reach nearly 3 feet in length, have a wonderful deep flavor and a firmer
texture than ordinary green beans. They're excellent in both Hot Sichuan-
style Green Beans (*page 242*) and Roasted Long Beans with Herb Butter
(*page 243*).

Some of the most interesting recipes in our pages were invented by immigrants to the West who re-created the flavors of home using Western produce. Asparagus *Talasani* (*page 240*) came to us from the kitchen of an
Indian reader who substituted asparagus for a vegetable known as drumstick, a long, slender green pod with a tough skin and tender interior (they
do, in fact, taste similar). Bacon and Kale Adobo (*page 250*) was created by a
Filipino chef in San Francisco who used kale instead of hard-to-find water
spinach. Sometimes in our cross-cultural recipes it's the method that gets
tweaked: On *page 271*, for example, we've included a sweet-potato casserole
that could be Southern except that it contains no sugar—only herbs—and
instead of the customary mini-marshmallow top, there's a pouf of golden
meringue.

In this chapter we've brought all corners of the vegetable universe to you.
Now it's your turn to explore.

Vegetables on the Side

Sautéed Baby Artichokes

Baby artichokes are actually fully mature artichokes that grow farther down on the stem, shaded from the sun. Unlike their heftier siblings, which grow at the top of the stem, baby artichokes are entirely edible.

SERVES 6 to 8 | **TIME** 1½ hours

36 baby artichokes
1 tbsp. salt, plus more to taste
1 oz. pancetta, chopped
2 garlic cloves, sliced
¼ cup *each* dry white wine and chopped mint leaves
Freshly ground black pepper
Grated parmesan cheese

1. Trim outer leaves and stems from artichokes, leaving just the tender yellow-green leaves. Trim bottoms and thorny tips.
2. Bring a large pot of water to a boil and add salt. Simmer artichokes in boiling water until tender when tops are poked with a knife, 10 to 20 minutes. Cut any larger ones in half.
3. Set a frying pan over medium-high heat. Add pancetta and cook, stirring, until fat is rendered. Add garlic and cook 1 minute, stirring. Add wine and artichokes. Cook until wine has almost evaporated. Add mint and salt and pepper to taste. Serve topped with parmesan.

PER SERVING: 117 cal., 17% (20 cal.) from fat; 7.3 g protein; 2.3 g fat (0.6 g sat.); 22 g carbo (11 g fiber); 473 mg sodium; 3.1 mg chol.

Asparagus *Talasani*

When reader Abhaya Karangutkar moved to California from Goa, India, she substituted fresh asparagus for the vegetable known as drumstick—the tender, tough-skinned green pod of *Moringa oleifera*, a tree native to northwest Indai. (*Talasani* is a style of stir-fry.)

SERVES 4 to 6 | **TIME** 15 minutes

1½ lbs. asparagus
1 tbsp. vegetable or olive oil
½ tsp. cumin seeds
1 garlic clove, minced
¼ tsp. turmeric
Salt

1. Snap off and discard tough stem ends from asparagus. Cut stalks diagonally into 2-in. lengths. You should have about 3 cups.
2. Heat oil in a 10- to 12-in. frying pan over medium-high heat until hot. Add cumin and stir until seeds are a shade darker, about 30 seconds. Stir in garlic and turmeric; add asparagus and stir until coated. Pour in 3 tbsp. water.
3. Cover pan, reduce heat to low, and cook until asparagus is tender-crisp to the bite, 3 to 4 minutes. Season to taste with salt.

PER SERVING: 34 cal., 65% (22 cal.) from fat; 1.8 g protein; 2.4 g fat (0.3 g sat.); 2.4 g carbo (0.6 g fiber); 1.5 mg sodium; 0 mg chol.

Artichokes and Castroville

For a vegetable, the artichoke has had its share of drama. The story starts quietly, with the first artichokes planted during the 1890s by immigrant Italian farmers in Half Moon Bay, about 30 miles south of San Francisco. A decade or so later, growers began shipping them to New York, where they became a prized delicacy.

Mobbed-up Chokes
The business in baby artichokes was so profitable that it attracted the Mafia, which began harassing distributors and shopkeepers and even destroying artichokes in the fields. Finally, in the 1930s, New York City's mayor, Fiorello La Guardia,

banned the sale, display, and possession of baby artichokes in the city, declaring, "A racketeer in artichokes is no different than a racketeer in slot machines." La Guardia lifted the ban after only a week, saying that he loved them with mayonnaise.

Chokes Come to Castroville
By 1922, artichokes had taken root a bit farther down the California coast, in Castroville, where they thrived in the well-drained soil and abundant fog. Castroville became the leading producer, eventually growing 75 percent of the nation's artichokes. In honor of its main cash crop, the town has held a big festival every

May since 1947, when a young, relatively unknown Marilyn Monroe was crowned its first Artichoke Queen (for festival details, see *artichoke-festival.org*).

Winter's Sweet Kiss
The main commercial variety has always been the buttery, nutty-tasting Green Globe, originally brought from Italy. You can identify it by its pointed, thorny leaf tips (leaves on other varieties are flatter and smoother). Frost turns the leaves slightly bronze or brown, but don't pass up a browned artichoke: This "winter kiss" actually makes the flavor even nuttier and sweeter.

La Super-Rica Pinto Beans

According to Isidoro Gonzalez, owner of La Super-Rica in Santa Barbara, California, these simple beans have maintained their popularity since they were added to the menu in 1981.

MAKES About 10 cups; 8 to 10 servings | **TIME** 2 hours, plus at least 2 hours to soak beans

1 lb. dried pinto beans, sorted for debris and rinsed
1 tsp. salt, plus more to taste
3 slices bacon, chopped
½ lb. uncooked Mexican chorizo (see Quick tips below)
1 poblano chile, seeds and ribs removed and finely chopped

1. Soak beans as directed in *Dried-bean Basics, page 242.*
2. Put beans in a 5- to 6-qt. pan. Add 2½ qts. water. Cover and bring to a boil over high heat; reduce heat and simmer, stirring occasionally, until beans are tender to the bite, 1¼ to 1½ hours. Add salt.
3. Meanwhile, in an 8- to 10-in. frying pan over medium-high heat, cook bacon, stirring frequently, until browned, 8 to 10 minutes. With a slotted spoon, transfer bacon to a bowl.
4. Remove and discard chorizo casings. Crumble sausage into frying pan. Cook, stirring frequently, until browned, 4 to 5 minutes. Add poblano and cook, stirring, until softened, 3 to 4 minutes.
5. To sausage mixture add cooked bacon and ½ cup bean cooking liquid; cook, stirring occasionally, 5 minutes. If beans seem very wet, drain off some of liquid (keep in mind that they will stiffen as they cool). Stir sausage-bacon mixture into beans and simmer to blend flavors, about 5 minutes. Add more salt to taste.
Quick Tip: Buy the best-quality lean chorizo you can find, preferably from a butcher or Mexican market. Avoid the kind that is very soft and sold in plastic casings—it tends to break down too much in cooking. (If you can't find good chorizo, substitute another spicy uncooked sausage.)
Make Ahead: Up to 3 days, chilled; up to 1 month, frozen airtight.

PER SERVING: 300 cal., 39% (117 cal.) from fat; 16 g protein; 13 g fat (4.9 g sat.); 30 g carbo (5.6 g fiber); 567 mg sodium; 25 mg chol.

Spicy Baked Beans

Making baked beans from scratch is a noble but time-consuming enterprise. Santa Fe–based barbecue experts Bill Jamison and Cheryl Alters Jamison like to offer a simpler alternative with dressed-up store-bought beans. Serve this zingy dish with Grilled Skirt Steak *(page 485)*. It's also a tasty accompaniment to grilled burgers, hot dogs, and sausages.

SERVES 6 to 8 | **TIME** 1½ hours

7 oz. bacon, diced
1 large onion, finely chopped
2 cans (28 oz. each) barbecue-flavored baked beans, such as Bush's
¼ cup bottled chili sauce
2 tbsp. *each* Worcestershire sauce and prepared yellow mustard
1½ tbsp. sweet smoked Spanish paprika (see Quick Tip below)
½ tsp. ground cumin
Kosher salt (optional)

1. Preheat oven to 350°. Grease a 2½- to 3-qt. baking dish.
2. In a large skillet over medium heat, cook bacon until beginning to brown but still limp. Stir in onion and cook until it is soft and translucent and bacon is crisp, another 5 minutes.
3. Spoon mixture into prepared baking dish. Add baked beans, chili sauce, Worcestershire, mustard, paprika, and cumin. Stir, taste to check seasonings, and add salt to taste if using.
4. Bake beans, uncovered, until bubbly throughout, with a bit of browned crust around the edges of dish, about 45 minutes.
Quick Tip: Smoked Spanish paprika is available at well-stocked and specialty grocery stores.
Make Ahead: Through step 3, up to 2 days, chilled.

PER SERVING: 477 cal., 36% (171 cal.) from fat; 14 g protein; 19 g fat (6.4 g sat.); 63 g carbo (11 g fiber); 1,325 mg sodium; 21 mg chol.

Dried-bean Basics

• **SOAK BEFORE COOKING:** This drastically reduces cooking time. Sort beans for debris, then rinse. For every 2 cups dried beans, bring beans and 2 qts. water to a boil over high heat in a 5- to 6-qt. pan. Cover, boil for 2 minutes, and remove from heat. Beans are ready to cook after soaking for 2 hours but are more digestible after 4 hours. Or combine beans and water in a large pot and let sit overnight. To use, drain and rinse. If cooked without soaking, beans will require more liquid and more time.

• **ADD SALT AND ACIDIC INGREDIENTS AT THE END:** If stirred in too early, ingredients such as tomatoes, wine, and citrus juices can toughen beans and slow down cooking. Wait to add them until 15 to 30 minutes before the end of the cooking time. They'll season the beans deeply without affecting their texture.

• **HOW MUCH TO COOK:** 16 oz. (about 2¼ cups) dried beans yields 32 to 38 oz. (5 to 6 cups) cooked.

• **HOW LONG TO COOK:** It varies, depending on the type of bean and how long it's been on the shelf. Also, you may want them firm for some uses, softer for others. Most beans lose their shape as they get soft, so watch them carefully toward the end of the cooking time to get the texture you want.

Summer Beans with Preserved Lemon, Almonds, and Rosemary

Jesse Z. Cool, the Menlo Park, California–based chef-owner of Flea St. Café, the Cool Café, and Cooleatz Catering Company, likes to serve these beans at room temperature with slices of garden-ripe tomatoes, but they're also great chilled as a salad.

SERVES 6 | **TIME** 35 minutes

1½ lbs. green, yellow, or purple beans, trimmed
3 or 4 wedges preserved lemon (*see Quick Tip below*)
2 tbsp. *each* finely chopped rosemary leaves and
   extra-virgin olive oil
1 or 2 garlic cloves, minced
Salt and freshly ground black pepper
¼ cup sliced almonds, toasted (*see How to Toast Nuts,*
   page 134)

1. Add about 2 qts. water to a 5-to 6-qt. pan and bring to a boil over high heat. Add beans and cook just until barely tender to the bite, 3 to 6 minutes. Drain and rinse under cold running water until cool.
2. Rinse preserved lemon thoroughly under running water; discard seeds and pulp. Finely chop lemon and put in a large bowl. Stir in rosemary, oil, and garlic, then add beans and salt and pepper to taste.
3. Just before serving, mix in almonds.
Quick Tip: Find preserved lemons at Middle Eastern markets and other specialty-foods stores.
Make Ahead: Through step 2, up to 6 hours, chilled.

PER SERVING: 108 cal., 65% (70 cal.) from fat; 3.1 g protein; 7.8 g fat (1 g sat.); 10 g carbo (2.8 g fiber); 2,204 mg sodium; 0 mg chol.

Hot Sichuan-style Green Beans

If you use the maximum amount of chile flakes, the dish will be quite hot.

SERVES 8 to 10 | **TIME** 15 minutes

2 tbsp. soy sauce
1 tbsp. unseasoned rice vinegar
2 tsp. sugar
¼ to ½ tsp. red chile flakes
¼ tsp. ground white pepper
1 lb. green beans, trimmed and cut into 2- to 3-in. lengths
1 tbsp. vegetable oil
2 tbsp. *each* minced garlic and minced fresh ginger

1. In a small bowl, mix soy sauce, vinegar, sugar, chile flakes, and pepper.
2. Set a 10- to 12-in. frying pan over high heat. When pan is hot, add beans and ¼ cup water. Cover and cook, stirring once, until beans are bright green and slightly crunchy to the bite, 3 to 4 minutes. Uncover and cook until any remaining water has evaporated.
3. Add oil, garlic, and ginger to pan; cook, stirring, until green beans and garlic are lightly browned, 1 to 2 minutes. Stir soy mixture and add to pan; bring to a boil and cook until most of liquid has evaporated and sauce thickens and coats beans, 2 to 3 minutes. Serve hot or cool.
Make Ahead: Up to 2 hours; let cool, then cover and let stand at room temperature.

PER SERVING: 34 cal., 38% (13 cal.) from fat; 1 g protein; 1.4 g fat (0.2 g sat.); 4.9 g carbo (0.8 g fiber); 209 mg sodium; 0 mg chol.

vegetables on the side

Green Beans with Crisp Meyer Lemon Bread Crumbs

Adding the Meyer lemon bread crumbs gives this super-simple dish extraordinary flavor.

SERVES 10 | **TIME** 45 minutes

2 cups coarse fresh ciabatta bread crumbs
¼ cup extra-virgin olive oil, divided
Finely shredded zest of 2 small Meyer lemons, plus 1 tsp. juice
⅛ tsp. *each* kosher salt and freshly ground black pepper, plus more to taste
2½ lbs. green beans, trimmed

1. In a large frying pan over medium heat, cook crumbs in 2 tbsp. oil, stirring, 5 minutes. Stir in lemon zest, salt, and pepper. Cook, stirring, until crumbs are golden, 5 more minutes. Pour into a bowl.
2. In a large pot fitted with a steamer basket, steam beans over 1 in. boiling water, stirring once, 7 minutes for very crisp beans and 10 minutes for tender-crisp.
3. Combine remaining 2 tbsp. oil with the lemon juice and salt and pepper to taste. Drain beans, toss with dressing, and pour into a shallow bowl. Top with crumbs.

PER SERVING: 91 cal., 54% (49 cal.) from fat; 2.1 g protein; 5.6 g fat (0.8 g sat.); 9.4 g carbo (2.7 g fiber); 94 mg sodium; 0 mg chol.

Garlic Green Beans with Manchego

This recipe from Sean Yontz, chef-owner of Sketch and Tambien restaurants, in Denver, is a perfect side dish for entertaining.

SERVES 8 to 10 | **TIME** 15 minutes

2 tbsp. olive oil
2 lbs. green beans, trimmed
⅓ cup minced garlic
¼ cup *each* dry white wine and fresh lime juice
Salt and freshly ground black pepper
⅔ cup shredded manchego cheese

1. Heat oil in a 12-in. frying pan or 14-in. wok over medium-high heat. Add green beans and cook, stirring often, until tender-crisp and lightly browned, 10 to 12 minutes. Add garlic and cook just until fragrant, 1 minute.
2. Add wine, lime juice, and salt and pepper to taste; bring to a boil, then transfer to a serving dish and sprinkle with manchego cheese.

PER SERVING: 94 cal., 53% (50 cal.) from fat; 3.7 g protein; 5.5 g fat (2.3 g sat.); 7.9 g carbo (1.5 g fiber); 53 mg sodium; 8 mg chol.

Roasted Long Beans with Herb Butter

You can make this dish with regular green beans, but Chinese long beans (also called yard-long beans) make for a more impressive presentation.

SERVES 12 | **TIME** 1 hour

2 garlic cloves, peeled
¾ cup butter, softened
1 tbsp. Dijon mustard
½ cup coarsely chopped flat-leaf parsley
1 tbsp. fresh lemon juice
1 tsp. *each* kosher salt and freshly ground black pepper
3 lbs. Chinese long beans (yard-long beans) or regular green beans, trimmed
Coarse sea salt (optional)

1. Finely chop garlic in a food processor. Add butter, mustard, parsley, lemon juice, kosher salt, and pepper; blend until thoroughly combined. Transfer to a bowl.
2. Meanwhile, add a quarter of the beans at a time to a large pot of boiling water and cook until barely tender, about 3 minutes. Prepare a large bowl of ice and cold water while beans are cooking. Using tongs, immediately transfer beans to ice water and let cool, then transfer to a colander to drain; repeat three more times for remaining beans, letting water come back to a boil before adding the next batch and adding more ice to bowl if it all melts. Blot beans dry.
3. Preheat broiler with one rack 5 to 6 in. from heat and another rack below it. Arrange beans lengthwise in a single layer in two rimmed baking pans. Dot beans with butter mixture, using about a quarter for each pan.
4. Cook beans in oven 1 minute. Toss to coat with butter and switch positions of pans. Cook until beans in top pan are blistered and speckled brown, 4 to 9 minutes, then remove top pan from oven. Move second pan to top rack and broil until beans are blistered, 2 to 5 minutes.
5. Transfer beans to a platter and sprinkle to taste with sea salt if using. Serve with remaining butter mixture on the side if you like.
Make Ahead: Through step 2, up to 1 day; store beans in a resealable plastic bag and butter in an airtight container in refrigerator.

PER SERVING: 88 cal., 60% (53 cal.) from fat; 2.2 g protein; 6 g fat (3.7 g sat.); 8.3 g carbo (3.9 g fiber); 144 mg sodium; 15 mg chol.

Quick-cooked Pea Shoots

San Francisco cookbook author Niloufer Ichaporia King learned this method from a family in the Seychelles, where it's a popular way to cook greens. It works with all kind of greens (amaranth greens, for instance, are excellent cooked like this). If the greens are tough, blanch them first.

SERVES 4 to 6 | **TIME** 15 minutes

1 to 2 lbs. pea shoots *(see Quick Tip below)* or watercress
2 tbsp. vegetable oil
1 tsp. kosher salt
1 fresh red or green arbol, Thai, or serrano chile, stem on and slit lengthwise; or 1 dried arbol or cayenne chile
6 quarter-size slices fresh ginger, cut into thin slivers

1. Trim any tough stems from pea shoots or watercress (for watercress, see Quick Tip in Classic Cobb Salad, *page 169*).
2. Heat oil in a wok or large, heavy frying pan over high heat until hot. Throw in salt, whole chile, and ginger. When ginger starts to sear, immediately add pea shoots. Cook shoots, moving constantly with tongs, just until thoroughly wilted, 1 to 2 minutes. Serve immediately, with chile on top of greens or set aside.
Quick Tip: Pea shoots are sold at farmers' markets (generally February through early June) and at Asian markets under their Chinese name, *dou miao*. "Pea shoots" can refer either to tiny new sprouts or the tendriled top greens of a mature plant; both work in this recipe.

PER SERVING: 236 cal., 22% (51 cal.) from fat; 13 g protein; 5.6 g fat (0.8 g sat.); 43 g carbo (0.1 g fiber); 357 mg sodium; 0 mg chol.

Three Peas with Leeks, Mint, and Cream

This dish is tasty with salmon or roast chicken. It's also delicious using any single type of pea or two combined.

SERVES 4 to 6 | **TIME** 30 minutes

½ lb. sugar snap peas, trimmed
¼ lb. snow peas, trimmed
1 cup shelled fresh peas
1 leek (½ lb.), root end and dark green top removed
2 tbsp. butter
½ cup whipping cream
Salt and freshly ground black pepper
¼ cup slivered mint leaves

1. Bring a large pot of water to a boil, then add all the peas. Cook just until they start to turn a brighter green,

15 to 30 seconds; drain immediately. Rinse well under cold running water until cool, then drain again.
2. Cut leek in half lengthwise. Swish around in a large bowl of water to rinse off dirt; transfer to a colander, leaving dirt behind, and rinse again in fresh water if necessary. Thinly slice crosswise.
3. In a frying pan over medium heat, melt butter. When it's foamy, add leek and stir until soft, about 5 minutes. Pour in cream, increase heat to medium-high, and cook, stirring often, until liquid is reduced by about half, 3 to 4 minutes. Add salt and pepper to taste.
4. Add all the peas and half the mint and cook, stirring, just until heated through, about 1 minute. Sprinkle with remaining mint.

PER SERVING: 147 cal., 61% (90 cal.) from fat; 3.6 g protein; 10 g fat (6.2 g sat.); 11 g carbo (2.8 g fiber); 52 mg sodium; 32 mg chol.

Miso-glazed Eggplant *(Nasu Miso)*

Reader Scott Lorenz, of Scotts Valley, California, created this version of the popular Japanese dish. Use slender, purple-black Japanese eggplant *(nasu)* if possible—it's sweeter and more tender than the bulky globe (Italian) type, and it doesn't need peeling. Serve with rice.

SERVES 4 | **TIME** 20 minutes

3 tbsp. vegetable oil
4 Japanese eggplants (1½ lbs. total), cut in half lengthwise and flesh scored in a crosshatch ¼ in. deep
⅓ cup yellow or red miso *(see Quick Tips below)*
2 tbsp. *each* firmly packed light brown sugar and sake or white wine
¼ tsp. red chile flakes
¼ cup cilantro leaves
1 tsp. toasted sesame seeds *(see Quick Tips below)*

1. Preheat broiler. Heat oil in an ovenproof frying pan over high heat. Add eggplants, flesh side down, and cook until flesh browns and softens, about 4 minutes.
2. In a small bowl, combine miso, brown sugar, sake, and chile flakes. Turn eggplants flesh side up and brush mixture over them.
3. Broil eggplants in pan 4 in. from heat until glaze starts to brown, about 3 minutes. Sprinkle with cilantro and sesame seeds.
Quick Tips: Look for miso in the supermarket refrigerator section, near the tofu. Buy toasted sesame seeds, or toast them yourself in a dry frying pan over medium heat until golden, about 5 minutes.

PER SERVING: 221 cal., 49% (108 cal.) from fat; 4.7 g protein; 12 g fat (1.6 g sat.); 24 g carbo (3.9 g fiber); 838 mg sodium; 0 mg chol.

vegetables on the side

Eggplant Intelligence

• **PICK A GOOD ONE AND STORE IT PROPERLY:** The best eggplants have fresh calyxes (the flower sepals beneath the stem) and smooth and unbruised skin with a good sheen. They should give slightly when pressed; very spongy ones have been on the shelf too long, while rock-hard eggplants have been left on the plant too long. Another sign of overmaturity is a color change: Purple varieties turn bronze; white and green ones turn yellow. Eggplants can be chilled a couple of days in paper bags.

• **AVOID BITTERNESS:** Selection and judicious trimming are more effective than salting. With globe (common purple or Italian) eggplants, larger ones tend to be more bitter, so go for the little guys. Globe types also contain a slightly bitter-tasting pigment—anthocyanin—in the skin and just beneath it; for the mildest flavor, trim these portions. Or choose milder purple, white, or green-skinned types (other than Lao Green Stripe, which is naturally assertive). Any variety, if overripe, will acquire a strong taste as seeds enlarge and get bitter.

• **PREVENT GREASINESS:** Raw eggplant can soak up oil like a sponge, but it doesn't have to. For grilling, lightly brush eggplant with oil to keep slices moist. Before sautéing, steam eggplant to eliminate the need for lots of oil: Put eggplant slices or cubes in a wok or 12-in. frying pan with a little water (¼ cup per 1 lb. of eggplant), then simmer, covered, until eggplant is tender when pierced, about 5 minutes. To sauté, uncover, add 2 tsp. oil per lb. of eggplant, and turn often until browned, 8 to 10 minutes.

Roasted Tomatoes and Peppers

This recipe is based on a dish we had at the home of Joan and Sid Cross in Vancouver, British Columbia. It was part of a lavish dinner starring local food: marinated spot prawns, pesto salmon, and ice cream sundaes made with blackberries picked not far away.

SERVES 8 | **TIME** 50 minutes

4 yellow or red bell peppers
2 firm-ripe red tomatoes
2 firm-ripe yellow tomatoes
2 or 3 garlic cloves, thinly sliced
2 tbsp. fresh thyme leaves or 2 tsp. dried thyme
¼ cup extra-virgin olive oil
Kosher or sea salt and freshly ground black pepper

1. Preheat oven to 400°. Cut each pepper in half lengthwise through stem. Remove seeds and ribs. Arrange peppers in a single layer, cut sides up, in two 9- by 13-in. pans.
2. Peel red and yellow tomatoes, core, and cut into ½-in. wedges. Divide between pans of peppers. Scatter garlic and thyme over peppers and tomatoes, then drizzle liberally with olive oil. Season with salt and pepper.
3. Bake until peppers are soft and some of the tomato edges are browned, 40 to 50 minutes. Serve hot, warm, or at room temperature.
Make Ahead: Up to 4 hours, at room temperature.

PER SERVING: 103 cal., 62% (64 cal.) from fat; 1.9 g protein; 7.4 g fat (1.1 g sat.); 9.7 g carbo (1.9 g fiber); 17 mg sodium; 0 mg chol.

Roasted Red Peppers with Garlic and Olive Oil (Pebrots Escalivats)

In this recipe from Eva Bertran, executive vice president of Gloria Ferrer Caves & Vineyards in Sonoma, California (and a native of Catalonia, Spain), you can roast the peppers either in the oven or on the grill. Make sure they are cooked until softened but not too charred.

SERVES 6 to 8 | **TIME** 1½ hours

8 red bell peppers
2 garlic cloves (see Quick Tip below), minced
1 tsp. kosher or sea salt
¼ cup extra-virgin olive oil

1. Preheat oven to 400°. Put peppers in a large baking pan and bake until soft when pressed, 40 to 50 minutes. Let cool 10 to 20 minutes to loosen skin.
2. Meanwhile, with a mortar and pestle, mash garlic with salt into a paste (or mash garlic with salt with the flat side of a chef's knife, then put into a small bowl). Stir in oil to blend.
3. Peel and seed peppers, then cut lengthwise into ¾-in.-wide strips. Arrange peppers on a platter and drizzle with garlic oil, scraping it out of mortar or bowl to get all the garlic. Serve warm or at room temperature.
Quick Tip: Be sure to use very fresh garlic; old garlic will taste bitter and strong.
Make Ahead: Through step 2, up to 1 day, chilled. Let come to room temperature and drain off excess liquid.

PER SERVING: 81 cal., 80% (65 cal.) from fat; 0.7 g protein; 7.2 g fat (1.1 g sat.); 5 g carbo (1.2 g fiber); 246 mg sodium; 0 mg chol.

Santa Fe Corn Pudding

This savory, custardy pudding studded with roasted chiles and crowned with a buttery crumb topping came from Santa Fe–based barbecue experts Bill Jamison and Cheryl Alters Jamison. It's best made with fresh corn at its ripest, but the dish is still mighty tasty with frozen corn.

SERVES 6 to 8 | **TIME** 1¼ hours

4 cups fresh corn kernels (from about 6 ears), divided
2 eggs
1½ cups half-and-half
1 tsp. kosher salt
½ cup chopped roasted green chiles (see Quick Tip below)
1 cup crushed buttery salted crackers (such as Ritz or Carr's Croissant Crackers), divided
¼ cup butter, melted, divided
½ cup finely shredded Monterey jack or pepper jack cheese

1. Preheat oven to 350°. Grease a 2-qt. baking dish.
2. Put 1¾ cups corn kernels in the bowl of a food processor. Pulse until corn is puréed but still a bit chunky, about 5 pulses. Set aside.
3. In a large bowl, whisk together eggs, half-and-half, and salt. Add whole and puréed corn kernels, chiles, ¼ cup cracker crumbs, and 3 tbsp. melted butter. Stir to combine. Spoon mixture into prepared baking dish and scatter cheese over the top.
4. In a small bowl, mix together remaining ¾ cup crumbs and 1 tbsp. melted butter. Sprinkle over cheese.
5. Bake pudding until puffed and golden brown, 45 to 50 minutes. The edges should be a bit crusty and the center still a little jiggly.
Quick Tip: Fresh or frozen roasted green chiles (such as Anaheim or New Mexico varieties) will give the dish more flavor, but if these aren't available, you can substitute canned roasted green chiles.

PER SERVING: 288 cal., 59% (171 cal.) from fat; 8.7 g protein; 19 g fat (10 g sat.); 24 g carbo (2.5 g fiber); 427 mg sodium; 107 mg chol.

Tomatoes in Spicy Yogurt Sauce

A recipe from Northern California cooking teacher and cookbook author Joanne Weir provided the inspiration here. The Indian-influenced tomatoes are warmed but not fully cooked in the sauce, leaving their softly solid texture intact. Serve them alongside broiled, grilled, or steamed fish and be sure to have plenty of rice to soak up the sauce.

SERVES 4 to 8 | **TIME** 30 minutes

8 ripe but firm tomatoes (about 2 lbs. total)
1 tsp. vegetable oil
2 tsp. cumin seeds
1 tsp. brown mustard seeds
2 tbsp. butter, cut into small pieces
¼ tsp. each turmeric and cayenne
6 garlic cloves, minced
2 serrano chiles, seeds and ribs removed and finely chopped
1 tsp. salt
1 cup plain whole-milk yogurt
Cilantro sprigs (optional)

1. Bring a large pot of water to boil. Meanwhile, fill a large bowl with cold water and a few ice cubes and set it near the pot. Put tomatoes in boiling water for 10 seconds each, then use a slotted spoon to transfer them to the ice water. Drain tomatoes and pat dry. Core and peel tomatoes (leave them whole). Set aside.
2. In a large frying pan, heat oil over high heat until hot. Add cumin and mustard seeds and reduce heat to medium-high. Cover and cook until seeds start to pop, about 2 minutes. Remove cover and add butter. When butter is melted, add turmeric and cayenne and cook, stirring, until fragrant, about 1 minute. Add garlic, chiles, and salt and cook, stirring, until fragrant, about 1 minute. Reduce heat to low. Add yogurt and stir in one direction until smooth. Add tomatoes. Gently stir to coat with sauce. Cook until tomatoes are just warm, about 5 minutes.
3. Garnish with cilantro if using and serve warm, with plenty of sauce.

PER TOMATO: 78 cal., 56% (44 cal.) from fat; 2.2 g protein; 4.9 g fat (2.5 g sat.); 7.5 g carbo (1.5 g fiber); 344 mg sodium; 11 mg chol.

8 Fast, Fresh Ideas for Side Dishes

1. Stir-fried Brussels Sprout Leaves
Trim the base, then peel the leaves off a batch of **brussels sprouts**, slice the nubbly centers thinly, and stir-fry leaves and bits in a little **vegetable oil** for 2 minutes with some minced **fresh ginger** and **red chile flakes**. When leaves are tender, stir in slivered **green onions**, finely shredded **lemon zest**, and a pat of **butter**.

2. Fava Bean Purée
Combine shelled and peeled **fresh fava beans** with some chopped **garlic** in **chicken or vegetable broth** to cover, then simmer until very tender. Purée beans and garlic in a blender with enough of the broth to make a thick paste. Season with **salt**. Delicious served with roast chicken or pork.

3. Fava Beans with Fresh Corn
Sauté shelled and peeled **fresh fava beans** in a bit of **butter** with chopped **bacon** and sweet **corn kernels**

sliced from their cobs. Add **salt** and freshly ground **black pepper** to taste.

4. Sautéed Sugar Snap Peas with Cream and Prosciutto
Sauté **sugar snaps** in **butter**, add a splash of **cream**, and cook until cream has thickened into a sauce (if you'd like it thick, cook it longer). Add julienned **prosciutto** or cooked, crumbled **pancetta**, then season with **salt**, **pepper**, and a pinch of freshly grated **nutmeg**.

5. Sesame-Garlic Peas
Heat a scant amount of **peanut or canola oil** in a wok or deep frying pan over high heat. Add some minced **garlic** and cook 10 seconds, then add shelled **fresh peas** and cook until bright green and crisp-tender, 2 to 3 minutes. Drizzle with **sesame oil** and sprinkle with **salt** and toasted **sesame seeds**.

6. Fried Green Tomatillos
Thickly slice husked **tomatillos**, dip

in beaten **egg**, dredge in **cornmeal** seasoned with **salt** and **pepper**, and fry in hot **oil** until browned. Drain, sprinkle with salt, and serve warm—with a dollop of **sour cream** if you like.

7. Garlic-Mint Roasted Potatoes
Toss 3 lbs. hot, freshly roasted **potatoes** with a generous handful of chopped **mint leaves** and 3 or 4 minced **garlic** cloves. Stir and let sit 10 minutes. Drizzle with **olive oil** and season with **salt** and freshly ground **black pepper**; serve warm or at room temperature.

8. Bacon-Rosemary Persimmons
Fry chopped **bacon** until crisp and leave some drippings in the pan. Sauté **Fuyu persimmon** wedges in the fat until golden; halfway through cooking, sprinkle in a bit of minced **rosemary** leaves, **salt**, and freshly ground **black pepper**. Stir in bacon.

Fresh Corn Cakes

These cakes from reader Lynn Lloyd of Santa Cruz, California, are delicious as a side dish smeared with butter. You can also dress them up with salsa and sour cream and serve as an appetizer.

MAKES 16 cakes | **TIME** 30 minutes

1 cup fresh corn kernels (from about 2 ears)
¼ cup chopped green onions
¼ cup vegetable oil, divided
2 eggs, separated
¼ cup *each* flour and yellow cornmeal
½ tsp. salt
¼ tsp. freshly ground black pepper

1. In a blender or food processor, pulse corn and green onions until chopped but not smooth. Transfer to a large bowl and stir in 2 tbsp. oil and the egg yolks.

2. In a small bowl, combine flour, cornmeal, salt, and pepper. Add to corn mixture and mix thoroughly but gently.
3. In a clean medium bowl, beat egg whites until soft peaks form. Fold into corn mixture.
4. In a large frying pan, heat 1 tbsp. oil over medium-high heat. Working in batches, drop large spoonfuls of corn mixture into pan (do not spread or flatten). Cook until edges begin to set and undersides are browned, about 2 minutes. Flip and cook until cakes are browned and cooked through. Cook remaining batter the same way, adding remaining 1 tbsp. oil as necessary.

PER CAKE: 63 cal., 60% (38 cal.) from fat; 1.5 g protein; 4.2 g fat (0.6 g sat.); 5.2 g carbo (0.4 g fiber); 83 mg sodium; 26 mg chol.

Stir-fried Asian Greens

This cooking method works well for larger greens cut into bite-size pieces.

SERVES 4 | **TIME** 8 minutes

1 lb. Asian greens, such as bok choy, choy sum, or Chinese mustard greens (*see A Guide to Asian Greens below*)
1 tbsp. *each* vegetable oil and chopped garlic
Salt

1. Remove and discard any yellow, damaged, or tough leaves from greens. Trim off and discard tough stem ends. For tough stalks, remove any thick side stems and the center stalk. Make additional cuts as follows: *For bok choy*, cut leaves and stalks diagonally or crosswise into ¼-in.-thick slices; separate leaves from stalks. *For choy sum or Chinese mustard greens*, if skin on stalks is tough, peel off and discard. Cut greens into 3-in. lengths, separating leaves and thin stems from thick stems or stalks. If any pieces are thicker than ½ in., cut to that thickness.

2. Set a 14- to 16-in. wok or 12-in. frying pan over high heat. When hot, add oil and garlic; cook, stirring, until garlic begins to brown, about 15 seconds. Stir in thicker stem or stalk pieces and 3 tbsp. water. Cover and cook until stems are tender-crisp, 2 to 3 minutes. Uncover,

A Guide to Asian Greens

Asian greens go by many names and transliterations, so it helps to know those you'll most often see in the market.

• **BABY BOK CHOY** (Shanghai bok choy): Small, curvaceous, jade green heads (4 to 10 in.) with mellow flavor.

• **BOK CHOY** (also called pak choi or Chinese white cabbage): Dark green leaves and smooth ivory stalks with a crisp, juicy texture and a mild, slightly cabbagelike flavor. Most supermarkets carry the mature sizes (up to 20 in.). Shorter heads (6 to 8 in.) are found mostly in Asian markets.

• **CHINESE MUSTARD GREENS** (gai choy, gai choy sum, juk gai choy, small gai choy, or leaf mustard): Several forms, with a mild-to-pungent mustard bite and jade green leaves and stems—some broad and smooth with ruffled leaves, others thin with smoother leaves.

• **CHOY SUM** (bok choy sum; yao, yau, yow, or yu choy; yao choy sum; or Chinese flowering cabbage): Literally, *choy sum* means "the heart of the vegetable," and it's not a type of green but rather the inner portion of several kinds of greens, including yoo choy (*see below*) and a miniature variety of bok choy with yellow flowers.

• **YOO CHOY** (yau, yow, or yu choy; choy sum; ching choy sum; flowering green; or flowering cabbage): Bright green, slender, fleshy, leafy stalks with tiny yellow buds or flowers and an earthy, slightly bitter mustard flavor. Young stalks of yoo choy are often labeled choy sum.

Yoo choy

Baby bok choy

Choy sum

Chinese mustard greens

Bok choy

add leaves and thin stems, and cook, stirring, until leaves are barely wilted, 1 to 2 minutes.

3. Add salt to taste.

PER SERVING: 49 cal., 65% (32 cal.) from fat; 1.9 g protein; 3.6 g fat (0.5 g sat.); 3.3 g carbo (1.2 g fiber); 74 mg sodium; 0 mg chol.

Pan-steamed Asian Greens with Shiitake Sauce

You can use just about any Asian green in this versatile recipe and it will be delicious. It's particularly good with fish or pork.

SERVES 4 | **TIME** 30 minutes

1 lb. Asian greens, such as bok choy, choy sum, or Chinese mustard greens *(see A Guide to Asian Greens, opposite page)*
1 oz. dried shiitake mushrooms
¼ cup dry sherry
2 tbsp. soy sauce
1 tbsp. minced garlic
2 tsp. *each* sugar and cornstarch

1. Remove and discard any yellow, damaged, or tough leaves from greens. Trim off and discard tough stem ends. For tough stalks, remove any thick side stems and the center stalk. Make additional cuts as follows: *For bok choy*, cut leaves and stalks diagonally or crosswise into ¼-in.-thick slices; separate leaves from stalks. *For choy sum or Chinese mustard greens*, if skin on stalks is tough, peel off and discard. Cut greens into 3-in. lengths, separating leaves and thin stems from thick stems or stalks. If any pieces are thicker than ½ in., cut to that thickness.

2. Rinse mushrooms and put in a bowl. Cover with 2 cups hot water. Let soak until soft, about 20 minutes. Lift mushrooms out, squeezing their liquid into bowl; reserve liquid. Cut off and discard stems; thinly slice caps.

3. Carefully pour ¾ cup of mushroom-soaking water into a 1- to 2-qt. pan, leaving grit behind. Add sliced mushrooms, sherry, soy sauce, garlic, and sugar. Bring to a boil over high heat, then cover, reduce heat, and simmer until mushrooms are tender, about 5 minutes.

4. In a small bowl, mix cornstarch with 2 tbsp. water until smooth; add to mushrooms and cook, stirring, until boiling.

5. Set a 5- to 6-quart pan over high heat. When hot, add ½ cup water and the greens; cover and cook until barely tender to bite, 3 to 5 minutes. Drain greens.

6. Arrange hot greens on a platter. Spoon mushroom sauce in a band over the top.

PER SERVING: 76 cal., 4% (2.7 cal.) from fat; 3 g protein; 0.3 g fat (0 g sat.); 13 g carbo (2.5 g fiber); 591 mg sodium; 0 mg chol.

Baby Bok Choy with Sesame Soy Sauce

Cut in half lengthwise and draped in a shimmering dark sauce, these baby bok choy look beautiful on a platter. Serve with teriyaki-seasoned grilled chicken or steak.

SERVES 8 | **TIME** 25 minutes

1 tbsp. sesame seeds
8 medium heads baby bok choy (about 1½ lbs. total), bottoms trimmed
1½ tbsp. Asian (toasted) sesame oil, divided, or more as needed
1 tbsp. minced fresh ginger
3 tbsp. *each* dry sherry and soy sauce
⅛ tsp. red chile flakes (optional)
¼ cup thinly sliced green onions

1. Toast sesame seeds in a large frying pan over medium-low heat, stirring, until golden, 3 to 5 minutes. Pour out of pan and reserve.

2. Cut bok choy in half lengthwise. Coat bottom of pan with 1½ tsp. oil; set over medium-high heat. When pan is hot, lay bok choy, as many as will fit in a single layer, cut side down in pan. Add 2 tbsp. water. Cover and cook just until bok choy wilts, about 2 minutes. Lift out of pan, drain briefly, and arrange cut side up on a deep platter. Remove any water from pan. Cook remaining bok choy the same way. Leave any residual water in pan.

3. Add 1 tbsp. oil and the ginger to the pan and cook, stirring, over high heat until ginger is lightly browned, about 30 seconds. Add sherry and bring to a boil. Remove from heat and add soy sauce and chile flakes if using.

4. Pour sauce over bok choy. Sprinkle with green onions and toasted sesame seeds.

Make Ahead: Bok choy, up to 4 hours at room temperature or chilled overnight; reheat in pan before serving. Sauce, up to 1 day, at room temperature, covered.

PER SERVING: 51 cal. (59% from fat); 2 g protein; 3.5 g fat (.5 g sat); 3.4 g carbo (1.1 g fiber); 435 mg sodium; 0 mg chol.

Curried Spinach with Fresh Cheese (Saag Paneer)

Paneer is a simple cheese that's easy to make at home. Its fresh flavor highlights the warm spices of a classic North Indian dish. Serve with flatbread or rice.

SERVES 6 | **TIME** 1½ hours, plus 3 hours to press *paneer*

8 cups whole milk
¼ cup plus 1 tsp. fresh lemon juice, plus more to taste
1 tbsp. plus 2 tsp. salt, plus more to taste
4 lbs. fresh spinach (*see Quick Tips, right*), thick stems removed
8 garlic cloves, peeled
2 onions, roughly chopped
2 serrano chiles, seeds and ribs removed
3-in. piece fresh ginger, roughly chopped
2 tbsp. vegetable oil
Seeds from 7 cardamom pods
3 whole cloves
2 bay leaves
1 cinnamon stick
2 tbsp. ground coriander
1 tbsp. ground cumin
1 tsp. turmeric
1 canned tomato, chopped
¼ cup plain whole-milk yogurt
2 tsp. garam masala (*see Quick Tips, right*)

1. Line a colander with two layers of cheesecloth and set in sink. Bring milk to a boil in a large pot over medium-high heat, stirring occasionally to prevent scorching. Let boil 30 seconds (remove from heat if it starts to boil over) and stir in ¼ cup lemon juice. Milk will curdle, separating into cheese curds and a clear yellow whey. Pour into cheesecloth-lined colander.
2. Rinse curds with cold water. Pull up edges of cheesecloth, gently squeeze out as much water as possible, and form curds into a 6-in. disk. Put the cheesecloth-wrapped disk on a large plate, top with a cutting board, and weigh down with a heavy pot. Refrigerate *paneer*, weighted with pot, at least 3 hours and up to overnight.
3. Bring a large pot of water to boil. Fill a large bowl with ice water and set aside. To boiling water, add 1 tbsp. salt and the spinach. Cook 1 minute, then drain spinach and transfer to ice water. Swirl around to cool; drain again. Squeeze water from spinach with your hands. Set aside.
4. In a blender, purée garlic, onions, chiles, ginger, and ¼ cup water to make a paste. Set aside.
5. Heat oil in a medium pot over medium-high heat. Add cardamom seeds, cloves, bay leaves, and cinnamon stick.

Cook, stirring, until spices darken, about 2 minutes. Add onion paste. Cook, stirring occasionally, until mixture thickens and darkens, about 15 minutes. If mixture starts to stick, add 1 tbsp. water at a time, stirring, to help loosen it.
6. Stir in coriander, cumin, and turmeric. Cook, stirring, until fragrant, about 2 minutes. Add tomato and yogurt. Cook until thickened slightly, about 3 minutes. Stir in spinach and remaining 2 tsp. salt. Turn heat to low and cover. Cook, stirring occasionally, until flavors are blended, about 30 minutes.
7. Cut *paneer* into ½-in. cubes and gently stir into spinach mixture. Cook until *paneer* is heated through, about 2 minutes. Add garam masala and remaining 1 tsp. lemon juice, plus more juice and salt to taste.

Quick Tips: *Saag paneer* requires a long cooking time for flavors to develop, so avoid using baby spinach, which will fall apart; instead, choose larger, more mature leaves. Garam masala is available in the spice section of many supermarkets; if you can't find it, substitute 1 tsp. cinnamon, ½ tsp. *each* ground cumin and freshly ground black pepper, and ¼ tsp. *each* ground cardamom, nutmeg, cloves, and cayenne.

PER SERVING: 337 cal., 45% (153 cal.) from fat; 19 g protein; 17 g fat (7.7 g sat.); 33 g carbo (6.9 g fiber); 1,233 mg sodium; 47 mg chol.

Bacon and Kale Adobo

Tim Luym, chef of the now-closed Poleng Lounge in San Francisco, gives this traditional Filipino dish a California twist by using kale instead of water spinach and substituting smoked bacon for pork belly.

SERVES 4 | **TIME** 1½ hours

6 oz. applewood-smoked bacon, finely chopped
1 small onion, finely chopped
3 large garlic cloves, lightly crushed
2 bay leaves
1 lb. kale, stems and ribs removed and leaves finely chopped
2 to 3 tbsp. reduced-sodium soy sauce, divided, plus more to taste
2 to 3 tbsp. coconut vinegar (*see Quick Tip, above right*) or 1 to 2 tbsp. cider vinegar, divided, plus more to taste
½ tsp. freshly ground black pepper
1 fresh Thai or serrano chile (optional), stemmed and crushed

1. In a 4- to 5-qt. pan over medium heat, cook bacon, stirring, until crisp, 8 to 10 minutes. Pour bacon and fat into a fine-mesh strainer set over a bowl. Return 5 tbsp. fat to pan; discard remainder.

2. Add onion, garlic, and bay leaves to pan and cook over medium-high heat, stirring often, until onion is pale golden, 5 minutes. Toss in kale; cook, stirring, until wilted. Add 1 cup water, half the bacon, 2 tbsp. each soy sauce and coconut vinegar, the pepper, and the chile if using. Simmer, covered, adding water if pan gets dry, until kale is very tender, about 1 hour. Taste; add more soy sauce and vinegar if it seems to need it. Serve sprinkled with remaining chopped bacon.

Quick Tip: Coconut vinegar is a cloudy white vinegar made from coconut water (the liquid within a fresh coconut); it has a mild, fruity kick. You can substitute cider vinegar, but use about two-thirds the amount called for.

PER SERVING: 243 cal., 70% (171 cal.) from fat; 7 g protein; 19 g fat (6.1 g sat.); 12 g carbo (2 g fiber); 677 mg sodium; 22 mg chol.

Sautéed Broccoli Rabe with Garlic and Chiles (*Rape Fritte*)

Italian cooking teacher Rosetta Costantino of Oakland, California, re-creates her native Calabria within her house and in her steeply sloped garden filled with peppers, eggplants, chiles, and fruit trees. Using chiles from her garden and locally grown broccoli rabe, she often makes *rape fritte* for Christmas Eve as part of *il cenone*, the traditional Calabrian feast of 13 dishes.

SERVES 8 | **TIME** 50 minutes

3 lbs. broccoli rabe (rapini; *see Quick Tip, above right*)
⅓ cup extra-virgin olive oil
8 garlic cloves, halved lengthwise if large
2 small dried hot red chiles, such as peperoncini, Thai, or Chinese, torn in half
½ tsp. kosher salt, plus more to taste

1. Trim broccoli rabe, removing tough parts of stems and any stems with a hollow core. Split stems (or quarter them if large) so they'll cook at same rate as florets.
2. Bring a large pot of water to a boil over high heat. Add broccoli rabe (you may have to add in batches, waiting until some of it cooks down) and cook until tender, 2 to 5 minutes. Scoop out and set aside about ¼ cup cooking water, then drain broccoli rabe in a colander. Let sit until cool enough to handle, about 15 minutes. Squeeze gently to remove excess moisture.
3. Heat oil in a 12-in. skillet over medium heat. Add garlic and chiles and cook, stirring, until garlic is golden, about 1 minute. Add broccoli rabe and salt and toss to coat with oil. Increase heat to high and cook until broccoli rabe is heated through and flavorful, about

5 minutes (if it looks dry, moisten with some of the reserved cooking liquid). Season with salt to taste. Serve hot or at room temperature.

Quick Tip: Buy broccoli rabe with firm green florets that show no sign of yellowing. Blanching the vegetable before sautéing removes some of its natural bitterness.

PER SERVING: 109 cal., 77% (84 cal.) from fat; 3.5 g protein; 9.3 g fat (1.3 g sat.); 6.1 g carbo (0.1 g fiber); 146 mg sodium; 0 mg chol.

Roasted Broccoli Rabe and Radicchio with Lemon

The bright citrus punch of lemon, coupled with the natural sweetening power of roasting, offsets the bitter edge of the broccoli rabe.

SERVES 4 to 6 | **TIME** 45 minutes

¾ lb. broccoli rabe (rapini)
½ head radicchio (about 4 oz.)
½ lemon
¼ lb. thickly sliced pancetta or bacon, chopped
3 tbsp. olive oil
¼ tsp. salt, plus more to taste
Freshly ground black pepper

1. Trim broccoli rabe, removing tough parts of stems and any stems with a hollow core. Cut broccoli rabe diagonally into 2-in. lengths. Core radicchio and cut head lengthwise into ½-in.-thick slices. Cut lemon half in half again lengthwise, then thinly slice crosswise, discarding ends and seeds.
2. Preheat oven to 400°. In an ovenproof frying pan, cook pancetta, stirring occasionally, over medium-low heat until crisp, 10 to 15 minutes. Add broccoli rabe, radicchio, lemon, oil, and salt.
3. Roast until broccoli rabe is tender when pierced and radicchio is wilted, about 10 minutes. Add salt and pepper to taste.

PER SERVING: 148 cal., 77% (114 cal.) from fat; 5.6 g protein; 13 g fat (2.9 g sat.); 3.9 g carbo (0.3 g fiber); 464 mg sodium; 17 mg chol.

Meet You at the Farmers' Market

A curiosity 20 years ago, the farmers' market is now a weekly part of life for many of us. It's where we discover new ingredients, find the freshest local and organic fruits and vegetables, and learn from the farmers about their produce (and what's in season when) and how to cook it. Increasingly, it's where we socialize with friends and nosh on handmade food—a crêpe, tamale, or freshly baked roll—as we browse the stalls.

The Trailblazers

The first farmers' market in the West (and one of the oldest in the country) was probably Seattle's Pike Place Market, which opened in 1907, followed by the Alemany Certified Farmers' Market in San Francisco and the Gardena Farmers' Market in Los Angeles. The Alemany market was started in 1943 by the Victory Garden Council during wartime to give farmers a way to sell surplus and blemished produce. Today, the Alemany market is one of California's largest and most diverse, and is known for offering hard-to-find specialty produce used in Asian and Latino cooking.

Farmers' markets in America nearly disappeared in the middle of the last century, mainly because of the rise of industrialized, wholesale produce. Before interstate highways went in and centralized retailing began, local, seasonal markets were a main source of fruits and vegetables. Afterward, produce could be transported hundreds of miles, fast—and it went to grocery stores. By 1970, only about 340 farmers' markets existed in the entire country.

A Flood of Farmers' Markets

The turning point came in 1976—that's when Congress passed the Farmer-to-Consumer Direct Marketing Act, helping small farmers sell to their communities. In California, governor Jerry Brown followed up by amending his state's rigorous produce-packing,

sizing, and shipping laws so farmers could sell at markets without any restrictions whatsoever. Tentatively, a few began to open, and they were hits: The Gardena Farmers' market, in Los Angeles, sold out within just a few hours on its opening day in 1979.

When the Santa Monica Farmers' Market started up two years later, it transformed a relatively seedy downtown area into a bustling hot spot and made farmers' markets chic. Its example—and a growing public craving for better food straight from the source—helped inspire the dozens, then hundreds, of markets that opened in the state. Today there are more than 5,000 farmers' markets in America, with more being founded every month. California has roughly 550, the most of any state. We Westerners seem especially to love our markets: According to the USDA, in the Far West (the entire Pacific coast, plus Hawaii and Nevada), annual sales

figures per market are much higher than in the rest of the country, and the number of weekly customers is more than twice the national average.

Some markets—like the Santa Monica market (now four locations), Pike Place, and San Francisco's Ferry Plaza market—are huge multi-vendor enterprises that are major tourist attractions as well as places to stock your kitchen for the week. Many hospitals and schools host weekly markets too. Chefs base their menus on what's freshest and best at the market (or sometimes the farm itself). Grocery stores often try to look more like markets, adding rustic bins to their produce sections or, in the case of Whole Foods, stocking some produce delivered from local farms. From the time the White House began to champion farmers' markets, in 2009, as a source of both healthy, fresh food and stronger communities, their presence in our lives has seemed destined to grow.

Orange and Walnut Broccoli,
page 265

Shaved Brussels Sprouts
with Pancetta, *page 266*

Miso-glazed Kabocha
Squash, *page 268*

Sweet Potato–Parsnip Latkes
with Gingered Sour Cream,
page 271

Salt-crusted Beets with
Avocado, Lavender, and
Thyme, *page 274*

257

Avocado Fries,
page 275

Split Pea–Squash Stew with
Basil and Serrano, *page 279*

Crusted Portabella "Burgers,"
page 284

Seven-vegetable Couscous,
page 287

Vegetable Ribbon Pasta Shells,
page 288

Stir-fried Eggplant and Tofu,
page 295

Leek and Chanterelle Tart,
page 298

Orange and Walnut Broccoli

Reader Laura A. Flynn of Littlerock, California, loves the combined flavors of orange peel and walnuts with spinach in a pork dish. Curious about how the flavors would complement other vegetables, she created a memorable side dish.

recipe pictured on page 253

SERVES 4 or 5 | **TIME** 15 minutes

1 orange
1 tbsp. vegetable oil
⅓ cup chopped walnuts
½ tsp. minced fresh ginger
1 tbsp. soy sauce
5 cups (¾ lb.) broccoli florets

1. With a vegetable peeler or small, sharp knife, pare zest from orange. Cut zest into very thin slivers. Squeeze juice from orange; measure ¼ cup and save the rest for other uses.
2. Heat oil in a 10- to 12-in. wok or frying pan over medium-high heat until hot. Add zest, walnuts, and ginger and stir often just until zest begins to brown slightly at edges, about 2 minutes.
3. Stir in ¼ cup orange juice and the soy sauce. Add broccoli and cook, stirring occasionally, until tender when pierced, about 5 minutes.

PER SERVING: 105 cal., 65% (68 cal.) from fat; 3.8 g protein; 7.6 g fat (0.8 g sat.); 6.1 g carbo (2 g fiber); 227 mg sodium; 0 mg chol.

Gorgonzola Broccoli Casserole

Everybody's Thanksgiving table needs a soothing, creamy casserole. This one, from Denise Marshall, owner of the Last Bite Cooking School in Eagle Point, Oregon, is a winner. It makes a satisfying side for other occasions too.

SERVES 12 to 14 | **TIME** 1¼ hours

3 lbs. broccoli
¼ cup butter plus 1 tbsp. melted butter
¼ cup flour
1 tsp. salt
2 cups milk
2 packages (3 oz. each) cream cheese, cut into
    ½-in. chunks
½ cup crumbled gorgonzola or other blue cheese
2 cups ½-in. cubes French or other firm white
    bread

1. Preheat oven to 350°. Bring 3 qts. water to a boil in a 5- to 6-qt. pot. Cut broccoli into 1-in. pieces. Add to boiling water and cook just until barely tender when pierced, 3 to 5 minutes. Drain.
2. Rinse and dry pot. Add ¼ cup butter and melt over medium heat. Stir in flour and salt and cook until bubbly, about 1 minute. Add milk and cook, stirring, over medium-high heat until boiling and thickened, about 3 minutes. Add cheeses; whisk until smooth. Stir in broccoli and transfer to a shallow 2½- to 3-qt. baking dish.
3. In a food processor, chop bread cubes into coarse crumbs (you should have about 1⅓ cups). In a bowl, mix crumbs with 1 tbsp. melted butter. Sprinkle evenly over broccoli mixture. Bake until casserole is hot and crumbs are golden, 20 to 30 minutes.

PER SERVING: 156 cal., 63% (99 cal.) from fat; 5.5 g protein; 11 g fat (6.8 g sat.); 9.9 g carbo (1.9 g fiber); 370 mg sodium; 33 mg chol.

Roasted Curry Cauliflower

In this recipe from reader Shelly Monfort of Los Gatos, California, sweet, nutty cauliflower is paired with the spicy warmth of curry powder.

SERVES 4 to 6 | **TIME** 45 minutes

2 tbsp. olive oil
1 tbsp. plus ½ tsp. fresh lemon juice
1 tbsp. curry powder
½ tsp. salt
¼ tsp. cayenne (optional)
1 head cauliflower, leaves and core removed, florets
    cut into ¼-in.-thick slices
Cilantro leaves

1. Preheat oven to 450°. In a large bowl, whisk together oil, 1 tbsp. lemon juice, the curry powder, salt, and cayenne if using. Add cauliflower slices and toss to coat. Spread cauliflower in a single layer in a large baking pan.
2. Bake until cauliflower is tender, chewy, and brown, 25 to 30 minutes. Sprinkle with remaining ½ tsp. lemon juice and garnish with cilantro.

PER SERVING: 65 cal., 78% (51 cal.) from fat; 1.2 g protein; 5.7 g fat (0.7 g sat.); 3.6 g carbo (1.7 g fiber); 241 mg sodium; 0 mg chol.

Shaved Brussels Sprouts with Pancetta

Brussels sprouts and pancetta are a classic pairing. Ambjorn Lindskog, chef-owner of Bistro Elan in Palo Alto, California, slices the sprouts very thinly in his version so they become extra-tender.

recipe pictured on page **254**

SERVES 8 to 10 | **TIME** 45 minutes

2 lbs. brussels sprouts
1 tbsp. vegetable oil
½ lb. pancetta, cut crosswise into ¼-in.-wide strips
Salt and freshly ground black pepper

1. Trim brussels sprouts at base and remove any damaged outer leaves. Using a sharp knife or mandoline (*see Quick Tip below*), thinly slice brussels sprouts crosswise. (The resulting sprout shavings should resemble confetti.)
2. Heat oil in a large pot or wok over high heat until hot but not smoking; add pancetta and cook, stirring constantly, until slightly crisp, about 5 minutes. Reduce heat to medium-high; add brussels sprouts and cook, stirring often, until sprouts are bright green and tender, 3 to 5 minutes. Add salt and pepper to taste.
Quick Tip: A mandoline works well for "shaving" the sprouts. Use a fork stuck in the core end of the sprout to keep your fingers away from the blade.

PER SERVING: 168 cal., 70% (117 cal.) from fat; 6.6 g protein; 13 g fat (5.6 g sat.); 9 g carbo (5.3 g fiber); 299 mg sodium; 14 mg chol.

Garlicky Sautéed Mushrooms

When mushrooms are cooked, they release a lot of liquid. Using high heat evaporates the juices, allowing the mushrooms to brown and develop flavor.

SERVES 4 to 6 | **TIME** 30 minutes

1 lb. wild or cultivated mushrooms
2 tbsp. olive oil
¼ tsp. sea salt, preferably *fleur de sel*, plus more for sprinkling
2 tsp. minced garlic
1 tbsp. chopped flat-leaf parsley

1. Trim mushroom stems and cut caps into bite-size pieces. Very small mushrooms can be left whole.
2. Set a 10- to 12-in. frying pan over high heat. When hot, add oil, swirl to coat bottom, and add mushrooms. Add salt and cook, stirring, until mushrooms stop releasing liquid and start to brown. Add garlic and cook, stirring, 2 to 3 minutes.
3. Remove from heat; stir in parsley. Sprinkle with more sea salt if you like.

PER SERVING: 59 cal., 69% (41 cal.) from fat; 1.8 g protein; 4.5 g fat (0.6 g sat.); 3.8 g carbo (0.9 g fiber); 96 mg sodium; 0 mg chol.

Soy-braised Mushrooms

The intense flavor and meatiness of these mushrooms make them an ideal side dish for grilled meat.

SERVES 8 to 10 | **TIME** 45 minutes

2 oz. dried whole shiitake mushrooms (2 to 3 in. wide; see *Quick Tip below*)
¼ cup *each* soy sauce and dry sherry
2 tbsp. sugar
8 quarter-size slices fresh ginger
3 garlic cloves, peeled
1 tsp. Asian (toasted) sesame oil
Thinly sliced green onions

1. Rinse mushrooms well and put in a 1½- to 2-qt. pan. Cover with hot water and let stand until soft, 15 to 20 minutes. Lift mushrooms out and trim off and discard tough stems. Slowly pour 2 cups of the soaking water into a glass measuring cup and reserve; discard remaining water with grit.
2. Rinse pan and return mushrooms and reserved soaking water to it; add soy sauce, sherry, and sugar. Lightly crush ginger and garlic with flat side of a chef's knife and add to pan. Cover and bring to a boil over high heat; reduce heat and simmer, covered, until mushrooms are tender, 15 to 20 minutes.
3. Uncover and boil over high heat until most of the liquid has evaporated, about 15 minutes. Remove ginger and garlic if you like. Stir in sesame oil. Serve hot or cool with green onions sprinkled on top.
Quick Tip: You can find dried shiitakes in Asian markets for far less than at a standard grocery store. Often you'll also find very plump ones with white cracks on the caps; these are delicious and you can use them, but they're more expensive and will require longer soaking to soften.
Make Ahead: Up to 1 day; let cool, then chill. Bring to room temperature and sprinkle with green onions to serve.

PER SERVING: 36 cal., 13% (4.5 cal.) from fat; 0.9 g protein; 0.5 g fat (0.1 g sat.); 7.7 g carbo (1 g fiber); 413 mg sodium; 0 mg chol.

vegetables on the side

Spaghetti Squash with Jalapeño Cream

We've tossed spaghetti squash with a spicy cream sauce and baked it, mac 'n' cheese–style, for a warming, hearty side dish that doubles easily and reheats beautifully. Keep this one in mind for Thanksgiving.

SERVES 8 | **TIME** 1¼ hours

1 spaghetti squash (about 3 lbs.)
2 cups milk
2 to 3 jalapeño chiles, seeds and ribs removed
   and chopped
2 tbsp. butter
3 tbsp. flour
1 tsp. salt
1 cup shredded jack cheese

1. Preheat oven to 375°. Cut squash in half lengthwise and use a spoon or melon baller to remove seeds and surrounding fiber. Put squash, cut side down, on a lightly buttered baking sheet and bake until flesh is tender when pierced with a fork, 30 to 40 minutes. Or poke several holes in skin of squash with a fork and microwave 10 minutes. If squash isn't tender when pierced with a fork, microwave at 1-minute intervals until it is. Let sit until cool.
2. Meanwhile, in a medium saucepan over medium heat, warm milk and jalapeños until bubbles form at the edges. Remove mixture from heat and let stand 15 minutes. Strain and discard jalapeños.
3. When squash is cool enough to handle, use a large spoon to scrape strands out of skin and into a large bowl.
4. In a medium saucepan over medium-high heat, melt butter. Whisk in flour and salt and cook, whisking, until flour smells cooked (like pie crust), about 3 minutes. Slowly pour in jalapeño-infused milk while whisking. Reduce heat to medium and continue whisking until mixture thickens slightly, about 3 minutes. Pour mixture over squash and stir to combine. Transfer mixture to a buttered 2-qt. baking dish. Sprinkle with cheese and bake until bubbling and brown on top, about 30 minutes.

PER SERVING: 168 cal., 53% (89 cal.) from fat; 6.7 g protein; 9.9 g fat (5.7 g sat.); 14 g carbo (2 g fiber); 447 mg sodium; 31 mg chol.

Baby Pumpkins with Garlic Custard

Although you can use any small edible pumpkins, the Baby Bear variety works best; other types don't hold as much custard.

SERVES 6 | **TIME** 1¼ hours

6 small edible pumpkins
⅓ cup *each* heavy whipping cream and whole milk
½ tsp. minced garlic
1 tbsp. finely shredded parmesan cheese
2 eggs
⅛ tsp. *each* salt and freshly ground white pepper

1. Preheat oven to 400°. Bake pumpkins on a baking sheet until just tender, about 20 minutes. Cut off tops and set aside to cool, then scoop out seeds.
2. In a bowl, whisk together cream, milk, garlic, parmesan, eggs, salt, and pepper. Pour into a measuring cup.
3. Arrange pumpkins in a baking dish large enough to hold them without crowding. Divide custard mixture among pumpkins and cover with tops. Pour enough water into dish to reach halfway up sides. Bake until custard jiggles only slightly, about 30 minutes. Remove from dish and let cool 5 minutes.

PER SERVING: 123 cal., 54% (66 cal.) from fat; 4.7 g protein; 7.4 g fat (4 g sat.); 12 g carbo (0.8 g fiber); 98 mg sodium; 91 mg chol.

3 Ways to Cook Winter Squash

1. MICROWAVE Poke squash all over with a fork. Microwave for 5 to 10 minutes, depending on size of squash. A fork should easily pierce both peel and flesh. If it doesn't, microwave squash in 1-minute intervals until it does. Let sit until cool enough to handle. Cut in half lengthwise and scoop out seeds. Works for all varieties.

2. ROAST/BAKE Preheat oven to 375°. Cut squash in half lengthwise. Using a soup spoon, scoop out and discard seeds. Oil or butter a baking sheet. Put squash, cut side down, on sheet and bake until tender when pierced with a fork, 15 to 45 minutes depending on size. Works for all varieties.

3. STEAM Peel, seed, and cut or slice squash and put in a steamer basket. Fill a pot with 1 in. water, bring water to a boil, and set basket in pot. Steam, covered, until tender to the bite, 10 to 20 minutes, depending on size of pieces. Best for squash that is smooth-skinned and easily peeled, such as butternut or kabocha.

Butternut Squash with Green Chile and Mustard Seeds

A fast, fun accompaniment to any simply grilled, broiled, or roasted meat. We particularly like it with a rotisserie chicken, some crusty bread, and Greek-style yogurt on the side. Save time and effort by using a 2-lb. bag of precut butternut squash.

SERVES 8 | **TIME** 30 minutes

2 tsp. vegetable oil
½ tsp. brown mustard seeds
3 garlic cloves, finely chopped
1 serrano chile, halved, seeds and ribs removed, and thinly sliced
1 medium butternut squash (about 2 lbs.), peeled, seeded, and cut into 1-in. cubes
Salt
Chopped cilantro (optional)

1. Pour oil and mustard seeds into a large frying pan. Cook over medium-high heat, covered, until seeds finish popping, about 1 minute. Add garlic and chile and cook, stirring, until garlic just starts to brown, about 1 minute.
2. Add squash and stir to coat with oil. Add ½ cup water, cover, and cook until squash is tender to the bite, 20 to 25 minutes. Sprinkle with salt to taste and garnish with cilantro if using.

PER SERVING: 56 cal., 21% (12 cal.) from fat; 1.1 g protein; 1.3 g fat (0.2 g sat.); 12 g carbo (2 g fiber); 4.1 mg sodium; 0 mg chol.

Miso-glazed Kabocha Squash

Dense, rich-tasting kabocha is one of our favorite squashes.

SERVES 8 | **TIME** 30 minutes

recipe pictured on page **255**

6 tbsp. white miso (*see Quick Tip, above right*)
3-in. piece fresh ginger, very finely grated
¼ cup sake or fino sherry
3 tbsp. vegetable oil
2 tbsp. *each* unseasoned rice vinegar, soy sauce, and firmly packed light brown sugar
½ kabocha squash (about 1½ lbs.), seeded and cut into ¼-in.-thick slices
2 tsp. Asian (toasted) sesame oil

1. Preheat oven to 375°. In a blender, purée miso, ginger, sake, vegetable oil, vinegar, soy sauce, and brown sugar until smooth.

2. In a large bowl, toss squash slices with miso mixture to coat thoroughly. Lift slices from sauce and arrange them, overlapping slightly, on a large baking sheet. Reserve sauce.
3. Bake 15 minutes. Brush slices with remaining sauce (you will have some left over) and cook until thick edges are tender when pierced with a fork, 5 to 10 more minutes. Drizzle with sesame oil and serve hot or warm.
Quick Tip: Look for white miso near the tofu in well-stocked supermarkets.

PER SERVING: 131 cal., 50% (65 cal.) from fat; 2.7 g protein; 7.2 g fat (0.9 g sat.); 13 g carbo (1.8 g fiber); 732 mg sodium; 0 mg chol.

Cranberry-Pomegranate Sauce

Cranberry sauce is a must-have at the Thanksgiving table—and it's appealing throughout winter. In our version, pomegranate molasses and seeds mellow cranberries' tartness and give a haunting depth to the sauce. It's a new classic in the crowded field of cranberry sauces.

MAKES 2½ cups; 12 servings | **TIME** 15 minutes

1 bag (12 oz.) cranberries, thawed if frozen
½ cup firmly packed light brown sugar
¼ cup pomegranate molasses (*see Pomegranate Molasses below*)
3 small thyme sprigs
1 cup pomegranate seeds

1. In a medium saucepan, bring cranberries, brown sugar, molasses, and thyme to a boil over medium-high heat, stirring frequently. Boil, stirring often, until most cranberries pop, about 5 minutes.
2. Remove from heat and stir in pomegranate seeds. Discard thyme.
Make Ahead: Up to 1 week, chilled. Add pomegranate seeds just before serving.

PER 3-TBSP. SERVING: 80 cal., 2% (1.9 cal.) from fat; 0.4 g protein; 0.2 g fat (0 g sat.); 20 g carbo (1.9 g fiber); 6.1 mg sodium; 0 mg chol.

■ Pomegranate Molasses

A tart, brownish syrup, pomegranate molasses is actually a concentrate made from the fruit's juice. Pomegranate molasses, a staple in Middle Eastern cuisines, is often used in meat marinades and *fesenjoon*, a dip or meat condiment. Look for it in well-stocked supermarkets and Middle Eastern grocery stores.

3 Ways With Zucchini Blossoms

The edible flowers of zucchini plants are gorgeous orange-yellow blossoms with a lovely, delicate flavor. You can often find them during the summer at farmers' markets. Choose specimens that look plump and fresh, make sure they are open if you plan to stuff them (it's hard to pry the petals apart without ripping them), and use them that day if possible. Here are three methods for cooking them:

1. BATTERED BLOSSOMS Dip 10 to 12 blossoms in a mixture of ⅔ cup **flour**, 1 cup **club soda**, 1 beaten **egg**, and ¼ tsp. **salt**. In **vegetable oil** (1 to 2 in. deep) heated to 375°, fry in small batches until golden. Drain on a cooling rack set over paper towels, sprinkle with **kosher salt**, and serve immediately.

2. STIR-FRIED BLOSSOMS Add blossoms to a wok full of summer vegetables.

3. STUFFED BLOSSOMS Fill each blossom with a bit of **goat, ricotta, or other soft cheese**. Twist ends closed; following directions above, dip in batter and fry. (Be careful: The cheesy interior can get very hot.)

Little Balsamic-glazed Onions

To save time peeling onions, choose large red pearl onions, or use fewer of them, along with the cipollini. The dish won't be as colorful, but it will be just as tasty. The garlic cloves are actually quite fast to peel—the skins slip right off after blanching.

SERVES 10 to 12 | **TIME** 2 hours

2½ lbs. *each* cipollini onions and red pearl onions
2½ heads garlic (optional), separated into cloves
3 tbsp. extra-virgin olive oil, divided
1 tbsp. fresh thyme leaves, plus several sprigs
½ tsp. *each* kosher salt and freshly ground black pepper
⅓ cup good-quality balsamic vinegar
1 cup reduced-sodium vegetable broth
1 bunch (about 8) green onions, trimmed and cut into
   2-in. lengths
3 tbsp. butter

1. Add half the cipollini to a pot of boiling water; blanch 1 minute, then transfer with a slotted spoon to a colander and immediately rinse with cold water. Repeat with remaining cipollini, then pearl onions (in two batches), then garlic if using.

2. With a small, sharp serrated knife, peel onions (and garlic), trying to keep them as intact as possible. Put in a bowl and drizzle with 1 tbsp. oil, the thyme leaves, salt, and pepper. Mix to coat.

3. In a large frying pan, heat remaining 2 tbsp. oil over medium-high heat. Add onions (and garlic) and cook, stirring often, until most are partly browned. Add vinegar and broth; reduce heat to medium-low and simmer, covered, until onions are tender and some are falling apart, 10 to 20 minutes.

4. Using a slotted spoon, transfer onions (and garlic) to a serving bowl. Stir in green onions and butter; cover. Boil sauce left in pan over high heat until syrupy and reduced to about ¾ cup, about 4 minutes, then stir gently into onion mixture. Top with thyme sprigs.
Make Ahead: Through step 3, up to 2 days, chilled. Reheat over low heat until onions are heated through.

PER SERVING: 133 cal., 42% (56 cal.) from fat; 1.4 g protein; 6.3 g fat (2.3 g sat.); 17 g carbo (3.6 g fiber); 161 mg sodium; 7.6 mg chol.

Caramelized Shallots and Walnuts

This side dish from chef Paul Canales of Oliveto in Oakland, California, is simultaneously sweet and savory, something like a relish served warm. The crunchy walnuts and silky, smooth shallots work especially well with beef.

SERVES 8 | **TIME** 45 minutes

¼ cup butter
2 lbs. shallots, peeled
½ tsp. salt
1 cup walnut halves
1 cup vin santo (Italian dessert wine; *see Quick Tip below*)
5 thyme sprigs

1. In a large frying pan over medium-high heat, melt butter. Add shallots and sprinkle with salt. Cook, stirring occasionally, until shallots are well browned all over, about 20 minutes.

2. Add walnuts, vin santo, and thyme. Bring to a boil, then reduce heat to low, cover, and simmer until shallots are tender, about 5 minutes.

3. Uncover, turn heat to medium-high, and cook until liquid is reduced and almost completely evaporated. Serve warm.

Quick Tip: Vin santo is sold at liquor stores; if you prefer, substitute madeira, marsala, port, or any other sweet wine.

PER SERVING: 234 cal., 58% (135 cal.) from fat; 4.8 g protein; 15 g fat (4.4 g sat.); 23 g carbo (1.6 g fiber); 220 mg sodium; 16 mg chol.

vegetables on the side

Glazed Carrots with Green Olives

In this delicious dish from cookbook author Paula Wolfert, carrots steam in melted butter and then are mixed with green olives, garlic, thyme, and cream. You can use a slow-cooker or prepare the carrots on the stove. For stovetop cooking, you'll need to use a heat diffuser or flame tamer under the pan to keep the heat low enough.

SERVES 8 to 10 | **TIME** 15 minutes, plus 2½ hours of unattended cooking

2 lbs. carrots, peeled
¼ cup butter or olive oil, divided
2 garlic cloves, sliced
2 tbsp. chopped flat-leaf parsley
1 cup (7 oz.) picholine or other mild green olives, pitted (see Quick Tip below)
4 thyme sprigs (4 in.)
Salt and freshly ground black pepper
6 tbsp. whipping cream

1. Cut carrots in half crosswise, then lengthwise into ½-in.-thick sticks. Put carrots and 2 tbsp. butter in an electric slow-cooker (4½ qt. or larger) or a heavy 12-in. frying pan.
2. *If using a slow-cooker,* cover and set heat to high. Cook, stirring twice, until carrots are very tender when pierced, 2 to 3 hours. Drain. *If using a heavy frying pan,* set on a heat diffuser over a burner on low heat. Add 3 tbsp. water, cover with a round of parchment paper (cut to just fit inside pan) and a tight-fitting lid, and follow the cooking instructions for slow-cooker.
3. About 10 minutes before serving, melt remaining 2 tbsp. butter in an 11- to 12-in. frying pan over medium heat. Add garlic and parsley and cook, stirring, until garlic softens, about 1 minute. Stir in carrots, olives, thyme, and salt and pepper to taste. Stir in cream, cover, and cook over medium-low heat until carrots are hot and cream has thickened and coats carrots, 5 to 7 minutes.
Quick Tip: To pit olives, gently tap each one with a wooden mallet or the flat side of a knife blade; halve the olive and pull out the pit.
Make Ahead: Through step 2, up to 1 hour before serving.

PER SERVING: 123 cal., 71% (87 cal.) from fat; 1.3 g protein; 9.7 g fat (4.9 g sat.); 8.9 g carbo (3.1 g fiber); 461 mg sodium; 23 mg chol.

Carrot and Sweet Potato Tzimmes

Napa Valley vegetable grower Amy Giaquinta roasts two root vegetables to sweetness for her version of this classic Jewish slow-cooked stew. It's wonderful alongside short ribs and a hit with her kids at Passover.

MAKES 6 cups; 12 servings | **TIME** 1¾ hours

2 lbs. carrots, cut into 1-in. pieces
2 lbs. orange-fleshed sweet potatoes (often labeled "yams"), peeled and cut into 1-in. pieces
¼ cup butter (see Quick Tip below)
3 tbsp. fresh thyme leaves
Kosher salt and freshly ground black pepper
4 green onions, trimmed and diagonally sliced

1. Preheat oven to 375°. Put carrots, sweet potatoes, butter, thyme, salt, and pepper in a 9- by 13-in. pan and cover tightly with foil. Bake 25 minutes.
2. Stir, then continue baking, covered, until carrots are very tender, about 50 minutes. Stir in green onions and bake until onions are wilted, about 5 minutes.
3. Coarsely mash vegetables in pan.
Quick Tip: For a nondairy kosher version, use extra-virgin olive oil in place of the butter.
Make Ahead: Up to 1 day, chilled. To reheat, microwave until hot, stirring occasionally.

PER ½-CUP SERVING: 122 cal., 30% (37 cal.) from fat; 1.7 g protein; 4.1 g fat (2.4 g sat.); 21 g carbo (4 g fiber); 167 mg sodium; 10 mg chol.

Okinawa Sweet Potatoes

Okinawa sweet potatoes, native to the Japanese island with that name, turn a stunning deep purple when cooked and have a dense, starchy texture. Our recipe is from Greg and Lynn Boyer of Oahu.

SERVES 10 to 12 | **TIME** 1 hour

4 lbs. Okinawa (purple) sweet potatoes (see Quick Tips, above right) or white sweet potatoes
2 limes
¼ cup butter
Hawaiian red salt (see Shaking Out the Salts, page 67) or sea salt

1. Bring a large pot of water to a boil over high heat. Prick sweet potatoes with a fork and boil until tender when pierced, 30 to 35 minutes. Drain.
2. While potatoes are boiling, finely shred zest from limes, then squeeze juice from limes; set aside.

3. When potatoes are cool enough to handle, peel and slice into ½-in.-thick slices. Arrange on a platter, cover with foil, and put in a 200° oven to keep warm.

4. Melt butter in a small saucepan over medium heat until foaming. Stir in lime zest and cook until fragrant, about 1 minute. Remove from heat and stir in lime juice. Drizzle over potatoes and sprinkle with salt to taste.

Quick Tips: Okinawa sweet potatoes, also called purple sweet potatoes, are available at some Asian-food markets and farmers' markets, and online at *melissas.com*. Find white sweet potatoes at well-stocked grocery stores.

PER SERVING: 136 cal., 29% (39 cal.) from fat; 2.6 g protein; 4.3 g fat (2.6 g sat.); 23 g carbo (2.1 g fiber); 50 mg sodium; 11 mg chol.

Sweet Potatoes with Meringue

By using meringue instead of marshmallows, Seattle chef Maria Hines of Tilth restaurant adds panache to a holiday favorite.

SERVES 10 to 12 | **TIME** 1¾ hours

4 lbs. orange-fleshed sweet potatoes (often labeled "yams"), peeled and cut into ¼-in. slices
¾ tsp. salt
½ tsp. freshly ground black pepper
1 tsp. minced thyme leaves
4 egg whites
¼ tsp. cream of tartar
½ cup sugar
½ tsp. vanilla extract

1. Preheat oven to 375°. Butter an 8-in. square baking pan. Arrange sweet potato slices in layers, sprinkling with salt, pepper, and thyme as you go. Cover with foil and bake until sweet potatoes are tender when pierced with a fork, 45 to 90 minutes.

2. Over high heat, bring 1 cup water to a boil in a medium pot. Reduce heat to maintain a simmer. Put egg whites and cream of tartar in a rimmed metal bowl just big enough to rest on rim of pot. Set bowl over pot and whisk egg whites constantly until hot but not cooking, 3 to 5 minutes. Remove from heat and beat with a mixer until firm peaks form. Sprinkle in sugar and vanilla and beat into stiff, shiny peaks. Spread over cooked sweet potatoes.

3. Broil 6 in. from heat until nicely browned.

Make Ahead: Through step 1, up to 1 day, chilled. Bring sweet potatoes to room temperature before reheating in a 375° oven until hot, about 15 minutes.

PER SERVING: 155 cal., 3% (4.5 cal.) from fat; 3 g protein; 0.5 g fat (0.2 g sat.); 35 g carbo (3.3 g fiber); 180 mg sodium; 0.4 mg chol.

Sweet Potato–Parsnip Latkes with Gingered Sour Cream

Earthy, crunchy, and sweet, these Hanukkah pancakes disappear quickly from the table. Sweet potatoes are less starchy than russets or Yukon Golds, so there's no need to rinse or squeeze the grated potatoes. *See Tips for Terrific Latkes, page 272.*

recipe pictured on page **256**

MAKES About 25 latkes | **TIME** 1 hour, 10 minutes

2 lbs. orange-fleshed sweet potatoes (often labeled "yams"), peeled
1 lb. parsnips, peeled
10 shallots, peeled
6 eggs, beaten
¾ cup plus 2 tbsp. matzo meal
1 tbsp. kosher salt
1 tsp. freshly ground black pepper
Vegetable oil for frying
Gingered Sour Cream (recipe follows)

1. Using the coarse side of a box grater or a food processor fitted with a medium-coarse grating disk, shred sweet potatoes, parsnips, and shallots. Toss together in a large bowl.

2. Add eggs, matzo meal, salt, and pepper and toss to mix well.

3. Pour ¾ in. oil into a 10- to 12-in. frying pan (with sides at least 2 in. high) and heat over medium-high heat. When oil reaches 350°, scoop ⅓ cup of sweet potato mixture from bowl, then gently turn onto a wide spatula. Press into a patty about ⅓ in. thick, then gently slide pancake into hot oil. Cook three or four pancakes at a time (do not crowd pan) until edges are crispy and well browned and undersides are golden brown, 2 to 3 minutes. Gently turn and cook until other sides are golden brown, 2 to 3 minutes longer.

4. Transfer pancakes to paper towels to drain briefly, then keep warm in a 200° oven while you cook remaining pancakes.

5. Serve latkes hot, with gingered sour cream.

PER LATKE: 123 cal., 39% (48 cal.) from fat; 2.7 g protein; 5.3 g fat (0.9 g sat.); 16 g carbo (2.1 g fiber); 256 mg sodium; 51 mg chol.

Gingered Sour Cream: In a small bowl, stir together 1 cup **sour cream**, 2 tbsp. **apple cider**, and 2 tsp. grated **fresh ginger**. Makes 1 cup.

PER TSP.: 11 cal., 82% (9 cal.) from fat; 0.2 g protein; 1 g fat (0.6 g sat.); 0.3 g carbo (0 g fiber); 2.6 mg sodium; 2.1 mg chol.

Herbed Yukon Gold Potato Latkes

These elegant latkes also make a great starter course or brunch main course. *See Tips for Terrific Latkes, above.*

MAKES 20 to 24 latkes | **TIME** 1 hour, 10 minutes

3½ lbs. Yukon Gold potatoes *(see Quick Tip, right)*, any
 brown spots or eyes removed
5 eggs, beaten
½ cup matzo meal, plus more if needed
¾ cup finely chopped chives
½ cup chopped flat-leaf parsley
2 tsp. *each* chopped thyme and rosemary leaves
1 tbsp. kosher salt
1 tsp. freshly ground black pepper
Vegetable oil for frying
9 to 12 oz. thinly sliced smoked salmon, cut into 20 to
 25 slices (optional)
Sour cream, thinly sliced red onion and/or 2-in. lengths
 of chives, and capers

1. Fill a large bowl three-quarters full with cold water. Using the coarse side of a box grater or a food processor fitted with a medium-coarse grating disk, grate potatoes, transferring them to the water as you go. Let potatoes stand in water 15 minutes.
2. Pour potatoes into a fine-mesh colander and rinse under cold running water until draining water is clear. Rinse bowl and wipe dry.
3. Take a large handful of potatoes and squeeze to remove some water. Pile onto a clean kitchen towel, gather towel corners up into one hand, and twist hard to wring out any remaining moisture. Repeat with rest of potatoes, using fresh towels if needed. Return potatoes to bowl.

4. In a medium bowl, stir together eggs, matzo meal, chives, parsley, thyme, rosemary, salt, and pepper, then pour over potatoes and toss to mix well. If at any time you notice a pool of liquid in bottom of bowl, toss in more matzo meal, 2 tbsp. at a time.
5. Pour ¾ in. oil into a 10- to 12-in. frying pan (with sides at least 2 in. high) or a large deep pot over medium-high heat. When oil reaches 350°, scoop a scant ¼ cup of potato mixture from bowl, then gently turn onto a wide spatula. Press into a patty about ⅓ in. thick, then gently slide pancake into hot oil. Cook three or four pancakes at a time (do not crowd pan) until edges are crispy and well browned and undersides are golden brown, 2 to 3 minutes. Gently turn and cook until other sides are golden brown, 2 to 3 minutes longer.
6. Transfer pancakes to paper towels to drain briefly, then keep warm in a 200° oven while you cook remaining pancakes.
7. Serve with sliced smoked salmon if using, sour cream, onion and/or chives, and capers.
Quick Tip: The skins of Yukon Golds are so thin that there's no need to peel them—just clean them well.

PER LATKE: 122 cal., 41% (50 cal.) from fat; 3.2 g protein; 5.6 g fat (0.9 g sat.); 14 g carbo (0.9 g fiber); 263 mg sodium; 44 mg chol.

Chipotle Corn Mashed Potatoes

Mashed potatoes are good just about any way, but here they're smoky, crunchy, and irresistible. Sean Yontz, chef-owner of Sketch and Tambien restaurants in Denver, gave us the recipe.

MAKES About 10 cups; 12 servings | **TIME** 45 minutes

4 ears corn, husks and silks removed
2 tsp. vegetable oil, plus more if needed
5 lbs. russet potatoes, peeled and cut into 2-in. chunks
¼ cup butter
¾ cup whole milk, plus more if needed, heated till hot
2 canned chipotle chiles (with no extra adobo sauce from
 can), minced
Salt and freshly ground black pepper

1. Prepare a charcoal or gas grill for direct medium heat *(see Direct Heat Grilling, page 436)*. Lightly rub corn with oil and grill, covered, turning often, until kernels are lightly browned all over, 9 to 12 minutes. Let stand until cool enough to handle. Holding corn upright in a deep bowl, cut kernels from ears with a sharp knife.
2. Meanwhile, in a 5- to 6-qt. pot over high heat, bring 3 qts. water to a boil. Add potatoes and cook until very tender when pierced, about 20 minutes. Drain and return to pot.

3. Add butter and hot milk and beat with a mixer or mash with a potato masher until smooth. Stir in corn and chipotles. Add more milk if you like, plus salt and pepper to taste.

PER SERVING: 207 cal., 25% (52 cal.) from fat; 5.3 g protein; 5.8 g fat (2.9 g sat.); 36 g carbo (3.3 g fiber); 95 mg sodium; 12 mg chol.

Horseradish Potato Purée

These smooth, creamy, innocent-looking mashed potatoes from San Francisco caterer Meme Pederson deliver an exhilarating hit of horseradish.

SERVES 12 | **TIME** 1¼ hours

5 lbs. russet potatoes, peeled and chopped into
    1-in. pieces
1¾ cups whipping cream
1 cup milk
½ cup unsalted butter
4 to 6 tbsp. cream-style prepared horseradish (see Quick
    Tip below)
1 tbsp. kosher salt
¼ tsp. white pepper

1. Bring a large pot of water to boil. Add potatoes, reduce heat to a simmer, and cook, covered, until very tender, about 25 minutes. Drain potatoes and return to pot over low heat. Stir over heat until potatoes are completely dry and starting to fall apart (this will make them soft and light when puréed).
2. Meanwhile, heat cream and milk in a heavy-bottomed pot over medium-low heat until just simmering.
3. Put potatoes, butter, and horseradish into bowl of a stand mixer with paddle attachment (or transfer them to a large bowl and use a handheld mixer) and beat on low until nearly smooth. While beating, drizzle enough of hot milk mixture into potatoes to make them soft and loose, keeping in mind that potatoes stiffen as they sit (you may not need all the milk and cream). Add salt and pepper and beat just until smooth (avoid overbeating, as purée will become gummy).
Quick Tip: This dish is wonderful when made with horseradish root instead—if you can find a good fresh one. Use ½ cup finely grated peeled fresh horseradish, add it to the heated cream-milk mixture, and let steep for 30 minutes, off the heat, before adding it to the potatoes.
Make Ahead: Up to 2 hours, chilled. Gently reheat in the microwave.

PER SERVING: 338 cal., 56% (189 cal.) from fat; 5.2 g protein; 21 g fat (13 g sat.); 33 g carbo (2.4 g fiber); 540 mg sodium; 71 mg chol.

Parmesan, Garlic, and Cajun Fries

In San Diego, Padres fans love the three choices of french-fry flavors at Petco Park. We couldn't pick just one, so we tossed them together for a triple play.

SERVES 8 | **TIME** 25 minutes

1 package (28 oz.) frozen shoestring french fries
½ cup finely shredded parmesan cheese
2 tbsp. minced garlic
½ tsp. Cajun seasoning
Kosher salt

1. Bake fries according to package directions.
2. Transfer hot fries to a large bowl. Add parmesan, garlic, and Cajun seasoning, tossing to coat well. Season to taste with salt.

PER SERVING: 203 cal., 31% (63 cal.) from fat; 5.3 g protein; 7 g fat (2.2 g sat.); 30 g carbo (2.6 g fiber); 198 mg sodium; 4.8 mg chol.

Cheesy Caraway-Bacon Potatoes

After reading a cookbook that recommended caraway seeds as a great match for potatoes, reader Jeff Mead of Hillsboro, Oregon, added them to his mother's favorite potato recipe—and liked their flavor and crunch.

SERVES 8 to 10 | **TIME** 1 hour, 50 minutes

½ tsp. salt
¼ tsp. freshly ground black pepper
4 lbs. russet or Yukon Gold potatoes, peeled and thinly
    sliced, divided
1 lb. bacon, cooked until crisp, then crumbled, divided
1½ cups finely shredded parmesan cheese, divided
1 tbsp. caraway seeds, divided
2 tbsp. butter

1. Preheat oven to 350°. In a small bowl, stir together salt and pepper. Arrange a third of potato slices in bottom of a buttered 9- by 13-in. baking dish. Sprinkle with ¼ tsp. salt-and-pepper mixture. Top with half the bacon, ½ cup parmesan, and 1 tsp. caraway seeds. Repeat to make a second layer. Arrange remaining third of potato slices on top. Sprinkle with remaining ¼ tsp. salt-and-pepper mixture, ½ cup parmesan, and 1 tsp. caraway seeds. Dot with butter, cover with foil, and bake 30 minutes.
2. Remove foil and bake until golden brown on top and cooked through, about 40 minutes.

PER SERVING: 315 cal., 40% (126 cal.) from fat; 14 g protein; 14 g fat (6.9 g sat.); 34 g carbo (2.7 g fiber); 642 mg sodium; 31 mg chol.

Golden Olive Oil–roasted Potatoes

Nothing more than good olive oil and crunchy sea salt turns super-simple potatoes into an irresistible side dish. This one comes from Maria Helm Sinskey, co-owner of Robert Sinskey Vineyards in Napa, California, and author of *The Vineyard Kitchen: Menus Inspired by the Seasons* and *Williams-Sonoma Family Meals: Creating Traditions in the Kitchen*.

SERVES 8 | **TIME** 1¼ hours, plus overnight to chill

5 lbs. large Yukon Gold potatoes
Salt
3 tbsp. extra-virgin olive oil
1½ tsp. sea salt, such as *fleur de sel*, plus more to taste

1. Peel potatoes and cut into 1½-in. cubes. Put in a large bowl, cover with cold water, and refrigerate overnight (*see Quick Tip below*).
2. Drain potatoes and preheat oven to 475°. Bring a large pot of lightly salted water to a boil over high heat. Add potatoes and cook until barely tender when pierced, about 10 minutes. Pour into a colander and let drain and dry 10 minutes.
3. Set potatoes in a single layer in a large rimmed baking pan. Drizzle with oil and sprinkle with sea salt; stir gently to coat. Bake potatoes until golden brown, 25 to 30 minutes, turning potatoes halfway through baking.
4. Sprinkle with more sea salt to taste.
Quick Tip: Soaking the potatoes at least 1 day (and up to 2 days) ahead makes them even crisper on the outside and creamier in the middle.

PER SERVING: 255 cal., 18% (47 cal.) from fat; 6 g protein; 5.2 g fat (0.8 g sat.); 45 g carbo (3 g fiber); 383 mg sodium; 0 mg chol.

Lavender in the Kitchen

Lavender is grown commercially in the West in California, Oregon, and Washington, as well as in Montana and Idaho. The dried buds of lavender can be used in the kitchen in many ways. In addition to incorporating them in our beet recipe (*right*), you can add them to salad dressings, perfume honey with them, make them a part of seasoning rubs for salmon or lamb, or add to breads and cookies.

The secret is to use lavender discreetly. You want to contribute an elusive floral note that makes the food taste distinctively different, but subtly so. Too much lavender can overwhelm other flavors and come off tasting like cheap cologne. Be sure to cook only with pesticide-free lavender grown for culinary use. Find it in the spice section of specialty-foods stores and some supermarkets.

Salt-crusted Beets with Avocado, Lavender, and Thyme

Chef Jeremy Fox, formerly at Ubuntu restaurant in Napa, California, roasts beets in an aromatic salt crust that infuses the kitchen and the beets with the fragrance of flowers and herbs.

recipe pictured on page 257

SERVES 6 | **TIME** 2½ hours

4 egg whites, beaten to blend
1 box (3 lbs.) plus ¼ tsp. kosher salt
⅓ cup chopped plus ½ tsp. minced fresh thyme leaves
¼ cup plus ¼ tsp. minced dried culinary lavender (*see Lavender in the Kitchen below left*)
2 tbsp. black peppercorns
3 *each* medium red and golden beets (1¾ lbs. total without tops), trimmed and gently scrubbed (*see Quick Tip, above right*)
3 tbsp. extra-virgin olive oil
1 tbsp. Champagne vinegar
1 tsp. minced shallot
¼ tsp. freshly ground black pepper
1 firm-ripe avocado, pitted, peeled, and cut into small wedges
2 cups (1¼ oz.) loosely packed mâche

1. Preheat oven to 425°. In a large bowl, combine egg whites, 3 lbs. salt, chopped thyme, ¼ cup lavender, the peppercorns, and ½ cup water, mixing with your hands until salt is evenly coated and feels like wet sand.
2. Spoon enough of salt mixture into a 9- by 13-in. baking pan to make a ¼-in. layer. Arrange beets on top without letting them touch. Mound remaining salt over each beet, pressing with hands to cover completely and make a crust.
3. Bake beets until very tender when pierced through salt, about 1¼ hours.
4. Poke tip of a table knife into salt crust about 1 in. from a beet and tap with a mallet to crack crust. Move and tap knife at ½-in. intervals in a circle around beet. Break beet free from crust and lift out. Repeat with remaining beets. Let beets stand until cool enough to handle.
5. In a medium bowl, whisk together oil, vinegar, shallot, pepper, the minced thyme, and the remaining ¼ tsp. salt and ¼ tsp. lavender to make the dressing. Spoon 1 tbsp. dressing into a second bowl and ½ tbsp. dressing into a third bowl.
6. Brush remaining salt off beets with a pastry brush. Peel beets and cut into thin wedges. Add golden beets and avocado to bowl with largest amount of dressing. Add red beets to bowl with 1 tbsp. dressing and mâche

vegetables on the side

to bowl with ½ tbsp. dressing. Gently mix each to coat and divide among salad plates.

Quick Tip: To keep the beets from getting too salty, trim and scrub them enough to remove dirt but not the skin. To loosen the baked salt from the pan, soak the pan in water.

PER SERVING: 157 cal., 69% (108 cal.) from fat; 2.1 g protein; 12 g fat (1.8 g sat.); 12 g carbo (1.7 g fiber); sodium N/A; 0 mg chol.

Avocado Fries

Crunchy on the outside, creamy and nutty inside, these fries are totally over the top. Our recipe comes from chef Trey Foshee at George's at the Cove restaurant in La Jolla, California.

recipe pictured on page **258**

SERVES 6 | **TIME** 30 minutes

Canola oil for frying
¼ cup flour
¼ tsp. kosher salt, plus more to taste
2 eggs, beaten to blend
1¼ cups panko (Japanese-style bread crumbs)
2 firm-ripe medium Hass avocados, pitted, peeled, and sliced into ½-in. wedges

1. Preheat oven to 200°. In a medium saucepan, heat 1½ in. oil until it registers 375° on a deep-fry thermometer.
2. Meanwhile, mix flour with salt in a shallow plate. Put eggs and panko in separate shallow plates. Dip avocado wedges in flour, shaking off excess. Dip in egg, then panko to coat. Set on two plates in a single layer.
3. Fry a quarter of the avocado wedges at a time until deep golden, 30 to 60 seconds. Transfer wedges to a plate lined with paper towels. Keep warm in oven while cooking remainder. Sprinkle with salt to taste.

PER SERVING: 271 cal., 70% (189 cal.) from fat; 5.5 g protein; 21 g fat (2.6 g sat.); 16 g carbo (2.1 g fiber); 119 mg sodium; 71 mg chol.

The Great Avocado Breakthrough

The green-skinned, mild-tasting Fuerte was the main avocado back in 1926, when Rudolph Hass, postman and amateur horticulturist, planted an avocado seedling of unknown origin in his grove in La Habra Heights, California. To his surprise, the tree bore a weird, almost black, pebbly skinned fruit with unusually deep, rich flavor. Hass never made much money on his namesake discovery—he died in 1952 having earned only $5,000 from it—but his tree's offspring now account for 80 percent of avocados sold commercially worldwide.

Oven-roasted Fall Vegetables

This recipe from San Francisco cookbook author Peggy Knickerbocker is great for a holiday buffet because it holds up well at room temperature. The following directions assume you have one oven. If you have two ovens, you can roast the batches simultaneously.

SERVES 10 to 12 | **TIME** 45 minutes, plus up to 2½ hours to roast

3 medium yellow onions, peeled and quartered (leave root ends intact)
3 medium russet potatoes, cut lengthwise into ½-in.-thick slices
3 medium turnips (1½ lbs.), peeled and cut into eighths
4 large carrots, cut into 3-in. lengths (cut thickest pieces in half lengthwise)
3 large parsnips, peeled and cut into 3-in. lengths (cut thickest pieces into halves or quarters lengthwise)
2 medium butternut squash, halved, peeled, seeded, and cut into 3- by 1-in. pieces
10 to 20 garlic cloves, loose papery outer skins removed, inner skins left on
2 medium orange-fleshed sweet potatoes (often labeled "yams"), peeled and cut into 3- by 1-in. pieces
About ¾ cup extra-virgin olive oil
1 tbsp. kosher salt, plus more to taste
1½ tsp. freshly ground black pepper, plus more to taste
7 rosemary sprigs (3 in. each)

1. Preheat oven to 400°. Put onions, potatoes, turnips, carrots, parsnips, squash, and garlic in a very large bowl; put sweet potatoes in a separate bowl. Drizzle bowls generously with oil and sprinkle with salt and pepper. Toss vegetables gently with your hands to coat.
2. Divide half the mixed vegetables between two large baking sheets, spreading them out into a single layer with space around each vegetable to ensure even browning. Break up 3 rosemary sprigs and sprinkle over vegetables. Roast vegetables 15 minutes. Stir vegetables gently with a metal spatula if they're sticking.
3. Divide half the sweet potatoes between the two pans and continue roasting, stirring every 15 minutes if necessary and changing pan positions to ensure even browning, until vegetables are browned and tender, 40 minutes to 1¼ hours. Remove from oven and set aside.
4. Repeat with remaining mixed vegetables, sweet potatoes, and 3 rosemary sprigs.
5. Season to taste with salt and pepper and garnish with remaining sprig of rosemary.

PER SERVING: 310 cal., 46% (144 cal.) from fat; 4.3 g protein; 16 g fat (2.3 g sat.); 42.5 g carbo (7.2 g fiber); 459 mg sodium; 0 mg chol.

vegetarian mains

When you live in the land of glorious produce, it's easy to make it the main focus of your meal.

Vegetarianism used to be motivated by ethics or religion or concerns about health. It still is, but there's another, very compelling reason to put vegetables at the center of the plate: They taste wonderful.

So good and varied are our vegetables, thanks in part to farmers' markets raising the bar, that we approach them with new respect. No longer do we throw together a medley of chopped-up vegetables and brown rice for the lone vegetarian at the table. Vegetable cooking is some of the most exciting food happening now, and a lot of us choose it for that reason alone.

Brilliant cooks are teasing out textures and flavors from vegetables to produce results so engaging and beautiful that even meat eaters are charmed (see Roasted Kohlrabi and Eggs with Mustard and Honey, *page* 292, and Seven-vegetable Couscous, *page* 287). Seasonings and techniques from India, Mexico, China, and other vegetable-savvy countries make our vegetable cooking more interesting too: Try Split Pea–Squash Stew with Basil and Serrano (*page 279*), for a dish that borrows from several cultures at once.

With hearty Lentil Stew with Winter Vegetables (*page* 279), Black Bean Chili (*page* 280), and a spectacular dish of Indian-style eggplant stuffed with peanuts, ginger, and cilantro (*page* 294), this chapter includes meat-free mains that work as the anchor of the day's eating. It also has lighter food, like Vietnamese Noodle Rolls (*page* 284) and "spaghetti" made of zucchini (*page* 296).

If a recipe qualifies as vegan, we've listed it in a handy index that gathers vegan recipes from all parts of this book (*page 751*). Whether you're a vegan, vegetarian, or omnivore, you'll find a lot to cook in this chapter.

Vegetarian Mains

vegetarian mains

Lentil Stew with Winter Vegetables

The satisfying combination of root vegetables, kale, squash, and lentils becomes vegan if you omit the goat cheese. Serve with crusty bread.

SERVES 4 | **TIME** 1 hour

2 tbsp. olive oil
1 medium onion, chopped
3 garlic cloves, minced
1 cup French green lentils, sorted for debris and rinsed
1 tsp. salt
¼ tsp. freshly ground black pepper
2 thyme sprigs
2 small turnips, cut into ½-in. cubes (about 1 cup)
1 bunch (about 5) baby golden or Chioggia beets, peeled (or 3 large beets, halved)
1 cup cubed peeled butternut squash (½-in. cubes)
4 cups chopped stemmed kale
1 bunch (about 5) baby carrots
½ cup minced flat-leaf parsley
3 oz. aged goat cheese (such as Le Chevrot or Bûcheron, cut into small pieces; *see Quick Tip below*)

1. Heat oil in a medium pot over medium-high heat until hot. Add onion and cook, stirring, until translucent, about 3 minutes. Add garlic, lentils, salt, pepper, thyme, and 4 cups water. Bring to a boil, then reduce heat to medium-low. Add turnips, beets, and squash and simmer gently, stirring occasionally, 20 minutes.
2. Add kale and carrots and cook until vegetables are tender and most of the liquid has been absorbed, about 10 minutes.
3. Remove from heat; stir in parsley and goat cheese.
Quick Tip: Semi-firm aged goat cheese, available at most cheese counters, has an assertive flavor that pairs well with winter greens and root vegetables. Its firmer texture holds up when heated.

PER SERVING: 416 cal., 30% (126 cal.) from fat; 23 g protein; 14 g fat (5.4 g sat.); 55 g carbo (10 g fiber); 813 mg sodium; 17 mg chol.

▪ Turnips

The peak season for turnips is October through February. Choose turnips that feel heavy for their size—these are the young ones and will be more delicately flavored and textured than older ones. The roots should be firm, and the greens should be bright and fresh-looking.

Split Pea–Squash Stew with Basil and Serrano

This fragrant, buttery stew makes a hearty vegetarian main dish. Serve with a green salad and *naan* (Indian flatbread) or fresh pita.

recipe pictured on page 259

SERVES 4 | **TIME** 45 minutes

1 cup yellow split peas, sorted for debris and rinsed
¼ tsp. turmeric
2 lbs. butternut squash, peeled, seeded, and cut into 1-in. cubes
2 tsp. salt
1 tsp. sugar
6 star anise pods
6 tbsp. butter
2 tsp. cumin seeds
2-in. piece fresh ginger, grated
2 serrano chiles (*see Quick Tips below*), halved, seeds and ribs removed, and thinly sliced
12 large basil leaves (*see Quick Tips below*), chopped

1. In a large pot, bring split peas, turmeric, and 4 cups water to a boil. Lower heat to a simmer, partially cover, and cook 15 minutes.
2. Add squash, salt, sugar, and star anise. Bring to a boil, lower heat to a simmer, and cook, uncovered, stirring occasionally, until squash is tender, about 15 minutes.
3. In a small frying pan, melt butter. When it stops foaming on top, turn heat to high, add cumin seeds, and cook, stirring, until browned and fragrant, about 2 minutes. Add ginger and chiles and cook, stirring constantly, another 2 minutes. Add basil. Stir to combine and cook until basil is wilted, about 30 seconds.
4. Serve stew hot, with the spiced butter poured over each serving. Or stir the spiced butter into pot of stew before serving.
Quick Tips: If you can't find serrano chiles, substitute 2 jalapeños. You can also use less common varieties of basil, such as Thai or lemon (double the number of leaves in the recipe if they're very small).

PER SERVING: 437 cal., 37% (162 cal.) from fat; 15 g protein; 18 g fat (11 g sat.); 60 g carbo (7.2 g fiber); 1,360 mg sodium; 47 mg chol.

Black Bean Chili

A simple chili with many layers of flavor, from garlic, cumin, fresh cilantro, chipotle, and rice vinegar. To make it vegan, leave off the sour cream topping.

MAKES 6 cups; about 4 servings | **TIME** 30 minutes

1 onion (½ lb.), chopped
2 tsp. *each* pressed or minced garlic and olive oil
3 cans (14.5 oz. each) black beans, rinsed and drained
1 can (14.5 oz.) crushed tomatoes
1½ tsp. ground cumin
¼ cup chopped cilantro
1 tbsp. *each* puréed canned chipotle chile and
    unseasoned rice vinegar
Salt
¼ cup reduced-fat sour cream
Tomato salsa (optional)

1. In a 3- to 4-qt. pan over medium-high heat, cook onion and garlic in oil, stirring often, until onion is softened and starting to brown, 6 to 8 minutes.
2. Add beans, tomatoes, cumin, and ½ cup water; bring to a boil, then reduce heat and simmer, stirring occasionally, to blend flavors, about 15 minutes.
3. Stir in cilantro, chipotle purée, and vinegar. Add salt to taste. Spoon chili into bowls and top each with 1 tbsp. sour cream and salsa if you like.

PER SERVING: 265 cal., 21% (56 cal.) from fat;14 g protein; 6.2 g fat (1.5 g sat.); 40 g carbo (10 g fiber); 709 mg sodium; 5 mg chol.

■ Chipotle Chiles

Chipotle chiles are smoked jalapeños; they are sold dried or canned in adobo sauce. The canned variety is packed with a lot of flavor but very little fat. Purée a can and keep the condiment in the refrigerator to have on hand for adding smoky heat to beans, soups, and meat stews; for stirring into mayonnaise to spread on sandwiches; or for adding spice and depth to any fresh or jarred salsa.

Greek Tortellini Salad

Reader Marilou Robinson, of Portland, Oregon, combined some of her favorite flavors in this rib-sticking main-dish salad. As a shortcut, use a store-bought salad dressing instead of the lemon-herb vinaigrette.

SERVES 8 | **TIME** 30 minutes, plus 2 hours to chill

1 package (20 oz.) fresh cheese-filled tortellini
½ cup extra-virgin olive oil
¼ cup *each* fresh lemon juice and red wine vinegar
2 tbsp. chopped flat-leaf parsley
1 tsp. dried oregano
½ tsp. salt
1 lb. baby spinach leaves
1 cup crumbled (about 6 oz.) feta cheese
½ cup slivered red onion
6 hard-cooked large eggs, peeled and quartered

1. In a 5- to 6-qt. pan over high heat, bring 2 qts. water to a boil. Add tortellini and cook, stirring occasionally, until tender to the bite, 3 to 5 minutes. Drain.
2. Meanwhile, in a large bowl, combine oil, lemon juice, vinegar, parsley, oregano, and salt. Add drained tortellini and mix to coat. Cover and chill at least 2 hours or up to 1 day.
3. Add spinach, feta cheese, and onion to tortellini and mix gently. Mound salad on a platter and arrange egg quarters around the edge.

PER SERVING: 485 cal., 50% (243 cal.) from fat; 18 g protein; 27 g fat (8.3 g sat.); 44 g carbo (4.4 g fiber); 780 mg sodium; 207 mg chol.

vegetarian mains

FROM THE PANTRY

Shiitake and Edamame Salad with White Miso Vinaigrette

Reader Laurel Swift, of Boulder, Colorado, dreamed up this recipe by making use of what was in her fridge. We liked her mix of textures and colors—meaty mushrooms, smooth beans, earthy beet greens—and the way she united them with a good miso vinaigrette.

SERVES 6 to 8 | **TIME** 40 minutes

⅓ cup orange juice
2 tbsp. *each* soy sauce, unseasoned rice vinegar, honey, and white miso (*see Quick Tip below*)
1 medium shallot, peeled
¼ cup vegetable oil, divided
3 tbsp. Asian (toasted) sesame oil
10 medium shiitake mushrooms, stems discarded and caps sliced ¼ in. thick
¼ tsp. salt
1 head butter lettuce, torn into bite-size pieces
2 cups baby beet greens or arugula
1 cup cooked shelled edamame (*see Quick Tip below*)
3 green onions (green part only), chopped
1 tbsp. sesame seeds

1. Purée orange juice, soy sauce, vinegar, honey, miso, and shallot in a blender. With blender running, pour in 3 tbsp. vegetable oil and the sesame oil and blend 10 seconds. Set vinaigrette aside.
2. Heat remaining 1 tbsp. vegetable oil in a large frying pan over high heat. Add shiitakes and salt and cook, stirring, until mushrooms are browned, about 3 minutes. Let cool.
3. In a large bowl, gently toss lettuce and beet greens with 2 tbsp. vinaigrette. Top with shiitakes, edamame, green onions, and sesame seeds. Serve remaining vinaigrette on the side.
Quick Tip: White miso and shelled edamame are usually available at large grocery stores.
Make Ahead: Vinaigrette, up to 1 week, chilled.

PER SERVING: 184 cal., 68% (126 cal.) from fat; 4.4 g protein; 14 g fat (2 g sat.); 11 g carbo (2.2 g fiber); 492 mg sodium; 0 mg chol.

Vegetable-box Salad

Reader Heather Ogston, of Roseville, California, composed a bountiful chopped salad after receiving a box of beautiful summer produce from a community farm. Chop the vegetables into pieces that are roughly the same size—each between ¼ and ½ inch.

MAKES 12 cups; about 4 main-dish servings
TIME 30 minutes

⅔ cup plain low-fat yogurt
⅓ cup mayonnaise
2 tbsp. *each* Dijon mustard and fresh lemon juice
1 tsp. celery salt
¼ tsp. *each* salt and freshly ground black pepper, plus more to taste
2 cups uncooked fresh white corn kernels
1½ lbs. ripe tomatoes, cored, seeded, and chopped
1 can (15 oz.) kidney beans, rinsed and drained
1 romaine lettuce heart (about ½ lb.), chopped
½ English cucumber (about ½ lb.), chopped
6 to 8 basil leaves, chopped
¼ lb. cheddar cheese, cut into ¼-in. cubes
3 hard-cooked eggs, shelled and chopped

1. In a small bowl, mix yogurt, mayonnaise, mustard, lemon juice, celery salt, salt, and pepper.
2. In a large bowl, mix corn kernels, tomatoes, kidney beans, lettuce, cucumber, basil, cheese, and eggs. Add dressing to bowl and mix gently to coat, or serve dressing separately, to spoon over individual servings. Add more salt and pepper to taste.

PER SERVING: 519 cal., 52% (270 cal.) from fat; 24 g protein; 30 g fat (9.8 g sat.); 38 g carbo (9.5 g fiber); 995 mg sodium; 202 mg chol.

Spicy Chickpea Sandwiches

In the streets of Palermo, Sicily, you'll find *panelle*, fried chickpea-flour patties served on a roll. Kevin Sandri adds a carrot slaw, salad greens, roasted squash, and spicy aioli for an exceptionally tasty vegetarian sandwich that he sells from his food cart, Garden State, in the Sellwood neighborhood of Portland, Oregon. Here's our simplified version.

SERVES 6 | **TIME** 1 hour

CHICKPEA PATTIES
1½ cups chickpea (garbanzo) flour *(see Quick Tip, right)*
1½ tsp. kosher salt
½ tsp. freshly ground black pepper
¼ tsp. *each* ground cumin and cayenne
¼ cup chopped flat-leaf parsley
SPICY LEMON MAYO
1 cup mayonnaise
2 tsp. minced garlic
⅛ tsp. cayenne
Finely shredded zest and juice of ½ lemon
CARROT SLAW
1 tbsp. *each* unseasoned rice vinegar and
    extra-virgin olive oil
½ tsp. kosher salt
¼ tsp. freshly ground black pepper
2 cups shredded carrots (⅔ lb.)
1 cup shredded radishes
COOKING & ASSEMBLY
6 ciabatta or *pane francese* rolls (3 oz. each)
2 tbsp. extra-virgin olive oil, divided
About ¼ tsp. kosher salt
¼ lb. salad mix (5 cups lightly packed)

1. Make chickpea patties: In a 3- to 4-qt. pan, mix chickpea flour and dry seasonings. Gradually whisk in 2½ cups water until smooth. Cook over medium heat, whisking often, until mixture begins to thicken, 3 to 5 minutes. Switch to a spoon and stir until mixture pulls away from pan bottom and mounds in center of pan, 4 to 6 minutes. Stir in parsley. Using an oiled spoon or fingers, evenly spread mixture in an oiled 9- by 13-in. pan. Let cool.
2. Make mayo: Mix all ingredients together in a small bowl. Chill, covered.
3. Make slaw: Whisk together vinegar, oil, salt, and pepper in a medium bowl, then gently stir in carrots and radishes.

4. Preheat broiler. Split rolls, leaving one side attached, and open up. Place rolls cut side up in a large rimmed baking pan; lightly brush with 1 tbsp. olive oil. Broil 4 in. from heat source until golden, about 1 minute. Tip onto counter and drape with foil.
5. Oil the baking pan. Brush chickpea mixture with remaining 1 tbsp. oil; sprinkle with salt. Cut into 12 rectangles and set, slightly separated, in oiled pan. Broil until golden, 4 to 6 minutes. Turn patties over and broil until golden on second side, about 2 minutes.
6. To assemble, generously spread spicy lemon mayo on cut sides of rolls. Place some salad greens on one side of each roll and top with some carrot slaw, then two chickpea patties.
Quick Tip: Find chickpea flour in the baking aisle of well-stocked grocery stores and at health food stores.
Make Ahead: Chickpea mixture (step 1) and mayo (step 2), up to 1 day, chilled.

PER SANDWICH: 655 cal. 65% (426 cal.) from fat; 14 g protein; 47 g fat (5.5. sat.); 62 g carbo (6.9 g fiber); 1,035 mg sodium; 22 mg chol.

Grilled Fresh Mozzarella and Apricot on Sourdough

Reader Bill Gaines, of Manteca, California, invented a delicious tangy-sweet sandwich to use the plentiful apricots from his neighbor's tree, which hung over the property line. "He told us we could have all the fruit on our side of the fence," Gaines explains.

MAKES 2 sandwiches | **TIME** 20 minutes

2 tbsp. butter, softened
4 slices sourdough bread
2 juicy firm-ripe apricots, pitted and thinly sliced
1 tbsp. sugar mixed with 1 tsp. cinnamon
4 slices fresh mozzarella cheese

1. Butter one side of each bread slice. Flip 2 slices over and top with apricots. Sprinkle with cinnamon sugar to taste. Top with mozzarella and remaining bread slices, buttered sides up.
2. Cook sandwiches in a large frying pan over medium heat, turning once, until golden and crisp on both sides, about 8 minutes total.

PER SANDWICH: 481 cal., 51% (243 cal.) from fat; 18 g protein; 27 g fat (17 g sat.); 40 g carbo (2 g fiber); 693 mg sodium; 81 mg chol.

Columbia Bar and Grill's Grain and Cheese "Burgers"

Tracy McIntosh of Newport Beach, California, led us to these vegetable burgers made of toasted rice, oats, and cheese. In its heyday—the late '80s through the '90s—the now-shuttered Columbia Bar and Grill in Hollywood was a TV and movie industry hangout, and these burgers were a favorite among its vegetarian customers.

MAKES 4 burgers | **TIME** 1 hour

1½ cups chopped shiitake mushroom caps
¾ cup chopped green onions (about 8)
1 tbsp. butter
½ cup *each* regular rolled oats and cooked brown rice
⅔ cup shredded sharp white cheddar cheese
⅓ cup chopped walnuts, toasted *(see How to Toast Nuts, page 134)*
3 tbsp. low-fat cottage or ricotta cheese
2 eggs
2 tbsp. chopped flat-leaf parsley
¾ tsp. kosher salt
½ tsp. freshly ground black pepper
3 tbsp. canola oil
Seeded hamburger buns, toasted
Mayonnaise (optional), red onion rings, and lettuce

1. In a 10- to 12-in. nonstick frying pan over medium heat, cook mushrooms and green onions in butter, stirring often, until both are limp, about 6 minutes. Add oats and cook, stirring, for 2 minutes. Remove from heat; let cool slightly, then stir in rice, cheddar cheese, walnuts, cottage cheese, eggs, parsley, salt, and pepper.
2. Pour oil onto a 12- by 15-in. rimmed baking sheet. Shape mixture into four patties, each ½ in. thick, and carefully lay on sheet. Broil 3 in. from heat until deep golden, using two spatulas to gently turn over once, 6 to 7 minutes total.
3. Serve on buns with mayonnaise, if using, plus onion and lettuce.

PER BURGER WITHOUT BUN OR CONDIMENTS: 509 cal., 45% (229 cal.) from fat; 28 g protein; 26 g fat (5.1 g sat.); 44 g carbo (9.7 g fiber); 654 mg sodium; 118 mg chol.

Lia's Walnut "Burgers"

Owner Lia Azgapetian closed the Mill Creek Station restaurant in Forest Falls, California, in 1986, but former customers still rave about these burgers.

MAKES 4 burgers | **TIME** 30 minutes

2 eggs
⅔ cup soft whole-wheat bread crumbs
½ cup *each* chopped walnuts, sliced green onions, toasted wheat germ, and small-curd cottage cheese
2 tbsp. chopped flat-leaf parsley
1 tsp. dried basil
½ tsp. *each* dried oregano and paprika
Garlic salt
4 slices (⅛ in. thick) jack cheese (3 oz.)
Toasted buns or bread
Thousand Island dressing, tomato and white onion slices, and lettuce

1. In a bowl, beat eggs to blend. Stir in bread crumbs, walnuts, green onions, wheat germ, cottage cheese, parsley, basil, oregano, and paprika. Add garlic salt to taste.
2. On an oiled 12- by 15-in. baking sheet, shape mixture into four patties, each ½ in. thick. Broil 3 in. from heat until deep golden, turning once, about 6 minutes total. Top with jack cheese and broil until melted, about 30 seconds more.
3. Serve burgers on buns with Thousand Island dressing, tomato, white onion, and lettuce.

PER BURGER WITHOUT BUN: 321 cal., 59% (189 cal.) from fat; 19 g protein; 21 g fat (6.4 g sat.); 16 g carbo; 301 mg sodium; 133 mg chol.

■ Walnuts

FROM THE PANTRY

One of humanity's most ancient foodstuffs, walnuts were carried to California by the Franciscan missionaries in the late 1700s. (Although America had its own native walnut, the black walnut, it wasn't common—and is still not grown much, owing to its thick, hard-to-crack shell.) The immigrant trees were common walnut, also known as Persian or English walnut, and are native to central Asia. They thrived in California's Mediterranean climate, and the first commercial orchard was planted in 1867, near Santa Barbara. Now California produces 99 percent of the U.S. crop and two-thirds of the world's export crop. (For more on Western nuts, *see page 617*.)

Crusted Portabella "Burgers"

Meaty portabellas get the fried cutlet treatment (well, actually baked, but you'd never know it from their crispy crunch).

recipe pictured on page **260**

MAKES 4 sandwiches | **TIME** 40 minutes

2 egg whites
1 tbsp. olive oil
⅓ cup Italian-style fine dried bread crumbs
2 tbsp. chili powder
4 portabella mushroom caps (5 in. wide; 1 to 1¼ lbs. total)
4 round sandwich buns (4 in. wide)
1 cup sour cream
2 tsp. minced canned chipotle chile in adobo sauce or hot sauce
¼ cup thinly sliced red onion
1 cup spinach leaves
Salt and freshly ground black pepper

1. In a bowl, beat egg whites and oil to blend. In another bowl, mix bread crumbs and chili powder.
2. Preheat oven to 450°. Coat each mushroom cap with egg mixture, drain briefly, then coat with crumbs, shaking off excess. Set caps, slightly separated and with gill sides down, on a 12- by 15-in. baking sheet. Lay bun halves, cut sides up, on another 12- by 15-in. baking sheet.
3. Bake portabellas until browned and flexible when pressed, about 20 minutes. About 3 minutes before portabellas are done, add buns to oven; bake until lightly toasted.
4. In a small bowl, mix sour cream and minced chipotle. Spread mixture on cut sides of buns. Layer onion and spinach on each bun bottom, top with a portabella, add salt and pepper to taste, and cover with bun top.

PER SANDWICH WITH BUN: 326 cal., 47% (152 cal.) from fat; 12 g protein; 17 g fat (7.2 g sat.); 36 g carbo (5 g fiber); 379 mg sodium; 25 mg chol.

Vietnamese Noodle Rolls

Serve these refreshing rolls for dinner—they're on the large side. They're also a little messy, so have a fork handy.

MAKES 10 rolls; 5 servings | **TIME** 35 minutes

3½ oz. rice vermicelli (thin dried rice noodles)
¼ English cucumber
½ large carrot
10 rice-paper wrappers (*bánh tráng*; 8½ in. wide; see *Quick Tip below*)
5 red lettuce leaves, torn in half crosswise
½ Granny Smith apple, peeled, cored, and very thinly sliced lengthwise
30 (about ¼ cup) mint leaves
40 (about ¼ cup) cilantro leaves
½ cup canned french-fried onions
Sweet and Spicy Sesame Sauce (*recipe follows*) or your favorite peanut sauce

1. In a large bowl, cover vermicelli with just-boiling water. Let noodles stand until tender, 5 to 8 minutes.
2. Meanwhile, cut cucumber and carrot into 4-in. lengths and then into matchsticks, using a mandoline or other handheld slicer, to yield ½ cup matchsticks of each (or cut cucumber into matchsticks with a knife and coarsely shred carrots).
3. Drain noodles and rinse with cold water. Spread noodles out on a baking sheet lined with a kitchen towel. Pat dry. Divide noodles into 2 long logs, then cut with scissors to total 10 equal portions.
4. Set out all ingredients except sesame sauce on a work surface. Pour very hot tap water into a large shallow bowl such as a pie pan. Submerge 1 rice-paper wrapper until moistened and softened slightly but not completely pliable (it will continue to soften as you work with it).
5. Lay wrapper on work surface and put a half lettuce leaf in the center. Mound one portion of noodles on lettuce followed by about one-tenth of cucumber, carrot, and apple slices; 3 mint leaves; 4 cilantro leaves; and a sprinkling of onions. Arrange ingredients into a rectangle about 4 in. long. Fold paper over short ends of filling, then roll up tightly from a long side. Repeat to make remaining rolls. Serve with sesame sauce.
Quick Tip: Find rice-paper wrappers in the Asian aisle of well-stocked supermarkets.
Make Ahead: Up to 1 day, chilled.

PER 2-ROLL SERVING: 119 cal., 12% (14 cal.) from fat; 1.8 g protein; 1.5 g fat (0.4 g sat.); 24 g carbo (1.1 g fiber); 29 mg sodium; 0 mg chol.

Sweet and Spicy Sesame Sauce: In a small bowl, whisk 3 tbsp. **hoisin sauce**, 1 tbsp. *each* **toasted sesame seeds**, **Asian (toasted) sesame oil**, and **soy sauce**, ½ tsp. **red chile flakes**, and ½ cup hot water. Keeps, covered and chilled, up to 1 week. Makes ¾ cup.

PER TBSP.: 27 cal., 52% (14 cal.) from fat; 0.2 g protein; 1.6 g fat (0.2 g sat.); 2.6 g carbo (0.1 g fiber); 165 mg sodium; 0 mg chol.

Linguine with Walnuts, Green Beans, and Feta

To make the dish come together quickly, start heating the oven and water before you prepare the ingredients.

SERVES 4 to 6 | TIME 30 minutes

¾ lb. linguine
¾ lb. slender green beans (each ¼ in. thick) such as haricots verts
1 tbsp. olive oil
Salt and freshly ground black pepper
¼ cup roasted walnut oil or extra-virgin olive oil
2 tsp. finely shredded lemon zest
1 cup crumbled (about 5 oz.) feta cheese
1 cup walnut halves or pieces, toasted (see *How to Toast Nuts, page 134*)

1. Preheat oven to 500°. In a covered 5- to 6-qt. pan over high heat, bring about 3½ qts. water to a boil. Stir in linguine and boil, uncovered, until barely tender to the bite, 8 to 10 minutes. Drain and return to pan.
2. Trim ends from green beans. In a 10- by 15-in. baking pan, combine olive oil and green beans; spread level in pan. Sprinkle generously with salt and pepper. Roast until green beans just begin to brown, 4 to 6 minutes.
3. In a large serving bowl, combine walnut oil, lemon zest, and feta. Add pasta, walnuts, and green beans; mix gently. Season to taste with more salt and pepper.

PER SERVING: 520 cal., 52% (270 cal.) from fat; 14 g protein; 30 g fat (5.9 g sat.); 51 g carbo (3.4 g fiber); 273 mg sodium; 21 mg chol.

■ Nut Oils

FROM THE PANTRY

A drizzle of walnut, hazelnut, or almond oil can add real depth of flavor to almost any dish. Nut oils also happen to be good for you; almond and hazelnut oils are rich in monounsaturated fats, and walnut oil supplies omega-3 fatty acids. Refrigerate nut oils after opening, as they turn rancid quickly at room temperature.

Ultimate Mac 'n' Cheese

Why "ultimate"? Because the sauce is creamy, not grainy; the dish is flavored with shallots, gruyère, and white wine, like fondue; and it's topped with crunchy sourdough bread crumbs.

SERVES 6 | TIME 50 minutes

½ lb. cavatappi, macaroni, or other tube-shaped pasta
3½ tbsp. butter, divided
½ cup finely chopped shallots
2 tbsp. flour
1¼ cups dry white wine
⅔ cup heavy whipping cream
7 oz. gruyère cheese, finely shredded
3 oz. aged gouda cheese (*see Quick Tip below*), finely shredded
2 tbsp. plus 1 tsp. minced chives
1 tbsp. Dijon mustard
½ tsp. kosher salt, divided
⅛ tsp. *each* cayenne and freshly grated nutmeg
¼ lb. crusty sourdough bread (about ¼ loaf), torn into large pieces

1. Preheat oven to 400°. Bring a large pot of boiling salted water to a boil and cook pasta until tender to the bite, 7 to 12 minutes. Drain, but do not rinse.
2. In a large frying pan over medium-high heat, melt 2 tbsp. butter. Add shallots and cook, stirring occasionally, until light golden, about 3 minutes. Sprinkle shallot-butter mixture with flour; cook, stirring often, 1 minute. Add wine and stir, scraping up any browned bits from bottom of pan. Add cream and stir well. Sprinkle in cheeses, one large handful at a time, stirring until each handful is mostly melted before adding the next. Stir in 2 tbsp. chives, mustard, ¼ tsp. salt, cayenne, and nutmeg. Stir drained pasta into cheese mixture, then pour the mixture into a 2-qt. baking dish.
3. In a food processor, pulse bread with remaining 1½ tbsp. butter, 1 tsp. chives, and ¼ tsp. salt until coarse bread crumbs form. Sprinkle bread crumbs over pasta and cheese and bake until top is browned and cheese is bubbling, 15 to 20 minutes.
Quick Tip: You can substitute romano, goat's-milk gouda, or more gruyère for the aged gouda.

PER SERVING: 586 cal., 49% (288 cal.) from fat; 21 g protein; 32 g fat (19 g sat.); 44 g carbo (1.6 g fiber); 739 mg sodium; 107 mg chol.

Zucchini Fusilli

Cutting the zucchini into strips allows them to twist and turn around the fusilli, clinging to the noodles and flavoring every bite. The pine nuts add richness to the plate, which—like all good pasta dishes—tastes greater than the sum of its parts. Following the recipe is an eggplant variation.

SERVES 6 | **TIME** 40 minutes

2 lbs. zucchini
2 garlic cloves, peeled
12 large basil leaves
⅓ cup pine nuts
2 tbsp. butter, divided
3 tsp. olive oil, divided
½ tsp. plus 1 tbsp. salt, divided
¾ lb. fusilli
1 cup finely shredded (about 2 oz.) parmesan cheese, divided

1. Bring a large pot of water to a boil. Meanwhile, trim and discard ends of zucchini. Cut each zucchini into 3- to 4-in. lengths; cut each length into ¼- to ½-in.-thick matchsticks and set aside. Chop garlic and set aside. Cut basil leaves into thin ribbons and set aside.
2. In a large frying pan over medium heat, toast pine nuts, stirring, until golden, about 2 minutes. Transfer to a small bowl and set aside. In the same pan, melt 1 tbsp. butter with 2 tsp. oil. Increase heat to high and add half of zucchini and ¼ tsp. salt. Cook zucchini, stirring frequently, until soft and browned, about 5 minutes. Transfer to a plate with a slotted spoon, leaving as much of the butter and oil in pan as possible. Repeat with remaining zucchini and ¼ tsp. salt. Set frying pan aside.
3. Add remaining 1 tbsp. salt and the fusilli to boiling water and cook until pasta is tender to the bite, 8 to 10 minutes. Drain and transfer to a large bowl.
4. Meanwhile, heat reserved frying pan with butter and oil over medium-high heat, add remaining 1 tsp. oil and the chopped garlic, and cook until fragrant but not browned, about 1 minute. Add reserved zucchini and pine nuts. Cook, stirring, until well combined. Add zucchini mixture and reserved basil to cooked fusilli and toss to combine. Add ½ cup parmesan and remaining 1 tbsp. butter. Toss until butter melts and ingredients are well combined.
5. Sprinkle with remaining ½ cup parmesan.

PER SERVING: 367 cal., 32% (117 cal.) from fat; 14 g protein; 13 g fat (5 g sat.); 49 g carbo (2.5 g fiber); 651 mg sodium; 17 mg chol.

Spicy Minty Eggplant Fusilli: Replace zucchini with 2 lbs. **eggplant**, cut into ½-in.-thick slices, then into ½-in.-thick strips, and cook until brown and soft, 5 to 10 minutes. Add ½ tsp. **red chile flakes** with chopped garlic. Instead of basil and parmesan, use **mint** and 1 cup shredded **ricotta salata cheese**.

Lemony Pasta Shells with Broccoli and Walnuts

Here's our definition of a perfect weeknight dish: a tasty, good-for-you pasta that comes together in less than half an hour. Start heating the water before you prep the ingredients.

SERVES 6 | **TIME** 25 minutes

1 lb. broccoli florets
¾ lb. whole-wheat pasta shells or penne
2 tbsp. olive oil, plus more to taste
3 garlic cloves, sliced
½ tsp. kosher salt, plus more to taste
¾ cup chopped walnuts, toasted (*see How to Toast Nuts, page 134*)
Juice and finely shredded zest of ½ lemon, plus more juice to taste
Finely shredded pecorino cheese

1. Bring a medium pot of water to a boil. Meanwhile, chop a third of the broccoli. Add pasta to boiling water and cook until tender to the bite. Drain.
2. While pasta is cooking, heat oil in a large frying pan over medium heat, add garlic, and cook, stirring until fragrant, about 1 minute. Add chopped broccoli and broccoli florets, ¾ cup water, and the salt. Cover; cook until broccoli is tender, 10 to 15 minutes.
3. Stir in walnuts and lemon juice and zest, then toss with drained pasta. Add more salt, lemon juice, and oil to taste. Serve with pecorino.

PER SERVING: 358 cal., 38% (135 cal.) from fat; 13 g protein; 15 g fat (1.6 g sat.); 50 g carbo (9.5 g fiber); 132 mg sodium; 0 mg chol.

vegetarian mains

Seven-vegetable Couscous

With layers of nuanced flavor, this beautiful dish gives a big payoff for relatively little time and effort.

recipe pictured on page 261

SERVES 4 to 6 | **TIME** 45 minutes

2 tbsp. olive oil
3 garlic cloves, minced
1 tbsp. *ras el hanout (see Quick Tips below)*
2 dried bird's-eye or arbol chiles
½ tsp. salt, plus more to taste
4 cups vegetable broth, divided
1 *each* medium carrot, parsnip, and potato, peeled and cut into ½-in. dice
1 *each* small turnip and orange-fleshed sweet potato (often labeled "yam"), peeled and cut into ½-in. dice
1 medium or 2 small zucchini, cut into ½-in. dice
1 can (14 or 15 oz.) chickpeas (garbanzos), drained and rinsed
2 ripe medium tomatoes (optional), cut into ½-in. dice
2 tbsp. chopped fresh flat-leaf parsley
2 cups couscous
1 preserved lemon (optional; *see Quick Tips below*), pulp removed, rind rinsed and finely chopped

1. In a large pot over medium-high heat, heat oil and garlic until fragrant, about 1 minute. Add *ras el hanout* and chiles and cook, stirring, 1 minute. Add salt, 3 cups broth, 2 cups water, the carrot, parsnip, potato, turnip, sweet potato, and zucchini. Bring to a boil. Add chickpeas, lower heat to produce a simmer, and simmer vegetables until just tender, about 15 minutes. Add tomatoes if using and parsley. Cook vegetables until tender, another 3 to 5 minutes. Add salt to taste.
2. Bring remaining 1 cup broth and 1¼ cups water to a boil in a medium pot. Add couscous, cover, and turn off heat. Let stand 5 minutes, then fluff with a fork.
3. Remove chiles from vegetables and discard. Serve vegetables over couscous, garnished with preserved lemon if using.
Quick Tips: *Ras el hanout*, a Moroccan spice mix, is available at Middle Eastern stores. To make your own, mix together ½ tsp. *each* ground ginger, turmeric, and coriander; ¼ tsp. *each* freshly ground black pepper, cinnamon, nutmeg, and saffron (optional); ⅛ tsp. *each* ground allspice, cloves, and mace; and crushed seeds from 6 cardamom pods (optional). Buy preserved lemons at specialty-grocery stores and Middle Eastern markets.

PER SERVING: 373 cal., 15% (55 cal.) from fat; 11 g protein; 6 g fat (.8 g sat.); 67 g carbo (7 g fiber); 661 mg sodium; 0 mg chol.

Whole-grain Penne with Walnuts, Caramelized Onions, and Ricotta Salata

The combination of flavors here plays up the nutty taste of whole-grain pasta.

SERVES 8 | **TIME** 1 hour, 20 minutes

7 medium onions (about 4 lbs.), thinly sliced
5 tbsp. olive oil, divided
¾ tsp. sugar
2 tsp. salt, plus more to taste
1¾ cups walnut halves, toasted (see *How to Toast Nuts*, page 134)
10 oz. whole-grain penne or fusilli
1 lb. ricotta salata cheese, crumbled
⅔ cup loosely packed flat-leaf parsley leaves, chopped
1½ tbsp. fresh lemon juice
1½ tsp. freshly ground black pepper

1. In a large frying pan over high heat, cook onions in 3 tbsp. oil with the sugar and salt, stirring and turning often, until onions begin to release their juice and turn golden, 10 to 13 minutes. Reduce heat to medium and cook, stirring occasionally, until onions turn a caramel color and become quite sweet, 35 to 40 minutes more. If onions begin to char or stick to the pan, reduce heat.
2. Meanwhile, put walnuts into a resealable plastic bag and lightly crush with a rolling pin. Set aside.
3. When onions are nearly done, bring a medium pot of salted water to a boil and cook pasta until tender to the bite, 9 to 12 minutes. Drain pasta, reserving about ½ cup cooking water.
4. Toss caramelized onions with pasta, walnuts, ricotta salata, parsley, reserved cooking water, lemon juice, pepper, and remaining 2 tbsp. oil. Season to taste with salt.

PER SERVING: 594 cal., 53% (315 cal.) from fat; 19 g protein; 35 g fat (11 g sat.); 56 g carbo (9.3 g fiber); 1,559 mg sodium; 50 mg chol.

■ Ricotta Salata

FROM THE PANTRY

Ricotta salata (also called "hard ricotta") is a firm white Italian cheese made by salting, pressing, and drying sheep's-milk ricotta. In flavor, it's like a very mild, nutty, less tangy feta, and it's good in pastas and salads (it can also be grated or shredded). Look for it at specialty-foods stores, Italian markets, or any supermarket with a good cheese department.

Vegetable Ribbon Pasta Shells

This is a wonderful end-of-summer pasta dish, with long shreds of zucchini and carrots in an herb-spiked sauce made from garden-fresh tomatoes.

recipe
pictured
on page
262

SERVES 5 | **TIME** 1½ hours

MARINARA SAUCE
1 medium onion, chopped
2 large garlic cloves, minced
1 tbsp. olive oil
2 lbs. ripe tomatoes, cored and coarsely chopped
2 tbsp. *each* chopped basil and marjoram leaves
1 cup dry red wine
¼ cup tomato paste (plain or with garlic)
½ tsp. *each* salt and freshly ground black pepper
PASTA & FILLING
20 jumbo pasta shells
¾ lb. zucchini
2 medium carrots, peeled
1 tbsp. chopped marjoram leaves
½ lb. part-skim mozzarella cheese, shredded
1 cup canned chickpeas (garbanzos), rinsed and drained
½ tsp. freshly ground black pepper
½ cup finely shredded parmesan cheese

1. Make sauce: In a 5- to 6-qt. pot over medium-high heat, cook onion and garlic in oil, stirring often, until golden, about 5 minutes. Stir in remaining sauce ingredients and bring to a boil. Reduce heat and simmer, stirring occasionally, until thick, 25 to 30 minutes. Measure sauce; you'll need 4½ cups. To reduce, simmer longer; to increase, just add water. Pulse sauce in a food processor into a coarse purée.

2. Meanwhile, preheat oven to 475° and prepare pasta and filling: Bring a large pot of salted water to a boil. Add shells and cook until tender to the bite. Drain and rinse under cold running water until cool enough to handle.

3. Using a mandoline or vegetable peeler, slice zucchini and carrots very thinly lengthwise. In a large bowl, toss vegetables with marjoram, mozzarella, chickpeas, and pepper.

4. Spread marinara sauce in a 9- by 13-in. baking dish. Generously fill each pasta shell with a scant ½ cup vegetable mixture, mounding filling, and set pasta filled side up in sauce. Cover tightly with foil.

5. Bake shells until mozzarella melts, 12 to 15 minutes. Uncover, sprinkle with parmesan, and bake until parmesan begins to brown, 10 to 12 minutes more. With a wide spatula, transfer shells and some sauce to plates. Serve with remaining sauce.

Make Ahead: Through step 4, up to 1 day, chilled. Preheat oven to 450° and heat shells, covered, until filling is hot (about 30 minutes). Continue as directed in step 5.

PER SERVING: 344 cal., 31% (108 cal.) from fat; 20 g protein; 12 g fat (5.6 g sat.); 42 g carbo (5.3 g fiber); 638 mg sodium; 27 mg chol.

Ravioli with Winter Squash and Sage

A quick variation of squash-filled ravioli with sage, a popular restaurant dish.

SERVES 3 or 4 | **TIME** 30 minutes

10 oz. unpeeled winter squash such as banana or Hubbard, or ½ lb. peeled butternut squash *(see Quick Tip below)*
2 tbsp. butter
1 tbsp. olive oil
16 sage leaves (2 in. each)
1 package (20 oz.) or 2 packages (9 oz. each) fresh cheese ravioli
¾ to 1 cup vegetable broth
⅓ cup whipping cream
Salt and freshly ground black pepper
Finely shredded asiago or parmesan cheese

1. Cut off and discard skin from winter squash. Chop squash into ¼-in. chunks.

2. In a 10- to 12-in. frying pan over medium heat, melt butter with oil. Add sage leaves and cook, turning once, until crisp and lightly browned, 5 to 7 minutes. Lift out leaves and drain on paper towels. Reserve butter and oil in pan.

3. In a 5- to 6-qt. pan over high heat, bring about 3 qts. water to a boil. Add ravioli, stir to separate, and cook until barely tender to the bite, 6 to 8 minutes. Drain.

4. Meanwhile, set reserved frying pan with butter and oil over medium-high heat. When pan is hot, stir in squash. Add ¾ cup broth, cover, and cook until squash is tender to the bite, about 5 minutes. Add cream and drained ravioli; stir gently until ravioli are hot, 1 to 2 minutes, adding more broth to moisten if you like. Add salt and pepper to taste. Garnish with fried sage leaves and add cheese to taste.

Quick Tip: For a shortcut, look for peeled chunks of butternut squash in your supermarket's produce section.

PER SERVING: 645 cal., 45% (288 cal.) from fat; 25 g protein; 32 g fat (16 g sat.); 65 g carbo (4.5 g fiber); 619 mg sodium; 160 mg chol.

vegetarian mains

What to Pour with Meatless Mains

Pairing a Cabernet with a steak is a no-brainer. But what to do when your main dish is a stew of split peas and winter squash, with serrano chiles thrown in (*page 279*)? This is territory where wine lovers really earn their food-pairing stripes—and have the most fun in the process.

The recipes in this chapter are built on legumes and grains and nuts, often studded with hearty vegetables or laced together with eggs and cheese. Pairing wine with such dishes is a matter of matching the weight and texture and mouthfeel of your cornerstone material while factoring in the main additions.

A full-bodied West Coast Chardonnay, for instance, would match textures with the split peas in the stew mentioned above; and with its apple and pear flavors, Chard is especially good with winter squash. The chiles are a wild card—if you have too high an alcohol level or too much tannin (from oak, in the case of Chardonnay), they'll start a fire in your mouth. But if your Chard is fruity enough so that it seems a little sweet, you're good with the chiles. On the other hand, a barely off-dry Riesling would handle the serranos easily, and have all the rich mouthfeel and good will toward squash required. Pour both!

Here are a few other natural starting points for exciting vegetarian pairings:

• **LEGUMES:** As with the split peas, the textures of legumes create some yummy partnerships. Lentils lean toward earthy Pinot Noir; beans love the soft tannins of Merlot; but if it's black beans you're talking about, a rustic, black-fruited Syrah is grand.

• **GRAINS:** Starchy pastas are set off well by Chardonnay or Pinot Gris (our pick with the Ultimate Mac 'n' Cheese, *page 285*, is Gris—or a sparkler).

Aromatic rice does well on both the texture and aroma fronts with Viognier. Corn—even in polenta form—is a natural with Chardonnay.

• **ROOT VEGETABLES:** Pour fruit-rich and/or aromatic whites—Chardonnay (again), Riesling, and Viognier.

• **MUSHROOMS:** Meaty portabellas and shiitakes call for red wine—loamy Pinot Noir or Merlot. But lighter types can even work with white wine; try a minerally Chardonnay with the Leek and Chanterelle Tart on *page 298*.

• **GREENS:** If lighter herbs and greens carry the dish, grassy Sauvignon Blanc is a good match, but hearty bitter greens like chard or kale, in partnership with legumes especially, can work with Merlot, which tends to have a more herbal side than Cab.

• **EGGS:** Very few wines stand up to the sulfurous quality of eggs, but Riesling, Gewürztraminer, and sparkling wine work beautifully.

• **CHEESE:** Red wine is not a natural here. Sauvignon Blanc, Viognier, Riesling, and sparkling are likelier bets. But if it's red you want—and the dish's other ingredients lean that way—Pinot Noir works across more cheeses than most other reds.

• **TOMATO SAUCE:** For all those red-sauced pastas, go for high-acid red wines—Sangiovese and Barbera are perfect (and, incidentally, they're staging a surge in the West).

A Sauvignon Blanc–Semillon blend will stand up to the tangy, bitter flavors of a pizza topped with ricotta cheese and broccoli rabe.

Tortellini with Soybeans and Pesto

Shelled soybeans, sold frozen in many markets, add great flavor and texture—as well as protein—to pasta dishes.

SERVES 3 or 4 | **TIME** 15 minutes

1 package (12 or 13 oz.) dried cheese tortellini or 1¼ lbs. fresh (*see Quick Tip below*)
1 cup frozen shelled soybeans (edamame)
⅓ to ½ cup Simple Pesto (*recipe follows*)
Salt and freshly ground black pepper
Grated parmesan cheese

1. In a 5- to 6-qt. pan over high heat, bring 3 qts. water to a boil. Add tortellini; cook, stirring occasionally, until barely tender to the bite, 10 to 11 minutes for dried, 4 to 5 minutes for fresh. Stir in soybeans 3 minutes before pasta is done. Drain, reserving 1 cup cooking water. Rinse and dry pan.
2. Return hot pasta to pan. Add pesto and salt and pepper to taste. Mix well, adding as much of reserved cooking water to moisten as desired. Mound on dinner plates or in a serving bowl. Add parmesan to taste.
Quick Tip: Dried and fresh tortellini vary in quality; for dried, we like Barilla's fresh-tasting filling and thin wrapping.

PER SERVING: 541 cal., 43% (234 cal.) from fat; 20 g protein; 26 g fat (11 g sat.); 54 g carbo (8.3 g fiber); 876 mg sodium; 65 mg chol.

Simple Pesto: In a food processor or blender, purée 3 cups lightly packed **basil leaves**, ½ cup *each* grated **parmesan cheese** and **extra-virgin olive oil**, and 2 peeled **garlic** cloves until smooth, stopping and pushing basil down into blades as needed if using blender. Add **salt** and freshly ground **black pepper** to taste. Cover if not using at once. Makes 1 cup, enough to coat 4 cups cooked linguine or similar-sized pasta (1 lb. dried).
Make Ahead: Make a few batches of pesto while fresh basil is in season and freeze to use throughout the year: Spoon it into ice cube trays, press plastic wrap onto the surface, and freeze. When solid, pop cubes from trays, wrap airtight, and freeze up to 6 months. Thaw before using. If surface gets dark, just stir to blend.

PER TBSP.: 87 cal., 89% (77 cal.) from fat; 2.5 g protein; 8.5 g fat (1.8 g sat.); 1.3 g carbo (0.9 g fiber); 83 mg sodium; 3.5 mg chol.

Whole-wheat Lasagna with Butternut Squash and Kale

Full of the lively flavor and color of midwinter vegetables, the lasagna is made with whole-wheat noodles, which add a slightly nutty flavor. It's even better the next day.

SERVES 8 | **TIME** 2 hours

¼ cup olive oil, divided
1 medium red onion, sliced
3 garlic cloves (1 minced, 2 peeled)
2 cans (14 oz. each) crushed tomatoes
1 tsp. dried oregano
1 tsp. *each* **salt and freshly ground black pepper, divided, plus more to taste**
6 cups ½-in. cubes peeled butternut squash (about 2 lbs.; *see Quick Tip, above right*)
½ tsp. dried thyme
1 lb. lacinato kale (also called dinosaur or Tuscan kale)
9 whole-wheat lasagna noodles (about ½ lb.)
1 container (15 oz.) part-skim-milk ricotta cheese
⅛ tsp. nutmeg
2 cups shredded (½ lb.) mozzarella cheese, divided

1. Preheat oven to 400°. Heat 2 tbsp. oil in a 2- to 3-qt. pot over medium heat. Add onion and minced garlic; cook, stirring occasionally, until onion is soft and translucent, about 5 minutes. Add tomatoes, oregano, and ½ tsp. each salt and pepper. Reduce heat and simmer until thick and flavors are combined, about 30 minutes. Set aside.
2. While sauce is cooking, in a 12- by 15-in. baking pan, sprinkle squash with thyme, remaining 2 tbsp. oil, and salt and pepper to taste. Add garlic cloves and toss squash mixture to coat with oil. Bake until soft, 10 to 15 minutes. Meanwhile, bring 3 qts. salted water to a boil in a large pot.
3. Reduce oven temperature to 350°. Transfer squash and garlic to a food processor and purée until smooth.
4. Tear kale leaves from center ribs and discard ribs. Boil leaves until soft, 5 to 8 minutes. Drain; let cool. Squeeze out as much water as possible and chop finely.
5. In the same pot, bring another 3 qts. salted water to a boil. Add noodles and cook until tender to the bite, about 10 minutes. Drain; rinse with cold water.
6. In a medium bowl, mix ricotta, nutmeg, 1 cup mozzarella, and remaining ½ tsp. each salt and pepper.
7. Coat bottom of a 9- by 13-in. baking pan with one-third of tomato sauce (about 1½ cups). Lay 3 noodles in a single layer over sauce. Top noodles with squash, spreading evenly. Sprinkle half of kale evenly over squash. Arrange 3 more noodles on kale and top with

ricotta mixture, spreading evenly. Top with remaining kale and noodles. Cover noodles with remaining tomato sauce and sprinkle with remaining 1 cup mozzarella.

8. Bake lasagna until juices are bubbling and cheese is melted, about 30 minutes. Let stand 10 minutes before slicing.

Quick Tip: For a shortcut, look for peeled chunks of butternut squash in your supermarket's produce section.

Make Ahead: Through step 7, up to 1 day, chilled (add 10 to 15 minutes to baking time). Freeze the lasagna, wrapped well in plastic wrap, up to 1 month; bake frozen (add 1¼ hours to oven time).

PER 4½-IN.-SQUARE SERVING: 424 cal., 38% (162 cal.) from fat; 20 g protein; 18 g fat (7.4 g sat.); 51 g carbo (8 g fiber); 659 mg sodium; 39 mg chol.

Sweet Potato Gnocchi with Mushrooms and Spinach

This spectacular main dish is the perfect vegetarian offering for Thanksgiving dinner—or any other special occasion.

SERVES 12 | **TIME** 3 hours

GNOCCHI

1 cup low-fat ricotta cheese

3 lbs. orange-fleshed sweet potatoes (often labeled "yams"), boiled until tender, peeled, and flesh puréed

3 tbsp. firmly packed light brown sugar

1 cup finely shredded parmesan cheese

2 tsp. kosher salt

½ tsp. freshly grated nutmeg

About 3 cups flour

TOPPING

¼ cup olive oil, divided

1 tbsp. minced garlic

¼ cup sliced shallots

1 lb. mixed mushrooms such as chanterelle, cremini, king trumpet, matsutake, and oyster *(see Quick Tip, right)*

2 cups vegetable broth

3 tbsp. butter

¾ lb. baby spinach leaves

1 tsp. kosher salt

½ tsp. freshly ground black pepper

1 tbsp. chopped thyme leaves

½ cup finely shredded parmesan cheese, divided

1. Make gnocchi: Drain ricotta in a fine-mesh strainer over sink, stirring occasionally, 1 hour.

2. In a large bowl, combine 3 cups sweet potato purée (save extra for another use), strained ricotta, brown

sugar, parmesan, salt, and nutmeg. Gently stir in flour, ½ cup at a time, until a soft dough forms.

3. Working on a lightly floured surface, divide dough into eight portions. Roll each portion with your hands into a 15-in. rope, then cut into 1-in. pieces, sprinkling dough with flour if it gets sticky. Transfer gnocchi to a rimmed tray lightly dusted with flour.

4. Bring a large pot of salted water to a boil. Reduce heat to medium-low. Working in batches of 15 to 20, drop gnocchi into water, stirring to prevent sticking, and cook until they are firm and float to top of water, about 5 minutes. Using a slotted spoon, transfer gnocchi to a strainer, then to a lightly oiled rimmed pan to cool.

5. Make topping: Heat 2 tbsp. oil in a large nonstick frying pan over medium-high heat. Add gnocchi to pan and cook, stirring often, until browned, 5 to 8 minutes. Transfer to a large serving dish.

6. Meanwhile, heat remaining 2 tbsp. oil in a second large frying pan over medium-high heat. Cook garlic and shallots, stirring, until fragrant, about 2 minutes. Add mushrooms and cook, stirring, until softened, about 5 minutes. Add broth, butter, spinach, salt, and pepper; cover and cook until spinach wilts, about 3 minutes.

7. Spoon vegetables over gnocchi and pour in broth. Sprinkle with thyme and half of parmesan. Serve with remaining parmesan.

Quick Tip: Try chanterelles and matsu-takes from the Northwest; Colorado is another great mushroom locale. Discard stems of oysters or shiitakes. Slice or quarter large, dense mushrooms like the cremini and king trumpets; no need to slice up soft mushrooms such as oysters.

Make Ahead: Through step 3, up to 3 days, chilled; up to 3 weeks, frozen (freeze in single layer on a cookie sheet to harden, then transfer to resealable freezer bags).

PER SERVING: 364 cal., 31% (114 cal.) from fat; 14 g protein; 13 g fat (5.3 g sat.); 49 g carbo (4.2 g fiber); 1,021 mg sodium; 24 mg chol.

Yams vs. Sweet Potatoes

The vegetables generally labeled "yams" in supermarkets are actually orange-fleshed sweet potatoes, such as the red-skinned Garnet and the brown-skinned Jewel. True yams are a starchy tuber that is a staple crop in many parts of the tropics; they come in many sizes and colors, and are seldom grown in the U.S. The great yam confusion arose in the 1930s, when U.S. growers developed the super-sweet orange-fleshed sweet potatoes and began marketing them as yams to distinguish them from the drier, paler sweet potatoes (also known as Japanese or Cuban sweet potatoes or *boniatos*) available up to that point.

Roasted Kohlrabi and Eggs with Mustard and Honey

When slow-roasted, kohlrabi—a type of cabbage with a gentle broccoli flavoróbecomes creamy, almost buttery. The eggs turn pale brown and take on faint popcorn flavor. Honeycomb, tart green sorrel, and a mustard vinaigrette add to the intrigue and beauty of this dish. Chef Jeremy Fox, a wizard with vegetables, created it for Sunset while heading the kitchen at Ubuntu, a vegetable-only restaurant in Napa, California.

SERVES 4 | **TIME** 30 minutes, plus 3 hours to roast

4 eggs
¼ cup olive oil
8 small purple or green kohlrabi bulbs (about
    2 in. diameter), leaves and stems trimmed
1 tsp. each yellow and brown mustard seeds
2 bay leaves, preferably fresh
2 tbsp. sherry vinegar
4 tsp. honey
1 tbsp. stone-ground mustard
Kosher salt
1 oz. chopped stemmed fresh sorrel (about √2 cup; *see
    Quick Tips, right*), plus several small leaves for garnish
4-in. piece honeycomb (*see Quick Tips, right*) or 2 tbsp.
    honey

1. Preheat oven to 250°. Put eggs in their shells in a bowl of warm water. Pour ¼ cup oil into an 8-in. square baking pan, add kohlrabi, and turn to coat. Cover tightly with foil.

2. Remove eggs from water and set directly on an ovenrack. Set pan of kohlrabi on another rack. Roast eggs and kohlrabi 2 hours (eggs will look freckled). Remove eggs, crack all over under cold water (but donít peel), and put in a bowl of cold water to cool.

3. Turn kohlrabi over in pan and cover tightly. Increase oven temperature to 375° and roast until butter-soft when pierced with a knife, about 1 hour. Uncover, turn kohlrabi over, and roast until crisp, aboout 30 minutes more.

4. Meanwhile, in a small saucepan, heat mustard seeds over medium-high heat until they just start to pop, 2 to 3 minutes. Add ½ cup water, the bay leaves, vinegar, and honey. Bring to a boil, then lower heat and simmer, covered, until mustard seeds are tender, 15 to 20 minutes.

5. Uncover the pan and boil sauce until reduced to ½ cup, 2 to 5 minutes. Remove from heat and whisk in stone-ground mustard. Season with salt to taste.

6. Peel eggs. Chop and mix with sorrel in a medium bowl.

7. While kohlrabi bulbs are still warm, tear some partway apart and some in half.

8. Divide egg mixture among plates or transfer to a big platter. Arrange kohlrabi on top, drizzle with honey-mustard sauce, and add a few small chunks of honeycomb (or drizzle with honey). Top with small sorrel leaves.

Quick Tips: Fox used red sorrel, wood sorrel, and sheep sorrel from Ubuntuís garden, but any kind of sorrel will work. Find honeycomb at well-stocked grocery stores and farmersí markets.

PER SERVING: 305 cal., 62% (189 cal.) from fat; 8.5 g protein; 21 g fat (3.8 g sat.); 23 g carbo (3.9 g fiber); 140 mg sodium; 212 mg chol.

Liquid Gold: California Olive Oil

The West produces some of the best olive oil in the world. Virtually all of it is produced in California, which has the kind of Mediterranean climate that olives love. The first trees planted in the state were brought by Spanish missionaries in the late 1700s. It's an enduring legacy: One of the most common varieties in California today is the Mission olive, descended from those original trees.

California olive oil production dropped around the turn of the last century due to an influx of cheaper imported oils. But a few oil makers stuck it out. In the 1980s, olive oil was rediscovered as a healthy, mono-unsaturated fat, and public demand for

it started to rise. Interest in high-quality olive oil began to increase too, both on the part of the consumers and the growers. To meet the need, the California Olive Oil Council (COOC) was founded in 1992 to raise the standards for the state's olive oil. This group of highly trained tasters sips and sniffs hundreds of oils every year, and only the flawless ones are officially certified as extra-virgin. Any oil with the COOC label, if properly stored, will be reliably good.

Olive oil is made by crushing the fruit of olive trees into a paste—pits and all—in a mill. Most producers use a giant tank mixer and a centrifuge to extract the oil from the paste.

Extra-virgin oil is produced from the first "pressing" of a batch of olives, without heat applied, and is unrefined.

Store your oil airtight in a cool, dark place, as heat and light can degrade its quality very quickly. Unlike wine, it does not improve with age; in fact, olive oil begins to lose quality just a few months after it's pressed (good oils will often have a harvest date on the bottle). Olive oil is best kept no more than a year at room temperature, although peppery varieties can last longer. And don't use your really good extra-virgin olive oil to cook; heat destroys its subtle flavors. Instead, use it for drizzling over food before serving or in salad dressings.

Spicy Hard-cooked Eggs

Eggs are wonderful in this creamy north Indian–style sauce. It's especially good with rice.

SERVES 4 | **TIME** 1 hour

1 large onion, finely chopped
2 tbsp. vegetable or canola oil
½ tsp. salt, plus more to taste
4 garlic cloves, minced
2-in. piece fresh ginger, finely shredded into mush
4 green onions, trimmed and chopped
1 jalapeño chile, seeds and ribs removed and finely chopped
2 tsp. ground coriander
¼ tsp. cayenne
¼ cup plain whole-milk yogurt
1 can (15 oz.) chopped tomatoes
2 tsp. garam masala (*see Quick Tips below*)
6 hard-cooked eggs (*see Quick Tips below*), halved lengthwise
¼ cup chopped cilantro (optional)

1. In a 6-qt. pot over medium-high heat, cook onion with oil and salt until onion is soft, about 2 minutes. Reduce heat to medium and cook, stirring occasionally, until onion starts to brown around edges, about 5 minutes.
2. Add garlic, ginger, green onions, and jalapeño. Increase heat to high and cook, stirring, until fragrant, about 1 minute. Add coriander and cayenne and cook, stirring, 30 seconds. Reduce heat to medium-high and stir in yogurt. Add tomatoes (with their juice) and 1 cup water. Bring to a boil, then reduce heat to maintain a steady simmer. Cook until flavors blend and sauce thickens a bit, about 10 minutes.
3. Stir in garam masala and add salt to taste. Set eggs, cut side up, on sauce. Spoon a bit of sauce over each egg and cook without stirring until hot and eggs are heated through, about 2 minutes. Serve garnished with cilantro if you like.

Quick Tips: Garam masala is available in the spice section of many supermarkets; if you cannot find it, substitute 1 tsp. cinnamon, ½ tsp. *each* ground cumin and freshly ground black pepper, and ¼ tsp. *each* ground cardamom, nutmeg, cloves, and cayenne. To hard-cook and peel eggs: Put 6 eggs in a medium saucepan. Cover with cold water by 1 in. Bring to a boil over high heat. Cover, remove from heat, and let stand 14 minutes. Transfer eggs to an ice bath (a bowl of ice and cold water) and let cool at least 10 minutes. When ready to peel, dip in hot water for 10 seconds to loosen shell. Remove shell.

PER SERVING: 242 cal., 52% (126 cal.) from fat; 12 g protein; 16 g fat (3.7 g sat.); 14 g carbo (2.3 g fiber); 568 mg sodium; 321 mg chol.

Asparagus, Spring Onion, and Morel Mushroom Sauté

Sweet asparagus and spring onions go so well with the woodsy flavor of morels. All you need is a bit of butter and some crème fraîche to finish the dish. If you can find fresh morels, they're worth the splurge. This is a light main course, so supplement with a hearty side or two.

SERVES 6 | **TIME** 45 minutes

⅓ lb. fresh morel mushrooms or 1 oz. dried (*see Quick Tips below*)
3 bunches asparagus, stem ends trimmed and stalks peeled (*see Quick Tips below*)
3 bunches green onions (white and pale green parts only), trimmed
¼ cup unsalted butter
½ cup crème fraîche
1 tsp. kosher salt
½ tsp. freshly ground black pepper

1. Bring a large pot of water to a boil. If using dried morels, put them in a small bowl, cover with 1 cup of the boiling water, and let stand 10 minutes. Lift out and pat dry.
2. Meanwhile, generously salt remaining boiling water. Fill a large bowl with ice and cold water and set near the stove. Add asparagus to boiling water and cook until crisp-tender, about 4 minutes. Remove from water and immediately plunge into ice bath to stop cooking. Repeat process with green onions. Drain asparagus and onions on paper towels, then cut asparagus spears in half crosswise.
3. In a large frying pan over medium-low heat, melt butter. Add morels, asparagus, and onions and cook 1 minute, tossing gently to coat with butter. Stir in crème fraîche and season with salt and pepper. Cook until heated through, about 4 minutes longer. Transfer to a serving dish.

Quick Tips: Be sure to clean either dried or fresh morels well before using, to avoid unpleasant sandy bites. We like to peel the tough outer skin from the asparagus for this dish. This not only makes it prettier but results in more tender stalks.
Make Ahead: For vegetables, blanch up to 1 day; chill, wrapped in moistened paper towels and then a plastic bag.

PER SERVING: 174 cal., 78% (135 cal.) from fat; 3.4 g protein; 15 g fat (9.5 g sat.); 7.6 g carbo (2 g fiber); 347 mg sodium; 37 mg chol.

Curried Red Kidney Beans and Cauliflower (*Rajma Masala*)

Red kidney beans are very nutritious. They are, however, harder to digest than other beans, which is why they're traditionally cooked with seasonings that help break them down, such as ginger. Use fresh spices for the most potent flavor. Serve with plain yogurt if you like.

SERVES 6 to 8 | **TIME** 1 hour

3 tbsp. vegetable oil
1 large onion, chopped
1 cinnamon stick (2 in.)
1 bay leaf
1 tbsp. *each* minced garlic and fresh ginger
1 tsp. *each* fennel seeds and cumin seeds
3 green cardamom pods, cracked open
½ tsp. *each* ground coriander, turmeric, and garam masala (see *Quick Tip below*)
¼ tsp. cayenne
1 can (14.5 oz.) whole peeled plum tomatoes, drained
1 serrano chile, seeds and ribs removed and minced
1 tsp. salt, plus more to taste
6 cups cooked red kidney beans (about four 14-oz. cans), rinsed and drained
½ head cauliflower, cut into ½- to 1-in. florets
1 to 1½ tbsp. fresh lemon juice
½ cup loosely packed cilantro sprigs, coarsely chopped
6 to 8 cups cooked brown rice

1. Heat oil in a heavy-bottomed 4- to 5-qt. pot or saucepan over medium-high heat. Add onion and fry, stirring occasionally, until slightly softened, 2 to 3 minutes. Stir in cinnamon, bay leaf, garlic, ginger, fennel, cumin, and cardamom and fry, stirring, 2 minutes. Add coriander, turmeric, garam masala, and cayenne and fry, stirring, 1 minute. Shred tomatoes into pot with your fingers. Stir in serrano chile, salt, kidney beans, cauliflower, and 1½ cups water. Lower heat to medium-low, cover, and simmer until cauliflower is tender and liquid has thickened into a velvety-looking sauce, about 20 minutes (add more water if necessary).

2. Season beans with salt to taste. Stir in lemon juice and cilantro. Serve over hot brown rice.

Quick Tip: Garam masala is available in the spice section of many supermarkets; if you cannot find it, substitute 1 tsp. cinnamon, ½ tsp. *each* ground cumin and freshly ground black pepper, and ¼ tsp. *each* ground cardamom, nutmeg, cloves, and cayenne.

PER SERVING: 281 cal., 22% (62 cal.) from fat; 15 g protein; 6.9 g fat (0.9 g sat.); 42 g carbo (7.1 g fiber); 437 mg sodium; 0 mg chol.

Indian Stuffed Eggplant with Peanuts and Spiced Yogurt

Reader Kusum Patel, of West Sacramento, California, contributed a deliciously spicy vegetarian main course from her native north India. If White Egg eggplant isn't available, look for the egg-size globe variety, or use pieces of any slender eggplant.

SERVES 4 | **TIME** 50 minutes

⅔ cup finely chopped roasted, salted peanuts
½ cup chopped cilantro, divided, plus more for garnish
3 tbsp. vegetable oil
2 tbsp. plus 1 tsp. minced fresh ginger
4 tsp. sugar
2 tsp. salt, plus more to taste
1 tbsp. *each* ground coriander and red chile flakes
1 tbsp. plus ½ tsp. cumin seeds
1¾ tsp. turmeric, divided
1¾ lbs. (8 to 12) White Egg eggplants (each about 2 in. wide, 3 in. long) or use 8 to 12 pieces slender eggplant (each about 1½ to 2 in. wide, 3 in. long)
1½ cups basmati rice
¾ cup plain yogurt

1. In a bowl, combine peanuts, 6 tbsp. chopped cilantro, oil, 2 tbsp. ginger, sugar, salt, coriander, chile flakes, 1 tbsp. cumin seeds, and 1½ tsp. turmeric.

2. Trim stems but not calyxes (which resemble green petals) from eggplants. From bottom end, quarter each eggplant lengthwise three-quarters of way to stem end. (If using slender eggplant, trim one end of each piece to sit flat, then quarter each piece lengthwise from untrimmed end three-quarters of way to trimmed end.) Gently open cuts in each eggplant and pack in peanut-cilantro filling. As filled, arrange eggplants upright in a 3- to 4-qt. saucepan; they must fit snugly.

3. Add ⅔ cup water to pan. Cover, bring to a boil over high heat, then reduce heat and simmer until eggplants are tender when pierced, 15 to 20 minutes (if overcooked they may fall apart).

4. Meanwhile, in a 3- to 4-qt. pan over high heat, bring 3 cups water to a boil. Add rice; reduce heat and simmer, covered, until liquid is absorbed, about 20 minutes.

5. While eggplant and rice cook, shake remaining ½ tsp. cumin in a small pan over high heat until seeds darken, 1 to 2 minutes. Coarsely grind with a mortar and pestle or in a clean coffee grinder, then combine with yogurt, ½ cup water, and remaining 2 tbsp. chopped cilantro, 1 tsp. ginger, and ¼ tsp. turmeric. Season to taste with salt.

6. Gently spoon eggplant into a dish, taking care to keep pieces together. If desired, skim and discard fat

vegetarian mains

from pan juices, then pour juices around eggplant. Serve eggplant over rice with yogurt sauce. Garnish with additional cilantro if you like.

PER SERVING: 466 cal., 49% (229 cal.) from fat; 13 g protein; 26 g fat (4 g sat.); 77 g carbo (9 g fiber); 1,395 mg sodium; 6 mg chol.

Spicy Lemongrass Tofu

This Vietnamese dish, adapted from a recipe by Sacramento, California-based cookbook author Mai Pham, has a wonderful interplay of tastes and textures—savory soy, aromatic basil, crunchy peanuts, piquant lemongrass, and the heat of fresh chiles.

SERVES 3 or 4 | **TIME** 40 minutes

1 package (12 to 16 oz.) firm tofu
2 stalks fresh lemongrass (10 to 12 in. each)
1½ tbsp. soy sauce
1½ to 2 tsp. minced fresh hot chile such as Thai bird
   or serrano
2 tsp. sugar
1 tsp. turmeric
½ tsp. salt, plus more to taste
1 tsp. vegetable oil
½ cup thinly sliced onion
2 tbsp. minced shallot
1 tsp. minced garlic
⅔ cup Thai or regular basil leaves
3 tbsp. chopped unsalted roasted peanuts, divided
4 cups cooked rice

1. Rinse tofu, drain in a colander for about 5 minutes, then pat dry with paper towels. Cut into ¾-in. cubes and lightly blot with more towels.
2. Cut off and discard tough tops and root ends from lemongrass; peel off and discard tough, green outer layers of stalks down to tender white core. Finely chop tender portions; you should have 4 to 7 tbsp.
3. In a medium bowl, mix lemongrass, soy sauce, chile, sugar, turmeric, and salt. Gently stir in tofu. Let marinate for 5 to 10 minutes, stirring occasionally.
4. In a 10- to 12-in. nonstick frying pan over medium heat, heat oil, add onion, shallot, and garlic, and cook, stirring, until fragrant, about 2 minutes; push to one side of pan. Add tofu mixture. Cook, gently turning cubes occasionally and stirring onion mixture, until tofu has browned around edges and onion is soft, 8 to 10 minutes.
5. Stir in basil and half of peanuts. Add salt to taste. Garnish with remaining peanuts. Serve with hot cooked rice.

PER SERVING: 413 cal., 26% (108 cal.) from fat; 21 g protein; 12 g fat (1.8 g sat.); 57 g carbo (2.2 g fiber); 692 mg sodium; 0 mg chol.

■ Lemongrass

FROM THE GARDEN

In the garden, lemongrass forms handsome clumps that reach 3 to 4 ft. tall and nearly as wide, with long, slender light-green leaves rising from swollen bases. When harvested, the bulbous stems look like green onions, but greenish yellow and more fibrous. When you cut them, the stems release essential oils, which perfume the air with the aroma of freshly cut lemon combined with the clean bite of ginger.

Thai and Vietnamese cooks use lemongrass in marinades, stir-fries, curries, and soups. To use lemongrass, discard the tough tops and root ends, then peel off and discard the more fibrous outer layers, down to the tender inner white core. You can find fresh lemongrass in larger supermarkets and in Asian grocery stores.

Stir-fried Eggplant and Tofu

With their meaty texture, the tofu and eggplant make this stir-fry from reader Jiranooch Shapiro, of Anchorage, Alaska, a great choice for a substantial dinner. Serve the stir-fry over rice.

recipe pictured on page **263**

SERVES 4 | **TIME** 25 minutes

3 tbsp. vegetable oil
1 package (18 oz.) firm tofu, drained, cut into 1½- by 2-in. chunks, and thoroughly dried on paper towels
2 garlic cloves, minced
1 lb. eggplant, cut into 1- by 3-in. strips
1 small red or green bell pepper, seeds and ribs removed and cut into 1-in. pieces
⅓ cup reduced-sodium soy sauce
2 tbsp. *each* sugar and vegetarian oyster sauce (*see Quick Tip below*)
¼ cup basil leaves

1. Heat oil in a large nonstick frying pan over medium heat until hot, add tofu, and gently cook, turning tofu occasionally, until browned slightly, about 10 minutes. Use a slotted spoon to transfer tofu to a plate.
2. Add garlic, eggplant, and bell pepper to pan and cook until softened, stirring occasionally, 12 to 15 minutes. Add soy sauce, sugar, and oyster sauce and cook until heated, another 2 minutes. Return tofu to pan and gently stir to coat. Remove from heat and stir in basil.
Quick Tip: Find vegetarian oyster sauce (made of mushrooms and vegetable proteins) in Asian grocery stores. If you're nonvegetarian, substitute regular oyster sauce if you like.

PER SERVING: 263 cal., 55% (144 cal.) from fat; 14 g protein; 16 g fat (2.4 g sat.); 21 g carbo (3.3 g fiber); 1,170 mg sodium; 0 mg chol.

Spicy Bok Choy with Fried Tofu

Each bite of baby bok choy offers the simultaneous crunch of the stems with the savory flavor of the deep green leaves, rich in vitamins A and C. Spoon the spicy bok choy over hot rice.

SERVES 2 | **TIME** 1 hour

6 to 8 oz. firm tofu
About ¾ lb. baby bok choy
1 tbsp. vegetable oil
2 garlic cloves, minced or pressed
4 green onions, trimmed and thinly sliced
1 (½ lb.) red bell pepper, seeds and ribs removed and cut into thin slivers
3 tbsp. reduced-sodium soy sauce
2 tsp. sugar
1 tsp. Asian hot sauce or Sriracha chili sauce
1 tsp. cornstarch mixed with 1 tbsp. water into a smooth slurry
2 cups cooked rice

1. Cut tofu into 1-in.-thick slices. Lay slices on kitchen towels and cover with more towels. Set a flat-bottomed pan on top of towels; put a 1-lb. can (such as beans or tomatoes) on pan. Let tofu drain 10 to 15 minutes.

2. Meanwhile, discard bruised or yellowed bok choy leaves. Cut each head in half lengthwise; if bases of bok choy pieces are thicker than 1 in., cut halves in half again lengthwise. Cut tofu into 1-in. cubes.

3. Heat oil in a 12-in. frying pan or a wok over medium-high heat until hot. Add tofu; cook, turning pieces with a spatula as needed, until cubes are golden brown all over. Transfer to paper towels to drain.

4. Add garlic, green onions, red pepper, bok choy, and 2 tbsp. water to pan. Cover and cook, stirring often, until bok choy stems are just tender when pierced, 3 to 5 minutes. Uncover and stir in tofu, soy sauce, sugar, hot sauce, and cornstarch mixture. Cook, stirring, until sauce is boiling.

PER SERVING: 545 cal., 25% (136 cal.) from fat; 24 g protein; 15 g fat (2.2 g sat.); 81 g carbo; 1,100 mg sodium; 0 mg chol.

Zucchini "Spaghetti"

From reader Shirley Blumberg, of Mammoth Lakes, California, comes a recipe that's a fun and tasty way to make use of an avalanche of zucchini from your garden.

SERVES 4 | **TIME** 20 minutes, plus 30 minutes to drain

6 large zucchini (about 2½ lbs. total)
½ tsp. kosher salt
2 tbsp. olive oil
2 or 3 garlic cloves, minced
2 cups spaghetti sauce (homemade or store-bought), heated until hot
Finely shredded parmesan cheese
Freshly ground black pepper

1. Trim ends off zucchini. Push zucchini lengthwise over a box grater, horizontally positioned with cutting side up, to make long thin strands, or use the julienne slicer on a mandoline.

2. In a colander, mix zucchini with salt and let drain 15 minutes. Rinse, spread on a kitchen towel, and roll up. Squeeze to absorb as much liquid as possible.

3. In a 10- to 12-in. frying pan, heat oil over high heat until hot. Add zucchini and garlic and cook, stirring often, until zucchini is hot, about 3 minutes. Pour zucchini into a colander in sink; let drain 2 to 3 minutes, or until most of liquid is gone.

4. Quickly transfer zucchini to a platter or wide bowl. Top with hot spaghetti sauce and mix to distribute a little. Sprinkle with parmesan and black pepper. Serve at once, with more cheese on the side.

PER SERVING: 174 cal., 44% (78 cal.) from fat; 9 g protein; 8.75 g fat (1 g sat.); 23 g carbo (5.75 g fiber); 838 mg sodium; 0 mg chol.

2 Ways with Summer Squash

Crisp, tender summer squash have a slightly sweet flavor that pairs well with rich and substantial ingredients, such as olive oil, garlic, and cheeses.

QUICK IDEA NO. 1: Sauté diced squash with garlic, olive oil, and herbs. Use the mixture to top toasted baguette slices spread with goat cheese. Sprinkle with dill, mint, or basil.

QUICK IDEA NO. 2: Roast long, thin slices of squash with garlic and olive oil until very soft. Layer in a pan along with goat cheese, pesto, and finely chopped sun-dried tomatoes. Serve with multigrain crackers.

vegetarian mains

Spaghetti Squash Stir-fry

A recipe from the spaghetti squash repertoire of reader Jane Shapton, of Portland, Oregon, who was introduced as a young girl to the vegetable by her mom and has been enjoying it ever since.

SERVES 6 | **TIME** 30 minutes

1 spaghetti squash (3 lbs.)
1 green bell pepper (6 oz.)
1 red bell pepper (6 oz.)
2 carrots (6 oz. total)
10 to 12 large basil leaves
1 tbsp. olive oil
½ cup vegetable broth
¼ tsp. freshly ground black pepper
Salt
¼ cup finely shredded parmesan cheese

1. Pierce squash in several places with a sharp knife. Microwave it until soft when pressed, 10 to 12 minutes; turn over after 5 minutes.
2. Meanwhile, remove seeds and ribs from green and red bell peppers. Peel carrots. Cut bell peppers and carrots into matchstick-size slivers.
3. When squash is tender, cut open and scoop out and discard seeds. Scoop out tender squash strands and reserve. Stack basil leaves and cut crosswise into slivers.
4. Set a 10- to 12-in. (not nonstick) frying pan over high heat. When hot, pour in oil, then immediately add bell peppers and carrots. Cook, stirring constantly, until carrots are tender-crisp, 5 to 7 minutes.
5. Add broth, basil, black pepper, and squash strands. Cook, stirring often, until squash is hot. Add salt to taste.
6. Transfer vegetables to a serving dish and sprinkle with parmesan.

PER SERVING: 116 cal., 33% (38 cal.) from fat; 4 g protein; 4.3 g fat (1.1 g sat.); 18 g carbo (4.3 g fiber); 183 mg sodium; 3.3 mg chol.

Supper Enchiladas

Here enchiladas are reinterpreted as mini casseroles served in ramekins. They are supremely comforting. For info on Mexican ingredients, *see Quick Tips, right*.

SERVES 6 | **TIME** 45 minutes

1 can (10 oz.) red enchilada sauce
1 jar (7 oz.) peeled roasted red peppers, drained and rinsed
½ cup refrigerated or canned salsa verde
1 cup canned green enchilada sauce
12 corn tortillas (blue or regular corn, 5 to 6 in. wide; *see Quick Tips, right*)

2 packages (10 oz. each) frozen chopped spinach, thawed and squeezed dry
6 oz. cream cheese or *panela*, cut into thin slices or small chunks (*see Quick Tips below*)
½ cup finely shredded parmesan cheese or packed crumbled *cotija* cheese, divided (*see Quick Tips below*)
6 or 12 eggs
1½ cups (6 oz.) shredded mild cheddar cheese
¾ cup thinly sliced green onions
6 tbsp. chopped cilantro
6 to 12 tbsp. sour cream or Mexican *crema*
Salt

1. In a blender, purée red enchilada sauce and roasted red peppers until smooth.
2. In a bowl, mix salsa verde with green enchilada sauce.
3. Set six ramekins (about 2 cups each, 5 to 6 in. in diameter) on large baking sheets. Divide red sauce mixture evenly among ramekins and tilt to coat bottoms. Cut tortillas into quarters. Arrange four pieces in each ramekin, overlapping edges to cover bottom and pressing tortillas down into sauce.
4. Scatter spinach, cream cheese, and ¼ cup parmesan evenly over tortillas. Lay another four pieces of tortilla over filling in each ramekin; overlap edges to fit. Spoon green sauce over tortillas, coating evenly.
5. Bake, uncovered, in a 375° oven until sauce is bubbling, about 25 minutes. Remove pan from oven and immediately, with the back of a large spoon, make one or two slight depressions for eggs near center of each ramekin. Break 1 or 2 eggs into each ramekin; sprinkle evenly with cheddar. Return to oven and bake 10 to 12 minutes longer for soft yolks (press yolk gently to test), 12 to 15 minutes for firm yolks.
6. Top each ramekin with green onions, cilantro, a spoonful of sour cream, and a sprinkling of remaining ¼ cup parmesan. Set ramekins on plates. Add salt to taste.
Quick Tips: Corn tortillas, particularly in Mexican supermarkets, come in a variety of sizes. If you can't find the size you want, trim larger ones and save the scraps for other uses. *Panela* (a fresh white quick-melting cheese), *cotija* (a dry, salty white cheese), and *crema* (a tangy thick cream) are all available at Mexican markets.
Make Ahead: Through step 4, up to 4 hours, chilled. Bake 25 to 30 minutes in step 5.

PER SERVING, WITH 1 EGG AND 1 TBSP. SOUR CREAM: 527 cal., 53% (279 cal.) from fat; 25 g protein; 31 g fat (17 g sat.); 40 g carbo (5.1 g fiber); 1,167 mg sodium; 285 mg chol.

Stacked Enchilada Pie

Soft, comforting, and rich, this stacked style of enchilada is popular in many parts of the West, and it never fails to satisfy. For a nonvegetarian version, substitute 2¼ cups shredded cooked chicken for the black beans.

SERVES 8 | **TIME** About 2 hours

1 onion (about ½ lb.), chopped
2 red bell peppers (about 1 lb. total), seeded and chopped
2 garlic cloves, pressed or minced
2 tsp. cumin seeds
About 1 tsp. vegetable oil
1 package (1 lb.) frozen corn kernels, thawed
2 cans (about 15 oz. each) black beans, rinsed and drained
½ cup chopped cilantro
1 can (19 oz.) red enchilada sauce
8 flour tortillas (10 in. wide)
3 cups shredded (about 9 oz.) pepper jack or plain jack cheese
1½ cups crumbled (about ½ lb.) *cotija* or feta cheese
1 firm-ripe avocado (about 6 oz.)
Cilantro sprigs

1. Preheat oven to 350°. In a 5- to 6-qt. nonstick pan over high heat, cook onion, bell peppers, garlic, and cumin seeds in 1 tsp. oil, stirring often, until onion softens, 5 to 7 minutes. Stir in corn, beans, and chopped cilantro; remove pan from heat.

2. Pour enchilada sauce into a 12-in. rimmed pizza pan or 10-in. pie pan. Dip a tortilla in sauce to coat both sides lightly; lift tortilla out, letting excess sauce drip back into pan. Set tortilla in an oiled 10-in. cheesecake pan with removable rim at least 3 in. tall *(see Quick Tip, above right)*. Spread one-seventh (about 1 cup) of vegetable filling level over tortilla. Sprinkle evenly with ⅓ cup jack cheese and 3 tbsp. cotija cheese. Repeat layers, making a total of seven; top with last tortilla. Reserve any leftover enchilada sauce and remaining jack and cotija cheeses. Cover pan with an oiled piece of foil, oiled side down. Set pan in a rimmed 10- by 15-in. baking pan.

3. Bake 30 minutes. Uncover and continue baking until hot (160°) in center, 30 to 40 minutes longer.

4. In a microwave oven, heat remaining enchilada sauce until hot, 20 to 30 seconds. Pit, peel, and slice avocado.

5. Run a knife between pie and pan rim to loosen. Remove rim, set pie on a platter, and drizzle with enchilada sauce. Arrange avocado slices in a ring on pie, sprinkle with remaining jack and cotija cheeses, and garnish with cilantro sprigs. Cut into wedges to serve.

Quick Tip: If the cheesecake pan rim is less than 3 in. tall, fold a 36- by 12-in. strip of foil in half twice lengthwise and oil one side. Line rim with strip, oiled side in and edge extending above rim.

Make Ahead: Through step 2, up to 1 day; chill pie, remaining enchilada sauce, and cheese separately. Bake, covered, for 1 hour; uncover and bake until hot in the center, 40 to 50 minutes longer.

PER SERVING: 597 cal., 41% (245 cal.) from fat; 27 g protein; 27 g fat (12 sat.); 66 carbo (7.2 g fiber); 1,784 mg sodium; 56 mg chol.

Leek and Chanterelle Tart

The simple salt-and-pepper crust of the tart is worth making from scratch. If you do use a ready-made crust, pick one without sugar.

recipe pictured on page **264**

SERVES 6 to 8 | **TIME** 1 hour, plus 30 minutes to chill

CRUST
1 cup flour
½ tsp. *each* salt and freshly ground black pepper
7 tbsp. butter, chilled and cut into small pieces
FILLING
3 leeks (white and very light green parts), halved lengthwise
3 tbsp. butter
½ tsp. salt
1 lb. chanterelle mushrooms *(see Quick Tip, right)*, cut into about 1-in. pieces
2 tsp. fresh thyme leaves
3 tbsp. heavy whipping cream
¼ tsp. freshly ground black pepper
1 cup finely shredded gruyère cheese, divided

1. Make crust: In a medium bowl, mix flour, salt, and pepper. Rub butter into flour until most of it looks like cornmeal but some larger pea-size pieces remain. Drizzle in 3 tbsp. ice-cold water while stirring quickly with a fork. Or pulse flour, salt, pepper, and butter in a food processor until a coarse, cornmeal-textured mixture forms, then drizzle in ice water until dough comes together. Turn dough onto a large piece of plastic wrap and use wrap to press dough into a 1-in.-thick disk. Wrap in plastic wrap and refrigerate at least 30 minutes.

2. Preheat oven to 375°. Lightly flour a work surface. Unwrap dough; with a lightly floured rolling pin gently roll it, turning dough 90° between each roll, into a 12-in. circle.

3. Place rolled-out dough in a 9½-in. tart pan. Trim edges flush with pan edges. Cover dough with a large

vegetarian mains

piece of foil and weigh down with pie weights, dried beans, or uncooked rice.

4. Bake crust 20 minutes. Lift foil and weights off crust and bake until beginning to turn golden, about 10 minutes. Let crust cool to room temperature.

5. Meanwhile, make filling: Swish leeks around in a large bowl of water to rinse off dirt; transfer to a colander, leaving dirt behind, and rinse again in fresh water if necessary. Thinly slice leeks. Melt butter in a large frying pan over medium-high heat. Add leeks and salt and cook, stirring, until leeks are soft, about 3 minutes. Turn heat to high and add mushrooms. Cook, stirring constantly, until mushrooms have released their liquid, 5 to 10 minutes. Stir in thyme, cream, and pepper, then turn off heat and let cool to room temperature.

6. Spread half of gruyère over tart crust. Spread leek-mushroom mixture on top and sprinkle with remaining gruyère. Bake until cheese is melted and golden, about 25 minutes. Let stand 10 minutes before cutting. Serve warm or at room temperature.

Quick Tip: Substitute button or cremini mushrooms for the chanterelles if you like.

Make Ahead: Dough, up to 2 days, chilled.

PER SERVING: 310 cal., 64% (198 cal.) from fat; 8.1 g protein; 22 g fat (13 g sat.); 22 g carbo (1.8 g fiber); 497 mg sodium; 62 mg chol.

Goat Cheese–Chive Soufflé

This soufflé is really nice for lunch or a light dinner, paired with a crisp green salad.

SERVES 4 or 5 | **TIME** 1 hour

¼ cup butter, plus more for buttering dish
¼ cup finely shredded parmesan cheese, divided
¼ cup flour
1½ cups milk
1 cup coarsely crumbled (about 5 oz.) fresh goat cheese *(see Quick Tip, above right)*
¼ cup minced chives
½ tsp. *each* kosher salt and cayenne
6 eggs, separated

1. Preheat oven to 375°. Butter a 2-qt. soufflé dish, then coat with 2 tbsp. parmesan.

2. In a medium saucepan over medium heat, melt ¼ cup butter. Add flour and cook, stirring often, until mixture begins to brown, about 4 minutes. Whisk in milk and continue whisking until mixture boils and thickens, about 5 minutes.

3. Remove pan from heat and stir in goat cheese, remaining 2 tbsp. parmesan, the chives, salt, and

cayenne. Stir in egg yolks one at a time, mixing well after each addition. Transfer mixture to large bowl.

4. In another bowl, with a mixer on high speed, beat egg whites until they hold stiff peaks. Stir one-fourth of whites into yolk mixture, then gently fold in the rest. Transfer mixture to prepared soufflé dish.

5. Bake soufflé until it is puffed and well browned and jiggles only slightly in the center when you shake pan gently, 30 to 35 minutes. Serve immediately, scooping out portions with a large spoon.

Quick Tip: Try a mild, fresh goat cheese from a Western producer such as Laura Chenel.

PER SERVING: 363 cal., 69% (252 cal.) from fat; 19 g protein; 28 g fat (16 g sat.); 9.7 g carbo (0.3 g fiber); 637 mg sodium; 316 mg chol.

Whip It Good: Soufflé Pointers

• Use a wire whisk attachment on your mixer to introduce air evenly into the whites, creating tiny, strong bubbles.

• Beat the whites just until stiff but moist-looking peaks form. If the whites are over-beaten, the walls of the air bubbles stretch out and may burst when heated, collapsing the soufflé.

• Fold the egg whites gently but thoroughly into the soufflé batter, using a flexible rubber spatula. Overmixing or folding with a heavy hand may collapse the egg-white bubbles, leaving your soufflé less than ethereal.

• Bake the soufflé in the right dish size for the best results. Measure your dish's capacity with water to determine its volume. Classic soufflé dishes aren't necessary; you can also use deep baking dishes or ovenproof bowls, though soufflés baked in bowls with sloping sides won't rise as high as those in straight-sided dishes. Buttering the sides also helps the soufflé rise easily.

fish
&
shellfish

Salmon, halibut, sardines, trout, crab, oysters, and more—here are the iconic seafoods of the West, cooked simply and well.

We have so many good fish in our Western waters, from the bays and rivers to the vast expanse of the Pacific and the Bering Sea, that we find cooking seafood endlessly exciting. Our fishes offer us a huge range of flavors and textures, and they lend themselves to all kinds of cooking methods: In this collection of recipes, we pan-fry, poach, salt-bake, sauté, roast, steam, braise, and parchment-bake.

Besides being versatile, seafood is extremely nutritious, a great source of lean protein and good-for-you omega-3 fatty acids. And—a boon to anyone busy, which means practically all of us—it's very fast to cook; more than half the recipes in this chapter can be prepared in less than 30 minutes (and the one for pan-fried sand dabs, on *page 325*, is ready in 5).

Over the generations, our wealth of seafood has produced some classic recipes that are as popular today as they ever have been, so we made sure to include them: cracked Dungeness crab (*pages 340*) and California roll (*page 337*), among others. We also added a DIY sushi party (*page 334*)—it's just more fun as a group activity.

The not-so-fun side of seafood is how fast stocks of many fish are declining, due to overfishing and pollution. So our recipes call for fish from well-managed waters, and wherever possible, we've given you tips for how to choose other sustainable species (for more on this ever-changing scenario, check the indispensable Monterey Bay Aquarium seafood guide, *seafood watch.org*). We figure that if we eat our wonderful seafood wisely, we can enjoy it in all the years to come.

Fish & Shellfish

Pan-roasted Black Cod with Thai Curry Sauce

Find the Asian ingredients for this creamy, mildly hot curry at well-stocked supermarkets and specialty-foods stores.

SERVES 4 | **TIME** 30 minutes

2½ tbsp. olive oil, divided
3 tbsp. minced shallots
2 garlic cloves, minced
2 stalks fresh lemongrass
1 tbsp. *each* Thai green curry paste and minced fresh ginger
¼ tsp. turmeric
1 can (13.5 oz.) coconut milk
1 tbsp. Thai or Vietnamese fish sauce (*nam pla* or *nuoc mam*)
1 tbsp. sugar
1 tsp. finely shredded lime zest
Salt
4 pieces skinned, boned black cod (sablefish) or sturgeon fillet (*see Quick Tip below*), 1 in. thick (5 oz. each)
Freshly ground black pepper

1. Preheat oven to 450°. Heat 1 tbsp. oil in a heavy-bottomed medium saucepan over medium heat until hot. Add shallots and garlic; cook, stirring often, until softened, about 2 minutes.
2. Trim ends from lemongrass stalks and peel off tough outer layers; crush with the flat side of a large knife, then cut into lengths that will fit in your pan. Stir curry paste, ginger, turmeric, and lemongrass into pan; cook until fragrant, about 2 minutes. Add coconut milk, fish sauce, sugar, and lime zest; simmer, stirring often, until slightly thickened, about 10 minutes. Remove lemongrass. Season with salt.
3. Meanwhile, sprinkle both sides of fish with salt and pepper to taste. Heat remaining 1½ tbsp. oil in a large ovenproof frying pan over medium-high heat until hot. Add fish and cook until browned on bottom, 3 to 4 minutes. Turn pieces and transfer pan to oven. Bake just until fish is opaque in center of thickest part, about 8 minutes.
4. Spoon curry sauce onto plates and top with fish.
Quick Tip: If you go with sturgeon, U.S.-caught is the best choice.

PER SERVING: 447 cal., 70% (315 cal.) from fat; 26 g protein; 35 g fat (21 g sat.); 9.8 g carbo (0.2 g fiber); 307 mg sodium; 85 mg chol.

Pan-roasted Black Cod with Mushrooms and Sour Cream

A bit of sour cream complements the rich texture of the black cod.

SERVES 4 | **TIME** 30 minutes

¼ cup olive oil, divided
½ lb. shiitake mushrooms, stems removed and caps cut into ½-in.-thick slices
1½ tsp. chopped thyme leaves
½ tsp. kosher salt, plus more for sprinkling fish
¼ tsp. freshly ground black pepper
½ cup dry white wine
1½ tbsp. finely chopped garlic
4 skinned, boned black cod (sablefish) fillets, 1 in. thick (about 1 lb. total)
3 tbsp. sour cream

1. Preheat oven to 375°. Heat 2½ tbsp. oil in a large, ovenproof frying pan over medium-high heat. Add mushrooms, thyme, salt, and pepper and cook, stirring, until mushrooms are crisp and brown, 8 to 10 minutes. Add wine and garlic and cook 1 minute more. Transfer to a bowl.
2. Wipe out pan; heat remaining 1½ tbsp. oil until hot. Salt fish lightly on skinned side and set skinned side down in pan. Cook 5 minutes on stove, then bake until fish is almost opaque, 3 to 6 minutes.
3. Transfer fillets to plates. Pour out liquid from pan, scrape pan clean, and set over medium-low heat. Reheat mushrooms, pour off any excess liquid, and stir in sour cream. Spoon mushrooms over fish.

PER SERVING: 385 cal., 38% (146 cal.) from fat; 25 g protein; 16 g fat (3.2 g sat.); 34 g carbo (5 g fiber); 316 mg sodium; 53 mg chol.

Black Cod

Also known as sablefish or butterfish, black cod is sweet and moist, with fat, pearly white flakes. It's a great substitute for the endangered Chilean seabass, which has a similar mouthfeel. Black cod is abundant in the Pacific Ocean, from California to Alaska, and is usually caught with ocean-friendly traps. Look for fresh or frozen fillets. It should have soft, lustrous flesh and an oceanlike aroma.

Cod with Red Pepper–Chorizo Ragout

Cod and chorizo are a classic pairing in Spain and Portugal. The spicy sausage infuses the mild but meaty fish with warmth, while red peppers add a hint of sweetness.

SERVES 4 | **TIME** 35 minutes

1 tbsp. olive oil
½ lb. fresh Mexican chorizo (about 1 link; *see Quick Tips below*), casing removed
2 large red peppers, seeds and ribs removed and cut into ⅛-in.-wide strips
6 garlic cloves, thinly sliced
½ cup dry white wine
1 can (15 oz.) white beans, such as cannellini or navy, drained and rinsed
½ cup chopped flat-leaf parsley
1 tsp. salt, divided
½ tsp. freshly ground black pepper, divided
3 tbsp. unsalted butter
1½ lbs. skinned, boned Pacific cod fillet, 1 in. thick (*see Quick Tips below*), cut into 4 pieces
½ cup flour

1. Heat oil in a large frying pan over medium-high heat until hot. Add chorizo and cook 2 minutes, stirring occasionally. Add peppers and garlic and cook until peppers are soft, about 5 minutes. Pour in wine, reduce heat to medium, and, using a wooden spoon, scrape any browned bits from bottom of pan.
2. Stir in beans, parsley, and half the salt and pepper. Cook until beans are heated through, about 2 minutes. Transfer ragout to a dish, tent with foil, and set aside.
3. Return pan to medium-high heat and add butter. Season cod with remaining salt and pepper and dredge in flour. Add fish to pan (do not crowd) and cook, turning once, until golden brown and cooked through, about 6 minutes total.
4. Divide ragout among plates and top each with a piece of fish.
Quick Tips: Buy the best-quality chorizo you can find, preferably from a butcher or Mexican market. Avoid the kind that is very soft and sold in plastic casings—it tends to break down too much in cooking. (If you can't find good chorizo, substitute with another spicy uncooked sausage.) Ask your fishmonger for cod from the thickest part of the fish so that the fillets cook evenly. Pacific cod from Alaska is the best choice in terms of sustainability; second best is trawl-caught cod from farther down the coast.

PER SERVING: 686 cal., 47% (324 cal.) from fat; 51 g protein; 36 g fat (14 g sat.); 33 g carbo (5.8 g fiber); 1,604 mg sodium; 146 mg chol.

Chilled Poached Halibut with Fresh Apricot Salsa

recipe pictured on page **313**

If you can find them, use fresh Blenheim apricots for this delicate poached halibut. Blenheims have a rich, tangy-sweet taste and a juicy, melting, deep-orange flesh. They're grown mostly in northern and central California and don't travel well, so farmers' markets there are the best sources. If you use supermarket apricots, mix in a little honey and extra lemon juice (*see Quick Tips below*).

SERVES 4 | **TIME** 30 minutes, plus 30 minutes to chill

2 tbsp. vegetable oil
2 tsp. brown mustard seeds (*see Quick Tips below*)
1 lb. apricots, preferably Blenheim
2 tbsp. fresh lemon juice
½ cup diced red onion, rinsed and drained
¼ cup coarsely chopped cilantro
¼ to ½ red jalapeño, seeds and ribs removed and cut into rings crosswise as thinly as possible, or ¼ to 1 tsp. minced seeded habanero chile
1 tbsp. kosher salt, divided, plus more to taste
½ lemon, thinly sliced
4 skinned, boned halibut fillets, ¾ in. thick (6 oz. each)

1. Put oil and mustard seeds in a skillet, cover, and heat over medium-high heat. The seeds will start popping wildly. When popping sounds die down, remove from heat. Let cool slightly, uncovered.
2. Halve and pit apricots; cut into ½-in. dice. Put diced apricots in a large bowl and toss gently with lemon juice, onion, cilantro, jalapeño, and mustard seeds with oil. Stir in 2 tsp. salt and chill for at least 30 minutes and up to 2 hours.
3. Wipe skillet clean with paper towels and fill half-full with water. Add remaining 1 tsp. salt and the lemon slices. Heat water over medium heat until gently simmering. Add fish and cook, covered, until just opaque in center (cut to check), 5 to 8 minutes.
4. Transfer fish with a spatula to a platter and chill at least 20 minutes. Season with salt to taste and serve cold with apricot salsa.
Quick Tips: Find brown mustard seeds at Middle Eastern, South Asian, and well-stocked grocery stores. If using supermarket apricots, increase lemon juice to 2½ tbsp. and mix it with 1½ tsp. honey before adding to salsa.

PER SERVING: 347 cal., 39% (135 cal.) from fat; 38 g protein; 15 g fat (1.9 g sat.); 15 g carbo (2 g fiber); 586 mg sodium; 54 mg chol.

fish & shellfish

What You Need to Know About Mercury & PCBs

Although fish is, in general, a very healthful food, some varieties contain high levels of mercury and the chemicals known as PCBs, and most kinds contain at least trace amounts.

Mercury

Most fish have at least trace amounts of mercury, a poisonous metal that is released into the environment primarily from industrial sources. When mercury accumulates in waterways, fish ingest it, and it builds up in their tissues. Trace amounts of mercury aren't of concern to most healthy people. But high levels are a health risk for everyone and can be especially harmful to fetuses, infants, and young children, as mercury targets developing nervous systems and kidneys.

You can't trim away or cook out mercury. The Food and Drug Administration, the Environmental Defense Fund, and other organizations advise us to limit mercury by following these guidelines.

• AVOID THE "BIG FOUR" FISH with the highest levels of mercury: king mackerel, shark, swordfish, and tilefish (older tuna also have high levels). Large, long-living, and predatory (they eat other fish that also contain mercury), these fish accumulate more of the toxin.

• EAT LOW-MERCURY FISH AND SHELLFISH. Good choices include catfish, herring, oysters, pollock, salmon, sardines, shrimp, and tilapia.

• CHOOSE SMALL FISH THAT ARE FAR DOWN ON THE FOOD CHAIN. Fish such as sardines and anchovies reproduce quickly and become food for bigger fish, so they don't have a chance to bioaccumulate much mercury.

• BE SMART ABOUT TUNA. Look for troll- or pole-caught fresh or canned albacore. These fishing methods catch younger tuna with lower mercury levels. Limit servings of fresh bluefin or ahi (yellowfin or bigeye) tuna and fresh and canned longline-caught albacore, as these fish contain a lot more mercury. Canned "light" tuna (mainly skipjack) has lower levels of mercury.

PCBs

Polychlorinated biphenyls (PCBs) are industrial chemicals that accumulate in rivers and coastal areas. Fish that live in these areas can build up PCBs in their fatty tissue, and humans who eat those fish can build up PCBs in *their* fatty tissue. The problem? These substances are considered likely human carcinogens. Lab animals exposed to high levels have shown damage to their circulatory, nervous, immune, endocrine, and digestive systems.

Limit your exposure to PCBs by trimming the skin and fat from raw and cooked fish and avoiding fried fish. The Environmental Defense Fund recommends that adults and kids limit their consumption of fish that are higher in PCBs.

In the following list, the portion size is 8 oz. for men, 6 oz. for women, 4.5 oz. for ages 6 to 12, and 3 oz. for ages 6 and under.

BLUEFIN TUNA: Women should avoid eating bluefin tuna entirely; men can eat a half-portion per month.

ENGLISH SOLE: Adults can eat more than four portions per month; three for ages 6 to 12; two for ages 6 and under.

RAINBOW TROUT: Eat no more than three portions per month; two for ages 6 and under.

ROCKFISH: Eat no more than two portions per month; one for ages 12 and under.

SALMON, FARMED (also known as Atlantic salmon): Eat no more than one portion per month; a half-portion for ages 6 and under.

SALMON, WILD (FROM ALASKA): Adults and children 6 and older can eat more than four portions per month; no more than four for ages 6 and under.

SALMON, WILD (FROM WASHINGTON): Eat no more than one portion per month; a half-portion for ages 6 and under.

For more information on mercury and PCBs in seafood, see *edf.org*, *gotmercury.org*, and *fda.gov* (search for "mercury").

Steamed Halibut or Salmon on Soft Tofu with Black Bean Sauce

Fish and pungent black bean–garlic sauce steam atop melt-in-your-mouth tofu in a recipe from Andy Wai, chef at Heaven's Dog restaurant in San Francisco.

SERVES 4 | **TIME** 30 minutes

1 package (18 oz.) water-packed soft tofu (*see Quick Tips, above right*)
1 tbsp. *each* Chinese black bean–garlic sauce (*see Quick Tips, above right*), Shaoxing rice wine or dry sherry, and Asian (toasted) sesame oil
2 tsp. soy sauce
2 tsp. dark soy sauce (*see Quick Tips, above right*); or 1½ tsp. regular soy sauce mixed with ½ tsp. molasses
1 tsp. minced garlic
¼ tsp. sugar
1 lb. skinned, boned halibut or salmon fillet, about ½ in. thick
1 tbsp. slivered fresh ginger
2 green onions, trimmed and cut into 2-in.-long slivers

1. Drain tofu and gently invert onto a thick layer of paper towels on a work surface. Pat dry and let drain about 5 minutes.
2. Meanwhile, make marinade: In a medium bowl, combine black bean–garlic sauce, rice wine, sesame oil, both soy sauces, garlic, and sugar. Set aside.
3. Pour 1 to 3 in. water into bottom of a steamer. Set rack at least 1 in. above surface of water. Cover and bring to a boil over high heat.
4. While water is coming to a boil, cut tofu in half lengthwise, then cut each half crosswise into rectangles about ½ in. thick. Lay tofu in a single layer in a 9- to 10-in. heat-resistant glass pie pan; save any pieces that don't fit for another use.
5. Cut fish into pieces about the same size as tofu. Add fish to reserved marinade and mix to coat. Lay fish on tofu and spoon marinade on top. Sprinkle ginger evenly over fish.
6. Set pie pan on rack. Cover and steam until fish in center is barely opaque in thickest part (cut to test), 6 to 8 minutes (fish will continue to cook after you remove it from heat).
7. Turn off heat. Carefully lift pie pan from steamer. If it's difficult to remove, slip a wide spatula under the pie pan to lift it up, then grasp pie pan with a pot holder (or use two sets of tongs). Sprinkle with green onions.

Quick Tips: Use water-packed soft tofu (sometimes labeled silken) rather than the tofu sold in aseptic packages. Black bean–garlic sauce, made from fermented salted black beans, can be found in many supermarkets and Asian grocery stores, as can Shaoxing rice wine, a cooking wine. Find dark soy sauce, also called black soy sauce, at Asian grocery stores; it's thicker, darker, and sweeter than regular soy sauce.

PER SERVING: 240 cal., 38% (90 cal.) from fat; 30 g protein; 10 g fat (1.3 g sat.); 5.9 g carbo (0.5 g fiber); 780 mg sodium; 36 mg chol.

Seared Halibut on Lemon Tabbouleh

Contributed by reader Deb Wandell, of Piedmont, California, this has become one of our favorite ways to cook good Pacific halibut.

SERVES 4 | **TIME** 40 minutes

1 cup bulgur
1¼ tsp. salt, divided
¼ cup extra-virgin olive oil
2 tsp. finely grated lemon zest
¼ cup fresh lemon juice
½ tsp. plus ⅛ tsp. freshly ground black pepper
1 cup chopped mint leaves (about 1 bunch)
2 cups chopped flat-leaf parsley
6 green onions, trimmed and thinly sliced
½ cup pine nuts, toasted (*see How to Toast Nuts, page 134*)
2 lbs. skinned, boned halibut fillet, cut into 4 pieces
1 tbsp. vegetable oil

1. In a large bowl, stir together bulgur and 1 tsp. salt, then pour 1½ cups boiling water over the mix. Cover and let sit until water is absorbed, 20 to 30 minutes. Fluff with a fork.
2. In a bowl, combine oil, lemon zest and lemon juice, ½ tsp. pepper, the mint, and parsley. Pour dressing over cooked bulgur and stir to coat. Stir in green onions and pine nuts.
3. Sprinkle both sides of halibut with remaining ¼ tsp. salt and ⅛ tsp. pepper. Heat a large frying pan over medium-high heat. Add oil, then halibut. Cook, turning once, until fish is opaque in thickest part (cut to test), about 10 minutes total per inch of thickness.
4. Mound tabbouleh on plates and top with halibut. Serve warm.

PER SERVING: 647 cal., 45% (291 cal.) from fat; 58 g protein; 32 g fat (4.6 g sat.); 36 g carbo (11 g fiber); 880 mg sodium; 73 g chol.

Steamed Halibut Packages

Because halibut is the star of this recipe, make sure that you use the freshest fish available.

SERVES 6 | **TIME** 1 hour

About 2 tbsp. salt, divided
2 bunches Swiss chard *(see Quick Tips below)*,
    stems removed and discarded
1 cup chopped flat-leaf parsley
2 tbsp. chopped thyme leaves
½ cup butter, divided
6 skinned, boned halibut fillets, 1 in. thick
    (6 to 8 oz. each)
Freshly ground black pepper
2 lemons, sliced paper thin *(see Quick Tips below)*
2 tbsp. minced shallot
¼ cup fresh lemon juice

1. Bring a large pot of water to boil and add 1 tbsp. salt. Fill a large bowl with ice and cold water and set aside. Select the 12 largest chard leaves (save remaining chard for another use) and cook in boiling water 1 minute. With tongs or a slotted spoon, transfer chard to ice water.

2. Drain chard and spread leaves out on clean, dry kitchen towels.

3. Arrange one large leaf on your work surface horizontally and arrange a second leaf on top of and perpendicular to the first. Sprinkle some of the parsley and thyme down the center of leaves, then top with 1½ tsp. butter. Generously season halibut with salt and pepper and set 1 fillet on butter and herbs. Arrange 4 lemon slices over top of fillet. Fold chard leaves around fish to enclose. Place packet seam side down in a steamer basket large enough to accommodate all six packets (or use a two-tiered bamboo steamer). Repeat with remaining 5 fillets.

4. Fill a large, high-sided frying pan or a wok with enough water to come ¾ in. up side and bring water to a boil. Add steamer basket and cover. Steam fish until just cooked through, 6 to 8 minutes. Very carefully cut into one packet to check fish for doneness.

5. While fish is steaming, make beurre blanc: Put shallot and lemon juice in a small nonreactive saucepan over medium heat. Cook until liquid is reduced to 1 tbsp. Remove from heat and whisk in remaining 5 tbsp. butter, 1 tbsp. at a time, until emulsified. Season with salt and pepper.

6. Serve fish packets immediately, topped with beurre blanc.

Quick Tips: You'll need two bunches of chard to get enough large leaves to wrap the fish, and a two-tiered bamboo steamer to steam it. It's essential that the lemons be sliced paper thin—a mandoline or very sharp knife works well.

PER SERVING: 396 cal., 45% (180 cal.) from fat; 45 g protein; 20 g fat (10 g sat.); 11 g carbo (4.5 g fiber); 1,728 mg sodium; 105 mg chol

Halibut Baked in Fresh Green Salsa

The creamy, delicately flavored salsa tastes equally good with salmon. Serve with rice.

SERVES 6 | **TIME** 40 minutes

1 tbsp. butter
2 tbsp. flour
¾ cup coarsely chopped tomatillos *(see Quick Tip below)*
½ cup coarsely chopped onion
2 poblano chiles (6 oz. total), seeds and ribs removed
    and coarsely chopped
¼ cup packed coarsely chopped cilantro, plus about
    2 tbsp. whole leaves
½ cup reduced-sodium chicken broth
¾ cup sour cream, divided
Kosher salt
1 to 2 tbsp. fresh lime juice
1 or 2 skinned, boned halibut or salmon fillets, about
    1 in. thick (1¾ lbs. total)

1. Preheat oven to 375°. In a large frying pan, melt butter over high heat. Stir in flour, remove from heat, and mix to form a smooth paste.

2. Scrape flour paste into a blender. Add tomatillos, onion, chiles, chopped cilantro, broth, and ½ cup sour cream. Blend until smooth. Pour salsa into frying pan; add salt and lime juice to taste.

3. Cut fish into six pieces and season with salt. Set pieces, slightly separated, in an 8- by 12-in. baking dish.

4. Bring salsa to a boil over high heat, stirring. Pour evenly over fish. Bake fish until it flakes but still looks moist in center of thickest part (cut to test), 15 to 20 minutes.

5. With a wide spatula, transfer fish to plates. Spoon salsa over portions, top with small spoonfuls of remaining sour cream, and sprinkle with whole cilantro leaves.

Quick Tip: To clean tomatillos, pull off and discard papery husks, rinse fruit well (it will be sticky), and rub dry.

Make Ahead: Salsa, up to 2 days, chilled.

PER SERVING: 255 cal., 39% (99 cal.) from fat; 30 g protein; 11 g fat (5.4 g sat.); 7.6 g carbo (1 g fiber); 157 mg sodium; 60 mg chol.

Mahimahi Fajitas

This sweet and mildly spicy dish from reader Rachael Pashkowski, of Orondo, Washington, makes a great filling for warm flour tortillas.

SERVES 4 to 6 | **TIME** 40 minutes

1 lb. skinned, boned mahimahi fillets
1 tbsp. *each* ground cumin and chili powder
2 tsp. minced garlic
½ tsp. salt, plus more to taste
1 red bell pepper (about ½ lb.)
1 green bell pepper (about ½ lb.)
1 yellow bell pepper (about ½ lb.)
1½ tbsp. vegetable oil, divided
1 onion (about ½ lb.), slivered lengthwise
½ cup mango juice or mango juice blend
2 tbsp. fresh lime juice
8 flour tortillas (8 in. wide), warmed

1. Cut fillets crosswise into 1-in.-wide strips. In a small bowl, mix cumin, chili powder, garlic, and salt. Rub fish all over with spice mixture. Remove seeds and ribs from bell peppers; cut lengthwise into ¼-in.-wide strips.

2. Heat 1 tbsp. oil in a 10- to 12-in. nonstick frying pan over medium-high heat until hot. Add onion and bell peppers and cook, stirring frequently, until softened, 5 to 6 minutes. Transfer to a plate. In same pan, heat remaining ½ tbsp. oil; add fish and cook, turning once, until browned on both sides, about 4 minutes total.

3. Add mango juice and bring to a boil. Cook until fish is opaque but still moist-looking in center of thickest part (cut to test), 2 to 3 more minutes. Add bell pepper mixture and lime juice and stir just until heated through. Season with salt to taste and serve with warm flour tortillas.

PER SERVING: 307 cal., 23% (71 cal.) from fat; 20 g protein; 7.9 g fat (1.1 g sat.); 40 g carbo (4 g fiber); 501 mg sodium; 55 mg chol.

Martini Mahimahi

Meaty mahimahi stands up to the bold brininess of the olives and the piney taste of gin.

SERVES 4 | **TIME** 25 minutes, plus 20 minutes to marinate

½ cup plus 1 tbsp. dry gin
¼ cup plus 1 tbsp. sweet vermouth
1 tbsp. finely shredded lemon zest, plus 2 tbsp. fresh lemon juice
8 garlic cloves, lightly crushed
4 skinned, boned mahimahi fillets (6 oz. each)
Kosher salt and freshly ground black pepper
2 tbsp. olive oil
1½ cups pimiento-stuffed green olives, each halved
¾ cup reduced-sodium chicken broth
2 tbsp. butter

1. Whisk together ½ cup gin, ¼ cup vermouth, lemon zest, and garlic in a small bowl.

2. Season fish with salt and pepper. Put in a 1-gal. resealable plastic bag and add marinade. Seal the bag and marinate at room temperature about 20 minutes (*see Quick Tip below*). Drain, saving garlic, and discard marinade. Blot fish and garlic with paper towels to avoid dripping alcohol near heat.

3. Heat oil in a large nonstick frying pan over medium-high heat until hot. Add fish, garlic, and olives. Cook until fillets are browned on one side, 3 or 4 minutes. Turn over and cook until cooked through but still moist in center, 2 to 3 minutes more. Remove pan from heat and transfer fish to a platter, leaving garlic and olives in pan.

4. Pour in lemon juice and broth and scrape up any browned bits from bottom of pan, then stir in remaining 1 tbsp. each gin and vermouth. Return pan to high heat and boil until liquid is reduced by half, about 3 minutes. Stir in butter to thicken. Pour sauce with olives and garlic over fish.

Quick Tip: Don't marinate for more than the recommended time; otherwise, the alcohol will "cook" the fish.

PER SERVING: 365 cal., 50% (182 cal.) from fat; 33 g protein; 20 g fat (5.5 g sat.); 3 g carbo (1.4 g fiber); 1,541 mg sodium; 140 mg chol.

Switching Fishes

Some of the fish we most enjoy eating are in serious trouble due to overfishing or habitat destruction. To allow them to recover, try these abundant, environmentally friendly alternatives.

IF YOU LIKE...	TRY...
Chilean seabass (firm, buttery)	Black cod (aka sablefish, butterfish)
Red snapper (mild, flaky, versatile)	Farmed striped bass, U.S.-farmed tilapia or rainbow trout
California or Oregon wild salmon (rich, meaty)	Alaska wild salmon, Arctic char
Bluefin tuna (meaty yet clean-tasting)	U.S.-caught bigeye tuna (ahi), Pacific albacore (troll- or pole-caught), U.S.-caught yellowfin tuna (also called ahi)

Striped Bass Fillets on Garlic Toasts with Arugula–White Bean Salad

This dish, from Los Angeles–based food stylist Valerie Aikman-Smith, is substantial but light, with a refreshing, summery salad underneath it. If you'd prefer skinless fillets, by all means use them, but be aware that the delicate edges may break up a bit without the skin there to hold them together.

SERVES 8 | **TIME** 1 hour

8 slices (1 in. thick) crusty bread, such as *pugliese*, **cut on a diagonal**
About ⅔ cup extra-virgin olive oil, divided, plus more for drizzling
¾ tsp. sea salt or kosher salt, plus more for sprinkling
¼ tsp. freshly ground black pepper, plus more for sprinkling
2 garlic cloves, cut in half
2 lemons
1 can (15 oz.) cannellini or other white beans, drained and rinsed
8 skin-on, boned striped bass or Pacific cod fillets (6 to 8 oz. each)
8 cups arugula leaves (about ⅓ lb.)
About 3 cups mixed red and yellow cherry tomatoes, halved
½ cup store-bought black olive tapenade
8 flat-leaf parsley sprigs

1. Preheat broiler. Put bread slices on a large baking sheet; brush both sides with oil, using about 6 tbsp. total, and sprinkle with salt and pepper to taste. Broil bread on both sides until golden and crunchy, about 2 minutes per side. When toasts are cool enough to handle, rub each on one side with garlic halves. Reset oven temperature to 325°.

2. Zest 1 lemon to yield 1 tsp. finely shredded zest, then cut lemon in half and squeeze to yield 2 tsp. juice. Cut other lemon into 8 wedges. In a large bowl, whisk together ¾ tsp. salt, ¼ tsp. pepper, lemon zest, lemon juice, and 2 tbsp. oil. Add beans and toss gently to mix. Set aside.

3. With a very sharp knife, make shallow slashes about 1 in. apart in skin of fillets. Season fillets with salt and pepper. Heat 1 tbsp. oil in a large nonstick frying pan over medium-high heat until hot. Add 4 fillets skin side down, reduce heat to medium, and cook 5 to 6 minutes, pressing often with a spatula to keep them as flat as possible; turn over and cook another 2 minutes. Transfer to a baking sheet and reserve pan juices in a bowl. Wipe pan clean with paper towels and cook remaining fillets the same way, using another 1 tbsp. oil, reserving pan juices, and transferring fillets to baking sheet. Put fish in oven and cook until done, about 8 minutes (cut to check).

4. Add arugula and tomatoes to beans and toss gently but thoroughly. Divide salad among plates.

5. Set toasts on salads, garlicky side up. Top with fillets, skin side up. Drizzle each fillet with a bit of pan juice, then top with 1 tbsp. tapenade, a parsley sprig, and a drizzle of oil. Garnish each plate with a lemon wedge. Drizzle some oil over each.

Make Ahead: Wash arugula the night before and chill, wrapped in a kitchen towel and stored in a resealable plastic bag. Make toasts (grilled instead of broiled if you like) a day ahead and keep in an airtight container. Vinaigrette can be made up to a week ahead and chilled. Fish can be seared (2 to 3 minutes per side in a hot pan) shortly before dinner, then all fillets put in a 350° oven on a baking sheet for about 8 minutes to finish cooking (an easy way to get all 8 servings ready at once).

PER SERVING: 510 cal., 46% (234 cal.) from fat; 46 g protein; 26 g fat (3 g sat.); 20 g carbo (3 g fiber); 916 mg sodium; 73 mg chol.

Salt-baked Striped Bass with Herbed Lemon-Chile Sauce
(Branzino Sotto Sale con Salmoriglio)

Cooking-school teacher Rosetta Costantino, who gives classes in Emeryville, California, makes this dish for Christmas Eve as part of *il cenone* ("the big dinner"). You might expect a whole fish baked in salt to taste salty, but it doesn't. It's exceptionally moist, because the salt crust allows the fish to cook in its own juice without any escaping.

SERVES 4 (recipe can easily be doubled) | **TIME** 1½ hours

2 whole striped bass (about 3 lbs. each; *see Quick Tips, right*), cleaned and scaled, with fins trimmed and tails trimmed to 1 in.

6 to 8 thyme sprigs

6 to 8 oregano sprigs, plus 1½ tbsp. finely chopped leaves

6 to 8 flat-leaf parsley sprigs, plus 1½ tbsp. finely chopped leaves

1 lemon, thinly sliced

4 medium garlic cloves, sliced, plus 1 large clove, minced

¾ cup plus 1½ tbsp. extra-virgin olive oil

6 lbs. plus 2 tsp. Diamond Crystal kosher salt (*see Quick Tips, right*)

8 egg whites

½ cup fresh lemon juice

2 small fresh or dried hot red chiles, such as peperoncini or Thai, stemmed and minced or sliced

1. Preheat oven to 425°. Set rack in middle of oven. Stuff cavity of each fish with thyme, oregano, and parsley sprigs and slices of lemon and garlic, dividing evenly. Coat fish with 1½ tbsp. oil.

2. In a very large bowl, combine 6 lbs. salt with the egg whites and 2 cups water. Mix with your hands, then add another 2 cups water, mixing, until salt feels like moist sand (you may need a little more water).

3. Line a large rimmed baking sheet with ½ in. of salt mixture. Arrange the 2 fish nose to tail on salt, leaving at least 1½ in. between them. Cover each with an even ½-in. layer of salt mixture, patting to adhere (no part of fish should remain exposed) and leaving a crevice between fish so they cook evenly. Bake until salt crust is very pale gold and hard to the touch, like ceramic, about 30 minutes.

4. Meanwhile, make sauce: Whisk together the remaining ¾ cup oil, the minced garlic, chopped oregano and parsley, the remaining 2 tsp. salt, the lemon juice, and chiles in a bowl. Set aside for at least 30 minutes to allow flavors to marry (but not more than 2 hours or herbs will lose their fresh taste).

5. Working with 1 fish at a time, tap hard salt crust with a small hammer or meat mallet to crack it. Lift off chunks of crust and brush any remaining salt off fish (a pastry brush is useful here).

6. With a large fork, carefully peel back skin, starting at spine and working toward belly. Lift off chunks of meat with fork and transfer to a platter. Lift out skeleton with head attached and discard. With fork, transfer rest of meat to platter.

7. Repeat dismantling of salt crust and filleting with remaining fish, adding meat to platter. Serve with sauce spooned over top and more served on the side.

Quick Tips: Order the bass from your fishmonger a few days ahead, since 3 lbs. is a bit bigger than average. Smaller fish (at least 2 lbs. each) are fine, but you may need to buy an extra one to make sure there's enough to go around. Also, not all kosher salts are created equal; we like flaky Diamond Crystal, which is more voluminous than other kosher salts and therefore covers the fish better. If you're using another brand, you may need as little as half the amount of water called for here.

PER HALF-FILLET WITH 1 TBSP. SAUCE: 231 cal., 55% (126 cal.) from fat; 25 g protein; 14 g fat (2.2 g sat.); 2 g carbo (0.2 g fiber); 776 mg sodium; 54 mg chol.

Signs of a Smart Fish Shop

Some seafood purveyors care not only about the quality of their fish but about conservation too. You'll know you're in such a place if you find at least a couple of the following:

• **A VARIETY OF SUSTAINABLE SEAFOOD CHOICES** (such as the fish in this chapter or those listed as Best Choices by the Monterey Bay Aquarium's Seafood Watch program (*seafoodwatch.org*)—and few, if any, endangered fish (the Seafood Watch program lists those too).

• **PEOPLE BEHIND THE COUNTER WHO CAN ANSWER ALL YOUR QUESTIONS**—especially about how fish were caught (and the environmental effects of those practices) and how they were processed afterward.

• **A LABEL ON EACH FISH** listing whether it's farmed or wild, how it was caught (e.g., pole- or troll-caught), and where it was caught (country-of-origin labels are now a U.S. requirement).

• **BROCHURES ON THE COUNTER** from sustainable seafood suppliers and organizations.

Braised Striped Bass with Ginger, Shiitake Mushrooms, and Chiles

Peruvian food is laced with Asian ingredients, the legacy of Chinese and Japanese laborers who came to Peru to work the plantations, mines, and railroads in the late 19th and early 20th centuries. The Peruvian restaurant Andina in Portland, Oregon, prepares this delicate, simple dish with mahimahi or halibut, but it can be made with any firm, white-fleshed fish.

SERVES 4 | **TIME** 30 minutes

4 skinned, boned striped bass fillets, preferably farm-raised (6 to 8 oz. each; *see Quick Tip below*)
Salt and freshly ground black pepper
1 tbsp. vegetable oil
4 cups vegetable broth
2 heads baby bok choy, ends trimmed and leaves separated
12 shiitake mushrooms, stems removed
2 tbsp. soy sauce
2 tsp. *each* minced fresh ginger, thinly sliced green onion, thinly sliced red jalapeño chile, and Asian (toasted) sesame oil

1. Season fillets with salt and pepper. Heat a frying pan over medium-high heat; add vegetable oil, then fillets. Cook until fillets start to brown on one side, about 2 minutes. Flip fillets and reduce heat to medium. Add broth, bok choy leaves, mushrooms, soy sauce, and ginger. Cover and cook until fish is opaque in center, about 3 minutes.
2. Divide the fish, mushrooms, and bok choy among deep, wide soup plates, then add the broth (depending on size of your plates, you may have some left over). Garnish with green onion and jalapeño and drizzle with sesame oil.
Quick Tip: Wild-caught striped bass populations are healthy but tend to have high levels of PCBs and mercury. Farm-raised striped bass do not.

PER SERVING: 246 cal., 28% (68 cal.) from fat; 35 g protein; 7.6 g fat (1.2 g sat.); 7.2 g carbo (1.2 g fiber); 1,600 mg sodium; 63 mg chol.

Pan-fried Sardines with Caramelized Onions, Pine Nuts, and Raisins

This recipe, based on the classic Sicilian *sardoni en saor* (marinated fried sardines), is a great introduction to sardines. The vinegar adds a mouthwatering acidity that balances the oiliness of the fish, the nuts provide crunch, and the raisins and onions contribute sweetness.

SERVES 4 to 6 | **TIME** 50 minutes, plus 1 hour to marinate

2 medium yellow onions
1 cup red wine vinegar
⅓ cup golden raisins
2 lbs. sardines, cleaned and filleted (*see Quick Tip below*), with heads removed
⅓ cup flour
⅓ cup olive oil, divided
1 tsp. kosher salt, divided
⅓ cup pine nuts, toasted (*see How to Toast Nuts, page 134*)
3 tbsp. coarsely chopped flat-leaf parsley

1. Cut onions lengthwise and slice into thin half-moons. Put vinegar in a measuring cup and add raisins.
2. Rinse sardines well inside and out, dry with paper towels, and roll in flour, shaking off excess.
3. Heat 3 tbsp. oil in a large frying pan over medium heat until hot. Fry sardines in two batches, 1½ minutes per side. Transfer to a large shallow serving dish or platter and sprinkle with ½ tsp. salt.
4. Wipe out pan with paper towels, return to heat, and add remaining 7 tsp. oil. When oil is hot, add onions and remaining ½ tsp. salt. Cook, stirring often, until onions are very soft and browned, about 20 minutes.
5. Add vinegar and raisins and cook, stirring, 10 minutes.
6. Pour onion mixture over sardines and sprinkle with pine nuts. Cover with plastic wrap and let marinate at least 1 hour at room temperature. Serve at room temperature, sprinkled with parsley. Eat by gently pushing fish off the bone with your fork.
Quick Tip: Order the prepared sardines from your fishmonger, or fillet them yourself (*see steps 1 through 3 in How to Clean and Fillet Sardines, page 191*).
Make Ahead: Up to 4 days, chilled.

PER SERVING: 505 cal., 56% (281 cal.) from fat; 35 g protein; 31 g fat (5.7 g sat.); 19 g carbo (4.4 g fiber); 1,596 mg sodium; 112 mg chol.

Green Onion and Sesame Parchment-baked Sole

Cooking in parchment seals in aromas and moisture as the food cooks, creating maximum flavor with minimal use of oil or fat—and it's fast, too. The technique is particularly good for cooking fish, since it protects the delicate flesh from direct heat and ensures even, gentle cooking. The natural juices of the fish and any vegetables do the work, simply by creating steam. Flavor combinations with fish are practically endless: herbs, flavored oils, fresh lemon juice or wine, and thinly sliced vegetables can be substituted or added as you like.

SERVES 4 | **TIME** 25 minutes

4 skinned, boned sole fillets, such as petrale or Rex
¼ tsp. salt
½ tsp. finely shredded fresh ginger (use a razor-sharp grater, such as a Microplane, or the fine holes on a box grater)
2 tsp. Asian (toasted) sesame oil
3 green onions, trimmed, cut into 3-in. lengths, and sliced thinly lengthwise

1. Preheat oven to 350°. Fold 4 pieces of parchment paper (12 by 14 in. each) in half to form 7- by 12-in. rectangles, then cut them into half-heart shapes as large as the paper allows. Unfold into hearts. Place a fish fillet to one side of center of each heart and sprinkle with a quarter of the salt. Spread each fillet with a quarter of the ginger. Drizzle with a quarter of the sesame oil and top with a quarter of the green onions. Fold papers over fillets and crimp edges to close (*see How to Make a Parchment Packet, above right*).
2. Put packets on a baking sheet and bake until fish is opaque and flakes easily in center, about 15 minutes (cut one packet open to check); if necessary, cook 5 minutes more.

PER SERVING: 179 cal., 22% (39 cal.) from fat; 32 g protein; 4.3 g fat (0.8 g sat.); 1 g carbo (0.3 g fiber); 283 mg sodium; 82 mg chol.

How to Make a Parchment Packet

Start with a piece of parchment paper about two and a half times the size of the food you'll be cooking. Fold the paper in half and cut it into a half-heart shape. Unfold, place the ingredients on one side, then fold over the other half to enclose.

Beginning at the top of the heart in the center of the dip, fold over about ¼ in. of the edge, then fold again. Continue to double-fold all around the edge. When you reach the bottom tip of the heart, twist the paper to seal.

You can use aluminum foil instead (simply fold it over the contents and crimp the edges to seal), but parchment makes an elegant presentation and can even puff up while cooking. In either parchment or foil, thin fillets like sole cook in 15 minutes. For thicker cuts, add 5 minutes for every ½ in. of thickness over ¾ in.

Almond-crusted Sole

This is a lot like fried fish sticks, only better.

SERVES 4 | **TIME** 20 minutes

4 skinned, boned sole fillets, such as petrale or Rex, (6 oz. each)
About ½ tsp. *each* kosher salt and freshly ground black pepper
3 tsp. olive oil, divided
Lemon wedges
½ cup *each* panko (Japanese-style bread crumbs) and finely grated parmesan cheese
⅓ cup slivered almonds
2 tbsp. minced flat-leaf parsley
1 tsp. finely shredded lemon zest

1. Preheat oven to 475°. Sprinkle both sides of fillets with ½ tsp. each salt and pepper, then set on a baking sheet lined with foil. Brush tops of fillets with 2 tsp. oil and squeeze a little lemon on top.
2. Combine panko, parmesan, almonds, parsley, lemon zest, remaining 1 tsp. oil, and a pinch each of salt and pepper. Evenly cover fillets with almond mixture. Bake on upper rack until fish is opaque in thickest part (cut to test), 6 to 8 minutes. Serve with more lemon.

PER SERVING: 325 cal., 39% (126 cal.) from fat; 39 g protein; 14 g fat (3.4 g sat.); 8 g carbo (1 g fiber); 492 mg sodium; 90 mg chol.

fish & shellfish

Chilled Poached Halibut
with Fresh Apricot Salsa,
page 304

Tilapia with Quinoa and
Black Beans, *page 326*

Grandmother's Chicken,
page 358

California Rolls, *page 337*

Spicy Mango Shrimp,
page 346

King Crab with Lemongrass-Ginger
Butter and Roasted Potatoes,
page 339

Chicken with Tomatoes,
Apricots, and Chickpeas,
page 361

Roast Chicken with
Meyer Lemon–Shallot
Sauce, *page 355*

Cracked Crab with Herbed
Avocado Sauce, *page 339*

Chicken Cashew Korma,
page 364

Oven-baked Salmon with Picholine Olive Sauce, *page 331*

Biscuit-topped Chicken
Potpies, *page 365*

Oven-browned Sole with Asparagus

Many kinds of delicious sole swim off the Pacific coast. Petrale sole, Rex sole, and sand dabs are the best known, but Western waters are also home to English sole, Dover sole, and starry flounder (all flatfish, including sole, are actually flounders). Our recipe works with any of them.

SERVES 4 | **TIME** 15 minutes

1½ lbs. asparagus (½ in. thick)
¼ cup flour
½ tsp. *each* salt and freshly ground black pepper
1 lb. skinned, boned sole fillets, such as petrale or Rex, ¼ in. thick
¼ cup butter, divided
1 cup dry white wine
3½ tbsp. coarsely chopped tarragon, divided

1. Preheat oven to 500°. Snap off and discard tough stem ends from asparagus.
2. In a plastic bag, combine flour, salt, and pepper. Shake 1 or 2 pieces of fish at a time in flour mixture to coat, shaking off excess as you lift fish from bag. Discard leftover flour mixture.
3. Put 1 tbsp. butter in a 10- by 15-in. baking pan and 2 tbsp. butter in another 10- by 15-in. pan. Set pans in oven until butter is melted, 1 to 2 minutes. Put asparagus in pan with smaller amount of butter; turn to coat spears. Put fish in remaining pan; turn to coat in butter and arrange in a single layer. Return pans to oven and roast until asparagus is tender-crisp to the bite and fish is opaque but still moist-looking in center of thickest part (cut to test), 4 to 5 minutes.
4. Transfer asparagus and fish to a platter and keep warm.
5. Pour wine into fish-roasting pan and add 3 tbsp. tarragon. Set pan over two burners on high heat and bring to a boil. Boil, stirring, until wine is reduced to ⅓ cup, about 2 minutes. Remove from heat and stir in remaining 1 tbsp. butter. Pour sauce into a bowl.
6. Scatter remaining ½ tbsp. tarragon over fish. Serve fish and asparagus with sauce on the side.

PER SERVING: 273 cal., 46% (126 cal.) from fat; 27 g protein; 14 g fat (7.8 g sat.); 12 g carbo (1.6 g fiber); 510 mg sodium; 87 mg chol.

3 Ways with Sand Dabs

The sand dab is a small flatfish found along the Pacific's sandy seafloor from Alaska to Baja California. It's sweet, light, and delicate, typically yielding thin fillets 4 to 5 in. long. You don't need to do much to it to have a fantastic meal. (The following cooking methods, by the way, also work for petrale and Rex sole.)

1. Bake in Parchment
Cut and fold parchment paper (or foil) for each fillet as instructed in *How to Make a Parchment Packet* (*page 312*). Top fillets with a dot or two of **butter**, very thinly sliced **mushrooms** (oyster mushrooms are delicious with sand dabs), chopped **parsley, salt and pepper**, and 1 tbsp. or so of **white wine**. Fold and crimp packets shut, put packets on a baking sheet, and bake at 350° until fish is opaque and flakes easily in center, about 15 minutes.

2. Broil
Brush the fillets liberally with melted **butter**, then broil 4 in. from heat until they just flake in the center, about 3 minutes.

3. Pan-fry
Dust fillets with **flour** (seasoned first with **salt** and freshly ground **black pepper**), then pan-fry them 2 minutes in a mixture of **butter** and **oil**, turning once. Serve with a mixture of melted butter, **fresh lemon juice**, and minced **flat-leaf parsley**.

Tilapia with Quinoa and Black Beans

This delicious combination of crispy fried fish, nutty quinoa, and black beans comes from reader Sal D'Amato, of San Carlos, California.

recipe pictured on page 314

SERVES 4 | **TIME** 30 minutes

1 cup quinoa, rinsed
3 tbsp. olive oil, divided
1 cup canned black beans, drained and rinsed
1 cup *each* chopped tomatoes and thinly sliced zucchini
2 tbsp. fresh lemon juice
1 tsp. paprika
4 skinned, boned tilapia fillets (about 1 lb. total)
Kosher salt and freshly ground black pepper
⅓ cup sliced green onions

1. Cook quinoa as package directs.
2. Meanwhile, heat 1 tbsp. oil in a saucepan over medium heat. Add beans, tomatoes, zucchini, lemon juice, and paprika and cook, stirring occasionally, until warm, about 5 minutes. Season vegetable mixture and fish with salt and pepper.
3. Heat remaining 2 tbsp. oil in a large frying pan over medium-high heat. Add fish and cook until browned underneath, 6 to 7 minutes; turn and cook until center just flakes, about 2 minutes more (test with a knife).
4. Serve fish with quinoa and vegetable mixture, sprinkled with green onions.

PER SERVING: 407 cal., 31% (126 cal.) from fat; 31 g protein; 14 g fat (2.2 g sat.); 41 g carbo (5.6 g fiber); 186 mg sodim; 55 mg chol.

Tilapia

Though tilapia is native to North Africa, this firm-textured, white-fleshed fish is now farm-raised all over the world. A lot of farmed tilapia comes from China and Taiwan, where, unfortunately, farms are major polluters. Central American tilapia is less problematic, but the most environmentally friendly tilapia farms are in the U.S.; ask at your fish shop about the source of the tilapia it sells.

Tilapia with Tomatoes and Garbanzos

Because tilapia is so mild-tasting, it works best with bold-flavored accompaniments like the ones in this dish.

SERVES 4 | **TIME** 45 minutes

1 tbsp. olive oil
½ cup slivered onion
1 head fennel (about 1 lb.), base and stalks trimmed, halved lengthwise, cored, and thinly sliced
1 can (14.5 oz.) crushed or diced tomatoes
1 can (15.5 oz.) chickpeas (garbanzos), drained and rinsed
1 tbsp. minced preserved lemon *(see Quick Tip below)*
¼ cup pitted oil-cured or other black olives
1½ tsp. ground cumin
½ tsp. *each* turmeric, paprika, salt, and freshly ground black pepper
4 skinned, boned tilapia fillets (about 1 lb. total)
1½ cups couscous
3 tbsp. chopped flat-leaf parsley

1. In a 10- to 12-in. frying pan (with sides at least 2 in. high), heat oil over medium-high heat until hot. Add onion and fennel and cook, stirring often, until softened, about 8 minutes.
2. Stir in tomatoes (with their juice), chickpeas, preserved lemon, olives, cumin, turmeric, paprika, salt, and pepper. Bring to a simmer. Lay fish over vegetables; cover and cook, turning fish once, until fish is opaque but still moist-looking in center of thickest part (cut to test), about 10 minutes.
3. Meanwhile, in a 2- to 3-qt. pan over high heat, bring 2 cups water to a boil. Stir in couscous, cover pan, and remove from heat. Let stand until water is absorbed and couscous is tender to the bite, about 5 minutes.
4. Fluff couscous with a fork and divide among wide bowls. Spoon fish and vegetables over couscous. Sprinkle with parsley.

Quick Tip: Preserved lemon is a salty, tangy condiment available in some well-stocked supermarkets and in stores that carry Middle Eastern ingredients. If you can't find it, substitute 1 tbsp. finely shredded lemon zest and an extra ¼ tsp. salt.

PER SERVING: 569 cal., 19% (108 cal.) from fat; 36 g protein; 12 g fat (1 g sat.); 79 g carbo (9.4 g fiber); 1,129 mg sodium; 57 mg chol.

Pan-fried Trout with Smoked Salmon

Janie Hibler, author of several cookbooks about Northwest food, invented this dish about 25 years ago while at her family's cabin in Washington's Cascade Range. The combination came about when she had smoked salmon in the fridge and her kids brought in fresh trout they'd caught at Swift Creek Reservoir.

SERVES 8 | **TIME** 40 minutes

8 whole trout (4½ lbs. total), cleaned and boned, at room temperature
1 tsp. kosher salt, divided, plus more to taste
8 thin slices smoked salmon (4 to 5 oz. total; *see Quick Tips below*)
½ cup cornmeal
5 to 7 tbsp. extra-virgin olive oil, divided
1 lb. (2 pts.) mini multicolored bell peppers, seeds and ribs removed and cut in half lengthwise (*see Quick Tips below*)
2 limes, cut into wedges

1. Preheat oven to 150°. Sprinkle inside of each trout with a little salt (use about ½ tsp. total). Stuff each with a single slice of smoked salmon. In a large, shallow dish, combine cornmeal and remaining ½ tsp. salt. Turn fish in cornmeal to coat evenly.

2. Pour 2 tbsp. oil into each of two 12-in. frying pans, preferably nonstick, and warm them over medium heat. (Or warm a large griddle over two burners.) Put 3 fish in each pan and cook, turning once, until golden brown outside and no longer translucent in the center, 8 to 9 minutes total; reduce heat if fish start to get too brown. Transfer fish to one or two large platters and keep warm in oven. Repeat cooking in one pan with 1 to 2 more tbsp. oil and remaining fish.

3. If pan (or griddle) is dry, add 1 more tbsp. oil. Set pan over medium-high heat and quickly cook peppers, stirring, until they're softened and lightly browned, about 5 minutes. Sprinkle with salt to taste and scatter on top of fish. Serve with lime wedges.

Quick Tips: Use soft, cold-smoked salmon, also called Nova-style salmon or Nova lox. Find mini bell peppers at Trader Joe's or farmers' markets, or use 1 lb. regular-size bell peppers, seeds and ribs removed and quartered.

PER SERVING: 290 cal., 53% (153 cal.) from fat; 23 g protein; 17 g fat (2.7 g sat.); 11 g carbo (1.2 g fiber); 512 mg sodium; 55 mg chol.

Fennel-crusted Trout with Lemon-Ginger Vinaigrette

This dish was inspired by one from San Francisco chef Harveen Khera, owner of the now-closed Tallula restaurant.

SERVES 4 | **TIME** 45 minutes

½ cup finely chopped fennel bulb
3 tbsp. white wine vinegar
1 tbsp. *each* minced shallot and grated fresh ginger
1 tsp. finely shredded lemon zest
½ tsp. salt, plus more for sprinkling
½ cup plus ½ tsp. olive oil, plus more for brushing
½ cup golden raisins
4 boned trout fillets (4 to 6 oz. each; *see Quick Tip below*)
2 tbsp. fennel seeds

1. In a bowl, mix fennel, vinegar, shallot, ginger, lemon zest, and salt. Whisk in ½ cup oil until combined, then stir in raisins.

2. Brush both sides of trout with oil, then sprinkle with salt and fennel seeds. Set a 12- to 14-in. nonstick frying pan over medium-high heat. Pour in remaining ½ tsp. oil, then wipe pan with a paper towel. Set fillets skin side down in pan. Cook, turning once with a spatula, until surface is lightly golden and fish is opaque in thickest part (cut to test), 5 to 6 minutes.

3. Transfer each fillet to a plate. Whisk vinaigrette to combine, then spoon over fillets.

Quick Tip: Trout may be sold whole; ask for boned, trimmed fillets.

PER SERVING: 479 cal., 66% (315 cal.) from fat; 25 g protein; 35 g fat (5 g sat.); 18 g carbo (2.5 g fiber); 359 mg sodium; 66 mg chol.

Farmed Rainbow Trout

Rainbow trout raised in tanks, ponds, and "raceways" (fast-moving channeled river water) not open to the sea are a good choice at the fish counter. These fish farms don't pollute or spread disease into the ocean. And because the fish feed on grain mixed into fishmeal, they don't deplete wild fish populations as much as larger fish do. Most of the farmed rainbow trout in this country come from farms along Idaho's crystalline, fast-moving Snake River.

Rainbow trout are generally sold fresh and whole, either bone-in or boned and butterflied. Look for fish with moist flesh, shiny skin and eyes, and a fresh, mild aroma.

Canned Fish Basics

What's the best fish to buy canned?

Wild salmon and pole- or troll-caught albacore tuna, both harvested and canned in the West. Most sardines and oysters are canned and imported from overseas and not subject to U.S. scrutiny.

Any advantages to canned?

It's cheaper than fresh; and with salmon, the soft and edible bones are included, boosting calcium content.

What to look for on a label

• **COUNTRY OF ORIGIN:** Where the seafood was caught or harvested. The United States is the best choice, because U.S. rules are relatively rigorous.

• **METHOD OF CATCH:** With tuna, look for poll- or troll-caught. All wild salmon–catching methods are considered acceptable and usually aren't listed.

• **DOLPHIN- AND TURTLE-SAFE:** This means that the catch method caused minimal harm to other sea animals. Longlines (which can snag other creatures) are not used.

• **MSC LOGO:** The Marine Stewardship Council (MSC) is an international certification program for sustainable fishing and seafood traceability. Products bearing the logo meet the toughest standards for the responsible catch of wild fish.

Roasted Salmon with Dill-Yogurt Sauce

This is a classic combination of flavors from reader Carolyn Larsen, of Kennewick, Washington. It's good served either hot or chilled.

SERVES 4 | **TIME** 25 minutes

½ **English cucumber, finely shredded and excess water squeezed out**
½ **cup** *each* **sour cream and plain yogurt**
2 **tsp. chopped dill, plus dill sprigs for garnish (optional)**
2 **garlic cloves, minced, divided**
2 **tbsp. fresh lemon juice, divided**
Salt and freshly ground black pepper
1½ **lbs. skin-on, boned salmon fillet, 1 in. thick**

1. Preheat oven to 350°. In a small bowl, stir together cucumber, sour cream, yogurt, chopped dill, half the minced garlic, 1 tbsp. lemon juice, and salt and pepper to taste. Set aside.
2. Line a baking pan with foil. Put salmon in pan, skin side down. Sprinkle with remaining garlic and 1 tbsp. lemon juice, and salt and pepper to taste. Bake until barely opaque in the center (cut to test), 10 to 15 minutes.
3. Serve salmon warm or cold with yogurt sauce. Garnish with dill sprigs if using.

PER SERVING: 381 cal., 57% (216 cal.) from fat; 35 g protein; 24 g fat (7.5 g sat.); 5.5 g carbo (0.7 g fiber); 131 mg sodium; 108 mg chol.

Curried Salmon Cakes with Lemon-Curry Aioli

Reader Erin Winemiller, of Portland, Oregon, created these cakes using sterile, shelf-stable pouches of boned, skinned salmon, but you can also use canned salmon if the pouches aren't available in your area.

SERVES 4 | **TIME** 25 minutes

½ **cup plus 2 tbsp. mayonnaise**
3 **tsp. curry powder, divided**
1 **tsp. finely shredded lemon zest plus 1 tbsp. fresh lemon juice**
1 **tsp. paprika, divided**
Salt
2 **eggs**
2 **pouches (about 7 oz. each) boned, skinned pink salmon, or 1 can (15 oz.) red or pink salmon, drained and skin removed**
½ **cup finely chopped apple**
¼ **cup** *each* **fine dried bread crumbs and thinly sliced green onions**
¼ **tsp. freshly ground black pepper**
1 **tbsp. vegetable oil**

1. In a small bowl, mix ½ cup mayonnaise, 2 tsp. curry powder, the lemon zest and juice, ½ tsp. paprika, and salt to taste. Set the aioli aside.
2. In a medium bowl, beat eggs with a fork. Add salmon and break up. Stir in apple, bread crumbs, green onions, the remaining 2 tbsp. mayonnaise, 1 tsp. curry powder, and ½ tsp. paprika and pepper. Shape into four cakes, each ¾ in. thick, and place on a piece of plastic wrap.
3. Set a 12-in. nonstick frying pan over medium heat. When hot, add oil, then salmon cakes. Cook until well browned on the bottom, 5 to 7 minutes. Turn cakes over and cook until browned on the other side, 3 to 5 minutes longer.
4. Serve cakes with aioli.

PER SERVING: 463 cal., 70% (324 cal.) from fat; 29 g protein; 36 g fat (5.3 g sat.); 10 g carbo (1.3 g fiber); 603 mg sodium; 170 mg chol.

Indian-spiced Salmon

This spicy-sweet glaze will shake you right out of your salmon cooking rut.

SERVES 4 | **TIME** 45 minutes

4 pieces skin-on, boned salmon fillet, about 1 in. thick
   (6 oz. each)
2 sweet onions such as Maui or Walla Walla (1 lb. total),
   slivered
2 tbsp. butter, melted
3 tbsp. firmly packed brown sugar
2 tsp. ground coriander
1 tsp. ground fennel seeds (see *Quick Tip, right*)
½ to ¾ tsp. cayenne
½ tsp. *each* ground cardamom, ground cumin, and salt
¼ tsp. *each* freshly ground black pepper, ground cloves,
   and cinnamon
1 tbsp. fresh lemon juice
2 tbsp. chopped cilantro
Lemon wedges

1. Preheat oven to 400°. Line a 12- by 18-in. baking pan with foil and set salmon pieces, skin side down, 1 in. apart in pan. Scatter onions around salmon.
2. In a small bowl, stir together butter, brown sugar, coriander, ground fennel, cayenne, cardamom, cumin, salt, pepper, cloves, and cinnamon. Stir in lemon juice. Brush mixture evenly over tops and sides of salmon pieces.
3. Bake salmon 5 minutes. Increase oven heat to broil; broil salmon 6 in. from heat until top is bubbling and well browned and fish is opaque but still moist-looking in center of thickest part (cut to test), 4 to 6 minutes.
4. With a spatula, transfer salmon pieces to a serving dish (leave skin behind) and surround with onions. Sprinkle with cilantro and garnish with lemon wedges.
Quick Tip: Grind fennel seeds in a clean coffee grinder or crush in a mortar.

PER SERVING: 418 cal., 50% (207 cal.) from fat; 32 g protein; 23 g fat (6.9 g sat.); 21 g carbo (1.9 g fiber); 456 mg sodium; 106 mg chol.

Wild Salmon vs. Farmed: Which to Eat?

Ever since the last Ice Age, adult salmon have left the ocean and battled their way up Western rivers—in some cases traveling more than a thousand miles—to spawn and die where they were born. It is an annual rite that has sustained bears, bald eagles, and other wildlife that feed on the returning salmon. And salmon have nourished many Native American tribes for countless generations—as food, as artistic inspiration, and as a religious symbol. The salmon is as much an icon of the West as the grizzly bear.

The Waning of Wild Salmon
It wasn't all that long ago that these fish were also the mainstay of a thriving fishing industry. Today, however, runs of wild salmon are fast disappearing from rivers in Washington, Oregon, and California. Overfishing, dams, development, pollution, and water diversions have all taken their toll. Alaska is the one remaining Western fishery that is still well managed, and its salmon populations are relatively healthy and abundant.

The Rise of the Farmed Fish
Most of the salmon we eat now in the United States is farmed (raised in open-net ocean pens)—as much as 90 percent by some estimates, the attraction being that it's so much cheaper than wild salmon.

   You'd think that farmed fish would provide an ecologically sound alternative, but in general that's not the case. Many salmon-farming practices pollute the ocean and endanger wild fish (when farmed fish escape, they can pass along diseases and parasites). And because salmon are carnivorous, farming them actually requires more pounds of smaller fish as feed than the poundage of salmon produced by the feeding—which isn't exactly efficient from a sustainability standpoint.

How It Shakes Out
For now, we think wild salmon is the best choice. The good news is that salmon-farming techniques are constantly being improved, and new land-based, closed-containment facilities may reduce some of the biggest problems with farmed salmon.

Wines for Fish

The dishes in this chapter are an invitation to revel in the enormous range of exciting white wines the West is producing now. Consider buttery Chardonnay to be only a starting point (and check out alternative styles of Chardonnay with less oak and less butter).

fish & shellfish

Sauvignon Blanc—crisp, herbal, and citrusy—has made great strides. Riesling, once considered a syrupy starter drink in this country (even though the rest of the wine world considers it one of the noblest white grapes of all) is now being made in drier styles with more complex aromatic stone fruit and minerality. Chenin Blanc, which had a slightly tarnished early reputation of its own, has shaped up, with lively tree fruit and bright citrus profiles. Pinot Gris—with herbs and minerals balancing delicate melon and stone fruit and grapefruit—has caught on (Pinot Grigio is the same grape). And the Rhône grape Viognier, rich and flamboyantly redolent of peach and honeysuckle, has entered the ranks of the West's great whites.

Some Pointers for Picking the Right Bottle

1. MATCH THE WINE TO THE MEATINESS OF YOUR FISH. With delicate sole, pour a lean, crisp white like Sauvignon Blanc (an especially great choice for the Oven-browned Sole with Asparagus, *page 325*, since its grassy, herbal side is emphasized by the tarragon and asparagus in the dish). With slightly fleshier seafood— striped bass, say—consider Pinot Gris (brilliant with the earthy but aromatic Braised Striped Bass with Ginger, Shiitake Mushrooms, and Chiles, *page 311*). And with very meaty and/or fatty species (halibut, black cod, and

salmon), go for the rich wine spectrum: Viognier and Chardonnay. A note about Riesling: Although it's generally zippy with acidity, don't be fooled into thinking it's a lightweight— the wine has a big (some say "oily") mouth-feel at the same time and can take on the meatiest of fish.

2. MATCH SEASONINGS AND SAUCES. No matter what the fish in the middle of the plate, if it's piled with green vegetables and herbs or sauced with citrus, you need an herbal, high-acid wine. (Principle: If your food has more acid in it than your wine, it will destroy the wine.) If aromatics set the personality of the dish—ginger in an Asian curry, say, or with a sushi roll—look to highly aromatic Riesling (our favorite with Pan-roasted Black Cod with Thai Curry Sauce, *page 303*, and the California Rolls, *page 337*). And the spicier the sauce, the sweeter the Riesling needs to be. Throw rich coconut milk into the picture, and you're in Viognier territory.

3. A NOTE ABOUT CRAB: There's no more quintessential California pairing than cracked Dungeness crab with drawn butter and buttery Chardonnay. But other whites are great with crab too, depending on what else is in the dish. It's Sauv Blanc's turn if the crab dish involves lemongrass and citrus; try Chenin Blanc or Pinot Gris should there be a lemony aioli, or a dry Riesling if there's avocado dip (*page 339*).

4. DON'T FORGET BUBBLES! Any dish in this chapter would taste great with a sparkling wine.

5. DON'T LIMIT YOURSELF TO WHITE. There's plenty of red territory here too: Meatier and more pungent fish—salmon and tuna, for example— go well with lighter-bodied reds like Pinot Noir, Grenache, and even Merlot, with its rounded-off tannins.

Oven-baked Salmon with Picholine Olive Sauce

Chefs Caprial and John Pence, of Portland, Oregon, gave us their recipe for salmon with a rich, delicious sauce. For the best flavor, prepare it with wild salmon.

recipe pictured on page **323**

SERVES 6 | **TIME** 45 minutes

2 garlic cloves, chopped
1 shallot, chopped
1 cup dry vermouth
½ cup chicken broth or fish stock
1 cup whipping cream
⅓ cup chopped pitted picholine olives (or other mild green olives; see *Quick Tip below*)
2 tsp. chopped thyme leaves, plus thyme sprigs for garnish
Salt and freshly ground black pepper
1 skinned, boned salmon fillet (3 lbs.)
1 tbsp. butter, cut into small pieces
½ cup dry white wine
1 tbsp. chopped tarragon, plus tarragon sprigs for garnish

1. In a 6- to 8-in. frying pan over high heat, boil garlic and shallot in vermouth until liquid is reduced by about half, 5 to 8 minutes. Add broth and bring to a boil again.
2. Add cream, olives, and chopped thyme. Boil, stirring occasionally, until sauce is thick enough to coat the back of a spoon and is reduced to about 1¼ cups, about 5 minutes. Add salt and pepper to taste. Cover and set aside.
3. Preheat oven to 400°. With tweezers, pull pin bones out of salmon. Lay fillet in a buttered 12- by 17-in. baking pan. Dot fillet with butter, drizzle with wine, and sprinkle with chopped tarragon. Sprinkle lightly with salt and pepper.
4. Bake until salmon is barely opaque but still moist-looking in thickest part (cut to test), 13 to 18 minutes. Slide salmon onto a platter.
5. If sauce is cool, stir over medium-high heat until hot. Drizzle fish with some of sauce; serve the rest on the side. Garnish fish with thyme and tarragon sprigs.
Quick Tip: To pit olives, crush slightly with the flat side of a knife blade, then remove pits.

PER SERVING: 567 cal., 62% (351 cal.) from fat; 44 g protein; 39 g fat (14 g sat.); 4.9 g carbo (0.3 g fiber); 356 mg sodium; 176 mg chol.

Crab-stuffed Salmon with Vermouth Cream

Michele and Norbert Juhasz, of C'est Si Bon restaurant in Port Angeles, Washington, specialize in French country classics, like chicken in mustard sauce and salmon in parchment. In season, they also offer this truly local pairing: wild salmon stuffed with Dungeness crab. Serve with simple parsleyed potatoes.

SERVES 4 | **TIME** About 1 hour

1 leek (about 6 oz.)
3 tbsp. butter, divided
6 oz. shelled cooked crab (¾ cup)
1 lb. skin-on, boned salmon fillet (7 to 8 in. wide)
2 cups dry vermouth
½ cup whipping cream
Salt and freshly ground black pepper
2 tbsp. thinly sliced chives (optional)
Lemon wedges (optional)

1. Preheat oven to 450°. Trim and discard stem end and tough green top from leek; cut leek in half lengthwise and hold each half under cold running water, separating layers to rinse well, then thinly slice. In a 10- to 12-in. ovenproof frying pan over medium heat, melt 1 tbsp. butter. Add leek and cook, stirring often, until softened, about 5 minutes. Transfer to a bowl.
2. Sort through crab and discard any bits of shell. Add remaining 2 tbsp. butter to pan; when melted, add crab and heat, stirring often, just until hot, 1 to 2 minutes. Push to one side of pan.
3. Holding a sharp knife at a 45° angle, cut salmon flesh crosswise off the skin into ⅛- to ¼-in.-thick slices; you should have about 12 slices (see *Quick Tip below*). One at a time, lay slices flat on a work surface and spoon about 1 tbsp. warm crab onto wide end. Starting at that end, roll salmon tightly around crab and place, seam down, in frying pan. Pour vermouth around rolls.
4. Bake until fish is opaque but still moist-looking in thickest part (cut to test), 12 to 15 minutes. With a slotted spoon, transfer salmon rolls to plates, cover loosely with foil or plastic wrap, and let stand in a warm place.
5. Add cream and leek to pan and boil over high heat until liquid is slightly thickened and reduced to about 1⅓ cups, 8 to 9 minutes. Season to taste with salt and pepper. Spoon sauce around salmon rolls and garnish with chives and lemon wedges if you like.
Quick Tip: To save time, you can have the salmon thinly sliced off the skin at your seafood market.

PER SERVING: 426 cal., 63% (268 cal.) from fat; 30 g protein; 30 g fat (13 g sat.); 8.4 g carbo (0.2 g fiber); 291 mg sodium; 159 mg chol.

Tuna Types and Tips

The Japanese, arguably the world's top tuna connoisseurs, rate tuna based on fat content and size, the higher-fat species and cuts being the most flavorful and tender. *Toro* is Japanese for tuna belly meat; *maguro* usually refers to a leaner cut taken from the fillet—although it's also the generic word for tuna. Look for troll-, pole-, or rod-and-reel-caught fish, and avoid buying the seriously endangered bluefin (*hon-maguro*).

BIGEYE (*mebachi maguro*; often called ahi): Deep ruby red flesh and high fat content. Availability can be spotty.

YELLOWFIN (ahi; sometimes labeled toro): Much like bigeye, but milder in flavor and slightly leaner and firmer. Widely available.

ALBACORE (*tombo*): Leanest and most affordable. Usually served cooked. The best choice for tuna from a sustainability standpoint is U.S. Pacific albacore.

Buying Tips
• Buy from a shop you trust. The way tuna is handled greatly affects its quality.
• Choose a store with quick product turnover. Japanese markets are often good bets.

• Select the fish with your nose: The fish should smell ocean-fresh or be odorless.
• Look for firm flesh with uniformly bright color.
• Avoid buying fish that feels slimy or granular.
• For sashimi (raw fish), ask for *maguro*—a tender cut that runs along the spine near the head—cut into *saku* blocks.

A Note on Safety
You don't have to worry about parasites in tuna. Do eat it as soon as possible, since it won't stay fresh long, and be sure to keep it well chilled.

Seared Tuna with Japanese-style Salsa

This recipe was one of Chicago chef Rodelio Aglibot's favorites when he was executive chef at Koi Restaurant in Los Angeles from 2002 to 2004. He used ponzu shoyu, a delicious soy sauce seasoned with citrus and seaweed, to flavor the salsa, but you can mix regular soy sauce and lemon juice for an easy alternative, as we've done here. Ponzu shoyu is available at Asian markets.

SERVES 2 | **TIME** 25 minutes

1 tsp. minced or pressed garlic
2 skinned, boned tuna steaks (bigeye, yellowfin, or albacore), about 1¼ in. thick (5 to 6 oz. each)
Salt and freshly ground black pepper
2 tsp. vegetable oil
¼ cup sake
2 tbsp. soy sauce, divided
¾ cup finely chopped tomatoes
2 tbsp. finely chopped green onion
1 tbsp. *each* chopped cilantro and fresh lemon juice
6 to 8 slices peeled firm-ripe avocado (3 to 4 oz. total)

1. Spread garlic on both sides of tuna steaks; sprinkle with salt and pepper. Heat oil in an 8- to 10-in. nonstick frying pan over medium-high heat until hot. Add tuna and cook, turning once, until lightly browned on both sides, about 1 minute per side. Pour sake and 1 tbsp. soy sauce around steaks; remove from heat. Let cool, turning fish often.
2. Meanwhile, in a small bowl, mix tomatoes, green onion, cilantro, lemon juice, and remaining 1 tbsp. soy sauce to make the salsa.
3. Lift tuna from sake mixture, reserving juices. Cut fish across the grain into ¼-in.-thick slices and lay on plates. Garnish with salsa and avocado slices. If desired, spoon pan juices over tuna.

PER SERVING: 340 cal., 48% (162 cal.) from fat; 32 g protein; 18 g fat (3.2 g sat.); 9.5 g carbo (1.9 g fiber); 1,093 mg sodium; 48 mg chol.

fish & shellfish

Seared Tuna with Papaya Salsa

A fresh tropical fruit salsa brightens up peppery ahi tuna steaks in this easy but stylish dish from reader Gail Durant of Sisters, Oregon.

SERVES 2 | **TIME** 15 minutes

1 firm-ripe papaya (about 1 lb.)
¼ cup finely diced red onion
1 jalapeño or serrano chile, seeds and ribs removed
  and minced
2 tbsp. chopped cilantro leaves
1 tbsp. fresh lime juice
Salt
2 ahi tuna steaks, 1 in. thick (5 to 6 oz. each)
2 tsp. olive oil
Coarsely ground black pepper

1. Peel and seed papaya; cut into ½-in. cubes.
2. In a bowl, mix papaya, onion, chile, cilantro, and lime juice. Add salt to taste. Set aside while preparing fish or cover and chill up to 4 hours.
3. Coat both sides of tuna steaks with oil and sprinkle all over with salt and pepper. Heat a 10- to 12-in. nonstick frying pan over medium heat; add fish and cook, turning once, until opaque on both sides but still pink in thickest part (cut to test), 8 to 10 minutes total. Transfer steaks to plates and spoon salsa over servings.

PER SERVING: 248 cal., 21% (53 cal.) from fat; 31 g protein; 5.9 g fat (1 g sat.); 18 g carbo (1.9 g fiber); 55 mg sodium; 57 mg chol.

Frozen Fish Basics

What's the best fish to buy frozen?
American seafood, preferably from the West Coast—from Alaska is even better—because our regulations on fishing and processing are among the most stringent in the world. Extra points if it has the Marine Stewardship Council logo, which verifies that it was processed in an eco-friendly way. Look for labels that overload you with good info, like where the fish was raised or caught.

Any advantages to frozen?
Fish that is quickly processed and frozen at sea may be in better condition than many fresh seafood products. Also, frozen fish transported by truck or ship has a smaller carbon footprint than air-freighted fresh fish.

BEST WAY TO THAW: Overnight in the refrigerator, to protect flavor and retain juices. **Shortcut:** Immerse sealed package in a container of cool water. Change water often until fish is thawed.

Tuna with Tomato-Caper Sauce

A friend's gift of freshly baked bread prompted reader Elizabeth Farquhar, of Portland, Oregon, to come up with this flavorful sauce for tuna—great for dunking good bread.

SERVES 2 | **TIME** 25 minutes

2 skinned, boned tuna steaks (albacore or yellowfin),
  about 1 in. thick (6 oz. each)
Salt and freshly ground black pepper
1 tbsp. olive oil
1 onion (½ lb.), halved lengthwise and thinly sliced
1 can (14.5 oz.) crushed tomatoes
½ cup dry red wine
3 tbsp. balsamic vinegar
1 tbsp. drained capers
1 tsp. dried oregano

1. Sprinkle tuna steaks lightly all over with salt and pepper. Heat oil in a 10- to 12-in. frying pan over medium-high heat until hot. Add onion and cook, stirring frequently, until softened, about 5 minutes.
2. Push onion to side of pan and add tuna steaks. Cook, turning once, just until browned on both sides, 6 to 8 minutes total. Stir in tomatoes, wine, vinegar, capers, and oregano. Reduce heat to maintain a simmer, cover, and cook until tuna is no longer pink in center (cut to test), about 15 minutes.
3. Transfer tuna to plates and top with sauce.

PER SERVING: 366 cal., 21% (76 cal.) from fat; 39 g protein; 8.4 g fat (1.3 g sat.); 24 g carbo (2.7 g fiber); 579 mg sodium; 68 mg chol.

Sushi Party
in 5 Easy Steps

Here's an easy plan for a DIY sushi party for six people. Your part is to cook the rice, prepare the fillings, set up a rolling station, and make the salad (steps 1 through 4). Your guests' job is to roll and wrap (step 5; *see page 336*). Round out the menu with items you can buy at Asian markets and many supermarkets, like frozen gyoza (potstickers), edamame (soybeans) in their pods, wasabi-flavored rice crackers, miso soup from a mix, and some mochi ice cream balls for dessert.

Nori (dried seaweed sheets), wasabi (powdered Japanese horseradish), and pickled ginger are available at well-stocked supermarkets and Asian grocery stores. Traditional bamboo sushi mats make rolling easy, but sheets of plastic wrap work surprisingly well. The mats, chopsticks, and rice paddles are available at Japanese markets, at other import stores, and online at *helensasiankitchen.com* and *surlatable.com*.

As for the fish itself, seek out the freshest, best-quality, fiber-free fish. "Sushi grade" or "sashimi grade," although not FDA-recognized terms, are most likely to have no parasites, often a concern when eating raw fish. Good seafood purveyors selling fish as sushi- or sashimi-grade follow the FDA's recommendations for freezing raw fish at very low temperatures (–4° for 7 days or –31° for 24 hours) to kill parasites (ahi is not prone to parasites, so can safely be eaten raw without special handling. Still, seek out sashimi grade for the best quality). You won't find this kind of fish at your grocery store; you'll have to shop for it at a Japanese market or a good fishmonger, or even through a fine online purveyor such as Catalina Offshore Products (*catalinaop.com*). Tell the fishmonger you intend to eat the fish raw, and keep it as cold as possible until you serve it.

1 Cook the Rice

You can make the rice up to 4 hours ahead; cover and let stand at room temperature.

SUSHI RICE
1. Combine ¾ cup **unseasoned rice vinegar**, 3 tbsp. **sugar**, and ¾ tsp. **salt** and stir until sugar and salt are dissolved.
2. In a fine-mesh strainer, rinse 4½ cups **short-grain white rice** under cold running water until water runs clear, 5 to 10 minutes. Put rice in a 4- to 5-qt. pan and add 5¼ cups water. Bring to a boil over high heat, then lower heat to maintain a simmer. Cover; cook until water is absorbed, 10 to 15 minutes.
3. Spread out rice in a shallow 12- by 16-in. baking pan and slowly pour vinegar mixture over it, turning rice gently and fanning it (Japanese cooks use a traditional fan, but you can use a piece of paper) until it cools to warm room temperature, about 15 minutes. Makes 9 to 10 cups.

radish sprouts · sushi rice · carrots · rice vinegar and water · enoki mushrooms · pickled ginger · wasabi · soy sauce · cucumber · chopsticks · smoked salmon · nori · bamboo rolling mat

2 Prepare Sushi Fillings

Choose five to seven items from this list of favorites. You can get them ready up to 4 hours ahead; chill airtight until you're ready to roll.

AHI: Rinse 3 oz. sashimi-grade **ahi tuna** (yellowfin or bigeye; *see Tuna Types and Tips, page 332*, for shopping tips); pat dry. Cut tuna into ¼-in.-thick strips about ½ in. wide and 3½ in. long. Just before serving, arrange raw fish on a bed of crushed ice on a rimmed plate.

ASPARAGUS: In a 5- to 6-qt. pan over high heat, bring about 1 qt. water to a boil. Snap off and discard tough stem ends from ½ lb. **asparagus**. Rinse asparagus and add to boiling water; cook until barely tender when pierced, 3 to 4 minutes. Drain and immediately immerse in a bowl of ice water. When cool, lift out and cut into 3½-in. lengths.

AVOCADO: Pit and peel 1 **firm-ripe avocado** (½ lb.); slice lengthwise into strips about ¼ in. thick and ½ in. wide. Put in a bowl with 2 tbsp. **fresh lemon juice**; turn to coat.

CARROT: Shred 1 **carrot** (3 oz.) or use ¾ cup shredded carrot.

CRAB: In a small bowl, mix ½ lb. shelled cooked **crab** or drained canned crab (squeeze out liquid) with ¼ cup **mayonnaise** and **soy sauce** to taste (about 2 tsp.). Makes about 1 cup.

CUCUMBER: Cut 1 **Japanese or English cucumber** (6 oz.) into 3½-in. lengths. Cut lengthwise into ¼-in.-thick slices, then stack two or three slices at a time and cut lengthwise into ¼-in.-thick sticks.

MUSHROOMS: Trim woody stem ends from 3 oz. **enoki mushrooms**. Rinse mushrooms briefly, drain, and gently pat dry.

SALMON ROE: Put 2 oz. **salmon roe** in a fine-mesh strainer and rinse gently under cold running water; mound in a small bowl.

SMOKED SALMON: Cut 3 oz. thinly sliced **smoked salmon** into ½-in.-wide strips.

SPINACH: In a 5- to 6-qt. pan over high heat, bring about 3 qts. water to a boil. Add 6 oz. **spinach leaves** and cook just until wilted, 1 to 2 minutes. Drain and immerse in a large bowl of ice water until cool. Drain again and spread on a clean kitchen towel. Roll towel and twist and squeeze tightly to remove as much liquid as possible.

SPROUTS: Gently rinse and drain 2 oz. (1½ cups) **radish or broccoli sprouts**; trim off any root ends.

3 Set up a Rolling Station

Arrange sushi components on the table or set up a station nearby.

1. Mix ¼ cup **unseasoned rice vinegar** with 4 cups water. Pour into small bowls for guests to moisten their hands while rolling sushi; the vinegared water will prevent the rice from sticking to skin.

2. Put 6 precut sheets of **nori** (7½ by 8 in.) in a covered serving container to keep dry; mound **sushi rice** (*recipe on opposite page*) and **fillings** on platters or in bowls (vegetables together, seafood separately). Put condiments—**soy sauce, pickled ginger** (1 cup), and **wasabi** (about 3 tbsp. prepared wasabi or ¼ cup wasabi powder mixed with about 2½ tbsp. water) —in separate bowls.

3. Arrange ingredients, along with bamboo mats or plastic wrap, on the table or station.

4 Make the Salad

The longer the cucumbers stand in the vinegar in the shrimp salad, the softer yet more flavorful they become. Chill salad up to 2 hours.

Shrimp Salad (Ebi Sunomono)

SERVES 6 | **TIME** 20 minutes

½ lb. medium peeled cooked shrimp (31 to 42 per lb.), tails removed *(see Quick Tip below)*
2 English cucumbers (about 1½ lbs. total)
⅓ cup unseasoned rice vinegar
2 tbsp. sugar
2 tsp. soy sauce
⅓ cup unsalted roasted peanuts, chopped

1. Cut shrimp in half lengthwise. Thinly slice cucumbers.
2. In a bowl, mix vinegar, sugar, and soy sauce. Add cucumbers and shrimp; mix to coat. Top with peanuts just before serving.
Quick Tip: For the most sustainable choice, buy shrimp farmed or caught in the U.S. or British Columbia.

PER SERVING: 115 cal., 35% (40 cal.) from fat; 11 g protein; 4.4 g fat (0.7 g sat.); 8.7 g carbo (2 g fiber); 200 mg sodium; 74 mg chol.

continued on page 336

5 Roll Your Sushi

Here are two different styles of rolls to try—the familiar cylindrical *futo-maki* (usually just called *maki*) and the free-form *temaki*, or hand roll, which is even easier.

Maki Sushi

MAKES 6 rolls; 6 to 8 servings
TIME 2 to 5 minutes per roll, depending on skill level

1. Place a sheet of **nori**, shiny side down, on a bamboo rolling mat (with slats running horizontally) or a piece of plastic wrap (about 10 by 12 in.). Align long side of nori with bottom edge of mat (the edge closest to you). Dip your hands in **vinegar-water mixture** *(see page 335)* and scatter 1½ cups **sushi rice** *(recipe on page 334)* over nori; pat into an even layer, spreading out to sides and bottom of nori but leaving a 2-in. strip bare along top edge.
2. With your finger, spread a thin stripe of **wasabi** horizontally across center of rice. Arrange three or four **sushi fillings** *(see page 335)* beside wasabi stripe (1); it's okay if some ends stick out. Moisten top edge of nori with vinegar-water mixture. Holding fillings down with your fingers, lift bottom edge of mat with your thumbs (2) and roll sushi to shape into a cylinder, rolling over bare nori edge to seal. Briefly press mat around roll (3).
3. Remove roll from mat. If desired, trim off any filling sticking out. With a sharp knife, cut roll into 6 or 8 pieces (4), rinsing knife in water between cuts.
4. Repeat with remaining nori, rice, and fillings.

PER PIECE OF CRAB, AVOCADO, AND CUCUMBER ROLL: 133 cal., 15% (20 cal.) from fat; 3.2 g protein; 2.2 g fat (0.4 g sat.); 25 g carbo (0.4 g fiber); 162 mg sodium; 7.2 mg chol.

PER PIECE OF SMOKED SALMON, ASPARAGUS, AND CARROT ROLL: 112 cal., 2% (2.7 cal.) from fat; 2.3 g protein; 0.2 g fat (0.1 g sat.); 24 g carbo (0.4 g fiber); 126 mg sodium; 0.5 mg chol.

Hand Rolls (*Temaki*)

Temaki is best eaten immediately, before the nori cone encasing fillings loses its crispness.

MAKES 8 dozen; 6 to 8 servings
TIME 2 to 5 minutes per roll, depending on skill level

1. With scissors, cut **nori sheets** into quarters (about 4 in. square).
2. Dot a square of nori with **wasabi** if you like, then spoon a rounded tbsp. of **sushi rice** *(recipe on page 334)* diagonally across nori. Top with 2 or 3 **sushi fillings** (1, below; *for fillings, see page 335*). Moisten one exposed corner of nori with **vinegar-water mixture**, pull opposite corner around fillings to form a cone, and overlap with moistened corner to seal (2).
3. Repeat with remaining nori, rice, and fillings.

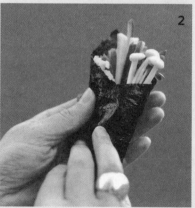

fish & shellfish

California Rolls

We wrap our version of the California roll with the nori on the outside. You can find the Japanese ingredients needed to make this in the Asian-foods aisle at most grocery stores.

recipe pictured on page **316**

MAKES 6 rolls; 36 to 48 pieces | **TIME** 1 hour

1½ cups short-grain white rice
¼ cup plus 1 tbsp. unseasoned rice vinegar
1 tbsp. sugar
¾ tsp. salt
6 sheets nori (dried seaweed; 7½ by 8 in.), toasted to
    soften (see *Quick Tip, right*)
2 tbsp. wasabi powder, mixed with 2 tbsp. water
1 firm-ripe avocado (½ lb.), pitted, peeled, and cut into
    ¼-in.-thick slices
½ lb. shelled cooked crab
Soy sauce and pickled ginger

1. In a fine-mesh strainer, rinse rice under cold running water until water runs clear, 5 to 10 minutes. Put rice in a 2- or 3-qt. pan and add 1½ cups water. Bring to a boil over high heat, then lower heat to maintain a simmer. Cover and cook until water is absorbed, 10 to 15 minutes.

2. Meanwhile, in a small bowl, combine ¼ cup vinegar, sugar, and salt and stir until sugar and salt are dissolved.

3. Spread out rice in a shallow 12- by 16-in. baking pan and slowly pour vinegar mixture over it, turning rice gently and fanning it (with a handheld fan or a piece of paper) until it cools to warm room temperature, about 10 minutes.

4. Mix remaining 1 tbsp. vinegar with 1 cup water. Pour into a small bowl to moisten your hands so rice doesn't stick to them while you're rolling sushi.

5. Place a sheet of toasted nori, shiny side down, on a bamboo rolling mat (with slats running horizontally) or on a piece of plastic wrap (about 10 by 12 in.). Align long side of nori with bottom edge of mat (the edge closest to you). Dip your hands in vinegar-water mixture and scatter ⅔ cup rice over nori; pat into an even layer, spreading out to sides and bottom of nori but leaving a 2-in.-wide strip bare along top edge.

6. With your finger, spread a thin stripe of wasabi paste (about 1 tsp.) horizontally across center of rice. Arrange 4 avocado slices along wasabi stripe (it's okay if slices overlap or if some ends stick out), then arrange about 2 tbsp. of crab on top of avocado.

7. Moisten top edge of nori with vinegar-water mixture. Holding fillings down with your fingers, lift bottom edge of mat with your thumbs (see *photo 2, far left*) and roll to shape sushi into a cylinder, rolling over bare nori edge to seal. Briefly press mat around roll (see *photo 3, far left*).

8. Remove roll from mat. If desired, trim off any fillings sticking out. With a sharp knife, cut roll into 6 or 8 pieces, rinsing knife in water between cuts.

9. Repeat with remaining nori, rice, and fillings. Serve with soy sauce, pickled ginger, and remaining wasabi paste.

Quick Tip: To toast nori, use tongs to wave each sheet over a gas or electric burner on high heat. Within a few seconds, the nori will soften and turn green.

PER PIECE (⅛ ROLL): 47 cal., 17% (7.8 cal.) from fat; 2.1 g protein; 0.9 g fat (0.1 g sat.); 7.7 g carbo (0.6 g fiber); 74 mg sodium; 4.8 mg chol.

The Story of the California Roll

A quintessential fusion food, the California roll was probably invented in the early 1970s at Tokyo Kaikan, a long-gone restaurant in L.A.'s Little Tokyo. Whereas traditional sushi focused on one pristine, perfect ingredient, plus rice, the California roll was a combo: avocado, cucumber, and crab (cooked, to make it more accessible to a timid new audience). Instead of exotic nori seaweed wrapping the roll, familiar white rice encased the exterior (with the nori buried beneath, wrapped around the other fillings).

Los Angeles loved it. Pretty soon, so did New York, San Francisco, and cities across the country. By the 1980s, the California roll was even in Japan, there called *kashu-maki*. Its impact set off a wave of fusion sushi that continues to flow to this day: the Philadelphia roll (smoked salmon and cream cheese), the Hawaiian roll (avocado, tuna, and pineapple), and the Cajun roll (deep-fried crayfish and cucumber). Here in Menlo Park, California, where *Sunset* is located, we even have cleverly filled multi-ingredient sushi named after Stanford professors teaching in nearby Palo Alto.

And, although imitation crab has crept into many versions of the California roll, do try it with the real thing—it's much better.

King Crab on the Half-shell

You can buy the large Alaska king crab legs in the shell, already cooked and usually frozen (or thawed from frozen). The meat is wonderful simply butter-basted and broiled on the half shell. Plan to buy about ¾ lb. king crab per serving. Thaw frozen crab overnight in the refrigerator.

SERVES 4 | **TIME** 15 minutes

4 cooked Alaska king crab legs (about 3 lbs.), thawed if
   frozen *(see the True Alaska King Crab below)*
¼ cup butter, melted
Kosher salt
Chopped flat-leaf parsley
1 lemon, cut into 8 wedges

1. Break crab legs at joints. (Wear thick, clean gloves—such as garden gloves—to protect yourself from the shell's many sharp points.) With scissors, cut along sides of shells and lift off the upper half of each. Arrange the crab legs, meat side up, on a baking pan and brush meat with melted butter. Sprinkle with salt to taste.
2. Broil crab 6 in. from heat until heated through, about 5 minutes. Serve several pieces (about 1 whole leg) to each person, sprinkled with parsley and served with a couple of lemon wedges.

PER SERVING: 292 cal., 44% (129 cal.) from fat; 37 g protein; 15 g fat (7.6 g sat.); 1.4 g carbo (0.4 g fiber); 2,133 mg sodium; 132 mg chol.

The True Alaska King Crab

Alaska king crab, the unwitting co-star of the Discovery Channel's documentary show *Deadliest Catch*, is sorely misrepresented in the Lower 48 by imported Russian king crab, an often illegally caught species that's sometimes marketed as Alaska king crab.

True Alaska king crab is pricier than Russian, but the meat is firmer, sweeter, and fresher tasting as a result of tighter management of the U.S. industry. (Both the Environmental Defense Fund and Monterey Bay Aquarium's Seafood Watch recommend consumers avoid buying imported Russian king crab because of that industry's overfishing and illegal fishing. Be sure to ask for source information when you shop.)

Nearly all Alaska king crab is shipped out cooked and frozen, but if you ever have the chance to try it fresh, you're in for a real treat.

Vietnamese-style Spicy Crab with Garlic Noodles

Don't plan on kissing anyone after eating this garlic-laden creation. Frying the crab is optional, but it adds superb flavor and makes the crabmeat more tender. The results will be even more transcendent if you start with raw crab (get it from a fishmonger, and fry it a minute or two longer than cooked crab) or partially cooked crab. If you elect not to fry the crab, skip steps 1 and 2, put 1 cup oil in a small saucepan over high heat, and start with step 3.

SERVES 4 to 6 | **TIME** 1½ hours

1 cup flour
1½ tbsp. salt, divided
1½ tsp. freshly ground black pepper, divided
½ tsp. cayenne
2 raw, partially cooked, or fully cooked Dungeness crabs
   (about 2 lbs. each; *see Quick Tip, right*), cleaned and
   cracked
3 tbsp. vegetable oil plus more for frying
10 garlic cloves, chopped
½ lb. spaghettini (thin spaghetti)
3 tbsp. butter, at room temperature
6 small dried red chiles
2 tbsp. grated fresh ginger
4 green onions, trimmed and chopped
4 serrano chiles, seeds and ribs removed and chopped
⅓ cup sake or other rice wine
1 cup basil leaves, chopped
½ cup mint leaves, chopped
½ cup cilantro leaves

1. Combine flour, 1 tsp. salt, 1 tsp. pepper, and the cayenne in a large bowl. Pat crab pieces dry with paper towels and toss (in batches) with flour mixture. Remove crab and shake off any excess flour. Set aside.
2. In a wok or large pot, heat 3 in. oil to 375°. Fry crab in batches (do not crowd wok) until golden, about 5 minutes per batch. Drain on paper towels.
3. Using the same hot oil, fry garlic until golden brown, 1 to 2 minutes. Remove with a slotted spoon and drain on paper towels. Set garlic aside; cool and discard oil.
4. Bring a large pot of water to a boil. Add 1 tbsp. salt and the spaghettini. Cook until tender to the bite, 5 to 8 minutes. Drain, transfer to a serving bowl, and toss with butter and half the fried garlic. Cover and put in a warm place.
5. Heat a wok or pot large enough to hold all the crab over high heat. Add 3 tbsp. oil, the dried chiles, and ginger. Cook, stirring constantly, until fragrant, about 30 seconds. Add green onions, chopped serrano chiles,

fish & shellfish

and remaining ½ tsp. salt. Cook, stirring, until onions wilt, about 1 minute. Add sake and cook, stirring, until sake is reduced by about half. Stir in crab and cover. Cook until crab is heated through, about 3 minutes.

6. Remove lid and cook, stirring, until any liquid evaporates. Stir in basil, mint, cilantro, and remaining ½ tsp. pepper. Cook, stirring, until herbs have wilted. Stir in remaining fried garlic. Transfer crab to a warm platter and serve with garlic noodles.

Quick Tip: You have three crab options. (1) Ask your fishmonger to clean and crack raw crabs, then cook as soon as possible that day. (2) Buy live crabs and cook as directed in *Dungeness Crab 101 (page 340)* but for only 3 minutes, then clean and crack. (3) Buy fully cooked, cleaned, and cracked crabs.

PER SERVING: 610 cal., 43% (261 cal.) from fat; 27 g protein; 29 g fat (7.1 g sat.); 56 g carbo (4.2 g fiber); 1,292 mg sodium; 105 mg chol.

King Crab with Lemongrass-Ginger Butter and Roasted Potatoes

recipe pictured on page **318**

Jack Amon, chef at the Marx Bros. Café in Anchorage, Alaska, serves Alaska king crab during the summer with a simple but zippy butter sauce and roasted potatoes. If you buy the crab legs thawed, you can have the fishmonger crack them for you, or thaw them yourself (in the refrigerator overnight) and use a nutcracker or wood mallet to crack the shell along each section of crab leg. Cracked Dungeness crab is also delicious prepared this way.

SERVES 6 | **TIME** 1½ hours

4 stalks fresh lemongrass (about ¼ lb. total)
1 cup butter
¼ cup minced fresh ginger
2 tbsp. minced garlic, divided
1¾ lbs. red thin-skinned potatoes (each about 2 in. wide)
2 tbsp. finely shredded parmesan cheese
2 tbsp. chopped flat-leaf parsley, divided
5 lbs. thawed Alaska king crab legs, cracked

1. Trim and discard tough tops and root ends from lemongrass. Remove and discard tough outer layers. With flat side of a knife, crush tender inner stalks; cut crushed stalks into 2-in. pieces. In a 1½- to 2-qt. pan over high heat, combine lemongrass pieces, butter, ginger, and 4 tsp. minced garlic. When butter is melted, turn heat to low and cook, stirring often, 15 to 20 minutes to blend flavors. With a slotted spoon, lift out and discard lemongrass.

2. Preheat oven to 400°. Cut each potato in half and brush cut sides with lemongrass-ginger butter, using about 1 tbsp. total. Set potatoes, cut side up, in a shallow 9- by 13-in. baking dish.

3. Bake potatoes 20 minutes. Turn cut side down and bake until well browned and tender when pierced, 20 to 30 minutes more.

4. In a small bowl, mix together parmesan, remaining 2 tsp. garlic, and 1 tbsp. parsley and sprinkle over potatoes. Cover with foil or a plate to keep warm.

5. Arrange crab legs in a single layer in an 11- by 17-in. pan. Brush with about ¼ cup lemongrass-ginger butter. Broil 4 to 6 in. from heat until meat is hot in center of thickest part of leg (cut where cracked to test), 8 to 10 minutes.

6. Transfer crab legs to a platter with potatoes and sprinkle with remaining 1 tbsp. parsley. Serve with remaining lemongrass-ginger butter.

Make Ahead: Lemongrass-ginger butter, up to 1 day, chilled. Reheat to serve.

PER SERVING: 386 cal., 32% (124 cal.) from fat; 41 g protein; 14 g fat (7.1 g sat.); 23 g carbo (2.4 g fiber); 2,189 mg sodium; 131 mg chol.

Cracked Crab with Herbed Avocado Sauce

recipe pictured on page **321**

This super-simple sauce was inspired by the tarragon tang and beautiful color of Green Goddess salad dressing.

SERVES 4 to 6 | **TIME** 15 minutes, plus 30 minutes for dressing to rest

2 firm-ripe avocados, pitted and peeled
½ cup olive oil
¼ cup white wine vinegar
½ tsp. salt, plus more to taste
½ cup finely chopped chives (about 2 bunches)
2 tbsp. finely chopped tarragon
2 Dungeness crabs, cooked, cleaned, and cracked
    (see *Dungeness Crab 101, page 340*)

1. In a blender, purée avocados, oil, vinegar, salt, and ½ cup water until smooth. Transfer to a bowl and stir in chives and tarragon. Cover and let sit 30 minutes at room temperature to let flavors blend.

2. Season sauce with salt to taste. Mound crab on a platter or on plates and serve with sauce.

PER SERVING: 413 cal., 76% (315 cal.) from fat; 19 g protein; 35 g fat (5.1 g sat.); 6.8 g carbo (1.7 g fiber); 482 mg sodium; 87 mg chol.

Dungeness Crab 101

Dungeness crabs are named after the town of the same name on Washington's Olympic Peninsula, where they were first harvested for commercial sale in the 1800s. Today they're caught in traps along a huge stretch of Pacific coast, from Alaska to central California, and are in season in winter, spring, and through most of the summer. If you've never cooked live crabs, the prospect can seem a little intimidating. But our paper-bag method for getting the critters in the water helps things go smoothly. Freshly cooked Dungeness crab is utterly delicious—one of the great culinary rewards of living in the West.

How to Cook

1. Keep live crabs chilled up to 12 hours in an open bowl or box, covered with damp paper towels. Fill a large pot with enough water to cover crabs by 2 to 3 in., leaving 3 to 4 in. of clearance below pot rim; bring to a boil.

2. Cut the handles off a sturdy paper bag. If the crabs are wrapped in newspaper or another material, gently unwrap them into the bag, putting in no more than two at a time. If the crabs are loose in a box, use tongs (*see right*) to lift each one up from the rear between the legs and put in the bag.

3. Holding the bag near the bottom, gently upend it (*see far right*) and let the crabs fall out into the water (avoid using tongs, which don't always give a steady grip if your crab starts to move); cover the pot. Cook, lowering the heat to a simmer once the water boils: 15 minutes for 1½- to 2½-lb. crabs, 20 minutes for bigger ones.

4. Lift out the crabs with tongs and rinse with cold running water until cool enough to handle.

How to Clean and Crack

1. Put a cooked crab, belly up, on a work surface. Pull off and discard the triangular flap (*see right*) and pointy appendages underneath it, plus the small paddles from the front of the crab.

2. Pry off the broad back shell from the rear end (*see far right*). Discard the liquid in the shell. Scoop out and save the soft, golden "butter" and white fat from the shell to eat with the crab, or discard with the back shell.

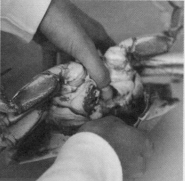

3. Turn the crab over. Pull off and discard any reddish membrane. Scoop out any remaining "butter." Pull off the long, spongy gills from the sides of the body. Rinse the body well.

4. Twist the legs and claws from the body. Using a nutcracker or wooden mallet, crack the shell of each leg and claw section. With a knife, cut the body into quarters.

How to Eat

Using a tip of a crab leg or a cocktail pick, remove the meat as you pull the legs and body sections apart. A cooked, cleaned crab yields about 25 percent of its weight in sweet, juicy meat, or about ½ lb. meat from a 2-lb. crab. A single serving is about ⅓ lb.

Cracked Crab with Lemongrass, Black Pepper, and Basil

A classic Southeast Asian balance of salty, sweet, hot, and aromatic. You can make the recipe with raw, partially cooked, or fully cooked crab. The first two options yield the most succulent meat.

SERVES 4 | **TIME** 1 hour, plus 15 minutes to chill

2 stalks fresh lemongrass, ends trimmed and coarse leaves discarded
2 tbsp. chopped fresh ginger
1 tbsp. chopped garlic
¼ cup *each* honey and reduced-sodium soy sauce
1½ tbsp. freshly ground black pepper
3 raw, partially cooked, or fully cooked Dungeness crabs (about 2 lbs. each; *see Quick Tip below*), cleaned, legs cracked, and bodies quartered
3 tbsp. peanut or vegetable oil
1 cup *each* loosely packed cilantro sprigs and Thai basil or small regular basil leaves

1. Chop lemongrass. Put in a food processor with ginger and garlic; chop until minced. Scrape into a large bowl and stir in honey, soy sauce, and pepper. Add crabs and stir to coat well. Cover, then chill at least 15 minutes and up to 1 hour.

2. Pour oil into a 14-in. wok or a wide 8- to 10-qt. pot over medium-high heat. With a slotted spoon, add crabs (reserve marinade). Cover and cook, stirring often, 5 minutes (omit this cooking time if using fully cooked crabs).

3. Uncover pan, add marinade, and cook, stirring often, until crab is steaming and meat is opaque, about 5 minutes more. Stir in cilantro and basil, then transfer crab and juices to a serving bowl.

Quick Tip: You have three crab options. (1) Ask your fishmonger to clean and crack raw crabs, then cook as soon as possible that day. (2) Buy live crabs and cook as directed in *Dungeness Crab 101 (left)* but for only 3 minutes, then clean and crack. (3) Buy fully cooked, cleaned, and cracked crabs.

PER SERVING: 351 cal., 35% (117 cal.) from fat; 35 g protein; 13 g fat (2.1 g sat.); 23 g carbo (2 g fiber); 1,060 mg sodium; 163 mg chol.

Spinach and Crab Enchiladas

Reader Christine Datian of Las Vegas serves these rich, tasty crab enchiladas with a sliced tomato and red onion salad. If vine-ripened tomatoes aren't available, use cherry tomatoes.

SERVES 8 to 10 | **TIME** 1 hour

1 tbsp. olive oil
1 onion (½ lb.), chopped
4 garlic cloves, minced
2 jalapeño chiles, seeds and ribs removed and minced
½ lb. shelled cooked crab or 3 cans (6 oz. each) lump crabmeat, drained
1 box (10 oz.) frozen chopped spinach, thawed and squeezed dry
3 cups shredded (¾ lb.) jack cheese, divided
½ cup *each* chopped black olives, chopped flat-leaf parsley, and mayonnaise
1 tbsp. Worcestershire sauce
1 tsp. chili powder
½ tsp. cayenne
Salt and freshly ground black pepper
2 cups tomato salsa or red enchilada sauce, divided
10 flour tortillas (7 to 8 in. wide)

1. Preheat oven to 350°. Heat oil in a 10- to 12-in. frying pan over medium-high heat until hot. Add onion, garlic, and jalapeños. Cook, stirring frequently, until onion is softened, 5 to 8 minutes.
2. In a large bowl, mix crab, spinach, 2 cups cheese, the olives, parsley, mayonnaise, Worcestershire, chili powder, cayenne, and onion mixture. Add salt and pepper to taste.
3. Spread about 1 cup salsa level in a 9- by 13-in. baking dish. Spoon about ½ cup crab mixture along center of a tortilla. Roll tortilla around filling. Repeat to fill remaining tortillas, then arrange them in a single layer over sauce in dish. Top evenly with remaining 1 cup salsa and remaining 1 cup cheese.
4. Bake until cheese is browned and bubbling, about 30 minutes. Let cool in pan about 5 minutes, then serve from pan with a wide spatula.

PER SERVING: 400 cal., 54% (216 cal.) from fat; 17 g protein; 24 g fat (8 g sat.); 28 g carbo (2.5 g fiber); 913 mg sodium; 65 mg chol.

Mendo Crabcakes

The point of a crabcake is pure crab flavor, not filler, according to Nicholas Petti, chef-owner of Mendo Bistro in Fort Bragg, California. He won the Mendocino Crab & Wine Days Crabcake Cook-off in both 2002 and 2003 with his simple, delicious cakes. Start the cabbage salad first, then make the aioli and crabcakes.

SERVES 4 as a main course or 8 as a first course
TIME 45 minutes

1 lb. shelled cooked crab (about 2¾ cups)
1¾ cups panko (Japanese-style bread crumbs) or other fine dried bread crumbs, divided
½ cup finely chopped green onions
Tarragon Aioli *(recipe follows)*
About ½ cup vegetable oil, divided
Champagne Cabbage Salad *(recipe follows)*

1. Sort through crab; remove and discard any bits of shell. In a bowl, combine crab, ¾ cup panko, and the green onions. Gently mix in ½ cup aioli just until mixture holds together.
2. Press mixture firmly into eight patties about 3 in. wide; set slightly separated on waxed paper or foil. Pour remaining 1 cup panko into a shallow bowl.
3. Preheat oven to 200°. Pour ⅓ cup oil into a 10- to 12-in. frying pan over medium-high heat. When hot, set each crabcake in panko, then, using a slotted spatula, turn, pressing gently to coat. Transfer a small batch of cakes to pan. Cook until golden brown on bottom, 3 to 4 minutes; turn gently and cook until browned on other side and hot in center, 3 to 4 minutes longer. Transfer cooked cakes, in a single layer, to a 12- by 15-in. baking sheet and keep warm in oven. Cook remaining cakes the same way, adding more oil as needed.
4. Divide cabbage salad among plates. Set crabcakes on salad, add a dollop of aioli, and serve immediately, passing remaining aioli to add to taste.

PER CRABCAKE: 138 cal., 31% (43 cal.) from fat; 13 g protein; 4.8 g fat (0.6 g sat.); 9.2 g carbo (0.6 g fiber); 197 mg sodium; 57 mg chol.

Tarragon Aioli: Combine 2 **egg yolks** *(see Quick Tip, above right)*, 3 peeled **garlic cloves**, ⅓ cup **fresh lemon juice**, and ½ tsp. **salt** in a blender; blend until mixture is smooth. With machine running, gradually pour in 1 cup **vegetable oil** (such as peanut) and ½ cup **extra-virgin olive oil** (or use all olive oil) in a slow, steady stream, blending until mixture is thick and smooth, 1 to 1½ minutes. Stir in ¼ cup chopped **tarragon**, ¼ to ½ tsp. **hot sauce**, and more lemon juice and salt to taste. Makes about 1⅔ cups.

Quick Tip: As a shortcut—or if you're concerned about possible bacteria in raw eggs—substitute 1½ cups store-bought mayonnaise mixed with ¼ cup chopped tarragon, 1½ to 2 tbsp. minced garlic, 2 tbsp. fresh lemon juice, and hot sauce and salt to taste.

PER TBSP.: 117 cal., 100% (117 cal.) from fat; 0.3 g protein; 13 g fat (1.8 g sat.); 0.4 g carbo (0 g fiber); 47 mg sodium; 16 mg chol.

Champagne Cabbage Salad: In a large bowl, mix 3 qts. finely shredded **cabbage** (about 1¼ lbs.) with 1½ tsp. **salt**; let stand 30 minutes. Mix with ⅓ cup finely chopped **chives** (about 1 bunch) and ¼ cup **Champagne vinegar**. Makes 1½ qts.

PER ¾-CUP SERVING: 19 cal., 5% (0.9 cal.) from fat; 0.9 g protein; 0.1 g fat (0 g sat.); 4.1 g carbo (1.8 g fiber); 449 mg sodium; 0 mg chol.

Mango-Mint Lobster Rolls

To make a dazzling main-dish salad, eliminate the rice-paper wrappers and increase the salad mix to 6 cups. Mound the salad mix on plates, top with lobster, mango, onion, mint, and cucumbers, then drizzle with the dipping sauce.

MAKES 12 rolls; 4 servings | **TIME** 45 to 50 minutes

1 spiny or rock lobster tail (about ¾ lb.), thawed if frozen
1 firm-ripe mango (about 1 lb.)
1 piece (5 in. long) English cucumber
¼ cup slivered red onion
⅓ cup mint leaves
12 rice-paper wrappers (*bánh tráng*; about 8 in. wide)
3 cups salad mix
Mint-Lime Dipping Sauce (*recipe follows*)

1. In a 4- to 5-qt. pan over high heat, bring about 2 qts. water to a boil. Add lobster tail; when boil resumes, reduce heat and simmer until meat is opaque but still moist-looking in center of thickest part (cut to test), about 10 minutes. Drain lobster, then immerse in ice water until cool to touch, about 5 minutes; drain again.

2. Meanwhile, cut pit and peel from mango and discard; cut fruit into small chunks. Cut cucumber lengthwise into thin slices; stack slices and cut lengthwise again to make ⅜-in.-wide sticks.

3. With scissors, snip underside of lobster shell free from back shell and lift off. Pull out lobster tail; discard shell. If vein is present, pull out and discard. Coarsely chop meat and put into a bowl. Add mango, onion, and mint; mix gently.

4. Immerse a rice-paper round in a large bowl of hot water, lift out, drain briefly, and lay on a work surface. Let stand until paper is soft and pliable, about 30 seconds. Repeat to moisten another rice-paper round and lay on work surface.

5. Working quickly, spoon about a twelfth of filling down center of each wrapper, leaving 1 in. of wrapper bare at both ends. Lay a twelfth of cucumber sticks parallel to filling and mound ½ cup salad mix on top.

6. Fold the 1-in. ends of each wrapper over filling, then, holding filling in place with your fingers, roll wrapper snugly around it. Press wrapper edges to seal; if edges are too dry to stick, moisten with a little more hot water. Set each roll, seam down, on a platter and cover airtight with plastic wrap.

7. Repeat steps 4 through 6 to fill remaining rice-paper wrappers (replace water in bowl as needed to keep hot).

8. Just before serving, cut each roll in half diagonally; if desired, stand rolls upright, cut ends up. Dip into mint-lime sauce to eat.

Make Ahead: Up to 3 hours, chilled.

PER SERVING: 293 cal., 2% (4.5 cal.) from fat; 14 g protein; 0.5 g fat (0.1 g sat.); 59 g carbo (3.2 g fiber); 184 mg sodium; 32 mg chol.

Mint-Lime Dipping Sauce: In a small bowl, mix ¼ cup *each* **fresh lime juice** and **seasoned rice vinegar**, 2 tbsp. finely chopped **mint leaves**, ½ to 1 red or green **jalapeño chile**, stemmed and minced, and 1 tbsp. *each* **Thai or Vietnamese fish sauce (*nam pla* or *nuoc mam*)**, minced **shallot**, and minced **garlic**. Makes ⅔ cup. Can be made up to 1 day ahead and chilled.

PER TBSP.: 12 cal., 15% (1.8 cal.) from fat; 0.4 g protein; 0.2 g fat (0 g sat.); 2.4 g carbo (0.1 g fiber); 180 mg sodium; 0 mg chol.

Roll-your-own Vietnamese Summer Rolls

A fun dish to serve when the weather is hot and you want to serve something light—and interactive: You set out the wrappers and fillings for diners to put together themselves, with store-bought peanut sauce on the side for dipping. Find the Vietnamese ingredients in the Asian-foods aisle of a well-stocked grocery store or at an Asian market.

MAKES 12 to 18 rolls; 4 servings | **TIME** 45 minutes

3½ oz. (half a 7-oz. pkg.) thin rice noodles
1 red bell pepper (6 oz.)
3 tbsp. Thai or Vietnamese fish sauce (*nam pla* or *nuoc mam*)
2 tbsp. sweet Asian chili sauce
1 tbsp. fresh lime juice
2 tbsp. chopped roasted peanuts
¾ lb. shelled cooked medium shrimp (31 to 42 per lb.), tails removed
½ lb. shredded cooked chicken
6 oz. mixed baby greens
1 English cucumber (10 oz.), halved lengthwise and thinly sliced into half-moons
2 carrots (½ lb. total), shredded
1 cup *each* loosely packed mint and cilantro leaves
12 to 18 rice-paper wrappers (*bánh tráng*; about 8 in. wide)

1. In a 4- to 5-qt. pan over high heat, bring 3 qts. water to a boil. Add rice noodles, stir to separate, and cook until tender to the bite, 3 to 5 minutes. Drain, rinse with cold water until cool, and drain again. Using scissors, cut noodles into about 3-in. lengths.
2. Meanwhile, remove seeds and ribs from bell pepper; cut lengthwise into ¼-in.-wide strips, then crosswise into 2-in. lengths. In a small bowl, stir together fish sauce, sweet chili sauce, and lime juice.
3. Mound rice noodles in center of a large platter. Drizzle 1 tbsp. fish sauce mixture over noodles, then sprinkle with peanuts. Mound bell pepper, shrimp, chicken, greens, cucumber slices, shredded carrots, mint, and cilantro around noodles (or put them on a separate platter if you like).

4. Pour 1 in. hot water into a large, shallow bowl. Immerse 1 or 2 rice-paper wrappers at a time until soft and pliable, about 30 seconds. Carefully remove and let drain briefly; stack on a plate.
5. Set out wrappers and fillings for diners to assemble their own rolls, with remaining sauce alongside for dipping. To roll, they arrange their choice of fillings down center of a wrapper, fold in sides over filling, then roll up tightly from closest edge, like a burrito.

PER SERVING: 606 cal., 15% (90 cal.) from fat; 44 g protein; 10 g fat (2.2 g sat.); 84 g carbo (8.2 g fiber); 892 mg sodium; 216 mg chol.

Golden Squash with Sautéed Shrimp

This is an unusual combination, but it works.

SERVES 4 | **TIME** 1 hour

2 tsp. curry powder
1 tsp. turmeric
½ tsp. cumin seeds
¼ tsp. cardamom seeds (*see Quick Tip, above right*) or ground cardamom
1 onion (½ lb.), chopped
1 red bell pepper (½ lb.), seeds and ribs removed and chopped
2 tbsp. minced fresh ginger
1½ cups chicken or vegetable broth, divided
3 cups cubed peeled butternut or other hard winter squash (1 lb.)
Salt
2 tsp. olive oil
1 lb. shrimp (21 to 30 per lb.), peeled and deveined
1 garlic clove, minced
½ cup plain yogurt
6 tsp. *each* finely chopped cilantro and dill

1. In a 10- to 12-in. frying pan over high heat, dry-roast curry powder, turmeric, cumin, and cardamom seeds until fragrant, 20 to 30 seconds. Add onion, bell pepper, ginger, and ½ cup broth; cook, stirring often, until liquid has evaporated, 5 to 8 minutes. Add remaining 1 cup broth and the squash. Cover, reduce heat, and simmer until squash mashes easily, about 15 minutes. Uncover, return heat to high, and stir until liquid has evaporated, 4 to 8 minutes.
2. Remove from heat and mash mixture with a potato masher or coarsely purée in a food processor. Add salt to taste. Keep warm.
3. Heat oil in 10- to 12-in. frying pan over high heat;

when hot, add shrimp and garlic. Stir-fry until shrimp are opaque in center (cut to test), about 3 minutes.

4. Spoon squash onto plates. Top each portion with 2 tbsp. yogurt, shrimp, and 1½ tsp. each cilantro and dill.

Quick Tip: To get cardamom seeds, crush ½ tsp. whole cardamom pods with the bottom of a glass; remove seeds and discard hulls.

PER SERVING: 262 cal., 16% (43 cal.) from fat; 30 g protein; 4.8 g fat (0.7 g sat.); 26 g carbo (4 g fiber); 516 mg sodium; 173 mg chol.

Wine-braised Seafood Choucroute

Comforting Alsatian choucroute—a tangle of seasoned sauerkraut, usually served with pork—is mighty hard on wine. But for centuries, Alsatians have been happily pairing choucroute with their own wines: dry Riesling and Gewürztraminer. Serve the choucroute with little red potatoes.

Serves 6 | **TIME** 2 hours

3 oz. bacon, chopped
2 medium onions, thinly sliced lengthwise
2 tbsp. chopped garlic
1½ qts. fresh sauerkraut (3 lbs.)
2 cups dry Riesling or Gewürztraminer, divided
1½ cups reduced-sodium chicken broth
2 bay leaves
1 tsp. dried juniper berries
½ tsp. freshly ground black pepper, plus more to taste
¼ cup each minced shallots and fresh Meyer or regular lemon juice
1 tbsp. Dijon mustard
½ cup olive oil, divided
Salt
1½ lbs. boned, skinned firm white-fleshed fish fillet, such as halibut or black cod
6 fresh seafood sausages (*see Quick Tip, above right*; about 1½ lbs.)
6 oz. hot-smoked salmon, skinned and broken into large chunks
Chopped chives

1. Preheat oven to 325°. In a large, wide ovenproof pot, brown bacon over medium-high heat, 4 to 5 minutes. Add onions and garlic; cook until onions are soft, about 5 minutes.

2. Rinse sauerkraut well in a colander; squeeze out as much moisture as possible. Stir sauerkraut into onion mixture. Add 1½ cups wine, the broth, bay leaves, juniper berries, and pepper. Bring to a boil, then cover and bake until sauerkraut is barely tender to the bite, about 1 hour.

3. In a small saucepan, boil shallots in remaining ½ cup wine until liquid is reduced by half. Remove from heat; whisk in lemon juice and mustard, then 6 tbsp. oil in a thin stream. Season with salt and pepper to taste and pour into a small pitcher.

4. Sprinkle fish all over with salt and pepper. Heat remaining 2 tbsp. oil in a large nonstick frying pan over medium-high heat. Cook fish, skinned side up, until browned on the bottom, about 6 minutes.

5. Nestle sausages into sauerkraut mixture and top with fish, browned side up. Cover and bake until sausages and fish are opaque but still moist-looking in center (cut to test), about 10 minutes.

6. Transfer fish and sausages to a warm plate. With a slotted spoon, mound sauerkraut on a warm platter; discard braising liquid. Tuck chunks of smoked salmon into sauerkraut and arrange fish and sausages around and on top. Sprinkle with chives and serve with shallot vinaigrette.

Quick Tip: Find seafood sausage at gourmet markets and seafood shops (you might have to order ahead). Or substitute 1½ lbs. peeled deveined raw shrimp (16 to 20 per lb.; tails left on); in step 5, stir shrimp into sauerkraut before adding fish.

PER SERVING: 620 cal., 49% (304 cal.) from fat; 62 g protein; 34 g fat (7.2 g sat.); 20 g carbo (6.8 g fiber); 0 mg sodium; 233 mg chol.

Spicy Mango Shrimp

Reader Heather Ripley, of Menlo Park, California, came up with this jazzy dinner. Serve with steamed jasmine rice.

recipe pictured on page **317**

SERVES 4 | **TIME** 25 minutes

3 tbsp. vegetable oil
1 cup chopped onion
2 tsp. minced garlic
1 tsp. red chile flakes
½ cup chopped basil leaves
2 tbsp. soy sauce
1 tbsp. fresh lime juice
About ¾ lb. medium shrimp (31 to 42 per lb.), peeled and deveined
2 cups cubed fresh (preferably unripe) or thawed frozen mango
¼ cup shredded unsweetened coconut, toasted (see Quick Tip below)

1. Heat oil in a large frying pan over medium heat until hot. Add onion and cook, stirring, until golden brown, 5 to 7 minutes. Add garlic, chile flakes, basil, soy sauce, lime juice, and shrimp; cook, stirring often, until shrimp turn pink, 3 to 5 minutes.
2. Add mango and cook until warm. Sprinkle with coconut.
Quick Tip: You can often find shredded coconut already toasted, but if you can't, spread coconut on a baking sheet and bake in a 325° oven until golden brown, 6 to 8 minutes. Let cool before using.

PER SERVING: 288 cal., 46% (132 cal.) from fat; 19 g protein; 15 g fat (3.9 g sat.); 22 g carbo (2.4 g fiber); 645 mg sodium; 129 mg chol.

Salt-and-Pepper Shrimp

A stir-fried version of the deep-fried Chinese dish that's both quick and light, yet keeps the intense flavor of the original.

recipe pictured on **cover**

Serves 4 to 6 | **TIME** 20 minutes

½ tsp. *each* black, green, red, and white peppercorns (*see Quick Tip below*)
2 lbs. shrimp, shells left on
2 tsp. salt, divided
2 tbsp. vegetable or peanut oil
4 garlic cloves, chopped
1 cup cilantro leaves, roughly chopped

1. Put peppercorns in a mortar and crush roughly with a pestle. Or put peppercorns in a large resealable plastic bag, spread out on a hard, flat surface, and crush with the bottom of a heavy frying pan or rolling pin.
2. Put shrimp, half the crushed peppercorns, and 1 tsp. salt in a large bowl and toss to coat shrimp evenly. Set aside.
3. Heat a wok or large (not nonstick) frying pan over high heat. Add oil, garlic, and remaining crushed peppercorns and 1 tsp. salt and cook, stirring constantly, until fragrant, about 1 minute. Add shrimp and cook, stirring constantly, until pink and cooked through, 3 to 4 minutes. Add cilantro, turn off heat, and toss to combine. Serve immediately.
Quick Tip: The different peppercorns add a subtle range of pepper flavor to this dish, but you can stick to just black peppercorns too; simply decrease the total amount to 1½ tsp.

PER SERVING: 209 cal., 34% (72 cal.) from fat; 30 g protein; 8 g fat (1.2 g sat.); 2.4 g carbo (0.3 g fiber); 685 mg sodium; 224 mg chol.

fish & shellfish

Spring Aioli with Shrimp

Aioli refers to both the garlicky mayonnaise of Southern France and to the ingredients it accompanies—which can range from simple vegetables to heaped platters like this one. The appearance of the first tender sugar snap peas and asparagus is the only excuse you need to prepare this celebration of the season.

Serve with both classic and green aioli, or shortcut versions of each that use store-bought mayonnaise instead of raw eggs (*recipes follow*).

SERVES 6 to 8 | **TIME** 1½ hours

1½ to 2 lbs. red thin-skinned potatoes (1 to 1½ in. wide)
1½ to 2 lbs. asparagus
1 lb. sugar snap peas
2 tbsp. fresh lemon juice or white wine vinegar
1 tbsp. olive oil
1 tsp. salt
3 or 4 artichokes (12 to 14 oz. each)
1 dozen radishes (about ½ lb.), trimmed
1½ to 2 lbs. peeled cooked large shrimp (21 to 30 per lb.)
6 to 8 hard-cooked eggs (optional), peeled
1½ to 2 cups aioli (*recipes follow*)

1. Put potatoes in a 5- to 6-qt. pan. Add 2 qts. water. Cover pan and bring to a boil over high heat, then reduce heat and simmer, covered, until potatoes are tender when pierced, 10 to 15 minutes. With a slotted spoon, lift potatoes out and let cool. Reserve cooking water in pan.
2. Meanwhile, snap off tough ends of asparagus. Peel any strings from outer edges of peas. Return water used for potatoes to a boil over high heat. Add asparagus and cook just until barely tender when pierced, 3 to 5 minutes. Lift out with tongs and immerse in a bowl filled with ice water. When cool, drain. Add peas to same boiling water and cook just until bright green, about 2 minutes. Pour peas and water into a colander, then immerse peas in ice water until cool; drain again.
3. Add about 3 qts. fresh water to the pan along with the lemon juice, oil, and salt. Cover and bring to a boil over high heat. Meanwhile, trim about 1 in. off tops of artichokes and discard. With scissors, trim remaining thorny tips off outer leaves. Trim off stems, then cut artichokes in half lengthwise. Immerse in boiling water and cover. When water returns to a boil, reduce heat and simmer, covered, until artichokes are tender when pierced in base, about 20 minutes. Drain and let cool.
4. Arrange potatoes, asparagus, peas, artichokes, radishes, shrimp, and peeled eggs (if using) on a platter. Serve with aioli.

Make Ahead: Through step 3, up to 1 day; chilled (store vegetables separately).

PER SERVING: 604 cal., 66% (396 cal.) from fat; 26 g protein; 44 g fat (6.3 g sat.); 28 g carbo (6.7 g fiber); 664 mg sodium; 206 mg chol.

Classic Aioli: In a blender, purée 1 **egg**, 2 tbsp. **fresh lemon juice**, 4 to 6 peeled cloves **garlic**, and ¼ tsp. **salt** until well blended. With machine running, gradually add 1 cup **extra-virgin olive oil** in a thin, steady stream until all is incorporated. Add more salt to taste. Makes about 1 cup. Can be made up to 1 week ahead, chilled. **Quick Tip:** If you're concerned about salmonella or bacteria in raw eggs, use a pasteurized egg. If using a pungent, peppery extra-virgin olive oil, start with ⅓ to ½ cup, then add a milder oil to make 1 cup total.

PER TBSP.: 125 cal., 100% (125 cal.) from fat; 0.4 g protein; 14 g fat (1.9 g sat.); 0.4 g carbo (0 g fiber); 40 mg sodium; 13 mg chol.

Green Aioli: Follow recipe for Classic Aioli, except add ½ cup loosely packed **basil** or **mint** leaves or coarsely chopped **flat-leaf parsley** and 1 tsp. finely shredded **lemon zest** to blender with egg mixture.

PER TBSP.: 127 cal., 99% (126 cal.) from fat; 0.6 g protein; 14 g fat (1.9 g sat.); 0.8 g carbo (0.3 g fiber); 41 mg sodium; 13 mg chol.

Quick Aioli: Omit egg and oil in Classic or Green Aioli and use 1 cup store-bought **mayonnaise** instead. Blend mayonnaise with lemon juice, garlic, and salt (and herbs and lemon zest for green aioli) until smooth.

PER TBSP.: 100 cal., 99% (99 cal.) from fat; 0.2 g protein; 11 g fat (1.6 g sat.); 0.7 g carbo (0 g fiber); 114 mg sodium; 8.1 mg chol.

Farmed vs. Wild Shrimp

Confused about which to choose? Either is fine, as long as you buy American (check the label on the package or the sign at the fish counter). Farm-raised shrimp and prawns from Asia and Latin America—representing the vast majority of the shrimp we eat—are often raised in badly managed, heavily polluted saltwater ponds that destroy the coast and spread disease. Also, in most parts of the world, wild shrimp are caught without regard to the turtles and fish that get snared in the nets used to haul them in. The United States has the highest production standards for harvesting wild shrimp; they are caught in relatively clean waters, with the conscientious use of devices that exclude bycatch.

Scallops with Miso, Ginger, and Grapefruit

Cookbook author and Californian Eric Gower, who specializes in innovative Japanese-Western fusion cooking, infuses sweet scallops with the tang of grapefuit.

SERVES 2 | **TIME** 40 minutes

1 Ruby grapefruit (1 lb.), cut in half
1 tbsp. *each* white miso, unseasoned rice vinegar, and sake
2 tbsp. *each* butter, minced shallots, and minced fresh ginger
Salt and freshly ground black pepper
1 tbsp. flour
1 tbsp. *each* chopped thyme and oregano leaves
½ lb. sea scallops (1 in. thick; *see How to Buy Scallops, right*)
2 tbsp. extra-virgin olive oil
1 tbsp. thinly sliced chives

1. Squeeze juice from a grapefruit half and reserve. With a small, sharp knife, cut peel from second half, down to flesh (discard peels), then cut between inner membranes and release half-segments into a small bowl.
2. In a blender, purée grapefruit juice, miso, vinegar, and sake until smooth.
3. In a 1- to 2-qt. pan over medium heat, melt butter. Add shallots and ginger and sprinkle with salt and pepper to taste. Cook, stirring often, until shallots are softened, 3 to 4 minutes. Pour in miso mixture and cook, stirring, until sauce is bubbling and slightly thickened, 2 to 3 minutes. Remove from heat.
4. On a plate, mix flour, thyme, oregano, and salt and pepper to taste. Coat scallops evenly in mixture.
5. Pour oil into a 10- to 12-in. frying pan over high heat and tilt pan to coat. When hot, set scallops in pan, spacing evenly. Cook, turning each scallop once with tongs, until golden brown on both sides and opaque but still moist-looking in center (cut to test), about 4 minutes total. Transfer to a serving plate.
6. Pour miso mixture into frying pan and stir, scraping browned bits from bottom of pan, until bubbling, about 1 minute. Pour sauce around scallops and top with reserved grapefruit segments and the chives.

PER SERVING: 409 cal., 59% (243 cal.) from fat; 22 g protein; 27 g fat (9.3 g sat.); 20 g carbo (1.3 g fiber); 616 mg sodium; 68 mg chol.

Scallops with Peppers and Corn

Reader Joyce Hannum, of Mason County, Washington, calls herself "the queen of clean-the-fridge cooking." This simple dish is the tasty result of her rummaging. Serve with couscous, pasta, or rice.

SERVES 6 | **TIME** 30 minutes

3 ears corn (about 2½ lbs. total), husked and silks removed
1¼ lbs. sea scallops (*see How to Buy Scallops below*)
Salt and freshly ground black pepper
2 tbsp. *each* butter and olive oil
2 red bell peppers (¾ lb. total), seeds and ribs removed and finely chopped
1 or 2 garlic cloves, minced
¼ tsp. ground cumin
⅓ cup *each* chopped basil leaves and cilantro

1. Holding each ear of corn upright in a deep bowl, cut kernels from cobs. Sprinkle scallops lightly all over with salt and pepper.
2. Melt 1 tbsp. butter with 1 tbsp. oil in each of two 10- to 12-in. frying pans over high heat. Add corn, bell peppers, garlic, and cumin to one pan; add scallops to the other. Cook, stirring vegetables often, until they are crisp-tender, about 3 minutes; cook scallops until they are browned on outside and barely opaque in center (cut to test), about 3 minutes, turning once halfway through.
3. Just before serving, stir basil into vegetable mixture and sprinkle cilantro over scallops. Add salt and pepper to taste to both. Mound vegetables in a wide, shallow bowl; top with scallops (and any pan juices).

PER SERVING: 231 cal., 39% (90 cal.) from fat; 19 g protein; 10 g fat (3.2 g sat.); 19 g carbo (2.8 g fiber); 203 mg sodium; 42 mg chol.

How to Buy Scallops

Avoid scallops that have been plumped up by a dip in sodium tripolyphosphate (STP) solution, which is also used to plump up ham. These scallops, when cooked, will ooze a copious amount of milky white liquid and will never caramelize; they'll just steam. Treated scallops are easy to recognize, because they'll be oozing STP liquid in the display case. Scallops that haven't been treated with this solution are often sold as "dry" scallops.

Abalone

It used to be easy to find abalone off the California coast, and anyone could wade out at low tide and nab a couple of plate-size beauties without much effort. Now the mollusk is extremely scarce, collecting them is the sport of the brave, and regulations are very strict—only a small area of the coast is open to sport divers. For most of us, the easiest way to taste this peerless sea creature is to order it from a farm. Our favorite source, the Abalone Farm in Cayucos, California, raises small (3- to 4-in.) California Red abalone, which it sells direct to consumers as frozen tenderized steaks ready for the grill or pan as well as live in the shell (find distributors at *abalonefarm.com*).

Proper Storage

If you're lucky enough to have snagged a large wild abalone from an abalone diver, or if you procured it yourself, keep it in a burlap sack soaked with saltwater in the refrigerator at least 1 day so it relaxes, but no more than 2 days. Farm-raised steaks should be prepared within 2 days of receiving them. If you plan to freeze fresh abalone steaks, be sure to tenderize them first (see step 5) or the meat will be tough and rubbery.

How to Prepare Whole Abalone

1. Force the tip of a cake spatula, sturdy knife, or sharp-edged soupspoon between the meat and shell near the shell's holes; shove it along the inside surface of the shell to sever the connector muscle.

2. Lift the meat and pull to separate it from the dangling saclike viscera on the side that was attached to the shell; or, using a sharp knife, cut off the sac (be careful not to break it, and put it in a plastic bag before discarding).

3. Set the abalone on a work surface. Pull or scrub off the frilly dark trim, or skirt, around the edges of the meat (save it for chowder or fritters; keeps best chilled, not frozen). With a wild abalone, trim off tough portions around the edges and the dark, tough bottom of the foot with a sharp knife.

4. If it's a large abalone, slice the meat across the grain in pieces ⅜ in. thick, holding the meat down firmly so it doesn't slide around. If it's a small abalone (and it will be, if it's farm-raised), leave it as is. If you're making chowder, you can dice the meat at this point.

5. To pound the abalone for frying or grilling, wrap each slice loosely in plastic wrap. If it's unsliced, put it foot side up. Gently pound with the toothed side of a wooden mallet. Use a light, rhythmic motion and pound evenly until the piece is velvety and limp enough to drape over your fingers.

3 Ways with Abalone

1. PAN-FRY

In a wide, shallow bowl, season **flour** with **salt** and freshly ground **black pepper** to taste. In a separate wide, shallow bowl, beat a couple of **eggs** with a spoonful of water to loosen. Put **fine dried bread crumbs or panko** (Japanese-style bread crumbs) in a third wide, shallow bowl. Dredge pounded **abalone steaks** (*see above*) in flour, then egg, then crumbs, and fry in hot **olive oil** 30 seconds to 1 minute per side, turning once. Serve with **lemon wedges**.

2. GRILL

Prepare a charcoal or gas grill for direct high heat (*see Direct Heat Grilling, page 436*). In a small saucepan, melt ¼ cup **butter** with 2 tsp. **fresh lemon juice** over low heat. Grill pounded **abalone steaks**, brushing frequently with butter mixture, 2 to 3 minutes. Turn over and grill, brushing with more butter, 2 to 3 minutes more. Add chopped **fresh herbs** or sliced toasted **almonds** to remaining butter and serve with steaks.

3. SAUTÉ, WITH MUSHROOM SAUCE

In a large frying pan, heat 1 tbsp. **butter** over medium-high heat until bubbling. Add 3 tbsp. chopped **green onion**, ½ tsp. minced **thyme leaves**, and 1 cup sliced **mushrooms** and cook, stirring occasionally, until mushrooms begin to brown. Add 2 tbsp. **white wine** and cook, stirring, 1 minute. Add ⅓ cup **whipping cream** and cook, stirring often, 2 minutes to thicken. Season to taste with **salt** and freshly ground **black pepper**. Pour into a heated bowl and cover to keep warm. Rinse pan and dry. Heat 1 tbsp. **olive oil** in pan over medium-high heat. Meanwhile, in a wide, shallow bowl, season **flour** with salt and freshly ground black pepper to taste. Dredge pounded **abalone steaks** in flour and fry in oil, 1 minute per side. Serve on heated plates with mushroom sauce and chopped **parsley** on top.

Scallop and Sugar Snap Pea Stir-fry

Creamy scallops and crunchy sugar snap peas make a wonderful contrast of tastes and textures. Serve with rice.

SERVES 4 | **TIME** 30 minutes

¾ **lb. sugar snap peas, trimmed**
¾ **lb. sea scallops** (*see How to Buy Scallops, page 348*)
½ **cup chicken broth**
2 **tbsp. mirin or rice wine**
1 **tbsp. cornstarch**
2 **tbsp.** *each* **vegetable oil and thinly sliced green onions**
1 **tbsp. minced garlic**
¼ **tsp. red chile flakes**
½ **cup slivered basil leaves**

1. Bring water to a boil in a large pan, then add sugar snap peas. Cook just until they start to turn a brighter green, 15 to 30 seconds, then drain immediately. Rinse well under cold running water until cool, then drain again.
2. Slice snap peas on the diagonal into ½-in. lengths. Cut scallops in half to form half-moon shapes.
3. In a small bowl, whisk broth, mirin, and cornstarch until well blended.
4. Heat oil in a 12-in. frying pan or 14-in. wok over high heat until hot. Add green onions, garlic, and chile flakes and cook, stirring, until fragrant, 30 to 45 seconds.
5. Add scallops and cook, stirring occasionally, until mostly opaque on surface, about 2 minutes. Stir in snap peas and pour in broth mixture. Cook, stirring, until sauce is thick and glossy and scallops are opaque but still moist-looking in center of thickest part (cut to test), 2 to 3 minutes.
6. Stir in half the basil, then pour into a serving bowl and sprinkle with remaining basil.

PER SERVING: 210 cal., 32% (68 cal.) from fat; 18 g protein; 7.5 g fat (0.9 g sat.); 14 g carbo (2.6 g fiber); 148 mg sodium; 28 mg chol.

Steamed Clams or Mussels in Seasoned Broth

Tailor our recipe to suit your tastes, using either clams or mussels and your choice of flavored broth and topping. Add crusty bread and a salad, and you've got a sensational dinner.

SERVES 2 | **TIME** 25 minutes

Seasoned broth (choices follow; *also see Quick Tip below*)
3 **dozen clams** (about 2½ lbs.) **or mussels** (1¼ lbs.)
Chopped flat-leaf parsley, green onions, or cilantro
Lemon wedges

1. In a covered 5- to 6-qt. pan over high heat, bring broth to a boil. Reduce heat to low and simmer while cleaning shellfish.
2. Meanwhile, scrub clams or mussels well; pull any beards off mussels. Discard open mollusks that don't close when tapped.
3. Return broth to a boil over high heat. Add mollusks, cover, and cook until shells pop open, 3 to 6 minutes. Discard any closed mollusks. Spoon mollusks and broth into bowls and sprinkle with garnish. Serve with lemon wedges.
Quick Tip: As the mollusks cook, they release their briny juices into the broth. Clams tend to be saltier than mussels; when cooking them, use water for the broth.

Creamy Tarragon-Shallot Broth: In pan, combine 1 cup water (for clams) or **clam juice** (for mussels), 1 cup **dry white wine**, ½ cup chopped **shallots**, ¼ cup **whipping cream**, and 1 tsp. **dried tarragon**.

PER SERVING WITH CLAMS: 265 cal., 34% (90 cal.) from fat; 13 g protein; 10 g fat (5.8 g sat.); 11 g carbo (0.3 g fiber); 328 mg sodium; 62 mg chol.

Garlic-Ginger Broth: In pan, combine 1 cup water (for clams) or reduced-sodium **chicken broth** (for mussels), 1 cup **sake or dry white wine**, 1 tbsp. *each* chopped **garlic** and **fresh ginger**, and ¼ tsp. **red chile flakes**.

PER SERVING WITH CLAMS: 154 cal., 5% (8.1 cal.) from fat; 12 g protein; 0.9 g fat (0.1 g sat.); 5.4 g carbo (0.2 g fiber); 56 mg sodium; 29 mg chol.

Tomato-Basil Broth: In pan, combine 1 can (14.5 oz.) **diced tomatoes** (with their juice), ½ cup water (for clams) or reduced-sodium **chicken broth** (for mussels), ½ cup chopped **onion**, 1 tbsp. minced **garlic**, and 2 tsp. **dried basil**.

PER SERVING WITH CLAMS: 131 cal., 11% (14 cal.) from fat; 14 g protein; 1.5 g fat (0.2 g sat.); 17 g carbo (2.4 g fiber); 386 mg sodium; 29 mg chol.

fish & shellfish

Mussels

Mediterranean mussels are larger, sweeter, and plumper than the common blue mussel. Both are farmed in the U.S., and—along with black and green mussels—cause little habitat destruction because they're usually grown on ropes suspended in the ocean. After scrubbing mussels to remove any sand or dirt, debeard them; the "beard" is the strands of tissue attached to the shell. Simply snip or pull the strands off. Mussels spoil quickly after debearding, so cook them immediately.

Wine-steamed Mussels with Aioli

Mussels have a sweet brininess that calls for a dry, bracing wine, but one with so much fruit flavor that it *seems* sweet. Pinot Gris is great on both counts and always good with aioli. If you have any aioli left over, it's excellent on sandwiches or blended with an avocado for a quick dip.

SERVES 4 to 6 | **TIME** 45 minutes

2 egg yolks
2 tsp. Dijon mustard
½ tsp. *each* kosher salt and freshly ground pepper
4 garlic cloves, crushed and divided
1 cup mild extra-virgin olive oil, or more as needed
2 tbsp. fresh lemon juice
2 cups Pinot Gris or other dry white wine
1 onion, halved lengthwise and thinly sliced
2 lbs. mussels in shells, scrubbed and beards pulled off
2 tbsp. butter
½ cup finely chopped flat-leaf parsley

1. In a food processor, purée egg yolks, mustard, salt, pepper, and 1 garlic clove until smooth. With motor running, add 1 cup oil in a thin, steady stream until mixture is emulsified. Add lemon juice and pulse to blend. If the aioli seems too thick, thin it with a bit more oil. Transfer aioli to a bowl, cover, and chill.
2. In a 4-qt. saucepan, combine wine, remaining 3 garlic cloves, and onion. Bring to a boil over high heat, then reduce heat and simmer 5 minutes. Add mussels, cover, and simmer until shells have opened, about 6 minutes.

3. With a slotted spoon, scoop mussels from pan into a serving bowl, discarding any that have not opened. Whisk butter into wine mixture until melted, then stir in parsley. Pour sauce over mussels and drizzle with aioli or serve it on the side. To drizzle aioli, put it in a resealable plastic bag, cut one corner, and squeeze it over the mussels.
Make Ahead: Aioli, up to 1 day, chilled.

PER SERVING: 370 cal., 71% (261 cal.) from fat; 7.5 g protein; 29 g fat (6.6 g sat.); 6 g carbo (0.7 g fiber); 328 mg sodium; 70 mg chol.

Yeo's Garlic Mussels

Although delicate in flavor and texture, mussels stand up surprisingly well to the intense black pepper–and–garlic sauce added to them at Straits Café restaurants in the San Francisco Bay Area. Chef Chris Yeo, head of Straits Restaurant Group, gave us the recipe for the remarkably quick-to-make five-ingredient Singaporean dish. Serve the mussels with sourdough bread for dunking if you like.

SERVES 4 | **TIME** 25 to 30 minutes

3 lbs. mussels, scrubbed and beards pulled off
3 tbsp. *each* butter and chopped garlic
1½ tbsp. cracked or coarse-ground pepper
6 tbsp. oyster sauce

1. Tap shells of any mussels that gape; if they don't close, discard them. Put mussels in a 5- to 6-qt. pan. Add ½ cup water, cover, and bring to a boil over high heat. Reduce heat and simmer until shells pop open, 5 to 10 minutes. Discard any closed mussels. Pour juices from pan and save.
2. In a 14-in. wok or frying pan or a 5- to 6-qt. pan over high heat, melt butter with garlic and pepper and stir until garlic is golden, about 30 seconds. Add oyster sauce and reserved mussel-cooking liquid. Boil over high heat, stirring often, until sauce is reduced to about 1 cup, 5 to 6 minutes.
3. Ladle mussels into bowls, top liberally with sauce, and stir once to coat.

PER SERVING: 207 cal., 48% (99 cal.) from fat; 15 g protein; 11 g fat (5.8 g sat.); 12 g carbo (0.8 g fiber); 1,444 mg sodium; 51 mg chol.

poultry & stuffing

Inventive recipes for everybody's favorite bird—chicken—plus great ways to cook turkey (with stuffing, of course) and even duck.

Tender, juicy, mild, and relatively inexpensive, chicken is the meat we eat the most. The great challenge with chicken, as with any staple food, is to keep it from getting boring. Fortunately, chicken is so versatile that we're always finding new ways to cook it, and this chapter is full of our discoveries and reinventions (as is our grilling chapter; *see page 432*). Some of our favorites are one-pot dishes like Grandmother's Chicken (*page 358*), a speedy version of a French classic with potatoes, bacon, and garlic; a soulful Moroccan *tagine* made with quick-cooking chicken thighs (*page 360*); and a lighter, simpler approach to tangy Filipino adobo (*page 360*). Another reason we're smitten with chicken is that these days it's easier to find really flavorful birds—almost always those raised under good conditions (look for labels that say pasture-raised, certified humane, or free-range). These birds cost more, but they're worth it on many levels.

As for turkeys, we've roasted and grilled hundreds over the years and distilled our expertise into a chart (*page 370*) that you can apply to any recipe for turkey. Because the breast meat tends to dry out by the time the dark is done, we've included a few appetizing ways to deal with this problem (see Dry-cured Rosemary Turkey, *page 371*, and Roast Turkey with Wine and Herbs, *page 385*). For meat that's almost impossible to dry out, try duck—utterly delicious cooked till the skin is golden brown and crisp (*page 389*).

You can't have turkey without stuffing. Our recipes run the gamut from traditional Western to intriguing versions influenced by India, China, and the Southwest—plus one of our most-requested recipes ever: Artichoke Parmesan Sourdough Stuffing (*page 394*).

Poultry & Stuffing

Roast Chicken with Meyer Lemon–Shallot Sauce

Shallots roast alongside the chicken; then they're puréed and browned with lemony pan juices to make a fragrant and naturally thick gravy—no flour or cornstarch necessary.

recipe pictured on page 320

SERVES 6 to 8 | **TIME** 2 hours, plus 3 hours to cure

1 chicken (4 to 5 lbs.)
1 tbsp. kosher salt
2 medium Meyer or regular (Eureka) lemons
2½ tbsp. olive oil, divided
1½ tsp. dried thyme
1 lb. shallots, unpeeled
¾ to 1 cup reduced-sodium chicken broth
⅓ cup dry white wine

1. Remove giblets from chicken and save for another use. Pull off and discard lumps of fat, then pat chicken dry. Loosen skin of breast and thighs and work some salt under skin. Rub remaining salt all over chicken and in cavity (*see Quick Tip, right*). Chill, uncovered, at least 3 hours and up to overnight.

2. Preheat oven to 400°. Finely shred zest of lemons. Slice 1 lemon; juice half the other and reserve.

3. Pat chicken dry, inside and out. Rub zest under as much of skin as possible and rub any remaining zest inside cavity. Rub chicken all over with 1 tbsp. oil and the thyme. Put lemon slices in cavity.

4. Set a V-shaped rack in a heavy roasting pan large enough to hold shallots. Put chicken in rack, breast side up. Add unpeeled shallots to pan and drizzle with remaining 1½ tbsp. oil, turning them to coat.

5. Roast chicken (*see 5 Secrets for Roasting a Chicken, page 356*), basting with pan juices every 30 minutes or so, until chicken leg moves easily, skin is brown and crisp, and a thermometer registers 170° when inserted through thickest part of breast to bone or 180° through thickest part of thigh at joint, 1 to 1½ hours (remove shallots after 1 hour and set aside). Tip chicken so juices from cavity pour into roasting pan. Transfer chicken to a carving board and let rest, covered with foil.

6. Meanwhile, make sauce: Pour pan drippings into a measuring cup with a pouring lip. Trim tops from shallots and squeeze soft insides into a blender. Discard all but about 1 tbsp. fat from pan drippings and add drippings to blender. Add ¾ cup broth and the wine and pulse until smooth.

7. Pour sauce into roasting pan. Cook over medium-high heat on your biggest burner (or straddling two burners), scraping any browned bits off bottom of pan and adding more broth if you want a thinner sauce, until sauce turns a nutty brown, about 10 minutes. Stir in 1 tbsp. reserved lemon juice, or more to taste. Pour sauce through a fine-mesh strainer into a serving bowl. Carve chicken, discarding lemon slices; serve with sauce.

Quick Tip: Salting the chicken hours ahead instead of just before cooking makes the meat more flavorful.

PER SERVING WITH 2 TBSP. GRAVY: 388 cal., 56% (216 cal.) from fat; 33 g protein; 24 g fat (6 g sat.); 11 g carbo (1.2 g fiber); 700 mg sodium; 101 mg chol.

How to Carve a Roasted Chicken

The Standard Way (8 pieces)

1. THIGHS AND DRUMSTICKS. With the chicken positioned breast up on a cutting board, pull a leg down and away from the body until the skin separates and you can see the thigh joint. Cut through the joint and meat with a sharp boning knife, then cut through the joint in the leg to separate the drumstick from the thigh. Repeat with the other leg.

2. WINGS. Gently twist them away from the carcass to expose the joint.

Cut through the joint with your knife. Cut off the wing tips (save for stock).

3. BREASTS. Gently but firmly, cut down one side of the breastbone, as close as possible to the bone and starting at the tail end. When you reach the wishbone at the front of the breast, follow its curve to free meat from the bone. Repeat on other side of the breastbone. Because breasts are often larger than other pieces, cut them in half crosswise or into thick slices if you like.

The Scissors Way (8 pieces)

If you're a little shaky in the carving department, take the easy route: With poultry shears or strong kitchen scissors, cut the legs off at the thigh joints; then cut through the joints in the legs. Snip the chicken on either side of the breastbone and remove the bone. Do the same with the backbone. Lastly, cut through the wing joints to separate wings from the breasts.

5 Secrets for Roasting a Chicken

When it's done right, a roast chicken is just about the best dinner a person could have—juicy, tender, crisp-skinned, and aromatic. Done wrong, it's a big disappointment. Follow our tips and you'll be very happy with the results.

1. The right oven temperature
Cook at 425° for the best browning, crispest skin, and most succulent meat. The high heat will create some spattering, but it results in a chicken so good it's worth dirtying the oven. (If you add a little water to the roasting pan it will reduce spattering considerably, though the skin won't be quite as crisp.) One note: If you're going to use a marinade or glaze with sugar in it or have other ingredients in your pan, you'll probably need to reduce the heat a bit to prevent scorching.

2. The right size
Big chickens—often labeled roasters (generally 6 to 8 lbs. and about 8 months old)—have deeper, richer, and more complex flavor than smaller ones. Of course, young chickens, also called broilers and fryers (under 6 lbs. and about 7 weeks old), can be roasted too, and since those are mainly what you'll find in the grocery store, our recipes tend to call for this size. The trouble with smaller birds is that by the time the skin is an appealing color, the breast meat is

usually cooked past its prime. A roaster, however, reaches perfection inside and out at the same time. To use one of them in any of our recipes, simply cook it longer.

3. A V-rack
We've tried roasting chickens directly in the pan and with different racks: a flat rack, a vertical roaster, even a spitlike suspension device. Starting with the bird positioned breast down then turning it over to brown doesn't keep the meat any moister, nor does rotating the chicken from side to side—and the skin doesn't get nicely colored in either case. In the end, we've found that the simple V-shaped rack produces the most even browning and juiciest meat.

4. No trussing
For the crispest skin and most evenly cooked meat, don't tie the legs together. Trussed legs may look tidy, but they stop the regular flow of hot air over and around the chicken.

5. A thermometer
This tool will help prevent you from overcooking your chicken. Insert it before cooking: When you have the bird positioned breast side up on your V-shaped rack, insert the thermometer through the thickest part of the breast to the bone (where the temperature is most consistent). Roast until the thermometer reaches 170° here, or 180° through thickest part of thigh at joint if you feel you need a second reading. We especially like the wand-style meat thermometer, which goes into the chicken and then threads out your oven door to a readout that beeps when the right temperature is reached (you can find these in any kitchenware shop). Or you can use an instant-read thermometer toward the end of cooking. When a chicken is done, the drumstick should wiggle easily, and the thigh meat should no longer be pink.

Soy-Ginger Roast Chicken with Shiitake Mushrooms

Marinating the chicken in soy sauce and brown sugar produces deep mahogany skin and aromatic meat. Serve the dish with rice cooked with coconut milk.

SERVES 6 to 8 | **TIME** 2 hours, plus 4 hours to brine

1¼ cups soy sauce, divided
1 cup firmly packed brown sugar
½ cup coarsely chopped fresh ginger, divided
10 garlic cloves, crushed, divided
1 chicken (6 to 8 lbs.)
½ cup chopped cilantro, divided
¼ cup cilantro sprigs
Salt and freshly ground black pepper
1 cup chicken broth
¼ cup *each* unseasoned rice vinegar and mirin *(see Quick Tip, right)* or sake
1 tbsp. *each* hoisin sauce and Asian (toasted) sesame oil
1 lb. green onions
2 lbs. fresh shiitake mushrooms (with 2-in. caps), stems discarded

1. In a 10- to 12-qt. pan, combine 1 cup soy sauce, brown sugar, ¼ cup ginger, 6 garlic cloves, and 4 qts. water; mix well.

2. Preheat oven to 425°. Remove giblets from chicken and save for other uses if you like. Pull off and discard lumps of fat. Pierce skin all over with a fork. Immerse chicken, breast down, in marinade; cover and chill at least 4 hours and up to 12 hours, turning several times.

3. Discard marinade and rinse chicken thoroughly under cold running water, rubbing gently; pat dry with paper towels. Set, breast up, on a V-shaped rack in an 11- by 17-in. roasting pan.

4. Starting at the neck, gently ease your fingers under skin to loosen it over the breast. Push ¼ cup chopped cilantro under skin and spread evenly over breast. Put cilantro sprigs, 2 tbsp. ginger, and remaining 4 garlic cloves in body cavity. Sprinkle chicken lightly with salt and pepper. Roast for 30 minutes.

5. Meanwhile, in a large bowl, mix remaining ¼ cup soy sauce, 2 tbsp. ginger, and ¼ cup chopped cilantro with broth, vinegar, mirin, hoisin, and sesame oil. Trim green onions; chop green tops and white bottoms separately and reserve ½ cup green tops. Mix mushrooms, the chopped white parts of onions, and all but reserved green tops with soy mixture. Lift out with a slotted spoon and distribute mushrooms and onions around chicken in pan; reserve soy mixture.

6. Continue to roast chicken, turning mushrooms and onions with a wide spatula after about 20 minutes, until

a thermometer registers 170° when inserted through thickest part of breast to bone or 180° through thickest part of thigh at joint, 45 minutes to 1¼ hours longer.

7. Insert a carving fork into body cavity, piercing carcass; lift bird and tilt to drain juices into pan. Set chicken on a rimmed platter. With a slotted spoon, arrange mushrooms and onions around chicken. Let rest in a warm place about 15 minutes.

8. Meanwhile, skim and discard fat from pan and set over two burners. Add reserved soy mixture and stir often over high heat, scraping up any browned bits, until reduced to ¾ cup, 10 to 12 minutes. Pour through a fine-mesh strainer into a small pitcher or bowl.

9. Sprinkle mushroom mixture with reserved ½ cup chopped green onion tops. Carve chicken and serve with mushrooms, onions, and pan juices. Add salt and pepper to taste.

Quick Tip: Find mirin (sweet sake) in the Asian section of many supermarkets and in Asian grocery stores.

PER SERVING: 508 cal., 44% (223 cal.) from fat; 47 g protein; 25 g fat (7 g sat.); 20 g carbo (2.7 g fiber); 703 mg sodium; 134 mg chol.

Oven-fried Chicken

Mickey Strang, a *Sunset* reader from McKinleyville, California, likes oven-fried chicken because it can be served warm or cold. She livened up her version with sharp cheddar cheese and ancho chile powder.

SERVES 4 | **TIME** 1¼ hours

6 slices day-old or slightly stale bread *(see Quick Tip below)*
½ cup finely shredded sharp cheddar cheese
¾ tsp. ancho chile powder or chili powder
½ tsp. salt
1 chicken (about 4 lbs.), cut into 8 pieces
2 eggs, beaten to blend

1. Preheat oven to 375°. Toast bread slices. Let cool, then tear into 1-in. chunks. Blend in a food processor to make coarse crumbs.

2. In a large shallow bowl, mix bread crumbs, cheddar cheese, ancho chile powder, and salt.

3. Dip chicken pieces in beaten egg and roll in crumb mixture to coat. Set on a foil-lined 12- by 15-in. baking sheet.

4. Bake until crumbs are browned and chicken is not pink at the bone (cut to test), 45 minutes to 1 hour.

Quick Tip: You can substitute 1½ cups store-bought fine dried bread crumbs.

PER SERVING: 446 cal., 48% (216 cal.) from fat; 43 g protein; 24 g fat (7.7 g sat.); 12 g carbo (0.6 g fiber); 512 mg sodium; 198 mg chol.

Grandmother's Chicken

We've created a modern granddaughter's version of the French *poulet grand-mère*, streamlining it so it comes together in little more than an hour, about half the time required for the original recipe. We leave the garlic unpeeled, in keeping with the homey nature of the dish. Once cooked, the cloves can be squeezed out of their skins and spread on bread.

recipe pictured on page **315**

SERVES 4 to 6 | **TIME** 1 hour, 20 minutes

1 chicken (4 to 5 lbs.), cut into 8 pieces
2 tbsp. olive oil
1 tsp. *each* salt and freshly ground black pepper
1 cup frozen pearl onions
6 large garlic cloves, unpeeled
2 thyme sprigs
1 lb. baby Yukon Gold potatoes, halved
3 slices thick-cut bacon, sliced crosswise into ¼-in.-wide pieces
1 lb. cremini or button mushrooms, quartered
2 cups reduced-sodium chicken broth

1. Save chicken wings for another use. Preheat oven to 375°. Heat oil in a heavy-bottomed 4- to 5-qt. oven-proof pot over medium-high heat until hot. Season chicken pieces with salt and pepper and add skin side down to pot. Cook without turning until skin is crispy and deeply browned, about 12 minutes. Remove chicken from pot and set aside.
2. Pour off all but 2 tbsp. fat from pot, reduce heat to medium-low, and add onions, garlic, and thyme. Cook, stirring often, for 5 minutes, then add potatoes and bacon. Cook, stirring occasionally, until mixture is well browned, about 8 minutes. Pour off all but a thin layer of fat.
3. Add mushrooms and broth, bring to a boil, and cook until liquid has reduced by a quarter. Arrange chicken, skin side up, on top of vegetables.
4. Transfer pot to oven and bake, uncovered, until chicken is cooked through, about 20 minutes.

PER SERVING: 772 cal., 56% (432 cal.) from fat; 57 g protein; 48 g fat (14 g sat.); 25 g carbo (2.5 g fiber); 1,013 mg sodium; 178 mg chol.

Japanese Soy-braised Chicken and Sweet Potatoes

Serve with rice to soak up the savory-sweet juices.

SERVES 6 | **TIME** 45 minutes

1 tbsp. vegetable oil
6 skinned, bone-in chicken thighs (6 oz. each)
2 cups chicken broth
¼ cup *each* soy sauce and mirin or cream sherry
1 tbsp. sugar
1 lb. orange-fleshed sweet potatoes (often labeled "yams"), peeled and cut crosswise into 1-in.-thick rounds
6 heads baby bok choy (3 oz. each), cut in half lengthwise

1. Heat oil in a 12-in. nonstick frying pan (with sides 2 in. high) or a 5- to 6-qt. pot over medium-high heat until hot. Add chicken thighs and cook, turning once, until browned on both sides, about 10 minutes total.
2. Add broth, soy sauce, mirin, and sugar; bring to a boil. Add sweet potatoes. Cover, reduce heat, and simmer, turning chicken and potatoes after about 10 minutes, until both are tender when pierced, 20 to 25 minutes total.
3. Lay bok choy halves over chicken and sweet potatoes; cover and simmer until bok choy is barely tender when pierced, 3 to 4 minutes.
4. Arrange chicken, sweet potatoes, and bok choy in wide bowls. Spoon broth over servings.

PER SERVING: 289 cal., 24% (68 cal.) from fat; 30 g protein; 7.5 g fat (1.6 g sat.); 22 g carbo (2.5 g fiber); 880 mg sodium; 103 mg chol.

■ Mirin

FROM THE PANTRY

Mirin, a staple in Japanese cuisine, is a low-alcohol rice wine that's similar to sake. Its slightly sweet taste is often used to enhance the flavor of a dish, especially those including fish and seafood. It should, however, be used in small amounts, as its flavor is fairly strong.

poultry & stuffing

Roy's Homestyle Chicken Curry

Roy Yamaguchi of Roy's Restaurant in Honolulu uses mild Thai Masaman curry paste—one of many prepared Thai curry pastes—to make this simple dish for his family.

SERVES 4 | **TIME** 50 minutes

4 whole chicken legs (thighs and drumsticks attached, about 2½ lbs. total)
1 tbsp. vegetable oil
1 stalk (12 to 16 in.) fresh lemongrass
1 can (13.5 oz.) coconut milk
1 tbsp. Masaman curry paste *(see Quick Tip below)*
1 tbsp. palm sugar *(see Quick Tip below)* or firmly packed brown sugar
2 tbsp. Thai or Vietnamese fish sauce (*nam pla* or *nuoc mam*), divided
4 quarter-size slices fresh ginger
2 garlic cloves, crushed
18 basil leaves (at least 2 in.)

1. Remove and discard chicken skin. Pat chicken dry.
2. Heat oil in a 10- to 12-in. nonstick frying pan over medium-high heat. Add chicken and brown on each side, about 5 minutes total. Transfer chicken to plate.
3. Meanwhile, trim and discard root end and coarse outer leaves of lemongrass. Cut stalk into 4-in. lengths and crush with a mallet or the blunt edge of a knife.
4. To pan, add coconut milk, curry paste, and sugar. Stir until mixture is smoothly blended. Stir in 1 tbsp. fish sauce and add lemongrass, ginger, and garlic. Heat until boiling.
5. Set aside 4 basil leaves for garnish; add rest to pan along with chicken. Cover and simmer over low heat for 15 minutes. Turn chicken over, cover, and continue to simmer until chicken is no longer pink at bone (cut to test), 10 to 15 minutes longer.
6. Lift chicken from sauce and put on a platter; keep warm. With a slotted spoon, remove lemongrass, garlic, ginger, and basil if you like (it's fine to keep them in too). If you want the sauce thick enough to coat chicken in a velvety layer, boil and stir to reduce slightly. Pour sauce over chicken and sprinkle with remaining basil leaves. Season with remaining 1 tbsp. fish sauce to taste.
Quick Tip: Look for Masaman (also spelled Massaman and Mussaman) curry paste and palm sugar at Asian markets. Some well-stocked supermarkets also carry the curry paste.

PER SERVING: 444 cal., 59% (261 cal.) from fat; 36 g protein; 29 g fat (21 g sat.); 11 g carbo (0.9 g fiber); 496 mg sodium; 130 mg chol.

Chicken with Rice (*Arroz con Pollo*)

Reader (and former *Sunset* employee) Eligio Hernández—who immigrated to California from Veracruz, Mexico—cooks chicken thighs on a chile- and mint-scented bed of rice to create a Mexican-style paella.

SERVES 4 | **TIME** 1¼ hours

8 bone-in chicken thighs (about 6 oz. each)
1 tbsp. chili powder
1 to 2 tbsp. vegetable oil
1 white onion (½ lb.), chopped
3 garlic cloves, minced
2 jalapeño chiles, stemmed and thinly sliced
1½ cups long-grain white rice
2 cups chicken broth
1 can (14.5 oz.) stewed tomatoes
1¾ cups (9 oz.) frozen corn kernels
⅓ cup chopped mint leaves, divided
Salt

1. Remove skin from chicken. Trim off and discard excess fat. Rub chili powder all over pieces.
2. Set a 12-in. frying pan (with sides 2 in. high) or a 5- to 6-qt. pan over medium-high heat. When hot, add 1 tbsp. oil and tilt pan to coat bottom. Add chicken in a single layer and turn as needed to brown on both sides, 10 to 12 minutes total (if necessary, brown in two batches, adding 1 tbsp. oil if needed). Transfer to a plate.
3. Add onion, garlic, and jalapeños to pan; cook, stirring often, until onion has softened, about 3 minutes. Reduce heat to medium and add rice; cook, stirring often, until rice is opaque, about 3 minutes. Add broth, tomatoes, corn, and ¼ cup mint. Bring to a boil over high heat.
4. Lay chicken pieces slightly apart in pan. Reduce heat to low, cover pan, and cook until rice is tender to the bite and chicken is no longer pink at bone (cut to test), 25 to 30 minutes. Sprinkle with remaining 4 tsp. mint and add salt to taste.

PER SERVING: 651 cal., 17% (108 cal.) from fat; 51 g protein; 12 g fat (2.6 g sat.); 83 g carbo (5.1 g fiber); 456 mg sodium; 161 mg chol.

Easy Chicken Adobo

Adobo, considered the national dish of the Philippines, is often made with pork and sometimes enriched with coconut milk. For everyday cooking we like this lighter, simpler version. Serve with rice.

SERVES 4 | **TIME** 45 minutes

1 tbsp. vegetable oil
6 skinned, bone-in chicken thighs
3 garlic cloves, minced
⅔ cup cider vinegar
⅓ cup soy sauce
1 tsp. black peppercorns
1 bay leaf

1. Heat oil in a medium frying pan over medium-high heat until hot. Add chicken thighs and cook until lightly browned, about 5 minutes, then turn over and cook an additional 5 minutes. Transfer chicken to a plate and set aside.
2. Pour off all but 1 tbsp. pan drippings and return pan to low heat. Add garlic and cook, stirring, until softened, about 1 minute. Add remaining ingredients and stir to incorporate. Return chicken to pan and cook, covered, for 20 minutes.
3. Uncover, increase heat to medium-low, and cook 15 to 20 minutes more, occasionally spooning sauce over chicken, until sauce thickens a bit and chicken is tender, cooked all the way through (cut to test), and nicely glazed with sauce.

PER SERVING: 251 cal., 35% (89 cal.) from fat; 34 g protein; 9.9 g fat (2.1 g sat.); 5.7 g carbo (0.2 g fiber); 1,501 mg sodium; 138 mg chol.

Chicken *Tagine* with Pine Nut Couscous

When prepared with quick-cooking chicken thighs, a *tagine* is relatively fast to make. Spices give this dish layers of flavor, and the cooked-down dried fruits create a silken richness.

SERVES 4 to 6 | **TIME** 1 hour, 20 minutes

2 tbsp. olive oil
6 skin-on, bone-in chicken thighs
1 medium onion, thinly sliced
4 large garlic cloves, minced
1 tbsp. minced fresh ginger
1 tsp. *each* cinnamon, turmeric, and ground coriander
¼ tsp. freshly ground black pepper
2 cardamom pods, lightly crushed
2 small dried red chiles, such as arbol
1 tsp. salt
15 *each* dried apricots and pitted prunes, halved
4 cups reduced-sodium chicken broth, divided
5 flat-leaf parsley sprigs plus ¼ cup minced parsley
1½ cups couscous
¼ cup pine nuts, lightly toasted (*see How to Toast Nuts, page 134*)
1 tsp. finely shredded lemon zest

1. Heat oil in a 6- to 8-qt. heavy-bottomed pot over medium-high heat until hot. Add half the chicken, skin side down, and cook until golden brown, 5 to 7 minutes. Turn over and cook 3 minutes more. Transfer to a plate; repeat with remaining chicken and set aside.
2. Drain all but 2 tbsp. oil from pot and reduce heat to medium. Add onion and cook, stirring, until golden, 5 to 7 minutes. Add garlic and ginger and cook, stirring constantly, for 3 minutes. Add cinnamon, turmeric, coriander, pepper, cardamom pods, chiles, and salt and stir to combine. Return chicken to pot and add apricots, prunes, 2 cups broth, and the parsley sprigs. Bring mixture to a boil, then reduce heat to medium-low. Cover and simmer 40 minutes.
3. Take pot off heat and remove parsley sprigs and chiles. Remove skin from chicken.
4. Bring remaining 2 cups broth to a boil. Turn off heat, stir in couscous, cover, and let sit 5 minutes. Uncover pan and fluff couscous with a fork. Stir in 2 tbsp. minced parsley, the pine nuts, and lemon zest and toss to combine. Mound couscous on a platter. Top with chicken thighs and pour sauce over the chicken. Sprinkle with remaining 2 tbsp. minced parsley.

PER SERVING: 793 cal., 40% (315 cal.) from fat; 46 g protein; 35 g fat (8.5 g sat.); 75 g carbo (6.2 g fiber); 1,043 mg sodium; 124 mg chol.

Macadamia Chicken with Orange-Ginger Sauce and Coconut Pilaf

The tropical flavors of this dish match up beautifully with Viognier's bright citrus and stone-fruit flavors.

SERVES 4 | **TIME** 1 hour

1 cup *each* **flour** and canned **coconut milk**
1 cup finely chopped roasted, salted **macadamia nuts** (about ¼ lb.; *see Quick Tips below*)
1 cup **panko** (Japanese-style bread crumbs) or other fine dried bread crumbs
4 skinned, boned **chicken breast halves** (6 to 7 oz. each)
Kosher salt and freshly ground **black pepper**
About 2 tbsp. *each* **butter** and **olive oil**
1 cup chopped **shallots**
1½ tbsp. *each* chopped fresh **ginger** and **garlic**
1 cup reduced-sodium **chicken broth**
½ cup **Viognier** or other dry white wine
½ cup fresh **orange juice** (*see Quick Tips below*)
Coconut Pilaf (*recipe follows*)

1. Preheat oven to 375°. Put flour and coconut milk in separate wide, shallow bowls. In another bowl, mix nuts and panko. Sprinkle chicken all over with salt and pepper.
2. Put 2 tbsp. each butter and oil in a large frying pan over medium heat. Dredge chicken in flour, shaking off excess; dip into coconut milk, letting excess drip off; then press into nut mixture to coat on all sides. Reserve coconut milk. Lay chicken in frying pan in a single layer and cook until golden brown on the bottom, 3 to 4 minutes. With a spatula, turn pieces (taking care not to break off the nut coating) and brown on other side, 2 to 3 minutes longer. Transfer chicken to a baking pan and bake until no longer pink in center of thickest part (cut to test), 15 to 20 minutes.
3. Meanwhile, wipe any scorched nuts from pan with a paper towel. If pan is dry, add 1 tbsp. each butter and oil, then shallots, ginger, and garlic. Cook over medium heat, stirring often, until beginning to brown, about 5 minutes. Pour in broth, wine, and orange juice. Boil until liquid is reduced by about half, 8 to 10 minutes.
4. Pour mixture into a blender and, holding lid down tightly with a towel, whirl until very smooth. Return sauce to frying pan and add ¼ cup reserved coconut milk (discard remainder) and salt and pepper to taste; stir over low heat until hot, then pour into a small bowl.
5. Top coconut pilaf with chicken, and serve with sauce.
Quick Tips: Pulse nuts briefly in a food processor. Zest the oranges before juicing them; save for the pilaf.

PER SERVING WITH 2 TBSP. SAUCE: 689 cal., 51% (351 cal.) from fat; 50 g protein; 39 g fat (12 g sat.); 33 g carbo (1.2 g fiber); 408 mg sodium; 119 mg chol.

Coconut Pilaf: Pour 2 tbsp. **olive oil** into a medium pot over medium-high heat. Add 1 cup chopped **onion** and cook, stirring often, until soft, about 4 minutes. Add 1½ cups **jasmine rice** and cook, stirring, 2 minutes. Add ¾ cup **Viognier or other dry white wine** and cook, stirring often, until absorbed, about 3 minutes. Add 1 cup **chicken broth**, ½ cup canned **coconut milk**, and ½ tsp. **salt**. Stir just to combine, then cover, reduce heat to low, and simmer until rice is tender to the bite, 20 to 25 minutes. Stir in 2 tbsp. finely shredded **orange zest**. Makes about 6 cups.

PER 1-CUP SERVING 405 cal., 19% (77 cal.) from fat; 4.2 g protein; 8.6 g fat (4.2 g sat.); 48 g carbo (0.4 g fiber); 301 mg sodium; 0 mg chol.

Chicken with Tomatoes, Apricots, and Chickpeas

The mix of ingredients here made us pause when we read this recipe from reader Catherine Swetland, of Scottsdale, Arizona. We made it, tasted it, and loved it.

recipe pictured
on page
319

SERVES 4 | **TIME** 30 minutes

4 skinned, boned **chicken breast halves** (about 2 lbs. total)
Kosher salt and freshly ground **black pepper**
1 tbsp. **olive oil**
2 tsp. ground **cumin**
1½ tsp. ground **coriander**
¼ tsp. **cayenne**
1 can (14.5 oz.) diced **tomatoes**
⅓ cup chopped dried **apricots**
1 tbsp. **sugar**
3 **garlic** cloves, minced
1 can (15.5 oz.) **chickpeas** (garbanzos), drained and rinsed
¼ cup chopped flat-leaf **parsley**

1. Sprinkle chicken all over with salt and pepper.
2. Heat oil in a large frying pan over medium-high heat until hot. Add cumin, coriander, and cayenne; cook 1 minute, stirring constantly. Add chicken and cook until golden brown underneath, about 3 minutes. Turn and cook until brown on other side, about another 3 minutes. Transfer to a plate.
3. Add tomatoes, apricots, sugar, and garlic to pan and stir. Bring to a boil, then reduce heat to a simmer and return chicken to pan. Cook, covered, until chicken is cooked through, about 10 minutes. Stir in chickpeas and parsley, and cook until heated through.

PER SERVING: 421 cal., 18% (76 cal.) from fat; 58 g protein; 8.4 g fat (1.3 g sat.); 27 g carbo (4.9 g fiber); 441 mg sodium; 132 mg chol.

Pan-roasted Chicken on Bacon Mushroom Ragout

Be very generous with the cracked pepper on the chicken; it makes a wonderful flavor bridge to the wine.

SERVES 6 | **TIME** 1½ hours

1 cup reduced-sodium chicken broth
½ oz. dried porcini mushrooms
3 oz. thinly sliced bacon or pancetta, cut into thin strips
½ lb. shallots, thinly sliced crosswise
About 1½ tbsp. olive oil, divided
1½ lbs. fresh mushrooms (wild, common, or a
    combination), thickly sliced
6 skin-on, boned chicken breast halves (about ½ lb. each)
Salt and freshly cracked black pepper
1 tbsp. butter
¾ cup Grenache or other dry red wine
1 tbsp. chopped lemon thyme or regular thyme leaves,
    plus sprigs for garnish

1. In a small saucepan, bring broth to a boil. Add dried porcini, remove from heat, and let stand until soft, about 15 minutes. Lift porcini from broth, squeezing out any extra liquid, and chop finely. Strain broth.
2. In a large frying pan over medium heat, cook bacon, stirring often, until fat is rendered. Add shallots; cook, stirring often, over medium-high heat until bacon begins to brown, about 5 minutes. With a slotted spoon, transfer shallots and bacon to paper towels. If pan is dry, add about ½ tbsp. oil. Add fresh mushrooms and chopped porcini; cook, stirring often over high heat until liquid has evaporated and mushrooms begin to brown, about 12 minutes.
3. Preheat oven to 375°. Sprinkle chicken on both sides with salt and cracked pepper. Heat butter and 1 tbsp. oil in a large, ovenproof frying pan over medium-high heat. Add chicken, skin side down, and cook until well browned on bottom, 5 to 7 minutes. Turn chicken and transfer pan to oven. Bake just until chicken is no longer pink in thickest part (cut to test), about 20 minutes.
4. Set chicken on a platter and keep warm. Pour wine into pan and bring to a boil over high heat, stirring to scrape up browned bits from bottom. Pour mixture into pan with mushrooms and add porcini-soaking liquid, bacon-shallot mixture, and chopped thyme. Cook, stirring often, over high heat until almost all liquid has evaporated, 8 to 10 minutes. Add salt and pepper to taste. Mound ragout on plates, top with chicken, and garnish with thyme sprigs.

PER SERVING: 585 cal., 54% (315 cal.) from fat; 53 g protein; 35 g fat (11 g sat.); 14 g carbo (2.4 g fiber); 365 mg sodium; 160 mg chol.

Drunken Chicken

Serve this as part of a multiple-dish Chinese dinner. To reach its "drunken" state, the chicken is simmered in the famous rice wine of Shaoxing, a province in Eastern China.

MAKES 8 to 10 small-plate servings | **TIME** 35 minutes, plus 3 hours to cool and chill

1 bottle (750 ml.) or 3 cups Chinese rice wine (Shaoxing)
    or dry sherry
2 skinned, boned chicken breast halves (6 to 8 oz. each),
    rinsed
2 tbsp. soy sauce
¼ cup *each* finely slivered green onions and coarsely
    chopped cilantro
2 tbsp. vegetable oil
3 tbsp. thinly slivered fresh ginger
2 tbsp. thinly slivered fresh red or green jalapeño or
    Fresno chiles

1. In a deep 3- to 4-qt. pan over high heat bring wine and 2 cups water to a boil. Add chicken and return to a boil. Remove from heat and cover tightly. Let stand until chicken is no longer pink in thickest part (cut to test), 15 to 18 minutes. Lift chicken from cooking liquid and let stand until chicken and liquid are cool, about 1 hour. Return chicken to cool liquid, cover, and chill for at least 2 hours or up to 1 day.
2. Lift chicken from liquid. Cut chicken crosswise into ¼-in.-thick slices. Arrange slices, slightly overlapping, on a small platter. In a small bowl, mix soy sauce with 3 tbsp. of cooking liquid; drizzle evenly over chicken. Reserve remaining cooking liquid to make broth, or discard.

■ Cilantro

FROM THE GARDEN

Sometimes called Chinese parsley, cilantro comes from the same plant that produces coriander seeds—hence its other name, fresh coriander. The green leaves have a distinctive flavor and aroma described as citrusy, waxy, and (occasionally) soapy. Cilantro is an integral part of cuisines throughout the world, including Asia, Mexico, India, the Caribbean, and North Africa. The leaves lose their flavor quickly, so rinse and chop just before you're ready to use them.

poultry & stuffing

3. Sprinkle green onions and cilantro over chicken. Pour oil into a 6- to 8-in. frying pan over high heat; when it ripples, in about 30 seconds, add ginger and chiles and stir until they sizzle, 10 to 15 seconds. Spoon mixture evenly over chicken.

Make Ahead: Through step 1 up to 1 day; the wine flavors the chicken more intensely when it stands overnight.

PER SERVING: 68 cal., 43% (29 cal.) from fat; 8.1 g protein; 3.2 g fat (0.5 g sat.); 1.3 g carbo (0.1 g fiber); 230 mg sodium; 20 mg chol.

Sticky Chile Chicken

We couldn't make enough of this sweet and spicy chicken to satisfy *Sunset* staffers. The recipe, from reader Fiona Lloyd of New Castle, Colorado, is a keeper.

SERVES 4 | **TIME** 1 hour

1 tbsp. vegetable oil
4 skin-on, bone-in chicken breast halves (2 lbs. total)
2 *each* dried ancho and chipotle chiles
½ cup *each* reduced-sodium soy sauce and white
   wine vinegar
⅔ cup sugar
¼ cup chopped cilantro

1. Heat oil in a large frying pan over medium-high heat until hot. Add chicken breasts in a single layer, skin side down, and cook until browned on that side, about 5 minutes. Remove with a slotted spoon and set aside. Discard oil in pan, leaving any browned bits on the bottom.
2. Wipe ancho and chipotle chiles with a damp cloth. Remove stems and seeds. Add chiles, soy sauce, vinegar, sugar, and 1½ cups water to pan; bring to a boil over high heat, then reduce heat and simmer until slightly thickened, about 5 minutes.
3. Return chicken, skin side up, to pan. Cover and simmer until no longer pink in center (cut to test), about 15 minutes. Transfer to a serving dish, cover with foil, and keep warm in a 200° oven. Meanwhile, simmer sauce until it has reduced and coats back of a spoon, about 25 minutes longer.
4. Remove chiles and discard. Spoon 1 tbsp. sauce over each chicken piece and sprinkle with cilantro. Serve remaining sauce on the side.

PER SERVING WITH 1 TBSP. SAUCE: 364 cal., 15% (56 cal.) from fat; 36 g protein; 6.3 g fat (1.3 g sat.); 41 g carbo (2.3 g fiber); 1,149 mg sodium; 90 mg chol.

Dijon Chicken with Panko Crust

Submitted by reader Christie Williams Katona, this weeknight favorite is extra-crunchy, thanks to the ultra-light Japanese-style bread crumbs that Williams Katona used for the crust.

Serves 4 to 8 | **TIME** 30 minutes

¼ cup butter, melted
¼ cup Dijon mustard
2 garlic cloves, minced or pressed
½ cup panko (Japanese-style bread crumbs; *see Quick
   Tip below*)
2 tbsp. grated parmesan cheese
1½ tbsp. minced flat-leaf parsley
8 skinned, boned chicken breast halves (6 to 7 oz. each)
Dijon Sauce *(recipe follows)*

1. Preheat oven to 500°. In a large bowl, whisk together butter, mustard, and garlic. In another bowl, mix panko, parmesan, and parsley.
2. One at a time, turn chicken breast halves in butter mixture to coat completely. Dip rounded side of each breast in panko mixture. Place breasts crumb side up in a 10- by 15-in. baking pan.
3. Bake chicken until crumbs are golden and breasts are no longer pink in thickest part (cut to test), about 15 minutes. Place 1 or 2 breast halves on each dinner plate. Accompany with Dijon sauce.
Quick Tip: Panko is available in well-stocked supermarkets and Asian grocery stores. If you can't find it, whirl two slices of firm-textured white bread (crusts trimmed) into coarse crumbs in a blender. Spread crumbs in a pie pan and bake in a 325° oven, stirring often, until crisp but not brown, 8 to 10 minutes.

PER SERVING: 355 cal., 53% (189 cal.) from fat; 33 g protein; 21 g fat (6.3 g sat.); 3.2 g carbo (0.2 g fiber); 666 mg sodium; 105 mg chol.

Dijon Sauce: In a bowl, mix ½ cup **mayonnaise**, ¼ cup **Dijon mustard**, ½ to 1 tbsp. **Asian (toasted) sesame oil**, and 1 tsp. **soy sauce**. Makes ¾ cup.

Chicken Cashew Korma

This elegant dish has warming-but-not-fiery spices, making it a comforting cold-weather main course. It's excellent with Viognier.

recipe pictured on page **322**

SERVES 4 to 6 | **TIME** 1½ hours

2 cups plain whole-milk yogurt
¾ cup unsalted roasted cashews, divided
2½ lbs. skinned, boned chicken thighs, cut into 1-in. pieces
1 tsp. kosher salt, plus more to taste
3 tbsp. olive oil
1 onion, halved lengthwise and thinly sliced
2 plum tomatoes, cored and diced
6 garlic cloves, minced
2 tbsp. finely grated fresh ginger
8 cardamom pods, crushed
2 cinnamon sticks
1½ tbsp. ground coriander
2 tsp. garam masala (*see Quick Tip below*)
1 tsp. cayenne
¼ cup *each* raisins and whipping cream

1. In a food processor, blend yogurt and ¼ cup cashews until nuts are finely ground. Sprinkle chicken with salt.
2. Heat oil in a large, deep frying pan over medium-high heat until hot. Add chicken and cook, stirring occasionally, until lightly browned all over, about 8 minutes. With a slotted spoon, transfer chicken to a bowl.
3. Add onion to pan; cook, stirring occasionally, until lightly browned, about 5 minutes. Reduce heat to medium; add tomatoes, garlic, ginger, cardamom, cinnamon, coriander, garam masala, and cayenne. Cook until tomatoes begin to soften, about 2 minutes.
4. Return chicken and juices to pan along with raisins, remaining ½ cup cashews, and the yogurt mixture. Reduce heat to medium-low, cover, and cook, stirring often, until chicken is no longer pink in the center (cut to test) and sauce has thickened slightly (it will look separated), 10 to 15 minutes.
5. Uncover, add cream, and stir over medium heat until sauce is smooth and hot, about 5 minutes. Add more salt to taste.
Quick Tip: Garam masala is available in the spice section of many supermarkets; if you can't find it, substitute 1 tsp. cinnamon, ½ tsp. *each* ground cumin and freshly ground black pepper, and ¼ tsp. *each* ground cardamom, nutmeg, cloves, and cayenne.

PER SERVING: 600 cal., 51% (306 cal.) from fat; 52 g protein; 34 g fat (9.8 g sat.); 22 g carbo (2.5 g fiber); 1,033 mg sodium; 216 mg chol.

Pan-roasted Chicken with Asparagus and Shiitakes

Meaty shiitakes, a good sear on the chicken, and a sprinkling of nutty parmesan cheese—not to mention sweet, tender-crisp asparagus—make this low-fat dish a winner. The recipe can be easily adapted to other vegetables or more mushrooms; see the variations that follow.

SERVES 4 | **TIME** 30 minutes

2 tbsp. olive oil
4 skinned, boned chicken breast halves (½ lb. each)
2 large shallots, minced
3 garlic cloves, minced
1 cup reduced-sodium chicken broth
3 thyme sprigs, plus chopped thyme leaves for garnish
½ lb. shiitake mushrooms, stems discarded and caps halved, or button mushrooms, halved
½ tsp. salt, plus more to taste
¼ tsp. freshly ground black pepper, plus more to taste
1 lb. slender asparagus, tough stem ends trimmed
¼ cup finely shredded parmesan

1. Preheat oven to 375°. Heat oil in a large, heavy oven-proof frying pan (not nonstick) over high heat until oil is hot but not smoking. Add chicken breasts, rounded side down, and cook until golden, 2 to 3 minutes. Turn chicken over.
2. Add shallots and garlic to pan with chicken and cook, stirring occasionally so garlic doesn't burn, until shallots are soft and translucent, 3 to 4 minutes. Add broth, thyme sprigs, mushrooms, salt, and pepper and cook until mixture begins to boil, about 1 minute.
3. Lay asparagus over chicken, cover pan, and put in oven. Bake until chicken is just cooked through (cut to test) and asparagus is tender (*see Quick Tip below*), 14 to 16 minutes. Transfer chicken to a plate.
4. Season asparagus-mushroom mixture with salt and pepper to taste. Divide vegetables among rimmed plates or shallow pasta bowls, top each with a piece of chicken, and spoon sauce over chicken. Garnish with chopped thyme and parmesan.
Quick Tip: If you prefer your asparagus more fully cooked, return it to the oven once you've lifted out the chicken and bake it 5 to 10 minutes more.

PER SERVING: 355 cal., 25% (88 cal.) from fat; 58 g protein; 9.8 g fat (1.7 g sat.); 8.3 g carbo (1.8 g fiber); 582 mg sodium; 132 mg chol.

Chicken with Haricots Verts, Potatoes, and Toasted Almonds: Substitute **haricots verts** (slender French green beans) for asparagus, 12 to 16 **baby**

red potatoes (first boiled for 6 minutes, then drained) for mushrooms, **tarragon** for thyme, and 4 tsp. toasted **slivered almonds** (see *How to Toast Nuts, page 134*) for parmesan.

Mushroom Lover's Chicken: Substitute reduced-sodium **beef broth** for chicken broth, omit asparagus, and add ¼ lb. mixed **fresh wild mushrooms**, whole or halved. Top with finely shredded **gruyère** instead of parmesan.

Biscuit-topped Chicken Potpies

For a grown-up take on a childhood favorite, we dropped the traditional pastry crust in favor of a no-fuss biscuit topping—then added cremini mushrooms and fresh thyme to the filling to give it some earthiness. You'll need six or seven 8- to 10-oz. ovenproof bowls or ramekins for this recipe.

recipe pictured on page **324**

MAKES 6 or 7 individual potpies | **TIME** 1¾ hours

2½ cups reduced-sodium chicken broth
3 carrots, finely chopped
2 medium Yukon Gold potatoes, finely chopped
1 stalk celery, finely chopped
¼ cup salted butter
1 medium onion, finely chopped
12 small cremini or button mushrooms, finely chopped
1 tsp. chopped thyme leaves
5 tbsp. plus 2 cups flour
1 cup plus 1 tbsp. milk
¼ tsp. freshly grated nutmeg
2 tsp. salt, divided
Freshly ground black pepper
2 tsp. finely chopped flat-leaf parsley
2½ cups chopped cooked chicken, preferably a mixture of white and dark meat (see *Quick Tip, right*)
¼ cup frozen peas
1½ tsp. baking powder
½ tsp. baking soda
5 tbsp. cold unsalted butter, cubed
½ cup finely shredded sharp cheddar cheese
2 tsp. minced sage leaves
1 egg plus 1 egg yolk
½ cup plus 2 tbsp. well-shaken buttermilk

1. In a medium saucepan over high heat, bring broth to a boil. Add carrots, potatoes, and celery. Lower heat to medium and cook until vegetables are tender, 5 to 7 minutes. Drain vegetables, reserving broth; set aside separately.

2. In a large, heavy-bottomed saucepan, melt salted butter over medium heat. Add onion and cook, stirring often, until golden, 6 to 8 minutes. Add mushrooms and cook, stirring often, 5 minutes. Add thyme and 5 tbsp. flour and cook 2 minutes. Slowly add 1 cup milk, whisking constantly, until combined, then add reserved broth and cook, stirring often, until mixture thickens, 8 to 10 minutes. Season with nutmeg, 1 tsp. salt, and pepper to taste. Add parsley, chicken, reserved cooked vegetables, and peas and divide filling among oven-proof bowls or ramekins, leaving top ¼ in. unfilled.

3. Preheat oven to 425°. To make biscuit topping, sift remaining 2 cups flour with baking powder, baking soda, and remaining 1 tsp. salt. Using your fingers or a pastry cutter, work in unsalted butter to form a coarse meal, working quickly to keep butter from warming up and melting into dough. Stir in cheddar cheese and sage. In a separate bowl, whisk together whole egg and buttermilk and add to flour mixture, stirring gently until a shaggy dough forms.

4. Lightly flour a counter, a rolling pin, and your hands. Divide dough into two balls. Roll out first ball to a ¼-in. thickness, then use a 2½-in. biscuit cutter to cut into rounds, scraping and re-rolling dough as needed. Repeat with second ball.

5. Place three rounds of dough on each potpie, overlapping as necessary (any unused rounds can be baked on their own as biscuits). Whisk egg yolk with remaining 1 tbsp. milk to make an egg wash. Brush dough with egg wash, put potpies on a cookie sheet lined with foil, and bake until biscuit crust is golden brown and filling is bubbling, 17 to 22 minutes.

Quick Tip: One standard-size rotisserie chicken (about 3½ lbs.) supplies just enough meat for the pies.

PER SERVING: 538 cal., 42% (225 cal.) from fat; 28 g protein; 25 g fat (13 g sat.); 51 g carbo (3.5 g fiber); 1,034 mg sodium; 160 mg chol.

Lemon-Artichoke Chicken

This dish from reader Charlotte Corkery, of Auburn, California, is simple to make but elegant enough for company.

SERVES 4 | **TIME** 1 hour

4 skinned, boned chicken breast halves (about ½ lb. each), pounded to an even thickness of ¼ to ½ in.
½ tsp. *each* salt and freshly ground black pepper
2 tbsp. butter
1 can (14 oz.) quartered artichoke hearts, drained
2 tbsp. *each* dry sherry and finely shredded lemon zest
2 tsp. fresh lemon juice
½ cup *each* whipping cream and grated parmesan cheese

1. Preheat oven to 350°. Sprinkle chicken on both sides with salt and pepper. In a 10-in. frying pan over medium-high heat, melt butter. Add chicken in batches and cook, turning once, until browned on both sides, about 4 minutes per side. Transfer chicken to a 9- by 13-in. baking dish and add artichoke hearts.
2. Add sherry, lemon zest, and lemon juice to remaining butter in frying pan; stir over medium heat until well blended and hot, 2 to 3 minutes. Add cream and stir. Remove from heat and pour sauce over chicken. Sprinkle with parmesan.
3. Bake until sauce is bubbling and golden brown on top, 20 to 25 minutes.

PER SERVING: 437 cal., 39% (171 cal.) from fat; 57 g protein; 19 g fat (11 g sat.); 6.6 g carbo (1.1 g fiber); 600 mg sodium; 184 mg chol.

Stir-fried Chicken and Asian Greens

Add chicken to stir-fried greens and you have a quick one-pan meal. Serve with hot rice.

SERVES 3 or 4 | **TIME** 40 minutes

¾ lb. skinned, boned chicken breast halves
2 tbsp. dry sherry
¾ cup chicken broth
1 tbsp. *each* soy sauce and cornstarch
¼ tsp. white pepper
1 lb. bok choy, choy sum, or Chinese mustard greens (*see A Guide to Asian Greens, page 248*)
1 tbsp. *each* vegetable oil, minced garlic, and minced fresh ginger
Salt

1. Cut chicken crosswise into strips about ⅛ in. thick and 2 to 3 in. long. In a bowl, mix chicken with sherry. In another bowl, mix broth, soy sauce, cornstarch, and white pepper.
2. Remove and discard any yellow, damaged, or tough leaves from greens. Trim off and discard tough stem ends. For tough stalks, remove any thick side stems and the center stalk. Make additional cuts as follows: *For bok choy*, cut leaves and stalks diagonally or crosswise into ¼-in.-thick slices; separate leaves from stalks. *For choy sum or Chinese mustard greens*, if skin on stalks is tough, peel off and discard. Cut greens into 3-in. lengths, separating leaves and thin stems from thick stems or stalks. If any pieces are thicker than ½ in., cut to that thickness.
3. Set a 14- to 16-in. wok or 12-in. frying pan over high heat. When hot, stir in thick stem or stalk pieces and 3 tbsp. water. Cover and cook until pieces are tender-crisp, 2 to 3 minutes. Add leaves and thin stems and cook, stirring, until leaves are barely wilted, 1 to 2 minutes; pour mixture into a bowl.
4. Return pan to high heat. When hot and any liquid has evaporated, add oil, garlic, and ginger; cook, stirring, until garlic begins to brown, about 30 seconds. Add chicken and cook until no longer pink in the center (cut to test), 2 to 3 minutes. Stir broth mixture and add to pan; cook, stirring, until boiling. Return greens to pan and stir until hot. Add salt to taste.

PER SERVING: 170 cal., 25% (42 cal.) from fat; 23 g protein; 4.7 g fat (0.7 g sat.); 6.1 g carbo (1.2 g fiber); 402 mg sodium; 49 mg chol.

poultry & stuffing

Chicken-Pesto Crêpes

Once you get the hang of cooking crêpes, they make a nice fast lunch or light dinner. Here we pair nutty buckwheat crêpes with a filling that requires no additional cooking.

MAKES 9 crêpes; 3 servings | **TIME** 30 minutes

3 eggs
⅓ cup *each* all-purpose flour and buckwheat flour (*see Quick Tip below*) or use all all-purpose flour
1 cup whole milk
About 2 tbsp. butter, melted, divided
½ cup plus 1 tbsp. store-bought pesto or homemade Classic Pesto (*page 208*)
1 cup shredded cooked chicken
⅓ cup thinly sliced roasted red peppers
½ cup finely shredded Swiss or parmesan cheese

1. In a blender, purée eggs, all-purpose and buckwheat flours, and milk until smooth, scraping down sides of container as necessary. The buckwheat flour may settle as batter stands; stir before cooking if necessary.
2. Using a heatproof pastry brush, brush butter across bottom of an 8-in. nonstick frying pan and heat over medium-high heat. When hot, wipe out excess with a paper towel.
3. Pour in ¼ cup batter, simultaneously tilting pan and swirling batter to coat bottom. Crêpe should set at once and form tiny bubbles. Cook crêpe until lightly browned at the edges and dry-looking on the surface, 1 to 3 minutes.
4. Run a wide spatula under crêpe edge to loosen. Turn crêpe over. Spread about 1 tbsp. pesto down center. Top with chicken, peppers, and cheese. Cook until bottom of crêpe is browned, about 1 minute, then fold two edges over filling, leaving a little of the filling exposed.
5. Repeat to make rest of crêpes, brushing more butter in the pan as needed.
Quick Tip: Buckwheat flour is available in many super-markets and in natural-foods stores.
Make Ahead: Crêpes, up to 1 day (cook through step 4, but without filling them). Reheat in a steamer basket over simmering water until hot, then fill.

PER 3-CRÊPE SERVING: 702 cal., 57% (401 cal.) from fat; 47 g protein; 45 g fat (18 g sat.); 29 g carbo (3.2 g fiber); 603 mg sodium; 331 mg chol.

Green Chile Chicken Enchiladas

Like all good New Mexico food, this dish is rustic and delicious. Its heat depends on the chiles; go with Anaheims if you scorch easily. You can also substitute our other recipe for New Mexico Green Chile Sauce (or try the red version) in this recipe if you like; *see page 367 for both.*

recipe pictured on page **373**

MAKES 10 enchiladas; 5 servings | **TIME** 50 minutes

1 lb. roasted, skin-on green New Mexico, poblano, or Anaheim chiles (*see Quick Tips below*)
2 tbsp. olive oil
1 tbsp. butter
5 large garlic cloves, finely chopped
½ tsp. *each* salt and freshly ground black pepper
3 cups reduced-sodium chicken broth, divided
10 corn tortillas (7 to 8 in. wide)
2 cups coarsely shredded cheddar or jack cheese, divided
2½ cups shredded cooked chicken (*see Quick Tips below*)
Sour cream

1. Preheat oven to 400°. Peel, seed, and chop chiles.
2. Heat oil and butter in a large frying pan over medium heat. Add garlic and cook until fragrant, about 30 seconds. Add chiles, salt, and pepper. Cook, stirring occasionally, 3 minutes. Add 1 cup broth and simmer until reduced by a third, about 10 minutes.
3. Meanwhile, prepare tortillas: In a small frying pan, bring remaining 2 cups broth to a gentle simmer. Very briefly dip a tortilla into broth to barely soften, then transfer it to a large baking sheet; repeat with remaining tortillas (you may need two or three baking sheets). Do not overlap or tortillas will stick.
4. Divide 1¼ cups cheese among tortillas and top each with the shredded chicken. Wrap tortilla around filling and transfer, seam side down, to a 9- by 13-in. baking dish.
5. Pour chile sauce over enchiladas and top with remaining ¾ cup cheese. Bake until cheese is bubbling and browned, 15 to 20 minutes. Serve with sour cream.
Quick Tips: Order fresh or frozen New Mexico chiles from the New Mexican Connection (*newmexican connection.com*). Or, to roast them yourself, broil the chiles until blackened all over; let sit until cool, then peel off skin with the help of a paper towel (don't wash it off; rinsing dilutes the flavor). For the chicken, you'll need about half the meat from a roasted 2½- to 3-lb. bird.
Make Ahead: Up to 1 month, frozen.

PER 2-ENCHILADA SERVING: 526 cal., 50% (261 cal.) from fat; 32 g protein; 29 g fat (13 g sat.); 38 g carbo (4.2 g fiber); 1,402 mg sodium; 117 mg chol.

The Green and Red Glories of New Mexico

Why are the chiles grown in New Mexico so good? High altitude, warm days, cool nights, and intense light create the robust flavors they're famous for. Picked green, the chiles taste fresh and lively, with a good kick. Left on the plant to fully mature, they turn red, developing a complex, earthy flavor and mellow heat as they dry. Together they are at the heart of traditional New Mexican cooking.

Southern New Mexico, from Hatch to Las Cruces, is home to the largest chile-growing region in the state. The dry valleys are best known for their meaty green chiles—high-yielding hybrids such as Sandia, Hatch, and NuMex Big Jim, developed for consistent flavor and thick, straight pods that are easy to peel after roasting. The chiles are used fresh or frozen in sauces and stews.

North of Santa Fe lies a smaller growing area known for its landrace chiles (strains or varieties adapted to specific geographic locations). These skinnier, more twisted native chiles are especially appreciated at the red stage, when they develop a more intense flavor with flowery aromas and varying heat levels. Smaller and thinner-fleshed than southern varieties, they dry more easily. These are the type traditionally strung on *ristras*, or ropes, to last throughout the year. Locals name them for the farming towns they come from: Dixon, Chimayo, Española. New Mexico cooks simmer dried red chiles in braises and use them whole or ground for sauces.

Stock up on chiles if you're in New Mexico during the summer-to-fall harvest season, or mail-order chiles any time of year. You can buy frozen roasted green chiles as well as whole and ground dried red chiles at *new mexicanconnection.com*; dried red chile and ristras at *cibolojunction.com* and ristras at *madeinnewmexico.com*.

Green or Red?

Chile colorado and *chile verde*, the two sauces on the opposite page, are ubiquitous in New Mexican cooking and are used in everything from stews to enchiladas. (In New Mexico's restaurants, you often get your choice of either green chile or red chile to accompany the dish you've ordered.)

New Mexico Red Chile Sauce
(*Chile Colorado*)

Red chiles make an earthy-sweet and intensely flavored sauce. For a richer flavor, some cooks like to use pork or chicken broth instead of water. To shave 20 minutes off the prep time, use the shortcut version that follows this recipe.

MAKES 1¼ cups | **TIME** 1 hour

3 oz. (7 to 12) dried New Mexico red chiles or California red chiles, stemmed, seeded, and rinsed
½ medium onion, chopped
2 garlic cloves, minced
1 tbsp. *each* vegetable or olive oil and flour
½ tsp. dried Mexican oregano
¼ tsp. ground cumin
½ tsp. salt, plus more to taste

1. Heat a wide 5- to 6-qt. pot over medium heat. Toast half the chiles at a time, turning occasionally, just until fragrant, about 2 minutes. Transfer chiles to a heatproof bowl, add 2 cups boiling water, and submerge chiles with a plate. Let stand until softened, 15 to 20 minutes. Drain, reserving water.
2. Meanwhile, in a medium saucepan, cook onion and garlic in oil over medium heat, stirring often, until onion is golden, 8 to 10 minutes. Sprinkle flour over onion and continue to cook, stirring, until mixture smells toasty, about 2 minutes. Remove from heat and stir in oregano, cumin, and salt.
3. Purée chiles in a blender with half the soaking liquid. Set a fine strainer over pan with onion mixture. Rub puréed chiles through strainer into pan. Discard contents of strainer.
4. Bring mixture to a simmer over medium heat, then reduce heat and simmer, uncovered, stirring occasionally, until flavors are well blended, 12 to 15 minutes; add more soaking liquid and water as needed (sauce should be thick enough to coat a spoon). Taste and add more salt if you like.
Make Ahead: Up to 3 days, chilled; or freeze.

PER ¼-CUP SERVING: 43 cal., 58% (25 cal.) from fat; 0.7 g protein; 2.9 g fat (0.3 g sat.); 4 g carbo (0.6 g fiber); 235 mg sodium; 0 mg chol.

Quick New Mexico Red Chile Sauce: Follow the directions above, but replace whole chile pods with ½ cup **ground New Mexico chiles** *(see opposite page)* and stir until smooth with 2 cups cold water. Omit steps 1 and 3. Stir chile mixture into onion mixture and proceed with step 4. Makes 1⅓ cups.

PER ¼-CUP SERVING: 98 cal., 45% (44 cal.) from fat; 2.7 g protein; 5 g fat (.31 g sat.); 11 g carbo (6.7 g fiber); 240 mg sodium; 0 mg chol.

New Mexico Green Chile Sauce
(*Chile Verde*)

If you have sensitive skin, wear gloves while working with chiles.

MAKES 2½ cups | **TIME** 40 minutes

½ cup chopped onion
2 garlic cloves, minced
2 tbsp. *each* vegetable or olive oil and flour
1½ cups chicken broth or water
1½ cups chopped stemmed, seeded, roasted green chiles, preferably New Mexico or poblano (from about 1¾ lbs. chiles; *see Quick Tip below*)
½ tsp. salt, plus more to taste

1. In a medium saucepan, cook onion and garlic in oil over medium heat, stirring often, until onion is golden, 8 to 10 minutes. Sprinkle flour over onion and continue to cook, stirring, until mixture smells toasty, about 2 minutes. Whisk in broth until smooth, then stir in chiles and salt.
2. Simmer sauce, uncovered, stirring occasionally, until flavors are blended, 15 to 20 minutes; add water if sauce gets too thick. For a smoother sauce, purée in a blender. Taste and add more salt if you like.
Quick Tip: Buy frozen roasted green New Mexico chiles *(see opposite page)* or roast your own: Arrange 2 lbs. fresh New Mexico green chiles or poblano chiles in a shallow pan. Broil, turning as needed, until chiles are charred all over, 10 to 15 minutes. Cool, then skin, seed, and chop.
Make Ahead: Up to 3 days, chilled; or freeze.

PER ¼-CUP SERVING: 62 cal., 44% (27 cal.) from fat; 2.2 g protein; 3.2 g fat (0.5 g sat.); 7.6 g carbo (1.1 g fiber); 140 mg sodium; 3.8 mg chol.

▪ Mexican Oregano

FROM THE PANTRY

Wildly aromatic Mexican oregano makes Mediterranean oregano seem meek. Each has its place, but for the cooking of New Mexico (and, of course, Mexico), we choose the wild stuff every time. Find it in Latin markets and in well-stocked grocery stores, and remember that dried herbs lose their punch after several months—so buy in small quantities.

Maple Mustard–glazed Cornish Hen With Sugar Snap Pea Couscous

The Cornish hen, often called a game hen, is actually a small chicken—a cross between Cornish and White Rock chickens. A single hen is just large enough to feed two people (or one hungry person).

SERVES 2 | **TIME** 1 hour

¼ cup *each* maple syrup and Dijon mustard
1 Cornish hen (about 1½ lbs.)
8 young, slender carrots with tops *(see Quick Tip below)*,
    greens trimmed to ½ in.
¾ cup chicken broth
½ lb. fresh sugar snap peas, trimmed
½ cup couscous
Salt and freshly ground black pepper

1. Preheat oven to 425°. In a small bowl, mix maple syrup and mustard. Remove neck and giblets from hen; reserve for another use. Pull off and discard any pockets of fat. With poultry shears or kitchen scissors, split bird in half lengthwise through breastbone and backbone. Brush hen halves with mustard mixture, turning to coat all sides. Set hen halves, skin side up and slightly apart, on a lightly oiled flat rack in a large, foil-lined rimmed baking pan. Arrange carrots, slightly separated, alongside.

2. Roast until hen is lightly browned, 25 to 30 minutes; remove from oven at halfway point to baste a second time with mustard glaze. Brush hen halves as well as carrots with mustard glaze, turning to coat all sides. Set halves, again skin side up, on rack and continue roasting with carrots until meat at thighbone is no longer pink (cut to test), 10 to 14 minutes longer.

3. About 8 minutes before hen is done, in a 1- to 1½-qt. pan over high heat, bring broth and snap peas to a boil. Stir in couscous. Cover pan and remove from heat; let couscous stand 5 minutes, then fluff with a fork.

4. Divide couscous and peas between plates. Set a hen half and carrots next to couscous. Season with salt and pepper to taste.

Quick Tip: Find slender young carrots with their greens attached at farmers' markets. You can also use 2 fully grown carrots and cut them in quarters.

PER SERVING: 757 cal., 32% (243 cal.) from fat; 46 g protein; 27 g fat (7.4 g sat.); 78 g carbo (7 g fiber); 625 mg sodium; 187 mg chol.

Trial by Turkey

Sometime in the 1960s, a bigger, meatier turkey waddled into the grocery store: the Broad-Breasted White (aka the Large White). It was fast growing and cheap to raise, its pale pinfeathers left no colored spots in the skin when plucked, and it had more white meat and a more tender texture than the slimmer, fuller-flavored standard turkeys (*see Heritage Turkeys, page 385*).

These busty new birds didn't cook the same, though. If you roasted them the traditional way (long and slow), you'd get cottony, dried-out white meat, and a lot of Thanksgiving feasters started to see turkey-eating as a chore.

By 1985, the Broad-Breasted White dominated the turkey market—and was still being cooked into cotton. *Sunset* decided there had to be a better way. Jerry Anne Di Vecchio, our food editor at the time, and her team held an epic turkey roast. Using hundreds of Broad-Breasteds, they experimented with cooking times, temperatures, and ways of measuring doneness. At the end, Di Vecchio distilled the findings into a handy little chart that we have used ever since (*see Turkey Basics below*). "I know so damn much about turkey, it's painful," she says. "When I die, my tombstone will read, DON'T OVERCOOK IT. BUY A THERMOMETER."

Turkey Basics (For oven-roasting or grilling)

Turkey weight with giblets*	Oven/grill temperature	Desired internal temperature**	Cooking time***
10–13 LBS.	350°	160°	1½–2¼ hours
14–23 LBS.	325°	160°	2–3 hours
24–27 LBS.	325°	160°	3–3¾ hours
28–30 LBS.	325°	160°	3½–4½ hours

*Allow 1 lb. (16 oz.) turkey per person (raw weight with bones) to yield ¼ lb. (4 oz.) neatly sliced meat per person, plus ample leftovers.

**To measure, insert a thermometer through the thickest part of breast until it touches the bone, where the temperature is most consistent (it will continue to rise after you remove the bird from the oven). *If stuffing the turkey*, use an instant-read thermometer to check it in several places; it should reach at least 165°.

***Times are for unstuffed birds. A stuffed bird may cook at same rate as an unstuffed one, but be ready to allow 30 to 50 minutes longer. Turkeys take about the same amount of time to roast as they do to grill, but a grill browns the bird more thoroughly.

Dry-cured Rosemary Turkey

This recipe from Helena Darling, of Ashland, Oregon, earned first-place honors for Best Turkey in our Thanksgiving in the West recipe contest in 2005.

SERVES About 14 (with leftovers) | **TIME** 3½ hours, plus 3 days to cure

3 tbsp. *each* sea salt or kosher salt, dried marjoram, dried thyme, and dried juniper berries
1 tbsp. black peppercorns
2 tsp. anise seeds
1 turkey (14 to 15 lbs.), not infused with broth or butter
12 rosemary sprigs (3 in. each)
12 garlic cloves, peeled
½ cup unsalted butter, at room temperature
Cooking-oil spray
Silky Pan Gravy *(recipe follows)*

1. Three days before serving, in a blender or spice grinder, finely grind salt, marjoram, thyme, juniper berries, peppercorns, and anise seeds.
2. Remove and discard leg truss from turkey. Pull off and discard any lumps of fat. Remove giblets and neck; save neck for gravy. Cut off wing tips to the first joint and reserve for gravy. Rub half of herb mixture all over turkey; sprinkle remaining in body cavity. Cover and chill 3 days.
3. Preheat oven to 325°. Put rosemary sprigs and garlic inside turkey body cavity. Gently push your hand between skin and turkey breast to separate skin from breast. Spread about half the butter over breast under skin. Melt remaining butter and brush lightly over top of turkey. Spray a V-shaped rack with cooking-oil spray and set in a 12- by 17-in. roasting pan. Put turkey, breast side down, on rack. Roast turkey for 1¾ hours.
4. Remove turkey from oven and turn breast side up. Return to oven. Roast until a thermometer inserted straight down through thickest part of breast to the bone registers 170°, 45 to 60 minutes longer.
5. Start making the gravy.
6. When turkey is done, tip it to drain juices from cavity into roasting pan (reserve juice and pan for finishing gravy). Transfer turkey to a platter and let stand in a warm place, uncovered, 15 to 30 minutes. Finish gravy, then carve turkey.

PER SERVING: 420 cal., 41% (171 cal.) from fat; 57 g protein; 19 g fat (5.7 g sat.); 1.7 g carbo (0.2 g fiber); sodium N/A; 167 mg chol.

Silky Pan Gravy: Pour 2 tbsp. **vegetable oil** into a 5- to 6-qt. pan over medium-high heat. Add **turkey wing tips and neck** and brown well, 4 to 7 minutes. Add 4½ cups reduced-sodium **chicken broth** and bring to a boil; cover, reduce heat, and simmer about 1 hour. Remove wings and neck. While turkey rests, pour juices from roasting pan into a 1- to 2-qt. glass measuring cup. Skim off and reserve fat. Add simmered broth to pan juices to make 4 cups; if you don't have enough, add water. Return ⅓ cup fat (if not enough, add enough melted butter to make up the difference) and 1 minced **garlic clove** to unwashed roasting pan; set over two burners at medium-high heat. Add ½ cup **flour** and cook, stirring, until bubbly and smooth. Stir in the 4 cups broth and 1 cup **whipping cream**; scrape pan sides and bottom to loosen browned bits. Cook gravy, whisking, until smooth and boiling, 4 to 7 minutes. Add **salt** to taste. Makes about 5½ cups.

PER ¼ CUP: 86 cal., 80% (69 cal.) from fat; 1.3 g protein; 7.7 g fat (3.2 g sat.); 2.8 g carbo (0.1 g fiber); sodium N/A; 15 mg chol.

Fixing Lumpy Gravy

There isn't a gravy that can't be fixed. Just reach for a strainer (medium weave). Set it over a bowl, pour in the gravy and stir. Voilà: Smooth gravy flows through, nasty lumps stay behind. Thin gravy can be boiled to the desired thickness; thick gravy can be thinned with hot broth or even water in a pinch.

Guajillo-Tamarind Turkey with Roasted Poblano Gravy

The glaze makes every bite of this turkey sweet, tangy, and hot all at once. The recipe is from Denver chef Sean Yontz.

SERVES 8 to 10 | **TIME** 4 hours, plus 30 minutes for turkey to rest

1 head garlic, plus 8 peeled cloves
12 dried guajillo chiles (3 oz. total; *see Quick Tip, right*), stemmed, divided
½ cup *each* tamarind concentrate and honey
1 cup loosely packed cilantro leaves
¼ cup fresh lime juice, plus 1 quartered lime
1 tsp. freshly ground black pepper
½ tsp. salt
1 turkey (12 to 18 lbs.)
1 onion (½ lb.), quartered
2 carrots (6 oz. total), cut into chunks
4 stalks celery (½ lb. total), cut into chunks
1 orange (½ lb.), quartered
2 lemons, quartered
6 thyme sprigs
Roasted Poblano Gravy *(recipe follows)*

1. Preheat oven to 350° and make glaze: Cut top ½ in. off garlic head; wrap head loosely in foil. Bake until soft when pressed, about 45 minutes. Let cool, then squeeze garlic from skins into a 3- to 4-qt. pan (discard skins). Wipe chiles clean with a damp cloth. Add 8 chiles, the tamarind concentrate, honey, cilantro, lime juice, pepper, salt, and 1 cup water to pan. Bring to a boil over medium-high heat, stirring often; remove from heat and let stand 10 minutes. Pour into a blender and purée until smooth.
2. Remove and discard leg truss from turkey. Pull off and discard any lumps of fat. Remove giblets and neck; discard or reserve for another use. Rub about a third of guajillo-tamarind glaze inside cavity. Set turkey, breast side up, on a V-shaped rack in a 12- by 17-in. roasting pan; pour remaining glaze into bottom of pan, then pour in 1 cup water. Arrange onion, carrots, celery, quartered lime, orange, lemons, 8 garlic cloves, 4 remaining chiles, and the thyme in roasting pan around and under rack.
3. Roast turkey according to chart on *page 370*, checking turkey every 30 minutes; if juices in bottom of pan threaten to scorch, add ½ cup water at a time. When a thermometer inserted through thickest part of breast to bone registers 155°, about 15 minutes before chart indicates turkey will be done, remove turkey from oven. Brush all over with juices in pan (if liquid is too thick to coat turkey in a thin, even layer, dilute with ½ cup more water). Continue roasting until turkey is well browned

and thermometer registers 160°, about 15 minutes longer.
4. Tip turkey to drain juices from cavity into pan. Transfer turkey to a platter. Let rest in a warm place for 30 minutes before carving. Pour pan juices through a fine-mesh strainer into a 2-cup glass measuring cup; discard solids and reserve juices for gravy. Make gravy, then carve turkey.
Quick Tip: Long, pointed, deep red dried guajillo chiles are available in Mexican markets. If you can't find them, substitute ancho chiles.
Make Ahead: Glaze, up to 1 week, chilled.

PER SERVING: 697 cal., 37% (261 cal.) from fat; 88 g protein; 29 g fat (8.3 g sat.); 18 g carbo (1 g fiber); 292 mg sodium; 255 mg chol.

Roasted Poblano Gravy: While turkey rests, skim fat from reserved pan drippings. Add **chicken broth**, if needed, to make 2 cups liquid. In a 3- to 4-qt. pan over medium heat, melt ¼ cup **butter**. Add 3 chopped, seeded, peeled, roasted **poblano chiles** (½ lb. total); stir for 1 minute. Turn heat to medium-low; whisk in 3 tbsp. **flour** until well combined. Whisking chile mixture constantly, slowly pour drippings mixture into pan. Whisk until gravy boils and thickens, 6 to 8 minutes. If gravy is thicker than you'd like, add more broth. Season to taste with **salt** and **pepper**. Makes about 2½ cups.

PER ¼ CUP: 218 cal., 66% (144 cal.) from fat; 1.7 g protein; 16 g fat (6.3 g sat.); 18 g carbo (0.8 g fiber); 119 mg sodium; 24 mg chol.

■ Tamarind Concentrate and Pulp

FROM THE PANTRY

The sticky, tart-sweet fruit of the tamarind tree, most widely grown in India, adds a wonderful flavor of dates and lemons to whatever it's in. Tamarind concentrate is a thick, dark-brown, seedless paste; it's easy to find in Indian and Latino markets. Better, though, is the packaged pulp with seeds, which has no additives and a fresher flavor, and is available at the same markets. To get ½ cup liquid from packaged pulp, soak ¼ cup pulp and seeds in ½ cup boiling water for 30 minutes; then strain through a fine-mesh strainer, pressing on pulp.

poultry & stuffing

Green Chile Chicken
Enchiladas, *page 367*

Coffee-braised Spoon
Lamb, *page 428*

Pinot-braised Duck with
Spicy Greens, *page 391*

**Port-braised Short Ribs with
Ginger and Star Anise,** *page 406*

Spicy Beef Cross-rib Roast
with Caramelized Clementine
Sauce, *page 403*

Cider-brined Pork Chops with
Sautéed Apples, *page 416*

Pineapple Satays with Coconut Caramel, *page 517*

Grass-fed Burgers with
Chipotle Barbecue Sauce,
page 466

Chorizo-Beef Dinner
Nachos, *page 423*

Champagne Ham with Brandy
Glaze, *page 424*

Cornbread-Chorizo Dressing,
page 393

383

Roast Turkey with Wine
and Herbs, *page 385*

Heritage Turkeys

Before the large, plump Broad-Breasted White turkey became ubiquitous in our grocery stores (*see Trial by Turkey, page 370*), we had a range of other turkey breeds, prized for their productivity and the beauty of their feathers. Among them were the Black, Bronze, Narragansett, Bourbon Red, White Holland, and Jersey Buff. They had long legs, slim bodies, and an even ratio of dark to white meat. Compared with the Broad-Breasted White, they were richer and fuller in flavor.

In the last several years, these birds—known as heritage turkeys—have made something of a comeback, thanks to the efforts of organizations like the American Livestock Breeds Conservancy (*albc-usa.org*) and to consumers' desire for less industrialized food. Unlike the Broad-Breasteds, which reach full size in about 18 weeks and usually can't live longer than a year, heritage turkeys grow slowly and can live as long as 7 years. Because they're genetically healthier, they're strong and fit enough to endure the outdoors, run and even fly, and mate naturally, none of which the factory-bred Broad-Breasted Whites can do.

If you're interested in tasting a turkey that's much closer to what the Pilgrims had for Thanksgiving, you might want to try a heritage bird. Since the supply is limited and the turkeys mature slowly, order early—in the spring. These lean, firm birds benefit from being brined first (*see Roast Turkey with Sage-Garlic Butter, page 388*, for a method) and from long, slow cooking.

Where to Find Heritage Turkeys

Order through gourmet grocery stores or try these sources:
• Mary's Free-Range Turkey, in Madera, California (delivers through local grocery stores in 42 states; *marysturkeys.com/storelocations3.htm*)
• LocalHarvest (search *localharvest.org* for heritage turkeys, and you'll get listings for turkey farmers in your area)

Roast Turkey with Wine and Herbs

recipe pictured on page **384**

Valerie Aikman-Smith, a Los Angeles–based food stylist, has a natural, easy grace in the kitchen. When she cooks turkey, she often buys the bird already cut up (or cuts it up herself), and then roasts the breast meat last so it doesn't dry out. This method not only results in moist meat but also means the meat is basically ready to go, right out of the oven—no carving at the table. Aikman-Smith likes to put a little individual pitcher of the turkey juices at each place so there's no need to pass a hot, sloshing gravy boat around the table.

SERVES 10 to 12 | **TIME** 2 to 2½ hours

1 turkey (12 to 14 lbs.), cut into pieces (*see Quick Tip, right*)
¼ cup olive oil
1 tbsp. *each* minced sage, rosemary, and thyme leaves, divided, plus sprigs for garnish
2 tsp. kosher salt, plus more to taste
1 tsp. freshly ground black pepper
2 cups white wine, divided
⅓ cup marsala
3 tbsp. red currant jelly

1. Preheat oven to 400°. In a large bowl, coat turkey all over with oil, 2 tsp. of each herb, salt, and pepper. Pour 1 cup wine into a roasting pan. Add drumsticks and wings. Roast 15 minutes, skin side down.

2. Turn drumsticks and wings over; add thighs and breast to pan, skin side up. Pour in remaining 1 cup wine. Roast until a thermometer inserted in thickest part of breast and thighs reads 160° and juices run clear, 45 minutes to 1 hour.

3. Transfer meat to a cutting board; tent with foil (any slight pinkness will fade as meat sits). Strain pan juices into a saucepan.

4. Add marsala, jelly, and remaining 1 tsp. of each herb; bring to a boil. Reduce heat and simmer 3 minutes; season with salt to taste. Spoon off fat. Pour juices into a pitcher (or individual pitchers) for serving if you like.

5. Carve thighs and breast meat into chunks or slices and arrange on a platter with legs and wings. Garnish with sprigs of herbs.

Quick Tip: Ask your butcher to cut turkey into 7 pieces (leave breast whole) and debone the thighs and breast.

PER SERVING: 290 cal., 46% (133 cal.) from fat; 32 g protein; 15 g fat (3.6 g sat.); 5.4 g carbo (0.1 g fiber); 404 mg sodium; 93 mg chol.

Turkey Carving
Made Easy

We love this method. The turkey looks good because the breast is cut into thick slices against the grain. Plus, it skips the interminable and messy slicing at the table: All the meat is carved in the kitchen and served neatly, ready to be eaten.

1. Cut off the thighs (with legs attached) and the wings; set aside. Slice off the breast halves lengthwise and set each to the side.

2. Carve each breast half across the grain into thick slices.

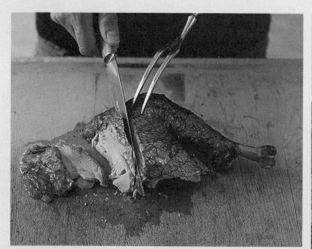

3. Slice the thigh meat off the bone and cut bone free from leg. Arrange sliced breasts, sliced thigh meat, and whole legs and wings on a platter.

Juniper-and-Herb Roast Turkey with Pine Nut Gravy

Presalting the turkey adds flavor and helps it stay moist during roasting; so does covering the breast and drumsticks with bacon. This recipe is from Seattle chef Maria Hines, of Tilth restaurant.

SERVES 10 to 12 | **TIME** 3 hours, plus 24 hours to brine

1 free-range organic turkey (12 to 14 lbs.)
3 tbsp. salt
1 tsp. *each* dried juniper berries, brown mustard seeds,
    and black peppercorns
½ cup butter, softened
⅓ cup minced thyme leaves
¼ cup minced sage leaves
2-in. rosemary sprig, leaves removed and minced
8 slices thick-cut bacon
1 cup dry white wine
Pine Nut Gravy (recipe follows)

1. Sprinkle turkey all over with salt, working some under the skin on breast and thighs. Put in a roasting pan, cover with foil or plastic wrap, and chill for at least 24 hours and up to 3 days.

2. Preheat oven to 400°. Unwrap turkey, discard any juices that have collected in pan, and pat turkey dry. Set aside. In a spice mill or clean coffee grinder, finely grind juniper berries, mustard seeds, and peppercorns. Rub spices all over turkey. In a small bowl, mix butter, thyme, sage, and rosemary until well combined. Massage mixture all over turkey and place bird in a large stovetop-safe roasting pan. Lay bacon slices over breast and drumsticks. Pour wine and ½ cup water into bottom of pan.

3. Roast turkey 1 hour, turning pan 180° halfway through. Reduce oven temperature to 350° and roast, turning pan every 30 minutes, until a thermometer inserted straight down through thickest part of breast to bone registers 155°, 1 to 1½ hours.

4. Transfer turkey to a carving board, loosely cover with foil, and let rest 30 minutes to 1 hour. Pour pan drippings into a glass measuring cup for Pine Nut Gravy, reserving pan to make gravy. Carve turkey and serve with gravy.

PER SERVING: 466 cal., 33% (153 cal.) from fat; 73 g protein; 17 g fat (6.2 g sat.); 0.3 g carbo (0.1 g fiber); 893 mg sodium; 198 mg chol.

Pine Nut Gravy

This nutty gravy is great with both roast turkey and stuffing. Or try it with mashed potatoes.

MAKES About 4½ cups | **TIME** 25 minutes, plus 1 hour to simmer stock

1 turkey neck
1 small onion, halved and peeled
2 bay leaves
½ cup pine nuts
Roasting pan and measuring cup of drippings from
    Juniper-and-Herb Roast Turkey (recipe precedes)
Up to ¼ cup butter if needed
¾ cup flour
Salt and freshly ground black pepper

1. In a medium saucepan over high heat, bring 6 cups water, turkey neck, onion, and bay leaves to a boil. Reduce heat to a simmer and cook, undisturbed, 1 hour. Take stock off heat and strain. Discard solids and set stock aside.

2. With a mortar and pestle, grind pine nuts into a rough paste; or in a food processor, pulse to a rough paste, being careful not to purée. Set paste aside.

3. Pour fat off pan drippings into a bowl and set aside (reserve juices left in measuring cup). Set roasting pan on top of stove so it spans two burners; turn them to medium low. Add ½ cup reserved fat (if you don't have enough, add butter to make ½ cup). Whisk in flour. Cook, whisking, until flour is deeply browned and has a nutty aroma, about 3 minutes.

4. Still whisking, pour in reserved pan juices and reserved stock. Use a wooden spoon to scrape up any browned bits from bottom of pan, then stir in reserved pine nut paste and whisk until gravy is smooth. Raise heat to high and bring to a boil. Boil until gravy is thick enough to coat the back of a metal spoon, 3 to 4 minutes. Season to taste with salt and pepper.

5. Pour into a gravy boat through a fine-mesh strainer, if you like, and serve immediately or keep warm (see Quick Tip below).

Quick Tip: You can keep the gravy warm by covering and resting it over a pan of barely simmering water for up to 2 hours. Whisk well before serving.

PER TBSP.: 39 cal., 82% (32 cal.) from fat; 0.6 g protein; 3.5 g fat (1.3 g sat.); 1.2 g carbo (0.1 g fiber); 117 mg sodium; 4.6 mg chol.

Roast Turkey with Sage-Garlic Butter

We are big believers in brining turkey before cooking. It helps the meat absorb moisture (and prevents the white meat from drying out before the dark meat is cooked) and makes the meat more flavorful overall.

SERVES 12 to 16 | **TIME** 2¾ to 3¾ hours, plus overnight to brine

1 cup kosher salt
1 turkey (12 to 18 lbs.)
1 cup unsalted butter, at room temperature
⅓ cup plus 1 tbsp. chopped sage leaves
2 tbsp. chopped garlic
½ cup flour
1 qt. reduced-sodium chicken broth, warmed

1. Make brine: Boil 1 qt. water with salt in a pot big enough to hold turkey, stirring until salt is dissolved. Add 2 qts. cold water and let cool to room temperature. Meanwhile, remove leg truss from turkey and discard. Remove neck, tail, and giblets and save for broth if you like. Pull off and discard lumps of fat. Rinse bird inside and out. Lower turkey into brine. If breast isn't submerged, make more brine, cool, and add. Chill, covered, at least 12 hours.
2. In a food processor, blend butter, ⅓ cup sage, and garlic until smooth.
3. Preheat oven to 350°. Lift turkey from brine, rinse, and pat dry. Set turkey on a V-shaped rack in a 12- by 17-in. or larger roasting pan (big enough so turkey fits inside rim).
4. Slide your fingers between skin and flesh of bird to make pockets of space on breast, back, and leg areas, turning bird as necessary. Still using your fingers, slide about 1 tbsp. sage-garlic butter at a time under skin in all the pockets. Place bird, breast side up, on rack.
5. Roast turkey, basting occasionally with pan drippings, until a thermometer inserted straight down through thickest part of breast to the bone registers 160°, 2 to 3 hours. Transfer turkey to a platter and tent with foil. Let rest in a warm place 15 to 30 minutes, then carve.
6. Meanwhile, make gravy: Scrape browned bits from bottom of pan and pour with drippings into a glass measuring cup. Skim fat off top; reserve ¼ cup and discard the rest. Measure drippings; add hot water if needed to make 1 cup total.

7. In a large frying pan, heat reserved fat over medium heat. Add flour and cook, whisking constantly, until golden brown, about 5 minutes. Add drippings, whisking into a smooth paste. Whisk in broth, about ½ cup at a time, letting mixture come to a boil between additions. Stir in remaining 1 tbsp. sage.
Make Ahead: Sage-garlic butter, up to 4 days, covered and chilled. Bring to room temperature before using.

PER SERVING: 288 cal., 45% (130 cal.) from fat; 33 g protein; 15 g fat (6 g sat.); 4 g carbo (0.1 g fiber); 581 mg sodium; 104 mg chol.

Turkey-Mushroom Meat Loaf

Karlyn Hochner, of Laguna Beach, California, updated her grandmother's meat loaf by using ground turkey and lots of fresh vegetables. Use a mix of dark and white turkey meat; all white makes the meat loaf dry.

SERVES 6 or 7 | **TIME** 1¼ hours

2 cups chopped mushrooms
1½ cups diced broccoli florets
1 cup *each* diced green bell pepper and carrots
½ cup diced onion
1 tsp. *each* minced garlic and vegetable oil
½ tsp. celery seeds
1 lb. ground turkey (mixed dark and white meat)
⅓ cup ketchup
3 tbsp. reduced-sodium soy sauce
2 tbsp. Dijon mustard
3 egg whites
1 cup fine dried bread crumbs

1. Preheat oven to 375°. In a 12-in. frying pan over medium-high heat, cook mushrooms, broccoli, green pepper, carrots, onion, garlic, oil, and celery seeds, stirring often, until carrots are tender-crisp, 8 to 10 minutes.
2. In a large bowl, combine vegetable mixture, turkey, ketchup, soy sauce, mustard, egg whites, and crumbs. Pat into a 8½- by 4½-in. loaf pan or 6- to 8-cup terrine, gently rounding top. Bake until firm to the touch, 40 to 45 minutes. For a browner crust, broil 3 in. from heat for a few minutes. Let stand 10 minutes before slicing.

PER SERVING: 216 cal., 27% (59 cal.) from fat; 17 g protein; 6.6 g fat (1.6 g sat.); 21 g carbo; 725 mg sodium; 47 mg chol.

poultry & stuffing

Turkey Enchiladas with Sour Cream

The original recipe for these rich and easy enchiladas came from the 1969 edition of the *Sunset Cook Book of Favorite Recipes*. Reader Donna Barasch, of Villa Park, California, adapted it with timesaving tricks, replacing the homemade chili-tomato sauce with a jar of medium-hot salsa; we tried both red and green salsas in our tests, as well as the New Mexico Red and Green Chile Sauces on *page 369*, and they were all delicious.

The recipe is a great way to use up leftover holiday turkey, but if you don't have turkey on hand, shredded cooked chicken is a good substitute.

SERVES 6 | **TIME** 40 minutes

3 cups shredded cooked turkey
2 cups sour cream
2 cups shredded (½ lb.) sharp cheddar cheese,
    plus more for sprinkling
1 tsp. salt
⅓ cup vegetable oil
12 corn tortillas (8 in. wide)
1 jar (16 oz.) medium-hot salsa

1. Preheat oven to 350°. In a large bowl, mix turkey, sour cream, cheddar cheese, and salt.
2. Heat oil in an 8- to 10-in. frying pan over low heat. Dip 1 tortilla at a time in hot oil just until limp, about 5 seconds each.
3. Fill tortillas with turkey mixture, roll up, and arrange side by side, seam down, in a 9- by 13-in. baking dish. Pour salsa evenly over the top. Bake until heated through, about 20 minutes.
4. Sprinkle more shredded cheese over hot enchiladas before serving.

PER SERVING: 677 cal., 60% (405 cal.) from fat; 35 g protein; 45 g fat (21 g sat.); 32 g carbo (2.6 g fiber); 1,308 mg sodium; 128 mg chol.

Rice with Duck or Geese (*Arroz con Patos o Gansos*)

We pulled this tasty nugget of a recipe from deep in our archives. It first appeared in 1954 in a column we called Chefs of the West, which featured recipes "by men...for men." It came from Jackson D. Arnold, who "served it first after a hunting trip into Mexico where he got his limit of wild geese and ducks." Given that geese are rarely on the table these days, we provide the recipe starring duck—but if a goose lands in your life, by all means try it here.

MAKES 3 ample servings | **TIME** 2 hours

3 duck breast halves (1 lb. each)
Salt and freshly ground black pepper
¼ cup olive oil
2 onions, finely chopped
1 garlic clove, minced or pressed
½ tsp. turmeric
2 cups white long-grain rice
5 cups beef consommé or chicken broth (*see Quick Tip below*)
1 bay leaf
½ cup jarred roasted red peppers, drained and chopped
¼ cup chopped parsley
½ cup slivered or sliced almonds, toasted (*see How to Toast Nuts, page 134*)

1. Preheat oven to 350°. Season duck with salt and pepper to taste. Put in a 9- by 13-in. baking dish at least 3 in. deep and bake, skin side up, 15 minutes; pour off excess fat. Transfer duck to a plate and scrape drippings into a frying pan. Return duck to baking dish.
2. Mix oil with drippings in pan and add onions, garlic, and turmeric. Cook over medium-high heat, stirring occasionally, until browned, about 5 minutes. Stir in rice and cook, stirring, 5 minutes.
3. In a separate pot, bring consommé with bay leaf to a boil. Stir into rice and onions. Pour rice mixture all over browned duck, scraping rice off meat into broth so it will cook. Add peppers and parsley and bake, uncovered, until meat pulls easily from bone (cut to test), about 45 minutes. Do not stir!
4. Carefully stir almonds into rice just before serving.
Quick Tip: To lower the salt content in the dish, buy reduced-sodium beef consommé or chicken broth.

PER SERVING: 1,107 cal., 37% (405 cal.) from fat; 55 g protein; 45 g fat (7.6 g sat.); 119 g carbo (4.5 g fiber); 1,220 mg sodium; 164 mg chol.

Tea-smoked Duck

Traditional Sichuan tea-smoked duck is made in three steps: The duck is first smoked over tea leaves, then steamed, then deep-fried. We've simplified the process by eliminating the steaming step and substituting roasting for deep-frying. It is still outrageously delicious. Serve slices of the duck tucked into steamed buns (recipe follows).

MAKES 2 or 3 servings | **TIME** 4 hours

Steamed Buns (*recipe follows*)
1 duckling (about 4 lbs.)
1 tsp. salt
1 tbsp. Sichuan peppercorns
2 tbsp. dry sherry
¼ cup *each* rice, firmly packed brown sugar, and black tea leaves
2 tbsp. coarsely chopped orange zest or dried tangerine peel
6 quarter-size slices fresh ginger, crushed
5 green onions, trimmed
Hoisin sauce
Cilantro sprigs

1. Prepare buns and set aside. Remove giblets and neck from duck; reserve for other uses or discard. Pat duck dry. Trim off and discard excess neck skin; with a fork, pierce remaining skin all over.
2. In a small frying pan over medium-low heat, cook salt and peppercorns, shaking pan often, until salt begins to brown and peppercorns become fragrant, about 10 minutes. Let cool, then coarsely grind with a mortar and pestle or crush with a rolling pin. Combine mixture with sherry; rub over duck, inside and out.
3. To smoke duck, you'll need a wok with a diameter of at least 14 in. (do not use an electric wok with a non-stick finish). Line wok with heavy-duty foil. In a small bowl, mix rice, brown sugar, tea leaves, and orange zest; pour into wok. Position a round cake rack or steamer rack in bottom of wok, at least 1 in. above tea mixture. Set duck on rack; place wok over high heat.
4. When wok mixture beings to smoke, cover pan tightly and smoke for 5 minutes. Reduce heat to medium and continue to smoke, without uncovering wok, for 15 minutes. Turn off heat and leave covered until smoke subsides, about 15 minutes. Remove duck. Discard tea mixture.
5. Preheat oven to 350°. Place ginger and 2 green onions inside duck cavity; fasten opening shut with a small skewer, if necessary. Place duck, breast side down, on a rack in a roasting pan. Bake for 1½ hours.

Drain and discard fat from pan and turn duck over; continue to bake until thigh feels soft when pressed, 45 minutes to 1 hour. Remove duck from oven; drain and discard all fat from pan. Increase oven temperature to 450°; return duck to oven and cook just until skin is crisp, about 5 minutes.
6. Slice duck meat from bones; cut remaining 3 onions into thin slivers. Steam buns for 5 minutes to reheat. Place duck slices in a warm bun; top with onions, hoisin, and cilantro, then close and eat out of hand.
Make Ahead: Through step 4, up to 1 day, chilled.

PER SERVING WITHOUT BUN: 303 cal., 48% (145 cal.) from fat; 34 g protein; 16 g fat (6 g sat.); 3.8 g carbo (0.9 g fiber); 940 mg sodium; 127 mg chol.

Steamed Buns

MAKES 12 buns | **TIME** 1 hour, plus 2 hours to rise

1 package (2¼ tsp.) active dry yeast
⅓ cup sugar
2 tbsp. vegetable oil
1 tsp. salt
3¼ cups flour

1. In a medium bowl, dissolve yeast in 1 cup warm (100° to 110°) water; blend in sugar, oil, and salt. Let stand 15 minutes. Add flour and mix until dough holds together. Place on a lightly floured board; knead until smooth and elastic, 8 to 10 minutes. Place in a greased bowl, cover, and let rise in a warm (about 80°) place until doubled, about 1¼ hours.
2. Turn dough out onto a lightly floured board; knead for 1 minute. Shape into a rectangle, then cut rectangle into 12 equal pieces. Roll each piece into a 4½-in. round; press edges to make them slightly thinner than rest of round.
3. Place each bun on a 3-in. square of foil. Cover and let rise in a warm place until puffy and light, about 30 minutes.
4. Set buns in a steamer over boiling water. Cover and steam until tops are glazed and smooth, 12 to 15 minutes. Serve warm.
Make Ahead: Up to 4 weeks, frozen. To reheat, steam frozen buns until hot, about 10 minutes.

PER BUN: 166 cal., 14% (23 cal.) from fat; 3.7 g protein; 2.7 g fat (0.3 g sat.); 32 g carbo (1 g fiber); 195 mg sodium; 0 mg chol.

poultry & stuffing

Pinot-braised Duck with Spicy Greens

Michael Wild, cofounder and chef-owner of Bay Wolf restaurant in Oakland, California, loves duck and Pinot Noir, and here he pairs them. Wild always recommends getting two bottles of wine for this dish: a reasonably priced Pinot Noir to cook with and the best one you can find—or a good red Burgundy—to drink with it (for drinking, he likes Pinot from Au Bon Climat, in Santa Barbara County, or Ponzi Vineyards, in Oregon's Willamette Valley). For a lighter sauce, and because it's easier to find, we've substituted chicken broth for the rich duck stock he uses.

recipe pictured on page **375**

SERVES 4 | **TIME** 2¼ hours

4 duck legs (about ½ lb. each)
Salt and freshly ground black pepper
1 tsp. herbes de Provence
About 1 bottle (750 ml.) Pinot Noir
2 tbsp. olive oil, divided
¼ cup minced shallots
4 cups reduced-sodium chicken broth
1 thyme sprig
1 bay leaf
1 tbsp. butter
1 onion (about ½ lb.), chopped
1 lb. broccoli rabe (rapini), trimmed and cut into about 1-in. pieces, or 1½ lbs. mustard greens, trimmed and sliced crosswise
2 garlic cloves, minced
1 flat anchovy (optional), minced
¼ tsp. cayenne
1 tbsp. fresh lemon juice

1. Preheat oven to 375°. Lay duck legs skin side up in a roasting pan that just holds them comfortably. Sprinkle with salt, pepper, and the herbes de Provence. Roast 1 hour.

2. Spoon fat from pan and save for other uses or discard. Pour wine over duck; it should be deep enough so meat is immersed but not so deep as to cover skin (skin should be exposed). Continue roasting until skin is golden red, about 30 minutes longer.

3. Meanwhile, pour 1 tbsp. oil into a 1½- to 2-qt. pan over medium-high heat; add shallots and cook, stirring often, until they begin to brown, about 2 minutes. Add broth, thyme, and bay leaf; boil, stirring occasionally, until reduced to about 1½ cups, about 45 minutes. When the duck is done, add 1 cup braising liquid to broth mixture and boil, stirring often, until mixture has reduced by a fourth, about 15 minutes. Pour through a fine-mesh strainer into a small pitcher or bowl.

4. While broth reduces, prepare broccoli rabe: In a 12- to 14-in. frying pan over medium-high heat, melt butter with remaining 1 tbsp. oil. Add onion and cook, stirring often, until it begins to brown, about 7 minutes. Add broccoli rabe and cook, stirring often, until tender to the bite, 3 to 5 minutes (if using mustard greens, add half, stir until wilted, then add remaining). Add garlic and anchovy if using and cook until fragrant, about 1 minute longer. Remove from heat and season to taste with salt, pepper, cayenne, and lemon juice.

5. Mound greens on plates and set duck legs on top. Serve pan juices alongside.

PER SERVING: 370 cal., 47% (175 cal.) from fat; 33 g protein; 20 g fat (5.4 g sat.); 16 g carbo (1.1 g fiber); 537 mg sodium; 106 mg chol.

Farm-raised vs. Wild Duck

Ducks harvested from the wild are generally pretty lean, with dark, rich-tasting meat. Because they're so lean, though, they overcook and dry out very easily, and must be cooked either hot and fast or slowly braised—and carefully watched. When pricked, their juices should run reddish pink.

Farm-raised ducks are milder, paler, and have a thick layer of fat, since they don't move much and their diet of corn and grain tends to plump them up. They need to be cooked more slowly so that the fat renders; when they're pricked, the juices should run clear.

Types of Farm-raised Duck

• **Pekin** (also known as White Pekin or Long Island): By far the most common breed, it's small, dainty, and the fattiest of the domestic ducks.

• **Muscovy:** Our favorite. It's big and meaty, with an appealingly musky flavor.

• **Moulard:** Large and usually leaner than either of the above types, this duck is typically raised for foie gras production.

Thyme-roasted Duck Breasts with Orange-Wine Sauce

When Washington chef Mike Davis was chef-owner of the Walla Walla restaurant 26 Brix (now closed), he served these duck breasts with mashed fingerling potatoes.

SERVES 6 | **TIME** 1¼ hours

2 tbsp. olive oil
1 cup *each* chopped carrots and celery
½ cup chopped shallots
¼ cup chopped garlic
1 bottle (750 ml.) dry red wine
1 cup orange juice
5 thyme sprigs, plus 1 tbsp. leaves
2 bay leaves
3 duck breast halves (about 10 oz. each)
Salt and freshly ground black pepper
½ cup heavy whipping cream
6 cups (5 oz.) baby arugula leaves

1. Preheat oven to 425°. Heat oil in a 12-in. ovenproof nonstick frying pan (with sides at least 2 in. high) over medium heat until hot. Add carrots, celery, shallots, and garlic; cook, stirring often, until vegetables are slightly softened and beginning to brown, about 7 minutes. Add wine, orange juice, thyme sprigs, and bay leaves; increase heat to high and boil, stirring occasionally, until liquid has reduced by about half and is slightly syrupy, about 15 minutes. Pour through a fine-mesh strainer into a glass measuring cup; you should have about 1 cup. Discard vegetables. Wipe pan dry and set aside reduction, covered.
2. Score skin of each duck breast half in a crosshatch pattern, making cuts about 1 in. apart, through skin into fat layer. Sprinkle lightly all over with salt and pepper. Set same frying pan over medium-high heat; when hot, lay duck breasts, skin side down, in pan. Cook until beginning to brown on bottom, 1½ to 2 minutes. Spoon out and discard any fat in pan. Turn breasts over and sprinkle with thyme leaves.
3. Transfer pan with duck to oven and roast until well browned on surface but still slightly pink in center of thickest part (cut to test), 20 to 25 minutes. Transfer duck to a rimmed cutting board and let rest in a warm place for 5 minutes. Skim off and discard fat from pan juices.
4. Set pan over medium-high heat and add orange-wine reduction and cream. Stir often, scraping up browned bits from bottom of pan, until sauce is boiling and coats the back of a spoon in a thin layer, 2 to 3 minutes. Season to taste with salt and pepper.

5. Divide arugula among plates. Slice duck breasts across grain and fan over arugula. Drizzle a little warm orange-wine sauce over duck and greens. Pour remaining sauce into a small pitcher for diners to add to taste. **Make Ahead:** Orange-wine sauce (through step 1), up to 1 day, chilled.

PER SERVING: 295 cal., 55% (162 cal.) from fat; 21 g protein; 18 g fat (7.1 g sat.); 12 g carbo (0.4 g fiber); 99 mg sodium; 131 mg chol.

Cornbread and Gorgonzola Dressing

This rich, moist concoction comes from reader Corry Kelly, of San Anselmo, California. It's really a cross between a dressing and a savory bread pudding.

SERVES 12 to 16 | **TIME** 1 hour, 40 minutes

⅓ cup plus ¼ cup butter
1½ cups flour
½ cup cornmeal
⅓ cup sugar
1 tbsp. baking powder
1½ tsp. salt, divided
5¼ cups milk, divided
8 eggs, divided
2 leeks, root ends and dark green tops removed
¼ lb. dried porcini mushrooms
3 garlic cloves, minced
2 shallots, minced
4 sage leaves, minced
¾ lb. baguette or similar French bread, cut into ½-in. cubes
10 oz. gorgonzola dolce cheese

1. Preheat oven to 350°. Butter two 9- by 13-in. baking dishes. Set aside. In a small saucepan over low heat, melt ⅓ cup butter. Set aside and cool slightly.
2. In a large bowl, combine flour, cornmeal, sugar, baking powder, and ½ tsp. salt. Stir in 1¼ cups milk, 2 eggs, and reserved melted butter. Pour batter into one buttered baking dish and bake until a toothpick inserted in center comes out clean, 30 to 35 minutes. Let cool and then cut cornbread into bite-size pieces.
3. Meanwhile, halve leeks lengthwise. Swish leeks around in a large bowl of water to rinse off dirt; transfer to a colander, leaving dirt behind, and rinse again in fresh water if necessary. Thinly slice white and light green parts. In a small bowl, soak porcini in 1¾ cups hot water for 15 minutes. With a slotted spoon, transfer porcini to a cutting board and roughly chop. Reserve porcini and soaking liquid.

4. Melt remaining ¼ cup butter in a large frying pan over medium-high heat. Add leeks, porcini, garlic, shallots, sage, and remaining 1 tsp. salt. Cook, stirring, until leeks and shallots are soft, about 5 minutes. Carefully pour in porcini soaking liquid, leaving behind any grit at bottom of bowl.

5. In a very large bowl, whisk together remaining 4 cups milk and 6 eggs. Stir in leek-porcini mixture. Add baguette cubes and stir. Add cornbread pieces and fold gently to mix. Transfer to second buttered baking dish and break gorgonzola into small pieces and scatter over top. Bake until set, about 40 minutes. Let stand 5 to 10 minutes before serving.

Make Ahead: Through step 4, up to 1 day. Cover bread cubes and cornbread and store at room temperature; cover and chill leek-porcini mixture, then bring to room temperature before resuming with step 5.

PER SERVING: 436 cal., 43% (189 cal.) from fat; 17 g protein; 21 g fat (12 g sat.); 43 g carbo (3.5 g fiber); 952 mg sodium; 174 mg chol.

You Say Dressing, I Say Stuffing

Although "dressing" is often thought of as the Southern term for the savory mix that traditionally fills a turkey, and "stuffing" the word used by the rest of the country, they're actually defined by how they're cooked, not by geography. Dressing is baked outside the bird, and stuffing is cooked within it. That said, it's doubtful that Southerners will ever spoon out steaming hunks of cornbread from the cavity of a turkey and comfortably call it stuffing. And Westerners will say "stuffing" even though they're serving right from a pan, not the bird. Sometimes tradition trumps the dictionary.

Cornbread-Chorizo Dressing

Sean Yontz, chef-owner of Mezcal and Tambien restaurants in Denver, gave us this recipe, and it's one of our most requested. It's great with Barbecued Glazed Turkey coated with Chile-Orange Glaze *(page 479)*.

recipe pictured on page **383**

Makes 12 cups; 16 servings | **TIME** 1 hour, plus time to make cornbread

1 lb. Mexican-style firm, fresh chorizo sausage *(see Quick Tips below)*, casings removed
½ cup butter
1 red onion (½ lb.), chopped
½ cup *each* chopped celery and carrot
6 garlic cloves, minced
¼ cup chopped cilantro
1 tbsp. *each* chopped thyme, oregano, and sage leaves
2 to 2½ cups reduced-sodium chicken broth, divided
12 cups ¾-in. cubes cornbread (*see Quick Tips below*)
Salt and freshly ground black pepper

1. In a frying pan over medium heat, cook chorizo, stirring, until crumbly and browned (leave some large chunks), about 5 minutes. Transfer to paper towels to drain.

2. Return pan to medium-high heat and melt butter. Add onion, celery, carrot, and garlic. Cook vegetables, stirring occasionally, until lightly browned, about 10 minutes. Add cilantro, thyme, oregano, and sage; cook until fragrant, 1 minute. Add chorizo and 2 cups broth and cook just until boiling. Remove from heat.

3. Preheat oven to 450°. In a large bowl, combine cornbread cubes and chorizo mixture. Stir until evenly moistened; season with salt and pepper. If mixture seems dry, moisten with about ½ cup additional broth. Spoon into a 9- by 13-in. baking dish.

4. Cover dressing and bake for 10 minutes; uncover and continue to bake until top is browned and dressing is heated through, 10 to 15 minutes longer.

Quick Tips: Buy firm, fresh chorizo in natural casings at well-stocked grocery stores or Latino markets. Very soft, bright red chorizo in plastic casings won't work in this dish. For the cornbread, bake two 8-in. square pans of your favorite cornbread or a boxed mix (you will have a little left over).

Make Ahead: Cornbread, up to 3 days, at room temperature. Through step 3, up to 2 days, chilled; bring to room temperature 3 hours before baking.

PER ¾-CUP SERVING: 376 cal., 53% (198 cal.) from fat; 12 g protein; 22 g fat (9.3 g sat.); 31 g carbo (1.8 g fiber); 959 mg sodium; 76 mg chol.

Artichoke Parmesan Sourdough Stuffing

Every November, we're asked again and again for this recipe, created by reader Leslie Jo Parsons of Sutter Creek, California (*Sunset* readers from all over the West have actually called Parsons to thank her for it). She makes the stuffing every year, and agrees with us: It's even better with extra parmesan, so we added some more here.

MAKES 10 cups; 12 servings | **TIME** 1½ hours

1 lb. mushrooms, trimmed and sliced
1 tbsp. butter
2 onions (¾ lb. total), chopped
1 cup chopped celery
2 tbsp. minced garlic
About 2 cups reduced-sodium chicken broth
1 loaf (1 lb.) sourdough bread, cut into ½-in. cubes
2 jars (6 oz. each) marinated artichoke hearts, drained and chopped
1 cup finely shredded parmesan cheese
1½ tsp. poultry seasoning
1½ tbsp. minced fresh rosemary leaves or ¾ tsp. crumbled dried rosemary
Salt and freshly ground black pepper
1 egg

1. Preheat oven to 325° to 350° (use the temperature your turkey requires). In a 12-in. frying pan over high heat, cook mushrooms, butter, onions, celery, and garlic, stirring often, until vegetables are lightly browned, about 15 minutes. Transfer to a large bowl. Add a bit of broth to pan and stir to scrape browned bits from bottom of pan. Add to bowl.
2. Pour 2 cups broth into bowl and add bread, chopped artichokes, parmesan, poultry seasoning, and rosemary; mix well. Add salt and pepper to taste. Make a well in stuffing. Drop egg in well and beat egg with a fork to blend; mix egg with stuffing. Spoon stuffing into a shallow 3-qt. (9- by 13-in.) baking dish.
3. For moist stuffing, cover baking dish with foil; for crusty stuffing, do not cover. Bake until hot (at least 150° in center; check with an instant-read thermometer) or lightly browned, about 50 minutes.
Make Ahead: Through step 2, up to 1 day, chilled. Allow about 1 hour to bake.

PER SERVING: 195 cal., 29% (56 cal.) from fat; 9 g protein; 6.2 g fat (2.5 g sat.); 26 g carbo (2.7 g fiber); 554 mg sodium; 27 mg chol.

Italian Chard Stuffing

If we could have only one other dish besides turkey for Thanksgiving, this would be it: a stuffing full of juicy sausage, good bread, and lots of chard. Former *Sunset* food editor Jerry Anne Di Vecchio got it from her mother-in-law.

MAKES 12 cups; 16 servings | **TIME** 1½ hours

¾ loaf (¾ lb.) French bread
1½ cups nonfat milk
2 lbs. Italian sausage, casings removed
1 cup chopped parsley
1 garlic clove, minced or pressed
1 medium onion, chopped
½ cup finely chopped celery
1½ lbs. green Swiss chard, stems trimmed and coarsely chopped
1½ cups finely shredded parmesan cheese
1½ tsp. dried basil
¼ tsp. *each* rubbed sage and dried rosemary
Salt

1. Cut bread into ½-in.-thick slices. Put slices in a large bowl and add milk. Mix gently with a spoon to saturate with milk and let stand about 30 minutes. Stir occasionally.
2. Meanwhile, preheat oven to 325° or 350° (use the temperature your turkey requires). Set a 6- to 8-qt. pot over high heat. Add sausage to pot. Cook meat, stirring often to crumble, until lightly browned, 10 to 15 minutes; discard fat. Add parsley, garlic, onion, and celery. Cook, stirring often, until vegetables are lightly browned, 5 to 8 minutes. Add chard and ½ cup water and cook, stirring often, until wilted, about 5 minutes.
3. With your hands, squeeze bread slices to break them into tiny pieces. Add cooked meat mixture, parmesan, basil, sage, and rosemary. Season with salt to taste.
4. Spoon stuffing into turkey or a shallow 3-qt. (9- by 13-in.) baking dish. If cooking in a baking dish, cover with foil for moist stuffing; leave it uncovered if you want it crusty. Bake until hot (at least 165° in center if cooking in turkey; check with an instant-read thermometer) or lightly browned, at least 30 minutes.
Make Ahead: Through step 3, up to 1 day, chilled. Allow 45 minutes to 1 hour to bake.

PER ¾-CUP SERVING: 318 cal., 59% (189 cal.) from fat; 15 g protein; 21 g fat (8.3 g sat.); 16 g carbo (1.6 g fiber); 815 mg sodium; 51 mg chol.

Chinese Rice Stuffing

Some of the best Thanksgiving recipes we've ever published have been cross-cultural creations. This one, from Rebecca Parker and her husband, Wei Chiu, of Palo Alto, California, is really wonderful—savory, moist, and studded with bits of sweet-salty Chinese sausage and crunchy water chestnuts. It can be eaten as a separate side dish or used to stuff turkey, chicken, or Cornish hens.

SERVES 8 to 10 | **TIME** 1 hour, plus 2 hours to soak rice

2 cups sweet rice
1 cup jasmine rice
½ tsp. salt
8 to 10 dried medium shiitake mushrooms
6 Chinese sausages (*lop chong*; about 9 oz. total)
1 can (8 oz.) sliced water chestnuts
6 tbsp. oyster sauce
1 tbsp. sugar
3 tbsp. vegetable oil
2 garlic cloves, minced
1 medium onion, diced
4 green onions, trimmed and thinly sliced, divided

1. In a large bowl, wash sweet rice well in several changes of water until water runs clear. Cover with plenty of cold water and soak at least 2 hours. Drain rice in a colander. Meanwhile, in a medium bowl, wash jasmine rice in a few changes of water until water runs clear. Put jasmine rice in a small saucepan with 1½ cups water and the salt and bring to a boil, covered, over high heat. Lower heat and simmer, covered, until water is absorbed, 10 to 15 minutes. Let stand 5 minutes.
2. Soak shiitakes in 1¾ cups warm water until softened, 15 to 30 minutes. Meanwhile, quarter sausages, then dice; put in a bowl. Dice water chestnuts and add to sausages. When shiitakes are softened, lift from water (reserve water) and remove and discard stems. Dice caps and add to bowl.
3. Pour 1¼ cups mushroom water into a measuring cup, leaving grit behind. Stir in oyster sauce and sugar.
4. Heat oil in a large frying pan or wok over medium heat. Add garlic and cook, stirring, until slightly browned, about 30 seconds. Add diced onion and cook, stirring, until translucent, about 5 minutes. Stir in sausage mixture and drained sweet rice. Cook, stirring often, until heated through, about 5 minutes.

5. Stir in oyster sauce mixture and cook, stirring, until bubbling, about 2 minutes. Stir in half the green onions, reduce heat to low, and simmer, covered and stirring occasionally, until rice is translucent and liquid is absorbed, about 20 minutes.
6. Gradually stir in jasmine rice, 1 to 2 cups at a time, until thoroughly mixed; heat until hot, about 4 minutes. Transfer stuffing to a serving bowl and sprinkle with remaining green onions.
Quick Tip: If you have a rice cooker, you can cook the sweet and jasmine rices together after soaking the sweet rice (follow rice cooker instructions). Stir warm mixed rice into pan with other stuffing ingredients in step 6.
Make Ahead: Soak sweet rice up to 1 day at room temperature, covered. Cook jasmine rice 1 day ahead and chill.

PER SERVING (ABOUT ¾ CUP): 262 cal., 38% (100 cal.) from fat; 6.1 g protein; 11 g fat (3.1 g sat.); 35 g carbo; 451 mg sodium; 0 mg chol.

To stuff a Cornish hen, chicken, or turkey:
Rub a terikayi-style sauce all over the bird and let marinate overnight. Bring to room temperature, then fill the cavity loosely with hot, just-cooked stuffing right before roasting. As soon as the bird comes out of the oven, scoop stuffing into a bowl—and chill the leftovers separately, not in the bird.

■ Sweet Rice

FROM THE PANTRY

Sweet rice (also known as sticky or glutinous rice) has a very short grain and is sold at many specialty-foods stores. We like Nishiki, Koda Farms, and Lundberg Family Farms' sweet rices for their satisfying, sticky chewiness, which makes them easy to pick up with chopsticks. All must be washed in several changes of water before cooking.

Basmati Rice Dressing with Dried Fruit, Toasted Almonds, and Coconut

A longtime maker of Indian pilafs, Lynn Lloyd of Santa Cruz, California, wanted to create a special one a couple of years ago. Her family all stood around the stove with forks, tasting and suggesting. "After I added the cinnamon, everyone said, 'Stop! This is it.'"

SERVES 10 to 12 | **TIME** 1½ hours

2 cups brown basmati rice
2 cups dried apricots, cut into quarters
1 cup *each* sweetened dried cranberries and
    unsweetened flaked dried coconut
2 cups slivered almonds
¾ cup butter
2 cups chopped onion
½ cup *each* chopped red and green bell peppers
2 tsp. *each* finely grated fresh ginger, minced garlic, curry
    powder, ground cumin, and salt
1 tsp. *each* freshly ground black pepper and ground
    cardamom
1 tsp. *each* finely shredded orange zest and lime zest
½ tsp. cinnamon

1. In a 2- to 2½-qt. pan over high heat, bring 3½ cups water and the rice to a boil. Reduce heat to low, cover, and simmer until water is absorbed and rice is tender to the bite, about 45 minutes.
2. Meanwhile, in a bowl, combine dried apricots and cranberries. Cover with boiling water and let stand until fruit is plump, about 15 minutes. Drain.
3. Preheat oven to 350°. Put coconut and almonds in two separate 10- by 15-in. baking pans. Bake, stirring occasionally, until golden, 4 to 5 minutes for coconut, 8 to 10 minutes for almonds.
4. In a 6- to 8-qt. pan over medium-high heat, melt butter. Add onion and red and green bell peppers; cook, stirring occasionally, until onion is softened, about 5 minutes. Reduce heat to medium and add ginger, garlic, curry powder, cumin, salt, pepper, cardamom, orange and lime zests, and cinnamon; stir just until spices are aromatic, about 30 seconds. Remove from heat. Stir in cooked rice, plumped fruit, almonds, and coconut. Spoon into a shallow 3-qt. baking dish and cover with foil.
5. Bake until hot in the center, about 30 minutes.
Make Ahead: Through step 4, up to 1 day, chilled. Before baking, let dressing stand at room temperature for 1 hour; bake until hot, about 45 minutes.

PER SERVING: 481 cal., 52% (252 cal.) from fat; 8.9 g protein; 28 g fat (11 g sat.); 54 g carbo (4.2 g fiber); 514 mg sodium; 31 mg chol.

Savory Bread Pudding with Sausage and Escarole

Filled with protein, iron, and calcium, this tasty alternative to dressing is practically a meal on its own. In fact, you could cut up your extra escarole and use it for a side salad with tomatoes, garbanzos, and an herb-garlic vinaigrette.

SERVES 6 to 8 | **TIME** About 1 hour

2 tbsp. olive oil
1 onion (10 oz.), cut in half and thinly sliced crosswise
2 garlic cloves, minced or pressed
1 lb. mild or hot Italian sausage (about 4 links), casings
    removed
¼ lb. escarole (*see Quick Tip below*), tough white parts
    discarded and thinly sliced
2 cups milk
4 eggs
1 cup shredded gruyère or Swiss cheese
10 cups cubed (1- to 2-in.) French or country-style bread
    (from a 1-lb. loaf; crusts removed)
1 tsp. salt
¼ tsp. freshly ground black pepper
⅛ tsp. freshly grated nutmeg

1. Butter a 9- by 13-in. baking dish. Pour oil into a 10- to 12-in. frying pan over medium-high heat. Add onion and stir often until limp and slightly golden, about 5 minutes. Stir in garlic and crumble sausage into pan. Stir often until meat is no longer pink, 7 to 10 minutes, using a wooden spoon to break it up if necessary.
2. Add escarole to sausage mixture in pan and reduce heat to low. Stir until escarole is wilted, 1 to 2 minutes. Remove pan from heat.
3. In a large bowl, whisk milk and eggs until combined. Stir in gruyère, bread cubes, salt, pepper, and nutmeg. Add sausage mixture and stir to mix well. Scrape mixture into baking dish and spread level.
4. Bake in a 375° oven until top is golden and a knife inserted in center comes out mostly clean, 35 to 45 minutes. (If top is brown after 30 minutes, cover loosely with foil and continue to bake.) Serve hot.
Quick Tip: If you can't find escarole, choose another leafy green, such as spinach or chard.
Make Ahead: Through step 3, up to 1 day ahead; chilled. Bring to room temperature before baking or increase baking time by 10 to 15 minutes.

PER SERVING: 515 cal., 56% (288 cal.) from fat; 22 g protein; 32 g fat (12 g sat.); 34 g carbo (2.2 g fiber); 1,130 mg sodium; 174 mg chol.

Portuguese Sausage Dressing

In a spin on the familiar Thanksgiving sausage and bread dressing, this version uses linguiça (Portuguese sausage), a common ingredient in Hawaii. Greg Boyer, who owns a landscape-design business in Oahu, serves this with his Hawaiian-Portuguese Smoked Turkey. You'll need 1 cup of the turkey marinade to prepare this.

SERVES 16 | **TIME** 1 hour, plus 30 to 40 minutes to bake

Marinated giblets and 1 cup marinade from Hawaiian-Portuguese Smoked Turkey (*page 476*)
½ cup butter
3 cups finely chopped celery
2 cups chopped onions
1¾ cups low-sodium chicken broth, divided
1 tsp. *each* poultry seasoning and minced sage leaves
1 tbsp. minced garlic
½ lb. linguiça (Portuguese sausage)
16 cups cubed (¾-in.) crusty white bread
½ cup chopped flat-leaf parsley

1. In a small saucepan, bring giblets and marinade to a simmer over medium heat, cover. Cook giblets until cooked through, about 20 minutes. Let cool; finely chop. Reserve ½ cup cooking liquid.
2. Preheat oven to 375°. Melt butter in a 10- to 12-in. skillet over medium-high heat. Add celery, onions, and chopped giblets and cook, stirring occasionally, 2 minutes. Add ¾ cup chicken broth, the poultry seasoning, sage, and garlic. Lower heat to medium-low and cook, stirring occasionally, until celery and onions are tender, about 20 minutes. Meanwhile, cut linguiça in half lengthwise, then slice into ¼-in.-thick half-moons.
3. Put bread cubes in a large bowl and stir in celery mixture, linguiça, and parsley. Stir in ½ cup giblet cooking liquid and remaining 1 cup chicken broth.
4. Spoon dressing into a 4- to 5-qt. baking dish and cover loosely with foil. Bake 25 minutes, uncover, and cook until browned on top, 10 to 20 minutes more. Serve hot.
Make Ahead: Up to 1 day ahead, chilled.

PER SERVING: 270 cal., 40% (108 cal.) from fat; 8.3 g protein; 12 g fat (5.5 g sat.); 33 g carbo (2.5 g fiber); 1,243 mg sodium; 25 mg chol.

Pancetta, Sourdough, and Apple Stuffing

Tangy Western sourdough bread makes this stuffing mouthwatering.

SERVES 16 | **TIME** 1¼ hours

1 lb. pancetta, cut into ½-in. cubes
1 tbsp. *each* olive oil and minced garlic
1 cup chopped celery
1½ cups chopped onion
2 Golden Delicious apples, peeled, cored, and thinly sliced
2 cups reduced-sodium chicken broth
5 qts. cubed (1-in.) sourdough bread (from a 1½-lb. loaf)
⅓ cup chopped flat-leaf parsley
1 tbsp. chopped thyme leaves

1. Grease a 9- by 13-in. baking dish. Brown pancetta in oil in a large frying pan over medium heat, stirring often, about 10 minutes. Add garlic, celery, and onion; sauté about 4 minutes. Add apples; stir to coat. Transfer to a large bowl. Add broth to pan; stir to scrape up browned bits from bottom. Pour into bowl. Stir in bread, parsley, and thyme. Spoon stuffing into baking dish, pressing down lightly to fill pan.
2. Bake in a 350° oven until browned and crusty, about 45 minutes.
Make Ahead: Through step 1, up to 1 day, chilled. Bake about 1 hour.

PER SERVING: 253 cal., 38% (96 cal.) from fat; 11 g protein; 11 g fat (3.4 g sat.); 29 g carbo (2 g fiber); 872 mg sodium; 25 mg chol.

meats

Whether you're looking for a grand holiday roast or a quick steak dinner, you'll find it in this collection of beef, pork, and lamb dishes—along with a few surprises.

From the high plains of Colorado to the inland valleys of California, ranches sprawl across the Western landscape. Beef is practically our birthright, and we raise excellent pork and lamb too—more and more of it on pasture, as we're learning how good grass is for the animals and, by extension, for us. In another positive development, long-neglected breeds (especially of pig) are slowly being revived, rewarding us with their more complex, rich flavors.

Elegant special-occasion dishes lend panache to this chapter—see Salt- and Herb-crusted Prime Rib with Fresh Horseradish Sauce (*page 404*) or Crown Roast of Pork (*page 415*). Even so, our hearts belong to the recipes that transform tough, usually cheap cuts into spectacular food: Put a clodhopper of a beef cross-rib roast (a type of pot roast) in a pan to slow-cook with clementines, chile, and ginger, and you get tender Spicy Beef Cross-rib Roast with Caramelized Clementine Sauce (*page 403*). And pork shoulder stuffed with figs and garlic and simmered in Pinot Noir (*page 417*) is one of the most succulent meals in our recent memory. To complement our slow food, we've included plenty of fast-cooking meats—steaks, chops, kebabs, stir-fries, meatballs, and scaloppine. If grilled meat is what you're after, turn to *page 432*, the beginning of reams of additional recipes awaiting you.

Looking for a bit of adventure? Check out the recipes at the end of this chapter. All are for very mild-tasting, lean meats that are getting more popular in the West. One is even lower in fat than skinned chicken breast (hint: It's the most widely eaten meat in the world).

Meats

Pepper Steaks with Balsamic Onions

Sometimes you just have to give in to the tried and true—a good steak and a glass of Cabernet. The only possible improvement: coating that steak with crunchy, pungent peppercorns and loading it with tangy balsamic onions.

SERVES 4 | **TIME** 45 minutes

2 tbsp. butter, divided
2 tbsp. olive oil, divided
2 sweet onions (1½ lbs. total) such as Walla Walla or Maui, slivered lengthwise
½ tsp. salt, plus more for sprinkling
½ tsp. sugar
2 tbsp. balsamic vinegar
1 tbsp. fresh thyme leaves, divided
4 boned tender beef steaks, 1 to 1½ in. thick (9 to 12 oz. each), such as top loin (New York strip) or rib eye
¼ cup cracked multicolored peppercorns (see *Quick Tip below*)

1. Melt 1½ tbsp. butter with 1½ tbsp. oil in a 12-in. frying pan over medium heat. Add onions and stir in salt. Cover and cook, stirring occasionally, until onions are softened, about 8 minutes. Uncover and sprinkle with sugar. Increase heat to medium-high and cook, stirring often, until onions begin to brown, 5 to 7 minutes. Add vinegar and 1½ tsp. thyme; cook, stirring often, until liquid has evaporated, 1 to 2 minutes longer.

2. Preheat oven to 375°. Pat steaks dry. Sprinkle both sides lightly with salt, then coat with cracked pepper. Melt remaining ½ tbsp. butter with remaining ½ tbsp. oil in a 12-in. ovenproof frying pan over medium-high heat (divide between two pans if there's not enough room for all the steaks in one). Add steaks and cook until well browned on bottom, 4 to 5 minutes. Turn steaks over and cook until beginning to brown on other side, about 2 minutes. Transfer pan to oven and bake until medium-rare (still pink in center; cut to test), 7 to 8 minutes, or until as done as you like (steaks will continue cooking for a few minutes after you take them out of the oven).

3. Transfer steaks to warm plates. Spoon onions over top and sprinkle with remaining 1½ tsp. thyme.

Quick Tip: To crack peppercorns, blend briefly in a spice mill or clean coffee grinder or crush with the bottom of a heavy glass or a small heavy saucepan.

PER SERVING: 813 cal., 65% (531 cal.) from fat; 52 g protein; 59 g fat (23 g sat.); 19 g carbo (4.2 g fiber); 503 mg sodium; 186 mg chol.

Steak Diane

An old recipe, but so fast to make—and tasty—that it belongs in our repertoire today.

SERVES 6 | **TIME** 20 minutes

1½ lbs. narrow end of beef tenderloin, fat trimmed
1 to 1½ tbsp. coarsely ground black pepper
¾ cup finely chopped shallots or onion
2 tbsp. butter, divided
½ cup beef broth
¼ cup *each* white wine vinegar and dry white wine
2 tbsp. dry mustard
1 tbsp. Dijon mustard
⅓ cup whipping cream
2 tbsp. *each* dry sherry and brandy
Salt

1. Cut thickest part of beef across the grain into 1½-in.-long pieces. Cut thinnest end into 2-in.-long pieces. Turn each piece onto a cut side and press down firmly to flatten. Sprinkle meat on each side with pepper, pressing it onto the surface.

2. In a large frying pan, combine shallots and 1 tbsp. butter. Cook, stirring, over high heat until shallots are limp, about 1½ minutes. Add broth, vinegar, wine, dry mustard, Dijon mustard, and cream. Boil over high heat, stirring, until reduced by half, 5 to 7 minutes. Pour sauce into a small bowl and set aside. Rinse pan and wipe dry.

3. Return frying pan to high heat. When hot, add remaining 1 tbsp. butter and swirl until it melts, then add meat (so that pieces aren't overlapping). Brown beef on one side, about 2½ minutes. Turn over and continue to cook until brown, about 2½ minutes more for rare.

4. Transfer beef to a warm plate. Add sherry, brandy, and sauce to pan. Stir until bubbling. Pour the sauce and any juices from the meat onto plates. Top with the beef. Add salt to taste.

PER SERVING: 298 cal., 51% (153 cal.) from fat; 25 g protein; 17 g fat (8.3 g sat.); 5.1 g carbo (0.4 g fiber); 174 mg sodium; 95 mg chol.

How to
Read a Beef Label

Most beef sold in markets comes from animals that spent much of their lives packed into feedlots, being fattened quickly on grain. The resulting "corn-fed" beef is marbled with fat that carries the flavor Americans have come to love. But shoulder-to-shoulder feedlot conditions and an unnatural grain diet (it actually makes cattle sick) require constant doses of antibiotics. And the desire for quick profits motivates many operators to use growth hormones. Alternative beef is increasingly available. Here's what the labels mean.

Free-range
Not an official term. Generally means that the animal was not confined to a feedlot. Hormones or antibiotics are not necessarily avoided.

Grass-fed
The animal's main diet was grass, not grain. Grass-fed beef is leaner than grain-fed; it has less saturated fat and more omega-3 fatty acids. Some meat labeled "grass-fed" is finished on grain, but if you see "USDA Process Verified," that means the cow was fed only grass and forage—no grain—during its lifetime with the exception of milk prior to weaning. It doesn't preclude use of hormones or antibiotics or confinement. Products bearing the American Grassfed Association (AGA) logo are from free-range cattle that are grass-fed until harvest; they are also antibiotic- and hormone-free.

Natural
According to the USDA, all raw beef is natural because it's minimally processed and contains no artificial ingredients or preservatives. In practice, though, most producers of "all natural" beef avoid giving their animals hormones, antibiotics, and feed containing animal by-products; some finish the cattle on grain (without additives) in a feedlot. Specifics vary by producer; check individual labels for explanations.

USDA Organic
Animal was raised without antibiotics or growth hormones, had access to a pasture, and was fed organically produced, plant-based feed (could be grain or grass). Vaccines are allowed. Certification based on standards in USDA's National Organic Program.

Certified Humane Raised & Handled
Animal was treated humanely from birth through slaughter according to a set of standards created by animal scientists and farm veterinarians. Certified animals have enough space to move naturally (i.e., they are not confined in cages, crates, or tie stalls); are gently handled; and are not subjected to routine cruel treatments, like tail-docking. The animals also have plenty of fresh water and good (though not necessarily organic) food and are not given antibiotics or hormones. All producers must reapply and be inspected annually in order to be certified.

Spicy Beef Cross-rib Roast with Caramelized Clementine Sauce

Chinese orange-peel beef was the inspiration for this roast.

SERVES 6 to 8 | **TIME** 2¼ hours

recipe pictured on page 377

2½ lbs. clementines, divided
1 to 2 tsp. red chile flakes
3 tbsp. coarsely chopped fresh ginger
4 garlic cloves, peeled
1 tsp. kosher salt
3 tbsp. vegetable oil
1 boned beef cross-rib (chuck) roast or boned chuck roast (about 3½ lbs.), tied with kitchen twine as a roast (*see Quick Tip below*)
6 tbsp. *each* sugar and soy sauce
3 tbsp. dry sherry
3 green onions, trimmed and cut into 2-in. matchsticks

1. Preheat oven to 450°. Finely shred zest from 2 large clementines. In a food processor, mince zest, chile flakes, ginger, garlic, and salt. Blend in oil.
2. Put meat in a 12- by 17-in. roasting pan, rub all over with chile mixture, and set fat side up. Roast beef until browned, 20 to 25 minutes. Reduce oven temperature to 325° and cook until a thermometer inserted into thickest part of roast registers 90°, about 20 minutes.
3. While beef roasts, cut clementines in half and juice them. Bring a large saucepan of water to a boil. Add peels and boil gently 5 minutes, stirring occasionally. Drain; rinse with cool water. Scrape out and discard pulp and white pith. Cut peels in half, then stack a few at a time and cut into long, thin strips. In a bowl, combine peel strips, sugar, soy sauce, sherry, and ⅔ cup juice.
4. When meat reaches 90°, pour juice-soy mixture around it. Cook, stirring sauce occasionally, until meat reaches 130° for medium-rare, 30 to 40 minutes; as pan juices begin to caramelize, stir in a few tbsp. juice if needed to prevent scorching.
5. Transfer beef to a cutting board and let rest, tented loosely with foil, 15 minutes. Pour remaining juice into roasting pan, set pan over high heat, and cook, stirring often, until juices are thickened and shiny, about 7 minutes. Scrape sauce into a bowl.
6. Snip twine from roast. Thinly slice meat crosswise and sprinkle with green onions. Serve with sauce.
Quick Tip: The chuck lies between the ribs and the neck, and includes the shoulder. It yields a number of different roasts. The cross-rib roast (aka English roast) is a relatively tender boneless roast from the shoulder. Other chuck roasts, as long as they're boneless, will also work in this recipe. You can ask your butcher to tie the roast, or do it yourself: Using kitchen twine, tie the roast crosswise at 1½- to 2-in. intervals, then twice lengthwise.

PER SERVING: 441 cal., 45% (199 cal.) from fat; 40 g protein; 22 g fat (7 g sat.); 19 g carbo (0.7 g fiber); 1,072 mg sodium; 129 mg chol.

Sonia's Special Steaks

A simple drizzle of balsamic vinegar and soy sauce takes ho-hum grilled steaks to another level, thanks to reader Sonia Ottusch, of Malibu, California. Serve with crusty bread to sop up extra sauce.

SERVES 4 | **TIME** 30 minutes.

10 large garlic cloves, chopped
2 tbsp. olive oil
¼ cup *each* balsamic vinegar and soy sauce
2 rib-eye steaks (each about 1 in. thick and 20 oz., cut in half crosswise)
Kosher salt and freshly ground black pepper

1. In a medium frying pan over low heat, cook garlic in oil, stirring often, until golden, about 3 minutes. Drain garlic on paper towels; save oil for other uses.
2. Preheat broiler. Combine vinegar and soy sauce. Lay steaks flat; using a paring knife, cut a 2-in.-wide pocket in the side of each steak. Spoon one-quarter of garlic into each pocket. Generously sprinkle steaks with salt and pepper.
3. Place steaks on broiler pan and spoon 1 tbsp. vinegar mixture over each. Cook steaks 4 in. from heat, turning once, 5 to 7 minutes total for medium-rare (cut to test). Serve with remaining vinegar sauce.

PER SERVING: 409 cal., 66% (270 cal.) from fat; 28 g protein; 30 g fat (10 g sat.); 5.3 g carbo. (0.2 g fiber); 1,098 mg sodium; 87 mg chol.

Salt- and Herb-crusted Prime Rib with Fresh Horseradish Sauce

Packing a rib roast in a salt crust keeps it moist and makes those richly seasoned end pieces worth vying for at the table. (The term "prime" is used out of habit, since it's a grade of meat that's rarely sold to the public any more.) This recipe comes from Maria Helm Sinskey, co-owner of Robert Sinskey Vineyards in Napa, California, and author of *The Vineyard Kitchen: Menus Inspired by the Seasons* and *Williams-Sonoma Family Meals: Creating Traditions in the Kitchen*.

SERVES 8, with plenty of leftovers | **TIME** 3 hours, plus overnight to marinate and 1½ hours to rest

1 four-rib beef rib roast (about 8 lbs.), fat trimmed to ¼ in.; or 1 tied boned beef cross-rib roast (4 to 6 lbs.; *see Quick Tips, right*)
8 garlic cloves, slivered lengthwise
½ cup extra-virgin olive oil
¼ cup *each* chopped fresh rosemary and thyme leaves, or 2 tbsp. *each* dried rosemary and thyme
3 tbsp. cracked black peppercorns (*see Quick Tips, right*)
1 cup coarse sea salt
Fresh Horseradish Sauce (*recipe follows*)

1. With a small, sharp knife, make small slits all over meat and insert a piece of garlic in each.
2. In a small bowl, combine oil, rosemary, thyme, and cracked pepper. Rub mixture all over beef; wrap meat airtight in plastic wrap and chill overnight.
3. Remove beef from refrigerator 1 hour before roasting. Preheat oven to 450°. Set roast, fatty side up, in a roasting pan. In a small bowl, mix salt with 2 tbsp. cold water to moisten. Press mixture over fatty side and ends of meat.
4. Roast for 25 minutes, then lower oven temperature to 350°. Continue roasting until a thermometer inserted into thickest part of roast registers 125° for rare (or 130° for medium-rare; the ends will be more done), 1½ to 2 hours longer. Let rest in a warm place 30 to 40 minutes.

5. Scrape as much salt off roast as you can. If it's tied, cut twine holding meat and bones together. Transfer roast to a cutting board, cut meat into ⅓- to ½-in.-thick slices, and arrange on a platter. Cut between bones, if you have them, and add to platter. Serve with fresh horseradish sauce.

Quick Tips: For easy carving, have the butcher cut the rib-eye muscle from the bones, then tie the meat and bones back together for roasting. To tie the cross-rib roast yourself, use kitchen twine to tie it crosswise at 1½- to 2-in. intervals, then twice lengthwise. Cross-rib roast, a type of pot roast, is a more budget-friendly cut than beef rib roast. Be careful not to cook it past an internal temperature of 125°, though, or it may be a bit tough; also, slice it thinner than you would a beef rib roast. To crack peppercorns, blend briefly in a spice mill or clean coffee grinder or crush with the bottom of a heavy glass or a small heavy saucepan.

PER 6-OZ. SERVING WITHOUT SAUCE: 427 cal., 53% (225 cal.) from fat; 47 g protein; 25 g fat (9 g sat.); 1.7 g carbo (9 g fiber); 859 mg sodium; 136 mg chol.

Fresh Horseradish Sauce: Peel ¼ lb. **fresh horseradish root** (buy at specialty-foods stores or farmers' markets) with a vegetable peeler. Grate finely or finely chop in a food processor. In a small bowl, mix horseradish with 2 tbsp. **white wine vinegar**. (Or substitute ¼ to ½ cup prepared horseradish and omit vinegar.) In another bowl, whisk 1½ cups **crème fraîche or sour cream** until slightly thickened. Stir in horseradish mixture or prepared horseradish, 3 tbsp. chopped **flat-leaf parsley**, and **salt** and freshly ground **black pepper** to taste. Tastes best if made 1 day ahead to let flavors develop; keep chilled. Makes about 2 cups.

PER TBSP.: 44 cal., 84% (37 cal.) from fat; 0.5 g protein; 4.1 g fat (2.6 g sat.); 1 g carbo (0 g fiber); 7.9 mg sodium; 9.4 mg chol.

Slow-cooker Merlot Pot Roast

Excellent with Horseradish Potato Purée *(page 273)*.

SERVES 6 to 8 | **TIME** 8½ to 9½ hours on low, 5½ to 6½ hours on high

1 tied boned beef chuck roast (3½ lbs.; *see Quick Tip below*)
Freshly ground black pepper
1 tbsp. olive oil
3 carrots (¾ lb. total), peeled
1 onion (½ lb.), chopped
⅔ cup chopped celery
3 garlic cloves, minced or pressed
½ tsp. dried thyme
¼ tsp. black peppercorns
1 bay leaf
1 cup Merlot or other dry red wine
⅓ cup tomato paste
1½ tbsp. cornstarch
1 tbsp. minced flat-leaf parsley
1 to 2 cups watercress sprigs (optional)
Salt

1. Pat beef dry and sprinkle generously all over with pepper. Heat oil in a 10- to 12-in. frying pan over medium-high heat until hot. Add beef and brown well on all sides, 6 to 8 minutes total.
2. Meanwhile, cut carrots into sticks about ⅜ in. thick and 2 in. long. In a 4½-qt. (or larger) slow-cooker, combine carrots, onion, celery, garlic, thyme, peppercorns, and bay leaf. Set beef on vegetables; add drippings from pan. In a small bowl, mix wine and tomato paste; pour over meat and vegetables.
3. Cover and cook until beef is very tender when pierced, 8 to 9 hours on low, 5 to 6 hours on high. If possible, turn meat over halfway through cooking.
4. With two slotted spoons, transfer meat to a platter; remove twine and keep meat warm. Skim and discard any fat from cooking liquid. Turn cooker to high (if not already on high) and cover. In a small bowl, blend cornstarch with 1½ tbsp. water; pour into cooker and cook, stirring often, until sauce is bubbling, 10 to 15 minutes.
5. With a slotted spoon, arrange vegetables beside meat. Sprinkle with parsley. Garnish platter with watercress if using. Spoon sauce over meat. Slice meat and serve with vegetables and sauce, adding salt to taste.
Quick Tip: Any kind of roast from the chuck—an area between the shoulder and neck—makes a good pot roast; usually it will be labeled as such. To tie it yourself, use kitchen twine and tie it crosswise at 1½- to 2-in. intervals, then twice lengthwise.

PER SERVING: 314 cal., 40% (126 cal.) from fat; 34 g protein; 14 g fat (5.6 g sat.); 11 g carbo (2.3 g fiber); 256 mg sodium; 115 mg chol.

Beef Brisket with Onion-Lemon Marmalade and Sweet Potatoes

Port, lemon, and onion flavor the meat as it cooks, then they're reduced to a shiny marmalade topping.

SERVES 8 to 10 | **TIME** 1 hour, plus 4 hours unattended cooking time

1 beef brisket (5 to 6 lbs.)
2 medium onions, thinly sliced
2 medium lemons, thinly sliced, divided
1 cup *each* port and firmly packed brown sugar
1 tbsp. dried marjoram or 2 tbsp. chopped fresh marjoram
1 tsp. freshly ground black pepper
8 to 10 medium orange-flesh sweet potatoes (often labeled "yams"; about 5 lbs. total)

1. Preheat oven to 300°. Trim excess fat from brisket. Put onion slices and three-quarters of lemon slices in a 12- by 18-in. roasting pan; chill remaining lemon slices. Lay brisket on top of onions and lemons.
2. In a medium bowl, mix together port, brown sugar, and marjoram; stir until sugar dissolves, then pour over brisket. Sprinkle brisket with pepper and cover pan tightly with foil. Bake brisket until very tender when pierced, about 4 hours.
3. About 1½ hours before brisket will be done, pierce each sweet potato with a fork a few times and set on oven rack alongside brisket or on rack above it.
4. When brisket is tender, uncover pan and brown meat slightly, about 15 minutes. Transfer brisket to a platter and set in a warm place, covered. When potatoes are soft when pressed, remove from oven and add to brisket platter.
5. Skim off and discard fat from pan juices. Set pan over two burners on high heat and boil, uncovered, stirring often. As mixture thickens, reduce heat to medium. Cook, stirring constantly, until thick and shiny and reduced to about 1½ cups, 20 to 30 minutes. Spoon marmalade over brisket and top with reserved lemon slices. To serve, slice brisket across the grain.
Make Ahead: Through step 5, up to 1 day, chilled.

PER SERVING: 882 cal., 64% (560 cal.) from fat; 39 g protein; 63 g fat (28 g sat.); 42 g carbo (5.6 g fiber); 1,598 mg sodium; 165 mg chol.

Paley's Place Double-chile Brisket

Vitaly Paley, of Paley's Place in Portland, Oregon, is known for his eclectic style and interesting twists on comforting favorites. This recipe is based on one in *The Paley's Place Cookbook*.

SERVES 8 to 10 | **TIME** 3 to 3½ hours

7 or 8 dried mild New Mexico chiles *(see Quick Tips below)*, seeded
5 dried pasilla negro chiles *(see Quick Tips below)*, seeded and broken into pieces
1 star anise pod
1 tsp. fennel seeds
1½ tsp. salt
½ tsp. black peppercorns
1 beef brisket (5 to 6 lbs.), fat and membrane trimmed
½ cup sherry vinegar
3 tbsp. olive oil
1 medium onion, diced
1 can (14.5 oz.) peeled whole tomatoes
1 cup beef or chicken broth

1. Preheat oven to 350°. In a medium bowl, pour 3 cups boiling water over New Mexico chiles and let soak until softened, about 30 minutes. Drain, reserving 1 cup liquid.
2. Meanwhile, grind pasilla negro chiles, star anise, fennel seeds, salt, and peppercorns in a spice mill or clean coffee grinder. Rub brisket with spice blend; set aside.
3. Purée soaked chiles, vinegar, and reserved chile liquid in a blender. Set aside.
4. Heat a large roasting pan (not nonstick) over medium-high heat (set it over two burners if necessary). Add oil, swirl in pan, and add brisket. Cook brisket until well browned on one side, about 3 minutes. Turn and brown on remaining sides, adjusting heat to keep brisket sizzling but not burning. Remove and set aside.
5. Add onion to pan and cook, stirring, until soft, about 3 minutes. Chop tomatoes and add with juice. Add chile purée and broth. Bring to a boil. Add brisket, cover, and bake until fork-tender, 2 to 3 hours.
6. Set brisket on a serving platter, cover with foil, and set in a warm place. Purée pan juices in a blender until smooth. Slice brisket thinly and serve hot, with blended pan juices on the side.
Quick Tips: Whole dried New Mexico chiles are available at specialty-foods stores and through *newmexican connection.com*. Find pasilla negro chiles at Latino markets. If the chiles are dusty, wipe with a damp cloth before cooking with them.

PER SERVING: 458 cal., 10% (47 cal.) from fat; 54 g protein; 24 g fat (7.2 g sat.); 5.2 g carbo (1.4 g fiber); 647 mg sodium; 156 mg chol.

Port-braised Short Ribs with Ginger and Star Anise

recipe pictured on page **376**

Serve these ribs and their flavorful sauce with cooked white rice.

SERVES 4 | **TIME** 2¾ to 3¼ hours

4 lbs. beef short ribs, cut through bone into 2½- to 3-in. pieces
Salt and freshly ground black pepper
1 cup *each* diced onion, carrots, and celery
2 tbsp. minced fresh ginger
1 tsp. black peppercorns
2 star anise pods or ½ tsp. anise seeds
1 cinnamon stick (1½ to 2 in.)
5 rosemary sprigs (about 4 in. each), divided
3 cups beef broth
1 cup fresh tangerine or orange juice
¾ cup ruby port
1 tangerine or orange, thinly sliced crosswise

1. Preheat oven to 450°. Pat beef ribs dry; trim off and discard excess fat. Sprinkle ribs lightly all over with salt and pepper and set in a single layer, bones down, in a 12- by 17-in. roasting pan. Roast until meat begins to brown, 15 to 20 minutes.
2. With tongs, turn ribs over. Add onion, carrots, celery, and ginger around ribs, then mix to coat with fat in pan; spread vegetables level. Roast until ribs are well browned and vegetables are beginning to brown, 15 to 20 minutes longer.
3. Meanwhile, wrap peppercorns, star anise, cinnamon stick, and 2 rosemary sprigs in a double layer of 10-in.-square cheesecloth; tie closed with heavy cotton string. To pan add broth, tangerine juice, port, and spice bundle. Stir gently to mix and scrape browned bits from bottom of pan. Cover pan tightly with foil.
4. Reduce oven temperature to 325° and braise ribs until meat is very tender when pierced, 2 to 2½ hours. Uncover pan and discard spice bundle. With tongs, transfer ribs to a rimmed platter; cover and keep warm in a 200° oven. Skim and discard fat from pan juices. Set roasting pan over two burners on high heat and boil juices, stirring often, until reduced to 2½ cups, about 10 minutes. Add tangerine slices and cook just until heated through, about 1 minute.
5. Pour sauce over ribs on platter. Garnish with remaining rosemary sprigs. Add salt and pepper to taste.

PER SERVING: 434 cal., 39% (171 cal.) from fat; 41 g protein; 19 g fat (8.1 g sat.); 23 g carbo (2.8 g fiber); 216 mg sodium; 110 mg chol.

Cabernet-braised Short Ribs with Dried Apricots

Even though there's quite a time lapse between browning and serving short ribs, very little of it involves work. This version fills your house with especially enticing smells. Serve the ribs with creamy mashed potatoes, polenta, or crusty bread.

SERVES 6 to 8 | **TIME** 2¾ hours

4 lbs. beef short ribs, cut through bone into
   2½- to 3-in. pieces
½ cup flour
1 tbsp. *each* salt and freshly ground black pepper,
   plus more to taste
1 tbsp. *each* butter and olive oil
1 onion (about 10 oz.), chopped
5 garlic cloves, chopped
2½ cups Cabernet Sauvignon
2 tbsp. Dijon mustard
1 cup dried apricots

1. Pat short ribs dry. In a paper bag, combine flour with salt and pepper. Drop ribs into bag and shake to coat. Lift ribs out, shaking off excess flour mixture.
2. In a heavy 6-qt. pan over medium-high heat, melt butter with oil (*see Quick Tip below*). Working in batches, add ribs in a single layer and turn to brown on all sides, about 5 minutes total per batch. With tongs, transfer ribs to a bowl. Discard all but about 2 tbsp. fat in pan.
3. Reduce heat to medium and add onion and garlic to pan; cook, stirring often, until onion is softened, about 6 minutes. Stir in wine, mustard, and apricots, then return short ribs to pan. Cover and bring to a simmer; reduce heat to maintain a low simmer and cook, turning ribs once or twice to submerge meat, until very tender when pierced, 2 to 2½ hours.
4. With tongs or a slotted spoon, transfer short ribs to individual wide, shallow bowls or a serving bowl. Skim off and discard any fat from pan juices. Boil juices over high heat until reduced to about 3 cups. Season to taste with more salt and pepper. Pour juices over ribs.
Quick Tip: Browning meat in a mixture of olive oil and butter, rather than just butter, allows you to cook at a higher temperature without scorching, producing better color and texture.

PER SERVING: 650 cal., 70% (458 cal.) from fat; 26 g protein; 51 g fat (21 g sat.); 21 g carbo (2.1 g fiber); 745 mg sodium; 110 mg chol.

Green Chiles Stuffed with Beef, Almonds, and Raisins

Raisins, nuts, spices, and a slightly sweet tomato sauce soften the citrusy heat of the chiles.

SERVES 5 or 6 | **TIME** 1¾ hours

15 to 18 green New Mexico or Anaheim chiles
   (*see Quick Tips below*)
1 tbsp. olive oil
8 large garlic cloves, minced, divided
¾ cup chopped onion
1 lb. ground beef
1½ tsp. salt, divided
1 tsp. *each* cinnamon, ground cumin, and
   freshly ground black pepper
⅓ cup raisins
½ cup fine dried bread crumbs
2 tbsp. chopped oregano leaves
⅓ cup plus ¾ cup slivered almonds, toasted
   (*see How to Toast Nuts, page 134*)
½ lb. *queso fresco* (*see Quick Tips below*), crumbled
1 can (28 oz.) crushed tomatoes
2 tbsp. honey

1. Slice off chile stems. With a spoon or melon baller, scoop out and discard seeds and white membranes (avoid slitting chiles). Preheat oven to 375°.
2. Add oil to a frying pan over medium-high heat. Add half the garlic and the onion and cook, stirring often, until onion is translucent, about 3 minutes. Add beef, 1 tsp. salt, the cinnamon, cumin, and pepper and cook, breaking up beef, until it is cooked through, about 10 minutes. Add raisins and cook, stirring, 3 minutes. Add bread crumbs, oregano, ⅓ cup almonds, and the *queso fresco*. Cook, stirring, 2 minutes; remove from heat.
3. Carefully pack each chile with beef filling. Arrange chiles in a large baking pan and bake until chiles are browned and beginning to blister, 35 to 45 minutes.
4. Meanwhile, make sauce: In a large frying pan over medium heat, bring tomatoes, honey, remaining garlic, and ½ tsp. salt to a gentle simmer. Cook until most of liquid has evaporated, about 15 minutes. Stir in remaining ¾ cup toasted almonds. Transfer sauce to a blender, add ½ cup water, and blend sauce until very smooth, about 1 minute. Drizzle sauce over chiles.
Quick Tips: Find chiles at farmers' markets in New Mexico and online at *newmexicanconnection.com*. *Queso fresco* is a mild, crumbly Mexican cheese sold in Latino markets and some supermarkets; if you can't find it, substitute farmer's cheese or feta.

PER 3-CHILE SERVING: 568 cal., 52% (297 cal.) from fat; 31 g protein; 33 g fat (11 g sat.); 40 g carbo (4.4 g fiber); 1,202 mg sodium; 76 mg chol.

Shredded Beef Enchiladas

Beef braised until it's so tender it can easily be torn into fine shreds is known throughout the Spanish-speaking Caribbean and parts of Latin America as *ropas viejas*—"old clothes" or rags. This flavorful meat is a classic filling for enchiladas. Reader Belinda Freitas, of Suisun City, California, gave us her version.

SERVES 6 | **TIME** 1¼ hours

1½ lbs. boned beef chuck roast, fat trimmed
2½ tbsp. red wine vinegar
1¼ cups beef broth
2 tbsp. chili powder
1½ tsp. salt, divided
2 tsp. ground cumin, divided
3 tbsp. vegetable oil, plus more for frying
1 medium white onion, chopped
3 cans (7 oz. each) diced green chiles, drained
1½ tbsp. flour
2 cups sour cream, divided
3½ cups shredded (about ¾ lb.) jack cheese, divided
12 corn tortillas (6 to 7 in. wide)
Bell Pepper Salsa (*recipe follows*), Salsa Ranchera (*page 568*) or Roasted Green Chile Chipotle Salsa (*page 25*)

1. Put roast in a 3- to 4-qt. pan with ¼ cup water. Cover and cook over medium heat 30 minutes. Uncover and cook until liquid boils away and meat is well browned, turning as needed, about 10 minutes. Lift out meat.
2. Add vinegar to pan; scrape any browned bits off bottom. Stir in broth, chili powder, and 1 tsp. each salt and cumin. Return meat to pan, bring to a boil, cover, and simmer over medium heat until meat is very tender and easily pulled apart, about 2 hours. Let meat cool, then tear into shreds. Mix with pan juices.
3. In a large frying pan, combine oil, onion, chiles, and remaining 1 tsp. cumin. Cook, stirring occasionally, over medium heat until onion is soft, about 15 minutes. Mix in flour, then blend in 1 cup sour cream and cook, stirring, until simmering. Remove from heat and blend in remaining ½ tsp. salt and 1½ cups cheese.
4. Preheat oven to 375°. Pour ½ in. oil into a 7- to 8-in. frying pan. Heat oil over medium-high heat until hot (*see Quick Tip, above right*). Cook 1 tortilla at a time until surface bubbles but tortilla is still limp, 5 seconds on each side. Lay tortillas flat on paper towels to drain.
5. Spoon about ⅓ cup chile mixture and ¼ cup shredded beef down center of each tortilla; roll to enclose.

Set enchiladas, seam side down, in a 9- by 13-in. baking pan or dish (it will be a tight fit).
6. Bake enchiladas—uncovered if you like crisp edges, covered if you prefer them very moist—until hot in center, about 15 minutes. Sprinkle remaining 2 cups cheese evenly on top. Return to oven and bake until cheese melts, about 5 minutes more.
7. Use a wide spatula to transfer enchiladas to dinner plates. Serve with remaining sour cream and salsa.
Quick Tip: An easy way to check the oil temperature is to stand a wooden spoon handle in the hot oil. If tiny bubbles immediately begin to form around the handle, the oil is hot enough for cooking.

PER SERVING: 882 cal., 64% (560 cal.) from fat; 39 g protein; 63 g fat (28 g sat.); 42 g carbo (5.6 g fiber); 1,598 mg sodium; 165 mg chol.

Bell Pepper Salsa

A suave blend of tomatoes and ripe red bell peppers, this salsa is more like a sauce. It's good drizzled over eggs too.

Makes 1 cup | **TIME** 1¼ hours

1 cup each coarsely chopped firm-ripe tomatoes
    and red bell peppers
2 garlic cloves, chopped
1 tsp. olive oil
½ cup chopped cilantro
⅓ cup chopped green onions
1½ tsp. balsamic vinegar
¼ tsp. sugar
Salt

1. Preheat oven to 350°. In an 8- or 9-in. square baking pan, combine tomatoes, bell peppers, garlic, and oil. Cover tightly with foil and bake until tomatoes mash easily, 50 to 60 minutes.
2. Pour vegetable mixture into a blender or food processor. Add cilantro, green onions, vinegar, and sugar; purée. Add salt to taste.
Make Ahead: Up to 2 days, chilled. Bring to room temperature before using.

PER TBSP.: 9 cal., 33% (3 cal.) from fat; 0.2 g protein; 0.3 g fat (0 g sat.); 1.4 g carbo (0.3 g fiber); 1.1 mg sodium; 0 mg chol.

Porcini Mushroom Meat Loaf with Mushroom Gravy

If free-form meat loaf is new to you, here's why we prefer it to the baked-in-a-bread-pan kind: It produces delicious pan drippings that become the base for a quick, mushroom-rich gravy.

SERVES 6 to 8 | **TIME** 2 hours

1½ oz. dried porcini mushrooms *(see Quick Tips, right)*
1 cup milk
1½ cups small bread cubes (from 2 slices hearty bread, crusts removed)
1 lb. *each* ground beef, veal, and pork *(see Quick Tips, right)*
⅓ cup *each* chopped shallots and flat-leaf parsley
2 eggs
1½ tsp. salt
1 tsp. freshly ground black pepper
1 medium carrot, finely chopped
1 stalk celery, finely chopped
1¾ cups chicken broth, divided
1 cup white wine
6 tbsp. butter

1. Preheat oven to 350°. Put mushrooms in a small bowl and pour 2 cups simmering water over them. Stir and let mushrooms sit 15 minutes. In another small bowl, pour milk over bread cubes. Squeeze bread with your fingers to soften completely.
2. Break meats into small chunks, then toss together in a large bowl. Add shallots, parsley, eggs, salt, and pepper.
3. Use a slotted spoon to remove mushrooms from water; reserve soaking liquid. Finely chop mushrooms and add about three-quarters to meat mixture; set rest aside. Gently squeeze bread to remove excess milk and add it to meat mixture; discard milk. Using your hands, gently mix seasonings, mushrooms, soaked bread, and meat until blended. Form mixture into a ball, transfer to a large, heavy-bottomed metal roasting pan, and pat into a rounded loaf.
4. Sprinkle carrot, celery, and remaining mushrooms in bottom of pan around meat loaf. Pour in ¾ cup each of mushroom soaking liquid (strain out any sediment, if necessary) and broth. Bake until outside of loaf is browned and a thermometer inserted into center registers 180°, about 1½ hours.
5. Transfer meat loaf to a platter. Set roasting pan over two burners on high heat. Pour in wine and, using a wooden spoon, loosen vegetables and browned bits off bottom of pan. Add remaining mushroom soaking liquid and 1 cup broth and simmer until liquid has reduced by half. Reduce heat to medium and whisk in butter; sauce will thicken slightly. Serve alongside meat loaf.
Quick Tips: Look for dried porcini mushrooms in Italian markets and other specialty-foods stores. We recommend buying veal from markets that guarantee humane farming practices (or look for the Certified Humane Raised & Handled sticker; *see How to Read a Beef Label, page 402,* for more information). If you prefer not to eat veal, use 1½ lbs. *each* ground beef and ground pork instead.

PER SERVING: 654 cal., 66% (432 cal.) from fat; 41 g protein; 48 g fat (21 g sat.); 12 g carbo (2.3 g fiber); 963 mg sodium; 247 mg chol.

Stuffed Chipotle Meatballs

The recipe for these lusciously saucy meatballs, each with a hidden surprise in the center, was handed down to reader Laura Granados of Glendale, California, from her mother and grandmother. Serve with white rice to absorb the delicious spicy sauce.

SERVES 4 | **TIME** 40 minutes

1 lb. ground beef
1 egg
1 tbsp. long-grain white rice
1 tsp. salt
½ cup finely diced onion
3 hard-cooked eggs, peeled and quartered
1½ cups reduced-sodium chicken broth
1 cup canned tomato sauce
2 canned chipotle chiles in adobo sauce
1 garlic clove, minced
1 bay leaf
3 tbsp. chopped cilantro

1. In a medium bowl, combine beef, egg, rice, salt, and onion; mixture will be soft. Form meat into 12 thin patties, each about 3 in. wide. Put a wedge of hard-cooked egg in center of each patty, then press meat around egg to form a ball. Cover and refrigerate while you prepare sauce.
2. In a blender or food processor, combine broth, tomato sauce, chipotles, and garlic; blend until smooth. Pour sauce through a fine-mesh strainer into a medium saucepan; add meatballs and bay leaf. Bring sauce to a boil, then reduce heat to a simmer. Cover pot and cook meatballs, turning occasionally, until they are cooked through, about 25 minutes. Sprinkle with cilantro.

PER SERVING: 430 cal., 59% (253 cal.) from fat; 29 g protein; 28 g fat (10 g sat.); 9.6 g carbo (2.3 g fiber); 1,390 mg sodium; 292 mg chol.

Braised Veal Shanks with Romano Beans and Roasted Grapes

Although the combination of flavors may sound odd, it's actually delightful. This is a simplified version of a dish from Restaurant Zoë in Seattle.

SERVES 6 | **TIME** 3½ hours

1 lb. seedless red grapes, stemmed
¼ cup olive oil, divided
2 tsp. plus ¼ cup fresh thyme leaves
¼ tsp. table salt
1¼ tsp. freshly ground black pepper, divided
6 veal shanks (4½ to 5 lbs. total), fat trimmed
2 tbsp. kosher salt
1 cup *each* dry white wine and cider vinegar
2 cups chopped onions
1 cup *each* chopped carrot, fennel head, peeled celery root, and leeks (white and pale green parts only; *see Quick Tip, right*)
¼ cup minced fresh ginger
5 bay leaves
2½ tbsp. tomato paste
2 tbsp. minced garlic
1 tbsp. *each* finely shredded orange and lemon zests
4 cups chicken broth
1 lb. romano beans, trimmed and cut into 1-in. pieces
1 tbsp. butter
1 tbsp. chopped sage leaves

1. In a 12- by 15-in. baking pan, mix grapes, 1 tbsp. oil, 2 tsp. thyme, table salt, and ¼ tsp. pepper. Roast, uncovered, shaking pan occasionally, until grapes begin to blister, 15 to 18 minutes. Set aside. Reduce oven temperature to 325°.
2. Sprinkle shanks with kosher salt. Heat remaining 3 tbsp. oil in a 6- to 8-qt. ovenproof pot or a 13- by 16-in. roasting pan over medium-high heat until hot. Add shanks in a single layer (work in batches if necessary). Cook, turning until richly browned on both sides, 10 to 12 minutes total; transfer to a plate.
3. Preheat oven to 400°. Add wine and vinegar to pot and bring to a boil; boil, uncovered, until liquid has almost evaporated, stirring to loosen browned bits from bottom, 5 to 8 minutes. Add onions, carrot, fennel, celery root, leeks, ginger, 3 tbsp. thyme, the bay leaves, remaining 1 tsp. pepper, tomato paste, garlic, orange and lemon zests, broth, and shanks. Cover pot (with foil if using a roasting pan). Braise in oven until meat is very tender when pierced, 2½ to 3 hours.
4. In a 5- to 6-qt. pot over high heat, bring 3 qts. water to a boil. Add beans; cook until tender-crisp, 1 to 2 minutes. Drain, plunge in ice water to cool, and drain again.

5. With tongs, transfer shanks to a plate; cover with foil. Remove bay leaves and skim fat from pot used to cook shanks. Working in batches, purée liquid and vegetables in a blender.
6. Melt butter in a 10- to 12-in. frying pan over medium-high heat. Add beans, grapes, sage, and remaining 1 tbsp. thyme; cook, stirring, until hot, about 3 minutes. Put each shank in a bowl; top with sauce and bean mixture.
Quick Tip: Clean leeks before chopping: Trim root ends, then cut in half lengthwise. Swish around in a bowl of water to rinse off; transfer to a colander, leaving dirt behind, and rinse again in fresh water if necessary.
Make Ahead: Veal shanks, through step 3, up to 1 day, chilled; reheat in a 350° oven until hot, 25 to 30 minutes. Grapes, through step 1, up to 4 hours, at room temperature.

PER SERVING: 525 cal., 31% (162 cal.) from fat; 54 g protein; 18 g fat (4.3 g sat.); 39 g carbo (5.6 g fiber); 2,421 mg sodium; 177 mg chol.

Bubble-sauced Veal Scaloppine

The key to success with scaloppine is in not overcooking the veal—less than 1 minute per side in a hot pan is all it needs.

SERVES 4 | **TIME** 30 minutes

¼ cup flour
⅛ tsp. *each* ground white pepper and nutmeg
1 lb. veal scaloppine, cut from the leg into ¼-in.-thick slices, membrane trimmed
½ cup unsalted butter, divided
3 tbsp. olive oil
¼ cup (about 1 oz.) minced prosciutto or cooked ham
¼ lb. mushrooms, thinly sliced
½ cup beef broth
⅔ cup sparkling white wine, divided

1. In a shallow dish, mix flour, pepper, and nutmeg. Coat veal with flour mixture; shake off excess and lay pieces side by side on a work surface.
2. In a 10- to 12-in. frying pan over medium-high heat, melt 2 tbsp. butter with the oil. Add veal without crowding, in batches if necessary, and brown lightly, about 45 seconds per side. Transfer to a platter as cooked; keep warm.
3. Add 2 more tbsp. butter to frying pan along with the prosciutto and mushrooms. Cook, stirring, until juices have evaporated; spoon mixture over veal.
4. Add broth and ½ cup wine to frying pan; boil rapidly, uncovered, until reduced to ½ cup. Add remaining ¼ cup butter and cook, stirring constantly, until incorporated.

5. Divide veal among warmed dinner plates; pour sauce over meat. At the table, pour remaining wine over veal.

PER SERVING: 479 cal., 67% (319 cal.) from fat; 28 g protein; 36 g fat (17 g sat.); 8.4 g carbo (0.4 g fiber); 327 mg sodium; 153 mg chol.

Veal Scaloppine with Pears

A wonderfully satisfying dish for a crisp night.

SERVES 6 | **TIME** 1 hour

1¾ lbs. boned veal, cut into ½-in.-thick slices, membrane and fat trimmed
¾ tsp. ground sage
¼ cup flour
½ cup butter, divided
3 tbsp. canola or safflower oil, divided
2 cups whipping cream
⅔ cup dry white wine
⅓ cup pear liqueur or rum (optional)
¾ tsp. Dijon mustard
Salt
1 garlic clove, minced or pressed
6 slices dark rye bread, crusts trimmed and cut in half diagonally
1 tbsp. fresh lemon juice
3 small firm-ripe pears

1. Place veal slices well apart on plastic wrap; sprinkle tops with sage. Cover with a second piece of plastic wrap, then pound with a flat-surfaced mallet until about ¹⁄₁₆ in. thick; veal will approximately triple in size. Coat both sides with flour and shake off excess.
2. Melt 1 tbsp. butter with 1 tbsp. oil in a 10- to 12-in. frying pan over medium-high heat. When butter begins to brown, add veal without crowding. Cook until browned on both sides, 2 to 4 minutes total, scraping pan as needed. Lift out meat and lay pieces side by side on a rimmed 10- by 15-in. baking sheet.
3. Brown remaining veal in batches, adding butter and oil as needed (up to 2 tbsp. more of each).
4. Preheat oven to 450°. Drain any juices from baking sheet into frying pan and stir to loosen browned bits from bottom of pan. Add cream, wine, liqueur if using, and mustard; boil, uncovered and stirring often, until reduced to 1½ cups. Add salt to taste.
5. Blend 3 tbsp. butter with garlic; spread on one side of each bread slice. Arrange bread, buttered side down, in a 9- by 12-in. baking pan.
6. Melt remaining 2 tbsp. butter with the lemon juice in a 9-in. square baking pan. Peel, core, and halve pears; put in pan, cut side down. Spoon butter over pears to coat.

7. Bake pears, veal, and bread, uncovered, until pears are warm, veal hot, and bread sizzling, about 10 minutes. Return sauce to a boil over medium heat, stirring often.
8. Divide veal slices among plates and drizzle with sauce. Add toast and pears to plates and serve with remaining sauce on the side.
Make Ahead: Through step 4, up to 3 hours at room temperature or up to 1 day chilled.

PER SERVING: 738 cal., 67% (493 cal.) from fat; 33 g protein; 55 g fat (30 g sat.); 29 g carbo (3.7 g fiber); 391 mg sodium; 254 mg chol.

Lacquered Five-spice Pork

This recipe is an adaptation of one in *Florence Lin's Chinese Regional Cookbook*. You'll need one 12-in. metal skewer to make it. We like to serve the pork with white rice or a bowl of soba noodles sprinkled with black sesame seeds.

SERVES 4 | **TIME** 1 hour, plus 2 hours to marinate

3 garlic cloves, crushed
1 tbsp. firmly packed light brown sugar
1 tsp. *each* salt and Chinese five-spice powder
¼ cup plus 1 tbsp. soy sauce
4 boned center-cut pork loin chops, about 1 in. thick (about 2 lbs. total)
¼ cup light corn syrup

1. In a medium bowl, mix garlic, brown sugar, salt, five-spice powder, ¼ cup soy sauce, and 2 tbsp. water. Add pork chops to marinade, cover, and refrigerate 2 hours, turning several times.
2. Preheat oven to 325°. Fill a roasting pan with 1 in. water and put on bottom rack of oven. Insert the skewer through all 4 chops, about ½ in. from edge of meat. Space chops about 1 in. apart on skewer. Pull top rack of oven out halfway, making sure rack is still supported and level, and very carefully lower skewer crosswise onto rack so meat goes between the bars and the skewer rests on the rack. Slowly push rack back into oven, then move pan of water directly beneath hanging meat.
3. Bake chops 30 minutes. Increase oven temperature to 425° and roast 10 minutes more.
4. Pour corn syrup and remaining 1 tbsp. soy sauce into a shallow dish and mix to combine. Transfer pork chops from skewer to corn syrup mixture, turning to coat them, then thinly slice each chop.

PER SERVING: 483 cal., 41% (198 cal.) from fat; 50 g protein; 22 g fat (8.2 g sat.); 19 g carbo (0.1 g fiber); 1,186 mg sodium; 140 mg chol.

meats

Vietnamese Skewered Pork and Onions

Serve with thinly sliced cucumbers marinated in seasoned rice vinegar for a wonderful light weeknight dinner. You'll need four 8- to 10-in.-long metal skewers for cooking the meat.

SERVES 4 | **TIME** 45 minutes

1 pork tenderloin (1 lb.), fat and membrane trimmed
3 green onions, trimmed
¼ cup soy sauce
2 tbsp. honey
2 garlic cloves, pressed or chopped
1 tsp. freshly ground black pepper
1½ cups long-grain white rice
3 tbsp. *each* orange marmalade and unseasoned rice vinegar
12 green- or red-leaf lettuce leaves

1. Cut pork crosswise into ½-in.-thick slices and put in a resealable plastic bag.
2. Coarsely chop enough white part of the green onions to make ⅓ cup; cut remaining green tops into 1½-in. lengths and set aside. In a blender or food processor, blend white part of green onions, soy sauce, honey, garlic, and pepper until smooth. Pour marinade over pork and seal bag; turn to mix well. Let stand 10 to 15 minutes.
3. Meanwhile, in a 2- to 3-qt. pan, combine rice and 2¾ cups water. Bring to a boil over high heat and cook until most of water is absorbed, 7 to 10 minutes. Reduce heat to low, cover, and simmer until rice is tender to the bite, 10 to 15 minutes longer.
4. While rice cooks, lift pork from marinade; reserve marinade. Thread meat onto each skewer so slices lie flat, with a reserved green onion piece perpendicular to skewer between slices.
5. Set skewers in a single layer on a foil-lined 10- by 15-in. broiler pan. Broil 3 in. from heat, turning once, until pork is browned on both sides and no longer pink in center (cut to test), 6 to 8 minutes total.
6. In a 1- to 2-qt. pan over high heat, bring reserved marinade, any pan juices, marmalade, and vinegar to a boil. Pour into a bowl.
7. Serve skewers with lettuce, rice, and marmalade-vinegar sauce. Put a spoonful of rice and a piece of meat on a lettuce leaf, drizzle with sauce to taste, and wrap up to eat with your hands.

PER SERVING: 468 cal., 7.9% (37 cal.) from fat; 28 g protein; 4.1 g fat (1.4 g sat.); 78 g carbo (1.4 g fiber); 1,097 mg sodium; 68 mg chol.

Hoisin Pork with Hot Mustard

A dish with big flavors. It's designed to be part of a communal meal with lots of small plates on the table to share. Serve warm or at room temperature.

MAKES 4 to 6 main-course servings; 8 to 10 small plates
TIME 1 hour, plus 1 hour to marinate

¼ cup hoisin sauce
2 tbsp. *each* white wine vinegar and sugar
1 tbsp. soy sauce
½ tsp. Chinese five-spice powder
1 pork tenderloin (1 lb.), fat and membrane trimmed
3 tbsp. dry mustard
1 tsp. Asian (toasted) sesame oil
Cilantro sprigs

1. In a small bowl, mix hoisin, vinegar, sugar, soy sauce, and five-spice powder. Put pork in a 1-gal. resealable plastic bag. Add half the hoisin mixture, seal bag, and gently rotate to coat pork with marinade. Chill at least 1 hour and up to 1 day. Cover and chill remaining marinade.
2. Preheat oven to 425° and line a 9- by 13-in. baking pan with foil. Transfer pork to baking pan (discard the used marinade) and roast 20 minutes. Baste with reserved marinade and continue roasting, basting occasionally, until a thermometer inserted into thickest part of tenderloin registers 155°, 20 to 30 minutes longer. Let rest at least 5 minutes.
3. Meanwhile, in small bowl, mix dry mustard with 2 tbsp. cold water until smooth. Let stand 5 minutes. Stir in sesame oil.
4. Slice pork thinly across the grain and arrange on a platter. Garnish with cilantro sprigs. Serve warm or at room temperature, with spicy mustard for dipping.
Make Ahead: Through step 2, 1 day, chilled. Bring to room temperature before serving.

PER SERVING: 96 cal., 33% (32 cal.) from fat; 9.8 g protein; 3.5 g fat (0.9 g sat.); 5 g carbo (0 g fiber); 195 mg sodium; 30 mg chol.

■ Hoisin Sauce

FROM THE PANTRY

This thick, sweet, red-brown sauce is made from soybeans, vinegar, sugar, garlic, and spices. Use it in stir-fries and marinades or as a barbecue sauce (brush it on near the end of cooking, as its sugar content makes it brown fast). Hoisin sauce is especially good with pork, poultry, and lamb.

Spice-rubbed Pork Tenderloins

This recipe from San Francisco–based food writer Peggy Knickerbocker works really well for a festive buffet dinner, because it's just as delicious cold as it is hot. The fragrant spice rub is good on chicken and spareribs too. Make extra and store in an airtight container for up to a few weeks—as Peggy says, it's like money in the bank.

Serves 8 to 10 | **TIME** 1 hour, 40 minutes

3 pork tenderloins (1 lb. each), fat and membrane trimmed
Coarse salt for sprinkling
2 tbsp. *each* star anise (about 8 pods crushed with the back of a heavy saucepan), coriander seeds, and fennel seeds
2 tsp. Chinese five-spice powder
1 tsp. *each* ground ginger, cinnamon, red chile flakes, and coarse salt
½ tsp. freshly ground black pepper
2 tbsp. olive oil, plus more as needed
Good-quality balsamic vinegar for drizzling

1. Liberally sprinkle tenderloins with salt. Coarsely grind star anise, coriander, and fennel using a mortar and pestle or a spice grinder. Add five-spice powder, ginger, cinnamon, chile flakes, salt, and black pepper; pound or whirl to combine. Rub spice mixture on pork until thickly coated on all sides (save remainder for another use). Let pork stand at least 1 hour (at cool room temperature, covered) or up to 1 day (covered and chilled).
2. Heat 1 tbsp. oil in a 10- to 12-in. heavy frying pan over medium-high heat. Add 2 tenderloins and brown well on all sides, 10 to 15 minutes, drizzling in additional oil as needed. Meat is done when an instant-read thermometer inserted in thickest part registers 140° (cut to test—it should be cooked but still rosy). If meat is not done, cover pan, lower heat to medium, and cook until thermometer registers 140° (*see Quick Tip below*), up to 10 minutes more.
3. Remove tenderloins from pan, cover with foil, and let rest at least 10 minutes. Cook remaining tenderloin the same way, but brown it over medium heat and check temperature after 10 minutes. Slice meat into ¾-in.-thick rounds and drizzle with vinegar.
Quick Tip: Pork is best when still a bit rosy and juicy. (Trichinosis in pigs is nearly nonexistent in the United States now, but if you are concerned about it, cook the pork until well done—155° instead of 140°. Its temperature will rise another 10° as it rests after cooking.)

PER SERVING: 194 cal., 43% (83 cal.) from fat; 236 g protein; 9.3 g fat (2.6 g sat.); 0.6 g carbo (0.2 g fiber); 295 mg sodium; 82 mg chol

Pork Milanese with Arugula, Fennel, and Parmesan Salad

"Milanese" refers to meat (or a thinly sliced vegetable, like eggplant) that has been pounded thin, dunked in egg, dredged in a mixture of bread crumbs and grated parmesan cheese, and fried. Although it's not traditional, we like using panko (Japanese-style bread crumbs), because it makes a crunchier crust.

SERVES 4 | **TIME** 40 minutes

4 boned center-cut pork loin chops, about ¾ in. thick (1½ lbs. total)
1 cup panko
¼ cup freshly grated parmesan cheese plus ¼ cup shavings from a block of parmesan (use a vegetable peeler)
½ tsp. *each* salt and freshly ground black pepper, divided
2 eggs
4 cups arugula
1 head fennel, bulb and stalks trimmed and thinly sliced
3 tbsp. plus ½ cup olive oil
Juice of ½ lemon

1. Trim excess fat from chops. Cut each chop in half horizontally to make a total of eight thin pieces. Working with two pieces at a time, sandwich pork between sheets of plastic wrap and use a rolling pin or flat side of a meat mallet to pound pork to an even ¼-in. thickness. Combine panko, grated parmesan, and ¼ tsp. each salt and pepper on a large plate. In a small bowl, lightly beat eggs. Dip each piece of pork in egg; transfer to panko mixture and coat completely with crumbs. Set aside.
2. In a large bowl, combine arugula, fennel slices, and parmesan shavings. Drizzle salad with 3 tbsp. oil and the lemon juice. Toss, season with remaining ¼ tsp. each salt and pepper, and toss again.
3. In a 12-in. nonstick frying pan, heat remaining ½ cup oil over medium-high heat until hot. Add 2 pieces of pork and cook, turning once, until deep golden brown and crisp, 4 to 6 minutes total. Transfer chops to a plate and keep warm. Repeat with remaining chops.
4. Cut each chop in half diagonally and arrange on a serving platter with salad.

PER SERVING: 725 cal., 65% (468 cal.) from fat; 46 g protein; 52 g fat (14 g sat.); 18 g carbo (3.5 g fiber); 726 mg sodium; 229 mg chol.

Pork Scaloppine with Sweet-tart Shallots

Try pairing this dish with a Riesling; the wine's rich mouthfeel makes it a good foil for pork's chewy texture, and its acid and fruit complement the tanginess of the sauce.

SERVES 4 | **TIME** 45 minutes

4 boned center-cut pork loin chops, about ¾ in. thick (1½ lbs. total)
1 tsp. *each* **kosher salt and freshly ground black pepper, plus more to taste**
1 cup flour
¼ cup olive oil, divided
2 tbsp. butter, divided
1 lb. shallots, halved lengthwise
2 tbsp. red wine vinegar
1 tbsp. sugar
½ cup *each* **chicken broth and dry white wine, such as Riesling** *(see Quick Tip, above right)*

1. Trim excess fat from chops. Cut each chop in half horizontally to make a total of eight thin pieces. Working with two pieces at a time, sandwich pork between sheets of plastic wrap and use a rolling pin or flat side of a meat mallet to pound pork to an even ¼-in. thickness. Season on both sides with salt and pepper. Pour flour into a wide, shallow bowl. Dip each piece of pork in flour, turning to coat completely and shaking off excess. Discard remaining flour.
2. In a medium frying pan over medium heat, combine 2 tbsp. oil with 1 tbsp. butter. When melted and hot, add shallots and cook, turning occasionally, until lightly browned, about 5 minutes. Reduce heat to medium-low and add vinegar and sugar. Cook, stirring occasionally, until shallots are well browned and soft when pierced, about 20 minutes.
3. About 5 minutes before shallots will be done, combine remaining 2 tbsp. oil and 1 tbsp. butter in a large frying pan over medium-high heat. When melted and hot, add pork in a single layer (in batches if necessary) and cook, turning once, just until lightly browned on both sides and no longer pink in center (cut to test), about 4 minutes total per batch.
4. Transfer pork to a warm platter and cover with foil. Add broth and wine to pan and scrape up any browned bits from bottom. Boil until liquid has reduced by a quarter, about 2 minutes. Season to taste with salt and pepper, then add shallots to pan. Mix to coat, then pour around pork.

Quick Tip: If you pair this dish with the same Riesling you used as an ingredient in the cooking, you'll create a very good match; just make sure your wine is on the dry side.

PER SERVING: 646 cal., 57% (369 cal.) from fat; 38 g protein; 41 g fat (13 g sat.); 27 g carbo (1 g fiber); 366 mg sodium; 130 mg chol.

Pork Chops with Fresh Green and Red Cabbage

Here's a hearty, tangy dish for a chilly autumn night. Pork, cabbage, and caraway—a classic German combination—go well with crisp, dry Riesling.

SERVES 4 | **TIME** 45 minutes

½ tsp. fennel seeds
1½ tsp. caraway seeds, divided
1 tsp. coarse kosher salt
½ tsp. freshly ground black pepper
4 bone-in center-cut pork chops, each about 1 in. thick (about 2¼ lbs. total)
¼ lb. thick-cut bacon, cut crosswise into ¼-in. slices
2 cups *each* **shredded green and red cabbage**
1 tbsp. sherry vinegar or cider vinegar

1. Combine fennel seeds, 1 tsp. caraway seeds, salt, and pepper in a mortar *(see Quick Tip below)* and coarsely crush with pestle. Sprinkle mixture over pork chops and set chops aside.
2. In a large frying pan over medium-high heat, cook bacon until browned and crisp, about 7 minutes. With a slotted spoon, transfer bacon to paper towels to drain.
3. Add pork chops to pan and cook, turning once, until browned on both sides and cooked through (cut to test), about 8 minutes total. Transfer pork chops to a rimmed plate and tent with foil to keep warm.
4. Add cabbage to pan and cook, stirring frequently, until wilted, about 3 minutes. Stir in remaining ½ tsp. caraway seeds, the vinegar, and bacon; cook 2 minutes.
5. Pile cabbage on a platter and arrange pork chops on top. Pour on any accumulated pork juices and serve immediately.
Quick Tip: If you don't have a mortar and pestle, you can crush your spices in a spice grinder or a clean coffee grinder.

PER SERVING: 516 cal., 66% (341 cal.) from fat; 37 g protein; 38 g fat (13 g sat.), 4.7 g carbo (2 g fiber); 647 mg sodium; 132 mg chol.

Crown Roast of Pork

This stately cut comes from the loin of the pig. The butcher ties two center-cut rib sections (typically 7 to 9 ribs each) into a circle, ribs facing outward, to form a "crown." Traditionally, the center is filled with stuffing, but the stuffing can take ages to cook that way and you risk overcooking the meat. We've "stuffed" our crown roast with a head of garlic instead.

SERVES 16 | **TIME** 3 hours

One 16-rib crown roast of pork (8 to 11 lbs.), fat trimmed
2 tsp. kosher salt, plus more to taste
1 tbsp. freshly ground black pepper, plus more to taste
2 tbsp. finely chopped thyme leaves
1 tbsp. *each* finely chopped rosemary and sage leaves
2 tbsp. extra-virgin olive oil
1 large head garlic
6 to 8 cups reduced-sodium chicken broth, divided
5 tbsp. flour

1. Preheat oven to 350°. Season pork all over with salt, pepper, thyme, rosemary, and sage. Set pork in a roasting pan and drizzle with oil. Cut top off garlic head so cloves are exposed and place in center of pork, cut end up. Cover top of each bone with a small cap of foil to prevent blackening in oven. Pour 2 cups broth into roasting pan.

2. Roast pork, basting every 30 minutes with accumulated pan drippings. (If pan begins to look dry, gradually add up to 2 cups additional broth.) Cook until a thermometer inserted horizontally through thickest part of roast registers 145°, 1½ to 2½ hours (*see Quick Tip, above right*). If garlic isn't soft by then, put it in a small ovenproof dish and cook for up to 30 minutes more. Transfer pork to a carving board, tent with foil, and let rest.

3. Meanwhile, pour pan juices into a large measuring cup; let stand until fat rises to top. Spoon off and reserve ¼ cup fat; discard rest. Measure 1 cup juices (add broth if necessary to make 1 cup).

4. Set roasting pan over two burners. Put reserved fat in pan and whisk in flour. Cook over medium-low heat, whisking, until flour develops a nutty aroma and is deeply browned. Gradually whisk in reserved juices and 3 cups broth. With a wooden spoon, scrape up any browned bits, then resume whisking until gravy is smooth. Increase heat to high and bring to a boil, whisking. Boil until gravy is thick enough to coat back of a metal spoon, 3 to 5 minutes. Add salt and pepper to taste; pour through a strainer into a gravy boat.

5. Pop garlic cloves out of their skins into a small serving bowl. Remove string from roast and foil covers from bones. Serve with roasted garlic and gravy. Carve between bones with a sharp knife.

Quick Tip: Order the crown roast a few days ahead from your butcher. Cooked pork is at its best when taken out of the oven at 145°, while still a bit rosy and juicy; its temperature will rise as it rests after cooking. Trichinosis from eating commercially raised pork is now nearly nonexistent in the United States, but if you're worried about it, cook the pork until well done (160°).

PER SERVING: 313 cal., 49% (153 cal.) from fat; 35 g protein; 17 g fat (5.5 g sat.); 3.7 g carbo (0.3 g fiber); 546 mg sodium; 88 mg chol.

Quick Tomatillo Pork

Reader Janet Urman Wohl of Mountain View, California, invented this easy, spicy pork dish out of necessity on a busy weeknight. Serve it over hot cooked rice with corn tortillas.

SERVES 4 | **TIME** 30 minutes

2 tbsp. vegetable oil
1½ lbs. pork tenderloin, fat and membrane trimmed and cut into 1-in. cubes
1 onion (about ½ lb.), chopped
¾ lb. mushrooms, sliced
2 garlic cloves, minced
1 can (28 oz.) green enchilada sauce
2 cans (7 oz. each) tomatillo salsa (salsa verde)

1. Heat oil in a 5- to 6-qt. pan over medium-high heat until hot. Add pork and cook, stirring often, until browned on all sides, about 12 minutes. Transfer pork to a plate.

2. Add onion, mushrooms, and garlic to pan. Cook, stirring often, until onion is softened, about 5 minutes. Add enchilada sauce, salsa, and pork to pan and bring to a simmer. Reduce heat to medium-low and cook, stirring occasionally, until pork is no longer pink in center (cut to test), about 15 minutes.

PER SERVING: 413 cal., 37% (153 cal.) from fat; 39 g protein; 17 g fat (4.2 g sat.); 22 g carbo (1.9 g fiber); 419 mg sodium; 100 mg chol.

Stir-fried Greens with Pork, Shiitakes, and Black Bean Sauce

A super-satisfying, any-night combo, cooked with earthy, robust seasonings. A bowl of short-grain brown rice is a must for soaking up the sauce.

SERVES 4 | **TIME** 50 minutes, plus 2 hours to freeze pork

2 boned pork chops (½ lb. total), fat trimmed
12 dried shiitake mushrooms
1¼ cups warm reduced-sodium chicken broth
2 tbsp. black bean–garlic sauce (*see Quick Tips below*)
¾ lb. *each* broccolini or Chinese broccoli and baby bok choy or choy sum (*see Quick Tips below*)
3 tbsp. peanut or canola oil, divided
½ large onion, cut lengthwise into slivers
2 tbsp. fresh ginger, cut into thin matchsticks

1. Put pork chops on a sheet of plastic wrap and wrap airtight. Freeze just until firm to touch, at least 2 and up to 3 hours. Cut into very thin diagonal slices.
2. In a small bowl, soak mushrooms in warm broth until soft and pliable, 20 to 30 minutes; occasionally work mushrooms with your fingers to release any grit. Lift mushrooms from broth, squeezing out liquid. Gently fold each mushroom in half, gill side out; trim off hard stems.
3. Pour ½ cup soaking broth into a measuring cup, leaving any grit behind, and set aside. Pour ¼ cup soaking broth into another measuring cup, leaving grit behind; stir in black bean sauce.
4. Meanwhile, trim ends from green vegetables. Peel broccolini stems, then cut into 3-in. lengths (if wider than ⅓ in., also halve lengthwise). Cut remaining green vegetables into 3-in. lengths, separating clusters of bok choy into single stalks.
5. Set a wok or 5- to 6-qt. pan over high heat. When hot, pour in 2 tbsp. oil and swirl to coat. Add pork, onion, and ginger and fry, stirring occasionally, until meat is mostly cooked but still a bit pink, 1 to 1½ minutes. Transfer ingredients to a plate with a slotted spoon.
6. Add broccolini stems, shiitakes, and reserved ½ cup soaking broth to pan and cover quickly. Cook until stems are barely tender-crisp, 1 to 2 minutes. Uncover and add remaining 1 tbsp. oil and rest of green vegetables. Cook, stirring, until leaves and flowers wilt, 1 to 1½ minutes. Return pork mixture to pan along with black bean sauce mixture; cook until bubbling.
Quick Tips: Look for black bean–garlic sauce in the Asian-foods section of a supermarket. Buy Chinese broccoli and choy sum at a farmers' market or an Asian market. For more information, *see A Guide to Asian Greens, page 248.*

PER SERVING: 278 cal., 45% (126 cal.) from fat; 20 g protein; 14 g fat (2.7 g sat.); 21 g carbo (4.1 g fiber); 934 mg sodium; 36 mg chol.

Cider-brined Pork Chops with Sautéed Apples

Brine the pork a few hours ahead; the rest comes together quickly.

recipe pictured on page **378**

SERVES 6 | **TIME** 30 minutes, plus 3 hours to brine

4¾ cups apple cider, divided
¼ cup plus ½ tsp. kosher salt, divided
2 bay leaves
2 garlic cloves, crushed
1 tsp. red chile flakes
6 bone-in pork loin chops, ¾ to 1 in. thick
3 tbsp. butter, divided
¾ cup chicken broth
2 tbsp. whole-grain mustard
½ cup crème fraîche
½ tsp. freshly ground black pepper
Sautéed Apples (*recipe follows*)

1. In a large bowl, mix 4 cups cider, 2 cups cold water, ¼ cup salt, the bay leaves, garlic, and chile flakes. Add pork chops, cover bowl, and chill, turning meat occasionally, at least 3 hours and up to 1 day.
2. Preheat oven to 325°. Remove pork chops from brine and blot dry. Melt 2 tbsp. butter in a large frying pan over medium-high heat. Add pork chops (in two batches if necessary) and cook until well browned on bottom, 3 to 5 minutes. Flip chops and cook until browned on other side, another 3 to 4 minutes. Layer chops in a 9- by 13-in. baking pan and bake until barely pink in the center (cut to test), 15 to 20 minutes.
3. Meanwhile, pour remaining ¾ cup cider into hot frying pan; with a wooden spoon, scrape any browned bits from bottom of pan. Add broth, turn heat to high, and boil until liquid has reduced to about ½ cup, 8 to 10 minutes. Remove from heat and stir in remaining 1 tbsp. butter and the mustard. When sauce is no longer bubbling, stir in crème fraîche. Season with remaining ½ tsp. salt and pepper.
4. Spoon a generous amount of sauce over each pork chop. Serve topped with sautéed apples.

PER SERVING WITH APPLES: 435 cal., 62% (270 cal.) from fat; 22 g protein; 30 g fat (15 g sat.); 16 g carbo (1.5 g fiber); sodium N/A; 113 mg chol.

Sautéed Apples: Peel and core 3 large **apples** (any variety) and cut into ¼-in.-thick wedges. In a medium nonstick frying pan over medium heat, cook apples with 2 tbsp. *each* **butter** and **cider vinegar** and ¼ tsp. **salt**. Cook, stirring occasionally, until apples are soft and golden but not mushy, 4 to 6 minutes.

Pork Shoulder Roast with Figs, Garlic, and Pinot Noir

Stuffing this roast with figs and garlic slivers will make you feel like a modern-day Julia Child, and the results are stunning: mosaic-like meat slices infused with rich fruit and wine flavors.

SERVES 6 or 7 | **TIME** 3¼ hours

1½ cups (10 oz.) dried Mission figs, stemmed
    and halved lengthwise
1 tbsp. sugar
½ tsp. anise seeds
2 tbsp. plus ½ tsp. chopped thyme leaves, divided,
    plus thyme sprigs
1 bottle (750 ml.) Pinot Noir, divided
1 boned pork shoulder (butt roast; about 3½ lbs.)
8 garlic cloves, cut into large slivers
1½ tsp. kosher salt, plus more to taste
½ tsp. freshly ground black pepper, plus more to taste
3 tbsp. olive oil
About 1 tsp. fresh lemon juice (optional)

1. Put figs, sugar, anise seeds, 1 tbsp. thyme, and 1 cup wine in a medium saucepan. Cover and bring to a boil over high heat. Reduce heat and simmer, covered, until figs are just tender when pierced, 10 to 12 minutes. Let cool.

2. With a small, sharp knife, make 16 evenly spaced lengthwise cuts into roast, each cut about 1 in. long and 1 in. deep. Insert a garlic sliver, then a fig half into each cut, closing meat over figs; make cuts a little bigger if needed. Set aside remaining garlic and figs and their liquid.

3. Preheat oven to 325°. Using kitchen twine, tie pork crosswise at about 1½-in. intervals and lengthwise twice to form a neat roast. In a small bowl, combine 1 tbsp. thyme, the salt, pepper, and oil. Rub all over roast.

4. Heat a 12-in. frying pan over medium-high heat. Brown pork all over, turning as needed, 8 to 10 minutes total; adjust heat if needed to keep meat from scorching. Transfer pork, fat side up, to a 9- by 13-in. baking pan.

5. Reduce heat to medium. Add reserved garlic to frying pan; cook, stirring often, until light golden, about 1 minute. Pour in remaining wine from bottle and bring to a boil, scraping browned bits from bottom of pan with a wooden spoon. Pour mixture over pork and cover tightly with foil.

6. Bake pork until almost tender when pierced, 2½ hours. Stir reserved fig mixture into pan juices; bake, covered, until meat is tender, 15 to 20 minutes more.

7. Spoon pan juices over pork to moisten, then transfer meat to a cutting board and tent loosely with foil. Skim fat from pan juices. Pour juices with figs into a large frying pan and boil over high heat until reduced to 2 cups,

about 5 minutes. Stir in remaining ½ tsp. thyme. Taste and season with lemon juice if using and more salt and pepper. Remove twine from pork, then cut meat crosswise into thick slices. Garnish with thyme sprigs and serve with sauce.

Make Ahead: Through step 3, up to 1 day, chilled.

PER SERVING: 498 cal., 50% (247 cal.) from fat; 32 g protein; 28 g fat (8.4 g sat.); 32 g carbo (4.2 g fiber); 526 mg sodium; 107 mg chol.

Braised Pork with Pears and Chiles

Sweet pears highlight the gentle heat of the dried chiles and become soft and a bit savory while cooking in the pork juices. With a side of greens, this is one of our favorite fall dinners.

SERVES 8 | **TIME** 3 hours, plus overnight to chill

2 tsp. salt
½ tsp. freshly ground black pepper
1 boned pork shoulder (butt roast; about 3½ lbs.;
    see Quick Tip below)
3 tbsp. vegetable oil
½ cup dry white wine
2 tbsp. fresh lemon juice
½ cup chicken broth
8 to 12 garlic cloves
2 dried arbol chiles
1 large mild dried chile, such as New Mexico
6 Bosc or Anjou pears

1. Rub salt and pepper all over pork. Cover with plastic wrap and chill overnight.

2. Preheat oven to 350°. Heat oil in a large ovenproof pot over high heat until hot. Add pork and brown well on all sides, about 4 minutes per side, adjusting heat to keep pork sizzling but not burning. Transfer pork to a plate or platter.

3. Reduce heat to medium and add wine and lemon juice, scraping browned bits from bottom of pot. Add broth, garlic, and all the chiles (wipe them with a damp cloth first if they look dusty). Return pork to pot and bring liquid to a boil. Cover pork and bake in oven until tender when pierced with a fork, about 2 hours.

4. Quarter, core, and peel pears. Add pears to pot, cover, and bake until pears are cooked through, about 30 minutes. Serve hot, with pan juices.

Quick Tip: Ask your butcher to tie the roast for you, or do it yourself: Using kitchen twine, tie the roast crosswise at 1½- to 2-in. intervals, then twice lengthwise.

PER SERVING: 568 cal., 59% (333 cal.) from fat; 36 g protein; 37 g fat (12 g sat.); 22 g carbo (3.6 g fiber); 747 mg sodium; 141 mg chol.

Lupe's Pork Tamales

Every Christmas, Lupe Coronel and her family, residents of La Quinta, California, make these fantastic tamales, based on a traditional recipe from Durango, Mexico. (We're not the only ones who think they're exceptional: They won first prize at the Indio International Tamale Festival in Indio, California, in 1994.) When you make the tamales, remember two things: Don't cut back on the salt or the lard (and don't substitute shortening for lard), or the taste and texture will suffer; and do have a few other people help you assemble the tamales, because it's time consuming. The good news is you can make a big batch and freeze part of it for later.

Makes 4 to 4½ dozen tamales | **TIME** 6 hours (with 3 people helping to assemble)

4 lbs. boned pork shoulder (butt), most of fat trimmed
3 oz. dried California or New Mexico chiles (*see Quick Tips, opposite page*)
1½ oz. dried pasilla chiles
¼ cup flour
2 large garlic cloves
2 tsp. *each* **coriander seeds and dried oregano**
1 tsp. cumin seeds
⅔ cup *each* **chopped tomato and onion**
½ cup *each* **chopped green bell pepper and chopped seeded Anaheim chiles**
3 cups (1⅓ lbs.) fresh lard (*see In Praise of Real Lard, page 649*)**, divided**
2 tbsp. instant beef bouillon
2 tsp. garlic salt
½ cup *each* **chopped cilantro sprigs and sliced green onions**
5 lbs. fresh masa (*masa fresca*, **dough made from ground dried corn kernels and no lard or salt); or 8 cups dehydrated masa (also sold as corn flour, masa harina, or instant corn masa mix), mixed until smooth with 5¼ cups warm water**
2 tsp. baking powder
2 tbsp. salt
1½ lbs. russet potatoes
¾ lb. dried cornhusks (*see Quick Tips, opposite page*)
1 jar (10 oz.) small pimiento-stuffed green olives, drained
2 cans (7 oz. each) sliced pickled jalapeño chiles, drained
Salsa, store-bought or homemade (*try Salsa Ranchera, page 568; Roasted Green Chile Chipotle Salsa, page 25; or in Sea Bass with Salsa Verde, page 504*)

1. Put pork in a 5- to 6-qt. pan with 3 qts. water; bring to a boil over high heat. Reduce heat; simmer, covered, until meat is tender when pierced, about 2 hours. Drain and reserve broth; skim off fat. Let meat stand until cool; tear into chunks, discarding fat. Return meat to pan.

2. Meanwhile, discard stems and seeds from all the dried chiles, then rinse well. Put in a 3- to 4-qt. pan with 1 qt. water and bring to a boil over high heat. Cover, reduce heat, and simmer, stirring often, until chiles are soft when pressed, 20 to 25 minutes. Drain, reserving 2 cups liquid. In a blender, purée chiles with liquid until very smooth; set aside.

3. In a 1- to 2-qt. pan over medium heat, cook flour, stirring, until deep tan, 5 to 6 minutes; pour into a bowl. When pork is cooked, stir ½ cup reserved broth into flour; scrape into pan with meat.

4. In a blender, whirl garlic, coriander seeds, oregano, cumin, and 1½ cups reserved broth until seasonings are very finely ground. Pour through a fine-mesh strainer into pan with meat, pushing on solids to extract as much liquid as possible. Discard seasonings.

5. To meat add 1½ cups chile purée, the tomato, onion, bell pepper, Anaheim chiles, ¼ cup lard, the bouillon, and garlic salt. Bring to a simmer over medium-high heat, stirring. Cook, stirring often, for 10 minutes to blend flavors. Stir in cilantro and green onions. With a fork, break any meat chunks into shreds.

6. Prepare masa: In a large bowl, break up masa with your hands. Add baking powder and salt; mix well. Heat remaining 2¾ cups lard in a 2- to 3-qt. pan over medium-high heat until melted; let stand until cool enough to touch. Pour into masa, add remaining chile purée, and mix with your hands or a heavy spoon. Mix masa vigorously with a spoon (or beat half at a time in a stand mixer) until very smooth and no lumps of masa remain.

7. Peel potatoes and cut into 48 sticks, each 4 to 5 in. long and ¼ to ⅓ in. thick (save scraps for other uses). Put sticks in a 3- to 4-qt. pan with water to cover. Bring to a boil over high heat; reduce heat and simmer, covered, until tender-crisp, about 3 minutes. Drain and set aside.

8. Separate cornhusks and discard any silks. Select 5½ dozen large outer husks (5 to 6 in. wide across middle and 7 to 8 in. long; trim larger husks to this size). Soak husks in a sink with hot water to cover until they are pliable, about 20 minutes. Rinse, removing any grit; drain and put in a large bowl. Tear about 12 of the husks into long, thin strips. (If assembly takes more than a few hours and husks dry out, briefly resoak.)

9. Assemble tamales: On a large work surface, arrange masa and whole husks at one end, followed by fillings (meat, potatoes, olives, and jalapeños) and husk strips, leaving some space at the other end for tying and stacking tamales.

10. For each tamale, lay a husk fairly flat with smooth side up. Spoon ¼ cup masa in center. Hold husk with one hand; using quick flicks of back of a soup spoon or a small spatula, evenly spread half of masa from center to one long edge (leave a 1-in. border bare at edge of husk). Repeat on other half of husk, again leaving a 1-in. border bare at edge. Spread 2 to 3 tbsp. meat filling in a band 1 in. from one long edge of masa. Place a potato piece, 2 olives, and a jalapeño piece over meat. Fold long edge of husk closest to fillings over them, then roll up snugly. If husk doesn't quite meet to enclose filling, patch with a piece of another husk. Using husk strips, tie tamale as tightly as possible at both ends, then just to hold in center. (If needed, knot two strips together to make a longer tie.) Repeat to make remaining tamales.

11. To steam 2 dozen tamales, set a rack on supports at least 1½ in. above bottom of an 8- to 10-qt. pot. Fill pot with 1 in. reserved pork broth or water. Arrange first layer of tamales in one direction on rack; change direction of tamales 90° with each additional layer.

12. Cover and bring to a boil over high heat, then simmer until masa no longer sticks to husks, 1 to 1¼ hours, occasionally adding boiling water to maintain level of liquid. Serve with salsa.

Quick Tips: Find dried chiles, cornhusks, and fresh masa at a Mexican market or well-stocked grocery store. You can also buy fresh masa from a tortilla company.

Make Ahead: Pork, through step 5, up to 2 days, chilled. Masa (step 6), up to 4 hours, covered at room temperature; up to 2 days, chilled (bring to room temperature before using, 4 to 5 hours). Uncooked tamales can be frozen up to 2 months; no need to thaw before cooking, but increase steaming time to 1½ to 1¾ hours.

PER TAMALE: 245 cal., 59% (144 cal.) from fat; 8.9 g protein; 16 g fat (5.5 g sat.); 18 g carbo; 673 mg sodium; 33 mg chol.

Slow-roasted Pork Shoulder

Turn your oven into a slow-cooker to make this meltingly tender pork shoulder, adapted from a recipe in Paula Wolfert's cookbook *The Slow Mediterranean Kitchen.*

SERVES 8 to 10 | **TIME** 30 minutes, plus 9 to 10 hours of mostly unattended roasting

1 bone-in, skin-on fresh pork picnic shoulder (6 to 7 lbs.;
    see Quick Tips, right)
1 head garlic (2½ oz.)
1 tbsp. coarse salt
1½ tsp. dried oregano
1 tsp. dried thyme
½ tsp. freshly ground black pepper
1 onion (10 oz.), sliced

1 carrot (¼ lb.), sliced
½ cup oloroso or cream sherry, divided
4 cups chicken broth, divided
¼ tsp. red chile flakes
1½ tsp. sherry vinegar or balsamic vinegar

1. Preheat oven to 450°. Score skin of pork in a crisscross diamond pattern, making ⅛-in.-deep cuts about 1 in. apart. Separate and peel garlic cloves. Using a mortar and pestle, crush garlic, salt, oregano, thyme, and pepper into a coarse paste (or mince garlic, then mix with salt, herbs, and pepper). Rub garlic paste all over roast. Set roast, skin side up, on a V-shaped rack in an oiled 9- by 13-in. roasting pan. Roast until deep golden brown, 40 to 45 minutes.

2. Remove pan from oven and scatter onion and carrot slices around pork. Pour ¼ cup sherry and 2 cups broth into pan. Add chile flakes. Baste pork with some of pan juices. Reduce oven temperature to 225° and roast until a thermometer inserted through thickest part of roast to the bone registers 160° to 165°, 7 to 8 hours (do not insert thermometer before last hour of roasting). If pork is done before you're ready to serve, reduce oven temperature to 160° and hold in oven for up to 4 hours (*see Quick Tips below*).

3. About 30 minutes before serving, transfer pork to a carving board. (For extra-crisp pork skin cracklings, *see Quick Tips below.*) Cover pork loosely with foil and set in a warm place. Pour remaining ¼ cup sherry and 2 cups broth into roasting pan (drippings will be dark) and set over two burners on high heat. Bring to a boil, scraping up browned bits from bottom of pan. Boil, stirring occasionally, until liquid has reduced by about half, 7 to 10 minutes. Pour through a fine-mesh strainer into a bowl, pressing on vegetables to extract as much liquid as possible (discard vegetables); you should have 1 to 1⅓ cups drippings. Skim off and discard fat. Stir in vinegar.

4. Lift skin off pork and cut it into bite-size chunks or strips; pile on a platter. Slice meat across the grain and add to platter. Drizzle about a quarter of pan juices over meat; serve the rest on the side to add to taste.

Quick Tips: You may need to order a fresh picnic shoulder from your meat market in advance. If you hold the roast in the oven after it is done, check to make sure oven is still on after 12 hours of continuous use; some ovens turn off automatically. For extra-crisp cracklings, pull skin off cooked pork, separate into bite-size pieces, and put in a shallow pan. Bake in a 400° oven until crisp and puffy, about 10 minutes.

PER SERVING: 521 cal., 66% (342 cal.) from fat; 37 g protein; 38 g fat (14 g sat.); 4.6 g carbo (0.3 g fiber); 578 mg sodium; 138 mg chol.

Salsa Verde Braised Pork

Braising the pork—simmering it for a long time in liquid under cover—makes it fork-tender. Browning it in a hot oven adds flavor. Serve with tortillas.

SERVES 6 | **TIME** 4 hours

3½ lbs. bone-in pork shoulder (butt)
1 bottle (15 oz.) salsa verde, plus more for serving
1 medium onion, finely chopped
3 cups reduced-sodium chicken broth
2 tsp. *each* cumin seeds and coriander seeds
1 tsp. dried oregano
½ cup chopped cilantro, plus some leaves
Salt

1. Trim excess pork fat. Put meat in a heavy, large pot or Dutch oven with salsa, onion, broth, cumin seeds, coriander seeds, and oregano. Bring to a boil over high heat; reduce heat, cover, and gently simmer until pork is very tender when pierced, about 3 hours.
2. Preheat oven to 375°. With two wide spatulas, transfer meat to a rimmed baking sheet. Bake until richly browned, about 30 minutes.
3. Meanwhile, skim and discard fat from cooking juices. Boil juices, stirring, until reduced to 2¾ cups, 8 to 10 minutes.
4. With two forks, tear meat into large shreds. Add to pot and stir in chopped cilantro. Season with salt. Spoon into a serving bowl and sprinkle with cilantro leaves. Serve with more salsa verde on the side.

PER SERVING: 571 cal., 63% (360 cal.) from fat; 36 g protein; 40 g fat (14 g sat.); 16 g carbo (0.8 g fiber); 1,101 mg sodium; 147 mg chol.

Slow-cooker Salsa Verde Pork: Put trimmed pork in a slow-cooker (5- to 6-qt.) and set on high. In a pan, bring salsa, onion, broth, cumin seeds, coriander seeds, and oregano to a boil. Pour over pork, cover, and cook until meat is very tender when pierced and registers at least 165° on an instant-read thermometer, 7 to 9 hours. Continue recipe with step 2, using a large pot for step 3.

Mexican Braised Pork Ribs

Former *Sunset* Books employee Eligio Hernández, of Newman, California, serves this spicy dish with rice and beans.

SERVES About 8 | **TIME** 1¾ hours

2 tsp. cumin seeds
5 lbs. country-style pork ribs, preferably shoulder
1 tsp. salt, plus more to taste
7 or 8 Roma tomatoes (1½ oz.)
5 or 6 jalapeño chiles (5 to 6 oz. total)
1 onion (about 6 oz.), chopped
2 garlic cloves
½ tsp. dried oregano
Chopped cilantro

1. In a 12-in. frying pan (with sides at least 3 in. high) or a 5- to 6-qt. pot over medium heat, toast cumin seeds, stirring, until lightly browned, about 3 minutes. Transfer to a small bowl.
2. Pat ribs dry and trim excess fat. Add ribs to pan and sprinkle with 2 tbsp. water and the salt. Cover and cook over medium-high heat, turning occasionally, until meat is very juicy, about 20 minutes. Uncover, increase heat to high, and cook, turning meat often, until juices have evaporated and meat is browned, 15 to 20 minutes. Drain off fat.
3. Meanwhile, lay tomatoes and chiles on a 10- by 15-in. rimmed baking sheet in a single layer and broil 4 in. from heat, turning to char on all sides, 10 to 15 minutes total. Remove from sheet as done. When cool enough to handle, pull off skins and remove stems, seeds, and ribs from chiles (*see Quick Tip, above right*).
4. In a blender or food processor, smoothly purée tomatoes, chiles, cumin seeds, onion, garlic, and oregano. Add along with 1½ cups water to ribs. Bring to a boil, then reduce heat, cover, and simmer, stirring occasionally, until meat is tender when pierced, 40 to 45 minutes.
5. Skim off and discard fat. Add salt to taste. Garnish with cilantro.

PER SERVING: 469 cal., 61% (288 cal.) from fat; 36 g protein; 32 g fat (12 g sat.); 7.3 g carbo (1.7 g fiber); 388 mg sodium; 128 mg chol.

Oven-barbecued Pork Back Ribs

Reader Mary Lou Nuffer, of Orange, California, says these ribs have been served at her church's annual luau fellowship dinner for at least 30 years. She gives Evelyn Smith credit for the original recipe. The ribs are easier to bake than grill because the sticky sauce is inclined to burn.

SERVES 5 or 6 | **TIME** 1½ hours, plus 2 hours to marinate

¾ cup *each* soy sauce and orange marmalade
½ cup pineapple juice
¼ cup honey
3 garlic cloves, minced or pressed
2 tbsp. minced fresh ginger
1 tbsp. fresh lemon juice
2 tsp. chopped fresh rosemary leaves or crumbled dried rosemary
¼ tsp. freshly ground black pepper
4 to 5 lbs. pork loin back (baby back) ribs , fat trimmed

1. Mix soy sauce, orange marmalade, pineapple juice, honey, garlic, ginger, lemon juice, rosemary, and pepper.
2. Divide ribs between two 1-gal. resealable plastic food bags. Pour half the soy sauce mixture into each bag; seal, turn to coat ribs with marinade, and set in a large bowl. Chill 2 hours or up to 1 day, turning occasionally.
3. Preheat oven to 350°. Line a rimmed baking pan (11 by 17 in. or 12 by 15 in.) with foil (the drippings char). Set a flat rack in pan. Lift ribs from marinade and arrange on rack in a single layer, edges curving down. Pour marinade into a bowl.
4. Bake, basting with marinade every 20 minutes for the first hour, until meat is well browned and pulls easily from bones, about 1¼ hours total. Transfer ribs to a platter and cut apart between bones.

PER SERVING: 716 cal., 54% (389 cal.) from fat; 38 g protein; 43 g fat (16 g sat.); 45 g carbo (0.2 g fiber); 2,219 mg sodium; 172 mg chol.

Sticky Ribs

Brush a sweet, tangy glaze over ribs coated with a mix of spices, then roast instead of grill to get crispness and good flavor without the risk of burning. You can cut this recipe in half if you like.

SERVES 10 to 12 | **TIME** 1¼ hours

4 racks pork loin back (baby back) ribs or 2 racks pork spareribs (about 8 lbs. total)
3 tbsp. *each* chili powder and kosher salt
2 tbsp. cumin seeds
1 cup honey
6 tbsp. fresh lime juice
Cooking-oil spray or vegetable oil

1. Preheat oven to 425°. Trim fat from ribs.
2. In small bowl, mix chili powder, salt, and cumin seeds to make the spice rub. In another small bowl, mix honey and lime juice for the glaze.
3. Rub spice mixture over both sides of ribs.
4. Line two 12- by 17-in. baking pans with foil. Set a flat rack in each and lightly coat with cooking-oil spray or oil. Set ribs, meaty side up, in a single layer on racks and roast until lightly browned on top, 20 to 30 minutes. Turn slabs over and switch pan positions. Roast until other side is browned, 20 to 30 minutes longer.
5. Brush generously with glaze. Continue to roast, basting occasionally, until glaze is browned and bubbly, 6 to 12 minutes. Turn ribs over and brush generously with more glaze. Roast, basting occasionally, until glaze is browned and meat between ribs is no longer pink in center (cut to test), 6 to 12 minutes longer.
6. Transfer ribs to a board. Let rest 5 minutes. Cut between ribs.

PER SERVING: 639 cal., 62% (396 cal.) from fat; 36 g protein; 44 g fat (16 g sat.); 26 g carbo (0.8 g fiber); 1,310 mg sodium; 172 mg chol.

Curried Ribs with Apricot-Mustard Glaze:
Follow recipe for Sticky Ribs but substitute 3 tbsp. *each* **kosher salt** and **curry powder** and 1 tbsp. *each* **ground ginger** and **ground coriander** for the rub. For the glaze, substitute 1⅓ cups **apricot jam** and ½ cup *each* **Dijon mustard** and **white wine vinegar** puréed in a blender until smooth.

Eggplant, Pork, and Tofu Stir-fry

Reader Kim Johnston of Molokai, Hawaii, was inspired to modify a friend's recipe to create this easy stir-fry with spicy garlic sauce. Serve it with rice.

SERVES 4 | **TIME** 30 minutes

1 lb. eggplant
1 tbsp. *each* vegetable oil, Asian (toasted) sesame oil, minced fresh ginger, and minced garlic
½ lb. ground pork
¼ cup soy sauce
1 tbsp. *each* sugar and unseasoned rice vinegar or white wine vinegar
1½ tsp. Asian red chili paste
2 tsp. cornstarch
½ lb. extra-firm tofu, drained and cut into 1-in. cubes
¼ cup thinly sliced green onions

1. Cut eggplant crosswise into 1-in.-thick rounds. Cut rounds into 1-in.-wide strips.
2. Heat vegetable and sesame oils in a 12-in. nonstick frying pan or a 14-in. wok over medium-high heat until hot. Add eggplant and cook, stirring frequently, until lightly browned and soft when pierced, about 8 minutes. Transfer eggplant to paper towels to drain.
3. Add ginger and garlic to pan and cook, stirring frequently, until fragrant, about 1 minute. Add pork and cook, stirring, until crumbled and brown, about 5 minutes.
4. In a small bowl, mix soy sauce, sugar, vinegar, chili paste, cornstarch, and ¼ cup water. Add to pan and cook, stirring, until mixture is simmering and thickened, about 1 minute.
5. Gently stir in tofu, eggplant, and green onions and cook until heated through.

PER SERVING: 334 cal., 62% (207 cal.) from fat; 18 g protein; 23 g fat (6 g sat.); 16 g carbo (2.2 g fiber); 1,082 mg sodium; 41 mg chol.

■ Hominy

Plump, starchy kernels of hominy look like corn kernels for giants. Hominy is prepared by boiling dried field corn with slaked lime (calcium hydroxide, a white, powdery substance also known as mason's or builder's lime—and a component of seashells) until the kernels swell and slough off their skins (the germ is removed too). Ground hominy is used to make masa, the fresh corn dough for tortillas, and, in the southern U.S., hominy grits. It's also an essential ingredient in the Mexican stew called posole.

Sausages with Hominy and Spinach

If you've had hominy—big, starchy corn kernels with the hull and germ removed—only in posole, you'll be amazed at how delicious and satisfying it is all on its own. Here we cook it in seasoning left in the pan by sausages to maximize flavor. The recipe is easily adapted; variations are on *opposite page*.

SERVES 4 | **TIME** 25 minutes

1 tbsp. olive oil, divided
4 cooked sausages (about 1 lb. total; *see Quick Tip below*)
½ cup dry white wine or chicken or vegetable broth, divided
1 can (29 oz.) hominy, drained and rinsed
¼ tsp. plus ⅛ tsp. salt, plus more to taste
¼ tsp. freshly ground black pepper, plus more to taste
2 garlic cloves, slivered
¼ tsp. red chile flakes
10 oz. fresh spinach leaves

1. Preheat oven to 200°. Put a large frying pan (not nonstick) over medium-high heat. When hot to the touch, add 1 tsp. oil and the sausages. Cover and cook 4 minutes. With tongs or a spatula, turn sausages over, cover, and cook until heated through (cut to test), about 4 minutes. Transfer sausages to a rimmed baking sheet, cover with foil, and put in oven to keep warm.
2. Add ⅓ cup wine to pan; with a wooden spoon or spatula, scrape up any browned bits left by sausages. Add hominy, ¼ tsp. salt, and the pepper. Cook, stirring occasionally, until all liquid has evaporated and hominy is hot and starting to stick to pan. Transfer hominy to baking sheet with sausages, piling it next to them. Add remaining wine to pan, scrape up any browned bits, and pour over hominy. Re-cover baking sheet with foil and return it to oven.
3. Increase heat to high and add remaining 2 tsp. oil, the garlic slivers, chile flakes, and remaining ⅛ tsp. salt to pan. Cook, stirring, until fragrant, about 30 seconds. Add spinach and cook, stirring, until wilted and cooked through.
4. Divide spinach among plates. Add hominy and sausage, plus more salt and pepper to taste.
Quick Tip: Use any sausage you like—Italian (spicy or sweet), knockwurst, andouille, or chicken apple, for example—as long as it's cooked.

PER SERVING: 590 cal., 63% (369 cal.) from fat; 21 g protein; 41 g fat (14 g sat.); 33 g carbo (7.1 g fiber); 1,539 mg sodium; 86 mg chol.

Variations: Customize this very flexible recipe to your taste or according to what you've got in your fridge or pantry.

• *Make creamed hominy.* Skip step 2 and put hominy in a separate pan with 1 tbsp. **butter**, 3 tbsp. **heavy whipping cream**, and **salt** and freshly ground **black pepper** to taste. Cook over medium heat, stirring occasionally, until hot, 5 to 7 minutes.

• *Vary the greens.* Use chard, kale, or other hearty greens in place of the spinach. Bring a large pot of water to a boil, and add 10 oz. trimmed **greens** and 1 tbsp. **salt**; cook for 2 minutes, drain, and chop greens. Add instead of spinach in step 3.

• *Try a different starch.* Instead of hominy, use cooked **white beans, pinto beans, or cranberry beans**.

• *Use a different meat.* We love the intense flavor this dish gets from sausage, but any quick-cooking meat will work; try **pork chops, chicken breast halves, or hanger steak**.

Chorizo-Beef Dinner Nachos

Our super-stacked version of nachos has tangy chorizo, juicy chopped steak, black beans, guacamole, and crisp lettuce.

recipe pictured
on page
381

SERVES 6 | **TIME** 45 minutes

5 oz. beef skirt steak, chopped; or ground lean beef
5 oz. Mexican-style firm, fresh chorizo sausage (*see Quick Tip, right*), casings removed and finely crumbled
1 medium onion
1 large garlic clove
1 tsp. ground cumin, divided
1½ cups plus 1 tbsp. salsa verde, store-bought or homemade (*for a recipe, see Sea Bass with Salsa Verde, page 504*)
1 can (15 oz.) black beans, drained and rinsed
½ tsp. dried oregano
1 can (4 oz.) diced green chiles, drained
1 large firm-ripe avocado
1 tbsp. fresh lime juice
2 tbsp. chopped cilantro, divided
Kosher salt
9 cups tortilla chips
2 cups shredded (½ lb.) jack cheese
4 cups finely shredded iceberg lettuce

1. Preheat oven to 400°. In a large frying pan over medium-high heat, brown steak and chorizo, stirring, about 5 minutes. Meanwhile, chop onion and mince garlic. Add onion and all but ⅛ tsp. cumin to pan. Cook, stirring often, until onion is soft, 4 to 5 minutes. Reduce heat to medium; stir in 1½ cups salsa. Simmer until thick, 8 to 10 minutes, stirring occasionally.
2. While steak mixture simmers, combine black beans, ¾ cup water, oregano, 1 tsp. garlic, and the chiles in a small saucepan. Bring to a boil over high heat; reduce heat and simmer until all but about ¼ cup liquid has evaporated, about 10 minutes.
3. Meanwhile, make guacamole: Pit and peel avocado. In a bowl, mash avocado with remaining 1 tbsp. salsa, ⅛ tsp. cumin, remaining garlic, and the lime juice. Stir 1 tbsp. cilantro into guacamole and add salt to taste.
4. Line a large rimmed baking sheet with parchment paper. Arrange chips in a 12-in. circle. Sprinkle with jack cheese. Bake until cheese melts, 3 to 4 minutes.
5. While chips are baking, arrange lettuce around rim of a large serving platter (at least 16 in. wide). With a wide spatula, loosen chips from parchment. Carefully lift parchment from pan, then slide chips off paper into center of platter. Spoon meat mixture over chips. With a slotted spoon, top with beans. Spoon guacamole over center of nachos and sprinkle with remaining 1 tbsp. cilantro.
Quick Tip: Buy firm, fresh chorizo in natural casings at well-stocked supermarkets or Latino markets. Very soft, bright red chorizo in plastic casings isn't nearly as good.

PER SERVING: 795 cal., 55% (441 cal.) from fat; 29 g protein; 49 g fat (16 g sat.); 63 g carbo (8.4 g fiber); 1,271 mg sodium; 75 mg chol.

The Story of Nachos

Nachos, the ultimate crowd-pleaser, were invented in 1943 by a maître d' at the Victory Club in Piedras Negras, Coahuila, Mexico (just across the border from Eagle Pass, Texas). Ignacio "Nacho" Anaya, the only restaurant employee on-site when a group of U.S. military wives came in for a snack, cobbled together a pile of tortilla chips topped with melted cheese and jalapeños. His creation became hugely popular, paving the way for massive concession-stand revenues across America.

Champagne Ham with Brandy Glaze

From reader Warren Stevens, of Boise, Idaho, comes this very festive sweet, tender ham, which considerately uses only a portion of a bottle of sparkling wine—leaving some for sipping.

recipe
pictured
on page
382

SERVES About 12 | **TIME** 2½ hours

1 fully cooked shank half ham (6 to 8 lbs.; *see Quick Tip below*)
Whole cloves
1¼ cups dry sparkling wine, or more as needed
⅓ cup Dijon mustard
¾ cup firmly packed brown sugar
3 tbsp. brandy

1. Preheat oven to 325°. Cut off and discard any tough, leathery skin from top of ham. Score fat in a crisscross diamond pattern and stud with cloves. Put ham in a 10- by 15-in. roasting pan and pour wine over it. Bake, uncovered, basting frequently with pan drippings and adding more wine if needed to keep at least ¼ in. of liquid in pan, until a thermometer inserted into thickest part of ham (not touching bone) registers 140°, 2 to 3 hours (allow 20 to 22 minutes per lb.). If ham starts to look too dark, loosely cover with foil.

2. Meanwhile, in a 1- to 1½-qt. pan, combine mustard, brown sugar, and brandy. Set over low heat and cook, stirring, until sugar dissolves. Brush ham with mustard mixture several times during last 30 minutes of baking. Let ham rest 15 minutes, then slice and serve with remaining mustard sauce.

Quick Tip: A shank half ham is taken from the lower portion of the hind leg and is half the size of a full ham.

PER SERVING: 323 cal., 19% (60 cal.) from fat; 51 g protein; 6.7 g fat (2 g sat.); 16 g carbo (0 g fiber); 1,790 mg sodium; 127 mg chol.

Herb-crusted Ham

Picnic hams come from the shoulder of the pig rather than the hind leg, so they are smaller than regular hams. They're usually sold with the skin on.

SERVES 10 (with leftovers) | **TIME** 3 hours, plus 45 minutes to cool

1 fully cooked shank-end picnic ham (5½ to 6½ lbs.)
¼ tsp. *each* fennel seeds, black peppercorns, dried thyme, and rubbed sage
¼ cup fine dried bread crumbs

1. Preheat oven to 350°. Set ham on a V-shaped rack (with thickest layer of fat under skin on top) in a 12- by 15-in. roasting pan. Bake until a thermometer inserted into thickest part of ham (not touching bone) registers 140°, about 2 hours.

2. Meanwhile, coarsely grind fennel seeds, peppercorns, thyme, sage, and bread crumbs in a clean coffee grinder (or crush spices with a mortar and pestle and mix with crumbs).

3. Remove ham from oven and let rest about 30 minutes; it will still be quite warm, but you should be able to touch it. If ham has any hard skin on top, remove it with scissors and a sharp knife (keeping layer of fat under skin); discard skin or save for another use.

4. Pat seasoned crumbs evenly over fat on ham. Return to oven and continue to bake until thermometer registers 160°, about 45 minutes. If crumbs begin to darken more than you like, lay a piece of foil over dark area. Let ham rest at least 15 minutes or until cool, then slice.

Make Ahead: Up to 2 hours. Serve ham at room temperature.

PER SERVING: 183 cal., 32% (59 cal.) from fat; 27 g protein; 6.5 g fat (2.1 g sat.); 3.8 g carbo (0.2 g fiber); 1,683 mg sodium; 132 mg chol.

Lamb Chops with Little Red Potatoes and Lamb's Lettuce

Smooth, small potatoes add substance without disrupting the delicacy of this dish. The chops are also excellent grilled fast over a hot fire.

SERVES 4 | **TIME** 40 minutes

8 lamb rib chops (about 2 lbs.), fat trimmed
1 tsp. kosher salt, plus more for salting water
½ tsp. freshly ground black pepper
2 large garlic cloves, minced
2 tsp. *each* finely shredded lemon zest and minced oregano leaves
¼ cup extra-virgin olive oil, divided
1 lb. small red or yellow potatoes (often labeled "creamer" or "new"), cut in half
2 tsp. whole-grain mustard
1 small shallot, minced
1 tbsp. *each* fresh lemon juice and white wine vinegar
1 package (3.5 oz.) lamb's lettuce

1. Pat lamb chops dry and season with salt and pepper. In a small bowl, combine garlic, lemon zest, oregano, and 1 tbsp. oil. Rub mixture over both sides of chops.
2. Put potatoes in a medium pot and add water to cover. Bring to a boil over high heat. Generously salt water, then reduce heat to a simmer and cook potatoes, covered, until tender, 8 to 10 minutes. Drain and let cool until just warm.
3. Meanwhile, whisk together mustard, shallot, lemon juice, and vinegar in a small bowl. Gradually whisk in remaining 3 tbsp. oil until dressing is emulsified.
4. Preheat broiler to high. Arrange chops on broiler pan and set pan 2 in. from heat. Broil chops, turning once, until browned and medium-rare inside (cut to test), 8 to 10 minutes.
5. Put lamb's lettuce in a salad bowl and add slightly warm potatoes. Drizzle three-quarters of dressing over salad and toss to coat. Divide salad among plates and top each serving with 2 chops. Spoon on remaining dressing.

PER SERVING: 628 cal., 69% (432 cal.) from fat; 28 g protein; 48 g fat (16 g sat.); 21 g carbo (2.5 g fiber); 617 mg sodium; 112 mg chol.

Lamb Chops with Spiced Salt Rub

Use a good sea salt in this recipe; it will really make a difference.

SERVES 4 to 6 | **TIME** 20 minutes, plus 4 hours to chill

3 tbsp. coriander seeds
2 tbsp. *each* fennel seeds and fine sea salt
1 tbsp. dried thyme
1½ tsp. coarsely ground black pepper
6 lamb loin chops (6 to 8 oz. each)
1 tbsp. vegetable oil

1. In a spice mill or clean coffee grinder, finely grind coriander seeds and fennel seeds. Add salt, thyme, and pepper; grind to combine. Rub about ½ tbsp. spice mixture over each lamb chop. Wrap airtight and chill at least 4 hours and up to 1 day.
2. Unwrap lamb chops. Pour oil into a 10- to 12-in. non-stick pan over medium-high heat and swirl pan to coat. Add chops and cook, turning occasionally, until surface is brown and center is pink (cut to test), 8 to 12 minutes.

PER SERVING: 400 cal., 67% (266 cal.) from fat; 30 g protein; 30 g fat (12 g sat.); 3.2 g carbo (2.3 g fiber); 2,331 mg sodium; 115 mg chol.

■ Lamb's Lettuce

FROM THE GARDEN

Sweet, nutty, and a little bit wild-tasting, lamb's lettuce (also known as mâche or corn salad) is a multitasker. Its delicate round leaves make a fresh background for other spring vegetables, and its hearty texture lets it work equally well as a cooking green. It is often sold prewashed in bags or with its roots in a potting medium. Lamb's lettuce doesn't keep well, so don't buy it more than a day ahead. If you can't find it, substitute watercress.

Crown Lamb Roast with Green Herb Couscous

Behind the fanfare of its form, a spectacular-looking crown roast is like any other roast—you just stick it in the oven and let it cook. Moreover, it's easy to carve. A crown is made from two or more loin roasts, from the choice muscle that's tucked alongside the backbone and back ribs. The backbone is sawed off to make the roasts flexible enough to curve and tie together—a task a professional at the meat market can take care of. To serve the crown, simply cut between the ribs.

SERVES 8 | **TIME** 1 hour

2 lamb rib racks, 8 ribs each (4½ to 5 lbs. total), tied together to make a crown *(see Quick Tip, right)*
½ tsp. ground cumin
½ tsp. *each* salt and freshly ground black pepper, plus more to taste
1 onion (½ lb.), finely chopped
2 Italian pork sausages (about ½ lb. total), casings removed
2 cups chicken broth
1 cup *each* frozen petite peas and couscous
½ cup *each* coarsely chopped flat-leaf parsley, mint leaves, and dill
¼ cup pine nuts, toasted *(see How to Toast Nuts, page 134)*

1. Preheat oven to 450°. Pat lamb dry and set on a flat rack in a shallow pan (at least 10 in. square). Mix cumin, salt, and pepper; rub over roast, inside and out.
2. Bake lamb until a thermometer inserted horizontally through roast into thickest part registers 145° to 150° for rare, 35 to 40 minutes, or 155° for medium-rare, 40 to 45 minutes. If bone tips start to scorch, drape with foil.
3. Meanwhile, in a 10- to 12-in. frying pan over high heat, cook onion and sausages, stirring frequently and breaking meat into small pieces, until lightly browned, about 10 minutes. Add broth and cover; when boiling, stir in peas and cover. When boiling again, stir in couscous, cover, and remove from heat. Let stand in a warm place 10 to 20 minutes.
4. In a food processor or with a knife, finely chop parsley, mint, and dill and mix.
5. Transfer roast to a platter; keeping it warm, let it rest 5 to 10 minutes. Stir herb mixture into hot couscous; fill center of roast with some of couscous and spoon remainder around meat. Sprinkle couscous with pine nuts. Cut lamb between ribs and serve chops with couscous. Add more salt and pepper to taste.

Quick Tip: Two lamb rib racks, joined, are enough for a table of eight or fewer. Racks vary in size, so order by weight. Some markets include ruffled paper or foil cuffs to slip on the rib bone tips. It's wise to order the lamb rib racks a few days ahead. Have your butcher trim the fat from the meat, trim the bone ends, cut off the backbone for easy carving between ribs, and tie the racks together to make a crown roast.
Make Ahead: Couscous, through step 4, but don't add peas; chill up to 1 day. To reheat, microwave with peas until steaming, 3 to 4 minutes, stopping to stir once or twice.

PER 2-CHOP SERVING: 455 cal., 45% (207 cal.) from fat; 35 g protein; 23 g fat (7.8 g sat.); 25 g carbo (3.6 g fiber); 482 mg sodium; 100 mg chol.

Lamb Shanks Adobo

Jeff Smedstad, chef-owner of Elote Cafe in Sedona, Arizona, learned the secrets for making great adobos (chile-rich sauces) in the markets of central Mexico. This lamb dish is adapted from a recipe in his book, *The Elote Cafe Cookbook*.

SERVES 4 | **TIME** 2¾ hours

8 garlic cloves, unpeeled
6 dried ancho chiles *(see Quick Tip, right)*, wiped clean with a damp cloth and seeded
4 cups fresh orange juice
2 tbsp. *each* firmly packed brown sugar, dried oregano (preferably Mexican; *see Quick Tip, right*), and cider vinegar
1 tbsp. *each* kosher salt and freshly ground black pepper, divided
2 tsp. ground cumin
⅛ tsp. ground cloves
1 stick *canela* (Mexican cinnamon; *see Quick Tip, right*) or regular cinnamon (about 3 in.)
2 bay leaves
4 lamb shanks (about 1 lb. each)
2 tbsp. canola oil
Finely chopped white onion and cilantro

1. Make adobo: In a dry, heavy-bottomed medium saucepan over medium heat, roast garlic, turning occasionally, until softened and speckled brown, 12 to 15 minutes. Remove from pan. Add chiles to pan and toast, turning once, until fragrant, about 30 seconds, taking care not to let them burn.
2. Carefully pour orange juice into pan with chiles. Add brown sugar, oregano, vinegar, 2 tsp. each salt and pepper, the cumin, cloves, canela, and bay leaves. Peel garlic

and add to pan. Cover and bring to a boil. Reduce heat and simmer, covered, until chiles are softened, about 10 minutes.

3. Remove canela and bay leaves and reserve. Cool adobo slightly, then purée in a blender until very smooth.

4. Preheat oven to 325°. Sprinkle lamb shanks with remaining 1 tsp. each salt and pepper. Heat oil in a heavy-bottomed, large pot over medium-high heat until hot. Brown 2 shanks at a time, turning occasionally, until golden brown, 7 to 8 minutes per batch. As each has browned, transfer to a 9- by 13-in. baking dish.

5. Discard fat from pot, then add adobo and reserved canela and bay leaves; bring to a boil over high heat, stirring. Pour over shanks. If needed, add hot water so liquid comes halfway up shanks. Seal dish with foil. Braise, turning shanks every hour, until meat is very tender when pierced, about 2 hours.

6. Transfer shanks to a platter and cover with foil. Pour adobo into a saucepan. Skim and discard fat. Boil over medium-high heat until thick enough to coat meat, about 10 minutes. Uncover shanks, pour sauce on top, and sprinkle with onion and cilantro.

Quick Tip: Find ancho chiles, Mexican oregano, and canela in the Latino-foods aisle or spice aisle of a supermarket or at a Latino market.

Make Ahead: Through step 5, up to 1 day, chilled. Reheat for 1½ hours at 325° before continuing.

PER SERVING: 897 cal., 45% (405 cal.) from fat; 76 g protein; 45 g fat (15 g sat.); 51 g carbo (7 g fiber); 1,064 mg sodium; 241 mg chol.

Lamb Shanks and Parsnips with Sherry-Onion Sauce

Lamb shanks and parsnips are cooked until they're succulent and sweet, then browned. A mix of fresh lemon zest and parsley brightens the dish just before you serve it.

SERVES 6 generously | **TIME** 3½ hours

6 lamb shanks (about 1 lb. each)
14 oz. frozen small onions
2 cups reduced-sodium chicken broth, or more as needed
1 cup plus 2 tbsp. dry sherry
2 tbsp. soy sauce
Freshly ground black pepper
½ cup minced flat-leaf parsley
2 tsp. finely shredded lemon zest (use small holes of a box grater)
Kosher salt
12 small parsnips (2 to 2½ lbs. total), peeled
1½ tbsp. olive oil

1. Preheat oven to 350°. Trim excess fat from lamb shanks. Lay shanks in a single layer in a large roasting pan. Distribute onions around them. Pour in 2 cups broth, 1 cup sherry, and the soy sauce; sprinkle with pepper to taste. Cover pan tightly with foil and bake 1½ hours.

2. Meanwhile, mix parsley and lemon zest in a bowl with salt and pepper to taste. Chill, covered, until ready to serve.

3. Tuck parsnips into pan around shanks. Bake, covered, until meat is very tender when pierced, about 1 hour more.

4. Increase oven temperature to 400°. With tongs, transfer shanks and parsnips to a large rimmed baking sheet (set pan with juices and onions aside). Brush shanks and parsnips with oil. Bake until shanks are browned, 15 to 20 minutes; turn off oven and keep shanks warm until ready to serve.

5. While shanks are browning, skim and discard fat from pan juices. Measure juices with onions; you need about 2½ cups (if necessary, supplement with more broth). Set pan over two burners on high heat and bring to a boil. Stir in remaining 2 tbsp. sherry.

6. With a wide spatula, loosen shanks and parsnips from baking sheets. Transfer shanks with tongs to a platter and arrange parsnips and onions around them. Pour pan juices on top. Sprinkle with two-thirds of parsley-zest mixture; serve with remaining parsley-zest mixture on the side.

PER SERVING: 930 cal., 51% (477 cal.) from fat; 71 g protein; 53 g fat (22 g sat.); 38 g carbo (8.4 g fiber); 767 mg sodium; 243 mg chol.

■ Parsnips

FROM THE GARDEN

Parsnips look like cream-colored, fat, broad-shouldered carrots. They have a similar sweetness and a lovely nutty, vaguely anise-like flavor. They're also starchy, like potatoes, and the two mashed together make an intriguing side dish. The center cores of parsnips tend to be tough and woody, though, so if you're mashing, be sure to cut them out.

Coffee-braised Spoon Lamb

Spoon lamb gets its name from the texture of the meat when it has finished cooking: so tender, you can cut it with a spoon. This slow-cooking technique breaks down the tough muscles in the leg of lamb, and the acidity of the coffee offsets the richness of the meat. The sauce made from the drippings is fantastic with polenta or potatoes.

recipe pictured on page **374**

SERVES 8 | **TIME** 1¼ hours, plus 5 hours largely unattended cooking time

6 garlic cloves
1 bone-in leg of lamb (about 7 lbs.), fat trimmed
Kosher salt and freshly ground black pepper
1 large onion, quartered
4 large carrots, cut into chunks
2 shallots, peeled
1 ripe tomato, cored and quartered
¼ cup olive oil
1 cup dry red wine
3 cups freshly brewed strong coffee, divided
¼ cup chopped flat-leaf parsley

1. Preheat oven to 400°. Mince 2 garlic cloves and rub over lamb, spreading evenly. Generously sprinkle lamb with salt and pepper. Put lamb on a V-shaped rack in a large roasting pan. Surround rack with onion, carrots, shallots, tomato, and remaining 4 garlic cloves. Drizzle oil over vegetables and lamb. Roast 30 minutes. Reduce oven temperature to 350° and cook another 30 minutes.
2. Reduce oven temperature to 250°. Transfer lamb to a plate and remove rack from roasting pan. Set pan on a burner over high heat; add wine and boil, using a wide metal spatula to stir and scrape up caramelized vegetables from bottom of pan, until wine has reduced by half. Stir in 2 cups coffee. Remove from heat. Set lamb back in pan (without rack); spoon juices over it. Cover tightly with foil.
3. Return pan to oven and cook until lamb is tender and pulling away from the bone, about 5 hours, turning lamb halfway through cooking.
4. Transfer lamb to a platter and cover with foil. Reheat remaining 1 cup coffee. Pour with liquid and vegetables from pan into a blender and pulse until smooth, working in batches if needed. Pour sauce through a fine-mesh strainer set over a bowl, using back of a spoon or ladle to push it through if needed. Season sauce with salt and pepper. Pour half the sauce over lamb and serve the rest in a bowl. Sprinkle lamb with parsley.

PER SERVING: 469 cal., 42% (198 cal.) from fat; 55 g protein; 22 g fat (6.2 g sat.); 10 g carbo (0 g fiber); 156 mg sodium; 170 mg chol.

Dolmas Pilaf

Instead of making time-consuming dolmas (stuffed grape leaves), reader Leilani McCoy of Seattle invented this flavorful pilaf using all the traditional dolmas ingredients.

SERVES 4 to 6 | **TIME** 45 minutes

3 tbsp. olive oil
1 lb. ground lamb
1 onion (½ lb.), chopped
2 cups long-grain white rice
1 cup rinsed, chopped preserved grape leaves, plus 2 tbsp. brine from jar
2 tbsp. *each* chopped flat-leaf parsley and dill
½ cup *each* pine nuts and dried currants

1. Heat oil in a 4- to 6-qt. pot over medium-high heat until hot. Add lamb and onion and cook, stirring frequently, until lamb is crumbly and browned, 5 to 7 minutes.
2. Add rice, grape leaves and brine, parsley, dill, pine nuts, currants, and 4 cups water. Bring to a boil. Reduce heat to maintain a simmer, cover, and cook until rice is tender to the bite, 20 to 25 minutes.

PER SERVING: 615 cal., 45% (279 cal.) from fat; 21 g protein; 31 g fat (9.6 g sat.); 63 g carbo (2.5 g fiber); 279 mg sodium; 55 mg chol.

Mediterranean Lamb- and Couscous-stuffed Peppers

Roasted peppers overflowing with lamb and couscous make a light yet satisfying meal.

SERVES 4 | **TIME** 35 minutes

4 red, green, and/or yellow bell peppers (2 lbs. total)
1½ cups chopped onions
1 tbsp. minced garlic
1½ tsp. *each* fresh thyme leaves, minced mint leaves, and minced rosemary leaves
1 tsp. olive oil
½ lb. ground lamb
5 tbsp. fresh lemon juice, divided
1⅔ cups chicken broth
1¼ cups couscous
1 cup chopped flat-leaf parsley
Salt
2 tbsp. crumbled feta cheese

1. Preheat oven to 450°. Slice bell peppers in half lengthwise through stems (keep stems) and remove seeds and ribs. Put halves, cut side down, in a 12- by

17-in. baking pan. Roast, uncovered, until lightly browned and tender when pierced, 13 to 18 minutes.

2. Meanwhile, in a 10- to 12-in. frying pan over medium-high heat, cook onions, garlic, thyme, mint, and rosemary in oil, stirring occasionally, until onions are softened and beginning to brown, about 5 minutes. Add ground lamb and 3 tbsp. lemon juice. Cook, stirring, until lamb is browned and crumbly, 2 to 3 minutes. Stir in broth, couscous, and remaining 2 tbsp. lemon juice. Bring to a boil, then cover and remove from heat; let stand until liquid has been absorbed and couscous is tender to the bite, 3 to 4 minutes. Stir in parsley; add salt to taste.

3. Turn pepper halves over. Fill each with about ⅔ cup lamb mixture. Sprinkle feta cheese evenly over filling. Bake until cheese is slightly melted, 3 to 5 minutes.

PER SERVING: 498 cal., 29% (144 cal.) from fat; 24 g protein; 16 g fat (6.7 g sat.); 65 g carbo (6.6 g fiber); 134 mg sodium; 45 mg chol.

Braised Kid Goat with Black Olives, Rosemary, and Wine

Having very little fat, kid goat can get tough unless it's cooked correctly. Braising is a great technique because the meat slowly tenderizes and stays moist. Reader F. P. Cronemiller, of Los Altos, California, contributed the recipe.

SERVES 6 to 8 | **TIME** 2 hours

¼ cup olive oil
1 kid goat hindquarter (about 4 lbs.; for buying information, *see the Global Goat, right*), cut into 2-in. pieces by butcher
1 medium onion, finely chopped
4 garlic cloves, finely chopped
2 tsp. finely chopped rosemary leaves
½ cup white wine
1 small can (8 oz.) tomato sauce
1 tsp. salt
½ tsp. freshly ground black pepper
½ lb. pitted ripe black olives, drained
⅓ cup finely chopped flat-leaf parsley

1. Heat oil in a 5- to 6-qt. heavy-bottomed pot over medium-high heat until hot. Brown goat pieces in oil, working in batches if necessary so as not to crowd meat; transfer to a plate as browned. Stir in onion, garlic, and rosemary and cook, stirring often, until onion softens, about 3 minutes.

2. Pour in wine and scrape browned bits from bottom of pan, then simmer until wine has almost evaporated, about 6 minutes. Add tomato sauce, salt, and pepper.

Reduce heat to a simmer and cook, covered, until meat is almost tender, 40 minutes to 1 hour.

3. Add olives and cook about 10 minutes more. Stir in parsley.

PER SERVING: 382 cal., 40% (153 cal.) from fat; 48 g protein; 17 g fat (2.6 g sat.); 7.5 g carbo (1.1 g fiber); 852 mg sodium; 129 mg chol.

The Global Goat

To beef lovers, it may come as a surprise that more goat is eaten around the world than any other meat. It's especially popular in Greece, southern Italy, the Indian subcontinent, Mexico, and the Caribbean. Why is this the case? Goats can survive in hot, rocky climates that would kill a cow or pig, and their meat is relatively healthy; it's lower in fat and calories than beef, lamb, or even chicken. And kid goats, if well raised, are tender and delicious—milder-tasting than lamb.

In the U.S., goat consumption is on the rise, and more American ranchers and farmers are raising goats—particularly the chunky Boer goats—for their meat. So far it's been mainly immigrant populations that have driven the market, but a tipping point may be coming as goat meat (also called chevon) makes its way onto fine-dining menus.

To try it yourself, seek out a rancher in your area. California now has a number of goat farmers; we've ordered good meat online from Copeland Family Farms, near the Oregon border (*goatmeats.com*). Or buy meat from a Mexican, Italian, or Greek market or a halal butcher (the halal meat tends to be milder-tasting). Most kid goats sold for meat are no more than 6 months old. *Cabrito*, the Spanish word for kid goat, often refers to milk-fed goats between the ages of 4 and 8 weeks. Meat from goats older than 1 year is tougher and gamier.

One thing to remember when cooking goat is that because the meat is so lean, it benefits from long marination before grilling, or from being cooked in liquid—i.e., braised or stewed. At *Sunset*, we've found that the best cuts for grilling are marinated chops or steaks, cooked fast over direct high heat. Larger, tougher cuts such as legs (or even the cubed meat from tougher muscles) are most tender when oven-braised. *Birria*, the popular Mexican goat stew using leg, is a great example.

Venison Loin Roast

Because venison tenderloin cooks so quickly, pan-brown it first to caramelize the surface. Then, when it finishes roasting, use the pan drippings to make sauce; we've provided you with two tasty choices.

SERVES 6 | **TIME** 30 minutes

2 venison tenderloins (about 1½ lbs. total), fat and
    membrane trimmed
2 tsp. canola or safflower oil
Blackberry-Orange Pan Sauce or Brandy-Peppercorn
    Pan Sauce *(recipes follow)*

1. Preheat oven to 450°. Pat tenderloins dry. Heat oil in a 10- to 12-in. ovenproof frying pan over medium-high heat until hot. Add venison and brown well on all sides, 4 to 5 minutes total.
2. Roast venison in frying pan in oven until done to your liking (125° on a thermometer for rare, 6 to 9 minutes), turning meat once. Transfer to a platter and let rest at least 5 minutes. Make sauce as directed below.
3. Slice meat, adding juices to sauce. Serve meat with sauce.

PER SERVING WITHOUT SAUCE: 136 cal., 18% (24 cal.) from fat; 26 g protein; 2.7 g fat (1.1 g sat.); 0 g carbo; 58 mg sodium; 96 mg chol.

Blackberry-Orange Pan Sauce: Heat frying pan with drippings over high heat. Add 1½ cups **beef broth**, 3 tbsp. **seedless blackberry jam**, 2 tbsp. **balsamic vinegar**, 1 tbsp. minced **orange zest**, and 2 tsp. **prepared horseradish**. Boil, stirring, until reduced to ⅔ cup, about 8 minutes, and season with **salt** to taste.

PER TBSP.: 19 cal., 0% from fat; 0.8 g protein; 0 g fat; 4.2 g carbo (0.1 g fiber); 14 mg sodium; 0 mg chol.

Brandy-Peppercorn Pan Sauce: Set frying pan with drippings over high heat. Add 1 tbsp. **butter**, ⅔ cup minced **shallots**, and 1½ tbsp. jarred **green peppercorns** (rinsed, drained, and crushed with the bottom of a heavy glass or skillet). Cook, stirring, over high heat until shallots are lightly browned, about 2 minutes. Add ¾ cup reduced-sodium **beef broth** and ¼ cup *each* **brandy** and **whipping cream**. Boil, stirring, until reduced to ⅔ cup, about 3 minutes.

PER TBSP.: 102 cal., 66% (67 cal.) from fat; 3.1 g protein; 7.4 g fat (4.6 g sat.); 2.6 g carbo; 82 mg sodium; 31 mg chol

Venison, Elk, or Caribou with Wild Mushroom and Juniper Berry Sauce

Venison, mainly imported from New Zealand, is relatively easy to get through a butcher. Elk (one of the largest deer species) is raised in several Western states, including Oregon, Idaho, and Colorado, and can be purchased online. Caribou and reindeer (the names are used interchangeably) generally come from Alaska, Canada, and northern Scandinavia. Look for sources online.

SERVES 12 to 14 | **TIME** 1 hour, 20 minutes, plus 2 hours to marinate

1 boned venison, elk, or caribou loin (4 to 6 lbs.)
¼ cup canola oil
1¾ cups dry red wine, such as Merlot, divided
1 small onion, minced
1 garlic clove, minced
1 bay leaf
2 tbsp. dried juniper berries, divided
½ tsp. dried thyme
¼ tsp. ground cloves
1 tbsp. coarsely ground black pepper
¼ cup butter
⅓ to ½ lb. chanterelle or button mushrooms, thinly sliced
2 cups beef broth
⅓ cup red currant jelly
1 cup whipping cream

1. From loin, trim off or scrape free and discard all fibrous sinew, silvery membrane, and tough bits of cartilage (if present). Reserve scraps of meat for other uses. To make an evenly shaped roast, tie loin snugly at 1½- to 2-in. intervals with cotton string, tucking thin end of meat under roast, if needed.
2. In a 2-gal. resealable plastic bag, combine oil, ¾ cup wine, the onion, garlic, bay leaf, 2 tsp. juniper berries, the thyme, and cloves. Add loin, seal bag, and rotate to coat meat with marinade. Set bag in a pan and chill at least 2 hours and up to 1 day; turn meat occasionally.
3. Preheat oven to 475°. Lift meat from marinade; drain briefly. Put on a flat rack in a 12- by 17-in. roasting pan; if meat is too long, cut in half, and place pieces well apart on rack. Pat pepper all over meat. Roast venison or elk until a thermometer inserted into thickest part of loin registers 125° for rare, about 25 minutes (check after 15 minutes; thinner roasts cook faster). Roast caribou until very rare (thermometer registers 120° to 123°), 15 to 20 minutes (check after 15 minutes). Put meat on a platter; keep warm.

4. Melt butter in same roasting pan over medium-high heat. Add mushrooms and cook, stirring often, until softened and just beginning to brown, 4 to 5 minutes. Add remaining 1 cup wine and 1 tbsp. plus 1 tsp. juniper berries, the broth, and jelly; bring to a boil over high heat, scraping browned bits from bottom of pan. Boil, uncovered, until reduced by half, about 20 minutes. Drain any juices from meat into pan. Add cream; boil until reduced to 2 cups, 6 to 8 minutes longer. Pour sauce into a small bowl.

5. Slice meat crosswise; offer sauce to add to taste.

PER SERVING: 352 cal., 45% (158 cal.) from fat; 38 g protein; 18 g fat (8 g sat.); 8.5 g carbo (0.5 g fiber); 160 mg sodium; 168 mg chol.

Soy Mustard–glazed Buffalo

Despite the animal's impressive size and intimidating burliness, buffalo (bison) is extremely mild in flavor and very lean.

SERVES 10 to 12 | **TIME** 1¼ hours

1 whole buffalo tenderloin (4 to 5 lbs.; *see Quick Tip below*)
1 cup Dijon mustard
⅓ cup firmly packed brown sugar
3 tbsp. *each* dry sherry, soy sauce, minced fresh ginger, and Asian (toasted) sesame oil

1. Preheat oven to 425°. Trim off or scrape free and discard all fibrous sinew and silvery membrane (if present) from buffalo tenderloin. Reserve any scraps of meat for other uses. To make an evenly shaped roast, tie snugly at 1½- to 2-in. intervals with a cotton string, tucking thin end of meat under roast, if needed.

2. In a small bowl, mix mustard, brown sugar, sherry, soy sauce, ginger, and sesame oil. Rub meat all over with a third of mustard sauce; reserve remaining sauce.

3. Place meat on a flat rack in a 12- by 17-in. roasting pan. Roast for 30 minutes. Brush to coat with some of reserved mustard sauce. Continue to roast until a thermometer inserted in thickest part of roast registers 130° for rare (do not overcook buffalo or it will be very dry), 10 to 25 minutes longer.

4. Transfer roast to a platter and let rest in a warm place 10 to 15 minutes. Pour remaining mustard sauce into a small serving bowl. Slice meat crosswise and offer sauce to spoon over each portion.

Quick Tip: Order the buffalo ahead of time from your butcher. If you can't find buffalo tenderloin, you can use beef tenderloin instead.

PER 3-OZ. SERVING: 265 cal., 19% (51 cal.) from fat; 42 g protein; 5.8 g fat (1.3 g sat.); 11 g carbo (0.1 g fiber); 760 mg sodium; 105 mg chol.

Bison: The Most Western Meat

As we continue to look for healthier and more sustainable meat options, bison is frequently the answer. This massive, shaggy-headed icon of the West, commonly known as American buffalo, is leaner and more delicate in flavor than beef; the meat is also an excellent source of protein and is low in fat and cholesterol (lower, actually, than skinless chicken).

Once plentiful, bison were driven nearly extinct by settlers and pioneers who hunted them for their hides, bones, and tongues, wasting the rest rather than using all parts of the animal as the Native Americans did. It's taken a long time, but bison are making a comeback. More small private ranchers are raising the animals and selling the meat, particularly in the mountain states of the West.

Antibiotics are prohibited in the bison industry, and the animals are most often grass fed, making bison meat an attractive choice for eco- and health-conscious consumers. Many grocery stores and butcher shops now carry a variety of bison roasts and steaks, as well as ground bison for burgers. Be sure not to overcook the meat; because it's so lean, it cooks much more quickly than beef.

the
fire
outside

We give you our tips—and top recipes—for the quintessentially Western way to eat.

If you live in West, the urge to grill goes with the territory. It's not just the smell of smoke and succulence that draws you in. Grilling is a good excuse to stay outside in gorgeous weather. It's also a quick way to cook a lot of food for a party or even just for your family. (We say "grill" because most of our cooking is fast; "barbecue" usually means long, slow Southern or Texas pit–style.) Plus, because it requires only casual monitoring rather than constant attention, it's easy to have conversations while you grill.

Grilling stands for so much of what's true about Western cooking: It's relaxed, friendly, fairly simple, and flavorful because the ingredients are fresh and good. The truth is, you can grill like a Westerner anywhere, as long as the weather permits. And pretty much any kind of food can be grilled, as this chapter makes clear: everything from appetizers through whole turkeys, fish, steaks and roasts, even soup, salad, pizza, and dessert. Some of the West's finest contributions to national gastronomy are in these pages, like barbecued (grilled) oysters (*page 444*), grilled artichokes (*page 440*), and juicy, charred tri-tip, a cut of beef that falls somewhere between a steak and a roast (*page 486*).

We acknowledge our frontier history here, too. Utah carries the torch for Dutch oven cooking (*page 518*), reminding us that generations after the covered wagons passed through, this sturdy pot is probably still the single most useful tool for cooking outdoors. Planked salmon (*page 506*), from the Native Americans of the Northwest, is enduringly delicious. And an old (even primal) form of cooking—roasting whole animals—is new again, revived by conscientious chefs who don't want to waste meat. No reason home cooks can't join them (*see page 496*)!

The Fire Outside

Grilling Basics

Charcoal or gas, direct or indirect heat, a searing blast or a gentle glow: Grillers have a lot of choices when it comes to building a fire. Here's how to create the setups specified in the recipes in this book.

Gas or Charcoal?

It's your choice. Cooking with gas versus charcoal is a little like driving an automatic versus a stick, and both have their fans. Gas is easy—just turn it on and you're good to go. With charcoal, you have to interact with the fire to keep the food cooking at the right temperature—adjusting the air flow, moving the coals, adding a bit more fuel, and doing a lot of impromptu shifting of the food to whichever spot is at the right heat. Some cooks feel that charcoal gives food a more "grilled" flavor, but gas aficionados tend to disagree.

Direct Heat Grilling

When a recipe calls for direct heat, that means the fire is right beneath the food—ideal for grilling smaller items such as steaks, burgers, and kebabs, plus seafood and vegetables; they'll be cooked all the way through by the time the outside is nicely browned.

DIRECT HEAT WITH GAS

Open the lid, press the ignition, turn all burners to high, close the lid, and wait 10 minutes or so for the grill to get hot. Then adjust the burners for the temperature range you need. As you cook, keep the lid closed as much as possible.

DIRECT HEAT WITH CHARCOAL

Ignite the charcoal. Our favorite way to start a charcoal fire is the chimney starter: Stash a few pieces of crumpled newspaper or a few paraffin cubes in its base, then fill with enough charcoal to cover the cooking grate in a single layer—usually to the top of the chimney starter for a standard kettle grill (*see Charcoal Choices, opposite page*).

Set the chimney on the firegrate (the bottom grate) and open the vents underneath the grill. Ignite the paper or cubes and let the fire burn until all the charcoal ignites, 15 to 20 minutes. You can buy a charcoal chimney starter at most hardware or barbecue stores.

Spread it out. Protecting your hands, dump the charcoal onto the firegrate and spread it out with tongs. Then put the cooking grate in place to preheat and let the coals burn to the heat specified in your recipe—usually 5 to 10 minutes for high, longer for medium to low (*see Taking Your Grill's Temperature, below*). If you can spare the grill space, leave about one-quarter of the firegrate clear of coals. This will give you a cool zone where you can temporarily move any foods that start to get too brown.

Add food. Arrange your food on the cooking grate; grill with the lid on (and its vents open) for the most even cooking, or keep the lid off for easy access—if, say, you're flipping a lot of burgers.

Adjust the vents. If you need to reduce the fire's temperature, partially close the vents in the lid and at firegrate level. (That will limit the oxygen that feeds the fire.)

Indirect Heat Grilling

In a recipe that calls for indirect heat, the fire burns to one side of the food or all around it rather than directly beneath. Large items such as turkey, long-cooked food like ribs, flammable

---

Taking Your Grill's Temperature

Some grills have built-in thermometers to guide you, but if not, use the following "hand test." Measure the temperature often; on a charcoal grill, it can fluctuate quite a bit (your cue to move the food to a hotter or cooler spot, or to add coals). You may have to move food to several different spots before it has finished cooking.

VERY HIGH 550° to 650°; you can hold your hand 5 in. above the cooking grate only 1 to 2 seconds.

HIGH 450° to 550°; you can hold your hand 5 in. above the cooking grate only 2 to 4 seconds.

MEDIUM 350° to 450°; you can hold your hand 5 in. above the cooking grate only 5 to 7 seconds.

LOW 250° to 350°; you can hold your hand 5 in. above the cooking grate only 8 to 10 seconds.

meats such as fat-rich duck, and anything glazed in sweet barbecue sauce all benefit from the more gentle, radiant heat of this method.

INDIRECT HEAT WITH GAS

Set a drip pan *(see the Drip Pan, below right)* on one burner, either on the side of the grill or in the middle—it doesn't really matter. With the grill lid open, ignite all the burners and turn them to high. Close the lid and wait 10 minutes or so for the grill to get hot. Turn off the burner with the drip pan on it and adjust the other burners to get the temperature you need. When the grill is at the right heat, set the food over the drip pan. As you cook, keep the lid closed.

INDIRECT HEAT WITH CHARCOAL

Ignite the charcoal. Following the steps under *Direct Heat Grilling (opposite page)*, light charcoal—usually about two-thirds of what you would need
to cover the entire firegrate.
Bank it. When coals are thoroughly ignited, after 15 to 20 minutes, bank them on opposite sides of the firegrate (bottom grate). Set a drip pan in the empty area *(see the Drip Pan, right)* and set the cooking grate in place to preheat. Let the coals burn to the heat specified in your recipe, usually 5 to 10 minutes for high, longer for medium to low *(see Taking Your Grill's Temperature, opposite page.)*
Add food. The area over the section cleared of coals is the indirect-heat area; set food on the cooking grate above cleared section. Cover the grill, being sure all vents are open.
Maintain the heat. If you're cooking longer than 30 minutes, add 10 to 12 briquets to the fire every 30 minutes, and leave the fire uncovered for a few minutes to help them light. At the same time, sweep ash from the firegrate by moving the outside lever; this keeps vents clear and air flowing.
Adjust the vents. If needed, reduce the fire's temperature by partially closing vents in the lid and firegrate.

Charcoal Choices

• **BRIQUETS** Briquets are the most common fuel for charcoal grillers. These compressed pillows—made of crushed charcoal, a starch binder, and often coal products to make the heat last—provide reliable, even cooking. Kingsford, the major manufacturer, has in recent years reformulated its briquets, and now they light faster and burn faster. For long cooking, you will probably need to replenish the coals every 30 minutes. Hardwood, or natural, briquets (made purely from charcoal) contain no additives and burn out even faster. Avoid briquets with lighter fluid added; they're bad for the environment and give food an off flavor.

• **LUMP CHARCOAL** Irregularly shaped pure hardwood chunks, lump charcoal gives food a nice smokiness. Compared with standard Kingsford briquets, lump charcoal lights faster, gets hotter, and loses heat more quickly—so be generous when adding fuel if you're cooking more than 30 minutes.

• **BRIQUETS AND CHARCOAL** Some grillers like to use a mix of briquets and lump charcoal for high, consistent heat and good flavor.

THE DRIP PAN

Whenever you grill indirectly, before beginning to cook, set a metal drip pan on the burner you intend to turn off (on a gas grill) or in the space cleared of coals (charcoal) underneath the cooking grate. The pan—ideally the same size as the food above it—helps prevent flare-ups by catching flammable falling bits. For extra-incendiary fatty foods (duck, some sausages), add water to the pan to fill it at least halfway. We also add water for long-cooking foods (ribs, turkey), to help keep them moist and to even out the temperature circulating inside the grill.

Basic Bruschetta on the Grill

This recipe for bruschetta with a selection of tempting toppers comes from Jennifer McIlvaine, who used to run a food stand at Seattle-area farmers' markets and now teaches cooking in Umbria, Italy. Use best-quality ingredients and you'll be rewarded with outstanding flavor.

MAKES 8 bruschettas | **TIME** 15 minutes

8 slices (¼- to ½-in. thick) good-quality bread
  (see Quick Tip below)
2 tbsp. olive oil
1 garlic clove, halved
Sea salt

1. Prepare a charcoal or gas grill for direct high heat (see Direct Heat Grilling, page 436), or set a rack 4 in. from a broiler on high. Lightly brush both sides of bread slices with oil. Toast, turning as necessary, until both sides are crisp and browned, 3 to 4 minutes.
2. Remove bread from grill or oven and rub each slice with a cut side of the halved garlic clove. Sprinkle with salt to taste. Eat plain or add one of the toppings that follow.
Quick Tip: Choose a good bread without too many large holes that would let the topping drip through. McIlvaine uses hominy bread, but we found that a bâtard or pane pugliese also worked well.

PER BRUSCHETTA: 81 cal., 56% (45 cal.) from fat; 1.3 g protein; 5 g fat (0.7 g sat.); 7.6 g carbo (0.5 g fiber); 333 mg sodium; 0 mg chol.

Tomato and Basil Topping

Here is a simple way to showcase fresh summer tomatoes at peak ripeness. Mix and match varieties for flavor and color.

MAKES Topping for 8 bruschettas | **TIME** 10 minutes

4 ripe medium tomatoes, diced
4 basil leaves, chopped
2 tbsp. extra-virgin olive oil, plus more for drizzling
1 garlic clove, thinly sliced
½ tsp. sea salt
⅛ tsp. freshly ground black pepper
Basic Bruschetta on the Grill (recipe above)

In a medium bowl, mix tomatoes, basil, oil, garlic, salt, and pepper. Spoon onto bruschettas and drizzle with oil.

PER TOPPED BRUSCHETTA: 125 cal., 62% (78 cal.) from fat; 1.9 g protein; 8.7 g fat (1.3 g sat.); 11 g carbo (1.3 g fiber); 461 mg sodium; 0 mg chol.

Chickpea and Octopus Topping

Rich and rustic, this topping made converts of Jennifer McIlvaine's most octopus-phobic customers at the food stand, Bruschettina, she ran in Seattle. It was also the hands-down favorite topping of Sunset's staff.

MAKES Topping for 8 bruschettas | **TIME** 1½ hours

1 lb. cleaned baby octopus (see Quick Tip below)
½ cup red wine vinegar
1 tbsp. salt
¼ cup olive oil
4 garlic cloves, roughly chopped
1 anchovy fillet
1 can (14.5 oz.) chickpeas (garbanzos), rinsed and drained
¼ cup dry white wine
Basic Bruschetta on the Grill (recipe, left)
Extra-virgin olive oil for drizzling

1. In a large pot, cover octopus with cold water. Add vinegar and salt and bring to a boil. Reduce heat to keep liquid at a slow boil and cook until a knife easily pierces meat, 45 to 60 minutes. Drain octopus, let cool, and chop into chickpea-size pieces.
2. Meanwhile, in a small pan, heat olive oil and garlic over low heat. Cook, stirring occasionally, until garlic is soft but not brown, about 10 minutes. Remove from heat, add anchovy, and mash thoroughly with a fork.
3. Put octopus, chickpeas, and garlic-anchovy oil in a large frying pan over high heat and cook, stirring and mashing chickpeas slightly, until mixture starts to brown. Add wine and scrape up any browned bits from bottom of pan. Remove from heat, spoon onto bruschetta, and drizzle with extra-virgin olive oil.
Quick Tip: Octopus is often available cleaned and frozen at specialty grocery stores, fishmongers, and some Asian markets.

PER TOPPED BRUSCHETTA: 255 cal., 56% (144 cal.) from fat; 12 g protein; 16 g fat (2.2 g sat.); 15 g carbo (1.9 g fiber); 700 mg sodium; 28 mg chol.

Eggplant with Mint Topping

Bright mint, spicy chile, and rich eggplant meld together into an almost creamy spread. For an even smoother texture, peel the eggplant before cooking.

MAKES Topping for 8 bruschettas | **TIME** 30 minutes

⅓ cup olive oil
1 small red onion, diced
1 garlic clove, thinly sliced
1 medium eggplant, diced
½ tsp. *each* sea salt and red chile flakes
⅛ tsp. freshly ground black pepper
6 mint leaves, chopped
Basic Bruschetta on the Grill *(opposite page)*
Extra-virgin olive oil for drizzling

1. Heat olive oil in a large frying pan over medium heat. Add onion and cook, stirring once or twice, until softened, about 4 minutes. Add garlic and cook another minute, then add eggplant, salt, chile flakes, and pepper. Stir to coat with oil. Reduce heat to medium-low and cook, stirring every few minutes, until eggplant is soft, about 20 minutes.
2. Stir in mint. Let mixture cool to room temperature and spoon onto bruschettas. Drizzle with extra-virgin olive oil.

PER TOPPED BRUSCHETTA: 284 cal., 79% (225 cal.) from fat; 2.3 g protein; 25 g fat (3.5 g sat.); 13 g carbo (1.7 g fiber); 459 mg sodium; 0 mg chol.

Mixed Herb Topping

McIlvaine likes to change her pestos with the seasons—stinging-nettle pesto in spring, basil and mixed herb in summer and fall, and hearty greens in winter. The recipe is flexible enough to allow experimentation; try it with a variety of favorite herbs.

MAKES Topping for 8 bruschettas | **TIME** 20 minutes

1 tbsp. salt, plus more to taste
6 cups loosely packed basil leaves
2 cups loosely packed tender green herbs, such as Thai basil, mint, parsley, summer savory, and/or tarragon
¼ cup grated parmesan cheese
¼ cup extra-virgin olive oil, plus more for drizzling
2 garlic cloves, chopped
Freshly ground black pepper
Basic Bruschetta on the Grill *(opposite page)*

1. Stir salt into a large pot of boiling water. Add basil and other herbs; cook for 10 seconds, then drain. Plunge herbs into a large bowl of very cold water (to preserve the bright green color). Drain and gently squeeze out excess water.
2. In a food processor, purée herbs with parmesan, oil, garlic, and 2 tbsp. water to make a paste. Add salt and pepper to taste. Spoon onto bruschettas and drizzle with extra-virgin olive oil.

PER TOPPED BRUSCHETTA: 201 cal., 72% (144 cal.) from fat; 4.8 g protein; 16 g fat (2.6 g sat.); 13 g carbo (4.5 g fiber); 680 mg sodium; 2 mg chol.

Braised Pepper Topping

Cook down bell peppers until they become soft and sweet.

MAKES Topping for 8 bruschettas | **TIME** 35 minutes

¼ cup olive oil
3 red, yellow, or orange sweet bell peppers, seeds and ribs removed and thinly sliced
1 garlic clove, thinly sliced
¼ tsp. sea salt
8 basil leaves, chopped
Basic Bruschetta on the Grill *(opposite page)*
Extra-virgin olive oil for drizzling

1. Heat olive oil in a large frying pan over medium heat. Add peppers, garlic, and salt. Cook, stirring occasionally, until peppers are very soft and sweet but not brown, about 30 minutes. Remove from heat. Stir in basil and let mixture cool to room temperature.
2. Spoon onto bruschettas and drizzle with extra-virgin olive oil.

PER TOPPED BRUSCHETTA: 149 cal., 72% (108 cal.) from fat; 1.6 g protein; 12 g fat (1.6 g sat.); 9.6 g carbo (1 g fiber); 334 mg sodium; 0 mg chol.

■ Rainbow Bell Peppers

FROM THE GARDEN

Many bell peppers start out green and mature to red or orange. Others begin life yellow, purple, or white. Varieties like bright orange Ariane and red Socrates Hybrid are very sweet. Golden Bell keeps its yellow color. Most supermarkets carry yellow and red bell peppers in addition to the familiar green; look for other colors and varieties at local farmers' markets.

Grilled Pancetta-Radicchio Wraps with Goat Cheese

Here's a brilliant Italian-style recipe that takes practically no time, requires just four ingredients, and is completely delicious.

SERVES 6 | **TIME** 15 minutes

6 oz. fresh goat cheese
6 radicchio leaves (about 3 by 5 in. each)
6 slices pancetta (1½ to 2 oz. total)
2 tbsp. balsamic vinegar

1. Divide goat cheese among radicchio leaves, placing a dollop in center of each leaf. Fold one edge of each leaf over cheese, then roll up gently to enclose. Wrap a slice of pancetta around each roll and secure with one or two toothpicks (it's okay if pancetta tears a little).
2. Prepare a charcoal or gas grill for direct medium-high heat *(see Direct Heat Grilling, page 436)*. Lay radicchio rolls on hot cooking grate (close lid on gas grill). Turn the rolls as needed until pancetta is lightly browned and crisp on all sides, 5 to 8 minutes total.
3. Set rolls on a platter and drizzle with vinegar. Serve warm or at room temperature.

PER SERVING: 112 cal., 75% (84 cal.) from fat; 6.5 g protein; 9.3 g fat (5.6 g sat.); 1.3 g carbo (0.1 g fiber); 185 mg sodium; 17 mg chol.

Grilled Artichokes with Green-olive Dip

The char of fire-roasting adds an extra layer of flavor to the artichokes and the pungent, salty olive dip.

recipe pictured on page **457**

SERVES 6 | **TIME** 1½ hours

6 artichokes
1 tbsp. plus ½ tsp. salt
Juice of 1 lemon, plus 2 tbsp. more juice
3 garlic cloves, minced
3 tbsp. olive oil
¼ tsp. freshly ground black pepper
Green-olive Dip *(recipe follows)*

1. Slice tops off artichokes, pull off small outer leaves, trim stems, and snip off thorny tips. In a large pot, bring 1 to 2 in. water to a boil. Add 1 tbsp. salt, juice of 1 lemon, and artichokes; cover and steam until artichoke bottoms pierce easily, 20 to 40 minutes, depending on their size. Drain artichokes. When cool enough to handle, cut each in half lengthwise and scrape out fuzzy center.

2. In a small bowl, combine garlic, oil, remaining 2 tbsp. lemon juice and ½ tsp. salt, and the pepper. Brush artichokes with garlic mixture.
3. Prepare a charcoal or gas grill for direct medium heat *(see Direct Heat Grilling, page 436)*. Grill artichokes, turning once, until lightly browned, 8 to 11 minutes.
4. Serve with olive dip.
Make Ahead: Artichokes through step 1, up to 2 days, chilled. Green olive dip, up to 2 days, chilled.

PER SERVING WITHOUT DIP: 126 cal., 51% (64 cal.) from fat; 4.3 g protein; 7.3 g fat (1.2 g sat.); 14 g carbo (7 g fiber); 317 mg sodium; 0.9 mg chol.

Green-olive Dip: In a blender, purée ½ cup chopped flat-leaf **parsley**, 5 tbsp. **extra-virgin olive oil**, 2 tbsp. chopped **green olives**, 1 tbsp. drained **capers**, 1 tbsp. **fresh lemon juice**, ½ tsp. **Dijon mustard**, ¼ tsp. **freshly ground black pepper**, and ⅛ tsp. **salt** until coarsely puréed.

PER TBSP.: 54 cal., 96% (52 cal.) from fat; 0.1 g protein; 6.1 g fat (0.9 g sat.); 0.4 g carbo (0.2 g fiber); 78 mg sodium; 0 mg chol.

Chèvre and Mango Steak Bites

If possible, grill the steak over charcoal—it makes a big difference in flavor here.

MAKES 30 to 34 rolls | **TIME** 1½ hours, plus 45 minutes to freeze steak

1 beef flank steak (1½ to 1¾ lbs.), fat trimmed
1 tbsp. olive oil
Kosher salt and freshly ground black pepper
About 2 tbsp. milk
½ cup packed (4 to 5 oz.) fresh goat cheese (chèvre)
30 to 34 small mint leaves
About 15 dried mango pieces, cut into 30 to 34 slivers (each ¼ by 1 in.)

1. Rub steak liberally with oil and salt and pepper.
2. Prepare a charcoal or gas grill for direct high heat *(see Direct Heat Grilling, page 436)*. Grill steak (close lid on gas grill), turning once, until firm when pressed on thin end but still quite pink inside (cut to test), 8 to 10 minutes. Transfer steak to a plate and let cool at least 30 minutes. About 45 minutes before slicing, put steak in the freezer (it will be easier to slice thinly).
3. On a grooved cutting board (to catch juices) and using a very sharp knife, cut steak across grain, straight up and down and as thinly and evenly as possible (less than ¼ in. thick), to make 30 to 34 slices. Save narrow and uneven ends for another use. If steak is wet, blot with paper towels and transfer to a dry plate.

4. Measure accumulated meat juices and add enough milk to make 2 tbsp.; pour into a bowl. Crumble goat cheese into bowl and mash into a smooth paste.

5. Working with one steak strip at a time, spread each with about ¾ tsp. cheese mixture, then lay 1 mint leaf and 1 mango piece at one end of strip (placed so they will poke up jauntily from the steak when it's rolled up); roll to enclose. Let stand at room temperature at least 10 minutes before serving.

Make Ahead: Up to 6 hours, chilled.

PER ROLL: 46 cal., 46% (21 cal.) from fat; 3.9 g protein; 2.3 g fat (1.1 g sat.); 2.2 g carbo (0.1 g fiber); 25 mg sodium; 9.7 mg chol.

Ginger Beef Mini Skewers

Cal Stamenov, chef at the Bernardus Lodge in Carmel Valley, California, gave us his recipe for little beef skewers. You'll need 20 small wooden skewers (each 4 to 4½ in.); buy these online, at *pickonus.com*.

MAKES 18 to 20 appetizer skewers | **TIME** 40 minutes, plus 8 hours to marinate

¾ lb. beef tenderloin
1 tbsp. thinly sliced fresh ginger, plus 1 tbsp. finely grated
½ head garlic, cloves thinly sliced, plus 1 tbsp. finely grated garlic
2 green onions, trimmed and thinly sliced
½ cup extra-virgin olive oil
2 tbsp. seasoned rice vinegar
¼ cup soy sauce
Salt and freshly ground black pepper
4 to 6 chives, thinly sliced

1. Cut tenderloin into ½-in.-thick slices and lightly pound each with flat side of a meat mallet until about ¼ in. thick. Each piece should be rectangular (about 1½ by 2½ in.); trim off any ragged bits for another use, such as a stir-fry. Stir together sliced ginger, sliced garlic, green onions, and oil in a bowl. Add beef, toss to coat, cover, and marinate in refrigerator at least 8 hours. Soak skewers in water at least 20 minutes and up to 4 hours.

2. Prepare a charcoal or gas grill for direct high heat (*see Direct Heat Grilling, page 436*). Whisk grated ginger, grated garlic, vinegar, and soy sauce in a bowl. Thread beef slices onto skewers and season with salt and pepper.

3. If using coals, mound to one side to reach about 4 in. below the cooking grate so that heat is extra-intense.

4. Grill skewers (close lid on gas grill) just until seared, turning once, about 30 seconds per side. Serve skewers drizzled with ginger-soy sauce and garnished with chives.

PER SKEWER: 66 cal., 74% (49 cal.) from fat; 3.3 g protein; 5.4 g fat (1.4 g sat.); 1.2 g carbo (0.1 g fiber); 255 mg sodium; 10 mg chol.

Ginger Shrimp Mini Skewers: Follow recipe (*left*) for Ginger Beef Mini Skewers, but substitute 24 large **shrimp** (21 to 30 per lb.), peeled with tails left on and deveined; reduce marinating time to between 30 minutes and 2 hours. Grill shrimp until just opaque, about 1 minute per side, and omit chives. Makes 24 skewers.

PER SKEWER: 35 cal., 66% (23 cal.) from fat; 2.3 g protein; 2.5 g fat (0.4 g sat.); 1.1 g carbo (0.1 g fiber); 211 mg sodium; 15 mg chol.

Peppered Beef Skewers with Red Onion–Horseradish Marmalade

These skewers have big flavor. You'll need eight slender metal skewers (each at least 8 in. long).

SERVES 8 as an appetizer; 4 as a main course
TIME 40 minutes, plus 1 hour to marinate

3 garlic cloves, minced
2 tbsp. soy sauce
1½ tsp. freshly ground black pepper
1 lb. tender beef, such as top sirloin or loin (¾- to 1-in. thick), fat trimmed
Red Onion–Horseradish Marmalade (*recipe follows*)

1. In a medium bowl, mix garlic, soy sauce, and pepper.

2. Cut beef into ¼-in.-thick strips about 3 in. long. Add to bowl and turn to coat. Chill, covered, at least 1 hour and as long as overnight.

3. Prepare a charcoal or gas grill for direct high heat (*see Direct Heat Grilling, page 436*). Weave skewers through meat, keeping strips flat. Grill skewers, turning to brown evenly, about 4 minutes total. Serve with marmalade.

PER APPETIZER SERVING: 104 cal.; 52% (54 cal.) from fat; 11 g protein; 6 g fat (2.3 g sat.); 1.3 g carbo; 282 mg sodium; 34 mg chol.

Red Onion–Horseradish Marmalade: Thinly slice 1 lb. **red onions**. In a large frying pan over medium-high heat, heat 1 tbsp. **extra-virgin olive oil**. Add onions and 2 tbsp. firmly packed **light brown sugar** and cook, covered, stirring occasionally, until juices have evaporated and onion is golden brown, about 8 minutes. Add ½ cup *each* **red wine vinegar** and **white wine** and 2 tsp. **prepared horseradish**. Cook, uncovered, stirring often, until liquid has evaporated, about 6 minutes. Serve warm or cool. Can be made up to 3 days ahead, and chilled. Makes about 1 cup.

PER TBSP.: 28 cal.; 32% (9 cal.) from fat; 0.3 g protein; 1 g fat (0.1 g sat.); 4 g carbo; 2 mg sodium; 0 mg chol.

Honey-Hoisin Grilled Chicken Wings

Sticky sweet replaces blazing Buffalo with these tasty wings. We serve them as finger food for an outdoor party or, paired with seasonal sides, as dinner.

SERVES 6 to 8 as an appetizer; 2 as a main course
TIME 1 hour

½ cup soy sauce
1 tbsp. *each* minced fresh ginger, minced garlic, and
    Asian chili paste
2 lbs. chicken wings, tips trimmed and separated at joint
½ cup honey
1½ tsp. hoisin sauce
2 tbsp. sesame seeds, toasted *(see Quick Tip below)*
1 green onion, trimmed and chopped

1. In large bowl, mix soy sauce, ginger, garlic, and chili paste. Add chicken and toss to coat. Let marinate at room temperature, stirring often, 15 minutes.
2. Prepare a charcoal or gas grill for direct medium heat *(see Direct Heat Grilling, page 436)*. Lay chicken wings on grill, close lid on grill, and grill wings, turning often, until golden, 10 to 15 minutes.
3. Meanwhile, in a small bowl, combine honey and hoisin sauce. Using a pastry brush, generously glaze wings and continue to grill, turning as glaze starts to caramelize, about 5 minutes more (turn often to keep glaze from burning).
4. Transfer to a platter; sprinkle with sesame seeds and green onion.
Quick Tip: To toast sesame seeds, heat them in a dry pan over medium heat until golden, stirring occasionally.

PER APPETIZER SERVING: 201 cal., 44% (88 cal.) from fat; 13 g protein; 9.8 g fat (2.5 g sat.); 16 g carbo (0.6 g fiber); 759 mg sodium; 37 mg chol.

Yakitori

Charcoal-grilled chicken skewers, or yakitori, are a popular Japanese street food that's part of the *izakaya* (Japanese pub) scene in the West. The sauce also works well on pork, fish, or beef. You will need eight wooden or metal skewers (each 10 in.).

SERVES 8 as an appetizer | **TIME** 35 minutes, plus 1 hour to marinate

1 cup mirin
⅓ cup sake
½ cup superfine sugar
2 tbsp. minced fresh ginger
2 tsp. minced garlic
¼ cup soy sauce
2 lbs. boned, skinned chicken thighs, fat trimmed and
    cut into 1½-in. pieces

1. If you're using wooden skewers, soak in water 30 minutes. Meanwhile, in a medium saucepan, combine mirin, sake, sugar, ginger, garlic, and soy sauce. Bring to a boil over high heat and cook until sugar has dissolved and sauce has thickened slightly, about 8 minutes. Remove from heat and let cool completely.
2. Put chicken in a large bowl, pour marinade over it, and turn to coat. Chill at least 1 hour and up to 3 hours.
3. Prepare a charcoal or gas grill for direct medium heat *(see Direct Heat Grilling, page 436)*. Thread chicken onto skewers. Transfer marinade to a small saucepan and boil over high heat until it has consistency of barbecue sauce, about 15 minutes.
4. Grill skewers (close lid on gas grill), basting with thickened marinade and turning frequently to prevent scorching, until chicken is caramelized and no longer pink in center (cut to test), about 6 minutes.

PER SKEWER: 274 cal., 15% (41 cal.) from fat; 23 g protein; 4.5 g fat (1.1 g sat.); 26 g carbo (0 g fiber); 613 mg sodium; 94 mg chol.

■ Soy Sauce

This dark, aromatic, and full-bodied sauce is brewed from fermented soybeans and wheat. There are distinct flavor differences between Japanese- and Chinese-made soy sauces, and also between different brands. Flavored soy sauces such as mushroom soy (infused with the essence of mushrooms) can be fun to try too.

Barbecued Bacon Shrimp

Kim Stephens of Novato, California, and her mother, Ven Kruebbe, of New Orleans, collaborated on this totally irresistible appetizer, which was a finalist in a *Sunset* grilling contest. You'll need toothpicks for this recipe.

SERVES 8 | **TIME** 30 minutes, plus 30 minutes to soak toothpicks

1 lb. medium shrimp (32 to 36 per lb.), peeled and deveined
16 to 18 slices bacon (16 to 18 oz.; see *Quick Tips below*), cut in half crosswise
Cooking-oil spray or vegetable oil
Mom's Barbecue Sauce (*recipe follows*)

1. Preheat oven to 450°. Count shrimp; for each, you need ½ slice bacon and 1 soaked wood toothpick.
2. Arrange bacon slices in single layers in two pans, each 10 by 15 in. Bake until bacon begins to brown on bottom (lift to check), 4 to 8 minutes. As bacon is browned, transfer to towels to drain. Discard fat in pans.
3. Wrap one bacon strip around each shrimp; secure with a toothpick. Spritz inside of an 11- or 12-in. square hinged grill basket with cooking spray (*see Quick Tips below*). Arrange wrapped shrimp in a single layer in basket; close basket. Cook in batches, if needed.
4. Prepare charcoal or gas grill for direct medium-high heat (*see Direct Heat Grilling, page 436*). Lay basket on grill and turn as needed to brown bacon lightly, 2 to 3 minutes total. Remove basket from heat, open, and baste bacon-wrapped shrimp with about one-quarter of Mom's Barbecue Sauce (proportionately less if cooking in batches). Close basket, flip over, open basket, and baste shrimp with another one-quarter of sauce (less if cooking in batches). Close basket, return to grill, and cook, turning once, until shrimp is opaque but still moist-looking in center of thickest part (cut to test) and bacon is well browned, 2 to 3 minutes longer.
5. Transfer bacon-wrapped shrimp to a platter. Pour remaining sauce into a bowl. Dip shrimp into sauce to eat.
Quick Tips: Hinged grill baskets are sold at barbecue supply stores; choose one with handles that will fit in your barbecue. You can also use a cooking grate (also sold at barbecue supply stores) with small holes; watch closely and turn shrimp often to brown evenly. Buy regular—not thick-sliced—bacon.

PER SERVING: 215 cal., 37% (80 cal.) from fat; 17 g protein; 8.9 g fat (3 g sat.); 14 g carbo (0.5 g fiber); 1,240 mg sodium; 100 mg chol.

Mom's Barbecue Sauce: In a 2- to 3-qt. pan, combine 1 cup **ketchup**, ¼ cup *each* **soy sauce** and **cream sherry**, 2 tbsp. *each* **fresh lemon juice** and firmly packed **brown sugar**, 4 tsp. minced **fresh ginger**, 2 tsp. **Dijon mustard**, and 1 tsp. *each* minced **garlic** and finely shredded **lemon zest**. Stirring occasionally, bring to a boil over high heat; reduce heat and simmer, stirring often, until sauce is slightly thickened and reduced to 1½ cups, about 20 minutes.

PER TBSP.: 64 cal., 1% (0.6 cal.) from fat; 1 g protein; 0.1 g fat (0 g sat.); 14 g carbo (0.5 g fiber); 903 mg sodium; 0 g chol.

Spicy Soy-Ginger Grilled Sea Bass

Variations of this dish make frequent appearances at the Linkery, a San Diego restaurant known for its craft beers and farm-to-table cooking.

SERVES 6 as a first course; 3 as a main course
TIME 40 minutes

2 tbsp. reduced-sodium soy sauce
2 tbsp. fresh lemon juice, divided
1½ tsp. *each* sugar, minced fresh ginger, and ground ginger
½ tsp. red chile flakes
¼ cup canola oil
1 bunch (about 1 lb.) asparagus, tough stem ends trimmed
¾ lb. Pacific sea bass, striped bass, or other firm white fish, cut into six 2-oz. pieces (or three 4-oz. pieces for main-course servings)
Kosher salt and freshly ground black pepper
1 tbsp. extra-virgin olive oil

1. In a blender, blend soy sauce, 1 tbsp. lemon juice, the sugar, fresh and ground ginger, and chile flakes. With machine running, slowly pour in canola oil and blend until emulsified, about 30 seconds. Spread asparagus on a rimmed baking pan, pour half of marinade over it, and toss to coat. Reserve remaining marinade.
2. Prepare a charcoal or gas grill for direct high heat (*see Direct Heat Grilling, page 436*). Pat fish dry. Season on both sides with salt and pepper and drizzle with olive oil and remaining 1 tbsp. lemon juice.
3. Put fish on cooking grate skin side down. Grill 3 minutes, then turn and continue grilling until fish is no longer translucent inside (cut to test), 2 to 3 minutes longer. Transfer to a clean plate and tent with foil to keep warm.
4. Grill asparagus spears, turning once or twice, until tender and browned, 5 to 6 minutes. Divide fish among plates and top each with asparagus spears. Use a spoon to drizzle with some of reserved marinade.

PER FIRST-COURSE SERVING: 179 cal., 65% (117 cal.) from fat; 13 g protein; 13 g fat (1.3 g sat.); 4.6 g carbo (0.6 g fiber); 241 mg sodium; 23 mg chol.

Barbecued Oysters with Chipotle Glaze

This recipe is from Dory Ford, former executive chef at Portola Restaurant at the Monterey Bay Aquarium. Seafood Watch, the aquarium's guide to sustainable seafood, recommends farmed oysters, which can be grown in protected areas and harvested with minimal environmental impact.

recipe pictured
on page
455

SERVES 8 as an appetizer | **TIME** 30 minutes, plus 30 minutes to marinate

2 tbsp. plus 2 tsp. fresh lime juice
2 tbsp. olive oil
1 tbsp. tequila
1 tsp. minced cilantro
1 tsp. coarse sea salt or kosher salt, divided
¼ tsp. freshly ground black pepper
2 dozen oysters on the half-shell, with their juices *(see Quick Tips, above right)*
¼ cup unsalted butter, softened
2 tbsp. mayonnaise
1 canned chipotle chile in adobo sauce, minced, plus 1½ tsp. sauce
1 tsp. minced lime zest
At least 2 cups rock salt for lining platter
Canola-oil cooking spray

1. Whisk 2 tbsp. lime juice with oil, tequila, cilantro, ½ tsp. sea salt, and the pepper in a medium bowl. Add oysters and their juices, reserving bottom shells. Marinate oysters 30 to 45 minutes in refrigerator; drain, reserving about 1½ cups marinade.
2. Meanwhile, soak shells in water for 30 minutes. Drain on a kitchen towel and pat dry.
3. Prepare a charcoal or gas grill for very high direct heat *(see Direct Heat Grilling, page 436)*.
4. In a small bowl, whisk together butter, mayonnaise, chile and sauce, lime zest, remaining 2 tsp. lime juice, and remaining ½ tsp. sea salt. Set glaze aside *(see Quick Tips, above right)*.
5. Spread rock salt on a platter large enough to hold oysters in a single layer. Arrange oyster shells on a large baking pan and spray insides lightly with cooking spray.
6. Set half of shells on cooking grate (balance on bars so they won't roll over). Heat shells 30 seconds. Spoon 1 oyster into each shell with 1 tbsp. reserved marinade and cook (close lid on gas grill) until juices are bubbling, 2 to 3 minutes. Drizzle 1 tsp. glaze onto each oyster and cook 30 seconds more. Using tongs, carefully transfer oysters to platter, keeping them level so

juices don't spill, and nestle them in the salt. Grill remaining oysters the same way.

Quick Tips: Have your fishmonger shuck the oysters if you like; just ask that the juices stay in the shells to keep the oysters moist. (To shuck them yourself, *see How to Shuck an Oyster, page 47*.) Keep them cold and as level as possible in transport to avoid losing the liquid, and use them as soon as you can. If the glaze stiffens, set glaze on the hot cooking grate for a minute.

PER 3-OYSTER SERVING: 146 cal., 86% (126 cal.) from fat; 3.3 g protein; 14 g fat (4.7 g sat.); 2.9 g carbo (0.2 g fiber); 320 mg sodium; 41 mg chol.

Hog Island Oyster Co. Barbecued Oysters 3 Ways

At Napa's Oxbow Public Market, the Hog Island Oyster Co. serves the bivalves hot off the grill, with a rotating lineup of toppings. Executive chef Ian Marks shared three topping recipes with us.

SERVES 8 as an appetizer | **TIME** 15 minutes, plus 1 hour for butter to chill

2 dozen large oysters on the half-shell *(see Quick Tip below)*, such as Hog Island Sweetwaters or Fanny Bays
Topping of your choice *(recipes follow)*
At least 2 cups rock salt for lining platter
Lemon wedges

1. Prepare a charcoal or gas grill for direct medium-high heat *(see Direct Heat Grilling, page 436)*. Spread rock salt on a platter large enough to hold oysters in a single layer.
2. Set oysters in shells on cooking grate (balance on bars so they won't roll over) and top each with about 1½ tsp. topping (about ¼-in. slice of log). Close lid on grill and cook oysters just until juices are bubbling around the edges, 4 to 5 minutes.
3. Meanwhile, line a platter with rock salt. With tongs, carefully lift oysters from grate, keeping them level so juices don't spill, and nestle them in the salt. Garnish with lemon wedges and serve hot.

Quick Tip: Have your fishmonger shuck the oysters if you like; just ask that the juices stay in the shells to keep the oysters moist. (To shuck them yourself, *see How to Shuck an Oyster, page 47*) Keep them cold and as level as possible in transport to avoid losing the liquid, and use them as soon as you can.

Bagna Cauda Butter: In a mortar with a pestle or on a cutting board using a fork, mash 1 large **garlic** clove, peeled, with ¼ tsp. **kosher salt** into a paste. Add 1 canned **anchovy fillet** and continue mashing until incorporated. Scrape into a bowl and add ½ cup room-temperature **unsalted butter**, ¼ cup chopped **flat-leaf parsley**, and 1 tbsp. chopped **capers**. Mix well. Spoon across a piece of plastic wrap and roll up into a 1½-in.-thick log. Chill at least 1 hour and up to 1 week. With a sharp knife, cut into slices about ¼ in. thick to top oysters. Makes about ¾ cup, enough to top 2 dozen oysters.

PER OYSTER WITH 1½ TSP. TOPPING: 49 cal., 82% (40 cal.) from fat; 1.6 g protein; 4.4 g fat (2.5 g sat.); 1 g carbo (0 g fiber); 97 mg sodium; 22 mg chol.

Casino Butter: In a medium frying pan over medium-high heat, cook 2 slices **thick-cut bacon**, turning as necessary, until browned but not completely crisp, 4 to 5 minutes. Transfer to paper towels to drain; when cool, finely chop. In a bowl, mix chopped bacon with ½ cup room-temperature **unsalted butter**, 3 tbsp. minced **shallots**, 2 tsp. **sweet smoked Spanish paprika** (find at gourmet grocery stores) or **sweet Hungarian paprika**, and 1 tsp. chopped **thyme** leaves. Spoon across a piece of plastic wrap and roll up into a 1½-in.-thick log. Chill at least 1 hour and up to 1 week. With a sharp knife, cut into slices about ¼ in. thick to top oysters. Makes about ¾ cup, enough to top about 2 dozen oysters.

PER OYSTER WITH 1½ TSP. TOPPING: 55 cal., 78% (43 cal.) from fat; 1.8 g protein; 4.8 g fat (2.7 g sat.); 1.1 g carbo (0 g fiber); 38 mg sodium; 23 mg chol.

Langosta Butter: In a medium bowl, mix ½ cup room-temperature **butter**, ⅓ cup (2 oz.) chopped **cooked lobster meat**, ¼ cup chopped **cilantro**, and 2 tsp. finely shredded **Meyer or regular lemon zest**. Spoon across a piece of plastic wrap and roll up into a 1½-in.-thick log. Chill at least 1 hour and up to 3 days. With a sharp knife, cut into slices about ¼ in. thick to top oysters. Makes about 1 cup, enough to top about 2 dozen oysters, with some left over.

PER OYSTER WITH 1½ TSP. TOPPING: 51 cal., 78% (40 cal.) from fat; 2 g protein; 4.4 g fat (2.5 g sat.); 0.9 g carbo (0 g fiber); 72 mg sodium; 24 mg chol.

Barbecued Oysters by the Bay

Six oyster farms operate in and around Tomales Bay, a 12-mile-long sliver of water separating Point Reyes National Seashore from the mainland, about an hour's drive north of San Francisco. Oysters do well in (and taste best from) a pristine environment, and Tomales Bay, one of the cleanest bodies of water on the West Coast, produces briny-sweet oysters. The area has been oyster country for centuries; the indigenous Coast Miwok were eating tiny wild Olympia oysters, now rare, out of the bay thousands of years ago.

HOT AND SIZZLING. Today, Tomales Bay is famous not just for its oysters (primarily Pacifics, *Crassostrea gigas*), but also for its preferred preparation: barbecued—which is to say, grilled.

Like so many good foods, a Tomales Bay barbecued oyster is super-simple. The oyster, ideally freshly plucked from the bay, is shucked and nestled on the half-shell between the bars of a hot cooking grate. It sizzles for a minute, maybe two. While it's cooking or just afterward, a squirt of barbecue sauce goes onto the tender meat. Bubbling and spitting a little, the hot, fragrant oyster is quickly transferred with tongs onto a plate with several more of its kind and immediately served to the waiting diner.

PICK YOUR FAVORITE. Restaurants up and down both sides of the bay serve barbecued oysters, each slightly differently. Tony's Seafood, in Marshall, slathers giant 4-inchers with plenty of dark, sweet-spicy sauce; at the Marshall Store, daintier Pacifics, harvested from the owner's own beds nearby, get a fat drop of homemade barbecue sauce and a drizzle of herbed garlic butter. There's also the DIY BBQ oyster: At Hog Island Oyster Company and Tomales Bay Oyster Co., you buy the oysters in a big dripping bag, then cook them yourself on little grills set up in a picnic area for that purpose. The sauce is up to you.

Grilled Corn and Pepper Bisque

The only cooking involved in this soup from reader Roxanne Chan, of Albany, California, takes place on the grill.

MAKES 6 cups; 4 to 6 servings | **TIME** 1 hour, plus 1 hour to chill

4 ears corn (2½ lbs. total), husked and silks removed
1 lb. red bell peppers, halved lengthwise and seeds and ribs removed
2 green onions (white and pale green parts only), trimmed
1 jalapeño chile, halved lengthwise and seeds and ribs removed
About 2 tsp. olive oil
¼ cup sour cream
2 tbsp. chopped cilantro
1 tsp. ground cumin
2 cans (14.5 oz. each) chicken broth
1 tbsp. fresh lime juice
Salt and freshly ground black pepper
1 firm-ripe avocado (6 oz.)

1. Prepare a charcoal or gas grill for direct high heat (*see Direct Heat Grilling, page 436*). Rub corn, bell peppers, green onions, and jalapeño lightly with oil. Lay vegetables on hot grill (close lid on gas grill). Cook, turning occasionally, until slightly charred, about 5 minutes total for green onions and jalapeño, 10 to 12 minutes total for other vegetables. Let cool.
2. Cut corn kernels from cobs; chop bell peppers, green onions, and jalapeño. In a blender, purée sour cream, cilantro, cumin, green onions, jalapeño, half the broth, and half the corn until smooth. Pour into a bowl. Stir in remaining broth and corn, the lime juice, bell peppers, and salt and pepper to taste.
3. Chill soup until cold, at least 1 hour and up to 1 day. Just before serving, pit, peel, and dice avocado. Ladle soup into bowls and top with avocado.

PER SERVING: 167 cal., 41% (69 cal.) from fat; 8.2 g protein; 7.7 g fat (2.1 g sat.); 20 g carbo (3.8 g fiber); 64 mg sodium; 4.2 mg chol.

Grilled Yellow Squash and Zucchini Pasta Salad

Here's a great way to use summer's abundant squashes. Toasted pine nuts and briny kalamata olives make this salad a standout. You'll need 10- to 12-in. metal skewers.

SERVES 15 as a side dish | **TIME** 1 hour

1 lb. farfalle (bow tie) pasta
1 lb. yellow summer (crookneck) squash, cut into 1-in. chunks
1 lb. zucchini, halved lengthwise and cut into 1-in. chunks
½ cup olive oil, divided
Salt
2 tbsp. Champagne vinegar
½ tsp. freshly ground black pepper
2 tbsp. chopped oregano leaves
¼ to ½ cup pine nuts, toasted (*see How to Toast Nuts, page 134*)
¼ cup chopped pitted kalamata olives

1. Prepare a charcoal or gas grill for direct medium heat (*see Direct Heat Grilling, page 436*). Meanwhile, cook pasta in a large pot of boiling salted water until tender to the bite, 9 to 12 minutes. Drain and rinse thoroughly under cold running water until completely cool.
2. Thread squash and zucchini chunks onto skewers and place on a baking sheet. Brush vegetables with ¼ to ⅓ cup oil on all sides and sprinkle with salt to taste. Transfer skewers to cooking grate (reserve baking sheet with oil). Grill skewers (close lid on gas grill), turning occasionally, until vegetables are very tender, 10 to 15 minutes.
3. Meanwhile, whisk together remaining oil, the vinegar, and pepper in a small bowl.
4. With a fork, push vegetables off skewers back onto reserved baking sheet with oil and stir to coat vegetables. In a large bowl, toss pasta, vegetables, oregano, pine nuts, and olives. Add dressing and salt and pepper to taste; toss. Serve warm or cold.
Make Ahead: Prep vegetables and cook pasta up to 1 day; chill (add 1 tbsp. extra-virgin olive oil to cooked pasta). Toss everything together just before serving.

PER 1-CUP SERVING: 207 cal., 41% (86 cal.) from fat; 5.1 g protein; 9.5 g fat (1.3 g sat.); 26 g carbo (1.4 g fiber); 212 mg sodium; 0 mg chol.

the fire outside

Grilled Lettuces with Manchego

Little Gem, a type of miniature romaine lettuce, is perfect for this recipe because its leaves are long and closely stacked rather than loose and floppy. Hearts of regular romaine work too.

SERVES 4 as a side dish | **TIME** 20 minutes

3 canned anchovy fillets, drained and finely
   chopped
2 to 2½ tbsp. extra-virgin olive oil
1 tbsp. fresh lemon juice
Salt and freshly ground black pepper
2 whole small Little Gem lettuces or 4 hearts
   of romaine
2 oz. manchego cheese, shaved into thin curls with
   a vegetable peeler
1 lemon, cut into wedges

1. With flat side of a knife, mash anchovies to a paste. In a small bowl, whisk together oil, lemon juice, anchovy paste, and salt and pepper to taste.
2. Cut lettuces in half lengthwise, keeping leaves attached to cores. Brush all over with 1½ to 2 tbsp. anchovy dressing.
3. Prepare a charcoal or gas grill for direct medium-high heat *(see Direct Heat Grilling, page 436)*. Grill lettuces (close lid on gas grill), turning once, until they are softened and streaked brown, about 8 minutes.
4. Place lettuces cut side up on a platter. Drizzle remaining dressing over lettuces and top with manchego curls. Serve with lemon wedges.

PER SERVING: 149 cal., 79% (117 cal.) from fat; 6.2 g protein; 13 g fat (4.8 g sat.); 5.2 g carbo (2.7 g fiber); 206 mg sodium; 17 mg chol.

■ Spring Lettuces

FROM THE GARDEN

At the same time that Little Gem lettuce starts showing up at farmers' markets, look for these other lovely varieties: *black-seeded Simpson*, a fast-growing old-fashioned variety with a pale-green hue; *perilla* (its Spanish name means "knob"), which grows in tight round clusters; *Forellenschluss*, a thick-leafed variety from Austria (its name is German for "speckled trout," which describes its maroon spots); and *brunia*, a French variety of red oak-leaf lettuce and one of the prettiest, with slender, deeply notched leaves tinged reddish bronze.

Grilled Eggplant with Tomato-Caper Vinaigrette

The salty capers and vinegar nicely offset the rich flavor of the eggplant.

SERVES 6 as a salad; 12 as an appetizer
TIME 1 hour

recipe pictured on page 452

2 eggplants (about 1 lb. each)
About ¾ cup olive oil, divided
1 Roma tomato (about ¼ lb.)
2 tbsp. *each* red wine vinegar and sherry
   vinegar
1½ tsp. minced capers
1 tsp. *each* chopped shallots, chopped garlic,
   and chopped basil leaves
Salt and freshly ground black pepper
Basil sprigs

1. Prepare a charcoal or gas grill for direct medium heat *(see Direct Heat Grilling, page 436)*. Cut eggplants crosswise in ⅜-in.-thick rounds and brush slices lightly with about ¼ cup oil.
2. Grill eggplant (close lid on gas grill), turning once, until very soft, 8 to 10 minutes.
3. Finely chop tomato and mix with remaining ½ cup oil, both vinegars, capers, shallots, garlic, and chopped basil.
4. Arrange eggplant slices on a platter and drizzle with tomato dressing. Season with salt and pepper and top with basil sprigs.
Make Ahead: Through step 2, up to 3 hours at room temperature and up to 1 day, chilled. Vinaigrette, up to 1 day, chilled.

PER SALAD SERVING: 282 cal., 86% (242 cal.) from fat; 1.8 g protein; 27 g fat (3.8 g sat.); 9.7 g carbo (5.4 g fiber); 26 mg sodium; 0 mg chol.

Grilled Chicken on Greens with Creamy Harissa Dressing

We breathed new life into the bistro standby of sliced chicken on greens by adding harissa, a fiery Tunisian chile paste laced with coriander, garlic, cumin, and caraway.

SERVES 4 as a main course | **TIME** 1 hour, plus 3 hours to marinate

1 lb. skinned, boned chicken breast halves (2 to 3 halves)
1 tsp. finely shredded lemon zest
1 tbsp. olive oil
¾ tsp. *each* salt and freshly ground black pepper, divided
½ tsp. sweet smoked Spanish paprika (*see Quick Tips, above right*) or hot Hungarian paprika
½ tsp. ground cumin
½ medium red onion, halved crosswise and thinly sliced into half-moons
1 cup plain low-fat yogurt
About 1 tsp. harissa (*see Quick Tips, above right*)
1 tbsp. chopped mint leaves, plus more for garnish
2 tsp. fresh lemon juice
8 cups loosely packed mixed baby greens
1 cup 2-in.-long carrot matchsticks (from 1 medium carrot)
½ red bell pepper, seeds and ribs removed and very thinly sliced lengthwise into strips
¼ cup quartered, pitted kalamata olives

1. Make a slice through each chicken breast half parallel to the work surface, slicing from the side to the center, and open up like a book. One at a time, put each piece between sheets of plastic wrap and pound with a meat mallet or the back of a small, heavy saucepan until ¼ in. thick. Whisk together lemon zest, oil, ½ tsp. each salt and pepper, paprika, and cumin in a small bowl. Put chicken breasts in a large, wide bowl and add marinade, rubbing all over to coat. Cover and chill at least 3 hours and up to overnight. Allow chicken to come to room temperature before grilling. Meanwhile, rinse onion and blot dry with paper towels.
2. Prepare a charcoal or gas grill for direct medium heat (*see Direct Heat Grilling, page 436*). Grill chicken (close lid on gas grill), turning once, until cooked through (cut to test), 6 to 8 minutes. Transfer chicken to a plate or cutting board, tent with foil, and let rest 5 minutes.
3. Meanwhile, whisk together yogurt, harissa, mint, remaining ¼ tsp. each salt and pepper, and the lemon juice in a small bowl. Slice chicken on a diagonal across the grain into ¼-in.-thick strips.
4. In a large bowl, toss together greens, carrot, bell pepper, onion, and olives with ½ cup dressing until just coated.

5. Divide salad among plates and top with chicken. Drizzle remaining dressing over salads and garnish with mint.
Quick Tips: You can buy smoked paprika and harissa at specialty-foods stores. The heat level of harissa depends on the brand, so start with a little and add more from there.

PER SERVING: 274 cal., 27% (73 cal.) from fat; 32 g protein; 8.1 g fat (1.7 g sat.); 17 g carbo (3.9 g fiber); 739 mg sodium; 69 mg chol.

Grilled Chicken Pita Salad

The flavors of the Mediterranean come together in a lovely salad. We prefer the chicken grilled and sliced, but if you're pressed for time, you can easily substitute 2 cups shredded rotisserie chicken from the deli.

recipe pictured on **cover**

SERVES 4 | **TIME** 30 minutes

2 skinned, boned chicken breast halves (1 lb. total)
About 6 tbsp. extra-virgin olive oil, divided
2 tbsp. fresh lemon juice
1 tbsp. fresh oregano leaves
½ tsp. freshly ground black pepper
1 bunch asparagus, trimmed and cut in half lengthwise
¼ lb. block feta cheese, broken into chunks
2 cups halved grape tomatoes
½ cup pitted kalamata olives
2 cups pita chips
2 cups loosely packed baby arugula

1. Prepare a charcoal or gas grill for direct high heat (*see Direct Heat Grilling, page 436*). Coat chicken breasts with 1 tbsp. oil and cook, turning once, until no longer pink in the center (cut to test) and grill marks appear, about 7 minutes total. Let rest 10 minutes, then slice.
2. Meanwhile, in a small bowl, whisk lemon juice, remaining 5 tbsp. oil, the oregano, and pepper; set aside. Bring a medium pot of salted water to a boil, drop in asparagus, and cook until bright green, about 2 minutes. Drain and rinse thoroughly with cold water.
3. In a medium bowl, combine chicken, feta, asparagus, tomatoes, olives, and pita chips. Pour dressing over mixture and toss gently to coat. Add arugula and toss once more just to combine before serving.

PER SERVING: 563 cal., 55% (309 cal.) from fat; 35 g protein; 35 g fat (7.3 g sat.); 29 g carbo (3.9 g fiber); 978 mg sodium; 91 mg chol.

Grilled Cilantro Chicken
with Pickled Tomato and
Avocado Salsa, *page 473*

449

Barbecued Glazed Turkey,
page 479

Chili-Lime Corn on the Cob,
page 513

Grilled Eggplant with
Tomato-Caper Vinaigrette,
page 447

Grilled Rib-eye Steaks with Miso Butter and Sweet Onions, *page 482*

Cedar-planked Salmon,
page 506

Barbecued Oysters with Chipotle Glaze, *page 444*

Santa Maria–style Grilled
Tri-tip, Salsa, Grilled Garlic
Bread, and Pinquito Beans,
page 486

Grilled Artichokes with
Green-olive Dip, *page 440*

Salt-cured Ouzo
Shrimp, *page 510*

Herb-rubbed Baby Back Ribs
with Cherry–Zinfandel
Barebecue Sauce, *page 492*

Crazed Mom's Easy Steak
and Garam Masala
Naan-wiches, *page 461*

Hot Flank Steak Salad with Chinese Black Bean Dressing

This lively, colorful dish takes a West Coast approach to Eastern flavors.

SERVES 6 | **TIME** 1 hour

1 beef flank steak (1½ to 1¾ lbs.), fat trimmed
5 tbsp. soy sauce, divided
1 tbsp. vegetable oil
1 cup reduced-sodium chicken broth
¼ cup rinsed salted fermented black beans (*see Quick Tip below*)
3 tbsp. *each* dry sherry and minced fresh ginger
6 tbsp. unseasoned rice vinegar
2 tbsp. cornstarch, blended smoothly with 2 tbsp. water
1½ tbsp. light brown sugar
½ cup salted peanuts
About 15 large romaine leaves
¾ cup finely diced red bell pepper
½ cup thinly sliced green onions
½ cup cilantro leaves

1. Rub steak with 1 tbsp. soy sauce and the oil.
2. Prepare a charcoal or gas grill for very high direct heat (*see Direct Heat Grilling, page 436*). Grill (close lid on gas grill), turning once, until firm when pressed on thin end but still quite pink inside (cut to test), 8 to 10 minutes. Transfer steak to a plate. Let cool at least 30 minutes.
3. On a board with a sharp knife, cut steak across the grain, straight up and down, into very thin slices, keeping slices in place. Cut steak lengthwise to divide slices into halves or quarters (if slices are very long).
4. Combine remaining 4 tbsp. soy sauce, the broth, black beans, sherry, ginger, vinegar, cornstarch mixture, and brown sugar. In a large frying pan, stir dressing over high heat until boiling. Add steak and juices; stir until hot, about 2 minutes. Remove from heat.
5. Put peanuts in a resealable plastic bag and coarsely crush with a meat mallet or bottom of a small, heavy skillet. Stack lettuce leaves and cut thinly crosswise.
6. Mound lettuce in wide salad or soup bowls. Spoon hot steak and dressing onto greens; sprinkle with bell pepper, green onions, and peanuts. Garnish with cilantro.
Quick Tip: Find salted fermented black beans in Asian markets.
Make Ahead: Grill steak up to 1 day ahead and chill; dressing, 1 day ahead, chilled (stir well before using).

PER SERVING: 296 cal., 49% (144 cal.) from fat; 24 g protein; 16 g fat (4 g sat.); 13 g carbo (2.1 g fiber); 1,404 mg sodium; 45 mg chol.

Crazed Mom's Easy Steak and Garam Masala *Naan*-wiches

recipe pictured on page **460**

Question: Is it possible to make dinner in about an hour while simultaneously grocery shopping for the week? Yes—if you throw a flank steak (very thin, fast-cooking) in a marinade, get someone else in your family to light the fire and set the table, rush off to a nearby grocery store and careen through aisles while piling food in the cart, zoom back home, and toss the meat on the grill. While it's cooking, make sauce from the marinade, warm up the bread, and put watercress in a bowl. Slice the meat and sit down to eat!

SERVES 6 | **TIME** 20 minutes, plus 1 hour to marinate

¼ cup olive oil
1½ tbsp. fresh lemon juice
1½ tsp. garam masala (*see Quick Tip below*)
½ tsp. salt, plus more to taste
½ tsp. freshly ground black pepper
1 beef flank steak (about 1 lb.), fat trimmed
6 *naan* breads, about 3½ by 8 in. (1½ lbs. total)
3 cups very loosely packed watercress sprigs

1. In an 8- or 9-in.-square baking dish, mix oil, lemon juice, garam masala, salt, and pepper. Turn steak in mixture and marinate at room temperature 1 hour.
2. Prepare a charcoal or gas grill for very high direct heat (*see Direct Heat Grilling, page 436*). Preheat cooking grate for at least 10 minutes.
3. Pour marinade into a small pan and bring to a simmer; remove from heat. Pour 1 tbsp. water into a blender, turn on, drizzle in marinade, and blend to emulsify.
4. Lay steak on cooking grate, close lid on grill, and grill steak, turning once, about 5 minutes for medium-rare (cut to test). Transfer to a board and loosely cover with foil.
5. Grill *naan*, turning once, until hot and slightly crusty, 1 to 2 minutes. Transfer to board.
6. Thinly slice steak across grain. Let each person arrange meat and watercress over half of each *naan*. Drizzle sauce on top, sprinkle with salt to taste, and fold *naan* in half to make a sandwich.
Quick Tip: Garam masala is available in the spice section of many supermarkets; if you cannot find it, substitute 1 tsp. cinnamon, ½ tsp. *each* ground cumin and freshly ground black pepper, and ¼ tsp. *each* ground cardamom, nutmeg, cloves, and cayenne.

PER NAAN-WICH: 457 cal., 41% (189 cal.) from fat; 25 g protein; 21 g fat (6.9 g sat.); 28 g carbo (2.9 g fiber); 764 mg sodium; 38 mg chol.

Vietnamese-style Steak Salad

We tested this salad using grass-fed beef, which is leaner than regular beef and cooks a lot faster. Because it's so lean, don't cook it beyond medium-rare—otherwise it will be tough.

SERVES 4 | **TIME** 1¾ hours, plus 1 hour to marinate

RUB & STEAKS

3 stalks fresh lemongrass
2 quarter-size slices fresh ginger
1 garlic clove, quartered
1 medium shallot, sliced
1 tbsp. vegetable oil
1¼ tsp. kosher salt, divided
2 New York beef strip steaks (½ lb. each), fat trimmed, or 1 beef skirt steak (1 lb. total), preferably grass fed

VINAIGRETTE

½ cup vegetable oil
8 large garlic cloves, very thinly sliced
⅓ cup fresh lime juice (from 3 or 4 large limes)
2 tsp. sugar
2 tbsp. Thai or Vietnamese fish sauce (*nam pla* or *nuoc mam*)

SALAD

¼ lb. thin rice-stick noodles (*see A Brief Guide to Asian Noodles, page 215*)
½ cup shredded carrot
1 cup thinly sliced cucumber
2 qts. chopped napa cabbage
¼ cup *each* chopped cilantro, mint leaves, and green onions

1. Make rub: Pull off tough outer layers of lemongrass and cut off stem end and coarse leaves. Chop tender inner stalk and very finely chop in a food processor, scraping down bowl sides as needed. Add ginger, garlic, and shallot and process until a paste forms, 2 to 3 minutes more. Add oil and ¼ tsp. salt; pulse to combine.
2. Sprinkle steaks with remaining 1 tsp. salt, then cover both sides with lemongrass rub. Chill at least 1 hour and up to 6.
3. Make vinaigrette: Heat oil in a medium frying pan over medium heat. Add garlic and cook until light golden, stirring gently, being careful not to burn (it will continue to darken off the heat). Pour garlic and oil through a strainer into a small, heatproof mixing bowl. Lift out garlic chips, reserving oil, and drain chips on paper towels. After oil has cooled slightly, whisk in lime juice, sugar, and fish sauce.
4. Make salad: In a 4-qt. saucepan, bring 2 qts. water to a boil and add rice noodles. Cook until tender, 3 to 5 minutes. Drain and put in a large bowl. Add carrot, cucumber, cabbage, cilantro, mint, and green onions.

5. Prepare a charcoal or gas grill for direct high heat (*see Direct Heat Grilling, page 436*). Grill steaks (close lid on gas grill), using a wide spatula to turn once (keeping as much of crust on steaks as possible), about 8 minutes total for medium-rare. Transfer steaks to a cutting board, tent with foil, and let rest at least 5 minutes.
6. Pour vinaigrette over salad and toss thoroughly. Divide salad among bowls. Slice steaks (trying to keep crust on slices) and arrange over salads. Sprinkle with garlic chips.
Make Ahead: Rub, vinaigrette, and salad, several hours ahead; toss salad together while steaks grill.

PER SERVING: 584 cal., 59% (342 cal.) from fat; 24 g protein; 38 g fat (6.5 g sat.); 37 g carbo (3.5 g fiber); 729 mg sodium; 49 mg chol.

Grilled Ahi Citrus Salad

Reader Mickey Strang, of McKinleyville, California, likes to serve this quick salad with classic accompaniments—crusty, buttery sourdough bread and a glass of Sauvignon Blanc or Pinot Gris.

SERVES 4 | **TIME** 30 minutes

2 tbsp. *each* honey and Dijon mustard
4 ahi tuna steaks (*see Quick Tip below*), about 6 oz. each
⅓ cup olive oil
2 tbsp. *each* Champagne vinegar and fresh lime juice
6 oz. mixed baby greens (3 qts. lightly packed)
½ cup thinly sliced sweet onion, such as Walla Walla or Maui
¼ tsp. *each* kosher salt and freshly ground black pepper
2 navel oranges, peeled and cut into half-moons
2 large firm-ripe avocados, pitted, peeled, and sliced

1. In a small bowl, combine honey and mustard. Rub tuna with mixture and let marinate at room temperature 10 minutes.
2. Prepare a charcoal or gas grill for direct medium heat (*see Direct Heat Grilling, page 436*). Grill tuna (close lid on gas grill) just until grill marks appear but tuna is still rare inside, 1 to 2 minutes on each side. Cut each steak across the grain into ¼-in.-thick slices.
3. In a small bowl, combine oil, vinegar, and lime juice. In a medium bowl, combine greens, onion, salt, pepper, oranges, avocados, and two-thirds of vinaigrette; toss to coat. Divide salad among plates and arrange tuna slices on top. Serve with remaining vinaigrette on the side.
Quick Tip: Look for troll- or pole-caught tuna; it's more sustainably fished than longline.

PER SERVING: 695 cal., 58% (405 cal.) from fat; 44 g protein; 45 g fat (7.6 g sat.); 30 g carbo (5 g fiber); 339 mg sodium; 65 mg chol.

Grill-roasted Vegetable Pita Sandwiches with Grilled Lamb

Roasting summer produce—eggplant, tomato, zucchini, and peppers—on a baking sheet on the grill yields silky, melt-in-your-mouth vegetables (and the baking sheet keeps the pieces from falling through the grate). We tuck the vegetables into pita pockets with or without chunks of skewer-grilled lamb. You'll need four metal skewers (each 10 to 12 in.).

MAKES 8 to 10 mini pita sandwiches or 4 or 5 regular-size pita sandwiches | **TIME** 1½ hours, plus 3 hours to marinate

9 tbsp. extra-virgin olive oil, divided
¼ cup soy sauce
2 tbsp. Worcestershire sauce
½ cup red wine
3 tsp. kosher salt, divided
1½ tsp. freshly ground black pepper, divided
2 lbs. lamb (leg, shank, neck, or loin) cut into
   1½-in. chunks
2 red bell peppers, seeds and ribs removed and cut into
   ¾-in.-wide wedges
2 red onions, cut into 1-in.-wide wedges
1 large eggplant, quartered lengthwise and cut into
   1-in.-thick slices
2 small zucchini, cut crosswise into ¼-in.-thick slices
3 Roma tomatoes, quartered lengthwise and seeded
3 garlic cloves, chopped
3 tbsp. balsamic vinegar
¼ cup coarsely chopped walnuts, toasted (see
   How to Toast Nuts, page 134)
½ cup crumbled feta cheese
8 to 10 mini pitas or 4 or 5 regular pitas, halved

1. In a large bowl, whisk together 2 tbsp. oil, the soy sauce, Worcestershire, wine, 1 tsp. salt, and ½ tsp. pepper. Stir in lamb and refrigerate 3 hours or overnight.
2. Prepare a charcoal or gas grill for indirect medium heat (*see Indirect Heat Grilling, page 436*).
3. In a large bowl, toss peppers, onions, eggplant, zucchini, tomatoes, and garlic with remaining 7 tbsp. oil, 2 tsp. salt, and 1 tsp. pepper. Transfer vegetables to a rimmed baking sheet (not nonstick).
4. Put baking sheet on indirect-heat area and cook until vegetables begin to get very tender, 30 to 60 minutes, tossing vegetables every 15 minutes. Drizzle vegetables with vinegar, toss to coat, and cook 15 minutes more. Remove baking sheet from grill and let vegetables cool.
5. Prepare grill for lamb: If using gas, turn all burners to medium-high. If using charcoal, add about 5 briquets

(if coals look significantly burned down) to bring heat back to medium-high.
6. Meanwhile, toss toasted walnuts with feta and cooled vegetables.
7. Thread lamb onto skewers and grill 5 minutes per side for medium (if using charcoal, grill over direct heat). With a fork, push lamb off skewers and into a bowl.
8. Spoon vegetable mixture into halved pita and top with lamb.

Make Ahead: Grill vegetables up to a day ahead and chill. Allow to come to room temperature and toss in feta and walnuts before serving.

PER MINI SANDWICH: 467 cal., 54% (252 cal.) from fat; 26 g protein; 28 g fat (8.2 g sat.); 29 g carbo (3 g fiber); 987 mg sodium; 77 mg chol.

Grilled Open-face Ham, Brie, and Arugula Sandwiches

Reader Karen Biggs, of Lake Forest Park, Washington, came up with these salad-topped yet luxurious sandwiches. You can make a lot of them in a hurry, so it's a good lunch for feeding a crowd.

MAKES 20 sandwiches | **TIME** 20 minutes

¼ cup olive oil, plus more for grilling bread
Juice and finely shredded zest of 1 lemon
1 garlic clove, minced
1 tsp. sugar
Salt and freshly ground black pepper
20 slices (½- to ¾-in. thick) ciabatta (from 1 loaf)
1 lb. brie cheese, cut into ¼- by 2-in. slices
¾ lb. ham, thinly sliced
About ½ lb. arugula

1. In a blender, pulse oil, lemon juice and zest, garlic, sugar, and salt and pepper to taste to combine.
2. Preheat a charcoal or gas grill for direct medium heat (*see Direct Heat Grilling, page 436*). Brush oil on both sides of bread and put on cooking grate; sprinkle with salt and pepper. Grill 2 minutes. Turn over, top with brie and close lid on grill. Grill until cheese melts, 1 to 2 minutes.
3. Top cheese with ham slices. In a large bowl, toss arugula with vinaigrette and arrange a handful on each sandwich. Drizzle remaining vinaigrette over sandwiches.

PER SANDWICH: 245 cal., 59% (144 cal.) from fat; 12 g protein; 16 g fat (4.9 g sat.); 22 g carbo (1.2 g fiber); 580 mg sodium; 32 mg chol.

Luau: The Ultimate Island Feast

Huge celebratory feasts have long been a tradition in Polynesia, of which Hawaii is geographically and culturally a part. And the luau—originally known as *'aha'aina* ("gathering")—was the way 19th-century Hawaiian royalty showed hospitality to guests. The word *luau* was, it's said, popularized by some of those guests: European sailors and traders who attended the lavish meals, which could last for weeks, noted a dish called "leuhow" or "loohow"—young, tender taro leaves (luau), mixed with chicken, fish, or pork and baked in coconut milk.

PIG IS KING As captivating as luau chicken seems to have been, the best-known item at today's luau (a version of which is usually included on the "Hawaiian plate" at restaurants across the state) is *kalua* pig. *Kalua*, meaning "the hole," refers to an underground oven. The traditional recipe involves digging a large hole, starting a fire with guava branches, and adding lava rocks to retain the heat. A whole pig is set in the hole, and other ingredients—such as sweet potatoes and fish—are often roasted with it. Damp banana or large, glossy *ti* leaves are layered into the pit to create steam, and the whole thing is covered with wet burlap bags and soil. The cooking process can take up to two days, but the succulent results are well worth the wait.

FILLING OUT THE FEAST At early luaus, the meal was eaten off fresh ti leaves set, along with elaborate floral arrangements, on mats on the ground. Guests helped themselves from large platters of food and ate with their hands—a key part of the pleasure of the feast. In fact, another luau staple—poi, the glutinous porridge of pounded taro—was described in terms of how many fingers it took to scoop it up: three-, two-, or one-finger poi. (Looser, one-finger poi is preferred today.)

Poi is still indispensable at luaus. Other foods include *lomi* salmon (fish crushed with tomatoes and sweet Maui onions), *laulau* (pork and/or fish steamed in taro or ti leaves, as in our Mahimahi Laulau, *page 66*), and *haupia* (coconut custard). And despite Hawaii's last 130 years of melting-pot cuisine—in which Chinese, Japanese, Portuguese, German, Filipino, and Korean flavors and foods have mingled—the old island tradition of the luau is still very popular. Beyond the tourist versions, it remains a meaningful ceremony for celebrating a range of special events, especially a first birthday and graduation from high school.

the fire outside

Char Siu–glazed Pork and Pineapple Buns

Chinese-style barbecued pork, or *char siu*, is popular throughout the Hawaiian Islands. We like to serve these tangy-sweet, meaty little buns at a cocktail-party version of the luau—along with Pineapple Drop cocktails (*page 76*), Caramelized Maui Onion Dip (*page 23*), Papaya and Avocado Salads (*page 142*), and Chocolate Liliko'i Parfaits (*page 693*).

SERVES 12 | **TIME** 1 hour, plus 3 hours to brine

¼ cup *each* kosher salt and packed light brown sugar
1 tbsp. Hawaiian vanilla extract *(see Quick Tip, above right)*
2 pork tenderloins (about 1 lb. each)
½ cup *each* ketchup and hoisin sauce
2 tbsp. *each* Asian (toasted) sesame oil, minced garlic, minced fresh ginger, and low-sodium soy sauce
12 slices peeled, cored fresh pineapple
24 King's Hawaiian sweet rolls or other small soft rolls, warmed on the grill if you like
1 cup cilantro sprigs

1. Make brine: In a large pot, bring 3½ cups water to a boil. Stir in salt, brown sugar, and vanilla. Chill until cool.

2. Put pork in a 9- by 13-in. pan and pour on brine. Chill at least 3 hours and up to 12.

3. Make char siu glaze: In a small bowl, mix together ketchup, hoisin, sesame oil, garlic, ginger, and soy sauce. Pour half of sauce into another small bowl.

4. Prepare a charcoal or gas grill for indirect medium heat *(see Indirect Heat Grilling, page 436)*. Lay pork over indirect-heat area, close lid on grill, and cook until an instant-read thermometer inserted into thickest part registers 135°, 15 to 20 minutes.

5. Using a pastry brush and one bowl of glaze, cover pork with glaze, reserving 2 tbsp. for pineapple. Cook pork (if you're using charcoal, add 6 to 8 briquets to maintain temperature), turning occasionally, until glaze has caramelized slightly and meat registers 145°. Transfer grilled pork to a cutting board, tent with foil, and let rest 15 minutes.

6. Lay pineapple on direct-heat area of grill, brush with reserved glaze, and cook, turning once, until grill marks appear. Remove slices from grill and cut in half.

7. Cut pork into ½-in.-thick slices. Cut a deep diagonal slit across top of each roll. Fill each roll with a piece of pork, a grilled pineapple slice, a cilantro sprig, and ½ tsp. glaze from second bowl. Serve rolls with remaining glaze for drizzling.

Quick Tip: Find aromatic Hawaiian vanilla extract at gourmet grocery stores and *hawaiianvanilla.com*; non-Hawaiian vanilla extract works too.

Make Ahead: Brine pork and make char siu glaze up to 1 day ahead and chill.

PER SERVING: 424 cal., 25% (108 cal.) from fat; 26 g protein; 12 g fat (5.2 g sat.); 53 g carbo (3.2 g fiber); 823 mg sodium; 87 mg chol.

Grilled Pizza

This dough produces crisp crust every time. Try this at your next backyard party—the pizzas can be partially grilled ahead of time, then finished in a few minutes.

MAKES 6 individual-size pizzas | **TIME** 1 hour, plus 2 hours for dough to rise

1 package (2¼ tsp.) active dry yeast
6 tbsp. olive oil, divided
4 cups flour
1½ tsp. salt
Your choice of toppings (*recipes follow*)

1. In the bowl of a stand mixer, stir yeast into 1½ cups warm water (100° to 110°). Let stand until yeast dissolves, about 5 minutes. Add ¼ cup oil, the flour, and salt. Mix with dough hook on low speed to blend, then mix on medium speed until dough is very smooth and stretchy, 8 to 10 minutes. If you don't have a stand mixer, mix in the oil, flour, and salt with a wooden spoon, then turn out on a lightly floured work surface and knead vigorously for 8 to 10 minutes, until dough is very smooth and stretchy. Cover dough; let rise at room temperature until doubled in bulk, about 1½ hours.

2. Punch down dough and let rise again until doubled, 30 to 45 minutes. Meanwhile, cut six pieces of parchment paper, each about 12 in. long. Prepare a charcoal or gas grill for direct medium heat (*see Direct Heat Grilling, page 436*).

3. Turn dough out onto a work surface and cut into six portions. For each pizza, lay a sheet of parchment on work surface and rub with 1 tsp. oil. Using well-oiled hands, put each portion of dough on a parchment sheet. Flatten dough portions, then pat into 9- to 10-in. rounds. If dough starts to shrink, let rest 5 minutes, then pat out again. Let dough stand until puffy, about 15 minutes.

4. Flip a round of dough onto cooking grate, dough side down. Peel off parchment. Put on one or two more dough rounds. Close lid and cook until dough has puffed and grill marks appear underneath, 3 minutes. Transfer rounds, grilled side up, to baking sheets. Repeat with remaining dough. (Grilled rounds can stand at room temperature up to 2 hours; reheat grill to continue.)

5. Arrange pizza toppings on grilled sides of dough. With a wide spatula, return pizzas, two or three at a time, to cooking grate and close lid on grill. Cook until browned and crisp underneath, rotating pizzas once for even cooking, 4 to 6 minutes.

Make Ahead: Complete dough through step 1, then chill, covered, at least 3 hours and up to 2 days (dough will double in size, and flavor will develop as it chills).

Coppa, Ricotta, and Arugula Pizza: Coppa, sometimes called capicola, is a delicious Italian-style cured meat eaten very thinly sliced. You can also use prosciutto, bresaola, or thinly sliced salami. Evenly spread 2 heaping spoonfuls (⅓ cup) **ricotta cheese** onto each half-grilled dough round in step 5 of Grilled Pizza, then top each pizza with 3 slices of **coppa**. Grill as directed. In a bowl, combine about 2 tbsp. **extra-virgin olive oil**, a squeeze of **fresh lemon juice**, and a pinch *each* of **salt** and **freshly ground black pepper**; toss with 5 cups (2½ oz.) **arugula**. About 1 minute before pizzas are done, scatter a generous amount of dressed arugula onto pizzas; close lid on grill and finish grilling, about 1 minute.

PER PIZZA: 643 cal., 45% (288 cal.) from fat; 22 g protein; 32 g fat (9.7 g sat.); 67 g carbo (2.8 g fiber); 980 mg sodium; 49 mg chol.

Pizza Bianca: Scatter a few slices of **white onion** and a large handful of shredded **mozzarella cheese** over each half-grilled dough round in step 5 of Grilled Pizza, then sprinkle with chopped **rosemary leaves** and a little **salt**. Grill as directed.

PER PIZZA: 587 cal., 41% (243 cal.) from fat; 20 g protein; 27 g fat (9.4 g sat.); 66 g carbo (2.6 g fiber); 796 mg sodium; 44 mg chol.

Pizza Margherita: Spread each half-grilled dough round in step 5 of Grilled Pizza with about 2 tbsp. **Ripe Tomato Pizza Sauce** (recipe follows). Evenly space 5 or 6 slices drained water-packed **fresh mozzarella cheese** over sauce. Grill as directed, then top with small whole or torn **basil leaves**.

PER PIZZA: 725 cal., 45% (324 cal.) from fat; 27 g protein; 36 g fat (14 g sat.); 73 g carbo (4.7 g fiber); 1,001 mg sodium; 67 mg chol.

Ripe Tomato Pizza Sauce: Heat 1 tbsp. **olive oil** in a saucepan over medium heat. Add 1 tbsp. minced **garlic** and cook, stirring, until fragrant, about 1 minute. Stir in 4 large chopped **tomatoes**, 1 tsp. **sugar**, ¼ tsp. **red chile flakes**, and ½ tsp. *each* **kosher salt** and **freshly ground black pepper**. Bring to a boil, reduce heat to low, and simmer, stirring often, until very thick, about 1½ hours. Stir in 1 tbsp. chopped **oregano leaves**. Makes 1 cup.

PER 2-TBSP. SERVING: 44 cal., 43% (19 cal.) from fat; 1.1 g protein; 2.1 g fat (0.3 g sat.); 6.4 g carbo (1.5 g fiber); 83 mg sodium; 0 mg chol.

Grass-fed Burgers with Chipotle Barbecue Sauce

You'll have plenty of the spicy, tangy sauce left over—try it with grilled chicken or ribs.

recipe pictured on page **380**

MAKES 4 burgers | **TIME** 35 minutes

CHIPOTLE BARBECUE SAUCE
¼ cup firmly packed light brown sugar
½ cup ketchup
2 tbsp. canned chipotle chiles in adobo sauce (about 3 chiles), plus 1 tbsp. sauce
1 tbsp. Worcestershire sauce
2 tbsp. *each* molasses and thawed orange juice concentrate
1 tsp. minced garlic
BURGERS
1¼ lbs. grass-fed ground beef (*see Better Burgers, page 468*)
2 tsp. *each* kosher salt and freshly ground black pepper, divided
1 red onion, cut ¼ to ½ in. thick crosswise
3 tsp. vegetable oil, divided
4 slices Swiss cheese
4 sesame-seed hamburger buns
4 slices ripe tomato
4 butter or romaine lettuce leaves

1. Make chipotle barbecue sauce: Purée all sauce ingredients in a blender or food processor until very smooth.
2. Make burgers: In a medium bowl, combine beef and 1½ tsp. each salt and pepper. Form into four patties, each about ¾ in. thick and slightly thinner in the center (burgers will even out while cooking). Put on a plate, cover, and chill until ready to grill.
3. Prepare a charcoal or gas grill for direct medium heat (*see Direct Heat Grilling, page 436*).
4. Sprinkle onion slices with remaining ½ tsp. each salt and pepper and 1 tsp. oil. Grill, covered, until softened, turning once, about 8 minutes total.
5. Meanwhile, rub burgers with remaining 2 tsp. oil and lay on grill. Close lid on grill and cook burgers, turning once, about 6 minutes total for medium-rare. In last few moments of cooking, lay a slice of cheese on each burger. Lay bun halves, cut side down, on cooking grate to toast slightly.
6. Transfer buns to a platter and add burgers and onions to bun bottoms. Spoon about 1½ tbsp. barbecue sauce on top of each and add a slice of tomato, a lettuce leaf, and bun tops.
Make Ahead: Sauce, 1 week, chilled.

PER BURGER, WITH 1½ TBSP. SAUCE AND TRIMMINGS: 612 cal., 50% (306 cal.) from fat; 36 g protein; 34 g fat (14 g sat.); 41 g carbo (2.3 g fiber); 1,175 mg sodium; 112 mg chol.

Gold Nugget Burger

The "gold nugget" is a thin slice of good cheddar that's tucked into the center of the patty. It oozes out with your first bite.

MAKES 4 burgers | **TIME** 30 minutes for burgers, plus 40 minutes for sauce and guacamole

1½ lbs. ground beef sirloin or chuck (*see Quick Tip below*)
½ tsp. salt, plus more to taste
¼ tsp. freshly ground black pepper, plus more to taste
8 slices (¼- by 1- by 2-in.) good-quality cheddar cheese
1 red onion (about ½ lb.), cut into ½-in.-thick slices
4 kaiser, onion, or crusty round rolls (4 in. wide), split
Sweet-and-Spicy Sauce (*recipe follows*)
1½ cups shredded iceberg lettuce
1 firm-ripe tomato (about ½ lb.), cored and thinly sliced
Classic Guacamole (*page 159*)

1. In a medium bowl, gently mix ground beef, salt, and pepper.
2. Divide meat mixture into eight equal portions and form each into a 4-in. round. Top each of four rounds with 2 slices of cheddar cheese. Lay another patty on top of each and press edges together to seal.
3. Prepare a charcoal or gas grill for direct high heat (*see Direct Heat Grilling, page 436*). Lay burgers and onion slices on hot cooking grate (close lid on gas grill). Grill burgers, turning once, until browned on both sides and done to your liking (cut to test), about 7 minutes total for medium-rare. Cook onion, also turning once, until browned on both sides, 7 to 8 minutes total. Remove from grill.
4. Lay buns, cut side down, on grill and cook until lightly toasted, 30 seconds to 1 minute.
5. Spread sauce on bun bottoms, reserving extra sauce to serve on the side. Add lettuce, tomato, burger, onion, and a dollop of guacamole to each. Set bun tops in place. Serve with remaining guacamole, sauce, and salt and pepper to add to taste.
Quick Tip: If you like your burgers on the rare side, buy the ground beef from a high-quality source or grind it yourself (*see Better Burgers, page 468*).

PER BURGER MADE WITH 10% FAT GROUND BEEF: 589 cal., 41% (243 cal.) from fat; 47 g protein; 27 g fat (12 g sat.); 38 g carbo (2.9 g fiber); 856 mg sodium; 133 mg chol.

Sweet-and-Spicy Sauce: In a 1½- to 2-qt. pan, combine ¾ cup **ketchup**, ½ cup **orange juice**, ¼ cup *each* **Worcestershire sauce** and **raisins**, 2 tbsp. **fresh lime juice**, 1 tbsp. *each* minced **fresh ginger** and **garlic**, and ½ tsp. **cayenne**. Bring to a simmer over medium heat, then reduce heat so mixture barely simmers and cook, uncovered, stirring often, until sauce is thick and reduced to 1 cup, 25 to 30 minutes. Purée mixture in a blender. Serve warm or cool. Chill airtight up to 2 weeks. Makes about 1 cup.

PER TBSP.: 27 cal., 3% (0.9 cal.) from fat; 0.5 g protein; 0.1 g fat (0 g sat.); 6.8 g carbo (0.3 g fiber); 175 mg sodium; 0 mg chol.

Grilled Rosemary Lamb Burgers with Pea and Mint Relish

Hugo Matheson, chef and co-owner of the Kitchen, in Boulder, Colorado, makes his juicy burgers with grass-fed local lamb.

MAKES 6 burgers | TIME 20 minutes, plus 2 hours to chill

1½ lbs. ground lamb
1 tbsp. chopped rosemary leaves
¼ cup chopped roasted piquillo or other red peppers *(see Quick Tip below)*
1¼ tsp. salt
Freshly ground black pepper
1 wide, crusty loaf, such as a bâtard
2 tbsp. olive oil
Pea and Mint Relish *(recipe follows)*

1. In a large bowl, mix lamb, rosemary, roasted peppers, salt, and pepper to taste. Form into six patties about ¾ in. thick. Put on a plate, cover, and refrigerate 2 hours.
2. Cut 12 slices, each about ½ in. thick, from bread; save rest of loaf for another use. Lightly brush slices all over with oil.
3. Prepare a charcoal or gas grill for direct high heat *(see Direct Heat Grilling, page 436)*. Lightly toast bread on grill, turning once, and transfer to a platter.
4. Lay burgers on cooking grate (close lid on gas grill). Grill burgers, turning once, until done to your liking, about 6 minutes for medium-rare. Set each burger on a slice of grilled bread. Top with pea relish, then remaining bread.
Quick Tip: Roasted piquillo peppers, available at specialty-foods stores and online, add a sweet, clean taste to the burgers, but you can use regular roasted red peppers instead.

PER BURGER: 418 cal., 47% (198 cal.) from fat; 24 g protein; 22 g fat (7.5 g sat.); 29 g carbo (1.8 g fiber); 890 mg sodium; 76 mg chol.

Pea and Mint Relish

This relish looks like guacamole, so the mild, fresh flavor of peas and mint is a surprise.

MAKES About ¾ cup | TIME 25 minutes

1 cup shelled fresh peas *(see Quick Tip below)*
2 tbsp. packed fresh mint leaves
1 tbsp. *each* chopped seeded red or green Fresno or jalapeño chile and extra-virgin olive oil
1½ tsp. fresh lemon juice
Salt and freshly ground black pepper

1. Blanch peas in boiling water for 30 seconds, drain, and transfer to a bowl of ice water. When cool, drain and pat dry.
2. Finely chop mint in a food processor. Add peas, chile, oil, and lemon juice. Pulse until finely chopped. Season to taste with salt and pepper.
Quick Tip: You'll need about 1 lb. pea pods for 1 cup shelled peas.
Make Ahead: Up to 2 hours, chilled.

PER 2-TBSP. SERVING: 42 cal., 52% (22 cal.) from fat; 1.5 g protein; 2.4 g fat (0.3 g sat.); 4 g carbo (1.5 g fiber); 2.7 mg sodium; 0 mg chol.

Try a Lamb Burger

It's tempting to fall back on tried-and-true fast-cooking food—like burgers—when time is tight. But ground beef doesn't have to be your only option. Ground lamb cooks as quickly as beef, and it has its own unique character that teams well with a different spectrum of seasonings, including mint, rosemary, and oregano. Ground lean lamb is available in most supermarkets. Its fat content varies, but it's usually similar to that of ground beef chuck.

USE IT OR FREEZE IT: Like any ground meat, ground lamb has a short storage life. For the freshest flavor, cook within 24 hours of purchase. Or, for future quick meals, season the meat, shape your burgers, and freeze them for up to three months.

DON'T OVERCOOK: For moist, juicy results, grill lamb burgers just until barely pink in the center. Otherwise the meat will be dry.

Better Burgers

There are burgers, and there are really good burgers. It's not hard to take burger-making to the next level. Here's how:

1. Buy the right meat. For juicy burgers, get ground chuck with a fat content of at least 18 percent. Lean and extra-lean meat make tough, dry burgers. Also, the more freshly ground the meat is, the more tender and flavorful the burger: If your store has butchers, ask them to grind the meat fresh for you. (Or just grind your own, following our no-fuss method at right.)

2. Mix in seasonings very, very gently. The more you handle the meat, the tougher your burger will be. In a large bowl, pull the meat apart into small chunks, add salt, pepper, and/or other seasonings, and toss gently with fingers spread apart until loosely mixed.

3. Use wet hands to form patties. This keeps your hands from getting sticky. It also allows the meat to come together faster, which will prevent overhandling.

4. Make patties thinner in the center. Divide meat into equal portions; form patties about ¾ in. thick at the edges and ½ in. thick in the center. They'll shrink and even out while cooking.

5. Keep meat cold until it goes on the grill. Chill the patties while the grill heats up. This helps retain more of the meat's flavor-carrying fat.

6. Use a clean, well-oiled, preheated grill. Bits of debris encourage sticking, as does an unoiled surface and too low a temperature; you want your burgers to quickly sizzle, firm up, and release from the grill.

7. Keep the grill at a steady high heat (450° to 550°; you can hold your hand 1 to 2 in. above grill level for 2 to 4 sec-onds). If using charcoal, you want ash-covered coals to produce even heat. With a gas grill, keep the lid closed while cooking; with a charcoal grill, leave the lid off.

8. Flip burgers once and at the right time. Constant turning will toughen and dry out meat, and if you flip too soon, burgers will stick. Wait until they release themselves from the grill, then flip. Cook 2 minutes per side for rare, 3 for medium-rare, 4 for medium, and 5 for well-done.

9. Don't press on the burgers while they're cooking. The juice you're pressing out holds most of the flavor and moisture.

10. Let burgers rest a few minutes before eating. This lets them finish cooking and allows their juices, which have collected on the surface during grilling, to redistribute throughout patty.

The Real Secret: Grind Your Own Meat

Grinding meat at home is not only easier than most people think, it also makes the moistest and most flavorful burgers. And, given the periodic safety concerns about commercially ground meat, home-ground is the way to go if you like your burgers cooked rare or medium. Manual meat grinders are available at kitchen supply stores, and grinder attachments for standing mixers work very well.

HOW TO GRIND MEAT:

1. For four 6-oz. burgers, buy 1½ lbs. chuck roast or sirloin, keeping a thin layer of fat on the meat.

2. For added safety, bring a large pot of water to a boil and boil the roast for 30 to 60 seconds (this kills any surface bacteria). Remove meat and rinse with cold water.

3. Cut the meat into 1-in. pieces. In a large bowl, toss meat pieces with 1 tsp. salt. Cover and refrigerate overnight.

4. Chill the grinder for 30 minutes before starting (a cold grinder works more efficiently).

5. Set up grinder according to manu-facturer's instructions, using the coarse plate or setting. Feed meat into funnel and grind, stopping to clear the grinder if necessary. Put ground meat through grinder once more and proceed with step 2 (*far left*).

Lucques Pork Burger

Chef-owner Suzanne Goin—of the Los Angeles restaurants Lucques, A.O.C., and Tavern—serves her pork burgers with an addictive chipotle aioli. For an easy version of the aioli, blend one or two canned chipotle chiles into 1 cup of mayonnaise.

MAKES 4 burgers | **TIME** 50 minutes

1½ lbs. ground pork
¼ lb. firm Spanish-style chorizo or hot Italian sausage, casing removed and crumbled
2 slices bacon, finely chopped
¼ cup *each* olive oil and minced shallots
2 tbsp. chopped flat-leaf parsley
2 tsp. fresh thyme leaves
1 tsp. ground cumin
4 hamburger buns, toasted

1. In a large bowl, mix pork, chorizo, bacon, oil, shallots, parsley, thyme, and cumin. Form mixture into four patties about ¾ in. thick.

2. Prepare a charcoal or gas grill for direct medium-high heat (*see Direct Heat Grilling, page 436*). Grill burgers (close lid on gas grill), turning once, just until no longer pink in center (except for pieces of chorizo; cut to test), 13 to 15 minutes total. Set burgers on buns.

PER BURGER: 751 cal., 64% (477 cal.) from fat; 42 g protein; 53 g fat (16 g sat.); 24 g carbo (1 g fiber); 742 mg sodium; 138 mg chol.

Double Salmon Burgers

Salmon is a welcome alternative to beef in burgers for summertime grilling. Try chum, pink, or coho—tasty salmon varieties that are less expensive than king (chinook)—for burgers.

MAKES 4 burgers | **TIME** 35 minutes

1 lb. skinned, boned salmon fillet
6 tbsp. chicken or vegetable broth
¼ cup fine dried bread crumbs
1 tbsp. chopped fresh dill or 1 tsp. dried dill
½ tsp. salt
1 egg
Vegetable or olive oil
4 soft potato rolls or English muffins (4 in. wide), cut in half horizontally
4 to 6 tbsp. smoked-salmon cream cheese spread
Butter lettuce leaves
Cucumber–Hearts of Palm Relish (*recipe follows*)

1. Cut salmon into ½-in. chunks. Pulse several times in a food processor to coarsely grind, scraping down container sides once or twice between pulses. In a bowl, with a fork, mix ground salmon with broth, bread crumbs, dill, salt, and egg until mixture is thoroughly blended.

2. With heavy-duty foil, make four strips 5 to 6 in. wide by 10 in. long. Fold each strip to form 5- to 6-in. squares, then fold in edges to seal layers. Coat one side of each foil square with oil. Divide salmon mixture into four equal portions, place a portion on oiled side of each foil square, and shape each into an evenly thick 4-in.-wide patty.

3. Prepare a charcoal or gas grill for direct high heat (*see Direct Heat Grilling, page 436*). Put salmon patties on foil on cooking grate. Close lid on grill and grill patties until firm when pressed and pale pink in center (cut to test), about 10 minutes. When patties are almost done, lay rolls, cut side down, on cooking grate and toast until golden, 1 to 2 minutes.

4. Spread toasted sides of rolls with smoked-salmon cream cheese. Layer bottom of each roll with lettuce and a salmon patty; top with relish and set roll tops in place.

Make Ahead: Through step 2 up to 1 day ahead; chill.

PER BURGER: 442 cal., 41% (180 cal.) from fat; 32 g protein; 20 g fat (5.3 g sat.); 31 g carbo (2 g fiber); 1,143 mg sodium; 130 mg chol.

Cucumber–Hearts of Palm Relish: In a bowl, combine ½ cup diced (¼ in.) seeded **English cucumber**, ½ cup thinly sliced canned **hearts of palm**, ¼ cup **unseasoned rice vinegar**, 2 tbsp. chopped **green onions**, 2 tsp. **sugar**, and ½ tsp. **salt** (or to taste). Mix and let stand at least 5 minutes or cover and chill up to 1 day. Serve with a slotted spoon. Makes about 1 cup.

PER TBSP.: 2 cal., 0% from fat; 0.2 g protein; 0.4 g carbo (0.2 g fiber); 20 mg sodium; 0 mg chol.

How to Control Flare-ups

If flames suddenly shoot up and around your food, move the food to a cooler spot on the grill and close the lid, cutting off the fire's oxygen supply. If a charcoal grill needs more flame control, close the vents on the lid and firegrate. We don't recommend squirting the fire with water because it sprays ash onto the food.

Peppered Buffalo Burgers with Relish

We're always looking for interesting ways to serve buffalo, and reader Clara Megraw, of Santa Ana, California, came through with this one. For more information on buffalo, see *Bison: The Most Western Meat, page 431.*

MAKES 4 burgers | **TIME** 1 hour, plus 2 hours to freeze butter

3 tbsp. butter, chilled in freezer 2 hours
1½ lbs. ground buffalo meat
½ tsp. *each* kosher salt and freshly ground black pepper
1 to 1½ tbsp. black peppercorns
Black-eyed Pea Relish *(recipe follows)*

1. Grate frozen butter on the coarse side of a box grater. In a large bowl, gently toss buffalo meat with butter and salt. Divide into four portions and form each into a 1-in.-thick patty that is slightly thinner in center. Put on a baking sheet or large plate and chill 30 minutes.
2. Prepare a charcoal or gas grill for direct high heat (*see Direct Heat Grilling, page 436*; alternatively, preheat broiler). Crush peppercorns with a mortar and pestle or with the bottom of a small pan. Sprinkle each patty all over with pepper.
3. Grill burgers, turning once, 2 to 3 minutes per side. Alternatively, broil burgers 2 to 3 minutes per side. Let rest a few minutes before eating. Serve with black-eyed pea relish.

PER BURGER WITHOUT RELISH: 309 cal., 57% (177 cal.) from fat; 33 g protein; 20 g fat (10 g sat.); 0.7 g carbo (0.3 g fiber); 463 mg sodium; 114 mg chol.

Black-eyed Pea Relish: Drain and rinse 1 can (15 oz.) **black-eyed peas**. In a bowl, combine peas with 1 small **onion**, diced; 3 **garlic cloves**, minced; ¼ cup *each* **olive oil** and **cider vinegar**; 2 tbsp. chopped **flat-leaf parsley**; and **salt** and **freshly ground black pepper** to taste. Relish keeps, chilled, up to 4 days.

PER TBSP.: 28 cal., 57% (16 cal.) from fat; 0.6 g protein; 1.8 g fat (0.3 g sat.); 2.4 g carbo (0.5 g fiber); 42 mg sodium; 0 mg chol.

Spice-rubbed Smoke-roasted Chicken

The wood chips and spice rub give this chicken a pervasive but gentle smokiness.

SERVES 6 | **TIME** 1¾ hours, plus 30 minutes to soak wood chips

1 cup (about 3 oz.) hickory, mesquite, or applewood chips (optional)
12 garlic cloves, peeled
1 tbsp. chili powder
⅓ cup *each* chopped thyme and rosemary leaves
¼ cup olive oil
1 tbsp. *each* salt and freshly ground black pepper
1 chicken (4 to 5 lbs.), giblets removed

1. In a medium bowl, soak wood chips, if using, in water. Let soak at least 30 minutes; drain just before they go on the grill.
2. Meanwhile, in a food processor, combine garlic, chili powder, thyme, rosemary, oil, salt, and pepper. Process until mixture forms a paste.
3. Pat chicken dry. Press down on breastbone to flatten bird slightly; rub skin with paste.
4. Prepare a charcoal or gas grill for indirect medium heat (*see Indirect Heat Grilling, page 436*). If using a gas grill, place all chips in metal smoking box or in a foil pan directly on heat in a corner. If using a charcoal grill, scatter half of wood chips over coals.
5. Place chicken over drip pan, breast side down; close lid on grill. If using a charcoal grill, adjust vents so they're open halfway. Cook 40 minutes, then turn chicken over (if using charcoal, scatter another 20 briquets over coals, along with remaining wood chips). Close lid on grill again.
6. Continue cooking chicken until an instant-read thermometer inserted into thickest part of breast to bone registers 170°, about 40 minutes longer. Transfer to a board or platter, tent with foil, and let rest 10 minutes. Carve to serve.

PER SERVING: 417 cal., 60% (252 cal.) from fat; 38 g protein; 28 g fat (6.8 g sat.); 1.8 g carbo (0.9 g fiber); 996 mg sodium; 118 mg chol.

Chicken Piri-piri

A spicy grilled dish common in southern Portugal and in Portuguese-style restaurants in Africa (*piri-piri* is a small hot chile). Traditionally, piri-piri includes a splash of lemon and a hint of garlic with its roundup of herbs and spices; we're more generous with both in our version.

SERVES 6 to 8 | **TIME** 1 hour, plus 4 hours to marinate

1 cup fresh lemon juice
¾ cup olive oil
¼ cup minced garlic
2 tbsp. red chile flakes
2 tsp. dried oregano
1 tsp. *each* dried thyme, ground cumin, and salt
2 chickens (3½ to 4 lbs. each), each cut into 8 pieces
   (see Quick Tips below)
½ cup butter
Lemon wedges

1. In a 1-qt. glass measure or a bowl, mix lemon juice, olive oil, garlic, chile flakes, oregano, thyme, cumin, and salt.
2. Trim and discard excess fat from chicken pieces. Put chicken in a large bowl. Stir piri-piri marinade, pour over the chicken, and turn to coat. Cover and chill at least 4 hours or up to 1 day, turning chicken occasionally.
3. Prepare a charcoal or gas grill for direct medium heat *(see Direct Heat Grilling, page 436)*. With tongs, lift chicken from marinade, drain well, and lay on cooking grate; close lid on gas grill. Cook, turning occasionally, until skin is well browned and meat at bone is no longer pink (cut to test), 35 to 40 minutes total; brush occasionally with marinade until about 10 minutes before chicken is done. As pieces are done, transfer to a platter and cover loosely with foil to keep warm.
4. Pour remaining marinade into a 1½- to 2-qt. pan over medium-low heat *(see Quick Tips below)*. Stirring occasionally, bring mixture to a simmer; adjust heat to maintain simmer. Add butter and stir until melted and incorporated; turn heat to low and stir occasionally until ready to serve. Pour sauce into a small bowl or pitcher.
5. Garnish chicken with lemon wedges and serve with sauce.
Quick Tips: Buy the chicken already cut into pieces or have your butcher cut it. It's important to bring the marinade to a simmer in step 4 to ensure that you have killed any bacteria from the raw chicken.
Make Ahead: Marinade (step 1), up to 3 days, chilled.

PER SERVING: 719 cal., 70% (504 cal.) from fat; 48 g protein; 56 g fat (17 g sat.); 4.7 g carbo (0.4 g fiber); 560 mg sodium; 185 mg chol.

Spatchcocked Chicken

"Spatchcocking" a chicken means splitting the bird down the back and flattening it out so it cooks more evenly and quickly. The word spatchcock, thought to have come from Ireland, refers to the speedy "dispatch" of the bird—i.e., the cooking of it—with this technique. "Butterflying" is another word for the method.

SERVES 4 | **TIME** 1 hour, plus 1 hour to marinate

1 chicken (4 to 5 lbs.), giblets removed
3 shallots (about ¼ lb.)
3 garlic cloves
½ cup flat-leaf parsley sprigs
1 tbsp. *each* herbes de Provence and fresh rosemary
   leaves
1½ tsp. kosher salt
1 tsp. freshly ground black pepper
Finely shredded zest and juice of 1 lemon
¼ cup Dijon mustard
½ cup extra-virgin olive oil

1. Pat chicken dry and put, breast side down, on a cutting board. Using poultry shears (or sturdy kitchen scissors), cut along both sides of backbone; remove backbone and open the chicken like a book. Reserve backbone for stock or discard. Turn chicken breast side up and, using heel of your hand, press firmly against breastbone until it cracks. Tuck wing tips under (toward cavity) so they don't burn on grill. Put chicken in a large rimmed baking pan.
2. In a food processor, combine remaining ingredients and pulse to make a thick paste. Transfer 1 cup paste to a separate bowl and rub over both sides of chicken. Cover chicken with plastic wrap and chill 1 hour. Set aside remaining paste.
3. Prepare a charcoal or gas grill for indirect medium heat *(see Indirect Heat Grilling, page 436)*.
4. Place chicken, skin side down, over direct heat; close lid on grill and cook until chicken has browned, about 8 minutes. Turn chicken over and move to indirect-heat area. If using charcoal, add 12 more briquets to fire to maintain medium heat. Continue cooking chicken, with the grill lid closed, turning as needed for even browning, until an instant-read thermometer inserted into thickest part of breast to bone registers 170°. Remove chicken from grill and let rest 5 minutes, then cut into quarters and serve with reserved paste.

PER SERVING: 823 cal., 65% (531 cal.) from fat; 63 g protein; 59 g fat (13 g sat.); 7.3 g carbo (0.9 g fiber); 988 mg sodium; 198 mg chol.

Grilled Chicken Thighs with Peas and Shallots

Served with shallots, pancetta, and fresh springtime peas, the chicken from the wood-fired oven of the Kitchen, in Boulder, Colorado, pairs extremely well with Belgian-style ale. (For more on pairing beer with food, *see Craft Beer in the West, page 77.*)

SERVES 6 | **TIME** 1½ hours, plus 6 hours to marinate

12 skin-on, bone-in small chicken thighs or 6 large (about 3 lbs. total), fat trimmed
3 tbsp. thin slices garlic, divided
3 tbsp. chopped rosemary leaves, divided
2 tbsp. extra-virgin olive oil
1½ tsp. kosher salt, divided
¾ tsp. freshly ground black pepper, divided
1 lb. shallots, separated into cloves and peeled
3 lbs. English peas in pod, shelled (about 3 cups), or 3 cups frozen peas *(see Quick Tip, above right)*
½ cup *each* chopped pancetta and red onion
2 tbsp. *each* chopped flat-leaf parsley and butter
3 or 4 tbsp. fresh lemon juice

1. Arrange chicken in a single layer in a 9- by 13-in. baking dish. Scatter 1½ tbsp. garlic slices over chicken, then sprinkle with 1½ tbsp. rosemary. Drizzle chicken with oil and sprinkle with 1 tsp. salt and ½ tsp. pepper. Turn to coat; chill, covered, at least 6 hours and up to overnight.
2. Prepare a charcoal or gas grill for indirect medium heat *(see Indirect Heat Grilling, page 436).*
3. Bring a large pot of salted water to a boil. Add shallots and cook until tender, 10 to 15 minutes. With a slotted spoon, transfer to a bowl and let cool; cut any large cloves into halves or quarters. Bring water back to a boil, add peas, and cook until just tender, 2 to 4 minutes. Drain peas; transfer to a bowl of ice water. When cool, drain again.
4. Pat chicken thighs dry and lay them, skin side down, over indirect-heat area; close lid. Cook 10 minutes (12 for large thighs). Turn over, close lid on grill, and cook, 10 minutes more. Move chicken over direct heat and cook, turning once, until skin is well browned and no longer pink at bone (cut to test), 3 to 5 minutes. Transfer chicken to a pan and tent with foil to keep warm.
5. In a large frying pan, cook pancetta over medium heat until fat begins to render and pancetta starts to become crisp, about 5 minutes. Add remaining 1½ tbsp. garlic, 1½ tbsp. rosemary, ½ tsp. salt, and ¼ tsp. pepper, the onion, parsley, and shallots to pancetta.

Cook, stirring, 2 minutes. Stir in peas and butter and cook until peas are heated through, about 2 minutes.
6. Divide chicken among warm plates. Sprinkle lemon juice over peas and shallots. Stir and spoon onto plates alongside chicken.
Quick Tip: If using frozen peas, don't cook them in step 3; add, still frozen, to pancetta mixture in step 5.

PER SERVING: 519 cal., 52% (270 cal.) from fat; 37 g protein; 30 g fat (10 g sat.); 25 g carbo (4.7 g fiber); 484 mg sodium; 126 mg chol.

Grilled Buttermilk Chicken

Grilled chicken is an all-American summer classic, but when you soak it in a buttermilk brine for extra-moist results and add subtle Indian-inspired seasonings, it becomes special.

SERVES 6 | **TIME** 30 minutes, plus 4 hours to brine

1 qt. buttermilk
½ cup *each* chopped shallots, chopped garlic, kosher salt, and sugar
1 tbsp. ground cumin
1 tsp. freshly ground black pepper
6 chicken thighs (about 2½ lbs. total), fat trimmed
6 chicken drumsticks (about 1¾ lbs. total), fat trimmed

1. In a large bowl, mix buttermilk, shallots, garlic, salt, sugar, cumin, and pepper.
2. Submerge chicken pieces in buttermilk brine. Cover and refrigerate for at least 4 hours and up to 1 day.
3. Lift chicken from brine; discard brine. Wipe excess from chicken with paper towels.
4. Prepare a charcoal or gas grill for direct medium heat *(see Direct Heat Grilling, page 436).* Grill chicken pieces (close lid on gas grill), turning frequently, until browned on both sides and no longer pink at bone (cut to test), 20 to 30 minutes. Serve hot or cold.
Make Ahead: Brine chicken up to 1 day before grilling; grill up to 1 day before serving and chill airtight. If grilling away from home, transport in brine, well chilled in an ice chest.

PER SERVING: 402 cal., 51% (207 cal.) from fat; 43 g protein; 23 g fat (6.4 g sat.); 4 g carbo (0.1 g fiber); 670 mg sodium; 149 mg chol.

Grilled Cilantro Chicken with Pickled Tomato and Avocado Salsa

We're nuts about this flavorful, unusual chicken recipe from Mary Sue Milliken and Susan Feniger of Ciudad in Los Angeles and Border Grill in Santa Monica and Las Vegas. The chefs marinate the chicken very simply and then spoon an addictive Indian-style pickled salsa on top.

recipe pictured
on page
449

SERVES 4 | **TIME** 1½ hours, plus 1 hour to chill salsa

PICKLED TOMATO AND AVOCADO SALSA

1 lb. medium beefsteak-type tomatoes, quartered and seeds squeezed out
2 serrano chiles, stemmed and thinly sliced
½ cup *each* thinly sliced green onions and distilled white vinegar
2½ tbsp. firmly packed brown sugar
1½ tsp. kosher salt
4 tsp. minced fresh ginger
1 tbsp. minced garlic
2 tsp. *each* mustard seeds, freshly cracked black pepper, and ground cumin
1 tsp. cayenne
½ tsp. turmeric
½ cup extra-virgin olive oil
2 firm-ripe avocados, pitted, peeled, and cut into ¾-in. chunks

CILANTRO CHICKEN

¼ cup *each* extra-virgin olive oil and fresh lime juice
½ cup chopped cilantro
1 tbsp. ground cumin
½ tsp. *each* kosher salt and freshly ground black pepper
4 skin-on, bone-in chicken breast halves (2½ lbs. total)

1. Make salsa: In a large bowl, combine tomatoes, chiles, and green onions. In a medium saucepan over high heat, bring vinegar to a boil. Add brown sugar and salt and cook, stirring, until dissolved, about 1 minute. Remove from heat. Put ginger, garlic, and dry spices in a bowl. In another medium saucepan, heat oil over medium-high heat until rippling. Add ginger mixture and cook, stirring, until fragrant, 1 minute. Remove from heat, stir in seasoned vinegar, and pour over tomato mixture.

2. Let salsa cool, then cover and chill at least 1 hour and up to 4 hours. About 1 hour before serving, stir avocados into salsa and bring to room temperature.

3. Make chicken: In a large bowl, combine oil, lime juice, cilantro, cumin, salt, and pepper. Turn chicken in mixture to coat. Let stand at room temperature, turning occasionally, for 30 to 45 minutes.

4. Prepare a charcoal or gas grill for direct high heat (*see Direct Heat Grilling, page 436*). Lift chicken from marinade (discard marinade) and grill (close lid on gas grill), turning often to prevent scorching, until no longer pink at bone (cut to test), 15 to 20 minutes.

5. Transfer chicken to a platter and spoon salsa on top, saving half of liquid for another use (it makes an appealing salad dressing).

PER SERVING: 746 cal., 64% (477 cal.) from fat; 50 g protein; 53 g fat (9.2 g sat.); 23 g carbo (4.9 g fiber); 591 mg sodium; 129 mg chol.

Tamil Chicken Wings

Reader Elagupillai Mageswari of Harbor City, California, seasons chicken wings with a fragrant Sri Lankan paste and serves them with a lively and refreshing cucumber salad.

SERVES 4 | **TIME** 35 minutes, plus 1 hour to marinate

1 stalk fresh lemongrass or 3 strips (3 by ½ in. each) lemon zest, chopped
¾ cup cilantro sprigs
8 garlic cloves
1 tsp. *each* salt and turmeric
½ tsp. freshly ground white or black pepper
8 chicken wings (about 1¾ lbs. total), fat trimmed
Cucumber Salad (*recipe follows*)

1. Trim stem end and tough outer layers from lemongrass. Cut tender inner stalk into chunks; put in a food processor with cilantro, garlic, salt, turmeric, and pepper and finely mince. Pat mixture over chicken wings. Cover and chill at least 1 hour and up to 1 day.

2. Prepare a charcoal or gas grill for direct medium heat (*see Direct Heat Grilling, page 436*). Grill chicken (close lid on gas grill), turning occasionally, until no longer pink at bone (cut to test), about 15 minutes. Serve with cucumber salad.

PER SERVING: 261 cal., 52% (135 cal.) from fat; 22 g protein; 15 g fat (4.2 g sat.); 9.5 g carbo (0.8 g fiber); 658 mg sodium; 63 mg chol.

Cucumber Salad: Shortly before serving chicken, in a bowl, combine 1 **cucumber** (about ¾ lb.), peeled and thinly sliced; ¼ cup thinly sliced **red onion**; 1 **jalapeño chile**, seeds and ribs removed and thinly sliced; 2 tbsp. **plain yogurt**; and 1 tbsp. **fresh lime juice**. Mix and add **salt** to taste.

PER SERVING: 17 cal., 19% (3.2 cal.) from fat; 0.9 g protein; 0.4 g fat (.17 g sat.); 2.9 g carbo (0.6 g fiber); 31 mg sodium; 1 mg chol.

Habanero-Lime Chicken Fajitas

These fajitas are more than just hot—the lime juice, cumin, oregano, and garlic give them layers of flavor.

MAKES 8 fajita tacos | **TIME** 50 minutes

¼ **cup fresh lime juice**
3 **tbsp. tequila**
1 **tbsp. olive oil**
½ **tsp.** *each* **ground cumin and dried oregano**
6 **tbsp. habanero chile hot sauce, plus more to taste**
2 **garlic cloves, minced**
1½ **lbs. skinned, boned chicken breast halves, fat trimmed**
3 **onions (1 lb. total), quartered lengthwise**
1 **cup chopped ripe tomatoes**
8 **flour tortillas (8 in. wide)**
1 **can (about 1 lb.) black beans, heated and drained**
1 **cup sour cream**
Lime wedges

1. In a 1-gal. resealable plastic bag, combine lime juice, tequila, oil, cumin, oregano, 6 tbsp. hot sauce, and garlic. Add chicken and onions, seal, and chill at least 15 minutes and up to 2 hours, turning occasionally.
2. Meanwhile, combine tomatoes and ¼ to 1½ tsp. hot sauce; set aside.
3. Prepare a charcoal or gas grill for direct high heat *(see Direct Heat Grilling, page 436)*. Lift onions from marinade and place on cooking grate (close lid on gas grill). Grill onions 3 minutes, turn over, cook a couple more minutes, then turn over and baste with marinade.
4. Add chicken to cooking grate (close lid on gas grill). Turn and baste chicken and onions occasionally until onions are soft and browned and meat is no longer pink in center (cut to test), about 8 minutes. Transfer chicken and onions to a board and keep warm.
5. Heat tortillas on grill, turning once, until softened and lightly speckled brown, 30 to 60 seconds.
6. Slice chicken crosswise. Pile with onions and beans into tortillas if you like, with tomatoes, sour cream, and a squeeze of lime—or have the tortillas alongside.

PER TACO: 389 cal., 29% (111 cal.) from fat; 25 g protein; 12 g fat (4.5 g sat.); 40 g carbo (4.9 g fiber); 860 mg sodium; 59 mg chol.

Grilled Chipotle-Chicken Quesadillas

Grilling adds a mildly smoky note that complements big flavors like lime, cilantro, and chile. Serve with store-bought pico de gallo or other salsa. Or, if you have a little more time, make our fresh pico de gallo.

MAKES 4 quesadillas | **TIME** 35 minutes

4 **skinned, boned chicken breast halves, fat trimmed**
1 **tbsp. olive oil**
Salt and freshly ground black pepper
1 **canned chipotle chile in adobo sauce, minced**
¼ **cup** *each* **sour cream and mayonnaise**
1 **tbsp.** *each* **fresh lime juice and chopped cilantro**
8 **corn tortillas (6 in. each)**
2 **cups finely shredded Monterey jack cheese**
Pico de Gallo *(recipe follows)* **or other salsa**

1. Brush chicken breasts with oil and sprinkle with salt and pepper.
2. Prepare a charcoal or gas grill for direct medium heat *(see Direct Heat Grilling, page 436)*. Grill chicken until no longer pink in center (cut to test), 4 to 5 minutes per side. Cut cooked chicken breasts into ¼-in.-thick slices. Keep grill hot.
3. In a small bowl, whisk together chipotle chile, sour cream, mayonnaise, lime juice, and cilantro.
4. Spread 1 tbsp. chipotle-lime sauce on one side of each tortilla. Top each of 4 tortillas with ½ cup cheese and one-quarter of chicken slices, then cover with remaining tortillas (sauce side down). Put each quesadilla on a plate.
5. Slide quesadillas off plates onto cooking grate over medium heat (you may need to grill quesadillas in batches). Grill, turning once, until cheese has melted and both sides are golden, about 2 minutes per side (use a large spatula and tongs to flip quesadillas). If grilling in batches, keep finished quesadillas warm in a 200° oven until ready to serve.
6. Slice each quesadilla into wedges and serve with salsa on the side.

PER QUESADILLA: 615 cal., 54% (333 cal.) from fat; 45 g protein; 37 g fat (14 g sat.); 26 g carbo (2.8 g fiber); 615 mg sodium; 143 mg chol.

Pico de Gallo: In a medium bowl, mix 2 cups diced ripe **tomatoes**, ½ cup diced **onion**, ¼ cup minced **cilantro**, 2 tbsp. *each* minced **jalapeño chiles** and **fresh lime juice**, and 1 tsp. **garlic**. Add **salt** to taste. Makes about 2½ cups.

PER TBSP.: 3.8 cal., 0% from fat; 0 g protein; 0.1 g fat (0 g sat.); 0.9 g carbo (0.2 g fiber); 1.3 mg sodium; 0 mg chol.

Yogurt-marinated Chicken Kebabs with Pearl Couscous

The yogurt marinade gives the chicken in this recipe—from reader Margee Berry, of Trout Lake, Washington—a delicious tang; it also tenderizes the meat. You'll need four metal skewers (each 8 in.).

SERVES 4 | **TIME** 45 minutes

1½ cups plain low-fat yogurt, divided
2 tsp. garam masala (*see Quick Tips below*)
1 tsp. Madras curry powder
2 garlic cloves, minced
1 tsp. plus 1 tbsp. salt
½ tsp. freshly ground black pepper
1½ lbs. skinned, boned chicken breast, cut into
    1½-in. cubes
⅓ cup crumbled feta cheese
3 tbsp. minced red onion
1 tsp. finely shredded fresh lemon zest
2 tbsp. chopped mint leaves, divided
1½ cups pearl couscous (*see Quick Tips below*)
2 tsp. olive oil
2 medium red bell peppers, seeds and ribs removed
    and cut into 1½-in. pieces

1. Combine 1 cup yogurt, the garam masala, curry powder, garlic, 1 tsp. salt, and the pepper in a large resealable plastic bag. Add chicken, seal bag, and shake to coat. Let marinate 20 minutes at room temperature.
2. Meanwhile, in a small bowl, stir together remaining ½ cup yogurt, the feta, onion, lemon zest, and 1 tbsp. mint; set aside.
3. Bring 2 qts. water to a boil and add remaining 1 tbsp. salt. Add couscous and cook until tender, 12 to 15 minutes. Drain, return to pot, and add oil. Cover to keep warm.
4. Prepare a charcoal or gas grill for direct medium-high heat (*see Direct Heat Grilling, page 436*). Thread chicken and bell peppers onto skewers and discard marinade. Grill skewers (close lid on gas grill), turning once, until chicken is browned and no longer pink in center (cut to test), about 10 minutes. Pile couscous on a platter, sprinkle with remaining 1 tbsp. mint, and arrange kebabs around it. Serve with yogurt-feta sauce.
Quick Tips: Garam masala is available in the spice section of many supermarkets; if you cannot find it, substitute 1 tsp. cinnamon, ½ tsp. *each* ground cumin and freshly ground black pepper, and ¼ tsp. *each* ground cardamom, nutmeg, cloves, and cayenne. Find pearl (also called Israeli) couscous at specialty grocers.

PER SERVING: 569 cal., 14% (77 cal.) from fat; 55 g protein; 8.6 g fat (3.5 g sat.); 64 g carbo (3.4 g fiber); 1,275 mg sodium; 114 mg chol.

Grilled Chicken Kebabs with Romesco Sauce

Romesco sauce comes from the Spanish province of Catalonia. Although the mixture has lots of variations, most combine roasted red peppers, nuts, garlic, and crusty bread to make a thick sauce that often tops grilled fish. We've gone ahead and paired it with chicken, and it's a wonderful dish. You'll need eight metal or wooden 8-in. skewers for this.

SERVES 4 | **TIME** 40 minutes

2 lbs. skinned, boned chicken breast halves,
    cut into 1½-in. cubes
½ cup chopped cilantro
½ cup extra-virgin olive oil, divided
2 tbsp. fresh lime juice
2 tsp. plus 1 tbsp. minced garlic
1 tsp. *each* kosher salt and sweet smoked Spanish
    paprika (*see Quick Tip below*)
½ tsp. freshly ground black pepper
¾ cup roasted red peppers
¼ cup whole almonds or hazelnuts, toasted
    (*see How to Toast Nuts, page 134*)
1 slice crusty bread, toasted and cut into cubes
1 tbsp. sherry vinegar
2 bunches green onions, trimmed

1. If using wooden skewers, soak in cold water at least 30 minutes. In a large bowl or resealable plastic bag, combine chicken, cilantro, 3 tbsp. oil, the lime juice, 2 tsp. garlic, the salt, smoked paprika, and pepper. Toss to coat, then marinate, chilled, 25 minutes.
2. Meanwhile, put roasted peppers, nuts, bread, vinegar, remaining 1 tbsp. garlic, and ¼ cup oil in a food processor and purée; sauce will be thick.
3. Prepare a charcoal or gas grill for direct medium-high heat (*see Direct Heat Grilling, page 436*). Thread chicken onto skewers, discarding marinade. Drizzle green onions with remaining 1 tbsp. oil. Lay skewers on cooking grate (close lid on gas grill) and grill 4 minutes. Turn skewers over, then lay green onions on grill. Grill until chicken is browned and no longer pink in center (cut to test) and onions are charred in places, about 4 minutes. Serve hot, accompanied by sauce.
Quick Tip: Smoked Spanish paprika is available at well-stocked and specialty-foods stores.

PER SERVING: 533 cal., 47% (252 cal.) from fat; 56 g protein; 28 g fat (4.2 g sat.); 14 g carbo (2.9 g fiber); 495 mg sodium; 132 mg chol.

Tandoori Kebabs

Hema Alur-Kundargi, a talented home cook from Cupertino, California, guided us through a local Indian grocery store one day. We came back loaded with tasty ingredients and several easy-to-make recipes; this was one of them. For vegetarian kebabs, Alur-Kundargi uses Indian *paneer* cheese or *nigari* (firm-pressed) tofu instead of chicken. You'll need eight 10-in. metal or wooden skewers.

SERVES 8 | **TIME** About 1 hour, plus 30 minutes to marinate

2 cups plain nonfat yogurt
1 red bell pepper (10 oz.)
1 red onion (6 oz.)
1 lb. peeled, cored fresh pineapple
1 lb. boned, skinned chicken breast halves (see
   Quick Tip below)
1 tbsp. Tandoori Masala, store-bought or homemade
   (recipe follows)
Raita (recipe follows)

1. If using wooden skewers, soak in cold water at least 30 minutes. Line a colander with a double layer of cheesecloth or four layers of paper towels; set colander in a sink or over a large bowl. Empty yogurt into lined colander and let drain about 30 minutes.
2. Meanwhile, stem and seed bell pepper; cut into 1-in. squares. Cut onion into 1-in. chunks, separating layers. Cut pineapple into 1-in. chunks. Cut chicken (or cheese or tofu, if using) into 1-in. chunks.
3. In a large bowl, mix drained yogurt with tandoori masala. If using chicken, scoop out ½ cup yogurt mixture and combine with chicken in a small bowl. Gently mix bell pepper, onion, and pineapple (or cheese or tofu if using) into yogurt mixture in large bowl. Cover and chill at least 30 minutes or up to 2 hours. Thread vegetables, pineapple, and chicken (or cheese or tofu) onto metal or soaked wooden skewers, alternating items.
4. Prepare a charcoal or gas grill for direct high heat (*see Direct Heat Grilling, page 436*). Lay kebabs on an oiled grill; close lid on gas grill. Cook, turning once, until vegetables are browned on both sides and chicken is no longer pink in center (cut to test), 8 to 10 minutes. Serve hot or warm, with raita to add at the table.
Quick Tip: Substitute Indian paneer cheese or nigari (firm-pressed) tofu for the chicken if you like.
Make Ahead: Through step 3, up to 2 hours; cover and chill.

PER SERVING WITH CHICKEN: 156 cal., 7% (11 cal.) from fat; 18 g protein; 1.2 g fat (0.3 g sat.); 18 g carbo (1.7 g fiber); 246 mg sodium; 34 mg chol.

Tandoori Masala: In a small bowl, combine 1 tsp. *each* **ground cumin** and **coriander**, ¼ tsp. *each* **ground cloves** and **cayenne**, and ⅛ tsp. *each* **nutmeg, freshly ground black pepper**, and **cinnamon**; mix well.

Raita: In a bowl, mix ¾ cup **plain nonfat yogurt** with ½ tsp. *each* **ground cumin, sugar**, and **salt**. Gently stir in ¼ cup *each* finely chopped **cucumber, tomato**, and **onion**. Makes about 1¼ cups.

Hawaiian-Portuguese Smoked Turkey

A wave of Portuguese came to Hawaii in the late 1800s to work the sugarcane fields, and over time their cooking traditions fused with those of other cultures in the islands, including Chinese and Japanese. Greg Boyer, who owns a landscape-design business in Oahu, picked up this recipe from a Hawaiian Portuguese acquaintance some 30 years ago. Boyer serves it with Portuguese Sausage Stuffing (*page 397*).

Serves 18 to 20 | **TIME** 4 to 5 hours, plus 2 days to marinate, plus 30 minutes to soak hickory chips

1 turkey (18 to 20 lbs.; see Turkey Basics, page 370),
   thawed if frozen (see Quick Tips, right)
1 tbsp. *each* coarsely chopped ginger and garlic, plus
   ¼ cup *each* minced garlic and ginger
4 cups soy sauce
1 cup apple vinegar
2 tbsp. light brown or turbinado sugar
6 cups hickory chips
2 cups chicken broth
2 large onions, quartered lengthwise
Hawaiian-Portuguese Turkey Gravy (recipe follows)

1. On day 1 (2 days before Thanksgiving), remove giblets from turkey and rinse turkey inside and out. Set turkey, breast side down, in a large disposable roasting pan set on a rimless baking sheet. Add giblets to pan (discard neck). Into cavity of turkey, sprinkle coarsely chopped ginger and garlic. In a bowl, whisk together minced garlic and ginger, soy sauce, vinegar, and brown sugar; pour over turkey. Cover turkey with plastic wrap and marinate 2 days, basting 3 to 5 times a day.
2. On day 3 (Thanksgiving Day), remove giblets. About 4 hours before serving, remove turkey from refrigerator. Let stand for 30 minutes in pan; meanwhile, soak hickory chips in water 30 minutes.

3. Remove turkey from pan and pour marinade into a bowl. (If you're making the Portuguese Sausage Stuffing, set 1 cup of the marinade aside.) Add broth and set aside. Return turkey to pan, breast side up, and add onions (put 2 or 3 quarters inside turkey). Truss turkey, tying drumsticks together tightly with kitchen twine; truss wing tips together the same way. Cover wing tips and drumsticks with heavy-duty foil "caps," molding them snugly to prevent scorching. Cover entire pan loosely with a double layer of foil, extending foil beyond turkey like an umbrella.

4. Prepare a charcoal or gas grill, large enough to hold the turkey, for indirect cooking: *For a charcoal grill*, ignite about 60 charcoal briquets. When coals are spotted with ash (about 20 minutes), bank evenly on opposite sides of firegrate. To each mound, add 5 unlit briquets and ½ cup drained soaked wood chips now and every 30 minutes during smoking. *For a gas grill* (with at least 11 in. between indirect-heat burners), put ½ cup drained soaked wood chips in a drip pan directly on heat in a front corner and add ½ cup chips through grate every 30 minutes during smoking. Turn heat to high and adjust gas for indirect cooking (*see Indirect Heat Grilling, page 436*). Close lid and preheat grill 10 minutes.

5. Carefully slide pan with turkey from baking sheet onto center of grill. Pour in marinade and broth. Close grill lid. (If your grill has a lip on it, rest pan at an angle on grill, then carefully slide pan onto grill.) Smoke turkey, basting every 30 minutes, until an instant-read thermometer inserted straight down through thickest part of breast to bone registers 150°, about 2½ hours (begin checking after 2 hours). Ladle marinade from pan into a heatproof bowl and reserve for Hawaiian-Portuguese Turkey Gravy.

6. Slide baking sheet under turkey pan, ease baking pan onto sheet, and lift pan with turkey off grill. Let turkey rest, covered with foil, at least 20 minutes (internal temperature will rise to 160°) before carving.

Quick Tips: Boyer starts with a frozen turkey and marinates it for 3 days; our version starts with a thawed or fresh bird. It's helpful to have a friend or relative assist you in easing the turkey on and off the grill.

PER SERVING: 368 cal., 39% (144 cal.) from fat; 50 g protein; 16 g fat (4.5 g sat.); 3.8 g carbo (0.3 g fiber); sodium N/A; 141 mg chol.

Hawaiian-Portuguese Turkey Gravy

The soy sauce in the turkey marinade turns this gravy an appetizing deep brown color.

MAKES About 4 cups; 16 servings | **TIME** About 20 minutes

6 tbsp. turkey fat (skimmed from cooked marinade of Hawaiian-Portuguese Smoked Turkey; *see recipe, opposite page*) **or 6 tbsp. unsalted butter**
6 tbsp. flour
4 to 4½ cups reduced-sodium chicken broth
⅓ cup defatted cooked marinade from Hawaiian-Portuguese Smoked Turkey, strained

Heat fat or butter in a medium heavy-bottomed saucepan over medium heat and whisk in flour. Cook, whisking, until roux is nut brown, 10 minutes. Whisk in 4 cups broth and marinade (if thick, add remaining ½ cup broth). Serve hot.

PER SERVING: 61 cal., 70% (43 cal.) from fat; 1.3 g protein; 4.8 g fat (1.4 g sat.); 3.1 g carbo (0.1 g fiber); 423 mg sodium; 4.9 mg chol.

When You Want Smoke with Fire

To add a delicious smoky taste to food, soak hardwood or fruitwood chips in water for about 30 minutes, then drain and add as recipes direct. Almost always, you'll be cooking over indirect heat.

FOR GAS: Put chips in a metal smoker box, if your grill has one, or a small shallow foil pan (find it at the grocery store) set directly on a turned-on burner in a corner of the grill.
FOR CHARCOAL: Sprinkle chips evenly over coals.

Wine-smoked Turkey

A recipe inspired by California wine country, this is the one you want to serve visitors from the East Coast—preferably outside, for a full-on Western-style Thanksgiving. Wine-infused wood chips, a heady herbal marinade, and apple, onion, and more herbs stuffed inside give this crisp-skinned grilled turkey fantastic flavor. Wine shows up in the velvety Zinfandel gravy too.

SERVES 16 to 18, with ample leftovers | **TIME** 3 to 3½ hours

4 to 6 cups lightly packed wine-infused wood chips or shavings *(see Quick Tip, right)*
3 tbsp. olive oil
2 tbsp. minced fresh sage leaves or 2 tsp. dried sage
1 tbsp. minced parsley
2 tsp. minced fresh marjoram leaves or ½ tsp. dried marjoram
½ tsp. freshly ground black pepper
1 turkey (16 to 18 lbs.; see Turkey Basics, page 370)
1 Golden Delicious apple, cored
1 medium onion, peeled
Zinfandel Gravy *(recipe follows)*
Sage and marjoram sprigs

1. Soak wine-infused chips or shavings in water at least 20 minutes. In a small bowl, mix oil with sage, parsley, marjoram, and pepper.
2. To prepare turkey, remove and discard leg truss. Pull off and discard any lumps of fat; remove giblets and neck and set aside for making Zinfandel gravy. Pat turkey dry. Brush turkey all over with 2 tbsp. oil mixture. Cut apple and onion into 1-in. chunks, stir into remaining oil mixture, and spoon apple mixture into body cavity. Put foil caps on drumstick tips and wing tips. Insert a meat thermometer straight down through thickest part of breast to bone (if using an instant-read thermometer, insert later).
3. Prepare a charcoal or gas grill for indirect medium-low heat *(see Indirect Heat Grilling, page 467). For a charcoal grill,* light 40 briquets on firegrate. When fully ignited, bank evenly on opposite sides of firegrate and let burn to medium. Place a drip pan filled halfway with warm water between banks of coals. To each mound of coals, add 5 briquets and ½ cup soaked wood chips or shavings now and every 30 minutes while cooking; if needed, keep grill uncovered for a few minutes to help briquets ignite. *For a gas grill,* remove cooking grate and turn all burners to high. Put 1 cup soaked wood chips or shavings in grill's metal smoking box or in a small, shallow foil pan set directly on burner in a corner. Close lid and heat 10 minutes. Then turn off one burner and lower other(s) to medium. Set a metal or sturdy foil

drip pan, filled halfway with water, on turned-off burner. Add another 1 cup wood chips or shavings now if first ones have burned away (add 1 cup chips every hour or so while cooking). Replace cooking grate.
4. Set turkey, breast up, on cooking grate over drip pan and close lid on grill. Cook until an instant-read thermometer inserted straight down through thickest part of breast to bone registers 160°, 2½ to 3 hours; during cooking, loosely tent turkey with foil if it starts to get too dark.
5. Drain juices and remove apple and onion from cavity; reserve for gravy. Place turkey on a platter and let rest 15 to 30 minutes. Remove drip pan from grill; skim and discard fat from juices. Reserve juices for Zinfandel gravy. Garnish platter with herb sprigs.
Quick Tip: Buy wine-infused chips from Just Chips (*justinwine.com*). Or soak mesquite or applewood chips in equal parts red wine and water and omit soaking in step 1.

PER ¼-LB. SERVING (WHITE AND DARK MEAT WITH SKIN): 250 cal., 43% (108 cal.) from fat; 32 g protein; 12 g fat (3.2 g sat.); 1.4 g carbo (0 g fiber); 82 mg sodium; 93 mg chol.

Zinfandel Gravy

A rich, delicious gravy that works especially well if you use the same wine that you plan to drink with dinner.

MAKES 6 cups; 18 servings | **TIME** 2 hours

Giblets and neck from a 16- to 18-lb. turkey
2 large onions, quartered
2 large carrots, cut into chunks
1 cup sliced celery
4½ cups reduced-sodium chicken broth, divided
2¾ cups Zinfandel, divided
2 strips orange zest (3 in. each)
½ tsp. freshly ground black pepper
Cooked apple mixture and fat-skimmed turkey pan juices from Wine-smoked Turkey *(left)*
½ cup cornstarch
Salt

1. In a 5- to 6-qt. pan, combine giblets, neck, onions, carrots, celery, and ½ cup broth. Cook, covered, over medium-high heat, 20 minutes. Uncover; cook over high heat, stirring often as liquid evaporates, until giblets and vegetables are browned and browned bits stick to bottom of pan, 5 to 8 minutes. Add another ½ cup broth and stir to loosen browned bits. Cook and brown, uncovered, as before.
2. Add remaining 3½ cups broth, 2 cups Zinfandel, the orange zest, and pepper to pan. Cover and simmer over low heat for 1 to 1½ hours.

3. Add apple mixture from turkey cavity; bring to a boil. Lower heat and simmer, covered, 5 minutes.

4. Pour broth mixture through a fine-mesh strainer into a bowl. Discard contents of strainer. Measure broth; if needed, add enough turkey pan juices to make 5½ cups. In pan, mix cornstarch with ¼ cup water and remaining ¾ cup wine. Stir in broth mixture and cook, stirring, over high heat until boiling, about 5 minutes. Season with salt to taste.

PER ⅓-CUP SERVING: 34 cal., 5% (1.8 cal.) from fat; 1.8 g protein; 0.2 g fat (0 g sat.); 6.1 g carbo (0 g fiber); 163 mg sodium; 3.8 mg chol.

Barbecued Glazed Turkey

One method, three flavor choices: Just pick the seasonings that go best with the rest of your feast. Grilling gives the bird a really crisp, brown skin—plus it frees up your oven so you can cook everything else.

recipe pictured on page 450

SERVES 12 to 24, depending on size of turkey, with ample leftovers | **TIME** 2 to 3 hours, plus 15 to 30 minutes to rest

1 turkey (12 to 24 lbs.; see Turkey Basics, page 370)
Olive or vegetable oil
Glaze (recipes follow)

1. Remove and discard leg truss from turkey. Pull off and discard any lumps of fat. Remove giblets and neck. Pat turkey dry. Rub skin with oil. Insert a meat thermometer straight down through thickest part of breast to bone (if using an instant-read thermometer, insert later).

2. Prepare a charcoal or gas grill for indirect medium heat, using a drip pan (see Indirect Heat Grilling, page 436).

3. Set turkey, breast up, on cooking grate over drip pan and close lid on grill. Cook turkey according to glaze directions.

4. Using two large spatulas, transfer cooked turkey to a platter. Cover loosely with foil and let rest 15 to 30 minutes.

5. Carve bird. If thighs are still pink at the joint, microwave them until pinkness disappears, 1 to 3 minutes.

Sage Butter Glaze: In a small bowl, mix ¼ cup melted **butter**, 2 tbsp. **fresh lemon juice**, and 1 tsp. minced **sage leaves**. When turkey has about 45 more minutes to cook (breast temperature at bone will be about 135° for birds up to 18 lbs. and about 145° for larger ones), baste often with sage butter. Cook, sliding folded strips of foil between bird and grate if edges of turkey begin to get too dark, until an instant-read thermometer registers 160°.

PER ¼-LB. SERVING (WHITE AND DARK MEAT WITH SKIN AND SAGE BUTTER GLAZE): 243 cal., 44% (108 cal.) from fat; 32 g protein; 12 g fat (3.9 g sat.); 0.1 g carbo (0 g fiber); 97 mg sodium; 97 mg chol.

Chile-Orange Glaze: In a small bowl, combine 3 tbsp. **ground dried New Mexico or California chiles**, 1 can (12 oz.; 1½ cups) thawed **orange juice concentrate**, 2 tbsp. finely shredded **orange zest**, and 1 tsp. **ground cumin**. When turkey has about 20 more minutes to cook (breast temperature at bone will be about 150° for birds up to 18 lbs. and about 155° for larger ones), coat generously with glaze. Cook, sliding folded strips of foil between bird and grate if edges of turkey begin to get too dark, and draping any other dark areas with foil, until an instant-read thermometer registers 160°.

PER ¼-LB. SERVING (WHITE AND DARK MEAT WITH SKIN AND CHILE-ORANGE GLAZE): 245 cal., 37% (90 cal.) from fat; 32 g protein; 10 g fat (3 g sat.); 3.7 g carbo (0.2 g fiber); 87 mg sodium; 93 mg chol.

Brown Sugar Crackle Glaze: In a small bowl, mix 2 cups firmly packed **light brown sugar**, 5 tbsp. **Dijon mustard**, and 2 tsp. **coarsely ground black pepper**. When turkey has about 45 more minutes to cook (breast temperature at bone will be about 135° for birds up to 18 lbs. and about 145° for larger ones), spread with half the glaze. Cook 20 minutes. Brush with remaining glaze and cook, sliding folded strips of foil between bird and grate if edges of turkey begin to get too dark, and draping any other dark areas with foil, until an instant-read thermometer registers 160°.

PER ¼-LB. SERVING (WHITE AND DARK MEAT WITH SKIN AND BROWN SUGAR CRACKLE GLAZE): 265 cal., 34% (90 cal.) from fat; 32 g protein; 10 g fat (3 g sat.); 9 g carbo (0 g fiber); 123 mg sodium; 93 mg chol.

Turkey, the Second Time Around

Whether you smoke, grill, or roast a turkey, you're likely to have leftovers—and that's a good thing. Make delicious reuse of your big-bird bounty in any of these recipes:

- Turkey Sandwiches with Shallots, Cranberries, and Blue Cheese (page 176)
- Golden Gate Grilled Turkey and Cheese (page 189)
- Vietnamese-style Turkey Subs (page 176)
- Yucatecan Tostadas (Salbutes) (page 194)
- Use instead of chicken in any of the main-course chicken salads beginning on page 168
- Use instead of chicken in Coconut-Lime Chicken and Rice Soup (page 96)
- Sunset Turkey Tetrazzini (page 215)
- Turkey Enchiladas with Sour Cream (page 389)

Grilled Butterflied Turkey with Rosemary Garlic Gravy

Butterflying the turkey—removing the backbone so it lies flat—makes it cook faster. Brining keeps it juicy and moist.

SERVES 10 to 12 | **TIME** 3½ hours, plus 12 hours to brine

BRINE & TURKEY
1½ cups kosher salt
6 large rosemary sprigs (7 in. each)
5 garlic cloves, crushed
1 turkey (12 to 14 lbs.; see *Turkey Basics, page 370*), butterflied (see *Quick Tip, right*), neck, back, and giblets reserved for gravy
About 2 tbsp. canola oil

ROSEMARY GARLIC GRAVY
Neck, back, and giblets from turkey
7 cups reduced-sodium chicken broth
1 cup dry white wine or reduced-sodium chicken broth
3 carrots, chopped
1 onion, chopped
2 stalks celery, chopped
1 tsp. *each* salt and freshly ground black pepper, plus more to taste
3 garlic cloves, crushed, plus 2 cloves mashed
2 large rosemary sprigs (7 in. each), plus 2 tsp. minced rosemary leaves
¾ cup flour

1. Make brine: Boil 1½ qts. water with salt in a pot big enough to hold the turkey, stirring until salt dissolves. Add rosemary, crushed garlic, and 3 qts. cold water; let cool. Add turkey. Chill, covered, at least 12 hours or overnight; turn once.

2. Make turkey broth for gravy: In a large pot, bring to a boil all gravy ingredients except mashed garlic, minced rosemary, and flour; simmer until giblets are tender, about 1 hour. Strain; discard solids. Chill.

3. Put a rack in a large rimmed pan. Set turkey on rack and drain 30 minutes at room temperature. Pat dry and rub all over with oil.

4. Meanwhile, prepare a gas or charcoal grill for indirect medium-high heat, using a drip pan filled halfway with warm water (see *Indirect Heat Grilling, page 436*).

5. Set turkey, skin side up, on cooking grate over drip pan and close lid on grill. Cook until an instant-read thermometer inserted into thickest part of thigh registers 175°, about 1½ hours. Transfer turkey to a cutting board. Tent loosely with foil and let rest in a warm place 15 to 30 minutes.

6. Meanwhile, make gravy: Skim any fat that has accumulated on surface of turkey broth, then reheat broth. In a 5- to 6-qt. pot, toast flour over medium heat, whisking, until deep golden brown, 7 to 10 minutes. Gradually pour in 3 cups turkey broth (from step 2), whisking to a smooth paste. Whisk in rest of turkey broth, mashed garlic, and minced rosemary; bring to a boil, then simmer about 10 minutes, whisking often. Season with salt and pepper.

7. To carve, cut through thigh joint, then cut drumstick from thigh. Slice thigh meat off bone (save bones for stock). Repeat with other leg. Cut off wing tips and save for stock; cut wings from breast. Divide breast into halves and cut into thick slices across the grain. Arrange drumsticks, wings, and sliced breast and thigh meat on a platter and serve with rosemary garlic gravy.

Quick Tip: Ask your butcher to butterfly the turkey for you, or do it yourself. Put turkey, breast side down, on a cutting board. Using poultry shears or sturdy kitchen scissors, cut along both sides of backbone; remove backbone and open up turkey like a book. Reserve the backbone for stock or discard. Turn turkey breast side up and, using the heel of your hand, press firmly against breastbone until it cracks. Tuck wing tips under (toward cavity) so they don't burn on grill.

PER SERVING: 350 cal., 38% (134 cal.) from fat; 43 g protein; 15 g fat (4.2 g sat.); 8 g carbo (0.5 g fiber); 1,105 mg sodium; 164 mg chol.

Thai-seasoned Turkey Thigh Roast with Fresh Herbs

This is an unusual way to cook turkey, we must admit, but it's so good that you'll return to it again and again, especially when you want a roast that's smaller than a whole bird.

SERVES 4 to 5 | **TIME** 1½ hours

¼ cup *each* chopped basil, cilantro, and mint leaves
3 garlic cloves, minced or pressed
1 tbsp. *each* firmly packed light brown sugar
    and soy sauce
2 tsp. *each* minced fresh ginger, Thai or Vietnamese fish
    sauce (*nam pla* or *nuoc mam*), and vegetable oil
½ tsp. Asian red chili paste
2 boned, skinned turkey thighs (about ¾ lb. each;
    see Quick Tip below)
Lime wedges
Salt

1. In a bowl, mix basil, cilantro, mint, garlic, brown sugar, soy sauce, ginger, fish sauce, oil, and chili paste. Spread about 2 tbsp. of the mixture evenly over boned side of 1 turkey thigh. Set remaining thigh, boned side down, over herb mixture, aligning with first thigh. Tie thighs together at 1-in. intervals with kitchen twine to create a cylinder about 3 in. wide and 7 in. long. With your fingers, pat remaining herb mixture evenly all over roast.
2. Prepare a charcoal or gas grill for indirect high heat (*see Indirect Heat Grilling, page 436*). Set roast over indirect heat area and cover grill; open vents for charcoal. Cook roast until an instant-read thermometer inserted in thickest part registers 170°, 40 to 45 minutes.
3. Transfer roast to a platter and, keeping it warm, let rest 5 to 10 minutes. Garnish platter with lime wedges. Cut roast into ½-in.-thick slices to serve. Squeeze juice from lime wedges over portions and add salt to taste.
Quick Tip: Have the turkey thighs boned and skinned at the meat market.
Make Ahead: Through step 1, up to 1 day, chilled (bring to room temperature before grilling). If you cover with plastic wrap and herb mixture sticks to wrap, scrape off and pat back onto roast.

PER SERVING: 209 cal., 33% (69 cal.) from fat; 28 g protein; 7.8 g fat (2.2 g sat.); 4.8 g carbo (0.5 g fiber); 400 mg sodium; 102 mg chol.

Boneless Breast of Mallard Duck

Grilling is probably our favorite way to cook duck. The fat drips away, leaving a crispy skin and basting the meat so it stays moist.

SERVES 4 to 8, depending on heartiness of appetite
TIME 1 hour, plus 24 hours to marinate

½ cup *each* soy sauce, white wine vinegar, and honey
2 garlic cloves, crushed
1½ tsp. ground ginger
1 tsp. dried tarragon
4 single duck breasts (1 lb. each)
About ¾ cup thin-cut orange marmalade
Parsley

1. Combine soy sauce, vinegar, honey, garlic, ginger, and tarragon in a large shallow pan and immerse duck breasts. Marinate 24 hours in the refrigerator.
2. Prepare charcoal or gas grill for indirect very high heat, using a drip pan filled ½ in. up sides with water (*see Indirect Heat Grilling, page 436*). Grill duck skin side down over cleared area (close lid and keep vent holes open), basting often with marinade, 6 minutes on each side. Move duck over direct heat and cook, skin side down, until skin is well browned and crisp and meat is medium-rare (cut to test), 5 to 10 minutes.
3. Place duck skin side up on an ovenproof platter and cover meat generously with marmalade. Broil in oven until marmalade bubbles and thickens. Garnish with parsley and serve.
Quick Tip: Take the duck off the grill while it's still quite rosy, since you'll be cooking it further under the broiler (grilled duck breast is at its juiciest and most tender when cooked medium rare). Duck breasts are usually available at gourmet grocery stores.

PER SERVING: 234 cal., 25% (59 cal.) from fat; 15 g protein; 6.5 g fat (1.7 g sat.); 30 g carbo (0.1 g fiber); 582 mg sodium; 82 mg chol.

Grilled Rib-eye Steaks with Miso Butter and Sweet Onions

Compound butter—made by blending such flavorings as herbs, wine, citrus juice, and garlic with butter—is a classic French accompaniment to meats and vegetables. Japanese miso paste adds an intriguing nuance to butter, giving it the savory, meaty quality called umami. Serve the steaks with Edamame-Orzo Salad (*page 149*) if you like.

recipe pictured on page **453**

SERVES 4 generously | **TIME** 40 minutes, plus 30 minutes to freeze butter

½ cup unsalted butter, softened
2 tbsp. plus 1 tsp. white or yellow miso paste
1 tbsp. finely minced chives
1½ tsp. minced garlic
4 boned rib-eye steaks (¾ to 1 in. thick)
Salt and freshly ground black pepper
4 sweet onions, such as Walla Walla or Maui
About 3 tbsp. olive oil, divided

1. In a small bowl, stir together butter, miso, chives, and garlic. Spoon butter mixture onto a square of plastic wrap, fold plastic over butter from top and bottom, and form it into a log about 1½ in. thick. Twist ends of plastic to close. Put in freezer until firm, about 30 minutes.
2. Meanwhile, pat steaks dry and season well with salt and pepper; let stand at room temperature 15 to 25 minutes. Cut onions in half crosswise. Trim about ½ in. from the rounded side of each onion half so that sides will lie flat on the grill. Rub onions with some oil and salt and pepper to taste.
3. Prepare a charcoal or gas grill for direct medium-high heat (*see Direct Heat Grilling, page 436*). Grill onions 2 minutes, then add steaks and grill until nicely browned, 3 to 4 minutes. Turn everything over. Onions will need another 6 to 8 minutes, until they're softened and browned. For steaks, cook an additional 2 to 4 minutes for rare, 5 to 7 minutes for medium-rare, and 8 to 15 minutes for well done (cut to test).
4. Remove plastic from miso butter; top each steak with 2 tsp. miso butter (you will have some butter left over). Serve with onions.

PER SERVING: 1,030 cal., 71% (729 cal.) from fat; 57 g protein; 81 g fat (35 g sat.); 19 g carbo (3.3 g fiber); 521 mg sodium; 237 mg chol.

Grilled Grass-fed Rib-eyes with Herb Lemon Butter

Nothing shows off the natural, clean flavor of grass-fed beef like a thick, juicy steak.

SERVES 4 | **TIME** About 15 minutes

4 grass-fed bone-in rib-eye steaks (1 lb. each and about 1 in. thick)
Kosher salt and freshly ground black pepper
Vegetable oil
Herb Lemon Butter (*recipe follows*)

1. Prepare a charcoal or gas grill for medium direct heat (*see Direct Heat Grilling, page 436*).
2. Sprinkle each steak generously with salt and pepper; rub with oil. Grill steaks, covered, turning once, until done the way you like, 10 to 12 minutes for medium-rare.
3. Transfer steaks to a large platter and top each with a slice of herb lemon butter.

PER SERVING WITHOUT BUTTER: 383 cal., 47% (180 cal.) from fat; 48 g protein; 20 g fat (8 g sat.); 0 g carbo; 117 mg sodium; 136 mg chol.

Herb Lemon Butter

Compound butter (butter blended with flavorings) is a great and simple way to add taste and texture to beef, chicken, fish, or vegetables.

MAKES 1 cup | **TIME** 20 minutes, plus 30 minutes to chill

½ cup unsalted butter, softened
¼ cup *each* chopped basil, cilantro, flat-leaf parsley, mint, and oregano leaves
2 tbsp. fresh lemon juice
Finely shredded zest of 1 lemon
¼ tsp. *each* kosher salt and freshly ground black pepper

1. Blend ingredients in a food processor until smooth, about 2 minutes.
2. Lay a piece of plastic wrap on a work surface. Using a rubber spatula, scrape butter lengthwise onto plastic. Lift top edge of plastic up and over butter to meet bottom edge of plastic. Roll butter toward you, forming a log about 4 in. long. Twist ends of plastic to close. Chill until firm, about 30 minutes.
3. Remove plastic and slice off ¼-in. portions (1 tbsp.) to serve over steaks.
Make Ahead: Up to 1 week chilled, or up to 1 month frozen, wrapped in several layers of plastic.

PER TBSP.: 54 cal., 96% (52 cal.) from fat; 0.2 g protein; 5.8 g fat (3.6 g sat.); 0.6 g carbo (0.2 g fiber); 1.7 mg sodium; 16 mg chol.

Tarragon-Mustard T-bone Steaks

In a T-bone, two cuts—loin and tenderloin—are separated by the bone. The porterhouse steak is almost identical to a T-bone, except that it has a larger tenderloin portion.

SERVES 4 | **TIME** 20 minutes, plus 30 minutes to marinate

⅓ **cup dry red wine**
3 **tbsp. Dijon mustard**
2 **tbsp.** *each* **minced shallots and olive oil**
1½ **tbsp. chopped fresh tarragon or 2 tsp. dried tarragon**
4 **beef T-bone steaks, 1½ in. thick (1 to 1¼ lbs. each), fat trimmed**
2 **cups (2 oz.) tender watercress sprigs**
Salt and freshly ground black pepper

1. In a small bowl, mix wine, mustard, shallots, oil, and tarragon. Pat steaks dry, then spread mixture thickly on all sides and stack steaks on a plate. Let stand at room temperature for at least 30 minutes, or cover and chill up to 1 day.
2. Prepare a charcoal or gas grill for direct high heat (*see Direct Heat Grilling, page 436*). Grill steaks (close lid on gas grill), turning once, until browned on both sides and done to your liking in center of thickest part (cut to test), 10 to 13 minutes for medium-rare.

3. Transfer steaks to plates. Let rest in a warm place for 3 to 5 minutes. Top each with ½ cup watercress. Add salt and pepper to taste.

PER SERVING: 490 cal., 48% (234 cal.) from fat; 57 g protein; 26 g fat (9 g sat.); 1.4 g carbo (0.4 g fiber); 342 mg sodium; 161 mg chol.

Korean Barbecued Beef (*Bulgogi*)

This recipe comes from Julie Chai, *Sunset*'s associate garden editor, whose father is Korean. Her family usually serves it with Korean Clear Noodles with Beef and Mixed Vegetables (*page 212*).

SERVES 6 | **TIME** 30 minutes, plus 30 minutes to marinate

1 **flank steak (1¾ to 2 lbs.)**
½ **cup soy sauce**
⅓ **cup thinly sliced green onions**
2 **tbsp. Asian (toasted) sesame oil**
3 **tbsp. sugar**
3 **garlic cloves, pressed or minced**

1. Pat steak dry. Cut at a 45° angle across the grain, cutting almost, but not completely, through. Make a parallel cut ¼ in. from first cut, cutting all the way through. Slice rest of steak similarly (*see Quick Tip below*). Open up butterflied slices and place in a large bowl.
2. Add soy sauce, green onions, sesame oil, sugar, and garlic to bowl; mix to coat. Cover and chill at least 30 minutes and up to 4 hours.
3. Prepare a charcoal or gas grill for direct high heat (*see Direct Heat Grilling, page 436*). Spread beef slices open and set on hot cooking grate (close lid on gas grill). Grill, turning once, until browned on both sides, 5 to 6 minutes total.
Quick Tip: Save hard-to-slice end pieces of uncooked steak to use in Korean Clear Noodles with Beef and Mixed Vegetables.

PER SERVING: 212 cal., 51% (108 cal.) from fat; 21 g protein; 12 g fat (4.4 g sat.); 4.6 g carbo (0.1 g fiber); 748 mg sodium; 52 mg chol.

Grass-fed Beef: Why to Buy and How to Cook

Americans are used to the rich taste of well-marbled, grain-fed beef. But we're growing more interested in beef fed mainly (or entirely) on grass, for a number of reasons: Grass-fed operations are easier on the environment than are grain feedlots, and are easier on the animals too (grass is, after all, a cow's natural diet). Plus, grass-fed beef is lower in saturated fats and higher in omega-3s and other essential nutrients, and it has a light, clean taste compared to the more mellow grain-fed. However, because it's so lean, it's easy to overcook—especially if you're used to cooking grain-fed. Follow these tips and you'll have no problems.

• **Lower the heat:** Instead of searing burgers and steaks over high heat, put them over a medium flame.
• **Add moisture:** With a larger cut (like a roast) that needs a longer cooking time, marinate or braise the meat to keep it from drying out.
• **Aim for rare to medium-rare:** At this level of doneness grass-fed beef is tender, but when medium to well-done, it's tough and chewy.

New York Strip Steaks with Orange and Oregano

Steaks cut from the top loin are usually called New York strip steaks. Here they get a Sicilian-style treatment with a marinade made with orange juice and vinegar. After cooking, they're sprinkled with fresh oregano.

SERVES 4 | **TIME** 20 minutes, plus 30 minutes to marinate

4 boned beef top loin steaks, 1½ in. thick
   (¾ to 1 lb. each), fat trimmed
¾ cup fresh orange juice
¼ cup red or white wine vinegar
2 tbsp. Worcestershire sauce
1 tbsp. olive oil
2 garlic cloves, minced
1½ tsp. coarsely ground black pepper,
   plus more to taste
¼ cup fresh oregano or marjoram leaves
Salt
1 orange (½ lb.), cut into 4 wedges

1. Pat steaks dry; put in a resealable plastic bag. Add orange juice, vinegar, Worcestershire, oil, garlic, and pepper. Seal bag and turn thoroughly to coat steaks with marinade. Chill for at least 30 minutes and up to 1 day.
2. Prepare a charcoal or gas grill for direct high heat (*see Direct Heat Grilling, page 436*).
3. Lift steaks from marinade (discard marinade) and wipe off excess. Grill steaks (close lid on gas grill), turning once, until browned on both sides and done to your liking in center of thickest part (cut to test), 10 to 13 minutes for medium-rare.

4. Transfer steaks to plates. Let steaks rest in a warm place for 3 to 5 minutes. Sprinkle with oregano and salt and more pepper to taste. Serve with orange wedges to squeeze over the top.

PER SERVING: 452 cal., 40% (180 cal.) from fat; 56 g protein; 20 g fat (7.2 g sat.); 7.9 g carbo (0.2 g fiber); 174 mg sodium; 148 mg chol.

Soy Sesame Grilled Flank Steak

This savory flank steak marinade with soy sauce, garlic, ginger, and sesame has been a favorite in Eugene, Oregon, reader Mary Massa's family for years. Because the steak marinates ahead of time, it can form the basis of a fast weeknight dinner.

SERVES 6 | **TIME** 30 minutes, plus 4 hours to marinate

½ cup soy sauce
¼ cup *each* olive oil, firmly packed brown sugar,
   and minced green onions
3 tbsp. sesame seeds
2 garlic cloves, crushed
½ tsp. *each* freshly ground black pepper and ground
   ginger
2 lbs. beef flank steak, fat trimmed

1. In a 1-gal. resealable plastic bag or a large bowl, mix soy sauce, oil, brown sugar, green onions, sesame seeds, garlic, pepper, and ginger. Add steak, seal bag or cover bowl tightly, and chill, turning meat occasionally, at least 4 hours and up to 2 days.
2. Prepare a charcoal or gas grill for direct medium-high heat (*see Direct Heat Grilling, page 436*). Lift steak from

How to Grill a Steak the Way You Like It

A good way to judge the doneness of a steak is to cut a tiny slit into the thickest part of the center to check the interior color. Or, with practice, you can tell by pressing the surface.

Rare. Red to pinkish red in the center; pale pink near the surface. *Touch test:* When you press the meat, it gives easily (like the flesh between your thumb and forefinger on the palm side, when your hand is relaxed).

Medium-rare. Very pink in the center; slightly gray toward the surface. *Touch test:* When you press the meat, it gives slightly (like the flesh between

your thumb and forefinger when your hand is halfway closed, into a loose fist).

Medium. Pink in the center; gray near the surface. *Touch test:* When you press the meat, it springs back (like the flesh between your thumb and forefinger when you make a fist).

Medium well to well done. Gray throughout. *Touch test:* The meat is completely firm when pressed, with very little if any spring (like the base of your thumb on the palm side when you touch your thumb to your ring finger or little finger).

Grilling Tips

Use the right level of heat. Most steaks range from 1 to 2 in. thick. Use high heat for thin steaks and lower heat for thicker steaks, to avoid charring the surface before the center is cooked.

Take it off early. Steaks usually continue to cook after you take them off the heat. For the juiciest meat, pull a steak off the grill just before it's done to your liking. If you prefer medium-rare, for instance, take it off when it reaches the rare stage, then let it rest for 3 to 5 minutes. The thicker the steak, the longer it will continue cooking from residual heat.

marinade and drain briefly. Grill steak (close lid on gas grill), turning occasionally to brown evenly, until medium-rare (cut to test), 9 to 12 minutes.
3. Transfer steak to a platter and let rest 10 minutes. Cut meat across grain into thin, slanting slices.

PER SERVING: 250 cal., 50% (126 cal.) from fat; 23 g protein; 14 g fat (4.3 g sat.); 6.6 g carbo (0.3 g fiber); 756 mg sodium; 55 mg chol.

Gin and Spice Flank Steak

The creamy gin sauce tastes delectable with hot charred steak. Serve the meat with an arugula salad.

SERVES 6 | **TIME** 45 minutes

4 tsp. dried juniper berries, divided
1½ tsp. *each* whole allspice and black peppercorns
1 tsp. kosher salt
1 beef flank steak (1½ to 1¾ lbs.), fat trimmed
1 tbsp. olive oil
1 cup reduced-sodium beef or chicken broth
¾ cup whipping cream
2 to 3 tbsp. gin

1. In a spice grinder, grind 2 tsp. juniper berries, allspice, and peppercorns until coarsely ground. Add salt and blend to mix.
2. Pat steak dry and rub all over with oil. Pat and rub spice mixture onto both sides of meat.
3. In a 2-qt. pot, bring broth and remaining 2 tsp. juniper berries to a boil over high heat and boil until reduced by three-quarters. Add cream and 2 tbsp. gin and boil over medium-high heat until reduced by half.
4. Prepare a charcoal or gas grill for direct high heat (*see Direct Heat Grilling, page 436*). Grill steak (close lid on gas grill), turning once, until firm when pressed on thin end but still quite pink inside (cut to test), 8 to 10 minutes. Meanwhile, reheat gin sauce over medium-low heat and, if more zip is desired, add remaining 1 tbsp. gin.
5. Transfer steak to a carving board with a well (to catch juices) and let rest 10 minutes. With a sharp knife, carve steak into thin, wide slices across grain, holding knife at a low angle to meat. Transfer steak to a warm platter; scrape drippings and juice from board into gin sauce. Serve meat slices with sauce.
Make Ahead: Through step 3 up to 6 hours ahead, chilled; sauce, up to 6 hours, chilled. Spice blend keeps several months, tightly covered.

PER SERVING: 266 cal., 68% (180 cal.) from fat; 19 g protein; 20 g fat (10 g sat.); 1.7 g carbo (0.1 g fiber); 467 mg sodium; 86 mg chol.

Grilled Skirt Steak (*Arracheras*)

Mexican *arracheras*, like Tex-Mex fajitas, are marinated skirt steaks cooked quickly over high heat to produce a nicely browned crust and pink interior. This recipe is from Santa Fe barbecue experts Bill Jamison and Cheryl Alters Jamison.

SERVES 6 to 8 | **TIME** 40 minutes, plus 5 hours to marinate

2 beef skirt steaks (1 to 1¼ lbs. each), fat and membrane trimmed
1 bottle or can (12 oz.) beer
¼ cup *each* fresh orange juice and lime juice
2 to 3 tbsp. chipotle hot sauce, such as Tabasco Chipotle Pepper Sauce, plus more for serving
2 tbsp. minced garlic
1½ tbsp. kosher salt
1½ tsp. ground cumin
3 large red onions, cut into ½-in.-thick slices
Vegetable-oil cooking spray
12 flour tortillas (8 in. wide), warmed
Lime wedges

1. Cut each steak in half crosswise. Put in a large resealable plastic bag. Stir together beer, orange juice, lime juice, hot sauce, and garlic, then pour over steaks. Seal bag and refrigerate at least 5 hours and up to overnight.
2. Prepare a charcoal or gas grill for direct medium-high heat (*see Direct Heat Grilling, page 436*). Drain meat and discard marinade. Blot dry with paper towels. Mix salt and cumin and rub into meat.
3. Spray onions lightly with oil and set, with steaks, on cooking grate. Do not cover. For medium-rare to medium doneness (cut to test), grill steaks 3 to 4 minutes per side if less than ½ in. thick; add 1 more minute per side if more than ½ in. thick. Turn steaks at least once while grilling (more if juice starts to pool on surface). Grill onions, turning once, until browned on both sides and cooked through, 8 to 10 minutes total.
4. Transfer steaks to a platter and let rest 5 minutes. With a sharp knife at a slight diagonal, cut across grain into thin strips. Serve meat and onions with tortillas, lime wedges, and hot sauce.

PER SERVING: 463 cal., 33% (153 cal.) from fat; 32 g protein; 17 g fat (5.1 g sat.); 43 g carbo (3.4 g fiber); 1,345 mg sodium; 58 mg chol.

The West Coast's Secret Steak: Tri-tip

Although relatively unknown elsewhere in the country, tri-tip—the pointy bottom end of the sirloin, sometimes called triangle roast—is enormously popular on the West Coast, especially California (it's the mainstay of Santa Maria–style barbecue; *opposite page*). For years it was regarded as a tough leftover from butchering. The secret most likely spread when, in the 1950s, a thrifty local butcher began cooking it up and giving samples to customers, who loved it and took the meat home to try. What makes tri-tip so appealing, besides its deep, beefy flavor, is its size—between 1½ and 3 lbs., perfect for 4 to 8 people—and its relatively low cost.

Grilled Tri-tip with Cuban *Mojo* Sauce

Mojo, Cuban garlic and orange sauce, is usually made with sour oranges, whose tartness complements meat. They can be hard to find, though, so we've substituted a mix of fresh lime and orange juices.

SERVES 8 | **TIME** 50 minutes, plus 30 minutes to marinate

1 beef tri-tip (2 to 2½ lbs.)
¼ cup olive oil, divided
2 tsp. ground toasted cumin seeds (*see Quick Tips, above right*), divided
1 tsp. dried oregano
1¾ tsp. salt, divided, plus more to taste
1 tsp. freshly ground black pepper, divided, plus more to taste
⅓ cup *each* fresh lime juice and orange juice; or ⅔ cup sour orange juice (*see Quick Tips, above right*)
2 tbsp. minced garlic
1 tsp. minced oregano leaves

1. Pat tri-tip dry, then rub with 1 tbsp. oil. Whisk together 1 tsp. cumin, dried oregano, 1¼ tsp. salt, and ½ tsp. pepper; massage into tri-tip. Let stand 30 minutes.
2. Meanwhile, make sauce: In a blender, froth juices with remaining 1 tsp. cumin, ½ tsp. salt, ½ tsp. pepper, 3 tbsp. oil, garlic, and fresh oregano. Season to taste with additional salt and pepper.
3. Prepare a charcoal or gas grill for indirect medium-high heat (*see Indirect Heat Grilling, page 436*). Grill tri-tip, turning to brown evenly, until an instant-read thermometer inserted into thickest part registers 125° to 130° for medium-rare, 25 to 30 minutes, or until done to your liking.

4. Transfer tri-tip to a cutting board, let rest 15 minutes, then cut across grain into thin, slanting slices. Serve with sauce.
Quick Tips: To toast cumin seeds, heat in a dry (not nonstick) frying pan over medium heat until fragrant and a shade darker, stirring occasionally, 3 to 5 minutes. Find sour or bitter oranges (also called Seville oranges) at Latino markets.

PER SERVING: 302 cal., 63% (189 cal.) from fat; 23 g protein; 21 g fat (6.4 g sat.); 3.2 g carbo (0.2 g fiber); 376 mg sodium; 72 mg chol.

Santa Maria–style Grilled Tri-tip

Grilling over red oak, the local wood in Santa Maria, gives the meat a wonderful rustic flavor. Using chips, which are easier to obtain for those of us outside the area, isn't quite the same as grilling over actual logs, but it's close. You can make a fine grilled tri-tip without them, but they do add flavor. Serve with pinquito beans, salsa, and garlic bread (*recipes follow*).

recipes pictured on page 456

SERVES 8 | **TIME** 1½ hours

2 tbsp. garlic powder
1½ tbsp. kosher salt
1 tsp. freshly ground black pepper
2 tsp. dried parsley
1 beef tri-tip (2 to 2½ lbs.), preferably with some fat on one side
2 cups red oak chips (optional; *see Quick Tip below*), soaked in water for at least 20 minutes

1. In a small bowl, mix garlic powder, salt, pepper, and parsley together; rub all over and into meat. Let stand 30 minutes at room temperature.
2. Meanwhile, prepare a charcoal or gas grill for indirect medium-high heat (*see Indirect Heat Grilling, page 436*) and add chips, if using, to grill. Set tri-tip over direct heat, fat side up, and sear until nicely browned (close lid on gas grill), 3 to 5 minutes; turn over and sear other side.
3. Move tri-tip over indirect-heat area and grill, turning every 10 minutes or so, until an instant-read thermometer inserted into thickest part registers 125° to 130°, 25 to 35 minutes.
4. Transfer tri-tip to a cutting board and let rest at least 15 minutes (keep grill going if you are making garlic bread; *see recipe on opposite page*). Slice meat across the grain as thin or as thick as you like.
Quick Tip: Find red oak chips online from Susy Q's Brand (*susieqbrand.com*).

PER SERVING: 290 cal., 50% (146 cal.) from fat; 32 g protein; 16 g fat (6.1 g sat.); 1.8 g carbo (0.3 g fiber); 1,158 mg sodium; 72 mg chol.

Santa Maria–style Pinquito Beans

Some Santa Maria cooks use diced ham instead of bacon, which is really good too.

SERVES 8 generously | **TIME** 2½ to 3 hours

1 lb. dried pinquito (small pink) beans *(see Quick Tip, right)*
8 slices (about ½ lb.) bacon, chopped
2 onions, chopped
2 garlic cloves, minced
½ cup *each* tomato purée and canned red chile or red enchilada sauce
1 tbsp. *each* firmly packed brown sugar and stone-ground mustard
1 tsp. salt

1. Pick over and rinse beans. Put in a 6-qt. pot and cover with water. Bring to a boil, cover, take off heat, and let stand 1 hour.

2. Drain beans. Cover with fresh water, bring to a boil, lower heat to a simmer, and cook, covered, until tender, anywhere from 40 to 90 minutes, depending on freshness of beans. Drain, reserving 1 cup cooking liquid along with beans.

3. In a 5-qt. pot over medium-high heat, cook bacon until crisp, stirring a few times. Pour off all but 1 tbsp. fat from pan. Add onions and garlic and cook, stirring, until onions just start to brown, about 4 minutes. Add tomato purée, red chile sauce, brown sugar, mustard, salt, beans, and reserved cooking liquid. Bring to a boil, stirring often; then lower heat and simmer for about 10 minutes to blend flavors.

Quick Tip: Find pinquito beans at grocery stores throughout Central California; small pink beans (different from pinto beans) are a fine substitute. You can also order pinquito beans online from Susie Q's Brand (*susieqbrand.com*).

PER 1-CUP SERVING: 296 cal., 19% (57 cal.) from fat; 16 g protein; 6.4 g fat (2.1 g sat.); 44 g carbo (8.2 g fiber); 678 mg sodium; 12 mg chol.

Santa Maria Salsa: Fresh and uncomplicated, this salsa goes with just about anything grilled. In a medium bowl, mix 4 chopped ripe **tomatoes** (1 lb. total); ½ cup *each* thinly sliced **green onions** and chopped **poblano chiles**; ¼ cup diced **celery**; 3 tbsp. chopped **cilantro**; 4 tsp. **red wine vinegar**; 1½ tsp. **kosher salt**; ¼ tsp. dried **oregano**; and a dash *each* **Tabasco** and **Worcestershire sauce**. Taste and add more salt, if needed. Makes about 3½ cups; 8 servings.

PER SERVING: 16 cal., 9% (1.5 cal.) from fat; 0.8 g protein; 0.2 g fat (0 g sat.); 3.5 g carbo (1 g fiber); 368 mg sodium; 0 mg chol.

Grilled Garlic Bread: Split a 14-in. loaf (1 lb.) soft **French-style bread** lengthwise almost in half, leaving the bread barely connected along its length. Slather with a mixture of ¼ cup softened **butter**, 1 tbsp. minced **garlic**, and ½ tsp. **kosher salt**. While tri-tip is resting, set garlic bread on grill, buttered side down, and grill until marks appear, 10 to 15 minutes. Serves 8.

PER SERVING: 202 cal., 32% (64 cal.) from fat; 4.6 g protein; 7.3 g fat (3.7 g sat.); 29 g carbo (1.5 g fiber); 519 mg sodium; 15 mg chol.

Santa Maria–style Barbecue

When Spanish settlers came to California, missions weren't all they established. In the Central Coast valley of Santa Maria, *rancheros*—owners of the huge cattle spreads called *ranchos*—cultivated a new tradition in outdoor cooking. After the annual calf branding, they hosted Spanish-style cookouts to feed those who had helped with the work—family, friends, and *vaqueros* (the original American cowboys). Besides beef, the menu included salsa, bread, and tiny local pinquito beans.

Those dishes are at the heart of what has become Santa Maria-style barbecue—a simple, quintessentially Western meal, flavored by the outdoors, and served all along the Central Coast and its inland valleys. The meat is either a thick cut of boned top sirloin or a tri-tip (*see the West Coast's Secret Steak: Tri-tip, opposite page*), usually seasoned with nothing more than salt, garlic salt, and black pepper; it's grilled over local red oak on a massive black grate that can be raised higher or lowered closer to the licking flames. The beef is nearly always served with fresh salsa, pinquitos, and buttered grilled French bread (the soft kind) for sopping up juices. A green salad usually appears, and sometimes macaroni salad or mac-'n'-cheese; often ice cream is dessert, or something involving local strawberries.

Plenty of nearby towns, notably Buellton and Casmalia, have Santa Maria barbecue on the menu, but the city of Santa Maria is its epicenter. You'll find it there at many restaurants and, especially on summer weekends, outside churches and schools and even in grocery store parking lots.

Shiraz-Soy Tri-tip

Tri-tip takes a savory dunk in a marinade of red wine, soy sauce, and balsamic vinegar in this recipe from Erik Olsen, winemaker at Clos du Bois Winery in Sonoma County, California. For a nice little side dish, marinate bell peppers and onions in the leftover marinade and grill next to the meat (grill them about 15 minutes, and don't brush with the marinade while cooking).

SERVES 8 to 10 | **TIME** 35 minutes, plus 2 hours to marinate

¾ cup Shiraz (Syrah) wine *(see Quick Tip below)*
⅔ cup soy sauce
¼ cup *each* vegetable oil, balsamic vinegar, and fresh lemon juice
2 tbsp. Worcestershire sauce
2 tsp. Dijon mustard
1½ tsp. minced garlic
1 beef tri-tip (about 2½ lbs.), fat trimmed

1. In a 1-gal. resealable plastic bag, combine Shiraz, soy sauce, oil, vinegar, lemon juice, Worcestershire, mustard, and garlic. Add tri-tip and seal bag. Chill at least 2 hours and up to 1 day, turning occasionally.
2. Prepare a charcoal or gas grill for direct medium heat *(see Direct Heat Grilling, page 436)*. Lift tri-tip from marinade and lay on hot cooking grate (close lid on gas grill); discard marinade. Grill tri-tip, turning every 5 minutes, until an instant-read thermometer inserted into center of thickest part registers 125° to 130° for medium-rare, about 25 minutes, or until done to your liking.
3. Transfer tri-tip to a cutting board, let rest 5 minutes, then cut across the grain into thin, slanting slices.
Quick Tip: Shiraz and Syrah are the same grape (Shiraz is what it's called in Australia, and Syrah is its French name—and what it's most commonly called in the U.S.).

PER SERVING: 151 cal., 38% (57 cal.) from fat; 21 g protein; 6.3 g fat (1.9 g sat.); 0.8 g carbo (0 g fiber); 342 mg sodium; 59 mg chol.

Grilled Beef Tenderloin with Fresh Herbs

Buttery, fancy tenderloin from the grill is a special-occasion treat.

SERVES 8 | **TIME** 1¾ hours, plus 1 hour to bring beef to room temperature

1 center-cut beef tenderloin (3 to 4 lbs.)
2 tbsp. Dijon mustard
12 large basil leaves
12 sage leaves
1 tbsp. fresh thyme leaves
6 to 9 garlic cloves, minced
2 tsp. sea salt, divided, plus more to taste
½ tsp. freshly ground black pepper, divided, plus more to taste
2 tbsp. olive oil
Sage, basil, or thyme sprigs

1. Bring meat to room temperature, about 1 hour. Trim any excess fat from meat and discard. Cut through meat lengthwise (parallel to the work surface) to within ½ in. of other side. Lay meat open like a book and spread with mustard. Lay basil and sage leaves on mustard. Sprinkle with thyme leaves, garlic, 1 tsp. salt, and ¼ tsp. pepper.
2. Bring cut sides together and tie roast with cotton string at about 1-in. intervals to secure. Rub beef all over with oil and sprinkle with remaining 1 tsp. salt and ¼ tsp. pepper.
3. Meanwhile, prepare a charcoal or gas grill for indirect medium heat, using a drip pan filled halfway with warm water *(see Indirect Heat Grilling, page 436)*. Grill beef over indirect-heat area, covered, until an instant-read thermometer inserted into thickest part registers 130° to 135° for rare, 60 to 70 minutes. Transfer beef to a platter and let rest in a warm place 20 minutes.
4. Remove string from beef. Garnish with herb sprigs. Slice and season with salt and pepper to taste.
Make Ahead: Through step 2, up to 2 hours (but work with chilled meat rather than bringing to room temperature first).

PER SERVING: 408 cal., 58% (237 cal.) from fat; 38 g protein; 26 g fat (9.9 g sat.); 2.1 g carbo (0.2 g fiber); 728 mg sodium; 129 mg chol.

the fire outside

Beef Rib Roast and Yorkshire Pudding from the Grill

Bob House, of Scottsdale, Arizona, received an award in a *Sunset* grilling contest for this unusual recipe. House rubs the roast with an herb-flavored oil and then grills it, catching the drippings in a pan. He pours Yorkshire pudding batter into the drip pan, where it puffs in the hot fat and browns from the heat of the coals.

SERVES 5 to 7 | **TIME** 1½ hours

1 center-cut bone-in beef rib roast (4 to 5 lbs.), surface
    fat trimmed to no more than ¼ in. thick
Garlic-Herb Oil (*recipe follows*)
1 cup *each* low-fat milk and flour
3 eggs
¾ tsp. salt
Melted butter (if necessary)
1 large bunch watercress, tough stems trimmed
Freshly ground black pepper

1. Pat beef dry and coat all over with garlic-herb oil.
2. Prepare a charcoal or gas grill for indirect medium heat, using an 8-in. square drip pan filled with 1 cup water (*see Indirect Heat Grilling, page 436*). Set roast, bones down, on cooking grate over drip pan. Close lid on grill (open vents on charcoal grill). Grill roast 45 minutes.
3. Meanwhile, in a blender, mix milk, flour, eggs, and salt until batter is smooth.
4. Transfer roast to a platter. Protecting your hands, lift off cooking grate and remove drip pan. Pour drippings through a fine-mesh strainer into a bowl. *If using a charcoal grill*, return 1 tbsp. drippings to pan; discard the rest. Return pan to firegrate and pour in batter. Replace cooking grate, set roast back over pan, close lid on grill (keeping vents open), and cook roast until an instant-read thermometer inserted into center of thickest part registers 135° for medium-rare, 30 to 50 minutes longer, or until done to your liking. Cook pudding until well browned, 40 to 50 minutes. *If using a gas grill*, return 3 tbsp. drippings (adding melted butter, if needed, to make this amount) to pan and pour in batter. Set another drip pan on firegrate, replace cooking grate, and set roast over pan. Set pudding next to roast and close lid on grill. Cook roast until medium-rare (an instant-read thermometer inserted into thickest part registers 135°), 30 to 50 minutes longer, or until done to your liking. Cook pudding until well browned, 20 to 30 minutes.
5. Transfer roast to a platter; let roast rest in a warm place for juices to settle, at least 10 minutes. If pudding is done before roast is ready to carve, close charcoal grill vents and leave pudding on grill to keep warm, or turn off gas grill and keep pudding warm with lid down.
6. Carve roast. Divide watercress among plates and serve slices of beef on top of watercress, with scoops of pudding on the side.

PER SERVING: 934 cal., 68% (639 cal.) from fat; 53 g protein; 71 g fat (27 g sat.); 18 g carbo (0.8 g fiber); 426 mg sodium; 269 mg chol.

Garlic-Herb Oil: In a food processor, finely chop ¼ cup **garlic cloves** with 3 tbsp. **olive oil** and 1½ tsp. *each* **dried rosemary**, **dried savory**, **dried thyme**, and **freshly ground black pepper**. Makes ⅓ cup.

Korean Barbecued Short Ribs (*Kalbi*)

Koreans have a wonderful way of cutting short ribs so that they open up thin and flat—and consequently cook well on a grill.

SERVES 6 | **TIME** 40 minutes, plus 4 hours to marinate

1 cup soy sauce
⅓ cup sugar
2½ tbsp. *each* minced garlic and fresh ginger
⅓ cup *each* crushed toasted sesame seeds (*see Quick
    Tips below*) and Asian (toasted) sesame oil
⅔ cup thinly sliced green onion
4 lbs. lean beef short ribs, cut into 2- to 3-in. pieces,
    each piece sliced to open flat (*see Quick Tips below*)

1. Mix all ingredients except beef in a large bowl. Add beef and turn to coat. Chill, covered, turning ribs a few times, at least 4 hours and up to 24.
2. Prepare a charcoal or gas grill for direct high heat (*see Direct Heat Grilling, page 436*). Lift ribs from marinade and grill until browned on both sides, 5 to 10 minutes total.
Quick Tips: To toast sesame seeds, heat them in a dry pan over medium heat until golden, stirring occasionally. Korean markets sell beef short ribs already cut for grilling, but you can also ask your butcher to cut the ribs—or do it yourself: Set a short rib (2 to 3 in. long) on a short side. Starting about ¼ in. from bone, slice straight down and parallel to bone, cutting almost but not all the way through (to within ¼ in. of end of piece) Turn rib over and make a similar cut about ½ in. from the first cut, so that the meat opens like an accordion. Spread the meat out in a long, flat strip.

PER SERVING: 355 cal., 58% (204 cal.) from fat; 27 g protein; 23 g fat (7.4 g sat.); 9.5 g carbo (0.9 g fiber); 1,252 mg sodium; 76 mg chol.

Pork Tenderloin with Pumpkin-seed Sauce

Reader Paul Heitzenrater, and his partner, John Farnam, who live in Denver, often host fund-raising dinners, with Heitzenrater as cook. One year, Heitzenrater was casting around for a party dish when he remembered a pumpkin-seed sauce he'd gone crazy for in Puerto Vallarta. He concocted one and dolloped it onto pork tenderloin medallions, adding layers of flavor with toasted pumpkin seeds and pumpkin-seed oil. (Sometimes he includes squash blossoms from his garden.)

SERVES 4 to 6 | **TIME** 40 minutes, plus 2 hours to marinate

4 canned chipotle chiles in adobo sauce, chopped, plus 2 tbsp. sauce
¼ cup orange juice
1 tbsp. firmly packed light brown sugar
2 lbs. pork tenderloin, fat and membrane trimmed
¾ cup hulled pumpkin seeds, divided
1 cup heavy whipping cream
1 garlic clove, minced
1 tsp. chipotle chile powder
½ tsp. salt
1 tbsp. pumpkin-seed oil *(see Quick Tip below)*

1. In a small nonreactive bowl, combine chiles, adobo sauce, orange juice, and brown sugar. Put pork in a baking dish and add marinade, turning pork to coat. Cover and refrigerate at least 2 hours and up to overnight.
2. Preheat oven to 375°. Toast pumpkin seeds on a baking sheet until they have popped and are just starting to brown, 7 to 11 minutes. Let cool. In a food processor, grind ½ cup of seeds into a paste.
3. Prepare a charcoal or gas grill for direct medium-high heat *(see Direct Heat Grilling, page 436)*. Lift pork out of marinade (discard marinade) and grill, turning once, until an instant-read thermometer inserted into thickest part registers 160°, about 10 minutes per side. Let pork rest 10 to 15 minutes. Reserve juices.
4. Meanwhile, in a medium pan over medium heat, combine pumpkin-seed paste, cream, garlic, chile powder, and salt. Cook, whisking until thickened, 3 to 5 minutes. Stir in reserved pork juices.
5. Slice pork into ½-in.-thick medallions. Drizzle with sauce and pumpkin-seed oil and garnish with remaining ¼ cup toasted pumpkin seeds.
Quick Tip: Find pumpkin-seed oil at well-stocked grocery stores.

PER SERVING: 411 cal., 59% (243 cal.) from fat; 33 g protein; 27 g fat (13 g sat.); 8.7 g carbo (0.9 g fiber); 414 mg sodium; 150 mg chol.

Sage-rubbed Pork Tenderloins with Sage Butter

Grilling gurus Bill Jamison and Cheryl Alters Jamison created this recipe for us using a two-level fire setup. Brown the tenderloins over high heat, then finish cooking on a cooler part of the grill. Drizzle with a simple sage-scented sauce.

SERVES 8 | **TIME** 1 hour

2 tbsp. crumbled dried sage
1½ tsp. *each* brown sugar and kosher salt
1 tsp. *each* garlic powder and freshly ground black pepper
2 pork tenderloins (¾ to 1 lb. each), fat and membrane trimmed
6 tbsp. unsalted butter
2 tbsp. olive oil
¼ cup packed fresh sage leaves, plus sprigs for garnish (sprigs optional)
1 garlic clove, slivered
1 tsp. mashed anchovy fillet, or salt to taste
Olive-oil or vegetable-oil cooking spray

1. Stir together dried sage, brown sugar, salt, garlic powder, and pepper and massage into tenderloins. Let stand, covered, at room temperature 25 to 30 minutes.
2. *For a charcoal grill*, light a chimneyful of charcoal. When all coals are lit, mound them against one side of the firegrate in a slope. Let coals burn until the crest is at high heat *(see Taking Your Grill's Temperature, page 436)* and the lower part of the slope at medium. Set clean cooking grate on top to preheat and oil well with a wad of oiled paper towels. *For a gas grill*, set one burner to high and the other to medium; make sure cooking grate is clean, and oil it well with a wad of oiled paper towels.
3. In a small saucepan over medium-low heat, cook butter, oil, fresh sage leaves, and garlic about 10 minutes; stir in anchovy and remove from heat. Let stand 10 minutes. Strain butter through a fine-mesh strainer and keep warm.
4. Spray tenderloins generously with cooking spray. Set on cooking grate over high heat, angling thinner ends of meat away from hottest part of fire. Grill, turning occasionally, until browned on all sides, about 5 minutes total. Move tenderloins over medium heat (close lid on gas grill) and grill, turning occasionally, until an instant-read thermometer inserted into thickest part registers 150° and center has a touch of pink remaining (cut to test). Time depends on meat's thickness: Thin tenderloins (about 1½ in. thick) require 8 to 10 minutes; plump tenderloins (up to 2½ in. thick) may need twice that long. Remove from grill, tent with foil, and let pork rest 10 minutes before carving.

5. Cut into thin slices, garnish with sage sprigs if you like, and serve with sage butter.

PER SERVING: 256 cal., 67% (171 cal.) from fat; 20 g protein; 19 g fat (7.8 g sat.); 1.9 g carbo (0.1 g fiber); 525 mg sodium; 86 mg chol.

Grilled Pork Chops with Onion-Peach Marmalade

Because modern pork is very lean, the meat can easily dry out. Using a brine adds moisture and flavor.

SERVES 4 | **TIME** 1 hour, plus overnight to brine

½ cup plus 1 tsp. kosher salt
½ cup firmly packed light brown sugar
1 sprig plus 2 tsp. chopped rosemary leaves
3 tsp. black peppercorns, divided
4 bone-in center-cut pork chops (1¾ lbs. total), fat trimmed
3 tbsp. olive oil, divided
4 cups sliced white onions
2 cups chopped peeled ripe peaches (see Quick Tip below)
⅓ cup granulated sugar
3 tbsp. sherry vinegar

1. In a large pot, bring 7 cups water to a boil. Remove from heat and add ½ cup salt, the brown sugar, rosemary sprig, and 2 tsp. peppercorns, stirring until salt and sugar are dissolved. Add 1 cup ice cubes and chill until cold. Immerse pork in brine and set a plate on top of pork to keep meat completely submerged. Cover with plastic wrap and chill overnight.
2. Heat 2 tbsp. oil in a large frying pan over medium heat. Add onions and cook, stirring often, until transparent and starting to brown, 10 to 15 minutes. Turn heat to low; add peaches, granulated sugar, vinegar, and remaining 1 tsp. peppercorns. Cook, stirring often, until marmalade is caramelized and sticky, about 40 minutes. Stir in remaining 1 tsp. salt and 2 tsp. rosemary.
3. Prepare a charcoal or gas grill for direct medium heat (see Direct Heat Grilling, page 436). Remove pork from brine and pat dry. Brush chops all over with remaining 1 tbsp. oil. Lay pork on cooking grate. Close lid on grill and cook pork, turning once, until done to your liking, about 10 minutes for medium (an instant-read thermometer inserted into center of thickest part registers 145°). Transfer pork to a platter, tent with foil, and let rest 5 to 10 minutes. Serve with warm marmalade.
Quick Tip: If you can't find fresh peaches, use frozen.
Make Ahead: Marmalade, 1 day, chilled; reheat to serve.

PER SERVING: 526 cal., 41% (216 cal.) from fat; 34 g protein; 24 g fat (6.5 g sat.); 44 g carbo (4.3 g fiber); sodium N/A; 88 mg chol.

Applewood-smoked Spareribs with Paprika Chili Spice Rub

Right before the end of cooking, Tyler Florence—the Northern California–based Food Network chef—sprinkles his ribs with a little more rub for an extra pop of flavor.

SERVES 6 to 8 | **TIME** 2¾ hours

3 cups applewood chips
1½ slabs pork spareribs (about 8 lbs. total)
6 tbsp. each hot paprika and chili powder
2 tbsp. garlic powder
1½ tbsp. each dried oregano and freshly ground black pepper
1 tbsp. kosher salt
2 tsp. celery seeds
⅓ cup distilled white vinegar
2 tbsp. fresh lemon juice

1. Soak chips in water 20 to 40 minutes. Meanwhile, prepare a charcoal or gas grill for indirect low heat, using a drip pan filled halfway with warm water (see Indirect Heat Grilling, page 436). Set cooking grate aside.
2. Cut the full slab of ribs in half. Make dry rub: Combine paprika, chili and garlic powders, oregano, pepper, salt, and celery seeds. Rub three-quarters of dry rub onto both sides of ribs. Set remaining one-quarter of rub aside.
3. Drain wood chips. If using a charcoal grill, sprinkle 1 cup chips over coals (keep rest wet) and set cooking grate on top. If using a gas grill, put 1 cup chips in a metal smoking box or small shallow foil pan and set directly on heat in corner; set cooking grate on top. Lay ribs on cooking grate over drip pan.
4. Smoke ribs, covered, 45 minutes to 1 hour. If using charcoal, add 8 to 10 briquets to lit coals (enough to keep heat constant) and 1 cup chips. If using gas, add ½ cup chips. Turn ribs over. Cook, covered, 45 minutes to 1 hour longer; add another 8 to 10 briquets (if using charcoal) and 1 cup chips (½ cup chips for gas). Turn ribs and cook for 30 minutes to 1 hour longer, until meat starts to pull away from tips of bone.
5. Meanwhile, make wet rub: Mix vinegar, 1 tbsp. water, and the lemon juice in a small bowl.
6. When meat is almost done, use a spray bottle or paper towels to thoroughly baste top of ribs with wet rub, then sprinkle with remaining dry rub. Cook ribs a few minutes more. Transfer to a cutting board and let rest 15 minutes before slicing and serving.
Make Ahead: Dry rub can easily be doubled or even tripled. Store it at room temperature, airtight, up to a month.

PER SERVING: 752 cal., 66% (500 cal.) from fat; 54 g protein; 56 g fat (20 g sat.); 9.8 g carbo (2.3 g fiber); 661 mg sodium; 214 mg chol.

Harissa Pork Ribs

Seattle chef Christopher Hartfield cuts prep time by marinating ribs in harissa, a Tunisian spice paste, which imparts a warm heat.

SERVES 8 | **TIME** 1 hour, plus 8 hours to marinate

¾ cup harissa paste (see Quick Tip below)
3 tbsp. fresh lemon juice
1 tbsp. minced garlic
2 slabs baby back ribs (about 1½ lbs. each)
Kosher salt and freshly ground black pepper
2 bottles (12 oz. each) of beer, any type

1. In a bowl, stir together harissa, lemon juice, and garlic.
2. Use a dull butter knife to loosen thin papery membrane that runs along underside of ribs, then pull it off with your fingers. Rub ribs generously on both sides with salt and pepper, then slather all over with harissa rub. Wrap ribs in plastic wrap and marinate, refrigerated, for at least 8 and up to 24 hours.
3. Prepare a charcoal or gas grill for indirect medium heat (see *Indirect Heat Grilling, page 436*). Place ribs, bone side down, on cooler part of the grill; close lid. Cook, basting gently with beer on both sides every 10 minutes (keep ribs bone side down), until ribs are tender and cooked through and meat has shrunk back from ends of the bones, 40 to 50 minutes total. Try to keep harissa paste on the ribs while basting. Serve ribs hot, with salad.
Quick Tip: Find harissa at gourmet markets and Middle Eastern markets.
Make Ahead: Marinate ribs 2 days ahead, grill the day before, then reheat on the grill to serve.

PER SERVING: 330 cal., 71% (234 cal.) from fat; 20 g protein; 26 g fat (9 g sat.); 3.2 g carbo (0 g fiber); 242 mg sodium; 97 mg chol.

Herb-rubbed Baby Back Ribs

The pepper in the rub picks up on the black-pepper notes in the Zinfandel sauce.

recipe pictured on page 459

SERVES 6 to 8 | **TIME** 2 hours

¼ cup paprika
3 tbsp. dried thyme
1 tbsp. salt, plus more to taste
1½ tbsp. freshly ground black pepper
3 racks pork baby back ribs (7 to 8 lbs. total)
Cherry-Zinfandel Barbecue Sauce (recipe follows)

1. Mix paprika, thyme, salt, and pepper. Pat ribs dry, then rub herb mixture over both sides of each rack, pressing so it sticks. Wrap each rack in heavy-duty foil.

2. Prepare a charcoal or gas grill for indirect medium heat, using a drip pan filled halfway with warm water (see *Indirect Heat Grilling, page 436*).
3. Lay foil-wrapped ribs on grill, meaty (convex) side up, over indirect heat area; overlap slightly if necessary. Close lid on grill and cook until tender when pierced (through foil), 1 to 1¼ hours.
4. Carefully remove foil from ribs. Brush meaty side of each rack lightly with barbecue sauce, turn over, and cook until sauce is browned, about 10 minutes. Brush bone (concave) sides, turn again, and cook until browned on that side, about 10 minutes longer.
5. Transfer ribs to a board and cut between bones into individual ribs. Season to taste with salt and serve with remaining barbecue sauce.
Make Ahead: Through step 1, up to a day, chilled; bring to room temperature before grilling.

PER SERVING: 813 cal., 69% (558 cal.) from fat; 51 g protein; 62 g fat (23 g sat.); 11 g carbo (0.6 g fiber); 1,229 mg sodium; 242 mg chol.

Cherry-Zinfandel Barbecue Sauce

This sauce is packed with the flavor of Zinfandel—dried cherries, anise seeds (Zin often has faint licorice flavors), black pepper—and lots of the wine itself.

MAKES 3½ cups | **TIME** 40 minutes

1 tbsp. olive oil
1 medium onion, chopped
2 tbsp. chopped garlic
1½ cups dry red Zinfandel
1 cup ketchup
⅔ cup dried tart cherries
3 tbsp. *each* cider vinegar, Worcestershire sauce, and lightly packed light brown sugar
2 tbsp. *each* Dijon mustard and chopped fresh ginger
1 tsp. *each* anise seeds and freshly ground black pepper
¼ tsp. cayenne
2 tbsp. fresh lemon juice, plus more to taste

1. Heat oil in a medium saucepan over medium-high heat until hot. Add onion and garlic and cook, stirring often, until limp, 3 to 4 minutes. Add remaining ingredients except lemon juice. Bring to a boil, then reduce heat and simmer, stirring occasionally, until liquid begins to thicken slightly, about 20 minutes. Let cool slightly.
2. Pour mixture into a blender, add lemon juice, and purée. Taste and add more lemon juice if you like. Use warm or at room temperature.
Make Ahead: Up to 3 days, chilled; bring to room temperature before using.

PER ¼ CUP: 70 cal., 14% (10 cal.) from fat; 0.8 g protein; 1.1 g fat (0.1 g sat.); 15 g carbo (0.5 g fiber); 294 mg sodium; 0 mg chol.

West Coast Wines for Food from the Grill

Where there's smoke, pour wine—red or white—with mouth-filling textures and exuberant flavors. Juicy fruit in a wine is a delicious contrast to a little char on seafood, meat, and vegetables. And rustic wines fit the backyard bill. The West Coast is in luck when it comes to making that match, because the wines produced here, using grapes from all around the globe, tend to have generous quotas of fruit flavors. And if the grapes have been grown in the right (cool enough) places, the wines will have held onto their acidity and juiciness.

Favorite Reds

ZINFANDEL. With rich, jammy berry and plum flavors, often seasoned with black pepper, Zin is a natural for barbecue. If pork ribs are involved, it's a must (test the theory with our Herb-rubbed Baby Back Ribs, *opposite page*). And you almost can't go wrong pouring it with hamburgers. Just be a little careful about the alcohol level in your Zin: Grown in mighty warm places and allowed to get über-ripe, the wine can creep up to 16 percent and above, and if your food has any spice to it, its heat combined with that of the alcohol can spark an inferno.

SYRAH. A grape from France's Rhône Valley, it's typically meaty (even leaning toward bacon), herbal, and underpinned with smoky tobacco notes. But West Coast versions layer lush berries and plums over the earthiness, making them perfect for the grill. If your hamburger has bacon on it, go for Syrah. And absolutely give it a try with Santa Maria–style barbecue *(page 487)*.

SANGIOVESE AND BARBERA. The Italians are coming on strong in the West and offer a lot to like when you're firing up the grill. Both have an earthy side, a naturally high level of acidity (great with anything involving tomatoes), and warm spices that make them great matches for not only Italian dishes but also flavors from the Far East. Dusty-berried Sangio would be great with the Classic Cioppino *(page 126)*. Spicy-cherried Barbera would handsomely cover everything from our Grilled Pizza *(page 465)* to Ginger Beef Mini Skewers *(page 441)* to *Char Siu*–glazed Pork and Pineapple Buns *(page 464)*.

PETITE SIRAH. Not little and not Syrah, this is a wine that can pack a wallop of dark fruit, spice, and tannin, so it's tasty with serious charred and chewy meats—grilled leg of lamb, say.

TEMPRANILLO. The main red variety in Spain—tangy, dark-fruited, and smelling of the earth—is on the winemaking radar here. Give one a try if your beef or lamb is marinated in balsamic vinegar with lots of herbs.

Choice Whites

On the white-wine front, think beyond Chardonnay and even Sauvignon Blanc when you're grilling. Here are the whites that deliver the combination of full body and bright fruit plus herbs and aromatics that set off what we're cooking on the grill these days.

RIESLING. Forget those syrupy versions from the '70s and '80s; Riesling has gone drier and crisper lately. With sweet but briny fruit and bright acidity, a great choice for our Barbecued Oysters with Chipotle Glaze *(page 444)*. But it's rich enough to handle that char siu–glazed pork too.

VIOGNIER. The main full-bodied, aromatic white (expect peaches and apricots and earth) from the Rhône, Viognier wraps around meaty, smoky, sweet combos like our Halibut Kebabs with Grilled Bread and Pancetta *(page 505)*.

Think Pink

You can let go of the old rules of pairing when you're cooking over fire; don't worry about pouring white wine with fish and chicken, or sipping red wine with all the rest. Slap ahi tuna (as in the Grilled Ahi Citrus Salad, *page 462)* or chicken on the grate, and your best bets are bright, fruity reds—or rosé. Give pink wine a chance! The rosés coming out of West Coast wineries today are dry and crisp, loaded with bright red fruit and refreshing citrus. Look for rosés made of Grenache, Syrah, and Mourvèdre in particular—they're shockingly perfect matches for the all-time favorites: barbecued chicken, ribs, and hot dogs.

Achiote-and-Orange Pulled Pork

Real, slow-cooked barbecue takes time, but this dish is truly worth it. Santa Fe barbecue experts Bill Jamison and Cheryl Alters Jamison pile the succulent meat on *bolillos* (hard Mexican-style rolls) or other small rolls that they've smeared with mayonnaise, then top with *queso fresco*, avocado slices, and a squeeze of lime. We also like layering the sandwiches with their Chipotle Coleslaw *(page 155)*.

SERVES 8 to 14, depending on size of pork shoulder
TIME 5 to 7 hours, plus 8 hours to marinate

MEAT & GRILLING

1 boned pork shoulder (also called butt; 4 to 6 lbs.)
2 to 3 cups cherry or hickory wood chips *(see Quick Tips, right)*

ACHIOTE SEASONING PASTE

3 oz. (6 tbsp.) orange juice concentrate
3 tbsp. achiote paste *(see Quick Tips, right)*
2 tbsp. *each* kosher or sea salt and coarsely ground black pepper
1 tbsp. *each* garlic powder and crumbled dried oregano
1 tsp. cayenne

ORANGE "MOP" SAUCE

3 oz. (6 tbsp.) thawed orange juice concentrate
2 cups cider vinegar or distilled white vinegar
2 tbsp. butter
1 tsp. kosher or sea salt

SERVING & CONDIMENTS

½ cup *each* thinly sliced green onions and chopped cilantro
Chipotle Coleslaw *(page 155)*
Rolls, mayonnaise, crumbled *queso fresco (see Quick Tips, right)*, sliced avocado, lime wedges, and/or hot sauce

1. The night before you plan to barbecue, cut pork shoulder lengthwise into two equal pieces (to speed up cooking), removing excess fat as needed. Combine seasoning-paste ingredients in a small bowl. Massage pork well with paste, then transfer to a large resealable plastic bag and refrigerate at least 8 hours.
2. About 45 minutes before you're ready to begin barbecuing, remove pork from refrigerator and let stand in plastic bag at room temperature (this will speed up cooking and help the meat cook evenly).
3. Put wood chips in a bowl, cover with water, and soak at least 30 minutes.
4. Combine "mop" ingredients with 1 cup water in a saucepan and warm over low heat. Set aside ¾ cup sauce.
5. Prepare a charcoal or gas grill for indirect low heat, using a drip pan filled halfway with water and ⅔ cup drained wood chips *(see Indirect Heat Grilling, page 436)*.
6. Lift meat from marinade and lay meat on cooking grate directly over drip pan. Cover grill and cook meat 1 hour. Using a heatproof brush, baste meat all over with mop sauce. If using charcoal, add 10 to 15 briquets to fire (or more if coals have burned down significantly) and another ⅓ cup drained wood chips (don't add more if using gas). Check water level in drip pan for either grill type; add more water as needed to keep filled halfway. Cover grill and keep smoking meat, maintaining grill temperature. Repeat process (mopping meat, adding 10 to 15 briquets and ⅓ cup chips if using charcoal grill, checking water level) every hour, turning meat occasionally, until an instant-read thermometer inserted into thickest part of each piece registers 190° and meat shreds easily, 1½ hours per lb. (3 to 5 hours total). If thermometer registers 190° but meat isn't tender, cook 30 minutes more.
7. Lift meat from grill and wrap in a double layer of heavy-duty foil, sealing tightly. Let meat steam at room temperature for about 30 minutes, then unwrap it, reserving any juices that have accumulated in foil.
8. When meat is cool enough to handle, pull it apart into large pieces. Discard excess fat. Shred meat with your fingers or a pair of forks. Toss shredded meat with green onions and cilantro and drizzle with reserved juices and reserved mop sauce to taste. Serve pork with coleslaw and your choice of condiments.

Quick Tips: You'll need 2 to 3 cups wood chips for charcoal grilling, but only about a cup for gas grilling. Find the chips at barbecue stores, some grocery stores, or online. Achiote paste is made from ground achiote seeds (also called annatto), vinegar, salt, and spices; it's often sold in bar form. *Queso fresco* is a fresh Mexican cheese. Find both in Latino markets and the Latino-foods aisle of large supermarkets.

PER SERVING: 481 cal., 54% (261 cal.) from fat; 39 g protein; 29 g fat (10 g sat.); 12 g carbo (64 g fiber); 1,110 mg sodium; 165 mg chol.

Tracking Temperature

While true barbecue is often cooked at temperatures as low as 175°, we found it more manageable to maintain a temperature between 250° and 300° on a home-style grill. Because it's hard to gauge such low temperatures with the hand test *(see Taking Your Grill's Temperature, page 436)*, we monitor the temperature of the grill using the grill's built-in thermometer or, for charcoal, a "smoker" thermometer poked through a top vent in the lid (choose a heatproof model that reads up to at least 400°; we found ours on *amazon.com*).

the fire outside

Spicy Pork Skewers

Moroccan meat skewers, or *kefta*, are made with beef and formed into sausage shapes. Our variation uses pork rolled into little meatballs. You'll need eight (10-in.) skewers for this.

SERVES 4 to 6 | **TIME** 20 minutes, plus about 20 minutes to soak skewers if using wooden

1¼ lbs. ground pork
1½ tbsp. minced garlic
2 tsp. *each* ground cumin and paprika
⅓ cup finely chopped onion
1½ tsp. salt
1 tsp. freshly ground black pepper

1. If using wooden skewers, soak in water for at least 30 minutes.
2. Meanwhile, in a medium bowl, stir together pork, garlic, cumin, paprika, onion, salt, and pepper. Form into small meatballs, each about the size of a golf ball, then thread meat onto skewers.
3. Prepare a charcoal or gas grill for direct medium heat (*see Direct Heat Grilling, page 436*). Grill skewers (close lid on gas grill), turning once, until browned on both sides and no longer pink in center (cut to test), about 8 minutes. Serve warm.

PER SERVING: 206 cal., 61% (126 cal.) from fat; 17 g protein; 14 g fat (5 g sat.); 2.5 g carbo (0.4 g fiber); 631 mg sodium; 61 mg chol.

Grilled Beer-cooked Sausages

San Franciscan James Bullard simmers these sausages, which he serves at his annual Oktoberfest bash, in beer, so they grill quicker and guests get fed faster. We love them smeared with coarse-grain mustard on crusty rolls. The onions take on a lot of the ale's flavor, including its slight bitterness. Leave them off your sausage if you're sensitive to bitter flavors.

SERVES 12 | **TIME** 40 minutes

6 bottles (12 oz. each) medium- to heavy-bodied ale
12 bratwursts (*see Quick Tip below*)
1 large onion, halved lengthwise and sliced crosswise

1. Bring beer to a boil in a large, wide pot. Add sausages and onion slices and simmer 15 minutes. Cover, remove pot from heat, and let stand until ready to grill, up to 1 hour.
2. Prepare a charcoal or gas grill for direct medium heat (*see Direct Heat Grilling, page 436*). Using tongs or a slotted spoon, transfer sausages to hot cooking grate. Grill sausages, turning once, until browned on both sides, about 8 minutes. Meanwhile, drain onions and set aside. Serve sausages hot or warm, with onions on the side for people to add if they like.
Quick Tip: You can add up to 8 more sausages without increasing the amount of beer or onion.

PER SERVING: 350 cal., 75% (261 cal.) from fat; 16 g protein; 29 g fat (11 g sat.); 4.3 g carbo (0.3 g fiber); 633 mg sodium; 68 mg chol.

Cooking on Sticks

Skewers—whether you call them kebabs, satay, or brochettes—are just plain fun, and versatile too: You can pop them on the grill or run them under the broiler, and serve them as appetizers or as a main course. Plus, they're tasty: Whatever you're skewering has been cut into small pieces, so once you apply a marinade or glaze, you get a high flavor-to-bite ratio.

Here's a list of the other kebab and skewer recipes in the book.

- Roasted Brussels Sprout and Prosciutto Skewers (*page 34*)
- Sweet-Hot Coconut Shrimp (*page 62*)
- Peppered Beef Skewers with Red Onion–Horseradish Marmalade (*page 441*)
- Ginger Beef Mini Skewers (*page 441*)
- Ginger Shrimp Mini Skewers (*page 441*)
- Yogurt-marinated Chicken Kebabs with Pearl Couscous (*page 475*)
- Grilled Chicken Kebabs with Romesco Sauce (*page 475*)
- Tandoori Kebabs (*page 476*)
- Vietnamese Skewered Pork and Onions (*page 412*)
- Grilled Lamb Brochettes with Lemon and Dill (*page 502*)
- Grilled Moroccan Lamb Kebabs with Grapes (*page 503*)
- Halibut Kebabs with Grilled Bread and Pancetta (*page 505*)
- Tandoori Shrimp in Green Marinade (*page 509*)
- Lemon-Garlic Shrimp Skewers (*page 510*)
- Salt-cured Ouzo Shrimp (*page 510*)

Cooking (and Eating) from Nose to Tail

Whole-animal cooking, the obsession of many a top chef in America, has set off a wave of interest in the subject around the country. Urbanites used to buying meat in plastic-wrapped portions are signing up for butchery demonstrations, willingly ordering unfamiliar cuts like trotters, jowls, and kidneys in restaurants that serve every part of an animal, and crowding into meat-tasting parties where whole animals lie around on display while cocktails are sipped. For those who grew up with whole-animal roasts as part of their heritage—in Hawaii, with *kalua* pig; Mexico, with *cabrito* (kid goat); Greece and Italy, with Easter lamb; the Philippines and Cuba, where roast pig is celebration food; or on farms and ranches—none of this is new. But for many others, it's a fascinating way to learn about meat and eat it with less waste.

Why Cook a Whole Animal Yourself?

Cooking whole animals at home takes the adventure to the next level. Here's why you might want to consider it:

• You can figure out where those supermarket cuts come from: the tenderloin, the chops, the rack of ribs. It's helpful to look at a meat chart as a guide. The best charts currently online are at *porkfoodservice.org* (click on "Cuts of Pork") and *americanlamb.com* (click on "Lamb 101").

• You can compare the tastes and textures of all the different pieces of the beast. One revelation, for us, was the supreme tenderness of the thin layer of meat over the pork belly.

• Roasted right, it yields incredibly crisp and delicious skin.

• From a sustainability standpoint, it makes sense to eat every part of the animal, instead of buying only the most familiar cuts—which encourages large-scale underutilizing of the rest.

• A whole grilled animal makes for a much more memorable party than do burgers, steaks, and hot dogs.

• You can feed a crowd for far less than if you bought individual cuts of meat.

• Because it *is* more affordable to cook this way, it's easier to consider spending extra to buy higher quality meat from local farms that raise animals humanely.

The Cooking Method: Consider a Caja China

Over the years, *Sunset* has published several articles about whole-animal cooking. In 1970, we dug up part of our lawn and constructed a genuine *imu* (Hawaiian-style earth oven), complete with burlap, hot rocks, and Hawaiian *ti* leaves, and cooked a Basque-style roast lamb that required making a fire wall and a rack out of fence posts.

A later story, in 1982, gave readers instructions on how to make a pig-roasting spit from steel plumbing pipe, using vises and C-clamps and sledges.

Both those approaches seem incredibly arduous today, when few people have the know-how—or the time—to build pits and spits. You can always rent a spit, but getting the animal onto the thing can be challenging, and renting the spit is pricey. So we decided to update whole-animal roasting to fit how we cook and live today. And that led us to the Caja China.

SELF-CONTAINED COOKING. The Caja China, a Cuban-style roasting box, is the easiest possible way to cook a whole animal, especially if you're a first-timer. It requires no special knowledge or skills, is portable, and leaves your garden unscathed. And it can cook a whole pig in about four hours—half the typical time for a pit roast. Plus, it's affordable: The biggest size, which can hold a 70-lb. dressed pig, costs about twice what you'll pay for a onetime spit rental. Best of all, though, are the fragrant, succulent, crisp-skinned results.

Made by La Caja China, a Cuban American company in Miami (*lacajachina.com*), the Caja China looks like a box crossed with a wheelbarrow. It's made of plywood and lined with aluminum, with wheels under one end and two sturdy, looping handles at the other. A drip pan rests on the bottom of the box, and the animal (butterflied by your butcher and then clamped between two racks by you) goes in over the drip pan. The top of the box consists of a large steel tray with a rack that you fill with lots of charcoal, so the meat cooks beneath the heat rather than over it. Because of its wheels, you can situate the Caja China anywhere, as long as you're on a nonflammable surface. And it isn't hard to assemble: With two people, we put our Model 2—the biggest size—together in less than an hour.

CUBAN, NOT CHINESE. So what is Chinese about the Caja China? It comes from Cuba, but no one is sure who invented it. According to Maricel Presilla, a Cuban American chef in Hoboken, New Jersey, and an authority on pan-Latin cooking, in Cuba anything especially clever or inventive is automatically dubbed "Chinese"—a likely explanation of how this ingenious device got its name. Similar boxes exist in other parts of the Caribbean, and also in Louisiana, where they're affectionately called Cajun microwaves.

A Whole-animal Roast Timeline

2 TO 3 WEEKS AHEAD: Order the Caja China
This will allow plenty of time for it to reach you (order at *lacajachina.com* or at 800/338-1323).

A FEW DAYS TO 3 WEEKS AHEAD: Order the meat
You can usually get lambs and pigs through a butcher shop with just a few days' notice, since many shops receive whole carcasses anyway. Explore ordering from a local farmer too—some of the best meat in the country is raised on small farms (try *localharvest.org* for listings of farms near you). However, with a small farm you may have to put in your request several weeks ahead and arrange a pickup at a farmer's market or from the farm itself. Ordering online is another option: McReynolds Farms, in Phoenix, sells whole pigs, lambs, and goats (*mcreynoldsfarms.com*) from its website, and Nicky USA, in Portland, Oregon, sells hazelnut-fed pigs (*nickyusa.com*).

When you order the animal, ask that it be butterflied, and that it be cut through the backbone at top and bottom so it lies as flat as possible. Lambs are sold with heads off; pigs typically come with the head. If you order yours head-on, ask that the head be butterflied as well, so that it cooks evenly.

A FEW DAYS TO 1 DAY AHEAD: Assemble the Caja China and gather supplies
Put the Caja China together, following the instructions included in the box. Other supplies you'll need:
• A brining syringe if you're cooking pig (optional; this comes with the Caja China)
• Matches or a gas grill lighter
• Instant-read thermometer and/or digital probe thermometer with wire, such as a Polder (optional)
• About 50 lbs. charcoal briquets. We used standard Kingsford charcoal; the directions that come with the Caja China were written before Kingsford's reformulation of its briquets (they now light faster and burn faster), so you'll need more of them than the product directions say.
• Lighter fluid (the meat is separated from the coals by the tray, so it won't pick up the taste of the fluid)
• Grilling or oven mitts
• A garden rake or trowel, for leveling the coals
• A metal dustpan or garden shovel, for removing ash from top tray
• A metal trash can or tub with some sand or dirt in it, for disposing of the hot ashes

DAY BEFORE OR MORNING OF: Pick up the meat
If you order from a butcher shop, it's ideal to pick up your whole animal the morning of the day you want to cook it so that you don't have to stash it at home. If you want or need to keep it overnight but lack a very large chest freezer or walk-in fridge, you can use a large plastic storage box—or even, if your family is willing, your bathtub. Line either one with ice, add the carcass, and cover with more ice (you will need lots of ice). Bring the meat to room temperature before cooking (about 2 hours).

If you decide to brine the meat, do it an hour after you've taken the meat out to warm up; then let it sit another hour after brining and before cooking. The roasting itself will take 3 to 5 hours (lamb is quicker than pig). So, as long as you get the preparations under way by midmorning, you'll be done by dinnertime. If you start very early, you can aim for lunch.

Spice-rubbed Whole Roast Pig

We used a large Caja China, capable of roasting a pig with a market weight of up to 100 lbs. (70 lbs. dressed). This recipe will also work with the midsize model and a smaller pig (70 lbs. market weight, about 45 lbs. dressed); just use less of the rub and brine and be prepared to finish cooking a little sooner. Some cooks prefer to brine, feeling it seasons the meat and gives it moisture; others like the natural taste of the meat itself, with seasoning on the outside only. Either way, the pig will taste wonderful. And if you have any uncrisped skin left over, cut it into pieces and deep-fry it to make addictive, crunchy pork rinds (called *chicharrones* in Mexico). Please read *Cooking (and Eating) from Nose to Tail (page 496)* before beginning this recipe; note the supplies called for in the timeline.

SERVES 50 | **TIME** 7 hours, including 2 hours to bring pig to room temperature and for rubbing and/or brining, and 4 to 5 hours to rack and cook

1¼ cups *each* star anise pods (crushed with the back of a heavy saucepan), coriander seeds, and fennel seeds
½ cup Chinese five-spice powder
2 tbsp. freshly ground black pepper
4 tbsp. *each* ground ginger, cinnamon, and red chile flakes
1 cup table salt (optional)
1 whole pig, including head (50 to 60 lbs. dressed weight), butterflied by butcher (*see Quick Tips, opposite page*), at room temperature
¾ cup kosher salt

1. In batches, coarsely grind star anise, coriander, and fennel using a mortar and pestle or a spice grinder. Add five-spice powder, black pepper, ginger, cinnamon, and red chile flakes; pound or grind to combine.
2. To make brine, bring 4½ cups water, the table salt, and ½ cup spice rub to a boil over high heat. Simmer, stirring, until salt dissolves. Remove from heat, pour into a bowl, and set in a larger bowl of ice water to quickly cool to room temperature. Pour through a cheesecloth-lined strainer into another bowl.
3. Lay pig on a large work surface, skin side down. Fill a large brining syringe with brine, if using, by immersing the needle and pulling back the plunger. Inject the pig with brine every 3 to 4 in. (you will have brine left over).
4. Add kosher salt to remaining spice rub, stir to blend well, and rub meat with enough spice rub to coat thoroughly. Turn pig over and rub skin the same way (save any remaining rub for another use). Let pork stand at room temperature at least 1 hour.

5. Clamp the pig between the racks using the supplied S-hooks (this is a two-person job: One pushes down while the other secures the hooks). If the pig is wider than the rack, you may have to cut through the meat and push the S-hook through so it can hook onto both the top and bottom racks, with the pig sandwiched in the middle.
6. Lay the racked pig, skin side down, over the drip pan. Insert the wired probe for the digital thermometer, if using, into the thickest part of the thigh and put the digital readout underneath the Caja China (it will stay completely cool, because all the heat is on top of the box). Top with the tray and charcoal rack. Following directions supplied with the Caja China (*see Quick Tips, right*), mound 16 lbs. of charcoal in two or three heaps on the rack and light them using lighter fluid. Follow the directions, but add 1 lb. (about 18) unlit briquets to coals whenever you see the coals starting to collapse into ash (every 30 minutes or so) and reduce the amount of briquets that are added at the second-hour mark to 9 lbs., and at the 2½-hour mark to 10 lbs. Whenever ash builds up, lift the charcoal rack, shake it gently to release ash, and rest it on the Caja China's handles while you scoop ash from the tray beneath and into the partly sand-filled metal tub. Replace the charcoal rack on the tray to continue cooking.
7. At the 2½-hour mark, remove the lid and flip the pig over (the handles on the rack make it easy). Score the skin every 4 to 6 in. in a crosshatch pattern. Replace lid, add another 1 lb. briquets, and cook until skin is crisp and meat is done (a digital or instant-read thermometer should register at least 165° and up to 187°; continue cooking, checking every 10 minutes, until done), at least 30 minutes longer. Lift pig onto a counter or table covered with several sheets of foil (turn up the edges to catch juices).
8. To serve: Either let people serve themselves from the roast itself, using tongs and/or a carving knife and fork, or carve the pig and put the meat on platters. The first way is better if you have a crowd of people interested in choosing their own choice bits straight from the animal. If your guests are slightly squeamish, they'll probably like the carved-and-plattered option better.
9. To carve, cut hind legs free at joints. Trim any crisp skin and place on platter. Cut away fat and less appealing skin from legs and slice (or pull) meat into serving pieces. Along backbone on each side, break ribs free and lift out the two tenderloins that run the length of the ribs; slice into serving portions. Cut the ribs into three or four sections. Trim the flank of fat and skin, lifting out the moist, long-fibered sections of meat. Separate the shoulders at the joints and pull or cut meat from the bone. Trim fat and skin away from neck

and, cutting as close to bone as you need to, lift out the meaty sections on either side and slice in pieces. Save the bones for stock if you like.

Quick Tips: Ask the butcher to split the backbone at top and bottom so the pig lies flat. We've adapted the Caja China directions for use with grooved Kingsford briquets, which burn faster and hotter than the original smooth-surfaced briquets (now discontinued).

PER SERVING, BRINED: 485 cal., 40% (195 cal.) from fat; 66 g protein; 21.7 g fat (7.5 g sat.); 3 g carbo (1.4 g fiber); 2,085 mg sodium; 189 mg chol.

Whole Roast Lamb with Rosemary and Garlic

Roasted over a simmering pan of rosemary, garlic, and white wine, lamb done in the Caja China is moist and fragrant. Save the juices from the pan and thicken them to serve with the meat, if you like. Please read *Cooking (and Eating) from Nose to Tail (page 496)* before beginning this recipe; note the supplies called for in the timeline.

SERVES 40 | **TIME** 5 hours, including 2 hours to bring lamb to room temperature and for seasoning, and 3 hours to cook

¼ cup minced rosemary leaves, plus 12 branches
   (6- to 8-in.)
¼ cup kosher salt
3 tbsp. freshly ground black pepper
½ cup minced garlic, plus 3 heads garlic
1½ cups olive oil
1 lamb (50 lbs. dressed weight), butterflied by butcher
   (see Quick Tips, right), at room temperature
3 bottles dry white wine
⅓ cup cornstarch (optional; for gravy)

1. In a large bowl, mix minced rosemary, salt, pepper, minced garlic, and oil. Lay lamb on a large work surface and rub all over with rosemary mixture.

2. Clamp the lamb between the racks using the supplied S-hooks (this is a two-person job: One pushes down while the other secures the hooks). If the lamb is wider than the rack, you may have to cut through the meat and push the S-hook through so it can hook onto both the top and bottom racks with the lamb sandwiched in the middle.

3. Separate out cloves from garlic heads and crush cloves. Pour wine into drip pan and add 2 quarts water, the rosemary branches, and crushed garlic. Lay the racked lamb, rib side down, over the drip pan. Insert the wired probe for the digital thermometer, if using, into the thickest part of the thigh and put the digital read-out underneath the Caja China (it will stay completely cool, because all the heat is on top of the box). Top with the tray and charcoal rack.

4. Mound 16 lbs. of charcoal in two or three heaps on the rack and light them using lighter fluid (*see Quick Tips below*). When coals are fully ignited, about 15 minutes, spread evenly over rack and cook lamb 30 minutes.

5. Spread 1 lb. (about 18) unlit briquets over coals and cook lamb 30 minutes more. Then lift charcoal rack and tray to handles of box and flip lamb over (the handles on the rack make it easy). Replace rack and lid; add 8 lbs. briquets to rack in an even layer and cook 30 minutes.

6. Lift charcoal rack and shake gently to release ash. Rest rack on Caja China's handles while you scoop out ash from the tray beneath and into the partly sand-filled metal tub. Replace the charcoal rack on the tray, add 1 lb. briquets, and cook 30 minutes more.

7. Add another 8 lbs. briquets and cook until digital or instant-read thermometer registers 150° for medium. Lift lamb onto a counter or table covered with several sheets of foil (turn up the edges to catch juices).

8. Make gravy if you like: Scoop 10 cups juices from drip pan (surprisingly, it's not very hot) and pour through a fine-mesh strainer into a large pot. Heat juices until hot. In a separate bowl, whisk 1½ cups juices with cornstarch until smooth. Whisk cornstarch mixture into the pot and bring to a boil, whisking. Boil until thickened, 2 to 3 minutes. Pour into a pitcher to serve with lamb.

9. To serve lamb: Either let people serve themselves from the whole roast using tongs and/or a carving knife and fork, or carve the lamb and put the meat on platters. The first way is better if you have a crowd of people interested in choosing their own choice bits straight from the animal. If your guests are slightly squeamish, they'll probably like the platter option better.

10. To carve, cut hind legs and forequarters free at joints, then slice meat from bone or pull off. Along backbone on each side, break ribs free and lift out the two tenderloins that run the length of the ribs; slice into serving portions. Cut the ribs into three or four sections. Put the meat on platters and serve with gravy if you like.

Quick Tips: Ask the butcher to split the backbone at top and bottom so the lamb lies flat. We've adapted the Caja China directions for use with grooved Kingsford briquets, which burn faster and hotter than the original smooth-surfaced briquets (now discontinued).

PER SERVING: 532 cal., 46% (244 cal.) from fat; 64 g protein; 27 g fat (8.5 g sat.); 2.6 g carbo (0.1 g fiber); 608 mg sodium; 209 mg chol.

Grilled Leg of Lamb with Yogurt-Mint Sauce

Christina Orchid, former chef-owner of Christina's restaurant on Orcas Island—one of the San Juan Islands off the Washington coast—likes to serve locally raised grass-fed lamb. She ties her leg of lamb, but we left it untied in our recipe so it cooks faster and gets nicely charred—making a good counterpoint to tangy yogurt-mint sauce.

SERVES 8 to 10 | **TIME** 1½ hours, plus 2 hours to marinate and 1 hour to bring to room temperature

1 yellow onion (6 oz.), quartered
7 garlic cloves
2 tbsp. roughly chopped rosemary leaves
½ cup fresh lemon juice
2½ tsp. salt
⅔ cup olive oil
1 boned leg of lamb (4 to 5 lbs.), butterflied and fat trimmed
1 red onion (6 oz.), thinly sliced
2 bunches radishes, trimmed
Yogurt-Mint Sauce *(recipe follows)*

1. In a blender, purée yellow onion, garlic, rosemary, lemon juice, and salt. With blender running, slowly pour in oil.
2. With a small knife, make small slashes (1 in. long, 1 in. deep) all over lamb, and put it in a nonreactive dish. Coat lamb with onion marinade, making sure mixture gets into slits. Cover and chill at least 2 hours and up to overnight, turning occasionally.
3. Remove lamb from refrigerator about 1 hour before you plan to cook it.
4. Prepare a charcoal or gas grill for direct medium heat *(see Direct Heat Grilling, page 436)*. Spread lamb flat on oiled cooking grate and close lid on grill. Cook lamb, turning once and brushing with marinade, until an instant-read thermometer inserted into thickest part registers 140° for medium-rare, about 40 minutes, or until done to your liking.
5. Transfer meat to a platter and cover. Let rest 15 to 20 minutes. Thinly slice lamb, garnish with sliced onion and radishes, and serve with yogurt-mint sauce.

PER SERVING: 210 cal., 45% (95 cal.) from fat; 25 g protein; 11 g fat (2.9 g sat.); 2.4 g carbo (0.5 g fiber); 210 mg sodium; 78 mg chol.

Yogurt-Mint Sauce: In a blender, purée ¼ cup **plain whole yogurt**, 1 **garlic clove**, minced, ⅔ cup packed **mint leaves**, 1 tsp. *each* **salt** and **fresh lemon juice**, ¼ tsp. **freshly ground black pepper**, and ⅛ tsp. **cayenne** until smooth. Transfer to a serving bowl and stir in an additional ¾ cup plain whole yogurt. Makes a little more than 1 cup.

PER TBSP.: 12 cal., 38% (4.5 cal.) from fat; 0.7 g protein; 0.5 g fat (0.3 g sat.); 1.4 g carbo (0.5 g fiber); 155 mg sodium; 1.8 mg chol.

Grilled Apricot-stuffed Leg of Lamb

The dried apricots swell and soften with the Moroccan-spiced juices of the roasting lamb.

SERVES 8 to 10 | **TIME** 3 hours, plus 6 hours to marinate

1 boned leg of lamb (4 to 5 lbs.), butterflied and fat trimmed
3 tsp. kosher salt, divided
½ cup plus 3 tbsp. olive oil
2 small onions, roughly chopped
5 garlic cloves, roughly chopped
2 tbsp. *ras el hanout (see Quick Tip below)*
1¼ to 1¾ cups dried apricot halves, preferably Blenheim

1. Unfold lamb and slash ½-in.-deep cuts about 1 in. apart all over both sides of lamb. Season all over with 1½ tsp. salt. Put in a baking dish just large enough to hold meat when unfolded.
2. Pour ½ cup water and ½ cup oil into a blender; add onions, garlic, *ras el hanout*, and remaining 1½ tsp. salt. Pulse to blend into a loose paste and pour over lamb. Cover and refrigerate at least 6 hours and up to 1 day. Let lamb come to room temperature before grilling, about 45 minutes.
3. Prepare a charcoal or gas grill for indirect low heat, using a drip pan *(see Indirect Heat Grilling, page 436)*.
4. Wipe marinade off lamb and arrange apricot halves in a single layer over meat, leaving about a ½-in. border on all sides. Roll up meat jelly-roll style and tie at 1-in. intervals with kitchen twine. Trim ends of twine. Rub lamb with remaining 3 tbsp. oil.
5. Grill lamb on oiled cooking grate over indirect-heat area, turning over once halfway through, until an instant-read thermometer inserted in thickest part registers 140° for medium-rare, 1½ to 2½ hours, or until done to your liking. Let lamb rest, covered with foil, 15 to 20 minutes. Slice and serve.
Quick Tip: *Ras el hanout* is a Moroccan spice mix available at well-stocked grocery stores or Middle Eastern markets. You can make your own blend if you like: Whisk together 1 tsp. *each* ground cardamom, coriander, ginger, and turmeric; ½ tsp. *each* freshly ground black pepper, cinnamon, nutmeg, and saffron (optional); and ¼ tsp. *each* ground allspice, cloves, and mace.

PER SERVING: 390 cal., 37% (144 cal.) from fat; 44 g protein; 16 g fat (4.8 g sat.); 16 g carbo (2 g fiber); 431 mg sodium; 135 mg chol.

the fire outside

Grilled Lamb Loin with Cabernet-Mint Sauce and Garlic Mashed Potatoes

This recipe is from Humberto Huizar, formerly chef at Cafe Chardonnay, in Ballard, California (the restaurant is now called the Ballard Inn Restaurant).

SERVES 3 or 4 | **TIME** 1½ hours, plus at least 4 hours to marinate

1 rolled and tied boned lamb loin (about 1 lb.; *see Quick Tip, right*)
30 garlic cloves, divided
½ cup plus ½ tbsp. extra-virgin olive oil
½ cup *each* balsamic vinegar and chopped shallots
2 tbsp. fresh thyme leaves or 1 tbsp. dried thyme
1 tbsp. chopped flat-leaf parsley
½ tsp. salt, plus more to taste
¼ tsp. freshly ground black pepper, plus more to taste
2 cups Cabernet Sauvignon or other dry red wine
3 cups reduced-sodium beef broth
½ cup plus 1 tbsp. butter
2 tbsp. chopped mint leaves
1¾ lbs. Yukon Gold or russet potatoes, peeled and cut into 1½-in. chunks
½ cup whipping cream
Milk (optional)

1. Pat lamb loin dry. Chop 10 garlic cloves. In an 8- by 10-in. baking dish, mix half of chopped garlic, ½ cup oil, the vinegar, shallots, thyme, parsley, salt, and pepper. Add lamb and turn to coat. Cover and chill at least 4 hours and up to 1 day, turning occasionally.

2. On a 12-in.-square sheet of foil, add remaining ½ tbsp. oil to 20 whole cloves garlic to coat; seal foil around garlic. Bake in a 350° oven until cloves are soft when pressed, about 45 minutes, turning packet over halfway through baking.

3. While garlic is baking, in a 10- to 12-in. frying pan over high heat, boil wine until reduced to 1 cup, about 10 minutes. Add broth and boil, stirring occasionally, until mixture is reduced to about 1½ cups, about 20 minutes. Whisk in 1 tbsp. butter, then stir in mint and roasted garlic. Set aside.

4. In a 5- to 6-qt. pan, combine potatoes and remaining chopped garlic; add water to cover. Bring to a boil over high heat; cover, reduce heat, and simmer until potatoes mash easily when pressed, 20 to 25 minutes.

5. Meanwhile, microwave cream with remaining ½ cup butter, stirring at 20-second intervals, until butter is melted and mixture is steaming (do not boil), about 1½ minutes total.

6. Drain potatoes and garlic. Mash with a potato masher or a mixer until almost smooth. Add cream mixture and mash to desired consistency; if potatoes are thicker than you like, add a little milk. Add salt and pepper to taste. Keep warm over low heat if necessary.

7. Meanwhile, prepare a charcoal or gas grill for direct medium-high heat (*see Direct Heat Grilling, page 436*). Lift lamb from marinade and drain well (discard marinade). Grill lamb (close lid on gas grill), turning occasionally, until lamb is browned on all sides and an instant-read thermometer inserted into thickest part registers 135° for medium-rare (pink in center), 20 to 25 minutes, or until done to your liking. Transfer lamb to a cutting board and let rest in a warm place at least 5 minutes. Meanwhile, gently reheat Cabernet-Mint Sauce.

8. Mound mashed potatoes on plates. Cut and remove string from lamb; slice loin crosswise and fan slices over potatoes. Spoon sauce with garlic around meat and mashed potatoes.

Quick Tip: Have the butcher bone a lamb loin (1¾ to 2 lbs.; make sure you don't get a tenderloin or the sirloin) and roll and tie it into a roast about 8 in. long and 2½ in. wide.

Make Ahead: Marinate lamb and prepare sauce through step 3 up to 1 day ahead and chill; bring sauce to a simmer over low heat before serving.

PER SERVING: 738 cal., 62% (459 cal.) from fat; 33 g protein; 51 g fat (26 g sat.); 39 g carbo (3.4 g fiber); 500 mg sodium; 178 mg chol.

How to Keep Food from Sticking: 4 Crucial Tips

1. Start with a clean cooking grate. Charred bits of old food will not only impart nasty flavors to whatever you're cooking, they'll make it stick too. Use a stiff-bristled wire grill brush to scrub the grates clean at the end and beginning of grilling—and if there's a serious amount of stuck-on gunk, put the grate in the sink or on the ground and scrub and rinse (no soap, though).

2. Preheat the cooking grate. Food set on a hot grate will brown better and stick less.

3. Oil the cooking grate. A light coat of oil on the food you're grilling may be enough to keep it from sticking, but for most recipes, you should oil the cooking grate too (especially for delicate, easy-to-tear foods like fish, thin meats, and some vegetables). Pour some vegetable oil onto a wad of paper towels, then oil the hot grate with them, using long-handled tongs.

4. Don't turn food too often. If you let food develop a brown crust before turning, it will naturally release itself from the grill.

Lamb Chops with Roasted Salsa

This simple, terrific dish is from Christina Savinos, *Sunset* reader and resident of Athens, Greece.

SERVES 4 | **TIME** 25 minutes

2 garlic cloves, chopped
3 tbsp. chopped mint leaves (preferably peppermint; see *Quick Tip, above right*)
Finely shredded lemon zest from 1½ lemons
½ cup olive oil, divided
2 tsp. *each* kosher salt and freshly ground black pepper, divided
8 lamb rib chops
1 ripe tomato
1 small red onion, cut in half
1 *each* red and green bell pepper, seeds and ribs removed and quartered
¼ cup chopped flat-leaf parsley
2 tsp. fresh lemon juice

1. In a large resealable plastic bag, combine garlic, mint, lemon, ¼ cup oil, and 1 tsp. *each* salt and pepper. Add lamb chops and mix to coat.
2. Prepare a charcoal or gas grill for direct high heat (*see Direct Heat Grilling, page 436*). Grill tomato, onion, and bell peppers, turning twice, until soft and blackened, about 6 minutes.

3. Lift chops from marinade (discard marinade) and grill, turning once, 5 minutes total for medium-rare.
4. Chop vegetables; mix with remaining ¼ cup oil, the parsley, lemon juice, and remaining 1 tsp. each salt and pepper. Spoon over lamb.
Quick Tip: Dark-stemmed, pointy-leaved peppermint, which has a much stronger flavor than typical grocery-store spearmint, is wonderful in this recipe.

PER SERVING: 578 cal., 78% (450 cal.) from fat; 23 g protein; 50 g fat (15 g sat.); 8.4 g carbo (2.1 g fiber); 521 mg sodium; 99 mg chol.

Grilled Lamb Brochettes with Lemon and Dill

The final spritz of lemon juice on these lamb skewers calls for a high-acid, citrusy wine, like a Sauvignon Blanc. Serve with hot cooked rice. You'll need seven or eight (10-in.) skewers.

SERVES 6 to 8 | **TIME** 20 minutes, plus 1 day to marinate, plus 20 minutes for soaking skewers if using wooden

½ cup olive oil
Finely shredded zest and juice from 1 lemon
¼ cup plus 1 tbsp. chopped dill, divided
2 tbsp. minced garlic
1½ tsp. salt
1 tsp. freshly ground black pepper
1 boned leg of lamb (2½ lbs.), fat trimmed and cut into 1-in. cubes
Lemon wedges

1. In a large bowl, mix oil, lemon zest and juice, ¼ cup dill, garlic, salt, and pepper. Add lamb and mix to coat thoroughly. Cover and chill overnight (*see Quick Tip below*).
2. If using wooden skewers, soak in water for 20 to 30 minutes.
3. Thread cubes of lamb onto skewers.
4. Prepare a charcoal or gas grill for direct medium-high heat (*see Direct Heat Grilling, page 436*). Grill skewers (close lid on gas grill), turning as needed, until lamb is browned on all sides but still pink in center (medium-rare; cut to test), 5 to 6 minutes, or just barely pink in center (medium), 6 to 7 minutes.
5. Transfer skewers to a platter. Sprinkle with remaining 1 tbsp. dill and serve with lemon wedges for a final squeeze of juice.
Quick Tip: The lamb is best if you marinate it overnight, but it also tastes good if you only have 2 hours or so.

PER SERVING: 266 cal., 51% (135 cal.) from fat; 30 g protein; 15 g fat (3.9 g sat.); 0.7 g carbo (0.1 g fiber); 291 mg sodium; 95 mg chol.

Grilled Moroccan Lamb Kebabs with Grapes

The grapes on these kebabs caramelize on the grill, and the result—along with the complex spices on the lamb—calls for a spicy, juicy wine like Zinfandel. Serve the kebabs with hot couscous (we love the large Israeli variety, also called pearl couscous). You'll need six or seven (10-in.) skewers.

SERVES 4 or 5 | **TIME** 30 minutes, plus 1 hour to marinate and 20 minutes for soaking skewers if using wooden

¼ cup olive oil
1 tbsp. fresh lemon juice
2 garlic cloves, minced
2 tbsp. minced flat-leaf parsley, divided
1½ tsp. salt
1 tsp. curry powder
¾ tsp. *each* paprika and ground cumin
½ tsp. *each* dried thyme and ground coriander
¼ tsp. *each* red chile flakes and freshly ground black pepper
1½ lbs. boned leg of lamb, fat trimmed and cut into 1-in. cubes
1 lb. red and/or green seedless grapes

1. In a large bowl, combine oil, lemon juice, garlic, 1 tbsp. parsley, salt, curry powder, paprika, cumin, thyme, coriander, chile flakes, and pepper. Add lamb and mix to coat thoroughly. Cover and chill at least 1 hour and up to 1 day.
2. If using wooden skewers, soak in water for 20 to 30 minutes.
3. Thread cubes of lamb alternately with grapes onto skewers.
4. Prepare a charcoal or gas grill for direct medium-high heat (*see Direct Heat Grilling, page 436*). Grill kebabs (close lid on gas grill), turning as needed, until lamb is browned on all sides but still pink in center (medium-rare; cut to test), 5 to 6 minutes, or just barely pink in center (medium), 6 to 7 minutes.
5. Transfer kebabs to a platter and sprinkle with remaining 1 tbsp. parsley.

PER SERVING: 314 cal., 40% (126 cal.) from fat; 30 g protein; 14 g fat (3.8 g sat.); 17 g carbo (1.6 g fiber); 422 mg sodium; 91 mg chol.

Grilled Kid Goat Shoulder Chops, Afghan-style (*Kebab e Chopan*)

Kid has a mild flavor (milder than lamb in many cases) and can be delicious if prepared right. Because it's so lean—it has less fat than skinned chicken breast—it's most flavorful and tender when braised or, in the case of thin cuts like chops, marinated and grilled over a fairly hot fire. We learned to make these crisp, garlicky chops from Shujau Siddiqi, whose halal butcher shop in Santa Clara, California, does a brisk business in goat meat. For more on goat, the most widely consumed meat in the world, see *the Global Goat, page 429*.

SERVES 4 | **TIME** 15 minutes, plus 3 hours to marinate

6 garlic cloves
1 tsp. kosher salt
½ tsp. freshly ground black pepper
2 tbsp. olive oil
8 kid goat shoulder or loin chops (1 to 1½ lbs. total; see *Quick Tip below*)

1. Mince garlic, sprinkle with salt, and mash to a paste with the flat side of your knife. Put garlic paste in a large bowl with pepper and oil and whisk to blend. Add chops, rubbing on all sides with marinade, and chill at least 2 hours. About 45 minutes before cooking, take chops out of refrigerator and let come to room temperature.
2. Meanwhile, prepare a charcoal or gas grill for direct medium-high heat (*see Direct Heat Grilling, page 436*). Brush off marinade and grill 3 minutes; turn over and grill another 3 minutes for medium-rare (cut to test). Don't overcook the chops; they'll be tough.
Quick Tip: Find kid goat at Mexican markets, halal and Middle Eastern markets, and some Italian and Greek markets. More ranchers are starting to raise goat in the U.S. (California has a number of farms), and some sell their meat online; one of our favorites is Copeland Family Farms (*goatmeats.com*).

PER SERVING: 196 cal., 31% (61 cal.) from fat; 30.9 g protein; 6.8 g fat (1.5 g sat.); 0.8 g carbo (0.08 g fiber); 338 mg sodium; 85 mg chol.

Herbed Grilled Kid Goat Chops: In a large bowl, whisk together 2 tbsp. *each* **fresh lemon juice** and minced **oregano leaves**, 1 tbsp. *each* minced **rosemary** and **thyme leaves**, ½ cup **olive oil**, 2 tsp. **kosher salt**, and 1 tsp. **freshly ground black pepper**. Add 8 **kid goat shoulder or loin chops** and turn to coat well. Marinate at least 3 hours and up to 1 day. Bring to room temperature and grill as directed in step 2 above. This marinade is also excellent on lamb.

PER SERVING: 285 cal., 53% (151 cal.) from fat; 31 g protein; 17 g fat (2.9 g sat.); 0.8 g carbo (0.1 g fiber); 578 mg sodium; 85 mg chol.

Grilled Bass with Salsa Verde

Tomatillos and fresh chiles give the salsa a bright, "green" flavor, and toasting the ingredients contributes a smoky element (plus it loosens the chiles' skins). Mexican cooks traditionally use a griddle or *comal* to toast salsa ingredients, but a broiler chars the chiles more evenly.

SERVES 2 | **TIME** About 45 minutes

SALSA
¼ **lb. tomatillos** *(see Quick Tips, right)*, **husked and rinsed**
1 **thick onion slice**
1 **small poblano chile** *(see Quick Tips, right)*
1 **serrano chile**
1 **tbsp.** *each* **chopped cilantro, basil, and mint leaves**
1 **small garlic clove**
1 **tbsp. fresh lime juice**
¾ **tsp. kosher salt**

FISH
2 **whole small butterflied striped bass or trout with bones and heads removed**
1 **tbsp. olive oil**
Salt and freshly ground black pepper
Chopped mint leaves

1. Make salsa: Preheat broiler. Line a rimmed baking pan with foil and set tomatillos, onion, poblano, and serrano in it.
2. Broil vegetables 3 in. from heat, turning as needed, until tomatillos and onion are speckled brown and chiles are black all over, 12 to 15 minutes; as vegetables are done, transfer to a bowl. Cover vegetables with a plate or foil and let stand about 5 minutes for chile skins to loosen.
3. Pull off stems and blackened skins from chiles; for best flavor, don't rinse chiles (a few blackened bits are okay to leave on). Open poblano and remove seeds.
4. In a food processor, pulse vegetables and any juices, cilantro, basil, mint, and garlic until coarsely puréed. Scrape into a bowl and stir in 2 tbsp. water, the lime juice, and salt.
5. Pat fish dry, then rub all over with oil, salt, pepper, and mint. Set each fish, skin side down, on a double sheet of well-oiled heavy-duty foil.
6. Prepare a charcoal or gas grill for direct medium-high heat *(see Direct Heat Grilling, page 436)*. Grill fish on foil, covered, until just opaque, about 3 minutes.
7. Spoon salsa onto plates. Carefully slide fish off foil and onto salsa.

Quick Tips: Tart-tasting tomatillos look like green tomatoes with papery husks. Poblanos (sometimes mislabeled as pasillas) are large, meaty, deep green chiles with a fairly mild flavor; find them in your grocery store's produce section.
Make Ahead: Salsa, up to 2 days, chilled.

PER SERVING: 421 cal., 33% (138 cal.) from fat; 58 g protein; 15 g fat (2.7 g sat.); 11 g carbo (3.4 g fiber); 944 mg sodium; 255 mg chol.

Grilled Trout Fillets with Crunchy Pine-nut Lemon Topping

Firm, meaty rainbow trout is one of our most sustainably raised fish, and most of it is grown on clean "farms" in Idaho. Because it's dense, with a fair amount of oil in the flesh, it's less likely to stick to the grill than white fish such as cod and halibut. You'll need four 10-in. metal skewers for the radicchio.

SERVES 4 | **TIME** 30 minutes

2 **tbsp. pine nuts**
¼ **cup extra-virgin olive oil, divided, plus more for brushing**
½ **cup panko (Japanese-style bread crumbs)**
2 **canned anchovy fillets, minced**
1 **tbsp. minced garlic (3 medium cloves)**
¾ **tsp. salt, divided, plus more to taste**
1 **tbsp. finely chopped flat-leaf parsley**
2 **tsp. very finely shredded lemon zest**
2 **medium heads radicchio**
4 **skin-on, boned trout fillets, about ½ in. thick**
3 **tsp. fresh lemon juice, divided**
Freshly ground black pepper

1. Toast pine nuts in a wide (not nonstick) frying pan over medium heat until lightly toasted, about 5 minutes. Transfer to a medium bowl and set aside.
2. In the same pan, heat 1 tbsp. oil over medium heat until just warm and add panko. Toast panko, stirring occasionally, until a shade darker, about 5 minutes. Add anchovies and garlic; stir to combine well. Add panko mixture to pine nuts. Stir in ¼ tsp. salt, parsley, and lemon zest.
3. Prepare a charcoal or gas grill for direct high heat *(see Direct Heat Grilling, page 436)*. Cut each radicchio head in half, cut each half into three wedges, and brush cut sides with oil. Thread wedges onto skewers, three per skewer. Grill radicchio skewers (close lid on gas grill), 2 minutes.

4. Turn radicchio skewers over. Brush trout fillets on both sides with oil. Grill, skin side down (close lid on gas grill), until fillets are opaque (cut to test) and loosen easily, 3 to 4 minutes. Using two spatulas, gently turn fish over (close lid on gas grill) and cook 1 minute more. Transfer fillets to plates and radicchio to a cutting board.

5. Remove skewers from grilled radicchio and chop roughly. Toss with 2 tsp. lemon juice and remaining ½ tsp. salt. Stir remaining 3 tbsp. oil into bread crumbs. Season fish with salt, pepper, and remaining 1 tsp. lemon juice. Spoon panko mixture over flesh side of fish. Serve fish with radicchio.

PER SERVING: 476 cal., 59% (279 cal.) from fat; 39 g protein; 31 g fat (4.9 g sat.); 9.4 g carbo (1.1 g fiber); 633 mg sodium; 100 mg chol.

Halibut Kebabs with Grilled Bread and Pancetta

With its big flakes, halibut holds up well on the grill. The pancetta bastes the fish as it cooks, keeping it moist and infusing it with meaty flavors. You'll need four metal skewers (each 10 in.).

SERVES 4 | **TIME** 30 minutes

¼ cup olive oil
1 tbsp. coarsely chopped rosemary leaves
1 tsp. *each* salt and freshly ground black pepper
1½ lbs. skinned, boned halibut fillet, cut into 2-in. chunks
4 cups crusty bread, such as ciabatta, cut into
   1½-in. cubes
3 oz. paper-thin slices pancetta

1. In a large bowl, combine oil, rosemary, salt, and pepper. Add halibut and bread and toss to coat; set aside 5 minutes.

2. Weave the pancetta around fish and bread: Skewer one end of a pancetta strip, then thread on a fish cube. Lay the pancetta strip over the fish cube and push it back onto skewer on other side of cube. Thread on a bread cube, then lay pancetta over bread cube the same way, so that pancetta strip is weaving between the cubes. Repeat skewering and weaving two more times; then repeat with remaining skewers.

3. Prepare a charcoal or gas grill for direct medium heat (*see Direct Heat Grilling, page 436*). Grill kebabs, turning often, until fish is cooked through and bread is browned, 6 minutes.

PER SERVING: 516 cal., 56% (288 cal.) from fat; 42 g protein; 32 g fat (6.9 g sat.); 22 g carbo (1.2 g fiber); 1,117 mg sodium; 66 mg chol.

Grilled Sardines with Bean Salad

Grilling is an excellent way to cook the delicious Pacific sardine. The oils in the fish keep it moist over high heat, and the smokiness of the grill has a tempering effect on sardines' assertive flavor. Using the dressing as a marinade for both the sardines and the bean salad helps flavors meld.

SERVES 4 | **TIME** 30 minutes

1 tsp. minced garlic
¼ cup fresh lemon juice
½ cup extra-virgin olive oil, plus more for cooking grate
2 tsp. kosher salt
½ tsp. freshly ground black pepper
8 whole sardines (1¼ lbs. total), cleaned, heads off,
   and spines removed (keep fish whole)
2 cans (15 oz. each) cannellini beans, rinsed and drained
1 cup *each* curly parsley leaves and halved grape tomatoes

1. Prepare a charcoal or gas grill for direct high heat (*see Direct Heat Grilling, page 436*). In a medium bowl, whisk together garlic, lemon juice, oil, salt, and pepper. Pour ¼ cup dressing over sardines in another medium bowl and let stand 10 minutes.

2. Meanwhile, add beans, parsley, and tomatoes to remaining dressing and toss to coat.

3. Using a wad of oiled paper towels and tongs, oil cooking grate. Lay sardines on cooking grate, skin sides down, and grill, turning once, until cooked through and dark grill marks appear, about 5 minutes.

4. Divide bean salad among plates and top with sardines.

PER SERVING: 520 cal., 49% (252 cal.) from fat; 22 g protein; 30 g fat (12 g sat.); 28 g carbo (9.5 g fiber); 1,019 mg sodium; 39 mg chol.

Pacific Sardines

Plentiful in the Pacific Ocean, with their reach extending from the coast of Baja California to southeastern Alaska, sardines have a rich, strong, slightly minerally flavor. They're caught using methods that have little impact on the surrounding habitat, with almost no unintentional harvest of other species, so they're an eco-friendly choice. And sardines are good for you, too—full of omega-3 fatty acids, phosphorus, and iron, and they don't concentrate pollutants in their flesh.

How to Choose and Prepare: Sardines are sold fresh and whole. Look for fish with bright eyes, shiny skin, and a mildly fishy aroma. Cook them within a day. If your fishmonger doesn't sell sardines already cleaned, it's easy to do yourself: *See How to Clean and Fillet Sardines, page 191.* They're also good marinated.

Herb- and Mustard-glazed Grilled Salmon

Fresh-caught, richly flavored Alaska salmon—from cold waters like those around Kodiak Island—is best when cooked simply. Grill the fish with a brown-sugar, mustard, and thyme glaze.

SERVES 8 to 10 | **TIME** 50 minutes

3 tbsp. butter, melted
¼ cup *each* firmly packed brown sugar, dry white wine, and fresh lemon juice
2 tbsp. Dijon mustard
1 tbsp. chopped thyme leaves
1 tsp. salt
½ tsp. freshly ground black pepper
1 skin-on, boned salmon fillet (3½ to 4 lbs.)

1. In a small bowl, whisk together butter, brown sugar, wine, lemon juice, mustard, thyme, salt, and pepper.
2. Prepare a charcoal or gas grill for indirect medium heat *(see Indirect Heat Grilling, page 436)*. Grill salmon, skin side down, on heavy-duty foil over indirect-heat area, brushing with glaze every 5 minutes, until just opaque but still moist-looking in thickest part (cut to test), 25 to 30 minutes.

PER SERVING: 279 cal., 42% (118 cal.) from fat; 31 g protein; 13 g fat (3.7 g sat.); 6.8 g carbo (0.1 g fiber); 399 mg sodium; 93 mg chol.

Spicy Ponzu Salmon on Greens

Amiko Gubbins, formerly chef of Café Japengo, in San Diego, uses the Japanese citrus-soy sauce called ponzu to make an all-purpose condiment that's great not just with salmon but also with other foods. Try it as a marinade, basting sauce, salad dressing, or dipping sauce.

SERVES 4 to 6 | **TIME** 45 minutes

½ cup soy sauce
¼ cup ponzu sauce
1 tbsp. Asian (toasted) sesame oil
¾ tsp. oyster sauce
½ tsp. *each* black bean sauce, Asian red chili paste, minced fresh ginger, and minced garlic
1 skin-on, boned salmon fillet (1½ to 2 lbs.)
3 qts. (9 oz.) salad greens

1. In a small bowl, mix soy sauce, ponzu sauce, sesame oil, oyster sauce, black bean sauce, chili paste, ginger, and garlic.
2. Coat fish with half of ponzu mixture. Let stand about 10 minutes, then discard marinade.

3. Prepare a charcoal or gas grill for direct high heat *(see Direct Heat Grilling, page 436)*. Grill salmon, skin side up (close lid on gas grill), turning once, until opaque but still moist-looking in thickest part (cut to test), 6 to 8 minutes. Remove from grill.
4. Mix salad greens with remaining ponzu mixture and serve with fish.
Make Ahead: Sauce, up to 1 month, chilled.

PER SERVING: 205 cal., 42% (86 cal.) from fat; 24 g protein; 9.6 g fat (1.4 g sat.); 4.1 g carbo (0 g fiber); 1,500 mg sodium; 1.4 mg chol.

Cedar-planked Salmon

A technique developed by Northwest Native Americans, planking salmon gives the fish a deep, woodsy taste and keeps it moist by protecting it from the flames. You will need an untreated cedar board, ½ to ¾ in. thick and big enough to accommodate your fish. Find planks at a well-stocked fish shop, barbecue store, or online.

recipe pictured
on page
454

SERVES 6 | **TIME** 45 minutes, plus 2 hours to soak plank

2 tbsp. table salt
1 tsp. vegetable oil
1 skin-on, boned salmon fillet (2 to 2½ lbs; see *Quick Tip* below)
½ tsp. kosher or sea salt
¼ tsp. freshly ground black pepper
1 tsp. butter

1. Put 8 cups hot water and table salt in a pan big enough to hold the plank; stir to dissolve salt. Soak plank at least 2 hours.
2. Meanwhile, prepare a charcoal or gas grill for indirect medium-high heat *(see Indirect Heat Grilling, pages 436-7)*.
3. Wipe water off plank and rub it with 1 tsp. oil. Set it over direct heat and toast it, covered, until it starts to smoke and char, 5 to 10 minutes.
4. Meanwhile, season salmon fillet with kosher or sea salt and pepper. Turn plank over, set over indirect heat, and set fillet, skin side down, on charred side. Dot with butter.
5. Close lid on grill and cook salmon until center of fillet flakes, 30 to 40 minutes.
Quick Tip: Look for (or ask for) a long, narrow fillet that fits your board. If all you can find is a short, wide fillet, just divide it down the center and lay the pieces end to end on the board to fit.

PER SERVING: 322 cal., 55% (176 cal.) from fat; 34 g protein; 20 g fat (4.3 g sat.); 0.1 g carbo (0 g fiber); 258 mg sodium; 98 mg chol.

Grilled Miso Salmon and Eggplant

Inspired by the classic Japanese recipe for miso-marinated black cod. If you have a perforated grill pan, you can use it instead of foil—just oil the pan well.

SERVES 4 | **TIME** 45 minutes, plus 8 hours to marinate

⅓ cup *each* sake and mirin (sweet sake)
1 cup white miso *(see Quick Tips, right)*
½ cup sugar
2 tbsp. grated fresh ginger
4 Japanese eggplants *(see Quick Tips, right)*
4 skin-on, boned, center-cut salmon fillets
   (6 to 8 oz. each)
About ⅓ cup canola oil
¼ cup finely chopped chives

1. In a small saucepan, bring sake and mirin to a boil and boil 30 seconds. Lower heat to medium and add miso, whisking until dissolved. Add sugar and ginger and whisk until sugar dissolves. Pour half of miso mixture into a large bowl and other half into a medium baking dish and let cool, about 10 minutes.

2. Slice eggplants on a diagonal into ¼-in.-thick ovals and add to miso mixture in bowl, turning to coat. Nestle salmon fillets, skin side up, in miso mixture in baking dish to coat the flesh but not the skin. Cover both bowl and dish with plastic wrap and refrigerate at least 8 hours and up to overnight.

3. Prepare grill as instructed in *How to Grill Crisp-skinned Salmon Fillets below.*

4. Shake marinade off eggplant slices. Oil a sheet of heavy-duty foil with canola oil and arrange eggplant on it in a single layer. Drizzle with remaining oil and grill over indirect-heat area until soft, 15 to 20 minutes. Set aside.

5. With paper towels, wipe marinade off salmon and grill as directed in *How to Grill Crisp-Skinned Salmon Fillets below.* While salmon is finishing on direct heat, reheat eggplant on foil over indirect heat. Serve salmon and eggplant sprinkled with chives.

Quick Tips: Find white miso in Asian and natural food markets and in well-stocked grocery stores. Japanese eggplant is smaller and more slender than bulbous Italian eggplant.

PER SERVING: 549 cal., 52% (288 cal.) from fat; 41 g protein; 32 g fat (5 g sat.); 21 g carbo (2.9 g fiber); 744 mg sodium; 111 mg chol.

How to Grill Crisp-skinned Salmon Fillets

The trickiest part about grilling salmon is preventing it from sticking, especially if you like crispy, delicious skin that stays on the fillet instead of gluing itself to the grill. But you can make perfect grilled salmon if you keep a few key points in mind: Use both direct and indirect heat; cook on perforated, oiled foil briefly set on the grill to preheat; use narrow, center-cut fillets, which, because they have less skin, are less likely to stick; and get the fillets good and sizzling (like a steak hitting a hot frying pan) on the foil before you shift them to indirect heat. You don't need special tools, but an offset cake spatula—thin but sturdy—will slide neatly between the salmon and the foil. Here are our steps to crisp-skinned salmon to serve 4.

1. Prepare a charcoal or gas grill for indirect medium heat *(see Indirect Heat Grilling, page 436).*

2. Fold two 12- by 18-in. pieces of heavy-duty foil in half widthwise to form rectangles. Using the tip of a small knife, make holes in rectangles about 2 in. apart and widen each hole to the size of a dime. Grease foil with olive oil; set over direct heat for 2 minutes.

3. Meanwhile, pat dry 4 skin-on, boned, center-cut salmon fillets (6 to 8 oz. each). Either cook the fillets just lightly oiled, or prepare them according to one of the recipes that follow. Brush skins with olive oil and set 2 fillets, skin side down, on each foil rectangle. Close lid on grill (if using charcoal, open vents on lid)

and cook fish until skin is light brown and really sizzling, 5 to 6 minutes. Slide foil to indirect heat, cover, and cook until all but top ¼ in. of fish is cooked, 3 to 8 minutes. Slide fish back over direct heat, cover, and cook until fish is cooked through (cut to test) and skin is browned and crisp, about 3 minutes.

4. Transfer foil with salmon to a baking sheet and, sliding an offset cake spatula or other thin spatula between salmon skin and foil, very gently free fish from foil. Finish each fillet as directed in the following recipes, or season with kosher salt and a few drops of fresh lemon juice.

Grilled Lemon-Dill Salmon with Cucumber Salad

Western salmon meets Scandinavia in this light, refreshing recipe.

SERVES 4 | **TIME** 40 minutes, plus 2 hours to marinate

2 or 3 lemons
4 skin-on, boned, center-cut salmon fillets
    (6 to 8 oz. each)
2½ tbsp. finely chopped dill, divided
1 English cucumber
½ cup drained bottled cocktail onions
2 tbsp. cider vinegar
1 tsp. sugar
½ tsp. salt, plus more to taste

1. Zest lemons to yield 2 tbsp. finely shredded zest. Sprinkle salmon fillets with 1½ tbsp. zest (set aside remaining zest and whole lemons) and 1½ tbsp. dill, dividing evenly among fillets and patting to adhere. Wrap fillets in plastic wrap and refrigerate at least 2 hours and up to overnight.
2. Slice cucumber paper-thin on a mandoline or other handheld slicer. Cut each onion in half. In a bowl, whisk together vinegar, sugar, and salt. Add cucumber, onions, remaining lemon zest and 1 tbsp. dill, and toss gently to coat. Taste and adjust seasonings, if necessary.
3. Grill salmon as directed in *How to Grill Crisp-skinned Salmon Fillets (page 507)*. Serve with cucumber salad.
Make Ahead: Salad, up to 8 hours, chilled.

PER SERVING: 375 cal., 48% (180 cal.) from fat; 39 g protein; 20 g fat (4.1 g sat.); 6.7 g carbo (1.6 g fiber); 980 mg sodium; 111 mg chol.

Almond and Spice-crusted Grilled Salmon

The crust on this salmon is similar to *dukka*, an Egyptian mix of spices, chopped nuts, and sometimes chickpeas. Serve with a simple herbed couscous if you like.

SERVES 4 | **TIME** 45 minutes

¼ cup slivered almonds
1 tbsp. plus 2 tsp. coriander seeds
1 tbsp. *each* cumin seeds and sesame seeds
¼ tsp. dried thyme
1 tsp. kosher salt, divided
½ tsp. freshly ground black pepper
4 skin-on, boned, center-cut salmon fillets
    (6 to 8 oz. each)
1 egg white

1. In a skillet over medium-high heat, toast almonds, stirring constantly, until golden brown, about 5 minutes. Let cool, then chop finely and transfer to a bowl.
2. In same skillet, toast coriander and cumin seeds until fragrant, about 2 minutes, stirring once or twice. Let cool, then grind coarsely in a spice grinder or clean coffee grinder. Toast and grind sesame seeds the same way. Add ground spices and sesame seeds to almonds along with thyme, ¾ tsp. salt, and pepper. Mix to combine.
3. Season salmon with remaining ¼ tsp. salt. Brush flesh side of fillets with egg white, then coat with almond-spice mixture, pressing slightly so it adheres to fish.
4. Grill salmon as directed in *How to Grill Crisp-skinned Salmon Fillets (page 507)*.

PER SERVING: 396 cal., 48% (189 cal.) from fat; 46 g protein; 21 g fat (2.8 g sat.); 4.3 g carbo (1.7 g fiber); 482 mg sodium; 119 mg chol.

Fennel-spiced Wild Salmon

Dory Ford, former executive chef at Portola Restaurant at the Monterey Bay Aquarium, prefers to work with wild Alaska salmon. Alongside this dish, he serves Chanterelle-Potato Salad with Pancetta, Shallots, and Thyme *(page 157)*.

SERVES 8 | **TIME** 20 minutes

2 tsp. fennel seeds
1 tsp. coarse sea salt or kosher salt
½ tsp. freshly ground black pepper
8 skinned, boned wild Alaska salmon fillets,
    1 in. thick (5 oz. each)
2 tbsp. canola oil

1. In a small, unoiled frying pan over medium heat, toast fennel seeds, stirring occasionally, until fragrant and a shade darker, 3 to 5 minutes. Put fennel seeds, salt, and pepper in a spice grinder or clean coffee grinder and grind until coarsely ground.
2. Pat salmon dry. Dust each fillet generously with spice mix, then rub it in gently. Pour oil onto a platter and lightly coat fillets.
3. Prepare a charcoal or gas grill for direct medium heat *(see Direct Heat Grilling, page 436)*. Grill salmon, skinned (outer) sides up, 3 minutes (close lid on gas grill). Turn salmon over and grill until moist and only slightly reddish pink in thickest part (cut to test), about 3 minutes longer. Let salmon rest 3 to 5 minutes before serving.

PER SERVING: 255 cal., 49% (126 cal.) from fat; 30 g protein; 14 g fat (2.2 g sat.); 0.3 g carbo (0.2 g fiber); 313 mg sodium; 88 mg chol.

Tandoori Shrimp in Green Marinade

Though your grill won't get as hot as the traditional tandoor Indian clay oven (which reaches 800°), these Indian-spiced skewers will still have fabulous flavor. They're from Neela Paniz, cookbook author and chef-owner of Neela's, in Napa, California. You'll need six to eight metal skewers.

SERVES 6 to 8 | **TIME** 45 minutes

1 tbsp. cumin seeds
1 cup coarsely chopped cilantro
10 garlic cloves, peeled
⅓ cup coarsely chopped fresh ginger
3 tbsp. thinly sliced serrano chiles
1 tbsp. garam masala *(see Quick Tip below)*
¼ to ½ tsp. cayenne
2 tbsp. vegetable oil
1 tsp. salt
2½ to 3 lbs. colossal shrimp (8 to 12 per lb.),
   peeled and deveined
Lime wedges
Mint Chutney *(recipe follows)*

1. In a 6- to 8-in. frying pan over medium heat, cook cumin seeds, stirring often, until lightly toasted, 2 to 4 minutes. Grind cumin seeds in a spice grinder or clean coffee grinder until finely ground.
2. In a blender, purée ground cumin, cilantro, garlic, ginger, chiles, garam masala, and ¼ tsp. cayenne into a smooth paste, adding ⅓ to ½ cup water as needed. Taste and add more cayenne if you like. Scrape into a bowl.
3. Shortly before serving, add oil and salt to cilantro paste; mix well. Add shrimp and toss until well coated with green marinade. Thread shrimp onto skewers, piercing shrimp through the center so they lie flat in a row.
4. Prepare a charcoal or gas grill for direct high heat *(see Direct Heat Grilling, page 436)*. Grill shrimp (close lid on gas grill), turning once, until opaque but still moist-looking in center (cut to test), 3 to 5 minutes per side. Transfer to a platter and serve with lime wedges and mint chutney.
Quick Tip: Garam masala is available in the spice section of many supermarkets; if you cannot find it, substitute 1 tsp. cinnamon, ½ tsp. *each* ground cumin and freshly ground black pepper, and ¼ tsp. *each* ground cardamom, nutmeg, cloves, and cayenne.

PER SERVING: 168 cal., 30% (50 cal.) from fat; 24 g protein; 5.6 g fat (0.8 g sat.); 4.1 g carbo (0.4 g fiber); 465 mg sodium; 175 mg chol.

Mint Chutney

A lively, refreshing condiment that goes well with seafood and grilled meats.

MAKES About 1 cup | **TIME** 20 minutes

2 tbsp. thinly sliced serrano chiles
1 onion (6 oz.), cut into 1-in. chunks
1 or 2 garlic cloves
1½ cups firmly packed mint leaves
½ cup chopped cilantro
¼ cup fresh lime juice
1 tsp. ground toasted cumin *(see step 1,*
   Tandoori Shrimp in Green Marinade, left)
½ tsp. salt, plus more to taste

1. In a blender, purée chiles, onion, and garlic into a smooth paste, adding 2 to 3 tbsp. water as needed.
2. Add mint, cilantro, lime juice, cumin, and salt; purée until smooth, adding 1 to 2 tbsp. water as needed. Scrape into a bowl and add more salt to taste.

PER TBSP.: 17 cal., 11% (1.8 cal.) from fat; 1 g protein; 0.2 g fat (0 g sat.); 3.5 g carbo (1.9 g fiber); 81 mg sodium; 0 mg chol.

Handling Chiles

A chile's heat comes from capsaicin (kap-*say*-i-sin), a compound found primarily in its seeds and spongy white ribs. As chiles ripen and develop more fruit flavors, they may seem smoother or sweeter, but they're still hot.

When handling chiles (fresh or dried), if you have sensitive skin and/or if you're handling a super-hot chile like a habanero, protect your hands. Wear rubber gloves or hold chiles with the tines of a fork.

If chiles burn your skin, rinse the area with rubbing alcohol. If chile juice sprays into your eyes or you touch your eyes with capsaicin-coated hands, flush your eyes well with water. To assess a chile's heat level for cooking, *see How Hot Is Your Chile, page 421.*

Chopping lots of fresh hot chiles? Work in a ventilated area. Otherwise your chest may tighten and you may start coughing.

To soothe a burning tongue, try ice cream, milk, or yogurt. Milk products lower the surface temperature of your tongue and contain casein, which washes away the capsaicin.

Lemon-Garlic Shrimp Skewers

A brief cure in salt and sugar adds flavor to the shrimp and makes them more tender. You will need six to eight (10-in.) skewers for this recipe.

SERVES 6 to 8 as a first course | **TIME** 1 hour, plus 45 minutes to cure

2 tbsp. *each* kosher salt and sugar
2 to 2½ lbs. colossal shrimp (12 to 15 per lb.), peeled and deveined
¼ cup *each* olive oil and chopped parsley
1 tbsp. finely shredded lemon zest
2 or 3 garlic cloves, minced
½ tsp. freshly ground black pepper
Lemon wedges

1. In a large bowl, mix salt and sugar. Add shrimp and stir gently to coat. Cover and chill 45 minutes to 1 hour. Meanwhile, if using wooden skewers, soak them at least 30 minutes.
2. Rinse shrimp well and drain; rinse and dry bowl. Return shrimp to bowl. Add oil, parsley, lemon zest, garlic, and pepper. Mix to coat. Thread shrimp on metal or wooden skewers, running skewer through body once near tail and once near head end of each shrimp, so it looks like the letter C.
3. Prepare charcoal or gas grill for direct high heat *(see Direct Heat Grilling, page 436)*. Lay shrimp skewers on an oiled hot cooking grate (close lid on gas grill). Grill, turning once, until shrimp are bright pink and opaque but still moist-looking in center (cut to test), 5 to 6 minutes total. Serve with lemon wedges to squeeze over shrimp.
Make Ahead: Assemble skewers through step 2 up to 1 day ahead; chill.

PER SERVING: 161 cal., 47% (75 cal.) from fat; 19 g protein; 8.3 g fat (1.2 g sat.); 1.6 g carbo (0.2 g fiber); 259 mg sodium; 140 mg chol.

Salt-cured Ouzo Shrimp

These shrimp have a two-punch licorice hit of anise seeds and ouzo. You'll need six metal or wooden skewers.

recipe pictured on page **458**

SERVES 6 | **TIME** 15 minutes, plus 45 minutes to cure

1½ tbsp. sugar
1 tbsp. kosher salt
1½ tsp. anise seeds, divided
1½ lbs. jumbo shrimp (16 to 20 per lb.), peeled, with tails left on, and deveined
1 tbsp. olive oil
2 tbsp. anise-flavored liqueur such as ouzo, plus more for drizzling
1½ tsp. minced garlic

1. In a medium bowl, mix sugar, salt, and ¾ tsp. anise seeds. Add shrimp and stir gently to coat. Cover and chill 45 minutes to 1 hour. Rinse both shrimp and bowl well and drain. Meanwhile, if using wooden skewers, soak them at least 30 minutes.
2. Return shrimp to bowl. Add remaining ¾ tsp. anise seeds, oil, ouzo, and garlic; mix to coat shrimp. Thread shrimp on skewers, running skewer through body once near tail and once near head end of each shrimp so it looks like the letter C.
3. Prepare a charcoal or gas grill for direct high heat *(see Direct Heat Grilling, page 436)*. Grill skewers, turning once, until shrimp are bright pink and opaque but still moist-looking in center (cut to test), 2 to 3 minutes total. Transfer to a platter. Drizzle more ouzo over shrimp if you like.

PER SERVING: 150 cal., 26% (39 cal.) from fat; 23 g protein; 4.3 g fat (0.7 g sat.); 3.3 g carbo (0 g fiber); sodium N/A; 173 mg chol.

Grilled Corn and Bay Shrimp Risotto

If there's ever a time for a buttery California Chardonnay, it's when you're eating sweet, crunchy corn. The wine's generous fruit makes it seem sweet, but it's balanced with creamy lemon, which whets your appetite for another bite of corn.

SERVES 6 | **TIME** 1 hour

3 medium ears corn, husked
3 tbsp. olive oil, divided
2 qts. reduced-sodium chicken broth
½ cup chopped shallots
1½ cups risotto rice (*see the Right Rice for Risotto, page 230*)
1 cup Chardonnay or other dry white wine
¾ lb. cooked bay shrimp, rinsed and drained
2 tbsp. *each* butter, chopped tarragon, and fresh lemon juice
1 tbsp. coarsely shredded lemon zest
1 tsp. freshly ground black pepper
Salt

1. Prepare charcoal or gas grill for direct high heat (*see Direct Heat Grilling, page 436*). Rub corn with 1 tbsp. oil. Lay ears on cooking grate (close lid on gas grill). Grill corn, turning occasionally, until lightly browned all over, 8 to 10 minutes total. Remove and let cool. Holding ears upright in a deep bowl, cut kernels from cobs with a large knife.
2. Meanwhile, in a medium saucepan, bring broth to a simmer. Pour remaining 2 tbsp. oil into a large saucepan over medium-high heat. Add shallots and cook, stirring often, just until softened, 2 to 3 minutes. Add rice and cook, stirring often, until grains are slightly translucent at edges, about 3 minutes more.
3. Add wine and cook, stirring often, until almost absorbed by rice. Add hot broth, one ladleful at a time, cooking and stirring after each addition until almost absorbed. Continue adding broth and stirring until rice is just tender to the bite and mixture is creamy, about 25 minutes (you will have broth left over).
4. Stir in corn, shrimp, butter, tarragon, lemon juice lemon zest, pepper, and salt to taste and cook, stirring often, until heated through, about 3 minutes. Add more broth if risotto gets too thick.
5. Spoon risotto into wide, shallow bowls and serve immediately.

PER SERVING: 377 cal., 31% (117 cal.) from fat; 21 g protein; 13 g fat (3.6 g sat.); 47 g carbo (4.5 g fiber); 894 mg sodium; 97 mg chol.

Grilled Marinated Calamari

The key to grilling squid is to cook it quickly; a few minutes too long and you've got rubber.

SERVES 4 | **TIME** 30 minutes, plus 1 hour to marinate

2 lbs. cleaned calamari (squid), tubes and tentacles separated but whole
1 tbsp. minced garlic
1½ tsp. red chile flakes
¼ cup chopped flat-leaf parsley
⅔ cup extra-virgin olive oil, divided
¼ cup fresh lemon juice, divided
1 tsp. sea salt, divided
½ loaf crusty bread such as ciabatta, cut in half horizontally

1. In a medium bowl, combine squid, garlic, chile flakes, parsley, ⅓ cup oil, 2 tbsp. lemon juice, and ½ tsp. salt. Chill, stirring often, 1 to 5 hours.
2. Pour squid and marinade into a colander over a bowl. Brush marinade over cut sides of bread.
3. Prepare a charcoal or gas grill for direct high heat (*see Direct Heat Grilling, page 436*). Grill bread on each side until grill marks appear, 3 to 5 minutes. Cut into slices.
4. Set calamari tubes perpendicular to cooking grate and grill, turning once, just until firm, about 3 minutes. Meanwhile, using tongs, drop tentacles in clumps onto grill just to firm up, then spread out to cook evenly, 4 minutes total.
5. Put squid in a dish and drizzle with remaining ⅓ cup oil, 2 tbsp. lemon juice, and ½ tsp. salt. Serve with bread.

PER SERVING: 707 cal., 57% (402 cal.) from fat; 39 g protein; 46 g fat (7.4 g sat.); 36 g carbo (1 g fiber); 998 mg sodium; 500 mg chol.

California Squid (Calamari)

Despite being heavily fished, squid swim in great numbers off the West Coast. They are caught with purse-seine nets, a method that has no habitat impact and produces little unintentional harvest of other species. Squid are found primarily in the Pacific Ocean off California, though they sometimes venture as far north as Oregon.

HOW TO CHOOSE AND PREPARE: Most squid are frozen soon after they're caught. Buy squid still frozen or thawed. They may come whole, or cleaned and separated into tubes and tentacles. Cleaned squid should be firm, have a mild aroma, and be white and glistening. They're mild and faintly sweet, like scallops, and quite versatile—they can be marinated and grilled, fried, or sautéed.

Grilled Seafood and Chorizo Paella

Few dishes are as dramatic as an enormous paella. You can let your guests share the limelight and put them to work chopping, prepping seafood, making the *allioli*, and taking a turn at the grill. Or you can do it yourself, easily; the key is to do all the prep work before you head to the grill, so you get the timing right for the rice and seafood.

SERVES 12 | **TIME** 2 hours

2 lbs. ripe tomatoes, cut in half
1 medium onion, chopped
1 *each* red and green bell pepper, seeds and ribs removed and chopped
2 tbsp. minced garlic
5 tsp. sweet Spanish paprika
2 tsp. kosher salt
4 cups Spanish Valenciano *(see Paella Pantry, page 513)* or Arborio rice
24 mussels, scrubbed, debearded
24 small littleneck clams, scrubbed
24 medium shrimp (¾ lb.), shelled with tails left on and deveined
1¼ lbs. fully cured or semi-cured Spanish chorizo *(see Paella Pantry, page 513)*, cut into thin diagonal slices
1 tsp. saffron threads
9 cups chicken broth, divided
2 cups dry white wine
7 tbsp. olive oil, divided
Coarsely chopped flat-leaf parsley
Allioli **(recipe follows)**

1. Coarsely grate tomatoes into a bowl and discard skins. Put onion and bell peppers in another bowl. Measure garlic, paprika, and salt into a small bowl. Put rice in a bowl, seafood in another, and chorizo in a third.
2. Prepare a charcoal or gas grill for direct medium heat *(see Direct Heat Grilling, page 436)*. Toast saffron in a large saucepan over medium heat, stirring, until fragrant, about 2 minutes. Add 6 cups broth and the wine, cover, bring to a boil over high heat, and keep warm. In a small saucepan, bring remaining 3 cups broth to a boil; keep warm. Carry all ingredients, a long-handled wooden spoon, slotted spoon, and oven mitts to grill.
3. For charcoal, add 15 briquets to fire just before cooking and cook with lid off until step 7. For gas, keep lid closed as you cook. Heat a 17- to 18-in. paella pan on grill. Add 3 tbsp. oil to pan, then chorizo, and brown, stirring occasionally, about 5 minutes. Using slotted spoon, transfer chorizo back to bowl.

4. Sauté onion and peppers in pan until onion is softened, about 5 minutes. Stir in tomatoes and cook, stirring often, until liquid evaporates and paste turns a shade darker, 10 to 12 minutes. Stir in the remaining ¼ cup oil and the garlic mixture; cook, stirring, for 30 seconds. Stir in rice until evenly coated, then pat out level.
5. Carefully pour hot saffron liquid over rice and scatter chorizo on top. Check to be sure grill and liquid in pan are level. If needed, reduce gas or airflow (for charcoal grill) to maintain a steady simmer. Cook for 12 minutes.
6. Pour enough hot plain broth over paella so rice is just covered in liquid (you may not use it all). Arrange mussels around rim of pan, almost touching, pushing them into liquid. Arrange any remaining mussels, the clams, and then the shrimp over paella in liquid.
7. Cover grill and cook until clams and mussels open and rice is *al punto* (al dente), another 6 to 10 minutes. Carefully remove paella from grill, drape with paper towels, and let stand about 5 minutes. Sprinkle with parsley. Serve with *allioli*.

PER SERVING: 692 cal., 38% (262 cal.) from fat; 35 g protein; 29 g fat (8.7 g sat.); 63 g carbo (3.6 g fiber); 1,162 mg sodium; 123 mg chol.

Allioli

The Spanish version of aioli, with the same garlicky hit.

SERVES 12 or 13 (makes 1⅔ cups) | **TIME** 5 minutes

1 cup extra-virgin olive oil
⅓ cup canola oil
4 large garlic cloves
1 egg plus 1 egg yolk
2 tbsp. fresh lemon juice, plus more to taste
1 tsp. kosher salt, plus more to taste

Pour oils into a container with a spout. In a food processor, whirl remaining ingredients into a smooth paste. With motor running, add oil in a slow stream until incorporated. Add more lemon juice and salt if you like.
Make Ahead: Up to 1 week, chilled.

PER 2-TBSP. SERVING: 209 cal., 98% (204 cal.) from fat; 0.8 g protein; 23 g fat (3 g sat.); 0.7 g carbo (0 g fiber); 32 mg chol.

Paella Pantry

You can buy nearly everything you need for paella at a well-stocked grocery store, but you can also order all of these things from *spanishtable.com*.

PAELLA PAN We like enamelled or stainless ones best (avoid carbon steel—it'll react with the tomatoes). These wide, shallow pans come in different sizes; for the recipe at left, get a 10-serving pan (17 in./42 cm.).

SPANISH RICE For good paella, you need short- to medium-grain rice that will absorb lots of liquid without losing its pleasing springiness. Spanish Valenciano fits the bill, or you can substitute Italian Arborio.

SPANISH CHORIZO Unlike the crumbly Mexican kind, the Spanish sausage, flavored with smoked paprika, holds its shape. Either of the two basic varieties works here. Fully cured is quite firm; we like smoky Palacios brand. Semi-cured is softer (like kielbasa); try Bilbao, a Basque-style chorizo with a tart edge.

Chili-Lime Corn on the Cob

Cooking corn on the cob in its de-silked husk keeps the kernels moist and adds a nice grassy flavor. You can also fully husk the corn and wrap it in foil. This recipe is from California restaurateur and Food Network personality Guy Fieri.

recipe pictured on page **451**

SERVES 6 | **TIME** 35 minutes, plus 30 minutes to soak

¼ cup butter, softened
1 tsp. *each* finely shredded lime zest and chili powder
½ tsp. salt, plus more for serving
½ tsp. freshly ground black pepper
¼ tsp. granulated garlic
6 ears unhusked corn

1. Combine butter, lime zest, chili powder, salt, pepper, and garlic in a small resealable plastic bag. Mush around to combine thoroughly.
2. Pull back husk from each ear without detaching from bottom of cob. Remove as much silk as possible. Spread evenly with butter mixture. Fold husks back over ears and tie in place with kitchen string or strips torn from outer husks.
3. Prepare a charcoal or gas grill for indirect medium heat (*see Indirect Heat Grilling, page 436*). Set corn over indirect-heat area and close lid on grill; cook corn until

tender and charred, about 20 minutes. Serve with salt for sprinkling.
Make Ahead: Through step 2 up to 24 hours, chilled.

PER SERVING: 112 cal., 39% (44 cal.) from fat; 3 g protein; 4.9 g fat (2.5 g sat.); 17 g carbo (2.5 g fiber); 150 mg sodium; 10 mg chol.

Grilled Ratatouille

A tasty, timesaving way to avoid having to skewer vegetables. Serve it in pita halves, over pasta, or with grilled lamb, beef, or chicken.

SERVES 8 as a side dish | **TIME** 2 hours

2 bell peppers (red or yellow), seeds and ribs removed and cut into ¾-in.-wide wedges
2 red onions, cut into 1-in.-wide wedges
1 large eggplant, cut into 1-in. chunks
2 small yellow zucchini or crookneck squash, cut into ¼-in.-thick rounds
3 Roma tomatoes, cored and quartered lengthwise
3 garlic cloves, chopped
5 tbsp. extra-virgin olive oil
1 tbsp. *each* finely chopped oregano leaves and flat-leaf parsley
2 tsp. kosher salt, plus more to taste
1 tsp. freshly ground black pepper
3 tbsp. balsamic vinegar
⅓ cup pine nuts, toasted (*see How to Toast Nuts, page 134*)
½ cup crumbled fresh goat cheese

1. Prepare a charcoal or gas grill for indirect medium heat (*see Indirect Heat Grilling, page 436*).
2. In a large bowl, toss together all ingredients except for vinegar, pine nuts, and goat cheese. Spread vegetables on a large rimmed baking sheet (not nonstick).
3. Set vegetables over indirect-heat area, close lid on grill, and cook until very tender, about 1 hour (for charcoal, add 4 briquets to each side every 30 minutes and keep measuring heat), gently stirring every 15 minutes.
4. Drizzle vegetables with vinegar, stir, and cook 15 minutes more. Let vegetables cool.
5. Put in a medium bowl, toss with pine nuts and salt to taste, and sprinkle with cheese.

PER SERVING (ABOUT ¾ CUP): 295 cal., 46% (135 cal.) from fat; 8.9 g protein; 15 g fat (3.5 g sat.); 35 g carbo (3.5 g fiber); 547 mg sodium; 6.7 mg chol.

The Griller's Guide to Vegetables

By grilling one or two vegetables with your main course, you can serve an entire meal from the grill. Before grilling, prepare vegetables as directed in the chart on these two pages; some vegetables need to be pre-cooked. Then coat with the Marinade (*see opposite page*)—or just use the basting sauce or marinade that you're putting on your main course—and grill as directed.

Vegetable	Prep	Grilling Directions & Cooking Time
ARTICHOKES	Trim away stem and coarse outer leaves; cut off top third. Trim thorny tips. Cook in boiling water to cover until stem end is tender when pierced, 20 to 40 minutes. Drain and cut in half lengthwise; scrape out fuzzy choke in center	Grill 8 to 12 minutes
ASPARAGUS	Trim tough stem ends	Set crosswise on cooking grate and grill about 5 minutes
BELL PEPPERS & CHILES	Leave whole (seasoning is optional—peppers are good with or without)	Grill 5 to 10 minutes
CABBAGE (red or green) & RADICCHIO	Cut cabbage into quarters lengthwise; cut radicchio in half	Grill 6 to 10 minutes
CARROTS	Cook whole medium peeled carrots in boiling water to cover until just tender, about 10 minutes. Drain	Set crosswise on cooking grate and grill 8 to 10 minutes
CORN IN HUSKS	Pull off outside dry husks; leave light green inner husks. Tear a few outer husks into strips to use as ties if you like. Gently pull back inner husks; remove and discard silks. Drizzle corn with marinade (or just butter and salt if you like). Put inner husks back in place around corn; tie with strips of husks or kitchen twine at top to enclose	Grill 18 to 20 minutes
CORN OUT OF HUSKS	Strip off any stray silks. Enclose in foil, if you like, with butter and salt or marinade	Grill 8 to 10 minutes
EGGPLANT	Cut off stem end. Cut Asian eggplants in half lengthwise; cut small globe (regular) eggplants crosswise into ½-in.-thick slices	Grill until meltingly soft, 8 to 12 minutes
FENNEL	Cut off and discard woody stems. Cut vertically into four slices	Grill 20 to 30 minutes
LEEKS (at least 1 in. wide)	Trim root ends; trim tops, leaving 2 in. of green leaves. Split lengthwise to within ½ in. of root ends. Rinse well; drain	Set crosswise on cooking grate and grill 8 to 10 minutes

Vegetable	Prep	Grilling Directions & Cooking Time
MUSHROOMS (button, cremini, portabella, shiitake)	Trim any tough stem ends (for portabellas and shiitakes, remove stems entirely)	Grill 10 to 15 minutes (start large mushrooms gill side down; turn once halfway through)
ONIONS, GREEN	Trim root ends and 2 in. of green tops (seasoning is optional—green onions are good with or without)	Grill 3 to 5 minutes
ONIONS (red, white, yellow)	Do not peel. Cut small onions in half lengthwise and larger ones into quarters, then marinate. Thread onto skewers with onions arranged as flat as possible	Grill 15 to 30 minutes
POTATOES (russet)	Poke a few times with a fork, then marinate (for a moister potato, enclose in foil before grilling)	Grill, turning and basting with more marinade every 10 minutes or so (if not in foil), until tender when pierced with a sharp knife, 30 to 60 minutes depending on size of potato
SQUASH, SUMMER (crookneck, pattypan, zucchini)	Leave small squash (1 in. or less in diameter) whole. Cut larger squash in half lengthwise	Grill 10 to 15 minutes
SQUASH, WINTER (acorn, kabocha)	Cut squash in half, scoop out seeds, and cut halves ½ in. thick	Grill 10 to 12 minutes, turning once
SWEET POTATOES or YAMS	Cut small sweet potatoes in half, large ones lengthwise into 1-in.-wide wedges	Grill 18 to 20 minutes
TOMATILLOS	Strip off papery husks and rinse well. Brush with olive oil (rather than marinade) and sprinkle with salt	Grill 10 to 12 minutes
TOMATOES	Cut in thick slices	Grill 8 to 12 minutes

The Marinade

In a medium bowl, whisk together 2 tbsp. chopped **thyme, rosemary, oregano, or tarragon leaves** (optional); **kosher or sea salt** and **freshly ground black pepper** to taste; and ⅓ to ½ cup **olive oil, vegetable oil, or melted butter**. Makes enough marinade for 2 lbs. vegetables; 6 to 8 servings.

THE METHOD

1. Prepare a charcoal or gas grill for direct medium heat (*see Direct Heat Grilling, page 436*). Indirect medium-high heat works too, if that's what's needed for the protein you're grilling; turn the vegetables less often, though, and let them cook a bit longer. If using wooden skewers, soak skewers in hot water for 30 minutes first so they won't burn on the grill.

2. Put prepared vegetables in a bowl or on a rimmed baking sheet, depending on their shape and size, and drizzle with marinade. Turn vegetables to coat. If your vegetables are small or cut into pieces, thread onto skewers, making sure vegetables lie flat.

3. Oil hot cooking grate quickly and carefully with a wad of oiled paper towels. Set vegetables on cooking grate and grill, turning frequently, until they're streaked with brown, crisp-edged, and tender when pierced (for specific directions and cooking times, see chart left and above).

4. Serve vegetables hot or at room temperature.

Grilled Red Potatoes

Tangy, slightly charred potatoes are fantastic with any kind of grilled meat or fish. You can easily double the marinade and use it on your protein, and grill both at the same time. Use a grilling basket or long metal skewers (each at least 12 in.).

SERVES 6 to 8 | **TIME** 45 minutes

3 to 3½ lbs. small (each about 1½ in. diameter) red thin-skinned potatoes
¼ cup balsamic or red wine vinegar
1½ tbsp. Dijon mustard
2 tsp. olive oil
Chopped flat-leaf parsley

1. Put potatoes in a 5- to 6-qt. pan and add water just to cover. Bring to a boil over high heat, covered, then simmer until potatoes are just barely tender when pierced, about 20 minutes. (You can keep potatoes warm in water, off the heat, up to 45 minutes.) Drain potatoes.
2. Prepare a charcoal or gas grill for direct medium-high heat (see Direct Heat Grilling, page 436).
3. Stir together vinegar, mustard, and oil. Add marinade to potatoes in pan; mix well. Put potatoes in a grilling basket. Alternatively, thread on skewers, using a fork to guide hot potatoes; push a second skewer through potatoes, parallel to and about ½ in. from first, to keep potatoes from spinning when you turn them.
4. Grill potatoes (close lid on gas grill), turning and basting often with marinade, until potatoes are browned and tender when pierced, about 20 minutes. Serve sprinkled with parsley.

PER SERVING: 149 cal., 0.01% (2 cal.) from fat; 3.5 g protein; 1.4 g fat (0.2 g sat.); 31 g carbo (3.1 g fiber); 80.4 mg sodium; 0 mg chol.

Grilled Fingerling Potatoes with Dill

Try making these at Thanksgiving for an unexpected alternative to traditional mashed. The dish has the additional advantage of freeing up stove and oven space.

SERVES 12 | **TIME** 45 minutes

6 lbs. fingerling potatoes, halved lengthwise (if very small, keep whole)
¼ cup extra-virgin olive oil
1½ tsp. kosher salt
1 tsp. freshly ground black pepper
¼ cup each softened butter and roughly chopped dill
Coarse sea salt, for finishing (optional)

1. Prepare a charcoal or gas grill for direct medium heat (see Direct Heat Grilling, page 436). In a large bowl, toss potatoes with oil, kosher salt, and pepper.
2. Oil four sheets of heavy-duty foil (each about 12 by 26 in.), shiny side down. Divide potatoes among sheets, arranging them cut side down in a single layer on short half of each sheet. Fold other half of each sheet over potatoes and crimp edges together to seal.
3. Lay packets, crimped sides up, on cooking grate. Close lid on grill and cook packets, rotating on grill halfway through cooking, until potatoes are tender when pierced through foil, about 20 minutes. Open packets; if potatoes aren't brown on cut sides, cook longer.
4. Transfer potatoes to a large bowl. Toss with butter and dill. Arrange on a platter; sprinkle with coarse sea salt if you like.
Make Ahead: Up to 3 days ahead, grill potatoes, remove from foil, and chill. Reheat in an oiled baking pan in a 450° oven until hot, about 15 minutes, then proceed with step 4.

PER SERVING: 233 cal., 33% (77 cal.) from fat; 4.4 g protein; 8.7 g fat (3.1 g sat.); 36 g carbo (3.9 g fiber); 281 mg sodium; 10 mg chol.

Grilled Spicy Sweet-potato Packets

Be sure to use heavy-duty foil for your packets, as regular foil may tear on the grill.

SERVES 6 | **TIME** 40 minutes

1½ lbs. orange-fleshed sweet potatoes (often called "yams"; about 2 medium), peeled, halved lengthwise, and cut into ¼-in.-thick half-moons
¾ lb. red onion (about 1 large), halved and cut into ⅓-in.-thick wedges
⅓ cup olive oil
2 tbsp. ketchup
2 tsp. each chili powder, salt, and chopped thyme leaves
1 tsp. freshly ground black pepper
1 lime, cut into 6 wedges

1. In a large bowl, toss sweet potato and onion wedges with oil, ketchup, chili powder, salt, thyme, and pepper.
2. On a work surface, set out six 12- by 14-in. sheets of heavy-duty foil, shiny side down. Distribute potato mixture evenly among sheets, spooning into center of each sheet. Fold top edge of each foil sheet down over potato mixture. Crimp edges together to create a tight seal.
3. Prepare a charcoal or gas grill for indirect medium heat (see Indirect Heat Grilling, page 436). Set potato packets over indirect-heat area, overlapping slightly if needed, and cover grill. Cook until potatoes are tender when pierced, 25 to 30 minutes.

4. Remove packets from grill. Let cool 10 minutes, then serve potatoes and onions with wedges of lime to squirt over vegetables.

PER SERVING: 224 cal., 48% (108 cal.) from fat; 2.5 g protein; 12 g fat (1.6 g sat.); 28 g carbo (3.8 g fiber); 861 mg sodium; 0 mg chol.

Grill-baked Apple Crisp

Traditional apple crisp gets a Western update on the grill. The recipe makes a lot, but we like having any left-overs for breakfast. You can substitute crème fraîche or freshly whipped cream for the vanilla ice cream. And if you love the flavor of smoke, you can actually smoke the crisp *(see Smokin' Apple Crisp, below)*.

SERVES 8 to 10 | **TIME** 1¼ hours

½ cup butter
10 apples (about 5 lbs. total), preferably a mix
 of Granny Smith and Golden Delicious
2 cups flour
1 cup sugar
2 tsp. *each* cinnamon and baking powder
¾ tsp. salt
2 eggs
Vanilla ice cream (optional)

1. Melt butter over low heat; set aside.
2. Peel, core, and cut apples into ⅓-in.-thick slices. Put apples in a foil pan or a foil-wrapped 9- by 13-in. baking pan; spread level.
3. In a bowl, mix flour, sugar, cinnamon, baking powder, and salt. Drop in eggs and mix with a pastry blender or fork until crumbly (mixture will resemble streusel). Spread topping evenly over apples. Drizzle with melted butter.
4. Prepare a charcoal or gas grill for indirect medium heat *(see Indirect Heat Grilling, page 436)*. Set apple crisp over indirect-heat area. Close lid on grill and cook until topping is browned, apples are tender, and butter is bubbling, 40 to 45 minutes. Serve warm with vanilla ice cream if you like.
Make Ahead: Up to 1 day, at room temperature.

PER SERVING: 376 cal., 26% (99 cal.) from fat; 4.2 g protein; 11 g fat (6.2 g sat.); 68 g carbo (4.3 g fiber); 379 mg sodium; 67 mg chol.

Smokin' Apple Crisp: Cover ⅓ cup **applewood chips** with water and soak for about 30 minutes, then drain. Just before you place apple crisp on grate, scatter chips over coals (if using a charcoal grill), or place chips in metal smoking box of your gas grill (or in a foil pan directly on heat in a corner).

Pineapple Satays with Coconut Caramel

Denser fruits like peaches, nectarines, and pineapples work much better on a grill than soft, small fruits like strawberries. When grilling fruit, be sure to thoroughly clean your grill beforehand so the fruit doesn't taste meaty. You'll need 16 wooden skewers (4 to 6 in. each).

recipe pictured on page **379**

SERVES 4 | **TIME** 35 minutes, plus 30 minutes to soak skewers if using wooden

1 ripe pineapple
1 cup sugar
¾ cup canned coconut milk
¼ cup unsweetened shredded coconut, toasted
 (see Quick Tip below)

1. Soak skewers 30 minutes. Trim ends from pineapple, then stand it on one end and cut off peel. Halve pineapple lengthwise; reserve half for another use. Halve remaining pineapple lengthwise and cut out core. Cut each pineapple quarter into 4 lengthwise slices, then cut each slice in half crosswise to make 16 thin wedges. Skewer each wedge lengthwise, dividing the wedges among skewers.
2. In a small saucepan, combine sugar with ½ cup water. Bring to a boil, swirling to dissolve sugar; boil, swirling occasionally (do not stir), until just golden and honeylike. Remove from heat and slowly whisk in coconut milk (mixture will bubble furiously).
3. Prepare a charcoal or gas grill for direct high heat *(see Direct Heat Grilling, page 436)*. Using a pastry brush, coat pineapple pieces with caramel sauce (you'll have sauce left over). Grill just until grill marks appear, then turn to grill other side until marked, 4 to 5 minutes total. Put skewers on a platter, sprinkle with toasted coconut, and serve with remaining caramel sauce.
Quick Tip: To toast coconut, spread in a shallow layer in a rimmed baking pan and heat in a 300° oven, stirring occasionally, until golden, about 10 minutes.

PER 4-SKEWER SERVING: 299 cal., 30% (89 cal.) from fat; 1.4 g protein; 9.9 g fat (8.3 g sat.); 56 g carbo (1.9 g fiber); 7.3 mg sodium; 0 mg chol.

The Dutch Oven: America's Original Outdoor Stove

For outdoor cooking, if you had your choice of just one piece of equipment, you'd probably want it to be a Dutch oven. Few kitchen items are as versatile as this sturdy cast-iron pot—it's a stewpot, a frying pan, and an oven all in one. A Dutch oven often has pointy little legs to raise it above the coals so the food cooks evenly instead of burning. It also frequently has a rimmed lid to hold more coals on top, to cook food from above as well as from below—re-creating the all-enveloping heat of a regular oven. The lid can also be inverted to form a griddle. You can make just about anything in the pot, really, from scrambled eggs to stews to cakes. All you need is an open fire. And if a Dutch oven is well-seasoned, it's even nonstick.

What's Dutch about Dutch Ovens?

Dutch ovens were prized by colonial cooks (they were often listed as valuable property in wills). Although not actually Dutch—similar pots have been used for centuries in many countries around the world—the cookware was sold by Dutch traders during colonial times, which may be how it got its name; another explanation is that at least some of the pots sold in the American colonies came from an English maker who borrowed metal-casting techniques from the Dutch. The ovens traveled West with the pioneers and explorers, including Lewis and Clark in 1805, and were indispensable to cowboys on the range.

A Western Favorite

The Dutch oven is still much loved in the West, especially in Utah, where it's an official state symbol. The International Dutch Oven Society, proud sponsor of the annual World Championship Dutch Oven Cook-Off, is in Logan, Utah. Why Utah? The state library's Utah State Cooking Pot web page offers this suggestion: "Perhaps it's because for Utahans, families have a special significance and particularly their pioneer forbearers. It's a unique and generational bonding experience for families to gather around a campfire after a meal from the same kind of Dutch ovens and tell the stories about and history of their pioneer ancestors."

TO SEASON A DUTCH OVEN: Wash it (with soap and hot water if it's waxed or otherwise coated; just with hot water if it's not) and dry it. Rub the pot and lid all over with vegetable oil. Set the pot and lid side by side in a 325° oven for 1 hour; as the pot heats, the "pores" in the metal open up and absorb the oil. (Open windows or turn on the vent, as this can get smoky.) Let cool, then wipe clean with paper towels. Every time you wash it thereafter (no soap, just hot water), dry it, coat it with oil, and wipe clean. Store the pot with the lid ajar, or with a paper towel inside to absorb moisture. After years of use and thorough oilings, a Dutch oven turns a smooth, glossy black and becomes a thing of beauty.

DUTCH OVEN SOURCES: Lodge Manufacturing Company (*lodgemfg. com*) is the country's biggest producer of traditional Dutch ovens; it also sells them preseasoned. Le Creuset and Staub make gorgeous modern versions designed for the oven, not the campfire.

Dutch Oven Cooking
(Bottom Heat Method)

Use this setup when you want to simulate the heat of a stovetop burner beneath the cooking pot. It's a great method for cooking stews and chili. If you have a Dutch oven with feet, you can skip the bricks and set the oven right over the briquets.

1. Spread 2 to 3 large sheets of heavy-duty foil, each at least 4 in. wider than the diameter of the oven, on a cleared and fireproof area (sand, bricks, tarmac) in a draft-free spot or in a firepit. (A two- or three-sided folding metal splash guard or wind-guard, a little higher than the pot, can block drafts; find these at hardware stores.)

2. Set 3 bricks, long narrow side down, in a Y formation; bricks should be about 4 in. high. Space bricks as shown in photo (*opposite page*).

3. About 15 minutes before you start cooking, ignite the number of briquets specified by the recipe in a chimney starter. If you need to add more later, ignite them about 15 minutes before you need them. When briquets are evenly ignited (about 15 minutes for grooved Kingsford briquets), heap

Bottom Heat Method

Top and Bottom Heat Method

them in the center of the brick Y (no higher than the bricks) and in between the bricks.

4. Set Dutch oven on the bricks so it rests over the coals; adjust position of coals, if necessary, so they are underneath the oven. Add 6 briquets every 30 minutes until cooking is done, and push away ashes every now and then with a poker or a stick to keep them from blocking air circulation.

Dutch Oven Cooking
(Top and Bottom Heat Method)

When you have coals arranged underneath the pot and on the lid, it creates an oven-like environment that works for cooking cakes, biscuits, and anything else that should get nice and brown on top. This method requires a Dutch oven with legs and a rimmed (flanged) lid.

1. Spread 2 or 3 large sheets of heavy-duty foil, each at least 4 in. wider than the diameter of the oven, on a cleared and fireproof area (sand, bricks, tarmac) in a draft-free spot or in a firepit. (A two- or three-sided folding metal splash guard or wind-guard, a little higher than the pot, can block drafts; find these at hardware stores.)

2. Trace around lid in center of foil. About 15 minutes before you start cooking, ignite the number of briquets specified by the recipe in a chimney starter. (We used standard Kingsford briquets, *shown above*, since they are widely available. In recent years, they've reformulated their briquets so that they light faster and burn baster. The Dutch oven recipes on the following pages were developed using Kingsford briquets.) If you need to add more briquets later, ignite them about 15 minutes before you need them.

3. Arrange about one-third of the coals inside the ring you have traced, spacing them evenly and keeping a border about ½ in. inside the ring free of coals. When baking doughs, leave the center of the ring clear to keep the dough from burning.

4. Set oven over coals (legs are only a little taller than a briquet) and arrange the remaining two-thirds coals evenly over the lid. Check the food every now and then to make sure it's cooking at an appropriate rate, lifting the coal-topped lid using a fireplace poker or long tongs that brace the lid as you lift it (or a Dutch oven lid-lifting tool, available from Lodge Manufacturing). Set the lid on a sheet of foil or a rimmed baking pan while you check the food.

5. To reduce heat, remove a few coals in a symmetrical pattern so heat remains even, and removing 2 coals from lid for every 1 coal from below. To increase heat, add ignited coals in a symmetrical pattern, 2 for the lid for every 1 from below. Push away ashes every now and then with a poker or a stick to keep them from blocking air circulation.

Dutch Oven Bacon, Onions, and Potatoes

If you've never cooked anything in a Dutch oven before, try this easy recipe. It tastes especially good after you've spent the day outdoors. To stir the contents, you'll have to carefully lift off the oven's coal-topped lid with a fireplace poker or long tongs that brace the lid as you lift it; set on a sheet of foil or a baking sheet.

SERVES 6 to 8 | **TIME** 45 minutes, including Dutch oven setup

½ lb. bacon, chopped
2 medium onions, chopped
2 lbs. Yukon Gold potatoes, sliced ¼ in. thick
Salt and freshly ground black pepper

1. Set up Dutch oven cooking area for *Top and Bottom Heat Method (page 519)*, igniting 60 coals. Add bacon to a 10-in. cast-iron Dutch oven with a rimmed lid and legs; put on lid. When coals are evenly ignited, spread one-third of them on foil. Set oven over coals (legs may be obscured by coals) and add remaining two-thirds of coals to lid.
2. Cook bacon, stirring once, until crisp, 8 to 10 minutes. Add onions; cover and cook, stirring once, until onions are softened, about 8 minutes. Mix in potatoes. Cover oven and cook until potatoes are tender when pierced, about 20 minutes. Spoon off fat if you like. Season to taste with salt and pepper.

PER SERVING: 234 cal., 49% (115 cal.) from fat; 6.3 g protein; 13 g fat (4.3 g sat.); 23 g carbo (1.8 g fiber); 99 mg sodium; 19 mg chol.

Pioneer Dutch Oven Pork Stew

This succulent stew was the main course at a dress-up dinner for 8-year-old girls in Woodland Hills, Utah, where Dutch oven cooking is a mainstay. Joyce Terry, who organized the outdoor party, gave us the recipe. You can also cook the stew on the stove. In either case, serve with warm bread to soak up the juices.

SERVES 6 to 8 | **TIME** 2 hours, including Dutch oven setup

2 lbs. boned pork shoulder (butt), excess fat trimmed and cut into 1-in. cubes
4 large carrots, cut into ¼-in.-thick slices
2 large russet potatoes, peeled and cut into 1-in. cubes
1 medium onion, chopped
6 garlic cloves, mashed
2 jars (15 oz. each) marinara sauce or other tomato-based pasta sauce
3 bay leaves
2 tsp. *each* red chile flakes, dried oregano, and dried thyme
1 tsp. cumin seeds, toasted *(see Quick Tip below)*
¼ tsp. freshly ground black pepper, plus more to taste
2 cups reduced-sodium beef broth or water, divided
Kosher salt to taste

1. Set up the Dutch oven cooking area for *Bottom Heat Method (page 518)*, igniting 60 coals. In a 10-in. cast-iron Dutch oven (or heavy pot), combine all ingredients except 1 cup beef broth (or water) and salt.
2. Cover oven and set over ignited briquets, or, if using a heavy pot, over low heat on the stovetop. Simmer stew, stirring occasionally, until meat is very tender when pierced, about 1¼ hours; add 6 more unlit briquets to pile of coals every half hour. If stew boils, spread out briquets slightly to lower heat, or lower heat on stove.
3. Season with salt and pepper to taste. If stew looks dry, add up to 1 cup broth or water. Serve with warm bread to soak up the juices.
Quick Tip: To toast cumin seeds, put in a dry (not non-stick) frying pan and toast over medium heat, stirring occasionally, until fragrant and a shade darker, 2 to 3 minutes.

PER SERVING: 384 cal., 14% (52 cal.) from fat; 25 g protein; 17 g fat (5.7 g sat.); 32 g carbo (5.4 g fiber); 640 mg sodium; 72 mg chol.

Helen's Dutch-oven Whole-wheat Beer Biscuits

These buttery, tender biscuits from Helen Vacek, a camp cook at Brush Creek Ranch, in Saratoga, Wyoming, can also be cooked in a conventional oven.

MAKES 8 to 9 | **TIME** 1¼ hours, including Dutch oven setup

2 cups all-purpose flour
1 cup whole-wheat flour
2 tbsp. sugar
4½ tsp. baking powder
1 tsp. salt
¾ cup butter
1 egg
1 cup beer

1. In a large bowl, combine both flours, sugar, baking powder, and salt. With a pastry blender or knives, cut in butter until mixture forms coarse crumbs.
2. Beat egg to blend; add to flour mixture along with beer. Stir with a fork just until dough holds together.
3. On a well-floured board, gently knead dough two or three times, until smooth. Pat dough 1 in. thick. Cut out biscuits with a floured 2- to 2 ½-in. biscuit or round cookie cutter, pressing straight down and lifting cutter straight up without twisting. Gently pat scraps together; cut out remaining biscuits.

4. To bake, set up the Dutch oven cooking area for *Top and Bottom Heat Method (page 519)*. Oil interior of a 10-in. cast-iron Dutch oven with a rimmed lid and legs; arrange biscuits in a single layer inside (you will have to squeeze them together). Put rimmed lid on oven. When briquets are fully ignited, evenly space 8 coals in a circle about ½ in. inside traced ring on foil on ground. Set oven over coals. Arrange remaining coals evenly on lid. Ignite another 12 to 15 briquets. After about 20 minutes, add 8 of the freshly ignited coals to lid. Bake another 15 minutes. Lift lid and check; if biscuits have not started to brown, add 4 to 6 more coals to lid. Continue baking until biscuits are browned, 10 to 15 minutes longer.
5. To bake in a conventional oven, arrange biscuits, slightly separated, on a greased 12- by 15-in. baking sheet. Bake in a 425° oven until browned, 18 to 20 minutes.
6. Serve biscuits warm or cool.

PER BISCUIT: 307 cal., 47% (144 cal.) from fat; 5.6 g protein; 16 g fat (9.8 g sat.); 35 g carbo; 623 mg sodium; 65 mg chol.

muffins,
rolls &
breads

Comfort comes in many forms. A fresh loaf of bread, its yeasty fragrance filling the house, is one of them. Warm, pillowy homemade cinnamon buns are another. Even the baking process itself—the rhythms of measuring, kneading, and punching down—is soothing.

Yet we never get around to baking. Why? We think it will swallow up the entire day. Or we worry that it's too hard, that it takes special skill to produce anything with a crust.

The good news is that, with rare exceptions, neither assumption is true. None of the bread recipes in this chapter takes more than 4 hours (several take less than an hour), and for most of that time the dough is rising on its own—you just check in now and then, while getting other things done around the house. Also, you can break up the time by chilling the dough overnight (it will keep rising, but more slowly). Or you can make a big batch of dough, create several different tempting rolls or pastries or a couple of loaves of bread, and freeze them until you're ready to bake (*see page* 538).

Other recipes require no more of you than an easy, 15- to 20-minute mixing of ingredients. Pop the batter in the oven and do something else until the timer rings. (Some favorites: Raspberry Streusel Muffins, *page* 525, and Buttermilk-Currant Scones with Lemon Glaze, *page* 528.)

On the other hand, if you enjoy immersing yourself in a bread project, we have a good one for you: sourdough, including its starter—a living "proto-bread" that you create and feed for a few days before using it to bake (*see page* 558). When you slide your first golden loaf out of the oven, you'll know the other joy of baking, besides comfort. It's pride.

Muffins, Rolls & Breads

Raspberry Streusel Muffins

Divinely tender and not-too-sweet muffins that came from the Steamboat Inn, a small lodge in pristine Oregon trout-fishing country on the North Umpqua River. The cooks used ripe, sweet local berries and fresh hazelnuts.

MAKES 14 muffins | **TIME** 1 hour, 20 minutes

⅓ cup hazelnuts, toasted *(see How to Toast Nuts, page 134)*, skins removed, and chopped

1¼ cups sugar, divided

3 tbsp. plus 1½ cups all-purpose flour

2 tbsp. butter, plus ⅓ cup melted

¼ tsp. nutmeg

½ cup whole-wheat pastry flour (or ¼ cup regular whole-wheat flour plus ¼ cup all-purpose flour)

2 tsp. baking powder

½ tsp. baking soda

¼ tsp. salt

1 egg

½ cup *each* milk and sour cream

1½ cups raspberries

1. Preheat oven to 400°. Butter 14 muffin cups (2¾ in. wide) or 8 ramekins (about 1-cup size). In a small bowl, combine nuts, ¼ cup sugar, 3 tbsp. all-purpose flour, 2 tbsp. butter, and the nutmeg, mixing with your fingers until crumbly. Set streusel aside.

2. In a medium bowl, combine remaining 1 cup sugar and 1½ cups all-purpose flour, the whole-wheat flour, baking powder and soda, and salt. In a large bowl, whisk egg, milk, sour cream, and ⅓ cup melted butter until smooth. Add flour mixture and stir just enough to moisten dry ingredients. Be careful not to overstir. Gently fold in raspberries.

3. Spoon batter into muffin cups or ramekins until two-thirds full. Top evenly with streusel; press lightly into batter. Bake until deep golden, about 25 minutes.

4. Loosen muffins from containers (if using ramekins, let cool completely first) and turn out onto a rack.

Make Ahead: Up to 3 days, at room temperature; up to a week, chilled; up to 2 months, frozen (double-bag in resealable plastic freezer bags).

PER REGULAR-SIZE MUFFIN: 253 cal., 39% (99 cal.) from fat; 3.6 g protein; 11 g fat (5.8 g sat.); 35 g carbo; 238 mg sodium; 39 mg chol.

Cornhusk Muffins

These rustic, nubbly-textured muffins go well with any chile-spiked egg dish. Because they're baked in cornhusks, you don't need paper baking cups to line the pan.

MAKES 12 muffins | **TIME** 50 minutes

6 to 8 dried cornhusks (6 to 8 in. each; *see Quick Tip below*)

2 cups flour

¾ cup yellow cornmeal or masa harina (*see Quick Tip below*)

1 tbsp. baking powder

½ tsp. salt

1¼ cups shredded (about 5 oz.) pepper jack cheese, divided

1 egg

¼ cup butter, melted

2 tbsp. honey

1 cup milk

1. Preheat oven to 375°. Grease 12 muffin cups (2¾ in. wide). Separate cornhusks. In a large bowl, pour boiling water over husks to cover; let soak until soft and pliable, about 10 minutes. Drain husks and pat dry. Tear lengthwise into 1½- to 2-in.-wide strips.

2. In a bowl, mix flour, cornmeal, baking powder, salt, and ¾ cup cheese. Make a well in center. In another bowl, beat egg, butter, honey, and milk until blended. Pour into well in flour mixture and stir just enough to moisten dry ingredients. Be careful not to overstir.

3. Arrange two or three strips of husk in a muffin cup, crossing centers in bottom so the ends fan out around sides. Fill cup two-thirds full with batter. Repeat to line and fill the remaining cups, one at a time. Sprinkle tops with remaining ½ cup cheese.

4. Bake until tops are golden, about 25 minutes. Lift out of pan; cool on rack. Serve warm or cool.

Quick Tip: Find dried cornhusks and masa harina (dehydrated corn dough; also labeled masa flour, corn flour, or instant corn masa mix) at well-stocked grocery stores or Latino markets.

Make Ahead: Up to 12 hours, at room temperature; up to 3 days, chilled; or up to 2 weeks, wrapped airtight and frozen (thaw unwrapped). Reheat at 350° until warm, 7 to 10 minutes.

PER MUFFIN: 219 cal., 35% (76 cal.) from fat; 6.8 g protein; 8.5 g fat (4.9 g sat.); 28 g carbo (1 g fiber); 328 mg sodium; 41 mg chol.

Blue Corn–Blueberry Muffins

Reader Louise Galen, of West Hollywood, replaced some of the flour in her favorite blueberry muffin recipe with blue cornmeal, creating an all-blue breakfast treat.

MAKES 12 muffins | **TIME** 1 hour

1 cup *each* **blue cornmeal** *(see Quick Tips, right)* **and flour**
½ cup **granulated sugar**
1 tsp. **baking soda**
½ tsp. *each* **baking powder and salt**
1¼ cups **buttermilk**
2 **eggs, lightly beaten**
½ cup **unsalted butter, melted and cooled**
1 cup **fresh blueberries**
2½ tbsp. **pearl sugar (optional;** *see Quick Tips, right***)**

1. Preheat oven to 400°. Generously grease 12 muffin cups (2¾ in. wide). Sift cornmeal, flour, granulated sugar, baking soda and powder, and salt into a medium bowl. In a separate bowl, whisk together buttermilk, eggs, and melted butter. Make a well in center of dry ingredients, pour liquid ingredients into well, and stir just enough to moisten dry ingredients. Be careful not to overstir. Fold in berries.

Blue Corn

A staple Native American food in the Southwest for centuries, blue corn appears there in everything from breads to stews to drinks. One of the more spectacular dishes comes from the Hopi, who use finely ground blue cornmeal to make *piki*, a crisp, tissue paper–thin bread rolled up like a scroll.

For many of us, though, blue corn is still waiting to be discovered. It is most commonly available as flour and cornmeal, in hues ranging from pale lilac to deep purple, and has a sweet, nutty flavor. Blue corn has several distinct health benefits, too: It's higher in protein (by at least 20 percent) than either white or yellow dent corn (the kind we eat most often) and may contain more zinc and iron. Its blue pigment, called anthocyanin, is thought to be a potent antioxidant.

In cooking, we like to use blue corn flour in equal proportion to all-purpose flour or wheat flour in pancakes and waffles. The cornmeal is great in muffins. And blue-corn tortillas can be used to make any kind of taco, burrito, or enchilada.

2. Fill each muffin cup two-thirds full with batter and sprinkle tops with pearl sugar if using. Bake until golden on top, about 25 minutes. Transfer pan to a rack and let cool 10 minutes before removing muffins.
Quick Tips: Look for blue cornmeal at natural-foods stores. Pearl sugar (available from King Arthur Flour, *kingarthurflour.com*) lends a pleasant crunch, but you can substitute 1 tbsp. granulated sugar if you like.
Make Ahead: Up to 3 days, at room temperature; up to a week, chilled; up to 2 months, frozen (double-bag in resealable plastic freezer bags).

PER MUFFIN: 209 cal., 39% (81 cal.) from fat; 4.1 g protein; 9 g fat (5.2 g sat.); 28 g carbo (1.1 g fiber); 263 mg sodium; 57 mg chol.

Banana-Nut Oat Bran Muffins

Reader Joan Stucey, of Klamath Falls, Oregon, often treats her co-workers to homemade muffins; they voted these the best.

MAKES 12 muffins | **TIME** 40 minutes

2 **oranges (about 1 lb. total)**
2 tbsp. **canola or safflower oil**
2 **eggs**
1 cup **mashed ripe bananas**
¼ cup *each* **honey and firmly packed light brown sugar**
2 cups **quick-cooking oat bran cereal**
2 tsp. **baking powder**
½ tsp. **salt**
½ cup **chopped walnuts**

1. Preheat oven to 400°. Oil 12 muffin cups (2¾ in. wide) or line with paper baking cups.
2. Finely shred 1 tbsp. zest from oranges. Cut oranges in half and ream juice. Measure ½ cup juice; save remainder for other uses.
3. In a large bowl, combine orange zest and juice, oil, eggs, bananas, honey, and brown sugar. Stir to mix well.
4. In a medium bowl, mix cereal, baking powder, salt, and walnuts. Add to egg mixture and stir just enough to moisten dry ingredients evenly. Be careful not to overstir. Fill each muffin cup two-thirds full.
5. Bake muffins until golden brown, 20 to 25 minutes. Loosen muffins from pan and turn out onto a rack. Serve hot, warm, or at room temperature.
Make Ahead: Up to 3 days, at room temperature; up to a week, chilled; up to 2 months, frozen (double-bag in resealable plastic freezer bags).

PER MUFFIN: 196 cal., 39% (77 cal.) from fat; 4.8 g protein; 8.5 g fat (1.1 g sat.); 30 g carbo (3.3 g fiber); 192 mg sodium; 35 mg chol.

Poppy-seed Muffins

Reader Karen Fukui, of Olympia, Washington, gave us this tender, cakelike muffin.

MAKES 12 muffins | **TIME** 1 hour

3 cups flour
⅓ cup poppy seeds
1 tbsp. baking soda
½ tsp. salt
½ cup butter, melted
1 cup granulated sugar
2 eggs
2 tbsp. finely shredded lemon zest
⅓ cup fresh lemon juice
⅔ cup milk

1. Preheat oven to 350°. Line 12 muffin cups (2¾ in. wide) with paper baking cups. In a medium bowl, mix flour, poppy seeds, baking soda, and salt.

2. In a large bowl, beat butter and granulated sugar until well blended. Add eggs and beat until incorporated. Beat in lemon zest and juice. Add half the flour mixture and stir just enough to moisten dry ingredients evenly, then stir in milk and remaining flour mixture. Be careful not to overstir. Spoon batter into muffin cups until two-thirds full.

3. Bake until tops are browned and toothpick inserted in center comes out clean, 15 to 18 minutes. Let pan stand on a rack 5 minutes, then remove muffins and let cool completely.

Make Ahead: Up to 3 days, at room temperature; up to a week, chilled; up to 2 months, frozen (double-bag in resealable plastic freezer bags).

PER MUFFIN: 294 cal., 34% (101 cal.) from fat; 5.7 g protein; 11 g fat (5.6 g sat.); 43 g carbo (1.4 g fiber); 485 mg sodium; 57 mg chol.

Cherry-Chocolate Scones

Generous chunks of milk chocolate are a decadent addition to dried-cherry scones.

MAKES 8 scones | **TIME** 50 minutes

3 cups flour
¼ cup sugar
1 tbsp. baking powder
½ tsp. salt
½ cup cold butter, cut into chunks
¾ cup half-and-half or light cream
1 egg
¼ lb. milk chocolate, cut into ½-in. chunks (about ½ cup)
½ cup *each* chopped pecans and dried cherries

1. Preheat oven to 350°. Butter a 12- by 15-in. baking sheet or line with parchment paper. In a large bowl or a food processor, mix flour, sugar, baking powder, and salt. Add butter to flour mixture. Cut in with a pastry blender or pulse until mixture resembles coarse crumbs. If using a food processor, scrape mixture into a bowl.

2. In a small bowl, whisk together half-and-half and egg. Reserve 2 tbsp. half-and-half mixture; add remaining to flour mixture along with chocolate, pecans, and cherries. Stir with a fork just until evenly moistened (dough will look crumbly).

3. Scrape dough onto a floured work surface and, with lightly floured hands, squeeze dough together into a ball. Pat out into a 7-in. round about 1¾ in. thick. Cut into 8 equal wedges.

4. Put wedges 2 in. apart on baking sheet. Brush tops of wedges lightly with reserved half-and-half mixture (discard any remaining).

5. Bake scones until tops are browned, about 25 minutes. Let cool about 10 minutes on baking sheet, then serve warm or let cool completely.

Make Ahead: Mix dry ingredients with butter ahead of time (step 1); seal mixture in a resealable plastic bag and chill for up to 1 week or freeze for up to 1 month (double-bag in resealable plastic freezer bags). Pour chilled or frozen mixture into a bowl and proceed with step 2.

PER SCONE: 486 cal., 46% (225 cal.) from fat; 8.1 g protein; 25 g fat (12 g sat.); 61 g carbo (2.1 g fiber); 480 mg sodium; 70 mg chol.

Cheese Dill Scones

These savory scones from reader Dorothy Reinhold, of Malibu, California, make a satisfying late-afternoon snack.

MAKES 8 scones | **TIME** 45 minutes

2 cups flour
2 tsp. dry mustard
1 tsp. baking powder
½ tsp. salt
½ cup cold unsalted butter, cut into chunks
1 cup shredded (¼ lb.) extra-sharp cheddar
¼ cup *each* finely shredded parmesan cheese, chopped chives, and chopped dill
½ cup low-fat milk

1. Preheat oven to 400°. Butter a 12- by 15-in. baking sheet or line with parchment paper. In a large bowl, combine flour, mustard, baking powder, and salt. With your fingers or a fork, work butter into flour mixture until it resembles cornmeal studded with a few pea-size pieces. Stir in both cheeses, the chives, and dill.
2. Add milk and stir to combine. Transfer dough to a floured work surface and gently knead two or three times, until it comes together. Pat into a 1-in.-thick disk and cut into 8 triangles. Arrange triangles about 2 in. apart on baking sheet. Bake until golden brown, about 20 minutes.
Make Ahead: Mix dry ingredients with butter ahead of time (step 1); seal mixture in a resealable plastic bag and chill for up to 1 week or freeze for up to 1 month (double-bag in resealable plastic freezer bags). Pour chilled or frozen mixture into a bowl and proceed with step 2. These scones are best the day they're made but freeze well. Unwrap and reheat frozen scones at 350° until warm, about 10 minutes.

PER SCONE: 314 cal., 54% (171 cal.) from fat; 10 g protein; 19 g fat (12 g sat.); 25 g carbo (0.9 g fiber); 551 mg sodium; 52 mg chol.

Buttermilk-Currant Scones with Lemon Glaze

Flaky and tender, with just the right balance of sweetness and lemony tang. Try them with butter and strawberry jam.

recipe pictured on page **543**

MAKES 8 scones | **TIME** 45 minutes

2½ cups flour
¼ cup granulated sugar
2 tsp. baking powder
½ tsp. salt
½ cup cold butter, cut into chunks
¾ cup buttermilk
1 egg
½ cup dried currants
1 tbsp. finely shredded lemon zest
⅔ cup powdered sugar
2 tbsp. fresh lemon juice

1. Preheat oven to 350°. Butter a 12- by 15-in. baking sheet or line with parchment paper. In a bowl or food processor, mix flour, granulated sugar, baking powder, and salt to blend. Add butter and cut in with a pastry blender or pulse until mixture resembles coarse crumbs. If using a food processor, scrape mixture into a bowl.
2. In a small bowl, whisk buttermilk and egg to blend. Add to flour mixture along with currants and lemon zest. Stir with a fork just until evenly moistened (dough will look crumbly).
3. Scrape dough onto a floured work surface and, with lightly floured hands, squeeze dough together into a ball. Pat into a 7-in. round about 1 ¾ in. thick. Cut into 8 equal wedges. Arrange wedges 2 in. apart on baking sheet.
4. Bake scones until tops are browned, 20 to 25 minutes. Let cool about 10 minutes on baking sheet. Meanwhile, in a small bowl, stir together powdered sugar and lemon juice until smooth. Drizzle glaze over warm scones. Serve scones warm or let cool completely.
Make Ahead: Mix dry ingredients with butter ahead of time (step 1); seal mixture in a resealable plastic bag and chill for up to 1 week or freeze for up to 1 month (double-bag in resealable plastic freezer bags). Pour chilled or frozen mixture into a bowl and proceed with step 2.

PER SCONE: 360 cal., 33% (117 cal.) from fat; 6.3 g protein; 13 g fat (7.5 g sat.); 56 g carbo (1.8 g fiber); 419 mg sodium; 58 mg chol.

Farmer John's Favorite Pumpkin Bread

Rich spice flavors shine in this tender, cakelike bread from Farmer John's Pumpkin Farm in Half Moon Bay, California.

MAKES 2 loaves (about 10 slices per loaf) | **TIME** 1¼ hours

2 cups flour
1¼ cups firmly packed dark brown sugar
1 cup *each* granulated sugar and coarsely chopped
    walnuts or pecans
½ cup raisins
1½ tsp. *each* baking soda and cinnamon
1¼ tsp. nutmeg
¾ tsp. *each* salt and ground cloves
½ tsp. *each* ground allspice and ground ginger
3 eggs
1¾ cups canned pumpkin or mashed fresh pumpkin
    (*see Try a New Kind of Pumpkin, right*)
¾ cup vegetable oil

1. Preheat oven to 350°. Oil two 8½- by 4½-in. loaf pans. In a large bowl, mix flour, both sugars, nuts, raisins, baking soda, cinnamon, nutmeg, salt, cloves, allspice, and ginger until well blended.
2. In a medium bowl, whisk together eggs, pumpkin, and oil until well blended.
3. Add wet ingredients to flour mixture and stir just until well blended. Divide between two pans.
4. Bake until bread pulls from pan sides and a toothpick inserted in center comes out clean, 50 to 60 minutes. Let bread cool in pans on a rack for about 15 minutes. Cut around outside edges of bread and invert onto rack. Cool thoroughly before slicing.
Make Ahead: Up to 3 days, at room temperature; or up to 3 months, wrapped well and frozen.

PER SLICE: 279 cal., 42% (117 cal.) from fat; 3.3 g protein; 13 g fat (1.7 g sat.); 38 g carbo (0.8 g fiber); 198 mg sodium; 32 mg chol.

Try a New Kind of Pumpkin

Most canned pumpkin is a variety called Dickinson's, which is in the same botanical category as butternut squash—perfectly fine stuff, but it can be fun to make your own mashed fresh pumpkin using other baking-worthy varieties, such as Sugar Pie (Sugar), Long Island Cheese, or Jarrahdale pumpkin—or kabocha squash. Here is a method given to us by Farmer John's Pumpkin Farm in Half Moon Bay, California.

Preheat oven to 350°. Cut a 3- to 9-lb. pumpkin in half vertically, starting along one side of stem; scoop out and discard seeds or reserve for another use. Rub inside with about 2 tsp. vegetable oil and lay, cut side down, in a 12- by 16-in. rimmed baking pan. Bake until squash is soft when pressed, 45 to 75 minutes. Scoop out and mash flesh; drain in a cheesecloth-lined colander if it's liquidy. Makes ¾ to 1¼ cups mashed pumpkin per 1 lb. raw. Can be chilled airtight up to 3 days or frozen up to 6 months.

Walnut-Zucchini Bread

Reader Mary Watson, of Scottsdale, Arizona, sent in this recipe. It's a great way to deal with at least part of a backyard garden bumper crop of zucchini.

MAKES 2 loaves (12 slices per loaf) | **TIME** 1¼ hours

3 eggs
2 cups sugar
1 cup vegetable oil
2 cups finely shredded zucchini
½ tsp. vanilla extract
3 cups flour
2 tsp. cinnamon
1 tsp. *each* salt, baking powder, and baking soda
¾ cup chopped walnuts

1. Preheat oven to 350°. Grease two 9- by 5-in. loaf pans.
2. In a large bowl, beat eggs until frothy. Add sugar, oil, zucchini, and vanilla and stir until well mixed. Add flour, cinnamon, salt, baking powder and soda, and walnuts; stir until just combined.
3. Pour batter into pans. Bake until a toothpick inserted in center comes out clean, 50 to 60 minutes. Cool loaves 10 minutes in pans, then turn out onto a rack and cool completely before slicing.

PER SLICE: 240 cal., 47% (112 cal.) from fat; 3.1 g protein; 13 g fat (1.5 g sat.); 30 g carbo (0.9 g fiber); 180 mg sodium; 26 mg chol.

Persimmon-Currant Bread

We pulled this recipe from deep in our archives; it was sent to us by a reader identified only as K.S., of Palo Alto, California. The moist, firm, fruit-filled bread keeps well in the refrigerator and the freezer. By adding more fruits, you can turn the recipe into a delicious dark fruitcake (if you like, poke a few holes over the top and drizzle it with ¼ cup brandy per week for 2 to 3 weeks).

MAKES 1 tube cake or 2 loaves (12 slices per loaf)
TIME 1¼ hours

2 cups thawed frozen Hachiya persimmon purée *(see Quick Tip below* and *Persimmons: Fall's Most Beautiful Fruit, page 73),* or 2 cups fresh persimmon purée mixed with 1 tbsp. fresh lemon juice
2 tsp. baking soda
2 cups *each* dried currants or raisins, chopped almonds, and sugar
2 tbsp. canola or safflower oil
3 cups flour
2 tsp. cinnamon
1 tsp. salt
¼ tsp. ground cloves
1 cup milk

1. Preheat oven to 325°. Grease a 10-in. tube pan (also called angel food cake pan) or two 8½- by 4½-in. loaf pans. Mix persimmon pulp with baking soda and set aside. In a large bowl, mix currants, almonds, and sugar. Stir in oil and persimmon pulp.
2. In a medium bowl, sift flour with cinnamon, salt, and cloves, then mix into persimmon mixture alternately with milk. Spoon batter into pan(s).
3. Bake until a toothpick inserted in center comes out clean, about 1½ hours for either cake or loaves. Cool in pan(s) 5 to 10 minutes. Turn out and cool on racks.
Quick Tip: To prepare persimmon purée, wait until the fruit is soft and almost jellylike throughout, then cut each persimmon in half and use a spoon to scoop out the flesh. Discard skin, seeds, and stem. Purée a little at a time in a blender or press through a food mill. To freeze purée, add 1 tbsp. fresh lemon juice to every 2 cups purée. Pack in freezer containers to within 1 in. of top and cover tightly or spoon into resealable plastic freezer bags.
Make Ahead: Up to 3 weeks, chilled; up to 2 months, frozen (wrap well in plastic and seal in a plastic freezer bag).

PER SLICE: 323 cal., 15% (49 cal.) from fat; 3.9 g protein; 5.5 g fat (0.6 g sat.); 67 g carbo (2.2 g fiber); 207 mg sodium; 1 mg chol.

Chocolate-Banana Bread

This recipe is adapted from one in *Cooking with the Seasons at Rancho La Puerta* by Deborah Szekely and Deborah M. Schneider. Guests who do the a 2-mile morning hike to La Cocina Que Canta, the resort's cooking school, are occasionally treated to this dense, moist bread as part of a garden breakfast. It tastes so rich you'd never guess it's made with prune purée instead of butter.

MAKES 1 loaf (20 slices) | **TIME** 1½ hours, plus 1 hour to cool

¾ lb. pitted prunes *(see Quick Tip below)*
¾ cup mashed ripe bananas (2 medium)
2 eggs
1 cup all-purpose flour or whole-wheat pastry flour (or ½ cup of each)
½ cup unsweetened cocoa powder
2 tsp. *each* baking powder and cinnamon
1½ tsp. baking soda
1 cup chopped walnuts
½ cup banana chips, coarsely chopped
1 cup semisweet chocolate chips

1. In a small saucepan, bring prunes and 2 cups water to a boil over high heat. Reduce heat and simmer, uncovered, until prunes are very soft, about 20 minutes. Drain.
2. Meanwhile, preheat oven to 350°. Lightly butter a 9- by 5-in. loaf pan and line bottom with a piece of parchment paper cut to fit.
3. In a food processor, purée prunes and bananas until very smooth. Add eggs and whirl to combine.
4. In a large bowl, sift together flour, cocoa, baking powder, cinnamon, and baking soda. Stir in banana mixture until evenly moistened. Stir in walnuts, banana chips, and chocolate chips. Scrape thick batter into pan and spread level.
5. Bake until a toothpick inserted in center comes out a little chocolaty but not gooey, 45 to 50 minutes. Loosen bread from pan with a knife and invert onto a rack. Lift off pan and remove parchment. Turn bread right side up and let cool at least 1 hour before slicing.
Quick Tip: You can substitute ¾ lb. (1½ cups) of unsweetened prune baby food for the pitted prunes, and omit water and cooking in step 1.

PER SLICE: 174 cal., 41% (71 cal.) from fat; 3.5 g protein; 7.9 g fat (2.7 g sat.); 27 g carbo (3.2 g fiber); 153 mg sodium; 21 mg chol.

muffins, rolls & breads

Cranberry-Orange Bread with Grand Marnier Glaze

A versatile, easy-to-make crowd pleaser, delicately laced with Grand Marnier and studded with tart dried cranberries and orange zest. You can substitute dried cherries and amaretto (*see the variation, right*) and/or vary the loaf size. You'll need a thin skewer to poke holes in the cake so the liqueur can seep into it.

recipe pictured on page **541**

MAKES 2 large loaves or 6 mini loaves (12 slices per large loaf) | **TIME** 1¾ hours

1½ cups unsalted butter, softened
1½ cups granulated sugar
4 eggs
1 cup *each* orange juice and sour cream
2 tbsp. finely shredded orange zest
2 tsp. vanilla extract
4 cups flour
1 tbsp. baking powder
½ tsp. salt
1½ cups dried cranberries
2 cups powdered sugar
7 to 8 tbsp. Grand Marnier or other orange-flavored liqueur

1. Preheat oven to 325°. Butter two 9- by 5-in. loaf pans or six mini loaf pans.
2. With a mixer on medium speed, cream butter and sugar together in a large bowl until pale and fluffy, about 3 minutes. Add eggs one at a time, mixing well after each addition. Add orange juice, sour cream, orange zest, and vanilla; mix until blended.

3. In a separate bowl, whisk together flour, baking powder, and salt. Add flour mixture and cranberries to wet ingredients and mix just until dry ingredients are moistened; do not overmix.
4. Pour batter into pans. Bake until a toothpick inserted in center comes out clean, 70 to 75 minutes for large loaves and 1 hour for mini loaves.
5. Meanwhile, in a small bowl, whisk together powdered sugar and 7 tbsp. Grand Marnier. Glaze should have consistency of thick maple or corn syrup. If it is too thick, thin with additional 1 tbsp. liqueur.
6. Let loaves cool in pans for 10 minutes, then remove from pans and transfer to a rack set over a large baking sheet. With a thin skewer or long toothpick, poke deep holes in tops of loaves. Drizzle with Grand Marnier glaze so that it coats top, runs down sides, and seeps into holes.
7. Let loaves cool completely, then slice and serve.
Make Ahead: Up to 1 month, frozen (wrap tightly with plastic wrap and put in resealable plastic bags). Thaw in refrigerator overnight, or a few hours, unwrapped, at room temperature.

PER SLICE: 344 cal., 39% (135 cal.) from fat; 3.7 g protein; 15 g fat (9 g sat.); 47 g carbo (1 g fiber); 133 mg sodium; 72 mg chol.

Cherry-Almond Bread with Amaretto Glaze:
Substitute **milk** for orange juice, omit orange zest, and substitute **almond extract** for vanilla. Substitute halved **dried tart cherries** for dried cranberries, and add 1 cup chopped **almonds** in step 3 when you add the cherries. Bake as directed. To make glaze, substitute 6 to 7 tbsp. **amaretto or other almond-flavored liqueur** for Grand Marnier.

PER SLICE: 375 cal., 43% (162 cal.) from fat; 5.1 g protein; 18 g fat (9.5 g sat.); 48 g carbo (1.2 g fiber); 139 mg sodium; 73 mg chol.

Fresh Fig Coffee Cake

Here's a recipe from reader Y.V., of Portland, Oregon, for those of you with your own fig tree or with access to great figs, period. This cake is rich, moist, and seriously scrumptious.

SERVES 12 | **TIME** 1¼ hours

1 lb. (about 15 large) fully ripe figs
2 tbsp. fresh lemon juice
¼ cup granulated sugar
1 tbsp. finely shredded lemon zest
½ cup raisins
1 egg
¾ cup firmly packed brown sugar, divided
½ cup canola or safflower oil
½ tsp. vanilla extract
2 cups flour
1 tbsp. baking powder
¾ tsp. cinnamon, divided
½ tsp. salt
¼ tsp. *each* ground cloves and ground ginger
¾ cup milk
1 cup lightly crushed cornflakes
½ cup chopped walnuts
3 tbsp. butter, melted

1. Preheat oven to 350°. Grease an 8-in. square baking pan. Cut stems and blossom ends off figs. Coarsely chop; you should have about 3½ cups. In a medium saucepan, combine figs with lemon juice, granulated sugar, lemon zest, raisins, and ¼ cup water. Cook over medium heat, stirring often, until thick and reduced to 3 cups, about 30 minutes (as mixture thickens, reduce heat to prevent scorching). Let cool.
2. In a large bowl, beat egg, ½ cup brown sugar, the oil, and vanilla until smooth.
3. In a medium bowl, stir flour, baking powder, ½ tsp. cinnamon, the salt, cloves, and ginger. Add flour mixture and milk alternately to egg mixture, blending well after each addition.
4. In a small bowl, combine cornflakes, walnuts, butter, and remaining ¼ cup brown sugar and ¼ tsp. cinnamon.
5. Spoon half the batter into pan. Spread fig mixture over top, then spoon remaining batter evenly over fig layer. Sprinkle cornflake mixture over top. Bake until a toothpick inserted in center comes out clean, 45 to 50 minutes. Cool slightly or completely. Cut into squares and serve warm or cooled.

PER SERVING: 433 cal., 35% (152 cal.) from fat; 5.4 g protein; 17 g fat (3.4 g sat.); 68 g carbo (3.8 g fiber); 326 mg sodium; 27 mg chol.

Blueberry–Cream Cheese Coffee Cake

A ribbon of cream cheese lies beneath sweet blueberries and sliced almonds. This recipe is from Margaret Fox, culinary director of Harvest Market in Fort Bragg, California.

MAKES 10 to 12 servings | **TIME** 1 hour

1 cup fresh or frozen blueberries
¼ cup apple juice
1 tsp. cornstarch
2 cups flour
1 cup sugar, divided
½ cup cold butter, cut into chunks
½ tsp. *each* baking powder and baking soda
¼ tsp. salt
1 tsp. finely shredded lemon zest
¾ cup plain low-fat yogurt
1 tsp. vanilla extract
2 eggs, divided
2 packages (3 oz. each) cream cheese, at room temperature
1 tsp. fresh lemon juice
½ cup sliced almonds

1. Preheat oven to 350°. Butter a 9-in. round cake pan with a removable rim. In a 1- to 2-qt. pan over medium heat, bring blueberries and apple juice to a boil. Lower heat and simmer, stirring occasionally, until blueberries have released their juices, about 3 minutes. In a small bowl, blend cornstarch and 2 tsp. water. Add to blueberry mixture; stir until it simmers and thickens, about 1 minute. Let cool to room temperature.
2. In a medium bowl or a food processor, mix flour and ¾ cup sugar. Add butter and cut in with a pastry blender or pulse until mixture resembles coarse crumbs. Reserve ½ cup. Pour remaining mixture into a large bowl and stir in baking powder and soda, salt, and lemon zest.
3. In a small bowl, mix yogurt, vanilla, and 1 egg until blended; stir into flour-lemon mixture until incorporated. Spread batter in pan.
4. In another medium bowl or a food processor (no need to wash from step 2), beat with a mixer on high speed or process cream cheese, remaining ¼ cup sugar, remaining egg, and the lemon juice until smooth. Spread over batter in pan, leaving a ½-in. border bare. Gently spread blueberry mixture over cream cheese mixture, leaving some of the mixture visible. Stir almonds into reserved ½ cup flour mixture and sprinkle over cake, concentrating most around edge of batter.

muffins, rolls & breads

5. Bake until center of cake barely jiggles when pan is gently shaken and top of cake is golden brown, 30 to 40 minutes. Let cool on a rack 15 minutes, then remove pan rim. Serve warm or at room temperature.

PER SERVING: 316 cal., 46% (144 cal.) from fat; 5.9 g protein; 16 g fat (8.7 g sat.); 37 g carbo (1 g fiber); 266 mg sodium; 73 mg chol.

Blueberry Cornbread

Reader Doug Case, of Portland, Oregon, calls his cake-like cornbread with blueberries "easy comfort food," and we have to agree. If you don't have masa harina, increase the cornmeal to 1⅓ cups.

MAKES 9 servings | TIME 40 minutes

2 eggs
1 cup buttermilk
¼ cup butter, melted
⅔ cup *each* all-purpose flour, yellow cornmeal, and masa harina *(see Quick Tip below)*
¼ cup sugar
1½ tsp. baking powder
½ tsp. salt
1 cup fresh blueberries

1. Preheat oven to 375°. Butter an 8-in. square baking pan. In a large bowl, beat eggs, buttermilk, and butter to blend.
2. In a medium bowl, mix flour, cornmeal, masa harina, sugar, baking powder, and salt. Stir flour mixture into egg mixture just until evenly moistened. Gently stir in berries.
3. Scrape batter into pan; spread level. Bake until a toothpick inserted into center comes out clean, 20 to 25 minutes. Let cool 10 minutes, then cut into 9 squares.
Quick Tip: Find masa harina (dehydrated corn dough; also labeled masa flour, corn flour, or instant corn masa mix) in the baking aisle of well-stocked grocery stores and at Latino markets.

PER SERVING: 206 cal., 31% (64 cal.) from fat; 5 g protein; 7.1 g fat (3.7 g sat.); 31 g carbo (1.8 g fiber); 307 mg sodium; 62 mg chol.

Southwest Cornbread

This slightly sweet cornbread tastes great with barbecue as well as Mexican-style grilled meat or chicken.

MAKES 9 to 12 servings | TIME 30 minutes

1 cup *each* flour and yellow cornmeal
⅓ cup plus 1 tbsp. sugar
2½ tsp. baking powder
¾ tsp. salt
2 eggs
1 cup buttermilk
¼ cup butter, melted and cooled
1 can (4 oz.) chopped green chiles, drained
¾ cup coarsely shredded jack cheese
1 tbsp. chili powder

1. Preheat oven to 400°. Butter an 8- or 9-in. square baking pan. In a large bowl, mix flour, cornmeal, ⅓ cup sugar, baking powder, and salt.
2. In a medium bowl, beat eggs to blend with buttermilk and butter. Stir in chiles and cheese. Pour egg mixture into flour mixture and stir just until evenly moistened.
3. Scrape batter into pan; spread level. In a small bowl, mix remaining 1 tbsp. sugar and the chili powder. Sprinkle evenly over batter.
4. Bake until bread springs back when lightly pressed in center and begins to pull from pan sides, 20 to 25 minutes. Let cool slightly or completely and cut into pieces. Serve warm or at room temperature.

PER SERVING: 192 cal., 35% (68 cal.) from fat; 5.7 g protein; 7.5 g fat (4.1 g sat.); 26 g carbo (1.2 g fiber); 402 mg sodium; 54 mg chol.

Savory Thanksgiving Popovers

The homemade popovers from reader Lorin Waldron, of Big Bear Lake, California, make delicious use of pan drippings from a roast turkey. Pouring the batter into every other muffin cup allows more air to circulate around the popovers, which helps them puff.

MAKES 12 popovers | **TIME** 45 minutes

2 tbsp. butter, melted
3 eggs, at room temperature
1 cup milk, at room temperature
1 cup flour
¼ cup plus 2 tbsp. grated parmesan cheese
3 tbsp. fat-skimmed turkey pan drippings (*see Quick Tip below*) or melted butter
½ tsp. salt
⅛ tsp. freshly ground black pepper

1. Preheat oven to 425°. Generously brush every other cup in two 12-cup muffin pans (2¾ in. wide) with melted butter (it will pool a bit in bottom of cups).
2. In a blender, purée eggs, milk, flour, ¼ cup parmesan, the pan drippings, salt, and pepper. Pour mixture into muffin cups until about half-full. Sprinkle evenly with remaining 2 tbsp. parmesan.
3. Bake until puffed and golden, about 20 minutes (don't worry if some popovers don't puff quite as high as others); reduce oven temperature to 350° and bake until popovers are firm, 10 to 15 minutes.
Quick Tip: To degrease the pan drippings, pour them into a glass measuring cup and let sit at room temperature until fat rises to the top. Skim off fat with a shallow spoon; or, conversely, pull up the juices from the bottom of the glass with a turkey baster and squirt them into a bowl.

PER POPOVER: 99 cal., 43% (43 cal.) from fat; 4.6 g protein; 4.8 g fat (2.5 g sat.); 9.1 g carbo (0.3 g fiber); 190 mg sodium; 63 mg chol.

Buttermilk Biscuits

Diane Rossen Worthington created this recipe for a 1995 *Sunset* cookbook called *Diner: The Best of Casual American Cooking*. In keeping with diner tradition, these are ultra-flaky biscuits that rely on shortening or lard for their texture. For a slightly softer crust, lightly brush the hot biscuits with melted butter when they come out of the oven.

MAKES 12 to 14 biscuits | **TIME** 25 to 30 minutes

2 cups flour
2½ tsp. baking powder
½ tsp. *each* salt and baking soda
½ cup cold solid shortening or fresh lard (*see In Praise of Real Lard, page 649*)
¾ cup cold buttermilk

1. Preheat oven to 450°. In a large bowl, stir together flour, baking powder, salt, and baking soda until well mixed. Add shortening and stir to coat with flour mixture. Using a pastry blender, two knives, or your fingertips and working quickly, cut or rub shortening into dry ingredients until mixture has consistency of coarse meal.
2. Make a well in center of flour mixture. Add buttermilk, then stir with a fork just until a soft dough forms that pulls from sides of bowl.
3. Gather dough into a ball and dust with flour on a lightly floured board. Knead very gently five or six times, just until the dough holds together. Gently pat or roll dough about ½ in. thick. Using a round 2- to 2½-in. biscuit or round cookie cutter, cut as many dough rounds as possible, pressing straight down and lifting cutter straight up without twisting. Put rounds about 1½ in. apart on a 12- by 15-in. baking sheet. Very gently knead scraps together two or three times and pat out and cut as before. Do not reroll any additional scraps.
4. Bake until evenly browned, 10 to 12 minutes. Serve hot.

PER BISCUIT: 139 cal., 49% (68 cal.) from fat; 2.4 g protein; 7.6 g fat (1.9 g sat.); 15 g carbo; 224 mg sodium; 0.5 mg chol.

Squash Dinner Rolls

Soft, cheerfully orange, and slightly sweet, the rolls from reader Angela Baker, of Bremerton, Washington, are a nice change of pace at the dinner table.

recipe pictured on page **546**

MAKES 2 dozen rolls | **TIME** 1½ hours, plus 1½ hours to rise

1½ cups warm (100° to 110°) milk
1 package (2¼ tsp.) active dry yeast
2 tbsp. sugar
1 tbsp. salt
1 egg, lightly beaten
¾ cup puréed cooked winter squash (*see Quick Tip below*) or canned pumpkin or squash
5 tbsp. vegetable shortening
4 to 5 cups flour
2 tbsp. butter, melted
2 tsp. poppy or sesame seeds

1. In a large bowl, combine milk, yeast, sugar, and salt. Let stand 5 minutes, then add egg and beat well to combine. Add squash and shortening; mash with a fork until shortening is in small pieces. Add 1½ cups flour and mix well with a wooden spoon. Gradually mix in more flour by the cupful until dough collects around spoon and pulls away from sides of bowl (you may not need all the flour).

2. Transfer to a lightly floured work surface and knead 2 minutes. Put dough in a greased bowl; cover with a kitchen towel. Let rise in a warm (about 80°) place until doubled in size, 1 to 1½ hours.

3. Punch dough down, turn out onto a lightly floured work surface, and knead until dough is smooth and supple, about 7 minutes. With a large knife, cut dough into four balls; cut each ball into six pieces. Roll each piece into a round and arrange rounds on a large buttered baking sheet so they barely touch. Brush with melted butter and sprinkle with poppy seeds; cover with plastic wrap and let rise 30 minutes.

4. Meanwhile, preheat oven to 400°. Bake rolls until golden brown, about 20 minutes. Let cool, then pull apart to serve.

Quick Tip: This is a great use for leftover cooked winter squash—acorn, butternut, or kabocha work equally well.

PER ROLL: 137 cal., 30% (41 cal.) from fat; 3.4 g protein; 4.5 g fat (1.7 g sat.); 20 g carbo (0.9 g fiber); 312 mg sodium; 14 mg chol.

Overnight Soft Herb Rolls

These rolls are so good, we could eat a dozen. Bradley Ogden created them when he was chef at the Lark Creek Inn (now the Tavern at Lark Creek) in Larkspur, California.

MAKES 12 rolls | **TIME** 1 hour, plus 45 minutes to rise

1 tbsp. active dry yeast
3 tbsp. sugar
1 tsp. table salt
1 tbsp. *each* minced flat-leaf parsley, dill, chives, and rosemary leaves
2 tbsp. butter, melted
1 egg plus 1 tbsp. lightly beaten egg
1 cup milk or half-and-half
3¼ cups flour
1 tbsp. kosher salt

1. In a large bowl, sprinkle yeast over ¼ cup cool (70°) water. Let stand 5 minutes. Stir in sugar, table salt, herbs, butter, whole egg, and milk; add flour and stir just until moistened.

2. Knead dough on a lightly floured work surface until elastic and not sticky, about 15 minutes; add flour as needed to prevent sticking. Shape into 12 equal-size balls and transfer to a well-buttered 9- by 13-in. baking pan.

3. Let dough rise in a warm (about 80°) place, covered loosely with plastic wrap or a kitchen towel, until doubled, 45 to 60 minutes. Meanwhile, preheat oven to 350°.

4. Brush rolls with beaten egg and sprinkle with kosher salt. Bake until deep golden, 25 to 30 minutes.

Make Ahead: Through step 2, up to 1 day, wrapped airtight and chilled (do not let rise before chilling). Proceed with step 3.

PER ROLL: 192 cal., 18% (34 cal.) from fat; 5.5 g protein; 3.8 g fat (2 g sat.); 33 g carbo (1.2 fiber); 604 mg sodium; 32 mg chol.

Chive and Thyme Pull-apart Rolls

Show off your garden herbs with these buttery rolls.

MAKES 20 rolls | **TIME** 1 hour, plus 2 hours to rise

1½ cups warm (100° to 110°) milk
1 package (2¼ tsp.) active dry yeast
2 tbsp. sugar
2 tsp. table salt
3 tbsp. chopped chives
1½ tbsp. chopped thyme leaves
3 eggs, at room temperature, divided
⅓ cup plus 1 tbsp. melted butter
5¼ cups flour
1 tsp. coarse sea salt

1. In a stand mixer or large bowl, combine milk, yeast, and sugar. Let stand 5 minutes. Add table salt, chives, thyme, 2 eggs, and ⅓ cup butter. If using a stand mixer, mix on low speed with a dough hook until blended. If mixing by hand, mix with a wooden spoon.
2. Blend in 5 cups flour. In a stand mixer, mix on medium speed until dough is smooth, stretchy, only slightly tacky, and pulling away from sides of bowl, 10 minutes. If mixing by hand, stir in flour with wooden spoon, then turn out onto a floured work surface and knead vigorously until dough is smooth and stretchy, 10 to 15 minutes. Put in a lightly oiled bowl. Cover and let rise in a warm (about 80°) place until doubled, about 1¼ hours.
3. Butter 20 muffin cups (2¾ in. wide). Punch down dough. On a lightly floured work surface, roll out dough to an even 30- by 9-in. rectangle. Brush with remaining 1 tbsp. butter. Cut dough into 6 long strips, each 1½ in. wide. Stack strips, then cut stack in half crosswise. With a serrated knife, gently cut each stack into 10 portions. Stand each portion in a muffin cup so the layers are oriented vertically.
4. Let rise at room temperature, loosely covered with plastic wrap or a kitchen towel, until puffy, about 45 minutes. Preheat oven to 350°.
5. Beat remaining egg, then gently brush over tops and sides of rolls. Sprinkle with sea salt. Bake rolls until golden brown, 20 to 25 minutes, switching pan positions halfway through baking. Let cool in pans on a rack 5 minutes, then gently lift out onto racks and serve warm or cool.
Make Ahead: Through step 3, wrapped loosely with plastic wrap and chilled overnight. Allow 1¼ hours for second rise.

PER ROLL: 183 cal., 28% (51 cal.) from fat; 5.2 g protein; 5.7 g fat (3.2 g sat.); 27 g carbo (1 g fiber); 360 mg sodium; 44 mg chol.

Grandma Carroll's Cinnamon Rolls

As the original chef-owner of Café Beaujolais in Mendocino, California, Margaret Fox turned breakfast into the most popular meal in that coastal town. A friend's grandmother introduced Margaret to these rolls.

MAKES 12 cinnamon rolls | **TIME** 1 hour, plus 3 hours to rise

1¼ cups milk
1 package (2¼ tsp.) active dry yeast
1¼ cups plus 3 tbsp. granulated sugar
¾ cup plus 2 tbsp. butter, at room temperature
1½ tsp. salt
About 5¼ cups flour, divided
¼ cup cinnamon
3 cups powdered sugar
1 tsp. vanilla extract

1. In a 2-qt. pan over medium heat, heat milk to lukewarm. In a large bowl, dissolve yeast in 1 cup warm (100° to 110°) water and let stand 5 minutes.
2. If using a stand mixer with paddle attachment, stir milk, 3 tbsp. granulated sugar, 2 tbsp. butter, salt, and 3½ cups flour into yeast mixture. Beat on high until slightly stretchy, about 2 minutes. Switch to dough hook and, on medium speed, beat in 1½ cups more flour until a stiff dough forms. Continue beating until dough pulls cleanly from sides of bowl, 5 to 7 minutes longer; if dough is still sticky, add more flour, 1 tbsp. at a time. To mix by hand, with a wooden spoon stir milk, 3 tbsp. granulated sugar, 2 tbsp. butter, salt, and 3½ cups flour into yeast mixture. Stir vigorously until slightly stretchy, 2 to 4 minutes. Stir in 1½ cups more flour until a stiff dough forms. Scrape onto a floured work surface and knead until smooth, elastic, and no longer sticky, about 8 minutes; add flour as required to prevent sticking. Return dough to bowl.
3. Cover bowl airtight and let dough rise at room temperature until doubled, 1 to 1½ hours.
4. Scrape dough onto a floured work surface and press gently to expel air. Divide in half. Roll each half into a 10- by 16-in. rectangle. Spread 6 tbsp. butter over each rectangle. In a small bowl, mix remaining 1¼ cups granulated sugar with the cinnamon. Sprinkle half the mixture over each rectangle.
5. Starting from a long edge, roll each rectangle into a tight cylinder. Cut each cylinder into six equal pieces (*see Quick Tip, above right*). Put cut side down and slightly apart in two 7- by 11-in. baking pans. Cover pans with plastic wrap or a kitchen towel and let stand at room temperature until rolls are almost doubled in size, 1 to 1½ hours.

6. Bake in a 350° oven until rolls are browned, 30 to 35 minutes. Cool in pan 10 minutes. Meanwhile, in medium bowl mix powdered sugar, vanilla, and ¼ cup water until smooth. Thin with more water if too thick. Drizzle icing over warm rolls and serve.

Quick Tip: For a clean cut, use a very sharp knife. If rolls get bent out of shape, reshape them as you set each one in the pan.

PER CINNAMON ROLL: 559 cal., 24% (135 cal.) from fat; 7.2 g protein; 15 g fat (9 g sat.); 100 g carbo (1.7 g fiber); 442 mg sodium; 40 mg chol.

Rich Refrigerator Doughnuts

The texture of fresh-from-the-oven homemade doughnuts is a revelation: ever so slightly crisp on the outside, light and cakelike inside. Letting the dough rise overnight in the refrigerator gives the doughnuts a rich and slightly tangy flavor.

MAKES 14 doughnuts, plus holes | **TIME** 1 hour, plus 4 hours to chill and rise

1 package (2¼ tsp.) active dry yeast
3¼ cups flour, divided
⅓ cup sugar
1 tsp. salt
1 egg, lightly beaten
⅓ cup butter, at room temperature
Vegetable oil for frying
Granulated sugar

1. In a large bowl, sprinkle yeast over 1 cup warm (100° to 110°) water. Let stand 5 minutes. Add 1½ cups flour, sugar, and salt. Beat for 2 minutes with a mixer or wooden spoon. Add egg and butter and gradually beat in remaining 1¾ cups flour by hand until the batter is smooth. Cover with plastic wrap and refrigerate dough for at least 2 hours and up to overnight.

2. Turn dough out onto a well-floured work surface. Roll dough ½ in. thick, flouring generously and turning dough 90° between rolls to keep it from sticking. Cut out rounds with a 2½ in. doughnut cutter. Alternatively, cut rounds with a 2½- or 3-in. biscuit or round cookie cutter, then cut out centers with a 1-in. round biscuit or cookie cutter. Put rounds and centers on two well-floured baking sheets at least 1 in. apart. Let dough rise, covered with plastic wrap or a kitchen towel, in a warm (about 80°) place until slightly puffy, about 2 hours.

3. Put racks over two empty baking sheets and set them near stove. Pour oil into a large pot to a depth of 2 in. and heat to 325° to 350° *(see Quick Tip below)*. To get a feel for the method and how the dough should look and act, start by frying the holes. Working in batches of 6 to 8 holes and then 3 or 4 doughnuts, fry just until golden brown, turning once, about 1 minute per side. (Doughnuts and holes should sink for 2 to 3 seconds before floating to surface; if they don't sink, the oil is too hot. Also, if doughnuts or holes take much more or less than 1 minute per side to cook, adjust oil temperature.) As doughnuts and holes brown, transfer with a slotted spoon to racks. After first batch, test a doughnut hole by breaking it open. It should be light and cakelike inside, not greasy. If it's greasy, either the oil wasn't hot enough or it cooked too long.

4. While doughnuts and holes are still slightly warm, dip in sugar.

Quick Tip: Experienced cooks know that the best frying results from watching the food and paying attention to how it looks and sounds—but if you're just learning to fry, use a candy or deep-fry thermometer to measure the temperature of the oil. Alternatively, dip the wooden handle of a kitchen spoon or spatula into the hot oil. It should take 2 seconds for 350° oil to bubble vigorously around the wood; more time and the oil is too cool, less time and it's too hot.

PER DOUGHNUT: 280 cal., 55% (153 cal.) from fat; 3.9 g protein; 17 g fat (4.3 g sat.); 29 g carbo (1 g fiber); 216 mg sodium; 27 mg chol.

Freezer Rolls, Homemade Breads & Breakfast Pastries

If you've tried frozen rolls and pastries, you may have wondered whether you could duplicate the make-ahead technique with homemade dough. You can. You'll enjoy it most if you make three or four batches of breads in one day of all-out baking, because the steps take on an efficient and pleasing flow. When you've finished the last batch of dough, the first should be about ready for the next step. By the end of the day, you'll have a freezer loaded with really good bread that you can quickly bake the day you want it.

Because all these doughs are frozen immediately after shaping—before their final rise—you have to let them thaw and rise before baking. This time varies from about 1½ to 2 hours at room temperature for rolls to about 5 hours for bread. Or you can let the dough thaw in the refrigerator overnight; then it will rise much quicker the next day. The recipes for each of the following breads include directions on how to thaw and bake them. If you'd like to bake any of the breads right after mixing the dough, don't freeze them; just let them double in bulk at warm room temperature (about 80°), then bake according to instructions.

Buttery Freeze-ahead Dinner Rolls

This dough is extremely easy to work with—you can make all kinds of shapes with it, and change up the flavor, too. Suggestions for variations follow the recipe.

MAKES 24 rolls | **TIME** 45 minutes, plus 2¼ hours to rise

1 cup milk
1 tbsp. active dry yeast
1 tsp. salt
¼ cup sugar
½ cup butter, softened
2 eggs, divided
3½ to 4 cups flour

1. Microwave milk, uncovered, until warm (100° to 110°), about 20 seconds at full power. Put in bowl of a stand mixer or a large bowl. Stir in yeast, salt, and sugar. Let stand 5 minutes.

2. If using a stand mixer, attach dough hook and, with mixer on low, stir in butter and 1 egg. Add flour, ½ cup at a time, until a stiff dough forms and pulls away from sides of bowl. If mixing by hand, stir in butter and 1 egg. Stir in flour, ½ cup at a time, until incorporated; then turn out onto a floured work surface and knead until a stiff dough forms.

3. Put dough into a greased bowl and turn to coat. Cover with a kitchen towel or plastic wrap and let sit until doubled in bulk, about 1½ hours. Meanwhile, butter two large baking sheets and set aside.

4. Punch down dough and turn it onto a floured work surface. Knead a few times, adding more flour if necessary to keep dough from sticking. Form dough into one of the shape variations on *page 539* or divide into 24 pieces, roll into 10-in. ropes and coil into flat spirals or pretzel shapes, then pinch ends in place (work with 1 piece at a time, keeping other pieces covered).

5. Put shaped rolls on baking sheets. Cover with plastic wrap or foil and set directly in freezer. As soon as they're completely frozen, you can remove rolls from baking sheets and store in resealable freezer bags. (If you're making variations, it's a good idea to label each package with the date and name of what's in it.)

6. Remove rolls from freezer about 2 hours before you plan to bake them. Arrange on greased baking pans about 1 in. apart. Cover loosely with a kitchen towel and set in a warm (about 80°) place to thaw and rise until almost doubled in size, 1½ to 2 hours. Meanwhile, preheat oven to 350°.

7. In a small bowl, beat remaining egg with 2 tbsp. water. Brush rolls with egg wash and bake until brown, about 20 minutes, rotating pans halfway through baking time to ensure even baking. Cool on wire racks. Serve warm or at room temperature.

Make Ahead: Through step 5, up to 2 months, frozen.

PER ROLL: 134 cal, 34% (46 cal.) from fat; 3.2 g protein; 5.1 g fat (2.9 g sat.); 19 g carbo (0.7 g fiber); 151 mg sodium; 30 mg chol.

FLAVOR VARIATIONS

Seed Rolls: After brushing rolls with egg wash in step 7, sprinkle them with 1 tbsp. **poppy seeds**, **sesame seeds**, or **onion seeds**.

Cheese Rolls: Add 1½ cups shredded **cheddar** or **gruyère cheese** to dough with the butter and egg in step 2. Sprinkle rolls with additional cheese before baking if you like.

Herb Rolls: Add 3 tbsp. minced **fresh herbs**—such as oregano, rosemary, thyme, or basil—to dough with the butter and egg in step 2.

Saffron Rolls: Add ½ tsp. **saffron threads** to the milk in step 1.

SHAPE VARIATIONS

Parker House: After kneading in step 4, roll dough ¼ in. thick. With a 2½-in. biscuit or round cookie cutter, cut into circles. With dull edge of knife, make crease in dough just off center. Brush with melted **butter** and fold larger part over smaller; press folded edge firmly. Freeze as directed in step 5.

Cloverleaf: After kneading in step 4, pinch off 1-in. pieces and, with your fingertips, shape each piece into a ball, tucking the edges under to make a smooth top. Arrange three balls carefully in each cup of a greased muffin tin. Freeze as directed in step 5.

Butterhorns: After kneading in step 4, roll dough into an 8-in. circle ¼ in. thick. Brush with melted **butter**. Cut circle into six wedges; roll each toward point. Put on greased baking sheet, point down. For crescents, shape like horseshoes. Freeze as directed in step 5.

Freeze-ahead Breads

You can use any bread recipe to make freezer loaves. Honey Wheat Bread *(page 561)* is especially good baked from frozen dough. As soon as you've shaped the loaves after their first rise, wrap them in plastic wrap or foil—baking pan and all—and freeze. If the bread dough is free-form, wrap and put it on a flat surface in the freezer so it will keep its shape. To bake a loaf, remove it from the freezer and let it thaw and rise in a warm (about 80°) place until almost doubled in size, about 6 hours for a standard-size loaf. Or thaw the loaf in your refrigerator overnight, then let it rise in a warm place about 2 hours. Bake as the bread recipe directs.

Freeze-ahead Breakfast Pastries

Treat your family or weekend guests to sweet breakfast rolls and yeasted coffee cake warm from the oven—without getting up before dawn to bake from scratch. From this one sweet dough recipe, you can have a choice of pastries ready and waiting in the freezer.Because it's so rich, this dough doesn't require much kneading—just enough to work about ¼ to ½ cup flour into the dough so it doesn't stick to your hands or work surface.

TIME 30 minutes, plus 2 hours to rise

¼ cup butter, cut into small pieces, plus 1 tbsp. softened butter for topping
1 tsp. salt
¼ cup sugar
1 cup milk, brought almost to a boil
1 package (2¼ tsp.) active dry yeast
1 egg, slightly beaten
4 cups sifted flour, plus more as needed

1. Put butter pieces, salt, and sugar in a large bowl; add hot milk and stir to dissolve sugar and salt and to melt butter; allow to cool to lukewarm. Soften yeast in ¼ cup warm (100° to 110°) water 5 minutes; then add, along with beaten egg, to cooled milk mixture. Stir in flour, 1 cup at a time, beating vigorously to blend. Scrape dough from sides of bowl and brush top of dough and sides of bowl with softened butter. Cover dough with plastic wrap or a kitchen towel and let rise in a warm (about 80°) place until almost doubled in bulk, about 2 hours.
2. Turn dough out onto a well-floured work surface and knead lightly, adding flour until dough is no longer sticky (do not use more than ¼ to ½ cup flour). Follow suggestions on *page 540* for shaping, filling, glazing, and baking.

continued on next page

Make-ahead Inside-out Cinnamon Rolls

Very light, tender, and not too sweet. Let them begin to thaw (and rise) overnight in the fridge; they'll double in bulk much faster in the morning.

1. Roll out **Freeze-ahead Breakfast Pastries** (*see page 539*) to a large rectangle, about 10 by 24 in. and ¼ in. thick; spread with softened **butter** (about 3 tbsp.). In a medium bowl, mix together ¾ cup firmly packed **dark brown sugar** and 2 to 3 tsp. **cinnamon**. Sprinkle cinnamon sugar over dough, then lightly press it into dough. Cut dough into strips about 10 in. long and 1 in. wide and roll each separately into a snail shape with sugar side out.
2. Put rolls 1 in. apart on a greased baking sheet and sprinkle tops with excess sugar that fell off dough; cover with plastic wrap and freeze. When frozen, remove from baking sheet and pack in resealable plastic freezer bags; they keep, frozen, up to 3 months.
3. Remove rolls from freezer about 2½ hours before they are to be baked. Put on greased baking sheets; let thaw and rise in a warm (about 80°) place until almost doubled in bulk. Bake in a 350° oven until golden, 18 to 20 minutes. Makes about 2 dozen rolls.

PER ROLL: 156 cal., 27% (42 cal.) from fat; 3 g protein; 4.8 g fat (2.8 g sat.); 26 g carbo (0.6 g fiber); 133 mg sodium; 20 mg chol.

Make-ahead Butter Nut Bubble Ring

Set this in front of your family and let them pull off the warm, buttery chunks with their hands.

1. Have ready ½ to ¾ cup chopped toasted **nuts** of your choosing (*see How to Toast Nuts, page 134*) and about ½ cup melted **butter**. Pinch off 1-in. pieces of **Freeze-ahead Breakfast Pastries** (*see page 539*) and, with your fingertips, shape each piece into a ball, tucking the edges under to make a smooth top. Put one layer of balls, about ½ in. apart, in a well-buttered 10-in. tube pan (also called angel food cake pan). Brush with about a third of melted butter and sprinkle with a third of nuts. Arrange two more layers, placing balls over spaces in layer below and topping each layer with melted butter and nuts. Wrap well with plastic wrap and freeze up to 3 months.
2. Remove bubble ring about 3 hours before it is to be baked; let thaw and rise in a warm (about 80°) place until almost doubled in size. Bake in a 350° oven until golden, 35 to 40 minutes.
3. Meanwhile, mix together ⅓ cup **dark corn syrup**, 2 tbsp. melted butter, and ½ tsp. **vanilla extract**. Pour this glaze over bubble ring when it comes out of oven. Let ring stand about 10 minutes before serving. Serves 12.

PER SERVING: 383 cal., 47% (179 cal.) from fat; 6.9 g protein; 20 g fat (10 g sat.); 45 g carbo (1.3 g fiber); 329 mg sodium; 60 mg chol.

Make-ahead Glazed Orange Rolls

The *Sunset* test kitchen went gaga over these tender, luscious rolls from our 1964 files. They're that good.

1. Prepare a filling mixture of ½ cup softened **butter**, 1 cup **sugar**, and 1 tbsp. finely shredded orange zest (from 2 medium **oranges**). Roll out **Freeze-ahead Breakfast Pastries** (*see page 539*) to a rectangle about ¼ in. thick; spread orange butter evenly over dough. Roll up dough as for a jelly roll and chill at least 1 hour.
2. Cut chilled dough into 1-in.-thick slices. Put slices in buttered muffin cups (2¾ in. wide) or 1 in. apart on greased baking sheets; wrap with plastic wrap and freeze. When frozen, store in plastic freezer bags for up to 3 months. (You can also store rolls right in muffin pans.)
3. Remove rolls from freezer 2½ to 3 hours before you want to bake them. Put in buttered muffin cups (if not already in them) or on greased baking sheets. (Rolls baked in muffin cups will be tall and those baked on baking sheets will be larger and flatter.) Allow rolls to thaw and rise in a warm (about 80°) place until almost doubled in bulk. Bake in a 425° oven until golden brown, 10 to 12 minutes. Serve warm, topped with glaze (*below*). Makes about 2 dozen rolls.

Orange Glaze:
Simmer together ½ cup **sugar** and ¼ cup *each* **light corn syrup** and **water** for about 10 minutes; add finely shredded zest of 1 **orange** (½ tbsp.). Cool slightly before glazing rolls.

PER ROLL: 215 cal., 32% (69 cal.) from fat; 3 g protein; 7.8 g fat (4.8 g sat.); 34 g carbo (0.5 g fiber); 157 mg sodium; 29 mg chol.

Cranberry-Orange Bread
with Grand Marnier
Glaze, *page 531*

Chocolate-Banana Bread,
page 530

Buttermilk-Currant Scones
with Lemon Glaze, *page 528*

Poached Eggs on Polenta with
Pesto and Crisp Prosciutto
(*Uova Benedetto*), page 574

Honey Wheat Bread,
page 561

Squash Dinner Rolls,
page 535

Paprika Tomatoes with
Poached Eggs (*Shakshouka*),
page 574

Lemon Flatbread,
page 556

Toffee French Toast with Pecans, *page 583*

New Mexican Red Chile
Breakfast Burritos,
page 571

Sourdough French
Bread, *page 557*

Cardamon Rolls,
page 553

Cardamom Rolls

Even die-hard cinnamon-bun fans will love this warmly aromatic cardamom version.

recipe pictured on page 552

MAKES 16 rolls | **TIME** 1½ hours, plus 1 hour to rise and overnight to chill

2 packages (4½ tsp. total) active dry yeast
1 cup unsalted butter, divided
½ cup granulated sugar
2 eggs
¾ cup milk, divided
4½ cups flour
1 tsp. salt
½ cup firmly packed light brown sugar
4 tsp. ground cardamom (see Quick Tip below)
¾ cup powdered sugar, divided

1. In a large bowl, sprinkle yeast over ½ cup warm (100° to 110°) water. Let stand 5 minutes. Meanwhile, melt ½ cup butter in a pan over low heat, then cool just until warm. Let remaining ½ cup butter soften in a warm place until spreadable.
2. To yeast, add melted butter, granulated sugar, eggs, ½ cup milk, flour, and salt. Stir or mix in a stand mixer with a dough hook until smooth, about 5 minutes. Cover with plastic wrap or a kitchen towel and let rise in a warm (about 80°) place until doubled in bulk, about 1 hour.
3. Butter two 9-in. round cake pans. When dough has doubled, punch it down and turn it out onto a lightly floured work surface. Roll dough into a 2-ft. square, spread with softened butter, and sprinkle with brown sugar and cardamom. Roll dough into a log, pinching seam to seal. Cut log into 16 slices and arrange, cut sides up, in a single layer in pans. Cover with plastic wrap and chill overnight.
4. Remove plastic wrap from rolls and bake in a 350° oven until golden brown and a toothpick inserted in center comes out clean, about 30 minutes. Let cool in pan 10 minutes.
5. Meanwhile, make glaze: Whisk together remaining ¼ cup milk and ½ cup powdered sugar in a small bowl until smooth. Remove rolls from pans and drizzle with half the glaze. Add remaining ¼ cup powdered sugar to remaining glaze and drizzle over rolls. Serve warm.
Quick Tip: Freshly ground cardamom makes a big difference in this recipe, and it's easy to prepare. Just remove cardamom seeds from pods and grind them in a clean coffee grinder or with a mortar and pestle.

PER ROLL: 330 cal., 35% (117 cal.) from fat; 5.4 g protein; 13 g fat (7.9 g sat.); 47 g carbo (1.2 g fiber); 286 mg sodium; 60 mg chol.

Kugelhopf

The tall, elegant, raisin- and almond-studded bread probably originated in Austria and is also widely baked in southern Germany, Switzerland, and the Alsace region of France. It's more like a coffee cake than a bread, yet isn't too sweet. Traditionally, kugelhopf (or *gugelhupf*) is baked in a special swirly-grooved kugelhopf pan; you can use any 10-in. tube pan.

SERVES 12 | **TIME** 1 hour, plus 2 hours to rise

1 package (2¼ tsp.) active dry yeast
¾ cup milk, scalded and cooled to lukewarm
¾ cup butter at room temperature
½ cup sugar
4 eggs, at room temperature
4 cups sifted flour
1 tsp. salt
1 cup golden raisins
1 cup slivered almonds, divided
1 tbsp. finely shredded lemon zest

1. In a small bowl, dissolve yeast in ¼ cup warm (100° to 110°) water and let stand 5 minutes. Add cooled milk and stir until blended. In a large bowl, with a mixer on medium speed, cream butter and sugar until light. Add eggs one at a time, beating after each addition and scraping down bowl as needed. Add yeast mixture and beat until well blended.
2. In a medium bowl, combine flour and salt, then sift into egg mixture. Beat on medium to low speed until batter is smooth. Stir in raisins, ½ cup slivered almonds, and lemon zest. Put remaining ½ cup almonds in a clean coffee grinder and pulse to grind finely (be careful not to grind into a paste).
3. Butter a large kugelhopf pan (see Quick Tip below) or a 10-cup tube pan and sprinkle with ground almonds, turning pan so bottom and sides are covered.
4. *For an airy, coarse-textured cake,* turn batter immediately into pan and let rise as directed in step 5. *For a fine-textured cake,* cover bowl loosely with plastic wrap or a kitchen towel and let rise in a warm (about 80°) place until doubled in bulk, about 2 hours. Beat batter down and turn into pan to rise.
5. Let rise in warm (about 80°) place until batter comes to about ¼ in. from top of pan, about 1 hour.
6. Bake in a 350° oven until a wooden skewer or long toothpick inserted in center comes out clean, 30 to 35 minutes. Let cool in pan, then invert onto a cake plate.
Quick Tip: Find kugelhopf pans online and at cookware stores.

PER SERVING: 441 cal., 45% (199 cal.) from fat; 11 g protein; 22 g fat (8.8 g sat.); 52 g carbo (3.7 g fiber); 308 mg sodium; 103 mg chol.

Do I Need to Proof My Yeast Every Time?

If you baked with the same batch of yeast within the past month and it hasn't undergone any drastic change in conditions since then (been exposed to very high temperatures, for instance), you can go ahead and add the yeast and the water measured for proofing in with the rest of the ingredients.

However, if it's been a while since you've used the yeast, or you have reason to think it might no longer be active, it's best to take the time to proof. Yeast that is still active will begin to foam after it's been combined with warm water. If it doesn't begin to foam within 5 minutes, pitch it out and get new yeast.

Western Nut Stollen

Stollen, a tender, brioche-like German sweet bread, looks like a giant Parker House roll. Traditionally, nuts and dried or candied fruits are strewn throughout the bread, but we find that the cavity formed as the oval of dough is folded makes an ideal spot for a toasty nut filling. Serve the loaf warm.

MAKES 1 loaf (12 slices) | **TIME** 1¼ hours, plus 1½ to 2 hours to rise

1 package (2¼ tsp.) active dry yeast
6 tbsp. granulated sugar
¼ tsp. salt
½ cup plus 4 tsp. milk, at room temperature
6 tbsp. butter, melted and cooled, plus 1½ tbsp. cold butter
3 egg yolks, plus 1 egg white, slightly beaten
3 cups flour
2 cups walnuts, toasted (*see How to Toast Nuts, page 134*), divided
¼ cup firmly packed brown sugar
¼ tsp. cinnamon
2 to 3 tbsp. apricot jam or orange marmalade
1 cup sifted powdered sugar

1. In a large bowl, sprinkle yeast over ¼ cup warm (100° to 110°) water. Let stand 5 minutes. Stir in granulated sugar, salt, ½ cup milk, 6 tbsp. melted butter, and the egg yolks, blending well. Beat flour with yeast mixture until evenly moistened, then turn dough onto a floured work surface and knead until smooth and velvety, working in as little additional flour as possible, about 5 minutes.

2. Put dough in a buttered bowl; turn dough over to grease top. Cover with plastic wrap or a kitchen towel and let rise in a warm (about 80°) place until doubled in bulk, about 1½ hours.

3. Chop 1¼ cups walnuts. In a wide frying pan over medium heat, melt remaining 1½ tbsp. butter. Add chopped nuts, brown sugar, and cinnamon; cook over low heat, stirring, until sugar melts. Set mixture aside until cool, then pulse in a food processor, a portion at a time, into a coarse powder; blend with jam. Set aside.

4. Knead dough on a lightly floured work surface to expel air bubbles; form into a smooth ball. Roll out to make a 10- by 12-in. oval and put on a greased baking sheet. Mound nut filling lengthwise down one half of dough; fold empty section over filling and pat gently in place. Lightly cover with plastic wrap and a thin kitchen towel and let rise in a warm (about 80°) place until puffy, about 30 minutes.

5. Meanwhile, preheat oven to 325°. Brush risen bread gently with egg white. Bake until well browned, about 45 minutes. Let cool on a rack until warm. Mix powdered sugar with remaining 4 tsp. milk to make glaze. Coarsely chop remaining ¾ cup walnuts. Spread glaze over surface and top with walnuts. Serve warm or cool, cut into slices.

Make Ahead: Baked, unglazed stollen, up to 2 months, wrapped airtight and frozen. To finish, unwrap and thaw at room temperature 2 hours, then wrap in foil and heat in a 325° oven for 25 minutes. Glaze and top with nuts.

PER SLICE: 418 cal., 47% (198 cal.) from fat; 8 g protein; 22 g fat (6.6 g sat.); 50 g carbo (2.3 g fiber); 118 mg sodium; 74 mg chol.

Quick Stollen

This shortcut version of stollen was given to us by a reader of German heritage identified only as G. B., of Palo Alto, California.

MAKES 1 loaf (10 slices) | **TIME** 1 hour

2½ cups flour
2 tsp. baking powder
¾ cup sugar
½ tsp. salt
¼ tsp. mace
⅛ tsp. ground cardamom
¾ cup ground blanched almonds
½ cup cold butter, plus 3 tbsp. melted
1 cup cottage cheese, puréed in a blender or forced through a fine-mesh strainer
1 egg
½ tsp. vanilla extract
¼ tsp. almond extract
2 tbsp. rum; or 1½ tbsp. water and ½ tsp. rum flavoring
½ cup *each* dried currants and golden raisins
¼ cup chopped candied lemon peel
2 tbsp. vanilla sugar *(see Quick Tip below)*

1. Preheat oven to 350°. Line a baking sheet with parchment paper. In a large bowl, combine flour, baking powder, sugar, salt, mace, cardamom, and almonds. Cut in cold butter with a pastry blender or two knives until mixture resembles coarse crumbs.
2. In a small bowl, blend cottage cheese, egg, both extracts, rum, currants, raisins, and lemon peel; stir into flour mixture until dry ingredients are moistened. Mold dough into a ball, put on a floured work surface, and knead 6 to 10 times, or until dough is smooth. Roll out dough to form an oval about 8½ by 10 in. With rolling pin, lightly crease dough just off center, parallel to 10-in. side. Brush dough with 1 tbsp. melted butter. Fold smaller section over larger.
3. Put on baking sheet and bake until well browned, 45 minutes (tent with foil after 35 minutes).
4. Brush with remaining 2 tbsp. melted butter and sprinkle with vanilla sugar. Slice warm or let cool.
Quick Tip: You can buy small envelopes of vanilla sugar in specialty-foods stores. To make your own, bury a split vanilla bean in 1 cup sugar and cover container tightly. Let sugar stand 2 or 3 days at room temperature before using.
Make Ahead: Up to 2 months, wrapped airtight frozen. To reheat, unwrap and thaw at room temperature 2 hours; wrap in foil and heat in a 350° oven for 30 minutes.

PER SLICE: 416 cal., 38% (157 cal.) from fat; 8.7 g protein; 18 g fat (8.7 g sat.); 58 g carbo (2.8 g fiber); 391 mg sodium; 57 mg chol.

Western Panettone

In Italy, panettone is baked in narrow, round, high metal molds or in decorative paper collars. A San Francisco reader identified as F. C. sent us this recipe for a panettone baked in a paper lunch bag—along with an explanation: "Inventive Italian cooks who came to the West without their panettone pans quickly discovered that a small paper bag was easier to use than a tied paper collar." The bread also doesn't rise as long as true Italian panettone, so its texture is more dense and cakelike. Use a paper bag that measures 3½ by 6 in. on the bottom.

MAKES 1 loaf (10 slices) | **TIME** 1½ hours

1 egg, plus 2 egg yolks
¾ cup sugar
½ cup butter, melted and cooled to lukewarm
1 tsp. finely shredded lemon zest
½ tsp. anise seeds
½ tsp. anise extract (optional)
¼ cup *each* pine nuts, raisins, and coarsely chopped candied lemon or orange peel
3 cups sifted flour
2 tsp. baking powder
½ tsp. salt
1 cup milk

1. Preheat oven to 350°. In a large bowl, with a mixer on medium-high speed, beat whole egg, egg yolks, and sugar until thick and pale yellow. Beat in melted butter, then stir in lemon zest, anise seeds, anise extract if using, pine nuts, raisins, and candied peel.
2. Into a medium bowl, sift flour, baking powder, and salt. Blend half the flour mixture into the batter. Stir in half the milk, add remaining flour mixture, and mix well. Add remaining milk and blend thoroughly.
3. Fold down top of a paper bag to form a 2¾-in. cuff. Butter inside of bag generously and pour in batter. Set on a baking sheet and bake until a wooden skewer or long toothpick inserted in center comes out clean, about 1¼ hours.
4. To serve hot, tear off paper bag and cut bread into wedges. To serve cold, wrap bread (still in bag) in a kitchen towel, then in foil, and let cool completely. To reheat slices, wrap bread in foil and warm in a 350° oven 45 minutes.

PER SLICE: 345 cal., 36% (125 cal.) from fat; 6.2 g protein; 14 g fat (7 g sat.); 50 g carbo (1.6 g fiber); 303 mg sodium; 90 mg chol.

Lemon Flatbread

Bright-tasting and slightly bitter salted lemon slices on this bread give it character. But you could also top it with cheese (about 1 cup shredded) or some fresh herbs The dough makes a good pizza crust too.

recipe pictured on page **548**

MAKES Two 10- by 15-in. flatbreads (30 pieces)
TIME 1½ hours, plus 1½ to 2 hours to rise

1 tbsp. active dry yeast
⅓ cup olive oil
4¼ cups flour
3 tbsp. salt (*see Quick Tip below*)**, divided**
3 lemons

1. In a large bowl, sprinkle yeast over 1¾ cups warm (100° to 110°) water. Let stand 5 minutes.
2. *If using a stand mixer,* attach dough hook and, on low speed, add oil, flour, and 4 tsp. salt. Mix until dough is smooth, about 2 minutes. *If kneading by hand,* in a large bowl mix oil, flour, and 4 tsp. salt with a wooden spoon until dough is smooth, about 2 minutes. (It will still be fairly sticky and won't pull away from sides of bowl.) Using a spatula or oiled hands, put dough in a large, oiled bowl. Cover with a kitchen towel or plastic wrap and let sit in a warm (about 80°) place until doubled in bulk, 1½ to 2 hours.
3. Meanwhile, slice lemons as thinly as possible. Discard any seeds. Put lemons and 1 tbsp. salt in a bowl. Let sit at room temperature at least 1 hour and up to 1 day.
4. Preheat oven to 425°. Lightly oil two 10- by 15-in. baking sheets. Punch down dough, divide in half, and put each half on a baking sheet. Flatten dough as much as possible, pushing gently from center out. (Dough will pull back toward center; don't worry if it doesn't stay in place.) Let rest 10 minutes, then flatten again, pushing edges and corners down to help them stay put (if it pulls back a bit, that's okay, but you want to make dough as thin and flat as possible).
5. Lift lemon slices out of their juices and lay them evenly over dough, pressing them in as much as possible. Sprinkle with remaining 2 tsp. salt. Bake until brown and crispy, about 25 minutes. While bread is still warm, cut each sheet into 15 pieces. Cool on wire racks.
Quick Tip: The final sprinkle of salt is a nice way to use *fleur de sel* or other fancy salt, if you have some.
Make Ahead: Through step 2, up to 1 day or overnight, covered and chilled.

PER PIECE: 91 cal., 29% (26 cal.) from fat; 2.1 g protein; 2.9 g fat (0.4 g sat.); 15 g carbo (1.1 g fiber); 545 mg sodium; 0 mg chol.

Onion Focaccia

Discover how easy it is to make focaccia with this recipe. Then experiment with herbs, cheese, and other flavorings.

MAKES 12 squares (4 in. each) | **TIME** 1½ hours, plus 2½ hours to rise

3 large onions, divided
5 tbsp. olive oil, divided
2 garlic cloves, minced
1½ tbsp. salt, divided
1 tbsp. active dry yeast
1 cup low-fat milk
2 tsp. sugar
6 cups flour

1. Finely chop 1 onion. In a large frying pan over medium-high heat, add 3 tbsp. oil, the chopped onion, garlic, and ½ tsp. salt. Cook, stirring occasionally, until onion is soft, about 3 minutes. Set aside.
2. Meanwhile, in a large bowl, sprinkle yeast over 1 cup warm (100° to 110°) water. Let stand 5 minutes.
3. *If using a stand mixer,* attach dough hook and, on low speed, add milk, 1 tbsp. salt, the sugar, and onion mixture to yeast. Work in flour, 1 cup at a time, until you have a smooth and elastic dough, about 3 minutes. *If kneading by hand,* put milk, 1 tbsp. salt, the sugar, and onion mixture in a medium bowl; stir to blend well, then add yeast mixture and stir to blend well again. Stir in flour, 1 cup at a time, until well blended. Turn out onto a floured work surface and knead until smooth and elastic.
4. Transfer dough to a large, oiled bowl. Cover with a kitchen towel or plastic wrap and let sit in a warm (about 80°) place until doubled in bulk, about 1½ hours.
5. Punch dough down, cover, and let sit until doubled in bulk again, about 1 hour.
6. Oil a large rimmed baking sheet (ideally 12 by 16 in.). Punch down dough again, transfer onto baking sheet, and use your hands to spread and gently push it into an even layer. Cover and let sit until soft and puffy, about 45 minutes.
7. Meanwhile, halve and thinly slice remaining 2 onions. In a large frying pan over medium-high heat, add remaining 2 tbsp. oil, the sliced onions, and ½ tsp. salt. Cook, stirring, until onions are soft and beginning to turn translucent, about 3 minutes. Set aside.
8. Preheat oven to 450°. Using your fingers, poke holes straight down into the risen dough. Spread cooked onion mixture evenly over top and sprinkle with remaining ½ tsp. salt. Bake until golden, 30 to 35 minutes. Cool in pan on a wire rack. Serve warm or at room temperature.

PER SQUARE: 320 cal., 21% (66 cal.) from fat; 8.2 g protein; 7.3 g fat (1.1 g sat.); 55 g carbo (2.9 g fiber); 886 mg sodium; 0.8 mg chol.

Sourdough French Bread

When *Sunset* published this recipe in 1973, the long, slender baguette was the only shape sourdough bakers were interested in. Professional and home bakers have branched out to additional forms, but the baguette remains the classic.

recipe pictured on page **551**

MAKES 1 loaf (20 slices) | **TIME** 30 minutes, plus up to 2½ hours to rise (and up to 24 hours for starter to ferment if you want a very sour dough)

1 cup sourdough starter, at room temperature (*see Sunset's Reliable Sourdough Starter, page 558, or Quick Tip, right*)
3 to 3½ cups bread flour, divided
1 package (2¼ tsp.) active dry yeast
1 tsp. *each* salt and sugar
Cornmeal

1. In a large bowl, stir together ½ cup warm (90°) water, the starter, and 1 cup flour until smooth. For sourest flavor, cover and let stand in a warm place until bubbly and sour smelling, 12 to 24 hours, before proceeding. (The longer you let it ferment, the more pronounced the sour flavor will be in the finished bread.) Soften yeast in ¼ cup warm (90°) water; stir into sourdough mixture with salt and sugar.

2. Using your method of choice, mix in remaining flour and knead:

By hand: Stir in enough flour to form a kneadable dough, about 2 cups. Turn dough out onto a lightly floured work surface and knead until smooth and elastic, 12 to 15 minutes; add as little flour as possible to keep dough from sticking. Put dough in a greased bowl; turn over.

In a stand mixer fitted with a dough hook: Mix in enough flour to form a somewhat stiff dough, about 2 cups. Beat on high speed until dough pulls cleanly from inside of bowl, about 8 minutes. If dough still sticks or feels sticky, add 1 tbsp. flour at a time until dough pulls free and isn't sticky. Leave in bowl.

In a food processor: Put 2¼ cups flour in processor with metal blade. With motor running, pour sourdough-yeast mixture into feed tube. Process until dough forms a ball and pulls from container, then process 45 seconds more. If dough feels sticky, add 1 tbsp. flour at a time and mix in short bursts. Put dough in a greased bowl; turn over.

3. Cover bowl with plastic wrap and let rise in a warm (about 80°) place until doubled in bulk, 1 to 2 hours.

4. Gently punch down dough. Turn out onto a lightly floured work surface and knead gently just until smooth. Roll with hands into a 3½- by 12-in. log. Generously sprinkle a piece of stiff cardboard with cornmeal; set dough on cornmeal. Cover lightly with plastic wrap and let rise in a warm place until puffy, 10 to 30 minutes.

5. Meanwhile, put a 12- by 15-in. baking sheet on lowest oven rack, then preheat oven to 400°.

6. With a flour-dusted razor blade or sharp knife, cut several ¾-in.-deep diagonal slashes on loaf's top. Slip loaf off cardboard onto hot baking sheet, keeping slashed side up. Mist bread all over with water from a spray bottle.

7. Bake for 5 minutes, and then mist again with water. Repeat after 5 more minutes, then bake until deep golden, 25 to 30 minutes more. Let cool completely on rack.

Quick Tip: Although it's gratifying to make your own sourdough starter, you can also order one online from *amazon.com*; we like Goldrush Sourdough starter.

PER SLICE: 119 cal., 4% (5.2 cal.) from fat; 4 g protein; 0.6 g fat (0.1 g sat.); 24 g carbo (0.9 g fiber); 123 mg sodium; 0.4 mg chol.

Variation: To form the dough into a round loaf, shape it after you have kneaded the dough in step 4, tucking the edges under and pushing them back up into the bottom of the dough (the top of the round should be slightly stretched). Put on a buttered baking sheet, cover, and let rise as directed, then bake as for a baguette.

Sourdough:
Wild Bread of the West

Since California's gold mining days, sourdough has been a Western staple, delighting generations with its tangy flavor in breads, pancakes, and other baked foods. The West didn't invent sourdough, of course. This style of baking goes back to the ancient Egyptians, and Europeans have baked with sourdough starters for centuries.

How Sourdough Works

A sourdough starter is a portion of dough that is allowed to ferment. When this happens, the wild yeast and bacteria in the flour, in the liquid, and even in the air break down natural sugars and produce carbon dioxide, which enables bread baked with the starter to rise. As it ferments, the starter also produces acidity—in the form of lactic acid and some acetic acid—creating the "sour" in sourdough.

Starters vary from place to place (because wild yeasts are different everywhere) and baker to baker. The ones that developed in the San Francisco area were uniquely sour. In fact, the bacterial strain that's responsible for that sour flavor was eventually identified and named *Lactobacillus sanfranciscensis* in honor of San Francisco.

Once established, a starter can be kept going for decades. Boudin Bakery, founded in San Francisco in 1849 and still operating, traces its sourdough starter to one begun more than 150 years ago by Isidore Boudin. (The Boudin starter was borrowed, so the story goes, from one of the actual "sourdoughs"—the name given to gold miners because they relied so heavily on sourdough starters for bread baking out in the gold fields.)

Sunset's Reliable Sourdough Starter

As with a classic starter, ours ferments flour and liquid—milk, in this case—with some yogurt, already packed with helpful bacteria to get things off to a good beginning. Yogurt also produces a very active, bubbly starter and gives a wonderful zesty flavor to the bread. After a few days' incubation in a warm place, the bacteria multiply to break down sugars in the flour and milk and give the characteristic sour smell and tang, and the starter is ready to use. Despite its terrific souring qualities, yogurt-based starters don't always have a reliable yeast component (their high levels of acidity can inhibit yeast's gas production), so we add dry yeast when baking. For best results, use milk (nonfat or low-fat for tangiest flavor) and yogurt that are as fresh as possible (check the sell-by date) and use them right after opening.

MAKES About 1⅓ cups starter | **TIME** 1 week

1 cup nonfat or low-fat milk
3 tbsp. plain yogurt (any fat level; use a brand with
    live cultures and no gelatin)
1 cup all-purpose or bread flour

1. In a 1-qt. pan over medium heat, heat milk to 90° to 100°. Remove from heat and stir in yogurt. Pour into a warm 3- to 6-cup container with a tight lid.

2. Cover and let stand in a warm (80° to 90°) place until mixture is consistency of yogurt, a curd has formed, and mixture doesn't flow readily when container is tilted. (It may also form smaller curds suspended in clear liquid.) The process takes 18 to 24 hours. If some clear liquid has risen to the top of the milk during this time, stir it back in. If liquid has turned light pink, discard batch and start again.

3. Once curd has formed, stir in flour until smooth. Cover tightly and let stand in a warm place until mixture is full of bubbles and has a good sour smell, 2 to 5 days. Again, if clear liquid forms during this time, stir it back into starter. If liquid turns pink, start over. To store, cover and refrigerate.

A Bread Revolution

In the 1980s, sourdough helped fire up an artisanal bread–making revolution when Steve Sullivan and his wife, Susie, founded Acme Bread Company in Berkeley, California; to create the leavener for their levain bread, which sets the standard for artisan-style bread in America, he created a starter inoculated with wild yeast from wine grapes.

Sourdough has been a standby at *Sunset* since 1933, when we published the first recipes. However, we discovered that capturing the right bacteria and yeasts to establish a good starter can be hit or miss—some mixtures never fermented at all, while others were weak or inconsistent. In 1973, staff food writer Kandace Reeves, working with microbiologist Dr. George K. York from the University of California, Davis, finally hit upon a truly dependable starter using yogurt. (*See Sunset's Reliable Sourdough Starter, opposite page.*)

Care and Feeding of Your Starter

To keep bacteria and yeasts healthy, the yogurt starter must be nourished occasionally with flour and milk.

ENVIRONMENT. When creating the starter, incubate it between 80° and 90°. Any hotter and the bacteria may die; any cooler and the starter could develop mold. Set it on top of your water heater, on a counter with a lamp warming it, or in an oven warmed with pans of boiling water. An established starter is stronger; after feeding, it can stand at room temperature.

TO FEED THE STARTER AND KEEP IT GOING. For best results, try to feed the starter at least once a month, even if you're not baking.

To feed, add warm (90° to 100°) nonfat or low-fat milk and all-purpose flour to the starter, each in quantities equal to what you'll be using in the recipe. For example, if the recipe calls for 1 cup starter, add 1 cup milk and 1 cup flour. (This is also the right amount for a monthly feeding even if you're not baking.) Cover tightly and let stand in a warm (80° to 90°) place until bubbly and sour-smelling and a clear liquid has formed on top, 12 to 24 hours. The clear liquid shows that the acid level has risen and is starting to break down milk protein, and high acid means sour flavor. Use at this point (just give it a stir first) or cover and chill.

To increase the starter supply (for gift-giving or quantity baking), you can add up to 10 cups *each* of milk and flour to 1 cup of starter (use a large container). The mixture may need to stand up to 2 days before the clear liquid forms on top.

Sourdough Starter FAQs

What if I neglect my starter?
Even with the best intentions, it's easy to forget to feed a starter, but they can be surprisingly resilient. If you rediscover yours in the back of the fridge, take its "pulse." An "old" smell, no bubbles at room temperature, a top layer of dark brown liquid, or slight mold growth indicate your starter isn't feeling its best. First spoon off and discard any mold, then stir the starter. Feed it 1 cup each of flour and milk and let stand as directed in *To Feed the Starter and Keep It Going, left*. After 24 hours, discard half the starter and repeat feeding and standing. Repeat a third time, if needed, until the starter bubbles and has a "fresh" sour smell. If, after repeated feedings, your starter still smells "off" and won't bubble, throw it away. Also begin a new starter if mold growth is heavy.

Can you use a starter too often?
Overuse isn't a problem per se; if you bake several times a week or feed your starter a lot all at once (to increase quantity), it may take longer than usual to regain normal sourness. After feeding, let it stand as directed in *To Feed the Starter and Keep It Going, left*.

Why do starters "die"?
The longer a starter stands without new food, the higher the acidity gets; too much acid, and beneficial bacteria can't survive. Mold infestations may also kill off good bacteria.

Can I freeze it when I'm not going to use it for a while?
Starters generally freeze successfully for up to a few months, but freezing does change the bacteria's cell structure. Longer freezing brings more changes and decreases the chance of success with the thawed starter.

Sourdough California Apricot Bread

The recipe from reader Nell Rogers Lane of Novato, California, combines two California culinary treasures—sourdough and apricots.

MAKES 1 loaf (25 slices) | **TIME** 1¼ hours (and up to 24 hours to ferment if you want a very sour dough)

½ cup sourdough starter, at room temperature (*see Sunset's Reliable Sourdough Starter, page 558, or Quick Tips, right*)
½ cup warm (90°) milk
1½ cups flour, divided
1 egg
½ cup *each* granulated sugar and firmly packed brown sugar
3 tbsp. canola or safflower oil or melted butter
1 tsp. baking powder
½ tsp. salt
¼ tsp. baking soda
½ cup *each* chopped dried apricots, preferably Blenheims (*see Quick Tips, right*), and chopped walnuts

1. In a small bowl, mix starter, milk, and ½ cup flour. For sourest flavor, cover and let stand in a warm place (80° to 90°) until bubbly and sour smelling, 12 to 24 hours, before proceeding.

2. Preheat oven to 350°. Grease a 9- by 5-in. loaf pan. In a large bowl, beat egg, both sugars, oil, and starter mixture until well blended. In a medium bowl, combine baking powder, salt, baking soda, remaining 1 cup flour, the apricots, and nuts; add to egg mixture and stir until evenly moistened.

3. Pour batter into pan. Bake until bread pulls from sides of pan, 55 to 60 minutes. Let cool in pan on a rack for 5 minutes, then turn out onto rack and let cool completely.

Quick Tips: Although it's gratifying to make your own sourdough starter, you can also order one online from *amazon.com*; we like Goldrush Sourdough Starter. The fresh Blenheim apricot is one of the most flavorful fruits in California; however, it doesn't ship well, so it has been slowly declining. Find dried California Blenheims online at *brfarms.com*.

PER SLICE: 112 cal., 31% (35 cal.) from fat; 2 g protein; 3.9 g fat (0.5 g sat.); 18 g carbo (0.6 g fiber); 87 mg sodium; 9.1 mg chol.

Baking with Sourdough

As you spend more time with sourdough, you'll learn tricks for coaxing out just the sour flavor you like and creating breads with a chewy texture and crackly crust.

SOURNESS. The greatest trick for increasing sour flavor is patience. The longer dough stands in the "sponge" stage, the more sourness you'll get— up to a point. A sponge is a mixture of starter and part of the liquid and flour called for in a recipe. Let it stand 12 to 24 hours before adding other ingredients; as it stands, bacteria multiply and produce acidity, or sourness. After about 24 hours, the sponge won't get much more sour. To mellow a too-sour starter, skip the sponge stage in the recipe and, after feeding the starter, let it stand only a few hours.

TEXTURE. Bread flour is what you want for traditional chewy sourdough texture. Compared with all-purpose flour, bread flour develops more gluten— the protein structure that forms when you knead dough, making it stronger and springier. For pancakes, muffins, and other breads that aren't kneaded and are softer in texture, all-purpose flour is a better choice.

For kneaded doughs, the correct amount of flour varies with weather and other factors. As you gain experience, you'll know when the kneaded dough feels right—it will still be tacky but not sticky (not enough flour) or dry (too much).

Sufficient kneading is also important for good bread texture. The dough should feel smooth and springy and have tiny bubbles just beneath the surface; underkneaded dough will be heavy when baked. Finally, for the best texture, be sure the dough rises enough. Because of their higher acid, sourdough loaves are naturally denser than other kinds.

CRUST. To achieve crisp crusts, professional bakers slide their sourdough loaves right onto the floor of hot ovens that also inject the chamber with bursts of steam. At home, you can use a preheated baking stone (pizza stone) and spray loaves with a mist of water as they cook.

A TIME-SAVING TIP. Sourdough bacteria multiply fastest between 80° and 90°, and slower the colder they are—so recipes call for starter that is at least as warm as room temperature. If you're skipping the sponge stage, you can use the starter cold.

Spiced Pecan Toasting Bread

Toasted and buttered, this bread reminds us of not-too-sweet, freshly baked cinnamon rolls.

MAKES 2 loaves (32 slices total) | **TIME** 1½ hours, plus 2½ hours to rise

2 tbsp. *each* active dry yeast and honey
3 eggs, divided
6 to 7 cups bread flour, divided, plus more as needed
½ cup *each* whole-wheat flour, firmly packed dark brown sugar, and low-fat or nonfat dried milk
4 tsp. salt
1 tbsp. vanilla extract
2 tsp. ground cardamom
1 tsp. cinnamon
½ tsp. freshly ground black pepper
¼ tsp. freshly grated nutmeg
1½ cups chopped pecans

1. In bowl of a stand mixer or a large bowl, dissolve yeast and honey in 1½ cups warm (100° to 110°) water and let stand 5 minutes.
2. *If using a stand mixer,* attach dough hook and, on medium speed, mix in 2 eggs, 2 cups bread flour, the whole-wheat flour, brown sugar, dried milk, salt, vanilla, cardamom, cinnamon, pepper, nutmeg, and pecans. Add remaining 4 to 5 cups bread flour, ½ cup at a time, until dough pulls away from sides of bowl. Knead on medium until smooth and elastic, adding more flour as necessary to keep dough from sticking too much. *If mixing by hand,* stir into yeast 2 eggs, 2 cups bread flour, the whole-wheat flour, brown sugar, dried milk, salt, vanilla, spices, and pecans. Stir in remaining 4 to 5 cups bread flour, ½ cup at a time; turn out onto a floured work surface and knead until smooth and elastic, adding more flour as necessary to keep dough from sticking too much. When ready, dough should feel a bit like an earlobe when you pinch it.
3. Transfer dough to a large, lightly buttered bowl. Cover and let sit in a warm (about 80°) place until doubled in bulk, about 1½ hours. Meanwhile, butter two 8½- by 4½-in. loaf pans and set aside.
4. Punch down dough, divide in half, and, on a lightly floured work surface, shape each half into an 8-in. oblong loaf. Put dough in pans, cover, and let sit in warm place until doubled in bulk, about 1 hour.
5. Preheat oven to 350°. In a small bowl, beat remaining egg with 2 tbsp. water. Brush dough with egg wash and bake until brown, about 35 minutes. Remove loaves from pans (they're done if they sound hollow when tapped on the bottom) and cool on racks before slicing.

PER SLICE: 176 cal., 24% (42 cal.) from fat; 5.1 g protein; 4.7 g fat (0.6 g sat.); 28 g carbo (1.4 g fiber); 305 mg sodium; 21 mg chol.

Honey Wheat Bread

A hearty, slightly sweet bread that's perfect for sandwiches or toasting.

recipe pictured on page 545

MAKES 2 loaves (32 slices total)
TIME 1½ hours, plus 2½ hours to rise

1 cup cracked wheat
⅓ cup honey
1½ tsp. salt
2 packages (4½ tsp. total) active dry yeast
2 cups whole-wheat flour
2½ to 3 cups bread flour, divided
2 tbsp. butter, melted

1. In a medium bowl, combine cracked wheat, honey, salt, and 2 cups boiling water. Cover with a kitchen towel or plastic wrap and let sit 30 minutes.
2. In a small bowl, sprinkle yeast over ¾ cup warm (100° to 110°) water. Let stand 5 minutes.
3. In bowl of a stand mixer (or a large bowl if mixing by hand), whisk whole-wheat flour and 2 cups bread flour together. Add cracked wheat mixture and yeast mixture.
4. Attach dough hook and, on low speed, mix to combine. Add remaining bread flour, ¼ cup at a time, until dough pulls away from sides of bowl. Continue mixing until smooth and elastic, adding more flour as necessary to keep dough from sticking too much. *If kneading by hand*, mix in bread flour to combine, then turn out onto a floured work surface and knead until dough is smooth and elastic. When it's ready, dough should feel a bit like an earlobe when you pinch it.
5. Butter a large bowl and put dough in it. Cover loosely and let sit in a warm (about 80°) place until dough has doubled in bulk, about 1 hour.
6. Punch down dough, cover, and let double again, about 1 hour.
7. Divide dough in half and shape each half into a rough 8-in.-long rectangle. Put dough in two buttered 8½- by 4½-in. loaf pans. Cover and let sit until doubled in bulk, 30 to 45 minutes.
8. Preheat oven to 350°. Brush butter onto tops of loaves. Using a razor or serrated knife, make a ¼-in.-deep slash lengthwise on top of each loaf and bake until browned, about 35 minutes. Remove loaves from pans (they're done if they sound hollow when tapped on bottom) and cool on racks.

PER SLICE: 103 cal., 12% (12 cal.) from fat; 3.1 g protein; 1.3 g fat (1 g sat.); 20 g carbo (2.1 g fiber); 120 mg sodium; 2.6 mg chol.

breakfast & brunch

Compared with people on the East Coast, we Westerners get up early, like birds. The day is bustling by 7 a.m., an hour when other places are barely opening their collective eyes. Maybe that's why we like breakfast so much—it fuels our jets.

There's nothing more invigorating than a healthy breakfast that tastes good. We've edited out lots of brown roughage and bowls of mush to bring you the zingy recipes that begin this chapter—great granola, unusual oatmeals, and cereals made from nutty wheat berries and amaranth, a sweet, grainlike seed packed with protein and calcium. You won't find a bore in the bunch.

That said, some of us are suckers for mighty, rib-sticking brunches, especially on weekends (of course, we plan to hike or bike ride beforehand). So we present morning glories like New Mexico–style breakfast burritos (*page 571*), Eggs Benedict with Crab (*page 575*), ethereal Buckwheat Belgian Waffles (*page 585*), Coffee and Brown Sugar Bacon (*page 587*), and sticky, gooey Toffee French Toast with Pecans (*page 583*).

Breakfast has focus: It offers us one plate or bowl of exactly what we want. Maybe that's why, more than any other meal, it so often hits the sweet spot. Breakfast makes us happy.

Breakfast & Brunch

Del's Grand Canyon Granola

Reader Elaine Bohlmeyer, of Payson, Arizona, gave us a recipe her husband created when they were planning a hiking trip to the bottom of the Grand Canyon. "The object was to get the most energy for the least amount of weight," says Bohlmeyer. "The added bonus is that it's delicious." (To turn the granola into a chocolate-covered bark candy, *see below.*)

MAKES 8 cups | **TIME** 45 minutes

2 cups rolled oats (regular or quick cooking)
1 cup pecans or walnuts
½ cup *each* wheat germ, unsweetened shredded dried coconut, slivered almonds, sunflower seeds, and roasted soy nuts *(see Quick Tip below)*
¼ cup *each* sesame seeds (optional) and nonfat dried milk
½ cup honey
¼ cup *each* maple syrup, firmly packed light brown sugar, and vegetable oil
1 tsp. vanilla extract
½ cup raisins

1. In a large bowl, mix together oats, nuts, wheat germ, coconut, seeds, soy nuts, and dried milk.
2. In a small saucepan, combine honey, maple syrup, brown sugar, oil, and vanilla and bring to a boil. Pour over dry mixture and mix together with a wooden spoon.
3. Preheat oven to 300°. Oil a rimmed baking sheet and pour mixture onto sheet. Bake 15 minutes. Stir granola and bake another 10 minutes. Sprinkle on raisins and bake 5 minutes more. (The granola will look wet and sticky but will dry out as it cools.)
4. Let granola cool completely on baking sheet.
Quick Tip: If you can't find roasted soy nuts, you can leave them out or use peanuts or pumpkin seeds.
Make Ahead: Up to 2 weeks, stored airtight at room temperature.

PER CUP: 535 cal., 49% (261 cal.) from fat; 11 g protein; 29 g fat (5.1 g sat.); 63 g carbo (5 g fiber); 21 mg sodium; 0.4 mg chol.

Chocolate Granola Bark Candy: In a medium bowl set over a saucepan of simmering water, melt ¾ lb. **semisweet chocolate chips**. Remove chocolate from heat while still a little chunky, then stir until smooth. Spread onto a baking sheet lined with parchment and sprinkle with 2 cups of Del's Grand Canyon Granola. Chill until set, at least 30 minutes. Break chocolate granola bark into pieces. Makes 1 lb., 1 oz.

PER 2-OZ. SERVING: 213 cal., 52% (111 cal.) from fat; 3.6 g protein; 12 g fat (4.3 g sat.); 26 g carbo (2.7 g fiber); 17 mg sodium; .04 mg chol.

Ranch Breakfast Muesli

Every morning at the breakfast buffet, guests at the Rancho La Puerta Spa, in Tecate, Mexico, look forward to this sweet-tart cereal full of refreshing apples. A flexible recipe, it works with or without nuts and more fruit.

SERVES 4 | **TIME** 15 minutes

1 cup regular rolled oats
3 tbsp. fresh lemon juice
2 firm tart apples, such as Granny Smith
¼ cup sliced almonds, toasted if you like *(see How to Toast Nuts, page 134)*
3 tbsp. agave syrup, maple syrup, or mild honey
¼ cup unsweetened shredded dried coconut, toasted if you like *(see Quick Tip below)*, or dried currants
1 cup plain low-fat yogurt (optional)

1. In a medium bowl, combine oats with ¾ cup water. Let stand while you prepare remaining ingredients.
2. Put lemon juice in another bowl. Peel and core apples, then cut eight very thin slices from 1 apple. Turn slices in lemon juice and lift out; set aside. Peel and coarsely shred remaining apples into lemon juice; mix immediately.
3. Stir shredded apples, almonds, syrup, and coconut into oats. Divide among bowls. Serve with yogurt if you like; garnish with apple slices.
Quick Tip: You can often find shredded coconut already toasted, but if you don't, here's how to toast it yourself: Spread coconut on a baking sheet and bake in a 325° oven until golden brown, 6 to 8 minutes. Let cool before using.
Make Ahead: In step 1, combine oats with 1½ cups water; chill at least 2 hours and as long as overnight, then drain (oats will be plumper than when short-soaked).

PER SERVING: 220 cal., 27% (59 cal.) from fat; 4.8 g protein; 6.6 g fat (2.3 g sat.); 38 g carbo (4.3 g fiber); 4.5 mg sodium; 0 mg chol.

■ Agave Syrup

FROM THE PANTRY

Agave syrup (also called agave nectar) is a sweetener made from the juice of several species of the agave plant. Its glycemic index is lower than sugar's, meaning it doesn't produce the same "rush" that sugar can. It is thinner and sweeter than honey. Find it at well-stocked grocery and natural-foods stores.

Toasty Baked Oatmeal

A delicious breakfast dish from reader Annis Henson, of Bend, Oregon, that can be prepped the night before. The next morning, add the pear and bake (see Make Ahead below).

SERVES 4 | **TIME** 1 hour

2 cups regular rolled oats
1½ tsp. baking powder
½ tsp. salt
⅓ cup *each* chopped almonds and chopped dried apricots
1 firm-ripe pear (½ lb.), cored and chopped into ¼-in. pieces
1½ cups milk
2 eggs
½ cup firmly packed brown sugar
3 tbsp. vegetable oil
½ tsp. cinnamon

1. Preheat oven to 325°. Butter an 8-in. square baking pan. In a large bowl, mix oats, baking powder, and salt. Stir in almonds, apricots, and pear.
2. In another bowl, whisk together milk, eggs, brown sugar, oil, and cinnamon. Pour over oat mixture and stir to combine.
3. Pour mixture into pan. Bake until liquid is absorbed and top is light golden, about 45 minutes. Spoon into bowls and serve warm.
Make Ahead: Up to 1 day. Mix oats, baking powder, salt, almonds, and apricots in a bowl; cover and let stand at room temperature. In another bowl, combine milk, eggs, brown sugar, oil, and cinnamon; cover and chill. The next morning, mix the two, stir in the pear, and bake.

PER SERVING: 572 cal., 39% (225 cal.) from fat; 15 g protein; 25 g fat (5.5 g sat.); 76 g carbo (7.5 g fiber); 573 mg sodium; 122 mg chol.

Aloha Oatmeal

Steel-cut oatmeal takes longer to make than instant or ordinary rolled oats, but the chewier texture and the deep, nutty flavor are worth the time spent. It also freezes well, so you can make a big batch, store by the cup, and defrost whenever you're craving good oatmeal (add the fruit after defrosting).

SERVES 4 | **TIME** 45 minutes

1 cup Irish steel-cut oats
½ cup golden raisins
2 tsp. sunflower or canola oil
¼ tsp. kosher salt
1 or 2 tbsp. honey, or to taste
¼ cup hot milk (optional), or to taste
½ ripe banana, chopped
½ cup diced fresh pineapple
¼ cup sliced almonds, toasted (see How to Toast Nuts, page 134)
¼ cup toasted sweetened shredded dried coconut (see Quick Tip below)

1. Cook oats according to package instructions but add ½ cup more water. As soon as the oats boil, add raisins, oil, and salt.
2. When oats are done, stir in honey and hot milk or water to get the consistency you like. Add banana, pineapple, and almonds. Top with toasted coconut.
Quick Tip: You can often find shredded coconut already toasted, but if you don't, here's how to toast it yourself: Spread coconut on a baking sheet and bake in a 325° oven until golden brown, 6 to 8 minutes. Let cool before using.

PER SERVING: 268 cal., 30% (81 cal.) from fat; 5.3 g protein; 9.1 g fat (2.9 g sat.); 45 g carbo (4.4 g fiber); 144 mg sodium; 1.5 mg chol.

Amaranth Fruit and Spice Cereal

For a change from your morning oatmeal, try amaranth, a high-protein grainlike seed that was a staple of the ancient Inca diet. Cooked amaranth contains more protein and calcium than oatmeal and has a pleasing, sweet taste.

SERVES 2 | **TIME** 20 minutes

½ cup amaranth grain (see Quick Tip, above right)
½ cinnamon stick
¼ cup *each* dried tart cherries and chopped dried apricots
2 tbsp. honey
½ cup nonfat Greek yogurt

breakfast & brunch

1. In a small saucepan, bring amaranth, cinnamon stick, and ⅔ cup water to a boil. Simmer, covered, 10 minutes. Let cool slightly.

2. Microwave cherries and apricots with honey and 2 tbsp. water until warm, about 30 seconds. Stir 1 tbsp. honey liquid into yogurt. Divide yogurt between dishes and top with amaranth, fruit, and remaining honey liquid.

Quick Tip: Buy amaranth in boxes or in bulk at well-stocked grocery and natural-foods stores.

PER SERVING: 359 cal., 8% (29 cal.) from fat; 13 g protein; 3.2 g fat (0.8 g sat.); 74 g carbo (8.7 g fiber); 34 mg sodium; 0 mg chol.

Wheat-berry Cereal

Whole-wheat kernels, or wheat berries, are one of the least-processed grain products; they're simply stripped from the stalk and separated from the chaff, their papery protective husks. Therefore, they retain fiber and nutrients and have an appealing chewiness. The other nice thing about wheat berries is that they freeze well. You can cook up a big batch, separate it into smaller portions, and freeze in resealable plastic bags; then thaw whenever you want cooked wheat berries.

SERVES 4 to 6 | **TIME** 20 minutes, plus 2½ hours to soak and cook wheat berries

1 cup wheat berries
2 tbsp. honey, plus extra for serving
½ cup chopped dried apricots or raisins, or some of each
¼ tsp. kosher salt
Plain yogurt (optional)

1. In a large saucepan, combine wheat berries and 5 cups water. Cover and let stand at least 8 hours or overnight. (Or bring to a boil, boil 2 minutes, and let stand off heat, covered, 1 hour.)

2. Without draining wheat berries, bring to a boil over high heat. Reduce heat to a simmer and cook, covered, until tender, about 1½ hours. Drain and cool. You should have about 3 cups.

3. In a 3-qt. pan, combine ½ cup water, honey, and apricots. Cover and bring to a boil. Stir in cooked wheat berries and salt; reduce to a simmer and cook, covered, until wheat berries are heated through and water is absorbed, about 10 minutes. Divide among bowls and serve with extra honey and yogurt to stir in if you like.

Make Ahead: Cooked wheat berries, through step 2, up to 1 week, chilled, and up to 2 months frozen.

PER SERVING: 161 cal., 4% (6.5 cal.) from fat; 5.1 g protein; 0.7 g fat (0 g sat.); 35 g carbo (4.1 g fiber); 82 mg sodium; 0 mg chol.

Creamy Rice Cereal with Oranges

Cooked rice cereal is anything but boring when you mix in some marmalade and top with crunchy granola.

SERVES 4 | **TIME** 20 minutes

3 cups lowfat milk
¾ cup quick-cooking rice cereal
1 tbsp. orange marmalade
½ tsp. finely shredded orange zest
¼ tsp. salt, plus more to taste
1½ cups orange segments (see *How to Cut Citrus into Segments,* page 135)
½ cup granola
Maple syrup

1. In a 1½- to 2-qt. pan, whisk milk with rice cereal, marmalade, orange zest, and salt to blend. Cook, whisking, over high heat until mixture is boiling, then continue cooking and whisking until thickened, about 30 seconds longer. Taste and add salt, if desired.

2. Pour cereal into bowls and top with orange segments. Sprinkle with granola and add maple syrup to taste.

PER SERVING: 299 cal., 14% (41 cal.) from fat; 10 g protein; 4.6 g fat (2.3 g sat.); 55 g carbo (2.6 g fiber); 245 mg sodium; 7.6 mg chol.

Tabbouleh Scramble

Reader Sonya Bavvai, of Palo Alto, California, makes this dish for weekend brunch or Sunday-night dinner and serves it with toasted pita bread. Buy prepared tabbouleh salad at a deli or make it using your own recipe or a boxed mix.

SERVES 4 | **TIME** 15 minutes

8 eggs
2 tbsp. diced drained oil-packed dried tomatoes, plus 1 tsp. oil from container
¾ cup prepared tabbouleh
Salt and freshly ground black pepper
2 to 4 tbsp. crumbled feta cheese

1. In a medium bowl, beat eggs lightly to blend.

2. Set a 10- to 12-in. frying pan over medium-high heat. When hot, add tomatoes and reserved oil, then add eggs and tabbouleh.

3. Cook, stirring constantly, until eggs are done to your liking. Add salt and pepper to taste. Spoon onto plates and sprinkle with feta cheese.

PER SERVING: 222 cal., 61% (135 cal.) from fat; 14 g protein; 15 g fat (4.3 g sat.); 8 g carbo (1.4 g fiber); 403 mg sodium; 429 mg chol.

Huevos Rancheros with the Works

Make the salsa, rice, and beans ahead of time, and you can put a restaurant-style bonanza together in less than half an hour.

SERVES 4 | **TIME** 25 minutes, plus 1 hour for make-ahead rice, salsa, and beans

2 cups Salsa Ranchera (*recipe follows*) or store-bought hot red salsa
Vegetable oil for frying
8 corn tortillas (5 to 6 in. wide)
8 eggs
1 cup coarsely shredded jack cheese, plus extra for sprinkling on beans and rice
¼ cup chopped green onions
3 tbsp. shredded *cotija* or parmesan cheese
2 tsp. dried Mexican oregano or 2 tbsp. chopped fresh cilantro
Chorizo Refried Beans (*recipe follows*)
Mexican Red Rice (*recipe follows*)

1. Put four heavy dinner plates in oven and preheat to 200°. Heat salsa in a small saucepan over low heat, covered.
2. Fill a large frying pan with ½ in. oil and heat over medium heat until handle of a wooden spoon bubbles when you stand it in oil. Remove plates from oven. Using tongs, fry each tortilla 2 seconds per side. Drain against side of pan, then overlap 2 tortillas on each warm plate. Pop in oven to keep warm.
3. Reduce heat to medium low. Cook 4 eggs, gently spooning oil over yolks to set them, about 2 minutes for firm whites and runny yolks.
4. Spoon about 3 tbsp. warm salsa onto each plate of tortillas. Using a slotted spatula or spoon, transfer 2 eggs to each of two warm plates, draining eggs against side of pan first; top each pair of eggs with another 3 tbsp. salsa. Keep warm in oven while frying and plating remaining 4 eggs. (You may have to increase the heat a little for second batch.)
5. Sprinkle eggs with jack cheese, then green onions, *cotija*, and oregano. Spoon beans and rice alongside and top with more jack cheese.

PER SERVING: 661 cal., 36% (238 cal.) from fat; 36 g protein; 26 g fat (11 g sat.); 71g carbo (16 g fiber); sodium N/A; 458 mg chol.

Salsa Ranchera

A good all-purpose salsa. Warm it up while you make the eggs.

MAKES 2 cups | **TIME** 15 minutes

2 tbsp. canola oil
½ white onion, finely chopped
2 cups canned fire-roasted tomatoes (such as Muir Glen brand)
2 garlic cloves, minced
2 serrano chiles, toasted in a dry skillet till brown spots appear all over, stemmed, and finely chopped
Mexican-style hot sauce (optional)

1. Put oil and onion in a medium pot over medium heat and cook until onion softens, about 5 minutes. Meanwhile, put tomatoes, garlic, and chiles in a blender and pulse a few times (leave mixture a bit chunky).
2. Pour tomato mixture into pot with onions and cook 5 minutes over high heat to thicken. Taste and add hot sauce if you like.

PER ¼ CUP: 48 cal., 66% (32 cal.) from fat; 0.7 g protein; 3.5 g fat (0.3 g sat.); 3.5 g carbo (0.7 g fiber); 146 mg sodium; 0 mg chol.

Chorizo Refried Beans

Chorizo makes these velvety beans extra-rich and savory. If you're in a real rush (or don't want chorizo), just microwave the beans, thinned with a bit of water, while you're making the huevos.

SERVES 4 to 6 | **TIME** 15 minutes

6 oz. Mexican chorizo (*see Quick Tip below*), squished out of casing and crumbled
¼ cup canola oil
2 cans (15 oz. each) refried pinto beans
¼ cup shredded jack cheese (optional)

Cook chorizo in oil in a large nonstick frying pan over low heat, mashing, until it starts to brown, about 5 minutes. Add beans and a few tbsp. of water to thin them if necessary. Heat for a few minutes, stirring occasionally. Turn out onto warm plates and top with cheese if you like.
Quick Tip: Good Mexican chorizo is available at butcher shops or Mexican markets. Avoid the very soft chorizo sold in plastic casings; it tends to break down in cooking and can have an unpleasant flavor.

PER SERVING: 310 cal., 61% (189 cal.) from fat; 13 g protein; 21 g fat (4.8 g sat.); 21 g carbo (7.6 g fiber); 546 mg sodium; 25 mg chol.

breakfast & brunch

Mexican Red Rice (*Arroz Rojo*)

This is exactly the kind of red rice you find in Mexican restaurants: slightly sweet, slightly sticky, and lip-smacking good.

MAKES 4 cups; 4 to 6 servings | **TIME** 1 hour

1 cup long-grain rice
2 tbsp. vegetable oil
1 white onion, chopped
1 garlic clove, minced
1 small serrano chile, stemmed and finely chopped
1 can (about 15 oz.) diced or chopped tomatoes, drained
1½ cups reduced-sodium chicken broth
¾ tsp. kosher salt

1. Put rice in a pot and cover with 1 in. cold water. Swish around until water is milky; pour off water. Repeat rinsing twice; then drain rice well in a colander and let dry 15 minutes.

2. Heat oil in a medium saucepan over medium-low heat. Add rice and cook, stirring, 2 minutes; increase heat to medium and cook until rice starts to turn golden, 6 to 8 minutes, stirring often.

3. Meanwhile, in a blender, purée onion, garlic, chile, and chopped tomatoes. Add tomato purée to rice, increase heat to high, and cook, stirring, until purée has been more or less absorbed, about 3 minutes (it will bubble and spatter). Stir in broth and salt and bring to a boil. Reduce heat to low, cover, and simmer until all liquid has been absorbed, 15 to 20 minutes. Let stand 10 minutes.

PER SERVING: 186 cal., 24% (45 cal.) from fat; 4.2 g protein; 5.3 g fat (0.9 g sat.); 30 g carbo (1.3 g fiber); 433 mg sodium; 6.3 mg chol.

The Egg Hunt

How to find the best eggs? Markets offer so many choices: Free-range, natural, cage-free, organic—it can be pretty confusing. Here is a brief guide.

ORGANIC: Hens have never been given antibiotics, and they've been fed organic feed. "Organic" doesn't otherwise describe how they are raised.

OMEGA-3: Hens eat a diet rich in algae, flax seed, or other foods with beneficial omega-3 fatty acids, which end up in their eggs. This label also doesn't describe how they are raised.

NATURAL: A loosely defined marketing term (not USDA-approved); often means the eggs are free-range and organic.

CAGE-FREE: Hens aren't squished into cages, as is common in conventional poultry operations. They can walk freely—but not necessarily outside or in a large space.

FREE-RANGE: Chickens are cage-free, with access to the outdoors. Means widely different things at different farms; an open door at the end of a barn can mean "access," even if the chickens never go through it.

PASTURE-RAISED: A fresh egg from a hen that spends most of its time pecking around in open pasture is a wonderful thing to eat—deeply flavorful, with a bright yellow (sometimes almost orange) yolk and a tender white. Besides having excellent flavor, pasture-raised eggs are most likely better for you than conventional eggs. Several studies suggest that they're higher in omega-3s and vitamins A, B12, and E and lower in fat and cholesterol. And the chicken gets to live as nature intended.

The nutritional difference, according to Jo Robinson, author of *Pasture Perfect* and founder of *eatwild.com*, comes from the chickens' feed. "Fresh grass is a very good source of omega-3 fatty acids and carotenoids," she says. "Eggs from chickens raised on good pasture have an intense yellow-gold color, most pronounced in the spring and early summer, when the grass is at its peak."

The shells, though, can be any color. Whether brown, white, or blue, the color simply indicates the breed of chicken, not what it ate.

The term "pasture-raised" isn't a government-approved definition, but it's generally accepted to mean that the chicken got most of its nutrition from foraging, with some grain to supplement. Although these eggs aren't widely available in stores, you can often find them at farmers' markets and at a few grocery stores (see *localharvest.org* or *eatwild.com* for sources).

Devil's Mess

This is a big, spicy scramble of eggs, hot pork sausage, vegetables, and chiles in which all the flavors remain distinct. It's from Big Sky Café in San Luis Obispo, California.

SERVES 6 | **TIME** 40 minutes

1 tbsp. olive oil
1 medium onion, chopped
½ lb. mushrooms, sliced
½ tsp. *each* kosher salt and freshly ground black pepper
1 cup chopped andouille sausage (about 6 oz.)
10 eggs
1 tbsp. minced garlic (about 3 cloves)
¼ tsp. red chile flakes, or to taste
6 oz. fresh spinach (about 2 qts.)
Hot sauce (optional)

1. Heat oil in a large nonstick frying pan over medium heat. Add onion, mushrooms, salt, and pepper, and cook, stirring often, until onion is light golden, about 10 minutes.
2. Increase heat to medium-high, add sausage, and cook, stirring often, until sausage has browned slightly and released some fat, about 5 minutes.
3. Meanwhile, in a medium bowl, whisk eggs with 3 tbsp. water.
4. Reduce heat to medium and add garlic and chile flakes to sausage mixture. Cook, stirring, until garlic is fragrant, about 1 minute. Add spinach to pan and toss with tongs until it has wilted, about 2 minutes. Transfer sausage-vegetable mixture to a bowl and wipe pan clean.
5. Add eggs to pan and scramble over medium heat just until set, 4 to 5 minutes, then gently stir in sausage-vegetable mixture. Serve with hot sauce if you like.

PER SERVING: 244 cal., 63% (153 cal.) from fat; 17 g protein; 17 g fat (4.9 g sat.); 7 g carbo (1.8 g fiber); 463 mg sodium; 370 mg chol.

Mesa Verde Breakfast Burritos

Here's a different way to enjoy eggs and sausage—wrapped in flour tortillas and topped with a chile-spiked, cheesy sauce.

SERVES 6 | **TIME** 35 to 40 minutes

½ lb. bulk pork sausage
1 onion (½ lb.), finely chopped
1 can (4 oz.) diced green chiles
10 eggs
½ tsp. *each* salt and freshly ground black pepper, plus more to taste
6 flour tortillas (10 in.; *see Quick Tips below*)
2 cups shredded (½ lb.) cheddar cheese
Chili con Queso Salsa *(recipe follows)*

1. In a 10- to 12-in. nonstick frying pan over medium-high heat, stir sausage, onion, and chiles until meat is crumbled and browned, about 15 minutes. Drain off and discard fat.
2. In a bowl, beat eggs to blend with ⅓ cup water, the salt, and pepper. Pour eggs into meat mixture in frying pan; with a wide spatula, stir over medium-high heat, scraping bottom of pan often, until eggs are set to your taste, about 3 minutes for creamy eggs.
3. Lay tortillas flat on a counter. Spoon an equal portion of the meat and egg mixture in a band down the center of each tortilla to within 1 in. of opposite edges. Sprinkle mixture evenly with cheese. To form each burrito, fold the bare 1-in.-wide tortilla edges over filling, then roll snugly from an open edge to enclose. Set burritos slightly apart, seams down, in a 10- by 15-in. pan; seal pan with foil.
4. Bake in a 200° oven until cheese is melted (cut a slit to test), 15 to 20 minutes (*see Quick Tips below*).
5. Set burritos on plates and ladle about ½ cup hot Chili con Queso Salsa on and around each. Season to taste with salt and pepper.

Quick Tips: Use fresh tortillas; stale ones will crack. You can also heat the burritos one at a time on a microwave-safe plate: Cover with microwave-safe plastic wrap and heat in a microwave oven until hot, about 1½ minutes.
Make Ahead: Through step 3, up to 1 day, chilled. Bake in a 325° oven until hot in the center, about 15 minutes.

PER SERVING: 714 cal., 55% (396 cal.) from fat; 39 g protein; 44 g fat (21 g sat.); 40 g carbo (2.8 g fiber); 1,502 mg sodium; 449 mg chol.

breakfast & brunch

Chili con Queso Salsa: In a 2- to 3-qt. pan over medium-high heat, melt 2 tbsp. **butter**. Add 2 tbsp. **flour** and stir until bubbling. Remove pan from heat and whisk in 2 cups **chicken broth** and 1 can (4 oz.) diced **green chiles**. Stir over high heat until boiling, 3 to 4 minutes. Add 1½ cups shredded (6 oz.) **cheddar cheese** and stir until melted. Serve hot, or let cool, cover, and chill up to 1 day; if chilled, heat, stirring, over high heat until steaming. Makes about 3 cups.

PER ½-CUP SERVING: 174 cal., 67% (117 cal.) from fat; 10 g protein; 13 g fat (8.4 g sat.); 3.5 g carbo (0.3 g fiber); 355 mg sodium; 40 mg chol.

New Mexican Red Chile Breakfast Burritos

Smothered in an earthy, medium-hot red chile sauce, these morning marvels are stuffed with scrambled eggs, country-style hash browns, and chorizo. Try them for dinner too.

recipe pictured *on page* **550**

MAKES 6 burritos | **TIME** 1¼ hours

1 tsp. corn oil
1 cup chopped yellow onion
2 garlic cloves, minced
2 tbsp. flour
⅔ cup ground New Mexico or California chiles
   (see Quick Tips, right)
1½ cups chicken broth
Salt
1½ lbs. thin-skinned potatoes
¾ lb. Mexican chorizo *(see Quick Tips, right)* or
   10 slices bacon
6 flour tortillas (10 in. wide)
Freshly ground black pepper
8 eggs
1 cup shredded sharp cheddar cheese
½ cup sour cream (optional)
⅓ cup sliced green onions

1. In a 1½- to 2-qt. pan over medium heat, heat oil; add yellow onion and garlic and cook, stirring, until onion is limp, 6 to 8 minutes. Add flour and ground chiles; toast, stirring, 1 to 2 minutes, until fragrant. Add broth and 1½ cups water and cook, stirring, until sauce is smooth and bubbling, about 8 minutes. Reduce heat to low and simmer, stirring occasionally, 10 minutes. Season to taste with salt. Set aside and keep warm.

2. Peel potatoes, halve lengthwise, and cut crosswise into ⅓-in.-thick slices. Put in a 2- to 3-qt. pan with water to cover and bring to a boil over high heat. Reduce heat and simmer, covered, until tender when pierced, about 6 minutes. Drain.

3. Meanwhile, remove casings from chorizo and crumble into a 10- to 12-in. frying pan (or cut bacon into 1½-in. pieces and put in pan). Over medium-high heat, stir often until meat is brown and crisp, 8 to 10 minutes. With a slotted spoon, lift meat to paper towels; drain fat from pan, reserving 4 tbsp. (If chorizo is very finely crumbled, drain fat through a strainer.) If necessary, add vegetable oil to equal 4 tbsp.

4. Preheat oven to 350°. Seal tortillas in foil and warm in the oven until hot, about 10 minutes.

5. Return 2 tbsp. reserved fat to frying pan. Over medium-high heat, add potatoes and turn occasionally until well browned, about 10 minutes (you may need to add another 1 tbsp. fat to pan). Season to taste with salt and pepper, remove from pan, and keep warm.

6. In a medium bowl, beat eggs to blend. Coat pan with 1 tbsp. fat. Add eggs; cook, stirring, over medium heat until softly set, about 2 minutes. Add salt and pepper to taste.

7. Lay tortillas flat. Toward one edge of each, fill with potatoes, eggs, and chorizo. Fold over sides and roll up tightly to enclose. Put each on a rimmed ovenproof plate and ladle chile sauce on top. Sprinkle with cheddar and bake just until cheese melts, 2 to 3 minutes.

8. Dollop sour cream on burritos, if you like, and sprinkle with green onions.

Quick Tips: For especially rich chile flavor, buy ground Dixon or Chimayo chiles, available from *peppahead.com*. It's crucial to use fresh chile powder in this recipe—anything over a year old will taste dusty and flat. Good Mexican chorizo is available at butcher shops or Mexican markets. Avoid the very soft chorizo sold in plastic casings; it tends to break down in cooking and can have an unpleasant flavor.

PER BURRITO: 618 cal., 44% (270 cal.) from fat; 26 g protein; 30 g fat (10 g sat.); 62 g carbo; 926 mg sodium; 317 mg chol.

Chorizo Soft Tacos

Why wait for lunch to have a taco? Scramble up some eggs and good Mexican chorizo, and fold them up in warm tortillas.

SERVES 4 | **TIME** 50 minutes

1 tbsp. vegetable oil
1 lb. Mexican chorizo *(see Quick Tip below)*
1 cup diced (¼ in.) peeled russet potatoes
¼ cup sliced mushrooms
1 tbsp. *each* chopped green onion and minced jalapeño chile
2 eggs
1 cup shredded jack cheese
Flour or corn tortillas
Shredded lettuce, sour cream, salsa, and chopped onions

1. Heat oil into a 10- to 12-in. frying pan over medium heat until hot. Add chorizo, potatoes, mushrooms, onion, and jalapeño; cook, stirring often, until meat is well browned and potatoes are tender when pierced, about 10 minutes (if potatoes aren't tender, add ¼ cup water, cover pan, and cook until tender, 8 to 12 minutes longer).
2. Pour in eggs, beaten to blend, and cook, stirring often, until eggs are firm, 1 to 2 minutes.
3. Remove pan from heat and stir in cheese. Serve with warm tortillas and lettuce, sour cream, salsa, and chopped onions.
Quick Tip: Unlike Spanish chorizo, which is usually cured and seasoned with brick-red Spanish paprika, Mexican chorizo is soft and uncooked, and seasoned with chiles and vinegar. Buy the best-quality lean chorizo you can find, preferably from a butcher or Mexican market. Avoid the kind that is very soft, very orange, and sold in plastic casings—it tends to break down too much in cooking. (If you can't find good chorizo, substitute another spicy uncooked sausage.)

PER SERVING: 745 cal. 53% (395 cal.) from fat; 37 g protein; 44 g fat (16 g sat.); 49 g carbo (3.4 g fiber); 895 mg sodium; 218 mg chol.

Scrambled-egg Taco (*Tacone*)

At Las Ventanas al Paraíso, a resort in Los Cabos, Mexico, the substantial breakfast burrito is called a *tacone* (big taco). Serve it with hot refried or cooked whole pinto beans.

SERVES 4 | **TIME** 25 minutes

9 eggs
¼ tsp. salt, plus more to taste
1 tbsp. olive oil
¼ lb. cooked ham, chopped
¼ lb. jalapeño chiles, seeds and ribs removed if you like, and chopped *(see Quick Tip below)*
1 onion (6 oz.), chopped
1 Roma tomato (¼ lb.), cored and chopped
1 cup shredded (¼ lb.) Oaxaca or jack cheese
4 flour tortillas (9 to 10 in. wide)
Tomato salsa
Freshly ground black pepper

1. In a medium bowl, whisk eggs, ¼ cup water, and salt until blended.
2. Set a 10- to 12-in. frying pan over high heat. Add oil, ham, chiles, onion, and tomato; cook, stirring often, until onion is limp, about 5 minutes. Reduce heat to medium-high. Add egg mixture, then sprinkle evenly with cheese. When a thin layer of egg is set on pan bottom, about 30 seconds, push cooked egg toward one side of pan with a wide spatula, letting uncooked egg flow underneath. Continue cooking and pushing egg mixture until eggs are softly set but still moist, 3 to 4 minutes total. Stir to turn eggs over. Remove pan from heat.
3. Wrap tortillas in paper towels and microwave just until hot and steamy, 15 to 30 seconds. Lay tortillas, one at a time, on a board and spoon about a fourth of egg mixture across each, just below center. Fold over sides and roll up tightly to enclose. Cut each burrito in half if you like and serve with salsa. Sprinkle with pepper.
Quick Tip: Remove all or some of seeds and ribs from chiles for less heat. If your skin is extra-sensitive, wear rubber gloves to protect your hands.

PER SERVING: 561 cal., 48% (270 cal.) from fat; 33 g protein; 30 g fat (10 g sat.); 39 g carbo (3 g fiber); 1,130 mg sodium; 525 mg chol.

breakfast & brunch

Eggs on Potato Chips

San Francisco food writer and historian Niloufer Ichaporia King, author of *My Bombay Kitchen: Traditional and Modern Parsi Home Cooking*, is known for her wonderful food. This dish never fails to enchant anyone who makes it. Have it for breakfast, lunch, or dinner.

SERVES 4 | **TIME** 30 minutes

1 tbsp. ghee (Indian-style clarified butter; *see Quick Tips below*); or a mixture of ½ tbsp. vegetable oil and ½ tbsp. butter
1 small onion, finely chopped
1 small garlic clove, minced, then mashed into a paste with ¼ tsp. kosher salt
½ tsp. finely shredded fresh ginger
2 or 3 fresh green arbol, Thai, or serrano chiles, stemmed and finely chopped
½ cup roughly chopped cilantro
4 large handfuls plain potato chips from a just-opened bag *(see Quick Tips below)*
4 eggs
Kosher or sea salt

1. Heat butter in a sturdy, well-seasoned medium frying pan, preferably cast iron, over medium heat. Add onion and cook, stirring occasionally, until softened and just beginning to brown. Stir in garlic paste, ginger, and chiles. Stir for a moment or two, then add cilantro. Crumble in chips, tossing or stirring contents of pan to combine them thoroughly.
2. Make 4 "nests" in surface of potato-chip mixture—they don't need to be perfect hollows—and crack an egg into each. Pour 1 tbsp. water down inside edge of pan to generate some steam. Cover skillet tightly and reduce heat to low. Let eggs steam just long enough to set whites (6 to 8 minutes; gently touch one with a spoon to see if it's done the way you'd like). Season to taste with salt and turn out onto waiting plates.
Quick Tips: To make ghee, heat at least ½ cup butter in a small saucepan over low heat until melted. Reduce heat to very low; heat butter until solids drop to the bottom of pan and have turned toasty but not dark brown (butter will smell nutty). Remove from heat, skim foam from surface, and carefully pour butter through a fine-mesh strainer into a jar, leaving solids behind. Ghee keeps at room temperature for 6 weeks, and up to 6 months chilled. Use best-quality potato chips—medium-thick and not too brown; otherwise the dish will taste burned.

PER SERVING: 384 cal., 61% (234 cal.) from fat; 10 g protein; 26 g fat (9 g sat.); 30 g carbo (2.9 g fiber); 489 mg sodium; 220 mg chol.

Hangtown Fry

We reached deep into our archives, back to 1969, for this recipe from Don Keebler. The parsley is our addition.

SERVES 1 | **TIME** 20 minutes

2 slices bacon
2 eggs
1 tbsp. milk
Salt and freshly ground black pepper to taste
1 tbsp. chopped flat-leaf parsley (optional)
Dash or two of Worcestershire sauce
5 oz. shucked medium oysters (at least 6 oysters)
Toast
Lemon wedges

1. In a frying pan over medium-high heat, cook bacon until brown and crisp; transfer to paper towels to drain.
2. Meanwhile, whisk together eggs, milk, salt, pepper, parsley if using, and Worcestershire. Chop oysters into ¾-in. pieces, add to bacon drippings, and cook about 1 minute; transfer to bowl of eggs.
3. Return bacon to pan, spacing slices about 3 in. apart, Pour egg mixture over top and, using 1 or 2 wide spatulas, keep the egg mixture pulled in toward the center of pan as it cooks. When omelet is set on bottom, carefully turn over, trying to keep it as intact as possible. This should expose the bacon on top. Cook about 1½ minutes longer. Transfer bacon-topped omelet to a warm plate and serve with toast and lemon wedges.

PER SERVING: 475 cal., 65% (307 cal.) from fat; 32 g protein; 34 g fat (11 g sat.); 8.9 g carbo (0 g fiber); 681 mg sodium; 526 mg chol.

The Story of Hangtown Fry

The pretty little town of Placerville, California, in the Sierra Nevada foothills near Lake Tahoe, went by the name of Hangtown during the relatively lawless Gold Rush because of three famous hangings that were conducted there. There are many stories about the origin of Hangtown Fry; the most oft-told one describes a just-struck-it-rich prospector rushing into the town's El Dorado Hotel, plunking his nuggets on the bar, and ordering the priciest dish in the place. On the spot, the cook invented a concoction of the three most expensive items in the larder: oysters (hauled in daily from San Francisco), bacon (shipped from the East), and eggs (also brought in daily).

No matter what the story, all recipes for Hangtown Fry agree on the inclusion of eggs and oysters. In fact, these days just about any combination of the two may be called Hangtown something-or-other.

Paprika Tomatoes with Poached Eggs (*Shakshouka*)

Traditionally, cooks in Tunisia and Israel use a lot of olive oil when making this one-pan tomato and egg meal (which is good for dinner too). We've cut back the amount of oil, but feel free to add more if you like. Serve *shakshouka* with crusty bread.

recipe pictured on page 547

SERVES 2 | **TIME** 45 minutes

1½ tsp. coriander seeds
1 tsp. cumin seeds
1½ tbsp. sweet Spanish or Hungarian paprika
½ tsp. kosher salt, plus more to taste
3 large garlic cloves, peeled
1 large poblano chile, seeds and ribs removed and chopped
1 to 2 tbsp. extra-virgin olive oil, divided
2 tbsp. tomato paste
1½ lbs. Roma tomatoes, halved lengthwise and cored
4 eggs
Freshly ground black pepper

1. Put coriander, cumin, paprika, and salt in a mortar and pound until crushed, or seal in a plastic bag and crush with a rolling pin. Add garlic and pound into a paste. Set aside.
2. In a 10-in. frying pan over medium heat, cook chile in 1 tbsp. oil, stirring often, until well browned, 10 to 12 minutes. Add spice mixture and tomato paste and cook, stirring, until fragrant, about 1 minute. Stir in ¾ cup water, then tomatoes. Cook, turning tomatoes occasionally, until softened, 10 to 20 minutes; add more water, ¼ cup at a time, if mixture starts to get dry (you should see juice around tomatoes).
3. With a wooden spoon, make four depressions in tomato mixture and crack an egg into each. Season with salt and pepper. Cover and cook until eggs are set but yolks are still runny, about 5 minutes.
4. Drizzle shakshouka with 1 tbsp. oil if you like, then scoop onto plates.

PER SERVING: 372 cal., 53% (198 cal.) from fat; 19 g protein; 22 g fat (4.8 g sat.); 30 g carbo (6.6 g fiber); 598 mg sodium; 424 mg chol.

Poached Eggs on Polenta with Pesto and Crisp Prosciutto (*Uova Benedetto*)

A recipe from reader Frank Darlington, of Seattle, *Uova Benedetto* is eggs Benedict's robust Italian cousin. It's comforting and elegant at the same time—the kind of thing to make for weekend brunch.

recipe pictured on page 544

SERVES 4 | **TIME** 1 hour

1 cup polenta
¼ cup butter, divided, plus more if needed
8 to 12 thin slices prosciutto
4 eggs
Basic Pesto, store-bought or homemade (*recipe follows*)

1. Butter an 8- or 9-in. square baking pan. In a 3- to 4-qt. pan over high heat, bring 3 cups water to a boil. Gradually stir in polenta. Reduce heat and simmer gently, uncovered, stirring frequently to prevent sticking, until mixture is very thick, about 25 minutes. Stir in 2 tbsp. butter. Spoon polenta into pan; spread evenly and let stand at least 10 minutes.
2. Cut polenta into four squares and gently remove from pan with a wide spatula. Melt remaining 2 tbsp. butter in a large frying pan over medium-high heat. Add polenta squares and cook, turning once, until crisp and lightly browned on both sides, about 10 minutes. Add more butter, if needed, to prevent sticking. Put on a warm platter; keep warm. Add prosciutto to pan, adding more butter to pan if needed, and cook until meat is lightly browned. Remove and keep warm.
3. Bring a large, deep frying pan of lightly salted water to a boil. Reduce heat to maintain a steady simmer. Crack 1 egg into a glass measuring cup, hold spout close to water's surface, and let egg slip gently into water. Repeat with rest of eggs. Cook until eggs are softly set, about 3 minutes.
4. Place 2 or 3 slices prosciutto on each polenta square. Gently lift out eggs with a slotted spoon and set a poached egg on each square. Spoon pesto over the top. **Make Ahead:** Through step 1, up to 1 day, chilled.

PER SERVING: 741 cal., 56% (414 cal.) from fat; 26 g protein; 46 g fat (17 g sat.); 58 g carbo (8.7 g fiber); 885 mg sodium; 287 mg chol.

Basic Pesto: In a blender or food processor, combine 1 cup loosely packed **basil leaves**, ½ cup finely shredded **parmesan cheese**, ⅓ cup **olive oil**, and 1 **garlic clove**, minced or pressed. Process until basil is finely chopped. Makes ½ cup.

PER TBSP.: 111 cal., 89% (99 cal.) from fat; 3 g protein; 11 g fat (2.4 g sat.); 1 g carbo (0.6 g fiber); 114 mg sodium; 4.8 mg chol.

breakfast & brunch

Eggs Benedict with Crab

If you have leftover crab on hand, there's no better use for it than this. Rich and creamy, bright with lemon, eggs Benedict with crab also makes a great supper, paired with a green salad. For an even richer dish, top each muffin half with a few slices of avocado before adding the crab.

SERVES 6 | **TIME** 45 minutes

HOLLANDAISE SAUCE
6 egg yolks
¼ cup fresh lemon juice
2 tbsp. Dijon mustard
1½ cups unsalted butter, melted
½ tsp. salt, plus more to taste
⅛ tsp. *each* freshly ground black pepper and cayenne, plus more to taste
EGGS
6 English muffins
3 cups shelled cooked Dungeness crab *(see Dungeness Crab 101, page 340)*, at room temperature
12 eggs

1. Make hollandaise sauce: In bottom of a double boiler or in a medium saucepan, bring 1 in. water to a simmer over high heat and adjust heat to maintain simmer. Put egg yolks, lemon juice, and mustard in top of a double boiler or in a round-bottomed medium bowl and set over simmering water. Whisk yolk mixture to blend.

2. Whisking constantly, add butter in a slow, steady stream (it should take about 90 seconds). Cook sauce, whisking, until it reaches 140° on a candy thermometer, then adjust heat to maintain temperature (remove from simmering water if necessary). Add salt, pepper, and cayenne and continue whisking until thick, about 3 minutes. Adjust seasonings to taste. Remove from stove and pour into a thermos to keep warm.

3. Preheat oven to 450°. Split English muffins and set on a baking sheet in a single layer. Bake until toasted, about 5 minutes.

4. Put two muffin halves on each plate and top them with crab.

5. Bring a large, deep frying pan of lightly salted water to a boil. Reduce heat to maintain a steady simmer. Crack 1 egg at a time into a glass measuring cup, hold spout close to water's surface, and let egg slip gently into water. Poach eggs, in two batches to keep them from crowding, 3 to 4 minutes for soft-cooked. Gently lift out eggs with a slotted spoon, pat dry with a paper towel, and place 1 egg on each crab-topped muffin half.

6. Top each egg with 2 to 3 tbsp. hollandaise sauce and serve hot.

PER SERVING: 833 cal., 68% (567 cal.) from fat; 36 g protein; 63 g fat (34 g sat.); 28 g carbo (1 g fiber); 949 mg sodium; 837 mg chol.

Poached Eggs with Smoked Trout and Potato Hash

Poaching is an easy way to enjoy the flavor of fresh eggs. These are served over a simple oven-roasted hash.

SERVES 2 | **TIME** 40 minutes

¾ lb. Yukon Gold potatoes, cut into ½-in. cubes
½ yellow onion (about ¼ lb.), chopped
1 tbsp. olive oil
¼ tsp. sea or kosher salt, plus more to taste
½ tsp. sweet smoked Spanish paprika
Freshly ground black pepper
2½ oz. skinned smoked trout fillet
2 tbsp. chopped dill
2 tsp. fresh lemon juice
4 eggs

1. Preheat oven to 400°. On a rimmed baking pan, mix potatoes with onion, oil, salt, paprika, and a few grinds of pepper. Bake, stirring a couple of times, until potatoes are tender, 20 to 25 minutes.

2. Break trout fillet into bite-size pieces as you add it to baking pan. Add dill and lemon juice and mix well, scraping up any browned bits from bottom of pan. Season hash with additional salt and pepper if you like and cover with foil to keep warm.

3. Bring a large, deep frying pan of lightly salted water to a boil. Reduce heat to maintain a steady simmer. Crack 1 egg into a glass measuring cup, hold spout close to water's surface, and let egg slip gently into water. Repeat with rest of eggs. Cook until eggs are softly set, about 3 minutes.

4. Divide hash between plates. Using a slotted spoon, gently lift out poached eggs, setting 2 on each plateful of hash; sprinkle with pepper to taste.

PER SERVING: 429 cal., 42% (180 cal.) from fat; 25 g protein; 20 g fat (4.9 g sat.); 36 g carbo (2.9 g fiber); 724 mg sodium; 431 mg chol.

Folding a Plain Cheese Omelet

1. As egg mixture sets on pan bottom, lift edge with a spatula and tilt pan to let uncooked egg flow underneath. Continue the process, working around the pan sides, until no uncooked egg mixture flows underneath and the top is still moist.

2. Sprinkle cheese in a strip down the center of the omelet, in line with the pan handle. With the spatula, fold one side over the strip of cheese.

3. Run spatula under omelet to loosen, and tip pan to slide omelet, folded edge first, onto a warm plate. Flip remaining edge over filling as omelet leaves the pan.

Folded Cheese Omelet

You're limited only by your imagination when it comes to omelet fillings. We provide the foundation recipe below, followed by a few filling ideas to get you started.

SERVES 1 | **TIME** 5 minutes

3 eggs
1 tbsp. whipping cream or milk
⅛ tsp. salt
1 tbsp. butter
⅓ cup shredded cheddar or Swiss cheese

1. In a bowl, whisk eggs, cream, and salt just until blended; do not overbeat.

2. Heat an 8-in. nonstick frying pan with sloping sides over medium-high heat for 1 minute. When hot, add butter and tilt pan to coat evenly. When butter is foamy, pour egg mixture into pan and swirl to spread it out to edges of pan.

3. As the egg mixture begins to set on bottom, lift one edge with a heatproof flexible spatula and tilt pan to let uncooked mixture on top flow underneath. Continue lifting edges of omelet and tilting pan, working your way around all sides, until no more uncooked egg mixture flows underneath and the top is just a little moist, about 2 minutes total.

4. Sprinkle cheese either in a strip down the middle, if you plan on folding the omelet into thirds, or over one half, if you're folding it in half. Loosen omelet with

spatula. For a third-fold, fold one edge over strip of cheese in the middle; tip pan to slide omelet, folded edge first, onto a warm plate, flipping remaining edge over filling as omelet leaves pan. For a half-fold, tip pan to slide omelet, cheese side first, onto warm plate; flip bare half over cheese as omelet leaves pan.

PER SERVING: 520 cal., 76% (396 cal.) from fat; 28 g protein; 44 g fat (23 g sat.); 2.7 g carbo (0 g fiber); 836 mg sodium; 724 mg chol.

Great Omelet Fillings

You can dress up a plain omelet in a mind-boggling number of ways. Some fillings seem natural for breakfast or brunch, others for lunch. And there's nothing like a gooey cheese-filled omelet for a late-night supper. Here are some of our favorite simple combos.

• Layer diced **roasted red peppers**, shredded **Swiss chard**, and grated **pecorino cheese**.

• Sauté thinly sliced **leeks** in **butter**; add along with sliced **Camembert or brie cheese**.

• Cut **cream cheese** into cubes and pair with sliced **green onions** and a couple of slices of **smoked salmon**.

• Make a hearty creation with a few slices of cooked **potato**, some **ricotta cheese**, and plenty of freshly ground **black pepper**.

• Liven up any omelet by adding 1 to 2 tbsp. chopped **herbs** to the egg mixture. Try thyme, parsley, chives, tarragon, and chervil, alone or combined.

Chiles Rellenos and Eggs with Tomato-Jalapeño Salsa

Cafe Pasqual's in Santa Fe is known for its inventive take on classic Mexican cuisine, and this breakfast twist on chiles rellenos is a good example. The restaurant uses Anaheim chiles, but we opted for poblanos because they're easier to work with. Still, roast a couple of extras in case any get torn when you peel them.

SERVES 6 | **TIME** 2 hours

SALSA

3 ripe medium tomatoes
¼ medium white onion, unpeeled
1 garlic clove, unpeeled
½ to 1 jalapeño chile
1 tbsp. finely chopped cilantro
1 tsp. *each* fresh lime juice and kosher salt

CHILES & EGGS

6 poblano chiles
¾ cup finely chopped onion
1½ cups shredded jack cheese
Vegetable oil for frying
11 eggs, divided
⅓ cup plus ½ cup flour
¼ tsp. kosher salt

1. Make salsa: Preheat oven to 400°. Line a baking sheet with foil and top with tomatoes, onion, garlic, and jalapeño. Bake until softened, about 25 minutes, turning ingredients halfway through baking. Remove from oven and let cool.

2. Core tomatoes, peel onion and garlic, and stem jalapeño. Put vegetables, cilantro, lime juice, and salt in a food processor and pulse just until chunky and combined. Transfer salsa to a bowl.

3. Prepare chiles: Preheat broiler. Arrange poblanos on foil-lined baking sheet in a single layer and broil 2 to 3 in. from heat until blackened, turning as needed, 10 to 12 minutes. Put chiles in a bowl, cover, and let stand 10 minutes to loosen skins.

4. Peel chiles, pull out stems (keeping chiles as intact as possible), and remove seeds with a spoon or your fingers. Blot with paper towels.

5. In a medium bowl, combine chopped onion and cheese. Squeeze handfuls of mixture to form six narrow logs. Carefully stuff logs into chiles through stem ends. Preheat oven to 200°.

6. Pour oil into a large pot to a depth of 2 to 3 in. and heat to 375° on a deep-fry or candy thermometer. Meanwhile, separate 5 eggs. With an electric mixer,

beat whites in a large bowl until soft peaks form. In another bowl, whisk yolks with ⅓ cup flour and the salt. Add a spoonful of whites to yolk mixture and whisk to combine, then gently fold yolk mixture into whites just until incorporated.

7. Put remaining ½ cup flour in a shallow bowl. Using tongs or your hands, dip a chile first into flour, then into egg batter, turning gently to coat. Gently lower chile into hot oil. Repeat with a second chile. Cook until browned, gently turning once with tongs, about 4 minutes total. Transfer chiles to a baking sheet lined with paper towels and keep warm in oven. Cook remaining chiles same way.

8. To poach remaining 6 eggs, bring a large, deep frying pan of lightly salted water to a boil. Reduce heat to maintain a steady simmer. Crack 1 egg into a glass measuring cup, hold spout close to water's surface, and let egg slip gently into water. Repeat with rest of eggs. Cook until eggs are done the way you like, 3 to 5 minutes for soft yolks with firm whites or 7 to 10 minutes for firm yolks and whites. Using a slotted spoon, transfer eggs to a plate.

9. Divide chiles among plates, top each with a poached egg and a spoonful of salsa, and serve remaining salsa on the side.

Make Ahead: Salsa, 1 day, chilled. Chiles, through step 5, up to 1 day, chilled.

PER SERVING: 396 cal., 55% (216 cal.) from fat; 21 g protein; 24 g fat (8.4 g sat.); 25 g carbo (2.9 g fiber); 522 mg sodium; 374 mg chol.

In Praise of Stuffed Chiles

Here and in Mexico, we've come across chiles stuffed with cheese, meat, fish, shellfish, vegetables, and other, less familiar ingredients. Sometimes the chiles are dipped in batter and fried; sometimes they are grilled, or baked with a topping, or layered with a filling. And the chile itself isn't always the same. Sometimes it's spicy; most times it's not.

In fact, almost anything goes—which troubles culinary traditionalists who favor specific combinations or a certain structure. To cooks like us, such flexibility is extremely appealing.

No matter what permutation, any chile relleno that oozes melted cheese is supremely comforting and cozy. It's as good for dinner as it is for brunch, paired with a crisp salad, more warm tortillas, and a glass of dry Riesling.

Baked Chiles Rellenos

Instead of coating each stuffed chile with egg and then painstakingly frying them, we laid all the chiles in a baking dish and surrounded them with rich, cheesy eggs. Bonus: You can make the dish a day ahead.

SERVES 8 | **TIME** 1¼ hours

8 poblano chiles
¾ lb. fresh Mexican chorizo *(see Quick Tips below)*
1 cup crumbled *cotija* cheese *(see Quick Tips below)*
1 tsp. minced oregano leaves
12 eggs
⅓ cup flour
1 tsp. baking powder
½ tsp. salt
1 cup finely shredded jack cheese, divided

1. Preheat broiler. Lay chiles in a single layer on a baking sheet. Broil about 4 in. from heat until chiles are blistering and black, about 5 minutes. Turn chiles over and broil until blistering and black all over, about 5 minutes. Put chiles in a large metal bowl and cover with foil or plastic wrap. Let sit 15 minutes.
2. Peel chiles and discard skins. Cut off stem ends and discard; remove seeds and ribs. Set chiles aside on layers of paper towels to dry.
3. Meanwhile, in a large frying pan over medium-high heat, cook chorizo, stirring occasionally to break up meat, until cooked through, about 4 minutes.
4. Preheat oven to 375°. In a large bowl, mix chorizo, *cotija*, and oregano. Stuff chiles with mixture and lay them in an 8- by 12-in. baking dish.
5. In a large bowl, whisk eggs until uniform in color and texture. Whisk in flour, baking powder, and salt. Sprinkle chiles with half the jack cheese. Pour egg mixture over chiles and sprinkle with remaining jack.
6. Bake until top starts to brown and eggs are set but still soft, about 30 minutes.
Quick Tips: Good Mexican chorizo is available at butcher shops or Latino markets. Avoid the very soft chorizo sold in plastic casings; it tends to break down in cooking and can have an unpleasant flavor. Find cotija, an aged, crumbly white Mexican cheese, at Latino markets and well-stocked grocery stores. If you can't find it, substitute finely shredded parmesan.
Make Ahead: Through step 5, up to 1 day, chilled (bake an extra 5 to 10 minutes).

PER SERVING: 444 cal., 63% (279 cal.) from fat; 28 g protein; 31 g fat (13 g sat.); 14 g carbo (1.4 g fiber); 1,093 mg sodium; 378 mg chol.

Swiss Chard and Ricotta Salata Egg Bake

Egg bakes are a brunch maker's best friend, since they're assembled the night before and then popped briefly into the oven the next morning.

SERVES 6 to 8 | **TIME** 1 hour

1 bunch Swiss chard
2 tbsp. butter
1 tsp. salt, divided
2 garlic cloves, minced
¼ tsp. white pepper
1½ cups shredded ricotta salata cheese
    (see Quick Tip below)
18 eggs
½ cup heavy whipping cream
¾ cup finely shredded gruyère cheese

1. Trim stem ends of Swiss chard. Cut out central stalk from leaves with a V-shaped slice or two that follow tapering shape of stalk. Thinly slice stalks and set aside. Chop leaves.
2. In a large frying pan over medium-high heat, melt butter. Add chard stalks and ½ tsp. salt. Cook, stirring occasionally, until tender. Add chard leaves and garlic. Continue to cook, stirring occasionally, until leaves are tender. Stir in pepper. Set aside and let cool slightly.
3. Butter a 9- by 12-in. baking dish. Spread cooked chard on bottom and sprinkle with ricotta salata. In a large bowl, whisk together eggs, cream, and remaining ½ tsp. salt. Pour over chard and ricotta salata. Sprinkle with gruyère, cover with plastic wrap, and chill overnight.
4. Preheat oven to 350°. Bake until set and top is golden brown, about 25 minutes. Serve hot, cut into squares.
Quick Tip: Find ricotta salata—a firm, slightly salty, mild sheep's-milk cheese—at well-stocked grocery stores or a cheese shop.
Make Ahead: Through step 3, up to 1 day ahead, chilled. Increase bake time to 40 to 45 minutes.

PER SERVING: 409 cal., 70% (288 cal.) from fat; 25 g protein; 32 g fat (16 g sat.); 6 g carbo (1 g fiber); 1,144 mg sodium; 611 mg chol.

Scallop-Bacon Tart

This is a wonderfully decadent brunch or supper dish. We recommend serving it with a creamy, full-flavored California Chardonnay or white Burgundy. Or, for a refreshing contrast, try a Chenin Blanc.

SERVES 6 | **TIME** 1¼ hours

PRESS-IN PASTRY
½ cup butter, cut into chunks
1½ cups flour
1 egg
FILLING
5 slices bacon, chopped
½ cup sliced green onions
1 tsp. minced fresh tarragon or ½ tsp. dried tarragon
½ lb. sea scallops
1½ tsp. cornstarch
2 eggs
¾ cup half-and-half
¼ tsp. *each* salt and freshly ground black pepper

1. Preheat oven to 325°. In a food processor (or bowl), process (or with your fingertips rub) butter into flour until mixture has consistency of fine crumbs. Add egg and process or stir with a fork until dough holds together. Press dough over bottom and up sides of a 10-in. tart pan with a removable rim. Bake until pale gold, about 25 minutes. Increase oven temperature to 400°.
2. Meanwhile, cook bacon, stirring often, in a 10- to 12-in. frying pan over medium-high heat until browned, 3 to 5 minutes. With a slotted spoon, transfer to paper towels. Discard all but ½ tbsp. fat from pan.
3. Add green onions to pan and cook until wilted, about 1 minute. Stir in tarragon. Spoon onion mixture into tart shell and spread evenly.
4. If needed, cut scallops horizontally so they're each about ½ in. thick. In a bowl, mix scallops with cornstarch to coat. Arrange on onion mixture.
5. In small bowl, whisk eggs, half-and-half, salt, and pepper to blend. Pour into tart shell over scallops. Scatter bacon on top.
6. Bake tart until custard no longer jiggles in center when pan is gently shaken, 22 to 25 minutes.
7. Let tart cool for 10 minutes. Run a knife inside pan rim, then remove rim. Cut tart into wedges.

PER SERVING: 403 cal., 56% (225 cal.) from fat; 16 g protein; 25 g fat (14 g sat.); 28 g carbo (1.1 g fiber); 448 mg sodium; 176 mg chol.

Creamy Baked Eggs with Asparagus and Pecorino

As soon as they come out of the oven, serve these smooth, rich eggs, with toast alongside.

SERVES 2 | **TIME** 1 hour

6 thin asparagus spears, tough stem ends trimmed
4 eggs
¼ cup *each* milk and lightly packed shredded pecorino cheese
Pinch of sea or kosher salt
Freshly ground black pepper

1. Preheat oven to 275°. Lightly butter two 4-oz. (½-cup) ramekins or ovenproof bowls and set in a baking pan just big enough to hold ramekins.
2. Slice asparagus thinly on a diagonal. Bring a small pot of water to a boil. Add asparagus; cook until just tender-crisp, 1 to 2 minutes, and transfer to a colander. Keep water boiling, covered.
3. In a medium bowl, beat eggs with milk until smooth. Stir in pecorino and salt. Divide mixture between prepared ramekins. Top each with half of asparagus and sprinkle with pepper.
4. Set ramekins in baking pan and put in oven. With oven door open, carefully pour the hot water into baking pan up to the level of eggs in ramekins. Bake until eggs are set in centers (touch to test), about 45 minutes.
5. To remove ramekins, carefully pull oven rack out partway; lift ramekins from pan with tongs and set aside. Push rack with pan back into the oven to cool.

PER SERVING: 236 cal., 65% (153 cal.) from fat; 20 g protein; 17 g fat (7.4 g sat.); 3.5 g carbo (0.3 g fiber); 384 mg sodium; 445 mg chol.

Layered Torta with Ham, Provolone, Spinach, and Herbs

This stunning savory pastry is loaded with flavor—it's a special dish that looks complicated but is actually quite easy to make.

SERVES 12 | **TIME** 2½ hours, plus 4 hours to chill and cool

DOUGH

2 cups flour
1 cup chilled unsalted butter, cubed
¾ tsp. salt

FILLING

2 tsp. olive oil
1 tbsp. minced garlic
1 lb. spinach leaves
1 tsp. kosher salt, divided
11 eggs
2 tsp. unsalted butter
1 tbsp. chopped oregano leaves
½ lb. sliced provolone cheese
1 cup basil leaves, stemmed and torn into bite-size pieces
¾ lb. thinly sliced smoked ham
1 jar (8 oz.) roasted red peppers, rinsed, drained, and patted dry (see Quick Tip, right)

1. Make dough: In a food processor, pulse flour, butter, and salt until butter is pea-size. Add ½ cup very cold water and pulse just until dough comes together, adding another tbsp. water if needed. Turn dough onto a work surface and press into a mound. Cut off one-fourth of dough, form both portions into flat disks, wrap airtight, and chill at least 1 hour.

2. Put larger piece of dough on a floured work surface. Roll into a circle about 14 in. across. Butter bottom and sides of an 8-in. springform pan. Lay circle of dough in pan, pressing into bottom and up sides and allowing excess dough to hang over edge.

3. Roll out smaller piece of dough a little bigger than pan, then cut to size of pan. Transfer pan-size circle to a plate, discarding scraps. Chill shell and circle until ready to use.

4. Make filling: Heat oil in a large nonstick pan over medium-high heat. Add garlic and cook, stirring, until fragrant, about 1 minute. Add half of spinach and cook, stirring, until it starts to wilt. Add remaining spinach and cook until all the leaves are wilted. Season with ½ tsp. salt. Spoon spinach into a strainer and let drain completely, then transfer to a paper towel and blot any excess liquid (see Quick Tip below).

5. Wipe frying pan with a paper towel. Reduce heat to medium-low. Crack 10 eggs into a bowl and stir with a fork just to break up. Melt butter in pan, then add eggs. Gently scramble eggs, stirring occasionally, until mostly solidified but still very wet (they'll cook more in the torta). Sprinkle with remaining ½ tsp. salt and the oregano, then transfer to a plate, spreading eggs evenly. Chill until cool.

6. Assemble torta: Spread half of eggs in bottom of dough-lined pan. Lay half of cheese over eggs, cutting slices if needed to make an even layer. Distribute half of spinach over cheese and sprinkle with half of basil. Cover with half of ham. Use a paper towel to blot peppers completely dry, then lay over ham, cutting peppers if needed to make an even layer. The peppers are the middle layer. From this point, layer remaining ingredients in reverse order: ham, then basil, spinach, cheese, and finally eggs.

7. Using scissors, trim edge of dough to a 1-in. overhang. Fold dough toward center of torta. Lay reserved dough circle on top, pressing down gently on torta with your hand to even out layers. Press edges of dough with your thumb along inside of pan to seal. Using a knife, cut a small X in center of the torta to let out steam during baking. Wrap torta in plastic wrap and chill at least 2 hours.

8. With a rack set on the lowest level, preheat oven to 375°. Whisk remaining egg and brush some over top of torta. Bake until golden brown, about 1 hour. Let cool on a rack at least 1 hour.

9. Run a knife between the sides of torta and pan, then loosen pan and lift pan off torta.

Quick Tip: To prevent a soggy crust, be sure to dry the peppers and spinach by blotting thoroughly with paper towels.

Make Ahead: Dough, up to 2 days, chilled; assembled torta, overnight, chilled; baked torta, up to 4 hours at room temperature.

PER SERVING: 415 cal., 63% (261 cal.) from fat; 20 g protein; 29 g fat (16 g sat.); 20 g carbo (1.9 g fiber); 935 mg sodium; 265 mg chol.

breakfast & brunch

Artichoke, Leek, and Fontina Frittata

Think of a frittata as an omelet made effortless: no fussing or folding. Just stir the ingredients together, pour into a skillet, briefly cook on the stove, and finish in the oven to create a crisp, golden top. Our cheesy version is studded with a savory blend of artichokes, leeks, and crisp bacon. You can also try it with sausage and potato (see right), or make it vegetarian by leaving out the meat altogether. And if you don't feel like shopping, simply improvise with what you have on hand.

SERVES 6 to 8 | **TIME** 40 minutes

4 slices thick-cut bacon, cut into ¾-in. pieces
8 eggs
½ cup milk
1 tbsp. chopped chives
¼ tsp. salt
½ tsp. freshly ground black pepper
½ lb. frozen artichoke hearts, thawed and roughly chopped (about 1 cup)
1 cup thinly sliced, well-washed leeks (white and light green parts)
¾ cup finely shredded fontina cheese, divided
¼ cup grated parmesan cheese

1. Preheat oven to 450°. In a 10-in. ovenproof frying pan or well-seasoned cast-iron skillet, cook bacon over medium-high heat until crisp, about 5 minutes. Transfer bacon with a slotted spoon to paper towels; reserve 2 tbsp. drippings in pan (discard the rest) and set aside.
2. In a medium bowl, whisk together eggs, milk, chives, salt, and pepper. Stir in bacon and artichoke hearts. Set aside.
3. Return frying pan to medium-high heat. Add leeks and cook in reserved bacon drippings, stirring, until softened, 1 to 2 minutes. Reduce heat to medium. Add egg mixture and stir to combine. Cook 1 minute, then gently stir in ½ cup fontina and the parmesan. Cook without stirring until edges of frittata are set and center is still a bit soft, about 2 minutes (edges should appear firm when pan is gently shaken; top layer should appear wet).
4. Sprinkle remaining ¼ cup fontina over top and transfer frying pan to oven. Bake until eggs are fully set and top is light golden brown, 5 to 7 minutes. If top has not browned, broil frittata about 5 in. from heat, keeping oven door ajar, until lightly golden, about 1 minute.
5. Slice frittata into wedges. Serve warm or at room temperature.

PER SERVING: 238 cal., 64% (153 cal.) from fat; 15 g protein; 17 g fat (7 g sat.); 6.3 g carbo (2.2 g fiber); 454 mg sodium; 268 mg chol.

Sausage and Potato Frittata: You can use any type of **cooked sausage** (pork or chicken) for this; we liked the andouille, Cajun-style, and sun-dried tomato varieties. Substitute 1 cup diced cooked sausage for bacon and cook, stirring, in 1 tbsp. **olive oil** over medium heat until lightly browned, 7 to 10 minutes. Transfer sausage with a slotted spoon to paper towels, reserving oil in pan. Proceed with step 2, but substitute 1 cup diced cooked **potato** for artichoke hearts. Proceed with steps 3 through 5.

PER SERVING: 267 cal., 61% (164 cal.) from fat; 17 g protein; 18 g fat (7.3 g sat.); 8.4 g carbo (0.6 g fiber); 587 mg sodium; 277 mg chol.

Wild Mushroom Egg Bake

The soft, velvety texture in the dish from reader Ruth Rush, of Coeur d'Alene, Idaho, comes from layering the cream with the eggs rather than beating them together.

SERVES 8 | **TIME** 1 hour

1½ cups shredded (6 oz.) havarti or jack cheese
2 tbsp. butter
½ lb. fresh morels or oyster mushrooms, stems trimmed and sliced
½ cup whipping cream
½ tsp. dry mustard
¼ tsp. *each* minced thyme leaves, salt, and freshly ground black pepper
6 eggs, lightly beaten

1. Preheat oven to 325°. Butter an 8-in.-square baking dish and sprinkle cheese over bottom. In a large frying pan over high heat, melt butter. Add mushrooms and cook, stirring often, until lightly browned, about 5 minutes.
2. In a small bowl, mix cream, mustard, thyme, salt, and pepper. Pour half of cream mixture over cheese in dish. Top with mushrooms and eggs. Pour remaining cream mixture over top. Bake until eggs are set, about 35 minutes.

PER SERVING: 184 cal., 73% (135 cal.) from fat; 9 g protein; 15 g fat (8.5 g sat.); 2.4 g carbo (0.4 g fiber); 271 mg sodium; 199 mg chol.

Chilaquiles

Made with torn-up leftover tortillas fried in oil and then simmered in spicy tomato or tomatillo sauce, soft, luscious chilaquiles are a breakfast staple in Northern Mexico, Southern California, and the Southwest—and are usually eaten with eggs. The name comes from the Nahuatl phrase *chil-a-quilitl* ("chile broth and herbs"). (By the way, Nahuatl, a Native American language of Mexico, also gave us the words "tomato" and "chocolate," among others.)

SERVES 4 | **TIME** 1 hour

12 dried California or New Mexico chiles (5 to 6 in. each, about 2½ oz. total)
2 cups chicken broth
1 onion (½ lb.), peeled
½ lb. firm-ripe Roma tomatoes
3 garlic cloves, unpeeled
½ tsp. *each* ground cumin and dried oregano
12 corn tortillas (6 in. wide)
Vegetable oil
6 oz. thinly sliced *asadero (see Quick Tip, above right)* or jack cheese
1 tbsp. minced cilantro
Salt

1. Preheat oven to 250°. Wipe chiles with a damp cloth. Discard stems and seeds. Lay chiles in a 10- by 15-in. baking pan. Bake until fragrant, about 3 minutes.
2. In a 3- to 4-qt. bowl, combine chiles and broth. Heat in a microwave until boiling, about 3 minutes. Let stand until chiles are soft, 10 to 15 minutes.
3. Meanwhile, cut onion crosswise into ½-in.-thick slices. Core tomatoes and cut in half lengthwise. Lay onion slices, tomato halves (cut sides up), and garlic cloves, slightly separated, in a 10- by 15-in. pan. Broil 4 to 6 in. from heat until vegetables are browned, 8 to 10 minutes; remove from pan as they are browned. Peel garlic.
4. In a blender, purée chiles and liquid until smooth (or purée chiles in a food processor, then gradually process in liquid). Rub mixture through a fine-mesh strainer back into bowl; discard chile residue.
5. Return chile purée to blender or food processor; add onion, tomatoes, garlic, cumin, and oregano and process until smooth; return mixture to bowl.
6. Stack tortillas and cut into ½-in.-wide strips. Heat ½ in. oil in a 10- to 12-in. frying pan over high heat until hot. Add about one-third of tortilla strips. Cook, stirring often, until strips are golden and crisp, about 2 minutes. With a slotted spoon, transfer strips to paper towels to drain. Repeat to cook remaining tortillas. Add tortilla strips to sauce in bowl and mix.
7. Preheat oven to 400°. Scrape mixture into a shallow 2-qt. baking dish. Cover evenly with cheese. Bake until cheese has melted and chilaquiles are hot in the center, 8 to 10 minutes. If desired, broil 4 to 6 in. from heat until cheese is lightly browned, about 4 minutes longer.
8. Sprinkle chilaquiles with cilantro. Add salt to taste.
Quick Tip: *Asadero* (grilling) cheese is a dryish fresh Mexican cheese that melts nicely when heated. Find it at Mexican markets.
Make Ahead: Sauce, through step 6, up to 1 day, chilled. Fry tortillas up to 1 day; store airtight at room temperature.

PER SERVING: 581 cal., 56% (324 cal.) from fat; 22 g protein; 36 g fat (10 g sat.); 51 g carbo (9.4 g fiber); 470 mg sodium; 37 mg chol.

Cherry Dutch Baby

Most likely based on the sweet, puffy German pancake called *Apfelpfannkuchen*, the Dutch (a mispronunciation of *Deutsch*, meaning German) baby is thought to have been invented at Manca's Café, in Seattle, sometime in the early 1900s. Until Manca's closed, in 1988, the Dutch baby remained a signature dish. The simple Yorkshire pudding–like crêpe is eaten with powdered sugar and a squeeze of fresh lemon. It's also wonderful with other fruits if cherries aren't in season.

SERVES 4 | **TIME** 30 minutes

¾ cup flour
2 tbsp. granulated sugar
¾ cup milk
3 eggs
¼ tsp. salt
¼ cup butter
2 cups pitted sweet cherries
Powdered sugar
Lemon wedges for serving

1. Preheat oven to 425°. In a blender, blend flour, granulated sugar, milk, eggs, and salt until smooth.
2. Melt butter in a 12-in. ovenproof frying pan over high heat. Add cherries; cook until warm, about 2 minutes. Pour in batter. Bake until golden brown and puffed, about 20 minutes. Serve with a dusting of powdered sugar and a squeeze of fresh lemon juice.

PER SERVING: 348 cal., 44% (152 cal.) from fat; 9.6 g protein; 17 g fat (9.4 g sat.); 41 g carbo (2.3 g fiber); 298 mg sodium; 194 mg chol.

breakfast & brunch

Chile Dutch Baby with Avocado Salsa

This savory version of a Dutch baby, from reader Mickey Strang, of McKinleyville, California, is a lot like chiles rellenos, but skips the work of filling and frying the chiles.

SERVES 4 | **TIME** 30 minutes

¼ cup butter

3 eggs

¾ cup *each* milk and flour

1½ tbsp. minced jalapeño or serrano chiles, divided

1 cup *each* chopped firm-ripe avocado and firm-ripe tomato

1 tbsp. *each* thinly sliced green onion and fresh lime juice

¼ tsp. cayenne (optional)

Salt

1. Preheat oven to 425°. Put butter in a shallow 2- to 3-qt. baking dish and heat in oven until melted, 3 to 4 minutes.

2. Meanwhile, in a blender or food processor, blend eggs and milk until blended. Add flour and blend until smooth, then add 1 tbsp. chiles and blend just to combine. Pour batter into hot baking dish.

3. Bake until Dutch baby is puffed and well browned, about 20 minutes.

4. Meanwhile, in a medium bowl, combine remaining ½ tbsp. chiles with avocado, tomato, green onion, and lime juice.

5. Dust baked Dutch baby with cayenne if you like. Cut into wedges. Add avocado salsa and salt to taste.

PER SERVING: 347 cal., 60% (207 cal.) from fat; 9.9 g protein; 23 g fat (11 g sat.); 26 g carbo (2 g fiber); 201 mg sodium; 198 mg chol.

Toffee French Toast with Pecans

The luscious sauce makes this French toast from the Kitchen, in Boulder, Colorado, taste like sticky toffee pudding. (Drizzle leftover sauce over ice cream if you like.)

recipe pictured on page 549

SERVES 4 | **TIME** 45 minutes

SAUCE

1 cup unsalted butter

1½ cups firmly packed light brown sugar

¾ cup heavy whipping cream

½ cup roughly chopped pecans

FRENCH TOAST

8 eggs

¼ tsp. nutmeg, preferably freshly grated

1 tsp. cinnamon

1½ tsp. vanilla extract

3 tbsp. orange-flavored liqueur, such as Grand Marnier, or orange juice

2 tbsp. salted butter, divided

8 thick slices (1 in.) brioche (about 1 lb.)

1. Prepare sauce: Melt unsalted butter in a medium saucepan over medium-low heat. Stir in brown sugar until well blended, then bring to a boil. Boil until sugar dissolves, 5 to 8 minutes. Carefully stir in cream (mixture may spatter) and pecans; reduce heat to low.

2. Make French toast: In a large shallow bowl, whisk together eggs, nutmeg, cinnamon, vanilla, and orange liqueur.

3. Preheat oven to 200°. Heat a large cast-iron skillet or nonstick frying pan over medium heat. Melt 1 tbsp. salted butter in skillet, tipping pan to coat. Quickly dip bread, 1 piece at a time, into egg batter, coating both sides but not drenching. Lay bread in skillet and repeat with another slice of bread. Cook until golden brown, 1½ to 2 minutes; then flip, add remaining 1 tbsp. butter, and cook until second side is golden brown, 1½ to 2 minutes more. Dip and cook remaining slices of bread, putting in oven on a baking sheet to keep warm.

4. Transfer French toast to plates, top with some of warm toffee sauce, and serve remaining sauce on the side.

Make Ahead: Sauce, up to 2 days, chilled (reheat in a microwave oven).

PER SERVING: 945 cal., 50% (468 cal.) from fat; 24 g protein; 52 g fat (24 g sat.); 93 g carbo (3 g fiber); 779 mg sodium; 570 mg chol.

Hazelnut-Cornmeal Pancakes

Serve these pancakes from reader David Beckstein, of Aptos, California, with butter, maple syrup, and cinnamon.

MAKES 12 pancakes | **TIME** 30 minutes

½ cup hazelnuts, toasted and skins removed (*see How to Toast Nuts, page 134*)
¼ cup cornmeal
1 cup flour
2 tbsp. sugar
1 tsp. baking powder
½ tsp. salt
2 eggs
1 cup milk
3 tbsp. butter, melted, divided

1. Finely grind hazelnuts in a food processor. Add cornmeal and blend to combine. Add flour, sugar, baking powder, and salt and blend to combine. Add eggs, milk, and 2 tbsp. butter. Pulse to just combine with dry ingredients.
2. Heat remaining 1 tbsp. butter in a large frying pan over medium-high heat. Ladle in 3-tbsp. portions of batter. Turn pancakes when bubbles appear on the surface, cooking about 3 minutes total per pancake.

PER PANCAKE: 147 cal., 52% (77 cal.) from fat; 3.7 g protein; 8.6 g fat (2.8 g sat.); 14 g carbo (0.8 g fiber); 189 mg sodium; 46 mg chol.

How to Make Perfect Pancakes

Follow these three simple rules to turn out outstanding pancakes every time.
1. Combine the dry ingredients first, then mix the liquid ingredients with the dry ingredients gently with a flexible spatula, just until evenly moistened. Avoid overmixing the batter, which can make for tough, rubbery pancakes.
2. Use the right pan and amount of oil. The outside texture of the pancake depends on the surface of the griddle or pan and how much oil you use. While some people prefer the dark rings produced by a cast-iron surface, we like the even-toned pancakes cooked on a nonstick surface that has been coated with oil, then quickly wiped nearly clean with a paper towel.
3. Heat the pan over medium-high heat until a small dollop of batter dropped in makes a sizzling noise. Lower the heat, add the first spoonful of batter, and observe how it cooks: By the time the edges of the pancake start to look dry and bubbles are forming and popping on top, the underside should be golden brown. Lower the heat if the pancake darkens too fast and raise it if the pancake is still too light when bubbles form.

Sourdough Pancakes

These pancakes, from reader Jennifer Roeser, of Mammoth Lakes, California, have a pleasant mild tang. The batter is very thin, and makes large, tender pancakes.

MAKES 10 or 11 pancakes; 4 servings | **TIME** 15 minutes

Overnight Starter (*recipe follows*)
2 tbsp. sugar
1 tsp. *each* salt and baking powder
3 tbsp. canola or safflower oil
2 eggs
½ tsp. baking soda
Butter
Maple syrup or powdered sugar

1. To overnight starter, add sugar, salt, baking powder, and oil; mix well. Add eggs and beat to blend. Mix baking soda with 1 tsp. water; stir into batter.
2. Heat griddle or large frying pan over medium heat; when hot, oil lightly. Pour batter in ⅓-cup portions onto griddle, spacing about 1½ in. apart. Cook until bubbles form on top of pancakes and bottoms are browned, about 1 minute. Turn with a wide spatula; cook until brown on bottom, about 1 minute longer. Serve hot with butter and syrup.

PER SERVING: 439 cal., 28% (123 cal.) from fat; 11.8 g protein; 13.9 g fat (1.8 g sat.); 65 g carbo (2 g fiber); 927 mg sodium; 107 mg chol.

Overnight Starter: In a large bowl, mix 2 cups **flour**, 1¼ cups warm (100° to 110°) **water**, and ½ cup *Sunset*'s Reliable Sourdough Starter (requires 1 week to make; *page 558,* or use ½ cup store-bought starter; *see Quick Tip below*). Cover with plastic wrap and let stand in a warm place (about 80°) at least 8 and up to 24 hours. Mix ½ cup overnight starter with sourdough starter to replenish it for future use. Use remaining overnight starter to make pancakes; cover sourdough starter and store it in refrigerator.
Quick Tip: Although it's gratifying to make your own sourdough starter, you can also order one online from *amazon.com;* we like Goldrush Sourdough Starter.

breakfast & brunch

Pumpkin-Ginger Pancakes with Ginger Butter

The pumpkin gives these lightly spiced pancakes a custardy texture and golden hue. The recipe comes from Margaret Fox, culinary director at Harvest Market in Fort Bragg, California, and former chef-owner of the legendary breakfast destination Café Beaujolais, in Mendocino, California.

MAKES About 8 pancakes; 2 or 3 servings
TIME 45 minutes

1 cup flour
2 tbsp. firmly packed brown sugar
1 tsp. baking powder
½ tsp. *each* baking soda, cinnamon, and ground ginger
¼ tsp. *each* ground nutmeg and salt
1 egg
¾ cup *each* milk and canned pumpkin
¼ cup plain low-fat or nonfat yogurt
2 tbsp. butter, melted
Candied-ginger Butter *(recipe follows)*
Maple syrup

1. In a large bowl, stir together flour, brown sugar, baking powder, baking soda, cinnamon, ginger, nutmeg, and salt. In a medium bowl, mix egg, milk, pumpkin, yogurt, and butter until well blended. Stir egg mixture into flour mixture just until evenly moistened.
2. Preheat oven to 200°. Heat a nonstick griddle or a 12-in. nonstick frying pan over medium heat; when hot, coat lightly with butter and adjust heat to maintain temperature. Spoon batter in ⅓-cup portions onto griddle and gently spread into 4-in. circles *(see Quick Tip below)*. Cook until pancakes are browned on bottom and edges begin to look dry, 2 to 3 minutes; turn with a wide spatula and brown other sides, 2 to 3 minutes longer. As pancakes are cooked, transfer to baking sheets and keep warm in oven.
3. Serve warm with Candied-ginger Butter and maple syrup.
Quick Tip: Our pancakes are standard-size, but Fox likes hers silver dollar–size, which she says makes them easier to flip.

PER PANCAKE: 211 cal., 51% (108 cal.) from fat; 3.9 g protein; 12 g fat (7.2 g sat.); 22 g carbo (1 g fiber); 346 mg sodium; 58 mg chol.

Candied-ginger Butter: With a wooden spoon, stir 2 tbsp. finely chopped **candied ginger** into ¼ cup softened **butter** (soften in a microwave oven for 5 to 10 seconds). Chill until firm before serving. Makes about ¼ cup.

PER TBSP.: 128 cal., 80% (102 cal.) from fat; 0.1 g protein; 12 g fat (7.3 g sat.); 6.9 g carbo (0 g fiber); 84 mg sodium; 31 mg chol.

Buckwheat Belgian Waffles

These incredibly light, crunchy waffles are from Nancye Benson of the food truck Moxie Rx in Portland, Oregon. She lets the batter stand overnight on the counter for slightly sour waffles. They're delicious, but if you prefer a sweet batter, chill it to keep it from developing a tang. In the summer, Benson adds seasonal toppings like plum-rose compote with mascarpone cheese.

SERVES 6 or 7 (makes 16 Belgian or 26 regular 4-in. waffles) | **TIME** 1 hour, plus overnight to rise

2½ tsp. active dry yeast
3 tbsp. sugar, divided
2 cups warm (100° to 110°) milk
½ cup butter, melted and cooled
1½ cups all-purpose flour
½ cup buckwheat flour
Cooking-oil spray
2 eggs
½ tsp. baking soda
¼ tsp. salt
1 tsp. vanilla extract
Cooking-oil spray
1 tsp. cinnamon
3 bananas, sliced
1¼ cups warm maple syrup
1½ cups vanilla yogurt (optional)

1. Sprinkle yeast and 1 tbsp. sugar into a medium bowl; pour over ½ cup warm (100° to 110°) water. Stir and let stand until foamy, about 8 minutes. Add milk, butter, and flours, then whisk until smooth. Cover bowl with plastic wrap and let rise overnight on counter (for slightly sour waffles) or chill (for sweet waffles).
2. In the morning, lightly spray grids on both sides of waffle iron with cooking-oil spray, then heat iron. Preheat oven to 200°.
3. Add eggs, baking soda, salt, and vanilla to batter and whisk until smooth. Ladle ¾ to 1 cup batter (or amount that waffle-iron maker directs) onto hot iron and cook until nicely browned and crisp, 4 to 5 minutes. Remove waffles and keep warm on a baking sheet in the oven. Repeat to cook remaining waffles.
4. Meanwhile, in a small bowl, combine remaining 2 tbsp. sugar and the cinnamon.
5. Break waffles into sections and divide among warm plates. Serve with bananas, maple syrup, cinnamon sugar, and yogurt if you like.

PER SERVING: 631 cal., 33% (209 cal.) from fat; 11 g protein; 23 g fat (12 g sat.); 100 g carbo (4.1 g fiber); 427 mg sodium; 123 mg chol.

BLT Waffles

Waffles are not just for breakfast at reader Mickey Strang's house in McKinleyville, California. This unusual combination makes an easy dinner as well as an intriguing brunch entrée.

SERVES 4 | **TIME** 30 minutes

1 cup flour
2 tsp. baking powder
½ tsp. salt, plus more to taste
1 cup milk
2 eggs, separated
½ cup oil-packed dried tomatoes, drained (reserve oil; if needed, add olive oil to measure 3 tbsp.) and chopped
Cooking-oil spray
4 slices bacon, cut in half lengthwise and crosswise
2 tsp. white wine vinegar
¼ tsp. Dijon mustard
Freshly ground black pepper
2 cups baby lettuce salad mix
12 cherry tomatoes, cut in half

1. In a large bowl, mix flour, baking powder, and salt. Add milk, egg yolks, dried tomatoes, and 2 tbsp. tomato oil; stir. In another large bowl, with a mixer on high speed, beat egg whites until soft peaks form. Fold whites into batter.
2. Preheat oven to 200°. Lightly spray grids on both sides of waffle iron with cooking oil spray, then heat iron. When hot, pour about half of batter (or amount that your waffle-iron maker directs) onto waffle iron. Lay 2 pieces of bacon over batter. Close waffle iron and bake until golden brown, 5 to 10 minutes. Remove waffles and keep warm on a baking sheet in the oven. Repeat to cook remaining waffles.
3. In a large bowl, whisk together remaining 1 tbsp. tomato oil, the vinegar, mustard, and salt and pepper to taste. Toss with baby lettuce and cherry tomatoes.
4. Top waffles with dressed salad.

PER SERVING: 520 cal., 66% (342 cal.) from fat; 12 g protein; 38 g fat (9.5 g sat.); 34 g carbo (1.6 g fiber); 1,412 mg sodium; 130 mg chol.

5 Simple Steps to Delicious Waffles

1. After heating, brush grids of waffle irons (even non-stick ones) with oil or melted butter, to prevent sticking. Or spray with cooking-oil spray before heating.
2. Wait until the iron is very hot, then pour batter into the center of each square—about ½ cup per 4-in. square. Pour the batter from a spouted glass measuring cup—rather than ladling it from a bowl—to prevent dripping.
3. Resist peeking too soon. Lifting the lid while the batter is still wet in the middle will pull the waffle apart.
4. Cook until the iron stops steaming. Belgian waffles can take up to 9 minutes, traditional ones 2 to 5.
5. Gently pry edges of waffle away from the iron with the tines of a fork if necessary.

Banana-Pecan Waffles with Chunky Pineapple Sauce

Margaret Fox—culinary director of Harvest Market in Fort Bragg, California, and former owner of Café Beaujolais in Mendocino—sometimes serves these waffles with a scoop of vanilla ice cream for dessert.

MAKES 8 to 10 Belgian waffles (4 in.); 4 to 6 servings
TIME 1 hour

1 cup flour
1 tbsp. sugar
1½ tsp. baking powder
½ tsp. *each* baking soda and cinnamon
¼ tsp. *each* nutmeg and salt
2 eggs, separated
¾ cup *each* low-fat milk and mashed ripe banana
½ cup sour cream
¼ cup butter, melted
¾ cup chopped pecans, toasted (*see How to Toast Nuts, page 134*)
Chunky Pineapple Sauce (*recipe follows*)
Maple syrup (*optional*)
Sliced bananas (*optional*)

1. In a large bowl, stir together flour, sugar, baking powder, baking soda, cinnamon, nutmeg, and salt. In a medium bowl, mix egg yolks, milk, banana, sour cream, and butter until well blended. Stir egg-yolk mixture into flour mixture just until combined. Stir in pecans.
2. In another large bowl, with a mixer on high speed, beat egg whites until soft peaks form. Gently fold into batter until no white streaks remain.

3. Preheat oven to 200°. Preheat a Belgian waffle iron; brush grids on both sides lightly with oil or melted butter. When hot, add about ½ cup batter per 4-in. square; close iron and cook until waffle is well browned (lift lid slightly to check), 6 to 9 minutes. Remove waffle; keep warm on a baking sheet in the oven up to 15 minutes. Repeat to cook remaining waffles.

4. Serve warm with pineapple sauce, maple syrup, and sliced bananas if you like.

PER WAFFLE: 313 cal., 49% (153 cal.) from fat; 4.6 g protein; 17 g fat (5.7 g sat.); 38 g carbo (1.6 g fiber); 271 mg sodium; 61 mg chol.

Chunky Pineapple Sauce: In a 1- to 2-qt. pan over medium heat, stir 1½ cups **fresh pineapple chunks** and ¾ cup **sugar** until sugar is dissolved and juices are bubbling, about 5 minutes. Let cool 5 minutes, then purée in a blender until smooth. Stir in 1 cup finely chopped fresh pineapple and 1 tbsp. **fresh lemon juice.** Makes 2 cups.

PER 2-TBSP. SERVING: 50 cal., 1% (0.3 cal.) from fat; 0.1 g protein; 13 g carbo (0.4 g fiber); 0.3 mg sodium; 0 mg chol.

Coffee and Brown Sugar Bacon

Everyone loves waking up to the smell of coffee and bacon, so it's not surprising that the flavors are wonderful together too. Add some molasses-y brown sugar, and you have bacon nirvana.

SERVES 8 | **TIME** 40 minutes

1 lb. thick-cut bacon
1 tbsp. ground coffee beans
½ cup firmly packed brown sugar
2 tbsp. freshly brewed coffee

1. Preheat oven to 375°. Line a rimmed baking pan with parchment or waxed paper and set a flat rack on top.

2. Lay bacon strips on rack, overlapping slightly if needed. Sprinkle top sides of strips with ground coffee. In a small bowl, combine brown sugar and brewed coffee, stirring just to blend into a paste. Brush top side of strips with half of sugar mixture.

3. Bake 15 minutes. Turn bacon over and brush with remaining sugar glaze. Bake until crispy, 10 minutes more.

PER SERVING: 144 cal., 49% (70 cal.) from fat; 4.9 g protein; 7.8 g fat (2.8 g sat.); 14 g carbo (0 g fiber); 259 mg sodium; 13 mg chol.

Hazelnut Breakfast Sausage

Reader Paul Pastina, of Richmond, California, created these easy pork patties to go with sweet breakfast dishes like pancakes.

MAKES 2 dozen 3-in. patties | **TIME** 1 hour

¾ **cup hazelnuts, toasted, skins removed, and cooled (see *How to Toast Nuts*, page 134)**
3½ **lbs. ground pork**
½ **cup chopped flat-leaf parsley**
¼ **cup hazelnut-flavored liqueur, such as Frangelico**
1 **tbsp. honey**
1 **tbsp. kosher salt, plus more to taste**
2 **tsp. freshly ground black pepper, plus more to taste**
1 **tsp. mace**

1. Put toasted hazelnuts in a food processor and pulse until they resemble coarse cornmeal.

2. Break pork into small chunks and put in a large bowl. Sprinkle ground hazelnuts, parsley, hazelnut liqueur, honey, salt, pepper, and mace over pork. Using your hands, gently mix ingredients together.

3. To check seasoning, cook a small amount of sausage in a frying pan over medium-high heat until browned and cooked through. Taste, then season pork mixture with more salt or pepper as desired.

4. Scoop out ¼-cup portions of sausage mixture and form into 3-in.-wide patties. Working in batches, cook patties in a large frying pan over medium-high heat until brown on one side, about 3 minutes. Flip patties, reduce heat to medium-low, partially cover, and fry until cooked through, about 5 minutes.

Make Ahead: Uncooked patties, well wrapped, frozen up to 2 months. Cook as directed (still frozen), adding 3 to 4 minutes to cooking time.

PER PATTY: 208 cal., 71% (147 cal.) from fat; 12 g protein; 16 g fat (5.4 g sat.); 2.2 g carbo (0.4 g fiber); 282 mg sodium; 48 mg chol.

Creamy Hash Browns (*Kugelis*)

A deeply comforting Lithuanian specialty of shredded potatoes, bacon, and onions from Sharon Miller, of the Cobblestone Inn in Carmel, California. Although Miller serves *kugelis* for breakfast, in Lithuania it's often a side dish or a stand-alone meal. Dollop your portion with extra sour cream for the full-on experience.

SERVES 9 to 12 | **TIME** 1½ hours

½ lb. bacon, cut into ½-in. pieces
3 eggs
1 cup sour cream
¼ cup half-and-half
4 large russet potatoes (2½ lbs. total)
1 large onion, minced
1 tsp. salt
¼ tsp. freshly ground black pepper

1. In a 10- to 12-in. frying pan, cook bacon over medium heat, stirring until crisp, about 15 minutes. With a slotted spoon, transfer bacon to paper towels to drain. Reserve fat from pan.
2. Preheat oven to 400°. Brush bottom and sides of a 9-in. square baking dish with some of the bacon fat. In a large bowl, beat together eggs, sour cream, and half-and-half until blended.
3. Peel potatoes and coarsely shred to make about 5½ cups. Stir potatoes, bacon, onion, and salt and pepper into egg mixture. Pour potato mixture into dish; spread evenly.
4. Bake 20 minutes, then reduce oven temperature to 350° and bake until browned, 45 to 50 minutes longer. Cut into squares.
Make Ahead: Up to 1 day, chilled. Reheat in a 350° oven until hot, about 15 minutes.

PER SERVING: 161 cal., 49% (79 cal.) from fat; 6.1 g protein; 8.7 g fat (3.9 g sat.); 15 g carbo (1.2 g fiber); 376 mg sodium; 71 mg chol.

Italian Oven-fried Potatoes

Crisp, herbaceous, and garlicky, these potatoes from reader Mickey Strang, of McKinleyville, California, can bake while you're getting the rest of brunch together.

SERVES 4 | **TIME** 45 minutes to 1 hour

2 lbs. red-skinned potatoes, cut into 1-in. chunks
1 to 2 tbsp. olive oil
2 tbsp. *each* minced oregano and basil leaves
1 garlic clove, minced or pressed
⅓ cup freshly grated parmesan cheese
Oregano and basil sprigs (optional)
Salt

1. Preheat oven to 475°. In a 10- by 15-in. pan, mix potatoes with oil. Bake until they are a rich brown, 35 to 45 minutes; do not disturb until potatoes begin to brown, then use a wide spatula to turn chunks over several times.
2. Pour potatoes into a warm bowl and sprinkle with oregano, basil, garlic, and about two-thirds of parmesan cheese. Mix, then sprinkle with remaining cheese; top with herb sprigs if you like. Season to taste with salt.

PER SERVING: 234 cal., 28% (65 cal.) from fat; 6.9 g protein; 7.3 g fat (1.9 g sat.); 37 g carbo (3.9 g fiber); 126 mg sodium; 4.8 mg chol.

Chocolate-Almond Croissants

Crispy, buttery plain croissants, fresh from the bakery, are a treat, but here's an easy way to jazz them up for a breakfast-in-bed surprise.

SERVES 4 | **TIME** 15 minutes

2½ oz. almond paste
2 tbsp. butter, melted
4 fresh croissants
¼ cup coarsely chopped semisweet or bittersweet
  chocolate

1. Preheat oven to 350°. Coarsely shred almond paste to make about ½ cup. In a bowl, stir almond paste and butter to form a soft paste.
2. Slice open croissants. Spread almond paste mixture on cut sides of bottom halves, then sprinkle chocolate over almond paste. Replace tops. Set croissants on a baking sheet and bake until chocolate starts to melt, 5 to 7 minutes.

PER SERVING: 414 cal., 56% (231 cal.) from fat; 6.8 g protein; 26 g fat (13 g sat.); 41 g carbo (3 g fiber); 468 mg sodium; 53 mg chol.

breakfast & brunch

Buttermilk Biscuits with Country Sausage Gravy

Chef Lisa Schroeder, of Mother's Bistro & Bar in Portland, Oregon, makes these tangy biscuits with whipping cream and extra butter on top, but we found them to be plenty rich made with half-and-half and a little less butter. They're amazing and worth the every-now-and-then indulgence.

SERVES 8 | **TIME** 45 minutes

BISCUITS
2 cups self-rising flour (*see Quick Tip, right*)
½ tsp. kosher salt
2 tbsp. sugar
¼ cup cold butter, plus 2 tbsp. melted
¾ cup buttermilk
¾ cup half-and-half or whipping cream
1 cup all-purpose flour
SAUSAGE GRAVY
¾ lb. bulk pork sausage
1½ cups half-and-half or whipping cream
1½ cups milk
¾ tsp. *each* garlic powder, onion powder, and freshly ground black pepper
2 tsp. minced thyme leaves, plus more for garnish
¼ to ½ tsp. cayenne
½ tsp. kosher salt, plus more to taste
3 tbsp. butter

1. Make biscuits: Preheat oven to 450°. In a large bowl, whisk together self-rising flour, salt, and sugar. Cut cold butter into small cubes and, using a pastry blender, cut butter into flour mixture until pieces are size of peas. Stir in buttermilk and half-and-half just until incorporated.
2. Put all-purpose flour in a shallow bowl or pie dish. Using an ice cream scoop or measuring cup, scoop one-eighth of dough and drop it into flour, tossing lightly to coat and shaking off excess. Put biscuits in an 8-in. cake pan. Repeat with remaining dough (biscuits will touch in pan). Reserve ¼ cup remaining flour.
3. Bake biscuits until deep golden brown and a toothpick inserted in center comes out clean, 20 to 25 minutes. Let cool 10 minutes. Brush with 2 tbsp. melted butter.
4. Make gravy: Put sausage in a saucepan over medium heat. Cook until lightly browned, 5 to 6 minutes, breaking it into small pieces with a wooden spoon. Transfer sausage to a plate with a slotted spoon, reserving any drippings.
5. Meanwhile, in another saucepan over medium-low heat, warm half-and-half, milk, garlic and onion powders, pepper, thyme, cayenne, and salt.
6. Add butter to sausage drippings and let melt. Add

¼ cup reserved flour and whisk until golden, 1 to 2 minutes. Gradually add warm milk mixture, whisking, until simmering. Stir in sausage and season to taste with salt. (For thicker gravy, simmer longer; for thinner gravy, add more milk.)
7. Halve biscuits and put on plates. Top with gravy; sprinkle with thyme.
Quick Tip: You can substitute 2 cups all-purpose flour mixed with 1 tbsp. baking powder and 1 tsp. kosher salt for self-rising flour.

PER BISCUIT MADE WITH HALF-AND-HALF AND ½ CUP GRAVY: 585 cal., 62% (360 cal.) from fat; 14 g protein; 40 g fat (20 g sat.); 42 g carbo (1.2 g fiber); 1,033 mg sodium; 96 mg chol.

PER BISCUIT MADE WITH WHIPPING CREAM AND ½ CUP GRAVY: 728 cal., 70% (513 cal.) from fat; 13 g protein; 57 g fat (31 g sat.); 41 g carbo (1.2 g fiber); 1,031 mg sodium; 163 mg chol.

Fruit-and-Nut Breakfast Bars

Easy to make and very tasty, these bars are pure fruit, nuts, and seeds—no pasty fillers. Take them on hikes, bike rides, or anywhere else you'll need a healthy snack.

MAKES 8 bars | **TIME** 30 minutes

¼ cup orange juice
½ cup whole Medjool dates (about 5), halved and pitted
1 cup unblanched almonds
½ cup dried apricots
¼ cup dried plums (prunes)
¼ tsp. salt
¼ cup *each* raw pumpkin seeds (*pepitas*) and sunflower seeds

1. Preheat oven to 300°. Line a baking sheet with parchment paper. Pour orange juice over dates and let soak 5 minutes.
2. Meanwhile, put almonds, apricots, and plums in a food processor and pulse a few times until coarsely chopped. Add salt and dates with orange juice and pulse until mixture starts to stick together. Add pumpkin and sunflower seeds, pulsing a few times just to incorporate.
3. Using wet hands, scoop mixture onto a work surface and form into a log about 1¾ in. wide and ½ in. thick. Use your palms to flatten into a bar, and cut bar into eight pieces.
4. Arrange pieces about 1 in. apart on baking sheet. Bake 8 minutes. Using a heatproof spatula, turn bars over and bake until nuts are toasted (but before fruit begins to burn), 8 minutes longer.
Make Ahead: Up to 4 days; store airtight.

PER BAR: 210 cal., 56% (117 cal.) from fat; 6 g protein; 13 g fat (1.4 g sat.); 22 g carbo (3.5 g fiber); 76 mg sodium; 0 mg chol.

cookies, bars & candies

Fill a jar with our great little cookies or glistening candies, or make someone happy with a gift.

The wonderful thing about cookies is they don't have to be perfect. A slightly overbrowned chocolate chip cookie or a lopsided gingersnap will still get gobbled up. It's one reason why cookies are the least intimidating of all baked goods to make—that and the fact that you can produce dozens of them in under an hour. They're also fun to make with kids, since most cookies don't demand a whole lot of dexterity.

Readers have given us some of our favorite cookie recipes. Check out David McCommack's Oatmeal–Peanut Butter–Chocolate Chip Cookies (*page 594*); they're the kind of giant chunky cookie that big industrial bakers keep trying to get right but never do. McCommack's, on the other hand, are home runs. Or Marisa DeSimone's Florentine Bars (*page 619*), which are supposed to cool completely before you eat them but rarely last that long.

Others come from Western chefs (be sure to try the knee-weakening Triple-threat Chocolate Cookies, *page 616*, from Oregon pastry chef Kir Jensen). And of course we've been baking up a storm ourselves. We love to make a master batch of dough and then turn it into several different types of cookies, ranging from homey to elegant (see what we've done with gingersnaps, for instance, on *page 599*)—it's a great return for not a lot of effort.

We dip into candies too, with a tempting collection that includes something for every taste, including fruity Candied Citrus Peels, *page 620*; crunchy Bite-size Honey Popcorn Balls, *page 619*; and chocolaty Salted Chocolate-Pecan Toffee, *page 621*. They're sweet gifts that are all the more charming because you took the time, in a hectic world, to make them.

Cookies, Bars & Candies

cookies, bars & candies

Sopaipillas

These light, airy pillows of fried dough, traditionally drizzled with honey or sprinkled with powdered sugar, are one of the Southwest's great treats. They're rewarding to make because the process seems magical: When you push the pieces of dough into the hot oil, they puff up like balloons. *(See Quick Tip below.)*

recipe pictured on page **604**

MAKES 2 dozen sopaipillas | **TIME** 1 hour, plus 1 hour to rise

1 package (2¼ tsp.) active dry yeast
1½ cups milk
3 tbsp. fresh lard or vegetable shortening
2 tbsp. granulated sugar
1 tsp. salt
4½ to 5 cups all-purpose flour, divided
1 cup whole-wheat flour
Vegetable oil
Powdered sugar and honey

1. In a large bowl, dissolve yeast in ¼ cup warm (100° to 110°) water for 5 minutes. In a 1½- to 2-qt. pan, combine milk, the lard, sugar, and salt; heat to 110° and add to dissolved yeast. With a wooden spoon or stand mixer fitted with a dough hook, stir 3 cups all-purpose flour and all the whole-wheat flour into the yeast mixture; beat until dough is stretchy. Stir in another 1 cup all-purpose flour to form a stiff dough.
2. Beat on medium speed until dough pulls cleanly from side of bowl and is no longer sticky (or knead until no longer sticky). If it's still sticky, add more all-purpose flour, 1 tbsp. at a time, and beat or knead until dough is smooth. Put dough in an oiled bowl and turn over to coat top.

3. Cover dough with plastic wrap and let stand in a warm (about 80°) place until doubled in bulk, about 1 hour. Punch down dough. If you're not ready to cut and fry dough, cover again and chill up to 1 day.
4. Knead dough on a lightly floured work surface to expel air. Cut into 4 equal portions. Working with 1 portion at a time, roll into a circle about ⅛ in. thick; with a floured knife, cut into 6 equal wedges and lay in a single layer on a floured rimmed baking sheet. Cover with plastic wrap and chill while you roll and cut remaining dough.
5. Pour enough oil into a 5- to 6-qt. pan to come 1½ to 2 in. up side of pan. Heat over medium-high heat until a deep-fry or candy thermometer registers 350°, then adjust heat to maintain temperature. Drop one or two pieces of dough into oil. With a slotted spoon, push them down into oil until they begin to puff. Fry until pale gold on both sides, turning over as needed to brown evenly, 2 to 3 minutes total. Drain in paper towel–lined pans. Fry remaining sopaipillas the same way.
6. Serve immediately, or keep first ones warm in a 200° oven until all are fried. Serve plain or dusted with powdered sugar, and set out honey for drizzling.

Quick Tip: For a shortcut, replace the homemade dough with two 1-lb. loaves of thawed frozen white or wheat dough; then, in step 4, cut each loaf in half and roll out thinly. The sopaipillas are quite large, so feel free to halve the recipe.

Make Ahead: Through step 3, up to 1 day, chilled; cut and fry dough the next day. Fried sopaipillas, up to 1 day, stored at room temperature; up to 2 months, frozen in resealable plastic freezer bags. To reheat fried sopaipillas, thaw (if frozen) and bake, uncovered, in a single layer on baking sheets in a 300° oven, turning once, just until warm, 5 to 8 minutes. Do not overheat or they'll harden.

PER SOPAIPILLA: 197 cal., 55% (108 cal.) from fat; 3.3 g protein; 11 g fat (2.1 g sat.); 20 g carbo (1.2 g fiber); 105 mg sodium; 3.7 mg chol.

Oatmeal–Peanut Butter–Chocolate Chip Cookies

These chunky kitchen-sink cookies flew off the counter when we made them. Reader David McCommack, of Mukilteo, Washington, created the recipe by combining a few others.

MAKES 5 dozen cookies | **TIME** 50 minutes

1 cup butter
½ cup granulated sugar
1 cup *each* firmly packed light brown sugar and smooth peanut butter
2 eggs
2 tbsp. vanilla extract
2 cups quick-cooking rolled oats
2½ cups flour
1 tsp. baking soda
1 package (12 oz.) semisweet chocolate chips

1. Preheat oven to 350°. In a medium bowl, with a mixer on medium speed, cream butter and both sugars until smooth. Add peanut butter and mix until combined; add eggs and vanilla and mix to combine, scraping down side of bowl as needed.
2. In another medium bowl, whisk together oats, flour, and baking soda. Add to butter mixture and mix on low speed until well incorporated. Stir in chocolate chips with a wooden spoon.
3. Drop dough by rounded tbsp. 1 in. apart onto ungreased baking sheets. Bake until lightly browned but still soft in the center, 10 to 12 minutes, switching pan positions halfway through baking. Transfer cookies to racks to cool.

PER COOKIE: 133 cal., 50% (66 cal.) from fat; 2.5 g protein; 7.3 g fat (3.4 g sat.); 15 g carbo (1 g fiber); 77 mg sodium; 15 mg chol.

Oatmeal-PB-Chocolate Chip Ice Cream Sandwiches:
Turn great cookies into superb ice cream sandwiches. Soften the **ice cream** of your choice, about 10 minutes. Spread ¼ cup onto flat side of a cookie and top with another cookie, flat side down, pressing lightly. Chill sandwiches in freezer about 10 minutes, just long enough to chill ice cream but not enough to harden cookies. Eat immediately.

Ginger-Chocolate Cookies

Inspired by a dessert that a guest brought to their annual Oktoberfest, James Bullard and Emily Watson, of San Francisco, created cookies that are part chewy molasses, part homey chocolate chip, and part spicy gingersnap.

MAKES About 3 dozen cookies | **TIME** 1 hour

2 cups flour
⅓ cup unsweetened cocoa powder (not Dutch-processed)
2½ tbsp. ground ginger
2 tsp. baking soda
1½ tsp. *each* cinnamon and freshly grated nutmeg
½ tsp. salt
¾ cup unsalted butter, softened
1 cup firmly packed light brown sugar
¼ cup molasses
1 egg
1 tsp. vanilla extract
8 oz. bittersweet chocolate, finely chopped
⅓ cup granulated sugar

1. Preheat oven to 350°. Butter a large baking sheet. In a medium bowl, whisk flour, cocoa, ginger, baking soda, cinnamon, nutmeg, and salt until thoroughly combined.
2. In a large bowl, beat butter and brown sugar until light and fluffy, about 3 minutes. Add molasses, egg, and vanilla; beat to combine.
3. Mix dry ingredients into butter mixture gently but thoroughly, scraping down side of bowl as necessary. (Batter will be thick.) Stir in chocolate until well combined.
4. Form batter into 2-tbsp. balls, roll each ball in granulated sugar, and place 12 balls on baking sheet. (If batter is too sticky, dampen your hands with water when forming balls.) Dip bottom of a cup or glass in water and use it to flatten balls to a thickness of about ¼ in., rewetting glass as necessary to prevent sticking.
5. Bake cookies 5 minutes, turn sheet 180°, and bake until just set, about 5 minutes more. Cool on sheet 5 minutes, then transfer cookies to racks. Bake remaining balls of dough.
Make Ahead: Up to 2 days, stored airtight at room temperature.

PER COOKIE: 133 cal., 44% (58 cal.) from fat; 1.5 g protein; 6.4 g fat (3.7 g sat.); 19 g carbo (0.6 g fiber); 108 mg sodium; 16 mg chol.

cookies, bars & candies

Homemade Fortune Cookies

Watching skilled workers in a fortune cookie factory in San Francisco convinced us that these cookies could be made at home. If you can shape the cookie in less than 15 seconds, you can make fortune cookies. That's about how long it takes the cookie—warm and pliable from the oven—to cool a little and become rigid. It's easier than you may think. Cotton gloves from a hardware store or garden shop (to handle the hot cookie quickly) and a muffin pan (to hold the folded cookie in shape for the few minutes it takes to cool) are about all you need, other than dexterity.

recipe pictured on page **608**

For the fortunes, rely on your own sense of humor or books of poetry or proverbs. Original messages are a good way to create entertainment, since fate has a curious way of matching fortunes and people. Write the fortunes on 3- by ½-in. slips of paper, then set them near the oven so they're ready to go into the hearts of the cookies.

MAKES About 20 cookies | **TIME** 1½ hours

1 cup flour, sifted
¼ tsp. salt
2 tbsp. cornstarch
6 tbsp. sugar
7 tbsp. canola oil
⅓ cup egg whites (from 2 or 3 eggs)

1. Preheat oven to 300°. Line a baking sheet with parchment paper or a silicone baking mat. In a medium bowl, whisk together flour, salt, cornstarch, and sugar. Stir in oil and egg whites; continue stirring until smooth. Gradually blend in 3 tbsp. water.

2. Drop four level 1-tbsp. portions of batter on baking sheet, spacing them at least 5 in. apart. Use the back of a small offset spatula or a butter knife to spread each evenly into a 4-in. circle. Bake until dark golden brown, about 25 minutes. (Homemade fortune cookies need to be a bit dark in order to bend properly, and will be a little speckled in appearance rather than uniformly gold.) Meanwhile, set a muffin pan (with cups 2¾ in. wide) next to the oven.

3. Using a wide spatula and wearing cotton gloves, remove a cookie from the oven and flip it onto one gloved hand. Place a fortune in center of cookie while bringing edges together to enclose (don't fold it too firmly in half). Grasp ends of cookie and bend corners down to form a crescent. If cookie hardens too fast or starts to crack, return it to oven for about 1 minute before continuing the fold. Once it's shaped, fit it, ends down, into a muffin cup to fix the shape as it cools. Shape other cookies the same way. Let cool completely. Repeat to bake and shape remaining cookies.
Make Ahead: Up to 1 week, stored airtight at room temperature.

PER COOKIE: 84 cal., 52% (44 cal.) from fat; 1 g protein; 5 g fat (0.4 g sat.); 8.9 g carbo (0.2 g fiber); 36 mg sodium; 0 mg chol.

The All-American Fortune Cookie

Fortune cookies are actually not Chinese. In fact, they are probably a variation on the Japanese *tsujiura senbei*, a fortune-stuffed cracker made of unsweetened sesame-miso batter. But the fortune cookie as we know it—made with butter and vanilla—came into being in California sometime in the late 1800s or early 1900s, and at least three different Asian Americans have laid claim to its invention: Makoto Hagiwara, designer of the Japanese Tea Garden in San Francisco's Golden Gate Park; David Jung, founder of the Hong Kong Noodle Company, in Los Angeles; and Seiichi Kito, one of the founders of the L.A. Japanese pastry shop Fugetsu-Do.

The association with Chinese food—in the United States and Canada at least—began during World War II, when most Japanese Americans were forcibly interned and Chinese Americans made inroads into the fortune-cookie business. Today, many consider fortune cookies the essential finale to a Chinese dinner. (They are now even made in China, where they are called many different things, including "good luck label cookie" and "divining cookie.")

Frosted Ginger Cookies

Reader Nancy Bolton-Rawles, of Eagle Point, Oregon, found this recipe in a collection of recipes her mother gave her. We love the cookies' soft texture and bright spice flavor.

MAKES 40 cookies | **TIME** 35 minutes

1 cup granulated sugar, plus more for rolling cookies
¾ cup butter, at room temperature
1 egg
3 tbsp. molasses
2 cups flour, sifted
1 tsp. baking soda
1½ tsp. ground ginger
1 tsp. cinnamon
½ tsp. *each* salt, ground cloves, and freshly grated
   nutmeg
1 cup powdered sugar
1 tsp. fresh lemon juice

1. Preheat oven to 350°. Grease a large baking sheet. In a large bowl, cream granulated sugar with butter until light and fluffy, about 3 minutes. Mix in egg and molasses.
2. In a medium bowl, stir together flour, baking soda, ginger, cinnamon, salt, cloves, and nutmeg. Add to butter mixture and blend well.
3. Fill a shallow bowl with granulated sugar. Break off walnut-size pieces of dough and roll into balls; roll balls in sugar. Arrange about 1 in. apart on baking sheet. Bake until golden brown, about 10 minutes. Transfer to racks to cool.
4. Meanwhile, make glaze: Combine powdered sugar with 1 tbsp. water and stir until smooth, then stir in lemon juice. Drizzle glaze over cooled cookies.

PER COOKIE: 102 cal., 33% (34 cal.) from fat; 0.8 g protein; 3.8 g fat (2.2 g sat.); 16 g carbo (0.2 g fiber); 98 mg sodium; 15 mg chol.

Honey Lace Crisps

These cookies look delicate but are extremely forgiving to work with—and here's a trick: If they begin to stiffen, put them back in the oven for a minute to rewarm and loosen up.

MAKES 20 cookies | **TIME** 45 minutes

¼ cup *each* unsalted butter and local honey
½ cup powdered sugar
⅛ tsp. salt
3 tbsp. flour

1. Preheat oven to 350°. Line two flat rimmed baking sheets with parchment paper. In a medium saucepan, melt butter with honey over medium heat. Add powdered sugar and salt and whisk until well combined. Add flour and continue to whisk until no lumps remain. Transfer to a small bowl and let cool slightly, about 5 minutes.
2. Spoon 1 heaping tsp. cookie batter onto sheets about 4 in. apart (they will spread a lot).
3. Bake until dark golden brown and small holes appear throughout, 10 to 12 minutes. Keep oven on.
4. Let crisps cool on tray until they start to firm up, 2 to 3 minutes. While cookies cool, use a paring knife to separate any cookies that have melted together and to shape each into a circle. Working in batches of 3 or 4, carefully peel cookies off paper and lay over a rolling pin. Let cool on pin until completely crisp, about 3 minutes. If cookies firm up before you can shape them, put baking sheet back in oven to warm slightly, about 1 minute.
Make Ahead: Up to 1 day; store airtight.

PER CRISP: 49 cal., 41% (20 cal.) from fat; 0.2 g protein; 2.3 g fat (1.5 g sat.); 7.3 g carbo (0 g fiber); 16 mg sodium; 6.1 mg chol.

Honey-Almond Lace Crisps: Follow directions for Honey Lace Crisps, *above*, through step 2. Bake until batter starts to bubble and spread, about 3 minutes. Sprinkle each crisp with 1 tsp. sliced **skin-on almonds** (about 1¼ cups total). Continue to bake, and then shape, as instructed in steps 3 and 4.

PER CRISP: 100 cal., 60% (60 cal.) from fat; 2.1 g protein; 6.7 g fat (1.8 g sat.); 9.3 g carbo (1.1 g fiber); 16 mg sodium; 6.1 mg chol.

Salted Honey Lace Crisps: Follow directions for Honey Lace Crisps through step 3. Immediately sprinkle the baked crisps with a pinch of **coarse sea salt** (about 2 tbsp. total). Shape as directed in step 4.

PER CRISP: 49 cal., 41% (20 cal.) from fat; 0.2 g protein; 2.3 g fat (1.5 g sat.); 7.3 g carbo (0 g fiber); 380 mg sodium; 6.1 mg chol.

Orange Cream–filled Honey Lace Crisps:
Follow directions for Honey Lace Crisps through step 3. In step 4, form hot cookies into a small cylinder around handle of a wooden spoon, holding until firm (a few seconds) and sliding off when cool. In a medium bowl, whisk together 2 cups **heavy whipping cream**, ¼ cup **granulated sugar**, and finely shredded **zest of 1 orange** until firm peaks form. Fill a large resealable plastic bag with cream. With scissors, snip off one corner of bag (about ¼ in.) and pipe cream into cookie cylinder from either end. Serve filled cookies immediately.

PER FILLED CRISP: 142 cal., 70% (100 cal.) from fat; 0.7 g protein; 11 g fat (7 g sat.); 11 g carbo (0.1 g fiber); 25 mg sodium; 39 mg chol.

Chocolate Decadence Cookies

Don't overbake these! They're best when slightly gooey. Our favorite Western bittersweet chocolate: Guittard (*guittard.com* or 800/428-2462), based in Burlingame, California.

MAKES About 40 cookies | **TIME** 30 minutes, plus 2 hours to chill

10 oz. bittersweet chocolate, chopped
2 oz. unsweetened chocolate, chopped
¼ cup unsalted butter, cut into chunks
3 eggs, at room temperature
1 cup sugar
¾ cup flour
¾ tsp. baking powder
¼ tsp. kosher salt

1. Put chocolates and butter in a medium metal bowl and set bowl over a pan filled with 1 in. of simmering water. Cook, stirring occasionally, until melted, then remove from heat and let cool slightly. Whisk in eggs and sugar, mixing until combined. Then whisk in flour, baking powder, and salt. Chill dough, covered, until firm, about 2 hours.
2. Let dough sit at room temperature 15 minutes. Meanwhile, preheat oven to 350° and line two baking sheets with parchment paper. Scoop 1 tbsp. portions of dough, rolling each into a ball, and put onto sheets 1 in. apart.
3. Bake cookies until they no longer look wet on top, about 8 minutes. Let cool on baking sheets.
Make Ahead: Dough (step 1), up to 1 day; baked cookies up to 2 days, airtight.

PER COOKIE: 86 cal., 56% (48 cal.) from fat; 1.4 g protein; 5.3 g fat (2.8 g sat.); 11 g carbo (0.8 g fiber); 27 mg sodium; 19 mg chol.

Double Chocolate Cookies: Stir 1 cup **white chocolate chips** into dough in step 1. Continue as directed.

PER COOKIE: 109 cal., 55% (60 cal.) from fat; 1.7 g protein; 6.7 g fat (3.7 g sat.); 13 g carbo (0.8 g fiber); 31 mg sodium; 20 mg chol.

Chocolate–Peanut Butter Thumbprint Cookies: Prepare Chocolate Decadence Cookies through step 2. Press your thumb into center of each cookie ball, making a small well. Fill a resealable plastic bag with ½ cup **peanut butter**. With scissors, snip off one corner of bag (about ¼ in.) and squeeze about ½ tsp. peanut butter from bag into each well. Bake as directed in step 3.

Chocolate–Peppermint Patty Cookies: Follow directions for Chocolate Decadence Cookies through step 2. Using palm of your hand, press dough balls into rounds ¼ in. thick. Bake cookies until they no longer look wet on top, about 8 minutes. Let cool on baking sheets. In a small bowl, mix 3 cups **powdered sugar**, ¼ cup **milk**, and ¾ tsp. **peppermint extract** until smooth. Spread 1 heaping tsp. peppermint icing onto flat side of a cookie. Top with flat side of a second cookie to form a sandwich, pressing together to squeeze filling to the edge. Roll edge of cookie in crushed **candy canes**. Repeat with remaining cookies. If you're in the mood for ice cream, substitute a spoonful of softened **mint gelato** for the mint filling, then roll edge in crushed candy canes. Makes 20 filled cookies.

PER SANDWICH COOKIE WITH PEPPERMINT ICING: 320 cal., 30% (96 cal.) from fat; 3 g protein; 11 g fat (5.8 g sat.); 58 g carbo (1.6 g fiber); 56 mg sodium; 38 mg chol.

4 Tips for Cookie Success

1. Start with soft butter. If the recipe calls for room-temperature butter, it should be soft but not runny. You can soften it for a few seconds in a microwave oven.
2. Measure flour accurately. Stir the flour to loosen it in the bin, then scoop it into the cup and level off the top of the cup with a metal spatula or knife.
3. Use cool baking sheets. Never put cookie dough on warm sheets. To cool sheets quickly, rinse with cold water; dry before using them again. Choose shiny, light-colored baking sheets; dark-colored ones retain heat and tend to burn the bottoms of cookies.
4. Rotate sheets halfway through baking time. Cookies will bake more evenly if they spend equal time on the top and bottom racks of the oven.

Vanilla-bean Leaf Cookies

Crisp, buttery cookies are just right when you want a small bite of something sweet after dinner.

MAKES About 2 dozen cookies | **TIME** 45 minutes

1 cup butter, at room temperature
¾ cup granulated sugar
1 vanilla bean (3 to 4 in.)
2¼ cups flour
½ tsp. baking powder
¼ tsp. salt
About 2 tbsp. coarse sugar (sometimes called sparkling sugar or sanding sugar; see Quick Tip below)

1. Preheat oven to 325°. Butter two or three baking sheets.
2. Put butter and sugar in a large bowl. Slit vanilla bean and, with knife tip, scrape seeds into bowl. With a mixer on medium speed, beat until smooth. In a medium bowl, whisk together flour, baking powder, and salt. On low speed, gradually mix flour mixture into butter mixture until blended. Beat on medium speed until dough forms a ball. Divide dough in half.
3. Transfer dough to a lightly floured work surface. With a lightly floured rolling pin, roll each half into a circle ⅛ in. thick. Cut out cookies with a floured 3- to 4-in. leaf-shaped cutter. Place cookies ½ in. apart on baking sheets. Re-roll scraps as needed.
4. With back of knife, lightly press a decorative vein pattern into cookies. Sprinkle with coarse sugar.
5. Bake cookies until edges just begin to brown, 12 to 15 minutes, switching pan positions halfway through baking. Cool completely on baking sheets.
Quick Tip: Find coarse sugar in the baking aisle of well-stocked grocery or specialty stores.
Make Ahead: Up to 2 days, stored airtight at room temperature.

PER COOKIE: 154 cal., 47% (72 cal.) from fat; 1.6 g protein; 8 g fat (4.9 g sat.); 19 g carbo (0.4 g fiber); 120 mg sodium; 30 mg chol.

Ginger Leaf Cookies: Follow directions for Vanilla-bean Leaf Cookies, except replace granulated sugar with firmly packed **dark brown sugar** and replace vanilla bean with 3 tbsp. minced **crystallized ginger** and 2 tsp. **vanilla extract**. Brush cookies with egg wash (1 **egg** lightly beaten with 1 tbsp. **milk**) before sprinkling with coarse sugar.

PER COOKIE: 154 cal., 47% (72 cal.) from fat; 1.6 g protein; 8 g fat (4.9 g sat.); 19 g carbo (0.4 g fiber); 120 mg sodium; 30 mg chol.

Coconut Cookies with Lemon Curd and Raspberries

These tartlike cookies can be baked ahead, then topped at the last minute with the pleasingly puckery lemon curd and sweet raspberries.

MAKES 2 dozen cookies | **TIME** 35 minutes, plus 1 hour to chill

¾ cup sweetened shredded dried coconut
⅔ cup unsalted butter, at room temperature
¾ cup sugar
1 egg
1 tbsp. milk
1½ cups flour
1 tsp. baking powder
½ tsp. salt
Lemon Curd (recipe follows)
1 pt. raspberries

1. Preheat oven to 325°. Spread coconut on a baking sheet and bake until golden brown, 6 to 8 minutes. Let cool before using. Set aside.
2. Increase oven temperature to 350°. In a large bowl, with a mixer on high speed, beat butter and sugar until light and fluffy. Beat in egg, coconut, and milk until well blended, scraping down side of bowl as necessary.
3. In a small bowl, whisk together flour, baking powder, and salt. Beat into butter mixture until well blended. Wrap dough in plastic wrap and chill until firm, at least 1 hour.
4. Unwrap dough and set on a lightly floured work surface. Roll out dough with a lightly floured rolling pin to ⅛ in. thick. Cut with a 3- or 4-in. flower-shaped or round cookie cutter and place cookies slightly apart on buttered or parchment paper–lined baking sheets.
5. Bake cookies until edges are golden, 10 to 14 minutes; if baking more than one sheet at a time, switch sheet positions halfway through baking. Transfer cookies to racks to cool.
6. Top each cookie with a dollop of lemon curd and several raspberries. Serve immediately.
Make Ahead: Dough, up to 3 days, chilled. Cookies, up to 2 days, stored airtight at room temperature. Lemon curd, up to 2 days, chilled.

PER COOKIE: 152 cal., 40% (61 cal.) from fat; 2.1 g protein; 6.8 g fat (4.1 g sat.); 21 g carbo (0.9 g fiber); 149 mg sodium; 49 mg chol.

Lemon Curd: In a heatproof bowl, whisk together 3 **eggs**, ½ cup **fresh lemon juice**, and ¾ cup **sugar** until well blended. Set over a pan of gently simmering water and cook, whisking constantly, until mixture begins to thicken noticeably, 5 to 8 minutes. Remove from heat immediately and stir in 3 tbsp. **butter**, 1 tbsp. at a time, until mixture is smooth and glossy. Cover bowl with a sheet of plastic wrap pressed against the curd's surface (to prevent a skin from forming) and refrigerate until cool, about 30 minutes.

Gingersnaps

This recipe makes a lot of cookies. You can halve it if you like, or—to get the most variety out of a full batch—use half the dough for Gingersnaps and the other half for Sugar- and Spice-dusted Ginger Chew Cookies or for sandwich cookies filled with dulce de leche or lemon meringue (*recipes follow*).

MAKES 100 cookies | **TIME** 1 hour, plus 3 hours to chill

1 cup butter, at room temperature
1 cup firmly packed brown sugar
½ cup unsulphured molasses
1 egg
3½ cups flour
1 tsp. baking soda
½ tsp. salt
2 tsp. ground ginger
1 tsp. cinnamon
**½ tsp. *each* ground cloves, nutmeg, and freshly ground
    black pepper**

1. In a large bowl, with a mixer on medium speed, beat butter and brown sugar together. Mix in molasses, then egg, until blended, scraping down side of bowl as needed.
2. In a medium bowl, combine flour, baking soda, salt, ginger, cinnamon, cloves, nutmeg, and pepper; add to butter mixture on low speed, mixing until combined.
3. Divide dough in half, shape each into a disk, wrap in plastic wrap, and chill until firm, about 3 hours.
4. Preheat oven to 350°. Line rimmed baking sheets with parchment paper. Unwrap dough. On a generously floured work surface, roll out each disk to ⅛ in. thick. Using a round 2½- to 3-in. cookie cutter, cut out dough and arrange circles about 1 in. apart on baking sheets (use a small spatula to transfer). Re-roll scraps as needed.
5. Bake cookies until dry-looking and just starting to brown at edges, about 8 minutes. Set sheets on racks and let cookies cool.
Make Ahead: Dough, up to 1 week, chilled. Cookies, up to 3 days, stored airtight at room temperature.

PER COOKIE: 46 cal., 37% (17 cal.) from fat; 0.5 g protein; 2 g fat (1.2 g sat.); 6.8 g carbo (0.2 g fiber); 39 mg sodium; 7 mg chol.

Sugar- and Spice-dusted Ginger Chew Cookies: Prepare Gingersnaps through step 3. In a small bowl, combine ½ tsp. **cinnamon** and ¼ cup **granulated sugar**. Pull off about 1 tbsp. of dough from disk, roll into a ball, and drop into cinnamon sugar bowl. Working in batches of 3 or 4, coat dough balls in sugar and arrange about 1 in. apart on baking sheets. Bake as directed in step 5.

PER COOKIE: 48 cal., 35% (17 cal.) from fat; 0.5 g protein; 2 g fat (1.2 g sat.); 7.3 g carbo (0.2 g fiber); 39 mg sodium; 7 mg chol.

Dulce de Leche Gingersnap Sandwiches: Dulce de leche—a staple sweet in many Latin American countries—is a thick, rich sauce made by reducing milk for hours. It's available at well-stocked grocery stores and Latino markets. Bake Gingersnaps as directed. On flat side of half the cookies, spread 1 scant tbsp. prepared **dulce de leche** (you'll need 3 cups total). Sandwich with remaining cookies. Makes 50 sandwich cookies. Cookies can be filled up to 5 hours ahead.

PER SANDWICH COOKIE: 145 cal., 28% (41 cal.) from fat; 2.1 g protein; 4.6 g fat (2.9 g sat.); 25 g carbo (0.3 g fiber); 100 mg sodium; 19 mg chol.

Lemon Meringue Gingersnap Snowflakes: Prepare Gingersnap dough, but use snowflake cutters in various sizes to cut out the dough. (Make sure you have an equal number of each size to form matching tops and bottoms.) Use a small cutter to remove centers from half the cookies (these will be the tops). Arrange snowflakes about 1 in. apart on baking sheets (use a small spatula to transfer). Bake as directed. Meanwhile, make lemon meringue: Mix ¾ cup **granulated sugar**, 2 tbsp. **fresh lemon juice**, and 3 **egg whites** in a medium metal bowl. Set bowl in a pan over 2 to 3 in. of simmering water (water should not touch bottom of bowl). Whisking constantly, heat mixture until egg whites are warm to touch and sugar has dissolved, about 4 minutes. Remove bowl from pan and use a mixer on medium speed to beat until cool and fluffy, about 10 minutes. Stir in finely shredded **zest of 1 orange**. Fit a 1-gal. resealable plastic bag with a star tip, snipping off one corner of bag and fitting tip snugly into it (or use a pastry bag). Half-fill bag with meringue. Gather bag at top and gently pipe about 2 tbsp. meringue onto flat side of a whole cookie. Sandwich with another cookie that has a cutout top. Repeat with remaining cookies. Dust cookies on both sides with **powdered sugar**. Makes 50 sandwich cookies. Cookies can be filled up to 5 hours ahead.

PER SANDWICH COOKIE: 105 cal., 32% (34 cal.) from fat; 1.3 g protein; 3.9 g fat (2.4 g sat.); 17 g carbo (0.3 g fiber); 82 mg sodium; 14 mg chol.

Cardamom–Brown Sugar Palmiers

Crunchy, spicy palmiers look hard to make—but actually, the opposite is true. This is a good recipe to make when you want to impress someone, but not work too hard at it.

recipe pictured on page **601**

MAKES 16 cookies | **TIME** 30 minutes, plus 1 hour to chill

½ cup firmly packed light brown sugar
2 tsp. ground cardamom
1 sheet frozen puff pastry dough (about ½ lb.), thawed

1. Combine brown sugar and cardamom in a small bowl. Unfold dough flat on a lightly floured work surface and sprinkle evenly with half the sugar mixture.
2. Using a rolling pin, lightly roll sugar into dough so that most of sugar sticks, being careful not to change shape of dough. Turn pastry over and sprinkle evenly with remaining sugar.
3. Beginning with side closest to you, fold in dough, 1 in. at a time, to center of rectangle. Repeat with opposite side. Fold one half on top of other as if closing a book. Wrap dough airtight in plastic wrap and chill at least 1 hour and up to 1 day (*see Quick Tip below*).
4. Preheat oven to 400°. Line two baking sheets with parchment paper. Using a sharp knife, cut dough crosswise into ½-in.-thick slices and lay slices flat about 2 in. apart on sheets.
5. Bake slices until doubled in size and golden, about 10 minutes. Let cookies cool completely on sheets.
Quick Tip: As with any super-buttery dough, chilling makes the dough much easier to slice.
Make Ahead: Unbaked palmiers, up to 2 weeks, frozen. Baked palmiers, up to 2 days, stored airtight at room temperature.

PER PALMIER: 111 cal., 47% (52 cal.) from fat; 1.1 g protein; 5.8 g fat (0.8 g sat.); 14 g carbo (0.2 g fiber); 41 mg sodium; 0 mg chol.

Buttery Semolina Currant Cookies

The sandy texture of these shortbreadlike cookies comes from semolina, made from durum wheat and usually used for pasta. Orange zest and currants give them lots of flavor.

MAKES About 2½ dozen cookies | **TIME** 40 minutes, plus 2 hours to chill

¾ cup dried currants
1½ cups flour
¾ cup fine semolina (*see Quick Tip below*)
½ tsp. salt
1 cup unsalted butter, softened
½ cup powdered sugar
1 egg
1 tbsp. finely shredded orange zest
About 2 tbsp. cornmeal

1. In a small bowl, cover currants with very hot water. Let sit for 10 minutes; drain.
2. Meanwhile, combine flour, semolina, and salt. In a large bowl, with a mixer on medium speed, beat butter and sugar until smooth. Add egg, scrape down side of bowl, and mix until combined. Add flour mixture, orange zest, and currants, mixing slowly until combined. Turn dough onto a lightly floured work surface and shape into a disk. Wrap in plastic wrap and chill at least 2 hours.
3. Preheat oven to 350°. Evenly sprinkle two rimmed baking sheets with about 1 tbsp. cornmeal each. Unwrap dough, place on a lightly floured work surface, and roll ⅓ in. thick. Cut dough with a 2-in. decorative cutter and place slightly apart on baking sheets, re-rolling scraps as needed.
4. Bake cookies until light golden brown, 10 to 12 minutes, switching sheet positions halfway through cooking. Transfer cookies to a rack to cool.
Quick Tip: Find semolina with the flour in your grocery store.
Make Ahead: Dough, up to 2 days, chilled. Cookies, up to 5 days, stored airtight at room temperature.

PER COOKIE: 115 cal., 50% (58 cal.) from fat; 1.6 g protein; 6.4 g fat (3.9 g sat.); 13 g carbo (0.6 g fiber); 42 mg sodium; 24 mg chol.

Cardamom-Brown Sugar
Palmiers, *page 600*

Candied Citrus Peels,
page 620

Florentine Bars,
page 619

Sopaipillas,
page 593

Caramelized Orange
Cheesecake, *page 642*

Strawberry Puff,
page 664

Candy Cane Cake,
page 636

Homemade Fortune
Cookies, *page 595*

Tres Leches **Cake with Raspberries,** *page 641*

Western Dried Fruits
Cake, *page 627*

Pear and Pecan Upside-
down Cake, *page 627*

Triple-threat Chocolate
Cookies, *page 616*

Butter Shortbreads

The rich butter flavor and crumbly texture of this cookie make it a staple of holiday baking. Plus, it's very versatile: You can create several different cookies with the same dough (variations follow).

MAKES 16 cookies | **TIME** 1¼ hours

2 cups flour
1 cup cold unsalted butter, cubed
½ cup granulated sugar
¼ tsp. salt
2 tbsp. coarse sugar (sometimes called sparkling sugar or sanding sugar; see Quick Tip below)

1. Preheat oven to 325°. Put flour, butter, granulated sugar, and salt in a medium bowl. With a mixer on low speed, mix until blended, then increase speed to medium and mix until dough is no longer crumbly and just comes together.
2. Press dough evenly into a 9-in. round cake pan. Sprinkle with coarse sugar.
3. Bake until golden brown, 30 to 40 minutes. Cut still-warm shortbread with a fork, tines down, into 16 wedge-shaped pieces with shaggy edges. Cool completely, then invert pan onto a clean work surface and carefully separate cookies.
Quick Tip: Find coarse sugar in the baking aisle of well-stocked grocery or specialty stores.
Make Ahead: Up to 1 week, stored airtight at room temperature.

PER COOKIE: 189 cal., 54% (103 cal.) from fat; 38 g protein; 12 g fat (7.3 g sat.); 20 g carbo (0.4 g fiber); 38 mg sodium; 31 mg chol.

Lemon-Rosemary Button Shortbreads: Prepare
Butter Shortbreads, adding finely shredded **zest of 1 lemon** and 1 tsp. chopped **rosemary leaves** to dough in step 1. Form dough into a disk and chill 30 minutes. On a lightly floured work surface, roll out dough to ½ in. thick. Cut dough into circles with a 1½-in. cookie cutter. Re-roll scraps as needed. Arrange on baking sheets 1 in. apart and chill 15 minutes. Bake until light golden brown, 12 to 15 minutes. Meanwhile, mix 1½ cups **powdered sugar**, 2 tbsp. **fresh lemon juice**, and finely shredded **zest of 1 lemon** until smooth. Spoon ½ tsp. glaze over each cooled cookie, spreading with the back of the spoon; then press 1 **rosemary sprig** into center of each cookie. Makes 32 cookies.

PER COOKIE: 115 cal., 45% (52 cal.) from fat; 0.9 g protein; 5.9 g fat (3.7 g sat.); 15 g carbo (0.3 g fiber); 19 mg sodium; 15 mg chol.

Raspberry Window Shortbreads: Prepare dough
for Butter Shortbreads through step 1. Form dough into a disk and chill 30 minutes. On a lightly floured work surface, roll out dough to ⅛ in. thick. Use a selection of 1½-in. decorative cutters to cut as many shapes as you can, making sure you have an equal number of each shape to form matching tops and bottoms and re-rolling scraps as needed. Arrange cookies 1 in. apart on baking sheets. Use a variety of smaller cutters to remove centers from half the cookies (these will be the tops). Chill on sheets 15 minutes, then bake until light golden brown, 12 to 15 minutes. When cool, spread each whole cookie with about ½ tsp. **raspberry jam** (you'll need about ¼ cup total). Sprinkle half the cutout tops evenly with ½ cup **powdered sugar**. Mix another 1 cup powdered sugar with 2½ tsp. **milk** to thin, then dip tops of remaining cutout tops with glaze. If you like, dip some glazed tops into coarse **sugar**. Set all tops on jam-covered bottoms. Makes 26 sandwich cookies.

PER SANDWICH COOKIE: 149 cal., 43% (64 cal.) from fat; 1.1 g protein; 7.2 g fat (4.5 g sat.); 21 g carbo (0.3 g fiber); 25 mg sodium; 19 mg chol.

Apricot-Pecan Crumb Bars: We used apricot jam
and pecans, but feel free to use whatever jam and nuts you like. Prepare dough for Butter Shortbreads through step 1. Reserve 1 cup dough. Press remaining dough into bottom of a buttered 9-in. square baking pan. Spread 1 cup **apricot preserves** over dough. In a small bowl, combine reserved dough with ¼ tsp. **cinnamon** and ½ cup **pecan halves** and evenly crumble mixture over preserves. Bake until golden brown and bubbling, about 50 minutes. Let cool completely, then cut into 16 squares.

PER BAR: 255 cal., 49% (126 cal.) from fat; 2.2 g protein; 14 g fat (7.6 g sat.); 32 g carbo (0.8 g fiber); 46 mg sodium; 31 mg chol.

Honey-Caramel Nut Bars: Prepare dough for
Butter Shortbreads through step 1. Press dough evenly into bottom of a buttered 9-in. square baking pan. Bake 10 minutes. Meanwhile, make topping: In a small saucepan, bring 3 tbsp. **butter**, ⅓ cup **honey**, and ⅓ cup **sugar** to a boil. Remove from heat. Stir in ¾ cup *each* toasted **whole almonds**, **pecan halves**, **salted cashews**, and **salted pistachios**. Carefully spoon mixture over shortbread and continue to bake until nuts are toasted and liquid is bubbling, about 30 minutes. Let cool completely. Use a serrated knife to cut into 16 squares, then cut each square diagonally to make 32 triangles.

PER BAR: 185 cal., 63% (117 cal.) from fat; 2.9 g protein; 13 g fat (5.1 g sat.); 16 g carbo (1.3 g fiber); 48 mg sodium; 18 mg chol.

Ev's Skorpas

Evelyn Mount's Swedish cookies—similar to biscotti—have been a holiday favorite in the family for as long as her daughter, *Sunset* reader Meredith Sage (of Colorado Springs, Colorado), can remember.

MAKES About 2 dozen cookies | **TIME** 1¾ hours

½ cup butter, cut into chunks, at room temperature
1 cup plus 2 tbsp. sugar
2 eggs plus 1 egg white
1 tsp. almond extract
3 cups flour
1 tbsp. ground cardamom (*see Quick Tip below*)
2 tsp. baking powder
⅓ cup half-and-half
¼ cup slivered almonds

1. Preheat oven to 350°. Butter and flour two 9- by 5-in. loaf pans. In a large bowl, with a mixer on medium speed, beat butter and 1 cup sugar until well blended. Beat in whole eggs and almond extract until completely incorporated, scraping down side of bowl as necessary.
2. In a medium bowl, stir together flour, cardamom, and baking powder; stir or beat flour into butter mixture along with half-and-half (dough will be stiff). Divide dough between pans and spread or pat level.
3. Beat egg white until foamy and brush over tops of dough. Sprinkle evenly with almonds and remaining 2 tbsp. sugar.
4. Bake until tops are golden, 25 to 30 minutes. Remove from oven and reduce temperature to 325°. Let cool in pans on a rack 5 minutes, then invert pans onto rack to release loaves. Let stand until cool enough to handle, about 20 minutes.
5. With a serrated knife, cut loaves crosswise into ¾-in.-thick slices and arrange on a large baking sheet. Bake until golden brown and firm to the touch, about 25 minutes longer. Transfer slices to rack and let cool completely.
Quick Tip: Use a fresh jar of ground cardamom if you can, or grind your own; the heady flavor of the spice will be well worth it.
Make Ahead: Up to 2 weeks, stored airtight at room temperature.

PER COOKIE: 148 cal., 34% (50 cal.) from fat; 2.7 g protein; 5.5 g fat (2.8 g sat.); 22 g carbo (0.5 g fiber); 89 mg sodium; 29 mg chol.

Apricot-Chocolate-Almond Biscotti

These biscotti are crumbly delivery systems for chewy apricot bits, hunks of dark chocolate, and crunchy almonds.

MAKES About 2 dozen biscotti | **TIME** 1½ hours

1¾ cups flour
1 cup sugar
½ tsp. baking powder
¼ tsp. salt
6 tbsp. unsalted butter, melted and cooled
½ tsp. vanilla extract
2 eggs
¾ cup diced dried apricots, preferably Blenheim (*see Quick Tip below*)
⅔ cup slivered almonds
4 oz. bittersweet chocolate, chopped

1. Preheat oven to 350°. Line a large baking sheet with parchment paper. In a food processor, pulse flour, sugar, baking powder, and salt 5 or 6 times to blend. In a small bowl, whisk together melted butter, vanilla, and eggs; add to flour mixture and pulse 10 to 12 times to form a dough.
2. Transfer dough to a large bowl. Add apricots, almonds, and chocolate and stir to mix thoroughly.
3. Put dough on baking sheet and form into two 12-in.-long loaves. Flatten tops slightly and bake until loaves are golden but give slightly when pressed, 25 to 30 minutes.
4. Remove loaves from oven and reduce temperature to 325°. Let loaves cool 5 minutes, then cut on diagonal into ½- to ¾-in.-thick slices. Arrange slices flat on baking sheet and bake until lightly browned, 10 to 15 minutes. Transfer cookies to racks to cool completely.
Quick Tip: The very flavorful, deep orange Blenheim apricot doesn't ship well, so it has been slowly declining. Find dried California Blenheims online at *brfarms. com*.
Make Ahead: Up to 1 week, stored airtight at room temperature. Dough, up to 2 days, chilled.

PER COOKIE: 152 cal., 41% (62 cal.) from fat; 2.7 g protein; 6.9 g fat (3 g sat.); 21 g carbo (0.8 g fiber); 41 mg sodium; 25 mg chol.

cookies, bars & candies

Chocolate-Hazelnut Domes

Reader Jayna Teisinger, of Fresno, California, created these nut-rich cookies with her daughter Emily. Dusted with powdered sugar, they look like snow-capped mountains.

MAKES 3 dozen cookies | **TIME** 45 minutes

12 oz. good-quality bittersweet chocolate, chopped
½ cup butter, at room temperature
2 cups granulated sugar
2 eggs
2 tsp. vanilla extract
2 cups flour
½ tsp. *each* baking soda and salt
¾ cup regular rolled oats
1½ cups hazelnuts, toasted *(see How to Toast Nuts, page 134)* and finely ground
¼ cup powdered sugar

1. Preheat oven to 350°. Line a large baking sheet with parchment paper. In a microwave or double boiler, melt chocolate.

2. In a large bowl, cream butter with granulated sugar until light and fluffy. Add eggs, vanilla, and melted chocolate and beat to combine. Add flour, baking soda, and salt and stir to combine. Stir in oats and hazelnuts.

3. Break off small pieces of dough, roll into 1½-in. balls, and arrange on baking sheet about 1 in. apart. Bake until puffed, about 9 minutes. Transfer cookies to a rack. When cool, sift powdered sugar over them.

PER COOKIE: 182 cal., 46% (84 cal.) from fat; 2.6 g protein; 9.3 g fat (3.7 g sat.); 24 g carbo (1 g fiber); 80 mg sodium; 19 mg chol.

Peppermint Layer Cookies

Fun, festive, and retro-cool.

MAKES About 70 cookies | **TIME** 2 hours, plus 1½ hours to chill

1 cup unsalted butter, at room temperature
1⅓ cups sugar
3 cups flour, plus more for rolling
½ tsp. *each* baking powder and salt
1 egg plus 2 egg yolks
2 tsp. vanilla extract
½ tsp. peppermint extract, divided
20 to 25 drops red food coloring
15 to 20 drops green food coloring
10 oz. white chocolate, finely chopped
5 oz. peppermint candy canes or peppermint candies, finely crushed

1. In the bowl of a stand mixer fitted with a paddle attachment, beat butter and sugar until pale and fluffy, about 4 minutes. Meanwhile, sift flour, baking powder, and salt into a separate bowl.

2. With mixer running, add egg and yolks one at a time to butter mixture, beating well after each addition. Add vanilla. Slowly add flour mixture and beat on low just until combined.

3. Divide dough into thirds. Shape one third into a disk; set aside. Return another third to mixer, raise speed to medium-low, and add ¼ tsp. peppermint extract and the red food coloring; shape into a disk and set aside. Clean bowl and paddle attachment. Put last third of dough in bowl and beat in remaining ¼ tsp. peppermint extract and the green food coloring; shape into a disk.

4. Draw a 6- by 8-in. rectangle on a sheet of waxed paper. Turn sheet over and lightly flour it. Working with one disk at a time, put dough in center of rectangle. Using a lightly floured rolling pin, your fingers, and a pastry scraper or a ruler, roll and shape each disk to fit rectangle. Layer each dough rectangle between sheets of waxed paper and chill at least 30 minutes and up to overnight. Let sit at room temperature for 5 minutes.

5. Line three baking sheets with parchment paper. Peel waxed paper from rectangles and put one sheet on counter; discard the rest. Set green dough on waxed paper. Top with red dough, lining them up as evenly as possible; gently press down. Top red dough with plain dough. Gently roll dough stack with a rolling pin to seal layers, then trim uneven edges with a very sharp knife.

6. Cut dough stack lengthwise into three 2-in.-wide columns. Cut each column crosswise into ⅓-in.-thick pieces. Lay pieces 2 in. apart on baking sheets. Freeze 30 to 45 minutes. Meanwhile, preheat oven to 350°.

7. Bake cookies 7 minutes; switch positions of baking sheets and bake until bottoms are light golden brown, 7 minutes more. (You may need to bake in two batches if your oven won't hold three baking sheets; keep cookies in freezer until ready to bake.) Cool cookies on wire racks.

8. Put chopped chocolate in a heatproof bowl that will fit over a pot with a few inches of water in it (bottom of bowl should not touch the water); set bowl aside. Bring water to a boil, turn off heat, and set bowl over water. Stir chocolate until melted and smooth. Dip each cookie about ½ in. into chocolate, then dip into or sprinkle with crushed candy. Set on waxed paper to harden (or chill in refrigerator 15 minutes).

Make Ahead: In an airtight container at cool room temperature or in refrigerator for up to 1 week; store peppermint ends up. Freeze cookies for up to 2 months.

PER COOKIE: 90 cal., 42% (38 cal.) from fat; 0.9 g protein; 4.2 g fat (2.5 g sat.); 12 g carbo (0.1 g fiber); 28 mg sodium; 17 mg chol.

Triple-threat Chocolate Cookies

Prepare to abandon all restraint when you try one of these cookies, made with melted chocolate and chocolate chips in the batter and layered with a chocolate ganache filling. Kir Jensen, a pastry chef who owns and operates a dessert food cart called the Sugar Cube in Portland, Oregon, calls them her secret weapon. The cookies are most irresistible when they're still soft after baking; test-bake one to judge how long they take in your oven.

recipe pictured on page **612**

MAKES 16 sandwich cookies | **TIME** 50 minutes, plus 2½ hours to chill and cool

COOKIES
10 oz. bittersweet chocolate, chopped
3 oz. unsweetened chocolate, chopped
¼ cup unsalted butter, cut into chunks
3 eggs, at room temperature
1 cup plus 2 tbsp. sugar
1 tbsp. instant espresso
2 tsp. vanilla extract
6 tbsp. flour
¾ tsp. baking powder
¼ tsp. kosher salt
1½ cups bittersweet chocolate chips
1 cup finely chopped toasted pecans (see *How to Toast Nuts*, page 134)

GANACHE
6 oz. bittersweet chocolate, chopped
¾ cup heavy whipping cream

1. Make cookies: Put chopped chocolates and butter in a medium metal bowl and set bowl over a pan of simmering water. Cook, stirring, until melted, then remove from heat and let cool slightly.

2. Whisk eggs, sugar, espresso, and vanilla into chocolate mixture. In a small bowl, stir together flour, baking powder, and salt. Stir into chocolate mixture until evenly mixed, then stir in chocolate chips and pecans. Wrap dough airtight and chill until firm enough to hold its shape, 50 to 60 minutes.

3. Meanwhile, make ganache: Put chocolate and cream in a medium metal bowl and set bowl over a pan of simmering water. Cook, stirring, until melted, then let cool. Cover and chill, stirring occasionally, until firm enough to spread, about 1¾ hours. If ganache becomes too firm to spread, transfer to a microwave-safe bowl and microwave for a few seconds to soften, then stir.

4. Preheat oven to 350°. Line two large baking sheets with parchment paper. Scoop 2-tbsp. portions of dough onto sheets, spaced about 1 in. apart. Press dough to flatten into even ½-in.-thick rounds. Bake until cookies no longer look wet and you can feel a slight crust on top, about 10 minutes (don't overbake); switch position of baking sheets halfway through. Let cookies cool on sheets on racks.

5. Generously spread flat sides of half the cookies with ganache, then top with remaining cookies. (You may have a little leftover ganache.)

Make Ahead: Ganache, up to 2 days, chilled. Filled cookies, up to 2 days, chilled; up to 2 months, frozen airtight. Serve at room temperature.

PER SANDWICH COOKIE: 433 cal., 64% (277 cal.) from fat; 5.9 g protein; 31 g fat (15 g sat.); 44 g carbo (2.3 g fiber); 60 mg sodium; 63 mg chol.

Caramel Brownies

Reader Chris Schaefer, of Everett, Washington, started with her grandmother's handwritten brownie recipe, then added caramels. We couldn't decide which we liked better, the crunchy outside pieces or the gooey inside ones. Leftovers are unlikely, but you can store the brownies airtight up to 1 day.

MAKES 35 squares | **TIME** 1¼ hours

1½ cups butter
3 cups sugar
5 eggs
1 tbsp. vanilla extract
1 tsp. *each* **salt and baking powder**
2 cups flour
1 cup unsweetened cocoa powder (not Dutch-processed)
14 oz. square caramel candies, such as Kraft or See's, unwrapped

1. Preheat oven to 325°. Butter a 12- by 20-in. piece of foil. Line a 9- by 13-in. baking pan with the foil, buttered side up, letting excess hang over pan ends. In a 3- to 4-qt. pan over medium-high heat, melt butter, stirring occasionally, about 4 minutes. Remove from heat.

2. Stir in sugar, then eggs and vanilla, until blended. Stir in salt and baking powder. Add flour and cocoa and stir until batter is smooth. Scrape batter into pan. Evenly space caramels over batter.

3. Bake just until a toothpick inserted in center (not in a caramel) comes out clean, 55 to 60 minutes. Set pan on a rack and let cool completely.

4. Lift brownies with foil from pan to a counter. Peel back sides of foil. With a long, hot knife, cut between caramels into 35 squares; occasionally rinse knife in very hot water and wipe clean.

PER BROWNIE: 224 cal., 40% (90 cal.) from fat; 2.7 g protein; 10 g fat (6.1 g sat.); 33 g carbo (1.1 g fiber); 200 mg sodium; 53 mg chol.

cookies, bars & candies

Triple-chocolate Brownies

If you like super-chocolaty, fudgy brownies, then this recipe from reader Anne-Marie Summerhays, of Portland, Oregon, is for you.

MAKES 16 brownies (2 in. each) | **TIME** 45 minutes

3 oz. bittersweet chocolate, chopped
½ cup butter
1 cup firmly packed light brown sugar
1 tsp. vanilla extract
2 eggs, beaten
½ cup flour
¼ cup unsweetened cocoa powder (not Dutch-processed)
½ tsp. salt
1 cup semisweet chocolate chips

1. Preheat oven to 350°. In a medium metal bowl set in a pan over 2 to 3 in. of simmering water (water should not touch bottom of bowl), melt chocolate and butter together. Stir in brown sugar and vanilla. Remove from heat. Add eggs and mix thoroughly. Add flour, cocoa, and salt, mixing until smooth. Stir in chocolate chips.

2. Pour batter into an 8-in. square baking pan. Bake until a toothpick inserted in center comes out with moist crumbs sticking to it, 20 to 25 minutes. Let cool in pan on a rack, then cut into 2-in. squares.

PER BROWNIE: 206 cal., 52% (108 cal.) from fat; 2.3 g protein; 12 g fat (6.7 g sat.); 27 g carbo (1.2 g fiber); 147 mg sodium; 42 mg chol.

In a Western Nutshell: Almonds, Macadamias, and More

From the dry slopes of the Colorado Plateau to the damp farms of western Oregon, from California's sunny Central Valley orchards to Hawaii's tropical plantations, the West is planted with just about every familiar nut except the peanut (which is actually a legume), the Brazil nut, and the cashew. Nut orchards in bloom are one of the pleasures of spring in the West, and the freshly harvested nuts are a delicious dividend of where we live.

ALMONDS Though 80 percent of the world's almond crop grows in California's Central Valley, the nuts originated in Central and Southeast Asia and have been cultivated since 4000 B.C. Almonds were even tucked into King Tut's tomb to sustain him in the afterlife. Sweet and mild, almonds are delicious both raw and toasted, and extremely versatile; they show up in everything from candies to curries.

HAZELNUTS French settlers introduced buttery-tasting hazelnuts (also called filberts) to Oregon in the mid-19th century, and now the state grows nearly 100 percent of the U.S. crop. Roasting (*see How to Toast Nuts, page 134*) brings out the hazelnut's rich flavor. The nut is especially good in salads and desserts.

MACADAMIAS We know macadamias as one of Hawaii's signature crops, but southern California grows plenty of them too. In fact, the first trees of this Australian native were planted in California two years earlier than in Hawaii, in 1879. Nothing matches the nut's lush, buttery flavor in baked goods, as a coating for fish fillets, or in tropical fruit salads.

PINE NUTS The tiny pine nut, or piñon, has been a significant part of the diet of the Hopi, Navajo, and other Native American peoples for thousands of years. Unlike most Western nuts, pine nuts are harvested from natural stands rather than farmed, and so the demand far exceeds the supply. Pinyon pines, widespread through the Colorado Plateau, stretch west to California's desert mountains and north to Wyoming. Compared with nuts from other species of pine tree—Italy's stone pine, with its long, slender nuts, and the Korean pine, with shorter, rounder nuts—the piñon nut is relatively large and easy to shell. To buy Western pine nuts in the shell, go to *pinenut.com*.

PISTACHIOS Originally from Asia Minor, pistachios were considered such a delicacy by the queen of Sheba that she hoarded the Assyrian supply for herself and her court. California produced its first commercial crop of pistachios in 1976, and today the state is the second-largest producer in the word. We especially love pistachios roasted and salted as a snack, in salads, and for dessert in pastries and ice cream.

WALNUTS Believed to be the oldest tree food known to people, walnuts date back to 7000 B.C. The Franciscan missionaries brought walnuts to the West in the late 1700s, where they thrived in the Mediterranean climate, and the first commercial planting was in 1867. Now California produces 99 percent of the U.S. crop and two-thirds of the world's export supply. Toasting mellows walnuts' bitterness, brings out their buttery flavor, and gives them a nice crunch.

STORING NUTS. Nuts' ample oil content means they can go rancid if not stored correctly. To keep nuts fresh, refrigerate them airtight for up to 6 months, or freeze in a double layer of resealable plastic bags for up to 1 year.

Mexican Chocolate Streusel Brownies

These cakelike brownies have a hint of cinnamon and a topping of Mexican chocolate streusel. Look for Mexican chocolate (which is flavored with cinnamon and sometimes almonds) in Mexican markets or well-stocked supermarkets. Or you can omit the streusel.

MAKES 32 brownies (2-in.) | **TIME** About 1¼ hours

¾ cup butter, cut into chunks
9 oz. unsweetened chocolate, finely chopped (about 2 cups)
1½ cups firmly packed brown sugar
1 cup granulated sugar
5 eggs
1½ tbsp. vanilla extract
1½ tsp. almond extract
1½ cups flour
1½ tsp. cinnamon
½ tsp. baking powder
¼ tsp. salt
Mexican Chocolate Streusel (*recipe follows*)

1. Preheat oven to 325°. Butter and flour a 9- by 13-in. baking pan. In a large bowl set over a pan of barely simmering water, stir butter and chocolate until melted and smooth. Remove from heat and whisk in brown sugar and granulated sugar. Add eggs one at a time, whisking well after each addition. Whisk in vanilla and almond extracts. Stir in flour, cinnamon, baking powder, and salt until well blended.

2. Spread batter level in pan. Squeeze handfuls of Mexican Chocolate Streusel until it sticks together, then crumble into chunks evenly over surface of batter.

3. Bake brownies until a toothpick inserted in center comes out with moist crumbs attached, 30 to 35 minutes. Let cool in pan on a rack for at least 20 minutes, then cut into 24 or 32 squares.

Make Ahead: Cool completely; do not cut into squares. Keeps 1 day, wrapped airtight.

PER SMALL BROWNIE: 229 cal., 47% (108 cal.) from fat; 2.7 g protein; 12 g fat (6.8 g sat.); 30 g carbo (1.4 g fiber); 105 mg sodium; 50 mg chol.

Mexican Chocolate Streusel: In a food processor or a bowl, whirl or stir ½ cup **flour** and ¼ cup firmly packed **brown sugar** until well blended. Add 5 tbsp. **butter** and whirl or rub in with your fingers until mixture forms coarse crumbs. Pulse in 4½ oz. (about 1½ tablets) coarsely chopped **Mexican chocolate** (some larger chunks will remain), or chop finely with a knife and stir into flour mixture. Use immediately or chill airtight for up to 1 week.

Peanut Butter–Cranberry Go-Bars

These not-too-sweet energy bars will withstand cold, heat, and being stuffed in a backpack or pocket. Natural peanut butters vary from brand to brand in terms of spreadability; we prefer Laura Scudder's Old Fashioned Nutty Peanut Butter because it makes a moister, chewier bar.

MAKES 16 bars (1½ in. each) | **TIME** 1 hour, plus 30 minutes to chill

Cooking-oil spray
1 cup regular rolled oats
⅓ cup oat bran
3 tbsp. flax seeds
1 cup whole-wheat flour
½ tsp. *each* baking powder and salt
½ cup *each* chopped roasted salted peanuts, dried cranberries, and finely chopped dried Mission figs
¾ cup natural chunky peanut butter
¼ cup low-fat milk
1 egg
½ cup honey
Finely shredded zest from 1 lemon
1 tbsp. fresh lemon juice

1. Line a 9- by 13-in. baking pan with plastic wrap, leaving an overhang on 9-in. sides, and coat with cooking-oil spray. In a large bowl, stir together oats, oat bran, flax seeds, flour, baking powder, salt, peanuts, cranberries, and figs until well blended.

2. In another large bowl, with a mixer on medium speed, beat together peanut butter, milk, egg, honey, and lemon zest and juice until well blended.

3. Add flour mixture to peanut butter mixture and beat until completely blended. Scrape dough into pan and, with wet fingers or a rubber spatula, pat to fill pan completely and evenly (dough is sticky, so you may need to wash your hands a few times). Chill dough until firm, about 30 minutes.

4. Meanwhile, preheat oven to 300°. Invert pan onto a clean work surface, lift off pan, and peel off plastic. Using a bench scraper or knife, cut straight down lengthwise through middle, then crosswise to make 16 bars, each 1½ in. wide. Place bars about 1 in. apart on a parchment paper–lined baking sheet.

5. Bake bars until lightly browned and somewhat firm to touch, about 20 minutes. Remove from oven and put pan on a rack to cool completely.

Make Ahead: Up to 2 weeks, stored airtight at room temperature; up to 3 months, frozen.

PER BAR: 227 cal., 40% (90 cal.) from fat; 7.4 g protein; 10 g fat (1.5 g sat.); 29 g carbo (4.1 g fiber); 160 mg sodium; 13 mg chol.

Cashew Bars: Follow directions for Peanut Butter–Cranberry Go-Bars but substitute chopped **roasted salted cashews** for the peanuts, an additional ½ cup chopped **dried Mission figs** for the cranberries, and **cashew butter** for the peanut butter.

PER BAR: 216 cal., 40% (87 cal.) from fat; 6.1 g protein; 9.7 g fat (1.8 g sat.); 30 g carbo (3.6 g fiber); 183 mg sodium; 13 mg chol.

Florentine Bars

Reader Marisa DeSimone, of Pasadena, California, makes these bars every year to give as Christmas gifts. In fact, she told us, "The one year I didn't, I never heard the end of it!"

recipe pictured on page **603**

MAKES 35 bars (2 in. each) | **TIME** 50 minutes, plus cooling time

1 cup salted butter, at room temperature
1¾ cups sugar, divided
1 egg plus 1 egg yolk
2½ cups cake flour
½ cup plus 6 tbsp. unsalted butter
⅓ cup *each* honey and heavy whipping cream
¾ lb. sliced almonds
½ cup raisins, finely chopped
½ cup dried apricots, preferably Blenheim *(see Quick Tip, above right)*, finely chopped
½ cup dried tart cherries, finely chopped

1. Preheat oven to 375°. In a large bowl, cream salted butter with ½ cup sugar until light and fluffy. Add whole egg and egg yolk and beat to combine. Gradually add flour and mix well (dough will be very soft).
2. Transfer dough to a floured 16- by 11-in. piece of parchment paper. With a floured rolling pin, roll dough to same size as parchment. Trim any overhang, then transfer dough (on parchment) to a large rimmed baking sheet. Bake until golden brown, about 12 minutes. Remove from oven (leave oven on) and set aside.
3. In a medium saucepan over medium heat, stir together unsalted butter, remaining 1¼ cups sugar, the honey, and cream. Cook mixture, stirring frequently, until the temperature registers 250° on a candy thermometer. Remove pan from heat and stir in almonds, raisins, apricots, and cherries.
4. Using a spatula, gently spread warm topping over shortbread. Bake until topping is caramelized and almonds are lightly browned, about 10 minutes. Remove from oven; while still warm, cut into 2-in. squares. Set sheet on a rack and cool completely.

Quick Tip: Find dried California Blenheims online at *brfarms.com.*

PER BAR: 256 cal., 57% (145 cal.) from fat; 3.2 g protein; 16 g fat (7.2 g sat.); 27 g carbo (0.9 g fiber); 59 mg sodium; 42 mg chol.

Bite-size Honey Popcorn Balls

The only quibble we have with popcorn balls is that they're usually too big to bite into. These miniature clusters, held together with caramelized honey, are just the right size.

MAKES 60 to 65 popcorn balls | **TIME** 1¼ hours

20 cups air-popped popcorn (from ⅔ to 1 cup kernels; see *Quick Tip below*)
1¼ cups butter, cut into chunks
1¼ cups honey
¾ tsp. salt
2 tsp. vanilla extract

1. Preheat oven to 325°. Put popcorn in a large roasting pan. Line a large baking sheet with parchment or waxed paper.
2. In a medium saucepan over medium heat, use a heat-proof spatula or wooden spoon to stir together butter, honey, and salt until butter is melted. Increase heat and boil honey mixture gently 1 minute, stirring constantly. Stir in vanilla.
3. Carefully pour honey mixture over popcorn in pan and stir gently to coat evenly. Bake popcorn, stirring every 5 minutes, until deep golden all over, about 25 minutes.
4. Let popcorn stand 5 minutes, or just until cool enough to handle. Working quickly with lightly buttered hands, press small handfuls of mixture into 1½-in. balls, occasionally loosening popcorn from bottom of pan with a spatula. If mixture cools too much to be malleable, return it to oven for about 45 seconds to soften.
5. Put popcorn balls on prepared baking sheet and let cool completely.
Quick Tip: If you don't have an air popper, you can pop the popcorn in the microwave. Working in two batches, put kernels in a brown paper bag (any size). Do not add oil. Fold the bag's opening several times to seal, then microwave in 1-minute increments, checking popcorn and removing popped kernels each time (they burn easily). Be careful when opening bag; it will release scalding hot steam.
Make Ahead: Up to 2 weeks, stored airtight at room temperature.

PER POPCORN BALL: 64 cal., 56% (36 cal.) from fat; 0.3 g protein; 4 g fat (2.4 g sat.); 7.3 g carbo (0.4 g fiber); 67 mg sodium; 11 mg chol.

Candied Citrus Peels

Citrus fruit is winter's gift, and candying the peels is an old Christmas tradition—especially in the Western citrus-growing states of California and Arizona. This recipe uses an unusual long-simmering technique.

recipe pictured on page **602**

MAKES About 6 cups peel | **TIME** 5 hours, plus 8 hours to dry

5 lbs. oranges (or grapefruits, lemons, limes, or any other kind of citrus), washed and dried
8 cups sugar, divided

1. Halve and juice fruit; reserve juice for another use. Put peels in a large pot and cover with cold water. Bring to a boil and cook 3 minutes. Drain. Return peels to pot, cover with cold water, bring to a boil, cook 3 minutes, and drain. Repeat once more.
2. Spread peels on baking sheets and let sit until cool enough to handle, 20 minutes.
3. Using a soup spoon, scrape inner membranes from peels and discard. Cut peels into ¼-in. strips and set aside.
4. In a large, heavy-bottomed pot over high heat, bring 8 cups water and 6 cups sugar to a boil. Add peels, then reduce heat to maintain a steady, gentle simmer; cook, stirring occasionally, until peels are tender, sweet, and translucent, about 3 hours. (Don't let sugar brown or caramelize.)
5. Drain peels and spread on racks set over baking sheets. Let sit until dry, at least 8 hours.
6. Toss a handful of peels at a time with remaining 2 cups sugar. Shake off excess sugar and put in an airtight container.
Make Ahead: Up to 2 weeks, stored airtight at room temperature.

PER ¼-CUP PEEL: 126 cal., 1% (0.9 cal.) from fat; 0.2 g protein; 0.1 g fat (0 g sat.); 32 g carbo (0 g fiber); 0 mg sodium; 0 mg chol.

Peanut-Raisin Bark

Chocolate-covered peanuts meet chocolate-coated raisins in this easy and addictive candy.

MAKES 3 dozen pieces (1 oz. each); 2¼ lbs. total
TIME 20 minutes, plus about 1½ hours to chill

1 lb. semisweet chocolate, chopped
2 cups (about ¾ lb.) roasted, salted, skinned peanuts
1½ cups (about ½ lb.) raisins

1. Line a large rimmed baking sheet with waxed paper. In a metal bowl set in a pan over 2 to 3 in. of simmering water (water should not touch bottom of bowl), melt chocolate, stirring until smooth. With a heatproof spatula or wooden spoon, stir in peanuts and raisins.
2. Scrape mixture onto baking sheet and spread to about ½ in. thick. Chill bark, uncovered, until firm, about 1½ hours.
3. Break chilled bark or cut into chunks.
Make Ahead: Up to 2 days, stored airtight at room temperature; up to 2 weeks, chilled.

PER PIECE: 133 cal., 58% (77 cal.) from fat; 3.2 g protein; 8.5 g fat (2.9 g sat.); 15 g carbo (1.9 g fiber); 43 mg sodium; 0 mg chol.

Chocolate-Pistachio Marshmallows

Kids will love to help dip the marshmallows into the melted chocolate and chopped nuts.

MAKES 2 dozen marshmallows | **TIME** 30 minutes, plus about 1 hour to chill

½ cup finely chopped pistachios
6 oz. bittersweet or semisweet chocolate, chopped
24 large marshmallows

1. Line a baking sheet with parchment or waxed paper. Put pistachios in a shallow bowl.
2. In a medium metal bowl set in a pan over 2 to 3 in. of simmering water (water should not touch bottom of bowl), melt chocolate, stirring until smooth. Set bowl on a counter.
3. Holding at one end, dip a marshmallow into chocolate, turning to coat about three-quarters of it. Use a knife to scrape excess chocolate off bottom and back into bowl. Hold marshmallow over bowl of pistachios and sprinkle nuts over chocolate.
4. Set marshmallow (nut side down) on baking sheet. Dip and sprinkle each remaining marshmallow and place on baking sheet. Chill marshmallows, uncovered, until chocolate is set, about 1 hour.
Make Ahead: Up to 2 weeks, stored airtight between sheets of waxed paper in refrigerator.

PER MARSHMALLOW: 73 cal., 47% (34 cal.) from fat; 1.2 g protein; 3.8 g fat (1.5 g sat.); 10 g carbo (0.4 g fiber); 3.5 mg sodium; 0 mg chol.

Chocolate-Pistachio Apricots: For a more grown-up treat, follow directions for Chocolate-Pistachio Marshmallows but substitute large **dried apricots** for marshmallows. Dip them in **semisweet chocolate** and sprinkle with pistachios.

PER APRICOT: 61 cal., 51% (31 cal.) from fat; 1 g protein; 3.4 g fat (1.4 g sat.); 8.1 g carbo (1.1 g fiber); 1.4 mg sodium; 0 mg chol.

Salted Chocolate-Pecan Toffee

An extra-crisp toffee with a spark of salt.

MAKES 40 squares (2 in. each) | **TIME** 1¾ hours, plus 1 hour to chill

2 cups pecan halves, toasted *(see How to Toast Nuts, page 134)*
3½ cups sugar
1½ cups butter
1 tsp. salt
1 tbsp. vanilla extract
12 oz. bittersweet chocolate
2 tsp. *fleur de sel (see Quick Tips, right)* or coarse sea salt

1. Coarsely chop pecans. Divide into two batches; chop one batch finely. Set both batches aside.

2. Put sugar, butter, salt, and ¾ cup water in a 4-qt. saucepan over medium heat *(see Quick Tips, right)*. When butter and sugar are melted, increase heat to medium-high and cook, stirring occasionally, until mixture is deep golden brown and the temperature registers 310° on a candy thermometer, about 20 minutes.

3. Remove pan from heat and carefully stir in vanilla (mixture will bubble up) and finely chopped pecans. Pour into a 10- by 15-in. rimmed baking sheet. Let toffee cool until set, at least 30 minutes. (For even pieces,

score toffee with a sharp knife after it has set for about 10 minutes, scoring into five strips lengthwise and eight strips crosswise to yield 40 pieces. Wipe knife clean with warm water after each line.)

4. Chop chocolate and put in a medium metal bowl. Fill an 8- or 10-in. frying pan with ½ in. of water and bring to a boil. Remove from heat and put bowl of chocolate in water. Let sit about 5 minutes. Stir chocolate until melted. Pour over toffee; with a knife or offset spatula, spread evenly. Sprinkle chocolate with roughly chopped pecans. Let sit until chocolate is cool but still a bit soft, about 20 minutes. Sprinkle with *fleur de sel*. Chill until set, about 1 hour.

5. To remove, gently twist sheet to release toffee, then chop or break into pieces. Store in an airtight container.

Quick Tips: *Fleur de sel* (French for "flower of salt") is the top layer of sea salt skimmed from seawater evaporation ponds and often has a delicious minerally flavor; find it at well-stocked grocery stores. Use caution when working with sugar syrup, as it can cause severe burns. Set out your baking sheet so it's ready to use, and keep ice water nearby to cool any burns.

Make Ahead: Up to 2 weeks, stored airtight at room temperature; up to 1 month, chilled.

PER SQUARE: 207 cal., 61% (126 cal.) from fat; 1.1 g protein; 14 g fat (6.2 g sat.); 23 g carbo (0.5 g fiber); 202 mg sodium; 19 mg chol.

Candymaking Tips

Follow these suggestions to get the best results.

MELTING CHOCOLATE. Fill a saucepan with 2 to 3 in. of water. Put finely chopped chocolate in a heatproof bowl that will fit over pan (the bottom of the bowl should not touch the water); set bowl aside. (Or use a double boiler if you have one, set up the same way.) Bring water to a boil, turn off heat, then set bowl over pan. Use a heatproof spatula or wooden spoon to stir the chocolate frequently and encourage even melting. Once the chocolate is melted, stir well and use immediately.

CARAMELIZING SUGAR. Your mantra should be "Watch closely." Sugar cooks quickly once it begins to brown,

so have your ingredients measured and your tools assembled before you start. Before bringing your sugar mixture to a boil, make sure you completely dissolve the sugar and melt the butter; stir the mixture with a flexible heatproof spatula over medium-low heat, running the spatula around the inside of the saucepan a few times to thoroughly mix everything together.

USING A CANDY THERMOMETER. It can be tricky to know when a sugar mixture has reached the temperature that will yield the texture you're after. Candy thermometers eliminate the guesswork. You'll find them at supermarkets and some hardware stores; make sure to choose one that measures temperatures up to 400°.

• Test it first. If you have an old thermometer in the back of your gadget drawer, test its accuracy by immersing it in boiling water; it should read 212°. (If it doesn't, get a new thermometer.) Look for one that is easy to read and will attach securely to the side of the pan.

• Read it accurately. Attach the thermometer to the side of the pan after the sugar mixture has come to a boil. The placement of the heat sensor varies among brands, but generally the bottom of the thermometer must be completely submerged in the sugar mixture to get an accurate reading. If the mixture is too shallow, carefully tilt the pan until liquid completely covers the bottom of the thermometer and hold it there until the indicator comes to a stop.

cakes

A bakery case of cakes awaits you: showstopper layer cakes and tender cupcakes, luscious cheesecake, homey sheet cake, and fruitcake that's a delicacy, not a doorstop.

At *Sunset*, we love to celebrate our colleagues' birthdays with cakes, and when they're homemade it causes a sensation. "You baked this?!" is the typical response, followed by thoughtful chewing, followed by enthusiastic praise. A cake says *ta-da*, all by itself.

Of course, the prettier the better if you're baking it for a special event. We offer several gorgeous choices, including Lemon Meringue Cake (*page 634*), a combo of cake and lemon meringue pie, and Caramelized Orange Cheesecake, topped with slices of shimmering, candylike oranges (*page 642*).

So what's Western about our cakes? We're not very traditional, for one thing. We put beer in our gingerbread (*see page 625*). Strawberry shortcake becomes Strawberry Tallcake (*page 635*). Instead of old-fashioned chocolate cake, we bake chile chocolate cake (*page 631*), and for Christmas, we slather angel food cake with whipped cream and crushed candy canes (*page 636*).

We showcase Western ingredients every chance we get: Meyer Lemon Cake (*page 629*) uses fragrant Meyer lemons, peel and all. Western Dried Fruits Cake (*page 627*), a mosaic of dates, apricots, raisins, and nuts, is so good there's no reason to wait till the holidays to make it.

We also like cakes that are easy. See the almond cake on *page 628* for a great example. Even the humblest of cakes, like Raisin Cake (*page 626*), has a certain glow just because it's cake. If you want to add luster to an occasion (and bask in glory), bake a cake.

Cakes

Butternut Squash Spice Cake

This remarkably moist and tender cake gets its warmth from spices like cinnamon, nutmeg, allspice, and a hint of black pepper. Whole-wheat pastry flour adds nutrients without compromising the taste or texture.

MAKES 1 cake (8 in.); 8 servings | **TIME** 1½ hours

1 small butternut squash
2 cups whole-wheat pastry flour (*see Quick Tips below*)
1 tsp. *each* ground allspice, cinnamon, freshly grated
   nutmeg, and baking powder
¾ tsp. salt
½ tsp. baking soda
¼ tsp. freshly ground black pepper
½ cup unsalted butter, at room temperature
1½ cups firmly packed light brown sugar
2 eggs
1 tsp. vanilla extract
Powdered sugar or whipped cream (optional)

1. Preheat oven to 350°. Cut squash in half lengthwise and remove seeds. Put squash halves, cut side up, in a baking pan and cover with foil; bake until tender when pierced with a fork, 20 to 30 minutes. Uncover and let sit until cool enough to handle, then use a spoon to scoop cooked squash from peel. Mash with a fork. Measure 1 cup squash and set aside any remaining for another use (*see Quick Tips below*).
2. Reduce oven temperature to 325°. Butter an 8-in. square baking pan.
3. In a small bowl, combine flour, allspice, cinnamon, nutmeg, baking powder, salt, baking soda, and pepper. Set aside.
4. In a large bowl, with a mixer on medium speed, cream together butter and brown sugar until smooth and a bit fluffy. Add eggs, one at a time, beating 30 seconds after each addition. Mix in vanilla.
5. Add half the flour mixture to butter mixture and stir to combine. Stir in reserved 1 cup squash. Add remaining flour mixture and stir just enough to combine. Pour batter into baking pan and bake until a toothpick inserted in center comes out clean, 50 to 60 minutes. Serve plain or with a dusting of powdered sugar or a dollop of whipped cream.
Quick Tips: Whole-wheat pastry flour is sold at natural-food and specialty baking stores as well as well-stocked grocery stores. Serve extra mashed squash hot with butter, salt, and pepper; stir it into soups or stews; or freeze for future cakes.

PER SERVING: 417 cal., 30% (126 cal.) from fat; 6.9 g protein; 14 g fat (8 g sat.); 70 g carbo (5.3 g fiber); 401 mg sodium; 85 mg chol.

Guinness Stout Gingerbread Cake

Dark beer, molasses, and crystallized ginger give this cake from San Francisco–based food writer Peggy Knickerbocker an uncommon depth of flavor. Candied-ginger whipped cream adds a spicy, surprising finish.

MAKES 2 cakes (8 in. each); 16 servings total | **TIME** 1 hour

1 cup *each* Guinness stout (not extra stout) and dark
   molasses (not blackstrap)
1 tsp. baking soda
2½ cups flour
2 tbsp. ground ginger
2 tsp. cinnamon
1 tsp. ground allspice
½ tsp. salt
1½ cups finely chopped crystallized ginger, divided
1½ cups unsalted butter, melted and cooled
1 cup firmly packed dark brown sugar
2 eggs, lightly beaten
1½ tbsp. finely shredded lemon zest (from 2 or 3 lemons)
Powdered sugar for dusting
1 cup heavy whipping cream
2 tbsp. granulated sugar

1. Preheat oven to 325°. Butter two 8-in. square glass or light-colored metal baking pans. Bring stout and molasses to a boil in a large, deep saucepan. Remove from heat and whisk in baking soda (it will foam up dramatically); let cool. In a small bowl, whisk together flour, ginger, cinnamon, allspice, and salt.
2. In a large bowl, combine 1 cup crystallized ginger, the butter, and brown sugar and stir together with a wooden spoon. Add eggs and lemon zest and stir once more. Gradually stir in dry ingredients in four batches, alternating with Guinness mixture. Pour batter into pans, dividing evenly.
3. Bake until a toothpick inserted into centers comes out clean, 30 to 40 minutes. Cool cakes in pans on a rack, then dust tops with powdered sugar. Cut each cake into 8 squares and arrange on a serving platter.
4. In a medium bowl, with a mixer, whip cream and granulated sugar together until cream holds soft peaks. Stir in all but 1 tsp. of remaining ½ cup crystallized ginger. Scoop whipped cream into a bowl, sprinkle with last bit of ginger, and serve with cake.
Make Ahead: Up to 2 days; cooled, covered with plastic wrap, and stored at room temperature.

PER SERVING: 357 cal., 44% (156 cal.) from fat; 2.5 g protein; 17.5 g fat (10 g sat.); 48.5 g carbo (1 g fiber); 146 mg sodium; 69 mg chol.

Raisin Cake

Reader Barbara Holt, of Paradise, California, sent this recipe to us. It came to her from her husband's grandmother; for that reason, it's known in the family as "Grandma O'Connor's Boiled Raisin Cake." We like its humble, homey appeal—it's the kind of cake you want to eat for breakfast or as an after-school snack on a rainy day.

MAKES 1 sheet cake; 12 servings | **TIME** 1 hour

Cooking-oil spray
2 cups raisins
½ cup butter, cut into chunks
2 cups *each* all-purpose flour, whole-wheat pastry flour, and sugar
1 tbsp. *each* Dutch-processed unsweetened cocoa powder, baking soda, and cinnamon
1 tsp. *each* ground cloves, ground allspice, and salt

1. Preheat oven to 350°. Coat a 9- by 13-in. baking pan with cooking-oil spray.
2. In a medium saucepan, bring raisins and 3 cups water to a boil. Reduce heat to maintain a steady simmer and cook, covered, until raisins are very tender, about 15 minutes. Remove from heat, add butter, and let sit until butter melts.
3. Meanwhile, in a large bowl, combine flours, sugar, cocoa, baking soda, cinnamon, cloves, allspice, and salt. Set aside.
4. Stir raisin-butter mixture into flour mixture. Transfer batter to pan and bake until a toothpick or knife inserted in center comes out clean, about 45 minutes. Serve cake warm or at room temperature, cut into pieces.

PER SERVING: 433 cal., 18% (77 cal.) from fat; 5 g protein; 8.5 g fat (4.9 g sat.); 87 g carbo (2.2 g fiber); 595 mg sodium; 21 mg chol.

Sweet (Liquid) Endings

Don't stop pouring when you clear away the main course. More and more West Coast winemakers are producing dessert wines (aka "stickies") that rival Europe's greatest—Bordeaux's honeyed Sauternes, Germany's ripest Rieslings. Mavericks as always, though, vintners here are playing fast and loose with the formulas, leaving all manner of grapes hanging on the vine for sweet, late-harvest versions (Gewürztraminer, Viognier, Chardonnay, and Zinfandel among them) and even making port out of Zinfandel.

Broadly speaking, dessert wines fall into three main categories, each with a set of characteristic flavors that matches some of our classic sweets. Just make sure that the wine is at least as sweet as your dessert and has enough acidity to balance its sugar.

Sweet Sparklers
These wines often carry apple, pear, berry, creamy citrus, or yeast flavors. Depending on the sweetness of the *dosage* (a blend of sugar and wine added before corking), they're called "extra dry," "sec," "demi-sec," or "doux," with doux being the sweetest.

GREAT PAIRINGS: Custard-fruit tarts, apple pie, buttery pastries, pumpkin pie, cheesecake, and English toffee.

Late-harvest Stickies
Made from grapes left on the vine past normal picking time, late-harvest wines have high levels of residual sugar (sugar remaining after fermentation has stopped) and concentrated fruit characters. The whites take on nectarlike stone-fruit flavors as well as hints of candied citrus and baked apple. If the grapes were affected by botrytis—the desirable fungus called "noble rot," which Sauternes relies on—all these flavors are coated in honey. (On the red side, late-harvest Zinfandel is full of dried cherries and chocolate.)

GREAT PAIRINGS: Any of the whites with cheesecake with berries, fruit tarts, apple pie, and carrot cake; late-harvest Zin is a natural with chocolate.

Port-style Reds
Ports—sweet wines fortified with brandy—are made here out of some of the traditional Portuguese grape varieties as well as the likes of Zinfandel and Syrah. They tend to have a core of dark cherry and dried-plum flavors layered with chocolate, coffee, and licorice.

GREAT PAIRINGS: All things chocolate (especially chocolate cake with a layer of jam) and mocha; pecan pie.

Pear and Pecan Upside-down Cake

When cooked, Bosc pears have an appealing density and graininess that is wonderful with the tender, moist bourbon-infused crumb of this cake.

recipe pictured on page **611**

MAKES 1 cake (9 in.); 8 servings
TIME 2 hours

2 Bosc pears, cored, peeled, and cut into ¼-in.-thick slices
1¼ cups granulated sugar, divided
1 cup chopped pecans, divided
⅓ cup bourbon
1 tsp. salt, divided
¾ cup unsalted butter
½ cup firmly packed light brown sugar
3 eggs
2 tsp. vanilla extract
1½ tsp. baking powder
½ tsp. baking soda
2 cups flour
¾ cup plain yogurt

1. Preheat oven to 350°. Generously butter a 9-in. round cake pan and arrange pear slices in a pattern on bottom.
2. Bring 1 cup granulated sugar and ½ cup water to a boil in a 10-in. frying pan over medium-high heat. Lower heat to maintain a steady simmer and cook, undisturbed, until mixture starts to brown (swirl pan to help mixture brown evenly). When mixture turns a medium amber color, add ½ cup pecans and cook until fragrant but not burning, about 30 seconds. Remove from heat and slowly stir in bourbon and ½ tsp. salt. Pour over pears in buttered pan.
3. Put butter, brown sugar, and remaining ¼ cup granulated sugar in a large bowl. With a mixer, beat on medium speed until smooth and a bit fluffy, about 3 minutes. Add eggs, one at a time, beating well after each addition. Beat in vanilla, baking powder and soda, and remaining ½ tsp. salt. Add half the flour and beat until combined. Beat in half the yogurt. Repeat with remaining flour and yogurt. Stir remaining ½ cup pecans into batter (it will be thick).
4. Drop spoonfuls of batter over pears in pan and sauce and spread evenly. Bake cake until golden and a toothpick inserted in center comes out clean, about 45 minutes.
5. Let cool on a rack 15 minutes. Run a knife between cake and pan sides and invert cake onto a plate or serving platter. Serve warm or at room temperature.

PER SERVING: 602 cal., 45% (270 cal.) from fat; 7.7 g protein; 30 g fat (13 g sat.); 79 g carbo (2.7 g fiber); 506 mg sodium; 130 mg chol.

Western Dried Fruits Cake

For a fruitcake you'll actually look forward to eating, try this one. It's solidly packed with good dried fruit, all of it grown in the West. A reader identified only as S.T., from Edmonds, Washington, gave us the recipe. The cake is good-looking, too—sliced, it shows off a mosaic of bright orange apricots, amber dates, and golden raisins.

recipe pictured on page **610**

Soak it in brandy if you like: With a toothpick, poke holes 1 in. apart over the top of the cooled cake and drizzle on ½ cup brandy or rum. Wrap the cake in cheesecloth, then in foil, and let it absorb the brandy for 1 week, chilled. Repeat the weekly drizzling at least once and up to three more times (for a total of 1 to 2 cups), depending on how boozy you want the fruitcake.

MAKES 1 loaf cake; 20 servings | **TIME** 2½ hours, plus 2 days to chill

1 package (8 oz.) pitted dates
2 cups quartered dried apricots
1 cup golden raisins
1½ cups *each* walnut pieces and blanched whole almonds, coarsely chopped
¾ cup *each* flour and sugar
½ tsp. baking powder
3 eggs
1 tsp. vanilla extract

1. Preheat oven to 300°. Butter a 9- by 5-in. loaf pan, line it with parchment or waxed paper, then butter the paper.
2. In a large bowl, combine dates, apricots, raisins, walnuts, and almonds. In a small bowl, stir flour, sugar, and baking powder to blend; add to fruits and mix evenly.
3. In a small bowl, beat eggs with vanilla to blend. Stir thoroughly into fruit mixture. Spoon batter into pan and spread evenly; press batter into corners of pan.
4. Bake until golden brown, about 2 hours. Cool in pan on a rack for 10 minutes, then invert onto a rack. Peel off paper and let cool. You can eat it right away, but it will be a bit crumbly; after 2 days in the refrigerator, wrapped in foil, it will slice neatly.
Make Ahead: Up to 2 months, chilled (whether brandied or plain).

PER SERVING: 266 cal., 42% (112 cal.) from fat; 6.3 g protein; 12 g fat (1.3 g sat.); 37 g carbo (3.1 g fiber); 31 mg sodium; 32 mg chol.

Easy Almond Cakes

Reader Karen Bagshaw, of San Francisco, got this recipe from her childhood friend Ginnie Beard at their 20th Girl Scout reunion. She says it's ideal for a large potluck since it's so easy and makes two cakes. You can quickly transform these modest cakes into showpieces by layering them. Use a serrated knife to carefully slice each cake horizontally into two even layers (see variation below).

MAKES 2 cakes (9 in. each); 16 servings total
TIME 45 minutes

Cooking-oil spray
1⅔ cups flour
1½ cups sugar
1 cup unsalted butter, melted
2 eggs, lightly beaten
2 tbsp. almond extract
¼ tsp. salt
2½ oz. (about ½ cup) sliced almonds

1. Preheat oven to 350°. Spray two 9-in. pie pans with cooking spray. In a large bowl, stir together flour, sugar, butter, eggs, almond extract, and salt.
2. Divide batter between pans and sprinkle each with half the almonds. Bake until light brown around edges, about 30 minutes. Serve warm or at room temperature.

PER SERVING: 263 cal., 49% (129 cal.) from fat; 3.2 g protein; 15 g fat (7.7 g sat.); 30 g carbo (1 g fiber); 47 mg sodium; 57 mg chol.

Easy Almond Layer Cakes: Slice each cake in half horizontally. In a large bowl, with a mixer on medium-high, whip 1 qt. **heavy whipping cream** with 1 cup **sugar** until stiff peaks form. Spread each bottom layer with 1 cup whipped cream and sprinkle with 1½ cups **fresh raspberries**. Add top layers and spread with remaining whipped cream; top each cake with another 1½ cups raspberries. (If you want to layer only one of the cakes, just halve the filling amounts.) Makes 8 servings each.

PER SERVING: 524 cal., 63% (330 cal.) from fat; 4.6 g protein; 37 g fat (22 g sat.); 46 g carbo (1.6 g fiber); 70 mg sodium; 139 mg chol.

Inside-out Carrot Cakes

With frosting in the middle, these tender, cookie-size cakes look like whoopie pies.

MAKES 10 to 12 individual frosted cakes | **TIME** 1 hour

¾ cup flour
½ tsp. baking soda
¼ tsp. kosher salt
1 tsp. ground ginger
½ tsp. cinnamon
Pinch ground cloves
⅛ tsp. *each* freshly grated nutmeg and freshly ground black pepper
6 tbsp. vegetable oil
½ cup firmly packed light brown sugar
1 egg
¼ cup sour cream
¼ tsp. vanilla extract
1½ medium carrots, shredded on fine side of a box grater (1 cup)
¼ cup unsweetened shredded dried coconut
Cream-cheese Frosting (*recipe follows*)

1. Preheat oven to 350°. Put a dab of butter in each corner of two large baking sheets and line with parchment paper.
2. In a small bowl, whisk together flour, baking soda, salt, ginger, cinnamon, cloves, nutmeg, and pepper. In a large bowl, whisk together oil, brown sugar, egg, sour cream, and vanilla; stir in dry ingredients until well combined. Add carrots and coconut, stirring until just combined.
3. Drop 1-tbsp. circles of batter about 1 in. apart on baking sheets. Bake until cooked through and browned slightly, 14 to 18 minutes. Cool on baking sheets.
4. Flip half the cakes over; spread each with about 1½ tbsp. frosting. Top with remaining cakes to sandwich the frosting.

PER CAKE: 248 cal., 58% (144 cal.) from fat; 2.6 g protein; 16 g fat (6.9 g sat.); 24 g carbo (0.6 g fiber); 134 mg sodium; 41 mg chol.

Cream-cheese Frosting: In a medium bowl, with a mixer on medium speed, beat 5 oz. softened **cream cheese** until very soft. Add 3 tbsp. softened **unsalted butter** and beat until smooth and well blended. Add ⅔ cup **powdered sugar** a third at a time, beating until smooth after each addition. Beat in 1 tsp. **heavy whipping cream or milk** and ½ tsp. **vanilla extract**. Makes about 1 cup.

PER 1½-TBSP. FROSTING: 106 cal., 67% (71 cal.) from fat; 1 g protein; 8 g fat (4.7 g sat.); 8.1 g carbo (0 g fiber); 43 mg sodium; 24 mg chol.

Meyer Lemon Cake

Reader Carolyn Grattan Eichin, of Campbell, California, contributed this wonderful, super-citrusy cake. Cooking the lemons before using them mellows their flavor.

MAKES 1 cake (9 in.); 10 servings | **TIME** 2 hours

1 lb. Meyer lemons plus 1 tbsp. fresh Meyer lemon juice
   (see Quick Tip, right) and 10 thin Meyer lemon slices
1½ cups whole skin-on almonds
½ cup flour
1 tsp. baking powder
½ tsp. salt
5 eggs, separated
1¼ cups granulated sugar
½ tsp. almond extract
¼ cup candied or crystallized ginger
½ cup powdered sugar

1. Put whole lemons in a large pot, cover with cold water, and bring to a boil over high heat, covered. Lower heat to medium and simmer until soft, about 30 minutes. Drain; transfer to a bowl of ice water. When lemons are cool, lift out of water, cut into quarters, and gently remove seeds, retaining as much juice as possible. Purée lemons in a food processor.

2. Meanwhile, preheat oven to 350°. Butter and flour a 9-in. springform pan. In a food processor, pulse almonds until nuts resemble coarse cornmeal. Put in a large bowl and add flour, baking powder, and salt. Stir to combine.

3. In another large bowl, whisk together egg yolks and granulated sugar until thick and pale yellow. Stir in lemon purée and almond extract. Add ground almond mixture and stir to combine. Finely dice candied ginger and stir into bowl. Set aside.

4. In another large bowl, with a mixer on medium-high speed, beat egg whites to form firm peaks. Gently fold egg whites into batter. Scrape batter into pan and spread evenly.

5. Bake until edges of cake begin to pull away from pan side, about 1 hour. Cool on a rack for 15 minutes, then run a knife between cake and pan rim, remove rim, and cool completely.

6. In a small bowl, combine powdered sugar and lemon juice to make glaze. Spread over cake. Garnish with lemon slices and serve.

Quick Tip: We also like the sharper flavor of regular lemons, which may be substituted in equal amounts.

PER SERVING: 333 cal., 36% (119 cal.) from fat; 8.3 g protein; 13 g fat (1.9 g sat.); 51 g carbo (4.7 g fiber); 209 mg sodium; 106 mg chol.

When Life Gives You Meyer Lemons

Frank Meyer was an agricultural explorer for the U.S. Department of Agriculture when he arrived in China in 1905. After battling heat, cold, and at least one assassin, he was traveling near Beijing when he encountered a dwarf lemon tree, most likely a hybrid between a lemon and an orange, with delicate, deep yellow, intensely fragrant fruit. He made sure to ship it back to America. Unfortunately, Meyer's life was short: He drowned mysteriously on a return expedition to China.

His namesake tree, however, won immortality. California growers deemed the lemons too soft for commercial use, but home gardeners appreciated the Meyer's nearly year-round bounty, and cooks fell in love with its wonderful aroma and tart-sweet flavor.

For decades the Meyer was a Western gardening secret, but now Meyer sorbets and soufflés star on menus in Manhattan and Miami, and growers in California's Central Valley are planting orchards to meet rising demand. If you live where the winters aren't frosty, you can grow a Meyer and have its wonderful fruit just steps from your house. Use them instead of standard Eureka lemons (both juice and zest), being mindful that they are not as tart, but more fragrant. Here are a few savory suggestions:

Spread it. Add a generous squeeze of fresh Meyer lemon juice and a minced clove of garlic to mayonnaise for a sandwich spread or a quick dip for cooked shrimp or crab.

Grate it. To make a version of Italian gremolata, combine the finely shredded zest of one Meyer lemon (use a razor-sharp grater, such as a Microplane, for best results) with one minced clove of garlic and a handful of chopped flat-leaf parsley. Stir it into braised meat dishes at the end of cooking.

Roast it. Add wedges of Meyer lemons alongside wedges of potatoes in a roasting pan for an unusual and flavorful side dish.

Spiced Cornmeal Pound Cake

Cornmeal gives this pound cake an appealing density. It's good toasted and spread with butter and honey.

MAKES 1 loaf cake; 6 to 8 servings | **TIME** 1½ hours, plus 1 hour to cool

¾ cup *each* **butter, at room temperature, and sugar**
3 eggs
¼ cup milk
1 tsp. vanilla extract
1½ cups flour
⅓ cup yellow or white cornmeal
1 tsp. baking powder
¼ tsp. *each* ground cinnamon, cloves, cardamom, and salt

1. Preheat oven to 325°. Butter and flour an 8½- by 4½-in. loaf pan. In a large bowl, with a mixer on medium speed, beat butter and sugar until well blended. Add eggs, one at a time, beating to blend well after each addition. Beat in milk and vanilla.
2. In a small bowl, mix flour, cornmeal, baking powder, cinnamon, cloves, cardamom, and salt. Add flour mixture to butter mixture and beat on medium speed just until well blended. Pour batter into pan and spread it level.
3. Bake until cake is golden on top and just begins to pull from pan sides, 60 to 70 minutes. Cool in pan on a rack for about 15 minutes, then invert cake onto rack and remove pan, turn cake upright, and let cool completely, about 1 hour.
Make Ahead: Up to 1 day, stored airtight at room temperature.

PER SERVING: 376 cal., 48% (180 cal.) from fat; 5.8 g protein; 20 g fat (12 g sat.); 43 g carbo (0.9 g fiber); 344 mg sodium; 129 mg chol.

Chocolate Zucchini Rum Cake

This boozy, tender, and very chocolaty cake from reader Andee Zetterbaum, of Modesto, California, gets some of its moistness from the zucchini, but otherwise the vegetable is undetectable. Health food it isn't, but it sure is delicious.

MAKES 1 tube cake; 16 to 20 servings | **TIME** 1½ hours

¾ cup butter, at room temperature
2 cups granulated sugar
3 eggs
2 cups loosely packed shredded zucchini
⅓ cup rum, brandy, or water
2½ cups flour
1 cup *each* semisweet chocolate chips and chopped walnuts
½ cup unsweetened cocoa powder (not Dutch-processed)
2½ tsp. baking powder
1½ tsp. baking soda
1 tsp. salt
¾ tsp. cinnamon
¼ cup milk
RUM GLAZE (OPTIONAL)
1⅔ cups powdered sugar
3 tbsp. rum

1. Preheat oven to 350°. Generously butter and flour a nonstick 10-cup plain or fluted tube pan (angel food cake pan). In a large bowl, with a mixer on medium speed, beat butter and granulated sugar until smoothly blended. Beat in eggs, one at a time, until fluffy. With a wooden spoon, stir in zucchini and rum.
2. In a medium bowl, mix flour with chocolate chips, walnuts, cocoa, baking powder and soda, salt, and cinnamon. Stir flour mixture and milk into egg mixture until well blended. Pour batter into tube pan and spread evenly.
3. Bake until cake begins to pull from pan sides and springs back when firmly pressed in center, 55 to 60 minutes. Let cool in pan on a rack about 15 minutes. Invert cake onto rack and let cool.
4. Make glaze if using: In a medium bowl, mix powdered sugar and rum together until smooth. Drizzle glaze over cake.
Make Ahead: Up to 2 days, at room temperature; up to 1 week, chilled.

PER SERVING: 299 cal., 45% (135 cal.) from fat; 4.5g protein; 15 g fat (6.7 g sat.); 41 g carbo; 352 mg sodium; 52 mg chol.

Pasilla Chile Chocolate Cake
(Pastel de Chocolate y Chile Pasilla)

This unusual recipe, with its mix of deep chocolate flavor and the hot spice of dried chiles, is from Agustín Gaytán, a San Francisco–based chef who also teaches classes on the cooking of his native Mexico.

MAKES 1 cake (9 in.); 12 servings | **TIME** 1 hour, plus 4½ hours to cool and chill

2½ oz. dried pasilla chiles (see Quick Tip, right); or
   2½ oz. dried ancho chiles plus ¼ tsp. cayenne
1 lb. bittersweet or semisweet chocolate, chopped
¾ cup butter, cut into ½-in. chunks, at room temperature
5 eggs, separated
2 tsp. vanilla extract
1½ tbsp. flour
½ cup firmly packed dark brown sugar or finely crushed
   piloncillo
¼ tsp. cream of tartar
Powdered sugar
1 cup whipping cream
1 tsp. vanilla extract or 1 tbsp. coffee-flavored liqueur,
   such as Kahlúa

1. Heat a large cast-iron frying pan over medium-high heat. When hot, lay chiles in pan in a single layer and toast just until pliable, about 2 minutes (you may have to toast in batches). Wearing rubber gloves, break off stems, shake out seeds, and break chiles into small pieces, dropping into a small bowl; discard stems and seeds. Cover chiles with warm water and let soak until soft, 5 to 7 minutes. Drain chiles and put in a blender with ⅓ cup water; purée, adding up to 1 tbsp. more water as needed to make a thick paste. Push purée through a fine-mesh strainer; discard residue. You need ⅓ cup chile purée. If using ancho chiles, stir cayenne into chile purée.

2. Preheat oven to 425°. Line bottom of a 9-in. round cake pan (with side at least 1½ in. high) with parchment paper.

3. In a medium metal bowl set over a pan of simmering water, combine chocolate and butter. Stir occasionally just until chocolate and butter are melted and mixture is smooth, about 8 minutes. Remove bowl from pan and whisk in the chile purée, egg yolks, vanilla, and flour until blended.

4. Pour brown sugar into a small bowl and stir or whisk to loosen it and break up clumps. In a large bowl, with a mixer on high speed, beat egg whites and cream of tartar until very frothy and foamy. Gradually add brown sugar to whites, beating until stiff, moist peaks form. With a whisk, fold a third of beaten whites into chocolate mixture until well incorporated. Then fold in remaining whites just until blended. Scrape batter into pan.

5. Bake cake until it appears set and center barely jiggles when pan is gently shaken, about 15 minutes. Let cool in pan on a rack for about 15 minutes.

6. Run a knife between cake and pan sides, then invert cake onto a serving platter. Lift off pan and peel off parchment. Let cake cool about 30 minutes, then reinvert and chill until firm and cold, at least 4 hours; cover cake with plastic wrap once completely chilled.

7. For best texture, let cake come to room temperature before serving, 45 minutes to 1 hour. Sift powdered sugar lightly over cake (for a pattern, lay a stencil on cake before sifting the sugar, then carefully lift it off).

8. In a medium bowl, beat cream until soft peaks form. Stir in vanilla. Cut cake into wedges and serve each with a dollop of whipped cream.

Quick Tip: Dried long, dark, skinny chiles labeled pasilla or chile negro give this dark chocolate cake a subtle fruit flavor with a hot finish. If these are not available, use ancho chiles (dried poblanos), which are sweet and fruity with little heat, and add cayenne to boost the spiciness.

Make Ahead: Up to 2 days, chilled.

PER SERVING: 434 cal., 71% (306 cal.) from fat; 6.5 g protein; 34 g fat (19 g sat.); 35 g carbo (2.2 g fiber); 155 mg sodium; 142 mg chol.

■ *Piloncillo* ....

FROM THE PANTRY

Piloncillo is a hard, unrefined Mexican brown sugar shaped into a cone. To use piloncillo, put it in a resealable plastic bag, cover with a kitchen towel, and pound it with a mallet or hammer until finely crushed. Find piloncillo in Latino markets.

Chocolate Chip Shortcakes with Berries and Dark Chocolate Sauce

Here's a fun twist on strawberry shortcake that uses blackberries and/or raspberries instead, but most any berry (as well as cherries) will work.

MAKES 6 shortcakes | **TIME** 1 hour

3 cups flour
6 tbsp. sugar, divided, plus more for sprinkling
1½ tbsp. baking powder
½ tsp. salt
½ cup cold butter, cut into chunks, plus about 1 tbsp. melted
1 cup whipping cream
¾ cup mini semisweet chocolate chips
4 cups blackberries and/or raspberries
¼ cup finely chopped mint leaves
Dark Chocolate Sauce (recipe follows)
Slightly sweetened softly whipped cream

1. Preheat oven to 375°. In a food processor, combine flour, 3 tbsp. sugar, the baking powder, and salt; process until blended. Add ½ cup butter and pulse until fine crumbs form. Add cream and pulse just until dough comes together when you squeeze a clump.
2. Turn dough onto a floured work surface and press to flatten slightly. Sprinkle chocolate chips over top, then knead until incorporated, six to eight turns. Pat dough out to 1¼-in. thickness. With a 2¾-in. biscuit or round cookie cutter, cut out shortcakes; gather dough and pat out again as needed to cut all 6 cakes, dusting surface with more flour as needed to prevent sticking. Set shortcakes slightly apart on a baking sheet, brush tops with melted butter, and sprinkle generously with sugar.
3. Bake shortcakes until golden brown, 22 to 25 minutes. Let cool on baking sheet at least 15 minutes.
4. Meanwhile, in a medium bowl, gently mix remaining 3 tbsp. sugar, the berries, and mint.
5. With a serrated knife, carefully slice shortcakes in half horizontally. Set bottoms on plates and top with berry mixture, chocolate sauce, and whipped cream. Set tops in place.
Make Ahead: Shortcakes, up to 1 day, cooled completely and stored airtight at room temperature.

PER SERVING: 719 cal., 49% (351 cal.) from fat; 9.1 g protein; 39 g fat (24 g sat.); 88 g carbo (7.5 g fiber); 754 mg sodium; 101 mg chol.

Dark Chocolate Sauce: In a medium saucepan over low heat, stir 1 cup **whipping cream** and 6 oz. **bittersweet or semisweet chocolate**, chopped, until smooth, about 15 minutes. Stir in 1 tsp. **vanilla extract**. Serve warm. Makes about 2 cups.
Make Ahead: Can be made up to 1 day ahead, chilled; to rewarm, heat gently over low heat.

PER ¼ CUP: 208 cal., 78% (162 cal.) from fat; 2.1 g protein; 18 g fat (11 g sat.); 13 g carbo (0.5 g fiber); 11 mg sodium; 41 mg chol.

Chocolate Citrus Almond Torte

"Guests always ask for the recipe," writes reader Trish Kruse, of Eagle, Idaho, "and beg to bring home leftovers!" No wonder: The combination of chocolate, orange, and almonds is terrific.

MAKES 1 cake (10 in.); 12 servings | **TIME** 1¾ hours, plus time to cool

Cooking-oil spray
1¼ cups blanched whole almonds, toasted (see How to Toast Nuts, page 134)
8 oz. good-quality bittersweet chocolate, coarsely chopped
½ cup unsweetened cocoa powder (not Dutch-processed), plus more for dusting cake
6 eggs, separated
1 cup sugar
½ cup orange juice
1 tbsp. finely shredded orange zest
2 tsp. finely shredded lemon zest
¾ cup plus 2 tbsp. butter, melted
½ tsp. salt

1. Preheat oven to 350°. Coat a 10-in. springform pan with cooking-oil spray.
2. In a food processor, pulse almonds and chocolate until finely ground. Add cocoa and pulse to combine.
3. In a large bowl, whisk together egg yolks, sugar, orange juice, and orange and lemon zests until mixture is thick and pale. Beat in chocolate-almond mixture and melted butter.
4. In another large bowl, with a mixer on medium-high speed, beat egg whites and salt until stiff peaks form; do not overbeat. Gently fold whites into chocolate mixture, then pour into pan.
5. Bake until cake pulls away from edges of pan and top is well browned, about 50 minutes. Let cool completely on a rack. To serve, run a knife between cake and pan rim, remove rim, and cut cake into wedges. Sprinkle with a light dusting of cocoa powder.

PER SERVING: 419 cal., 63% (265 cal.) from fat; 7.6 g protein; 30 g fat (15 g sat.); 36 g carbo (3.1 g fiber); 253 mg sodium; 141 mg chol.

Praline Pumpkin Torte

This showstopping dessert from reader Kathy Masur, of Broomfield, Colorado, was the creation of her Aunt Katy—"a wonder in the kitchen." Although her aunt passed away years ago, Masur still makes the pumpkin torte every year at Thanksgiving as a tribute.

MAKES 1 layer cake (9 in.); 12 servings | **TIME** 1 hour, plus 1½ hours to cool

¾ cup firmly packed light brown sugar
⅓ cup butter
3 tbsp. plus 1¾ cups whipping cream
1 cup chopped pecans, divided
4 eggs
1⅔ cups granulated sugar
1 cup vegetable oil
2 cups canned pumpkin
1 tsp. vanilla extract, divided
2 cups flour
2 tsp. baking powder
2 tsp. pumpkin pie spice; or ¾ tsp. *each* ground
    cinnamon, ginger, and nutmeg
1 tsp. *each* baking soda and salt
¼ cup powdered sugar

1. Preheat oven to 350°. Butter two 9-in. round cake pans. Line bottoms of pans with parchment paper. In a heavy-bottomed 1- to 2-qt. pan over low heat, stir brown sugar, butter, and 3 tbsp. cream until melted and blended, about 5 minutes. Divide brown sugar mixture between pans. Sprinkle evenly with ¾ cup pecans.
2. In a large bowl, with a spoon, beat eggs, granulated sugar, and oil until well blended. Stir in pumpkin and ½ tsp. vanilla. In a small bowl, whisk together flour, baking powder, pumpkin pie spice, baking soda, and salt to blend. Whisk dry ingredients into pumpkin mixture until well blended. Pour half the batter into each pan; smooth tops.
3. Bake until a toothpick inserted in center of cakes comes out clean, 30 to 35 minutes. Let cool in pans on racks about 5 minutes, then invert onto racks and remove pans and paper. Let cool completely, about 1½ hours.
4. In a large bowl, with a mixer on high speed, beat remaining 1¾ cups cream until soft peaks form. On low speed, beat in powdered sugar and remaining ½ tsp. vanilla just until blended. Set one cake layer, pecan praline side up, on a serving platter. Spread two-thirds of whipped cream mixture over top. Set second layer, praline side up, on top. Cover with remaining whipped cream mixture. Sprinkle with remaining ¼ cup chopped pecans.
Make Ahead: Cake layers (through step 3), up to 1 day, stored airtight at room temperature. Assembled layers, up to 6 hours, covered with a large inverted bowl or pan and chilled.

PER SERVING: 676 cal., 59% (396 cal.) from fat; 6.3 g protein; 44 g fat (14 g sat.); 66 g carbo (2 g fiber); 481 mg sodium; 129 mg chol.

Polenta and Pine Nut Torte

Reader Roxanne Chan, of Albany, California, serves lemon sorbet with this cakelike cornmeal torte, which can be eaten warm or cool.

MAKES 1 cake (9 in.); 8 to 10 servings | **TIME** 1 hour, plus 30 minutes to cool

½ cup sour cream
2 eggs
¼ cup olive oil
1 tsp. *each* finely shredded lemon zest and fresh lemon
    juice
¾ cup flour
½ cup polenta or yellow cornmeal
1 tsp. baking powder
¾ cup sugar, divided
½ cup pine nuts

1. Preheat oven to 350°. Oil a 9-in. fluted tart pan with a removable rim. In a large bowl, beat sour cream, eggs, oil, and lemon zest and juice until well blended. In a small bowl, stir together flour, polenta, baking powder, and ½ cup sugar. Stir or beat into sour cream mixture until well blended.
2. Pour batter into pan. Sprinkle pine nuts and remaining ¼ cup sugar evenly over top.
3. Bake until golden brown, about 35 minutes. Let cool about 30 minutes, then remove pan rim. Serve warm or cool, cut into wedges.

PER SERVING: 248 cal., 47% (117 cal.) from fat; 4.8 g protein; 13 g fat (3.1 g sat.); 29 g carbo (0.9 g fiber); 68 mg sodium; 48 mg chol.

Best Butter Cake

Simple, yummy, and extremely versatile, this cake could be your new dessert standby. To turn it into a birthday cake, frost it with Fudge Frosting *(recipe follows)*.

MAKES 2 cakes (8 in. each); 16 servings total
TIME 40 minutes, plus 45 minutes to cool

2¼ cups cake flour
2½ tsp. baking powder
1 tsp. salt
1¼ cups sugar
½ cup unsalted butter, at room temperature
2 eggs
2 tsp. vanilla extract
⅔ cup milk

1. Preheat oven to 350°. Butter and flour two 8-in. cake pans. Sift flour, baking powder, and salt into a medium bowl; set aside.
2. In a large bowl, with a mixer on medium speed, beat sugar and butter until creamy. Add eggs to butter mixture, one at a time, beating well after each addition, scraping down side of bowl as needed, and adding vanilla with last egg. Beat in flour mixture and milk in alternating batches, starting and ending with flour and making sure each addition is fully incorporated before adding the next.
3. Divide batter between pans.
4. Bake until golden brown and a toothpick inserted in center of each cake comes out clean, 20 to 25 minutes. Cool cakes 5 minutes. Invert onto a rack, remove pans, and let cool to room temperature, at least 40 minutes.
Make Ahead: Up to 2 days, wrapped airtight and chilled.

PER SERVING: 203 cal., 31% (62 cal.) from fat; 2.9 g protein; 6.9 g fat (4 g sat.); 32 g carbo (0.4 g fiber); 237 mg sodium; 43 mg chol.

PER SERVING WITH FUDGE FROSTING: 391 cal., 41% (162 cal.) from fat; 4 g protein; 18 g fat (11 g sat.); 58 g carbo (1.7 g fiber); 300 mg sodium; 60 mg chol.

Fudge Frosting: Melt 5 oz. chopped **unsweetened chocolate** in a medium metal bowl set in pan over simmering water, stirring until smooth. Let cool to room temperature, about 10 minutes. Add ½ cup **butter**, at room temperature, and beat with a mixer on high speed until light and fluffy, about 2 minutes. Add 3 cups **powdered sugar** and 6 tbsp. **milk**; beat until smooth. Add more powdered sugar if frosting seems too thin. Makes about 2 cups.

PER TBSP.: 93 cal., 47% (43.7 cal.) from fat; 0.7 g protein; 5 g fat (3.3 g sat.); 12.7 g carbo (0.74 g fiber); 00 mg sodium; 7.9 mg chol.

To frost a two-layer cake: Dollop 1 tbsp. frosting onto center of a cake stand (to hold cake in place). Set one cake layer on stand. Spread with about ¾ cup frosting. Top with second layer. Starting with top, then working down sides, frost cake with remaining frosting.

Lemon Meringue Cake

Our butter cake meets lemon meringue pie. We used a loaf pan to change the shape of the cake—a simple twist that dramatically alters the presentation.

MAKES 1 loaf cake; 12 servings | **TIME** 2¾ hours, plus 1 hour to chill

CAKE
Batter for Best Butter Cake *(left)*, prepared through step 2
2 tbsp. finely shredded lemon zest
LEMON CURD
½ cup *each* butter and fresh lemon juice (about 3 lemons)
¾ cup sugar
8 egg yolks
MERINGUE
1 cup *each* egg whites (from about 8 eggs) and sugar

1. Preheat oven to 350°. Butter and flour a 9- by 5-in. loaf pan. Stir zest into cake batter and pour into pan. Bake until a toothpick inserted in center comes out clean, about 45 minutes. Cool 5 minutes, then invert cake onto a rack. Remove pan and let cake cool to room temperature, at least 40 minutes.
2. Meanwhile, make lemon curd: In a heavy-bottomed medium saucepan, melt butter with lemon juice over high heat. In a medium bowl, whisk together sugar and yolks. Slowly whisk hot lemon butter into egg mixture, ½ cup at a time. Pour mixture back into saucepan and cook over high heat, whisking constantly, until mixture is very thick, 5 to 8 minutes.
3. Transfer lemon curd to a nonreactive container (glass, plastic, or stainless steel). Cover with plastic wrap, pressing it against surface of curd to prevent a skin from forming. Chill until cold, at least 1 hour.
4. Make meringue: Whisk whites and sugar together in a medium metal bowl. Set in a pan over simmering water and whisk constantly until mixture is warm to touch and sugar feels dissolved, about 2 minutes.
5. With a mixer on high speed, whisk whites until light and fluffy and sides of bowl feel cool to touch, about 2 minutes.
6. Assemble cake: Preheat broiler. Using a serrated knife, trim brown exterior from sides and top of cake. Slice cake horizontally into three even layers.

7. Place one cake layer, cut side up, on a rimmed baking sheet. Spread with half the lemon curd mixture. Repeat with second layer and remaining curd. Top with last layer. Using a spatula, cover entire cake with meringue.
8. Broil cake 7 in. from heat just until top is golden brown, being careful not to burn it, about 1 minute. Using two large pancake turners (sliding them under the cake to support it evenly), transfer cake to a serving plate.
Make Ahead: Lemon curd, up to 2 days, chilled.

PER SERVING: 504 cal., 36% (180 cal.) from fat; 8 g protein; 20 g fat (11 g sat.); 74 g carbo (0.6 g fiber); 432 mg sodium; 220 mg chol.

Strawberry Tallcake

We created this elegant, elongated version of strawberry shortcake by stacking cake layers with berries and whipped cream.

MAKES 1 layer cake (8 in.); 6 servings
TIME 35 minutes, plus 1 hour, 20 minutes to bake and cool butter cake

4 cups quartered strawberries
6 tbsp. sugar, divided
1 tbsp. *each* finely shredded lemon zest and fresh lemon juice
2 cups heavy whipping cream
Best Butter Cake *(opposite page)*, cooled
6 oz. good-quality strawberry jam (9 tbsp.)

1. Make filling: In a large bowl, combine strawberries, 2 tbsp. sugar, and the lemon zest and juice. Let sit 10 minutes.
2. In a medium bowl, with a mixer on medium-high speed, whip cream with remaining ¼ cup sugar until it holds a stiff peak.
3. Assemble cake: Using a serrated knife, slice both cake layers in half horizontally. Set rounded tops aside to use as middle layers. Dollop 1 tbsp. whipped cream onto center of a cake stand (to hold cake in place). Set one of the bottom layers on stand, cut side up. Spread with about 3 tbsp. jam. Sprinkle with about a quarter of sweetened strawberries, along with some juice. Then dollop a quarter of cream over strawberries. Repeat with second and third cake layers, using reserved rounded tops.
4. Place remaining bottom layer on top of cake, cut side down. Mound remaining whipped cream in center and spread to about 1 in. from edge, then sprinkle with remaining strawberries.

PER SERVING: 361 cal., 45% (162 cal.) from fat; 3.8 g protein; 18 g fat (11 g sat.); 48 g carbo (1.5 g fiber); 253 mg sodium; 84 mg chol.

Chocolate Peanut Butter Cake

An homage to Reese's Peanut Butter Cups. This cake is for the true peanut butter and chocolate lover.

MAKES 1 layer cake (9 in.); 16 servings | **TIME** 1 hour, plus 1 hour, 20 minutes to bake and cool butter cake

1¼ cups creamy peanut butter, divided
Batter for Best Butter Cake *(opposite page)*, prepared through step 2
1 package (8 oz.) cream cheese, at room temperature
1 cup powdered sugar
¼ cup milk
Fudge Frosting *(page 634)*
3 Reese's Peanut Butter Cups, quartered
¾ cup dry-roasted peanuts

1. Preheat oven to 350°. Butter and flour two 9-in. cake pans. Stir ½ cup peanut butter into cake batter and divide between pans. Bake until a toothpick inserted in centers comes out clean, about 45 minutes. Cool 5 minutes, then invert cakes onto a rack. Remove pans and let cakes cool to room temperature, at least 40 minutes.
2. Make peanut butter filling: In a medium bowl, with a mixer on medium speed, beat together remaining ¾ cup peanut butter, cream cheese, powdered sugar, and milk until smooth and fluffy.
3. Assemble cake: Dollop 1 tbsp. peanut butter filling onto a cake stand (to hold cake in place). Set one cake, right side up, on stand. Spread with remaining peanut butter filling. Top with second cake. Frost cake with Fudge Frosting, starting with top, then working down sides. Decorate top with candy pieces and peanuts.

PER SERVING: 603 cal., 51% (306 cal.) from fat; 11 g protein; 34 g fat (16 g sat.); 71 g carbo (3 g fiber); 445 mg sodium; 76 mg chol.

Chocolate Peanut Butter Cupcakes: Make batter for Chocolate Peanut Butter Cake *(see step 1 above)* but pour into 18 buttered muffin cups (2¾ in. wide). Bake cupcakes in a 350° oven until a toothpick comes out clean, about 20 minutes. While cupcakes are baking, make peanut butter filling *(step 2 above)*. Cool cupcakes, then frost thinly with filling. Make a batch and a half of **Fudge Frosting** and mound on top of cupcakes. Decorate with chunks of **Reese's Peanut Butter Cups** and **peanuts** if you like. Makes 18 cupcakes.

PER CUPCAKE WITHOUT FROSTING: 402 cal., 52% (210 cal.) from fat; 9.5 g protein; 23 g fat (8.7 g sat.); 42 g carbo (2 g fiber); 342 mg sodium; 52 mg chol.

Raspberry-Lemon Pudding Cakes

recipe pictured on page **679**

These yummy little cakes are based on a recipe sent to us by reader Jeannette Hennings, of Lake Havasu City, Arizona. As the cakes cook, they separate into layers: A tender berry cake rises to the top, while a layer of a creamy lemon pudding sinks to the bottom. You'll need six ramekins (⅔-cup size).

MAKES 6 individual cakes | **TIME** 50 minutes, plus 30 minutes to cool

2 eggs, separated
½ cup granulated sugar
3 tbsp. flour
2 tbsp. butter, melted
Finely shredded zest of 1 lemon
3 tbsp. fresh lemon juice
1 cup low-fat (1%) milk
⅛ tsp. cream of tartar
2⅔ cups raspberries (¾ lb.), divided
Powdered sugar

1. Preheat oven to 350°. Set ramekins in a 9- by 13-in. baking pan.
2. In a medium bowl, whisk together egg yolks and granulated sugar until thick and creamy. Whisk in flour, butter, lemon zest and juice, and milk until blended.
3. In a deep bowl, with a mixer on high speed, beat egg whites and cream of tartar until whites hold stiff, moist peaks. Stir a quarter of whites into yolk mixture until blended, then gently fold in remaining whites. Gently fold in half the raspberries.
4. Spoon batter into ramekins. Pour enough hot water into baking pan to come 1 in. up sides of ramekins.
5. Bake until cake layers are set and tops are golden, 30 to 35 minutes. Remove ramekins from water; let cool on rack at least 30 minutes. Serve with more berries on top and a dusting of powdered sugar.
Make Ahead: Up to 1 day, chilled (pudding layer will become more distinct).

PER SERVING: 189 cal., 30% (57 cal.) from fat; 4.4 g protein; 6.3 g fat (3.2 g sat.); 30 g carbo (2.9 g fiber); 83 mg sodium; 82 mg chol.

Candy Cane Cake

recipe pictured on page **607**

Angel food cake slathered with whipped cream and crushed candy has been a favorite dessert in Molly Watson's family for three generations. "It was my childhood birthday request year after year," says Watson, a former *Sunset* recipe editor. "Our topping was crushed toffee, but a few years ago at Christmas, I switched over to candy canes. It became our new holiday classic." For a shortcut version, start with a store-bought angel food cake.

MAKES 1 tube cake; 8 to 10 servings | **TIME** 1½ hours, plus 1 hour to cool

1 cup sifted cake or pastry flour
1¾ cups sugar, divided
12 egg whites, at room temperature
1 tsp. cream of tartar
¼ tsp. salt
1 tsp. *each* vanilla and almond extracts
½ lb. peppermint candy canes
2 cups heavy whipping cream

1. Preheat oven to 325°. Sift together flour and ¾ cup sugar. Sift again and set aside.
2. In a large bowl, with a mixer on medium-high speed, beat egg whites until foamy. Add cream of tartar and salt. Beat until soft peaks form. Add ¾ cup sugar and the vanilla and almond extracts. Continue beating until egg whites are firm but not dry.
3. Sift a third of flour-sugar mixture onto egg whites and, with a rubber or silicone spatula, gently fold mixture into egg whites. Add remaining flour-sugar in two batches, folding gently after each addition. Turn batter into a 10-cup tube pan (also called angel food cake pan) and bake until browned and firm to the touch, 50 to 60 minutes.
4. Invert cake (in pan) on a rack for at least an hour. When completely cool, run a long, thin, sharp knife between cake and pan sides to loosen, and remove cake.
5. Put candy canes in a large resealable plastic bag. Crush them into small pieces with a meat pounder, rolling pin, or bottom of a small frying pan. Sift crushed candy with a fine-mesh strainer and reserve candy dust for another use (*see Quick Tip, above right*). Set crushed candy aside.
6. In a large bowl, with a mixer with clean, dry beaters on medium-high speed, beat cream with remaining ¼ cup sugar until soft peaks form. Frost cake with whipped cream using a spatula to form swirls and

peaks. Sprinkle frosted cake with crushed candy canes just before serving (the moisture from the whipped cream makes the peppermint begin to "melt" after half an hour). To get candy on the cake's sides, hold your hand about 1 in. from cake and gently toss crushed candy at sides. Serve immediately, using a serrated knife to cut slices.

Quick Tip: The very fine candy "dust" left over from crushing the candy canes is delicious sprinkled on vanilla ice cream or stirred into hot cocoa.

PER SERVING: 498 cal., 36% (180 cal.) from fat; 7 g protein; 20 g fat (12 g sat.); 75 g carbo (0.2 g fiber); 174 mg sodium; 72 mg chol.

Chocolate Chiffon Cupcakes

These tender, deep chocolate cupcakes are from Elizabeth Falkner, chef-owner of Citizen Cake and Orson in San Francisco.

MAKES 17 or 18 cupcakes | **TIME** 50 minutes

1½ cups cake flour
½ cup plus 1 tbsp. unsweetened cocoa powder (not Dutch-processed)
1 tsp. baking powder
½ tsp. salt
¼ tsp. baking soda
4 eggs, separated
¾ cup vegetable oil
¾ cup plus 2 tbsp. sugar
About 1⅔ cups Creamy Chocolate Frosting (recipe follows) or frosting of your choice

1. Preheat oven to 325°. Butter 17 or 18 muffin cups (2¾ in. wide) or line with paper baking cups. Sift flour, cocoa, baking powder, salt, and baking soda into a large bowl.
2. In a medium bowl, whisk egg yolks, oil, and ⅓ cup water until blended. Whisk in ¾ cup sugar. Add egg-yolk mixture to flour mixture and stir until well blended.
3. In another medium bowl, with a mixer on high speed, beat egg whites until frothy. Gradually add remaining 2 tbsp. sugar, beating just until soft peaks form. Add egg-white mixture to batter and fold in with a rubber spatula until evenly blended.
4. Fill each muffin cup about three-fourths full with batter.
5. Bake until tops spring back when lightly touched in center, 20 to 25 minutes. Cool on racks 5 minutes; remove from pans. Cool completely before frosting.

Make Ahead: Frosted cupcakes, up to 4 hours, stored airtight at room temperature; up to 1 day, chilled. Frosting, up to 1 day, chilled; bring to room temperature before using.

PER UNFROSTED CUPCAKE: 182 cal., 54% (99 cal.) from fat; 2.8 g protein; 11 g fat (1.7 g sat.); 20 g carbo (1 g fiber); 124 mg sodium; 47 mg chol.

Creamy Chocolate Frosting

Although Elizabeth Falkner created this frosting for her Chocolate Chiffon Cupcakes, *left*, you can also spread it on chocolate wafers or graham crackers to make sandwich cookies.

MAKES About 3 cups (enough to frost about 32 cupcakes or a 9-in. double-layer cake) | **TIME** 20 minutes, plus 1½ hours to cool

1½ cups whipping cream
1½ tbsp. light corn syrup
12 oz. bittersweet or semisweet chocolate, chopped, or 2 cups chocolate chips
¼ cup butter, thickly sliced

1. In a 1½- to 2-qt. pan over high heat, bring cream and corn syrup to a boil, stirring occasionally, 3 to 4 minutes.
2. Put chocolate in a heatproof bowl. Pour hot cream mixture over chocolate. Let stand about 5 minutes, then stir until smooth. Add butter, then stir again until butter is melted and mixture is smooth.
3. Let frosting cool, stirring occasionally, until thick and spreadable, 2 to 3 hours at room temperature or about 1½ hours in the refrigerator.
Make Ahead: Up to 2 days, chilled. Bring to room temperature and stir until creamy and spreadable before using.

PER TBSP.: 67 cal., 76% (51 cal.) from fat; 0.7 g protein; 5.7 g fat (3.3 g sat.); 4.7 g carbo (0.2 g fiber); 13 mg sodium; 11 mg chol.

Cupcake Decorating Tips

Patric Gabre-Kidan, a Seattle pastry chef, shared some insider information with us on cupcake decoration. (We've added our favorite strategies as well.)

- **Make sure your frosting is soft and creamy.** This is especially important if you're piping it. Cold, stiff frosting will look dull and clumpy, not silky and smooth. If it's been chilled, let it come to room temperature before using it.
- **Use a lot of colors.** It will make each cupcake distinctive and turn a trayful into instant decorations for a party.
- **Don't think that sprinkles are cheesy.** They can actually elevate the look.
- **Mix simple decorations with more elegant ones.** Colorful sprinkles aren't lowbrow beside sifted cocoa.
- **Have fun with candies.** Some of our favorite toppings are chocolate sprinkles, jelly beans, miniature M&Ms, miniature chocolate chips, and peanuts. We also like chopped toffee, malted milk balls, or dark chocolate.
- **Try artistic touches.** Thin shreds of lemon or orange zest, candied lemon or orange peel, toasted coconut, candied ginger, and sugared rose petals are pretty flourishes. If using rose petals, lightly coat fresh, un-sprayed ones with pasteurized egg whites, then sugar, and let them dry before using.
- **Use peanut butter as frosting.** Stir it until creamy, then dollop on cupcakes; or swirl with chocolate frosting.
- **Add "architectural" elements.** Little meringues, miniature Oreos, or chunks of chocolate wafer cookies give drama to your tiny cakes.

Vanilla Frosting

This frosting from chef Elizabeth Falkner, of Citizen Cake and Orson, both in San Francisco, can be flavored many ways; see our variations following the recipe.

MAKES About 2½ cups (enough to frost about 27 cupcakes or an 8-in. double-layer cake)
TIME 10 minutes

1 cup unsalted butter, at room temperature
4 cups (1 lb.) powdered sugar, sifted, divided
⅛ tsp. salt
2 tbsp. milk
2 tsp. vanilla extract

In a large bowl, with a mixer (preferably fitted with a wire-whisk attachment) on low speed, beat butter, 2 cups powdered sugar, and the salt until blended. Add milk and vanilla; beat until blended. Add remaining powdered sugar, 1 cup at a time, beating until incorporated. Turn mixer to high speed and beat frosting until fluffy and smooth.
Make Ahead: Up to 2 days, chilled. Bring to room temperature and stir until creamy and spreadable before using.

PER TBSP.: 86 cal., 48% (41 cal.) from fat; 0.1 g protein; 4.6 g fat (2.9 g sat.); 11 g carbo (0 g fiber); 8.4 mg sodium; 13 mg chol.

Orange Frosting: Replace milk with **orange juice**, and vanilla with finely shredded **orange zest**.
Mint Frosting: Replace vanilla with 4 tsp. **crème de menthe** or 1 tsp. **mint extract** and 2 or 3 drops **green food coloring** if you like. Makes enough to frost 25 cupcakes.
Lemon Frosting: Replace milk with **fresh lemon juice**, and vanilla with finely shredded **lemon zest**. Makes enough to frost 26 cupcakes.
Coffee Frosting: Replace milk and vanilla with 4 tsp. **instant espresso powder** dissolved in 3 tbsp. hot water, then cooled. Makes enough to frost 27 cupcakes.

Coconut Cupcakes

Sunset reader Amber Burhans, of Grants, New Mexico, tells us that these buttery cupcakes are one of her signature dishes.

MAKES 30 cupcakes | **TIME** 45 minutes, plus 40 minutes to cool and frost

2¾ cups butter, at room temperature, divided
2 cups granulated sugar
4 eggs
2 tsp. *each* vanilla and almond extracts, divided
3 cups flour
½ tsp. *each* baking powder, baking soda, and salt
1 cup canned coconut milk
1½ cups sweetened shredded dried coconut, toasted if you like *(see Quick Tip, above right)*, divided
1 package (8 oz.) cream cheese, at room temperature
2¾ cups powdered sugar

1. Preheat oven to 350°. Line 30 muffin cups (2¾ in. wide) with paper baking cups. In a large bowl, cream together 2 cups butter and the granulated sugar until light and fluffy. Add eggs, one at a time, beating well after each addition. Mix in 1½ tsp. each vanilla and almond extracts.

2. In another large bowl, combine flour, baking powder and soda, and salt. Add to butter mixture in three batches, alternating with coconut milk. Stir 1 cup shredded coconut into batter.

3. Fill each muffin cup about two-thirds full with batter. Bake until a toothpick inserted into center of a cupcake comes out clean, 15 to 20 minutes. Cool for 10 minutes before removing muffins from pans. Cool completely.

4. Meanwhile, in a medium bowl, beat cream cheese and remaining ¾ cup butter and ½ tsp. each vanilla and almond extracts until smooth. Gradually beat in powdered sugar. Frost cupcakes and sprinkle with remaining ½ cup coconut.

Quick Tip: To toast coconut, spread it on a baking sheet and bake in a 325° oven until golden brown, 6 to 8 minutes. Let cool before using.

Make Ahead: Unfrosted cupcakes, up to 4 hours, stored airtight at room temperature. Frosting, up to 1 day, chilled; warm to room temperature before using. Frosted cupcakes, up to 1 day, chilled.

PER CUPCAKE: 359 cal., 58% (207 cal.) from fat; 3.1 g protein; 23 g fat (15 g sat.); 36 g carbo (0.6 g fiber); 282 mg sodium; 82 mg chol.

Strawberry-Kiwi Pavlova

The traditional Australian pavlova looks much like a classic meringue, but it has a crisp surface and a soft, almost marshmallow-like interior. You can either bake it in one large round, the usual way—or make individual pavlovas.

MAKES 1 large pavlova or 8 small ones; 8 servings
TIME 1 hour, 20 minutes for large; 1 hour, 10 minutes for small, plus 20 minutes to cool

¾ cup plus 2 tbsp. sugar
1 tbsp. cornstarch
4 egg whites (½ cup) or ½ cup refrigerated pasteurized egg whites *(see Quick Tip, above right)*
1 tsp. distilled white vinegar or white wine vinegar
1 tsp. vanilla extract
1 cup whipping cream
3 cups sliced strawberries (15 oz.)
1 cup sliced peeled kiwi fruit (½ lb.)

1. For one large pavlova, preheat oven to 250° and line one 12- by 15-in. rimmed baking sheet with parchment paper. For individual pavlovas, preheat oven to 300° and line two rimmed baking sheets.

2. In a small bowl, mix 1 tbsp. sugar with cornstarch. Set aside. In a large bowl, with a mixer (preferably fitted with wire-whisk attachment) on high speed, beat egg whites and vinegar until foamy. Gradually add ¾ cup sugar, about 1 tbsp. at a time, beating well after each addition and scraping down side of bowl as needed, until stiff, shiny peaks form. Add cornstarch mixture and vanilla and beat just until blended.

3. For one large pavlova, mound all meringue on the baking sheet and shape into a 7- to 8-in. round, with edges slightly higher than center. To make individual pavlovas, mound meringue in eight equal portions (a scant ½ cup for each) on sheets, spacing at least 3 in. apart. Shape each into a 4-in. round, with edges slightly higher than center. *(See Tips for Perfect Meringue, below.)*

4. Bake until a thin, crisp crust forms on surface but interior is still soft when gently pressed, 50 to 60 minutes for large pavlova, 20 to 25 minutes for individual pavlovas. Remove from oven and let cool completely on baking sheet(s). Carefully remove and transfer to a platter or plates (it's normal for crust to crack a little).

5. In a bowl, with a mixer on high speed, beat whipping cream just until soft peaks form. Turn mixer to low and beat in remaining 2 tbsp. sugar.

6. Just before serving, top pavlova(s) with whipped cream, strawberries, and kiwi fruit. Cut large pavlova into wedges.

Quick Tip: Since the egg whites in this recipe won't be completely cooked, consider using pasteurized whites if serving the pavlova to anyone with a compromised immune system (raw eggs can carry harmful bacteria).

Make Ahead: Baked pavlova(s), up to 1 day, stored airtight at room temperature.

PER SERVING: 206 cal., 42% (86 cal.) from fat; 2.8 g protein; 9.5 g fat (5.8 g sat.); 29 g carbo (2.3 g fiber); 37 mg sodium; 33 mg chol.

Tips for Perfect Meringue

1. Use the wire-whisk attachment on your mixer. It introduces air evenly into whites and creates small bubbles, which are both stronger and more flexible than big ones.
2. Make sure the bowl and beaters are clean; any fat can interfere with the formation of the foam.
3. Add an acid, like vinegar or cream of tartar, to the whites when beating; it helps coagulate the egg-white protein.
4. Beat the whites into stiff, shiny peaks. The mixture should feel smooth when you rub it between your fingers.

Banana Pecan *Dacquoise*

This knockout dessert is all about contrasts in texture: Crisp meringue layers alternate with soft, creamy filling. Make all the components ahead and assemble them shortly before serving, starting with step 9.

MAKES 1 layer cake (9 in.); 12 servings
TIME 2½ hours, plus 2 hours to chill

BANANA CARAMEL
1 cup sugar
1 tbsp. light corn syrup
4 ripe bananas, chopped
¼ cup whipping cream
1 tbsp. butter

PASTRY CREAM
1 cup whole milk
½ vanilla bean, split lengthwise
¾ cup sugar
3 tbsp. flour
¾ tsp. salt
4 egg yolks
2 tbsp. butter

NUT MERINGUES
3 cups pecan halves, toasted (*see How to Toast Nuts, page 134*), divided
1⅓ cups sugar, divided
2 tbsp. cornstarch
6 egg whites
Pinch salt

ASSEMBLY
1 cup whipping cream
3 firm-ripe bananas

1. Make banana caramel: In a medium saucepan, bring sugar, corn syrup, and ¾ cup water to a boil over high heat (do not stir). When sugar starts to darken in one spot, carefully swirl pan to caramelize evenly until medium amber in color.

2. Add chopped bananas and cream (mixture will bubble up furiously); stir to mix. Reduce heat and simmer, uncovered, stirring occasionally, about 30 minutes. Stir in butter. Let cool, then chill airtight at least 2 hours.

3. Make pastry cream: In a small pan, heat milk and vanilla bean over high heat until milk starts to boil. Remove from heat and let sit 15 minutes.

4. Whisk sugar, flour, and salt together in a small bowl. Whisk in egg yolks, then gradually whisk in warm milk mixture. Return mixture to pan and cook over medium heat, whisking constantly. When mixture boils, cook 2 more minutes, whisking (it should be very thick and stiff). Remove from heat, stir in butter, and remove

vanilla bean. Transfer pastry cream to an 8- or 9-in. baking pan and lay a piece of plastic wrap directly on surface to prevent a skin from forming. Chill at least 1 hour.

5. Make meringues: Preheat oven to 300°. Set a 9-in. plate or round cake pan on a piece of parchment paper (waxed paper won't work) and trace around plate with a pen or pencil. Lay paper on a greased baking sheet, marked side down. Repeat with two more pieces of parchment and two more baking sheets.

6. Reserve 1 cup of nicest-looking pecan halves for garnish. Put remaining 2 cups pecans, ⅔ cup sugar, and the cornstarch in a food processor. Pulse until mixture is fine and crumbly, about 30 seconds. Pour into a large bowl.

7. Put egg whites and salt in a large bowl; with a mixer (preferably fitted with wire-whisk attachment) on medium speed, beat until white and foamy. Increase speed to high and slowly sprinkle in remaining ⅔ cup sugar. Keep whisking until stiff, shiny peaks form. Using a rubber spatula, fold into nut mixture.

8. Using spatula, dollop meringue into centers of parchment circles, dividing evenly. With an offset metal spatula (*see Quick Tip below*) or butter knife, spread meringue outward to edge of circles. Bake meringues, in two batches if needed, until golden brown and crisp, about 45 minutes. Let cool completely on pans.

9. Assemble *dacquoise*: In a medium bowl, with the mixer on medium-high speed, whisk cream until it just holds a peak (it shouldn't be too stiff). Whisk half the whipped cream into chilled pastry cream.

10. Peel parchment from meringues. Set one meringue in center of a cake stand and spread with half the pastry cream. Spoon on half the banana caramel. Quarter 1 banana lengthwise and lay on top. Add second meringue, remaining pastry cream and caramel, and another banana.

11. Set last meringue on top and dollop remaining whipped cream in center. Quarter last banana lengthwise and lay over cream. Sprinkle with half the reserved pecan halves and put rest in a small bowl to pass at the table. Serve immediately, using a serrated knife to cut slices.

Quick Tip: Offset spatulas are great for spreading meringue or frosting, because the L-shaped blade helps you keep your wrist elevated above the meringue (a flat blade makes it hard to avoid a wrist-smear or two).

Make Ahead: Banana caramel and pastry cream, up to 4 days, chilled. Meringues, up to 2 days, stored airtight at room temperature.

PER SERVING: 576 cal., 52% (297 cal.) from fat; 6.9 g protein; 33 g fat (10 g sat.); 69 g carbo (3.6 g fiber); 141 mg sodium; 115 mg chol.

Tres Leches Cake with Raspberries

This layer cake from Thomas Schnetz, chef-owner of Doña Tomás restaurant in Oakland, California, is his take on the moist, rich Mexican sponge cake of the same name. Like the traditional cake, it's soaked in "three milks" (*tres leches*)—evaporated milk, sweetened condensed milk, and cream.

recipe pictured on page **609**

MAKES 1 cake (9 in.); 10 to 12 servings
TIME 1½ hours, plus 3 hours to cool and chill

CAKE
6 eggs
1 cup *each* granulated sugar and flour
6 tbsp. butter, melted
TRES LECHES SAUCE
1 can (12 oz.) evaporated goat milk (*see Quick Tip below*)
6 tbsp. granulated sugar
2 tbsp. light corn syrup
1 stick cinnamon (about 2 in.)
⅛ tsp. baking soda mixed with 2 tsp. water
⅔ cup canned sweetened condensed milk
1¼ cups whipping cream
FILLING AND FROSTING
1¾ cups raspberries
1½ tbsp. granulated sugar
2 cups whipping cream
2 tsp. vanilla extract
½ cup powdered sugar

1. Preheat oven to 350°. Butter and flour a 9-in. springform pan (with side at least 2 in. high). Put a medium bowl in the refrigerator to chill.

2. Make cake: Select a large stainless steel bowl (at least 10-cup capacity) that can nest comfortably in a large pot. Fill pot halfway with water and bring to a boil over high heat, then reduce heat to a gentle simmer. In bowl, combine eggs and granulated sugar. Set bowl over water; with a mixer on high speed, beat eggs and sugar until pale and thick enough to fall from a spoon in a wide ribbon, about 10 minutes.

3. Remove bowl from heat. Shake flour through a sieve over egg mixture and fold in gently. Add butter and fold in gently until no streaks remain. Scrape batter into pan.

4. Bake until cake is evenly browned, just begins to pull from pan sides, and springs back when lightly touched in center, about 40 minutes. Set pan on a rack and let cool at least 10 minutes. Run a thin knife between cake and pan rim. Remove rim and let cake cool completely.

5. Make *tres leches* sauce: In a large pot (at least 6-qt. capacity) over high heat, combine goat milk, granulated sugar, corn syrup, and cinnamon stick. Bring mixture to a boil. Stir in baking soda mixture (sauce will foam up), reduce heat, and simmer, stirring occasionally, until sauce turns a caramel color and has reduced to ¾ cup, 10 to 12 minutes.

6. Remove sauce from heat; discard cinnamon stick, and stir in condensed milk and cream. Use warm (*see Make Ahead below*).

7. With a long, serrated knife, cut cake in half horizontally. Leave bottom half on pan base. Lift off cake top and set, cut side down, on a flat plate.

8. Put cake bottom (with pan base) on a rack set over a rimmed baking sheet. Poke cake bottom all over with a toothpick, being careful not to poke all the way through. Slowly spoon enough warm tres leches sauce (about 1 cup) over cake bottom to saturate but not cause it to ooze. Let stand until cool, about 10 minutes.

9. Make filling: Reserve several raspberries to go on top of cake, then put remaining fruit in a bowl and mix gently with granulated sugar. Set aside. In a chilled bowl, using a mixer on medium-high speed, whip cream until it holds soft peaks and is thick enough to spread. Add vanilla and powdered sugar; mix well. Scoop about 1⅓ cups whipped cream onto cake bottom and spread level to edge. Dot with sugared raspberries, pushing them down into cream. Carefully set cake top, cut side down, onto cake bottom and neatly align. Poke top all over with a toothpick as before, then slowly spoon about 1 cup tres leches sauce evenly over cake top to saturate well. Smoothly frost top and sides of cake with remaining whipped cream; transfer to a clean serving plate. Cover cake without touching (invert a large bowl over it) and chill at least 2 hours. Cover and chill raspberries if held longer than 2 hours. Cover and chill remaining tres leches sauce.

10. Uncover cake and decorate with reserved raspberries. Serve with remaining tres leches sauce.

Quick Tip: Evaporated goat milk (Meyenberg is a popular brand) is sold in most grocery stores. Look in the baking aisle, near the condensed milk.

Make Ahead: Cake and tres leches sauce, up to 1 day, chilled; reheat sauce before drizzling over cake. Completed cake, up to 1 day, chilled (garnish with raspberries just before serving).

PER SERVING: 637 cal., 55% (351 cal.) from fat; 10 g protein; 39 g fat (24 g sat.); 62 g carbo (1.4 g fiber); 203 mg sodium; 244 mg chol.

Roasted Sweet Potato Cheesecake

Sunset reader Kari Bowers, of Bellevue, Washington, won the grand prize in our 2005 Thanksgiving recipe contest for this dessert.

MAKES 1 cheesecake (9 in.); 12 to 16 servings
TIME 2½ hours, plus 2½ hours to cool and chill

2 dark orange–fleshed sweet potatoes (often labeled "yams"; 1¼ to 1½ lbs. total)
1 tbsp. butter, melted
Pecan Crust (*recipe follows*)
2 tsp. fresh lemon juice
3 packages (8 oz. each) cream cheese, at room temperature
¾ cup granulated sugar
½ cup firmly packed light brown sugar
4 eggs
¼ cup *each* whipping cream, sour cream, and maple syrup
1½ tsp. cinnamon
1 tsp. *each* nutmeg and ground ginger
Maple Cream (*recipe follows*)

1. Preheat oven to 375°. Peel sweet potatoes and cut in half lengthwise. Put in a 9- by 13-in. baking pan and brush with butter. Bake until soft when pressed, 45 to 55 minutes.
2. Meanwhile, prepare crust. Bake it in oven with potatoes until lightly browned all over, 10 to 12 minutes.
3. Scrape any charred spots off potatoes, then cut potatoes into chunks. Purée in a food processor or mash in a bowl with lemon juice until smooth. Reserve 1 cup; save any extra for another use.
4. Reduce oven temperature to 325°. In a large bowl, with a mixer on high speed, beat cream cheese until fluffy. Gradually beat in both sugars until well blended, scraping down side of bowl occasionally. Add eggs, one at a time, beating well after each addition. Add sweet-potato mixture, whipping cream, sour cream, maple syrup, cinnamon, nutmeg, and ginger. Mix on low speed until well blended.
5. Wrap bottom of cheesecake pan with heavy-duty foil, pressing it up the sides. Pour batter over crust. Put cheesecake pan in a 12- by 15-in. roasting pan at least 2 in. deep. Set pans in oven and pour enough boiling water into roasting pan to come halfway up side of cheesecake pan.
6. Bake until cake barely jiggles in center when gently shaken, about 1 hour.
7. Remove pans from oven. Lift cheesecake pan from roasting pan and put on a rack. Run a thin-bladed spatula between cheesecake and pan rim (*see Quick Tip below*).

Let cool completely, about 1 hour, then chill until cold, at least 1½ hours; cover with plastic wrap once cold.
8. Up to 6 hours before serving, cut around inside of pan rim again to ensure release of cake; remove rim. Cut cake slices with a serrated knife, running knife under hot water and wiping clean after each slice. Serve with Maple Cream.
Quick Tip: Run a spatula around the inside of the pan just after baking to help the cheesecake firm up without cracking.
Make Ahead: Up to 3 days, chilled.

PER SERVING: 427 cal., 61% (261 cal.) from fat; 6.2 g protein; 29 g fat (17 g sat.); 38 g carbo (1.1 g fiber); 242 mg sodium; 133 mg chol.

Pecan Crust: Finely grind ¼ cup chopped **pecans** in a blender. In a bowl, mix pecans, 1¼ cups **fine graham cracker crumbs** (from about 17 squares), 2 tbsp. **granulated sugar**, and 5 tbsp. **melted butter**. Pour into a 9-in. springform pan (with side at least 2¼ in. high). Press mixture evenly over bottom of pan.

Maple Cream: In a medium bowl, using a mixer on high speed, beat ¾ cup **whipping cream** until stiff peaks form. On low speed, beat in ¼ cup **maple syrup** just until blended. Makes 1¾ cups.

Caramelized Orange Cheesecake

This snowy cheesecake has a glistening topping of candylike orange slices. It's easier to prepare than a lot of other cheesecakes, since you don't have to set the cake pan in a water-filled larger pan.

recipe pictured on page **605**

MAKES 1 cheesecake (9 in.); 12 servings
TIME 2¼ hours, plus 3½ hours to cool and chill

TOPPING
1 large firm thin-skinned orange, such as Valencia
1 cup sugar
2 tsp. fresh lemon juice
CHEESECAKE
1¼ cups graham cracker crumbs (from about 17 squares)
3 tbsp. butter, melted
3 packages (8 oz. each) cream cheese, at room temperature
¾ cup sugar
4 eggs, at room temperature
2 tbsp. flour
½ cup sour cream
1 tbsp. orange-flavored liqueur, such as Grand Marnier or Cointreau, or 2 tsp. vanilla extract
3 tbsp. fresh orange juice

cakes

1. Make topping: With a sharp knife, slice orange into thin rounds (between ⅛ and 1/16 in. thick; *see Quick Tip, right*), discarding ends and seeds. In a deep 10-in. frying pan or pot over medium-high heat, stir sugar, ¾ cup water, and lemon juice until sugar is dissolved. Add orange slices and bring to a simmer. Cover and simmer 5 minutes. Uncover and simmer gently, keeping slices in a single layer and turning occasionally, until they're slightly candied and translucent and liquid has consistency of a thin syrup, about 20 minutes (there should be about ½ cup liquid in pan; if less, add enough hot water to make that amount and shake pan to mix water into syrup). Let cool in pan. Cover and chill at least 15 minutes.

2. Make cheesecake: Preheat oven to 300°. Pour cracker crumbs into a 9-in. springform pan (with side at least 2¼ in. high); add butter and mix. Press mixture evenly over bottom and ½ in. up sides of pan.

3. In a large bowl, with a mixer on medium speed, beat cream cheese and sugar until smooth. Add eggs, one at a time, beating well after each addition. Beat in flour, sour cream, and liqueur just until incorporated. Pour into crust-lined pan.

4. Bake until center barely jiggles when cake is gently shaken, 60 to 70 minutes. Run a thin-bladed knife between cheesecake and pan rim. Cool completely at room temperature, then cover with plastic wrap and chill until cold, at least 3 hours.

5. Remove pan rim. If any moisture has collected on top of cake, gently blot dry with a paper towel. Gently lift candied orange slices from syrup, reserving syrup, and blot dry. Arrange slices, slightly overlapping, over top of cheesecake.

6. Bring reserved syrup to a boil over high heat. Stir occasionally until syrup is deep golden brown, 1 to 3 minutes. Remove from heat and carefully stir in orange juice (mixture will bubble up). Let cool to room temperature and generously brush over orange slices (you may have extra syrup).

7. Cut cake slices with a serrated knife, running knife under hot water and wiping clean after each slice.

Quick Tip: For the topping, slice the whole orange as thinly and evenly as possible (it helps to have a very fresh, firm orange). If this is difficult, cut it in half lengthwise, then crosswise in thin slices.

Make Ahead: Candied orange slices and cheesecake, up to 2 days, chilled. Glazed cheesecake, up to 2 days, chilled.

PER SLICE: 433 cal., 56% (243 cal.) from fat; 7.6 g protein; 27 g fat (16 g sat.); 41 g carbo (0.6 g fiber); 279 mg sodium; 145 mg chol.

The Challenges of Cheesecake

Cracking, sinking, curdling, slumping—we've made all the mistakes one can make with cheesecake and fixed them. Learn from us with these tips.

• **CRACKING IN THE CENTER.** The edges of the cheesecake cook first, tightening and pulling away from the softer, cooler center. If the oven is too hot, the temperature differential is great enough to cause a tug of war, and hence, a fissure.
Fix: Bake at a low-ish temperature—300° to 350° is a good range. Or put your cake in a water bath to equalize the heat penetration: Wrap the cake pan in foil if it's a springform (to prevent leaking), and then set it in a larger pan. Fill the larger pan with hot or boiling water up to the level of the cake; then bake.

• **GRAINY, WEEPY CHEESECAKE.** If the cake cooks too long, its protein structure tightens, squeezing out moisture and making the texture grainy; the cake will also ooze liquid when cut. When the cake shrinks, chances of cracking go up too.
Fix: To prevent overbaking, gently shake the cheesecake in the oven when it's supposed to be done. If the center just barely jiggles, it's ready. If it ripples, it's undercooked, and if it doesn't move, it's overcooked.

• **SUNKEN CENTER.** When you beat the cake batter, air bubbles are trapped within. If the oven is too hot, as the cake bakes, the bubbles expand quickly, pushing up the first-to-set parts of the cake—the rim; however, in the still-liquid center, the bubbles have no firmed-up cake to hold them in, so they burst, and the cake sinks.
Fix: Don't beat your batter at a high speed; you'll trap too many bubbles, which will increase the odds of sinkage. Also, if you bake the cheesecake at a lower temperature (300° to 350°), the bubbles won't swell as fast or get as big, preserving the light texture and the flat, even surface.

• **CURDLED OR LUMPY CHEESECAKE.** If eggs are added too quickly to the cream cheese batter, the mixture won't be smooth and will separate when baked.
Fix: Add the eggs, one at a time, and beat the batter until it's completely smooth after each addition.

pies, tarts & fruit desserts

Sweet, juicy fruit teams up with flaky pie crusts, streusels, biscuity toppings, and more, in desserts that celebrate the seasons.

One of the happiest days at *Sunset* is January 23, National Pie Day. We bring pies to the office and, at the designated hour (usually in the morning, because no one can wait very long), we cut them and contentedly eat big slabs. We like pie so much that we've instituted a second Pie Day, on 3.14 (the mathematical ratio pi, which does, of course, apply to pie).

So you can bet we spent a lot of time putting this chapter together. We lingered for several weeks over our pie chart (*page 654*), making triple-extra-sure that every combination of fruit fillings and crusts and pie sizes worked. (It wasn't exactly a chore.) We rediscovered the joy of real lard (*page 649*) and how crisp it can make a crust. Over and over again, we were grateful for the amazing fruit we have in the West, from sweet Colorado peaches to California figs, because they turn our pies, crisps, cobblers, and tarts into treasures.

Our consolation for leaving summer fruits behind? Sumptuous holiday pies, like Apple-Cranberry-Currant Pie with French Topping (*page 649*) and Salted Chocolate Tart (*page 661*), so elegant and rich that it fits any special occasion.

Sometimes, after a large dinner, all you want is fruit itself—but something more than plain fruit. Sparkling Oranges (*page 668*) or Blueberries in Black Pepper–Syrah Syrup (*page 670*) will do you nicely.

The next time you find beautiful fruit in peak season, buy a few pounds and try one of our recipes. It will be sensational, because you started right.

Pies, Tarts & Fruit Desserts

Pie Crust
Without Fear

For many beginners, pie crusts are the most intimidating part of pie-making. Don't let crust scare you. Store-bought crusts are easy to use, but the truth is, homemade is much better. You just have to accept that you won't make a perfect crust the first time around. As with so many things, practice makes perfect—and the following tips will help.

• **KEEP THE DOUGH COLD AND THE BUTTER CHUNKY.** For a flaky crust, keep the butter from melting into the dough before baking. Why? Those bits of butter—which should be fairly big, about the size of peas—are meant to melt in the oven, giving off steam, which creates flaky pockets. If the dough seems to be softening too much as you're working with it, throw it in the refrigerator for 15 minutes. As you roll out the dough, you should see veins of butter running through it.

• **ROLL OUT FROM THE CENTER.** It's much easier to roll dough into a circle if you work from the center out to the edge in all directions. Roll firmly but gently, using short strokes. Also, start lifting off the rolling pin as you roll over the rim, to avoid gluing it to the work surface. If edges split while rolling, press them back toward the center to smooth.

• **LOOSEN THE DOUGH FROM THE WORK SURFACE EVERY NOW AND THEN.** A couple of times while rolling, slide a long spatula or pastry scraper under the dough to keep it from sticking to your counter or table. Once it's loosened, you can lift it up and sprinkle a little more flour underneath to keep it loose.

• **DON'T OVERDO IT.** Overworking the dough and using too much flour can make a pie crust tough and dry. Try to keep a light hand with both, rolling just enough to reach your desired size and using only enough flour to keep the dough from sticking to the work surface. If this is tricky for you, see the next tip.

• **USE A PIE-CRUST BAG.** A flat, round plastic bag, this handy tool takes the strain out of rolling, allowing you to use less flour and avoid shaggy edges. Simply put your chilled dough in the bag, zip it up, roll out the dough, and transfer it to your pan. The bags come in different sizes for regular and deep-dish pies and are available from many online sources (such as *sugarcraft.com*).

• **EASE THE DOUGH INTO THE PAN.** If you're not using a pie-crust bag, fold the dough circle gently in half, lift gently without stretching, and lay the folded edge across the center of the pie pan. Gently unfold; without stretching the dough, ease it from the center of the pan out to the rim. (Pulling or stretching the dough makes it shrink back when baked.) If any cracks or holes appear, push them together with your fingers or use a bit of extra dough from trimming edge.

• **CRIMP THE EDGES.** Crimping or fluting the edges of a double-crust pie seals the dough and keeps the filling from leaking out during baking. Even on a single-crust pie, crimping can create a helpful dam effect. There are many good techniques, but our favorite is to pinch the dough around the index finger of one hand using the thumb and index finger of the other.

Rolling out dough using a pie-crust bag   **Crimping the edge of a pie crust**

Crunch-top Apple Pie

Apple pie has always been a popular topic with *Sunset* readers. This crumb-and-nut–topped one, from January 1953, is among our most requested desserts. Its simplicity may have a lot to do with its longevity.

MAKES 1 pie (10-in.); 8 or 9 servings | **TIME** 1½ hours

6 medium tart apples such as Granny Smith, peeled, cored, and sliced
10-Inch Pie Shell *(right)*
1 cup *each* sugar and graham cracker crumbs
½ cup *each* flour and chopped walnuts
½ tsp. cinnamon
½ cup butter, melted
1 cup whipping cream (optional)

1. Preheat oven to 350°. Arrange apples evenly in unbaked pie shell. Combine sugar, graham cracker crumbs, flour, walnuts, and cinnamon; sprinkle over apples. Drizzle butter over topping.

2. Bake until crust is well browned and apples are tender when pierced, about 1 hour. Meanwhile, whip cream, if using, in a medium bowl. Serve pie at room temperature or chilled, with whipped cream if you like.

PER SERVING (WITHOUT WHIPPED CREAM): 498 cal., 47% (235 cal.) from fat; 5.6 g protein; 26 g fat (12 g sat.); 62 g carbo (2.7 g fiber); 231 mg sodium; 41 mg chol.

The Best Apple for the Job

Below are our favorite apples for cooking (including some Western varieties), divided out by which are best for pie and which are best for applesauce (most varieties can do double duty). Two apples, 3 in. wide, weigh about 1 lb. Peeled and sliced, they yield 3½ to 4 cups.

VARIETY	SAUCE	PIE
CORTLAND	•	•
EMPIRE	•	•
GRANNY SMITH		•
GRAVENSTEIN	•	•
HONEY CRISP	•	
IDA RED	•	•
JONAGOLD		•
JONATHAN	•	•
MCINTOSH	•	
PIPPIN		•
PINK LADY		•
WINESAP	•	•

10-Inch Pie Shell

Shortening or lard makes a pie crust flaky, and butter gives it flavor. Double the recipe if you're also making pastry leaves or other shapes to decorate the edges or top *(see Quick Tip below)*.

MAKES 1 pie shell (10-in.) | **TIME** 20 minutes

About 1½ cups flour
¼ tsp. salt
¼ cup cold vegetable shortening or fresh lard (*see In Praise of Real Lard, opposite*), cut into chunks
¼ cup cold butter, cut into chunks

1. In a medium bowl, mix 1½ cups flour and salt. Add shortening and butter. With a pastry blender or two knives (one held in each hand and moved crosswise), cut fats into flour or rub in with your fingers until mixture forms pea-size crumbs.

2. Sprinkle 3 tbsp. ice water over crumbs and mix with your hands until evenly moistened. Gently squeeze a handful of dough into a ball; if it won't hold together, sprinkle dough with 1 more tbsp. water, then mix again until evenly moistened.

3. With lightly floured hands, form dough into a ball. Dust ball lightly with flour; flatten into a round about ¾ in. thick, pressing edges to smooth. On a lightly floured work surface with a lightly floured rolling pin, roll dough firmly but gently in short strokes from center outward to form a circle about 14 in. in diameter (about ⅛ in. thick); lift and turn dough occasionally, dusting underneath with more flour. If edges split while rolling, press them back toward the center to smooth.

4. Fold dough circle in half, lift gently without stretching, and lay folded edge across center of a 10-in. pie pan. Unfold and ease dough into pan (if you push or stretch it, it will shrink back when baked). Trim edge evenly 1 in. beyond pan rim; reserve scraps for other uses or discard. Fold edge under itself, making it flush with rim; flute decoratively. Cover and chill until ready to use.

Quick Tip: To make pastry leaves or other shapes, double the crust recipe. Roll out half of dough as directed for pie shell; roll other half into a ⅛-in.-thick circle and use a cookie cutter to make shapes, or place a leaf on the dough and cut around it. Set shapes on top of filling right before it goes into the oven.

PER ½ OF CRUST: 137 cal., 57% (78 cal.) from fat; 1.8 g protein; 8.7 g fat (3.6 g sat.); 13 g carbo (0.5 g fiber); 87 mg sodium; 10 mg chol.

In Praise of Real Lard

Fresh, real lard—consisting of nothing but rendered pork fat—produces incomparably crisp, flaky pie crust (and great tamales, tortillas, and fried chicken too). It is nothing like the stiff, snow-white hydrogenated lard sold in tubs, which is not only laden with dangerous trans fats but is tasteless (and sometimes rancid) besides.

Fresh lard is soft at room temperature and ranges in hue from off-white to pale beige. Being high in calories, it isn't exactly health food if you eat too much of it. However, it has no trans fats, has less saturated fat than butter (about 40 percent compared with nearly 60 percent), and its "good" monounsaturated fat is 45 percent, double that of butter's. Compared with shortening, which is full of trans fats, it's an excellent and delicious choice.

Unfortunately, fresh lard is hard to find because it's been slandered for decades. Farmers' markets and good butcher shops are the best places to look. You can also try rendering your own lard from pork fat (see right).

A tip about working with fresh lard: It's so soft at room temperature that you will have to freeze it before you can cut it into cubes for making pie dough. Once you've cut the lard, freeze it again until you're ready to use it.

How to Render Lard

All pork fat is not created equal. Leaf lard (which comes from the kidney area) is the best for pie crust, because its structure is more crystalline, but it's hard to find. Back fat is fine too, and can usually be ordered through a butcher. Pork belly, which has bits of meat in it, can be used if you're making tamales, but will give a distinctly porky flavor to pies. Other types of pork fat—from the loin or shoulder—won't taste as good or render as well, and we don't recommend them. All our methods below yield 1 to 1½ cups lard per lb. of fat. Lard keeps, chilled, up to 2 months; frozen, up to 1 year.

Stovetop method: Good for small batches (1 lb. or less). Cut fat into 1-in. cubes and put in a medium pot. Add ⅓ cup water for every 1 lb. fat. Heat fat over very low heat, stirring occasionally, about 4 hours, or until chunks of fat have liquified and reduced in size by at least half. Remove from heat and strain through a cheesecloth-lined fine-mesh strainer into a heatproof container. Let cool completely.

Oven method: Best for rendering amounts larger than 1 lb. Put cubed fat in an ovenproof pot along with ⅓ cup water for every lb. of fat. Cook at 225°, stirring every 30 minutes or so, until fat has liquified and reduced in size by at least half. This takes anywhere from 5 to 8 hours, depending on how much fat you're rendering. Strain and cool as directed above.

Slow-cooker method: Put the cubed fat, plus ⅓ cup water for every lb. of fat, in a crockpot and cook at 150° to 200° (or the lowest setting) until chunks of fat have liquified, reducing their size by at least half, but rendered fat is still clear. This will take 6 to 8 hours (it's a good overnight project). Strain and cool as directed above.

Apple-Cranberry-Currant Pie with French Topping

This delicious pie, with its tumble of fruits and buttery brown sugar top, is a breeze to make. We gave its creator, Beth Secrest, of Somers, Montana, the grand prize one year in a holiday dessert contest.

MAKES 1 pie (10-in.); 10 to 12 servings | **TIME** 2 hours, plus 1 hour to plump currants and 2½ hours to cool

¼ cup *each* brandy and dried currants
1¼ cups granulated sugar, plus more to taste
6 tbsp. plus 1 cup flour
1 tbsp. finely shredded orange zest
¾ tsp. cinnamon
½ tsp. nutmeg
¼ tsp. salt
1½ cups fresh or thawed frozen cranberries
6 cups sliced, peeled Granny Smith apples (about 2¼ lbs.)
10-Inch Pie Shell (*page 648*)
⅔ cup firmly packed brown sugar
½ cup butter, cut into chunks

1. In a small bowl, combine brandy and currants. Cover; let stand until currants are plump, at least 1 hour and up to 1 day.

2. Preheat oven to 375°. In a large bowl, mix granulated sugar, 6 tbsp. flour, the orange zest, cinnamon, nutmeg, and salt. With a slotted spoon, transfer currants from brandy (reserve brandy) to sugar mixture; add cranberries and apples and mix well. Add more granulated sugar if you like. Pour filling into unbaked pie shell; drizzle with reserved brandy.

3. In a medium bowl, mix remaining 1 cup flour and the brown sugar. Add butter and cut in with a pastry blender or rub in with your fingers until mixture forms small lumps. Sprinkle topping over filling. Set pie in a foil-lined 10- by 15-in. baking pan.

4. Bake on lower rack until juices bubble, 55 to 65 minutes; if pie starts to brown too quickly, cover loosely with foil. Set pie, uncovered, on a rack until cool, 2½ to 3 hours. Cut into wedges.

PER SERVING: 431 cal., 35% (153 cal.) from fat; 3.6 g protein; 17 g fat (8.4 g sat.); 69 g carbo (2.6 g fiber); 219 mg sodium; 31 mg chol.

Pumpkin Streusel Pie

It takes both restraint and imagination to improve on a classic, and that's exactly what Sharon Klein, of Milwaukie, Oregon, did with pumpkin pie. Her recipe was a runner-up in our reader holiday pie contest.

MAKES 1 pie (10-in.); 12 servings | **TIME** 2 hours, plus 2 hours to cool

FILLING & CRUST

½ cup *each* granulated sugar and firmly packed dark brown sugar

1 tbsp. flour

1½ tsp. cinnamon

½ tsp. *each* nutmeg and salt

¼ tsp. ground ginger

1 can (15 oz.) pumpkin

1 can (12 oz.) evaporated milk

2 eggs, beaten to blend

10-Inch Pie Shell *(page 648)*

WALNUT STREUSEL

½ cup each firmly packed brown sugar, regular rolled oats, and chopped walnuts

¼ cup *each* flour and butter

½ tsp. *each* cinnamon and nutmeg

1. Preheat oven to 375°. In a large bowl, mix sugars, flour, cinnamon, nutmeg, salt, and ginger. Add pumpkin, evaporated milk, and eggs; whisk until well blended. Pour mixture into unbaked pie shell.

2. In a medium bowl, mix streusel ingredients until crumbly. Sprinkle evenly over pie filling.

3. Bake on lower rack until a knife inserted in center comes out clean, about 1 hour. Let cool completely on a rack, about 2 hours.

PER SERVING: 397 cal., 43% (171 cal.) from fat; 7 g protein; 19 g fat (8 g sat.); 51 g carbo (1.7 g fiber); 277 mg sodium; 65 mg chol.

Ancho Chile Pumpkin Pie

Denver chef and restaurateur Sean Yontz puts a Latin spin on pumpkin pie by adding a healthy dose of warming ancho chile (it adds more spice than heat) to the traditional cinnamon and nutmeg. Serve with lightly sweetened whipped cream.

MAKES 1 pie (9-in.); 8 to 10 servings | **TIME** 1½ hours, plus 2 hours to cool

9-in. single-crust pie shell, store-bought or homemade *(see Best All-purpose Pie Crust, page 652; halve recipe)*

1 can (15 oz.) pumpkin

1⅔ cups whipping cream

3 eggs, beaten to blend

½ cup *each* granulated sugar and firmly packed brown sugar

1 tbsp. ground dried ancho chiles

1 tsp. cinnamon

½ tsp. *each* nutmeg and salt

1. Preheat oven to 375°. Top pie shell with foil and fill halfway with pie weights or dried beans. Bake pie shell on lower rack until edges are dry and barely golden, about 15 minutes. Remove from oven and carefully remove pie weights and foil. Reduce oven temperature to 350°.

2. Meanwhile, in a large bowl, whisk pumpkin, cream, eggs, both sugars, ground chiles, cinnamon, nutmeg, and salt until smooth.

3. Pour pumpkin mixture into hot crust and return pie to oven on center rack. Bake until center barely jiggles when shaken, about 45 minutes. Let cool to room temperature on a rack, at least 2 hours. Cut into wedges to serve.

Make Ahead: Up to 1 day, chilled.

PER SERVING: 329 cal., 52% (171 cal.) from fat; 3.3 g protein; 19 g fat (11 g sat.); 36 g carbo (0.9 g fiber); 232 mg sodium; 112 mg chol.

Spiced Blueberry Pie

Black pepper, nutmeg, and cloves play up the underlying spicy note of blueberries in this pie. Serve with freshly whipped cream if you like.

recipe pictured on page **684**

MAKES 1 pie (9-in.); 8 servings | **TIME** 3 hours

2¾ cups flour, divided
1 tbsp. plus ¼ to ½ cup granulated sugar
2½ tsp. salt, divided
½ cup very cold butter, cut into small pieces, divided
7 tbsp. very cold vegetable shortening, cut into pieces, or fresh lard (see In Praise of Real Lard, page 649)
¼ cup firmly packed light brown sugar
1 tbsp. quick-cooking tapioca
1 tsp. cinnamon
½ tsp. *each* freshly ground black pepper and freshly grated nutmeg
¼ tsp. ground cloves
2 pts. fresh or unthawed frozen blueberries
1 tbsp. fresh lemon juice

1. Mix 2½ cups flour, 1 tbsp. sugar, and 1½ tsp. salt in a large bowl. Drop in 7 tbsp. butter and the shortening. Using a pastry blender, your fingers, a fork, or two knives, work butter and shortening into flour mixture until particles are about size of peas and mixture looks like fresh, shaggy bread crumbs.
2. Using a fork, quickly stir in ½ cup very cold water. Turn chunks of dough and crumbs onto a lightly floured work surface. Knead just until dough starts to hold together, 5 to 10 times. Divide dough in half and pat each half into a 6-in. disk. Wrap in plastic wrap and chill 15 minutes and up to overnight.
3. Unwrap one disk of dough and put on a lightly floured surface. With a lightly floured rolling pin, roll dough into a 12-in. circle (about ⅛ in. thick), rolling outward from the center; occasionally lift and turn dough to loosen from surface (see *Pie Crust Without Fear, page 647*). Fold dough gently in half, lift gently without stretching, and lay folded edge across center of a 9-in. pie pan. Gently unfold; without stretching the dough, ease it from center of pan out to the rim. Trim dough edges to ¼ in. past rim of pie pan. Cover with plastic wrap and chill 15 minutes. Meanwhile, roll out second disk into an 11-in. circle. Cut into ten 1-in.-wide strips. Transfer to a baking sheet, cover with plastic wrap, and chill 15 minutes.
4. Preheat oven to 375°. While doughs chill, mix remaining ¼ cup flour, ¼ cup granulated sugar, the brown sugar, tapioca, remaining 1 tsp. salt, the cinnamon, pepper, nutmeg, and cloves in a large bowl. Add blueberries and lemon juice; toss. Taste and add more granulated sugar (up to ¼ cup) if you like. Pour berry mixture into shell and dot with remaining 1 tbsp. butter.
5. To weave a lattice crust, lay five strips of pie dough vertically across pie, spacing evenly. Take the top of every other strip and fold it back halfway. Lay a strip horizontally across center of pie, next to folds of vertical strips. Unfold vertical strips back over horizontal strip. Fold back vertical strips that were left flat last time, and repeat with a second horizontal strip, placing it above first strip (away from you). Repeat with a third horizontal strip above second. Repeat this process on lower half of pie, using remaining two strips of dough. (For a photo, see page 653.)
6. Fold bottom crust edge up over lattice edges and crimp edges together. Bake on lower rack until crust is browned and filling is bubbling in center, 1 to 1¼ hours. Cover edge with strips of foil if browning too quickly. Let cool until bottom of pie pan is at room temperature.

PER SERVING: 473 cal., 46% (216 cal.) from fat; 5.1 g protein; 24 g fat (10 g sat.); 62 g carbo (2.9 g fiber); 859 mg sodium; 31 mg chol.

Almond-Plum Cream Galette

For such a simple recipe, this free-form French-style tart has incredibly sophisticated flavor. Make it for a party when you don't have time to fuss—your guests will think you did.

MAKES 1 galette (9-in.); 12 servings | **TIME** 45 minutes

¼ cup almond paste
2 tbsp. firmly packed light brown sugar, plus more for sprinkling
¼ cup sour cream
9-in. single-crust pie pastry, store-bought or homemade (see *Best All-purpose Pie Crust, page 652; halve recipe*)
3 red plums, halved, pitted, and sliced
About 1 tbsp. whole milk

1. Preheat oven to 375°. In a food processor, blend almond paste, brown sugar, and sour cream. Roll out pie crust to a 13-in. circle and lay on a baking sheet.
2. Evenly spread almond mixture on dough, leaving a 2-in. border. Scatter plums evenly over top and fold dough edge over plums. Brush edge with milk and sprinkle more brown sugar on top of galette.
3. Bake until crust is golden, about 35 minutes.

PER SERVING: 114 cal., 46% (53 cal.) from fat; 1.6 g protein; 5.9 g fat (1.8 g sat.); 14 g carbo (0.8 g fiber); 64 mg sodium; 2.2 mg chol.

Fruit Pie
in 5 Easy Steps

A good fruit pie should be a knee-weakening combination of super-flaky, golden crust and juicy, ripe, seasonal fruit. Once you get the hang of making pie, you'll find yourself wanting to do it more and more often—the rolling of the dough, the slicing of the fruit, and the buttery sweet fragrance as it bakes are all deeply soothing pleasures. Plus, then you get to eat pie.

See our handy Pie Chart (*page 654*) for the filling proportions you need for just about any kind or size of fruit pie.

1 Make the pie dough

For helpful tips on making dough and rolling out pie crusts, see *Pie Crust Without Fear (page 647)*.

Best All-purpose Pie Crust

MAKES 1 double crust for a 9-in. pie (or 2 single-crust 9-in. pies); or 2 double crusts for 6-in. pies; or 4 double crusts for $4\frac{1}{2}$-in. pies (measurements are from inner rim to inner rim). Dough can also be halved. **TIME** 10 minutes, plus 20 minutes to chill

1. In a medium bowl, combine 2 cups **flour**, 1 tsp. **salt**, and $\frac{3}{4}$ cup cold **vegetable shortening** (or half shortening and half unsalted butter; the crust won't be quite as flaky, but the flavor will be good; or use all butter, which will be less flaky but very flavorful). You can also use fresh lard (not homogenized) instead of shortening (*see In Praise of Real Lard, page 649*).
2. With a pastry blender or two knives (one held in each hand and moved crosswise), cut shortening into flour until particles are about the size of peas and the mixture looks like fresh, shaggy bread crumbs. You can also use your fingers, lifting the mixture above the

bowl and rubbing the butter quickly into the flour, then letting it fall, so that everything stays loose and crumbly (if the butter starts melting, your hands are too warm; switch to one of the other methods).
3. Measure 6 tbsp. ice-cold water into a spouted measuring cup. Drizzle 4 tbsp. water over the mixture, stirring lightly and quickly with a fork until it just forms a dough. Gently squeeze a handful of dough into a ball; if it won't hold together, sprinkle dough with 1 to 2 more tbsp. water, then mix again until evenly moistened. Press into a ball with your hands and chill at least 20 minutes and up to 2 days; can also double-wrap and freeze up to 6 weeks. Meanwhile, make the filling.

2 Make the fruit filling

• **Taste the fruit.** Depending on how ripe and sweet it is, determine how much sugar and lemon juice to add (within the range suggested on the chart). Sugar increases the liquid in pie, so if you use the maximum quantity of sugar (or if your fruit is especially juicy), you should also use the maximum quantity of cornstarch or tapioca for thickening. In a pinch, you can use an equal amount of frozen fruit, thawed and drained, but, depending on the fruit and how it was frozen, it often gives off a lot more liquid than fresh fruit—so you will need more thickener; increas-

ing the cornstarch or tapioca by half is a good rule of thumb.
• **Put fruit in a bowl and add the sugar, cornstarch or tapioca, and lemon juice.** You could also add spices that seem appealing—cinnamon, allspice, and ginger are standbys for fruit pies (for a 9-in. pie, 1 to $1\frac{1}{2}$ tsp. total spice is about right, but feel free to experiment). In our experience, however, when fruit is at its peak, it's best not tampered with. Gently mix everything together and let stand (at least 15 minutes for tapioca, to soften it) while you finish the pastry. Raspberries are a special case: They must be mixed with the dry ingredients right before you fill the pie, or they'll liquefy.

3 Roll out the dough

• **Preheat oven to the temperature recommended on the chart.** Divide dough in as many portions as your pie(s) require and flatten each portion into a round on a lightly floured work surface. With a lightly floured rolling pin, roll dough from center outward in all directions to form a circle about $\frac{1}{8}$ in. thick and about 11 in. in diameter for a 9-in. pie, about 8 in. for a 6-in. pie, and about $6\frac{1}{2}$ in. for a $4\frac{1}{2}$-in. pie. Or roll the dough out in a nifty piecrust bag (*see Pie Crust Without Fear, page 647*)—it's easy to make a perfectly round and even crust using one of these.

• **Fold the circle gently in half, lift gently without stretching, and lay folded edge across center of pie pan.** Gently unfold; without stretching the dough, ease it from center of pan out to the rim. Trim edge evenly ½ in. beyond pan rim. If you're using a top crust, chill this bottom shell, then roll out dough for the top following step 1.

4 Fill the pie

• **Fill the pie shell with the fruit mixture, then dot with butter.** Fold second rolled-out dough (if using) into quarters, carefully transfer to pie, and gently unfold to cover filling. Trim overhang evenly 1 in. beyond rim, then fold edge under edge of bottom shell. Press edge with a fork to seal, or crimp with your fingers. Cut several 1-in. slashes in top to allow steam to escape.

5 Bake the pie

• **Loosely wrap edges of pie(s) with a thick strip of foil to keep them from getting too brown.** Set pie(s) on a rimmed baking sheet to collect any drips. Bake on the lower rack of oven for the time recommended. Check streusel-topped pies after 15 to 20 minutes; if they are browning too fast, loosely cover the streusel with foil.

• **About 15 minutes before baking time is finished, remove the foil strip.** (For a streusel pie, remove foil about 5 minutes before.) Bake until pie juices bubble vigorously in center and pastry is well browned.

• **Remove pie from oven;** let cool almost to room temperature on a rack (to help the filling set; the exceptions are apple and pear). Serve slightly warm, at room temperature, or cold.

Lattice-topped Pie

1. Make a double crust for each pie as directed in Best All-purpose Pie Crust *(opposite page)*. For a 9-in. pie, cut top dough circle into ten ½-in.-wide strips (we used a fluted pastry cutter for the photo below). For a 6-in. pie, make eight ½-in.-wide strips, and for a 4½-in. pie, make six ⅓-in.-wide strips (save leftover dough for another use if you like, such as impromptu pie-crust cookies sprinkled with cinnamon sugar and baked alongside the pie till golden).

2. Fill the pie shell with fruit and dot with butter, then lay five strips of pie dough vertically across pie, spacing evenly. Take the top of every other strip and fold it back halfway. Lay a strip horizontally across center of pie, next to folds of vertical strips. Unfold vertical strips back over horizontal strip. Fold back vertical strips that were left flat last time, and repeat with a second horizontal strip, placing it above first strip (away from you). Repeat with a third horizontal strip above second. Repeat this process on lower half of pie, using remaining two strips of dough.

3. Fold bottom crust edge up over top crust and crimp edges together.

Streusel-topped Pie

MAKES 2 cups (enough for one 9-in. pie, two 6-in. pies, or four 4½-in. pies)

1. Make a bottom shell for each pie and fit into pie pan as directed in Best All-purpose Pie Crust, *opposite page*, except trim overhang to 1 in., in step 3 crimp edge (see step 4), and hook edge slightly over rim. Chill while making streusel.

2. Combine 1 cup **flour**, ½ cup firmly packed **brown sugar**, ½ tsp. **cinnamon**, ¼ tsp. salt, and 6 tbsp. **unsalted butter**. Rub mixture through your fingers until butter lumps are no longer distinguishable. Stir in ½ cup chopped **nuts** if you like.

3. Fill pie with fruit filling (skip the butter). Squeeze handfuls of streusel into firm hunks, then crumble into large nuggets and scatter over fruit. Bake pie as directed; if streusel starts getting too dark, cover the top loosely with foil.

The *Sunset* Pie Chart

PIE SIZE	FRUIT (CUPS PER PIE)	SUGAR	CORNSTARCH OR TAPIOCA	LEMON JUICE	BUTTER	MINUTES TO BAKE AT 425°
APPLE (Granny Smith, Gravenstein, Jonathan, any good tart-sweet heirloom apple)—peel, core, and thinly slice						
9 in.	8	¾ to 1 cup	1½ to 2 tbsp.	1 to 1½ tbsp.	2 tbsp.	55 to 60
6 in.	3	⅓ to ½ cup	2 tsp. to 1 tbsp.	2 tsp.	1 tbsp.	40 to 50
4½ in.	1¼	2 tbsp.	¾ tsp.	1 tsp.	1 tsp.	35 to 40
APRICOT—use fully ripe; cut in quarters and remove pits (slice if large)						
9 in.	8	1¼ to 1½ cups	3½ to 4 tbsp.	1 tbsp.	2 tbsp.	55 to 60
6 in.	3	½ to ¾ cup	3 to 4 tsp.	2 tsp.	1 tbsp.	40 to 50
4½ in.	1¼	2 to 3 tbsp.	1 to 2 tsp.	1 tsp.	1 tsp.	35 to 40
BERRY (blackberry, blueberry, boysenberry, loganberry, olallieberry, raspberry)—use whole berries; mix in raspberries right before cooking						
9 in.	8	1½ to 1¾ cups	4 to 5 tbsp.	1 tbsp.	2 tbsp.	55 to 60
6 in.	3	⅔ to ¾ cup	2 to 2½ tbsp.	2 tsp.	1 tbsp.	40 to 50
4½ in.	1¼	3 to 4 tbsp.	1 to 1½ tbsp.	1 tsp.	1 tsp.	35 to 40
CHERRY, SWEET—remove pits (halve if large)						
9 in.	8	1 to 1¼ cups	3 to 3½ tbsp.	2 to 3 tbsp.	2 tbsp.	55 to 60
6 in.	3	⅓ to ½ cup	1½ to 2 tbsp.	1½ to 2 tbsp.	1 tbsp.	40 to 50
4½ in.	1¼	2 tbsp.	2 tsp. to 1 tbsp.	1 to 2 tsp.	1 tsp.	35 to 40
NECTARINE or PEACH—halve, pit, peel peaches (leave nectarines unpeeled), and thinly slice						
9 in.	8	¾ to 1 cup	3 to 3½ tbsp.	1 to 2 tbsp.	2 tbsp.	55 to 60
6 in.	3	4 to 5 tbsp.	1 to 1½ tbsp.	2 tsp.	1 tbsp.	40 to 50
4½ in.	1¼	2½ to 3 tbsp.	2 to 3 tsp.	1 tsp.	1 tsp.	35 to 40
PEAR (Bosc, Comice)—peel, core, and thinly slice						
9 in.	8	¾ to 1 cup	2½ to 3 tbsp.	2 tbsp.	2 tbsp.	55 to 60
6 in.	3	¼ to ⅓ cup	3 to 4 tsp.	1 tbsp.	1 tbsp.	40 to 50
4½ in.	1¼	2 tbsp.	2 tsp.	2 tsp.	1 tsp.	35 to 40
PLUM—halve, pit, and slice						
9 in.	8	1 to 1¼ cups	4 to 4½ tbsp.	2 tbsp.	2 tbsp.	55 to 60
6 in.	3	½ to ¾ cup	1 to 1½ tbsp.	1 tbsp.	1 tbsp.	40 to 50
4½ in.	1¼	2 to 3 tbsp.	2 tsp.	1 tsp.	1 tsp.	35 to 40

Rhubarb–Lemon Cream Pie

The double tang of rhubarb and lemon makes for a lively slice of pie.

MAKES 1 pie (9-in.); 8 to 10 servings | **TIME** 45 minutes, plus 3 hours to chill

5 tbsp. butter, cut into chunks
5 egg yolks
½ cup sugar
2 tsp. finely shredded lemon zest
½ cup fresh lemon juice
½ recipe Best All-purpose Pie Crust dough *(page 652)*
1 tsp. unflavored gelatin
1 cup whipping cream
Easy Rhubarb Compote *(page 671)*, chilled

1. In a 2- to 3-qt. pan over low heat, combine butter, egg yolks, sugar, lemon zest, and lemon juice. Stir constantly until mixture thickly coats the back of a wooden spoon, 10 to 12 minutes (do not boil). Pour into a small bowl; place a piece of plastic wrap directly against the surface of the lemon curd (it will keep a skin from forming) and chill until cold, at least 2 hours, or nest pan in a large bowl of ice water and stir mixture until cold, about 10 minutes.
2. Meanwhile, make pie crust: Preheat oven to 375°. With a lightly floured rolling pin, roll dough from center outward in all directions to form a circle about ⅛ in. thick and about 11 in. in diameter for a 9-in. pie. Fold the circle gently in half, lift gently without stretching, and lay folded edge across center of pie pan. Gently unfold; without stretching the dough, ease it from the center of the pan out to the rim. Trim edge evenly ½ in. beyond pan rim.
3. Top pie shell with foil or parchment paper and fill halfway with pie weights or dried beans. Bake pie shell on lower rack until edges are dry and barely golden, about 15 minutes. Remove from oven and carefully remove pie weights and foil. Reduce oven temperature to 350°, return pie shell to oven, and bake until evenly golden brown, 15 to 20 minutes more. Let crust completely cool on rack before filling.
4. In a heatproof 1-cup glass measure, sprinkle gelatin over 2 tbsp. cold water. Let stand until soft, 2 to 3 minutes. Put 1 in. of water in a small pan; bring to a boil over high heat, then remove from heat. Set measure in water in pan and stir until gelatin is dissolved, 2 to 3 minutes. Let cool.
5. In a large bowl with a mixer on medium-high speed, beat cream until slightly thickened. Beating constantly, pour in gelatin; continue beating until soft peaks form.

6. Stir about ½ cup whipped cream into cold lemon curd until well blended, then scrape mixture into remaining whipped cream and fold gently until incorporated. Spoon into pie crust and spread level. Cover with plastic wrap and chill until firm, at least 1 hour, or up to 1 day.
7. Pour rhubarb compote into a fine-mesh strainer set over a bowl. Let drain until dripping stops, then gently spoon rhubarb pieces over lemon cream pie. Cut pie into wedges.

PER SERVING: 421 cal., 47% (198 cal.) from fat; 4.1 g protein; 22 g fat (11 g sat.); 54 g carbo (0.3 g fiber); 174 mg sodium; 148 mg chol.

Creamy Pink Grapefruit Tart

Reader Jeanne Walker, of Oxnard, California, substituted grapefruit juice for lime in a traditional Key lime pie. For the best color, use a deep pink to red variety of grapefruit.

MAKES 1 pie (9- or 10-in.); 8 to 10 servings
TIME 1¼ hours, plus 1¼ hours to cool

1½ cups flour
½ cup butter, cut into chunks
4 eggs
1 tsp. finely shredded pink grapefruit zest
⅔ cup *each* pink grapefruit juice with pulp, sugar, and whipping cream
Sweetened whipped cream and peeled grapefruit segments

1. Preheat oven to 325°. In a food processor or bowl, combine flour and butter. Whirl or rub in with your fingers until fine crumbs form. Add 1 egg and whirl or stir with a fork just until dough holds together. Pat into a ball, then press evenly over bottom and up side of a 9- to 10-in. tart pan with a removable rim. Bake on lower rack until crust is pale gold, 25 to 30 minutes. Let cool.
2. Increase oven temperature to 350°. In a large bowl, whisk together remaining 3 eggs, grapefruit zest and juice, sugar, and cream. Set baked crust on oven rack and carefully pour in filling.
3. Bake pie until filling jiggles only slightly in the center when pan is gently shaken and tart is golden at edges, 25 to 30 minutes.
4. Let tart cool on a rack at least 45 minutes. Serve slightly warm or chilled, with sweetened whipped cream and grapefruit segments.
Make Ahead: Up to 1 day; chilled.

PER SERVING: 285 cal., 51% (144 cal.) from fat; 4.9 g protein; 16 g fat (9.5 g sat.); 30 g carbo (0.5 g fiber); 125 mg sodium; 128 mg chol.

Chunky Lemon Meringue Pie

In this adaptation of old-fashioned Shaker pie, thin slices of whole lemon are soaked with sugar overnight to soften and sweeten the peel. When mixed with eggs, they create a soft custard base with chewy lemon pieces and a pleasantly bitter edge.

MAKES 1 pie (9-in.); 8 servings | **TIME** 1½ hours, plus overnight to soak and 3½ hours to cool

3 lemons
2 cups sugar
½ recipe Best All-purpose Pie Crust dough *(page 652)*
4 eggs plus 1 egg yolk
6 egg whites
⅛ tsp. *each* salt and cream of tartar
3 tbsp. light brown sugar
2 tbsp. granulated sugar

1. Quarter lemons lengthwise. Slice quartered lemons crosswise as thinly as possible, discarding end pieces that are just peel and pith. Put lemon slices in a large bowl with the sugar. Toss to combine, cover, and let sit at least 24 hours and up to 2 days at room temperature.

2. Preheat oven to 450°. Lightly dust counter and rolling pin with flour, then unwrap dough. With short strokes from center outward, roll dough into a 12-in. circle (about ⅛ in. thick), turning 90° after every 3 or 4 passes of the rolling pin to keep it from sticking. Transfer dough to a 9-in. pie pan, letting it fall into place (if you push or stretch the dough, it will shrink back when baked). Trim overhang to ½ in., then tuck edge under. Cover with plastic wrap and refrigerate 20 minutes.

3. Meanwhile, whisk whole eggs and egg yolk in a medium bowl until frothy. Drain lemons (reserving liquid) and add lemon slices and 1¼ cups of the reserved liquid to the eggs. Stir to combine. Pour filling into crust. Cover with foil and bake 15 minutes on lower rack. Remove foil, reduce oven temperature to 325°, and bake another 20 minutes. Remove from oven and reposition rack to center, but leave oven on.

4. In a large clean bowl, beat egg whites, salt, and cream of tartar with a mixer until soft peaks form. Add brown and granulated sugars and beat until shiny, firm peaks form. Spread meringue in a mound over hot pie and set on center rack in oven. Bake until top is puffed and deep brown, about 25 minutes. Let cool completely, at least 3½ hours, before slicing.

PER SERVING: 458 cal., 28% (126 cal.) from fat; 8.7 g protein; 14 g fat (5.5 g sat.); 79 g carbo (2.4 g fiber); 387 mg sodium; 146 mg chol.

Triple Coconut Cream Mini Pies

At Tom Douglas's Seattle restaurants—which include Lola, Etta's, Dahlia Lounge, and Serious Pie—as well as his Dahlia Bakery, the triple coconut cream pie is a perennial bestseller. We love the miniature version (and made them even smaller here, since they're so rich).

MAKES 9 mini pies | **TIME** 1½ hours, plus 3 hours to chill pastry cream

COCONUT PASTRY CREAM
2 cups milk
2 cups sweetened shredded dried coconut
1 vanilla bean, split lengthwise
2 eggs
½ cup plus 2 tbsp. sugar
3 tbsp. flour
¼ cup unsalted butter, softened
PIE & TOPPING
9 Coconut Pie Shells (3½ in.; *recipe follows*), baked and cooled
2½ cups heavy whipping cream
⅓ cup sugar
1 tsp. vanilla extract
GARNISHES
1 chunk (3 oz.) white chocolate, at room temperature
1 cup unsweetened "chip" (or large-shred) coconut or ½ cup unsweetened shredded coconut, toasted *(see Quick Tip, above right)*

1. Make pastry cream: Put milk and coconut in a medium saucepan over medium-high heat. Scrape seeds from vanilla bean and add both seeds and bean to saucepan. Bring mixture to a gentle simmer, stirring occasionally.

2. In a medium bowl, whisk together eggs, sugar, and flour. While whisking, drizzle about one-third of hot milk mixture into egg mixture, then slowly whisk egg-milk mixture back into saucepan. Cook over medium-high heat, whisking, until pastry cream thickens and begins to bubble, 4 to 5 minutes. Remove from heat, stir in butter, and discard vanilla bean.

3. Spoon hot pastry cream into a bowl and set in a larger bowl of ice and cold water, stirring occasionally, until cooled to room temperature. Cover with plastic wrap, pressing it directly onto surface (to prevent a skin from forming) and chill until cold, at least 3 hours.

4. Fill pies: Carefully remove baked shells from brioche molds. Spoon pastry cream into shells, filling each a little more than halfway. In a large bowl, with a mixer on high speed, whip cream with sugar and vanilla extract until it holds stiff peaks. Fill a pastry bag fitted with a large star tip (no. 6) with whipped cream and pipe a double layer of cream onto each pie, or simply spoon it on (use all the cream—pies should look like beehive hairdos).

5. Garnish pies: With a vegetable peeler, scrape wide curls or shavings from chunk of white chocolate. Sprinkle curls or shavings over pies, and top with toasted coconut. Serve immediately.

Quick Tip: Chip (or large-shred) coconut, which is sold at natural-foods stores, looks like little curls and makes the prettiest garnish, but regular shredded dried coconut works just fine. Toast coconut in a 350° oven until golden, 10 to 15 minutes.

Make Ahead: Pastry cream, up to 2 days, chilled; unbaked formed pastry shells, up to a few weeks, frozen. Fill baked shells with pastry cream up to several hours ahead and keep chilled; top with whipped cream and garnishes just before serving.

PER MINI PIE: 746 cal., 66% (495 cal.) from fat; 8.1 g protein; 55 g fat (36 g sat.); 57 g carbo (2.7 g fiber); 186 mg sodium; 187 mg chol.

Coconut Pie Shells

You'll need nine 1½- by 3½-in. fluted nonstick brioche molds to make this recipe (*see Quick Tip, above right*).

MAKES 9 mini pie shells (3½-in.) | **TIME** 1 hour, plus 1½ hours to chill

1 cup plus 2 tbsp. flour
½ cup sweetened shredded dried coconut
½ cup cold unsalted butter, cut into ½-in. cubes
2 tsp. sugar
¼ tsp. kosher salt

1. In a food processor, pulse together flour, coconut, butter, sugar, and salt to form coarse crumbs. Add ice water 1 tbsp. at a time, pulsing after each addition, just until dough holds together when you pinch it (you'll use 3 to 5 tbsp. ice water total); dough will still look like crumbs.

2. Turn crumbs out onto work surface, form into a ball, and divide into nine equal portions, forming each into a small disk. Wrap each disk in plastic wrap and chill at least 30 minutes and up to 1 hour.

3. Unwrap disks and, working with one at a time, set on a lightly floured work surface. With a lightly floured rolling pin, using short strokes from center outward, roll dough into a 5-in. circle (about ⅛ in. thick). Ease dough into brioche mold, letting it fall into place (if you push or stretch the dough, it will shrink back when baked). Trim overhang flush with edge. Prick bottom lightly with a fork. Repeat with remaining dough disks and molds. Chill unbaked pie shells for 1 hour before baking.

4. Preheat oven to 400°. Lay a sheet of parchment paper in each pie shell and fill with pie weights or dried beans. Put shells on a rimmed baking sheet and bake on lower rack until medium golden brown, 10 to 12 minutes.

5. Remove pie weights and parchment paper; return shells to oven. Bake until crusts have golden brown patches, about 10 minutes. Let cool before filling.

Quick Tip: One source for fluted brioche molds is Sur La Table (*surlatable.com*).

Double-crust Cherry Tart

The thick cornmeal crust gives this tart a pleasantly crunchy texture. It's terrific with smooth, juicy summer cherries.

MAKES 1 tart (9-in.); 8 servings | **TIME** 1½ hours

1 cup butter, at room temperature
1 cup sugar, divided, plus more for sprinkling
2 egg yolks
2½ cups flour
⅔ cup yellow cornmeal
1 tsp. baking powder
¼ tsp. salt
1½ lbs. fresh sweet cherries, pitted
2 tbsp. quick-cooking tapioca
1 tbsp. fresh lemon juice

1. In a medium bowl, with a mixer on medium speed, beat butter with ¾ cup sugar until smooth; beat in egg yolks. Stir in flour, cornmeal, baking powder, and salt until well blended. Divide dough in half. Press one portion into bottom and up sides to rim of a 9-in. fluted tart pan with removable rim. Place other portion on a lightly floured piece of waxed or parchment paper. With a lightly floured rolling pin, roll out dough to a 10-in. circle. Slide circle onto a baking sheet. Chill tart shell and circle until firm, at least 30 minutes.

2. Preheat oven to 375°. In another medium bowl, mix cherries, tapioca, lemon juice, and remaining ¼ cup sugar. Let stand 10 minutes. Pour into chilled tart shell and spread level. Invert round over tart. Press edges into rim of tart pan, pinching off any excess. Sprinkle tart lightly with sugar.

3. Place tart pan on a rimmed baking sheet to catch any drips. Bake on lower rack until top is golden brown, 35 to 40 minutes, rotating tart halfway through baking time. Serve warm or at room temperature.

PER SERVING: 564 cal., 41% (234 cal.) from fat; 6.9 g protein; 26 g fat (15 g sat.); 79 g carbo (2.8 g fiber); 382 mg sodium; 115 mg chol.

Blueberry-Peach Tart

Blueberries and peaches are an inspired summer pairing, the blueberries offering up just a little pucker to offset the luscious sweetness of tree-ripened peaches. This recipe is from Erik Olsen, winemaker of Clos du Bois Vineyard in Sonoma County. Whole-wheat pastry flour makes a smooth-textured crust and gives it a delicious nuttiness.

MAKES 1 tart (9-in.); 8 to 10 servings
TIME 50 minutes, plus 45 minutes to cool

½ cup pecan halves, toasted and cooled (*see How to Toast Nuts, page 134*)
1¼ cups whole-wheat pastry flour (*see Quick Tip, right*) or all-purpose flour
¼ cup firmly packed brown sugar
6 tbsp. butter, cut into chunks
1½ tsp. vanilla extract
1 egg yolk
1 package (8 oz.) cream cheese, at room temperature
½ cup sour cream
¼ cup powdered sugar
2½ cups thinly sliced, peeled firm-ripe white or yellow peaches or thinly sliced nectarines
1 tbsp. fresh lemon juice
1 tsp. minced mint leaves (optional)
½ cup blueberries
3 tbsp. apricot jam

1. Preheat oven to 350°. In a food processor, blend nuts, flour, brown sugar, and butter until fine crumbs form. Add vanilla and egg yolk; blend until mixture comes together in a ball.
2. Press dough evenly into bottom and up side of a 10-in. tart pan with a removable rim. Bake on lower rack until deep golden, 15 to 20 minutes. Let cool.
3. In a medium bowl, with a mixer on medium speed, beat cream cheese, sour cream, and powdered sugar until smooth. In another medium bowl, mix peaches with lemon juice.
4. Spread cream cheese mixture over bottom of pastry. Sprinkle mint on top if using. Arrange peach slices, overlapping slightly, in a circular pattern over cream cheese. Scatter blueberries over peaches.
5. Put jam in a 1-cup glass measuring cup and heat in a microwave oven until melted, 30 to 45 seconds. Brush over fruit.
6. Serve tart or chill, uncovered, up to 1 hour. Remove pan rim and cut tart into wedges.

Quick Tip: Find whole-wheat pastry flour at Whole Foods markets and other natural-foods stores; some well-stocked grocery stores have it too.

PER SERVING: 329 cal., 60% (198 cal.) from fat; 5.2 g protein; 22 g fat (11 g sat.); 31 g carbo (3.2 g fiber); 150 mg sodium; 70 mg chol.

How to Thicken a Pie or Tart Filling

Most fruits start to dissolve when baked and will gush out in a flood of sweet syrup when you cut into a finished pie or tart—even when it's cooled. Thickeners give your filling the body it needs for a more or less clean slice. There are three main choices, and each has its virtues.

FLOUR. Nice because you always have some on hand and, if used judiciously, gives the filling a pleasantly floury taste while thickening it. However, it makes the filling opaque and can give it a pasty texture, and the floury flavor can interfere with the pure taste of the fruit. For those reasons, we've omitted it from our chart (*page 654*). If you're a flour lover, feel free to use it, doubling the amounts given for tapioca or cornstarch in the chart.

TAPIOCA (INSTANT). Tiny beads of dried starch from the root of the cassava plant, tapioca thickens at twice the power of flour, without leaving a floury taste or turning the filling opaque. However, it doesn't dissolve in cooking; if you look closely at the cooked filling, you'll see lots of soft little clear beads. Therefore tapioca is best used with fruits that are similar to it in texture, like raspberries or blueberries.

CORNSTARCH. Like tapioca, it has double the thickening power of flour—and, being powdery and white, is easy to mistake for flour, which could explain those pie fillings (we've all had them) that are so stiff they're like shellac. In the right amounts, though, silky white cornstarch—ground from the heart of the corn kernel—produces a lovely, glossy, just-thick-enough filling that shines with the color and flavor of the fruit.

Black Mission Fig Tart

If your guests can't figure out where they've tasted something like this rich, deep, spicy tart, from Maria Hines, chef-owner of Tilth restaurant in Seattle, just utter two words: "Fig Newton." Although the dessert isn't hard to make, it takes a while—so it's useful to apply the make-ahead tips *(right).*

recipe pictured on page **686**

MAKES 1 tart (10-in.); 10 to 12 servings
TIME 4½ hours

1 lb. dried black Mission figs
2 bottles (750 ml. each) light- or medium-bodied dry red wine (such as Pinot Noir)
1 cup plus 3 tbsp. sugar
¾ tsp. salt, divided
5 black peppercorns
1 cinnamon stick
3 whole allspice
2 whole cloves
1 tsp. vanilla extract
1½ cups flour
¾ cup very cold butter, cut into small pieces
8 oz. crème fraîche (about 1 cup)

1. Bring 6 cups water to a boil. Meanwhile, trim stems off figs, then cut into ⅛-in.-thick slices and put in a large heatproof bowl. Pour boiling water over figs and let stand 10 minutes. Drain. Put figs in a large pot over medium-high heat with wine, 1 cup sugar, and ½ tsp. salt. Bring to a boil. Meanwhile, tie up peppercorns, cinnamon, allspice, and cloves in a 6-in. square of cheesecloth and add to pot. Lower heat to maintain a simmer and cook until figs are soft and liquid is reduced to about ¾ cup, about 2 hours. Remove spices and discard. Stir in vanilla. Let figs and liquid cool to room temperature.
2. While figs are cooking, make and chill crust: In a large bowl, stir together flour and remaining 3 tbsp. sugar and ¼ tsp. salt. Drop in butter and work it into flour mixture with a pastry blender, your fingers, a fork, or two knives until it resembles coarse cornmeal with lots of pea-size chunks. Quickly stir in 2 tbsp. very cold water until dough starts to hold together (it will still be quite crumbly). Gently knead dough two or three times in bowl, then turn onto a large piece of plastic wrap, shape into a 6-in. disk, cover with wrap, and chill for at least 1 hour and up to 3 days.
3. Preheat oven to 350°. Put a 10-in. tart pan with a removable rim on a large baking sheet. Butter a large piece of foil. Unwrap dough and put on a lightly floured work surface. With a lightly floured rolling pin, roll dough into a 13-in. circle, occasionally lifting and turning to keep it from sticking. Fold in half and ease into tart pan, allowing dough to fall into place (if you push or stretch it, it will shrink back when baked). Trim edges ½ in. past rim of pan and fold down to double the thickness of the tart edge. Set foil, buttered side down, gently onto dough and top with pie weights or dried beans. Bake on lower rack 30 minutes. Remove weights and foil and bake until golden brown, about 15 minutes. Let cool completely, about 30 minutes.
4. Arrange cooled figs in cooled crust and pour fig-cooking liquid over them. Let stand at least 1 hour (at room temperature) and up to overnight (in refrigerator). Serve at room temperature, with crème fraîche.
Make Ahead: Figs through step 1, up to 1 day, chilled; dough through step 2, up to 3 days, chilled.

PER SERVING: 418 cal., 41% (171 cal.) from fat; 4 g protein; 19 g fat (12 g sat.); 60 g carbo (4.2 g fiber); 286 mg sodium; 48 mg chol.

Rustic Individual Pear Tarts

Fresh pears and purchased puff pastry add up to an incredibly easy seasonal dessert.

SERVES 6 | **TIME** 1¼ hours

1 sheet (about 10 by 12 in.) frozen puff pastry (14-oz. package), thawed
2 or 3 firm-ripe pears, such as Bosc or Comice
About ⅓ cup orange marmalade
1 egg, beaten to blend
About 2 tbsp. turbinado sugar
6 tbsp. crème fraîche
1½ tsp. granulated sugar

1. Preheat oven to 375°. Lightly butter two large baking sheets. On a lightly floured work surface with a floured rolling pin, roll out pastry to 16 by 18 in. Cut pastry in thirds lengthwise and in half crosswise. With a wide spatula, transfer six rectangles to baking sheets.
2. Core pears and cut into thin wedges. Arrange, slightly overlapping, on pastry rectangles, leaving a 1½-in. border bare (angle slices if necessary). Warm marmalade in a microwave oven to melt, then brush over pears. Fold pastry border over edge of pears, stretching slightly and pressing down to hold. Brush new edges with egg, then sprinkle turbinado sugar over tarts, especially pastry edges.
3. Bake until pastries are richly browned, 25 to 30 minutes. In a small bowl, whisk crème fraîche and granulated sugar until slightly thickened. Serve tarts warm or cool, with sweetened crème fraîche.

PER TART: 556 cal., 53% (297 cal.) from fat; 6.9 g protein; 33 g fat (8.1 g sat.); 60 g carbo (2.8 g fiber); 209 mg sodium; 51 mg chol.

Apricot-Nut Tart

This is a *Sunset* Thanksgiving favorite—it's easy to transport if you need to, and everyone loves its supremely buttery crust packed with crunchy nuts and soft, tangy apricots. Serve dolloped with whipped cream if you like.

MAKES 1 tart (10- to 11-in.); 12 servings
TIME 1¼ hours

1 cup (6 oz.) dried apricots, preferably Blenheim (*see Quick Tip below*)
⅔ cup dessert wine, such as orange Muscat, or orange juice, divided
½ tsp. finely shredded orange zest
⅔ cup honey, divided
3 eggs
1 tsp. vanilla extract
2 tbsp. butter, melted
1 cup *each* hazelnuts and blanched whole almonds, toasted (*see How to Toast Nuts, page 134*)
Butter Pastry (*recipe follows*)

1. In a medium saucepan, simmer apricots, ⅓ cup wine, orange zest, and 2 tbsp. honey over low heat, uncovered, stirring occasionally, until apricots are soft and liquid is absorbed, 10 to 25 minutes.
2. Preheat oven to 350°. In a medium bowl, whisk eggs, remaining wine and honey, the vanilla, and butter until blended. Stir in nuts.
3. Press pastry into bottom and up side of a 10- to 11-in. tart pan with a removable rim. Distribute apricots evenly over pastry. Pour nut mixture over fruit, arranging evenly.
4. Bake tart on lower rack until golden brown, 50 to 55 minutes. Cool in pan on rack, then remove pan rim to serve.
Quick Tip: Find the very flavorful, deep orange Blenheim apricot online at *brfarms.com*.
Make Ahead: Up to 1 day, chilled.

PER SERVING: 404 cal., 53% (216 cal.) from fat; 7.6 g protein; 24 g fat (7.5 g sat.); 45 g carbo (3.6 g fiber); 121 mg sodium; 96 mg chol.

Butter Pastry: In a food processor, combine 1⅓ cups **flour** and ¼ cup **sugar**. Add ½ cup **butter**, cut into pieces; blend until mixture forms fine crumbs. Add 1 **egg yolk**; blend until dough holds together. Makes one 10- to 11-in. tart crust.

Mascarpone Tart with Strawberries

For not a lot of effort, you get a showstopper dessert of bright red strawberries over a creamy, honeyed filling in a chocolate crust.

MAKES 1 tart (9-in.); 10 to 12 servings | **TIME** 1 hour, plus 1½ hours to cool and chill

About 9 oz. chocolate wafer cookies, broken into ½-in. pieces
½ cup butter, melted
2 tbsp. sugar
2 tsp. dried instant espresso
1 lb. mascarpone or cream cheese
⅓ cup honey
1 tsp. vanilla extract
2 eggs
2 tbsp. flour
¼ tsp. salt
2 cups strawberries

1. Preheat oven to 325°. Place cookies in a 1-qt. resealable plastic bag and seal. With a rolling pin, crush cookies into fine crumbs. Pour 2 cups crumbs into a bowl and mix with butter, sugar, and instant espresso. Press mixture evenly into bottom and up sides of a 10-in. tart pan with removable rim.
2. In a medium bowl, with a mixer on medium speed, beat mascarpone, honey, and vanilla until smooth. Add eggs, 1 at a time, beating well after each addition. Beat in flour and salt.
3. Set tart pan on a 12- by 16-in. rimmed baking sheet and pour filling into shell. Bake until filling is pale golden and barely set in center when you gently shake pan, 30 to 35 minutes.
4. Remove tart from oven and let cool on a rack about 30 minutes, then chill until cold, at least 1 hour.
5. Shortly before serving, remove rim from pan. Hull and thinly slice strawberries. Arrange in a circular or spiral pattern on top of tart, overlapping slices slightly.
Make Ahead: Through step 4, up to 1 day, chilled.

PER SERVING: 388 cal., 65% (252 cal.) from fat; 5.4 g protein; 28 g fat (17 g sat.); 30 g carbo (1.5 g fiber); 279 mg sodium; 88 mg chol.

pies, tarts & fruit desserts

Salted Chocolate Tart

Large flakes of Maldon sea salt look striking against the glossy chocolate surface, and its crunchy texture contrasts beautifully with the smooth, velvety filling.

MAKES 1 tart (9½-in.); 16 servings | **TIME** 1½ hours, plus 1½ hours to cool

CHOCOLATE CRUST

6 tbsp. unsalted butter, softened
¾ cup powdered sugar
1¼ cups flour
¼ cup unsweetened cocoa powder (not Dutch-processed)
5 egg yolks

CHOCOLATE FILLING

8 oz. extra-bittersweet top-quality chocolate, such as Callebaut or Valrhona, chopped
¾ cup unsalted butter
⅓ cup plus 1 tbsp. sugar
¼ cup brewed coffee
4 eggs

CHOCOLATE GLAZE

4 oz. extra-bittersweet top-quality chocolate, such as Callebaut or Valrhona, chopped
2 tbsp. light corn syrup
⅓ cup heavy whipping cream
2 tbsp. unsalted butter, softened
Maldon sea salt for sprinkling (see Quick Tip, above right)

1. Make crust: In a stand mixer with a paddle attachment, or with a handheld mixer, beat butter and sugar on medium speed until smooth. In a separate bowl, sift together flour and cocoa; add to butter mixture and mix on low speed at first, then on medium, until combined. Add yolks and mix on low speed just until dough comes together. If small pieces remain, knead dough to blend them in. Form dough into a disk and wrap in plastic wrap. Chill for at least 1 hour and up to 3 days.

2. Unwrap dough and set on a lightly floured work surface. With a floured rolling pin, using short strokes from center outward, roll into a 12-in. circle. Fold dough in half and transfer to a 9½-in tart pan. Unfold, ease into pan, and, using your thumb, press into sides. Trim dough flush with top edge. Line shell with parchment paper, completely fill with pie weights or dried beans, and chill at least 30 minutes. Preheat oven to 350°.

3. Bake on lower rack 10 minutes, then remove parchment and pie weights and return to oven until crust looks dry, about 5 minutes. Set on a rack to cool slightly.

4. Make filling: Put chocolate in a medium heatproof bowl. In a medium saucepan, combine butter, sugar, and coffee and bring to a boil over medium heat. Pour hot liquid over chocolate and let stand 3 to 4 minutes, then gently stir until smooth. Break eggs into a large bowl and slowly pour in warm chocolate mixture, whisking constantly until incorporated.

5. Pour warm filling into still-warm tart shell. Bake on center rack until filling has risen slightly, appears dry on surface, and seems firm when shaken slightly, about 10 minutes. Set on a rack and let cool completely.

6. Make glaze: Put chocolate and corn syrup in a medium bowl. In microwave, heat cream to boiling; pour over chocolate. Add butter and stir slowly until smooth, working in one direction to prevent air bubbles from forming (if butter doesn't melt completely, microwave in 5-second intervals to warm slightly).

7. Pour glaze onto center of tart and use a small metal spatula (preferably offset) or butter knife to push glaze to edges. Let stand at least 15 minutes to set before slicing. Serve with Maldon salt for sprinkling.

Quick Tip: Find Maldon sea salt at many grocery stores, or substitute a high-quality *fleur de sel*.

Make Ahead: Up to 8 hours, chilled; bring to room temperature before serving.

PER SERVING: 372 cal., 65% (243 cal.) from fat; 5.4 g protein; 27 g fat (15 g sat.); 33 g carbo (1.2 g fiber); 27 mg sodium; 165 mg chol.

4 Quick Fresh Fruit Desserts

1. Kumquat Bonbons

Cut **kumquats** in half lengthwise and hollow out halves with a small measuring spoon. Stir some softened **cream cheese** with minced **crystallized ginger** and **sugar** to taste. Spoon into kumquats. Top each with a sliver of **kumquat peel**.

2. Broiled Sugared Grapes

Fill a shallow ramekin with a single layer of halved **grapes**. Spread thickly with **whole-milk Greek yogurt**. Sprinkle generously with **dark brown sugar**. Broil 6 in. from heat until sugar is bubbling, 3 to 4 minutes.

3. Fresh Peaches in Rosé Wine

At the end of a meal, when you still have a little **wine** in your glass, add a few slices of **ripe peach**. Let stand for a few minutes, then sip and spoon the results. *Pictured on page 681.*

4. Roasted Strawberries

Halve **strawberries** and toss them with **brown sugar** and a bit of **ground cardamom**. Put strawberries in a buttered pie pan and bake at 400° until softened and a little darker, about 15 minutes. Serve with **vanilla-bean ice cream**.

Macadamia Nut Tart

This buttery tart from Greg Boyer, of Oahu, Hawaii, has just enough sweet filling to hold the nuts together, no more. Serve with vanilla or ginger ice cream if you like.

MAKES 1 tart (9-in.); 12 servings | **TIME** 1 hour, plus 1 hour to cool

1¼ cups flour
2 tbsp. plus ½ cup firmly packed dark brown sugar
½ tsp. salt, divided
¾ cup cold unsalted butter, cut into pieces, plus 2 tbsp. melted butter
1 egg yolk plus 1 egg
¼ cup light corn syrup
2 tbsp. dark rum
1⅓ cups unsalted macadamia nuts, coarsely chopped

1. Preheat oven to 375°. In a food processor, blend flour, 2 tbsp. brown sugar, and ¼ tsp. salt. Add cold butter and pulse until mixture resembles coarse crumbs. Add egg yolk and pulse to combine. Add 2 to 3 tbsp. ice water, pulsing until mixture begins to come together in a ball.
2. Press dough into bottom and up side of a 9-in. tart pan with a removable rim. Prick bottom of tart with a fork and chill in freezer 15 minutes. Bake crust on lower rack until medium golden brown, 15 to 25 minutes, and remove from oven (leave oven on).
3. Meanwhile, in a medium bowl, with a mixer on high speed, beat whole egg and remaining ½ cup brown sugar and ¼ tsp. salt until pale and ribbony, 7 to 10 minutes. Beat in melted butter, corn syrup, and rum.
4. Pour sugar mixture into tart shell and sprinkle with macadamia nuts. Bake tart on center rack until a knife inserted in center comes out clean, about 25 minutes. Cool tart on a rack at least 1 hour.

PER SERVING: 350 cal., 64% (225 cal.) from fat; 3.5 g protein; 25 g fat (10 g sat.); 28 g carbo (0.4 g fiber); 118 mg sodium; 72 mg chol.

■ Macadamia Nuts

FROM THE PANTRY

Native to Australia, the macadamia nut arrived in Hawaii in the late 1800s and began to be widely planted there in the 1920s. Rich and buttery, macadamias are delicious simply as a salted snack, as well as used in baked goods. To keep macadamia nuts fresh, refrigerate them airtight for up to 6 months, or freeze in a double layer of resealable plastic bags for up to 1 year. For more on Western nuts, *see page 617*.

Walnut-Caramel Tart

A fail-safe press-in crust makes this tart easy to pull off.

MAKES 1 tart (9-in.); 12 to 16 servings
TIME 1 hour, plus 4 hours to cool

¾ cup butter, at room temperature, divided
¼ cup firmly packed brown sugar
1 egg yolk
½ tsp. vanilla extract
1½ cups flour
¾ tsp. salt, divided
2¾ cups walnut halves, toasted and cooled (*see How to Toast Nuts, page 134*)
1¾ cups granulated sugar
2 tbsp. light corn syrup
½ cup crème fraîche or whipping cream

1. In a bowl, with a mixer on medium speed, beat ½ cup butter and the brown sugar until smooth. Beat in egg yolk and vanilla. Add flour and ¼ tsp. salt and beat until mixture forms a ball.
2. Press dough into bottom and up side to rim of a 9-in. fluted tart pan with a removable rim. Freeze until firm, about 15 minutes.
3. Preheat oven to 350°. Bake tart shell on lower rack until golden, 16 to 18 minutes. Transfer to a rack to cool. Meanwhile, chop 2 cups toasted walnuts; reserve remainder.
4. In a 3- to 4-qt. pan over medium heat, combine granulated sugar, corn syrup, and ¼ cup water. Stir until sugar is dissolved, then increase heat to high and boil, swirling mixture occasionally, until it reaches a deep golden brown, 10 to 15 minutes. Remove from heat and stir in crème fraîche and remaining ¼ cup butter and ½ tsp. salt (mixture will foam). Stir until smooth.
5. Spread chopped walnuts in tart shell, then pour in hot caramel; spread level with a rubber spatula. Garnish edge of tart with reserved walnut halves. Let tart cool until caramel is firm enough to slice, at least 4 hours. Cut into thin wedges.
Make Ahead: Up to 2 days, chilled; bring to room temperature before serving.

PER SERVING: 366 cal., 54% (198 cal.) from fat; 4.2 g protein; 22 g fat (8.2 g sat.); 40 g carbo (1.1 g fiber); 209 mg sodium; 43 mg chol.

Burnt-caramel Rum-Banana Tart

Try different fruits in this quick tart, and other syrups or glazes—cherries with chocolate sauce, for instance, or apricots with blueberry preserves, heated just until liquefied. Use fruits that aren't too juicy, or the crust will be soggy. The burnt-caramel sauce is also great on ice cream.

MAKES 2 tarts; 8 to 12 servings total
TIME 45 minutes, plus 2 hours to chill

½ cup *each* granulated sugar and heavy whipping cream
2 tbsp. dark rum
1 sheet (about ½ lb.) frozen puff pastry, thawed
4 firm-ripe bananas
Egg wash (1 egg whisked with 2 tbsp. water)
3 tbsp. firmly packed light brown sugar

1. Preheat oven to 375°. Put granulated sugar with ¼ cup water in a small, deep, heavy saucepan and, without stirring, bring to a boil over medium-high heat (*see Quick Tip below*). Using a pastry brush dipped in water, brush down sides of pan to dissolve any sugar granules. When sugar has dissolved and begins to darken, 6 to 8 minutes, tilt and swirl it to cook evenly. Cook, swirling pan occasionally, until sugar is a deep reddish brown, about 2 minutes more. Remove from heat and whisk in about 1 tbsp. of cream (sauce will foam up). Slowly whisk in remaining cream. Whisk in rum, let cool to room temperature, and chill at least 2 hours to thicken.
2. Meanwhile, on a lightly floured work surface and with a lightly floured rolling pin, roll pastry sheet out to a 10- by 14-in. rectangle. Cut pastry in half to form two 10- by 7-in. rectangles and place halves on a large, rim-less baking sheet. Lightly prick pastry halves with a fork, leaving a ½-in.-wide border.
3. Peel bananas, cut into ¼-in.-thick slices, and arrange on pastry. Brush borders with egg wash and sprinkle tarts all over with brown sugar.
4. Bake tarts on lower rack until crusts are medium golden brown (lift edges of tarts to check doneness of undersides), 15 to 17 minutes. Let cool slightly and drizzle generously with caramel sauce. Serve tarts warm or cool, each cut into 4 to 6 pieces.
Quick Tip: When making the caramel, it helps to use a regular stainless steel or other light-colored saucepan; the paler background lets you see the true color of the caramel as it darkens.
Make Ahead: Sauce, up to 1 week, chilled.

PER SERVING: 287 cal., 44% (126 cal.) from fat; 3.3 g protein; 14 g fat (4.2 g sat.); 38 g carbo (1.2 g fiber); 70 mg sodium; 37 mg chol.

Chinese Egg Tarts

A pleasingly dense filling in filo shells—a sweet ending to a dim sum brunch. The recipe doubles and triples easily.

MAKES 15 tartlets | **TIME** 30 minutes

1 package frozen mini filo tart shells (15 shells)
1 egg white
3 egg yolks
2 tbsp. *each* sugar and milk

1. Preheat oven to 325°. Arrange shells on a baking sheet and defrost at room temperature, about 15 minutes. Meanwhile, beat egg white until loose but not foamy.
2. With a fine-bristle pastry brush, generously brush inside of shells with egg white, gently working it into crevices. Bake until white is set, about 5 minutes.
3. In a large glass measuring cup (or other vessel with a spout), whisk yolks, sugar, and milk to combine. Skim off and discard any foam on top of mixture and let stand 5 minutes (this will ensure tarts with sunny, shiny tops). Pour into shells and bake until set, 8 to 10 minutes.

PER TARTLET: 41 cal., 46% (19 cal.) from fat; 1.3 g protein; 2.1 g fat (0.4 g sat.); 3.8 g carbo (0 g fiber); 14 mg sodium; 43 mg chol.

Apple-Cherry Turnovers

Frozen puff pastry is a real timesaver. These turnovers are a delicious dessert or midafternoon snack.

MAKES 4 turnovers | **TIME** 25 minutes

1 sheet frozen puff pastry (about ½ lb.), thawed and cut into 4 squares
1 Granny Smith apple, peeled, cored, and thinly sliced
2 tbsp. *each* firmly packed brown sugar and granulated sugar
¼ tsp. cinnamon
½ cup dried tart cherries

1. Preheat oven to 425°. Put puff pastry squares on a rimmed baking sheet lined with parchment paper.
2. In a small bowl, toss apple with brown and granulated sugars, cinnamon, and cherries. Place an equal amount of apple mixture in center of each square of pastry. Pull one corner over mixture to meet opposite corner and form a triangle, then press to seal the two touching corners, leaving sides open.
3. Bake turnovers until golden brown, about 15 minutes.
Make ahead: Baked turnovers, up to 1 day, at room temperature.

PER TURNOVER: 456 cal., 46% (209 cal.) from fat; 4.9 g protein; 23 g fat (3.3 g sat.); 57 g carbo (5.6 g fiber); 154 mg sodium; 0 mg chol.

Strawberry Puff

A cross between a cream puff and a cheesecake, this beauty is piled with strawberries. Substitute any peak-season fruit—and replace the strawberry sauce with drizzles of warm honey if you like, or sift on more powdered sugar.

recipe pictured on page 606

SERVES 6 to 8 | **TIME** 1 hour

5 tbsp. butter, cut into ½-in. chunks
1 tbsp. granulated sugar
⅔ cup flour
3 eggs
4 oz. cream cheese, at room temperature
1 tsp. finely shredded orange zest
½ tsp. vanilla extract
1 cup whipping cream
⅔ cup plus 1 tbsp. powdered sugar, sifted
2 cups sliced, hulled strawberries
Strawberry Sauce (*recipe follows*)

1. In a 2- to 3-qt. pan, combine ⅔ cup water, butter, and granulated sugar; bring to a boil over high heat. Add flour all at once and stir quickly until mixture pulls away from pan sides and clumps together. Remove from heat and stir until flour is incorporated and mixture is smooth. Let cool about 5 minutes, stirring occasionally.
2. Preheat oven to 400°. Butter a 9-in. cheesecake pan with removable rim. Stir eggs, 1 at a time, into warm butter mixture in pan, stirring with a wooden spoon after each addition until dough is smooth and satiny. (Or scrape warm butter mixture into a bowl, add eggs 1 at a time, and beat with a mixer on high speed after each addition just until smooth; do not overbeat.) Spoon dough into pan; spread evenly over bottom and about 1 in. up side.
3. Bake until puffed and golden, 25 to 30 minutes. Prick pastry crust with a toothpick in about 12 places, then return to oven and bake until golden brown, dry, and crisp, 5 to 10 minutes longer. Transfer pan to a rack and let cool completely. Run a knife around pan sides to release pastry, then remove pan rim.
4. In a medium bowl, with a mixer on high speed, beat cream cheese, orange zest, and vanilla until smooth. Add whipping cream and ⅔ cup powdered sugar; beat on low speed until blended, then on high speed just until mixture forms stiff peaks (do not overbeat).
5. Spoon filling into puff shell. Scatter sliced strawberries over filling. Sift remaining 1 tbsp. powdered sugar over top. Cut into wedges and serve with strawberry sauce to spoon over individual servings.

Make Ahead: Crust through step 4, up to 1 day, covered airtight, at room temperature. If crust loses its crispness, bake, uncovered, in a 400° oven 15 to 20 minutes, then cool. Filling (step 5) and sliced berries, up to 2 hours ahead; fill crust just before serving.

PER SERVING: 325 cal., 64% (207 cal.) from fat; 5.5 g protein; 23 g fat (14 g sat.); 24 g carbo (1.4 g fiber); 150 mg sodium; 148 mg chol.

Strawberry Sauce: Hull 1½ cups **strawberries** and purée in a blender. Blend in 2 to 3 tbsp. **sugar** (or to taste) and 2 tbsp. **orange-flavored liqueur**, such as Grand Marnier (optional). Makes about 1 cup.
Make Ahead: Up to 1 day, chilled.

PER 2-TBSP. SERVING: 23 cal., 4% (0.9 cal.) from fat; 0.2 g protein; 0.1 g fat (0 g sat.); 5.6 g carbo (0.9 g fiber); 0.4 mg sodium; 0 mg chol.

Blenheim Apricot Crisp

recipe pictured on page 678

Blenheim apricots are a fragile, deep-orange, extremely flavorful variety sold mainly at farmers' markets because it doesn't ship well. You can still use other apricots, but cut each into quarters, increase the lemon juice to 2 tbsp. and granulated sugar to ½ cup, and mix a pinch each of cinnamon, ground ginger, and nutmeg into the fruit before baking. For more about Blenheims, *see Queen of the Apricots, page 718.*

SERVES 8 | **TIME** 1 hour, plus 30 minutes to cool

½ cup flour
½ tsp. *each* cinnamon, ground ginger, and nutmeg
¼ tsp. *each* ground cloves and salt
⅓ cup firmly packed dark brown sugar
⅔ cup quick-cooking rolled oats
⅓ cup *each* golden raisins and chopped pecans
½ cup butter, melted and cooled
5 cups halved, pitted fresh apricots, preferably Blenheim (about 15 apricots)
1 tbsp. fresh lemon juice
¼ cup granulated sugar

1. Preheat oven to 350°. Grease an 8-in. square baking pan. In a medium bowl, whisk together flour, cinnamon, ginger, nutmeg, cloves, salt, and brown sugar. Stir in oats, raisins if using, and pecans, then stir in butter.
2. Toss apricots with lemon juice and granulated sugar. Spread apricot mixture in prepared pan. Squeeze oatmeal-spice topping into shaggy chunks and scatter over apricots. Bake until bubbling, 40 to 50 minutes; cool at least 30 minutes.

PER SERVING: 322 cal., 45% (144 cal.) from fat; 3.7 g protein; 16 g fat (7.8 g sat.); 44 g carbo (2.5 g fiber); 78 mg sodium; 32 mg chol.

Rhubarb Crisp

Because rhubarb is one of the earliest arrivals in spring, it gets a lot of attention in the *Sunset* test kitchen. Top it with scoops of vanilla ice cream or dollops of softly whipped cream.

SERVES 6 to 8 | **TIME** 1 hour

1 cup flour
1 cup granulated sugar, divided
¼ cup firmly packed brown sugar
½ cup chopped toasted almonds *(see How to Toast Nuts,*
    page 134)
1 tsp. finely shredded lemon zest
¾ tsp. cinnamon, divided
¼ tsp. salt
½ cup cold butter, cut into chunks
2 lbs. rhubarb stalks, trimmed and cut into ½-in. pieces

1. Preheat oven to 375°. In a medium bowl, mix flour, ¼ cup granulated sugar, the brown sugar, almonds, lemon zest, ½ tsp. cinnamon, and the salt. Add butter and stir in with a wooden spoon or rub it in with your fingers until mixture forms coarse crumbs and begins to come together.
2. In a large bowl, mix rhubarb and remaining ¾ cup granulated sugar and ¼ tsp. cinnamon. Pour into an 8-in. square baking pan and spread level. Sprinkle evenly with flour-almond mixture.
3. Bake until juices are bubbly and topping is golden brown, 45 to 50 minutes.

PER SERVING: 351 cal., 41% (144 cal.) from fat; 4.3 g protein; 16 g fat (7.6 g sat.); 50 g carbo (1.4 g fiber); 197 mg sodium; 31 mg chol.

Rhubarb: First Sign of Spring

Although most often used in sweet dishes, rhubarb is a vegetable—a relative of garden sorrel. Its leaves, which contain toxins including oxalic acid, shouldn't be eaten, but they're fine to touch; just cut them off. In the West, rhubarb grows best in the cool climates of Washington and Oregon.

Hothouse rhubarb shows up in early- to mid-spring, and has traditionally been the first spring "fruit" to appear on the scene. It has pale pink to pale red stalks and yellowish leaves. Deep red field-grown rhubarb is sweeter and richer-tasting, and comes a bit later. It's classically paired with strawberries in jams and pies but also partners nicely with ginger and even makes a lovely compote to spoon over dessert *(see Easy Rhubarb Compote, page 671)* or into hot cereal. Because it's intensely sour, you have to cook it with quite a bit of sugar.

Nectarine-Boysenberry Vanilla-Pecan Crisp

Although this is an especially wonderful combination, you can use any mix of stone fruits and berries that appeals to you. This crisp tastes best warm, but you can also serve it at room temperature.

SERVES 8 to 10 | **TIME** 1 hour

1½ lbs. firm-ripe nectarines
2 cups boysenberries or blackberries
¼ cup granulated sugar
2 tbsp. fresh lemon juice
¾ cup firmly packed brown sugar
⅔ cup flour
½ cup regular rolled oats
1 tsp. *each* vanilla extract and cinnamon
¼ tsp. *each* nutmeg and salt
½ cup cold butter, cut into ½-in. pieces
¾ cup pecans, chopped

1. Preheat oven to 350°. Cut nectarines off their pits into ½-in.-thick wedges and drop into a large bowl. Add berries, granulated sugar, and lemon juice and mix gently just until combined.
2. In a medium bowl, stir brown sugar, flour, oats, vanilla, cinnamon, nutmeg, and salt until well combined. Add butter and cut it in with a pastry blender or rub it in with your fingers until mixture resembles coarse cornmeal with lots of pea-size pieces. Stir in pecans.
3. Spread fruit mixture level in a shallow 2- to 2½-qt. baking dish. Sprinkle oat-pecan mixture over top. Bake until juices at edges of dish are bubbling and top is crisp and golden, 40 to 45 minutes.

PER SERVING: 309 cal., 44% (135 cal.) from fat; 3.1 g protein; 15 g fat (6.2 g sat.); 43 g carbo (3.2 g fiber); 158 mg sodium; 25 mg chol.

Huckleberry Skillet Cobbler

This is one of our all-time favorite desserts. It's from Janie Hibler, the author of several cookbooks on Northwest cooking, and has just a hint of spice to tease out the complex, wine-rich flavor of the huckleberries. (It's almost as good made with blueberries.) Hibler likes to eat the cobbler for breakfast.

SERVES 8 to 10 | **TIME** 1¾ hours, plus 45 minutes to cool

1½ cups plus 2 tbsp. sugar (if using blueberries, decrease to 1 cup plus 2 tbsp.), divided
⅓ cup quick-cooking tapioca
½ tsp. *each* cinnamon and ground cardamom
1 tbsp. fresh lemon juice
2 qts. (2½ lbs.) fresh or frozen huckleberries *(see Quick Tip, above right)* or blueberries
Butter and Cream Pastry *(recipe follows)*
½ tbsp. milk
1 cup crème fraîche

1. Preheat oven to 400°. In a 12-in. ovenproof frying pan or a 9- by 13-in. baking dish, combine 1½ cups sugar (1 cup if using blueberries), the tapioca, cinnamon, and cardamom. Gently mix in lemon juice and berries. Let stand, stirring occasionally, to allow tapioca to soften slightly, about 15 minutes (50 minutes for frozen berries; they'll start to look wet). Spread berries level.
2. On a lightly floured work surface with a floured rolling pin, roll out pastry to a 14-in. round or 10- by 14-in. rectangle (depending on whether using pan or dish), lifting up pastry and re-flouring underneath if needed to prevent sticking. Trim uneven edges with a knife. Slide a rimless baking sheet under pastry and ease it over berries. Fold edges of pastry under so they're flush with pan or dish, pressing together any cracks. Flute pastry edges with a finger and thumb to seal.
3. Brush crust (but not fluted edges) with milk and sprinkle with remaining 2 tbsp. sugar. Cut about six vents in crust to release steam. Bake until crust is golden brown and filling is bubbling through vents, 50 to 60 minutes; tent with foil if pastry starts to get too brown, and put a rimmed baking sheet underneath if the cobbler starts to bubble over.
4. Supporting cobbler underneath, carefully transfer to a rack and let cool at least 45 minutes. Serve warm or cool, with crème fraîche to spoon on top.

Quick Tip: Buy Western huckleberries from specialty produce markets or pick them yourself, from your garden if you grow them or in the wild in the Northwest. (For more on huckleberries, *see Berry Land, page 704*.)

PER SERVING: 499 cal., 47% (234 cal.) from fat; 4.5 g protein; 26 g fat (16 g sat.); 64 g carbo (3.3 g fiber); 307 mg sodium; 68 mg chol.

Butter and Cream Pastry: Put 2 cups **flour**; ¾ cup cold **butter**, cut into 1-in. pieces; 1 tsp. *each* **sugar** and **fresh lemon juice**; ½ tsp. salt; and ¼ cup plus 1 tbsp. **heavy whipping cream** in a food processor and process just until dough comes together and is evenly moistened. Gather into a ball, then shape into a flat disk.

Blackberry-Hazelnut Honey Crisp

Foods that grow in the same place tend to taste good together, as this pairing of blackberries and hazelnuts proves—Oregon is far and away the country's leading producer of both crops.

SERVES 8 | **TIME** 1½ hours, plus 30 minutes to cool

4 pts. fresh or frozen blackberries
3 tbsp. quick-cooking tapioca
¼ cup *each* berry-blossom or wildflower honey and fresh lemon juice
¾ cup hazelnuts, toasted *(see How to Toast Nuts, page 134)*
¼ cup *each* flour and sugar
½ tsp. salt
½ cup *each* butter and quick-cooking rolled oats

1. Preheat oven to 350°. In a large bowl, toss berries with tapioca. In a small bowl, combine honey, lemon juice, and 1 tbsp. boiling water. Stir to dissolve honey. Add to berries and toss to combine. Put berry mixture in an 8-in. square baking pan and set aside.
2. In a food processor, pulse hazelnuts until finely ground. Add flour, sugar, and salt and pulse to combine. Add butter and pulse until mixture forms a thick dough. Stir in oats. Drop nut-oatmeal topping in flattened 1-tsp. chunks over berries.
3. Bake crisp until topping is brown and berries are bubbling, about 1 hour. Let cool to set, about 30 minutes.

PER SERVING: 341 cal., 50% (171 cal.) from fat; 3.7 g protein; 19 g fat (7.7 g sat.); 43 g carbo (7.3 g fiber); 282 mg sodium; 31 mg chol.

pies, tarts & fruit desserts

Cobbler for a Crowd

Fruit cobblers are wonderful because they're so easy. This recipe works for crowds small and large; just pick your fruit and desired size on our chart *below*, and begin.

SERVES An 8-in. square cobbler serves 6; a 9- by 13-in. serves 12; an 11- by 17-in. serves 24 | **TIME** 1 hour, 20 minutes to 2 hours, depending on fruit and pan

1. Prepare fruit as directed in chart. Put in a bowl and crush about one-quarter of it with a potato masher. Gently mix in lemon juice (if called for), then sugar and tapioca or cornstarch (*see How to Thicken a Pie or Tart Filling, page 658*). Mix gently and, if using tapioca, set aside at least 15 minutes and up to 1 hour, stirring occasionally (the fruits' juices soften tapioca). Raspberries are the exception. They should be mixed with dry ingredients right before baking or they'll liquefy.

2. Preheat oven to 350°. In a bowl, mix flour with sugar, baking powder, and nutmeg. Cut butter into ½-in. chunks. With a pastry blender or your fingers, incorporate butter into flour mixture until mixture resembles coarse crumbs. Add cream; stir just until dough holds together.

3. Butter a baking dish and add fruit, spreading it level. Using your fingers, crumble dough evenly over fruit.

4. Bake cobbler (set on a larger rimmed pan to catch juices) until golden brown, 50 minutes to 1 ½ hours. Serve warm or cool. The 11- by 17-in. cobbler takes about 8 hours to cool and thicken up completely.

Make Ahead: 1 day, at room temperature. Serve as is or reheat, uncovered, in a 350° oven until warm in center, 15 to 25 minutes.

PAN SIZE	FRUIT	SUGAR	TAPIOCA OR CORNSTARCH	LEMON JUICE	SALT
BERRY (blackberry, boysenberry, loganberry, ollalieberry, raspberry)—use whole berries					
8-in. square	5½ cups	1⅛ cups	2 tbsp.	1 tbsp.	big pinch
9- by 13-in.	2¾ qts.	2¼ cups	6½ tbsp.	2 tbsp.	¼ tsp.
11- by 17-in.	5½ qts.	4½ cups	¾ cup	3 tbsp.	½ tsp.
BLUEBERRIES—use whole berries					
8-in. square	5½ cups	¼ cup	2 tbsp.	2 tbsp.	big pinch
9- by 13-in.	2¾ qts.	1½ cups	6 tbsp.	3 to 4 tbsp.	¼ tsp.
11- by 17-in.	5½ qts.	3 cups	¾ cup	⅓ cup	½ tsp.
PEACH—use firm-ripe to soft-ripe; pit, peel, and thinly slice					
8-in. square	5½ cups	⅓ cup	1 tbsp.	1 tbsp.	big pinch
9- by 13-in.	2¾ qts.	¾ cup	3 tbsp.	2 tbsp.	¼ tsp.
11- by 17-in.	5½ qts.	1½ cups	6 tbsp.	¼ cup	½ tsp.
PLUM—use firm-ripe to soft-ripe; pit and thinly slice					
8-in. square	5½ cups	¾ cup	3 tbsp.	1 tbsp.	big pinch
9- by 13-in.	2¾ qts.	1½ cups	6 tbsp.	2 tbsp.	¼ tsp.
11- by 17-in.	5½ qts.	3 cups	¾ cup	¼ cup	½ tsp.

DOUGH

PAN SIZE	FLOUR	SUGAR	BAKING POWDER	NUTMEG	COLD BUTTER	WHIPPING CREAM
8-in. square	1 cup	3 tbsp.	½ tsp.	¼ tsp.	⅓ cup	⅓ cup
9- by 13-in.	2 cups	⅓ cup	1 tsp.	½ tsp.	⅔ cup	⅔ cup
11- by 17-in.	4 cups	⅔ cup	2½ tsp.	1 tsp.	1⅓ cups	1⅓ cups

Summer Fruit Clafouti

Clafouti is an old French dessert, traditionally made in late spring with cherries, but equally good with other stone fruit. Serve it warm with vanilla ice cream.

SERVES 8 | **TIME** 1¼ hours

1½ lbs. apricots, pluots, or purple-skinned plums
¼ cup sweet white wine such as Muscat or late-harvest Riesling
3 eggs
1 cup whole milk
½ cup *each* granulated sugar and flour
5 tbsp. unsalted butter, melted
1 tbsp. vanilla extract
⅛ tsp. salt
Powdered sugar

1. Preheat oven to 325°. Butter a shallow 2-qt. baking dish. Cut apricots off pits into ¼-in.-thick wedges and drop into a bowl. Add wine and mix gently. Let stand 5 minutes.
2. In a blender, combine eggs, milk, granulated sugar, flour, butter, vanilla, and salt; blend until smooth.
3. With a slotted spoon, transfer fruit to prepared baking dish. Pour remaining wine and juices into egg mixture and blend. Pour egg mixture over fruit.
4. Bake clafouti in upper third of oven until puffed and set in the center (touch to test), 55 to 65 minutes. Serve warm (clafouti will settle slightly as it cools). Sprinkle powdered sugar over the top just before serving.

PER SERVING: 243 cal., 41% (99 cal.) from fat; 4.9 g protein; 11 g fat (6 g sat.); 32 g carbo (1.9 g fiber); 82 mg sodium; 105 mg chol.

Sparkling Oranges

This sophisticated yet easy dessert from San Francisco food writer Peggy Knickerbocker is especially refreshing after a rich main course. If you like, return the whole spices (cinnamon sticks, cloves, and star anise) to oranges just before serving to give your guests a clue to what's flavoring the fruit.

SERVES 10 to 12 | **TIME** 40 minutes, plus 30 minutes to cool

10 very firm oranges
5 tbsp. sugar
2 cinnamon sticks (3 in. each)
6 whole cloves
2 star anise pods
1 vanilla bean, split lengthwise
2 tbsp. fresh lemon juice
½ cup pomegranate seeds
About ½ cup prosecco or other sparkling wine

1. Using a very sharp five-hole zester, remove zest from 6 oranges. Bring 1 cup water to a boil in a small saucepan, add zest, and boil 30 seconds. Pour zest through a fine-mesh strainer into a bowl and return orange water to saucepan. Rinse zest with cold water and set aside.
2. Add sugar to orange water and bring to a simmer over medium-high heat. Lower heat to medium (adjust to maintain an active simmer) and add cinnamon sticks, cloves, star anise, and vanilla bean. Simmer 10 minutes. Add zest, remove from heat, and let cool 30 minutes.
3. Meanwhile, cut a thin slice from each orange bottom so oranges sit upright on a cutting board. With a very sharp, smooth-bladed paring knife, slice off peels and thick white pith from oranges. Cut oranges crosswise into ¼-in.-thick slices, removing seeds and discarding any fibrous end slices.
4. Remove spices from syrup (reserve for garnish if you like) and add lemon juice. Cover bottom of a large, shallow glass serving dish (13- by 9-in. is ideal) with a layer of orange slices and sprinkle 1½ to 2 tbsp. of syrup and several pomegranate seeds over oranges. Repeat layering with oranges, syrup, and pomegranate seeds until all oranges are used. Pour any remaining syrup over oranges.
5. Just before serving, top with prosecco and garnish with reserved whole spices if you like.
Make Ahead: Up to 3 days, chilled.

PER SERVING: 110 cal., 2% (2.7 cal.) from fat; 1.2 g protein; 0.3 g fat (0 g sat.); 26 g carbo (3.3 g fiber); 1.3 mg sodium; 0 mg chol.

A Golden Fruit for the Golden State

More than any other fruit, sweet, juicy oranges symbolize California's sunshine, vitality, and abundance. Both the thin-skinned summer-ripening Valencia and the thick-skinned, seedless winter navel orange arrived in the state in the 1870s—and it was the navel in particular that transformed Southern California.

It got its start when a couple named Luther and Eliza Tibbets, newly arrived in Riverside, California, requested from the Department of Agriculture plants suitable for growing in their climate. Before long, they received three navel orange trees, the last survivors of a batch from Brazil that the USDA had been nurturing in its garden.

The Navel: A Seedless Superstar

The Tibbetses waited five years for the trees to bear fruit. One died, but the remaining two produced oranges that blew away the small group of tasters—all orange farmers growing other, seedy varieties—with its sweet, juicy seedlessness. Word of these incredible oranges rapidly spread, and Luther Tibbets gave away hundreds of buds from his trees, reasoning that the navels had been given to him free by the government and therefore he shouldn't profit from them.

But others made millions. Within a few years thousands of acres of cattle-grazing land had been planted to oranges, using trees budded from the Tibbets navels. People poured into Southern California to get in on the orange action, and an orange-driven real estate boom created the towns of Pomona, Ontario, Redlands, Tustin, Monrovia, and many more in what came to be called Orange County. California navels were shipped across the country and became a strong part of the state's economy. Riverside was the wealthiest city in the state by the end of the 1800s.

As for the Tibbetses, Eliza succumbed to illness; and Luther, his money drained from travels he had taken with Eliza at the end of her life, and from battling litigation over water rights, lost his property in foreclosure. A New York Times story from 1902 described Luther looking out from the county poorhouse across a valley of green orange groves and beautiful homes. One hopes that he took some pleasure in knowing it had all come from his hand.

In any event, one of his original trees is still alive, planted in a park in Riverside—even though the glory days of the California orange have faded.

The Boom Subsides

In the 1960s, when real estate prices soared, orange ranchers sold out all over Southern California; groves were replaced by housing developments and shopping malls. More recently, competition from Australia and South Africa has hurt Southern California's citrus industry. But a group of determined growers is fighting to preserve California's oranges. The Inland Orange Conservancy, for one, has created a program called Share of the Crop, distributing to its members two 5-lb. bags of just-picked oranges every week during the harvest season. And some areas—like the town of Ojai, whose fierce zoning laws have protected its groves—raise wonderful and sought-after citrus. Some sunshine still warms the California orange.

Baked Apples with Cranberry-Molasses Bread Pudding

It's three desserts in one: baked apples, a gingerbread-like pudding, and ice cream and caramel sauce.

SERVES 12 | **TIME** 2¼ hours

1½ qts. cubed (½-in.) brioche or unseeded challah (about ¾ lb.)

12 Pink Lady or Golden Delicious apples (6 lbs. total), or some of each

¾ cup firmly packed light brown sugar

½ cup dark molasses

6 tbsp. butter, melted and cooled

2 eggs

1 cup half-and-half

1 tbsp. ground ginger

1½ tsp. vanilla extract

½ tsp. nutmeg

1¼ cups cranberries, cut in half

1½ cups coarsely chopped pecans, toasted (see How to Toast Nuts, page 134)

Vanilla ice cream and warm caramel sauce (store-bought or homemade; recipe follows)

1. Preheat oven to 200°. Toast bread cubes in a large rimmed baking pan until crisp, 40 to 45 minutes. Let cool.

2. Meanwhile, peel the top quarter of each apple and, using a melon baller, scoop out stem, core, and enough of inside so that walls of apple are about ½ in. thick (don't break through bottoms). If needed, trim bottoms slightly so apples sit upright.

3. In a large bowl, whisk brown sugar, molasses, butter, eggs, half-and-half, ginger, vanilla, and nutmeg to blend.

4. Add bread and cranberries to molasses mixture; toss to coat. Let stand, stirring occasionally, until two-thirds of liquid is absorbed, about 12 minutes. Stir in pecans.

5. Increase oven temperature to 325°. Generously stuff apples with bread mixture, mounding it. Set in a 9- by 13-in. baking dish plus a smaller shallow dish.

6. Bake on lower rack until each apple is very tender when pierced with a skewer, about 1 hour; check after 40 minutes and tent loosely with foil if they're getting dark. Serve warm in shallow bowls with ice cream and caramel sauce.

Make Ahead: Through step 5, up to 1 day, chilled. Bring to room temperature (2½ hours) before baking.

PER SERVING: 500 cal., 38% (188 cal.) from fat; 6.3 g protein; 21 g fat (6.7 g sat.); 79 g carbo (7.8 g fiber); 213 mg sodium; 72 mg chol.

Warm Caramel Sauce: In a saucepan over high heat, cook 3 tbsp. **butter** and ⅔ cup **sugar**, stirring, until mixture is caramel-colored, 2 to 4 minutes. Remove from heat and add ⅔ cup **whipping cream**; stir until blended (mixture foams). Return to high heat and stir until caramel sauce comes to a rolling boil, 1 to 2 minutes. Makes 1 cup.

Make Ahead: Up to 1 month, chilled.

PER TBSP.: 81 cal., 58% (47 cal.) from fat; 0.2 g protein; 5.3 g fat (3.3 g sat.); 8.7 g carbo (0 g fiber); 25 mg sodium; 17 mg chol.

Blueberries in Black Pepper–Syrah Syrup

Enough already with pairing wine with each dish—just put the wine right in the dessert. Syrah often has blueberry flavors; pour it over the real berries, along with a little black pepper to clinch the match. Serve with dark chocolate truffles if you like.

SERVES 6 | **TIME** 15 minutes, plus 2 hours to chill

1 bottle (750 ml.) Syrah

¼ cup sugar

1 tsp. vanilla extract

½ tsp. freshly ground black pepper

18 oz. blueberries

Twists of lemon zest

1. In a small pan, combine Syrah and sugar. Boil over medium-high heat (watch to make sure mixture doesn't boil over), stirring often, until reduced by about half, about 15 minutes. Stir in vanilla and pepper and let cool.

2. Put blueberries in a large bowl and pour Syrah mixture over them. Chill airtight for at least 2 hours.

3. Serve in small dessert bowls or glasses garnished with twists of lemon zest.

Make Ahead: Up to 1 day, chilled.

PER SERVING: 132 cal., 2% (2.7 cal.) from fat; 0.8 g protein; 0.3 g fat (0 g sat.); 23 g carbo (2 g fiber); 12 mg sodium; 0 mg chol.

Easy Rhubarb Compote

Cooking rhubarb in the oven is less work than cooking it on the stove and also better preserves its brilliant pinkish red color. Spoon the compote over ice cream, serve it chilled with shortbread cookies, or incorporate it into other desserts and into drinks—it's very versatile stuff. For five ways to use rhubarb compote, *see below*

MAKES About 4 cups | **TIME** 1 hour

2 lbs. rhubarb, trimmed and cut into ½-in. pieces
1½ cups sugar

1. Preheat oven to 350°. Mix rhubarb and sugar in a 9- by 13-in. baking dish and spread level. Cover dish tightly with foil.
2. Bake until rhubarb is very soft when pierced with a knife but just holds its shape, about 45 minutes. Serve warm or cool.
Make Ahead: Up to 1 week, chilled.

PER CUP: 333 cal., 1% (3.6 cal.) from fat; 1.8 g protein; 0.4 g fat (0 g sat.); 84 g carbo (0 g fiber); 8.9 mg sodium; 0 mg chol.

5 Ways to Serve Rhubarb Compote

1. Strawberry-Rhubarb Fool
Stir together chilled compote, sliced hulled **strawberries**, and unsweetened **whipped cream**; spoon into bowls and chill 2 hours.

2. Rhubarb-Orange Parfaits
Layer compote with **orange segments** and **vanilla ice cream** in tall glasses. Top with a bit of **orange zest**.

3. Rhubarb Sandwich Cake
Split a **sponge cake** horizontally and spoon compote between layers, using a slotted spoon; sprinkle cake with **powdered sugar** and serve with **whipped cream**.

4. Rhubarb Mimosas
Pour the compote through a fine-mesh strainer (reserve fruit for other uses); add a little of the syrup to glasses of **prosecco or sparkling wine** for a blushing pink drink.

5. Rhubarb Lemonade
Stir the strained syrup into **lemonade** for a new twist.

Caramelized Pears with Toasted Hazelnuts and Chocolate Sorbet

These stunning golden-brown pears are from Maria Helm Sinskey, cookbook author and co-owner of Robert Sinskey Vineyards in Napa.

SERVES 8 | **TIME** 2¼ hours

1 cup hazelnuts, toasted (see *How to Toast Nuts*, page 134)
3 tbsp. superfine sugar
8 to 10 large, firm-ripe Bosc pears with stems
¼ cup unsalted butter
1 cup *each* granulated sugar and brandy
1 tbsp. fresh lemon juice
2 pts. chocolate sorbet

1. Preheat oven to 350°. In a large ovenproof frying pan, mix hazelnuts with superfine sugar. Bake until sugar is lightly browned, about 20 minutes. Meanwhile, line a large rimmed baking pan with parchment paper. Remove nut mixture from oven and stir immediately. Set over medium-high heat on stove and cook, stirring constantly with a wooden spoon, until sugar is melted and golden brown, about 2 minutes. Pour immediately into lined pan and separate nuts gently with spoon. Let cool.
2. Peel pears. With large end of a melon baller, scoop out bottoms of cores; then with smaller end, dig and scoop out seeds. Cut a slice off bottoms so pears sit upright.
3. Increase oven temperature to 400°. Melt butter in a large ovenproof frying pan over medium-high heat. When it starts to brown, add pears and cook, gently turning occasionally with two wooden spoons, until golden brown all over, 5 to 7 minutes. Sprinkle pears with granulated sugar and continue to cook and turn pears until sugar is caramelized and thick, about 5 minutes.
4. Remove pan from heat and add brandy. Return to heat and boil until liquid is reduced to a thick, bubbly syrup, 10 to 12 minutes. Pour in ½ cup very hot water and set pears upright in pan. Bring liquid to a boil; transfer pan to oven. Bake, basting every 15 minutes, until pears are tender when pierced and liquid has thickened again and is dark gold, 25 to 30 minutes. If liquid reduces too quickly, add more water, ¼ cup at a time. Let pears cool slightly in liquid, basting often.
5. Transfer pears to shallow bowls. Stir lemon juice into syrup, then spoon over pears. Add a scoop of chocolate sorbet to each bowl and sprinkle with toasted hazelnuts.
Make Ahead: Baked pears (through step 4), up to 4 hours at room temperature. Warm over medium heat, basting pears with syrup, about 3 minutes.

PER SERVING: 608 cal., 37% (225 cal.) from fat; 4.9 g protein; 25 g fat (10 g sat.); 100 g carbo (9.9 g fiber); 60 mg sodium; 16 mg chol.

puddings, trifles & frozen delights

Soft, smooth, and luscious, these are the seducers of the dessert world. Few can resist their charms.

If you were blindfolded, the desserts in this chapter might give you the greatest pleasure of any in this book. Puddings, custards, trifles, and their kin are all about texture—a soft, irresistible silkiness. Ice creams, sherbets, and granitas are all about temperature—the riveting sensation of frozen sweetness melting in your mouth.

Puddings and custards are often thought of as bland, but any of the recipes in this chapter will overturn that impression. Velvety Dark Chocolate Pots de Crème (*page 676*) are so intense they're electrifying, and even gentle-sounding Old-fashioned Creamy Lemon Pudding (*page 675*) has a bright, fresh tang. Though it contains gelatin, sophisticated Yogurt Honey Jelly with Strawberries and Roses (*page 692*) is light-years away from Jell-O. Rice puddings are anything but ho-hum, thanks to the intersection of the world's cultures in the West: Try Coconut Brown Rice Pudding (*page 689*), an amazing dessert that is similar to sweet Thai sticky rice.

Western fruit plays a huge role in this chapter, giving us a rainbow of frozen desserts starring peaches, blueberries, figs, pineapple, tangerines, cherries, pears, and even avocado. Because you can't live by fruit alone when it comes to ice cream, we brought in other favorite flavors too, like chocolate and peanut butter. And for sheer kid appeal (and we include the eternal child in all of us), check out our blowout sundaes and deliciously drippy popsicles. For elegant occasions, we offer pear and Champagne sorbet (*page 706*) and Almond Nougat Semifreddo (*page 695*). Because they're fast and easy (usually 30 minutes or less to mix), because you can create such exciting flavors, and because they taste far better when fresh, frozen desserts are especially worthy of making at home.

Puddings, Trifles & Frozen Delights

puddings, trifles & frozen delights

Old-fashioned Creamy Lemon Pudding

Reader Sandra Krist, of Sherman Oaks, California, set out to make a creamy lemon pie and then ditched the crust—the filling mixture was good on its own as a pudding. Made with buttermilk, it has a tang reminiscent of lemon curd.

SERVES 4 to 6 | **TIME** 25 minutes

2 eggs
1 cup sugar
3 tbsp. cornstarch
2 tbsp. flour
2 cups buttermilk
½ tsp. finely shredded lemon zest
⅓ cup fresh lemon juice
¼ cup butter, cut into pieces
Lightly sweetened whipped cream (optional)

1. In a small bowl, whisk eggs to blend.
2. In a 2- to 3-qt. pan, mix sugar, cornstarch, and flour. Stir in buttermilk, then set mixture over medium heat and stir often until simmering, 10 to 12 minutes. Continue simmering, stirring often, 2 minutes longer.
3. Whisk half of hot buttermilk mixture into eggs, then return both to pan, along with lemon zest and juice and butter. Whisk over medium-low heat until pudding reaches 160° on an instant-read thermometer and coats a spoon very thickly, 4 to 6 minutes; do not boil.
4. Spoon pudding into bowls or heatproof glasses. Serve warm or cool, with whipped cream if you like.

PER SERVING: 285 cal., 32% (90 cal.) from fat; 5.2 g protein; 10 g fat (5.9 g sat.); 44 g carbo (0.1 g fiber); 192 mg sodium; 96 mg chol.

■ Mangoes

Native to the rain forests of South and Southeast Asia, mangoes are the favorite fruit in much of the tropics; India, China, and Thailand are the world's leading producers. For half the planet, rapturous memories of mangoes—gorging on the sugary, peachy flesh, juice dripping down the chin—are emblematic of home. In the United States, Florida, Hawaii, and California grow exquisite mangoes, but on a modest scale, and chiefly for local sale. Mangoes must be harvested firm and ripened off the tree, like pears, and are aromatic and give to gentle thumb pressure when ready to eat. A red blush is not an indicator of ripeness, as many fine mangoes have more of a yellow cast than a reddish one.

Cardamom Pudding with Mango

Sweet mango tops an aromatic cardamom-scented pudding.

SERVES 6 to 8 | **TIME** About 40 minutes, plus 1½ hours to chill

6 cardamom pods
4¼ cups whole milk, divided
½ cup sugar, divided
⅓ cup cornstarch
½ tsp. ground cardamom
About 2 lbs. ripe mango
2 tbsp. ginger-flavored liqueur (optional)
Mint leaves

1. Crack cardamom pods by gently pressing with a rolling pin. Combine with 4 cups milk in a 3- to 4-qt. pan; heat, stirring occasionally, over medium-high heat until milk is boiling, 9 to 15 minutes.
2. Meanwhile, in a small bowl, mix ¼ cup sugar, the cornstarch, and ground cardamom. Stir in remaining ¼ cup milk. When milk in pan is boiling, remove from heat and gradually whisk in cornstarch mixture. Return to medium-low heat and heat, stirring, just until mixture comes to a boil, 3 to 7 minutes. Pour through a fine-mesh strainer set over a bowl; discard residue. Ladle pudding into 6 to 8 small bowls or ramekins (¾- to 1-cup size). Let cool about 10 minutes, then cover and chill until cold and set, at least 1½ hours.
3. Pit and peel mangoes. Cut flesh into about 1-in. chunks (you need 2 cups). In a food processor, combine 2 cups mango, remaining ¼ cup sugar, and the ginger liqueur if using; whirl just until mango is coarsely puréed (mixture should be slightly chunky). Cover and chill.
4. Just before serving, spoon all of the mango mixture over puddings. Garnish with mint leaves.
Make Ahead: Through step 3 up to 1 day, chilled.

PER SERVING: 176 cal., 23% (41 cal.) from fat; 4.5 g protein; 4.5 g fat (2.7 g sat.); 31 g carbo (0.5 g fiber); 65 mg sodium; 18 mg chol.

Dark Chocolate Pots de Crème

This is a true chocolate-lover's dessert: rich, thick puddings topped with crushed chocolate wafers. Best of all, you can make the puddings with very little fuss using a microwave and a blender.

SERVES 8 | **TIME** 15 minutes, plus 30 minutes to chill

14 oz. (about 3 cups) semisweet or bittersweet
    chocolate, roughly chopped
2 eggs plus 2 yolks
2½ cups whipping cream
⅓ cup coffee-flavored liqueur
½ cup chocolate wafer crumbs

1. In a food processor, finely chop chocolate. Pour into a bowl. Put whole eggs and yolks in the processor.
2. In a 4-cup glass measure, heat whipping cream in a microwave oven until cream boils, 3 to 5 minutes.
3. With processor on high speed, add boiling cream to egg. Check temperature of mixture with an instant-read thermometer; if below 160°, pour mixture back into glass measure and reheat in microwave until it reaches 160°, stirring and checking at 15-second intervals.
4. Combine hot cream mixture, chopped chocolate, and liqueur in processor (or whisk the ingredients together in a large bowl); whirl until smooth, about 1 minute.
5. Pour chocolate mixture into 8 ramekins or glasses (½-cup size). Chill until softly set, 30 to 45 minutes. For creamiest texture, let desserts stand at room temperature about 30 minutes before eating.
6. Spoon 1 tbsp. wafer crumbs onto each pot de crème.
Make Ahead: Up to 1 day, chilled.

PER SERVING: 597 cal., 69% (413 cal.) from fat; 6.3 g protein; 46 g fat (27 g sat.); 45 g carbo (3.2 g fiber); 94 mg sodium; 209 mg chol.

Pumpkin Chai Pots de Crème

Reader Edwina Gadsby, of Great Falls, Montana, decided to incorporate the flavors of Starbucks' pumpkin latte into her favorite dessert, pot de crème. "My sister Leanne, a huge chai fan, suggested I try it with chai instead of coffee, and everyone loved it," she says.

SERVES 6 | **TIME** About 1¼ hours, plus 1½ hours to cool and chill

1 cup *each* whipping cream and whole milk
¼ cup firmly packed light brown sugar
6 egg yolks
¼ cup granulated sugar
½ cup canned pumpkin
⅓ cup chai tea concentrate or strong brewed chai tea
2 tsp. finely shredded orange or Meyer lemon zest
1 tsp. vanilla extract
Pumpkin Seed Brittle *(recipe follows)*

1. Preheat oven to 325°. In a 2- to 3-qt. pan over medium heat, stir cream, milk, and brown sugar until sugar is dissolved, 2 to 4 minutes. Remove from heat.
2. In a bowl, whisk egg yolks until light yellow. Add granulated sugar and whisk until blended. Gradually whisk one-fourth of hot cream mixture into egg mixture. Then slowly whisk in remaining cream mixture and the pumpkin, chai, orange zest, and vanilla.
3. Divide mixture among six ramekins (¾-cup size). Set in a 12- by 16-in. roasting pan at least 2 in. deep. Set pan in oven and pour in boiling water to halfway up sides of ramekins.
4. Bake until custards barely jiggle when gently shaken, 45 to 50 minutes. Lift ramekins out of water and let cool on racks for 30 minutes, then chill until cold, at least 1 hour. Cover when cold.
5. Shortly before serving, garnish with shards of pumpkin seed brittle.
Make Ahead: Custards, up to 1 day, chilled; pumpkin seed brittle, 1 day, stored airtight at room temperature.

PER SERVING: 382 cal., 57% (216 cal.) from fat; 8 g protein; 24 g fat (11 g sat.); 35 g carbo (0.7 g fiber); 48 mg sodium; 263 mg chol.

Pumpkin Seed Brittle: In a heavy 6- to 8-in. frying pan over medium-high heat, heat ⅓ cup **sugar** and ¼ cup water, stirring, until sugar is dissolved, 1 to 2 minutes. Cook without stirring, shaking pan often, until mixture is a deep amber color, 5 to 10 minutes. Remove from heat and stir in ½ cup **hulled roasted pumpkin seeds** (sometimes sold as *pepitas*). Pour onto a 12- by 15-in. piece of buttered foil and spread thin. Let cool until hard, 6 to 10 minutes. Cut or break brittle into about ½-in. shards.

Peanut Butter Chocolate
Ice Cream Sandwiches,
page 699

Blenheim Apricot Crisp,
page 664

Raspberry-Lemon Pudding
Cakes, *page 636*

Fig-Blackberry-Orange Quick Jam, *page 714*, and
Peach-Raspberry-Lavender Quick Jam, *page 715*

Fresh Peaches in
Rosé Wine, *page 661*

Mexican Chocolate Ice
Cream with Hot Fudge
Piñon Sauce and Spiced
Piñon Brittle, *page 698*

Canned Heirloom
Tomatoes, *page 722*

Spiced Blueberry Pie,
page 651

Cherry Sherbet,
page 703

Black Mission Fig Tart,
page 659

Pickled Green Beans with
Dill, Tarragon, Garlic, and
Peppercorns, *page 725*

Date Flan with Almond
Brittle, *page 690*

Coconut Brown Rice Pudding

This is our brown rice take on classic coconut sticky rice. Long cooking time yields an unctuous sauce that clings to the spoon. We love the sweet-tart dried apricots, but feel free to customize it with tropical fruit or berries.

SERVES 8 | **TIME** 2¼ hours

3 cans (13.5 oz. each) light coconut milk
1 cup brown sweet rice *(see Quick Tip below)*
½ cup sugar
½ tsp. salt
½ cup diced dried apricots (optional)

1. In a heavy-bottomed 3-qt. saucepan over medium heat, bring coconut milk, rice, sugar, and salt to a gentle boil. Partially cover and reduce heat to maintain a gentle simmer. Cook, stirring occasionally, until rice is tender to the bite and liquid thickens, about 2 hours.
2. Serve warm, at room temperature, or chilled. Top with fruit if you like.
Quick Tip: Brown sweet rice has a very short grain and is sold at many specialty grocery stores. We like Lundberg Family Farms' sweet rice (see *lundberg.com* for stores). You can use short-grain brown rice in place of it, but the result is a thicker, less silken pudding.

PER ½-CUP SERVING: 227 cal., 33% (76 cal.) from fat; 4 g protein; 8.4 g fat (4.9 g sat.); 38 g carbo (1 g fiber); 184 mg sodium; 0 mg chol.

Creamy Basmati Rice Pudding

Indian-style rice pudding (*kheer*) inspired this rich dessert.

SERVES 8 | **TIME** 30 minutes, plus 2 hours to cool and chill

¾ cup basmati rice
4 cardamom pods, crushed
½ tsp. salt
1 cup whipping cream
⅓ cup sugar
1 container (8 oz.) mascarpone cheese
¼ tsp. rose water (optional; *see Quick Tip, above right*)
Chopped pistachios (optional)

1. In a 2- to 3-qt. pan over high heat, bring rice, cardamom, salt, and 1½ cups water to a boil. Lower heat to maintain a simmer, cover, and cook until water is absorbed and rice is tender, 20 to 25 minutes. Fluff with a fork, cover, and let cool to room temperature. Discard cardamom pods.
2. In a large bowl, combine cream, sugar, mascarpone, and rose water if using. With a mixer on medium speed, whip until thickened. Stir in rice.

3. Spoon pudding into bowls or dessert glasses. Cover and chill until cold, at least 1 hour. Just before serving, sprinkle with chopped pistachios if you like.
Quick Tip: Find rose water in Middle Eastern markets and well-stocked supermarkets, and look for Middle Eastern, French, and Italian brands—which have better flavor—over Indian ones.

PER SERVING: 301 cal., 66% (198 cal.) from fat; 4.4 g protein; 22 g fat (14 g sat.); 24 g carbo (0.2 g fiber); 177 mg sodium; 57 mg chol.

Coconut Tapioca Pudding

This delicious Filipino-style dessert comes from Tim Luym (who was chef at the now-closed Poleng Lounge in San Francisco). Once it's chilled, he thins the pudding with the water inside a fresh young coconut, sold at Asian markets—if you can find one, by all means try it.

SERVES 4 | **TIME** 30 minutes, plus 1¼ hours to chill

⅓ cup small pearl tapioca *(see Quick Tips below)*
1 can (13.5 oz.) coconut milk
1 cup whole milk or soy milk, plus more if needed
¼ cup sugar
½ vanilla bean, split lengthwise
¾ cup unsweetened large-flake dried coconut, toasted
  (see Quick Tips below)
½ cup chopped, peeled fresh fruit, such as mango, papaya, or kiwi fruit

1. In a medium saucepan, cook tapioca in 1½ qts. boiling water until only slightly chewy to the bite, 5 to 8 minutes. Pour through a fine-mesh strainer.
2. Meanwhile, in another medium saucepan over medium heat, warm coconut milk, whole milk, sugar, and vanilla bean, pressing bean gently to loosen seeds, until steaming, 6 to 8 minutes.
3. Stir drained tapioca into coconut milk mixture. Cook, stirring often, until tapioca pearls are clear and just tender, 3 to 6 minutes.
4. Let pudding cool, then chill, stirring occasionally, at least 1¼ hours. Remove vanilla bean and stir in more whole milk if pudding seems too thick.
5. Spoon into tall glasses. Top with coconut and fruit.
Quick Tips: Find small pearl tapioca in the supermarket baking or Asian-foods aisle or at an Asian market. Get large-flake coconut at a natural-foods store; toast it in a 350° oven until light golden, 3 to 4 minutes.
Make Ahead: Up to 1 day, chilled.

PER SERVING: 412 cal., 66% (270 cal.) from fat; 4.9 g protein; 30 g fat (26 g sat.); 36 g carbo (1 g fiber); 107 mg sodium; 8.5 mg chol.

Date Flan with Almond Brittle

This recipe won Best Dessert in a contest we held to celebrate the flavors of the West. The creation of Connie Deady, of Santa Monica, California, the flan was creamy and perfect every time we made it and ingenious in its double use of caramel sauce.

recipe pictured on page **688**

MAKES 1 flan (8 in.); 6 to 8 servings | **TIME** 1 hour, plus 6 hours to chill

1¾ cups sugar, divided
⅓ cup sliced almonds
2 cups heavy whipping cream
1 vanilla bean, split lengthwise
3 eggs plus 2 egg yolks
Pinch salt
⅓ cup pitted Medjool dates, coarsely chopped

1. Butter a baking sheet. In a medium saucepan over medium-high heat, add 1¼ cups sugar to 3 tbsp. water and cook, without stirring, until sugar begins to melt. Cook, swirling pan, until syrup turns dark amber, 10 to 13 minutes.
2. Remove from heat and pour one-third of caramel into a 2-qt. custard mold, tipping mold so caramel covers bottom. Pour almonds into remaining caramel, quickly stir to mix, and pour almond caramel onto baking sheet. Once brittle has hardened, break it into shards and set aside in a cool, dry place.
3. Preheat oven to 325°. Bring a large pot of water to a boil and keep hot. Meanwhile, in a small saucepan, combine cream and vanilla bean and bring to a simmer, stirring occasionally (do not let boil).
4. In a large bowl, whisk together whole eggs, egg yolks, remaining ½ cup sugar, and salt. Remove vanilla bean from cream, scraping any remaining seeds into cream, and slowly pour cream into egg mixture, whisking constantly. Pour egg mixture into a blender, add dates, and purée.
5. Pour date custard mixture into caramel-coated mold. Set mold in a baking dish with sides at least 2½ in. high and pour hot water (from step 3) into baking dish until it comes halfway up sides of mold. Bake custard in water bath until custard is set and barely jiggles in center, about 40 minutes.
6. Remove pans from oven. Let custard cool in water bath. Remove, cover with plastic wrap, and refrigerate at least 6 hours.
7. Run a thin knife around edge of mold, put a serving plate on top, and invert it. Top custard with almond brittle or serve with brittle on side.
Make Ahead: Brittle, up to 3 days, stored airtight at room temperature. Flan, up to 2 days, chilled.

PER SERVING: 466 cal., 54% (252 cal.) from fat; 5.2 g protein; 28 g fat (15 g sat.); 52 g carbo (0.7 g fiber); 74 mg sodium; 215 mg chol.

Hot Dates

Dates are an incredibly ancient fruit—at least 50 million years old, according to fossil records. They're full of fiber, potassium, and minerals and have nourished humans for some 6,000 years in the Middle East. Spanish missionaries brought them to California in the late 1700s, but the U.S. date industry truly began only about a century ago, in the ferocious dry heat of California's Coachella Valley (which produces 95 percent of the U.S. crop) and in parts of southwestern Arizona.

An Astonishing Bounty
The fruit grows on huge clusters of branches that dangle down like fat brown earrings from each tree. Some clusters weigh close to 100 pounds, and nurturing them is an elaborate process that involves hacking off gigantic, tire-piercing thorns early in the season; shrouding the clusters in bags to protect them from rain, dust, birds, and insects; and then, if the tree is tall, hand-picking them while balancing on a mobile steel tower.

Roughly a dozen different varieties grow in date country. Most are picked when fully ripe (the *tamar* stage, in date lingo). However, at California and Arizona farmers' markets and some Middle Eastern markets, you can try two other stages of ripeness too: the just-ripe, crunchy, and faintly astringent *khalal*-stage dates, often sold still on the branch; and the tender, moist, lusciously caramelly *rutab* stage, when the dates are almost but not completely ripe.

Pick Your Date
These are some of our favorite varieties from American date country. To order by mail, try Oasis Date Gardens (*oasisdate.com*) or Flying Disc Ranch (*flyingdiscranch.com*), both in California's Coachella Valley.
• **BARHI.** Small, round, plump, and meltingly soft (especially in the rutab stage). Tastes of caramel and honey, sometimes with a brandy finish.
• **DAYRI (OR DHERRI).** Slender and extremely dark, with rich molasses flavor.
• **KHALASA.** Small, medium-brown, chewy-soft date with notes of cinnamon and cloves.
• **MEDJOOL.** The biggest of all dates (up to 3 in. long), with finely wrinkled, delicate skin and chewy-tender, dense fruit.

Sticky Toffee Pudding

Dates are the key ingredient in this moist, rich, cakelike dessert. Although the recipe probably originated in Britain, it shot to stardom in Australia and New Zealand. It's a spectacular use for luscious California and Arizona Medjools.

MAKES 1 loaf cake (8 to 10 servings) and about 2 cups sauce | **TIME** 2¼ hours, plus 2 hours to cool

SAUCE

6 tbsp. unsalted butter
1½ cups heavy whipping cream
¾ cup firmly packed dark brown sugar
3 tbsp. molasses (not blackstrap)
¾ tsp. vanilla extract
Pinch salt
CAKE
3 tsp. baking soda, divided
10 oz. Medjool dates (15 to 25 dates), halved, pitted, and coarsely chopped *(see Hot Dates, opposite page)*
1½ cups unbleached flour
¼ tsp. salt
¾ cup walnut halves (about 30), toasted *(see How to Toast Nuts, page 134)*
5 tbsp. softened unsalted butter, cut into chunks
1 cup firmly packed dark brown sugar
2 eggs, lightly beaten
1 tbsp. vanilla extract
1 tbsp. espresso granules dissolved in 1 tbsp. warm water

1. To make sauce, melt butter in a medium saucepan over medium-low heat. Add cream, brown sugar, and molasses and bring to a boil. Turn heat down to a low boil and cook, stirring occasionally, 5 minutes. Stir in vanilla and salt.
2. Preheat oven to 350°. Combine 1 tsp. baking soda with 1¼ cups water in a small saucepan and bring to a boil. Put dates in a heatproof bowl and pour baking-soda water over them. Stir and let cool.
3. Sift flour with remaining 2 tsp. baking soda and salt; set aside. Butter bottom of a 9- by 5-in. loaf pan and line bottom with parchment paper cut to fit, smoothing out any wrinkles with your fingers. Butter and flour sides of pan and parchment. Cover bottom with a layer of walnuts, rounded sides down, and pour ½ cup of sauce over nuts.
4. Meanwhile, in a stand mixer with the paddle attachment, blend butter and brown sugar on medium speed until thoroughly combined, 3 to 4 minutes. On medium-low speed, beat in eggs, vanilla, and espresso. On low speed, gradually beat in flour mixture. Stir in date mixture.

5. Pour batter over sauce and walnuts in pan. Bake cake just until no longer jiggly, 50 to 60 minutes. (It will look very dark when done.) Let cool 1 hour in pan on a rack, then invert onto a rimmed platter. Let cool completely.
6. Slice cake thickly (to get around most of walnuts) and serve at room temperature with remaining sauce.

PER SERVING WITH 2 TBSP. SAUCE: 620 cal., 47% (290 cal.) from fat; 5.8 g protein; 33 g fat (17 g sat.); 80 g carbo (2.9 g fiber); 494 mg sodium; 126 mg chol.

Rangpur Lime Soufflés

Resembling a small orange, the Rangpur lime is fruity and deliciously sour, like a mix of tangerine and lime. In this soufflé it produces ethereal, citrus-flavored clouds. The recipe is from Cal Stamenov, chef of Marinus restaurant at Bernardus Lodge in Carmel Valley, California.

SERVES 6 | **TIME** 40 minutes

¼ cup *each* **butter and flour**
1 cup half-and-half
⅔ cup sugar, divided
Finely shredded zest of 4 Rangpur limes or 2 large tangerines
6 tbsp. fresh Rangpur lime juice *(see Quick Tip below)*; **or ¼ cup fresh lime juice plus 2 tbsp. fresh tangerine juice**
6 eggs, separated
¼ tsp. cream of tartar

1. Preheat oven to 375°. Butter six ramekins (1¼- to 1½-cup). Set in a rimmed baking pan.
2. Melt butter in a medium saucepan over medium-high heat. Whisk in flour, then half-and-half and ⅓ cup sugar. Cook, whisking, until mixture boils; boil 30 seconds more. Remove from heat and whisk in zest and juice until smooth. Whisk in egg yolks.
3. In a large bowl, with a mixer on high speed, beat egg whites until frothy. Add cream of tartar and beat until soft peaks form. Gradually add remaining ⅓ cup sugar, beating until whites hold straight peaks when beaters are lifted.
4. Fold one-quarter of whites into yolk mixture, then fold all of yolk mixture into rest of whites. Spoon into ramekins (they'll be nearly full).
5. Bake until soufflés no longer jiggle when gently shaken, 15 to 18 minutes. Serve immediately.
Quick Tip: Find Rangpur limes at specialty-foods markets mainly in winter.

PER SERVING: 321 cal., 53% (171 cal.) from fat; 8.2 g protein; 19 g fat (10 g sat.); 31 g carbo (0.6 g fiber); 185 mg sodium; 252 mg chol.

Cran-Tangerine Layered Gelatin

This parfait is a stunner: ruby red cranberry gelatin on the bottom, chunky tangerine segments in the center, and a topping of tangerine gelatin made creamy with the addition of a little yogurt.

SERVES 8 | **TIME** 1¾ hours, plus about 1 hour to chill

1½ tsp. plus 1 envelope unflavored gelatin, divided
1 cup unsweetened cranberry juice, chilled
⅓ cup plus ½ cup sugar
1 tbsp. finely shredded tangerine zest
1 cup fresh tangerine juice (from about 4 tangerines)
Peeled segments from 5 tangerines, divided
½ cup nonfat plain yogurt

1. In a small saucepan, sprinkle 1½ tsp. gelatin over cranberry juice. Let stand until softened, about 5 minutes. Stir in ⅓ cup sugar and cook over medium-high heat until steaming, 3 to 5 minutes. Evenly divide mixture among eight heatproof glasses. Let cool 15 minutes, then chill until firmed slightly, about 70 minutes.
2. Meanwhile, in a small saucepan, sprinkle remaining 1 envelope gelatin over ¾ cup water. Let stand until softened, about 5 minutes. Stir in remaining ½ cup sugar and cook over medium-high heat until steaming, 3 to 5 minutes. Chill mixture until cool but still liquid, about 30 minutes, then whisk in tangerine zest and juice. Divide between two bowls.
3. Chop segments from 4 tangerines, drain, and stir into one bowl of tangerine gelatin. Spoon it gently and evenly over firmed cranberry layer in glasses and chill.
4. When tangerine-segment gelatin firms slightly, about 15 minutes, whisk yogurt into remaining tangerine gelatin (if it has firmed up, microwave until liquid but not hot). Spoon yogurt gelatin into glasses. Chill until firm, about 20 minutes. Garnish with remaining tangerine segments.
Make Ahead: Up to 1 day, chilled.

PER SERVING: 157 cal., 1.5% (2.4 cal.) from fat; 4.7 g protein; 0.3 g fat (0 g sat.); 36 g carbo (1.1 g fiber); 18 mg sodium; 0.3 mg chol.

Yogurt Honey Jelly with Strawberries and Roses

Bay Area cookbook author Niloufer Ichaporia got her inspiration for this dessert from a *Sunset* recipe from 1975 called Russian Cream, in which sour and whipped creams were sweetened, folded together, and set with gelatin, and a recipe called Athenian Jelly from English food writer Josceline Dimbleby. We used a 6-in. cake pan for the mold, but use anything from a metal mixing bowl to a fancy multifaceted pudding bowl. Or pour the yogurt into small bowls to make individual servings.

SERVES 6 | **TIME** 20 minutes, plus 1 hour to chill

1 envelope unflavored gelatin
½ cup heavy whipping cream
½ tsp. vanilla extract
¼ cup honey, or to taste
Pinch salt
1½ cups plain Greek yogurt
1 cup hulled strawberries, sliced lengthwise
1 tbsp. sugar
½ tsp. rose water (optional; *see Quick Tips below*)
¼ cup rose petals (*see Quick Tips below*)

1. Put gelatin and ½ cup water in a small saucepan and let soften for a few minutes. Meanwhile, pour cream and vanilla in a medium bowl; with a mixer on medium-high speed, whip cream into soft peaks.
2. Heat gelatin mixture over low heat until gelatin dissolves. Stir in honey and salt; remove from heat.
3. Whisk yogurt in a medium bowl. Whisk some yogurt into gelatin-honey mixture; whisk that mixture into rest of yogurt. Fold whipped cream into yogurt mixture and pour into a 6-in. cake pan. Cover with plastic wrap and chill until set, at least 1 hour.
4. Combine strawberries, sugar, and rose water in a small bowl and mix gently. (If you'd like a bit of syrup, let mixture stand for 20 to 30 minutes before serving.)
5. To unmold, dip bottom of cake pan in a large bowl of hot water for a minute or so. Remove from water and set a serving plate face down on top. Holding plate in place, quickly invert cake pan to release jelly (tap pan if necessary). Top with strawberries and rose petals.
Quick Tips: Find rose water in Middle Eastern markets and well-stocked supermarkets, and look for Middle Eastern, French, and Italian brands—which have better flavor—over Indian ones. Rose petals are edible if they're pesticide-free; pluck from your garden if you haven't sprayed, or find at your farmers' market.

PER SERVING: 207 cal., 57% (117 cal.) from fat; 5.7 g protein; 13 g fat (9.2 g sat.); 18 g carbo (0.7 g fiber); 51 mg sodium; 37 mg chol.

Chocolate *Liliko'i* Parfaits

Liliko'i (as the Hawaiians call passion fruit) is extremely tart. It tastes wonderful with brownies—decadent but surprisingly refreshing. You can buy the brownies and chocolate sauce or use your own favorite recipes; a 9- by 13-in. pan made from a boxed brownie mix would give you enough.

SERVES 12 | **TIME** 1 hour, plus 1½ hours to chill

¾ cup *each* passion fruit purée *(see Quick Tip below)* and butter
1 cup sugar
12 egg yolks
1½ cups whipping cream
2 lbs. brownies (store-bought or homemade; for a recipe, make brownies for Triple Cherry Chocolate Brownie Sundaes, *page 700*), cut into about 60 cubes (¾-in)
Hot fudge sauce (store-bought or homemade; for a recipe, see page *701*)

1. In a heavy-bottomed medium saucepan, heat passion fruit purée and butter over medium heat, stirring occasionally, until simmering. In a large bowl, whisk sugar and egg yolks together to form a paste. Slowly add hot liquid, whisking constantly, until combined. Pour mixture into pan and cook, whisking constantly, until it just reaches a simmer around edges, about 4 minutes. Transfer to a glass or ceramic bowl, cover with a piece of plastic wrap pressed against the curd's surface to prevent a skin from forming, and chill until cold and firm, about 1½ hours.
2. In another large bowl, with a mixer, whisk cream until soft peaks form. Whisk in one-third of cold curd; then, using a rubber spatula, fold in remaining curd. Put three or four brownie chunks in bottom of an 8-oz. juice glass or other, similar-size serving dish. Top brownies with about ¼ cup passion fruit cream, another three or four brownie chunks, then another ¼ cup cream. Repeat with 11 more glasses. Chill until ready to serve.
3. Heat chocolate sauce in microwave until it is warm and easily drizzles off back of a spoon. Spoon about 1 tbsp. chocolate sauce over each parfait and serve.
Quick Tip: Find passion fruit purée in the freezer section of most well-stocked supermarkets.
Make Ahead: Through step 2, 1 day, chilled.

PER SERVING WITHOUT CHOCOLATE SAUCE: 713 cal., 54% (387 cal.) from fat; 8.4 g protein; 43 g fat (20 g sat.); 79 g carbo (1.6 g fiber); 400 mg sodium; 297 mg chol.

Beeramisu

Pieter Vanden Hogen, former chef at the Pelican Pub & Brewery in Pacific City, Oregon, used the brewery's award-winning Tsunami Stout for this compelling version of tiramisu, but you can substitute another non-hoppy stout, such as Samuel Smith's Imperial Stout.

SERVES 6 to 8 | **TIME** 20 minutes, plus 8 hours to chill

1 container (8 oz.) mascarpone cheese
¾ cup heavy whipping cream
¼ cup coffee-flavored liqueur, such as Kahlúa
1 package (7 oz.) Italian-style crunchy ladyfingers (*savoiardi*)
1½ cups Pelican Tsunami Stout beer or other non-hoppy stout
1 tbsp. unsweetened cocoa powder (not Dutch-processed), plus more for garnish

1. Line a 9- by 5-in. loaf pan with plastic wrap, leaving at least a 1-in. overhang on all sides.
2. In a large bowl, with a mixer on low speed, beat mascarpone, cream, and liqueur until mixture is thick enough to spread (do not overbeat).
3. Stand 1 ladyfinger cookie upright against a long edge of loaf pan and trim it flush with rim of pan. Use it as a guide to trim 12 more cookies, reserving trimmed ends. Soak 1 trimmed ladyfinger at a time in beer, about 1 second per side; then arrange in rows along long sides of pan, picket fence–style. Arrange 4 soaked ladyfingers lengthwise on bottom of pan.
4. Spoon half of mascarpone mixture over bottom layer of ladyfingers and smooth evenly. Top with another layer of soaked ladyfingers (using reserved trimmed ends first), then top with remaining mascarpone mixture, smoothing evenly. Sift cocoa over top of cream. Wrap beeramisu and chill at least 8 hours.
5. To serve, use plastic wrap to lift cake out of loaf pan. Unwrap and slice crosswise. Dust each slice with additional cocoa if you like.
Make Ahead: Through step 4, up to 1 day, chilled.

PER SERVING: 334 cal., 57% (189 cal.) from fat; 4.3 g protein; 21 g fat (14 g sat.); 25 g carbo (0.4 g fiber); 85 mg sodium; 58 mg chol.

Gingerbread Pear Trifle

Amy Jackson, of Vancouver, Washington, created a trifle with all the flavors of holiday season—luscious ripe pears and spicy gingerbread, made festive with dollops of fresh whipped cream and the spark of brandy and crystallized ginger.

SERVES 16 | **TIME** 1½ hours

1½ cups flour
1 tbsp. baking soda
2 tsp. cinnamon
1½ tsp. ground ginger, divided
1 tsp. ground cloves
1 tsp. salt, divided
1¼ cups granulated sugar, divided
4 eggs
½ cup *each* applesauce and molasses
1 tbsp. plus ½ tsp. grated fresh ginger
1 tbsp. vegetable oil
¼ cup butter, softened, divided
3 Bosc pears, peeled, cored, and sliced
2 tbsp. firmly packed light brown sugar
2½ cups half-and-half
3 tbsp. cornstarch
1 tsp. vanilla extract
1 cup heavy whipping cream
2 tbsp. powdered sugar
3 tbsp. brandy
¼ cup crystallized ginger, finely chopped

1. Make gingerbread: Preheat oven to 350°. Butter an 8-in. square baking pan. In a small bowl, mix flour, baking soda, cinnamon, 1 tsp. ground ginger, cloves, and ½ tsp. salt. In a large bowl, whisk ¾ cup granulated sugar with 1 egg until thick and pale. Stir in applesauce, molasses, 1 tbsp. fresh ginger, the oil, and ¼ cup hot water. Stir in flour mixture until combined. Pour into prepared pan and bake until a toothpick inserted in center comes out clean, about 35 minutes. Let rest 5 minutes; turn out onto rack and let cool. Cut into 1-in. cubes.

2. Cook pears: Melt 2 tbsp. butter in a large frying pan over medium heat. Add pears. Cook, stirring occasionally, until soft, about 7 minutes. Stir in brown sugar, ¼ tsp. salt, and remaining ½ tsp. ground ginger.

3. Make custard: In a medium pan over medium heat, whisk half-and-half, cornstarch, and remaining 3 eggs, ½ cup granulated sugar, and ¼ tsp. salt until thickened, about 10 minutes. Remove from heat; stir in vanilla and remaining 2 tbsp. butter until butter melts.

4. Whip cream: In a medium bowl, with a mixer on high speed, beat cream, powdered sugar, and remaining ½ tsp. fresh ginger until soft peaks form.

5. Assemble trifle: Put half of gingerbread cubes in a trifle dish or glass bowl. Sprinkle with half of brandy. Spoon half of pears and their liquid over gingerbread. Pour half of custard over pears. Top with half of whipped cream and half of crystallized ginger. Repeat layers.
Make Ahead: Up to 1 day, chilled.

PER SERVING: 347 cal., 39% (135 cal.) from fat; 4.4 g protein; 15 g fat (8.5 g sat.); 48 g carbo (1.3 g fiber); 461 mg sodium; 96 mg chol.

Strawberry Zinfandel Trifle

The trifle from reader Maggie Kademian, of Westlake Village, California, is a classy dessert for a spring party.

SERVES 10 to 12 | **TIME** 20 minutes, plus 3 hours to cool and chill

1½ cups dry red Zinfandel
½ cup sugar, divided
1 tsp. vanilla extract
4 cups sliced hulled strawberries
1 plain or lemon-flavored pound cake (1 lb.)
2 cups whipping cream
A few whole strawberries

1. In a 3- to 4-qt. pan over high heat, bring wine and ⅓ cup sugar to a boil. Boil until reduced to 1 cup, about 5 minutes. Remove from heat and stir in vanilla and sliced strawberries. Let cool about 1 hour, stirring occasionally.

2. Cut cake into ½-in.-thick slices, then into 1½- by 2-in. pieces.

3. In a large bowl, with a mixer on high speed, beat cream and remaining sugar until soft peaks form.

4. Arrange a third of cake in bottom of a 2½- to 3-qt. straight-sided glass dish. Spoon one-third of sliced berries and wine over top. Spread about one-third of whipped cream over berries. Repeat layers twice, ending with cream.

5. Cover trifle loosely and chill at least 2 hours.

6. Garnish with whole berries. Scoop down into layers to serve.
Make Ahead: Through step 5, up to 1 day, chilled.

PER SERVING: 315 cal., 57% (180 cal.) from fat; 3.3 g protein; 20 g fat (12 g sat.); 32 g carbo (1.8 g fiber); 166 mg sodium; 128 mg chol.

Individual Plum and Wine Trifles

A concentrated spiced-wine syrup gives this easy layered dessert so much flavor that it tastes like it cooked for hours.

SERVES 4 | **TIME** 30 minutes

1 cup *each* Cabernet Sauvignon and fresh orange juice
½ cup plus 2 tbsp. sugar
½ tsp. ground cardamom
4 firm-ripe plums (1 lb. total), pitted and sliced
1 cup heavy whipping cream
12 sugar or shortbread cookies (5½ oz. total), such as Pepperidge Farm, broken into pieces

1. In a 3- to 4-qt. pan, boil wine, orange juice, ½ cup sugar, and the cardamom, stirring often, until reduced to ⅔ cup, 10 to 15 minutes. Remove from heat, stir in plums, and let stand 10 minutes, stirring often.
2. In a bowl, with a mixer on high speed, beat cream with remaining 2 tbsp. sugar until soft peaks form.
3. With a slotted spoon, lift three or four plum slices into each of four small bowls. Top each with a piece of cookie, then a spoonful of cream. Repeat layers twice. Serve trifles with syrup and any remaining fruit.

PER SERVING: 628 cal., 47% (297 cal.) from fat; 5.6 g protein; 33 g fat (18 g sat.); 78 g carbo (3.9 g fiber); 184 mg sodium; 97 mg chol.

Almond Nougat Semifreddo (Semifreddo al Torrone)

Torrone (hard almond nougat) is an Italian candy associated with winter and Christmas. Cookbook author Rosetta Costantino, of Oakland, California, chops it and then folds it into a semifreddo—a frozen custard dessert similar to ice cream—to give tradition a delicious twist. The chocolate sauce, says Rosetta, who teaches classes in Calabrian cooking, "is the simplest sauce in the world, just cream and chocolate. But you need good chocolate." She uses Valrhona.

SERVES 12 | **TIME** 1 hour, plus 6 hours to freeze

3 eggs, separated
½ cup sugar
¾ cup hot (about 125°) milk
2 cups finely chopped or crushed (7 oz.) Italian *torrone classico* (see Quick Tip, above right), divided
2 tbsp. almond-flavored liqueur, such as amaretto
¼ cup finely chopped (1½ oz.) bittersweet chocolate
1¾ cups whipping cream, divided
4 oz. bittersweet chocolate, coarsely chopped

1. Set a bowl of ice water near stove. Put egg yolks and sugar in a large bowl. With a whisk or a mixer on medium-high speed, beat until thick and pale yellow, 1 to 2 minutes. Slowly add hot milk, whisking or beating constantly. Pour mixture into a 1- to 2-qt. saucepan and cook over medium heat, stirring constantly, until it's thick enough to coat a metal spoon and reaches about 165° on an instant-read thermometer, 4 to 5 minutes. Do not let custard boil or it will curdle. Remove from heat and set pan in bowl of ice water; stir often until cold. Stir in 1 cup torrone and the liqueur.
2. Line a 9- by 5-in. loaf pan with a single sheet of plastic wrap, leaving a generous overhang on all sides. Sprinkle bottom first with remaining 1 cup torrone, then with the finely chopped chocolate, spreading them evenly.
3. In a medium bowl with clean beaters or a whisk, whip egg whites to stiff peaks. In another medium bowl, whip 1¼ cups cream to firm peaks.
4. Pour custard over egg whites and fold in gently. Fold in whipped cream until no white streaks remain. Pour mixture into loaf pan. Cover with overhanging plastic wrap. Freeze semifreddo until firm, at least 6 hours.
5. Make chocolate sauce: In a small saucepan, bring remaining ½ cup cream to a simmer. Put coarsely chopped chocolate in a small bowl and pour hot cream over it. Let stand until chocolate is softened, about 3 minutes, then whisk until smooth.
6. Remove plastic wrap covering loaf pan. Put a platter upside down over pan. Invert and remove pan and wrap. If you want to remove wrinkle marks, smooth them over using a thin metal spatula. Cut semifreddo into ½-in.-thick slices and place on dessert plates. Spoon chocolate sauce over and around the semifreddo. Serve immediately.

Quick Tip: Be sure to buy *torrone classico*, which is brittle, and not soft *torrone morbido*; the classico is available at Italian markets, some well-stocked supermarkets, and online.
Make Ahead: Semifreddo, up to 1 week, wrapped well and frozen; chocolate sauce, up to 2 days, chilled (warm up a little before serving if you'd like it to be thin).

PER SERVING, WITH 1 TBSP. SAUCE: 330 cal., 60% (198 cal.) from fat; 5.6 g protein; 22 g fat (12 g sat.); 26 g carbo (1.3 g fiber); 43 mg sodium; 104 mg chol.

Blueberry-Lemon Sour Cream Ice Cream

There are two main types of American ice cream: custard (aka French-style) and uncooked (aka Philadelphia-style or eggless). This easy uncooked ice cream has a light texture, but it's bursting with berry flavor.

MAKES 1 qt. | **TIME** 10 minutes, plus 3 hours to freeze

2 cups blueberries
1½ cups half-and-half
½ cup *each* **sugar and sour cream**
1 tbsp. *each* **finely shredded lemon zest and fresh lemon juice**
½ tsp. salt

1. In a blender, purée blueberries and half-and-half. Add sugar, sour cream, lemon zest and juice, and salt. Process until combined.
2. Pour mixture through a fine-mesh strainer into an ice cream maker (at least 1-qt. capacity). Freeze according to manufacturer's directions until mixture is firm enough to scoop.
3. Serve softly frozen or freeze in an airtight container until firm enough to scoop, at least 3 hours.
Quick Tip: As with all non-custard ice creams, this mixture freezes solid after a day in the freezer. Let it soften for 10 minutes at room temperature before serving.
Make Ahead: Up to 2 weeks, frozen airtight (although it's best when fresh).

PER ½-CUP SERVING: 159 cal., 47% (75 cal.) from fat; 2 g protein; 8.3 g fat (5.1 g sat.); 20 g carbo (0.9 g fiber); 174 mg sodium; 23 mg chol.

Easy Dreamy Peachy Ice Cream

San Joaquin Valley organic farmer Shelby Mayfield makes an ultra-refreshing plain vanilla ice cream and serves slices of his ripe California peaches on the side. We added the fruit right in and loved the results. You can substitute all kinds of mashed ripe fruits—such as berries or plums—for the peaches.

MAKES About 1 qt. | **TIME** 30 minutes, plus 2 hours to freeze

2 cups half-and-half
1 can (14 oz.) sweetened condensed milk
1 cup heavy whipping cream
1 tsp. vanilla extract
1 cup mashed, peeled very ripe peaches

1. In a large bowl, stir together half-and-half, condensed milk, cream, and vanilla.
2. Pour mixture into an ice cream maker (at least 1-qt. capacity). Freeze according to manufacturer's instructions. When mixture starts to look frozen, add peaches. Continue churning until it has a soft-serve consistency.
3. Transfer to an airtight container and freeze until firm enough to scoop, about 2 hours.
Make Ahead: Up to 2 weeks, frozen airtight (although it's best when fresh).

PER ½-CUP SERVING: 351 cal., 56% (198 cal.) from fat; 6.4 g protein; 22 g fat (14 g sat.); 33 g carbo (0.3 g fiber); 99 mg sodium; 80 mg chol.

Fresh Fig Ice Cream

When fat, juicy brown figs come into season at the end of summer, we love to put them in this ice cream, contributed in 1978 from a reader identified only as L.C. Curiously, the ice cream's flavor deepens if it's allowed to sit in the freezer for at least a day.

MAKES About 6 cups | **TIME** 25 minutes, plus 1½ hours to freeze

1 lb. (about 8 large) fully ripe figs
2 tbsp. fresh lemon juice
¾ to 1 cup sugar, divided
⅛ tsp. salt
1 tsp. vanilla extract
2 eggs *(see Quick Tip below)*
2 cups half-and-half

1. Cut stems and blossom ends off figs. Coarsely chop; you should have about 2 cups. In a blender, blend figs in two batches with lemon juice, ¼ cup sugar, the salt, and vanilla.
2. In a large bowl with a mixer on medium speed, beat eggs with remaining ½ cup sugar until thick and lemon colored. With mixer on low speed, gradually beat in half-and-half. Stir in fig mixture; taste, then add more sugar if you like.
3. Pour mixture into a 1½-qt. ice cream maker. Freeze according to manufacturer's directions until softly frozen.
Quick Tip: If you're concerned about eating raw eggs, use pasteurized eggs in lieu of fresh.
Make Ahead: Up to 2 weeks, frozen airtight (although it's best in the first few days).

PER ½-CUP SERVING: 151 cal., 33% (49 cal.) from fat; 2.4 g protein; 5.4 g fat (3 g sat.); 24 g carbo (1 g fiber); 53 mg sodium; 51 mg chol.

puddings, trifles & frozen delights

Lavender-Blueberry Ice Cream

A trip to a lavender farm inspired reader Jan Sousa, of Mt. Shasta, California, to infuse blueberry syrup with lavender flowers and turn the syrup into ice cream. For an elegant dessert, she spoons it into wineglasses, garnishes it with lavender blossoms, and sets lemon cookies on the side.

MAKES About 5 cups | **TIME** 30 minutes, plus 25 minutes to freeze

1 cup blueberries
¾ cup sugar
2 tbsp. dried culinary lavender blossoms
½ tsp. *each* cinnamon and vanilla extract
3 cups half-and-half

1. In a 1- to 1½-qt. pan over medium-high heat, cook blueberries, sugar, and ½ cup water, stirring, until berries begin to pop, 4 to 5 minutes. Pour mixture through a fine-mesh strainer set over a bowl. Put blueberries into a blender. Return berry syrup to pan.
2. Add lavender to syrup and stir over medium heat until syrup is infused with flavor, about 5 minutes. Strain into blender, pressing to extract liquid. Discard lavender.
3. Add cinnamon and vanilla to blender; purée. Pour into a bowl, nest in a larger bowl of ice water, and stir often until cold, about 15 minutes. Stir in half-and-half.
4. Pour chilled mixture into an ice cream maker (at least 1½-qt. capacity). Freeze according to manufacturer's directions until firm enough to scoop.
Make Ahead: Up to 2 weeks, frozen airtight (although it's best when fresh).

PER ½-CUP SERVING: 161 cal., 47% (75 cal.) from fat; 2.2 g protein; 8.3 g fat (5.2 g sat.); 20 g carbo (0.3 g fiber); 31 mg sodium; 27 mg chol.

Salted Caramel Peanut Butter Ice Cream

This ice cream contains no eggs. Instead, it relies on peanut butter to supply the rich creaminess that egg yolks would give. Using jarred caramel sauce makes the salted caramel swirl a snap. If you want an extra-peanutty ice cream, add ¼ cup chopped toasted peanuts in step 2. (*See page 699* to incorporate the ice cream into Peanut Butter Chocolate Ice Cream Sandwiches.)

MAKES 1 qt. | **TIME** 30 minutes, plus 8 hours to freeze

½ cup good-quality jarred caramel sauce
½ tsp. salt
¾ cup *each* crunchy peanut butter, at room temperature, and sugar
1¼ cups whipping cream
1 cup milk
1½ tsp. vanilla extract

1. In a small saucepan or microwave-safe container, heat caramel sauce until warm but not boiling, about 1 minute over medium heat or 20 seconds in microwave. Add salt and stir to combine. Set aside.
2. In a medium bowl, whisk together peanut butter, sugar, cream, milk, and vanilla until peanut butter is mostly dissolved. Let stand until sugar has dissolved, about 5 minutes, then whisk again.
3. Pour mixture into an ice cream maker (1-qt. capacity). Freeze according to manufacturer's directions. Add salted caramel for last 10 seconds of churning.
4. Transfer to an airtight, freezer-safe container and freeze at least 8 hours and up to 24, depending on how firm you would like the ice cream to be.
Make Ahead: Up to 2 weeks, frozen airtight (although it's best when fresh).

PER ¼-CUP SERVING: 215 cal., 59% (126 cal.) from fat; 4 g protein; 14 g fat (5.9 g sat.); 21 g carbo (0.8 g fiber); 163 mg sodium; 28 mg chol.

Mexican Chocolate Ice Cream

When Jen Castle and Blake Spalding opened Hell's Backbone Grill, in Boulder, Utah, in 2000, they found the town to be wary of them—especially since they are Buddhists, and Boulder is a traditional Mormon farming community. To warm things up, Castle and Spalding threw an ice cream social, with this recipe as part of the draw. Practically the entire town showed up, and the event has been an annual tradition ever since. For an over-the-top double-chocolate experience, serve this with hot fudge sauce and piñon brittle (recipes follow).

recipe
pictured
on page
682

MAKES 1½ qts. | **TIME** 1 hour, plus 6 hours to chill and freeze

½ **vanilla bean**
2 cups *each* **heavy whipping cream and whole milk**
9 oz. **Mexican chocolate (such as Ibarra; *see Quick Tip, above right*), coarsely chopped**
2 oz. **unsweetened chocolate, coarsely chopped**
2 **cinnamon sticks**
5 **egg yolks**
½ cup **sugar**
¼ tsp. **salt**

1. Split vanilla bean lengthwise and scrape out seeds. In a 4-qt. saucepan over medium heat, bring cream, milk, Mexican chocolate, unsweetened chocolate, cinnamon sticks, and vanilla seeds and pod to a simmer. Remove cream mixture from heat and let steep 20 minutes.
2. Meanwhile, in a medium bowl, with a mixer on medium-high speed, whisk egg yolks, sugar, and salt until mixture is thick and pale yellow, 2 to 3 minutes.
3. Return cream mixture to medium heat and bring just to a simmer. Remove from heat and pour through a fine-mesh strainer into a clean bowl; discard cinnamon sticks and vanilla pod. With mixer running on medium speed, pour ½ cup cream mixture into egg mixture. Slowly drizzle in remaining cream mixture, continuing to mix as you go.
4. Pour this custard into saucepan. Return to stove and cook over low to medium-low heat, stirring with a wooden spoon, until custard thickens a bit and reaches 170° on an instant-read thermometer.
5. Pour custard into a bowl and set in a larger bowl of ice water. Let cool 10 minutes, stirring occasionally. Cover with plastic wrap and chill for at least 1 hour and up to 1 day.

6. Freeze custard in an ice cream maker (2-qt. capacity) according to manufacturer's instructions. Transfer to an airtight plastic container and freeze until hardened, at least 5 hours.
Quick Tip: Mexican chocolate, usually described on the package as "Mexican chocolate drink mix," is a spiced chocolate bar that's commonly melted for hot chocolate. It gives the ice cream a pudding-like texture. Look for it (sold in boxes of 5 or 6 disk-shaped bars) at Latino markets or in the Latino-foods aisle of large supermarkets.
Make Ahead: Up to 2 weeks, frozen airtight (although it's best when fresh).

PER ½-CUP SERVING: 346 cal., 62% (216 cal.) from fat; 3.8 g protein; 24 g fat (13 g sat.); 30 g carbo (0.7 g fiber); 86 mg sodium; 149 mg chol.

Hot Fudge Piñon Sauce
The ground pine nuts lend a buttery flavor and pleasing texture.

MAKES 4 cups | **TIME** 35 minutes

1½ cups **shelled piñon or pine nuts (*see Quick Tip below*)**
½ cup **sugar**
¼ cup **unsweetened cocoa powder (not Dutch-processed)**
¼ tsp. **salt**
1¼ cups **heavy whipping cream**
1 cup **light corn syrup**
1 tbsp. **distilled white vinegar**
⅓ cup **semisweet chocolate chips**
2 oz. **unsweetened chocolate, coarsely chopped**
¼ cup **butter**
1 tbsp. **vanilla extract**

1. Pulse nuts in a food processor until coarsely ground (like the texture of couscous).
2. Sift sugar, cocoa, and salt into a medium saucepan. Add ¾ cup warm water and stir to combine. Bring to a simmer over medium heat, stirring until smooth.
3. Add cream, corn syrup, vinegar, and chocolate chips. Raise heat to medium-high and boil, swirling occasionally, until slightly reduced (mixture will be thin and sticky), 8 to 10 minutes; remove from heat. Stir in unsweetened chocolate, butter, vanilla, and pine nuts. Serve warm.
Quick Tip: Piñon nuts, grown in the Southwest's high desert, are the intensely flavored cousins of the more common Italian pine nut. Either variety works well here.
Make Ahead: Up to 1 week ahead, chilled. Gently rewarm over medium-low heat.

PER 2-TBSP. SERVING: 142 cal., 61% (86 cal.) from fat; 2 g protein; 9.6 g fat (4.4 g sat.); 14 g carbo (0.8 g fiber); 50 mg sodium; 17 mg chol.

puddings, trifles & frozen delights

Spiced Piñon Brittle

This crunchy topping gets a delicately spicy flavor from chili powder and cloves. Though the recipe isn't difficult, it does require vigilance. When cooking the sugar, be sure to stir constantly—it can burn easily.

MAKES 3 cups | **TIME** 30 minutes

¾ **cup shelled piñon or pine nuts** (*see Quick Tip for Hot Fudge Piñon Sauce, below left*)
1½ **cups sugar**
1 **tsp. chili powder**
½ **tsp.** *each* **ground cloves and salt**

1. Line a baking sheet with parchment paper and grease paper well.
2. In a small frying pan over low heat, toast nuts until light golden brown, 7 to 10 minutes.
3. In a nonstick frying pan over medium heat, combine sugar, chili powder, cloves, and salt. Cook, stirring constantly, until mixture is smooth and dark brown. If it darkens too quickly, remove from heat, stir well, then return to heat. When sugar has entirely melted, stir in nuts.
4. Quickly pour mixture onto parchment and spread ⅛ to ¼ in. thick. Let cool until hard, then break into pieces.
Make Ahead: Up to 2 weeks; store airtight at room temperature.

PER ¼-CUP SERVING: 147 cal., 28% (41 cal.) from fat; 2.1 g protein; 4.5 g fat (0.7 g sat.); 26 g carbo (0.5 g fiber); 99 mg sodium; 0 mg chol.

Coconut-Avocado Ice Cream

Silky smooth and luscious, this unusual ice cream is surprisingly good with chocolate sauce.

MAKES 1 qt. | **TIME** 40 minutes, plus 2 hours to freeze

2 **firm-ripe medium Hass avocados (about 1 lb. total), chilled**
¼ **cup sugar**
1½ **tbsp. fresh lemon juice**
1 **can (14 oz.) sweetened condensed milk**
1 **can (13.5 oz.) coconut milk** (*see Quick Tip, above right*)**, chilled**

1. Pit avocados. Scoop flesh into a food processor, add sugar and lemon juice, and purée. Add condensed milk and coconut milk and blend.
2. Pour mixture into an ice cream maker (at least 1 qt. capacity). Freeze according to manufacturer's instructions. Freeze a large bowl.
3. Scrape ice cream into cold bowl. Cover and freeze until firm enough to scoop, about 2 hours.

Quick Tip: For a delicate flavor, use coconut milk. For a bigger coconut hit, buy one made with coconut extract.
Make Ahead: Up to 2 weeks, frozen airtight (although it's best when fresh).

PER ½-CUP SERVING: 354 cal., 56% (198 cal.) from fat; 5.8 g protein; 22 g fat (13 g sat.); 38 g carbo (1.2 g fiber); 74 mg sodium; 17 mg chol.

Peanut Butter Chocolate Ice Cream Sandwiches

These soft, yielding cookies are the perfect foil for rich, gooey peanut butter ice cream.

recipe pictured on page 677

MAKES 8 ice cream sandwiches
TIME 40 minutes, plus 10 minutes to chill

6 **tbsp. butter, softened**
½ **cup firmly packed light brown sugar**
⅓ **cup granulated sugar**
1 **egg**
1 **tsp. vanilla extract**
1¼ **cups flour**
⅓ **cup unsweetened cocoa powder (not Dutch-processed)**
¾ **tsp. baking powder**
¼ **tsp.** *each* **baking soda and salt**
Vegetable oil for your hands
2 **cups (½ batch) Salted Caramel Peanut Butter Ice Cream** (*page 697*)**, softened slightly**

1. Preheat oven to 350°. Line two rimmed baking sheets with parchment paper. In a medium bowl, with a mixer on high speed, beat butter and sugars together until light and fluffy, about 2 minutes. Add egg and vanilla and beat until combined.
2. In another bowl, sift together flour, cocoa, baking powder and soda, and salt. With mixer on medium speed, add dry ingredients to butter mixture in two batches, beating 15 to 20 seconds after each batch to incorporate and scraping down side of bowl as needed.
3. Lightly oil your hands and use them to knead dough for 2 minutes. Then roll dough into 16 walnut-size balls. Evenly space balls on baking sheets and, using your palms, press each ball into a 2-in. disk.
4. Bake cookies until they have spread out and are cooked but still soft, about 10 minutes. Cool slightly, then transfer to a rack to cool completely.
5. To make ice cream sandwiches, spoon ¼ cup ice cream onto flat side of 8 cookies. Top with remaining cookies, flat side down, pressing lightly. Chill sandwiches in freezer about 10 minutes, just long enough to chill ice cream but not enough to harden cookies.

PER SANDWICH: 450 cal., 48% (216 cal.) from fat; 7.2 g protein; 24 g fat (12 g sat.); 57 g carbo (2.3 g fiber); 422 mg sodium; 78 mg chol.

Fresh Pineapple Sundaes

Here's a sweet ending to a dinner party—a sundae that comes together in minutes.

MAKES 10 sundaes | **TIME** 20 minutes

3 lbs. cored, peeled fresh pineapple
1½ cups dulce de leche *(see Quick Tips below)* or other caramel sauce
1⅓ cups sweetened shredded dried coconut
2½ qts. vanilla ice cream, scooped into balls *(see Quick Tips below)*

Cut pineapple into bite-size chunks. Layer pineapple, caramel sauce, coconut, and ice cream balls in 10 bowls.

Quick Tips: Find dulce de leche, the thick, caramel-like sauce of reduced sweetened cow's or goat's milk, in cans or jars at Latino markets or well-stocked supermarkets. It's often sold under its Mexican name, *cajeta*. Scoop balls of ice cream onto a baking sheet and freeze for easy serving.

PER SUNDAE: 503 cal., 32% (162 cal.) from fat; 6.2 g protein; 18 g fat (12 g sat.); 85 g carbo (2.3 g fiber); 304 mg sodium; 58 mg chol.

The Passing of the Western Pineapple?

Pineapples are synonymous with Hawaii, the only state in America with a climate lush enough to grow this tropical fruit. At one time, Hawaii grew almost 80 percent of the world's pineapples. Today, because of higher costs in growing, producing, and packing, Hawaii grows only about 2 percent of the pineapples sold; Thailand and the Philippines have become the world leaders.

However, all is not glum on the Hawaiian pineapple front, thanks to the rise of specialty varieties like Maui Gold, developed by the Maui Pineapple Co., and the Smooth Cayenne, both sweeter than the Red Spanish type grown in Central and South America. You can spot a Hawaiian pineapple by its large size, conical shape, smooth-edged leaves, and deep yellow flesh.

Triple Cherry Chocolate Brownie Sundaes

We couldn't get enough of these sundaes. Every layer has a sweet, tart cherry flavor and decadent chocolatiness. (The brownies are great on their own too, and work well for picnics.) The sundaes are especially good when made with cherry chocolate-chip ice cream.

SERVES 8 to 10 | **TIME** 1 hour for brownies, 2½ hours to cool, 10 minutes to assemble

1 lb. fresh Bing cherries, pitted and quartered
1 tbsp. plus 2 cups sugar
1 cup butter
8 oz. good-quality bittersweet chocolate, broken into large chunks
5 eggs
1 tbsp. vanilla extract
¼ tsp. salt
1⅓ cups flour
⅔ cup dried Bing cherries or any other dried cherry
1 cup semisweet chocolate chips
1 gal. cherry ice cream
1 cup Hot Fudge Sauce *(recipe follows)*

1. In a medium bowl, toss fresh cherries with 1 tbsp. sugar and set aside in refrigerator.
2. Preheat oven to 350°. Butter a 9- by 13-in. pan. In a medium saucepan, melt butter and bittersweet chocolate over very low heat, stirring constantly with a heatproof rubber spatula, until just melted. Do not let simmer. Remove from heat and let cool slightly, about 5 minutes.
3. In a large bowl, whisk together eggs, remaining 2 cups sugar, the vanilla, and salt. Slowly pour chocolate-butter mixture into egg mixture, whisking constantly. With spatula, thoroughly but gently fold in flour. Add dried cherries and chocolate chips and stir just until combined.
4. Spread batter evenly into prepared baking pan and bake until brownies are firm, beginning to pull away from sides of pan, and a toothpick inserted near center of pan (2 in. from edge) emerges with only a few crumbs clinging to it (try to avoid inserting it into a chocolate chip), 35 to 40 minutes.
5. Let brownies cool completely, then cut into 24 to 30 (1-in.) chunks (you will have about a half-pan of brownies left over).
6. Put 3 brownie chunks in each of 8 to 10 sundae dishes or shallow bowls, add a generous scoop of ice cream to each, and top with fudge sauce and fresh cherries.

PER SERVING: 705 cal., 47% (333 cal.) from fat; 8.9 g protein; 37 g fat (16 g sat.); 94 g carbo (2 g fiber); 232 mg sodium; 134 mg chol.

PER 3-IN. BROWNIE: 372 cal., 47% (174 cal.) from fat; 4.3 g protein; 19 g fat (11 g sat.); 50 g carbo (1.4 g fiber); 159 mg sodium; 87 mg chol.

Hot Fudge Sauce

Glossy and smooth, this uncomplicated sauce takes no time to whip up. You'll have extra for making more sundaes later, or even chocolate milk.

MAKES About 2 cups | **TIME** 10 minutes

1 cup heavy whipping cream
⅓ cup light corn syrup
8 oz. bittersweet chocolate, roughly chopped

1. Put cream and corn syrup in a small saucepan, stir, and bring to a boil over medium-high heat, stirring occasionally.
2. Remove saucepan from heat and whisk in chocolate until smooth.
Make Ahead: Up to 1 week, chilled. Reheat in small saucepan over low heat or in a glass bowl in microwave, stirring every 20 seconds.

PER 2-TBSP. SERVING: 140 cal., 67% (94 cal.) from fat; 1.3 g protein; 10 g fat (6 g sat.); 14 g carbo (0.3 g fiber); 19 mg sodium; 20 mg chol.

Cracker Jack Caramel Sundaes

No ball game would be complete without the traditional peanuts and Cracker Jack. These sundaes give you both, and they're fun to serve at a World Series party. You can use store-bought Cracker Jack or make your own with gourmet caramel corn and salty Spanish peanuts.

MAKES 8 sundaes | **TIME** 15 minutes

1¾ cups sugar, divided
1 tbsp. butter
2 cups whipping cream, divided
1 qt. vanilla ice cream
2 cups caramel corn and 1 cup salted roasted Spanish peanuts; or 3 cups Cracker Jack

1. In a medium saucepan, bring 1½ cups sugar and ¼ cup water to a boil over medium heat. Cook, without stirring, until mixture starts to turn a deep reddish brown, 6 to 8 minutes. Gently swirl pan to color evenly, remove from heat, and add butter and 1 cup whipping cream, stirring constantly (mixture will boil furiously). Let cool slightly.
2. In a medium bowl, with a mixer on medium-high speed, whisk remaining 1 cup whipping cream and ¼ cup sugar until soft peaks form.
3. Scoop about ½ cup ice cream into each serving bowl. Pour 2 tbsp. warm caramel sauce over ice cream (you will have a little extra), then top each with ¼ cup

caramel corn and 2 tbsp. peanuts. Dollop portions with whipped cream.

PER SUNDAE: 664 cal., 56% (369 cal.) from fat; 9 g protein; 41 g fat (21 g sat.); 71 g carbo (0.5 g fiber); 188 mg sodium; 115 mg chol.

Chocolate Peppermint Ice Cream Bonbons

When you dip the ice cream balls in chocolate, make sure you coat some of the skewer too, to keep the ice cream from sliding off as it melts. Experiment with other flavors of ice cream, such as coconut or chocolate, and coatings like flaked coconut or dark chocolate. You'll need 8 to 10 decorative skewers or picks.

SERVES 8 to 10 | **TIME** 40 minutes, plus 6 hours to freeze

½ cup vanilla ice cream, softened
¼ tsp. peppermint extract
8 oz. white chocolate, chopped
2 tbsp. vegetable shortening
½ cup crushed peppermint candies

1. In a small bowl, stir together ice cream and extract until blended. Freeze until firm, at least 2 hours. Meanwhile, line a baking sheet with parchment paper and freeze it also.
2. Using a large melon baller, quickly scoop the ice cream into balls and place them to one side of cold baking sheet. Freeze until firm, 1 to 1½ hours.
3. Insert a decorative skewer or pick into the center of each ice cream ball and return to the freezer to set, about 30 minutes.
4. Meanwhile, put chocolate and shortening in a small metal bowl. Set bowl in a slightly larger bowl of hot water and let stand until melted, stirring occasionally. Transfer chocolate mixture to a 1-cup glass measuring cup. Put crushed candies on a small plate.
5. Working with one ice cream ball at a time, dip into melted chocolate to coat, making sure chocolate reaches above ice cream onto skewer and letting excess chocolate drip off bottom. Roll ball in candy and set on clean side of baking sheet. Repeat with remaining balls, returning them to freezer if they start to soften. Freeze at least 2 hours before serving.
Make Ahead: Up to 1 day.

PER BONBON: 197 cal., 50% (99 cal.) from fat; 1.3 g protein; 11 g fat (5.9 g sat.); 24 g carbo (0 g fiber); 39 mg sodium; 5.6 mg chol.

Tart 'n' Tangy Fro-Yo

Why not make your own frozen yogurt when it's so easy? This is the refreshing, not-too-sweet kind of yogurt served at chains like Pinkberry and Red Mango. For a lemon variation, see *below*.

MAKES About 4¾ cups | **TIME** 25 minutes, plus 2 hours to freeze

1 container (32 oz.; about 4 cups) plain nonfat yogurt (*see Quick Tip below*)
¾ cup sugar, plus more to taste

1. In a medium bowl, whisk together yogurt and sugar until sugar dissolves. Taste and add more sugar if you like.
2. Spoon mixture into an ice cream maker (1½-qt. capacity). Freeze according to manufacturer's directions. Transfer yogurt to a freezer-safe container and freeze until firm, about 2 hours.
Quick Tip: The quality of the yogurt really matters; look for brands without unnecessary additives.
Make Ahead: Up to 1 week, frozen. Let soften at room temperature several minutes until easy to scoop, or microwave a few seconds until softened.

PER ½-CUP SERVING: 121 cal., 1% (1.8 cal.) from fat; 5.8 g protein; 0.2 g fat (0.2 g sat.); 24 g carbo (0 g fiber); 77 mg sodium; 2 mg chol.

Luscious Lemon Fro-Yo: Substitute ⅔ cup **lemon curd** (see Lemon Meringue Cake, *page 634*—make half the recipe for the curd) for sugar. Mixture will take longer to freeze until firm, about 3½ hours.

PER ½-CUP SERVING: 116 cal., 12% (14 cal.) from fat; 7 g protein; 1.5 g fat (0.2 g sat.); 22 g carbo (0 g fiber); 94 mg sodium; 2 mg chol.

Frozen Citrus Cups

Mary Canales, owner of the Berkeley ice cream shop Ici, created this meringue-topped ice cream dessert served in clementine "cups" as a refreshing end to a hearty feast. She layers homemade candied-tangerine ice cream with clementine sorbet in her cups, but we love them just as much with store-bought vanilla ice cream, as long as it is a rich, high-quality version.

SERVES 8 | **TIME** 1 hour, plus 1 hour, 20 minutes to freeze

8 clementines (*see Quick Tip below*)
Clementine Sorbet (*recipe follows*) or 1 pt. store-bought mango or lemon sorbet
1 pt. premium vanilla ice cream
4 egg whites, at room temperature
⅔ cup sugar
⅛ tsp. salt

1. Cut clementines in half crosswise and juice them, being careful not to tear peels; use juice to make clementine sorbet, or simply save for another use. With a small spoon, gently scrape out and discard remaining membranes. Place clementine cups on a baking sheet and freeze at least 20 minutes and up to overnight; cover with plastic wrap if freezing longer than 1 hour.
2. Make clementine sorbet, if using, or let store-bought sorbet stand at room temperature 5 to 10 minutes to soften. Fill each citrus cup halfway with sorbet. Return cups to freezer for at least 30 minutes.
3. Let ice cream stand at room temperature 5 to 10 minutes to soften. Spoon over sorbet to completely fill each citrus cup. Return cups to freezer for at least 30 minutes.
4. Make meringue topping: In a large, clean, dry bowl, with a mixer on high speed, whip egg whites until frothy, then slowly pour in sugar and salt. Continue whipping until whites are stiff and shiny. Pipe or spoon meringue on top of each citrus cup, covering all of ice cream.
5. When ready to serve, preheat oven to 350°. Place cups on the chilled baking sheet in hot oven and briefly bake until meringue is golden brown, about 3 minutes. Remove from oven and transfer two citrus cups to each dessert plate. Serve immediately.
Quick Tip: If you plan to make clementine sorbet, juice the clementines (as directed above and in sorbet recipe, above right), then choose the 16 best-looking clementine halves to use as serving cups; discard the rest. If using store-bought sorbet, use 8 clementines as directed *above*.

Make Ahead: Through step 4, up to 1 day, covered with plastic wrap if freezing longer than 1 hour.

PER SERVING: 283 cal., 21% (59 cal.) from fat; 4.2 g protein; 6.5 g fat (3.7 g sat.); 52 g carbo (0 g fiber); 85 mg sodium; 23 mg chol.

Clementine Sorbet: Cut 2½ lbs. (about 16) **clementines** in half crosswise and juice them. Stir ⅓ cup **sugar** into clementine juice. Taste and, if the mixture is sour, add more sugar. It should taste sweet-tart. Pour mixture into an ice cream maker (1 qt. capacity) and freeze according to manufacturer's instructions. This sorbet freezes very hard. Makes about 3 cups.

PER ½-CUP SERVING: 107 cal., 3% (3.6 cal.) from fat; 0.8 g protein; 0.4 g fat (0 g sat.); 25 g carbo (0 g fiber); 0.1 mg sodium; 0 mg chol.

Jasmine-Honey Sherbet

Although green tea with half-and-half would make a strange hot drink, it's great as a sherbet.

MAKES About 5 cups | **TIME** 30 minutes, plus 6 hours to chill and freeze

3½ cups **warm brewed green jasmine tea**
¾ cup *each* **half-and-half and honey**
¼ cup **sugar**
⅛ tsp. **fresh lemon juice**

1. In a large bowl, whisk together tea, half-and-half, honey, sugar, and lemon juice. Cover and chill until cold, at least 3 hours or up to 1 day.
2. Transfer mixture to an ice cream maker (at least 1½-qt. capacity). Freeze according to manufacturer's instructions. Transfer sorbet to an airtight freezer-safe container and freeze until firm, about 3 hours.
Make Ahead: Up to 2 weeks, frozen airtight.

PER ½-CUP SERVING: 121 cal., 16% (19 cal.) from fat; 0.6 g protein; 2.1 g fat (1.3 g sat.); 27 g carbo (0 g fiber); 11 mg sodium; 6.7 mg chol.

■ Regional Honey

FROM THE PANTRY

Honey's flavor, color, and aroma are a direct result of where bees gather pollen, and the West offers a delicious diversity of regional honey. You can pick from honey produced by bees that have feasted in the almond orchards of California or on wildflowers in the mountains of Colorado or the desert flowers or citrus trees of southern Arizona, their flavors running from sweet and mild to dark and wild. Experiment to see what flavors you like best.

Cherry Sherbet

recipe pictured on page **685**

This dense sherbet is subtly dark and elegant. The difference between sorbet and sherbet is that sorbet typically contains little more than fruit and sweeteners, while sherbet adds eggs or dairy products, such as milk or a splash of half-and-half.

MAKES 1 qt. | **TIME** 20 minutes, plus 5 hours to chill and freeze

2 cups **frozen sweet cherries (including juice)**
    or 3 cups **very ripe pitted fresh sweet cherries**
    (see Quick Tip below)
1 cup **sugar**
1½ cups **milk**
¼ cup **fresh lemon juice**
2 tbsp. **kirsch**

1. Put cherries in a small saucepan. Add ¼ cup water and bring to a boil over high heat. Lower heat to medium and cook, stirring, until cherries have released their juice and pulp has softened.
2. Transfer cherry mixture to a blender and pulse 3 or 4 times to purée. Pour through a fine-mesh strainer into a medium heatproof bowl, pressing down with a ladle or spatula to extract liquid. Discard solids. Add sugar to hot liquid and stir until dissolved completely. Cover and chill for at least 1 hour.
3. Add milk, lemon juice, and kirsch and stir to combine. Pour into an ice cream maker (1-qt. capacity). Freeze according to manufacturer's directions. Transfer to an airtight freezer-safe container and freeze at least 4 hours.
Quick Tip: Bing cherries will make a deep bluish red, almost purple sherbet; lighter-hued cherries produce a tangier, brighter red sherbet.
Make Ahead: Up to 2 weeks, frozen airtight.

PER ½-CUP SERVING: 176 cal., 10% (18 cal.) from fat; 2.2 g protein; 2 g fat (1.1 g sat.); 38 g carbo (0 g fiber); 23 mg sodium; 6.4 mg chol.

Berry Land

Like people, berries are happiest in places that are not too hot and not too cold. They like plenty of rain in the winter, and in summer, they prefer warm, dry days and cool nights. Much of the West is ideal for berries—especially the central California coast and Oregon's Willamette Valley, America's berry bowl. Raspberries, blackberries, and strawberries are what we're known for, and we grow cranberries and blueberries too. Then there are the wild berries—a staple of the Native American diet for centuries—found in woods all over the West: the tiny, intensely flavored purple-blue to bright red huckleberry, a pain to pick but worth the trouble; true wild blackberries, which grow on vines both trailing and upright; teardrop-shaped, dark blue salal berries; tart and seedy Oregon grape (related not to grapes but to barberries); and the sweet, delicate thimbleberry—pale red and so fragile it almost falls apart when you pick it. For more on cultivated and wild Western berries, pick up Janie Hibler's *The Berry Bible*. In the meantime, here are the main types you'll find in markets.

Varieties

Most of these berries are sold generically as raspberries, blueberries, and the like, but at farmers' markets you may see them labeled with specific varietal names, which helps with identifying their flavor nuances. Harvest times vary by location, with warmer, more southern areas ripening first.

BLACKBERRIES (May through September). Look for the following varieties in addition to fruit simply labeled "blackberries":

Boysenberry. A wild blackberry-raspberry cross—fat and luscious. First grown commercially in Southern California by Walter Knott, who made them famous at Knott's Berry Farm, and now grown in California and Oregon.

Loganberry. Another cross between a wild blackberry and raspberry; red-black and richly flavored, with good acidity. Developed in the 1880s, logans were a staple of the berry industry until the 1950s, when the marionberry was developed. Now they're less common; nearly all grow in Oregon.

Marionberry. The queen of blackberries, against whose deep tangy-sweet flavor all other blackberries are judged. Named for Marion County, Oregon, and grown exclusively in the Beaver State. Widely available frozen and, in Oregon, fresh.

Olallieberry. A long, slender blackberry, sweet and full-flavored, grown primarily along California's Central Coast. Developed by the USDA and Oregon State University in 1949. *Olallie* is the Chinook word for berry.

BLUEBERRIES (April through September). Oregon is the West's biggest producer (and third in the nation, after Michigan and New Jersey). With new low-chill varieties, California's San Joaquin Valley may be catching up.

CRANBERRIES (fall). Native to New England, cranberries were brought to the West in the late 1800s. The vines, which thrive in southern Oregon and southwest Washington, put down shallow roots in sandy bogs. Farmers harvest cranberries dry for the fresh market and flood the fields to gather floating berries for processing into juices and sauces.

RASPBERRIES (May through September). Unlike the solid-core blackberry, raspberries come away from the plant with a hollow center, and are therefore more fragile.

Black. (July only). Drier and seedier than red raspberries, this North American native is a bit tart, with a dusky, jammy flavor. Black raspberries rank especially high in antioxidants and cancer-fighting compounds. Most grow in Oregon.

Golden. Sweeter and more delicately flavored than red; Washington is the main source for golden raspberries.

Red. Medium to deeply colored, depending on variety. Red raspberries grow along the West Coast from California to British Columbia.

STRAWBERRIES (year-round; peak is April through June). California leads the world in commercial production, thanks to staggered planting cycles and varieties bred for shipability. However, berries have much better flavor and texture close to where they're grown, because they're picked when riper. More fragile varieties, including tiny Alpine strawberries (sometimes sold under the French term *fraises des bois*), are a revelation for their deep flavor; they're sold at farmers' markets.

Choosing and Storing Berries

Look for fully colored berries with shiny surfaces and no mold. Don't buy more than you can eat within a few days, because that's as long as they last. Store covered and unwashed in baskets in the refrigerator, and just before eating, rinse and dry gently with paper towels. To freeze, arrange rinsed, dried fruit in a single layer on a baking sheet and freeze until firm. Then put in heavy-duty plastic bags and freeze up to 1 year.

Fruit Pops

You can make popsicles with just about any fruit under the sun, and sweeten them as much or as little as you like. Use ice pop molds with a ¼- to ⅓-cup capacity, available at cookware and hardware stores and online. Molds come in a variety of shapes, including bars, cylinders, and even rockets. See *below* for a layered version.

MAKES 6 to 8 pops | **TIME** 10 to 15 minutes, plus 3 hours to freeze

Fruit mixture (*recipes follow*)

1. Pour fruit mixture into 6 to 8 molds. Attach covers firmly and insert sticks, leaving 1½ to 2 in. of each sticking out. Set molds in freezer, making sure they're level and upright, and freeze until firm, at least 3 hours.
2. To unmold, run warm water over the molds up to the rim, just until pops are released from sides, 5 to 15 seconds. Remove the covers and pull out the pops.
Make Ahead: Up to 2 weeks, frozen airtight.

Blackberry-Cardamom Pops: In a blender, purée 3½ cups **blackberries**. Push through a fine-mesh strainer into a 1-qt. glass measuring cup; discard seeds. Add ½ cup **apple juice**, 2 to 4 tbsp. **sugar** (to taste), and ⅛ tsp. **ground cardamom** to purée; stir until sugar is dissolved.

PER POP: 53 cal., 6% (3 cal.) from fat; 0.9 g protein; 0.3 g fat (0 g sat.); 13 g carbo (3.2 g fiber); 1.3 mg sodium; 0 mg chol.

Peach-Almond Pops: In a blender, purée 3 cups sliced peeled ripe **peaches**, ¾ cup canned **peach nectar**, 1 to 2 tbsp. **sugar** (to taste), 1 tbsp. **fresh lemon juice**, and ⅛ tsp. **almond extract**.

PER POP: 45 cal., 3% (1.4 cal.) from fat; 0.6 g protein; 0.2 g fat (0 g sat.); 11 g carbo (1 g fiber); 1.7 mg sodium; 0 mg chol.

Mango-Coconut Pops: In a blender, purée 1¼ cups **mango** chunks (about 1 in., from 1 lb. fruit), ¾ cup canned **coconut milk**, 1 to 2 tbsp. **sugar** (to taste), and 1 tbsp. **fresh lime juice**.

PER POP: 68 cal., 60% (41 cal.) from fat; 0.6 g protein; 4.6 g fat (4 g sat.); 7.5 g carbo (0.5 g fiber); 3.3 mg sodium; 0 mg chol.

Raspberry-Orange Pops: In a blender, purée 3 cups **raspberries**. Push through a fine-mesh strainer into a 1-qt. glass measuring cup; discard seeds. Add ⅔ cup **orange juice** and 3 to 4 tbsp. **sugar** (to taste) to purée; stir until sugar is dissolved.

PER POP: 55 cal., 6% (3.1 cal.) from fat; 0.7 g protein; 0.3 g fat (0 g sat.); 13 g carbo (3 g fiber); 0.7 mg sodium; 0 mg chol.

Strawberry-Cream Pops: In a blender, purée 2 cups hulled **strawberries**. Push through a fine-mesh strainer into a 1-qt. glass measuring cup; discard seeds. Return purée to blender and mix with ½ cup **light sour cream**, 2 to 3 tbsp. **sugar** (to taste), and 2 tsp. **fresh lemon juice**.

PER POP: 48 cal., 33% (16 cal.) from fat; 0.8 g protein; 1.8 g fat (1 g sat.); 7.9 g carbo (0.7 g fiber); 11 mg sodium; 5.4 mg chol.

Layered Pops: To create two-tone pops, make two different Fruit Pops recipes and use twice as many molds. Pour one mixture into all the molds and freeze until firm to touch on top, about 45 minutes, then pour second mixture over first and freeze completely.

Triple-berry Popsicles

We couldn't believe how simple it was to make these frozen treats. You can strain out the seeds if you like, but they give the pops great texture. Feel free to use boysenberries, pitted cherries, or other fruits instead of the combination here. You will need 10 (4-oz.) ice pop molds and 10 popsicle sticks (often labeled "craft sticks").

MAKES 10 popsicles | **TIME** 20 minutes, plus 8 hours to freeze

⅔ cup sugar (*see Quick Tip below*)
1 cup *each* blueberries and raspberries
1 cup strawberries, hulled and sliced
¼ cup fresh lemon juice

1. Put sugar and ⅓ cup water in a small saucepan and bring to boil over high heat, stirring until sugar is dissolved. Set simple syrup aside.
2. Purée berries and lemon juice in a blender, about 30 seconds. Add ⅓ cup simple syrup and blend just until combined. (Save remaining syrup for another use, such as sweetening iced tea.)
3. Transfer purée to pop molds and freeze 4 hours. Insert popsicle sticks and freeze until frozen solid, another 4 to 6 hours.
Quick Tip: Simple syrup makes the pops less icy and more velvety than sugar alone. (If you don't have time to make the syrup, just add ⅓ cup undissolved sugar to the purée in step 2.)
Make Ahead: Up to 2 weeks, wrapped well.

PER POPSICLE: 44 cal., 4% (1.8 cal.) from fat; 0.3 g protein; 0.2 g fat (0 g sat.); 11 g carbo (1.3 g fiber); 6.4 mg sodium; 0 mg chol.

Pear Sorbet

Light and refreshing, this sorbet is a delightful way to end a heavy meal. If you want to serve sparkling wine with it, choose a sweeter one than that in the sorbet. Pear juice may be substituted for the sparkling wine.

MAKES About 1 qt. | **TIME** 1 hour

2 lbs. ripe Bartlett or Anjou pears, peeled, cored, and chopped
1½ cups extra-dry or brut sparkling wine, divided *(see Quick Tip, above right)*
¾ cup sugar
2 tbsp. light corn syrup

1. Put pears and ¾ cup sparkling wine in a medium pan over medium-high heat. Bring to a boil, then lower heat to maintain a steady simmer. Cook, stirring occasionally, until pears are tender, about 10 minutes.
2. Transfer mixture to a blender, add the sugar and purée. Stir in corn syrup, cover, and chill until cold, at least 1 hour.
3. When mixture is cold, stir in remaining ¾ cup sparkling wine. Transfer to an ice cream maker (1-qt. capacity). Freeze according to manufacturer's instructions.

Quick Tip: Extra-dry sparkling wine is actually sweeter than brut.
Make Ahead: Up to 2 weeks, frozen airtight.

PER ½-CUP SERVING: 179 cal., 2% (3.6 cal.) from fat; 0.4 g protein; 0.4 g fat (0 g sat.); 39 g carbo (2.5 g fiber); 8.6 mg sodium; 0 mg chol.

Rosy Strawberry Sorbet

This juicy sorbet isn't merely rose-colored. It also contains rose water, which combines so beautifully with strawberries that its flavor seems like an extension of the fruit. Neither heavy nor perfumey, it gives the sorbet a delicate, aromatic sweetness.

MAKES 3 cups | **TIME** 30 minutes, plus 2 hours to chill and freeze

⅓ cup plus 1 tbsp. sugar
1 lb. strawberries, hulled
1½ tbsp. rose water *(see Quick Tips, right)*
2 tbsp. fresh lemon juice
⅛ tsp. salt

1. In a small saucepan over medium-high heat, bring sugar and ½ cup water to a simmer. Stir to dissolve

---

Pick Your Pear

Most of our nation's pears come from Oregon and Washington. Here's a guide to the types commonly grown and when they (versus imports) are in season and available in markets. Pears ripen from the inside out, so check the narrowest part of the pear—the neck—for ripeness by gently pushing on it; if it gives slightly, the pear is ripe. That said, some varieties, like Bartletts, are good even when quite firm.

ANJOU. Sweet and juicy, with a mild flavor and dense texture. Can be green or red. Good for eating raw or for cooking. *Green:* September–July. *Red:* September–May.

ASIAN. Its crisp (even crunchy) texture and delicate, refreshing flavor make this pear great for eating raw. There are many varieties of Asian

pears; most from the United States look like round, beige apples. July–August.

BARTLETT. The juiciest pear, it turns very soft and loses its shape when cooked. August–February.

BOSC. A crisp fruit with a soft, grainy texture, russet skin, long and tapered neck, and beautiful aroma, this is the most pear-shaped of all the pears. It holds its shape when cooked, making it a good candidate for poaching. September–April.

COMICE. Plump, almost swollen-looking, the Comice has a deeply indented blossom end, a finer texture than that of other pears, and a gentle sweetness. Very juicy and excellent for eating raw. September–March.

CONCORDE. A slender, elegant, long-necked golden-green pear. Floral, sweet, and very juicy, yet holds up well to cooking. September–February.

FORELLE. Small and chubby, with a freckled red blush over its green-gold skin. Crisp and slightly grainy, with a trace of mouth-puckering tannin in the skin. October–March.

SECKEL. A golden, elf-size pear with faint green freckles. Highly perfumed pale gold flesh with notes of jasmine flower. September–February.

STARKRIMSON. Deep rose-colored skin with dark red freckles. Pale white, very juicy flesh with tingling acidity beneath the sweetness. August–January.

sugar, then remove pan from heat and cool to room temperature, about 20 minutes *(see Quick Tips below)*.

2. Meanwhile, purée strawberries in a blender. Pour purée through a fine-mesh strainer into a medium bowl to remove seeds, pressing down with a ladle or spatula to extract liquid. Discard seeds.

3. In a medium bowl, combine sugar syrup, strawberry purée, rose water, lemon juice, and salt. Cover with plastic wrap and refrigerate until well chilled, at least 2 hours *(see Quick Tips below)*.

4. Stir mixture well and transfer to an ice cream maker (1-qt. capacity). Freeze according to manufacturer's directions.

Make Ahead: Up to 2 weeks, frozen airtight.

Quick Tips: Find rose water in Middle Eastern markets; look for Middle Eastern, French, and Italian brands which have the best flavor. To save time, you can quickly cool the sugar syrup in step 1 by setting the pan in an ice bath (a bowl of ice and cold water) and stirring until the mixture reaches room temperature, 2 to 5 minutes. Likewise, you can bypass chilling the mixture in the refrigerator in step 3 by setting the bowl in an ice bath and stirring until well chilled, about 12 minutes.

PER ½-CUP SERVING: 73 cal., 4% (2.7 cal.) from fat; 0.5 g protein; 0.3 g fat (0 g sat.); 18 g carbo (1.9 g fiber); 51 mg sodium; 0 mg chol.

Pink Grapefruit Granita

An icy dessert can be a nice finish for a hearty winter dinner. This one is tart and sweet at the same time.

SERVES 6 | **TIME** 30 minutes, plus 4 hours to freeze

3 pink grapefruit (10 to 12 oz. each), cut into segments *(see How to Cut Citrus into Segments, page 135),* **juice reserved**
4 cups store-bought unsweetened pink grapefruit juice
⅔ cup sugar

1. Coarsely chop grapefruit segments. Cover and chill until ready to use.

2. In a large bowl, stir fresh grapefruit juice, store-bought grapefruit juice, and sugar until sugar is dissolved. Pour into a 9- by 13-in. metal baking pan, cover with plastic wrap, and freeze until solid, at least 4 hours.

3. When juice mixture is frozen, quickly scrape with a fork to break it up and form fluffy crystals. Scoop granita into wineglasses or bowls. Top with chopped grapefruit segments and serve immediately.

Make Ahead: Up to 2 weeks; re-scrape just before serving.

PER SERVING: 170 cal., 0% (1.8 cal.) from fat; 1.2 g protein; 0.2 g fat (0 g sat.); 42 g carbo (0.4 g fiber); 1.9 mg sodium; 0 mg chol.

Watermelon Granita

Try this after a dinner of grilled salmon or burgers on a hot summer evening.

SERVES 4 | **TIME** 30 minutes, plus 8 hours to freeze

1 cup sugar
2 tsp. finely shredded lime zest
2 lbs. chopped, seeded watermelon (about 3 lbs. unpeeled)
1 tsp. fresh lime juice, plus more to taste

1. In a 1- to 2-qt. pan over high heat, combine 1 cup water, sugar, and lime zest and bring to a boil. Let cool, then pour through a fine-mesh strainer into a bowl.

2. In a blender, purée watermelon and 1 cup lime syrup until smooth. If there are seeds, pour mixture through strainer into a bowl. Stir in lime juice. Add more syrup and/or lime juice to taste (mixture will taste less sweet once frozen).

3. Pour purée into an 8-in. square metal baking pan. Cover with plastic wrap and freeze until mixture has started to freeze at edges but is still slushy, 2 to 3 hours.

4. Stir granita mixture thoroughly, scraping sides down. Cover and freeze until solid, at least 5 or 6 hours longer.

5. To serve, scrape granita with a fork to break it up and make large flakes. Scoop into chilled glasses or bowls.

Make Ahead: Up to 2 weeks; re-scrape just before before serving.

PER SERVING: 267 cal., 3% (9 cal.) from fat; 1.4 g protein; 1 g fat (0 g sat.); 66 g carbo (1 g fiber); 5.3 mg sodium; 0 mg chol.

preserves & pickles

Pause here for a primer on preserving, plus recipes for quick jams, salsas, pickles, and more.

The words "peak season" take on new meaning when you shop at a farmers' market, belong to a CSA, or tend your own backyard garden (or do all three). They describe a giant, juicy wave of perfection headed your way, and the best way to cope is to start canning.

For a few hours' worth of work, the rewards are sweet and long-lasting: A big box of peaches, turned into jam, brightens up your toast on a glum winter day with the taste of summer. And if those peaches are from your own yard, there's pride to enjoy along with the flavor.

Compared with store-bought canned goods, home-canned food usually costs less, and can be tailored to your tastes (less sugar, for instance, or an interesting herb or two). Also, in this era of food recalls, it's reassuring to know how it was processed: with your own two hands.

Although preserving does take some time, it's not difficult (see our primer, starting on *page* 712) or dangerous if you follow standard safety tips (*page* 713), and you can produce a year's supply of pickles or green beans, tomatoes, or raspberry jam in one fell swoop. Even if you don't have a lot of time, you can make our quick refrigerator jams (*page* 714) when you have beautiful fruit you can't bear to let spoil.

Turn the page and let the canning begin.

Preserves & Pickles

Pomegranate Jelly

Over the years, *Sunset* has published several recipes for pomegranate jelly. We like this fresh-tasting version the best.

MAKES About 7 half-pts. | **TIME** 1½ hours, plus 2 days to set up

10 large pomegranates
2 tbsp. fresh lemon juice
1 box (1.75 or 2 oz.) Sure-Jell dry pectin
6 cups sugar

1. Follow directions in *Canning ABCs: Get Ready (page 712)*, using 7 half-pint-size jars, plus matching rings and lids.
2. To extract juice, cut crowns off pomegranates and score peel of each in several places. Immerse pomegranates, one at a time, in cool water in a large bowl; working with your hands underwater, break into sections and separate seeds. Skim off floating peel and membrane; discard. Drain seeds.
3. In a 5- to 6-qt. pot over high heat, combine seeds and ½ cup water. Cover and cook until seeds are soft when pressed, about 10 minutes.
4. Set a colander lined with cheesecloth in a bowl. Pour in seeds and liquid. Tie cloth closed. Wearing rubber gloves, squeeze bag to extract remaining juice. Measure; you need exactly 4 cups (if amount is short, add water).
5. Combine pomegranate juice, lemon juice, and pectin in the 5- to 6-qt. pot. Bring to a boil over medium-high heat. Stir in sugar and bring to a boil so strong that it can't be stirred down; boil, stirring, exactly 2 minutes.
6. Fill jars as directed in *Canning ABCs: Fill and Seal Jars*, leaving ¼ in. headspace. Wipe rims and seal with lids and rings as directed.
7. Process as directed in *Canning ABCs: Process Jars*, boiling for 5 minutes (boil for 10 minutes at altitudes of 1,000 to 6,000 ft., 15 minutes above 6,000 ft.). Cool, check the seals, and let stand for 2 days for jelly to set. Store as directed (up to 1 year)
Quick Tip: To avoid getting stained with pomegranate juice—it tends to spurt out when you break the fruit apart—immerse chunks of the fruit in a big bowl of water and then separate out the seeds. The water contains the spurting juices, the seeds sink, and the membranes and other bits float to the top, making them easy to skim off.

PER TBSP.: 55 cal., 3% (1.5 cal.) from fat; 0.2 g protein; 0.2 g fat (0 g sat.); 14 g carbo (0.6 g fiber); 1.3 mg sodium; 0 mg chol.

Peach-Raspberry Jam

Reader Alice Cyr, of Bellingham, Washington, says this combination is "more delicate and less seedy than raspberry jam alone, with more pizzazz than plain peach."

MAKES 5 to 6 pts. | **TIME** 1 hour, 20 minutes

3½ lbs. ripe peaches, peeled *(see Quick Tips below)* and pitted
3½ cups raspberries (1 lb.)
½ cup fresh lemon juice
½ tsp. butter (optional; *see Quick Tips below*)
1 box (1.75 to 2 oz.) MCP or Sure-Jell dry pectin, or 2 boxes (1.75 oz. each) Ball Fruit Jell dry pectin
10 cups sugar

1. Follow directions in *Canning ABCs: Get Ready (page 712)*, using 6 pint-size jars, plus matching rings and lids.
2. Coarsely chop peaches; you should have 5½ cups. Coarsely chop or mash raspberries; you should have 2 cups.
3. In an 8- to 10-qt. pan, combine peaches, raspberries, lemon juice, butter if using, and pectin. Bring to a rolling boil over high heat, stirring often. Stir in sugar; when mixture resumes boiling, stir for exactly 4 minutes if using MCP pectin (1 minute if using Sure-Jell or Ball Fruit Jell). Remove from heat immediately. Skim and discard any foam from jam.
4. Fill jars as directed in *Canning ABCs: Fill and Seal Jars*, leaving ¼ in. headspace. Wipe rims and seal with lids and rings as directed.
5. Process as directed in *Canning ABCs: Process Jars*, boiling for 5 minutes (boil for 10 minutes at altitudes of 1,000 to 6,000 ft., 15 minutes above 6,000 ft.). Cool, check the seals, and store as directed (up to 1 year).
Quick Tips: To peel peaches, immerse in boiling water for about 30 seconds. Lift out with a slotted spoon, let cool, then pull off skin. Butter keeps foam from forming during cooking. If you leave it out, skim off foam before ladling jam into jars.

PER TBSP.: 45 cal., 0% (0 cal.) from fat; 0.1 g protein; 12 g carbo (0.2 g fiber); 0.7 mg sodium; 0 mg chol.

Canning ABCs

Canning is the best way to make summer's fresh produce last through the year. With just a few tools and basic techniques under your belt, you'll be on your way to a pantry and refrigerator filled with jewel-toned jams, rich red tomatoes, and piquant pickles to enjoy and share.

Get Ready

1. Gather equipment. Canning jars with matching metal lids and rings, a 20-qt. boiling-water canner with rack, a wide-mouthed funnel, tongs, and a jar lifter. Most hardware stores carry these basics.

2. Fill canner with water and heat it up. The canner should be two-thirds full for pint and half-pint jars; half-full for quart jars. Set rack on pan rim and cover pan. Over high heat, bring water to a boil (180° to 185° for pickles); this takes 30 to 45 minutes.

3. Meanwhile, wash canning jars and rings in a dishwasher and hand-wash lids; drain. For jelly and jam only, sterilize the washed jars too: When water in canner boils, place jars on rack, lower into water, and boil for 10 minutes (at elevations of 1,000 ft. or higher, add 1 minute for each 1,000-ft. increase above sea level). Reduce heat to a simmer and keep jars in water until needed.

Nest lids inside rings in a saucepan and cover with water. Heat until small bubbles form (about 180°; do not boil). Remove pan from heat and cover.

4. Rinse or wipe produce clean, then prepare as recipe directs.

Fill and Seal Jars

1. Put foods into jars through a wide funnel or arrange with fingers, leaving the headspace (the distance between jar rim and food) specified

Before getting started, assemble all your equipment.

Arrange the fruit or vegetables in the canning jars.

Run a knife around the inside of the jar to release any air bubbles.

by the recipe. If the last jar isn't completely full, let cool, then serve or chill; do not process.

2. Release air bubbles in chunky mixtures: Gently run a knife around inside of jars. Wipe jar rims and threads with a clean, damp cloth so that lids will seal.

3. Center clean lids on jars so the sealing compound on lids touches jar rims. Screw metal rings on firmly, but don't force.

Process Jars

1. Lower jars on rack into water. The water should cover jars by at least 1 in.; add hot water as needed during processing. Cover canner and return water to a boil. Cook for time specified in recipe.

2. Lift rack with jars onto edge of canner, using tongs and a hot pad. Using jar lifter, transfer jars to kitchen towels on a work surface. Don't tighten rings. Cool completely at room temperature. You may hear a "ping" as jars form a seal.

3. Press on the center of each lid. If it stays down, the jar is sealed. If it pops up, it isn't (you can still eat the food—chill it as you would leftovers). Label jars and store in a cool, dark place up to 1 year. Once opened, refrigerate; eat jams, chutneys, and relishes within 3 weeks, pickles within 2 months.

Can Safely

Home canning is not complicated, but for success and safety, you must precisely follow the recipes and certain guidelines.
• Do not double the recipes. If you want to make more, cook successive batches.
• Always use the processing method recommended in the recipe.
• Maintain safe levels of vinegar and sugar. Use the recommended amount of commercial vinegar or citric acid to prevent the growth of harmful bacteria. Using the full amount of sugar called for in jellies, jams, and chutneys is also vital for safe preservation, and it ensures the correct consistency.
• For more details on canning safety: Visit the National Center for Home Food Preservation (*uga.edu/nchfp*) for all the USDA canning guidelines on one handy site.

Remove a sterilized lid from the hot water and screw it onto the filled jar, firmly but without forcing it.

When the jars are filled, set them into the rack, lower it into the boiling water, and cover the canner.

After processing, remove the jars from the canner using a jar lifter.

Raspberry-Blackberry Jam

This sweet-tart spread has the bright flavor of raspberries, with just enough blackberries for a rich undertone. Add sugar to the boiling berry mixture (step 4) all at once; this helps the mixture gel properly.

MAKES 8 half-pts. or 4 pts. | **TIME** 1¾ hours

3 cups (¾ lb.) blackberries
2½ qts. (2⅔ lbs.) raspberries
5 cups sugar, divided
1 pkg. (1.75 oz.) Sure-Jell dry pectin labeled "for less or no-sugar needed recipes" *(see Quick Tips below)*
½ tsp. butter (optional; *see Quick Tips below*)

1. Follow directions in *Canning ABCs: Get Ready (page 712)*, using 8 regular or wide-mouthed half-pint-size jars or 4 pint-size jars, plus matching rings and lids.
2. Meanwhile, purée blackberries in a food processor. Rub through a fine-mesh strainer over a bowl to extract as much juice as you can. Discard seeds and scrape juice into an 8- to 10-qt. pot. Add raspberries and mash very coarsely with a potato masher.
3. Measure 4¾ cups sugar into a bowl; set aside. Put remaining ¼ cup sugar in another bowl and stir in pectin. Stir pectin mixture into pot with berries and add butter if using.
4. Over high heat, bring berry mixture to a full boil that you can't stir down, stirring constantly with a long-handled spoon and protecting your hands from spatters. Add reserved sugar all at one time and return to a full boil, continuing to stir. Boil, stirring, exactly 1 minute.
5. Fill jars as directed in *Canning ABCs: Fill and Seal Jars,* leaving ¼ in. headspace. Wipe rims and seal with lids and rings as directed.
6. Process as directed in *Canning ABCs: Process Jars,* boiling for 5 minutes (boil for 10 minutes at altitudes of 1,000 to 6,000 ft., 15 minutes above 6,000 ft.). If your canning rack doesn't hold all the jars at once, process them in two batches. Cool, check the seals, and store as directed (up to 1 year).
Quick Tips: Don't use regular Sure-Jell for this recipe; the one we call for has more gelling power, which is what you want in this case. Butter keeps foam from forming during cooking. If you leave it out, skim off foam before ladling jam into jars.

PER TBSP.: 39 cal., 2% (0.9 cal.) from fat; 0.1 g protein; 0.1 g fat (0 g sat.); 9.8 g carbo (0.6 g fiber); 5.6 mg sodium; 0 mg chol.

Fig-Blackberry-Orange Quick Jam

We love to stir this intensely fruity jam into yogurt, so we usually take it off the heat when the mixture is still a bit runny. Cook longer for a thicker consistency.

recipe pictured on page **680**

MAKES About 3 cups | **TIME** 25 minutes, plus 2 hours to chill

2 lbs. (about 2 pts.) ripe figs, stems trimmed and fruit cut into quarters
6 oz. (½ pt.) blackberries
¾ cup sugar
½ cup fresh orange juice
1½ tsp. finely shredded orange zest

1. In a 4-qt. pan over medium-high heat, combine figs, blackberries, sugar, and orange juice. Bring to a boil and cook, stirring often, until liquid has consistency of thick maple syrup, about 12 minutes. Stir in orange zest. Boil, stirring often, until mixture reaches desired thickness *(see Quick Tip below)*, about another 2 minutes.
2. Remove jam from heat and let cool at room temperature 15 minutes. Chill, covered, at least 2 hours in refrigerator before using.
Quick Tip: To see whether the jam has cooked long enough to thicken to your taste, put a tablespoonful onto a plate you've chilled for 20 minutes in the freezer. The jam will cool and thicken to its final consistency.
Make Ahead: Up to 1 month, chilled.

PER TBSP.: 29 cal., 3% (0.9 cal.) from fat; 0.2 g protein; 0.1 g fat (0 g sat.); 7.4 g carbo (0.8 g fiber); 0.2 mg sodium; 0 mg chol.

Quick Jams

Preserving summer-ripe fruits sometimes demands more time than anyone can spare. Quick jams are a wonderful alternative to canning. These simple, small-batch jams are basically fruit and sugar cooked down until thickened and glossy, and are meant to be kept in the refrigerator and consumed within a month. They won't be quite as thick as jams made with added pectin, but they will have a lovely silken texture.

Peach-Raspberry-Lavender Quick Jam

Lavender adds a floral note, but you can omit it if you like.

recipe pictured on page **680**

MAKES About 3 cups | **TIME** 45 minutes, plus 2 hours to chill

2 tsp. dried culinary lavender buds
1 lb. ripe peaches (about 5), peeled *(see Quick Tips below)*, pitted, and chopped into 1-in. pieces
3 oz. red raspberries
1½ cups sugar
3 tbsp. fresh lemon juice

1. Put lavender buds in a small bowl. Pour ¼ cup boiling water over buds and let steep 10 minutes. Strain scented water into a bowl and set aside; discard buds.
2. In a 4-qt. pan over medium-high heat, combine peaches, raspberries, sugar, and lemon juice. Bring to a boil and cook, stirring often, until liquid has consistency of thick maple syrup, about 14 minutes. Stir in lavender water and boil, stirring often, until mixture reaches desired thickness *(see Quick Tips below)*, about another 2 minutes.
3. Remove jam from heat and let cool at room temperature 15 minutes. Chill, covered, at least 2 hours before using.
Quick Tips: To peel peaches, immerse in boiling water for about 30 seconds. Lift out with a slotted spoon, let cool, then pull off skin. To see whether the jam has cooked long enough to thicken to your taste, put a tablespoonful onto a plate you've chilled for 20 minutes in the freezer. The jam will cool and thicken to its final consistency.
Make Ahead: Up to 1 month, chilled.

PER TBSP.: 28 cal., 0% (0 cal.) from fat; 0.1 g protein; 7.3 g carbo (0.2 g fiber); 0.1 mg sodium; 0 mg chol.

Fresh Cherry Refrigerator Preserves

Make this delicious jam with summer-sweet Bing cherries.

MAKES 2 cups | **TIME** 1 hour, plus 4 hours to chill

1½ lbs. fresh cherries, pitted and halved or very coarsely chopped
1 cup sugar
1 tbsp. fresh lemon juice
¼ tsp. almond extract

1. In a 3- to 4-qt. pan, combine cherries, sugar, and lemon juice. Stir over medium heat until sugar is dissolved and cherries are juicy, about 10 minutes. Adjust heat to maintain a low simmer and stir occasionally until mixture has thickened, about 40 minutes.
2. Stir in almond extract and pour preserves into a bowl. Chill, uncovered, until cold, about 4 hours, then cover.
Make Ahead: Up to 3 weeks, chilled.

PER TBSP.: 38 cal., 4% (1.5 cal.) from fat; 0.2 g protein; 0.2 g fat; 9.5 g carbo (0.3 g fiber); 0.1 mg sodium; 0 mg chol.

Sunset's Canning Tips

• Measure all the sugar into a bowl before beginning the recipe. Many canning recipes call for a large volume of sugar to be added when a mixture is already boiling; measuring ahead simplifies this step and prevents mistakes.
• Adding just a little bit of butter to jams and jellies prevents foam from forming during cooking. If you omit the butter, skim off the foam before ladling jam or jelly into jars. The recipe will yield about ¼ cup less.
• Use a ruler to measure volume. Some recipes call for a mixture to be reduced by a certain amount. To ascertain this easily, insert a clean wooden ruler into the pan before cooking and measure how far up the mixture comes. Then cook as directed until it has reduced by the percentage specified. For example, if the uncooked mixture measures 4 in. in the pan and the recipe says to reduce by half, cook it down to 2 in.
• Choose the best possible peak-season produce for canning. The flavor, months later, will reward you.
• Focus on one food per day if you're dealing with a bumper crop of something—say, beans for pickling, or berries for jam.
• Make several batches of one recipe on the same day (but don't double recipes) so you get a good payoff for your time.

Microwave Apricot–Grand Marnier Jam

Zapped in small quantities in the microwave, berries and pieces of other fruit retain their shape and fresh flavor better than when boiled for jam.

MAKES About 1 cup | **TIME** 30 minutes, plus 2½ hours to cool

1 to 1¼ lbs. ripe to firm-ripe apricots
2 tbsp. fresh lemon juice
½ cup sugar
2 tbsp. Grand Marnier or other orange-flavor liqueur

1. Pit and quarter the apricots; put in a 3- to 4-qt. microwave-safe bowl. Add lemon juice and sugar; mix.
2. Heat in a microwave oven until juices boil, 6 to 8 minutes. Stir gently to turn fruit pieces over; let mixture stand until cool, at least 1 hour or up to 3 hours. Microwave again until boiling, 5 to 6 minutes; let stand at least 1 hour or up to 3 hours.
3. Stir liqueur into apricot mixture, then microwave again until syrup forms big, shiny bubbles, 12 to 15 minutes, stirring gently every 4 to 5 minutes to turn fruit pieces over and prevent browning. The syrup around the apricots will be thinner than jam, but it thickens as it cools. Spoon into a jar or dish and let cool slightly. Serve warm or cool.
Make Ahead: Up to 2 weeks, chilled airtight. Discard if you see any sign of mold.

PER TBSP.: 39 cal., 2.3% (0.9 cal.) from fat; 0.4 g protein; 0.1 g fat (0 g sat.); 9.9 g carbo (0.3 g fiber); 0.7 mg sodium; 0 mg chol.

Shortcut Plum-Apricot Jam

This jam and its two flavor variations *(below and opposite page)*, start with store-bought preserves. Fresh fruit is added to give the mixture your own personal spin and a homemade taste. Storage couldn't be easier—just return the customized preserves to the original jars.

MAKES About 4¾ cups | **TIME** 30 minutes, plus 6 hours to cool

1 orange (½ lb.), thinly sliced (discard the end slices), seeded, and coarsely chopped (reserve any juice)
½ cup sugar
2 cups finely chopped firm-ripe red plums
4 jars (10 oz. each) apricot jam

1. In a 5- to 6-qt. pan, combine chopped orange and any juice, the sugar, and ¼ cup water. Bring to a boil over high heat, stirring often to prevent scorching, and continue to boil until liquid is almost gone, 4 to 5 minutes.
2. Remove from heat and add plums and apricot jam; set unwashed empty jam jars and lids aside. Return pan to high heat and stir until jam is melted. Stirring often to prevent scorching, boil for 10 minutes, then use the "sheet test" to see whether it's set enough: Dip a cool metal spoon into jam and lift above the steam, over pan. Turn spoon sideways so that jam runs off into pan. If it drips, it's not set enough; if it forms two thick droplets that flow together and hang there, or "sheet," then it's ready. Continue to boil until jam meets the sheet test, checking every minute or so.
3. Remove pan from heat and ladle the hot mixture into the unwashed jars to within ¼ in. of rims; pour any extra preserves into a small bowl or jar. Wipe jar rims clean and screw lids snugly into place. Let stand until cool, about 6 hours. Preserves will keep, airtight in the refrigerator. If any mold develops, discard the jam.

PER TBSP.: 45 cal., 0% from fat; 0.2 g protein; 0 g fat; 12 g carbo (0.3 g fiber); 6 mg sodium; 0 mg chol.

Shortcut Blueberry-Currant Jam: Follow
directions for Shortcut Plum-Apricot Jam, above, but substitute a **lemon** for the orange, **blueberries** for the plums, and **currant jelly** for the apricot jam. In step 2, boil until the berries begin falling apart before testing for firmness. Makes 4 cups.

PER TBSP.: 57 cal., 0% from fat; 0.1 g protein; 0 g fat; 15 g carbo (0.3 g fiber); 6.7 mg sodium; 0 mg chol.

Shortcut Peach-Ginger Marmalade: Follow directions for Shortcut Plum-Apricot Jam, left, but substitute a **lemon** for the orange and add ¼ cup minced **fresh ginger** along with the sugar and water in step 1. Substitute finely chopped peeled firm-ripe **peaches** for the plums and 2 jars (18 oz. each) **orange marmalade** for the apricot jam. Makes 4 cups.

PER TBSP.: 48 cal., 0% from fat; 0.1 g protein; 0 g fat; 13 g carbo (0.2 g fiber); 9 mg sodium; 0 mg chol.

Mango-Chile Jam

A sweet jam with a kick from reader Theresa M. Liu, of Alameda, California, who likes to serve it with poultry or fish. Liu does not water-process this jam. If you're uncomfortable with that, just let it cool, spoon into containers, cover, and store the jam in the refrigerator, where it will keep for up to 3 weeks. To store longer, pack into sturdy plastic containers instead of glass jars, leaving about 1-in. headspace, and freeze.

MAKES 4 pts. | TIME 40 minutes

6 to 10 (6 to 9 oz.) red or green jalapeño chiles
6 cups coarsely chopped peeled ripe mangoes
¾ cup fresh lemon juice
1 package (1.75 oz.) dry pectin for lower-sugar recipes
4 cups sugar, divided

1. Follow directions for sterilizing jars, rings, and lids in *Canning ABCs: Get Ready (page 712)*, using 4 pint-size jars, plus matching rings and lids.
2. Place chiles on a small baking sheet and broil 3 to 4 inches from heat, turning as needed, until chiles are charred and blistered all over, 10 to 12 minutes. Cool. Remove and discard skin, stems, and seeds. Coarsely chop chiles.
3. In a 6- to 8-qt. pan, combine mangoes, chiles, and lemon juice.
4. Mix pectin with ¼ cup sugar. Stir into mangoes. Stirring, bring to a rolling boil over high heat. Add remaining 3¾ cups sugar and stir until mixture returns to rolling boil. Stir and boil exactly 1 minute longer. Remove from heat.
5. Drain jars, rings, and lids. Fill jars as directed in *Canning ABCs: Fill and Seal Jars*, leaving ⅛-in. headspace. Wipe rims and seal with lids and rings as directed. Invert jars for 5 minutes, then turn upright. Let cool at least 24 hours. Check seals by pressing firmly on centers of the lids. If a lid pops back, it's not sealed; store it in refrigerator.

PER TBSP.: 33 cal., 0% from fat; 0.1 g protein; 0 g fat; 8.3 g carbo (0.1 g fiber); 25 mg sodium; 0 mg chol.

Preserved Kumquats

Preserving lemons with salt, a common practice in the Middle East and North Africa, turns them into a powerful seasoning agent. Treated the same way, little orange kumquats undergo a similar metamorphosis. They're also beautiful and make a lovely gift. Use them in any recipe that calls for preserved lemon, or serve them with chicken, pork, beef, lamb, or fish.

MAKES About 3 cups | TIME 15 minutes, plus 1 day to freeze and chill

1 lb. kumquats
2 to 3 tbsp. drained large capers
¼ cup kosher salt

1. Slit each kumquat lengthwise to the center. Put in a 3½- to 4-cup jar and add the capers and salt.
2. Screw on the jar's lid and freeze at least 8 hours.
3. Put jar upside down in the refrigerator and let stand 24 hours to develop flavor. Use, or chill up to 1 month, turning jar over every 2 or 3 days to keep salt distributed.

PER KUMQUAT: 6.2 cal., 0% from fat; 0.1 g protein; 0 g fat; 1.6 g carbo (0 g fiber); 108 mg sodium; 0 mg chol.

■ Kumquats

FROM THE GARDEN

The name means "gold citrus fruit" in Cantonese, and the kumquat looks like a tiny, oval version of its larger relatives. Unlike other citrus fruits, though, kumquats are enjoyed peel and all (the tender peel is the sweet part; the pulp packs a sour punch). Find them at farmers' markets in fall and winter, and at well-stocked grocery stores.

Golden Fruit Conserve

Reader Sher Bird Garfield, of Bellevue, Washington, serves her conserve (a jam containing nuts) with scones, in crêpes, and over ice cream.

MAKES About 4 pts. | **TIME** 1 hour

1¾ lbs. ripe peaches (about 5), peeled (*see Quick Tips below*)

1 lb. ripe nectarines (about 3)

½ lb. ripe apricots (about 4)

1 cup golden raisins

⅓ cup fresh lemon juice

½ tsp. butter (optional; *see Quick Tips below*)

1 box (1.75 to 2 oz.) MCP, Sure-Jell, or Ball Fruit Jell dry pectin

5¾ cups sugar

2 tbsp. dark rum (optional)

1 cup sliced almonds

1. Follow directions in *Canning ABCs: Get Ready (page 712)*, using 4 pint-size jars, plus matching rings and lids.
2. Pit and coarsely chop peaches, nectarines, and apricots; you should have 6 to 7 cups total.
3. In an 8- to 10-qt. pan, combine fruit, raisins, lemon juice, butter if using, and pectin. Bring to a rolling boil over high heat, stirring often. Stir in sugar; when mixture returns to a boil, stir for exactly 4 minutes if using MCP pectin (1 minute if using Sure-Jell or Ball Fruit Jell). Remove from heat.
4. Skim and discard any foam. Add rum if using and almonds. Stir occasionally for 5 minutes to distribute fruit and nuts.
5. Fill jars as directed in *Canning ABCs: Fill and Seal Jars,* leaving ¼ in. headspace. Wipe rims and seal with lids and rings as directed.
6. Process as directed in *Canning ABCs: Process Jars,* boiling for 5 minutes (boil for 10 minutes at altitudes of 1,000 to 6,000 ft., 15 minutes above 6,000 ft.). Cool, check the seals, and store as directed (up to 1 year).
Quick Tips: To peel peaches, immerse in boiling water for about 30 seconds. Lift out with a slotted spoon, let cool, then pull off skin. Butter keeps foam from forming during cooking. If you leave it out, skim off foam before ladling jam into jars.

PER TBSP.: 48 cal., 7.5% (3.6 cal.) from fat; 0.3 g protein; 0.4 g fat (0 g sat.); 11 g carbo (0.2 g fiber); 1.2 mg sodium; 0 mg chol.

Queen of the Apricots

It's not a perfect-looking apricot, the Blenheim. Its thin skin sometimes has a greenish hue. Being unusually delicate, it's often also slightly bruised.

None of this really matters—because inside, the fruit is the deep orange of a setting sun, with a silky texture and a taste so rich and tangy-sweet, it makes ordinary apricots difficult to take seriously. This extraordinary flavor is what made the Blenheim (sometimes called the Royal) the dominant variety in California until the 1950s.

That's when modern long-distance shipping began to require harder, more durable varieties, and the Blenheim—so named because it was thought to have emerged from the gardens of England's Blenheim Palace—began to fade from the market shelves, replaced by bigger, tougher, rosy-cheeked apricots that look beautiful but often taste like Styrofoam.

Most of our remaining Blenheims are grown in Northern and central California, and you can still find them fresh there, mainly at farmers' markets, during their brief season in late June and early July.

Apricot-Almond Chutney

Reader Jacqueline Johnson, of Fowler, California, teaches 4-H groups the art of canning. She won first prize at the California State Fair with this chutney.

MAKES 5 to 6 pts. | **TIME** 1¾ hours

2 lbs. *each* ripe apricots and red bell peppers

2 Valencia oranges (¾ lb. total)

2 lemons (½ lb. total)

1 cup blanched whole almonds, toasted until golden (*see How to Toast Nuts, page 134*)

2½ cups chopped onions

2 cups *each* sugar and cider vinegar

1 cup *each* golden raisins and chopped crystallized ginger

2 tsp. *each* salt, ground ginger, and minced garlic

1. Follow directions in *Canning ABCs: Get Ready (page 712)*, using 6 pint-size jars, plus matching rings and lids.
2. Pit and coarsely chop apricots; you should have 3⅓ cups. Stem, seed, and coarsely chop bell peppers; you should have 3⅓ cups. Seed and finely chop oranges and lemons (including peel); you should have 1⅓ cups oranges and 1 cup lemons, including juices.
3. In an 8- to 10-qt. pan, combine almonds, apricots, bell peppers, oranges, lemons, onions, sugar, vinegar, raisins, crystallized ginger, salt, ground ginger, and garlic. Measure volume (*see Sunset's Canning Tips, page 715*). Bring to a boil over high heat, stirring occasionally.

Reduce heat to medium and cook, stirring often, until mixture is thick and reduced by one-third, about 35 minutes.

4. Fill jars as directed in *Canning ABCs: Fill and Seal Jars,* leaving ½ in. of headspace in each jar (if any aren't completely full, refrigerate instead of processing). Process jars, boiling for 10 minutes (at altitudes of 1,000 to 6,000 ft., boil for 15 minutes; above 6,000 ft., boil for 20 minutes). Cool, check the seals, and store as directed (up to 1 year).

PER TBSP.: 25 cal., 14% (3.6 cal.) from fat; 0.3 g protein; 0.4 g fat (0 g sat.); 5.2 g carbo (0.3 g fiber); 26 mg sodium; 0 mg chol.

Apple-Ginger Chutney

Reader Celeste Adams, of Claremont, California, gives this chutney to family and friends for the holidays.

MAKES 6 to 7 pts. | **TIME** 2¾ hours

4 lbs. sweet-tart apples such as Jonathan or Gravenstein
2 lbs. red bell peppers
2 lemons (12 oz. total)
1 qt. cider vinegar
4 cups firmly packed brown sugar
2 cups raisins
½ cup chopped crystallized ginger
2 tsp. each minced garlic and salt
1 tsp. cayenne

1. Follow directions in *Canning ABCs: Get Ready (page 712),* using 7 pint-size jars, plus matching rings and lids.
2. Peel, core, and chop apples; you should have 2½ qts. Stem, seed, and chop peppers; you should have 1 qt. Cut off and discard peel and outer membrane from lemons. Finely chop lemons, discarding seeds; you should have ½ cup, including juices.
3. In an 8- to 10-qt. pan, combine apples, bell peppers, lemons, vinegar, brown sugar, raisins, ginger, garlic, salt, and cayenne. Measure volume *(see Sunset's Canning Tips, page 715).* Bring to a boil over high heat, stirring occasionally. Reduce heat to medium and boil gently, stirring often, until mixture is thick and reduced by one-quarter, 35 minutes to 1 hour.
4. Fill jars as directed in *Canning ABCs: Fill and Seal Jars,* leaving ½ in. of headspace in each jar (if any aren't completely full, refrigerate instead of processing). Process jars, boiling for 10 minutes (at altitudes of 1,000 to 6,000 ft., boil for 15 minutes; above 6,000 ft., boil for 20 minutes). Cool, check the seals, and store as directed (up to 1 year).

PER TBSP.: 26 cal., 0% (0 cal.) from fat; 0.1 g protein; 6.9 g carbo (0.2 g fiber); 23 mg sodium; 0 mg chol.

Spiced Peaches

Reader Susan Johnson, of Palo Alto, California, flavors her peaches with sweet spices and peppercorns. The syrup they're packed in is delicious over pancakes or ice cream.

MAKES 4 qts. | **TIME** 2 hours

5 cups sugar
2⅓ cups unseasoned rice vinegar
1 tsp. whole allspice
12 black peppercorns
4 cinnamon sticks (about 2½ in. long each)
4 cardamom pods, cracked *(see Quick Tips below)*
4 star anise pods
10 lbs. firm-ripe peaches (about 20), peeled *(see Quick Tips below)*, halved, and pitted

1. Follow directions in *Canning ABCs: Get Ready (page 712),* using 4 wide-mouthed quart-size jars, plus matching rings and lids.
2. In a 6- to 8-qt. pan, combine sugar, vinegar, allspice, peppercorns, cinnamon sticks, cardamom, and star anise. Stir over high heat until boiling; reduce heat, cover, and simmer for 5 minutes, stirring occasionally.
3. Turn heat under sugar mixture to high. Add one-third of peaches, cover, and stir occasionally until mixture returns to a boil and peaches are barely tender when pierced, 2 to 3 minutes. With a slotted spoon, transfer peaches to a large bowl. Repeat to cook remaining peaches. Remove syrup from heat.
4. Arrange spices and peaches, cut sides down, in jars. Return syrup to boiling over high heat.
5. Fill jars as directed in *Canning ABCs: Fill and Seal Jars,* ladling hot syrup over peaches, leaving ½ in. of headspace in each jar, and boiling jars for 25 minutes. (At altitudes of 1,000 to 3,000 ft., boil jars for 30 minutes; from 3,000 to 6,000 ft., boil for 35 minutes; above 6,000 ft., boil for 40 minutes.) Cool, check the seals, and store as directed (up to 1 year). Chill any extra syrup airtight up to 2 weeks.

Quick Tips: Crack cardamom pods slightly with your fingers, keeping seeds in pods. To peel peaches, immerse in boiling water for about 30 seconds. Lift out with a slotted spoon, let cool, then pull off skin.

PER ½ CUP: 168 cal., 0% (0.9 cal.) from fat; 0.8 g protein; 0.1 g fat (0 g sat.); 43 g carbo (1.7 g fiber); 0.4 mg sodium; 0 mg chol.

Range Fire Salsa

Reader Gayle Stover named her spicy salsa for the range fires common near her home in Hazelton, Idaho. If you like, you can tone down the heat by removing the seeds and veins from the jalapeños.

MAKES 6 to 7 pts. | **TIME** 4 hours

7¼ lbs. ripe tomatoes, peeled (*see Quick Tip below*)
2⅓ lbs. bell peppers (green and/or yellow)
3¾ lbs. onions
3½ oz. jalapeño chiles (about 5)
1¼ cups cider vinegar
¼ cup fresh lemon juice
2 tbsp. *each* minced garlic and salt
1 tbsp. red chile flakes
1½ tsp. *each* freshly ground black pepper and ground cumin

1. Follow directions in *Canning ABCs: Get Ready (page 712)*, using 7 pint-size jars, plus matching rings and lids.
2. Core and coarsely chop tomatoes; you should have 3 qts., including juice. Stem, seed, and coarsely chop bell peppers; you should have 1½ qts. Peel and coarsely chop onions; you should have 1½ qts. Stem and mince jalapeños; you should have ¾ cup.
3. In an 8- to 10-qt. pan, combine tomatoes, bell peppers, onions, jalapeños, vinegar, lemon juice, garlic, salt, chile flakes, pepper, and cumin. Measure volume (*see Sunset's Canning Tips, page 715*). Bring to a boil over high heat, stirring occasionally. Reduce heat to medium and cook, stirring often, 1 hour. Reduce heat to medium and stir often until thick and reduced by half, about 1 hour more.
4. Fill jars as directed in *Canning ABCs: Fill and Seal Jars*, leaving ½ in. of headspace in each jar (if any aren't completely full, refrigerate instead of processing). Process jars, boiling for 15 minutes (at altitudes of 1,000 to 6,000 ft., boil for 20 minutes; above 6,000 ft., boil for 25 minutes). Cool, check the seals, and store as directed (up to 1 year).
Quick Tip: To peel the tomatoes, immerse in boiling water until skins crack, about 15 seconds. Lift out with a slotted spoon and let cool, then pull off skins.

PER TBSP.: 7.1 cal., 13% (0.9 cal.) from fat; 0.2 g protein; 0.1 g fat (0 g sat.); 1.6 g carbo (0.3 g fiber); 64 mg sodium; 0 mg chol.

Lou's Chile Sauce

About 30 years ago, reader Margie Carothers, of Oro Valley, Arizona, received this recipe from a friend. It has become a family staple, set out whenever there's pot roast for dinner.

MAKES 6 to 7 pts. | **TIME** 3¾ hours

1 tbsp. whole allspice
7¾ lbs. ripe tomatoes, peeled (*see Quick Tip below*)
1¾ lbs. onions (about 4)
1⅓ lbs. *each* red and green bell peppers (about 3 each)
2 cups distilled white vinegar
1½ cups sugar
2 tbsp. salt
1 tbsp. *each* dry mustard, cinnamon, curry powder, nutmeg, ground ginger, and hot sauce
4 dried hot chiles (3 to 4 in. long each), such as arbol

1. Follow directions in *Canning ABCs: Get Ready (page 712)*, using 7 pint-size jars, plus matching rings and lids.
2. Enclose allspice in a double layer of cheesecloth and tie tightly with string.
3. Core and coarsely chop tomatoes; you should have 4 qts., including juice. Peel and coarsely chop onions; you should have 4½ cups. Stem, seed, and coarsely chop red and green bell peppers; you should have 3 cups of each.
4. In a 10- to 12-qt. pan, combine spice bag, tomatoes, onions, red and green peppers, vinegar, sugar, salt, mustard, cinnamon, curry powder, nutmeg, ginger, hot sauce, and chiles. Measure volume (*see Sunset's Canning Tips, page 715*). Bring to a boil over high heat, stirring occasionally. Reduce heat to medium and stir often until mixture is thick and reduced by half, about 2 hours. Lift out spice bag and discard.
5. Fill jars as directed in *Canning ABCs: Fill and Seal Jars*, leaving ½ in. of headspace in each jar (if any aren't completely full, refrigerate instead of processing). Process jars, boiling for 15 minutes (at altitudes of 1,000 to 6,000 ft., boil for 20 minutes; above 6,000 ft., boil for 25 minutes). Cool, check the seals, and store as directed (up to 1 year).
Quick Tip: To peel the tomatoes, immerse in boiling water until skins crack, about 15 seconds; lift out with a slotted spoon and let cool, then pull off skins.

PER TBSP.: 12 cal., 7.5% (0.9 cal.) from fat; 0.2 g protein; 0.1 g fat (0 g sat.); 2.7 g carbo (0.3 g fiber); 66 mg sodium; 0 mg chol.

preserves & pickles

Habanero Marmalade

Reader Ann Beck, of Tucson, Arizona, reached the finals of a *Sunset* cooking contest with this recipe (her category: chiles). "It's good spooned on soft lavash or cucumbers, brushed over meats during the last few minutes of barbecuing, even melted and poured over ice cream," she says. Beck doesn't use a water bath to process her marmalade, but if you feel uncomfortable not processing yours, just keep the marmalade in the refrigerator.

MAKES 7 jars; 1 cup each | **TIME** 45 minutes, plus 3 hours to cool

1¾ oz. (4 to 5) fresh habanero chiles
1½ lbs. red bell peppers
1½ cups distilled white vinegar, divided
6½ cups sugar
2 pouches (3 oz. each) liquid pectin

1. Follow directions for sterilizing jars, rings, and lids in *Canning ABCs: Get Ready (page 712)*, using 7 regular or wide-mouth canning jars (1-cup size), plus matching rings and lids.
2. Wearing rubber gloves, remove and discard stems and seeds from chiles. Cut off curved tops and bottoms from bell peppers; discard stems. Cut off and discard white membranes; save seeds. Slice sides of peppers into ⅛- by 2½-in. strips.
3. In a blender, smoothly purée chiles, bell pepper tops and bottoms, and ½ cup vinegar until smooth.
4. In an 8- to 10-qt. pan over high heat, bring chile purée, bell pepper seeds and slices, remaining 1 cup vinegar, and the sugar to a full, rolling boil, stirring constantly; then boil for exactly 3 minutes.
5. Add pectin to pan. Stirring constantly over high heat, return chile mixture to a full, rolling boil, then boil for exactly 1 minute.
6. Drain jars, rings, and lids. Fill jars as directed in *Canning ABCs: Fill and Seal Jars,* leaving ⅛-in. headspace. (Let any extra marmalade cool, then serve or chill airtight up to 2 weeks.) Wipe jar rims clean. Cover with hot rings and lids.
7. Protecting hands with pot holders, invert filled jars on a towel for 5 minutes. Turn right side up. Every 5 minutes, turn jars over until marmalade has set and seeds are evenly distributed, 45 to 60 minutes.
8. Let marmalade cool at least 2 more hours. Serve, or store up to 1 year.

PER TBSP.: 47 cal., 0% from fat; 0.1 g protein; 0 g fat; 12 g carbo (0.1 g fiber); 0.3 mg sodium; 0 mg chol.

Pickled Jalapeños (*Jalapeños en Escabeche*)

Elena Cota, a 78-year-old San Diego native and cooking teacher, serves this classic tangy-hot Mexican pickle as part of a buffet with tacos of all kinds, skirt steak, grilled shrimp, pinto beans, and salads.

MAKES 8 to 10 servings | **TIME** About 30 minutes

1 lb. jalapeño chiles
2 carrots (6 oz. total)
1 onion (6 oz.)
2 cups distilled white vinegar
½ cup vegetable oil
3 or 4 garlic cloves, peeled
1 tsp. dried oregano, crumbled
1 bay leaf
Salt and freshly ground black pepper

1. Pierce each jalapeño with a fork. Peel carrots and cut crosswise into ¼-in.-thick slices. Peel onion and cut vertically into ¼-in.-wide slivers.
2. In a 3- to 4-qt. pan over high heat, combine jalapeños, carrots, onion, 2 cups water, vinegar, oil, garlic, oregano, and bay leaf. Bring to a boil. Reduce heat and simmer just until carrots are tender-crisp when pierced, 5 to 8 minutes. Add salt and pepper to taste.
3. Pour into jars, cover, and chill at least 1 day. Use a slotted spoon to serve.
Make Ahead: Up to 2 months, chilled.

PER SERVING: 130 cal., 76% (99 cal.) from fat; 1 g protein; 11 g fat (1.4 g sat.); 8.8 g carbo (1.2 g fiber); 8.7 mg sodium; 0 mg chol.

Canned Heirloom Tomatoes

For this extra-easy recipe, adapted from the *USDA Complete Guide to Home Canning* (uga.edu/nchfp/index.html), you just squish raw, skinned tomatoes into jars. The cold-pack technique may cause fruit and liquid to separate a bit during processing, but the results still taste delicious.

recipe pictured
on page
683

MAKES 6 to 7 qts. | **TIME** 3 hours

17 lbs. ripe yellow or red heirloom tomatoes
14 tbsp. bottled ReaLemon lemon juice or 3½ tsp. citric acid such as Fruit Fresh *(see Quick Tip below)*
7 tsp. salt (optional)
7 thyme sprigs (3 to 4 in. long; optional)

1. Follow directions in *Canning ABCs: Get Ready (page 712)*, using 7 wide-mouthed quart-size jars, plus matching rings and lids.
2. Meanwhile, peel tomatoes: Fill a large saucepan three-quarters full of water and bring to a boil over high heat. Cook one layer of tomatoes at a time in water, just until skins split or will peel easily with a knife, 20 to 40 seconds. Remove from water with slotted spoon; let cool, then core, pull off skins, and trim any brown areas, working over a bowl to catch juice.
3. Put 2 tbsp. lemon juice or ½ tsp. citric acid in each jar. Add 1 tsp. salt if you like. Follow directions in *Canning ABCs: Fill and Seal Jars,* cutting tomatoes to fit through jar openings, if needed, and pushing them into jars to fill compactly; leave ½ in. headspace. Pushing will create juice; if needed, add more juice from bowl so tomatoes are covered. Using handle of a fork, poke 1 thyme sprig down side of each jar if you like. Release air, wipe rims, and seal with lids and rings as directed.
4. Process as directed in *Canning ABCs: Process Jars,* boiling for 1 hour and 25 minutes (add 5 minutes for every 3,000 ft. in altitude above sea level). It's okay if jars leak a little.
5. Turn off heat and let jars stand in water in canner for 5 minutes. Cool, check seals, and store as directed (up to 1 year).
Quick Tip: It's essential for food safety when working with plain tomatoes (recipes without added vinegar) that you acidify them with bottled (not fresh) lemon juice or citric acid, which has a standardized acidity, and that you do not increase the amount of herbs or add any other ingredients. Buy citric acid in your supermarket's baking aisle.

PER ½ CUP: 28 cal., 13% (3.6 cal.) from fat; 1.1 g protein; 0.4 g fat (0.1 g sat.); 6.3 g carbo (1.6 g fiber); 14 mg sodium; 0 mg chol.

Tomato Jam

Surprisingly good on ham and cheese sandwiches, and excellent with steak or chicken.

MAKES About 2 cups | **TIME** 1¾ hours

1½ lbs. cherry tomatoes (about 4 cups)
1¼ cups firmly packed brown sugar
¼ cup cider vinegar
½ lemon (3 oz. total), including peel, very thinly sliced
2 tbsp. minced fresh ginger
1 tsp. ground cumin
¾ tsp. cinnamon
½ tsp. salt, plus more to taste
⅛ tsp. ground cloves
⅛ tsp. freshly ground black pepper, plus more to taste

1. Put all ingredients in a medium saucepan and bring to a boil over medium heat, stirring often.
2. Reduce heat and simmer, stirring occasionally, until mixture is reduced to 2 cups and has the consistency of thick jam, about 1¼ hours. Season to taste with salt and pepper.
Make Ahead: Up to 2 weeks, chilled.

PER ¼-CUP: 153 cal., 2% (2.7 cal.) from fat; 0.9 g protein; 0.3 g fat (0 g sat.); 39 g carbo (1.6 g fiber); 167 mg sodium; 0 mg chol.

Denver Summer Relish

Former *Sunset* food editor Jerry Di Vecchio came up with this recipe after visiting her daughter, Angela, who lives in Denver with her family and has a bountiful supply of backyard tomatoes. The relish is good in toasted brie cheese sandwiches or alongside pork chops.

MAKES 3 cups | **TIME** 30 minutes, plus 20 minutes to cool

1 lb. Roma tomatoes, cored and cut into ¼-inch dice
2 cups diced (¼ in.) onions
1 cup golden raisins
1 cup white vinegar (distilled, rice, or wine)
1 cup sugar
2 tbsp. minced fresh ginger
2 jalapeño chiles, seeds and ribs removed and chopped
Salt

1. Put tomatoes, onions, raisins, vinegar, sugar, ginger, and chiles in a large saucepan and bring to a boil over high heat, stirring often, until mixture is reduced to 3 cups, about 20 minutes.

2. Let cool at least 20 minutes. Season to taste with salt; stir and serve.

Make Ahead: Up to 3 weeks, chilled.

PER TBSP.: 31 cal., 0% from fat; 0.3 g protein; 0 g fat; 7.9 g carbo (0.4 g fiber); 1.5 mg sodium; 0 mg chol.

Mixed Bread-and-Butter Pickles

Reader Stephanie Baldwin has fond memories of making these pickles as a child in New Zealand. She uses a mix of vegetables, incorporating 2 cups of each of the following: pickling cucumbers sliced ¼ in. thick, celery sliced ¼ in. thick, green beans cut into ½-in. lengths, coarsely chopped bell peppers, coarsely chopped cauliflower, and shredded cabbage.

MAKES 5 to 7 pts. | **TIME** 1½ hours, plus 12 hours to brine vegetables

3 qts. sliced or chopped vegetables (a mix or all pickling cucumbers; see above)
2¼ lbs. onions (about 4), halved lengthwise and thinly sliced crosswise
½ cup salt
1 qt. distilled white vinegar
2½ cups sugar
1 tbsp. mustard seeds
2 tsp. *each* celery seeds and ground turmeric

1. In a large bowl (at least 6 qts.), combine vegetables, onions, salt, and 2½ qts. water. Cover and chill at least 12 hours and up to 24 hours. Drain, rinse well, and drain again.

2. Follow directions in *Canning ABCs: Get Ready (page 712)*, using 6 pint-size jars (7 if making with cucumbers only), plus matching rings and lids.

3. In an 8- to 10-qt. pan over high heat, bring vinegar, sugar, mustard seeds, celery seeds, and turmeric to a boil, stirring often. Add vegetable mixture, cover, and return to a boil; reduce heat and simmer, stirring occasionally, until onions are limp, about 2 minutes.

4. Fill jars as directed in *Canning ABCs: Fill and Seal Jars*, leaving ½ in. headspace in each jar; be sure liquid covers vegetables (discard any leftover liquid). Bring water in canner to 180° to 185° (not boiling, or pickles will get soft) and process for 20 minutes (add 5 minutes for every 3,000 ft. in altitude above sea level). Cool, check seals, and store as directed (up to 1 year).

PER ¼ CUP, DRAINED: 57 cal., 1.6% (0.9 cal.) from fat; 0.6 g protein; 0.1 g fat (0 g sat.); 14 g carbo (0.8 g fiber); 293 mg sodium; 0 mg chol.

Quick Indian Pickles

Try serving the savory, spicy spears as an appetizer.

MAKES 24 spears | **TIME** 1 hour

1 tsp. vegetable oil
½ tsp. *each* brown mustard seeds, black peppercorns, coriander seeds, and whole allspice
1 tsp. cumin seeds
3 cardamom pods, split
2 small dried hot red chiles such as arbol or Thai, broken in half
¼ tsp. ground turmeric
1 cup distilled white vinegar
½ cup fresh lime juice
3 tbsp. firmly packed light brown sugar
1½ tbsp. kosher salt
4 garlic cloves, cut in half
1-in. piece fresh ginger, thickly sliced
6 Persian cucumbers, cut into 4 spears each, or 2 English cucumbers, each cut into thirds crosswise and then into 4 spears

1. Warm oil in a small saucepan over medium heat. Add mustard seeds and cook, covered, until they pop, about 2 minutes. All at once, add peppercorns, coriander, allspice, cumin, cardamom, and chiles and cook, stirring, until spices are very fragrant, about 1 minute. Add turmeric and stir just until sizzling. Carefully add ½ cup water, the vinegar, lime juice, brown sugar, salt, garlic, and ginger. Bring to a boil over high heat, then reduce heat and simmer 2 minutes.

2. Pack cucumber spears into a deep bowl. Pour pickling liquid over them, weight with a small plate to keep submerged, and let cool to room temperature, about 40 minutes. Lift pickles out of brine to serve.

Make Ahead: Up to 2 days, chilled (pickles will get more flavorful).

PER SPEAR: 13 cal., 12% (1.6 cal.) from fat; 0.3 g protein; 0.2 g fat (0 g sat.); 2.7 g carbo (0.3 g fiber); 181 mg sodium; 0 mg chol.

Refrigerator Sweet Zucchini Pickles

Reader Chuck Allen of Palm Springs, California, gives these zucchini pickles as a fine house gift.

MAKES 3 pts. | **TIME** 40 minutes, plus 1 day to chill

4 zucchini (¼ lb. each)
1 red onion (½ lb.)
1 tsp. salt
2 red or yellow bell peppers (or 1 of each; ½ lb. total)
2 cups cider vinegar
⅔ cup sugar
2 tbsp. pickling spice

1. Trim and discard zucchini ends. Thinly slice zucchini. Peel onion and cut in half lengthwise, then vertically into thin slivers. Mix zucchini, onion, and salt. Let stand 30 minutes. Rinse well and drain.
2. Meanwhile, stem, seed, and cut bell peppers into thin slivers about 2 in. long.
3. In a 4- to 5-qt. pan over high heat, bring vinegar, sugar, and pickling spice to a boil. Add bell peppers and zucchini-onion mixture. Remove from heat and mix well.
4. Spoon vegetables and liquid into 1-pt. jars, cover, and let cool. Chill at least 24 hours before eating.
Make Ahead: Up to 6 weeks, chilled.

PER ¼ CUP: 33 cal., 0% from fat; 0.4 g protein; 0 g fat; 8.6 g carbo (0.3 g fiber); 99 mg sodium; 0 mg chol.

Dill Pickle Spears

"The chiles give these pickles a kick," says reader Debbie Harpe, of Placentia, California.

MAKES 4 qts. | **TIME** 1 hour

¼ cup pickling spice
3½ cups distilled white vinegar
6 tbsp. sugar
¼ cup salt
5 lbs. pickling cucumbers (about 40; *see Quick Tips below*)
8 dill seed heads (2 to 3 in. wide; *see Quick Tips below*)
8 garlic cloves, peeled
12 small dried hot chiles (each 3 to 4 in. long; ¼ oz. total), such as arbol

1. Follow directions in *Canning ABCs: Get Ready (page 712)*, using 4 wide-mouthed quart-size jars, plus matching rings and lids.
2. Enclose pickling spice in a double layer of cheesecloth and tie tightly with string. In a 2- to 3-qt. pan over high heat, bring spice bag, 3½ cups water, vinegar, sugar, and salt to a boil, stirring often. Cover, reduce heat, and simmer, stirring occasionally, 15 minutes. Discard spice bag.
3. Meanwhile, discard any blossoms and stems from cucumbers. Quarter cucumbers lengthwise.
4. Place 2 dill seed heads, 2 garlic cloves, and 3 chiles in each jar. Pack cucumber quarters vertically into jars without forcing, pushing ½ in. below rim; cut off any tips of spears that stick above this level. Pour hot vinegar mixture over cucumbers, leaving ½ in. of headspace (be sure liquid covers cucumbers). Release air bubbles and seal jars.
5. Process as directed in *Canning ABCs: Process Jars,* but keep water at 180° to 185° (not boiling, or pickles will get soft), checking with a thermometer, for 20 minutes (add 5 minutes for every 3,000 ft. in altitude above sea level). Cool, check seals, and store as directed (up to 1 year). For best flavor, let the pickles stand at least 1 week before serving.
Quick Tips: For the best pickles, buy very fresh cucumbers 3 to 4 in. long—larger ones are more likely to have formed hollows and don't pack as neatly into jars. Dill seed heads are sold on the stalk; snip off and discard the stem.

PER 2 SPEARS, DRAINED: 9.5 cal., 9.5% (0.9 cal.) from fat; 0.2 g protein; 0.1 g fat (0 g sat.); 2.5 g carbo (0.3 g fiber); 262 mg sodium; 0 mg chol.

preserves & pickles

Cabbage Pickles with Daikon (Kimchi)

In Korea, *kimchi* is traditionally made in autumn, in batches large enough to last a family through the winter and spring. The spicy cabbage mixture is packed in large crocks, then allowed to ferment. You'll find *kimchi* sold in Asian markets and some supermarkets. Hotness and pungency vary from brand to brand, but most are quite potent—one good reason to consider making your own. By controlling the degree of fermentation and adjusting the amount of chile, you can make homemade *kimchi* as mild or bold as you like. Korean crushed red chile gives the *kimchi* an authentic flavor, but cayenne will still give it an exciting amount of heat. Strips of daikon make a slightly more pungent pickle; omit them if you prefer a milder version.

MAKES About 3½ cups | **TIME** 30 minutes, plus 3 to 4 hours to stand

1 medium head napa cabbage (1½ to 2 lbs.)
2½ tbsp. salt, divided
¼ lb. daikon (optional), peeled and cut into matchstick pieces
2 green onions, trimmed and cut into thin slivers
3 garlic cloves, minced or pressed
1 to 2 tsp. Korean crushed red chile (*see Quick Tip below*) or cayenne
2 tsp. sugar

1. Core and cut cabbage into chunks about 1 in. square; place in a large bowl and add 2 tbsp. salt. Mix well. Cover and let stand at room temperature until cabbage is wilted and reduced to about half its original volume, 3 to 4 hours.
2. Rinse cabbage thoroughly; drain. Return to bowl along with daikon if using, green onions, garlic, red pepper, sugar, and remaining ½ tbsp. salt; mix well.
3. Pack mixture loosely into a 1-qt. jar; cover with lid or plastic wrap and let stand at room temperature, tasting often, until fermented to your liking. (In warm weather, fermentation may take only 1 to 2 days; in cooler weather, count on 3 to 4 days.) Store in refrigerator, covered, for up to 2 weeks.
Quick Tip: Find Korean crushed red chile online at *koamart.com*.

PER ½ CUP: 28 cal., 3% (0.7 cal.) from fat; 1.5 g protein; 0.1 g fat (0 g sat.); 5.9 g carbo (1.5 g fiber); 512 mg sodium; 0 mg chol.

Pickled Green Beans with Dill, Tarragon, Garlic, and Peppercorns

These tart, snappy beans are just the thing with a Bloody Mary or burger. Processing the beans in the canner at 180° to 185° rather than at the boiling point keeps them crunchy.

recipe pictured on page **687**

MAKES 7 pts. | **TIME** 1¾ hours

4 lbs. haricots verts or 4½ lbs. regular green beans
14 *each* dill and tarragon sprigs (4 in. long)
7 garlic cloves, peeled
About 1¼ tsp. black peppercorns
1 qt. (32 oz.) white wine vinegar (5% acidity)
2 tbsp. plus 1 tsp. salt (optional)

1. Follow directions in *Canning ABCs: Get Ready (page 712)*, using 7 regular or wide-mouthed pint-size jars, plus matching rings and lids.
2. Trim stem ends from beans, keeping tips intact, so beans are 3½ to 4 in. long.
3. Pack jars: Holding each jar on its side, insert 2 dill sprigs, 2 tarragon sprigs, and a garlic clove. Fill snugly with beans, tips down. Sprinkle about 12 peppercorns into each jar.
4. In a large saucepan, bring vinegar, 4 cups water, and salt if using to a boil over high heat. Ladle liquid over beans to within ½ in. of rims; discard any extra liquid. Wipe rims and seal with lids and rings as directed.
5. Process as directed in *Canning ABCs: Process Jars*, but keep water at 180° to 185° (not boiling), checking with a thermometer, for 30 minutes (add 5 minutes for every 3,000 ft. in altitude above sea level). Cool, check seals, and store as directed (up to 1 year).

PER ¼ CUP: 14 cal., 0% (0 cal.) from fat; 0.7 g protein; 3.2 g carbo (0.6 g fiber); 2.6 mg sodium; 0 mg chol.

from tasting to touring:
getting to know
Western
wines

Your Wine Questions Answered

How can you tell if a wine is corked? What are legs? And is it okay to keep wine in your closet?

Is there an official way to taste wine to get the most out of it?

Official? No. But yes to the rest of the question. There are some actual mechanics that pull the most aroma and flavor from a wine.

1. Look. Tip your glass slightly and look at the wine's color (a white backdrop helps); the appearance of a wine usually corresponds to its taste. Red wine picks up color as it picks up flavor from the skins and seeds, so wine with dense color is likely to have fairly intense flavors. (Keep in mind that red wine lightens with age, and white wine darkens with age.)

2. Swirl. Gently swirl the wine in the glass to release the aromas.

3. Sniff. Get your nose right in the glass—you can't be polite about it. The first sniffs tell you the most, and you actually pick up more aromas with a few quick sniffs than with one long one.

4. Sip. Keep the wine in your mouth for 3 to 4 seconds (it takes that long to penetrate your taste buds), swirling it around all over your tongue. Pro tasters often pull air in through the wine while it's in their mouth, but reverse gurgling might raise some eyebrows at your average dinner party.

What's the best way to open wine?

Cut off the top of the foil cap first, using the knife on your corkscrew or an official foil cutter. It's not always easy to cut it cleanly, but if you run the knife around under the ridge of the bottle rim and begin pulling up the edge of the foil, the whole thing will release itself. As far as the corkscrew goes, use any wine opener with a screw mechanism (the "worm") shaped in a helix, as though it's been wrapped around a cylinder. That shape ensures that the screw follows the path of the point exactly, causing as little damage as possible to the cork.

A side note about the Butler's Friend: This two-pronged wine opener was used by 19th-century butlers to open wine without putting a hole in the cork. The butler could drink a little wine, fill the bottle with something else, and replace the cork without detection. It's a good tool for opening older bottles with fragile corks; on the other hand, it can also backfire and push the cork farther down into the bottle.

Do you really need different glasses for different types of wine?

No. One good set of wineglasses is fine. It's true that some glass shapes optimize the characteristics of certain varieties, but they aren't so much better that anyone should lose sleep over it. Just choose glasses that have big enough bowls to let you swirl wine—red or white—pretty vigorously without splashing it out. The one quality factor that does make a difference is the rim: A thin-rimmed glass (rather than the thick, rolled style) makes wine taste better. They tend to be more expensive, which leads to one last guideline: Never use a glass that's more expensive than you can afford to break!

What wines should be decanted?

Two categories of wine benefit from decanting: young, tannic reds and old reds that likely have thrown some sediment during their lifetime.

The first can stand to be splashed through the air into a decanter that gives the wine a lot of surface space in contact with oxygen. The oxidation process softens the tannins and opens up the flavors in the wine.

Old, fragile reds need different treatment. The purpose of decanting is to get them off their sediment, but too much oxygen, and the most fragile of them will breathe their last. Stand the bottle upright for a few hours to get the sediment to the bottom. Then pour very slowly and carefully into a decanter, stopping when the sediment gets to the edge of the bottle's lip. When professional sommeliers do this, it appears to involve a little bit of useful ceremony and a little bit of voodoo. They pour in front of a light source, often a candle. This looks a little mystical, but allows the sommelier to see the sediment in the neck of the bottle.

Most of us could stand to decant a lot more young red wines than we do. You don't need a fancy container for decanting; a clean mayonnaise jar will work just fine.

How much wine should your pour?
Most people pour too much. As a rule of thumb, fill the glass no more than one-third full. This leaves enough space to swirl the wine. (Of course, when you order wine by the glass at a restaurant, they often do a higher pour so you feel like you've gotten your money's worth. The best-case scenario: when a restaurant serves its wine in very large glasses so you're getting a generous pour, but still fills only a third of the glass.)

What are legs?
When you swirl wine in a glass, the residual that sticks to the side and slowly drips down is called the legs, or sometimes the tears. Common wisdom had it that the more substantial the legs, the better the wine. (Cue the jokes: "Look at those legs!") But wine legs are simply caused by changes in surface tension due to the differing evaporation rates of alcohol and water. They do provide a clue about a wine's alcohol content level but very little about its quality. Heavier legs indicate a higher alcohol level, but that's neither good nor bad. Whether high or low, it needs to be in balance with other elements in the wine.

Why do wine alcohol levels seem to be getting higher?
Today many wineries are asking growers to let the grapes hang on the vine longer for lusher, riper fruit flavors. But sugar levels rise as the grapes get riper. And since fermentation involves yeast turning sugar into alcohol, very ripe wines usually have correspondingly high alcohol levels (unless the winemaker has removed

some, which is legal). The issue is much discussed—both criticized and defended. So if your wine seems big and fruity, you might want to check the label for the alcohol level and maybe moderate your intake.

Are there rules of etiquette for receiving a bottle of wine in a restaurant?
Again, no rules. But there's a traditional process, part of which is just vestige from history, and part of which is useful. The waiter shows you the label of the bottle to make sure it's what you ordered. He or she will open it in front of you for full transparency—no shenanigans with the product. Then a little unnecessary action: He/she will put the cork on the table in front of you. You don't need to do anything with it but look at it (it's a sign of good storage if the bottle end is moist). The custom of placing the cork on the table started in the 1800s when restaurants were known for uncorking an expensive bottle of wine, selling it, and putting less expensive wine in the bottle. This prompted wineries to brand their corks. Waiters began putting the cork in front of the customer so they could check to make sure the brand on the cork matched the wine label.

Next, the server will pour a small amount of wine in the glass of whoever ordered it. This is to let you taste it to see if it's sound, not whether you like it.

There are two main reasons to send a wine back: if it's prematurely oxidized (it will smell and taste a little bit like sherry), which means it was probably not shipped or stored well. Or if it's what's called "corked"—tainted with a compound called TCA (trichloroanisole). A corked wine will smell musty, like a wet dog or old newspapers in the basement. A phenomenon that occurs in natural cork and ruins the wine, TCA isn't the fault of the restaurant or the winery, but the restaurant will gladly take back a bottle of corked wine. New methods of treating cork are reducing the number of corked bottles, but it still happens regularly.

What's the best way to pick out wine in the supermarket, if that's where you shop for wine?

Most supermarkets organize their wines in a way that's predictable. The expensive bottles are on the top shelf, midrange wines are on the middle shelf, and magnums and jug wines are on the lower shelf (or in a separate section). Don't rule out that bottom shelf; these days, with winemaking getting better and better across the board, you can find good-value bulk wines there.

In general, though, in the absence of a helpful wine clerk, go with better-known labels, the ones you've heard of. The supermarket isn't the best place to take a risk on obscure bottles. Do, though, look for special wine displays out on the floor or in end caps on the aisle. These are often the wines the store has gotten a good deal on and can be the best buy.

How should you store wine if you don't have a wine cellar?

You don't need perfect conditions to store wine. Many experts say that 55° is the ideal cellar temperature. But if you don't have a proper cellar, don't be discouraged for a minute. An inner closet in your home could work just fine.

SIMPLE STORAGE RULES

1. Keep wine where the temperature is fairly constant. A cool place is best, but what you really want to avoid is large temperature swings. A constant 70° is better than 60° to 85° 10 times a season.
2. Keep wine out of bright sunlight, which deteriorates it.
3. Store wine in a place that is fairly still. You wouldn't want to store wine on top of a refrigerator, for instance, because vibration deteriorates wine.
4. Store wine on its side or upside down to keep the wine in contact with the cork, keeping it moist. This prevents the cork from shrinking and drying out, which

can cause air to get in and oxidize the wine too fast. If you buy a case, set it on its side or turn it so the bottles are upside down.

How do you know when wine is ready to drink?

The truth is, most winemakers these days are producing wines that are very pleasant to drink as soon as the wine is released, which is when most of us drink them (after aging them in the backseat of the car all the way home from the supermarket).

That said, big, structured red wines get more interesting with age. The fruit flavors soften and slowly fade as secondary flavors like dried flowers, soy sauce, and leather come to the front. That profile isn't familiar to a lot of people, though, and many don't like older wines at all.

There's no trusty formula for how long to age an age-worthy wine. A good rule of thumb for West Coast Cabernets is between five years (about when the effect of aging kicks in) to 10 years. That's not gospel—some will still be beautiful at 25 years. They'll have all those secondary flavors going on with very little fruit, but will be fascinating still.

What constitutes an age-worthy red wine?

It needs three things in balance: great tannin structure, good acidity, and solid (complex) fruit flavors.

THE HALF-CASE EXPERIMENT

The only way to determine whether a red will age gracefully is by opening a bottle and trying it. If its tannin, acid, and fruit are a little out of balance now, it's not going to taste great 10 years down the line. If they are in balance, buy half a case.

The Long-range Tasting Plan

• Drink a bottle now, and make a few notes about your impression (the tough part: finding a place to keep those notes where they won't get lost or forgotten).
• Drink a bottle in three years as a sneak preview; add to your notes.
• Drink a bottle in five years (you get the idea about the notes).
• Drink a bottle at seven years. If it's tired, drink the last two too.
• If it's not, drink the fifth bottle in 10 years; if it still tastes good, hold the last bottle.
• Drink the final bottle at 20 years, and see what you have.

Pairing Wine with Food

Here are profiles of the West's most popular wines—plus general advice on pairing them with food and specific tips for great matchups with recipes in this book.

Red Wines

Cabernet Sauvignon
The king of reds, Cabernet is a big-structured, dark-fruited wine. The best Cabs become even more elegant with age.

Swirl and taste: Plums, blackberries, and black currant (cassis); sometimes violets or rose; often mint, mocha, and eucalyptus or cedar; firm tannins underneath.

Find your style: Some Cabs are made to be drunk tonight—with ripe fruit and subdued tannins. Others need years to mellow. Great Cabs, some argue, are balanced the day they're released and get better with time.

Pair with: Well-marbled beef • Hearty fowl like duck • Spice rubs and sauces with lots of black pepper • Mushrooms • Marinades with soy sauce • Long-braised stews • Pot roast • Grilled red meat

GREAT RECIPE PAIRINGS FOR CABERNET SAUVIGNON
- Thyme-roasted Duck Breasts with Orange-Wine Sauce (*page 392*)
- Pepper Steaks with Balsamic Onions (*page 401*)
- Salt- and Herb-crusted Prime Rib with Fresh Horse-radish Sauce (*page 404*)
- Peppered Beef Skewers with Red Onion–Horseradish Marmalade (*page 441*)
- Grilled Rib-eye Steaks with Miso Butter and Sweet Onions (*page 482*)
- Gin and Spice Flank Steak (*page 485*)
- Beef Rib Roast and Yorkshire Pudding from the Grill (*page 489*)
- Grilled Lamb Loin with Cabernet-Mint Sauce and Garlic Mashed Potatoes (*page 501*)

Merlot
The most popular red wine in the United States, Merlot has dark fruit flavors like Cabernet Sauvignon, but is generally a little rounder and softer.

Swirl and taste: Blackberries, blueberries, plums, cassis, and dried cherries combined with chocolate, cedar, and tobacco and sometimes hints of black olive.

Find your style: Merlot is the popular wine that it is partly because of its gentle reputation. But don't write Merlot off as less than serious! The variety can be deeply concentrated, with firm, Cab-rivaling tannins—especially Merlot from Washington.

Pair with: Tender, milder cuts of beef, such as tenderloin • Lamb • Meaty fish—salmon, tuna • Black olives • Mushrooms • Fresh herbs • Grilled foods • Meats with warm spices • Meats with fruit sauces—berries, dried cherries • Legumes

GREAT RECIPE PAIRINGS FOR MERLOT
- Spiced Beef Tenderloin (*page 69*)
- Spicy Beef Cross-rib Roast with Caramelized Clementine Sauce (*page 403*)
- Slow-cooker Merlot Pot Roast (*page 405*)
- Ginger Beef Mini Skewers (*page 441*)
- Korean Barbecued Beef (*page 483*)
- New York Strip Steaks with Orange and Oregano (*page 484*)
- Grilled Beef Tenderloin with Fresh Herbs (*page 488*)

Pinot Noir
A light-bodied, low-tannin, silky, sensual red, Pinot Noir was handed stardom in 2004 by the movie *Sideways*.

Swirl and taste: Red or dark berries, cherries, plums, violets, warm spices (cloves, cinnamon), herbs, and sometimes orange peel with an underside of cedar, smoke, leather, mushrooms, and loam.

Find your style: Pinot Noir can have an earthy Old World style (as in those from Burgundy, France—long on minerals, short on fruit). Or it can have a riper, more fruit-forward, New World style.

Some winemakers in Oregon's Willamette Valley and the cooler parts of California make a hybrid that's lean and earthy yet still has generous fruit. The leaner, cooler-weather versions tend to have lower alcohol levels; the riper, fruitier Pinots from warmer places can have alcohol levels that overwhelm this wine.

Pair with: Boldly flavored poultry and duck • Lamb • Venison • Hearty fish—salmon, tuna • Ham, spicy pork • Mushrooms • Earthy legumes like lentils • Warm spices—cinnamon, cloves, cumin, ginger • Sweet-salty marinades • Fruit-based sauces—with berries, dried cherries • Spiced Asian and eastern Mediterranean dishes • Many cheeses

GREAT RECIPE PAIRINGS FOR PINOT NOIR
- Mushroom Potstickers (page 43)
- Curried Salmon Cakes (page 328)
- Tuna with Tomato-Caper Sauce (page 333)
- Soy-Ginger Roast Chicken with Shiitake Mushrooms (page 357)
- Pinot-braised Duck with Spicy Greens (page 391)
- Pork Shoulder Roast with Figs, Garlic, and Pinot Noir (page 417)
- Double Salmon Burgers (page 469)
- Spice-rubbed, Smoke-roasted Chicken (page 470)
- Barbecued Glazed Turkey (page 479)
- Grilled Apricot-stuffed Leg of Lamb (page 500)
- Herb- and Mustard-glazed Grilled Salmon (page 506)
- Spicy Ponzu Salmon on Greens (page 506)

Zinfandel
The most American wine of all (it's grown very few other places), Zinfandel is a juicy, jammy, spicy red that loves to turn your teeth purple.

Swirl and taste: Intense dark berries, dried cherries, plums, chocolate, and black pepper—a mouth-filling wine.

Find your style: Zinfandel is mostly grown in warm places, and the grapes are allowed to get very ripe, producing the wine's signature jammy flavors—and high alcohol levels. If you don't love fruit bombs, look for Zins from cooler places, which are slightly leaner, often with interesting herbal notes.

Pair with: Barbecue (Zin loves pork ribs) • Hamburgers • Sausages • Pizza • Grilled foods—leg of lamb, steak, chicken • Long-braised stews • Slightly spicy foods • Southwest and Mexican dishes • Moroccan spices—coriander, cinnamon, cumin

GREAT RECIPE PAIRINGS FOR ZINFANDEL
- Green Chile (Chile Verde) (page 123)
- Shredded Beef Enchiladas (page 408)
- Stuffed Chipotle Meatballs (page 409)
- Mexican Braised Pork Ribs (page 420)
- Sticky Ribs (page 421)
- Lamb Shanks Adobo (page 426)
- Grilled Pizza (page 465)
- Gold Nugget Burger (page 466)
- Grilled Skirt Steak (Arracheras) (page 485)
- Applewood-smoked Spareribs with Paprika Chili Spice Rub (page 491)
- Herb-rubbed Baby Back Ribs with Cherry-Zinfandel Barbecue Sauce (page 492)
- Grilled Moroccan Lamb Kebabs with Grapes (page 503)

Syrah
Earthy and fruity at once, Syrah grows well in a wide range of climates and therefore comes in many different styles.

Swirl and taste: Dark fruit (blackberries, blueberries, and cherries), black olives, and herbs against a backdrop of earthy leather, tobacco, and meaty bacon, laced with black pepper.

Find your style: Syrah grown in the cooler parts of the West can be very lean, dark, and earthy. In warmer regions, the ripe fruit pops.

Pair with: Lamb • Sausages • Grilled meats of all kinds • Roast pork • Barbecue • Stews • Game—venison, squab • Black olives • Dishes with lots of black pepper • Dishes with pungent herbs and/or warm spices (Moroccan, Indian)

GREAT RECIPE PAIRINGS FOR SYRAH
- Crown Lamb Roast with Green Herb Couscous (page 426)
- Coffee-braised Spoon Lamb (page 428)
- Crazed Mom's Easy Steak and Garam Masala Naan-wiches (page 461)
- Grilled Rosemary Lamb Burgers with Pea and Mint Relish (page 467)
- Lucques Pork Burger (page 469)
- Grilled Tri-tip with Cuban Mojo Sauce (page 486)
- Santa Maria–style Grilled Tri-tip (page 486)
- Lamb Chops with Roasted Salsa (page 502)

Dry Rosé Wine

A crisp pink that combines the rich fruit of red wine with the refreshing, low-tannin nature of white—not to be confused with white Zinfandel.

Swirl and taste: Strawberries, cherries, watermelon, citrus, flowers, herbs, and spices.

Find your style: Dry rosés made from Pinot Noir (often called *vin gris*) have delicate red fruit and warm spices; those from Syrah, Grenache, and Mourvèdre (traditional in France) come with wilder berries, watermelon, and herbs; rosés made from Merlot and other Bordeaux grapes are generally darker and heavier.

Pair with: Fish and seafood • Chicken and turkey • Pork • Spicy or garlicky dishes • Sandwiches, picnic fare • Thanksgiving dinner • Southwest flavors • Chinese food • Indian food • Cheese

GREAT RECIPE PAIRINGS FOR DRY ROSÉ
- Spicy Seafood Stew (*page 125*)
- California Niçoise Sandwiches (*page 189*)
- Curried Salmon Cakes (*page 328*)
- Spring Aioli with Shrimp (*page 347*)
- Grilled Buttermilk Chicken (*page 427*)
- Bruschetta on the Grill (*page 438*)
- Honey-Hoisin Grilled Chicken Wings (*page 442*)
- Salt-cured Ouzo Shrimp (*page 510*)
- Grilled Seafood and Chorizo Paella (*page 512*)

White Wines

Chardonnay

With complex fruit flavors and a rich, creamy texture, Chardonnay is the most popular white wine in the United States to date.

Swirl and taste: Apple, pear, melon, creamy lemon, and sometimes pineapple, rounded out with butterscotch and vanilla.

Find your style: California winemakers have traditionally made Chardonnay in a rich, buttery style by fermenting and aging it in oak barrels. Too much oak can cover up the fruit, though, so some winemakers are starting to substitute stainless-steel tanks, for a leaner, crisper style.

Pair with: Sweet shellfish • White-fleshed fish—halibut, black cod (sablefish), sturgeon, mahimahi, tilapia • Chicken and turkey • Pork • Veal • Legumes • Winter squash • Corn • Nuts • Risotto and pasta • Cream and butter sauces • Mild Caribbean dishes with tropical fruit flavors • Pasta

GREAT RECIPE PAIRINGS FOR CHARDONNAY
- Ultimate Crabcakes (*page 62*)
- Crispy Shrimp with Arugula and Lemony Mayo (*page 64*)
- Hawaiian Steamed Mahimahi Wraps (Mahimahi *Laulau*) (*page 66*)
- King Crab with Lemongrass-Ginger Butter and Roasted Potatoes (*page 339*)
- Scallops with Miso, Ginger, and Grapefruit (*page 348*)
- Scallops with Peppers and Corn (*page 348*)
- Roast Chicken with Meyer Lemon–Shallot Sauce (*page 355*)
- Biscuit-topped Chicken Potpies (*page 365*)
- Sage-rubbed Pork Tenderloins with Sage Butter (*page 400*)
- Veal Scaloppine with Pears (*page 411*)
- Grilled Corn and Bay Shrimp Risotto (*page 511*)

Sauvignon Blanc

A lean, crisp white, Sauvignon Blanc is extremely flexible with food—a great alternative to Chardonnay.

Swirl and taste: Tart lemon, grapefruit, melon, and tropicals like passionfruit—even gooseberry—over a pleasant grassiness and herbal quality.

Find your style: The majority of West Coast Sauvignon Blancs are fermented in stainless steel and never touch oak. Winemakers are trying to retain the fresh fruit character and great acidity natural to the grape—traits that make the wine a good match for green vegetables, salads, and all sorts of cheeses (especially goat). A few vintners, though, ferment part of their Sauvignon Blanc in oak barrels, looking for a slightly rounder, richer style. A handful of these are labeled Fumé Blanc, a name—and style—invented by Robert Mondavi.

Pair with: Cheese (especially goat cheese) • Green vegetables (asparagus, zucchini, fresh peas, artichokes) • Oysters • Delicate fish like sole • Fresh herbs • Mild vinaigrettes • Dishes with tangy dairy ingredients • Herbal, briny sauces • Pesto

GREAT RECIPE PAIRINGS FOR SAUVIGNON BLANC
- Roasted Artichoke Salad with Lemon and Mint (*page 151*)
- Halibut Baked in Fresh Green Salsa (*page 307*)
- Oven-browned Sole with Asparagus (*page 325*)
- Scallop and Sugar Snap Pea Stir-fry (*page 350*)
- Lemon-Artichoke Chicken (*page 366*)
- Chicken-Pesto Crêpes (*page 367*)
- Grilled Artichokes with Green Olive Dip (*page 440*)
- Grilled Yellow Squash and Zucchini Pasta Salad (*page 446*)
- Grilled Lamb Brochettes with Lemon and Dill (*page 502*)
- Grilled Bass with Salsa Verde (*page 504*)
- Lemon-Garlic Shrimp Skewers (*page 510*)

Pinot Gris/Grigio

Pinot Grigio, as the Italians call it, is usually crisp, light, and steely, with great acidity; Pinot Gris (the same grape), as it's called in France, is often made into a rounder, more complex wine.

Swirl and taste: Pear, lemon (sometimes leaning toward lemongrass), melon, and sweet spice flavors often come with a flinty edge—imagine wet stones.

Find your style: U.S. winemakers can call this wine either Pinot Grigio or Pinot Gris. Their choice is generally an indication of whether they're shooting for the crisp Italian style or the more layered French style.

Pair with: Richer fish—tuna, salmon • Shellfish • Chicken • Pasta • Fresh herbs • Simple but rich sauces • Mild Asian dishes • Coconut milk–based curries • Some cheeses—gruyère is excellent

GREAT RECIPE PAIRINGS FOR PINOT GRIS/GRIGIO

- Crab and Smoked Trout Cakes with Herb Salad (page 61)
- Northwest Smoked Salmon Crêpes (page 68)
- Warm Chicken BLT Salad (page 185)
- Ultimate Mac 'n' Cheese (page 285)
- Pan-roasted Black Cod with Thai Curry Sauce (page 303)
- Oven-baked Salmon with Picholine Olive Sauce (page 331)
- Steamed Mussels in Creamy Tarragon-Shallot Broth (page 350)
- Spicy Soy-Ginger Grilled Sea Bass with Asparagus (page 443)
- Grilled Trout Fillets with Crunchy Pine-nut Lemon Topping (page 504)
- Halibut Kebabs with Grilled Bread and Pancetta (page 505)
- Lemon-Garlic Shrimp Skewers (page 510)

Viognier

An exotic, full-bodied, aromatic, floral white.

Swirl and taste: Honeyed tangerine, peach, and apricot with honeysuckle and citrus blossom aromas.

Find your style: Naturally aromatic and loaded with opulent fruit and floral qualities, Viognier from warmer regions, where the grapes ripen with abandon, can get blowsy, heavy-handed, and cloying.

In slightly cooler places, where the grapes hold on to their acidity, Viognier is leaner and less flabby—its richness balanced with crispness.

Pair with: Shellfish—crab, prawns, scallops, lobster • Rich fish such as black cod (sablefish) and sturgeon—especially with cream sauces • Spice-rubbed roast chicken and turkey • Braised or roasted root vegetables—carrots, turnips, squash • Sauces with warm, aromatic spices • Moroccan dishes—*tagines*, charmoula sauce • Mild curries—Indian, Southeast Asian • Fruity, spicy condiments like chutney

GREAT RECIPE PAIRINGS FOR VIOGNIER

- Thai Coconut Chili Clams and Mussels (page 48)
- Roasted Beet Salad with Oranges and Queso Fresco (Ensalada de Betabel) (page 152)
- Fried Chicken Sandwiches with Spicy Slaw (page 175)
- Mango-Mint Lobster Rolls (page 343)
- Spicy Mango Shrimp (page 346)
- Chicken Tagine with Pine-nut Couscous (page 360)
- Chicken Cashew Korma (page 364)
- Vietnamese Skewered Pork and Onions (page 412)
- Yogurt-marinated Chicken Kebabs with Pearl Couscous (page 475)
- Grilled Pork Chops with Onion-Peach Marmalade (page 491)
- Spicy Pork Skewers (page 495)
- Grilled Ahi Citrus Salad (page 562)

Riesling

An extremely crisp (high-acid), aromatic wine, Riesling is considered the noblest white of all by much of the wine world, and it pairs with just about everything.

Swirl and taste: Delicate white peach, green apple, and lime flavors—or riper apricot, nectarine, and mandarin orange. Riesling often has a pleasant minerality akin to wet stones and a haunting diesel-like aroma (if you can imagine that as a good thing).

Find your style: Riesling can be bone-dry to quite sweet. In the West it earned a bad reputation through the 1970s and '80s because winemakers were making it too sweet for the amount of acidity it had, and the result was simple, syrupy, uninteresting wine. Now, though, Western vintners are making drier and drier Rieslings. And the best have enough acidity to keep the wine lively no matter how sweet it is.

Pair with: Shellfish • Pork and ham • Salads and vegetables • Egg dishes • Sausages, salumi, and charcuterie—especially cured pork products • Barbecue • Asian dishes—Thai, Vietnamese, Chinese, Japanese (sushi!), Indian • Southwestern foods • Avocado

GREAT RECIPE PAIRINGS FOR RIESLING
- Chile Cheese Fondue (*page 30*)
- Avocados with Warm Bacon Parsley Vinaigrette (*page 33*)
- Deviled Eggs with Bacon (*page 41*)
- Green Chile (*Chile Verde*) (*page 123*)
- Best-ever Chinese Chicken Salad (*page 168*)
- Shrimp Pad Thai (*page 219*)
- Pan-roasted Black Cod with Thai Curry Sauce (*page 303*)
- Chilled Poached Halibut with Fresh Apricot Salsa (*page 304*)
- Cracked Crab with Herbed Avocado Sauce (*page 339*)
- Hoisin Pork with Hot Mustard (*page 412*)
- Pork Scaloppine with Sweet-tart Shallots (*page 414*)
- Cider-brined Pork Chops with Sautéed Apples (*page 416*)
- Eggplant, Pork, and Tofu Stir-fry (*page 422*)
- *Char Siu*–glazed Pork and Pineapple Buns (*page 464*)
- Grilled Cilantro Chicken with Pickled Tomato and Avocado Salsa (*page 473*)
- Achiote-and-Orange Pulled Pork (*page 494*)

Sparkling Wines

Made primarily from Chardonnay and Pinot Noir grapes, good-quality sparklers in this country get their bubbles from the traditional Champagne method: They're created by a second fermentation right in the bottle. Bubbly's great acidity makes it an excellent food wine (not just a sipper for celebrations).

Swirl and taste: Apple, lemon, lime, pear, strawberry, and cherry flavors with a pleasant yeastiness (like brioche baking) and earthy minerality.

Find your style: *Blanc de blancs* is 100 percent Chardonnay and generally shows off its apple, pear, and citrus flavors. A classic brut is a blend of Chardonnay and Pinot Noir, so brings some red fruit into the mix. *Blanc de noirs* is mostly Pinot Noir, leaning further toward red fruit flavors. And sparkling rosé has just been left on those Pinot Noir skins a tiny bit longer, to pick up more color, texture, and flavor.

Pair with: Caviar • Smoked salmon • Cheeses • Fish and shellfish • Cream sauces • Potpies, savory turnovers • Asian dishes of all kinds • Sausages—especially

There are full-on red sparklers out there—made out of the likes of Cabernet Sauvignon—and they can be fun food partners, especially for meat off the grill.

poultry, pork, and Polish • Tangy, fruity condiments • Salty foods • Deep-fried foods • Potato chips • Popcorn

GREAT RECIPE PAIRINGS FOR SPARKLING WINE
- Smoky Salmon Chive Spread (*page 26*)
- Caramelized Pear and Sage Crostini (*page 29*)
- Spicy Fried Chickpeas (*page 36*)
- Baby Ballpark Dogs (*page 38*)
- Blue Cheese Puffs (*page 41*)
- Pork and Shrimp Dumplings (*Shu Mai*) (*page 43*)
- Oysters on the Half-shell with Grapefruit Granita (*page 47*)
- Tuna Tartare in Spicy Sesame Oil (*page 69*)
- Fried Chicken Sandwiches with Spicy Slaw (*page 175*)
- Sushi (*page 334*)
- Mendo Crabcakes (*page 342*)
- Spring Aioli with Shrimp (*page 347*)
- Herb-crusted Ham (*page 424*)
- Barbecued Oysters with Chipotle Glaze (*page 444*)
- Grilled Sardines with Bean Salad (*page 505*)
- Tandoori Shrimp in Green Marinade (*page 509*)
- Grilled Seafood and Chorizo Paella (*page 512*)

Tasting Places: A Guide to Western Wines

The beauty of wine country is an enduring reason to visit, and there is no better way to understand and appreciate a wine than to sip it in the place where it's grown. But with some of the best wine in the world coming from the West to wine aisles all over the nation, it doesn't take a trip to wine country to enjoy the wealth. If you are going, though, below are some must-sees for wine lovers. And if you're headed to your local wine shop, use our descriptions of the best varieties in each region as a shopping guide.

California: Golden State of Wine

When an unknown Napa Cabernet was famously declared—by an all-French panel of judges—the top red in the Judgment of Paris tasting of 1976, besting Bordeaux legends, and a California Chardonnay beat out the white burgundies, California wine was catapulted onto the world stage. And since that time, successive generations of winemakers have energetically raised the bar on winemaking quality and passionately planted new grapes in new places, discovering what grows well where, until the state of the craft here is nothing short of astonishing.

With well over 2,000 wineries, California produces almost 85 percent of the country's wine. Even so, there's an enduring spirit of creativity and experimentation—and an unmistakable air of agriculture—in most of the state's wine-growing regions, layered under the sophistication and sheer beauty they all share. And now winemakers from all over the world have joined our homegrown talent, often because the level of innovation they find here isn't possible in their highly regulated Old World regions. Grapevines have also made their way here from all over the world (many tucked away in suitcases—Samsonite cuttings, they're called). The result is a diversity of winery personalities, wines, and winemaking styles that makes exploring California wine country (whether by car or in your local wine store) endlessly interesting.

Napa

For most of the world, "Napa Valley" is shorthand for all California wines, in the same way that Hollywood means American movies. It's home to some of California's grandest traditional wineries as well as its most jaw-droppingly extravagant contemporary ones. Roughly 30 miles long and 5 miles wide, the valley and the benchlands and mountain peaks that surround it contain, at last count, more than 400 wineries. Their right to the Napa Valley moniker on their labels gives every bottle a pedigree—and correspondingly higher price tag.

There's some justification for this. Since their triumphs at the Judgment of Paris tasting, Napa wines have been acknowledged to be on par with their

French counterparts. Today, the reputation of the region rides largely on one grape: Cabernet Sauvignon. Hundreds of grape varieties were planted in the valley's early years, and a few now make some pretty great wine—Merlot and other Bordeaux varieties especially, plus some Zinfandel, Sauvignon Blanc, and, in the cool-weather Carneros District, Chardonnay. But in Napa, Cab is king.

The heart of the valley, around Rutherford and Oakville, produces some of the most sought-after Cabs in the world—meaty, lush, layered, wonderful. But Napa Valley as an appellation or AVA (American Viticultural Area) is carved up into more than a dozen smaller AVAs. Attention is increasingly focused on the benchlands that lie against the Mayacamas Mountains to the west and the Vaca Range to the east (home to the legendary Stags' Leap District). And there's plenty of greatness to be found higher up, in the mountain sub-AVAs—Mount Veeder, Diamond Mountain, Spring Mountain, and Howell Mountain. For the wine-loving visitor, tasting across the AVAs of Napa Valley shouldn't be missed. Can you pick up traces of earthy, minerally "Rutherford dust"? Winemakers there swear by it. Stags' Leap District's "iron fist in a velvet glove"? Howell Mountain's tannic muscle and deep, dark berries? Grab a loaf of good bread and an untried bottle of Napa Valley wine, find a picnic spot, spread your blanket, and enjoy this very special corner of the world.

Sonoma

Sonoma County might be home to only about half as many wine producers as Napa Valley, its soft-rival sibling to the east, but it has the advantage of size. At more than 1,500 square miles, it's as big as Rhode Island. And while it's impossible not to attempt comparisons between the two preeminent wine regions in the state, the most that can be said is that Sonoma County takes great pleasure in not being Napa—and pride in wine diversity over a single signature grape.

Wildly disparate geography makes the region impos-

sible to summarize. The county sprawls through warm valleys shielded from any Pacific Ocean influence and cool ones defined by ocean wind and fog, over inland mountains cooled by altitude and coastal hills that poke above the fog for warmth. It is largely temperature that distinguishes Sonoma County's AVAs from one another, and determines the grapes that have become their various signature wines.

On the eastern side, the cooling breezes off San Pablo Bay make the Carneros region (which Sonoma shares with Napa) a great place for Pinot Noir and Chardonnay—both still and bubbly versions. The cooling effect peters out as you get into Sonoma Valley proper, so warmer-weather grapes thrive: Sauvignon Blanc, Cabernet, Zinfandel, Syrah. Farther north, in toasty Knights and Alexander valleys, gentle Cabs and Merlots reign. To the west, planting decisions are based on where you are in relation to the Petaluma Gap, which lets the Russian River out to the sea and sends cool air in the other direction. The Russian River Valley is a remote and beautiful home for Pinot Noir and Chardonnay. But follow the Russian River north into Dry Creek Valley, and Cab and Zin rule. New money, though, is on the very cold outer reaches of the Sonoma Coast appellation, where Pinot Noir, Chardonnay, and Syrah are becoming awfully interesting.

Sonoma is a place where ambitious young winemakers of all stripes still have a prayer of a chance of getting a foothold in the business. And the result is an eclectic range of personalities—and wines.

Mendocino

California's mainly Mediterranean climate confronts the wetter Pacific Northwest in Mendocino County. Valleys are greener, mountains steeper and more thickly covered with pine and fir. Vineyards are tucked between stands of coast redwoods and meadows of grazing sheep. Winemaking tends toward the intimate and idiosyncratic, and is very clearly shaped by the natural world.

For the traveler, Mendocino divides itself neatly into two regions: the wineries along State Highway 128 and those farther inland, along U.S. Highway 101. Possibly the most newsworthy are the former, in remote Anderson Valley, running along 128 north from Boonville through Philo, until it dives into the redwoods on its way to the sea. Where the Navarro River breaks through the trees, the ocean fog rolls in, establishing the valley as Pinot Noir and cool-weather white (Riesling, Gewürztraminer, Pinot Gris) territory. The French took note of the Anderson Valley back in the 1980s, when none other than Roederer saw the potential for Pinot Noir and Chardonnay—the two main grapes in Champagne—and established one of the best sparkling-wine houses in California. The valley floor is not the whole Anderson Valley story though.

There's a stealth region above the fog: Mendocino Ridge, unique as an AVA in being a noncontiguous collection of peaks that reaches above the 1,400-foot fog line to produce warmth-loving Zinfandel from vineyards planted by Italian immigrants in the late 1800s. The southern entrance to the valley also has its own appellation, the Yorkville Highlands, where interesting organic winemaking abounds.

Inland, running from Hopland north through Ukiah to Redwood Valley, Highway 101 takes you to the wineries of the upper Russian River area—the Sanel, Ukiah, and Redwood valleys. Some of these wineries lie just off the highway; others require detours over pretty country roads. What you'll find in these much warmer valleys is the roster of warm-weather reds, from the Bordeaux cousins (like Cabernet Sauvignon and Merlot) to the Rhône players (like Syrah and Mourvèdre) to the Italians (such as Sangiovese and Barbera) to good old California Zinfandel. Wine tasting in Mendocino County makes you appreciate not just a wine but the things that give us that wine—soil, rain, sun, sky.

Lake County

One of California's more intriguing new centers of winemaking is Lake County, whose grape history reaches back to the 19th century (as it does in many of the wine-producing parts of the state). Due north of Napa and east of Mendocino, it is classic interior California, a landscape of high, rounded, oak-studded hills, in this case dominated by an extinct volcano, Mount Konocti, which rises 4,300 feet, and 68-square-mile Clear Lake, which is the largest freshwater lake entirely within California. (Take that, Lake Tahoe!)

With nuanced microclimates, soils, and elevations, it's also a good place for wine grapes: Sauvignon Blanc, on the white front, is especially interesting here. On the red front, expect all the warm-weather lovers, but watch particularly for the Spanish grape Tempranillo. Lake County, it seems, has something in common with the Iberian Peninsula.

Tourism here has always centered on the lake itself, and you'll still want to bring your bathing suit and fishing rod. But don't be surprised if they languish for days at a time while you circle the perimeter tasting wine.

Sierra Foothills

In the 19th century, gold came first in these parts. Wine arrived soon after (specifically, some of the first Zinfandel vines in California). Demand—and necessity—generated supply, as would-be-rich miners were forced to return to more traditional ways of making a living from the earth. More recently an influx of creative new winemakers has turned this enclave of quaintly restored towns trading off a compelling historical past into one of the most interesting wine regions in California.

This is a big wine country: The Sierra Foothills AVA extends across eight counties, from Yuba in the north to Calaveras in the south. Within it are smaller appellations, notably El Dorado and Fair Play in El Dorado County and Fiddletown and Shenandoah Valley in Amador County. Despite its size and geographic diversity, the region for decades was mainly identified with one wine: Zinfandel. More than a few of the Zin vineyards here are not just old; they're ancient by California standards. Ironically, those old Zinfandel vines (intertwined with other grapes, we know now) survived in large part because of an enormous customer base that knew very little about true red Zin, but bought copious amounts of it in the form of sweet white Zinfandel (thank you, Sutter Home).

Now the nobler form of the variety has regained a passionate following. And Amador and El Dorado counties especially—with their infamously warm summer days and lesser-known temperature drops at night—are producing some of the state's most intense and powerful versions. Sierra Zins aren't for the timid. Their fruit is almost pruny ripe and earthy, with correspondingly high alcohol levels (often pushing past 15, even 16 percent). But the best are spectacular wines—in balance, with acid and tannins to match. And they've been joined by wines made from Rhône grapes (Syrah, Grenache, Mourvèdre, Viognier), Italian grapes (Barbera, Sangiovese), and, most recently, Spanish (Tempranillo)—all worth watching.

The Santa Cruz Mountains

The Santa Cruz Mountains are the San Francisco Bay Area's backyard wine country. Many of the region's wineries lie only 10 or 20 miles from the office parks and affluent suburbs of the San Francisco Peninsula and greater San Jose. But that geography is misleading. The roads twisting up from Silicon Valley take you to a land that is wilder than you could have imagined, where sunlight filters through old-growth redwoods and hairpin turns reveal surprising views of the sea. The Santa Cruz Mountains official AVA extends across 400,000 acres in three counties—Santa Cruz, Santa Clara, and San Mateo, with topography ranging from sun-splashed (and, alternately, fog-shrouded) meadows overlooking the ocean to deep, redwood-shaded canyons to drier hills. But only 1,500 acres of it are actually planted in grapes, which is the main reason Santa Cruz Mountains wine is rare on national shop shelves: There's very little of it. You have to come here to get at it.

Winemaking here—like the terrain—is a bit wild. There's a little more isolation and a little less convention in these hills than in most other California wine regions, inviting original characters and iconoclasts. Individualists all, they're not eager to hire high-powered wine consultants or follow beaten paths. If there's a dearth of familiar elegance in their wines due to this unwillingness to follow conventions, there's also a range of personality that more than fills the gap. Santa Cruz Mountains wines—led by chill-loving Pinot Noir and Chardonnay—are endlessly interesting, full of the complexities that stony soils, mountain elevations, and fog-driven hang time induce.

No other Santa Cruz Mountains visionary has made as big a mark on the international wine world, though, as Paul Draper of Ridge Vineyards, widely considered the dean of California winemaking. In the now-famous 2006 rematch of the aforementioned 1976 Judgment of Paris tasting, Draper's 1971 Ridge Monte Bello Cab won over the entire field (it came in fifth 30 years before). More than one wine writer has slipped and reported that, once again, Napa Cabs have proved they're every bit as good—and long-lived—as Bordeaux. But no, number one would be a Santa Cruz Mountains Cabernet.

Monterey

A wine powerhouse, Monterey County is planted with 40,000 acres of vineyards. But most of the best wine (most of the worst too, for that matter) doesn't come from near the well-known destinations by the water but from the length of the Salinas Valley east of the Santa Lucia Range. Here, the wind has legendary strength on summer afternoons (reportedly starting at 2 p.m.), pulling in an ocean chill from the north, where the valley angles into Monterey Bay.

Early on in this county, some planting mistakes were made. Cabernet Sauvignon—the main fine-red wine of choice in California for a long time (maybe still)—was widely planted throughout. But the north valley was just too cold for it, and Monterey Cabs got a bad rap for their "veggie" qualities. Growers have been sorting things out and replanting, though, putting cool-weather lovers like Pinot Noir and Chardonnay in the north valley and grapes with warmer needs to the south.

Along the way, a handful of very special regions has emerged. One of the most exciting is a narrow strip of benchland on the west side of the Salinas Valley: the Santa Lucia Highlands, where Pinot Noir, Chardonnay, and cool-weather versions of Syrah and other Rhône grapes are shining. The drive south from Salinas along River Road through the Santa Lucia Highlands is the new classic California, where vineyards are interspersed with lettuce and broccoli fields.

Directly across the valley, up in the Gabilan Range, the Chalone AVA produces distinctive Chardonnays, full of fruit and the flavors of the limestone-rich soil they're grown in. And due east of Monterey County, San Benito County is California's stealth wine region— respected by winemakers, little known by the public. From vineyards very close to the Chalone AVA, but on the east side of the mountains, San Benito Pinot Noir takes advantage of the limestone soil and sets standards for the variety.

But Monterey County is amazingly long, from north to south. Drive south toward Paso Robles, and you'll bisect vast vineyards devoted to Cabernet, Merlot... oodles of it—headed for respectable, great-value California bottles.

San Luis Obispo County

In wine terms the soul of California's Central Coast region, San Luis Obispo County, is as diverse as they come but most easily divided into north and south county sections. Due east across the Santa Lucia Mountains from San Simeon and its iconic rococo Hearst Castle spreads the vast 610,000-acre Paso Robles AVA (north county). Few wine areas in California have changed as much or as rapidly as this sprawling land of rolling, oak-dotted hills. Go back just a handful of decades, and it was cattle country; today it's home to hundreds of wineries.

No other California wine region is as hard to characterize as Paso Robles. There's just too much of it. The unifying condition is that it's warm here, but not as hot in its warmest parts as many people think, and cool enough in other parts to surprise wine-savvy outsiders. Two features determine temperature and wine-growing potential. The Santa Lucia Range blocks the cool ocean air from the stretch of the region east of the Salinas River (and Highway 101). In broad strokes, the east side, as it's known, is the hot, dry land of Cabs from large producers, some of whom make big red wines exceptionally well. On average, the east side temperature drops 40 degrees at night during the growing season, giving the area one of the greatest diurnal swings in California (propitious for wine).

There's a crack in the range called the Templeton Gap, which lets maritime breezes funnel into the west side of the Paso Robles AVA. Here, small producers are crafting Syrahs and white Rhône varieties that are among the best in the state. But geographically based judgments are way too simple. Many west-side winemakers get some of their grapes from growers on the east side, and vice versa. And all the reds here— Zinfandels, Cabs, Syrahs—share rich color, soft tannins, and ripe, juicy fruit flavors.

The county's other two main appellations—Edna Valley and Arroyo Grande Valley, comprising the south county—are more compact, stretching south from the city of San Luis Obispo. Here the chilly maritime influence is more noticeable, steering winemakers toward Pinot Noir, Chardonnay, and, increasingly, other crisp whites, from Riesling, Sauvignon Blanc, Pinot Blanc, and Pinot Gris to the likes of Spanish Albariño. Their versions are joining the leagues of the best in California, and in many cases leading.

Santa Barbara County

Given the fact that it produces world-class wines, you might think that the Santa Ynez Valley and its adjacent appellations, Sta. Rita Hills and the Santa Maria Valley, had been wine centers for aeons. In fact, only in the 1970s did pioneering winemakers see the potential for growing wine here and start planting vineyards. What they saw was a series of interconnected valleys that—unusual in California—run east to west, with rugged mountain ranges on three sides but open to the Pacific to the west. The offshore ocean current here is much colder than it is in the city of Santa Barbara itself, just to the south; dramatically cooling fog blows inland. Roughly speaking, for every mile you travel east from the coast, the average temperature rises by one degree.

Three main valleys are the wine beneficiaries of this marine influence: Santa Ynez, Santa Maria, and the Santa Rita Hills (the AVA is a valley, even if named for its surrounds, and its rightful legal name is Sta. Rita Hills, the result of an agreement with the very large Chilean winery Santa Rita, which objected to the use of its trademark). The easternmost, Santa Ynez, is the warmest, but even it has a wide variation from east to west. To the east, Bordeaux varieties— Cabernet Sauvignon, Merlot, and Sauvignon Blanc— shine. Moving west, Syrah and Grenache are thriving in slightly cooler conditions.

In contrast, to the west, the Santa Maria Valley is much colder and its output more focused. Pinot Noir and Chardonnay are the bread-and-butter grapes here—although anything but pedestrian.

Just south of Santa Maria, the Sta. Rita Hills AVA is as cold as its neighbor to the north but has different soils. A cluster of vintners in Lompoc has made the town a hot address for Pinot Noir, Chardonnay, and Syrah.

Santa Barbara wine country has been far from undiscovered ever since Miles and his *Sideways* chum, Jack, misbehaved on their Pinot Noir quest through the region in the 2004 movie. But the film got the mix of sophistication and unpretentiousness on the ground here right. The place is a wine lover's treat.

Temecula Valley

The southerly location of Temecula Valley has worked against the notion that it could produce quality wines. It's true that Temecula—in the rolling hills of southwestern Riverside County—is California's southernmost wine region, but it's just 25 miles from the Pacific Ocean, at an elevation of 1,500 feet. Days are warm and nights are cool, a combination that—along with the well-drained soil—can support many varieties typically grown farther north, including Gewürztraminer, Merlot, and Sauvignon Blanc.

But therein lies another problem: The valley produces so many different varieties that it's hard to know what to expect will be good. Let Temecula's latitude lead you to warm-climate varieties, which it's especially suited to—southern French, Italian, and Spanish grapes.

Temecula Valley is just an hour from San Diego and 90 minutes from Los Angeles, making it an easy wine country for Southern California wine fans to explore. And it is a SoCal scene—suburban strip malls stop just short of the vineyards. But sophisticated winemaking is taking hold. This is one to watch.

Oregon Wine

Latitude is destiny. That's what Oregon winemakers like to think.

The 45th parallel runs through Oregon's Willamette Valley. It runs through France's Burgundy region as well. In the 1960s, that geographical coincidence gave pioneering Oregon winemakers the nerve to think they could produce wines that might rival the best France had to offer.

Today the Willamette Valley AVA—which stretches from the Portland suburbs south to Eugene—contains some 400 wineries. Although the valley produces Chardonnay, Pinot Gris, and other varietals, Pinot Noir is its star, which doesn't

mean that it's an easy grape to grow here. Famously damp, cool, and gray much of the year, the Willamette Valley produces barely enough hours of light and degrees of heat to ripen grapes. In a bad year, that can result in wines that are underripe and thin. But in a good year, those seemingly unfavorable conditions nurture Pinots with lush, complex flavors that earn accolades (and high prices).

Oregon's other main wine region is a relative newcomer. Established in 2005, the Southern Oregon appellation includes the Umpqua, Rogue, and Applegate Valley AVAs—Applegate being a subregion of the Rogue. The climate across most of the region is noticeably warmer and sunnier—more Californian, if you like, so the region is best known for its Syrah- and Merlot-based blends. The exception to that is the multifaceted Umpqua (the most northerly of the Southern Oregon appellations): The region contains so many mini valleys and microclimates that it produces everything from Pinot Noir, Chardonnay, and Pinot Gris to Cabernet, Syrah, Viognier, Sangiovese, and Tempranillo.

Washington Wine

After California, Washington is the nation's second-largest wine producer. If that statistic surprises you, drive through the Yakima Valley near Toppenish, or take State Highway 12 near Walla Walla, and see the acre upon acre of vineyards.

Settlers began planting wine grapes in Washington as early as the 19th century, but serious winemaking began only in the 1960s. Today, although you can find small wineries scattered around Puget Sound, the vast majority of Washington grapes are grown in the higher, drier country east of the Cascade Mountains.

The region's relative aridity is one of the forces that shape Washington wines: Growers use irrigation to control how much water their vines get. Eastern Washington is also high enough in elevation that summer nighttime temperatures drop after scorching days, keeping the grapes' acid levels high. And its northerly latitude means that during growing season vineyards get about one more hour of sunlight a day than does the Napa Valley, giving grapes the chance to develop intense flavors.

With these influences, coupled with seriously talented winemakers, Washington is producing superbly structured Cabernets, Merlots, Syrahs, and some of the best Rieslings this side of Germany. Appellations to look for include Yakima Valley and Walla Walla Valley, and also smaller, rising subregions like Horse Heaven Hills.

Guadalupe Valley, Baja California

There's been winemaking in Mexico since before California vintners could say "new French oak." But it wasn't until a couple of decades ago that a special little valley in northern Baja California—just 90 minutes south of San Diego—began growing grapes capable of producing great wine. Now the Guadalupe Valley, which angles northeast from Ensenada, is becoming a bona fide "wine country" at an astonishing rate.

To the north, south, and east, the valley is cupped by dramatic mountain ranges that allow ocean breezes to flow in from the west and then be held there. As a result, the area doesn't get as hot as you might expect, so the grapes can retain their all-important acid. And because the growing season is long, winemakers can count on complex, concentrated flavors.

Everywhere you look in the Guadalupe Valley, you see new vineyards and new wineries. Those on the leading edge are determined to find out which grapes do well in what parts of the valley, and what specific traits each area brings to the fruit. The Mexican government has established a *Ruta del Vino* (Wine Route) that runs among the vineyards. Much of it might be washboard rough, but the Guadalupe Valley is an easy day-trip from the San Diego area, and U.S. Customs lets you bring back two bottles per person over the border.

The West's Wine Frontiers

When it comes to wine, Nampa, Idaho, isn't mentioned in the same breath as Napa, California. Sonoita, Arizona, won't be confused with Sonoma.

Give them time. A hallmark of 21st-century winemaking in the West is that it's being done in some very unexpected places. Some of these frontier vintages may be airport gift-shop curiosities. But many are already good enough to deserve much more attention than that.

One of the more established regions is Colorado's Grand Valley, near Grand Junction (winegrowing began here in the 1980s). Long famous for peaches, it now produces Viognier and some fine, muscular Cabernets.

Southeast of Tucson, Arizona, Spanish reds like Tempranillo thrive in the high (4,500 feet), dry (under 20 inches of rain a year) Sonoita AVA. And north of Phoenix, in Sedona's Verde Valley, Rhône varietals are coming on strong. In New Mexico, Gruet produces award-winning méthode Champenoise vintages from grapes grown near the town of Truth or Consequences.

Farther north, Idaho's Snake River Valley AVA—which stretches southeast and northwest from Boise—has more than 30 wineries, most focusing on white wines, notably Rieslings. And British Columbia's Okanagan Valley may be the most promising "new" wine region of all (it's not new at all, of course, but is enjoying a renaissance of wine development). Centered on Lake Okanagan, the 100-mile-long valley has enough microclimates to support an incredible range of cold- and hot-weather grapes, among them Merlot, Riesling, Sangiovese, and Mourvèdre.

Make It Your West

From world-renowned Napa Valley to Arizona's up-and-coming Verde Valley, Western regions are this country's mother lode of wine. A road trip through California's Central Coast or Oregon's Willamette Valley gives wine a riveting sense of place. Bottles from these regions can bring that to your table—along with considerable pleasure.

topical indexes

Essential Western Recipes

Although all the recipes in this book are part of how we eat in the West, these are the ones that most make us feel like we're home. They're listed here in order of their appearance in the book. Page numbers in regular type refer to the recipe; page numbers in boldface refer to a photograph of the dish.

Weeknight Meals

Here are all the main course recipes that can be prepared from prep to plate in 45 minutes or less. Whatever you're in the mood for, we've got it covered—soups, pastas, supper salads, or something for the grill. We've also included sandwiches and a few brunch selections, which make a nice change of pace for dinner. To complete your meal, check out the chapters Salads (*page 130*) and Vegetables on the Side (*page 236*) for recipes that can be put together in the time it'll take you to prepare your main course. They're listed here in order of their appearance in the book. Page numbers in regular type refer to the recipe; page numbers in boldface refer to a photograph of the dish.

Lean & Healthy Recipes

We put this recipe index together for those readers looking to cut down on their intake of calories, fat, and/or sodium. Generally, the recipes that follow adhere to the following nutritional guidelines per serving: *Appetizers and first courses (including first-course soups):* 150 cal., 8 g fat, 300 mg sodium; *main courses (including main-course salads and soups, as well as breakfast dishes and sandwiches):* 450 cal., 20 g fat, 500 mg sodium; *side dishes (including side salads and grain side dishes):* 200 cal., 10 mg fat, 300 mg sodium; *desserts:* 250 cal., 10 g fat, 300 mg sodium.

For those readers for whom sodium is less of a concern, we've also included recipes that are low in fat and calories but exceed the above guidelines in sodium. We've marked those with an asterisk (*). Recipes are listed in order of their appearance in the book. Page numbers in regular type refer to the recipe; page numbers in boldface refer to a photograph of the dish.

Vegan Recipes

The recipes in this index include no animal products—no fish, shellfish, poultry, meat, eggs, or dairy. Some vegans also avoid honey. We've chosen to include such recipes, but have indicated them with an asterisk (*) for your convenience. We've also included recipes that could be vegan if one or two optional ingredients are omitted or substituted (which we've indicated in a note after the recipe title). Recipes are listed in order of their appearance in the book. Page numbers in regular type refer to the recipe; page numbers in boldface refer to a photograph of the dish.

general
index

This overall index is a mix of recipe titles and general subject matter. Boldface words highlight main topics, and recipes within those topics are indented. Page numbers in regular type refer to the recipe; page numbers in boldface refer to a photograph of the dish.

Ev's Skorpas, 614

Photo Index

Photo Credits

Photographers

Iain Bagwell: front cover right, front cover left, 314
James Baigrie: 317
Noel Barnhurst: 477, 740
Edmund Barr: 368
Leigh Beisch: 42 all, 182, 264, 324, 386 all, 450, 543, 601, 603, 611
Annabelle Breakey: front cover middle, back cover, front flap, back flap top, spine, 24 all, 49, 50, 51, 52, 53, 54, 55, 56, 57, 58, 60, 110, 112, 114, 115, 116, 118, 119, 120, 177, 179, 180, 181, 184, 185, 186, 188, 253, 254, 255, 256, 257, 258, 260, 261, 263, 315, 316, 318, 319, 320, 323, 373, 374, 375, 376, 377, 379, 380, 381, 382, 383, 384, 449, 451, 452, 454, 455, 456, 457, 458, 459, 460, 541, 545, 548, 549, 550, 551, 602, 604, 605, 606, 607, 608, 609, 610, 612, 677, 679, 682, 683, 684, 685, 687, 688
Rob D. Brodman: 330, 728, 736 all, 739
James Carrier: 125 all, 248, 299, 371, 730, 737
Alex Farnum: 340 all, 341 all, 542
Sheri Giblin: 653
Dan Goldberg: 259, 321, 378, 453, 544
Leo Gong: back flap bottom, 109, 111, 113, 117, 183, 187, 262, 322, 546, 547
Thayer Allyson Gowdy: 334, 336 all
Jim Henkens: 686
Ngoc Minh Ngo: 178
Minh + Wass: 552
Scott Peterson: 59, 680, 681
David Prince: 647 all
Thomas J. Story: 200 all, 289, 313, 378, 425, 468 all, 577 all, 712 all, 727, 733, 735
E. Spencer Toy: 135 all, 519 all, 734

Food Stylists

Valerie Aikman-Smith: 178
Dan Becker: front cover left, front cover middle, 42 all, 111, 114, 186, 261, 314, 320, 322, 324, 378, 386 all, 450, 453, 468 all, 544, 605, 653
Merilee Bordin: 182, 264, 543, 611
Katie Christ: 552
Kevin Crafts: front cover right
Susan Devaty: 299
George Dolese: 477, 740
Randy Mon: back cover, back flap bottom, 109, 113, 116, 118, 185, 187, 200 all, 289, 317, 340 all, 341 all, 374, 379, 425, 458, 460, 542, 548, 549, 679, 684, 727, 733, 735
Laura Shafsky: 734
Karen and Barry Shinto: 334, 336 all
Karen Shinto: front flap, back flap top, spine, 24 all, 49, 50, 51, 52, 53, 54, 55, 56, 57, 58, 59, 60, 110, 112, 115, 117, 119, 120, 125 all, 177, 179, 180, 181, 183, 184, 188, 248, 253, 254, 255, 256, 257, 258, 260, 262, 263, 313, 315, 316, 318, 319, 321, 323, 371, 373, 375, 376, 377, 378, 380, 381, 382, 383, 384, 449, 451, 452, 454, 455, 456, 457, 459, 541, 545, 546, 547, 550, 551, 577 all, 602, 603, 604, 606, 607, 608, 609, 610, 612, 647 all, 677, 681, 682, 683, 685, 686, 687, 688, 712 all, 730, 737
Jen Straus: 259, 680

Photo Stylists

Natalie Hoelen: 178
Molly Hurd: 686
Emma Starr Jensen: front flap, back flap top, 49, 51, 52, 53, 54, 55, 56, 57, 58, 60, 112, 115, 119, 120, 177, 179, 180, 181, 184, 253, 254, 255, 256, 257, 260, 263, 318, 319, 323, 375, 376, 377, 380, 381, 382, 383, 384, 451, 452, 454, 455, 456, 457, 459, 541, 545, 550, 551, 602, 604, 606, 607, 608, 609, 610, 612, 677, 682, 683, 687, 688
Sara Slavin: 42 all, 182, 264, 324, 386 all, 450, 543, 601, 603, 611

Metric Equivalents

The information in the following charts is provided to help cooks outside the United States successfully use the recipes in this book. All equivalents are approximate.

Cooking/Oven Temperatures

	Fahrenheit	Celsius	Gas Mark
Freeze Water	32°F	0°C	
Room Temp.	68°F	20°C	
Boil Water	212°F	100°C	
Bake	325°F	160°C	3
	350°F	180°C	4
	375°F	190°C	5
	400°F	200°C	6
	425°F	220°C	7
	450°F	230°C	8
Broil			Grill

Liquid Ingredients by Volume

¼ tsp	=					1 ml	
½ tsp	=					2 ml	
1 tsp	=					5 ml	
3 tsp	=	1 tbl	=	½ fl oz	=	15 ml	
2 tbsp	=	⅛ cup	=	1 fl oz	=	30 ml	
4 tbsp	=	¼ cup	=	2 fl oz	=	60 ml	
5⅓ tbsp	=	⅓ cup	=	3 fl oz	=	80 ml	
8 tbsp	=	½ cup	=	4 fl oz	=	120 ml	
10⅔ tbsp	=	⅔ cup	=	5 fl oz	=	160 ml	
12 tbsp	=	¾ cup	=	6 fl oz	=	180 ml	
16 tbsp	=	1 cup	=	8 fl oz	=	240 ml	
1 pt	=	2 cups	=	16 fl oz	=	480 ml	
1 qt	=	4 cups	=	32 fl oz	=	960 ml	
				33 fl oz	=	1000 ml	= 1 l

Dry Ingredients by Weight

(To convert ounces to grams, multiply the number of ounces by 30.)

1 oz	=	¹⁄₁₆ lb	=	30 g
4 oz	=	¼ lb	=	120 g
8 oz	=	½ lb	=	240 g
12 oz	=	¾ lb	=	360 g
16 oz	=	1 lb	=	480 g

Length

(To convert inches to centimeters, multiply the number of inches by 2.5.)

1 in	=				2.5 cm	
6 in	=	½ ft		=	15 cm	
12 in	=	1 ft		=	30 cm	
36 in	=	3 ft	= 1 yd	=	90 cm	
40 in	=				100 cm	= 1m

Equivalents for Different Types of Ingredients

Standard Cup	Fine Powder (e.g. flour)	Grain (e.g. rice)	Granular (e.g. sugar)	Liquid Solids (e.g. butter)	Liquid (e.g. milk)
1	140 g	150 g	190 g	200 g	240 ml
¾	105 g	113 g	143 g	150 g	180 ml
⅔	93 g	100 g	125 g	133 g	160 ml
½	70 g	75 g	95 g	100 g	120 ml
⅓	47 g	50 g	63 g	67 g	80 ml
¼	35 g	38 g	48 g	50 g	60 ml
⅛	18 g	19 g	24 g	25 g	30 ml

How To Bake at
High Altitudes

Climb every mountain, and you're likely to find a frustrated baker. That's because most baking recipes, including ours, are developed and tested for use from sea level to about 2,000 feet. With the help of high-altitude baking authorities Pat Kendall, of the Colorado State University Cooperative Extension; Nancy Feldman, from the University of California Cooperative Extension; and the invaluable book *Pie in the Sky*, by Susan G. Purdy (William Morrow, 2005), we've assembled some guidelines that should help you bake successfully above 2,000 feet. If you live in one of the country's many high-altitude areas, consider buying Purdy's entertaining and exhaustively researched book—she tested every recipe at five different elevations.

Why Does Altitude Matter?

Liquids boil at lower temperatures (below 212°), and moisture evaporates more quickly at high altitudes—both of which significantly impact the quality of baked goods. Also, leavening gases (air, carbon dioxide, water vapor) expand faster. If you live at 3,000 feet or below, Kendall and Feldman suggest that you first try a recipe as is. Sometimes few, if any, changes are needed. But the higher you go, the more you'll have to adjust your ingredients and cooking times.

A Few Overall Tips

• Use shiny new baking pans. This seems to help mixtures rise, especially cake batters.

• Use butter, flour, and parchment to prep your baking pans for nonstick cooking. At high altitudes, baked goods tend to stick more to the pans.

• Be exact in your measurements (once you've figured out what they should be). This is always important in baking, but especially so when you're up high. Tiny variations in ingredients make a bigger difference at high altitudes than at sea level.

• Boost flavor. Seasonings and extracts tend to be more muted at higher altitudes, so increase them slightly.

• Have patience. You may have to bake your favorite sea-level recipe a few times, making different adjustments each time, until it's worked out to suit your particular altitude.

• Find out exactly how high you are with a topographic map from the U.S. Geological Survey (*usgs.gov* or 888/275-8747—ask for customer service).

Breads

• Cut back on the flour. Flours tend to be drier and will absorb more liquid in the low humidity of high altitudes. You may need less flour than the recipe calls for, so mix in about two-thirds, and then check the dough to see whether it looks and feels right before adding more.

• Keep an eye on the dough's rise, and let it rise twice, even three times if necessary. Yeast doughs rise more quickly—sometimes twice as fast—in the reduced pressure of higher altitudes. If dough rises much more than double, it could collapse. Check the rise after half the time specified in the recipe. The drawback of a short rise can be a muted flavor. If your bread doesn't have a good, full sourdough or yeast taste, the next time you make the recipe, punch the dough down after the first fast rise and let it rise a second (even a third) time before shaping.

• Pre-empt the last rise. Instead of letting dough rise until doubled in volume, only let it rise by about a third. That will compensate for its tendency to overexpand in the oven.

• Add moisture to the oven. As wheat products bake, they are lightened, or leavened, as the heated moisture in them swells and forms tiny bubbles encased by thin dough walls. At high altitudes, moisture evaporates more quickly, and the surface of the bread dries out and crusts over before the inside has fully cooked—preventing the loaf from rising. Putting a pan of water on the oven floor or spraying the hot oven walls with water creates steam, which stops the evaporation in the bread and allows the interior to fully expand.

• Baking at a slightly higher temperature can help too (*see baking chart below*).

Cakes

• At higher elevations, cakes are especially fragile. The adjustments you need to make depend on what makes the cakes rise.

• *Cakes leavened by trapped air.* Cakes such as chiffon, angel food, and sponge are leavened by air bubbles trapped in whipped eggs or egg whites. At higher altitudes, egg mixtures whipped to the maximum will collapse as the lower air pressure encourages the air cells to keep expanding. To account for this, whip the eggs a little less—to soft peaks instead of stiff ones for egg whites—to allow for expansion. Also, reduce the sugar slightly; this will help the whipped mixture to firm up at a lower temperature.

If the egg foam breaks, its drainage forms a rubbery layer—and the cake usually falls. A little additional flour will strengthen the cake, and baking at a slightly higher temperature will firm up the egg mixture faster.

• *Cakes leavened by baking powder or soda.* At high altitudes, a slight increase in egg and flour (along with the changes noted in the baking chart *below*) produces effective results. All-purpose flour, because it has a stronger protein structure that holds up better at high altitudes, is usually a better choice than weaker cake flour. Also, the baking powder and soda need to be reduced, because the gases they produce expand so much more freely at high altitudes; they'll burst through the cake's structure and cause it to fall the minute it leaves the oven.

Quick Breads

The batters and doughs for muffins, pancakes, biscuits, and other quick breads contain less fat and sugar than do those for regular cakes, and a minor reduction in baking powder may be all that is needed. But if results are unsatisfactory, try the other modifications suggested in the baking chart below.

Cookies

Cookies are relatively easy to make at high elevations. The main problem is that they tend to spread, especially if they contain a lot of fat, and their flavor may be more muted. Prescription: To slow down the spread, add a little more flour, slightly reduce the baking powder and soda, and bake at a higher temperature for a longer time. However, it sometimes also works to increase baking temperature and shorten the time; see chart below.

Pies

Crusts—especially the rims—tend to brown before the filling is cooked at higher altitudes, so shield the rim of your pie with foil (one easy way is to cut the center out of a square of foil and then set it over the pie). And the bottom crusts tend to get soggy, so you can either par-bake them before filling, or start the pie off on the bottom shelf (right above the heating element) in a hot oven for the first 15 minutes and then move it to the center rack and finish baking at a more moderate temperature.

Also, consider sticking to soft fruits, most of which will cook faster, before the crust burns, or parcooking the fruit before filling your pie shell. (The exception is berries, which actually cook slower at high altitudes. The lower boiling point means their juices won't heat as quickly to soften the starch needed for thickening the filling.)

Ingredient/Temperature Adjustments for High-altitude Baking

CHANGE	AT 3,000 FEET	AT 5,000 FEET	AT 7,000 FEET
Baking powder or baking soda	Reduce each tsp. called for by up to ⅛ tsp.	Reduce each tsp. called for by ⅛ to ¼ tsp.	Reduce each tsp. called for by ¼ to ½ tsp.
Sugar	Reduce each cup called for by up to 1 tbsp.	Reduce each cup called for by up to 2 tbsp.	Reduce each cup called for by 2 to 3 tbsp.
Liquid	Increase each cup called for by up to 2 tbsp.	Increase each cup called for by 2 to 4 tbsp.	Increase each cup called for by 3 to 4 tbsp.
Oven temperature	Increase 3° to 5°	Increase 15°	Increase 21° to 25°

Favorite Recipes Journal

Jot down your family's and your own favorite recipes for quick and handy reference. And don't forget to include the dishes that drew rave reviews when company came for dinner.

RECIPE	SOURCE/PAGE	REMARKS

RECIPE	SOURCE/PAGE	REMARKS

The *Sunset* Cookbook

ISBN-13: 978-0-376-02794-8
ISBN-10: 0-376-02794-0
Library of Congress Control Number: 2009943552
10 9 8 7 6 5 4 3 2 1
Printed in Thailand
First Printing October 2010

Oxmoor House

VP, Publishing Director: Jim Childs
Editorial Director: Susan Payne Dobbs
Brand Manager: Fonda Hitchcock
Managing Editor: Laurie S. Herr
Project Editor: Vanessa Lynn Rusch
Senior Designer: Emily Albright Parrish
Design Contributor: Allison Sperando
Production Manager: Terri Beste-Farley
Interns: Georgia Dodge, Perri Hubbard

Sunset Publishing

President: Barb Newton
VP, Editor-in-Chief: Katie Tamony
Creative Director: Mia Daminato
Photography Director: Yvonne Stender
Food Editor: Margo True

The Sunset Cookbook
Contributors

Editor: Pam Hoenig
Copy Editors: Tam Putnam (Chief), Julie Harris
Production Specialist: Linda M. Bouchard
Proofreaders: Lauren Brooks, Rhonda Richards
Indexer: Mary Ann Laurens

Front Cover Photography: Salt-and-Pepper Shrimp, page 346;
Roast Chicken with Meyer Lemon–Shallot Sauce, page 355;
Grilled Chicken Pita Salad, page 448.
For photography credits, see page 810.

To order additional publications, call 1-800-765-6400.
For more books to enrich your life, visit **oxmoorhouse.com**
Visit *Sunset* online at **sunset.com**
For the most comprehensive selection of *Sunset* books, visit **sunsetbooks.com**
To search, savor, and share thousands of recipes, visit **myrecipes.com**

Special thanks to the following people for their contributions to this book:
Susan Blank, Annabelle Breakey, Kimberley Burch, Sophie Egan, Erika Ehmsen, Jose Guzman,
Mark Hawkins, Lynne and Bill Hill of Hill Nutrition Associates, Michelle Lau, Alan Phinney,
Lorraine Reno, Karen Shinto, Johanna Silver, Margaret Sloan, Vanessa Speckman, Emma Star Jensen,
E. Spencer Toy, and our wonderful *Sunset* recipe retesters—Angela Brassinga, April Cooper,
Dorothy Decker, Sarah Epstein, Lenore Grant, Doni Jackson, Melissa Kaiser, Marlene Kawahata,
Eve F. Lynch, Rebecca Parker, Bunnie Russell, Laura Shafsky, Vicki Sousa, Linda Tebben, and Sue Turner.